MW01555013

Fortress Commentary on the Bible

THE
OLD TESTAMENT
AND **APOCRYPHA**

Fortress Commentary on the Bible

THE
OLD TESTAMENT
AND APOCRYPHA

Gale A. Yee

Hugh R. Page Jr.

Matthew J. M. Coomber

Editors

Fortress Press

Minneapolis

FORTRESS COMMENTARY ON THE BIBLE: The Old Testament and Apocrypha

Copyright © 2014 Fortress Press. All rights reserved. Except for brief quotations in critical articles and reviews, no part of this book may be reproduced in any manner without prior written permission from the publisher. Visit http://www.augsburgfortress. org/copyrights/contact.asp or write to Permissions, Augsburg Fortress, Box 1209, Minneapolis, MN 55440.

Unless otherwise noted, Scripture quotations are from New Revised Standard Version Bible, copyright © 1989 by the Division of Education of the National Council of Churches of Christ in the United States of America.

Advisory Board: Walter Brueggemann, William R. Herzog II, Richard A. Horsley, Elisabeth Schüssler Fiorenza, Gale A. Yee

Fortress Press Publication Staff: Neil Elliott and Scott Tunseth, Project Editors; Marissa Wold, Production Manager; Laurie Ingram, Cover Design.

Copyeditor: Jeffrey A. Reimer

Typesetter: PerfecType, Nashville, TN

Proofreader: David Cottingham

Library of Congress Cataloging-in-Publication data is available

ISBN: 978-0-8006-9916-1

eISBN: 978-1-4514-8966-8

The paper used in this publication meets the minimum requirements of American National Standard for Information Sciences— Permanence of Paper for Printed Library Materials, ANSI Z329, 48-1984. Manufactured in the U.S.A.

CONTENTS

CONTRIBUTORS

Volume Editors

Gale A. Yee
Nancy W. King Professor of Biblical Studies
Episcopal Divinity School
Ruth
1, 2 Kings

Hugh R. Page Jr.
Associate Professor of Theology and *Africana* Studies
Vice President, Associate Provost, and Dean of the First Year of Studies
University of Notre Dame
The People of God and the Peoples of the Earth
Song of Songs
Habakkuk

Matthew J. M. Coomber
Assistant Professor of Biblical Studies
St. Ambrose University
Reading the Old Testament in Ancient and Contemporary Contexts
Jonah
Micah

Wilma Ann Bailey
Professor of Hebrew and Aramaic Scripture
Christian Theological Seminary
Lamentations

Harold V. Bennett
President and Dean
Charles H. Mason Theological Seminary
Deuteronomy

Alejandro F. Botta
Associate Professor of Hebrew Bible
Boston University School of Theology
1, 2 Chronicles

M. Daniel Carroll R. (Rodas)
Distinguished Professor of Old Testament
Denver Seminary
Amos

Corrine L. Carvalho
Professor of Hebrew Bible
University of St. Thomas
Ezekiel
Judith

Richard J. Coggins
Emeritus Lecturer in Old Testament
King's College London
Malachi

J. Blake Couey
Assistant Professor of Religion
Gustavus Adolphus College
Haggai

Stacy Davis
Associate Professor of Religious Studies
Coordinator, Gender and Women's Studies
Saint Mary's College
Sirach

Carol J. Dempsey, OP
Professor of Theology (Biblical Studies)
University of Portland
Themes and Perspectives in the Prophets: Truth,
*   Tragedy, Trauma*

Thomas B. Dozeman
Professor of Old Testament
United Theological Seminary
Exodus

Amy Erickson
Assistant Professor of Hebrew Bible
Iliff School of Theology
Zechariah

Judy Fentress-Williams
Professor of Old Testament
Virginia Theological Seminary
Esther

Carole R. Fontaine
Taylor Professor of Biblical Theology and
    History
Andover Newton Theological School
Proverbs

Chris A. Franke
Professor of Bible and Theology Emerita
St. Catherine University
Isaiah 40–66

Christopher Frechette
Assistant Professor of Old Testament
Boston College School of Theology and
    Ministry
Prayer of Manasseh
Psalm 151

Norman K. Gottwald
Professor of Biblical Studies Emeritus
New York Theological Seminary
Themes and Perspectives in the Historical Writings

Jin Hee Han
Professor of Biblical Studies
New York Theological Seminary
Zephaniah
Malachi

Karina Martin Hogan
Associate Professor of Bible and Christianity
    in Antiquity
Fordham University
Baruch

Karl N. Jacobson
Teaching Pastor
Lutheran Church of the Good Shepherd
Edina, MN
Numbers

Vivian Johnson
Professor of Old Testament
United Theological Seminary
Esther (The Greek Additions)

Nyasha Junior
Assistant Professor of Hebrew Bible/Old
    Testament
Howard University School of Divinity
Susanna

Alice A. Keefe
Professor of Religious Studies
University of Wisconsin Stevens Point
Hosea

Micah D. Kiel
Associate Professor of Theology
St. Ambrose University
Ecclesiastes
Tobit

Robert Kugler
Paul S. Wright Professor of Christian Studies
Lewis and Clark College
Leviticus

Victor H. Matthews
Professor of Religious Studies and Dean of the
    College of Humanities and Public Affairs
Missouri State University
Judges

Michael S. Moore
Faculty Associate in Old Testament
Fuller Theological Seminary
1, 2 Maccabees

Kelly J. Murphy
Assistant Professor of Biblical Studies
Central Michigan University
Jeremiah

Alissa Jones Nelson
Acquisitions Editor, Religious Studies
De Gruyter Publishing
Job

Pekka M. A. Pitkänen
Senior Lecturer in Old Testament/Hebrew
    Bible
University of Gloucestershire
Joshua

Anathea E. Portier-Young
Associate Professor of Old Testament
Duke Divinity School
Daniel

Emerson B. Powery
Professor of Biblical Studies
Messiah College
Wisdom of Solomon

Hugh S. Pyper
Professor of Biblical Interpretation
The University of Sheffield
1, 2 Samuel

Rodney S. Sadler Jr.
Associate Professor of Bible
Union Presbyterian Seminary at Charlotte
Genesis

Timothy J. Sandoval
Associate Professor of Hebrew Bible
Brite Divinity School
Introduction to Wisdom and Worship: Themes and
    Perspectives in the Poetic Writings

Eileen M. Schuller
Professor of Religious Studies
McMaster University
Introduction to the Apocrypha

Joseph F. Scrivner
Assistant Professor of Religion and Theology
Stillman College
Obadiah

Sarah Shectman
Independent Scholar
San Francisco
*Themes and Perspectives in the Torah: Creation,
    Kinship, Covenant*

Ronald A. Simkins
Professor of Old Testament and Near Eastern
    Studies
Creighton University
Joel

Daniel L. Smith-Christopher
Professor of Theological Studies
Loyola Marymount University
*Reading the Christian Old Testament in the
    Contemporary World*
1 Esdras

Katherine E. Southwood
Associate Professor of Hebrew Bible
St. John's College, University of Oxford
Ezra
Nehemiah

W. Derek Suderman
Associate Professor of Religious Studies and
    Theological Studies
Conrad Grebel University College, University
    of Waterloo
Psalms

Marvin A. Sweeney
Professor of Hebrew Bible
Claremont School of Theology
Isaiah 1–39

Samuel I. Thomas
Associate Professor of Religion
California Lutheran University
3, 4 Maccabees

Patricia K. Tull
A. B. Rhodes Professor Emerita of Old
    Testament
Louisville Presbyterian Seminary
Letter of Jeremiah

Wilhelm J. Wessels
Professor of Old Testament
University of South Africa
Nahum

Lawrence M. Wills
Ethelbert Talbot Professor of Biblical Studies
Episcopal Divinity School
*Prayer of Azariah and the Song of the Three
    Young Men*
Bel and the Dragon

Robin Darling Young
Associate Professor of Theology and Religious
    Studies
The Catholic University of America
2 Esdras

ABBREVIATIONS

General

AT	Alpha Text (of the Greek text of Esther)
BOI	Book of Isaiah
Chr	Chronicler
DH	Deuteronomistic History
DI	Deutero-Isaiah
Dtr	Deuteronomist
Gk.	Greek
H	Holiness Code
Heb.	Hebrew
JPS	Jewish Publication Society
LXX	The Septuagint
LXX B	Vaticanus Text of the Septuagint
MP	Mode of production
MT	Masoretic Text
NIV	New International Version
NRSV	New Revised Standard Version
OAN	Oracles against Nations (in Jeremiah)
P.	papyrus/papyri
P	Priestly source
PE	Pastoral Epistles
RSV	Revised Standard Version
TI	Trito-Isaiah

Books of the Bible (NT, OT, Apocrypha)

Old Testament/Hebrew Bible

Gen.	Genesis
Exod.	Exodus
Lev.	Leviticus
Num.	Numbers
Deut.	Deuteronomy

Josh.	Joshua
Judg.	Judges
Ruth	Ruth
1 Sam.	1 Samuel
2 Sam.	2 Samuel
1 Kgs.	1 Kings
2 Kgs.	2 Kings
1 Chron.	1 Chronicles
2 Chron.	2 Chronicles
Ezra	Ezra
Neh.	Nehemiah
Esther	Esther
Job	Job
Ps. (Pss.)	Psalms
Prov.	Proverbs
Eccles.	Ecclesiastes
Song.	Song of Songs
Isa.	Isaiah
Jer.	Jeremiah
Lam.	Lamentations
Ezek.	Ezekiel
Dan.	Daniel
Hosea	Hosea
Joel	Joel
Amos	Amos
Obad.	Obadiah
Jon.	Jonah
Mic.	Micah
Nah.	Nahum
Hab.	Habakkuk
Zeph.	Zephaniah
Hag.	Haggai
Zech.	Zechariah
Mal.	Malachi

Apocrypha

Tob.	Tobit
Jth.	Judith
Gk. Esther	Greek Additions to Esther
Sir.	Sirach (Ecclesiasticus)

Bar.	Baruch
Let. Jer.	Letter of Jeremiah
Add Dan.	Additions to Daniel
Pr. Azar.	Prayer of Azariah
Sg. Three.	Song of the Three Young Men (or Three Jews)
Sus.	Susanna
Bel	Bel and the Dragon
1 Macc.	1 Maccabees
2 Macc.	2 Maccabees
1 Esd.	1 Esdras
Pr. of Man.	Prayer of Manasseh
2 Esd.	2 Esdras
Wis.	Wisdom of Solomon
3 Macc.	3 Maccabees
4 Macc.	4 Maccabees

New Testament

Matt.	Matthew
Mark	Mark
Luke	Luke
John	John
Acts	Acts of the Apostles
Rom.	Romans
1 Cor.	1 Corinthians
2 Cor.	2 Corinthians
Gal.	Galatians
Eph.	Ephesians
Phil.	Philippians
Col.	Colossians
1 Thess.	1 Thessalonians
2 Thess.	2 Thessalonians
1 Tim.	1 Timothy
2 Tim.	2 Timothy
Titus	Titus
Philem.	Philemon
Heb.	Hebrews
James	James
1 Pet.	1 Peter
2 Pet.	2 Peter
1 John	1 John

2 John	2 John
3 John	3 John
Jude	Jude
Rev.	Revelation (Apocalypse)

Journals, Series, Reference Works

ABD	*Anchor Bible Dictionary.* Edited by David Noel Freedman. 6 vols. New York: Doubleday, 1992.
ACNT	Augsburg Commentaries on the New Testament
AJA	*American Journal of Archaeology*
AJT	*Asia Journal of Theology*
ANET	*Ancient Near Eastern Texts Relating to the Old Testament.* Edited by J. B. Pritchard. 3rd ed. Princeton: Princeton University Press, 1969.
ANF	*The Ante-Nicene Fathers.* Edited by Alexander Roberts and James Donaldson. 1885–1887. 10 vols. Repr., Peabody, MA: Hendrickson, 1994.
ANRW	*Aufstieg und Niedergang der römischen Welt: Geschichte und Kultur Roms im Spiegel der neueren Forschung.* Edited by Hildegard Temporini and Wolfgang Haase. Berlin: de Gruyter, 1972–.
ANTC	Abingdon New Testament Commentaries
AOAT	Alter Orient und Altes Testament
AbOTC	Abingdon Old Testament Commentary
AOTC	Apollos Old Testament Commentary
A(Y)B	Anchor (Yale) Bible
BA	*Biblical Archaeologist*
BAR	*Biblical Archaeology Review*
BDAG	Bauer, W., F. W. Danker, W. F. Arndt, and F. W. Gingrich. *Greek-English Lexicon of the New Testament and Other Early Christian Literature.* 3rd ed. Chicago: University of Chicago Press, 1999.
BEATAJ	Beiträge zur Erforschung des Alten Testaments und des Antiken Judentum
Bib	*Biblica*
BibInt	*Biblical Interpretation*
BJRL	*Bulletin of the John Rylands University Library of Manchester*
BJS	Brown Judaic Studies
BNTC	Black's New Testament Commentaries
BR	*Biblical Research*
BRev	*Bible Review*
BSac	*Bibliotheca sacra*
BTB	*Biblical Theology Bulletin*
BZAW	Beihefte zur Zeitschrift für die alttestamentliche Wissenschaft
CAT	Commentaire de l'Ancien Testament

CBC	Cambridge Bible Commentary
CBQMS	Catholic Biblical Quarterly Monograph Series
CC	Continental Commentaries
CH	*Church History*
CHJ	*Cambridge History of Judaism.* Edited by W. D. Davies and Louis Finkelstein. Cambridge: Cambridge University Press, 1984–.
ConBNT	Coniectanea biblica: New Testament Series
ConBOT	Coniectanea biblica: Old Testament Series
CS	Cistercian Studies
CTAED	*Canaanite Toponyms in Ancient Egyptian Documents.* S. Ahituv. Jerusalem: Magnes, 1984.
CTQ	*Concordia Theological Quarterly*
CurTM	*Currents in Theology and Mission*
ExpTim	*Expository Times*
ETL	*Ephemerides Theologicae Lovanienses*
ExAud	*Ex auditu*
FAT	Forschungen zum Alten Testament
FC	Fathers of the Church
FRLANT	Forschungen zur Religion und Literatur des Alten und Neuen Testaments
HAT	Handbuch zum Alten Testament
HBT	*Horizons in Biblical Theology*
HNTC	Harper's New Testament Commentaries
HR	*History of Religions*
HSM	Harvard Semitic Monographs
HTKAT	Herders Theologischer Kommentar zum Alten Testament
HTR	*Harvard Theological Review*
HTS	Harvard Theological Studies
HUCA	*Hebrew Union College Annual*
HUCM	Monographs of the Hebrew Union College
HUT	Hermeneutische Untersuchungen zur Theologie
IBC	Interpretation: A Bible Commentary for Teaching and Preaching
ICC	International Critical Commentary
Int	*Interpretation*
JAAR	*Journal of the American Academy of Religion*
JAOS	*Journal of the American Oriental Society*
JBL	*Journal of Biblical Literature*
JBQ	*Jewish Bible Quarterly*
JECS	*Journal of Early Christian Studies*
JJS	*Journal of Jewish Studies*
JNES	*Journal of Near Eastern Studies*

JNSL	*Journal of Northwest Semitic Languages*
JQR	*Jewish Quarterly Review*
JRS	*Journal of Roman Studies*
JSem	*Journal of Semitics*
JSJ	*Journal for the Study of Judaism in the Persian, Hellenistic, and Roman Periods*
JSNT	*Journal for the Study of the New Testament*
JSOT	*Journal for the Study of the Old Testament*
JSOTSup	Journal for the Study of the Old Testament Supplement Series
JSQ	*Jewish Studies Quarterly*
JSS	*Journal of Semitic Studies*
JTI	*Journal of Theological Interpretation*
JTS	*Journal of Theological Studies*
JTSA	*Journal of Theology for Southern Africa*
KTU	*Die keilalphabetischen Texte aus Ugarit.* Edited by M. Dietrich, O. Loretz, and J. Sanmartín. AOAT 24/1. Neukirchen-Vluyn: Neukirchener, 1976.
LCC	Loeb Classical Library
LEC	Library of Early Christianity
LHB/OTS	Library of the Hebrew Bible/Old Testament Studies
LW	*Luther's Works.* Edited by Jaroslav Pelikan and Helmut T. Lehmann. 55 vols. St. Louis: Concordia; Philadelphia: Fortress Press, 1958–1986.
NAC	New American Commentary
NCB	New Century Bible
NCBC	New Cambridge Bible Commentary
NedTT	*Nederlands theologisch tijdschrift*
Neot	*Neotestamentica*
NICNT	New International Commentary on the New Testament
NICOT	New International Commentary on the Old Testament
NIGTC	New International Greek Testament Commentary
NovT	*Novum Testamentum*
NPNF[1]	*The Nicene and Post-Nicene Fathers*, Series 1. Edited by Philip Schaff. 14 vols. 1886–1889. Repr., Grand Rapids: Eerdmans, 1956.
NTL	New Testament Library
NTS	*New Testament Studies*
OBT	Overtures to Biblical Theology
OTE	*Old Testament Essays*
OTG	Old Testament Guides
OTL	Old Testament Library
OTM	Old Testament Message
PEQ	*Palestine Exploration Quarterly*
PG	Patrologia graeca [= Patrologiae cursus completus: Series graeca]. Edited by J.-P. Migne. 162 vols. Paris, 1857–1886.

PL	John Milton, *Paradise Lost*
PL	Patrologia latina [= Patrologiae cursus completus: Series latina]. Edited by J.-P. Migne. 217 vols. Paris, 1844–1864.
PRSt	*Perspectives in Religious Studies*
QR	*Quarterly Review*
RevExp	*Review and Expositor*
RevQ	*Revue de Qumran*
SBLABS	Society of Biblical Literature Archaeology and Biblical Studies
SBLAIL	Society of Biblical Literature Ancient Israel and Its Literature
SBLDS	Society of Biblical Literature Dissertation Series
SBLEJL	Society of Biblical Literature Early Judaism and Its Literature
SBLMS	Society of Biblical Literature Monograph Series
SBLRBS	Society of Biblical Literature Resources for Biblical Study
SBLSCS	Society of Biblical Literature Septuagint and Cognate Studies
SBLSP	*Society of Biblical Literature Seminar Papers*
SBLSymS	Society of Biblical Literature Symposium Series
SBLWAW	SBL Writings from the Ancient World
SemeiaSt	Semeia Studies
SJT	*Scottish Journal of Theology*
SNTSMS	Society for New Testament Studies Monograph Series
SO	Symbolae osloenses
SR	*Studies in Religion*
ST	*Studia Theologica*
StABH	Studies in American Biblical Hermeneutics
TD	*Theology Digest*
TAD	*Textbook of Aramaic Documents from Ancient Egypt.* Vol. 1: *Letters.* Bezalel Porten and Ada Yardeni. Winona Lake, IN: Eisenbrauns, 1986.
TDOT	*Theological Dictionary of the Old Testament.* 15 vols. Edited by G. Johannes Botterweck, Helmer Ringgren, and Heinz-Josef Fabry. Translated by David E. Green and Douglas W. Stott. Grand Rapids: Eerdmans, 1974–1995.
TJT	*Toronto Journal of Theology*
TNTC	Tyndale New Testament Commentaries
TOTC	Tyndale Old Testament Commentaries
TS	*Theological Studies*
TZ	*Theologische Zeitschrift*
VE	*Vox evangelica*
VT	*Vetus Testamentum*
VTSup	Supplements to Vetus Testamentum
WBC	Word Biblical Commentary
WSA	Works of St. Augustine: A Translation for the Twenty-First Century
WUANT	Wissenschaftliche Untersuchungen zum Alten und Neuen Testament

WUNT	Wissenschaftliche Untersuchungen zum Neuen Testament
WW	*Word and World*
ZAW	*Zeitschrift für die alttestamentliche Wissenschaft*
ZBK	Zürcher Bibelkommentare
ZNW	*Zeitschrift für die neutestamentliche Wissenschaft und die Kunde der älteren Kirche*

Ancient Authors and Texts

1 Clem.	*1 Clement*
2 Clem.	*2 Clement*
1 En.	*1 Enoch*
2 Bar.	*2 Baruch*
Abot R. Nat.	*Abot de Rabbi Nathan*
Ambrose	
Paen.	*De paenitentia*
Aristotle	
Ath. Pol.	*Athēnaīn politeia*
Nic. Eth.	*Nicomachean Ethics*
Pol.	*Politics*
Rhet.	*Rhetoric*
Augustine	
FC 79	*Tractates on the Gospel of John, 11–27.* Translated by John W. Rettig. Fathers of the Church 79. Washington, DC: Catholic University of America Press, 1988.
Tract. Ev. Jo.	*In Evangelium Johannis tractatus*
Bede, Venerable	
CS 117	*Commentary on the Acts of the Apostles.* Translated by Lawrence T. Martin. Cistercian Studies 117. Kalamazoo, MI: Cistercian Publications, 1989.
Barn.	*Barnabas*
CD	Cairo Genizah copy of the Damascus Document
Cicero	
De or.	*De oratore*
Tusc.	*Tusculanae disputationes*
Clement of Alexandria	
Paed.	*Paedogogus*
Strom.	*Stromata*
Cyril of Jerusalem	
Cat. Lect.	*Catechetical Lectures*
Dio Cassius	
Hist.	*Roman History*

Dio Chrysostom
    Or.   *Orations*
Diog.   *Diognetus*
Dionysius of Halicarnassus
    Thuc.   *De Thucydide*
Epictetus
    Diatr.   *Diatribai (Dissertationes)*
    Ench.   *Enchiridion*
Epiphanius
    Pan.   *Panarion (Adversus Haereses)*
Eusebius of Caesarea
    Hist. eccl.   *Historia ecclesiastica*
Gos. Thom.   *Gospel of Thomas*
Herodotus
    Hist.   *Historiae*
Hermas, *Shepherd*
    Mand.   *Mandates*
    Sim.   *Similitudes*
Homer
    Il.   *Iliad*
    Od.   *Odyssey*
Ignatius of Antioch
    Eph.   *To the Ephesians*
    Smyr.   *To the Smyrnaeans*
Irenaeus
    Adv. haer.   *Adversus haereses*
Jerome
    Vir. ill.   *De viris illustribus*
John Chrysostom
    Hom. 1 Cor. *Homiliae in epistulam i ad Corinthios*
    Hom. Act.   *Homiliae in Acta apostolorum*
    Hom. Heb.   *Homiliae in epistulam ad Hebraeos*
Josephus
    Ant.   *Jewish Antiquities*
    Ag. Ap.   *Against Apion*
    J.W.   *Jewish War*
Jub.   *Jubilees*
Justin Martyr
    Dial.   *Dialogue with Trypho*
    1 Apol.   *First Apology*

L.A.E.	*Life of Adam and Eve*
Liv. Pro.	*Lives of the Prophets*
Lucian	
Alex.	*Alexander (Pseudomantis)*
Phal.	*Phalaris*
Mart. Pol.	*Martyrdom of Polycarp*
Novatian	
Trin.	*De trinitate*
Origen	
C. Cels.	*Contra Celsum*
Comm. Jo.	*Commentarii in evangelium Joannis*
De princ.	*De principiis*
Hom. Exod.	*Homiliae in Exodum*
Hom. Jer.	*Homiliae in Jeremiam*
Hom. Josh.	*Homilies on Joshua*
Pausanias	
Descr.	*Description of Greece*
Philo	
Cher.	*De cherubim*
Decal.	*De decalogo*
Dreams	*On Dreams*
Embassy	*On the Embassy to Gaius (= Legat.)*
Fug.	*De fuga et inventione*
Leg.	*Legum allegoriae*
Legat.	*Legatio ad Gaium*
Migr.	*De migratione Abrahami*
Mos.	*De vita Mosis*
Opif.	*De opificio mundi*
Post.	*De posteritate Caini*
Prob.	*Quod omnis probus liber sit*
QE	*Quaestiones et solutiones in Exodum*
QG	*Quaestiones et solutiones in Genesin*
Spec. Laws	*On the Special Laws*
Plato	
Gorg.	*Gorgias*
Plutarch	
Mor.	*Moralia*
Mulier. virt.	*Mulierum virtutes*
Polycarp	
Phil.	*To the Philippians*

Ps.-Clem. Rec.	*Pseudo-Clementine Recognitions*
Pss. Sol.	*Psalms of Solomon*
Pseudo-Philo	
L.A.B.	*Liber antiquitatum biblicarum*
Seneca	
Ben.	*De beneficiis*
Strabo	
Geog.	*Geographica*
Tatian	
Ad gr.	*Oratio ad Graecos*
Tertullian	
Praescr.	*De praescriptione haereticorum*
Prax.	*Adversus Praxean*
Bapt.	*De baptismo*
De an.	*De anima*
Pud.	*De pudicitia*
Virg.	*De virginibus velandis*
Virgil	
Aen.	*Aeneid*
Xenophon	
Oec.	*Oeconomicus*

Mishnah, Talmud, Targum

b. B. Bat.	*Babylonian Talmudic tractate Baba Batra*
b. Ber.	*Babylonian Talmudic tractate Berakhot*
b Erub.	*Babylonian Talmudic tractate Erubim*
b. Ketub.	*Babylonian Talmudic tractate Ketubbot*
b. Mak.	*Babylonian Talmudic tractate Makkot*
b. Meg.	*Babylonian Talmudic tractate Megillah*
b. Ned.	*Babylonian Talmudic tractate Nedarim*
b. Naz.	*Babylonian Talmudic tractate Nazir*
b. Sanh.	*Babylonian Talmudic tractate Sanhedrin*
b. Shab.	*Babylonian Talmudic tractate Shabbat*
b. Sotah	*Babylonian Talmudic tractate Sotah*
b. Ta'an.	*Babylonian Talmudic tractate Ta'anit*
b. Yev.	*Babylonian Talmudic tractate Yevamot*
b. Yoma	*Babylonian Talmudic tractate Yoma*
Eccl. Rab.	*Ecclesiastes Rabbah*
Exod. Rab.	*Exodus Rabbah*
Gen. Rab.	*Genesis Rabbah*

Lam. Rab.	*Lamentations Rabbah*
Lev. R(ab).	*Leviticus Rabbah*
m. Abot	*Mishnah tractate Abot*
m. Bik.	*Mishnah tractate Bikkurim*
m. Demai	*Mishnah tractate Demai*
m. 'Ed.	*Mishnah tractate 'Eduyyot*
m. Git.	*Mishnah tractate Gittin*
m. Pesaḥ	*Mishnah tractate Pesaḥim*
m. Šeqal.	*Mishnah tractate Šeqalim (Shekalim)*
m. Shab.	*Mishnah tractate Shabbat*
m. Sotah	*Mishnah tractate Sotah*
m. Ta'an.	*Mishnah tractate Ta'anit*
m. Tamid	*Mishnah tractate Tamid*
m. Yad.	*Mishnah tractate Yadayim*
m. Yebam.	*Mishnah tractate Yebamot*
m. Yoma	*Mishnah tractate Yoma*
Num. Rab.	*Numbers Rabbah*
Pesiq. Rab.	*Pesiqta Rabbati*
Pesiq. Rab Kah.	*Pesiqta Rab Kahana*
S. 'Olam Rab.	*Seder 'Olam Rabbah*
Song Rab.	*Song of Songs Rabbah*
t. Hul.	*Tosefta tractate Hullin*
Tg. Onq.	*Targum Onqelos*
Tg. Jer.	*Targum Jeremiah*
y. Hag.	*Jerusalem Talmudic tractate Hagiga*
y. Pesaḥ	*Jerusalem Talmudic tractate Pesaḥim*
y. Sanh.	*Jerusalem Talmudic tractate Sanhedrin*

Dead Sea Scrolls

1QapGen	*Genesis apocryphon* (Excavated frags. from cave)
1QM	*War Scroll*
1QpHab	*Pesher Habakkuk*
1QS	*Rule of the Community*
1QSb	*Rule of the Blessings* (Appendix b to 1QS)
1Q21	*T. Levi*, aramaic
4Q184	Wiles of the Wicked Woman
4Q214	Levi[d] ar (*olim* part of Levi[b])
4Q214b	Levi[f] ar (*olim* part of Levi[b])
4Q226	psJub[b] (4Q *pseudo-Jubilees*)
4Q274	Tohorot A

4Q277	Tohorot B[b] (*olim* B[c])
4Q525	*Beatitudes*
4QMMT	*Miqṣat Maʿaśê ha-Torah*
4QpNah/4Q169	4Q Pesher Nahum
4Q82	*The Greek Minor Prophets Scroll*

Old Testament Pseudepigrapha

1 En.	*1 Enoch*
2 En.	*2 Enoch*
Odes Sol.	*Odes of Solomon*
Syr. Men.	*Sentences of the Syriac Menander*
T. Levi	*Testament of Levi*
T. Mos.	*Testament of Moses*
T. Sim.	*Testament of Simeon*

INTRODUCTION

The *Fortress Commentary on the Bible*, presented in two volumes, seeks to invite study and conversation about an ancient text that is both complex and compelling. As biblical scholars, we wish students of the Bible to gain a respect for the antiquity and cultural remoteness of the biblical texts and to grapple for themselves with the variety of their possible meanings; to fathom a long history of interpretation in which the Bible has been wielded for causes both beneficial and harmful; and to develop their own skills and voices as responsible interpreters, aware of their own social locations in relationships of privilege and power. With this in mind, the *Fortress Commentary on the Bible* offers general readers an informed and accessible resource for understanding the biblical writings in their ancient contexts; for recognizing how the texts have come down to us through the mediation of different interpretive traditions; and for engaging current discussion of the Bible's sometimes perplexing, sometimes ambivalent, but always influential legacy in the contemporary world. The commentary is designed not only to inform but also to invite and empower readers as active interpreters of the Bible in their own right.

The editors and contributors to these volumes are scholars and teachers who are committed to helping students engage the Bible in the classroom. Many also work as leaders, both lay and ordained, in religious communities, and wish this commentary to prove useful for informing congregational life in clear, meaningful, and respectful ways. We also understand the work of biblical interpretation as a responsibility far wider than the bounds of any religious community. In this regard, we participate in many and diverse identities and social locations, yet we all are conscious of reading, studying, and hearing the Bible today as citizens of a complex and interconnected world. We recognize in the Bible one of the most important legacies of human culture; its historical and literary interpretation is of profound interest to religious and nonreligious peoples alike.

Often, the academic interpretation of the Bible has moved from close study of the remote ancient world to the rarefied controversy of scholarly debate, with only occasional attention to the ways biblical texts are actually heard and lived out in the world around us. The commentary seeks to provide students with diverse materials on the ways in which these texts have been interpreted through the course of history, as well as helping students understand the texts' relevance for today's globalized world. It recognizes the complexities that are involved with being an engaged reader of the Bible, providing a powerful tool for exploring the Bible's multilayered meanings in both their ancient and modern contexts. The commentary seeks to address contemporary issues that are raised by biblical passages. It aspires to be keenly aware of how the contemporary world and its issues and perspectives influence the interpretation of the Bible. Many of the most important insights of contemporary biblical scholarship not only have come from expertise in the world of antiquity but have also been forged in modern struggles for dignity, for equality, for sheer survival, and out of respect for those who have died without seeing justice done. Gaining familiarity with the original contexts in which the biblical writings were produced is essential, but not sufficient, for encouraging competent and discerning interpretation of the Bible's themes today.

Inside the Commentary

Both volumes of *The Fortress Commentary on the Bible* are organized in a similar way. In the beginning of each volume, **Topical Articles** set the stage on which interpretation takes place, naming the issues and concerns that have shaped historical and theological scholarship down to the present. Articles in the *Fortress Commentary on the Old Testament* attend, for example, to the issues that arise when two different religious communities claim the same body of writings as their Scripture, though interpreting those writings quite differently. Articles in the *Fortress Commentary on the New Testament* address the consequences of Christianity's historic claim to appropriate Jewish Scripture and to supplement it with a second collection of writings, the experience of rootlessness and diaspora, and the legacy of apocalypticism. Articles in both volumes reflect on the historical intertwining of Christianity with imperial and colonial power and with indexes of racial and socioeconomic privilege.

Section Introductions in the Old Testament volume provide background to the writings included in the Torah, Historical Writings, Wisdom, Prophetic Writings, and a general introduction to the Apocrypha. The New Testament volume includes articles introducing the Gospels, Acts, the letters associated with Paul, and Hebrews, the General Epistles and Revelation. These articles will address the literary and historical matters, as well as theological themes, that the books in these collections hold in common.

Commentary Entries present accessible and judicious discussion of each biblical book, beginning with an introduction to current thinking regarding the writing's original context and its significance in different reading communities down to the present day. A three-level commentary then follows for each sense division of the book. In some cases, these follow the chapter divisions of a biblical book, but more often, contributors have discerned other outlines, depending on matters of genre, movement, or argument.

The three levels of commentary are the most distinctive organizational feature of these volumes. The first level, "The Text in Its Ancient Context," addresses relevant lexical, exegetical, and literary aspects of the text, along with cultural and archaeological information that may provide additional insight into the historical context. This level of the commentary describes consensus views where these exist in current scholarship and introduces issues of debate clearly and fairly. Our intent here is to convey some sense of the historical and cultural distance between the text's original context and the contemporary reader.

The second level, "The Text in the Interpretive Tradition," discusses themes including Jewish and Christian tradition as well as other religious, literary, and artistic traditions where the biblical texts have attracted interest. This level is shaped by our conviction that we do not apprehend these texts immediately or innocently; rather, even the plain meaning we may regard as self-evident may have been shaped by centuries of appropriation and argument to which we are heirs.

The third level, "The Text in Contemporary Discussion," follows the history of interpretation into the present, drawing brief attention to a range of issues. Our aim here is not to deliver a single answer—"what the text means"—to the contemporary reader, but to highlight unique challenges and interpretive questions. We pay special attention to occasions of dissonance: aspects of the text or of its interpretation that have become questionable, injurious, or even intolerable to some readers today. Our goal is not to provoke a referendum on the value of the text but to stimulate reflection and discussion and, in this way, to empower the reader to reach his or her own judgments about the text.

The approach of this commentary articulates a particular understanding of the work of responsible biblical interpretation. We seek through this commentary to promote intelligent and mature engagement with the Bible, in religious communities and in academic classrooms alike, among pastors, theologians, and ethicists, but also and especially among nonspecialists. Our work together has given us a new appreciation for the vocation of the biblical scholar, as custodians of a treasure of accumulated wisdom from our predecessors; as stewards at a table to which an ever-expanding circle is invited; as neighbors and fellow citizens called to common cause, regardless of our different professions of faith. If the result of our work here is increased curiosity about the Bible, new questions about its import, and new occasions for mutual understanding among its readers, our work will be a success.

Fortress Commentary on the Old Testament

Gale A. Yee
Episcopal Divinity School

Hugh R. Page Jr.
University of Notre Dame

Matthew J. M. Coomber
St. Ambrose University

Fortress Commentary on the New Testament

Margaret Aymer
Interdenominational Theological Center

Cynthia Briggs Kittredge
Seminary of the Southwest

David A. Sánchez
Loyola Marymount University

READING THE OLD TESTAMENT IN ANCIENT AND CONTEMPORARY CONTEXTS

Matthew J. M. Coomber

As students file into their desks on the first day of my "Introduction to the Old Testament" course, they are greeted with a PowerPoint slide that simply states, in bold red letters, "Caution: Dangerous Texts Ahead!" The students often respond with the mixture of chuckles and uneasy looks that I intend to provoke. To some extent, the slide is offered tongue in cheek, but not entirely. As with any wry statement, the cautionary slide holds an element of truth. The Old Testament contains powerful teachings and radical ideas that have moved the hearts and minds of both adherents and skeptics for millennia.

While the texts of the Old Testament have had a profound effect on societies and cultures for a long span of time, their texts often take a back seat to the Gospels and the Pauline Letters in popular Christian religion. Even though they constitute well over half of the content of Christian Bibles, very few of my students claim to have read much—if any—of the Old Testament or Apocrypha, despite the fact that I teach at a Roman Catholic university in which the vast majority of the students are Christian. In fact, only a handful of my students claim to have been exposed to the stories of the Old Testament outside of either Sunday school or in episodes of the popular cartoon series *Veggie Tales*. Due to this lack of exposure to the Old Testament, I feel compelled to give them fair warning about what they have gotten themselves into by signing up for what may seem like an innocuous required course. I take it as a professional responsibility to alert them to the fact that a keen examination of the ancient Near Eastern library that sits on their desks has the power to change their lives and forever alter the ways in which they experience the world.

5

Any collection of books containing calls to wage wars of conquest, to resist the temptation to fight while under threat, thoughts on God's role in governance, and meditations on what it means to live *the good life* has the potential to change lives and even inspire revolutions. To assume that the Bible is harmless is both foolish and irresponsible. After all, the Old Testament's contents have been used by some to support slavery and genocide while inspiring others to engage in such dangerous pursuits as enduring imprisonment, torture, and death in attempts to liberate the oppressed. And just as with using any powerful instrument, be it a car or a surgical blade, reading the Old Testament demands care, responsibility, and substantial consideration from those who put it to use.

Books that promote powerful ideas are complex tools that often belong to the readers as much as—if not more than—their authors. The level of consideration required to read, interpret, and actualize such books is magnified when approaching ancient texts such as those found in the Old Testament. These biblical books bridge multiple theological, cultural, and linguistic worlds, which demand multiple levels of understanding and interpretation. Readers must inhabit three worlds (contexts) when reading any of the books of the Old Testament or Apocrypha, from Genesis to 4 Maccabees: (1) the ancient contexts in which they were written, (2) the modern contexts into which the text is being received, and (3) all of those contexts in between wherein interpreters in each generation have shaped the reading of the texts for their own time and place. *The Fortress Commentary on the Bible: The Old Testament and Apocrypha* approaches these ancient texts with due reverence to this complexity. The purpose of this introduction is to explore a few of the many considerations that are required in reading this ancient Near Eastern scriptural library in its ancient and modern contexts.

A Few Considerations on Receiving Ancient Texts with Modern Minds

The word *context*, whether pertaining to events or a book, looks deceptively singular. A student trying to uncover the context of the US civil rights movement will find many contextual viewing points: those of African Americans who rose up against institutionalized oppression, those of segregationists who tried to maintain the status quo, those within the Johnson administration who worked to find a way forward without losing the Democrats' white voters in the South, and the list goes on.

Challenge of Finding an Ancient or Modern Context

The words *ancient context* and *modern context*, when applied to the Old Testament, also need to be considered in the plural. Considering the ancient context, the books of the Old Testament contain the theologies of diverse communities who lived, wrote, argued, and worked to understand their relationship with the divine under a wide variety of circumstances. An attempt to find a single context for the book of Isaiah, for example, is as complex as finding a single sociohistorical setting of the United States, from the colonial period to the present; it cannot be done. The same is true with the modern context. As these religious texts are received in Chicago or Mumbai, on Wall Street or on skid row, they flow into and take on very different meanings and contexts.

Differing Expectations and Intents of Ancient and Modern Histories

Readers in the age of science have certain expectations when reading a history, and these expectations inform how histories—whether written before or after this age—are received. Modern readers want to know, with scientific precision, when, why, and where events happened. Great value is placed on reconstructions of events that are backed up by reliable sources and with as little interpretive bias as possible. A *good* history of the Battle of the Bulge should include not only dates and locations but also eyewitness accounts of allied forces, Wehrmacht and SS divisions, and civilians. Expectations of accuracy and value in objectivity are a service both to the study of the past and to understanding how these events helped to shape the present. However, when dealing with the Old Testament it is easy to project our appreciation for accuracy and disdain for bias onto the ancient texts, which ultimately is not a fair way to approach these ancient texts.

Long before there was even a concept of "Bible," many of the texts of the Old Testament were passed down through oral tradition, only to be written down and finally canonized centuries later; this is evidenced in the repetitive Torah narratives, such as the creation refrain in Gen. 1:1—2:4a and the lyrical hymn of Deborah in Judges 5. To imagine the original texts as printed, bound, copyrighted, and collected works, as we hold them today, is both inaccurate and misleading. Moreover, assuming the intents and expectations of the oral historian to be akin to those of modern historians is misleading, and focusing on accuracy can limit the scope of a passage's message when the intent of the passage rests in the ideas it promotes. Cultures that employ oral tradition do not make dates, places, or accuracy a priority; rather, they are interested in the telling and retelling of a story to develop an understanding or identity that can answer the questions of the times into which they are received. Take the account of King Solomon's wealth in 2 Chron. 9:22-24, for example.

> King Solomon surpassed all the kings of the earth in wealth and wisdom. All the kings of the earth came to pay homage to Solomon and to listen to the wisdom with which God had endowed him. Each brought his tribute—silver and gold objects, robes, weapons, and spices, horses and mules—in the amount due each year (JPS).

Such an account served a purpose to the ancient author and his audience, but the account was certainly not accurate. Putting aside the issue of transoceanic travel for contemporary rulers in the Americas or the South Pacific, Israel held no such wealth in the tenth century BCE, and such superpowers as Egypt and Assyria would never have been compelled to offer tribute. While questions surrounding the reality of Solomon's wealth are not a center of contentious debate in the public sphere, questions pertaining to the creation of the universe are highly controversial; the front lines of this debate can be seen at the doors of the Creation Museum in Petersburg, Kentucky.

Founded by Ken Ham and Answers in Genesis (AiG), a Christian apologetics organization, the Creation Museum is a prime example of how scientific-age expectations are frequently placed on the ancient texts of the Old Testament. With the motto "Prepare to Believe," the museum promotes Gen. 1:1—2:4a as a scientific explanation for the creation of the cosmos, an event that is said to have occurred around 4,000 BCE, as determined through James Ussher's seventeenth-century-CE biblically based calculations. It is important to consider that the questions the Creation Museum seeks to answer do not likely match the agenda of the authors of Gen. 1:1—2:4a, which is connected to the Babylonian myth the *Enuma Elish* and/or the battle between the Canaanite god Baal and Yam, each of which centers on order's conquest of chaos. It also does not take into consideration that those who canonized the Torah followed this story with another creation story (Gen. 2:4b-25), which is juxtaposed with the first, making it unlikely that the ancient intent was to give a *scientific* account of our origins. Furthermore, the authors of the texts believed that the sky was a firmament that held back a great sky-ocean (Gen. 1:6-8), from which precipitation came when its doors were opened, and that the moon was self-illuminating (Gen. 1:14-18). A key danger in treating Old Testament books with modern historical and scientific expectations is not only receiving inaccurate messages about our past but also failing to realize the intent of the authors and the depth of meaning behind the messages they conveyed.

Projecting Modern Contexts onto the Ancient Past

The oft-repeated notion that only the winners write history is not entirely true, for readers rewrite the histories they receive by projecting their own personal and cultural perspectives onto them. The medievalist Norman Cantor stresses how individuals tend to project their own worldviews and experiences onto the past, thereby reinventing the past in their own image (156–58). Whereas Cantor dealt with issues of secular history, biblical history appears to follow suit, as found in such art pieces as Dutch painter Gerard van Honthorst's piece *King David Playing the Harp*. In the painting van Honthorst depicts the king with European-style attire and instrument. In contextually ambiguous passages, such as the land seizures in Mic. 2:1-4, we find scholars filling in the blanks with characters that make more sense in our time than in the ancient past, such as the mafia (Alfaro, 25). It is difficult for a reader not to project his or her own time and culture onto the text, for that is the reader's primary reference point; to escape doing so is likely not possible. But just as complete objectivity is not attainable, an awareness of its hazards can help readers exercise some degree of control regarding how much they project their present onto the past.

Bringing One's Ideology to the Text

Just as readers bring their notions of history to the Old Testament, so also they bring their ideologies. While attempts to view Old Testament texts through the biblical authors' eyes may be made, one's perceptions can never be entirely freed from one's own experiences, which help shape how a particular idea or story is read. This challenge is a double-edged sword. On one side of the sword, the ideology and experiences of the reader may cloud the text's original meaning and intent, causing unintended—and sometimes intentional—misreadings of a passage. When this occurs, the resulting interpretation often tells us more about the social or ideological location of the reader than the biblical characters who are being interpreted. Albert Schweitzer found that nineteenth-century biographies on the life of the "historical Jesus" turned out to be autobiographies of their authors; romantics uncovered an idealist Jesus, political radicals found a revolutionary, and so on (Schweitzer). On the other side of the sword, one finds an advantage shared by oral tradition. Reading a text through one's own experiences can breathe new life into the text and allow it to speak to current circumstances, as found in postcolonial, feminist, and queer interpretations. Since readers cannot fully remove themselves from their own ideological locations, it is important to acknowledge that a reader's ideas and biases are brought to the text and that much is to be learned by considering various interpretations.

Because ideology plays a role in interpretation, it should be noted that history—and biblical histories, in particular—do not exist in the past, but are very much alive and active in the present. YHWH's granting of land to Abraham's dependents, for example, plays a prominent role in the Israel-Palestine conflict. This is addressed by Keith Whitelam and James Crossley, who find the biblical text shaping modern perceptions of land via cartography. A post-1967 war edition of *The Macmillan Bible Atlas* contains a map of Israel with borders that look remarkably similar to the modern-day border with Gaza—despite great uncertainty surrounding ancient Israel's borders—and that is inscribed with Gen. 13:14-15: "The LORD said to Abram . . . 'Lift up your eyes, and look from the place where you are, northward and southward and eastward and westward; for all the land which you see I will give to you and to your descendants forever'" (RSV; see Whitelam 61–62; Crossley 176). Whether one sees this connection in a positive or negative light, clear political implications of the biblical past can be seen.

Differing Views on the Old Testament's History

Another factor to be considered, which is also highly political, is the lack of consensus pertaining to the historicity of biblical narratives and the state of ancient Israel, ranging from the exodus narrative to the Davidic monarchy. The degree to which these events and histories are *real histories* or *cultural memory* has been the subject of much debate and polemic within the academy. Many scholars agree that the story of the Hebrew exodus out of Egypt is cultural memory, with varying degrees of historical truth, ranging from seeing the Hebrews as an invading force to an indigenous movement within Canaan that rose up against exploitative rulers. But one of the most heated debates in the history of ancient Israel has revolved around the dating of the monarchy and the rise of Judah as a powerful state.

The traditional view, often referred to as the *maximalist* perspective, gives greater credence to the Bible's account of the monarchy's history. Scholars of this persuasion accept, to varying degrees, the Old Testament's stories of the rise of Israel beginning with King Saul and continuing on through the destruction of Israel and Judah. So-called *minimalists* give less credence to biblical accounts, relying more on archaeological and extrabiblical sources to develop their views of the monarchy and the presence of a powerful state, for which they find little evidence. While largely unnoticed outside the academy, the debate has caused great animosity within. Maximalist scholars have been accused of burdening archaeology with the task of upholding the biblical narratives (Davies), while minimalists have been accused of attempting to erase ancient Israel from world history (Halpern).

The purpose of addressing the maximalist/minimalist debate in this introduction is to emphasize that biblical scholarship contains diverse voices and points of view on the Bible's history, which will be seen in the commentaries of this volume. It is good that these different perspectives are aired. When approaching an area of history that is of such great importance to so many, yet with so little definitive information available, it is important to articulate and compare different ideas so as to produce and refine the historical possibilities of the Bible's contexts. In this way we see how differing views of biblical interpretation can work as a dance, where partners can complement each other's work, even if tempers can flare sometimes when partners step on one another's toes.

Reading the Old Testament in Its Ancient Context

It is apparent that contemplating the ancient contexts of the Old Testament requires several areas of consideration. While there is no end to the complexities involved with pursuing a greater understating of the world(s) out of which the books of the Old Testament developed, this section is intended to draw the reader's attention to some of the Old Testament's physical environments, political climates, and theological diversity.

Physical Environments of the Old Testament

The geography and ecology of ancient Palestine can easily be overlooked, but their value for understanding the Old Testament should not be underestimated. While the Old Testament represents diverse social settings that span hundreds of years, all of its authors lived in agrarian societies where land, climate, economics, and religion are inseparable. Due to agrarian societies' dire need to ensure successful and regular harvests—whether for survival or with the additional aspiration of building empire—farming practices become incorporated into religious rituals that end up dictating planting, harvesting, and land management. This strong connection between faith and farming led to rituals that served as an interface between spirituality and socioeconomic activities, effectively erasing the lines between religious and economic practice (Coomber 2013). In the end, the ritualization of agrarian economics helps shape perceptions of the deity or deities to which the rituals are connected: the Feast of Unleavened Bread (Exod. 23:14-17), the barley harvest festival incorporated in the Passover feast (Exodus 12; cf. John 19:29, the wheat-harvest Feast of Weeks, also known as Pentecost (Lev. 23:15-21; cf. Acts 2:1), and the fruit-harvest Feast of Booths (Lev. 23:33-36). Thus geography and ecology affected not only the way ancient Hebrews farmed but also how they came to understand God. Moreover, the geographical regions in which many of them farmed influenced these understandings.

Regions of Ancient Israel

Ancient Israel can be divided into a number of geographical areas, each of which presents its own unique environment. Furthest to the west is the *coastal plain*, which held great economic importance in the way of trade. This is especially visible in the development of manufacturing and shipping cities such as Ekron and Ashkelon. Due to the region's trade potential, it was usually controlled by foreign powers and is not frequently mentioned in the Old Testament (e.g., Judges 16; 2 Kings 16; Jer. 25:20; Amos 1:8; Zeph. 2:4).

The lowland *Shephelah* and the *highlands* are just east of the coastal plain, forming an important region of Israel, which is at the center of most of the Old Testament's stories. This fertile land, composed of low hills and valleys, is good for animal husbandry and the cultivation of grains, cereals, nuts, olives, and grapes. These areas were valuable for both subsistence farming and the production of trade goods, in which surrounding empires could engage. The agrarian potential of this area also made Shephelah and the highlands a target for foreign invasion. This region's political influence was heightened by the cities of Jerusalem, Samaria, and Lachish.

The *Jordan Valley*, east of the highlands, contains the lowest natural surface in the world and is part of a fault that extends into Africa. The valley follows the Jordan River from the city of Dan through the city of Hazor and the Sea of Galilee before flowing into the Dead Sea. Aside from the important role that the Jordan Valley plays in Ezekiel's vision of water flowing out of the temple to bring life to the Dead Sea (Ezekiel 47), the region is rarely mentioned.

To the east of the Jordan Valley is the *Transjordan highlands*, which is often referred to as "beyond the Jordan" (e.g., Josh. 12:1). Extending from the Dead Sea's altitude of 650-feet below sea level to the 9,230-foot peak of Mt. Hermon, this region contains a diverse range of topography and climates that allow for the cultivation of diverse agricultural goods, including grains, fruits, timber, and livestock. The agrarian potential of the area attracted a number of peoples, including the Moabites, the Ammonites, and the Edomites.

Whether valued for their sustaining, trade, or defensive capabilities, the topography of ancient Israel and its surrounding lands influenced its inhabitants' ability or inability to find sustenance and pursue their own interests. When empires such as Assyria and Babylon were on the rise, this region attracted their rulers who sought the earning potential of the land, and these events—or the cultural memories they inspired—influenced the Old Testament authors' stories of defeat and are reflected in their perceptions of God's attitudes toward them.

Climatic Challenges

While the land in and around Israel was some of the most sought after in the ancient Near East, its inhabitants endured serious meteorological challenges. The ancient Israelites lived at the crossroads of subtropical and temperate atmospheric patterns—producing rainy winter seasons and dry summers—and the effects of these patterns shaped the ways in which the Hebrews lived: the resulting erratic precipitation patterns result in a 30 percent chance of insufficient rainfall (Karmon, 27). The unpredictability of each growing season's weather pattern meant that the rainfall of a given season could play out in any number of ways, each demanding specific farming strategies for which farmers had little foresight or room for error. Subsequent failed seasons that diminished surpluses could lead to debt and the selling of family members into slavery or even the extinction of a family line.

Everything in society—from the interests of the poorest farmer to the king—depended on successful harvests and access to their crops, and the strong desire for divine assistance is reflected in Old Testament narratives that emphasize fidelity to YHWH. The seriousness placed on securing favorable rainfall and accessing harvests is clear in warnings against following other deities, such as the weather god Baal (e.g., Judg. 2:11; 2 Kings 3:2; Ps. 106:28; Hosea 9:10), God-given visions that foretell rainfall (Genesis 41), and the granting and withholding of rain as reward or punishment (Deut. 11:11-14; cf. 1 Kings 17–18). Additionally, there are strict rules to protect land access (Leviticus 25) and condemnation against abuses (1 Kings 21; Isa. 5:8-10; Mic. 2:1-4).

The physical environments of the Old Testament authors are an important consideration, because they not only affected the way the authors lived but also helped to shape their views of God and the world around them. From the development of the ancient Hebrews' religious rituals to finding either God's favor or wrath in agrarian events (see Zech. 10:1; 1 Kings 17–18), the topography and climatic environments that affected cultivation played key roles in how the biblical authors perceived and interacted with the divine.

Sociopolitical Contexts of the Old Testament

In addition to the challenges presented by Israel's geographic and climatic setting, its strategic location between the empires of Mesopotamia and northern Africa presented a recurring threat. As these empires invaded the lands of ancient Israel for military and economic reasons, the biblical authors and redactors received and transmitted these events into their religious narratives: foreign invasion was often perceived as divine punishment—with the notable exception of the Persians—and the defeat of foreign forces was perceived as a result of divine favor. Before addressing foreign influences on the Old Testament's ancient contexts, a brief overview of Israel's domestic structures should be considered.

Israel's Domestic Sociopolitical Contexts

While ancient Palestine's Mesopotamian neighbors developed cities and urban economies in the Early Bronze Age (3300–2100 BCE), Palestine largely remained a patchwork of scattered settlements that functioned as a peripheral economy, engaging in trade activity as neighboring empires made it lucrative, and receding into highland agriculture when those powers waned (Coomber 2010, 81–92). Adapting to the demands of waxing and waning empires—rather than taking significant steps toward powerful urban economies of its own—resulted in a marked reliance on subsistence strategies on into the seventh century BCE (Coote and Whitelam).

Biblical accounts of Hebrew societal structures present a patronage system that had its roots in small family units called the *bet av* ("father's house"), which together formed a *mishpahah* ("family" or "clan"), which expanded up to the tribe, or *shevet*. When the monarchy was established, the *malkut* ("kingdom") became the top rung. While the *malkut* and *shevet* held the top two tiers, the phrase "all politics is local" applies to ancient Israel: loyalty structures were strongest at the bottom.

Philip Davies and John Rogerson note that the *bet av*, "father's house," likely had a double meaning (32). While it indicated a family unit that included extended lineage and slaves—excluding daughters who left the family at marriage—it likely also denoted the descendants of a common ancestor, who may not have lived under a single roof (e.g., Gen. 24:38). While the *bet avim* grew through the births of sons and the accumulation of wives and slaves, the danger of collapse due to disease, war, and a lack of birth of sons presented a constant threat. Debt was also a threat to a *bet av*, inspiring legal texts that protected its access to arable land (Leviticus 25; Deut. 25:5). It was the patriarch's responsibility to care for the family's economic well-being, as well as to pass on traditions, the history of the nation, and the laws of God (Deut. 6:7; 11:8-9; 32:46-47). The *bet av* also had power over such judicial matters as those of marriage and slave ownership.

Mishpahah denotes a level of organization based on a recognizable kinship (Numbers 1; 26). It had territorial significance, as seen in tribal border lists of Joshua 13–19, and was responsible for dividing the land. While *mishpahah* is difficult to translate, Norman Gottwald offers the useful definition, "protective association of extended families" (Gottwald 1999, 257). If the immediate or extended families of a citizen who had to sell himself to an alien could not redeem him, the *mishpahah* became the last line of protection from perpetual servitude (Lev. 25:48-49).

Shevet refers to the largest group and unit of territorial organization, which was primarily bound together by residence. Military allegiances appear to have belonged to this level, against both foreign and domestic threats—as seen in the Benjamite battles of Judges 12 and 20–21. Gottwald sees the *shevet* as more of a geographic designation pertaining to clusters of villages and/or clans that gathered for protective purposes rather than as representative bodies within a political system (Gottwald 2001, 35).

The *malkut*, or kingdom, is a source of continued contention in the so-called minimalist/maximalist debate mentioned above. The Old Testament account claims that the kingdom of Israel was founded when Saul became king over the Israelite tribes (1 Samuel 9) and continued through the line of David, after Saul fell out of favor with God. Israel's united monarchy is reported to have spanned 1030 to 930 BCE, when King Rehoboam was rejected by the northern Israelites (1 Kgs. 12:1-20; 2 Chron. 10:1-19), leading to the period of the divided monarchy, with Israel in the north and Judah in the south. These two kingdoms existed side by side until Israel was destroyed by Assyria (734–721 BCE). Judah entered into Assyrian vassalage in the 720s and was destroyed by the Babylonians around 586 BCE. Those who give less credence to the biblical account take note that there is little extrabiblical evidence of a monarchy prior to King Omri, aside from the Tel Dan Stele, which refers to "the House of David," which may refer to a king.

While Israel's domestic organizational landscape played a major role in the development of biblical law and narrative, the biblical authors' interactions with surrounding peoples had profound effects on the stories they told. The main imperial influences, from the premonarchical period to the fall of the Hasmonean Dynasty, were Egypt, Philistine, Assyria, Babylon, Persia, the Greeks, and the Romans.

Israel's Foreign Sociopolitical Contexts

The Egyptian Empire played an important role in the development of the Torah, as seen in the stories of Abram and Sarai (Genesis 12), Joseph (Genesis 37–50), and throughout the entire exodus narrative, interwoven into many areas of the Old Testament. The authors of Exodus used the backdrop of Egypt's powerful *New Kingdom* (1549–1069 BCE) to display their faith in YHWH's power, and other books draw on this narrative as a recurring reminder of the Israelites' debt and obligations toward their god (e.g. Deut. 5:15, 24:17-22, 23:7-8; Ps. 106:21; Ezekiel 20; Amos 2:10; Mic. 6:4), and as a vehicle of praise (Psalms 78; 81; 135; 136). The Jewish holiday of Passover, which is referred to throughout the Old Testament, has its roots in this anti-Egyptian epic. A later and weaker Egypt returns to play a role in the story of Judah's lengthy downfall: King Hezekiah (d. 680s) enters into a failed anti-Assyrian alliance with Egypt (Isaiah 30–31; 36:6-9), and King Zedekiah (d. 580s) enters into a failed anti-Babylonian alliance with Pharaoh Hophra (Ezek. 17:15; Jer. 2:36).

While their point of origins are in dispute (Amos 9:7 puts their origin at Caphtor), the Philistines tried to invade Egypt in 1190 BCE, but were repelled by Ramses III, who settled them in the coastal towns of Gaza, Ashkelon, and Ashdod (Deut. 2:23). From there, they continued their incursions along the coastal plain and perhaps even drove out their Egyptian rulers, under the reign of Ramses IV (d. 1149 BCE). They play a key adversarial role in the book of Judges, as found in the stories of Shamgar (Judg. 3:31) and Samson (Judges 13–16). Their military competencies are reflected in the story of their capture of the ark of the covenant in 1 Sam. 4:1—7:2. Fear of the Philistine threat helped influence the people's decision to choose a king to unite the tribes (1 Sam. 8–9). The biblical authors continued to portray the Philistines as a threat to the Israelites, but Philistine influence in the highlands faded as the power of Assyria grew.

Assyria's fearsome power and influence in the region gave them a villain's role in the Old Testament. The biblical authors perceived Assyria's incursions into Israel and Judah as YHWH's punishment for such transgressions as idolatry and social injustice. While archaeological evidence of Philistine-Israelite interaction is scant, there is plenty of archaeological and extrabiblical evidence of Assyria's impact on Israel and Judah.

From the start of its ninth-century conquests, Assyria was feared for its ruthless force. The psychological impact of Assyria's powerful conscripted forces, iron chariots, siege engines, and public mutilations surface in the writings of the Old Testament authors. The Assyrians enforced submission through power and fear, deporting conquered rulers to prevent uprisings (2 Kings 17:6, 24, 28; 18:11). When uprisings occurred, Assyrian troops were deployed from strategically positioned garrisons to flay, impale, and burn the perpetrators, as portrayed in Assyrian palace-reliefs.

In the late eighth century, both Israel and Judah felt the full weight of Assyria's might. The northern kingdom of Israel was destroyed in 721 BCE after joining an alliance of vassals that stopped paying tribute to Assyria. At the end of the century, King Hezekiah entered Judah into a similar alliance with Egypt (Isaiah 30–31), which resulted in the invasion of his kingdom and the siege of Jerusalem. According to 2 Kgs. 18:13-16, the siege was broken when Hezekiah sent a message of repentance to the Assyrian king, Sennacherib, at Lachish, promising to resume his tribute obligations. Other texts in 2 Kings suggest that Sennacherib abandoned the siege to deal with political unrest at home (19:7, 37) or a plague (19:35-36). Despite his efforts to subvert Sennacherib's dominance of Judah, Hezekiah and his successors continued to rule as vassals.

Under the rule of King Nebuchadnezzar, the Babylonian Empire captured Nineveh in 612, destroyed the Egyptians at the battle of Carchemish in 605, and captured Jerusalem in 597, deporting many inhabitants. After a rebellion by King Zedekiah in 586, the Babylonians destroyed Jerusalem and the temple and deported a significant portion of Judah's population (2 Kings 24; 2 Chronicles 36). The prophets Ezekiel, Jeremiah, and Habakkuk saw Nebuchadnezzar's conquest as YHWH's punishment for the sins of the Judean state (Ezekiel 8–11; Jer. 25:1-14; Hab. 1:6-10). The events of the Babylonian conquest are largely supported by archaeology and extrabiblical literature (Grabbe, 210–13).

Biblical claims of the removal of all Judeans but the poorest "people of the land" (2 Kgs. 24:14-16; 25:12; Jer. 52:16, 28-30) are reflected in the archaeological record, which indicates that inhabited sites decreased by two-thirds, from 116 to 41, and surviving sites shrank from 4.4 to 1.4 hectares, suggesting a population collapse of 85 to 90 percent (Liverani, 195). Such a massive exile plays a formidable role in the Old Testament, as described in the stories of significant characters such as Ezekiel and Daniel. Rage associated with this event is found in Psalm 137, which recounts the horrors of the exile and ends with the chilling words "a blessing on him who seizes your [Babylonian] babies and dashes them against the rocks!" (137:9 JPS). The exiled Hebrews who returned to Palestine after the Persians conquered the Babylonians returned to a destroyed Jerusalem that no longer enjoyed the security of a defensive wall. Some of the returnees helped to reshape Judaism with a flourishing priesthood and the composition of scholarly works and biblical texts. While exile is portrayed in negative terms, many Jews remained in the lands to which they had been deported; this had the effect of spreading Judaism outside the confines of Palestine.

After overthrowing his grandfather King Astyages of the Medes in 553 BCE, Cyrus of Persia (d. 530) rapidly expanded his empire, moving westward into Armenia and Asia Minor and east toward India, and defeated Babylon in 539. But unlike previous conquests, the Old Testament treats Persian dominance as a time of hope. As successor to the Babylonian Empire, King Cyrus instituted a policy of allowing victims of Babylonian exile to return to their homelands, where he sponsored their local religions. To the biblical authors, this policy was met with celebration and as a sign of YHWH's love for his people. The authors of 2 Chron. 36:23 and Ezra 1:2 portray King Cyrus as crediting YHWH with his victories and with the mandate to rebuild the temple in Jerusalem; Ezra 1:7 even portrays the Persian king personally returning the vessels that Nebuchadnezzar had seized from the temple four decades before. While the Bible treats Cyrus's policy of return as inspired by YHWH, Davies and Rogerson note that the practice was neither new nor disinterested, as it served to restore the national culture of a large and culturally varied empire (59). It is important to note the great shift in how the biblical authors treated King Cyrus of Persia, as opposed to the kings of the Assyrians and Babylonians, whom they disdained. In Isaiah 40–50, Cyrus is championed as the great savior of the Judean deportees and of the rebuilding of Jerusalem. In fact, while oracles against foreign nations are a key theme in prophetic oracles, none are directed against Persia. Even when their rulers are compliant with the murder of Jews, they are portrayed as either acting against their own desires or out of ignorance (Daniel 6; Esther).

Like the exile, itself, the return from exile plays an important role in the politics and religion of the Old Testament. Accounts of these events are found in the books of Ezra and Nehemiah. While the Bible presents the return as a blessing from God and a time of joy, it does not seem to have been without its hardships. It can be deduced from Ezra and Nehemiah that resettlement involved various tensions; in Ezra 3:3, those who had remained in Judah during the exile, along with other neighboring peoples, take the Canaanites' role in the book of Joshua: "an evil influence which will, unless strenuously rejected, corrupt the 'people of God'" (Davies and Rogerson, 88). It was during the Persian period that the Jerusalem temple was rebuilt and the priesthood gained power and influence.

The long march of succeeding empires continued with the rise of Alexander the Great, who seized control of the Greek city-states in 336 BCE and conquered the Persian Empire before his death in 323. Unlike previous empires that might make their subjects worship a particular deity or relocate to a different region, the Greek ideal of *Hellenism* posed a particular cultural threat. Hellenism promoted a view in which people were not citizens of a particular region, but of the world, enabling the integration of Greek and regional cultures, thus breaking down barriers that separated local peoples from their foreign rulers. Within a hundred years, Koine Greek had become the lingua franca, and Greek philosophy, educational systems, art and attire, politics, and religion permeated the empire. The consequences of Hellenization had profound linguistic, political, and theological effects on the biblical authors who lived and wrote during this period. Jews who lived outside of Israel became more familiar with the Greek language than Hebrew. By the second century CE, Greek had become so widely spoken among the Jewish community in Alexandria, Egypt, that the Hebrew Bible was translated into Koine Greek, which came to be called the Septuagint.

Greek rule eventually led to the severe oppression of the Jewish people at the hands of the usurper king Antiochus IV (d. 164 BCE), who sought to weed out cultural diversity in the Seleucid Empire. King Antiochus, who called himself *Epiphanes* ("god made manifest"), was known for his erratic character, which manifested itself in his brutal hatred of the Jews. Even his allies referred to him by the nickname *Epimanes*—a play on Epiphanes—meaning "the crazy one." He is known for looting the Jerusalem temple to fund his battles against the Ptolemies and for forbidding the Jewish rite of circumcision and sacred dietary laws.

King Antiochus was also known for instigating treachery among the Jewish leadership, giving Jason—of the pro-Greek Onias family—the high priesthood in return for complying with Antiochus's plans to Hellenize Jerusalem by building a gymnasium and enrolling its people as citizens of Antioch (2 Macc. 4:7). Further strife erupted when Menelaus, another aspirant for the high priesthood, offered Antiochus even greater gifts for the office. The rivalry of Jason and Menelaus led to the sacking of Jerusalem, slaughtering of its citizens, and the looting of its temple (2 Macc. 5:11-23; Josephus 12.5.3 §§246–47). The horrors of life under King Antiochus IV are reflected in the horn that emerges from the fourth beast in the apocalyptic vision of Dan. 7:7-8, and is then slain by the "Ancient One" (7:11).

From stripping the temple to pay for his wars to setting up an altar for Zeus in the temple, King Antiochus IV's brutality against the Jews led to a revolt that started in the Judean village of Modein in 167 BCE and spread rapidly throughout the region—as chronicled in 1 and 2 Maccabees and in Josephus's *Antiquities of the Jews* (c. 100 CE). A guerrilla warfare campaign that was led by Judas Maccabeus eventually liberated and purified the temple—an event celebrated today in the Jewish festival of Hanukkah. The Maccabean revolt drove out the Greeks and expanded the borders to include Galilee. While the revolt was successful in ushering in a period of self-rule, the resulting Hasmonean Dynasty fell prey to the lust for power. As civil conflict broke out between two rival claims to the throne, the Roman general Pompey invaded Judea in 63 BCE, seizing control of the region for his empire. In 40 BCE, the Roman Senate appointed an Edomite convert to Judaism, *Herod the Great*, as king of Judea. Despised by his people, the puppet king had to take Jerusalem by force, from where he ruled harshly.

Each of these empires, vying for control over the Southern Levant, brought with them challenges that helped to shape the Hebrew people by influencing the ways they viewed themselves, their God, and their religious practices.

Religious Contexts of the Old Testament

Despite common perceptions of the Bible as a univocal work, the Old Testament represents diverse theologies of communities that spanned centuries and were influenced by the religious systems of their contemporaries. Babylonian and Canaanite musings over the power of order over chaos, as found in the *Enuma Elish* and Baal narratives, are present in Gen. 1:1—2:4a and referenced in Ps. 74:12-17. The authors of the Bible's Wisdom literature exchanged ideas with their foreign neighbors, as found in parallels between the Babylonian story I Will Praise the Lord of Wisdom and the book of Job, and passages from Proverbs that mirror the words of the Egyptian thinkers Ptah-Hotep and Amen-em-opet (e.g., Prov. 22:4; 22:17—24:22). Understanding the diversity of theological perspectives in the Old Testament can aid both exegesis and hermeneutics by giving the reader greater insight into the biblical authors' ideas of God and uncovering layers of meaning that might otherwise go unnoticed.

Monotheism and Henotheism

It should not be assumed that all Old Testament authors were monotheists: many were *henotheists*. Henotheism promotes a multi-god/dess universe in which the adherent gives allegiance to a supreme primary deity. Elements of this outlook appear to be found in God's decision to create humanity "in our image, after our likeness" (Gen. 1:26 RSV), and in YHWH's anxiety over the man that he created becoming "like one of us" in Gen. 3:22. YHWH also expresses his disgust in that the *sons of God* mated with human women, resulting in the birth of the nephilim (Gen. 6:2-4). In the *Song of Moses*, Moses poses the rhetorical question, "who is like you, O LORD, among the gods?" (Exod. 15:11). The writer of Ps. 95:3 proclaims, "YHWH is a great God, the king of all divine beings," while 97:9 asserts that YHWH is "exalted high above all divine beings." These examples pose a number of questions about the biblical authors' views on the divine. Two that will be briefly addressed here concern the identity of God and the role of the other deities being inferred. The supreme deity of the ancient Hebrews is given several names and titles, representing different personality traits and theological views.

Elohim

The name or title *Elohim*, which is usually translated from the Hebrew into English as "God," makes its first appearance in Genesis 1. The name Elohim is used to identify the Hebrews' supreme deity in several Old Testament texts, including those found in the books of Genesis, Exodus, Psalms, and Job. As in the Bible's priestly creation story (Gen. 1:1—2:4a), Elohim is portrayed as an all-powerful, confident, commanding, and somewhat distant deity, whose supremacy and majesty are emphasized.

YHWH

YHWH is an anthropomorphic god who exhibits tendencies toward both kindness and severity and is self-described as a jealous god who, unlike other ancient Near Eastern gods, demands the exclusive allegiance of his followers. The name YHWH, which is often translated into English as "the LORD"—from the Hebrew *adonay*—makes its first appearance in the second creation story (Gen. 2:4b). The name YHWH carries a sense of mystery. Derived from the Hebrew verb *hawah*, meaning "to be," YHWH is difficult to translate, but means something like "he who is" or "he who causes what is." Some believe that YHWH's origins can be traced to the god YHW, who was worshiped in the northwestern region of the Arabian Peninsula known as Midian: this is where Moses first encounters YHWH (Exodus 3).

YHWH has strong associations with Canaanite culture, which highlights discrepancies between biblical directions for the deity's worship and how the deity was worshiped in popular religion. Whereas the biblical authors convey strict messages that YHWH should be worshiped alone, the remains of Israelite homes reveal that other gods and goddesses, such as Asherah—whom the author(s) of Jeremiah refers to as *the queen of heaven*—were worshiped alongside YHWH (Dever, 176–89). Jeremiah 44 appears to give a glimpse into the popular polytheistic or henotheistic religion of sixth-century-BCE Judah. After YHWH threatens the people for worshiping other gods, the women say that they will not listen but will continue the traditions of their ancestors and give offerings to the queen of heaven, who protected them well (Jer. 44:16-17). Further biblical evidence of Asherah's popularity is found in the biblical authors' continual condemnation of her worship, often symbolized through the presence of pillars and poles, as they worked to direct the people toward monotheism (Deut. 7:5; Judg. 3:7-8; 1 Kgs. 14:15, 23; Jer. 17:17-18).

El

The name or title *El* appears around two hundred times in the Old Testament, with frequent use in the ancestor stories of Genesis and surfacing throughout the Old Testament. Its presence poses some interesting questions.

On one level, El is a common Semitic title for "divine being," and can be read as an appellative for "divinity," often compounded with other words such as *el-shadday* ("God Almighty" [Gen. 17:1; Exod. 6:3; Ezek. 10:5]) and *el-elyon* ("God Most High" [Gen. 14:22; Deut. 32:8-9; Ps. 78:35]). In addition to a title referring to God, El is also the name of the chief god of the Canaanite pantheon. Often portrayed as a bearded king on his throne, and referred to as the "Ancient One," El was worshiped in Canaan and Syria both before and after the emergence of Israel. The frequent use of El for God—and the Canaanite god's prominence in Israel—has led many to conclude that El developed into YHWH. Mark Smith asserts, "The original god of Israel was El. . . . Isra*el* is not a Yahwistic name with the divine element of Yahweh, but an El name" (Smith, 32; emphasis on *el* in "Israel" is mine). A cross-pollination of Canaanite and Hebrew religion is found in the use of Canaanite El imagery to describe the "Ancient One" in Dan. 7:9-10 who sits on a throne with white garments and hair as pure as wool. Furthermore, the description of "one like a human being coming with the clouds of heaven," who "came to the Ancient One and was presented before him" (Dan. 7:13), dovetails with images of the Canaanite god Baal coming before El. Whether or not the authors of Daniel 7 envisioned El, the imprint of Canaanite religion appears to have been stamped on ideas of God and passed down through the generations. While not accepted by biblical authors, popular religion in ancient Israel appears to have had a complex network of deities that fulfilled various roles in daily life. (For a helpful overview on differences between "popular" and "official" religion in ancient Israel, see Stavrakopoulou.)

The idea that El was absorbed into YHWH is also supported by the fact that the chief god of the Canaanite pantheon is never condemned in the Old Testament, but his son Baal, consort Asherah, and other gods face vicious condemnation (Num. 25:2; Deut. 4:3; Judg. 6:30; 1 Kgs. 16:31—18:40). Why would the biblical authors attack lesser Canaanite deities but leave the head god unscathed? One possible answer is that El had become synonymous with YHWH; both share a compassionate disposition toward humanity (Exod. 34:6; Ps. 86:15), use dreams to communicate (Gen. 31:24; 37:5; 1 Kgs. 3:5-15), and have healing powers (cf. *KTU* 1.16.v–vi with Gen. 20:17; Num. 12:13; Ps. 107:20 [Smith, 39]).

The Divine Council

As El served as chief of the Canaanite pantheon, YHWH was head of the *divine council*, whose members were often referred to as "the sons of gods." In Gen. 28:12; 33:1-2; Pss. 29:1 and 89:6-9, we find YHWH at the head of subordinate divine beings who are collectively referred to as the "council of Lord" (Jer. 23:18 and the "congregation of El" (Ps. 82:1). In Psalm 82, God attacks the congregants for their oppressive acts against humanity, for which they are doomed to die like mortals (vv. 5-7). In Job 1:6-7, Job's troubles begin when the divine council convenes with YHWH, and God asks "the satan" where he has been. The satan also appears on the divine council in Zechariah, where YHWH delivers judgment between two members of his entourage. The clearest depiction of the divine council's function is in 1 Kgs. 22:19-22, where YHWH seeks guidance and direction from the council, the members of which confer in open discussion before one spirit approaches YHWH with a proposal. Following a common motif in ancient Mediterranean literature, humans are sometimes transported before God and the divine council, as found in a party feasting with Elohim in Exod. 24:9-11 and Isaiah's commission as prophet in Isaiah 6 (Niditch 2010, 14–17).

Concluding Words on the Complexities of the Ancient Context

Reading the Old Testament in its ancient contexts requires a variety of considerations and an understanding that there are divergent views on these contexts. But this complexity should not discourage readers of the Bible from contemplating the origins of the Old Testament books, because a better understanding of their origins results in a broader understanding of their meanings and potential applications to our modern contexts. The authors of this volume's commentaries have worked to give the reader the best possible overview of the sociohistorical contexts that underlie the books of the Old Testament, opening its texts in new ways so that new meanings can be derived. While this section has highlighted some of the many considerations that need to be addressed when reading the "Very Dangerous Texts Ahead," the variety of contexts out of which the Old

Testament's books emerged is paralleled by the diversity of cultures, faiths, and societies into which they have been received.

Reading the Old Testament in Its Contemporary Contexts

Actively engaging the Old Testament in both its ancient and modern contexts enables readers to discover new levels of meaning that would otherwise go unnoticed. Through acknowledging an Old Testament text's historical setting, exploring how it has been interpreted through the millennia, and noticing the questions and challenges that it raises for our contemporary settings, engaged readers are better able to receive multiple levels of meaning that aid the reader in better understanding the biblical authors' intentions and discerning the passage's potential relevance to conversations that are unfolding today.

The Challenge of Bringing Ancient Context in Line with Modern Contexts

To participate in this process, however, is not a simple task. Beyond working to discern the various levels of meaning within the Old Testament, it is of paramount importance for readers to also acknowledge the preconceptions and biases they bring with them as they work to connect the ancient writings to their own world—an issue that is explored at length below.

As humorously demonstrated in A. J. Jacobs's book *The Year of Living Biblically*, it is important to remember that the texts of the Old Testament were not written for twenty-first-century audiences, but for citizens of the ancient world. As he recounts in his book, Jacobs tried to live as literally as possible according to the laws of the Hebrew Bible for one year. His experiment revealed that to live by the rules of the Hebrew Bible is to live as an outlaw in much of the modern world, whether because the Hebrew Bible calls for the execution of people who wear mixed fibers or because it mandates sacrificing animals in urban centers. This clash of ancient and modern cultures occurred in a very serious way in the tragic murder of Murray Seidman. Mr. Seidman's killer referenced Lev. 20:13 as his motivation for stoning the elderly and mentally disabled man (Masterson).

Conversely, some people, like Charlie Fuqua, assert that engaging with the Old Testament's historical contexts is not required. During the 2012 United States election, Fuqua ran for a seat on the Arkansas state legislature and released a book titled *God's Law: The Only Political Solution*. In his book, Fuqua calls for the creation of legal channels that will facilitate the execution of disobedient children, as commanded in Deut. 21:18-21 (2012, 179). While Fuqua's views represent a fringe group of theomonists that include such Christian reconstructionists as Cornelius Van Til and Rousas John Rushdoony, his example illustrates the importance of contemplating the important differences that exist between the biblical authors' societies and those into which their writings are received today. One must ask questions such as, Did the authors of Deut. 21:18-21 actually seek the execution of disobedient children, or did they pose an extreme example to illustrate a point on child rearing? Another important question to consider is, Did Deut. 21:18-21 originate at a time when resources were so scarce and the production of food so difficult that a child who didn't contribute to—but rather threatened——the common good posed a threat to the community's survival? Growing and cultivating food could certainly be a matter of life and death. Fuqua's failure to engage Deut. 21:18-21, choosing instead to blindly subscribe to the text at face value, is a very serious and dangerous matter, especially considering his aspirations for political office. But while vast differences separate the cultures and societies of the Old Testament authors and the world that we inhabit today, a surprising number of connections do exist.

Whether a Judean farmer or an American physician, we all share such aspects of the universal human experience as love, hate, trust, betrayal, fear, and hope—all of which are reflected both in the Old Testament and in our daily lives. Such themes as women working to find justice in societies that offer little, the quest for love along with its dangers and rewards, and people's struggle to understand their relationships with power, whether personal or political, are all found in the stories of the Old Testament and are still highly relevant to us today.

It should be pointed out, however, that earnestly engaging the Old Testament in its ancient and modern contexts is difficult, even hazardous. Several key considerations that help in an engaged reading of the books of the Old Testament are included here, including issues of biblical ownership, methods of interpretation, and approaches to the reception of its texts.

Whose Bible Is It, Anyway?

While the texts of the Old Testament are commonly used with an air of authority and ownership, their ownership is open to question. So, to whom do they belong? Now that their authors are long dead—and their works have passed through generations and around the world—who is the heir of these works? To which community would they turn and say, "The keys are yours"? One problem with answering this question is that the Old Testament's authors and editors did not represent a unified tradition through which a unified voice could be offered. Furthermore, the faiths and cultures of the twenty-first century CE are so far removed from the ancient authors' that they would most likely be utterly unrecognizable to them. On one level, it is a moot question. Those authors are dead, and they do not get a say regarding who uses their works, or how. Be that as it may, it is an important question to consider, for recognizing that the Old Testament has a number of spiritual heirs with divergent views of the divine underscores the vast interpretive possibilities these texts contain. While many faith traditions draw on the books of the Old Testament, the three largest—in order of appearance—are Judaism, Christianity, and Islam.

The Hebrew Bible (the *Tanakh*) of Judaism is composed of twenty-four books, which are divided into the Torah (Law), the Nebiim (Prophets), and the Ketubim (Writings). The Torah gives accounts of the creation, the establishment of the Hebrew people, and their movement out of captivity in Egypt toward the land that was promised to their ancestors. The public reading of the Torah is a religious ritual that culminates with the annual holiday of *Simchat Torah*, which celebrates its completion. Although the Tanakh forms the whole of Jewish biblical literature, it is supplemented by other interpretive collections.

The Christian *Old Testament*, sometimes referred to as the *First Testament*, sets the books of the Tanakh in a different order and serves as the first section of the *Christian Bible*, as a whole. Canonization of the Old Testament varies among different Christian traditions. Roman Catholicism,

Eastern Orthodoxy, and some Protestant groups include the seven additional books in their canon, as well as additions to the books of Esther and Daniel; these additions are called the *deuterocanon* ("second canon") or *Apocrypha* ("hidden"). Many of the books of the Old Testament are popularly seen as a precursor to the coming of Jesus and his perceived fulfillment of the law.

Islam incorporates many of the figures of the Old Testament into its sacred writings, the Holy Qur'an. Giving particular reverence to the Torah and the Psalms, the Qur'an honors Abraham, Isaac, and Moses as prophetic predecessors to the faith's final and greatest prophet, Muhammad (d. 632 CE).

While each of these traditions draws deep meaning and conviction from the Hebrew Scriptures, they also use them in different ways to reflect their own unique spiritual paths and theologies. The question of which group is the rightful heir of the biblical authors is impossible to answer definitively, since each claims to be in fact the rightful heir. The fact that such a diverse pool of people turns to these texts as sacred Scripture amplifies the many possibilities for Old Testament interpretation.

Evolving Views of the Old Testament and Its Interpretation

Whether or not it is done consciously, all readers of the Old Testament are engaged in some level of interpretation; there are no passive readers of the Bible. When people read the books of the Old Testament, they do so actively, bringing their own presuppositions, experiences, and cultural norms to a text. In essence, readers of the Old Testament bridge the ancient to the modern by way of exegesis and hermeneutics.

Exegesis looks at the texts in their ancient contexts, while hermeneutics works to discern how they relate to a modern reader's situation. Biblical scholars and readers have developed a number of methods for bringing the ancient and the modern together, often with specific objectives and theological motives in mind.

Biblical Literalism

Biblical literalism—which asserts that the Bible is the inerrant word of God, unaltered and untainted by human agency during its transmission from God to humanity—is a prevalent form of interpretation in the United States, practiced commonly within fundamentalist and some evangelical communities. The literal meanings of individual biblical texts were long considered alongside allegorical, moral, and mystical interpretations; it was not until the Reformation's second wave, in the seventeenth century, that literalism became a way to approach the Bible as a whole.

Protestant Christians who broke from the authority of Roman Catholicism found a strong sense of liberation in the idea of gaining access to God's direct word through the Scriptures. If an adherent could access God directly through a Bible, what need did they have for such individual or institutional arbitrators as priests, popes, or the Roman Church? Whereas early Reformers like Martin Luther and John Calvin viewed Scripture as being inspired by God with human involvement in its transmission, some of the second wave of Reformers, such as Amandus Polanus (d. 1610) and Abraham Calov (d. 1686), placed even greater emphasis on the Bible's inerrancy. The movement known as Protestant Scholasticism promoted the idea that any human involvement in the creation of the Bible was strictly mechanical; those who wrote the words were merely tools used by God. This was the first time that the idea of the inerrancy of Scripture as a literal interpretive approach was applied to the Bible—as a whole.

Despite the many developments in biblical interpretation that have occurred between the seventeenth and twenty-first centuries CE, many North American Christians still self-identify as biblical literalists. However, almost nobody practices biblical literalism in the strictest sense, for it would be an almost untenable position. The various contributions by the different religious communities that went into the writing of our biblical texts have resulted in contradicting versions of similar content (cf. Exod. 21:2-8 with Deut. 15:12-13). Given these challenges, how could A. J. Jacobs's experiment in living in strict accord with biblical law have any hope of being tenable, or even legal?

Historical Criticism

The influence of the Enlightenment—with its emphases on reason and searching for facts—gave rise to *the historical-critical movement*, which works to reconstruct the ancient contexts of the Bible. Baruch Spinoza (d. 1677) argued that the same scientific principles that were being applied to other areas of knowledge should be applied to the Bible as well. The results, which are still highly influential on how biblical scholarship is conducted today, have challenged such traditionally held Old Testament notions as the Genesis account(s) of the creation, Moses' composition of the Torah, and the historical validity of the Hebrew exodus out of Egypt, to name a few. Scrutinizing a particular text's origins through asking such questions as, Who wrote the text? For what purpose? and, Under what circumstances? Historical critics work to better understand what lies beneath the text.

Historical criticism's influence on biblical scholarship has shaped the way that many theologians read the Bible by adding to our understanding of the ancient contexts behind biblical texts. *Religionsgeschichte* ("history of religions") is a tool of historical criticism that reads biblical texts in their ancient religious contexts. Another historical-critical tool is *form criticism*, which has gleaned new meaning from such passages as the Song of Deborah (Judges 5) by considering their oral prehistory, reconstructing the *Sitz im Leben* ("original setting"), and analyzing their literary genres.

Social-Scientific Criticism

In the late 1970s—with the publication of Norman Gottwald's *The Tribes of Yahweh*—biblical scholars began to look at the books of the Old Testament through the lens of their sociological settings. Since then, numerous scholars have used societal patterns both to fill in many of the hidden contexts that are simply not addressed in the texts themselves and to better understand the societal motivations behind the Old Testament authors' messages.

One advantage to the social-scientific method of interpretation is its ability to inform hermeneutics (again, the application of biblical texts to modern circumstances). Social-scientific models have proven to be of particular use in shedding light on the contexts and motivations behind biblical texts while opening new ways of understanding how those texts might relate to the modern world (Chaney; Coomber 2011). A tempting misuse of social-scientific models of interpretation, however, is to treat the findings gained through social-scientific models as hard evidence that can stand on its own. Social-scientific models that deal with tribalism, urban development, religious-political interactions, or economic cycles can provide insight into how humans—and their systems—are expected to behave; they do not, however, prove how humans and systems did behave. It is for this reason that social-scientific approaches should be used in tandem with all available data, be it archaeological or literary.

Commenting on the great value of using social-scientific models in the interpretation of biblical texts, Philip Esler writes that their use "fires the social-scientific imagination to ask new questions of data, to which only the data can provide the answers" (Esler, 3). In other words, these models are useful for the interpretation of evidence, not as evidence in and of themselves. Social-scientific criticism has proven especially useful in the development of contextual readings of the Old Testament, which address issues ranging from political interpretations of the Bible to interpretations within such minority groups as LGBT (lesbian, gay, bisexual, and transgender) and disabled communities.

Contextual and Reception Readings and Criticisms

Contextual readings of the Old Testament provide excellent examples of how the ancient stories and ideas of the Old Testament can speak to the modern contexts of diverse communities. These forms of criticism, like social-scientific or literary criticism, often take on an interdisciplinary nature. While a plethora of contextual topics have been covered biblically, those that address issues of empire, gender, and race are briefly covered here.

Empire

Just as issues of empire were integral in the formation of the Old Testament, as addressed in the "Reading the Old Testament in Its Ancient Contexts" section above, Old Testament texts continue to influence the ways people approach issues of empire today. On the one hand, the imagery that celebrates conquest in the invasion of Canaan (Joshua) and the glory of Solomon's kingdom (e.g., 1 Kings 4) could be used to support the building of empire. On the other hand, those who challenge the rise or expansion of empires can draw on anti-imperial readings that condemn the conduct of royals and their exploitation of the citizenry (e.g., Micah 3), and legislation against economic injustice in the Torah, Writings, and Prophets.

Pro-imperial readings of the Old Testament can be seen in the building and expansion of US influence, such as the idea of *Manifest Destiny*, which portrays the Christian European settlement of the United States as God's divine will. Manifest destiny involved a reimagining of the Pilgrims—and later European settlers—as the new Hebrews, pushing aside the Native American peoples—who took on the role of Canaanites—in order to create a new Israel. The Rev. Josiah Strong's publication *Our Country* echoes this sentiment in its assertion that God was charging European Christianity "to dispossess the many weaker races, assimilate others, and mold the remainder" (Strong, 178). Reverberations of the Old Testament–rooted Manifest Destiny still surface in aspects of American exceptionalism, which influences the US political spectrum and can be seen in such approaches to foreign policy as "the Bush Doctrine," which works to spread American-style democracy as a path to lasting peace.

Just as the Old Testament has been used for empire building, it has also been used to challenge empire and its institutions. While the exodus narrative helped to shape the idea of Manifest Destiny, it also became a powerful abolitionist force in attacking the institutions of slavery and segregation. During the abolitionist movement, the powerful imagery of the exodus story gave hope and power to free African Americans and slaves alike. The power of the story was harnessed again in the mid-twentieth century, giving strength to those who struggled for racial equality (Coomber 2012, 123–36). Recent biblical scholarship has also turned to the Old Testament to address various issues of modern-day economic exploitation and neoimperialism (e.g., Gottwald 2011; Boer, ed.; West 2010).

A highly influential outcome of the crossing of Bible and empire has been *postcolonial interpretation*. As European empires spread throughout the world, they brought the Bible and Christianity with them. With the twentieth-century waning of European imperialism, colonized and previously colonized peoples have found their own voices in the Bible, resulting in a variety of new interpretations and new approaches to major Old Testament themes. Postcolonial interpretation has enriched the field from Mercedes García Bachmann's use of Isaiah 58 to address issues of "unwanted fasting" (105–12) to raising questions about whether the Christian canon should be reopened to include the folk stories and traditions of colonized Christian communities that feel unrepresented by the current Bible (Pui Lan).

Gender

Studies in gender have also revealed a wide range of interpretive possibilities and have come to the forefront of biblical scholarship during the past four decades. While often treated as the sex of the body, the word *gender* is a complicated term that addresses a variety of factors of embodiment, including mental and behavioral characteristics. *Masculinity* and *femininity*, for example, take on different attributes and expectations depending on the society or culture in which they exist. While gender is an area of study that is continually developing into various branches, both within and outside of biblical studies, one of its most predominant manifestations in biblical studies is found in *feminist criticism*.

Women have been longtime readers and commentators on biblical texts, even though their work has rarely been given the same consideration as their male counterparts, who have long served as the vanguard of the academy. Hildegard of Bingen (d. 1179) authored a commentary on Genesis 1–2 (Young, 262); R. Roberts (d. 1788) composed numerous sermons on a range of texts for a clergyman acquaintance (Knowles, 418–19); and abolitionist Elizabeth Cady Stanton (d. 1902) helped to publish *The Woman's Bible*. These three women serve as but a few examples of women who have made important contributions to biblical studies, though their work is unknown to many.

Feminist criticism continues to be a very effective mode for recovering women's insights, perspectives, knowledge, and the feminine principle in biblical texts, often rescuing those voices and interpretations from centuries of marginalization by patriarchal and even misogynistic interpretation. Elisabeth Schüssler Fiorenza claims that, unlike many other forms of biblical criticism, feminist biblical studies does not owe its existence to the academy but to social movements for change, and also to a desire for the ongoing pursuit of equal participation and equal rights, which have in practice been restricted to a small group of elite men (Schüssler Fiorenza, 8–9). Schüssler Fiorenza argues that since the Bible has most often been used in these struggles for either "legitimating the status quo of the kyriarchal order of domination *or* for challenging dehumanization, feminist biblical interpretation is best articulated as an integral part of wo/men's struggles for authority and self-determination" (9). Like so many forms of contextual and received readings, feminist criticism can serve as a liberating force by revealing perspectives within the Bible's texts that have otherwise gone unnoticed.

An example of recovering the woman's perspective in the Old Testament is found in feminist commentaries on such texts as Isa. 42:14, in which God says,

> For a long time I have held my peace,
>   I have kept still and restrained myself;
> now I will cry out like a woman in labor,
>   I will gasp and pant.

Patricia Tull has highlighted the way in which YHWH adopts the power of a woman in labor to emphasize God's own divine power of creation (Tull, 263). Another example of uncovering women's voices to find justice in patriarchal cultures—which work to subvert women's voices and rights—is found in Sharon Pace Jeansonne's treatment of Tamar as a woman who seizes power to find justice in a society that is set up to stop her from doing so (Jeansonne, 98–106).

Feminist criticism—as with most any other form of biblical criticism—is polyvocal, with a broad spectrum of biblical views, including those who have argued that the Bible might be best left alone (Bal, 14). Male scholars have also engaged with feminist-focused readings of Old Testament texts. Daniel Cohen's midrash on Genesis 3, for example, addresses misogynistic interpretations of the Garden of Eden story (Cohen 141–48).

Similar to some of feminist criticism's attempts to reclaim the women's voice in the Bible and address misogynistic interpretation, *queer criticism* works to uncover LGBT perspectives in the Old Testament and messages that are of importance to LGBT communities. Queer interpretation has addressed a number of such topics, including K. Renato Lings's work on homophobic critiques of the destruction of Sodom in Genesis 19—a text often used to condemn homosexuality—in which he argues that attaching homosexuality to the sin of Sodom was a later interpretive development, unrecognized by biblical authors (Lings, 183–207). Others have shed new light on the ways in which biblical texts are interpreted to affect modern-day political decisions, such as the issue of same-sex marriage (see Stahlberg).

Conclusion

To be an engaged reader of the Old Testament involves simultaneously navigating the worlds of the biblical authors and redactors, as well as all those who have interpreted its texts. It is through approaching a biblical text or idea through these multiple angles that the multilayered meanings of the Old Testament books can be unlocked, not only in regard to the authors' intentions, but also in ways that the biblical writers may have never been able to foresee. These multiple intersections with the biblical text help people to have meaningful conversation and debate on topics ranging from climate change, to same-sex marriage, to the international banking crisis, and more. Naturally, being an engaged reader requires considerable effort, but it is through deliberating on biblical texts in all of their complexity that deeper meaning can be found, and more honest—or at least informed—readings of the Bible's contents can be gleaned.

In this volume, the contributors' commentaries provide a tool through which people can develop their engagement with the books of the Old Testament and Apocrypha. Whether approaching this volume as a researcher, educator, member of the clergy, or student, it is the intent of the *Fortress Commentary on the Old Testament* to inform readers about the Old Testament books' historical contexts, interpretive histories, and the modern contexts with which they engage, while also serving as an opening through which the conversation can be expanded.

Works Cited

Alfaro, Juan I. 1989. *Justice and Loyalty: A Commentary on the Book of Micah*. Grand Rapids: Eerdmans.

Bachmann, Mercedes L. García. 2009. "True Fasting and Unwilling Hunger (Isaiah 58)." In *The Bible and the Hermeneutics of Liberation*, edited by A. F. Botta and P. R. Andiñach, 113–31. Atlanta: SBL.

Bal, Mieke. 1989. *Anti-Covenant: Counter-Reading Women's Lives in the Hebrew Bible*. Sheffield: Almond.

Boer, Roland, ed. 2013. *Postcolonialism and the Hebrew Bible: The Next Step*. SemeiaSt 70. Atlanta: SBL.

Cantor, Norman F. 1992. *Inventing the Middle Ages: The Lives, Works, and Ideas of the Great Medievalists of the Twentieth Century*. Cambridge: Lutterworth.

Chaney, Marvin L. 1999. "Whose Sour Grapes? The Addressees of Isaiah 5:1–7 in the Light of Political Economy." In *The Social World of the Hebrew Bible: Twenty-Five Years of the Social Sciences in the Academy*, edited by Ronald A. Simkins and Stephen L. Cook. *Semeia* 87:105–22.

Cohen, Daniel. 2007. "Taste and See: A Midrash on Genesis 3:6 and 3:12." In *Patriarchs, Prophets and Other Villains*, edited by Lisa Isherwood, 141–48. London: Equinox Publishing.

Coomber, Matthew J. M. 2010. *Re-Reading the Prophets through Corporate Globalization: A Cultural-Evolutionary Approach to Understanding Economic Injustice in the Hebrew Bible*. Piscataway, NJ: Gorgias.

———. 2011. "Caught in the Crossfire? Economic Injustice and Prophetic Motivation in Eighth-Century Judah." *BibInt* 19, nos. 4–5:396–432.

———. 2012. "Before Crossing the Jordan: The Telling and Retelling of the Exodus Narrative in African American History." In *Exodus and Deuteronomy: Texts @ Contexts*, edited by Athalya Brenner and Gale A. Yee, 123–36. Minneapolis: Fortress Press.

———. 2013. "Debt as Weapon: Manufacturing Poverty from Judah to Today." *Diaconia: Journal for the Study of Christian Social Practice* 4, no. 2:141–55.

Coote, Robert B., and Keith W. Whitelam. 1987. *The Emergence of Early Israel in Historical Perspective*. Sheffield: Almond.

Crossley, James G. 2008. *Jesus in an Age of Terror: Scholarly Projects for a New American Century*. London: Equinox.

Davies, Philip. 2000. "What Separates a Minimalist from a Maximalist? Not Much." *BAR* 26, no. 2:24–27, 72–73.

Davies, Philip, and John Rogerson. 2005. *The Old Testament World.* 2nd ed. Louisville: Westminster John Knox.

Dever, William G. 2008. *Did God Have a Wife? Archaeology and Folk Religion in Ancient Israel.* Grand Rapids: Eerdmans.

Esler, Philip F. 2005. "Social-Scientific Models in Biblical Interpretation." In *Ancient Israel: The Old Testament in Its Social Context,* edited by Philip Esler, 3–14. London: SCM.

Fuqua, Charles R. 2012. *God's Law: The Only Political Solution.* Salt Lake City: American Book Publishing.

Gottwald, Norman. 1999. *The Tribes of Yahweh: A Sociology of the Religion of Liberated Israel, 1250–1050* BCE. Sheffield: Sheffield Academic Press.

———. 2001. *The Politics of Ancient Israel.* Louisville: Westminster John Knox.

Grabbe, Lester L. 2007. *Ancient Israel: What Do We Know and How Do We Know It?* London: T&T Clark.

Halpern, Baruch. 1995. "Erasing History: The Minimalist Assault on Ancient Israel." *BRev* 11: 26–35, 47.

Jacobs, A. J. 2007. *The Year of Living Biblically: One Man's Humble Quest to Follow the Bible as Literally as Possible.* New York: Simon & Schuster.

Jeansonne, Sharon Pace. 1990. *The Women of Genesis: From Sarah to Potiphar's Wife.* Minneapolis: Fortress Press.

Josephus, Flavius. 1854. *The Works of Flavius Josephus: Comprising the Antiquities of the Jews, a History of the Jewish Wars, and Life of Flavius Josephus, Written by Himself.* Translated by William Whiston. Philadelphia: Jas. B. Smith.

Karmon, Yehuda. 1971. *Israel: A Regional Geography.* London: Wiley-Interscience.

Knapp, A. Bernard. 1988. "Copper Production and Eastern Mediterranean Trade: The Rise of Complex Society in Cyprus." In *State and Society: The Emergence and Development of Social Hierarchy and Political Centralization,* edited by J. Gledhill, B. Bender, and M. T. Larsen, 149–72. London: Unwin Hyman.

Knowles, Michael P. 2012. "Roberts, R. (ca. 1728–88)." In *Handbook of Women Biblical Interpreters,* edited by M. A. Taylor and A. Choi, 418–20. Grand Rapids: Baker Academic.

Kwok Pui-lan. 2003. "Discovering the Bible in the Non-Biblical World." In *Searching the Scriptures: A Feminist Introduction,* edited by Elisabeth Schüssler Fiorenza, 276–88. New York: Crossroad.

Lings, K. Renato. 2007. "Culture Clash in Sodom: Patriarchal Tales of Heroes, Villains, and Manipulation." In *Patriarchs, Prophets and Other Villains,* edited by Lisa Isherwood, 183–207. London: Equinox.

Liverani, Mario. 2007. *Israel's History and the History of Israel.* Translated by Chiara Peri and Philip Davies. London: Equinox.

Masterson, Teresa. 2011. "Man, 70, Stoned to Death for Being Gay." *NBC10 Philadelphia.* Accessed October 14, 2013. http://www.nbcphiladelphia.com/news/local/Man-70-Stoned-to-Death-for-Homosexuality-Police-118243719.html.

Niditch, Susan. 2010. "Experiencing the Divine: Heavenly Visits, Earthly Encounters and the Land of the Dead." In *Religious Diversity in Ancient Israel and Judah,* edited by Francesca Stavrakopoulou and John Barton, 11–22. London: T&T Clark.

Schüssler Fiorenza, Elisabeth. 2013. *Changing Horizons: Explorations in Feminist Interpretation.* Minneapolis: Fortress Press.

Schweitzer, Albert. 1968. *The Quest of the Historical Jesus: A Critical Study of Its Progress from Reimarus to Wrede.* New York: Macmillan.

Smith, Mark S. 2002. *The Early History of God: Yahweh and the Other Deities in Ancient Israel.* Grand Rapids: Eerdmans.

Stahlberg, Lesleigh Cushing. 2008. "Modern Day Moabites: The Bible and the Debate About Same-Sex Marriage." *BibInt* 16:422–75.

Stavrakopoulou, Francesca. 2010. "'Popular' Religion and 'Official' Religion: Practice, Perception, Portrayal." In *Religious Diversity in Ancient Israel and Judah*, edited by Francesca Stavrakopoulou and John Barton, 37–58. New York: T&T Clark.

Strong, Josiah. 1885. *Our Country: Its Possible Future and Its Present Crisis*. New York: The American Home Missionary Society.

Tull, Patricia K. 2012. "Isaiah." In *Women's Bible Commentary: Twentieth-Anniversary Edition*, edited by C. A. Newsom, S. H. Ringe, and J. E. Lapsley, 255–66. Louisville: Westminster John Knox.

West, Gerald. 2010. "The Legacy of Liberation Theologies in South Africa, with an Emphasis on Biblical Hermeneutics." *Studia Historiae Ecclesiasticae* 36, Supplement: 157–83.

Whitelam, Keith W. 2007. "Lines of Power: Mapping Ancient Israel." In *To Break Every Yoke: Essays in Honour of Marvin L. Chaney*, edited by R. B. Coote and N. K. Gottwald, 40–79. Sheffield: Sheffield Phoenix Press.

Young, Abigail. 2012. "Hildegard of Bingen (1098–1179)." In *Handbook of Women Biblical Interpreters*, edited by M. A. Taylor and A. Choi, 259–64. Grand Rapids: Baker Academic.

THE PEOPLE OF GOD AND THE PEOPLES OF THE EARTH

Hugh R. Page Jr.

The Bible Is Just the Beginning

The Bible is preeminently a book about people. That may strike some as a rather odd assertion given the stature enjoyed by the Bible as sacred text containing, in many faith traditions, everything one needs to know about God and salvation. Nonetheless, some of the more important foci of the Old and New Testaments have to do with the saga of the human family and the women and men that are dramatis personae in this unfolding drama. In the twenty-first century CE, our appreciation of how Scripture narrates that story is much more nuanced than it was perhaps a generation or two ago. We are much more aware of the processes by which traditions are shaped and preserved. We have a deeper understanding of the myriad stages through which the inspired words of prophets, poets, and sages proceed before being canonized: as well as of the place the Bible occupies in the global ecology of sacred texts. Moreover, we recognize that many of the world's sacred texts have important things to say about the human condition. Thus perspectives on what it means to be "people of God," women and men in a special relationship with a transcendent being, or members of a large and diverse human family sharing a common terrestrial abode vary widely. Moreover, in today's world, scholarship in fields such as genetics and anthropology is changing the way we think about human origins and notions of personhood.

It is because of new ideas about humanity and its origins that responsible readers of the Bible must, therefore, examine biblical conceptions of personhood, while keeping in mind the ways in which both the human family in general and those individuals called into special relationship with the God of Israel are construed. In so doing, they must also look at how such ideas have shaped, and continue to influence, notions about the world and its inhabitants today; are related to comparable ideas about personhood in other faith traditions; relate to what scientific evidence reveals about the human family; have been complicit in the exploitation of colonized peoples; and stand in relationship to those ideas about the human family articulated in documents such as the United Nations Declaration of Human Rights and the Declaration on the Rights of Indigenous Peoples. Such a task is necessary if we are to enhance the extent to which the Bible can be deployed as a resource in building a more just and equitable global community. Failure to do so may limit the extent to which members of faith communities for which the Bible is authoritative are able to join in meaningful dialogue about the future of our global community and the institutions that support it. It may also inadvertently lend credence to the idea that religious texts and traditions have no place in conversations about those ideals on which a cosmopolitan global community should be based in the future.

The Earth and Its Peoples—A View from the Ethnographic Record

Science has revealed that modern human beings are the result of a remarkable evolutionary process. We share common African ancestry, and our diversity at this point in time bears witness to an array of migratory, climatic, and genetic adaptations that span hundreds of thousands of years. Our cultural landscape is vast and remarkable in its variation. For example, the comprehensive cultural database maintained by Human Relations Area Files at Yale University (see http://www.yale.edu/hraf/collections.htm) contains information on several hundred cultures.

The *Ethnographic Atlas*, a massive project undertaken by George Peter Murdock (1969) and ultimately brought to full fruition in the 1970s, contains information on more than one thousand distinct groups. As an ethnologist, Murdock was particularly interested in both the comparative study of cultures and the identification of behavioral traits that manifest locally, regionally, and internationally (see especially Murdock 1981, 3). His work calls attention to the breadth of lifeways characteristic of peoples around the world. Scholarship continuing in the vein of Murdock's has led to the identification of some 3,500 cultures on which published data are readily available (see, e.g., Price, 10). Such studies have also resulted in the development of templates for comparing social organization, religious beliefs, and other information about the world's disparate peoples (see Ember and Ember; and Murdock et al.). Needless to say, the vision of the human family derived from this research is remarkable. Social scientists see this diverse collage of languages, customs, and religious traditions as the end result of developmental forces that have been operational for *aeons*. It is also for them a mystery to be probed using the critical tools at their disposal. Ethnographic investigations and theory testing have laid bare and will continue to reveal its undiscovered truths. However, humankind has not revealed, and is not likely to yield, the sum total of its secrets to even the most dogged of investigators. Like the stories of primordial reality we encounter in the biblical book of Genesis, such research offers a place from which to begin pondering what it means to be human.

Human life is, of course, dynamic. New social and religious groups are born constantly. The first two decades of the current millennium have even witnessed the dissolution of geopolitical boundaries, the creation of new nation states, and the birth of new religious movements. Thus notions of culture and personhood in our era are anything but static. Our human family continues to grow and with each passing day becomes more diverse and increasingly complex. Research in the social sciences has increased our understanding of how culture and identity evolve. We know more today than ever before about the ways language, physical environment, and other factors contribute to ideas about what it means to be a fully actualized self and to be in relationship with those other selves that are one's family members, friends, and neighbors. It has also shed light on the role that the collection and preservation of religious lore play in this process. Sacred traditions and texts serve as the repositories for stories about how people and the groups in which they are embedded came to be. They also function as points of reference for the nurture of persons and the communities in which they live.

The challenge we face in an era when such traditions are often read narrowly or uncritically—without an eye toward their implicit limitations—is to create charitable and inclusive approaches that allow us to engage and appropriate them. Such strategies necessitate that we become well versed in the ways that stories, both ancient and modern, shape our identities, beliefs, and relationships with one another. Whether one has in mind venerable tales such as the Babylonian *Enuma Elish* and the so-called Priestly account of creation (Gen. 1:1—2:4a), or modern cinematic myths like the *Matrix* or *Prometheus* sagas, narratives of one kind or another provide a context for understanding who we are and how we choose to live. Returning to the Bible itself, it is arguable that one of its central aims is to inform us of what it means to be finite beings that are threads in a sacred cosmic fabric woven, as it were, by a divine and ineffable artisan.

Ancient Near Eastern Lore and Conceptions of Personhood

In the late nineteenth and early twentieth centuries, scholars such as James Frazer and Stith Thompson began looking seriously at cultural practices and folklore from various parts of the world. The results were remarkable, though not without some degree of controversy. Frazer's efforts included his Victorian-era classic *The Golden Bough* (Frazer 1981) and an equally important, if less celebrated, three-volume work titled *Folk-Lore in the Old Testament* (Frazer 1918a; 1918b; 1918c); and Thompson's work on folklore motifs was pioneering insofar as it laid important groundwork for the comparison of tales from around the world. Although questions remain about the aims and theoretical presuppositions of these early works, their efforts, and those of the scholars following in their immediate footsteps, set the stage for much of the social-scientific research we have seen in the twentieth and twenty-first centuries, even in the field of biblical studies.

Among biblical scholars, the pioneers of form criticism and the so-called myth and ritual school found in this body of information—and other information gathered from ancient Near Eastern sources—a treasure trove useful for contextualizing and interpreting key portions of the Old Testament. Among form critics, Hermann Gunkel must be noted. His collection of essays in *What Remains of the Old Testament* and topical studies of literary *Gattungen* ("forms") as such pertain to the Bible in *The Legends of Genesis* and *The Folktale in the Old Testament* repay—even today—careful reading

(1928; 1964; 1987). Among myth and ritual adherents, Sigmund Mowinckel's work deserves pride of place, especially his *Psalmenstudien* (1966). These pioneers' use of ethnological resources in the study of Scripture were paralleled by those of Johannes Pedersen in his two-volume study of ancient Israelite culture (1926–1940) and extended in subsequent generations by Theodor Gaster's efforts to reclaim and expand the work of Frazer (1950; 1959; 1969); Mary Douglas's exploration of the body as social map (1966); Bruce Malina's use of a circum-Mediterranean paradigm to understand the roles of women and men in the Bible (1989); and others whose work has explored the intersections of Jewish, Christian, Mediterranean, and other cultural traditions both ancient and modern.

Several lessons can be gleaned from this body of research. The first is that people are in some ways "hardwired" to create and tell stories. These stories help in making sense of life crises such as birth, maturation, and death. They are also pivotal in defining the self and the social networks into which individual selves are embedded. A second lesson is that one particular genre, creation stories—whether they focus on the birth of deities (theogonies), the universe (cosmogonies), humanity, tribal confederations, monarchies, or all of the aforementioned—have a direct impact on the ways people understand their place in the world. Creation stories define social and ethnic boundaries, reify social and political hierarchies, and ascribe status based on age, gender, and other ontological and ascribed markers. These two factors should inform the ways information about individuals and groups embedded in poetry, rituals, royal inscriptions, and other texts is understood. A few examples from the ancient Near East are particularly illustrative.

The Mesopotamian flood tradition encountered in the Atrahasis myth has, among its more important purposes, articulation of a basic theological anthropology—one that is based on an understanding of the mutable and immutable dimensions of an, at times, capricious cosmos. Human beings are oddly situated in this power-filled and unstable environment. They are remarkable for three reasons. The first is because they are made of the flesh and blood of a divine insurgent and sacrificed because he led a rebellion against the harsh labor imposed on a subset of deities in the pantheon.

> When the gods themselves were men,
> They did the work. They endured the toil.
> The labor was onerous.
> Massive was the effort. The distress was exceedingly great. (Lambert and Millard, 42
>   [tablet 1.1.1–4], translation my own)

> Let them sacrifice the divine leader.
> Let the gods purify themselves by immersion.
> With his essence—flesh and blood—let Nintu mix the clay,
> So that divinity and humanity may be thoroughly
> Blended in the amalgam.
> For all time let us hear the drumbeat.
> In the flesh of the god let the ghost remain.
> Let her [Nintu] inform him [the slain god] of his token.
> So that there will be no forgetting,
> The spirit will remain. (Lambert and Millard, 58 [tablet 1.4.208–17], translation my own)

The human heartbeat is the "drum" reminding women and men for all time of the immortal lineage that is uniquely their own. The second reason that people are special is due to their being extended kin, as it were, of Atrahasis, the "exceedingly wise one," who managed to survive the great deluge by which all of humanity was destroyed. To them belongs the empowering, yet dangerous, model of this *liminal* ancestor. As William Moran noted more than four decades ago: "The Atrahasis Epic is an assertion of man's importance in the final order of things. It is also a strong criticism of the gods" (Moran, 59).

Humans are also special (see Moran, 60–61) for a third reason: because they are living proof of the imprudence of the gods and goddesses they serve. Created to assume the day-to-day labor deemed too difficult for immortals to bear, the din of their daily existence proved far too disruptive of their divine patrons' and matrons' sleep. Their death was decreed because they were, in a word, "noisy" (Lambert and Millard, 66 [tablet 1.7.354–59]). It is only through the quick-witted intervention of Enki, his personal god, that Atrahasis and his family are able to escape the inundation. Atrahasis is a powerful symbol of what can happen when human perseverance and divine subterfuge are allied.

The Atrahasis myth suggests that people are made of supernatural "stuff" and are heirs to a distinctive lineage. It also emphasizes that in a world filled with danger, the gods who are in control of the fates of women and men do not always have the best interest of the human family in mind. Although all mortals are in a sense beings belonging to and dependent on the gods, the implication of the sobering reality revealed in this myth is that in order to survive, women and men would do well to leverage their inner resources while at the same time relying, should all else fail, on timely divine intervention by those deities with whom they have a special relationship. Such assertions are, of course, in conversation with anthropologies articulated in other lore across a wide spectrum of genres. For example, Gilgamesh—particularly the Old Babylonian version of this Akkadian classic—focuses attention on the unique challenges confronted by one species of individual: monarchs. Of particular interest in this epic are their socialization, capacity to form friendships, quest for lasting renown, and insecurities about death. royal inscriptions, of which exemplars are too numerous to mention, continue in this vein and further define the traits of kings and those subject to their authority. Suzerainty treaties can be said to function in a comparable manner by defining the relationships of sociopolitical aggregates to one another. Sets of laws, like those found in the Code of Hammurabi, reify social status through taxonomies that identify insiders (e.g., king, free men, and those acquitted of offenses) and outsiders (e.g., criminals, widows, and orphans).

Another story, that of the travails of the god Ba'lu from the ancient city of Ugarit, offers a slightly different perspective on human life—this time from West Semitic lore. Unlike the story of Atrahasis, the Ba'lu myth is concerned primarily with how the enigmatic god of the fructifying rains—mainstays of human life—secures his place as head of the pantheon. Although the primary concern of this tale is Ba'lu's contest with rivals for ascendancy to the throne, it lifts the veil concealing the ongoing cosmic struggle between two such forces that inscribe the parameters for human existence: that is, life/fertility, represented by Ba'lu as numen of the storm, and Môtu, the embodiment of death and dissolution. At one point in this saga, he voluntarily submits himself to the authority and power of Môtu. His death, emblematic of nature's cyclic periods of aridity, leads his father 'Ilu, head of the pantheon, and his sister 'Anatu, to bewail its impact on the world. Both give voice to a lament intended, no doubt, to sum up the anguish of all affected by the storm god's departure.

> Ba'lu has died. What is to become of humanity?
> Dagan's child is no more. What will happen to earth's teeming masses? (CAT 1.5.6.23–24;
>   1.6.1.6–7)

The world and its inhabitants are part of the background landscape against which this divine drama unfolds. Nonetheless, as the narrative progresses, one realizes that each episode has a profound, if at times only partially articulated, impact on the peoples of the earth. Ba'lu returns to life, largely through the intervention of his sister 'Anatu. Eventually, he and Môtu have a fateful encounter that reveals, in no uncertain terms, that they are—and shall remain—in an interminable struggle.

> They fight each other like heroes
> Môtu is strong, as is Ba'lu
> Like raging bulls, they go head to head
> Môtu is strong, as is Ba'lu
> They bite one another like serpents
> Môtu is strong, as is Ba'lu
> Like animals, they beat each other to a pulp
> Môtu falls, Ba'lu collapses. (CAT 1.6.6.16–22)

The two battle to a virtual draw: an indication that the struggle between life and death is ongoing. The hope for "earth's teeming masses" is that the forces of life are able—at the very least—to withstand Death's furious and unrelenting onslaught. To be engaged nobly in the struggle is, therefore, to participate heroically in an age-old struggle that unites every member of the human family as kin. The warp and weft of day-to-day existence finds its ultimate significance in this ongoing cosmic battle. We see a stunning reflex of this mythology in the biblical Song of Songs, where the protagonists are anthropomorphized hypostases of Love ('ahăbâ) and Death (māwet).

> Seal me to your heart.
> Brand me on your arm.
> Love is equal to Death in its strength.
> Passion rivals Sheol in its ferocity.
> Its flames are a blazing fire.
> It is an eternal inferno. (Song of Songs 8:6, author's own translation)

Additional textual examples from Egypt and Anatolia could be cited, but the above suffice to show how implicit and explicit messaging about people—their nature, connection to one another, and relationship to the divine forces responsible for their creation and support—is conveyed in expressive culture.

The Hebrew Bible, Personhood, and Identity

Biblical references to the earth and its peoples are very much in conversation with these ancient Near Eastern traditions. The opening chapter of the Hebrew Bible contains a remarkable assertion in what scholars have traditionally designated the Priestly account of creation (Gen. 1:1—2:4a): that the world and everything in it is "good." It uses the Hebrew word *ṭôb* to describe its fundamental essence, a word whose semantic range connotes something sweet and pleasurable. Human beings are an important part of the created order. Made on the sixth day, they are distinguished only by gender: male and female. Neither ethnic nor regional markers are noted. All are made according to the divine "form" (*ṣelem*) and "pattern" (*dĕmût*)—that is, God's "image and likeness" according to the NRSV. Theirs are the tasks of reproducing and exercising control of the earth (1:26–28). The word used to describe what will be involved to reach this desired outcome (*kābaš*) connotes a process requiring forceful effort (Oswalt, 430). Also implied here is the idea that this is a laborious enterprise that is both collective and collaborative.

Following this masterful cosmogonic hymn, readers encounter in the remainder of Genesis a "mixed bag" of traditions about the earth's populace representing several sources: fragments of archaic poetry (2:23; 3:14-19; 4:23-24; 49); a descanting creation narrative (2:4b-24); etiological tales (11:1-9); ethnohistorical musings about the origins of particular peoples (4:17-22); an epic about the peregrinations of Israel's ancestors (11:31—36:43); and an extensive novella dealing with a key figure in the national saga: Joseph (37–50). While these materials can be read—as scholarly literature attests—from a variety of perspectives, one thing is very clear: together they tell the story of the God of Israel's relationship with the world and its peoples, some of whom—namely, Abraham, Sarah, and their descendants—are called to take on special responsibilities for the entirety of the human family (12:1-3). In fact, it could be argued that a significant portion of the Genesis tradition (1:1—11:32) has been intended as a creative "riff" on, or response to, Sumero-Akkadian lore (like that found in Atrahasis) about the origins of humanity.

One of the unifying threads holding together the narrative tapestry of Genesis and the remaining books of the Torah/Pentateuch is the story of how the world is affected by the shifting, strained, at times tumultuous, dynamic, and constantly evolving relationships among those who are the offspring of the primordial family. While highlighting theological themes such as *calling* (Exod. 3:1-15); *covenant* (Exod. 6:1-8; 20:1-17); *sin and redemption* (Exod. 32:1-35); *divine immanence and transcendence* (Exod. 25:1—31:18); *holiness* (Lev. 10:3; 20:26); *significant individuals* (Exod. 2:10; 15:20; 2:21; 3:1); *groups* (Exod. 3:8; 6:19); and *events* (Exodus 15; Num. 3:14-16; 9:15-16); these books also articulate a gestalt ("general sketch") for comprehending what it means to be part of a human family. This can entail struggling both to recognize its connectedness and to honor its diversity. It can also involve wrestling with the challenge of managing intergroup crises that influence the welfare of peoples living in proximity; competing for limited resources; and dealing with those changing geopolitical realities that generate population shifts, form new social movements, and give rise to diasporas. It is for this reason that one of the foci of these books, and the sources used therein, is the establishment of social, religious, and other boundaries that determine personhood, group affiliation, and status. For example, the Priestly creation story (Gen. 1—2:4a) can be said to inscribe broad and inclusive parameters for personhood. Since all human beings bear the imprint of the creator's "form" and "pattern," they can be said to belong to a single unified group, for which gender is the only subclassification (1:26-27). The implication of this is that everyone created *by* God belongs *to* God and is therefore part of the "people of God."

Genealogical tables, such as that found in Genesis 10, offer a more nuanced view of group identity based on location, language, and kin group (e.g., 10:5). The story of the Tower of Babel goes a step further in its linkage of linguistic heterogeneity to human hubris and a divine response to quell it (Gen. 11:5-7). Although it can be read simply as an entertaining etiology accounting for the diversity and spread of languages, it does contain a polemical strain resistant to linguistic solidarity, centralized government, and the conscription of resources needed to build monumental structures and to maintain the places—that is, cities—where they are most likely to be found in antiquity. Thus the story seems to be suggesting, on one level, that diversity and difference are preferable to a homogeneity whose consequences, intended or unintended, are to transgress the boundary separating mortals from God.

The block of material inclusive of the ancestral epic and the story of Joseph's rise to Egyptian prominence offers an even more complex picture of the "people of God." On the one hand, the "yes" given by Abram/Abraham to the call of YHWH (Gen. 12:1-3), and the covenant made with him (Gen. 15:18; 17:1-27) by YHWH, serve to distinguish him and his descendants among the "people of God"—that is, as a conduit of blessing to the entirety of the human family (Gen. 12:3). On the other hand, an inversion of status—from "temporary sojourner" to "inheritor" of Canaan (17:6-8)—is also promised, one that sets the stage for what is later described in Joshua and Judges. The story of Joseph's tensions with his brothers, as well as that of the peculiar circumstances leading Jacob and his kin to go to Egypt, set the stage for further musing on several issues. The first is how the kin group through whom all of the "people of God" are to be blessed understands its internal subdivisions (Genesis 49; Deuteronomy 32–33). The second has to do with how the kin group's liberation, covenant at Sinai, sojourn in the wilderness, and occupation of Canaan (Exod. 4:1—20:21; 32:1—35:29; Num. 1:1—36:13; Joshua; and Judges) are construed, particularly in terms of how these sources present Israel's relationship to its neighbors, both as stewards of a unique revelatory experience and part of a larger family of divine offspring. The third concerns the final book of the Pentateuch—Deuteronomy—that serves as the transitional bridge to the Former Prophets. From a literary standpoint, it is a rearticulation and expansion of core precepts first articulated in Exod. 20:1-17. It inscribes very narrow parameters for Israel's self-understanding and relationship to its neighbors. "When you come into the land that the LORD your God is giving you, you must not learn to imitate the abhorrent practices of those nations" (Deut. 18:9).

The book of Deuteronomy has very strict stipulations for the centralization of worship (12:1-28), prophetic practice (18:15-22), the conduct of war (20:1-20), and the care of those without material support (24:14-15, 17-18). All of these grow out of a particular self-understanding, stated most succinctly in what Gerhard von Rad long ago identified as a short creedal statement.

> A wandering Aramean was my ancestor; he went down into Egypt and lived there as an alien, few in number, and there he became a great nation, mighty and populous. When the Egyptians treated us harshly and afflicted us, by imposing hard labor on us, we cried to the LORD, the God of our ancestors; the LORD heard our voice and saw our affliction, our toil, and our oppression. The LORD brought us out of Egypt with a mighty hand and an outstretched arm, with a terrifying display of power, and with signs and wonders; and he brought us into this place and gave us this land, a land flowing with milk and honey. (Deut. 26:5-9)

Israel's identity as an "alien" subject to "hard labor" and "oppression," now liberated by YHWH, is the backdrop against which Deuteronomy's exclusive covenantal obligations are formulated. The jealousy of YHWH (Deut. 4:24) establishes impermeable cultural and ethical borders separating Israel from its neighbors. Deuteronomy and the historical narrative of the occupation of Canaan and the flowering of the monarchy are written in accordance with its principles. This so-called Deuteronomistic History (abbreviated Dtr by some scholars) consists of Joshua, Judges, the books of Samuel, and 1 and 2 Kings. It offers a far more complex, yet ultimately less inclusive, vision of the "people of God."

For example, we encounter the technical designation 'am yhwh ("YHWH's people") in the Pentateuch's oldest strata (e.g., Judg. 5:11, 13—an ancient Hebrew poem; and Num. 11:29; 16:41). Here it refers to either the members of Israel's tribal confederation (Judges) or the Israelite community on the march through the wilderness following its flight from Egypt (Numbers). It is present much more frequently in Dtr, where it denotes those faithful bound by the Deuteronomic covenant (Deut. 27:9—lĕ'am layhwh); Israel before the establishment of the monarchy (1 Sam. 2:24); the fallen military contingent that supported Jonathan and Saul (2 Sam. 1:12); and as an *ethnonym* for those under the reign of David (2 Sam. 6:21), Jehu (2 Kgs. 9:6), and Jehoida (2 Kgs. 11:17). We also find the terms 'am hā'ĕlōhîm or 'am 'ĕlōhîm ("people of God") used in reference to the Israelite tribal contingent armed for battle (Judg. 20:2) and to those under David's sovereign rule (2 Sam. 14:13). Beyond these references, we encounter the term "YHWH's people" in 2 Chron. 23:16 (paralleling 2 Kgs. 11:17). Another enigmatic reference—to "the God of Abraham's people"—is found in Ps. 47:9, a poem asserting the universal kingship of 'ĕlōhîm ("God").

Although references to "Yahweh's people" and "people of God" do not appear in the Latter Prophets (Isaiah, Jeremiah, Ezekiel, and the Book of the Twelve) or the Writings (outside of the Chronicler), we can certainly detect a keen interest in the world's peoples in many of these books. In some instances, the focus is decidedly polemical. The pointed critique of Israel's neighbors in prophetic oracles is an excellent example (e.g., Isaiah 14–19; Ezekiel 26–30). The bimodal subdivision of humanity in Proverbs (between those who heed Wisdom's voice and others who do not in Proverbs 8–9). A third case in point is the distinction made between "those who lead many to righteousness" in Dan. 12:3) and their opponents. In others, there is an affirmation of the God of Israel's keen interest in building an inclusive eschatological community (e.g., Isa. 66:18-21) and questioning a culture of entitlement and condemnatory rhetoric among Israelite prophets (Jon. 4:9-11). In Jewish apocryphal literature, we also see an interest expressed in the relationship among peoples. In the Greek Addition F to Esther, an editor has called attention to the different "lots" God has assigned to "the people of God" and to "all the nations" (10:10). The author of the Wisdom of Solomon takes a slightly different tack. While adopting a rhetoric that accentuates the difference between the "righteous" and the "ungodly" (Wisdom), it also calls attention to the common ancestry of humanity:

> there is for all one entrance into life, and one way out. (Wis. 18:9)

What we have, therefore, in the Hebrew Bible are multiple visions of what it means to be "people of God" and "peoples of the earth." Some are narrow. Others are selectively inclusive. All must be read with an eye toward genre, the setting in which the text was produced, and the social, political, and religious circumstances it seeks to address.

It goes almost without saying that biblical writers and their initial audiences were concerned with theological issues such as Israel's election and the implications such issues have on the community's holiness and distinctiveness when compared to its neighbors. In light of this special calling, as it were, boundaries—their creation, maintenance, and occasional erasure—take on particular significance. Maintenance is a sign of covenantal fidelity (Deut. 7:1-6) and purity (Lev. 10:1-3). Periodic transgression is, at least in some instances, a necessary survival strategy. Judges is an excellent case in point (see Page). We see evidence in this book of the crossing of bodily, cultural, and other borders as part of what characterizes Israelite life during that bittersweet epoch when "there was no king in Israel" and "people did what was right in their own eyes" (Judg. 21:25). Israel's identity as a people with a unique identity, mission, and teleological objective is, thus, variously articulated in the Hebrew Bible. These overlapping, competing, and complementary ideas of what it means to be a "people of God" among "the earth's peoples" require attentiveness to the religious objectives, political aims, and eschatological foci of the books in which they are found. Therefore, any attempt to fully reconcile all aspects of these disparate conceptions is likely to meet with frustration. Instead, it is perhaps better to recognize that the Hebrew Bible does not speak with a single voice on the issue of what it means to be part of the human family.

Looking beyond the Bible

One could argue that this absence of uniformity in the Hebrew Bible is an invitation not simply to read, but also to query and "talk back to" its books. Among the questions we should ask is what sources—in addition to Scripture—we ought to consult in making sense of who we are, what our relationship should be to one another, and what our place is in the universe. This process is far more involved than turning to Genesis or some other biblical book for a "proof text" (the practice of using a specific text as the final authoritative word on a given issue). Instead, it requires taking into consideration modern geopolitical realities such as globalization and what the pure, applied, and social sciences are telling us about our biological origins, diversity, and connectedness.

It also makes it incumbent on Bible readers to be aware of how documents such as the United Nations Declaration on Human Rights (1948) and the United Nations Declaration on the Rights of Indigenous Peoples (2007) influence how we think about our rights and responsibilities as people of faith and citizens of the world. For example, article 1 of the former states that "all human beings are born free and equal in dignity and rights. They are endowed with reason and conscience and should act towards one another in a spirit of brotherhood" (United Nations General Assembly 2000, 326). An affirmation of this kind shapes the way one thinks about religious texts and traditions that qualify human freedom, equality, dignity, or rights endowed at birth. Furthermore, according to article 18 of the Declaration, "Everyone has the right to freedom of thought, conscience, and religion; this right includes freedom to change his religion or belief, and freedom either alone or in community with others and in public or private, to manifest his religion or belief in teaching, practice, worship, and observance" (United Nations General Assembly 2000, 327). Such texts can't help but influence our reading and deployment of those parts of the Bible that affirm behaviors that affirm or disagree with these statements and the ideals they represent. In the case of those that run counter, a hermeneutic inclusive of exegesis and critical engagement is warranted. Article 7 section 2 of the United Nations Declaration on the Rights of Indigenous Peoples states that "indigenous peoples have the collective right to live in freedom, peace and security as distinct peoples and shall not be subjected to any act of genocide or any other act of violence, including forcibly removing children of the group to another group" (United Nations General Assembly 2007, 5). Moreover, article 8 section 1 affirms that "indigenous peoples and individuals have the right not to be subjected to forced assimilation or destruction of their culture" (United Nations General Assembly 2007, 5). The reading or deployment of biblical passages that appear to celebrate or support behaviors of this kind can be neither ignored nor interpreted in a way that treats lightly the ways they have been used to justify policies that abrogate the rights of indigenous peoples around the world.

Thus, in our current era, perhaps the Bible should be seen less as the single authoritative source from which the final word on what it means to be "people of God" and "people of the earth" is to be found, and more as one of several interlocutors—including lived experience—informing our consideration of what is an unfolding *mystery* about the larger human experience that we are invited to prayerfully ponder.

Works Cited

Douglas, Mary. 1966. *Purity and Danger*. London: ARK.

Eilberg-Schwartz, Howard. 1990. *The Savage in Judaism: Anthropology of Israelite Religion and Ancient Judaism*. Bloomington: Indiana University Press.

Ember, Melvin, and Carol R. Ember, eds. 1999. *Cultures of the World: Selections from the Ten-Volume Encyclopedia of World Cultures*. New York: Macmillan Library Reference USA.

Frazer, James. 1981. *The Golden Bough*. 1890. Reprint, New York: Grammercy.

———. 1918a. *Folk-Lore in the Old Testament*. Vol. 1. London: Macmillan.

———. 1918b. *Folk-Lore in the Old Testament*. Vol. 2. London: Macmillan.

———. 1918c. *Folk-Lore in the Old Testament*. Vol. 3. London: Macmillan.

Gaster, Theodor H. 1950. *Thespis: Ritual, Myth, and Drama in the Ancient Near East*. New York: Harper & Row.

———, ed. 1959. *The New Golden Bough*. New York: Criterion.

————. 1969. *Myth, Legend and Custom in the Old Testament*. New York: Harper & Row.

Gunkel, Hermann. 1928. *What Remains of the Old Testament and Other Essays*. Translated by A. K. Dallas. New York: Macmillan.

————. 1964. *The Legends of Genesis: The Biblical Saga and History*. Translated by W. H. Carruth. Reprint of the introduction to the author's 1901 *Commentary on Genesis*. New York: Schocken.

————. 1987. *The Folktale in the Old Testament*. Translated by M. D. Rutter. Translation of the 1917 ed. Sheffield: Almond.

Lambert, W. G., and A. R. Millard, eds. 1999. *Atra-Hasis: The Babylonian Story of the Flood*. 1969. Reprint, Winona Lake, IN: Eisenbrauns.

Malina, Bruce. 1989. "Dealing with Biblical (Mediterranean) Characters: A Guide for U.S. Consumers." *BTB* 19:127–41.

Moran, William L. 1971. "Atrahasis: The Babylonian Story of the Flood." *Bib* 52:51–61.

Mowinckel, Sigmund. 1966. *Psalmenstudien: 1921–1924*. Amsterdam: Grüner.

Murdock, George Peter. 1969. *Ethnographic Atlas*. 3rd ed. Pittsburgh: University of Pittsburgh Press.

————. 1981. *Atlas of World Cultures*. Pittsburgh: University of Pittsburgh Press.

Murdock, George Peter, C. S. Ford, A. E. Hudson, R. Kennedy, L. W. Simmons, and J. W. M. Whiting. 1987. *Outline of Cultural Materials*. 5th ed. New Haven: Human Relations Area Files.

Oswalt, J. N. 1980. "Kabash." In *Theological Wordbook of the Old Testament*, edited by R. Laird Harris, Gleason L. Archer, and Bruce K. Waltke, 1:430. Chicago: Moody Press.

Page, Hugh R., Jr. 1999. "The Marking of Social, Political, Religious, and Other Boundaries in Biblical Literature—A Case Study Using the Book of Judges." *Research in the Social Scientific Study of Religion* 10:37–55.

Pedersen, Johannes. 1926–1940. *Israel: Its Life and Culture*. 4 vols. London: Oxford University Press.

Price, David H. 2004. *Atlas of World Cultures: A Geographical Guide to Ethnographic Literature*. 1989. Reprint, Caldwell, NJ: Blackburn.

Rad, Gerhard von. 1966. *The Problem of the Hexateuch and Other Essays*. London: SCM.

Thompson, Stith. 2001. *Motif-index of Folk-Literature: A Classification of Narrative Elements in Folk-tales, Ballads, Myths, Fables, Mediaeval Romances, Exempla, Fabliaux, Jest-Books*. Rev. ed. 6 vols. Bloomington: University of Indiana Press.

United Nations General Assembly. 2000. "Universal Declaration of Human Rights (1948)." In *Sourcebook of the World's Religions: An Interfaith Guide to Religion and Spirituality*, edited by J. Beversluis, 325–28. Novato, CA: New World Library.

————. 2007. *United Nations Declaration on the Rights of Indigenous Peoples*. http://www.un.org/esa/socdev/unpfii/documents/DRIPS_en.pdf.

READING THE CHRISTIAN OLD TESTAMENT IN THE CONTEMPORARY WORLD

Daniel L. Smith-Christopher

In nineteenth-century Charleston, South Carolina, the Old Testament seemed to assure Episcopal clergyman Frederick Dalcho that slavery was consistent with Christian faith. The same Old Testament, however, particularly Josh. 6:21, just as powerfully inspired fellow Charleston resident and former slave Denmark Vesey to plan a slave revolt. Those involved in the slave revolt felt assured that God would help them "utterly destroy all in the city, both men and women, young and old, with the edge of the sword" (Edgerton 1999, 101–25). In 2010, Steven Hayward, at that time F. K. Weyerhaeuser Fellow at the American Enterprise Institute, published an essay in which he read the story of Joseph in Egypt as a dire warning against government intervention, and suggested that his reading of these texts from Genesis served as a defense of a free-market, private-property economic system. Also in 2010, John Rogerson, professor of Scripture at Sheffield University, began his book on Old Testament theology, written because he, too, believed that the "Old Testament has something to say to today's world(s)," by stating that he wrote as "an Anglican priest . . . a humanist and a socialist" (Rogerson, 11). Dr. James Edwards, of the Center for Immigration Studies, reads some of the Mosaic laws of the Old Testament as defending firm national borders, low tolerance for immigration rights, and concerns for cultural corruption by outsiders (Edwards 2009 n.p., online), while Dr. Lai Ling Elizabeth Ngan of Baylor University, an Asian American scholar, finds that the Old Testament story about God's listening to the prayers of the "foreign woman," namely Hagar, "redefines boundaries that others have inscribed for her"; the story suggests that modern Christians should uphold the dignity of all peoples and resist denigrating people because of physical or racial differences (Ngan 2006, 83).

These are six Christians, all reading their Old Testament in the contemporary world. The fact that not all of these voices are biblical scholars, however, only serves to highlight the fact that reading the Christian Old Testament in the contemporary world is a complex mixture of the scholarly as well as the popular, stereotyped traditional views as well as innovative new insights, and that reading the Old Testament often strikingly divides readers into quite seriously opposing social and political views. Does this mean that reading the Christian Bible (Old or New Testament) in the modern world is a parade example of Cole Porter's 1934 song "Anything Goes"? Is it a matter of some disappointment that we can still agree with Leo Perdue's 1994 observation that "no commanding contemporary theology has yet appeared to form a consensus" (Perdue 1994, 8)?

I would argue that there is no cause for despair. Quite to the contrary! One of the most fascinating aspects of reading the Christian Old Testament in the contemporary world is not simply that there is unprecedented enthusiasm and diversity among scholars and viewpoints in the field but also that *this diversity itself is part of an ongoing debate and discussion*. At the outset, however, we should clarify that we are interested in thinking about serious readings of the Christian Old Testament, and not merely social or political propaganda that lightly seasons its rhetoric with a few Bible verses.

Marketplaces vs. Museums

Biblical scholarship is separated from religious propaganda not only by the fact that biblical scholarship presumes a basic orientation in the relevant historical contexts of the ancient world, familiarity with a diversity of texts both ancient and modern, and the ability to recognize a good argument supported by credible evidence or reasonable suggestions. These are all essential, of course. What really separates biblical scholarship from propaganda is the fact that biblical scholarship in the contemporary world is part of an ongoing discussion—a discussion that knows *and listens* to the challenges of others and seeks to contribute one's own insights *as part of the discussion*. As in all fields of discovery and intellectual endeavor, the success of biblical scholarship is not to be measured by the achievement of some dominant unanimity, but rather is judged by the quality and results of the participation in the scholarly tasks at hand and the *shared perception* that progress is taking place. We are seeing and understanding biblical texts in ever more profound and provocative ways. However, one of the most striking aspects of the rise of simplistic or propagandist use of the Bible is precisely its refusal to engage in dialogue, self-correction, or even acknowledgment of rival views, beyond the occasional ad hominem dismissal of arguments based solely on their association with groups identified by politicized generalizations—for example, "those liberals."

What we are suggesting is that there is an essential *dialogue* in modern, serious reading of the Bible. So, if this essay on reading the Christian Old Testament is not to be a rehearsal of some of the grand theories generally agreed on, now and forever (like a quiet museum tour of accomplishments), it is time for a new guiding image. I am intrigued by suggestions of the Cuban American New Testament scholar Fernando Segovia, who celebrates diversity in dialogue over the Scriptures. Segovia has famously suggested the "marketplace of ideas," rather like Wole Soyinka's discussion of the Silk Road market town Samarkand, as an image of modern sharing and exchanging of multicultural ideas and friendships (see Segovia and Tolbert; Segovia; Soyinka). An introduction to reading the Christian Old Testament in the contemporary world does not need to provide a historical survey of the "great ideas" that led to the present. Good surveys already exist, if European-dominated ideas are one's particular interest (e.g., Ollenburger; Rogerson 1984; Hayes and Prussner). Marketplaces can be elusive, however. They exist within the totality of the lives of people from everywhere, people who set up stalls and shop. Like the night markets of Auckland, New Zealand, or Darwin, Australia, they appear at designated places, at the designated hours, but otherwise there is only quiet. In short, the image of the marketplace suggests that we need a guidebook.

Laura Pulido, Laura Barraclough, and Wendy Cheng have recently published a marvelous, politically informed tour guide titled *A People's Guide to Los Angeles* (2012). The introduction itself is worth the price of admission. In these preliminary observations, the authors reflect on guidebooks and Los Angeles itself.

> *A People's Guide to Los Angeles* is a deliberate political disruption of the way Los Angeles is com-
> monly known and experienced. . . . Guidebooks select sites, put them on a map, and interpret
> them in terms of their historical and contemporary significance. All such representations are
> political, because they highlight some perspectives while overlooking others. Struggles over who
> and what counts as "historic" and worthy of a visit involve decisions about who belongs and who
> doesn't, who is worth remembering and who can be forgotten, who we have been and who we
> are becoming.

They continue,

> Mainstream guidebooks typically describe and interpret their sites through the story of one
> person—almost always a man, and usually the capitalist who invested in a place, or its architect
> or designer. In doing so, they reinforce an individualized and masculinist way of thinking about
> history. Meanwhile, the collectives of people who actually created, built, or used the space remain
> nameless.

It would be difficult to think of a better series of thoughts to begin an essay on reading the Christian Old Testament in the contemporary world, because biblical analysis is rarely, if ever, written without some contemporary concerns in mind. Modern biblical theologies, for example, now usually identify the perspective of the author in the contemporary world (e.g., Brueggemann 1997; Rogerson 2010). Thus I am quite certain that part of the reason I agree with this need for a new image is that I write as a Christian who was born into, and very self-consciously remain informed by, the Quaker tradition. I also learned a great deal of biblical history, language, and theology from my fellow Christian sectarians the Mennonites, and I was first inspired to think seriously about biblical theology in high school by reading Vernard Eller, a theologian from yet another of my sister sectarian movements, the Church of the Brethren (informally known as the Dunkers). This means that I write as a Christian raised on "counterhistories" of the Christian movement—George Fox on Pendle Hill, Margaret Fell at Swarthmore, Conrad Grebel in Zurich, and Alexander Mack in Philadelphia—in addition to the canonical events of Christian history, such as the councils, the division between Rome and the Eastern Orthodox, Calvin, Luther, Wesley, and so on. I am thus well aware that texts, like towns, are susceptible to decisions about which locations are worthy of a visit, and which locations ought to be "memorialized" as deeply important. We could visit the old, established halls memorializing conquest or power—or we can find the marketplaces where we can encounter new ideas, argue with the "stall keepers" (the authors), make offers and listen to the counteroffers. In short, Christian biblical scholarship is tolerant of a variety of particular views of biblical texts, grammar, history, or theological interpretation. It is quite properly intolerant of the refusal to participate in dialogue with others. One of the hallmarks of propagandist abuses of the Bible in the modern world is the virtual absence of dialogue with other serious students of the Bible—a refusal to appear in the marketplace where ideas are examined and challenged.

It might seem that all this "marketplace" talk runs the risk of privileging process rather than results, and thus avoiding the hard work of evaluating whether ideas are good or bad, and then promoting the good. It is a uniquely contemporary heresy, however, to privilege solitary ideas or accomplishments while overlooking the long processes that often lead to any achievements worthy of celebration. Furthermore, to celebrate dialogue in the development of Christian thought about the Bible has sometimes been thought to be a uniquely modern phenomenon. That is already a mistake. What constitutes the "Old Testament," and even whether to have one, have both been matters of serious debate in Christian history.

The Christian Old Testament as a Product of Dialogue

Let us begin with a deceptively simple question: What constitutes the Old Testament? Christians do not even agree on this! Before the early Christian movement that historians now routinely refer to as "orthodox" arose victorious, the determination of what would be the authorized and foundational writings for Christian faith was a lively debate. The so-called *Festal Letter* 39 of Athanasius, which includes the earliest authoritative "list" of a canon of the Christian Bible, is dated to (a surprisingly late) 367 CE. Before then, debates about texts clearly ranged widely, and this does not even address the interesting continued use of noncanonical lore in popular, pre-Reformation medieval theater in the streets and churches of Europe (see Muir).

Furthermore, Athanasius's fourth-century declaration did not really settle the matter. Protestant, Catholic, and Orthodox Christians have each determined to authorize slightly different Old Testaments. Catholics, staying with the collection of Jewish writings that appeared in some of the old Greek translations known as the Septuagint (LXX), have included a series of books in the Old Testament that Protestants do not recognize, which Catholics call "deuterocanonical," and the Orthodox have chosen to include even a few more of these later Jewish (but still pre-Christian) writings. Protestants usually refer to these works as "the Apocrypha." Having said this, however, the difference between Christian canons has fewer implications for biblical scholarship than one might suspect at first. This is primarily because academic biblical studies, including biblical theological work, now tends to overlook specific church doctrines regarding the categories of "canonical," "deuterocanonical," and "noncanonical" writings. In the biblical studies marketplace, no text, artifact, ancient translation, or geographical context is "off limits" to research, comment, and consideration.

Canonical works obviously get the most attention—but it is hardly exclusive—and commentaries and critical analysis of *noncanonical* writing often make significant contributions to the further understanding of the canonical work as well. But we aren't finished with dialogue in relation to the existence of the Old Testament.

In fact, Christianity was marked by diversity in dialogue from the very beginning, as any sober reading of the arguments discussed in the book of Acts clearly reveals. One reason that dialogue is such an important context for thinking about the Old Testament is the fact that *the very existence of a "Christian Old Testament" was not a matter of widespread agreement in the earliest history of Christianity*. The early Christian convert Marcion (c. 85–160) famously proposed that true Christianity ought to discard any connection whatsoever to Judaism and the Jewish tradition; he embraced only a limited number of writings to represent this clean break between Jesus and the Jewish tradition (he proposed only a version of Luke, and ten Pauline epistles). However, the reaction was furious and widespread. W. H. C. Frend argues that Marcion holds the distinction of being "one of the very few opponents of orthodoxy whom Greek and Latin theologians united in damning. For nearly a century after his death . . . he was the arch-heretic" (212). Clearly, not every idea in the marketplace survives. We can stop cynically humming Porter's "Anything Goes" now.

The first Christian centuries, therefore, bequeath a task to all subsequent generations of readers of the "Christian Old Testament," namely, to take these writings into serious consideration when determining the nature of Christian faith. Furthermore, the vast majority of modern Christian communities (Protestant, Catholic, and Orthodox) have agreed with the church fathers and mothers of the first centuries that Christianity does indeed have a "canon," and that the Hebrew writings are part of it. Is this a settled issue, then? Hardly. Before we can speak of ways the Christian Old Testament is being read in the contemporary world, it is important to acknowledge, however briefly, that there are still ways it is *not* being read, and that it is even effectively ignored, in Christian faith and practice. Marcion still haunts us.

Tourism vs. Engagement: Ignoring the Marketplace?

As Aidan Nichols has recently acknowledged for the Catholic Church (2007), and as many others have suggested for other churches (Jenkins 2006, 42–47), a serious tendency remains among many Christian traditions in the modern world to overlook the larger part of their Bible before the Gospel of Matthew begins. Effectively ignoring the witness of the Old Testament for modern Christian faith and practice has sometimes been referred to as "Neo-Marcionism" (Nichols, 81). Even though few modern Christians would explicitly admit to it, the lack of effective education or preaching in Old Testament/Hebrew Bible studies is an alarming prospect for Christian faith and practice. A Christian theology cannot be true to the historic legacy of the faith tradition if it perpetuates such a neo-Marcionite subordination of these texts. This can happen in a number of ways, but it is more typical of popular and/or propagandist readings of the Bible than in biblical scholarship. In fact, some ways of "reading the Christian Old Testament" are simply ways to avoid it!

For example, there is a huge market for "Bible prophecy" books in the United States. One of the most significant criticisms of this popular literature is not only its total neglect of serious biblical scholarship on the prophetic books of the Old Testament but also its exclusive interest in how the books of the Bible may be "decoded" so that they can be understood to refer to contemporary events—as if the eighth-century-BCE book of Amos were actually speaking about twentieth-century Russia, or second-century-BCE portions of the book of Daniel were actually speaking about the twentieth-century ayatollahs of Iran. This "decoding" process usually neglects the historical content of the Old Testament book at hand in favor of what it is "understood" to be saying about modern times. In short, the actual content is merely a code. Its decoded meaning has nothing to do with what is actually written, when it was written, or who may have written it. One effective way of entirely ignoring a biblical book, then, is to completely reconstruct it without regard to its actual content as a historical work. This may not be Marcion's original idea, but he would clearly approve. This radical transformation of the work has little to do with actual study of it, nor is this part of the serious dialogue taking place about how the books of the Old Testament ought to inform contemporary Christian faith and practice.

This case of wildly popular literature on Bible prophecy in the modern world is particularly ironic. While some Christians frequently fault biblical scholars for not accepting the "plain sense" of the biblical text, it is astounding how carefully the various approaches to Bible prophecy omit any engagement with the most straightforward, or "plain," messages of the prophets of ancient Israel, namely, God's concern for the poor and the judgment threatened against the rich and powerful, those who, in the unforgettable images of Amos and Isaiah,

> trample the head of the poor into the dust of the earth,
>   and push the afflicted out of the way (Amos 2:7)

or who

> join house to house,
>   who add field to field,
> until there is room for no one but you,
>   and you are left to live alone
>   in the midst of the land! (Isa. 5:8)

No decoding seems necessary here. Radically altering the Old Testament texts beyond any credible historical or theological contexts in the process is clearly to do violence to those texts.

Another even more problematic way to virtually ignore the Old Testament in the Christian tradition is the Christian idea that the Old Testament is "old" and therefore largely replaced by the New Testament. Jesus is thus understood to have so reformed Jewish thought, very much as in Marcion's original proposal, that very little of the Old Testament is left of any real importance for Christian theology (save, perhaps, for the Ten Commandments). The dangers of such a "de-Semiticized" Jesus are legion, beginning with the problem of failing to understand Jesus' own faith tradition. For example, the event universally known as the "cleansing of the temple" is incomprehensible apart from recognizing that Jesus cites two Hebrew prophets in the act (Jer. 7:11 and Isa. 56:7). The reactions to Jesus' famous "reading" in his home synagogue in Luke 4 are equally incomprehensible apart from carefully noting the Old Testament references therein. Such examples can be multiplied throughout the New Testament.

Finally, the Hebrew tradition in both its historic and contemporary expressions is revered by a living people. Contemporary Christian scholarship is increasingly open to dialogue with Jewish biblical scholarship. Even though all Christians share most of the books of the Jewish canon with Judaism, there has been historically a significant difference in Jewish study of the Bible as opposed to Christian study (see summaries in Sommer 2012). One of the important characteristics of modern Christian readings of the Old Testament is that Jewish, Roman Catholic, Orthodox, and Protestant Scripture scholars are all in dialogue and discussion with each other in biblical studies on levels unprecedented before the twentieth century, and these dialogues continue in a variety of academic contexts in the twenty-first century.

Exorcising the ghost of Marcion from contemporary Christian scholarship of the Old Testament properly insists that taking the Old Testament seriously for Christian faith and practice involves a consideration of what Old Testament writings can say to the Christian tradition, not vice versa; Christian tradition should not use the Old Testament to buttress predetermined doctrinal ideas derived from the New Testament. Dictating terms to the Old Testament will never allow it to speak to Christian faith and practice in new and challenging ways. That isn't the way a marketplace works, after all, and trying to fix prices and control commodities only leads to other marketplaces.

The Role of Historical Events in the Old Testament for Christian Faith and Practice

We have already determined that the adjective *Christian* in our title means that we are interested in how the Old Testament speaks to Christian faith and practice, and therefore we are interested in discussing the role of "biblical theology." Here we encounter one of the loudest sectors of our marketplace. There are contemporary scholars (see Barr) who maintain an older tradition that suggests Old Testament scholarship should never be primarily "religious" or "theological," but rather historical, examining texts and other ancient evidence and then handing the results over to the theologians. Thus some scholars believe that biblical theology seeks to identify an exclusively *historical* expression of *past* belief (e.g., What did the ancient Israelites believe?). Indeed, the famous inaugural lecture of Johann Gabler in 1787, considered by some to be the "founding document" of this understanding of biblical theology (Gabler, 497), argued quite forcefully for maintaining a clear separation between biblical theology, defined as an exclusively historical enterprise, on the one hand, and systematic ("dogmatic") theology on the other.

It should be acknowledged that many modern biblical scholars would insist on this same separation between the historical and the theological approaches to Old Testament study and firmly place themselves in the "historical questions only" camp. Some scholars, again citing the late James Barr, have no objection to doing Christian theology based on biblical ideas, but believe that the formulation of these religious ideas ought to be a separate task from the exclusively historical task of Old Testament study. There are others who have doubts about religious belief in general or about the viability or validity of the specific religious traditions that make religious use of these writings. Some biblical scholars self-identify as atheists, for example, and there are even contemporary biblical scholars who openly condemn the very notion of a viable contemporary belief informed by the Bible (e.g., Avalos).

Both versions of the "historical analysis only" argument would maintain that it is not only possible but also necessary for a scholar of biblical texts to refrain from allowing contemporary interests or commitments (religious or otherwise) to "bias" or "interfere" with the task of historical analysis. This proposed form of historical analysis is represented as an activity that seeks to emulate scientific methodology as much as possible. The goal of this approach is thus described as "objective knowledge," or at least a close approximation of objective knowledge, even if these scholars were to acknowledge that certain influences or limitations of a time period certainly apply, such as the state of historical, archaeological, and textual studies at the time. In either case, the result is similar: a form of biblical studies that would be understood entirely as an aspect of historical investigation, no different in kind from determining what Shakespeare or Isaac Newton may have "believed," on religious (or any other) questions. Thus, while some may think or hope that their work could contribute to Christian faith and practice, they would carefully leave that task to others.

Interest-Free Biblical Analysis?

Recent debates, however, forcefully challenge many of the methodological assumptions that a bias-free analysis of historical texts is even a possible, much less laudable, goal. The term *postmodernism* is normally assigned to such challenges. Especially since the work of Thomas Kuhn (who gave us the concept of a "paradigm shift," 1996) and Paul Feyerabend (who calls for an "anarchist theory of knowledge," 2010), even the notion of an "objective" *scientific* analysis (science being the purported, even if largely self-appointed, model of objective analysis for all fields of inquiry) has been largely abandoned as both claim and goal. Motivations or interests do not necessarily poison results, but in the postmodern age, we are always vigilant about their influence, and thus the tendency in postmodernism is to declare such "interests" in the work itself. Does this preclude the possibility of doing biblical theology for modern Christian faith and practice? I contend that the postmodern criticism of a "bias-free" analysis of the Bible not only allows an enterprise of biblical theology but also positively encourages it.

The endless debates about the precise meaning of postmodernism need not distract us from a useful insight associated with this term: *all knowledge is contingent.* What we "know" usually depends on what we seek to know, and thus the questions we think to ask. Furthermore, what we investigate is influenced by own concerns, and we also sort out and determine which of our results are the most important. This is all part of the dialogue of diversity and, in twenty-first-century study of the Christian Old Testament, is now a widely acknowledged working assumption. Few would deny the importance of not only the identification of one's own working interests and assumptions in thinking about how the Christian Old Testament can speak to the modern age but also the retrospective work of placing older Old Testament theological writings in important social and historical contexts in ways that deepen our appreciation of their achievements and limitations (Rogerson 1984).

Is There a "Collapse of History" in Christian Old Testament Study?

There is an interesting debate going on in another sector of the marketplace. In his recent important monographs on the problems of Old Testament biblical theology, Leo Perdue refers to a "collapse of history" in recent biblical studies. One of the ways he formulates this point is to ask: Can these predominantly religious texts really help us reconstruct historical events in ancient Israel? If not, how can it be said that Israel's experience is important for contemporary readers who are seeking to read these texts as a guide to events that inform contemporary faith and practice? Perdue alludes to an important ongoing debate that began in the late twentieth century, a debate about our ability to know much actual history from what is available to us both in the Old Testament texts and in the relevant archaeological work (both ancient texts and artifacts) that supplements the study of biblical texts.

Especially after the publication of Thomas L. Thompson's widely cited monograph *The Historicity of the Patriarchal Narratives* (1974), fiery debates ensued between scholars who were divided (often unfairly) into "camps" called "minimalists" and "maximalists." These terms referred to those who despaired of the ability to be confident about historical events at all (thus "minimalists") and those who thought there was actually a great deal more evidence for biblical history than was often acknowledged (so Dever 2001; 2003). An interesting summary view of some of the historical debates is provided by Grabbe.

However, as some contemporary scholars have pointed out (see Brueggemann), these debates about historical events and biblical narratives mask the importance of answering a previous question, namely, whether *establishing that an event happened—or precisely how it happened—automatically dictates a corresponding religious significance to that event.* Clearly, it does not. Even if I can be convinced, for example, that the measurements of the temple provided in Ezekiel 40–48 are precise, accurate dimensions of the Jerusalem temple during the first millennium BCE, this does not strike me as having monumental importance for Christian faith and practice. It may have quite fascinating historical interest, but *theological* significance? This can also apply to less obscure issues. For example, determining that the texts in the opening chapters of the book of Exodus give us a more or less "historically reliable" report of the actual events of Israelites departing from Egypt does not thereby answer the question: Of what significance is the departure from Egypt *for contemporary Christian faith and practice*? Simply agreeing on the *historical* reliability of a biblical passage leaves considerable ground to cover on questions of *significance*. Simply agreeing on the historical details of the exodus, for example, does not thereby make one a liberation theologian. In fact, precious little of the powerful writings of liberation theology, beginning with the 1968 gathering of bishops in Medellín, Colombia (CELAM), actually debated the historical details of the book of Exodus. It is not that the historical story is insignificant; but rather its historical significance, if any, needs to be *part* of the theological argument, and not the entire task.

What happens when different perspectives can no longer be united on a particular reading of biblical events, especially on the accompanying significance of those events? Dominant and influential Old Testament theologies of the past depended on accepting an assigned weight to particular passages or biblical events that were considered central or guiding concepts, and thus critically important for modern theology. For example, Walter Eichrodt proposed that the idea of God's establishing agreements or "covenants" with God's people represents the central notion of the entire Hebrew Bible (Eichrodt 1961; 1967; the original German volumes were published in 1933 and 1935). Gerhard von Rad's equally influential Old Testament theology (Rad 1962; 1965; German 1957 and 1960) argued for the central importance of certain narratives of faith that Israelites allegedly repeated (he used the term "creeds") as indications of their faith, and thus suggested that Israelites were people who identified with such narratives. There is little doubt that such theological arguments, based on readings of the Old Testament, exerted a powerful influence on Christian theological education throughout the Western world in the twentieth century.

However, what if differing perspectives on the part of modern readers of the Bible—especially influenced by differing life situations (ethnicity, gender, etc.)—suggest to some modern readers that different biblical "events" in the Old Testament (whether unquestionably historical or not) are more important than others? Examples are not difficult to cite. On the one hand, after 1968, Latin American biblical scholars (especially Roman Catholic scholars) determined that the Moses and Exodus stories had a powerful message for them in their modern-day circumstances of economic poverty. On the other hand, Native American (Osage) professor of American studies Robert Allan Warrior famously challenged biblical theologians who celebrated the exodus and the entry to a "promised land" by noting that Native Americans frankly had more in common with the beleaguered Canaanites, reminding us that indigenous peoples continue to have an ambiguous relationship with the legacy of the book of Joshua (see Warrior). Nineteenth-century African American slaves also determined that the Jonah and Daniel stories had powerful messages for them in their circumstances of oppression and suppression (Levine; Cone 1992). Finally, recent suggestions view the conquest of Jerusalem in 587 and the subsequent exile of thousands of Judeans (Albertz; Ahn) as a biblical event with serious theological implications (Brueggemann; Smith-Christopher 2002). Nineteenth-century Maori Christians in New Zealand determined that the prophets were powerful examples of a new form of pantribal leadership that had new potential to unite previously fragmented tribal peoples in opposition to growing European settlement, and some even looked to the Davidic monarchy as a model for a new and culturally unprecedented Maori king, and thus an answer to the power and authority of the British Crown (Elsmore 1985; 1989). Is all this also a "collapse of history"? Or is it really the collapse of *dominant readings* of history in the face of alternative decisions about central ideas, events, and themes?

There is little doubt that some Christian biblical scholars and theologians lament the absence of the dominant Old Testament readings. Such a view arguably represents a kind of wistfulness for the "good old days" when a dominant perspective seemed to influence writing and doing (and teaching!) Old Testament theology in Christian institutions of higher learning. Not only does this "hoped-for dominant" perspective do violence to those who were never part of the "dominant perspective" (because they were either gender or cultural minorities, e.g., women, African American,

Asian American, Latino/Latina, or theological minorities such as Anabaptists, Quakers, or Pentecostals), but it is also arguably built on a largely discredited model of intellectual progress that mimics seventeenth- to twentieth-century Western imperial politics and social values—namely, the (intellectual) goal of domination and the vanquishing of opposition.

Surely an alternative to dominance or conquest is concord, dialogue, and cooperation in common causes. If we are to read the Christian Old Testament, and consider it theologically significant, then that theological significance will have to extend to the entire world. The *emerging* Christian world is now based in the Southern Hemisphere (Jenkins 2002). Reading the Christian Old Testament is thus by necessity a global enterprise. The modern marketplace is diverse indeed, and there are a number of ways to recognize this diversity.

Contemporary Worlds in Dialogue

We have seen that Segovia's "marketplace of ideas" does not so much despair of speaking of the past at all, much less signal a "collapse of history." The issue is not whether history can be written any longer. Rather, the issue is how different histories, and different texts, can be understood to matter in differing contexts. Marketplaces can resist organization. Nevertheless, there are perhaps two general ways of sorting the diversity in view. One way is to focus on the identities of the participants themselves, especially in those cases when they consciously and explicitly draw on these identities in their reading of the Bible. The other is to focus on challenges to the human enterprise in local or global contexts. Many of these challenges will require that we marshal our collective wisdom in order to survive as a species, and there are hardly more urgent reasons for biblical scholars to make their contribution to the ideological, spiritual, and political will of people to act in positive ways.

Text and Experience: The Feminist Pioneering of New Questions

New Testament scholar Elisabeth Schüssler Fiorenza points out that it was early feminist critical studies that largely opened up critical readings of both the New and Old Testaments from a perspective informed by particular "interests" (see Schüssler Fiorenza). One of first of these interests was reviewing the long-presumed subordination of women in the narratives of the Bible. It is interesting to see how this work progressed in a variety of different directions, all inspired by gender-related questions. For some feminist readers of the Bible, restating the often unacknowledged positive and powerful roles of women in the Bible is an important corrective to assumptions about the exclusive biblical focus on men (Gafney; Meyers 1988/2013). Phyllis Trible, on the other hand, pioneered the role of an unvarnished focus on destructive texts featuring violence against women, calling them "texts of terror" and thus highlighting dangerous tendencies within historical biblical cultures themselves (see Trible). Renita Weems, similarly, opened a line of investigation on the prophetic use of violent language associated with feminized subjects and objects that also betrayed violent attitudes (e.g., "Lady Jerusalem," Weems 1995). Kathleen O'Connor, Elizabeth Boase, and Carleen Mandolfo have taken this conversation further, suggesting that there is evidence of an ongoing dialogue with "Lady Jerusalem" that began with the violent imagery noted by

Weems in Hosea and Ezekiel, but then continued to Lamentations and Deutero-Isaiah, suggesting that there is acknowledgment of and even repentance for this violence (see O'Connor; Boase; Mandolfo). There are many other directions that studies can go, many of which explicitly identify as feminist, or gender-interested, analysis (see, e.g., Yee 2003).

The feminist approach, far from being a limiting perspective, has moved methodologically from an interest in one formulation of a "minority" perspective—namely, the role of women—to a comparative interest in how this critical approach relates to other issues of "gendering" and "embodiment" in the Bible (homosexuality, prostitution, especially the vexed question of temple prostitution, foreign wives of mixed marriages, gender in relation to slavery, etc.). This approach can also move beyond questions of gender. These early feminist perspectives quite logically moved toward an interest in those who are considered "marginalized" in Hebrew texts—for example, Edomites, Egyptians, Moabites, those lumped together as "aliens" in the Mosaic laws, foreign workers—for other reasons. Interesting work indeed. But what does it have to do with Christian faith and practice?

While not all feminist analysis of the Bible is done with the hope that it will contribute to a more equitable and egalitarian Christian movement in the contemporary world, a considerable amount is.

Cultural Identities and Social Situations in the Marketplace

Feminism is not the only "contemporary interest" that has driven new questions in Christian biblical analysis. Especially those who hope biblical analysis will affect Christian faith and practice have made significant contributions. Already in narratives of freed slaves in North America, African American readers of the Bible were reflecting on their own insights, especially as a countertheology to the European preachers who constantly preached obedience and subservience (see Raboteau; Hopkins and Cummings). In fact, it is possible to trace a twentieth-century flowering of these early readings, some of which began by reexamining the role of explicitly identified Africans in biblical history (see Felder) in a manner similar to those who reexamined the Old Testament stories explicitly about women. One clear goal was to highlight African presence in the Bible that had been neglected in the face of racial prejudice in the modern world against those of African descent. However, in the wake of important calls for a more assertive black theology in the twentieth century (Cone 1970), this project then expanded in different directions in ways very similar to the expansion of gender-related questions (and often intersecting with gender questions, e.g., in "womanist" analysis; see Weems 1991). In the African American context, the appearance of the groundbreaking work *Stony the Road We Trod* (Felder) was a major contribution to the maturing of contemporary, consciously African American biblical scholarship. Included in this collection were essays that dealt not only with historical-critical analysis of the Bible from an African American perspective, but with the use of the Bible in the history of African American interpretation. Further work on African American history of interpretation (Callahan; Wimbush) continues to make important contributions to unique insights into both the later use of Scripture, but also arguments contributing to historical understanding of the texts themselves. Not only is the role of the Bible in African American history itself the subject of important analysis, but African American biblical analysis is also interested in examining texts that have been used historically to suppress both those of explicitly African descent (for example, to defend slavery) and many non-European peoples. A convergence in methods, and sometimes goals, began to emerge that sought to forge alliances across explicitly named cultural or ethnic categories.

So, even though it has followed a different trajectory than African American scholarship, Latino/ Latina literature now also holds an important place in the context of the United States. For example, Justo González, Jean-Paul Ruiz, and Miguel De La Torre (2002; 2007) have published monographs and commentaries on Old Testament themes. Interestingly, however, De La Torre has taken a somewhat pessimistic attitude as to whether cross-cultural analysis of the text will influence the general discipline. De La Torre is clear—Euro-Americans are largely not to be trusted for biblical analysis, because "Euroamerican Christians, either from the fundamentalist right or the far liberal left, probably have more in common with each other and understand each other better than they do Christians on the other side of the racial and ethnic divide" (De La Torre 2007, 125). Nevertheless, serious contributions continue to challenge biblical scholars to take seriously the contributions of those who write Old Testament analysis from an openly acknowledged perspective. Gregory Lee Cuéllar, for example, compares passages of Isaiah to the Mexican and Mexican American folk music style known as the *Corrido*, not only to suggest ways that the biblical texts can be understood in contemporary Mexican American communities, but also to propose potential new readings for the book of Isaiah itself (Cuéllar 2008).

While there have been a number of important works from Asian American biblical scholars in the late twentieth century that consciously draw on Asian themes and identity, a significant milestone was the publication in 2006 of the collected volume *Ways of Being, Ways of Reading*. This volume was comparable in many ways to the impact of the 1991 work *Stony the Road We Trod* in the African American scholarly context. It includes retrospective and survey essays, even very personal reflections on academic work (e.g., Yee 2006), as well as examples of contemporary work of some of the most prominent American scholars using cross-cultural approaches.

Finally, in terms of the American context, it is notable that Randall Bailey, Tat-siong Benny Liew, and Fernando Segovia have initiated a dialogue between Latino/a American, Asian American, and African American scholarship, hoping to find common ground in "minority" analysis of the Bible (Bailey, Liew, and Segovia), suggesting the possibilities of a convergence and maturing of methods of analysis, even as they reject any sort of false consensus on similarity of cultural contexts.

Although it is fair to say that readings explicitly related to specific cultural and ethnic identities and traditions continue in the century, attention has tended to turn toward social, political, and economic locations as another significant source of issues that influence the reading of Scripture. In the last quarter of the twentieth century, a number of Old Testament scholars consciously incorporated sociological and anthropological analysis in their ancient historiography of the Bible (Gottwald; Overholt 1992, 2003), and this dialogue with social sciences certainly continues (Chalcraft). Exegetical issues of the most recent writing in Old Testament studies soon converged on a series of questions closely associated with the influence of Edward Said's classic work *Orientalism*, which further built on the early social theories and the observations of the postcolonial theorists Frantz Fanon and Albert Memmi. Once this dialogue with Said's influence was articulated powerfully in the many works of R. S. Sugirtharajah, the rise of postcolonial approaches to Scripture became a significant movement in the early twenty-first century. Sugirtharajah's now classic compendium *Voices from the Margin* signaled a new energy in "interested perspectives" in the reading of the Bible.

The Rise of Postcolonial Biblical Analysis

We have already noted that Christianity—and its Bible—is seeing profound growth in the Southern Hemisphere in the twenty-first century. Twentieth-century Christians in developing societies, especially India, South America, and Africa, began to assert their own perspectives in the analysis of the Bible. After Said's influential work, they began to identify ways in which previous European scholarship contained certain social and cultural assumptions about Western superiority. They then began readings of the Bible within their past experiences of European colonial presence. In the process of reasserting a cultural and/or national identity, however, they soon realized that a reconstruction of cultural identity in the new world could never go back to a purified "precolonial" state, but must always be in dialogue with the social, political, and philosophical realities of having been deeply affected by Western thought and practice. Although in the context of religion and the Bible, one might better speak of "post-Western-missionaryism," the discussions in biblical studies borrowed a term from social and cultural theory to identify their new reviews of the Bible in their own contexts: *postcolonialism*. Postcolonial biblical exegesis provided special tools for Christians in formerly colonized states (or among indigenous peoples in Western European settled lands, North and South America, Australia, and New Zealand). The questions whether, and to what extent, largely imported biblical scholarship was (and is) tainted by imperial goals of control and economic expansion raised serious concerns about those readings of Scripture that seemed deeply involved in that imperial process (De le Torre 2002). A prime example of attempting to counter Western domination was the Latin American assertion that the exodus is the prime event of the Old Testament—and thus liberation is the prime theological theme. However, it is important to note that these questions were being raised largely by Christian Bible scholars. Not all criticism of colonial and missionary policies rejected Christianity and the Bible as an unwanted imposition (see Roberts); sometimes it rather engaged in the more creative task of rereading the texts.

If "postcolonial" contexts include minorities living in multicultural nations, then Fernando Segovia's "Diasporic" approach to reading Scripture becomes especially suggestive. In the American context, this obviously can include African American, Asian American, and Mexican American readings of particular texts that resonate with themes, motifs, or elements of minority existence such that they lead to expositions of Old Testament texts that are suggestive for all readers of the Bible—and not only to fellow members of particular ethnic or cultural groups.

Ethnic and culturally informed readings challenge the notion that European scholarship has a privileged position in biblical scholarship generally, and in the construction of Christian theologies built from Old Testament texts particularly. What we have learned about diversity in dialogue is that the Christian reading of the Old Testament in the contemporary world will be richer, more learned, and more convincing in both textual and historical analysis only if our marketplace grows in its resemblance to the actual diversity of our worlds. What new insights into particular Old

Testament texts await the future BA, MA, or PhD theses and papers written by young Tibetan, Chinese, Navajo, Roma, or Aboriginal Australian students and scholars? What will they see that the rest of us have too quickly dismissed or completely overlooked? In the twenty-first century, we are likely to benefit from an increase of book titles like that of Senegalese American biblical scholar Aliou Niang: *Faith and Freedom in Galatia and Senegal: The Apostle Paul, Colonies, and Sending Gods.*

Let us reaffirm that diversity ought always to lead to dialogue. Agreements, shared insights, and common convictions that we are all learning from the dialogue ought to deliver even the most cynical from the simplistic hope that we Bible scholars would just please get to "the bottom line." Marketplaces don't have a bottom line! Dialogue and haggling over texts is simply the reality. The invitation, therefore, is to listen and learn. Incidentally, lest Christians think that all this is somehow radically new, those familiar with classic rabbinic dialogue and argumentation over religious texts are aware that dialogue with God and with each other is at the heart of theology.

Issues Driving Contemporary Biblical Analysis

Questions from identities and cultural experiences are not, however, the only major and significant sources of urgency in reading and rereading the Christian Old Testament. A number of contemporary global crises have inspired a renewed examination of the ways in which the Bible can be reread. The modern interest in trauma as the psychosocial reality of a world in crisis has recently gained ground in biblical analysis (see O'Connor; Janzen; Kelle). The millions of humans who flee wars and crises as international refugees have also influenced biblical analysis on ancient exile and deportation (see Ahn). The potential list of pressing issues is depressingly long, of course, but it is possible to examine a few examples to illustrate how this section of the marketplace can be organized. In fact, we can move from an example that is already very old but critically ongoing, war and peace in the Old Testament; to an issue that arguably has its roots in the twentieth century, environmentalism; and finally note the signs of a rising issue so new that it has barely begun to generate serious thought among biblical scholars: evolutionary philosophy, transhumanism, and the nature of the person.

War, Peace, and Violence and the Old Testament

Since the fourth century CE, the Christian church has been faced with direct responsibility for violence. The monarchical descendants of the Roman emperor Constantine made Christianity the official religion of the empire, leading into the Byzantine Empire. Biblical study was now intimately connected to the foreign policy of a powerful military machine, and would continue to have foreign policy implications from that time to the present. The continued relevance of the Bible to issues of war and peace is not difficult to discern in the writings of the Christian warriors and their chaplains on the one hand, and the Christian peacemakers and their communities on the other, throughout Western history especially. A clear majority in this debate has supported more violent interpretations, however regretfully they are sometimes offered.

The Jesus who said, "Love your enemies and pray for those who persecute you" (Matt. 5:44), and the Paul who exhorted, "live peaceably with all" (Rom. 12:18), were effectively trumped in Christian faith and practice very early on by an uncritical admiration for the genocidal Joshua and the conquering David (see Davies). There have been a variety of ways in which Christians have responded to the use of the Old Testament as a moral trump over the pacifist Jesus. Once again, the similarities to the methods of feminist biblical analysis are instructive.

For example, especially since the churches in twentieth-century Europe began to mobilize an opposition to the Cold War threats in their own backyards, innumerable monographs have attempted to reexamine the actual practices of Old Testament violence and warfare, either with explicit admiration (so, famously, Yadin), or appropriate levels of horror (Craigie; Niditch; Collins). In modern Old Testament study, then, one is hopefully exposed to the potential dangers of a casual and unguarded use of biblical texts that are so clearly contrary to contemporary moral judgments and international standards of justice.

Finally, similar to those who sought to lift up exemplary moments previously overlooked, there are those who seek to highlight strongly peaceful passages in the Bible that may even have been in critical dialogue with more violent episodes in the canon and thus reveal an internal dialogue or debate that reveals stronger peace voices among the canonical choir (Enz; Smith-Christopher 2007). This approach articulates how a certain form of Hebrew nonviolence would have been a logical expression of theological tendencies that had their roots in the Servant Songs of Second Isaiah and the universalism of the book of Jonah, where we find openness to the repentance of national enemies like the Assyrians, who are portrayed as repenting ". . . of the violence of their hands." Further developments can affirm the wisdom ethic of peacefulness—an ethic that frequently contrasts self-control over against brute force and earnestly recommends a sober, wise consideration of counsel and diplomacy (Prov. 16:7, 32; 17:27; 24:5-6). In fact, the Wisdom tradition may itself represent precisely a staging place for international discussion, given that wisdom values are as universal in the ancient Near East as any literary themes can be. Ancient Egyptian wisdom, Mesopotamian wisdom, and Greek wisdom all compare quite favorably to ancient Israelite forms.

Texts that reflect an Israelite "exilic" lifestyle, lived in "active nonconformity to the world" (as the famous 1955 Mennonite Church statement puts it), would also build on biblical protests against narrow ethnocentrism (e.g., the book of Ruth, Jacob's apology to Esau, Isaiah 56 and 66, and the striking affirmation in Zechariah 9 of a mixed-race people of God). In fact, there is evidence of a rising protest against violence and narrow self-centeredness (e.g., Ezekiel 40–48) that can be seen to affirm the Deuteronomic critique of the monarchy, and especially the condemnation of the monarchy in the penitential prayers of Ezra 9, Nehemiah 9, and Daniel 9. Thus the fact that there are passages where God is alleged to have called for the massacre of foreign cities does not necessarily cancel out or trump the fact that there are more hopeful passages on this subject as well, texts that openly question whether the stance of the Hebrews toward foreign peoples should be hostile and that envision a different and more peaceful reality (Isaiah 2; 19; Micah 4).

Regrettably, offering a more peaceful reading of the Old Testament will not likely bring about world peace. But if the late Colonel Harry Summers of the Army War College is correct that "it is the passions of the people that are the engines of war" (Summers, 75–76), then perhaps careful biblical analysis will remove at least one major ideological prop and provocation that has certainly been used in the past to excuse quite reprehensible behavior among those who honor the Scriptures (see Trimm).

Environmentalism

Biblical analysis that is driven by ecological concerns can be clearly dated to responses to the famous 1967 article in *Science* by Lynn White, accusing Christianity for providing the "roots" of the ecological crisis in God's injunction to the first couple in Gen. 1:28 to "subdue" and "have dominion" over nature. The late twentieth century then saw an increase of literature that highlighted ways that the Hebrew Bible/Old Testament affirmed a spirituality of care and responsibility for the earth as God's creation. Much of this work owes a great deal to the early writings of Australian biblical scholar Norman Habel (see also Hallman; so now Craven and Kaska; Deane-Drummond). The often-cited "this-worldly" emphasis of much Old Testament ethical discussion, and even the imagery of deep fascination with and appreciation of the created world (Job 38–41; Psalm 147–48), however, continues to inspire further development in pioneering biblical theologies. Genesis portrays God involving Adam in the naming of other creatures (Gen. 2:19) and further records God's intention to "re-create" the world in the Hebrew version of the flood narrative, the basic outlines of which were clearly known to the Jewish people by the time of the Babylonian captivity, and most likely borrowed from Mesopotamian traditions.

A related development is in the direction of animal rights. Concern for animal welfare is not absent from Hebrew law or narrative (Deut. 25:4; Numbers 22). The flood story, of course, involves the considerable responsibility of Noah to preserve animals. The Old Testament strikingly expresses certain visions of peace by referring to changes in the animal kingdom (Isa. 11:6: the wolf living with the lamb) and even hinting that in their first created state, humans were vegetarian (before Gen. 9:4, where eating meat is first explicitly mentioned). Psalm 148 portrays the created animals of the world praising God, and Job famously portrays God's careful attention and knowledge of the details of the animal kingdom (Job 39; on animal rights work, see Linzey 1995; 2009; Miller).

Work in environmentalism more generally, and animal rights specifically, have been parts of a move to appreciate biblical themes that buttress a more responsible care for the earth (Toly and Block). There are, however, some serious economic and even political issues at stake here. On the issue of environmentalism particularly, there has been a serious backlash from those with business interests who see strong environmentalist movements as potential threats to their expansion of industry. Not unexpectedly, then, this reaction has motivated more conservative Christian scholars to reassert a strongly pragmatic and typically short-term ethic of consumption unmitigated by strong concerns for conserving resources in the long term. Christians in this tradition, rarely biblical scholars themselves, are clearly not impressed with nuanced arguments about responsibility for species and their survival. Nor are they likely to be impressed by arguments based largely on Old Testament passages, especially if that concern is perceived as requiring economic sacrifices. An interesting example of this reaction is the work of Steven Hayward, from the conservative think tank the American Enterprise Institute. In a published essay titled "Mere Environmentalism" (the title itself is an homage to evangelical hero C. S. Lewis) and subtitled "A Biblical Perspective on Humans and the Natural World," Hayward suggests that the Genesis narratives promote the hierarchy of creation with humanity at the top. He therefore construes a biblical mandate, not for preservation of the environment, but for a "stewardship" that promotes responsible use of resources and a free-market-driven effort to conquer the "untamed wilderness," and furthermore as free of government intervention as possible. Indeed, Hayward further argues that the story of Joseph in Pharaoh's household is a warning against centralized state control, because Joseph's centralization of resources for the Pharaoh leads directly to the enslavement of the Hebrews. Environmental degradation, therefore, may be a matter calling for repentance, but definitely not for government regulation (33). Finally, Noah offers sacrifice of animals after the flood, Hayward notes, so this story provides no basis for simple preservation, and certainly suggests that animals were to be used for human benefit.

The twenty-first century is likely to see more, rather than less, of this polemical exchange in biblical scholarship. Although more propagandistic approaches have tended to avoid participation in scholarly organizations like the Society of Biblical Literature, we are likely to see more direct engagement over the use, and abuse, of Scripture on various issues of social, and especially economic, importance.

The Nature of the Person: The Rise of Evolutionary Social Science and Philosophy

Finally, it is important in the context of this essay to speculate about issues that may well emerge more fully as the twenty-first century develops. In the wake of Daniel Dennett's polemical 1996 assertion of atheist scientism, titled "Darwin's Dangerous Idea," there is a rise of perspectives represented by the following: "If you believe in a traditional concept of the soul, you should know that there is little doubt that a fuller appreciation of the implications of evolutionary theory . . . is going to destroy that concept"; and, "we must openly acknowledge . . . the collapse of a worldview that has sustained human energies for centuries" (Stanovich, 3). Will biblical studies also be challenged by evolutionary thought? If so, in what way?

In Christian theology and biblical studies, the classic beginning point for discussion of the nature of the human person is the concept of the *imago Dei*, the creation of humanity in the image and likeness of God (Gen. 1:26-27). J. Richard Middleton, for example, seeks to rethink the *imago Dei* debates in a modern context, noting that older Christian theological uses of Genesis 1 were rather strained, and usually presumed that the significance of "the image" and "likeness" of God was precisely human *reason*. Recent discussion has emphasized the royal context of these terms, suggesting that humans are portrayed as royally deputized representations of divine authority and responsibility in the world. Middleton even suggests that the *imago Dei* is, in fact, a politically sophisticated as well as theologically loaded term in Genesis, because here we find the textual staging ground for a narrative culture war against Mesopotamian hegemonic narratives of conquest and subservience. These Mesopotamian narratives were weapons in a philosophical/ideological war that accompanied the invading and conquering armies that conquered both the northern kingdom (722 BCE) and Jerusalem and Judah (597/587).

While it is quite possible to celebrate the theological importance of all humanity from an explicitly evolutionary view of the emergence of *homo sapiens*, it is also clear that some interpretations of human evolution threaten to radically debase and reduce humanity to a mere "sack of genes," with little inherent worth, whose values, art, and faith are mere "spandrels" (that is, accidental and irrelevant by-products) that accompany the real work of genetic reproduction. The value of life is thus no longer inherent in creation, but purely instrumental, as some humans serve as sexual slaves, soldiers, and workers for the shrinking and increasingly ruthless elite. The masses are already once again being pacified by the modern equivalent of bread and circus: ever smaller and more inexpensive sources of digital pornography, graphic violence, and (contra Kant's imperative) the view of fellow humans as means rather than ends.

In this context, religious faith (including, of course, the Bible) is strongly dismissed as "nothing but" the result of evolutionary mechanisms for survival. We perceive deities only because of our ancient and genetically honed "agency detection devices" (instincts that perceive potential threats in the environment). Others suggest that religion was merely a part of a sophisticated social "mate selection" mechanism whereby mates with trustworthy values could be quickly identified. In short, religion is a neural response pattern.

The interesting question is no longer, "Can a biblical scholar believe in evolution and teach Genesis"? Of course they can, and do. What is new is the rising insistence of a form of evolutionary social thought that would dismiss all religious speculation as irrelevant. Such a radically reductionist anthropology seeks to replace the "Eden myth" with an equally implausible and comprehensive "African Savannah myth" that subsumes all humanity into categories of neural survival mechanisms driven by reproductive genes. Does the Old Testament have anything to say in this decidedly modern discussion?

The resources of Wisdom literature and its emphasis on sober assessments of God's moral patterns in the created world provide a foundation beyond Genesis for seeking dialogue with naturalists and biologists. But the issues will continue to press, and will no longer be simply the leisure-time, science-fiction reading of those whose day jobs are in biblical studies. Seeking biblical guidance on the nature of the human person will become increasingly pressing in this century in the light of (1) increased emphasis in the human sciences on "transhumanism," according to which humans can be enhanced by further evolutionary merging with technology; (2) manipulation of genetic information to favor certain human traits (already taking place passively by rejecting human eggs in artificial insemination processes that bear indications of undesired genetic traits); (3) progress in artificial intelligence such that ethical questions are becoming increasingly prominent (when does turning off a machine consist of killing a living being? etc.); (4) further work in cloning; and (5) the location and identification of personhood as directly (and some would say: *only*) a function of neural brain activity, thus raising the possibility of "downloading" human persons into hardware.

Are these exclusively theological issues? Do they have any implications for biblical analysis? Will a biblical analysis arise, for example, driven in part by the prescience of the science fiction writer Philip K. Dick, who anticipated many ethical issues dealing with modern technology? It is possible that biblical scholars will simply suggest that radically new technologies are not the business of textual analysis. However, when those technologies raise serious questions about the nature and value of the human person, it is hard to resist the notion that biblical analysis has something to say to this issue.

Return to the Beginning: Does the Marketplace Matter? Are There Any Real People There?

Finally, we can pick up on a discussion that was left aside at the very beginning of this essay. What about the clashes among various readings of the Old Testament? Is biblical studies hopelessly mired in disagreements such that, in the end, an individual must simply hum along with Porter's "Anything Goes"?

Appearances, especially in the contemporary world, can be deceiving. The reality of extensive and exciting discussion and debate in biblical studies does not mean that the field is wandering aimlessly. Furthermore, the impressive level of publication and discussion does not mean that there is no consensus of methods or results among biblical scholars. Biblical scholars, like professionals in other fields such as medicine, engineering, or astronomy, certainly stay in touch with each other's work, and through international organizations (the largest being the Society of Biblical Literature) continue to pursue common interests, projects, and even enjoy continued debates and disagreements. It is hardly the case, as philosopher Alvin Plantinga somewhat sourly suggests, that biblical scholars can never agree on anything, explaining (for Plantinga, presumably) why Christians usually do not take their work seriously.

Plantinga may be surprised, however. The influence of biblical scholarship on wider Christian practices might be slow in manifesting itself, but it is absolutely clear. Plantinga should be impressed with the articulate, profound, and serious assessment of the importance of biblical analysis in the 1994 document of the Pontifical Biblical Commission titled "The Interpretation of the Bible in the Church." Calling the historical-critical method of biblical analysis "indispensable for the scientific study of the meaning of ancient texts," the document critically assesses, both positively and negatively, many current approaches to biblical analysis common in universities and biblical scholarship, and recommends much of modern biblical scholarship to the Catholic world more widely. Furthermore, the document famously refers to fundamentalist readings of Scripture as "intellectual suicide." Unimpressed with official declarations by hierarchies? One need only examine the textbooks for Catholic *high school* students, including those explicitly recommended by the bishops, to see the profound impact of biblical scholarship on questions of multiple authorship, historicity, the dangers of literalism, and so on.

Only the most conservative Christians today believe that the only way to treasure the significance of the narratives of Genesis is to take them literally, or believe that Moses wrote every word of the Pentateuch. Only the most fundamentalist Christians today would think that the book of Jonah is about surviving in the gullet of a marine animal, or that nearly one-fifth of the entire population of ancient Egypt left with Moses in the thirteenth century BCE. Furthermore, what many Christians in the church pews and Sunday schools *do* know is that a profound Christian faith can be enriched by learning that an unnamed second prophet we call "Second Isaiah" likely reapplied some of the thought of the eighth-century Isaiah of Jerusalem, but also proclaimed radically new thoughts in the late sixth-century BCE when the Persian emperor Cyrus lived. Furthermore, Christians today know much more about the horrific tragedy of the destruction of Jerusalem in 587, and how Lamentations is a powerful poetic response to that tragedy, and how Psalms contains religious poetry from long after the time of David. None of these ideas are shocking to Christians in the churches any more, and none of them are destructive of anything but the most simplistic of readings of the Old Testament.

Finally, what Christians in the churches surely know is that the Bible invites—indeed nearly demands—the careful attention of many different cultures, genders, ages, and contexts who are brought into dialogue as they listen, read, discuss, and debate the meanings and importance of these texts of the Old Testament. There is important historical information we can know, but there is so much more to ask. For those who love only quiet museum tours of "certainties" enclosed in glass cases so that the masses can be enlightened, biblical studies in the contemporary world is not for them. The marketplace is teaming, ebullient, and alive.

Works Cited

Ahn, John. 2010. *Exile as Forced Migrations: A Sociological, Literary, and Theological Approach on the Displacement and Resettlement of the Southern Kingdom of Judah.* Berlin: de Gruyter.

Albertz, Rainer. 2003. *Israel in Exile: The History and Literature of the Sixth Century* B.C.E. Atlanta: Society of Biblical Literature.

Avalos, Hector. 2007. *The End of Biblical Studies.* New York: Prometheus.

Bailey, Randall, Tat-siong Benny Liew, and Fernando F. Segovia, eds. 2009. *They Were All Together in One Place? Toward Minority Biblical Criticism.* Atlanta: Society of Biblical Literature.

Barr, James. 2000. *History and Ideology in the Old Testament: Biblical Studies at the End of a Millennium.* Oxford: Oxford University Press.

Boase, Elizabeth. 2006. *The Fulfillment of Doom? The Dialogic Interaction between the Book of Lamentations and the Pre-Exilic/Early Exilic Prophetic Literature.* London: T&T Clark.

Brueggemann, Walter. 1997. *Theology of the Old Testament: Testimony, Dispute, Advocacy.* Minneapolis: Fortress Press.

Callahan, Allen Dwight. 2006. *The Talking Book: African Americans and the Bible.* New Haven: Yale University Press.

Chalcraft, David. 2006. *Social-Scientific Old Testament Criticism.* London: T&T Clark.

Collins, John J. 2004. *Does the Bible Justify Violence?* Minneapolis: Fortress Press.

Cone, James H. 1970. *A Black Theology of Liberation.* Maryknoll, NY: Orbis.

———. 1992. *The Spirituals and the Blues: An Interpretation.* Maryknoll, NY: Orbis Books.

Craigie, Peter. 1979. *The Problem of War in the Old Testament.* Grand Rapids: Eerdmans.

Craven, Toni, and Mary Jo Kaska. 2011. "The Legacy of Creation in the Hebrew Bible and Apocryphal/Deuterocanonical Books." In *Spirit and Nature: The Study of Christian Spirituality in a Time of Ecological Urgency,* edited by Timothy Hessel-Robinson and Ray Maria McNamara, RSM, 16–48. Eugene, OR: Pickwick.

Cuellar, Gregory L. 2008. *Voices of Marginality: Exile and Return in Second Isaiah 40-55 and the Mexican Immigrant Experience.* New York: Peter Lang.

Davies, Eryl. 2010. *The Immoral Bible: Approaches to Biblical Ethics*. London: T&T Clark.

Deane-Drummond, Celia. 2008. *Eco-Theology*. London: Darton, Longman & Todd.

De La Torre, Miguel. 2002. *Reading the Bible from the Margins*. Maryknoll, NY: Orbis.

———. 2007. *Liberating Jonah: Forming an Ethic of Reconciliation*. Maryknoll, NY: Orbis.

Dennett, Daniel. 1996. *Darwin's Dangerous Idea*. New York: Simon & Schuster.

Dever, William G. 2001. *What Did the Biblical Writers Know and When Did They Know It?* Grand Rapids: Eerdmans.

———. 2003. *Who Were the Early Israelites and Where Did They Come From?* Grand Rapids: Eerdmans.

Edwards, James. 2009. *A Biblical Perspective on Immigration Policy*. Washington, DC: Center for Immigration Studies. http://www.cis.org/ImmigrationBible

Egerton, Douglas R. 1999. *He shall go out free : The lives of Denmark Vesey*. Madison, WI: Madison House, 1999

Eichrodt, Walter. 1961. *Theology of the Old Testament*. Translated by J. A. Baker. Vol. 1. London: SCM.

———. 1967. *Theology of the Old Testament*. Translated by J. A. Baker. Vol. 2. London: SCM.

Elsmore, Bronwyn. 1985. *Like Them That Dream: The Maori and the Old Testament*. Wellington, New Zealand: Tauranga Moana Press.

———. 1989. *Mana from Heaven*. Auckland: Reed.

Enz, Jacob. 2001. *The Christian and Warfare: The Roots of Pacifism in the Old Testament*. Eugene, OR: Wipf & Stock (reprint).

Fanon, Frantz. 1963. *The Wretched of the Earth*. New York: Grove.

Felder, Cain Hope, ed. 1991. *Stony the Road We Trod*. Minneapolis: Fortress Press.

Feyerabend, Paul. 2010. *Against Method*. New York: Verso.

Foskett, Mary F., and Jeffrey Kah-jin Kuan, eds. 2006. *Ways of Being, Ways of Reading: Asian American Biblical Interpretation*. St. Louis: Chalice.

Frend, W. H. C. 1984. *The Rise of Christianity*. Minneapolis: Fortress Press.

Gabler, Johann P. "An Oration on the Proper Distinction between Biblical and Dogmatic Theology and the Specific Objectives of Each." In Ollenburger, *Old Testament Theology*, 497–506.

Gafney, Wilda C. 2008. *Daughters of Miriam: Women Prophets in Ancient Israel*. Minneapolis: Fortress Press.

González, Justo L. 1996. *Santa Biblia: The Bible through Hispanic Eyes*. Nashville: Abingdon.

Gottwald, Norman. 1979. *The Tribes of Yahweh*. Maryknoll, NY: Orbis.

Grabbe, Lester. 2007. *Ancient Israel: What Do We Know and How Do We Know It?* New York: T&T Clark.

Habel, Norman. 1993. *The Land Is Mine: Six Biblical Land Ideologies*. Minneapolis: Fortress Press.

Hallman, David G. 1994. *Ecotheology: Voices from South and North*. Maryknoll, NY: Orbis.

Hayes, John H., and Frederick Prussner. 1984. *Old Testament Theology: Its History and Development*. Atlanta: John Knox.

Hopkins, Dwight N., and George C. L. Cummings, eds. 2003. *Cut Loose Your Stammering Tongue: Black Theology in the Slave Narratives*. Louisville: Westminster John Knox.

Janzen, David. 2012. *The Violent Gift: Trauma's Subversion of the Deuteronomistic History's Narrative*. LHB/OTS 561. London: T&T Clark.

Jenkins, Philip. 2002. *The Next Christendom: The Coming of Global Christianity*. New York: Oxford University Press.

———. 2006. *The New Faces of Christianity: Believing the Bible in the Global South*. New York: Oxford University Press.

Kelle, Brad. 2013. *Ezekiel*. New Beacon Bible Commentary. Kansas City: Beacon Hill.

Kuhn, Thomas. 1996. *The Structure of Scientific Revolutions*. 3rd ed. Chicago: University of Chicago Press.

Levine, Lawrence. 1977. *Black Culture and Black Consciousness.* New York: Oxford University Press.

Linzey, Andrew. 1995. *Animal Theology.* Urbana: University of Illinois Press.

———. 2009. *Creatures of the Same God.* New York: Lantern.

Mandolfo, Carleen. 2007. *Daughter Zion Talks Back to the Prophets.* Atlanta: Society of Biblical Literature.

Meyers, Carol. 1988/2013. *Rediscovering Eve: Ancient Israelite Women in Context.* Oxford: Oxford University Press.

Middleton, J. Richard. 2005. *The Liberating Image: The Imago Dei in Genesis 1.* Grand Rapids: Brazos.

Miller, David. 2011. *Animal Ethics and Theology.* New York: Routledge.

Muir, Lynette R. 1995. *The Biblical Drama of Medieval Europe.* Cambridge: Cambridge University Press.

Niang, Aliou. 2009. *Faith and Freedom in Galatia and Senegal.* Leiden: Brill.

Nichols, Aiden. 2007. *Lovely Like Jerusalem: The Fulfillment of the Old Testament in Christ and the Church.* San Francisco: Ignatius.

Niditch, Susan. 1993. *War and the Hebrew Bible: A Study in the Ethics of Violence.* Oxford: Oxford University Press.

Ngan, Lai Ling Elizabeth. 2006. "Neither Here nor There: Boundary and Identity in the Hagar Story." In Foskett and Kuan, *Ways of Being,* 70–83.

O'Connor, Kathleen. 2002. *Lamentations and the Tears of the World.* Maryknoll, NY: Orbis.

Ollenburger, Ben, ed. 2004. *Old Testament Theology: Flowering and Future, Sources for Biblical and Theological Study.* Winona Lake, IN: Eisenbrauns.

Overholt, Thomas. 1992. *Cultural Anthropology and the Old Testament.* Minneapolis: Fortress Press.

———. 2003. *Channels of Prophecy: The Social Dynamics of Prophetic Activity.* Eugene, OR: Wipf and Stock.

Perdue, Leo. 1994. *The Collapse of History: Reconstructing Old Testament Theology.* Minneapolis: Fortress Press.

Plantinga, Alvin. 2009. "Two (or More) Kings of Scripture Scholarship." In *Oxford Readings in Philosophical Theology,* vol. 2, *Providence, Scripture, and Resurrection,* ed. Michael C. Rea, 266–301. Oxford: Oxford University Press.

Pulido, Laura, Laura Barraclough, and Wendy Cheng, eds. 2012. *A People's Guide to Los Angeles.* Berkeley: University of California Press.

Raboteau, Albert J. 1978. *Slave Religion: The Invisible Institution in the Antebellum South.* New York: Oxford University Press.

Rogerson, John. 1984. *Old Testament Criticism in the Nineteenth Century: England and Germany.* London: SPCK.

———. 2010. *A Theology of the Old Testament.* Minneapolis: Fortress Press.

Roberts, Nathaniel. 2012. "Is Conversion a 'Colonization of Consciousness'?" *Anthropological Theory* 12:271–94.

Ruiz, Jean-Pierre. 2011. *Readings from the Edges: The Bible and People on the Move.* Maryknoll, NY: Orbis.

Said, Edward W. 1979. *Orientalism.* New York: Vintage.

Schüssler Fiorenza, Elisabeth. 2009. *Democratizing Biblical Studies.* Louisville: Westminster John Knox.

Segovia, Fernando F. 2000. *Decolonizing Biblical Studies: A View from the Margins.* Maryknoll, NY: Orbis.

Segovia, Fernando F., and Mary Ann Tolbert, eds. 1985. *Reading from this Place,* vol. 1, *Social Location and Biblical Interpretation in the United States.* Minneapolis: Fortress Press.

Smith-Christopher, Daniel. 2002. *A Biblical Theology of Exile.* Minneapolis: Fortress Press.

———. 2007. *Jonah, Jesus, and Other Good Coyotes: Speaking Peace to Power in the Bible.* Nashville: Abingdon.

Sommer, Benjamin, ed. 2012. *Jewish Concepts of Scripture: A Comparative Introduction.* New York: New York University Press.

Soyinka, Wole. 2003. *Samarkand and Other Markets I Have Known*. New York: Methuen.

Stanovich, Keith. 2004. *The Robot's Rebellion*. Chicago: University of Chicago Press.

Sugirtharajah, R. S., ed. 2006. *Voices from the Margin: Interpreting the Bible in the Third World*. 3rd ed. Maryknoll, NY: Orbis.

Summers, Harry G. 1984. "What Is War?" *Harper's*, May, 75–78.

Toly, Noah J., and Daniel I. Block, eds. 2010. *Keeping God's Earth: The Global Environment in Biblical Perspective*. Downers Grove, IL: IVP Academic.

Thompson, Thomas L. 1974. *The Historicity of the Patriarchal Narratives: The Quest for the Historical Abraham*. Berlin: de Gruyter.

Trible, Phyllis. 1984. *Texts of Terror: Literary-Feminist Readings of Biblical Narratives*. Minneapolis: Fortress Press.

Trimm, Charles. 2012. "Recent Research on Warfare in the Old Testament." *Currents in Biblical Research* 10:171–216.

Rad, Gerhard von. 1962. *Theology of the Old Testament*. Vol. 1. New York: Harper & Row.

———. 1965. *Theology of the Old Testament*. Vol. 2. New York: Harper & Row.

Warrior, Robert Allen. 1996. "Canaanites, Cowboys, and Indians." In *Native and Christian: Indigenous Voices on Religious Identity in the United States and Canada*, edited by James Treat, 93–104. New York: Routledge.

Weems, Renita J. 1991. "Reading Her Way through the Struggle: African American Women and the Bible." In Felder, *Stony the Road We Trod*, 57–77.

———. 1995. *Battered Love: Marriage, Sex, and Violence in the Hebrew Prophets*. Minneapolis: Fortress Press.

White, Lynn, Jr. 1967. "The Historical Roots of Our Ecological Crisis." *Science* 155:1203–7.

Wimbush, Vincent L., ed. 2000. *African Americans and the Bible: Sacred Texts and Social Textures*. New York: Continuum.

Yadin, Yigael. 1963. *The Art of Warfare in Biblical Lands*. London: Weidenfield & Nicolson.

Yee, Gale A. 2003. *Poor Banished Children of Eve: Woman as Evil in the Hebrew Bible*. Minneapolis: Fortress Press.

———. 2006. "Yin/Yang Is Not Me: An Exploration into an Asian-American Biblical Hermeneutics." In Foskett and Kuan, *Ways of Being*, 152–63.

THEMES AND PERSPECTIVES IN TORAH: CREATION, KINSHIP, AND COVENANT

Sarah Shectman

The first five books of the Hebrew Bible (the Christian Old Testament)—Genesis, Exodus, Leviticus, Numbers, and Deuteronomy—occupy a primary place in the biblical canon, not just because they come first, but also because they are likely the earliest part of the Bible to have been canonized. Sometimes these books are referred to as the Pentateuch, from the Greek *pente*, "five," and *teuchos*, "book." In Jewish tradition, the books are referred to as the *Torah*, a Hebrew word that literally means "teaching" or "instruction." The Torah itself uses the Hebrew term *torah* to refer specifically to the laws ("instructions") that YHWH (the proper name of the biblical deity) gives the Israelites through Moses (see, for example, Exod. 24:12; Deut. 4:44), not to the whole collection of five books. Outside of the Torah, the term may refer to YHWH's laws or to more general instruction or teaching, as from a parent (for example, Prov. 1:8); it also appears in phrases such as "the book of the teaching of Moses" (*sefer torat moshe*), which may have a broader meaning (see, for example, Neh. 8:1), perhaps encompassing the text of the Torah more or less as we know it. Thus though the biblical text says only that Moses wrote down the laws (*torot*; singular, *torah*) that YHWH instructed him at Sinai, later the term *torah* comes to encompass the whole collection of books, not only the laws, and the whole is understood as a larger written "Law."

Part 1: Perspectives on Reading the Torah

In the first part of this essay, we will consider two questions: First, What is the Torah? And second, Who wrote it?

What Is the Torah?

The material in the Torah falls into two main categories: narrative and law. The narrative begins in Genesis with the creation of the universe and the Garden of Eden. As humans proliferate after Adam and Eve's expulsion from the garden, their behavior deteriorates, prompting YHWH to obliterate them in the flood and start over with the lineage of Noah. Humans once again proliferate, this time culminating in the lineage of Abraham, who becomes the first ancestor of the Israelites when YHWH tells him to go to the land of Canaan and promises to make him a great nation there. YHWH then makes a covenant with Abraham, a central theme in the following narrative. The remainder of Genesis contains stories about the Israelite ancestors Abraham and Sarah; Isaac and Rebekah; Jacob, Leah, and Rachel; and Jacob's children, particularly Joseph. This family history is punctuated by the passing down of YHWH's promise and covenant to Abraham's descendants. Genesis ends with the descent of Joseph and then the rest of Jacob's family to Egypt.

The story in Exodus picks up sometime later, the Israelites having become numerous and been enslaved in Egypt. YHWH selects Moses to be the savior of the people, leading them out of Egypt after a great show of destructive and miraculous plagues. At Mount Sinai, YHWH renews the Abrahamic covenant with the Israelites, delivering numerous laws covering a wide variety of topics, not just religious but also civil, social, agricultural, and military. The Israelites are on their way to conquer Canaan, the land promised to Abraham and his descendants by YHWH, but the people immediately begin to question the leadership of both Moses and YHWH, prompting YHWH to punish them by keeping them in the wilderness for forty years, until the entire exodus generation has died. The Israelites move from place to place in the wilderness, fighting various battles and beginning the initial stages of their conquest of the promised land in the region across the Jordan River from Canaan. There, on the plains of Moab, Moses makes his farewell speech, recounted in the book of Deuteronomy, and then dies; with his death, the Torah comes to an end.

The law, as this narrative summary shows, is an integral part of the story: the connection of the law with the exodus event and with Sinai is deeply embedded in the narrative. But most of the legal sections also stand apart from the narrative flow, pausing events in order to recount the various stipulations that YHWH requires of the Israelites in order to maintain the covenant. The legal material thus stands on its own as a genre. But the whole of the Pentateuch, both narrative and law, has come to be understood as law (*torah*) in some sense—even the narrative material. Thus the narrative parts are often understood to be instructional as well and to provide a set of guiding principles.

This characterization reveals one of the primary issues in understanding the Torah, namely, the question of genre. The Torah presents itself as a history, in the sense that it provides a more-or-less continuous narrative recounting the origins and early events in the lives of the Israelite people. But it is not always clear that the Torah is meant to be understood in the way modern readers understand history. One obvious way in which it is unlike modern histories is in its inclusion of miracles and other supernatural events that do not withstand scientific scrutiny. Should the Torah thus be classified as fiction rather than history?

The question of whether these stories are purely fictional or whether they might have a historical kernel is a vexing one. There is no clear evidence for any of the people mentioned in the Torah in any outside sources or in the archaeological record, which are the primary means of testing the historicity of ancient texts. But does this mean that there is no history behind the Torah? It is difficult to say. Given the absence of evidence for this question, it is perhaps more useful to think in terms of the function of the text for an ancient Israelite audience. The narratives present a particular worldview (or worldviews), and thus they seem intended to be understood not exactly as history but as ancient Israel's understanding of its constitution as a nation and of YHWH's place in the national self-image. In this vein, scholars sometimes refer to the Torah as the "foundation document" of ancient Israel, the story of its creation and its relationship to its deity, YHWH. In such an analysis, rather than focusing on the issue of whether the story is myth or history, scholars choose to focus on the key themes of the Torah, in order to understand what those themes tell us about the Israelites' understanding of themselves and of their God.

Although the Torah stands on its own as one division of the Hebrew Bible, it is not clear that it was originally intended to be a self-standing unit. Though it forms a mostly continuous narrative, the storyline continues without interruption in the next book of the Bible, Joshua, with the conquest of the promised land and thus the fulfillment of the promise made to the ancestors in the Torah. However, Deuteronomy contains the last of the laws and ends with the death of Moses, which also suggests a strong break between the Torah and the following material. Complicating the matter further, Deuteronomy is in many ways different from the first four books of the Torah, giving a sort of retrospective view of the story so far and focusing in particular on certain theological issues such as idolatry and the centralization of worship at a single sanctuary. These themes feature prominently in the following books (Joshua, Judges, 1–2 Samuel, and 1–2 Kings) as well, prompting many scholars to refer to Deuteronomy–2 Kings as the Deuteronomistic History, a composition distinct from Genesis–Numbers. The book of Deuteronomy in particular, then, is a kind of "hinge" connecting the first four books with the following six.

Although the narrative of the Torah continues in Joshua–2 Kings, only certain episodes from the Torah are mentioned in those books. The exodus from Egypt, for example, is mentioned frequently, not just in the Deuteronomistic History but also in the prophets, Psalms, and many other books. Likewise, the subjects of Moses, covenant, and law appear often in other biblical books. But other episodes do not. Adam and Eve are not mentioned again outside of the first few chapters of Genesis; the Garden of Eden and Noah and the flood are mentioned only rarely, as are the ancestors who feature so prominently in Genesis. It seems, then, that the Torah contains a particular set of traditions that were not necessarily as important, or perhaps even known, to the authors of other books of the Hebrew Bible. Most of these authors also do not seem to have been aware of a book called the Torah (the Torah of Moses, see above)—though the author of the book of Nehemiah apparently did (see Neh. 8:1). By the time some of the later books of the Bible were written, a self-standing Torah may have existed and been known to those books' authors; but this was likely not the case for the majority of the books of the Bible.

The question of the Torah's original audience is a difficult one. Though the law is presented as having been related to the Israelites of the exodus generation directly by YHWH or indirectly through Moses, the rest of the material is told from a later vantage point and thus cannot have been initially composed for this generation. Furthermore, the historicity of these events has been seriously questioned and can no longer be taken for granted, and so we must judge the identity of the audience based on the content and themes of the Torah, or of its component parts. Large sections of Leviticus, for example, may have been intended as instructions for priests or for people bringing sacrifices to the temple. Other parts of the Torah, such as the stories about the ancestors in Genesis, may have been written for a more general Israelite audience, as they provide a national "foundation history" and emphasize themes relevant to ancient Israelite self-understanding, perhaps in the period of the monarchy or later (tenth century BCE and after). The laws about kingship in Deuteronomy 17, though addressed in the narrative to all Israel, were likely intended for the king specifically, as a check on his powers.

It is unlikely that the Torah was intended to be picked up and read by the average Israelite, not least because literacy was probably not very common in ancient Israel. Copies of written works would also have been available only to a few people, mainly those in larger cities with a political or religious establishment, or both. The Torah's contents may not have been known at all to most people for much of the biblical period. However, there is some evidence that the Torah or parts of it were meant to be read aloud to the Israelites on a regular basis. The book of Deuteronomy (Deut. 31:10-13; and see Deut. 6:7) instructs the Israelites to recite the *torah* (probably just law, but later meaning the whole five books) regularly, and Nehemiah 8–9 recounts one such public reading in a later period.

Over the centuries, though, especially with the rise of Christianity and its inclusion of the Hebrew Bible in its sacred Scriptures, the Torah became more widely known. With time, too, the Torah's audience changed, and different communities have derived different meanings from it. The Torah was translated into Greek in the second century BCE so that the community of Jews in Alexandria, Egypt, would have access to it, and we can imagine that the story of the Israelites' sojourn in Egypt would have resonated differently for that audience than it did for one remaining in Jerusalem. Similarly, the laws relating to sacrifice and the temple would have gained new meaning with the destruction of the temple by the Romans in 70 CE. In later periods, too, the Torah's stories would have taken on different significance in changing historical circumstances; thus, for example, slaves in antebellum America found deep meaning in the story of the Israelites' delivery from slavery, and modern women seeking equal rights saw an example of a female leader in the figure of Miriam, who challenges the authority of her brother as sole leader of the Israelites (Numbers 12).

Who Wrote the Torah?

Although tradition holds that Moses was the author of the whole Torah (hence the title "Torah of Moses"), the Torah itself does not say who wrote it. Moses is said to have written down certain parts of the law (Exod. 24:4; 34:28; Deut. 31:9, 24); YHWH is said to have written the Ten Commandments on the tablets of stone (Exod. 24:12; 31:18; Deut. 4:13; 5:22; 9:10). However, there are indications within the text itself that neither Moses nor any other single person wrote the whole thing. The first problem, noticed by scholars already in the medieval period, is that Moses dies just before the end of Deuteronomy—so he cannot have written the last few verses! And it hardly seems likely that Moses would have (or could have) boasted, "Never since has there arisen a prophet in Israel like Moses, whom the LORD knew face to face. He was unequaled for all the signs and wonders that the LORD sent him to perform in the land of Egypt" (Deut. 34:10–11).

But these are only minor problems, easily (if not convincingly) solved by the traditional suggestion that Joshua, Moses' successor, wrote the last few verses after the great leader's death. More problematic are the repetitions, contradictions, and gaps that appear throughout the Torah and that are much more difficult to reconcile with the idea of a single author composing a single, continuous narrative. For example, there are two creation stories, one appearing in Gen. 1:1—2:4a and the other in Gen. 2:4b—3:24. Moreover, these two stories differ about the order of creation, humans being created before the animals in the first story and after them in the second. The flood story in Genesis 6–9 also contains two narrative strands, which differ regarding such details as the length of the flood and the numbers of animals brought into the ark. Some parts of the Torah recognize a multiplicity of holy sites, whereas others insist that there can be only one. Some depict YHWH in human terms, but others insist on the deity's transcendence and incorporeality.

By the medieval period, scholars had begun to notice some of these issues and come up with alternatives to the hypothesis that Moses wrote the whole Torah. Beginning in the nineteenth century, a model that posited multiple authors, none of whom were Moses, began to take hold. This model holds that the Torah is composed of four main narrative strands, termed J, E, D, and P. E (Elohist), named for its use of the divine name *Elohim*, is the most fragmentary of the sources and is considered by some to be the oldest. J (Yahwist), so named for its exclusive use of the divine name YHWH, or *Jehovah*, in the German of the theory's originator, is generally thought to be a little later than E. D (Deuteronomist) appears mostly in the book of Deuteronomy, though some scholars see evidence of some D editing in other books of the Torah. P (Priestly) is the sparest narrative but contains the most extensive legal material, especially concerned with sacrificial and other cultic matters.

Early proponents of this source theory, called the Documentary Hypothesis, argued that an editor or editors, possibly also from a priestly school like P, were responsible for the combination of the material, which until that point had been independent written sources. Many scholars hold that J and E were combined first and separately, and then joined with P and then D. A growing number of scholars, especially in Europe, reject the distinction between J and E and instead see in this material a complex layering that accrued in stages over several centuries; often this material is referred to simply as "non-Priestly." Scholars have likewise continued to reevaluate the P and D material, and especially the nature of P as an independent source, though there is more agreement about what material belongs to the Priestly and Deuteronomic collections than there is about the non-Priestly material traditionally. The differences between these sources go beyond the use of divine names, which disappears as a distinction after Exodus 6, when all the sources start using the name YHWH. Some of these differences will be discussed below in the context of specific themes and theologies of the Torah.

Aspects of the sources' material suggest that they came from different times and places: E focuses on northern tribes and places, hinting at composition in the north in the period before the fall of the northern kingdom in 722 BCE. J's focus on the south suggests a time when the kingdom of

Judah was thriving, likely sometime in the seventh century BCE (as is indicated by the archaeological evidence). P's focus on the sacrificial cult suggests a time when the temple existed, either before or after the Babylonian exile. D's focus on centralization suggests a location in Jerusalem, which was the central locus of worship in the seventh century and also in the postexilic period.

Of course, the Torah is about a time much earlier than any of these proposed dates—the earliest of which is sometime during the period of the northern kingdom of Israel (ninth and eighth centuries BCE). According to the Bible's chronology, Moses lived well before this, sometime around 1400 BCE. The ancestors, Abraham and Sarah and their descendants, lived several centuries earlier. How do we know that the Torah, or at least parts of it, was not written in this period? The main reason is that the archaeological record provides no evidence that a people known as "Israel" existed before about 1200 BCE. There are no references to them in outside sources before the first mention in an Egyptian text known as the Merneptah Stela, dated to around 1200 BCE. In addition, the archaeology of the land of Israel does not indicate the appearance of a new people on the scene before this time. The culture that can be identified archaeologically as Israel only begins to emerge in the late second millennium BCE, and as it emerges, it shows remarkable continuity with the Canaanite culture that precedes it, indicating that the people called "Israel" were indigenous to the land of Canaan, not a group that conquered it from outside (Finkelstein and Silberman).

The production of a literary work as expansive as the Hebrew Bible would depend on the kind of social structures that only appear with urban culture and a strong central government (Schniedewind). But the need for such social structures relates only to the written work; it is likely that the Torah also contains some earlier oral traditions. A few texts bear the markers of oral composition; the existence of multiple versions of a story, such as the wife/sister stories in Genesis 12, 20, and 26, indicates that some traditions developed independently, in different times and places, before being brought together in the final written work. Likewise, the focus of traditions on certain geographical areas—especially where those traditions tend to be clustered into one or another of the sources identified in the Documentary Hypothesis—suggests the development of local traditions before the written composition of the Torah itself began. And evidence of archaic Hebrew indicates earlier composition for some texts as well.

The Torah also shows the influence of the literary traditions of the surrounding cultures: the treaties, laws, and myths of the Babylonians, Assyrians, Hittites, and Egyptians. Scholars debate when and how this influence happened, and as with the development of the sources and their traditions, it seems to have taken place over a lengthy span of time. All of these factors indicate that the composition of the Torah was a complex process. And though the Torah bears clear marks of its gradual composition, it works well together as a whole. It is unified not only by a fairly continuous plot arc but also by a number of narrative and theological themes. It is also important to keep in mind that, despite the fracturing in the text, someone did finally put the whole thing together, and this whole has been meaningful to numerous people for millennia. Though modern scholars have developed historical-critical methods of reading the Bible, using tools such as archaeology and source criticism, others have developed new ways of reading the final form of the text, seeking meaning from the fact that the whole exists as it does, contradictions and all (see, for example, Childs). In particular, the final form of the text serves as a striking narrative of the nation of Israel's birth and development, its special relationship with YHWH, and YHWH's powerful role in history. Its various themes are knit together in such a way that the story has continued to resonate with people of different religious faiths, ethnicities, and nationalities for over two millennia.

Part 2: Themes in the Torah

The key themes of the Torah can be grouped into three main categories: creation, kinship, and covenant. Each of these categories is established early in the Torah and is a focus of a particular part of the whole, but each also continues throughout the Torah. So, for example, creation is highlighted at the beginning of the Torah, in the story of the creation of the world in Genesis 1–3. However, the theme of creation repeats in the story of the creation of the nation of Israel through the ancestor Abraham and his descendants; this creation in turn is a twofold creation, beginning in the period of the ancestors and culminating in the period of the exodus generation.

Kinship likewise runs as a thread throughout the Torah. The stories of Genesis are focused on family history—on a particular kinship group, beginning with Abraham and continuing through his grandson Jacob's children, the ancestors of Israel's twelve tribes. Outside of Genesis, kinship concerns are manifest in stories about the roles and relationships of the tribes, and the narrative is punctuated throughout by genealogical lists that make clear the importance of kinship—and the close connections between various kinship groups in and around ancient Israel.

The Torah narrative is marked by three covenants: the covenant with Noah, the covenant with Abraham, and the covenant with all Israel. These covenants mirror the three periods of creation in the Torah, from the primeval period, to the ancestral period, and into the larger nation of Israel. It is the covenant that constitutes the creation of the people of Israel and illustrates their special relationship to YHWH. The covenant is passed down generationally, from father to son. A primary component of the covenant is the promise of land, progeny, and blessing first made to Abraham; this promise is left unfulfilled at the end of the Torah, however, as the Israelites have not yet entered the promised land.

Creation

The theme of creation figures in the Torah in a number of ways, not only in the most obvious, the creation of the world at the beginning of Genesis. The whole of the Torah is a much larger creation story, of the nation of Israel. The role of YHWH in the world and especially in the history of Israel is a key and related theme, as is the theme of divine presence and absence that goes along with it.

The well-known beginning of the book of Genesis details the creation of the world, land, water, sky, plants, and animals, including humans. Unlike the other animals, humans are created "in the image of God" and are the culmination of the creation account in Genesis 1. Their purpose is to exercise dominion over creation and to "be fruitful and multiply," setting the stage for the unfolding narrative in the rest of the Torah. Genesis 2–3, which provides a slightly different account of creation, also makes humans paramount, though in this case the focus is on the relationship of the humans to one another and to YHWH.

The story continues with a long genealogical list of the ensuing long-lived generations—the results of the humans' being fruitful and multiplying. Unhappy with the state of things, however, YHWH destroys this first attempt at creation, saving only Noah and his family and rebuilding from that line. Another genealogical list follows, this time outlining the numerous other nations and peoples that surrounded the ancient Israelites and were seen as descending from this common ancestor.

As noted above, there are two creation stories side by side at the beginning of Genesis; both emphasize the deity's role in creation, but in different ways. Both also focus on the creation of humans, but again they differ in how they do this. They also diverge in the divine name they use: the first employs Elohim ("God") and the second YHWH ("Lord"). The first story describes the creation of humans as "in the image of God," suggesting a close connection between deity and humanity. The question of just what "in the image of God" means, however, is a perplexing one with major implications. Is it a literal comparison, or figurative? Does it suggest that humans are literally godlike in some way? Does it apply only to men, or to both men and women? Historically, the verse has been used to justify numerous entitlements and obligations of the human race (see Jónsson).

The humans seem to be given dominion over all creation in a fashion parallel to God's power. But Genesis 1 also depicts a God who is quite separate from creation. Unlike the deity in Genesis 2–3, this one does not come down and walk around on the earth, forming humans by hand, nor does God in Genesis 1 speak directly with the humans as YHWH does in the second creation story. God in Genesis 1 is depicted as transcendent, existing above and acting on the world. Thus the "image of God" in Genesis 1 may not refer to human form. It may instead indicate the place of God in creation: above it and the master of it, as humans are in relation to their own environment, over which they are given dominion by God. Many interpreters have also taken "image of God" to mean something moral or ethical: humans are like God (and unlike the animals) in that they have an ethical sense, though this view is problematic because the Hebrew term for "image" usually means something more physical or concrete.

If Genesis 1 has been important for understanding the place of humans in the world, then Genesis 2–3 have had a major impact on the status of women in relationship to men. The creation of the woman after the man in this story has been taken to indicate that she is of inferior status to him. Despite the creation of the man and woman simultaneously as the final act of creation, and both "in the image of God," in Genesis 1, interpreters have seen in Genesis 2–3 a prescription for women's subordinate status to men. More than the derivative status of woman in Genesis 2, however, Genesis 3 has been used in various ways to justify women's secondary status. First, women are blamed for the "fall from grace," "original sin," and the expulsion from the garden. Yet, a closer look at the text shows that "fall" and "sin" are terms that never appear in this episode. True, the woman is punished for transgressing YHWH's edict, but the man is punished as well. And as modern scholars have shown, the woman is not "cursed" with subordination to man but rather is punished with difficult labor and childbirth and with hard toil—as is the man (see Meyers).

Women's subordinate status and sinful nature were thus seen as having been encoded in the natural order of things at the creation. These chapters of Genesis were therefore fundamental to the women's rights movement from its inception. Beginning in the medieval period, women recognized the role of these texts in their subordination and moved to reject the traditional interpretations.

In the late nineteenth century, the suffragist movement had to tackle these texts; and the feminist movement in the 1970s likewise required a rejection of sexist interpretations of the story. Many feminists moved toward a rejection of the Bible as a whole, seeing these texts as irredeemably patriarchal (see Daly); but other feminists offered alternative readings, seeing in Genesis 1 a depiction of equality between the sexes and in Genesis 2–3 an empowering depiction of an intellectually curious woman (see Trible).

These chapters have also been important for the understanding of humanity's place in creation. The command in Genesis 1 to humans to have "dominion" over the earth and to "subdue" it was taken as justification for human exploitation of the world and of all its resources. More recently, the text has been used instead as an argument for environmental stewardship and for people's responsibility toward the world and toward all people "in the image of God."

In addition to the creation of the world and everything in it, the Torah is also the story of the creation of the nation of Israel, YHWH's own covenant people. This story begins with the selection of Abraham, the first ancestor of the Israelites. YHWH tells Abraham (at first named Abram) to leave his home and go to Canaan, a land that YHWH promises to give to Abraham and his descendants, who will be as numerous as the stars of the sky. After Abraham's arrival in Canaan, YHWH makes a covenant (treaty) with him and reiterates the promise as the content of this covenant, which is predicated on Abraham and all the men of his household being circumcised. Thus the nation of Israel is born, though it is not until Abraham's grandson Jacob (also called Israel) that the nation gets its namesake. It is Jacob's twelve sons (and two of his grandsons) after whom the various tribes of the nation are known.

An important aspect of the theme of the creation of the nation of Israel is the threat to its existence that the nation continually faces. The ancestors and their wives are frequently threatened with death by those around them. All of the matriarchs are barren at one point or another, creating narrative tension about the ability of the fledgling nation to survive. Not only that, but the patriarchs repeatedly put their wives and children in questionable situations, risking their ability to have children and for those children to live to adulthood. In each case, though, with YHWH's help, the line of Abraham continues and even flourishes.

These narrative details probably reflect not only real aspects of life in ancient Israel, such as infertility and infant mortality, but also the precarious situation of the Israelites at many points during their history. Archaeological evidence reveals that the Israelites emerged as a subgroup from within an indigenous Canaanite population, rather than invading and conquering (as the biblical narrative itself depicts). So the early Israelites must have had to develop customs, habits, and other markers of identity to distinguish themselves from the nations, especially the Canaanites, around them (see Killebrew). Further, they were surrounded at nearly all times by great and expansionistic empires. The threat of assimilation and destruction would have been real throughout most of Israel's history.

Unlike the initial slate-wiping and re-creation with Noah, however, YHWH does not reject this chosen line, even when its members are disobedient. The role of YHWH in Israel's history is thus paramount. The message comes through clearly throughout the Torah: YHWH takes an active interest in the survival of the nation of Israel, ensuring that barren wives become fertile, that children survive, that wealth is accrued, that slaves are freed, and that enemies are vanquished. YHWH has power not only over Israel but over all people. Beginning the story with the creation of the entire world demonstrates the extent of YHWH's power. Other ancient Near Eastern creation stories also show that the gods (a whole pantheon of them) create the world, and they may occasionally take an interest in a special person. Likewise, ancient Near Eastern histories certainly mention gods as having enabled a king, for example, to perform various feats, and the gods are invoked as parties to treaties and oaths. But in no other contemporary texts is the activity of any deity—much less only one deity—incorporated in the same fashion that it is here in Israel's foundational story.

As a result, the theme of divine presence and absence is critical to the Torah. Israel owes its success to its special relationship with YHWH, which is manifested in the deity's presence among the people—either physically or metaphysically, depending on the text. The importance of YHWH's presence also has a flip side: YHWH's potential absence, which is seen as the abandonment of the people. This problem is especially evident in the Priestly material, particularly in the book of Leviticus. Leviticus is concerned with the sacrificial system and the ideas of purity and impurity, all of which are mentioned as safeguards for the purity of the Israelite encampment, where YHWH is understood to be present. Impurity will force YHWH to leave and thus to abandon and imperil Israel, inviting catastrophe. Such a catastrophe was realized with the Babylonian exile, which many Israelites understood as YHWH's abandonment of them—an understanding expressed, in retrospect by the postexilic Priestly author, as YHWH's threat at the beginning of the covenant relationship: "the land will vomit you out for defiling it, as it vomited out the nation that was before you" (Lev. 18:28; see also Ezekiel 8–10).

This theme also appears at the very beginning of the Torah: YHWH is initially present in the Garden of Eden, walking in it and interacting with the man and woman. They are in close relationship with one another. But after the humans disobey YHWH's command not to eat the fruit of the knowledge of good and evil, this relationship is severed. The humans are now fundamentally alienated from the divine; having "become like" YHWH by gaining knowledge, they are forever separated from YHWH, lest they also achieve immortality by eating the fruit of the tree of life and become, for all intents and purposes, divine themselves. Having become too much like YHWH, they are forever removed from YHWH's presence, and reentry is blocked. In the future, additional barriers will be set up to maintain the separation (but also the mutual coexistence) of the human (common) and the divine (holy) spheres, as in Leviticus. Thus the story of the Torah is one of alienation from the divine and the ongoing efforts of YHWH and the Israelites to maintain their special relationship.

The tensions between divine presence and absence differ somewhat in different parts of the Torah, however. In the earlier (non-Priestly) material, although human and divine are seen as fundamentally separated from one another, as recounted in the Garden of Eden story, YHWH moves about on the earth, interacting directly or through intermediaries with numerous people. Though the Israelites' frequent misbehavior threatens YHWH's allegiance to the people, YHWH's permanent abandonment of them seems to be less of a concern. In the Priestly and Deuteronomic material, in contrast, YHWH is seen as present in a less physical, though no less real, fashion. In P, YHWH is present among the people as the cloud of fire that descends on and dwells in the tabernacle (see

Num. 9:15-23). The elaborate Priestly cultic system is meant to ensure YHWH's presence there by maintaining the purity of the land. Deuteronomy also has some concern with the purity of the land (for example, Deut. 23:13-15), though YHWH's presence is linked more to the idea of covenant than to purity specifically. Deuteronomy also develops a theology linked to YHWH's *name* dwelling in the land, rather than YHWH being physically present in an embodied sense.

The ideas of divine presence and absence or alienation from the divine have continued to reverberate through the ages. In Judaism, alienation from the divine after creation is addressed through the concept of *tikkun olam*, or repairing the world. Jewish mystical belief holds that vessels containing divine light shattered after creation, and performing commandments (*mitzvot*) is a way of gathering the sparks and restoring the divine (Robinson, 383). According to this principle, right relationship with the divine is restored through positive action. In some modern Jewish denominations, this idea has been expanded to include social justice, environmentalism, and other movements, expressing the divine through common experience with all people.

Kinship

The Torah begins as a universal history, narrows its focus to become a family history, and ends as a national one. The theme of kinship is thus of primary importance, whether it is kinship among all peoples of the earth, among a single clan or tribe, or within an entire nation conceived of as descended from a common ancestor. Indeed, all of humanity is depicted as descended from a common ancestry—first from Adam and Eve and then from Noah and his wife. Large portions of Genesis and other books are genealogical lists, also emphasizing the genetic connection.

Immediately after the creation story, Genesis begins to describe history in terms of families, beginning with the family of Adam and Eve, thereby emphasizing the importance of this theme (Petersen, 8). After the primeval history, which focuses on the families from which all humanity is descended, the narrative moves to the family history of Abraham, tracing his descendants from Isaac to Jacob to Jacob's twelve sons, the eponymous ancestors of the tribes of Israel. A key feature of this narrative is the threefold promise by YHWH to Abraham of progeny, land, and blessing (Gen. 12:1-3). While Abraham is dwelling in Haran (in northern Mesopotamia), YHWH appears to him and tells him to leave his extended family and travel to a land that YHWH will show him, promising to give him that land on his arrival. Abraham takes his wife Sarah and his nephew Lot and sets out. When he arrives in Canaan, YHWH announces that this is the land he will receive and that will be passed down to his son. But though Abraham and his descendants live in this land (with minor forays to Egypt for Abraham and to Aram for Jacob), things take a turn with Jacob's sons, who all end up in Egypt. When Exodus picks up the story, the Israelites have been enslaved to the Egyptians. Moses appears and takes the descendants of Jacob, now called the Israelites, out of Egypt and slavery and back to the promised land, but the Torah ends before they actually get there. Thus this promise is unfulfilled at the end of the Torah, though the people are perched on the edge of the land, ready to move in and take it over.

Along with the promise of the land, Abraham receives a promise that he will be the forebear of numerous offspring. In the Priestly material, this promise is linked to the command made to

Adam at creation that he "be fruitful and multiply" (Gen. 1:28). This promise initially looks to be unfulfilled too, as Abraham's wife Sarah is barren. Abraham has a child, Ishmael, with Sarah's slave Hagar, but Ishmael is excluded from the promise by YHWH; it is only Sarah's son who will be the heir of the promise. Sarah finally conceives, with YHWH's aid, and bears Isaac. Isaac's wife Rebekah is also initially barren and requires divine assistance in order to have her two sons, the twins Jacob and Esau. Jacob, the heir, likewise has wives who are barren at various points, though between them and their two slaves they manage to bear twelve sons and a daughter. Barrenness and difficulty in childbirth thus serve in the Torah to emphasize both the power of YHWH and the special nature of the sons born out of such circumstances. And despite all these apparent setbacks, Genesis ends with the promise of progeny already well fulfilled; the overproliferation of the Israelites at the beginning of Exodus, to the extent that the Egyptian pharaoh is concerned that the Egyptians will be overrun, leaves the reader in no doubt about YHWH's power to fulfill the promise.

Though kinship is important in the Torah, it is only certain lineages in the larger Abrahamic kinship group that are deemed to be the "right" kinship lines. Abraham and Isaac both have two sons, but only one son is allowed to inherit the promise and with it the covenant, the formalization of the relationship between Abraham and YHWH that includes the promises (Genesis 17). Abraham's son Ishmael is excluded from becoming the heir, and thus from inheriting the promise, when Sarah objects to the son of her slave inheriting alongside her own son (or when YHWH informs Abraham that Ishmael will not inherit; compare Genesis 17 and 21). Likewise, Rebekah helps ensure that her favorite, Jacob, will inherit the promise and covenant, to the exclusion of his twin brother, Esau. Esau also seems to disqualify himself through his own actions, giving away his birthright and marrying the wrong women (Gen. 26:34); for this generation, as for the one before, a woman from Abraham's lineage in Aram is required for the "right" heir. With Jacob's sons, though, we move into a broader definition of the lineage; all of his sons inherit the promise and the land (and are no longer required to marry women from a specific family). The correct lineage having been identified, it can now proliferate and thus fulfill the progeny part of the promise.

This emphasis on lineage appears elsewhere in the Torah, too, though it does not receive quite the same emphasis elsewhere that it does in Genesis. It reappears as a theme especially in the genealogies interspersed throughout the Torah; these genealogies are manifestations of fulfillment of the command to "be fruitful and multiply" and the promise to Abraham of countless progeny (Exodus 6; Numbers 26). The genealogies primarily trace lines of male descent (from fathers to sons)—the tradition of matrilineal descent in Judaism developed much later. Women do figure into genealogies on occasion, especially where there is more than one wife and the author considers it important to note which woman is the mother of which child.

The third and final aspect of the promise, blessing, is a little harder to quantify. YHWH tells Abraham that he will be blessed and that "in you all the families of the earth shall be blessed" (Gen. 12:3). But just what does this mean? It has often been taken to refer to Abraham's role as a medium of blessing for all humanity, through his own relationship with YHWH. But it might simply mean that Abraham, owing to the fulfillment of the other aspects of the promise, will be invoked as a blessing by those who wish to achieve the same kinds of success. In either case, though, the Torah story seems to be a mixed bag as far as blessing is concerned. The Israelites do end up numerous and on the verge of possession of the land, but it is a long and rocky road that they take to get there.

YHWH's choice of Israel for the covenant, which involves the promise of numerous offspring, is closely connected to—even requires—the emphasis on lineage, as the covenant becomes a generational promise that is passed down within the line of a single son for two generations before being expanded to include all twelve of Jacob's sons. There is never an expansion of the genealogy to include non-Jacobite (non-Israelite) lineages in the covenant. In reality, other groups of people were absorbed into the Israelite nation, and the Torah does allow for the admission of others into the "community of Israel," but the concept of Israel as a separate and selected people remains one premised on the idea (if not the reality) of genealogical purity (see Cohen). It is for this reason that the Torah includes numerous genealogies; they detail the kinship between Israel and other peoples, but they also serve to delineate Israel's own genealogy specifically. The lists of member clans and families are carefully enumerated, not only for the purposes of census taking but also for outlining the roles of certain groups, especially in the tribe of Levi.

Genealogies are a special favorite of the Priestly author, who uses them to structure the narrative and divide it into portions. These genealogies are mostly concerned with men, but women are introduced into them from time to time; the inclusion of women in the genealogies is linked in particular to validating certain lineages (Exod. 6:14-25)—the pedigree of a lineage is indicated not only by the male line but also by the wives and mothers (see Shectman, 148–53).

Though these long lists of "begats" can seem tedious at first, the genealogies are an integral part of the narrative. They provide a framework for much of it, functioning as summaries at key junctures in the narrative (Genesis 10; 25; 36; Numbers 1–3). In addition to lists of general kinship or national groups (in the so-called Table of Nations in Genesis 10–11) and specifically Israelite tribes and clans, genealogical notices also appear for other, non-Israelite groups. The largest of these is a detailed genealogy of the descendants of Jacob's twin brother, Esau, who becomes the ancestor of the Edomites, one of ancient Israel's close neighbors. The inclusion of this list, the similar tribal structure of the Edomites, and the relationship between the characters of Esau and Jacob all suggest that these two groups had similar social structures and close affinities—and perhaps also that the biblical authors, through narratives and genealogies, wanted to differentiate the two (very similar) nations from one another.

The genealogies record births but also some marriages. As was noted above, marriages are important because they are one of the ways that a person establishes the "right" lineage: Isaac must marry a woman from Abraham's family (Genesis 24). Esau disqualifies himself from receiving his father's blessing and covenant by, among other things, repeatedly marrying the wrong women (Gen. 28:6-9). That one of his wives is an Ishmaelite—a descendant of Abraham's other son—further proves his inappropriateness as heir. Jacob, like Isaac, also marries women from his extended family (his cousins on his mother's side—a common phenomenon and not considered incest in many cultures, even today). Miriam and Aaron challenge Moses' authority by complaining that he has married a Cushite woman (Numbers 12).

Although we might expect the emphasis on Israelite lineage and inheritance to extend to a general prohibition on marriage with outsiders—or exogamy—this is not the case in the Torah. Though certain groups are prohibited—namely, Moabites and Edomites—there is no blanket prohibition on outside marriage. Wives from specific kinship groups are required only for certain figures: Isaac and Jacob in particular, figures from the early part of the narrative, when the nation is still being established and thus the need for self-differentiation is greater. Although in some instances the choice of a wife from a specific tribe or clan appears to help validate a particular lineage (see especially Aaron's line in Exodus 6), many major figures marry exogamously. Judah, the ancestor of one of the largest and most important tribes, marries a Canaanite woman—a member of a group that Israelites are elsewhere forbidden to marry (see Deut. 7:1-4). Joseph marries Asenath, the daughter of an Egyptian priest (Gen. 41:45). And Moses' Cushite wife is vindicated when Miriam is punished for challenging the marriage.

The most rigid marriage restrictions apply to the priests (Leviticus 21) and are related to cultic purity (see below) and to the purity of the priestly lineage. Priests are not allowed to marry prostitutes or divorced women; the high priest must marry a virgin "of his own people," probably meaning any Israelite woman, not only a woman from the priestly tribe of Levi. Marriage between members of different tribes seems not to have been a problem, though for logistical reasons it may not have been widespread. Especially in rural areas and in the earlier part of Israel's history, people are likely to have married fairly locally, from neighboring villages within their larger clan, but less likely from other tribes (Meyers, 142). There is only one case in which marriage within a close kinship group is required of any Israelites: the case of daughters of a man with no sons (Num. 27:1-11; 36:1-12), who hold temporary rights of inheritance when their father dies. In order to ensure that the land they temporarily inherit does not pass out of their clan's holdings, such women are required to marry within their clan (Shectman, 162–64).

Archaeological evidence indicates that the Israelites were very closely related to their Canaanite neighbors. Even though some biblical authors might have forbidden intermarriage with Canaanites in order to differentiate the Israelites from them, in reality it is likely that once the Israelites emerged as a distinct group around 1200 BCE, they intermarried with neighboring peoples frequently. We see remnants of these marriages in the text, despite the prohibitions against them. The marriages of early ancestors such as Judah and his son Simeon (Exod. 6:15) to Canaanite women, though likely not historical, may reflect a recognition by the biblical author that in the past the groups intermarried. There are also indications that the Israelites sought to make alliances with their neighbors through marriage. Jacob's objection to the episode involving his daughter Dinah and a Canaanite prince in Genesis 34 seems to focus not on her near-marriage to a Canaanite but to the souring of relations with the Canaanites when Dinah's brothers Simeon and Levi retaliate for what they see as an affront to their honor. Similarly, as the Israelites go from Egypt to the promised land, they attempt to move peacefully through the territories of some of their non-Canaanite neighbors (Num. 20:14-21; 21:21-32; but compare Deuteronomy 2), though they are not always granted these terms. It is only the Canaanites—the Israelites' closest neighbors—who are slated for complete annihilation even before the Israelites reach their territory, though again, both the biblical and the archaeological evidence suggests that such complete destruction did not take place (see Moore and Kelle).

In the early period of Israel's history, this creation of distinctions between the Israelites and Canaanites would have been quite important, as the nascent Israelite nation sought to establish its own independent identity. The archaeological evidence suggests that the early Israelites mostly lived in rural areas, and so they probably did not have frequent contact with non-Canaanite people. A broader prohibition on exogamy would therefore not have been necessary. It is not until the later period of Israelite history, with the Babylonian exile and afterward, that broader prohibitions on intermarriage appear in the biblical text. In this period, the Israelites in exile would have been in contact with an increasing number of people; without their own political structure and territorial autonomy, the threat of assimilation and intermarriage would have been greater. Thus, in later books such as Ezra and Nehemiah, we see broader prohibitions on exogamy, which are developed more fully in the rabbinic period (see Cohen). But most of the Torah seems to have been written before this view took hold.

A variety of types of marriage exist in the Torah, among them monogamy, polygyny (multiple wives), concubinage, and levirate marriage, the latter of which requires that a childless widowed woman's brother-in-law marry her and that their first son count as the deceased husband's heir (Deut. 25:5-10). There is thus no single concept of "biblical marriage," despite the frequent use of this phrase in modern society. Perhaps because Gen. 2:24 says, "Therefore a man leaves his father and his mother and clings to his wife, and they become one flesh," many people believe that a "biblical" marriage is a marriage between one woman and one man. But nowhere does the Torah say that a marriage *must* look like this, and the marriages of Abraham, Jacob, and perhaps even Moses (if Zipporah and the Cushite wife are indeed two different wives) do not conform to such a model.

Furthermore, the families modeled in the Torah, especially in Genesis, do not conform to our modern idea of a nuclear family. Including as they do multiple wives and their children, the families exist as small communities of their own. These families are filled with rivalries, younger sons usurping older ones, daughters seducing fathers, wives fighting over husbands, and sisters challenging brothers. These are not the kinds of "family values" that we often hear touted as the biblical model. Nevertheless, these stories do impart certain lessons. Beyond theological messages about faith in YHWH, the stories emphasize the importance of family and of hospitality to strangers, and they provide numerous models for nonviolent conflict resolutions (see Petersen).

Covenant

YHWH makes a series of covenants with various people over the course of the Torah's narrative. What is a covenant? It is an agreement between two parties, rather like a treaty. Indeed, the biblical covenant resembles the political treaties we know of from other ancient Near Eastern cultures, especially the Hittites and the Assyrians. These political treaties are typically between a sovereign and a vassal and outline the obligations of both parties. Various deities are invoked as "witnesses" to the treaties, and the documents conclude with long lists of punishments in the case that the vassal party breaks the treaty, much like the lists of blessings and curses in Leviticus 26 and Deuteronomy 27–28.

So, too, the covenants in the Torah are between a suzerain (YHWH) and a vassal (Israel), but the content of these treaties varies. The first treaty is between YHWH and Noah and "every living creature of all flesh"—that is, all the animals as well! YHWH prohibits eating meat with blood in it and shedding human blood (Gen. 9:4-6); Noah is also given dominion over all the animals and is commanded to "be fruitful and multiply," in terms reminiscent of the same command made to Adam in Genesis 1, though in that case the term *covenant* is not used. In return, YHWH promises never again to destroy the world with a flood and sets the rainbow in the sky as a sign of this covenant.

The second covenant is made with Abraham; there are actually two covenants with Abraham. The first is made in Genesis 15 and is often referred to as the "covenant between the pieces" as it involves the ritual killing and dismembering of animals to solemnize the pact. In this case, YHWH reiterates the promise to give Abraham and his offspring the land of Canaan. Nothing is required of Abraham in return according to this covenant's terms.

Two chapters later, YHWH makes another covenant with Abraham (Genesis 17). Genesis 15 and Genesis 17 are probably two originally independent versions of a single covenant, from two separate sources. This covenant too includes YHWH's promise to fulfill the original promise to Abraham of land and numerous progeny; YHWH also assures the still-childless Abraham that he will have a son through Sarah, his first wife; Ishmael, his son by the Egyptian slave Hagar, will not be the inheritor of this promise and covenant. In this covenant, unlike the one in Genesis 15, Abraham is required to do something in return: he and all the males of his household must be circumcised. This rule applies even to Ishmael and other members of the household who will not actually be part of the covenant—that is, they are not part of the lineage that ultimately becomes Israel and for whom the promise will be fulfilled. This covenant is also called an "everlasting covenant" (Gen. 17:19), which suggests that it can never be broken. Indeed, so far none of these covenants have involved any stipulations about what happens if one party or the other breaks the terms of the treaty. Thus these covenants are generally seen as eternal and unbreakable.

Abraham is often referred to as the "first Jew" because the covenant and circumcision are connected to the idea that the Israelites, and later the Jews, are YHWH's "chosen" people. Yet the term "chosen" (Hebrew *yivhar*) is never used in reference to Abraham. In fact, this idea does not appear in the Torah until near its end, in the book of Deuteronomy (Deut. 4:37; Seebass, 83). Nevertheless, the selection of Abraham and the inheritance of the covenant by his son Isaac and his grandson Jacob establishes a particular lineage with a special relationship to YHWH, a covenant that the deity has promised will be eternal. This proved to be a problem with the rise of Christianity, with its claims that a new covenant had been established. Very early Christianity was a movement within Judaism, so initially there was no theological problem. But as Christianity increasingly became a religion of gentiles, separating itself from other Jewish movements, Christian leaders like the apostle Paul began to reject the idea that they must follow all of the laws of the Torah (that is, the stipulations of the covenant; see below). Thus, in the letter to the Galatians, Paul offers a radical new reading of the promise to Abraham. The promise, Paul says, is passed down through faith, rather than being hereditary (see Galatians 3). Just as Abraham has faith in YHWH's promise (Gen. 15:6), so do Christians who have faith inherit the promise, and thus the covenant. Circumcision and other legal observances are not required. The blessing also becomes the key aspect of the promise, rather than the promises of progeny and land that are emphasized in the Torah: blessing (that is, salvation) is conveyed to Christians through faith, not through observance of the law. According to this interpretation, the new covenant (or "testament") in Christ supersedes the Jewish covenant initiated with Abraham.

The covenant with Abraham having been made and passed down through the generations to Jacob's sons, the new nation of Israel finds itself, at the beginning of the book of Exodus, enslaved to the Egyptians. Now quite numerous (the promise of numerous progeny being fulfilled), the Israelites pose a threat to the Egyptians, who use oppressive measures to arrest the population's growth. At this point, YHWH is notably absent from the narrative, apparently paying little attention to Israel in the centuries that pass between the end of Genesis and the beginning of Exodus and allowing the Israelites to become enslaved. Yet there is no indication in the text that YHWH has broken the covenant by allowing the Israelites' enslavement or that the Israelites are being punished for breaking their side of the agreement. Indeed, it is not until Exod. 2:24 that we read, "God remembered his covenant with Abraham, Isaac, and Jacob."

The Egyptians' attempts at oppression do not serve their intended purpose, but they do cause the Israelites to cry out. YHWH hears the Israelites' cries and determines to save the people, commissioning Moses to lead them to freedom. The Israelites escape to the Sinai wilderness, headed to the promised land and the fulfillment of the promise of the land. At Sinai, YHWH appears to the people and makes the third and final covenant of the Torah, this time with the entire nation of Israel. Now, though, the covenant takes on a very different form: it becomes a collection of laws, beginning with the Ten Commandments and expanding from there. The promises of land and progeny play less of a role in the making of this covenant in Exodus–Numbers, though they feature more prominently in the book of Deuteronomy, which is framed as a retrospective on the preceding narrative. Instead, the key features of this covenant are that the Israelites are to worship YHWH and only YHWH and that they are to observe all of the ritual, ethical, and social stipulations of the various collections of laws gathered together in the books of Exodus through Deuteronomy.

The new content of the covenant, the laws (Hebrew *torah*), occupy considerable space in the Torah. The bulk of the laws appear in Exodus and Leviticus, at the narrative point where the Israelites are encamped near Mount Sinai. YHWH appears and delivers most of the laws, some directly to the people and the rest to Moses, who ascends the mountain to receive them. A reiteration of many of these laws, as well as additional ones, also appears in the book of Deuteronomy. The laws cover a range of topics: religious laws governing various aspects of belief, worship, and sacrifice; criminal laws covering crimes such as murder and theft; and civil laws covering institutions such as marriage, inheritance, and slavery. The laws in Exodus include the Ten Commandments as well as numerous other social and religious precepts, along with instructions on how to build the tabernacle, the wilderness shrine that is a stand-in for the later Jerusalem temple. The laws of Leviticus are largely focused on the sacrificial cult and the system of purity and impurity that is the particular focus of the priesthood. The laws in these two books and in Deuteronomy appear as fairly coherent legal collections that have been inserted into the narrative. In Numbers, the interplay between law and narrative is more complex; the two are not always as clearly delineated from one another as they are in Exodus and Leviticus. In part, this may be due to the fact that in Numbers the Israelites depart from Mount Sinai, and thus the narrative loses its strong connection between place and lawgiving that allowed for the large sections of legal material to appear in the earlier narrative.

The covenant becomes explicitly conditional at this point: not only do many laws carry punishments, including the death penalty in some cases, for the person who breaks them, but if the Israelites do not obey the laws of the covenant, then YHWH will also abandon them to their enemies and they will be exiled from the promised land. It is noteworthy that exile from the land is the ultimate punishment for the people's breaking the covenant. The final curse in Deuteronomy for violation of the covenant speaks of a dispersed and miserable life for the people in places such as Egypt, where they will not even be able to sell themselves as slaves, so awful will their situation be (Deut. 28:64-68).

Despite the fact that the Israelites' foundational history included a period spent as slaves, the Torah's stance on slavery is mixed. As noted, the period of slavery in Egypt is not a punishment of the people, though the experience is certainly viewed as a terrible episode in their history, and YHWH's deliverance of the people from Egypt is one of the most frequently cited of the deity's miraculous and salvific acts. However, in the very same book, biblical laws condone slavery—and not only of foreign war captives or people perceived as Israel's enemies but also of other Israelites (Exod. 21:2-11). Thus the Torah has been used both as a justification for the institution of slavery and, in the past two centuries, as a source of liberation theology, which encourages freedom from political oppression.

Much of the legal material covers, broadly speaking, what is called the "cult"—that is, the system of Yahwistic religious observance. This includes broad stipulations such as the First Commandment (the First and Second Commandments in Jewish tradition): "I am the LORD your God, who brought you out of the land of Egypt, out of the house of slavery; you shall have no other gods before me" (Exod. 20:2-3). It also includes rules related to the priests and the temple. The biblical authors understood the sacrificial system to be a key part of Yahwism, beginning with Noah's first sacrifice after the flood. We read of ancestors setting up altars and making offerings in the book of Genesis (12:8; 26:25), even before the Israelites have been instructed in the specific details of the sacrificial system, which appear mostly in Leviticus. According to some biblical authors, then, the sacrificial system has more or less always been in operation. Even before the laws stipulating that sacrifices be performed only at certain places appeared, sacrifices could be performed almost anywhere. According to the Priestly author, however, sacrifice only begins with the revelation of the law at Sinai; before this time, the Priestly narrative does not depict anyone offering a sacrifice—they could not have done so, after all, without having yet been told how to do it! Similarly, the author of Deuteronomy insists that sacrifice can only be performed at a single location, which most scholars believe was likely Jerusalem; according to this view, Deuteronomy was written in Jerusalem in the later part of the Judean monarchy (eighth–seventh centuries BCE) as a means of centralizing worship at Jerusalem's temple. Other sources seem to assume that sacrifices continued to be offered in multiple locations even after the temple was built. Archaeological evidence also reveals that sacrifice was an Israelite practice even in the earliest history of the people—as it was for most ancient Near Eastern people—and that it continued at multiple Israelite sites even after the building of the Jerusalem temple.

Sacrifices were to be offered for a variety of reasons; there were a number of different types of them, some offered in the temple daily and others brought by individuals only on certain occasions.

The animals or other items for sacrifice were mostly brought by the people, but the process of sacrifice itself was officiated by the priests, who according to the Torah belonged to the lineage of Aaron, Moses' brother and a member of the tribe of Levi. They were assisted by Levites who were not from the Aaronide line. Only the Aaronide priests had access to the inside of the temple (analogized in the portable wilderness shrine—the tabernacle, or "tent of meeting"—in the Torah).

The purpose of sacrifice in many cultures is the feeding of the deity, and this aspect of sacrifice is retained at some level in the Torah, despite the attempts by some authors, especially P, to deanthropomorphize YHWH. Thus, in Gen. 8:21 (a non-Priestly text), YHWH smells the "pleasing odor" of Noah's offering, and Lev. 3:11 (a P text) says, "The priest shall turn these into smoke on the altar *as food*, an offering by fire to the Lord" (author's translation). However, sacrifices in the Torah have an additional and more important function as well: they are meant to absolve the people of culpability from their sins and to purify the temple. In the biblical view, the world was separated into two domains, holy and common, and two states, pure or impure. Purity had to do with abstract concepts rather than with physical characteristics such as dirtiness. Common things were allowed to be in either of these two states, though the pure state was preferred. But holy things, primarily meaning the temple and the things in it—including, in the innermost sacred area, YHWH—had to remain always in a state of cultic purity.

There were various causes of impurity, some of them physical (contact with a corpse, sexual intercourse, certain illnesses) and some of them moral (idolatry, bloodshed, and certain other ethical transgressions; see Klawans). Impurity was dangerous not only because it was incompatible with the holy but also because it was contagious and thus had to be stopped before it could spread too far. Ritual impurity was the more easily purged, generally through sacrifice and often through ritual bathing and the washing of clothes; moral impurity was harder to remedy, and its steady accrual would eventually cause the land to become so impure that YHWH would abandon the covenant, causing the nation to be exiled.

It is important to distinguish purity and impurity from *sin*, an idea that pertains to moral transgressions rather than cultic ones. Impurity is not inherently sinful—indeed, it can even result from obeying certain commandments—though a deliberate failure to rectify it is. The primary biblical root typically translated as "sin" does not always carry the same sense of moral transgression that the word has come to have in modern English, especially as a result of Christian theologies of "original sin" and a "fall from grace." In particular, the *hatta't* sacrifice, often translated "sin offering" (see Leviticus 4), is meant as a means of ritual purification and does not have an overt moral meaning. (And it should be noted that no biblical term for sin appears in Genesis 2–3, the story of so-called original sin; the idea that Adam and Eve "sinned" is based on later interpretations, both Jewish and Christian.) Though there is certainly a concept of sin in the Torah, cultic impurity and culpability are not necessarily dependent on sin—impurity accrues in the course of a normal life and would continue to do so even if everyone lived without sin.

Once YHWH has rescued the Israelites from slavery, delivered the laws to them, and renewed the covenant (all of which takes about a year), we might expect that things would go smoothly and the Israelites would move swiftly on to the conquest of the promised land. But of course, that is not what happens; instead, the Israelites wander in the desert for thirty-nine more years before entering the land of Canaan, occasionally engaging in battle but only beginning the process of conquest. When they finally do enter the land, Aaron, Miriam, and Moses have all died, and Moses' successor Joshua now leads the people. How does this happen? The remainder of the Torah narrative, in which the Israelites wander the wilderness, is peppered with episodes of complaint and conflict on the part of the Israelites. And this is not a new theme: Genesis and the early parts of Exodus, too, are littered with conflict between characters.

The conflicts in the Torah are of two main types: those between humans and those between humans and YHWH. Conflicts between humans include issues such as inheritance, water rights, the right to lead the people, and rivalries between wives. Those between humans and the divine appear especially in the wilderness narrative and tell of the Israelites' doubt that YHWH (and Moses) will in fact lead the people safely into the promised land. In perhaps the most egregious episode, the Israelites abandon YHWH altogether, making a molten calf to worship as a god instead (Exodus 32). It is only after Moses' intercession that YHWH relents from utterly destroying the people in punishment.

Though at one level such stories might make the Israelites look ungrateful and badly behaved in the face of divine benevolence, they also help to explain to an Israelite audience the frequent ups and downs in the course of Israel's history in the period of the monarchy, through the Babylonian exile, and afterward. They reveal an Israelite self-understanding that is based not only on YHWH's love of the people but also on the people's constant conflicts with the deity and with others. Indeed, the very name *Israel* is given an etymology based on struggle. In Gen. 32:28, Jacob struggles all night with a divine being; when Jacob prevails, the man says, "You shall no longer be called Jacob, but Israel, for you have striven [from the Hebrew root *srh*] with God and with humans, and have prevailed." Israel is a sort of permanent underdog, constantly striving, which may well reflect their status historically, in a region where they were continually dominated by larger and often oppressive powers. But this self-understanding also carries hope: YHWH has always looked out for the nation and has promised them continuing love, despite their misbehavior.

Through these themes—creation, kinship, and covenant—the Torah presents the foundational story of the Israelite nation. These themes are all connected to a larger idea of relationships: the relationship of humans to the world, of YHWH to the Israelites, and of the Israelites to one another. The narrative material details the history of these relationships, replete with conflict though they may be, and the laws supply the tools with which the covenant people are to maintain them. It is easy to see how this text resonated with and reassured an audience reading the Torah following the destruction of the Jerusalem temple by the Romans in 70 CE, and how it continues to resonate for Jews, Christians, and Muslims, all of whom trace their lineage, in one way or another, to Abraham. Though the text may have come together in stages from the hands of multiple authors with multiple worldviews, in the end the individual *torot* become a Torah that is greater than the sum of its parts.

Works Cited

Childs, Brevard S. 1979. *Introduction to the Old Testament as Scripture*. Philadelphia: Fortress Press.

Cohen, Shaye J. D. 1999. *The Beginnings of Jewishness: Boundaries, Varieties, Uncertainties*. Hellenistic Culture and Society 31. Berkeley: University of California Press.

Daly, Mary. 1973. *Beyond God the Father: Toward a Philosophy of Women's Liberation*. Boston: Beacon.

Finkelstein, Israel, and Neil Asher Silberman. 2001. *The Bible Unearthed: Archaeology's New Vision of Ancient Israel and the Origin of Its Sacred Texts*. New York: Free Press.

García López, F. 2006. "הרֹות, *tôrâ*." *TDOT* 15:609–46.

Jónsson, Gunnlaugur A. 1988. *The Image of God: Genesis 1:26–28 in a Century of Old Testament Research*. ConBOT 26. Lund: Almqvist & Wiksell.

Killebrew, Ann E. 2005. *Biblical People and Ethnicity: An Archaeological Study of Egyptians, Canaanites, Philistines, and Early Israel 1300–1100* B.C.E. SBLABS 9. Atlanta: Society of Biblical Literature.

Klawans, Jonathan. 2004. "Concepts of Purity in the Bible." In *The Jewish Study Bible*, edited by Adele Berlin and Marc Zvi Brettler, 2041–47. New York: Oxford University Press.

Meyers, Carol. 2013. *Rediscovering Eve: Ancient Israelite Women in Context*. New York: Oxford University Press.

Moore, Megan Bishop, and Brad E. Kelle. 2011. *Biblical History and Israel's Past: The Changing Study of the Bible and History*. Grand Rapids: Eerdmans.

Nicholson, Ernest W. 1986. *God and His People: Covenant and Theology in the Old Testament*. Oxford: Clarendon.

Petersen, David L. 2005. "Genesis and Family Values." *JBL* 124, no. 1:5–23.

Robinson, George. 2000. *Essential Judaism: A Complete Guide to Beliefs, Customs, and Rituals*. New York: Pocket Books.

Schniedewind, William M. 2004. *How the Bible Became a Book*. New York: Cambridge University Press.

Seebass, Horst. 1975. "רחַב@f *bāchar*." *TDOT* 2:73–87.

Shectman, Sarah. 2009. *Women in the Pentateuch: A Feminist and Source-Critical Analysis*. Hebrew Bible Monographs 23. Sheffield: Sheffield Phoenix Press.

Trible, Phyllis. 1978. *God and the Rhetoric of Sexuality*. OBT. Philadelphia: Fortress Press.

Weinfeld, Moshe. 1975. "תירבְּ@; *bᵉrith*." *TDOT* 2:253–79.

GENESIS

Rodney S. Sadler Jr.

Introduction

A division of Genesis into two major sections (1–11 and 12–50) represents well the major concerns of this book. The initial section (1–11), which may be discussed under the heading "The Founding of a World: The Genealogical Journey from Adam to Abram," introduces the reader to God, the world, and humanity and frames the relation among these three principal "characters" of the tale that will unfold throughout the rest of the Hebrew Bible and the Christian Testament. It can be subdivided as follows:

1:1—2:25	Providence Introduced: God's Creation of the World
3:1—5:32	Providence Thwarted: Fractures of the Initial Family
6:1—11:32	Providence Restored: Flood and New Creation

The second section, "The Founding of a Family: The Circuitous Journey from Haran to Egypt," focuses readers' attention on the development of one specific family, the family of Abram/Abraham and Sarai/Sarah, who descend from the line of Shem the son of Noah, and their circuitous trek to Egypt. It can be subdivided as follows:

12:1—25:18	Providence Heeded: Abram/Abraham the Faithful's Cycle
25:19—37:1	Providence Manipulated: Jacob/Israel the Trickster's Cycle
37:2—50:26	Providence Manifest: Joseph/Zaphenath-paneah and the Redemption Novella

Together, these two basic sections constitute the book we know as Genesis and are the appropriate introduction to Exodus inasmuch as they offer insight into the making of a world, the founding of a family, and the trek of that family from the northernmost regions of the Fertile Crescent to the two lands of Egypt, whence our story will continue.

In this exploration of Genesis, the concept of providence relates to the notion of God's gracious control of the cosmos and human destiny. This theme seems to be at the heart of the larger story in Genesis. Thus in this division, providence is revealed in two basic moves. Initially it is offered in relation to the cosmos and the first humans universally. Herein it is offered by YHWH/God, rejected by humanity, and then finally restored in a new creation by means of the divine reassertion of authority represented by the flood narratives. Subsequently, providence governs the lives of those in the Abramic/Abrahamic line and is revealed in the lives of three eponymous ancestors. First, Abram/Abraham, who lives faithfully under God's control, frequently seeks to realize the divine promises made to him through his own actions, but learns that it is only by God's hand that they will be manifest; second, Jacob, whose story reveals the consequences of human manipulation of God's providence in the fractures of his familial relationships; and third, Joseph, whose novella reveals the activity of God at work amid the seemingly random and often devastating events of his life. The concept of providence is quintessential in this account, since through his trials and tribulations and several nadirs, he is eventually exalted in a manner that only becomes evident in his own hindsight (50:20). Theologically, this book serves as an exemplar of the notion of providence as God's ultimate control over the cosmos, and human destiny rests at the heart of each of its narratives. As such, it would have served as a "primer on providence" to its initial audience, and in its present location in the canon, it continues to play that role in the lives of subsequent believers in the "God of Abraham."

Genesis 1-11: The Founding of a World: The Genealogical Journey from Adam to Abram

The founding of the world, or the primordial history (chaps. 1–11), introduces the reader to God, the world, and humanity. It is from this section of the larger book that we first encounter the chief protagonist in the biblical narratives, God. God, introduced by several names (e.g., Elohim, YHWH Elohim, YHWH, El Shaddai, El Elyon) and described with various character traits, is shown to be at the center of this book and, indeed, the entire created order. It is God who alone is able to create, the sole subject of the Hebrew verb *bārā'* ("create") in the Hebrew Bible. As Creator, God stands alone in authority, autonomy, and in awesomeness; this quality is used in numerous instances in Scripture to authenticate God's right to act in the world (see chaps. 37–40, where God's creative power serves to legitimate his ability to act unabated by human consideration).

In Genesis, we are introduced to God by a distinctive name as well. In 2:4b, for the first time, we encounter the name YHWH. This brief abbreviation, called the Tetragrammaton because it is often presented as four Hebrew letters *yôd, hê, wāw, hê,* identifies the particular deity of the Hebrew Bible. YHWH or YHWH God is not just a god; YHWH is presented as the one deity to whom allegiance is due; even when other deities are referenced, the distinctive attributes of YHWH set this deity apart as uniquely worthy of devotion and fealty. YHWH is the central character of the primordial history, and this collection of eleven chapters is our introduction to this transcendent being.

The primordial history also introduces us to the world in which the biblical narratives will unfold. It is a strange world, an alien world to those of us who live in the scientific, postmodern, Westernized world. It is a world that is covered with a *rāqia'*, or "dome" (1:6) like a glass terrarium; where the sun, moon, and stars are pressed into the dome (1:16-17); where the great seas are gathered together in a single *miqwēh*, or "collecting vessel"; where dry grounds are watered by an ethereal *'ēd*, or "mist" (2:6). Yet it is our world, defined as essentially good, carefully crafted to meet the needs of all of its inhabitants, but most particularly its human inhabitants (1:28-30). It is our world that is repeatedly described in the first chapter as "good," the product of God's thoughtful, creative proclamation in Gen. 1:1—2:4a, the product of YHWH God's careful crafting and tactile manipulation in Gen. 2:4b-17. It is a world made ready for us to *kābaš*, or "tame," and *rādâ*, or "administer," as we are set as stewards of this YHWH's artistic masterpiece we call earth.

And the third member of this triumvirate of characters is, well, us. Humanity is also introduced in the primordial history. We are *'ādām*, or "earthlings," taken from the dust of the *'ādamâ*, or the "earth" (2:7). We are vested with a hint of divinity, in one instance described as reflecting the *ṣelem*, or "image," of God (1:26-27) and in another described as animated by the *nĕšāmâ*, or "breath," of YHWH God (2:7). We are special, set apart, singled out in creation for distinctive glory. It is only after we are created that God declares the world to be "very good" (1:31). Yet we are also found to be disobedient (Genesis 3), murderous (Genesis 4), and capable of total depravity (Genesis 6). Still, despite our shortcomings, which are legion, YHWH will continue to be gracious to us, forgiving us when we have fallen, protecting us when we have made ourselves vulnerable, and redeeming a righteous remnant when we seem to have all but lost our way.

In part, the primordial history is the beginning of a dramatic love story, a story that unfolds as a romance between YHWH and humanity, complete with instances of heartfelt commitment interspersed with instances of serial infidelity. It is a passionate affair that leads to violence, separation, reconciliation, and eventually forgiveness and restoration. At the end of this section in chapter 11 of Genesis, we will finally meet the human partner who will follow faithfully YHWH's call and who will eagerly assent to the providential covenantal relationship that YHWH has sought with humanity.

Genesis 1–2: Providence Introduced: God's Creation of the World

▮ The Text in Its Ancient Context

Genesis 1–2 contains the two primary stories associated with the creation of the world and introduces the reader to God's providence by means of demonstrating God's authority over and care of creation. Historically, the two chapters have been taken as a single narrative, yet a closer investigation demonstrates that they are actually two distinct narratives composed for different reasons and likely at different times.

The initial Priestly (P) narrative, in Gen. 1:1—2:4a, is the most famous of the two stories and occurs as a formulaic description of the creation of the cosmos from an originally watery earth. In the space of six days, the story asserts that God (*'ĕlōhîm*) creates the heavens and the earth in a fairly methodical and extraordinarily orderly set of events. The formula of creation unfolds in a repetitive process that generally begins with God's statement "Let there be *x*," followed immediately by an assertion that *x* comes to be, that *x* is called by a name, that *x* is evaluated as "good," and then some sort of acknowledgment of the passing of time, "and there was evening and there was morning, day *y*." The formula recurs over the course of six days, with subtle alterations in each day. For example, there is no evaluation on day two, and the complexity of God's action tends to increase over each day; but the general flow of the formula persists until the sixth day.

On the sixth day, the earth is populated by living land creatures in complexity increasing beyond the birds of the fifth day. This process culminates with the creation of the *'ādām*, or "earthling," in 1:26. The earthling's creation violates the general pattern in several ways. First, it occurs after the daily evaluation of the creation of other living creatures in verse 25. Second, its creation is offered in conjunction with a divine self-reflection: "Let us make humankind [earthlings] in our image." This phrase alone could bear considerable analysis, for the nature of the *ṣelem*, or "image," held in common between the *'ĕlōhîm* and the earthling is never clearly explicated, nor is the suddenly plural quantification of the deity, who though represented by the theoretically plural term *'ĕlōhîm* is consistently associated with singular verbs in all other instances except in this verse. Because of the common image, however, the earthling is vested with considerable authority over creation to both "subdue" and exert "dominion" over it. Finally, in verse 31, God offers an assessment of the entire creation with the addition of the earthling, and only now does the assessment merit the evaluative statement "very good."

From this it is clear that this is not just a general statement about creation. It is an anthropocentric assessment that celebrates creation in a way that emphasizes our own role in it as God's crowning glory. The orderly and potent deity crafts a world that is only assessed to be "very good" (1:31) once we are included in it. Further, the overall narrative ends up as a metaphor focused on the comparison between God and humanity. Creation unfolds over six days, allowing God the opportunity to *šabbāt*, or "rest," on the seventh day, and thus, by analogy, human beings should also *šabbāt* on this day that God has "hallowed" (2:3).

At the end of this first creation story, the original audience could have seen the narrative's overall purposes. It has confirmed that God is orderly and morally "good," that the world is orderly and "good," and that with the inclusion of humanity the overall schema is "very good." This positive assessment of theology, cosmology, and anthropology marks this narrative in a way that would have been clear to its early audience. Perhaps finding its final form as an address to a community that experienced exile in the aftermath of the Babylonian captivity in the latter sixth to early fifth centuries BCE, this story was intended to contrast the creation narratives of the Babylonians (Brueggemann, 25), whose stories of creation posited that the world was the by-product of the slain corpse of Tiamat, the goddess of the sea, and that humans were crafted from the blood of Kingu, her illegitimate spouse, to be slaves to a host of spiteful deities. This narrative offers a distinct view of God, the world, and humanity that would have answered its initial audience's questions quite well. Further, by cohering with the seven-day paradigm for a week that culminates in Sabbath, which would have already been known to the original audience, this narrative would have validated the world as they knew it.

Here Brueggemann's caution that this is not a scientific description but a theological affirmation should be heard (Brueggemann, 25; cf. Sarna, 3–4). This is a story told to resolve distinctive concerns of a particular audience at a particular time and was not intended to bear the burden of being the final universal statement about the scientific creation of the world. If we remember that point, the narrative can speak to us with renewed pertinence as a theological statement about the nature of God, the world, and humanity.

The second, Yahwistic (J) creation narrative, in Gen. 2:4b-24, describes creation in an arid land, by a deity described in much more anthropomorphic terms, who is called *yhwh ʾĕlōhîm*. With the different moniker comes a deity who does not create by word in six days but who creates the world by manual manipulation in a single day (2:4b), who forms the earthling as the first act of creation (2:7) and intimately performs CPR on it to bring it to life, and who fashions the rest of creation in response to the needs of the earthling. Instead of creating by divine command, *yhwh ʾĕlōhîm* "planted a garden" (v. 8), "took" and "put" the earthling in it (v. 15), "formed" from the earth other living creatures (v. 19), and finally performs an elaborate surgical procedure wherein the deity bifurcates the earthling (vv. 21-23), taking its *ṣēlaʿ*, best read not as a single "rib" but as its "side." From this "side," *yhwh ʾĕlōhîm* forms the earthling's appropriate counterpart. It is only then that the earthling is described with the gendered terms *ʾîš*, or "man," and *ʾiššâ*, or "woman," in the narrative (Meyers, 72–94; cf. Sadler 2010, 72).

This second narrative would have served the early audience not simply as a creation account but also as an elaborate etiology, or "origin story," for the institution of marriage, justifying this institution on the basis that the original earthling was split into two and can only become whole when united with its counterpart in a paired unit. And so this section ends with the statement, "Therefore a man leaves his father and his mother and he clings to his woman, and they become one flesh" (v. 24).

▌ THE TEXT IN THE INTERPRETIVE TRADITION

These two narratives have been combined over the years of Christian interpretation to form a single narrative, often ignoring the definitive fissures in the accounts. In part, this has led to wonderful and poetic retellings like James Weldon Johnson's "Creation," wherein the poet weaves the two stories together masterfully, demonstrating the common understanding of the creation story. In part, this has contributed to the idea that there is just one story of creation and fueled the debates that pit the biblical creation narrative (read as singular) against scientific perceptions of the big bang and evolution.

Lost in such interpretive decisions is the fact that these accounts deftly address questions posed by the original audience about the nature of God, the world, and humanity; about the reason for a seven-day week and Sabbath rest; about the intimate relationship between the deity and the human creature; and about the reason human beings marry. Subsequent Judeo-Christian communities have often lost sight of these narratives' original concerns and replaced them with our own issues and our own concerns. In the process, we have lost sight of the rhetorical power wielded by these stories for their initial audiences.

■ THE TEXT IN CONTEMPORARY DISCUSSION

There are a number of issues that these texts still present for contemporary communities. The concerns about the nature of God, the world, and humanity are still issues with which we wrestle today, and these texts provide incredibly useful insight into these questions, positing a careful and good Creator who developed a good world in which we are integral members. Today questions of ecology are also at the forefront of our concerns as we seek to determine whether the instructions from Gen. 1:28 to "subdue" and exercise "dominion" entitle us to do to creation whatever we will or if the narrative instead, in light of global climate change and the growing scarcity of our natural resources, charges us to be stewards of what God has granted to us.

Perhaps no issues are more pressing from the initial narrative than those that have to do with the importance of the "image of God." This compelling notion, revisited in Gen. 9:6 and offered as a reason for the valuation of human beings and the prohibition of taking human life, has served as the theological basis of many contemporary struggles for liberation and equality. What would this world be like if every human being truly began to appreciate what it means that we humans are all vested with the image of God? As Martin Luther King Jr. notes, "Man is a child of God made in His image, and therefore must be respected as such" (King, 255). May we all one day appreciate this core value and its implications for establishing interpersonal and social justice!

The second narrative continues to be relevant today as the concept of permanent-pair bonding is much less prevalent as a social institution than it has been in previous generations. That this was deemed a core concern of the ancestors of our faith traditions, significant enough to grant it a location at the outset of the biblical narratives, should not be lost on us. The notion of the attainment of wholeness through lifelong pair bonding should not be ignored as we consider these texts. To the contrary, these texts have also been used as "clobber texts" on the LGBT community, noting that they establish the basis of the relationship between "Adam and Eve, not Adam and Steve." As we appropriate these texts in the contemporary world, we will have to revisit anew how these texts continue to inform our relationships in the contemporary world.

Genesis 3–5: Providence Thwarted: Fractures of the Initial Family

■ THE TEXT IN ITS ANCIENT CONTEXT

This section of Genesis introduces us to the individual personalities of the first family and suggests the initial instance of human rebellion against the providence of God. Starting in chapter 3, these flat characters begin to take shape as more rounded characters with depth and dimension. This chapter begins with the story of the "tempting" of the original pair. To the original audience, this story is more than simply a morality tale; it is also a joke. It begins in verse 1 by introducing us to a serpent that is described as being *ārûm*, or "cunning" or "crafty," and climaxes in verse 7 with the first pair learning that they are *'ĕrummîm*, or "naked." In their attempt to gain the power of the knowledge of everything, literally all that lies between the two extremes of good and evil, in their attempt to become wise and powerful like *yhwh 'ĕlōhîm*, who has forbidden them from eating from the fruit of the tree of the knowledge of good and evil (2:17), they have found themselves vulnerable; they have realized they are naked. The irony of the end of this action would not have been lost on the original audience, which may have both chuckled and sighed at the consequence of the protagonists' actions.

For this community, the serpent would have been understood to be a wise creature and would have served as a metaphor for wisdom; it was clearly a "beast of the field" as it is identified in the narrative, not a spiritual or angelic figure (i.e., Satan, a figure only evident by name in 1 Chronicles, Job, and Zechariah in the Hebrew Bible; see Brueggemann, 47; De La Torre, 66–68). Along the lines of the story of Gilgamesh, which contains in tablet 1 column 4 the account of the wild man Enkidu, who is taught by sexual relations with a wise female figure, Shamhat, to be a wise human (Dalley, 55–56), this narrative provides an etiology for the cognitive ability of human beings, distinguishing them from the other animals (cf. Eccles. 3:18-19). This is evident by the couple's realization of their nakedness in verse 7, a reversal of the prior assessment about their status in 2:25. Yet it is also a story of loss, as the consequence (3:14-24) for the actions of these previously oblivious creatures is that the females will bear children in pain, the males will live only by the sweat of their brows, that all of humanity will be forbidden from accessing the tree of life and the garden paradise, and that they will all eventually die (see Meyers, 72–94).

This loss is the result of their rebellion against YHWH's instruction. The stated penalty for the action of eating the fruit in 2:17 and 3:3 is death, making their choice to eat the fruit consequential. We should note, however, that this choice is nowhere in this passage deemed "sin." Hebrew equivalents for this term (ḥaṭṭāʾt) do not occur in the text until 4:7, when the concept is introduced in YHWH's warning to Cain about his feelings toward his brother Abel.

Subsequently, YHWH God not only utters curses but also lifts up the fallen human beings, fashions clothing for them, and makes provision for them to have not the death associated with rebellion but a life outside the Garden of Eden. As we end this story, our vision of God has expanded, for God is not only the powerful, careful Creator of Genesis 1 or the intimate, hands-on Creator of Genesis 2 but also the forgiving, gracious God who can see flawed humanity and find a way to redeem us in spite of our rebellion against God's providence.

It is important to recognize that the initial audience would not have thought the woman was "tempted" in ignorance. Inasmuch as she was part of the original earthling, she received the same instruction as her male counterpart when they were together as a combined entity. The woman was not "tempted" in isolation; she gave the fruit to her husband who was "with her" (3:6). We should also note that the fruit is never identified as an apple either.

Further, the original audience would probably have realized that there does not appear to be any attempt to hierarchically relate men and women until after the curses are ascribed here (3:16). In this regard, such a state of disordered relationships can be described as a product of YHWH God's response to human disobedience; it was not a part of YHWH God's intention for the created order.

As the story continues, the original earthlings give birth to the next generation. The story in Genesis 4 is probably best remembered because of the line "Am I my brother's keeper?" uttered by the antihero Cain in verse 9. This painful story begins as two brothers both try to please YHWH

God, and ends describing the further failings of humanity fostered by the first recorded instance of a human being competing for God's favor; in this brief narrative is the seed that will give rise to countless billions of deaths caused ostensibly by humanity's religious fervor. Ironically, the first murder is not over property rights, over sexual partners, over social status, over material goods, over a struggle for rights, over a struggle to survive; the first murder is predicated on an attempt to please God.

A few quick notes on this story might yield some insight into this brief but often misunderstood account:

- Though Abel the felled brother is often thought to be the key brother and the symbol of religious obedience and moral exemplar in this story, we should note that he never utters a word and is a fairly flat character. His name actually means "Vapor," suggesting his ephemeral nature in the narrative.
- His brother's name is "Cain," which in Hebrew would be similar to the English moniker "Smith" or "-smith," meaning one who crafts something from metal. In essence, it is the story of an agriculturalist that is cursed from the ground and then becomes a "craftsman" or "smith." It is an etiology or origin story for people who are neither shepherds nor farmers in an otherwise dimorphic society, but who live by the cunning of their hands.
- The well-known mark of Cain (4:15) is not a curse. It is actually the Lord's mark of protection on him so that he will not be killed (though the story is surprisingly silent about by whom he would have been killed). In essence, far from being a curse, the mark of Cain is a symbol of divine protection conferred by a caring God on an errant human character.

In the end, we are left with a further-developed picture of YHWH God, who again has forgiven humanity for its missteps, here even forgiving the capital offense of homicide (cf. 9:5-6). The narrative has also provided a means past the sinful nature (4:7) that human beings manifest. In part, this should serve as a reminder that the grace of God is not a "New Testament" innovation! No, God's grace, though not explicitly so named, is evident even in the earliest texts in the Old Testament.

The story in Genesis 5 merits less attention, but we should note that it is not insignificant. Many of the narratives in the first five books of the Bible relate to patronyms, or genealogical lists of male ancestors. This was significant for the people of ancient Israel/Judah because they wanted to be able to trace their familial roots back to the very beginning of the world. This continuity of the march of humanity is relevant to us as well, for in it we can see that the origins of human beings are said to be common; we are all ultimately related according to the Genesis narratives. Human beings all are described as being from one family emerging from one common ancestral lineage. There is no attempt to describe different origins of different racial types or different ethnic groups from different geneses. All of humanity comes from one source, and these genealogies affirm our ultimate kinship in the common origins of all human beings.

A final significant feature of chapter 5 is the introduction of Noah and his three sons, who will become key figures in the overall narrative in the next several chapters. Through them humanity will receive its second genesis.

■ The Text in the Interpretive Tradition

Genesis 3 has been historically understood as the "fall of humanity," an interpretive tradition that likely is fostered in the Christian tradition by Paul, who in Romans 5 and 1 Corinthians 15 brings together the notion of "sin" (*hamartia*) and this story of Adam. To this was added the instruction found in 2 Cor. 11:3 and 1 Tim. 2:13, both of which describe the deception of Eve. These texts give rise to the traditional interpretation that posits the fall of humanity into "sin" by means of the serpent's deception of the woman. In the traditional interpretation, the man has often been denied ultimate culpability because he is presumed to have been absent when the woman was "tempted" by the serpent. It goes without saying that the traditional reading has been employed to misogynistic ends.

In this interpretive tradition as well, the serpent is conflated with the devil and Satan, likely based on a reading of Rev. 12:9, where the great dragon is described in both tangible and transcendent ways (see Isa. 27:1). In this regard, the ancient Near Eastern account of the cunning serpent who was a "beast of the field" or a "wild animal" (3:1) who promises to make the humans wise has been reinterpreted as the story of the devil or Satan, a malevolent spiritual being in an antagonistic relationship with God whose goal is the destruction of humanity.

Thus the story of this initial act of human striving that leads to rebellion against YHWH God's providence has been recast as a story of the fall of humanity at the hands of God's great foe, Satan, and the subtle details of the extant narrative have been lost, obscured beneath strata of subsequent theological and ideological detritus. As the narratives continue to unfold over the next few chapters, human depravity will become a significant focus of the story, so the traditional interpretations are not without merit; still, interpreters must be careful not to conflate subsequent interpretive traditions that ascribe "sin," "Satan," and "the fall" to this etiological narrative that defines as realities of the world the earliest audiences would have known with its painful births, the need for human toil, growing patriarchy, and a healthy fear of serpents (see Sarna, 24–29; De La Torre, 66–68). More recent interpreters like Miguel De La Torre have offered a revised assessment of this text not as "the fall" but as an initial instance of "rebellion" (De La Torre, 72) as human beings exert their own autonomy in response to God's providence.

Traditional interpretations of chapter 4 tend to elevate Abel, who somehow becomes a moral exemplar in the narrative because of his offering of an appropriate sacrifice and his subsequent victimization at the hand of his own brother; he is even seen as a prefiguration of Jesus or the martyrs of the world (see Louth, 104–9). Historically, Genesis 4 has served as a narrative that epitomizes humanity's inhumanity, as it shows that the bitter resentments of those as close as two brothers can end in a homicidal rage with the shedding of innocent blood. This narrative has also been used to denote the rapid progression of sin in the world that quickly escalates from willful disobedience to God in chapter 3 to fratricide in chapter 4. This sets up the scenario we will encounter in chapter 6 as we discuss the nadir of human morality in preparation for the flood story.

The traditional interpretations of the account in chapter 5 focus on the saintly nature of Enoch and the extremely long lengths of human lives described herein (Louth, 118–22). The particularly long lifespan of Methuselah has become a well-known aspect of this story, and it has become a commonplace description for a person of advanced age to be deemed as "old as Methuselah."

◼ THE TEXT IN CONTEMPORARY DISCUSSION

Exploring these narratives in chapter 3, we should ponder the differences between the society for whom these narratives were initially composed and our own. How do those differences manifest differences in interpretive emphases? Does the interjection of early Christian interpretive traditions of "original sin" and the unifying metanarrative of the "Bible" complete with a theology describing sin's introduction in Adam and solution in Christ obscure the meanings that the initial audiences would have derived from these texts? How can we begin to appreciate these stories on their own merits without presuming a post-Pauline interpretive posture?

Looking at these narratives in chapters 4–5, how can we help but notice the prevalence of violence in our contemporary world? This narrative that describes the first murder as the result of sibling rivalry over religious fealty brings home the fact that we really are all related, we really are as human beings all siblings in an interdependent relationship with one another (Genesis 5). The passage of time has not lessened the poignancy of this account, nor have we yet learned to be each other's keepers over the millennia. The rhetorical question asked by Cain continues to resonate throughout the years and serves as a constant reminder that his presumed answer "no" was wholly antithetical to what should have been. As creatures of community who flock together in societies, we live in a symbiotic relationship with one another and our lives are dependent on the maintenance of our web of mutuality and on our efforts on behalf of each other. Our survival as a species depends on our recognizing the importance of each and every other human being and caring about their plight. In the end, may we all seek to answer Cain's question, "Am I my brother's keeper?" with a definitive yes!

Genesis 6:1—11:32: Providence Restored: Flood and New Creation

◼ THE TEXT IN ITS ANCIENT CONTEXT

After the initial manifestations of human rebellion in the prior section, God reasserts providence over a creation in disarray. The narratives in this section of Genesis present the path toward a new creation wherein YHWH God will definitively address human depravity and will reestablish order, manifesting particular affection for a distinctive line in Noah's progeny introduced at the end of chapter 11. Chapter 6 begins with a story most would categorize as a biblical mythology. Here, as in Greek mythology's stories of Heracles and Perseus, we find an account referring to sexual unions between human and divine beings. The offspring produced from these unions are, like those in Greek mythology, superhumans endowed with great ability, the "heroes of old" and "warriors of renown." The phrase *běnê hā'ělōhîm*, or "sons of God," in 6:2 seems to recall entities like those in Job 1:6 and to refer to undefined "heavenly beings." In this case, the "sons of God" are probably angelic creatures from the heavenly realm interacting with human beings and thereby producing semidivine progeny.

The Nephilim of 6:4 represent an interesting dimension in this narrative. They are thought to have been biblical giants who likely engaged in many miraculous tales known to the original audiences of this text, hence the reference to them being men of *hašēm*, "name" or "renown" (6:4). The term "Nephilim" may actually come from a Hebrew root, *npl*, that means "fallen," hence we could understand them to be the "fallen ones," which may have some bearing on the overall account of these great demigods fallen from the heavens who once ruled on earth. Though they do not appear to be present in the narratives that describe human wickedness (vv. 5-7, 11-12), the limitation of these figures to their brief appearance in the preflood narratives suggests that they too did not survive the flood.

Human life is limited here to 120 years. This is probably more of a general number than an actual time. This recalls the fact that human beings are said to have endured death in Genesis 3 and seems to expedite the period from the near thousand years of some of the characters mentioned in Genesis 5. It is odd that we see stories of such great longevity in these accounts since many speculate that contemporary people live longer than people in the ancient world may ever have lived. Perhaps the extraordinary lengths of these characters' lives served some function in the calculations of the calendars of ancient Israelite/Judahite peoples.

In verse 3, we note the potent concept of the *rûaḥ*, or "Spirit" of YHWH. Here we should recognize the obscure use of the Hebrew verb *dyn* used with *rûaḥ*, meaning likely "judge" or "contend" in relation to the Spirit of YHWH's action in human beings. The Septuagint's use of a form of the verb *katamenō* suggests that the Spirit's job was to animate human life; hence the reference to the limitation of the Spirit's presence leading to the reduction in the spans of life to 120 years. Though utilizing different terms than Gen. 2:7's *nišmat*, there does seem to be an allusion to this narrative in which human beings are vested with sacral significance by the "breath" of YHWH God. In this regard, the concept of God's indwelling spirit as the vivifying aspect of human life implies that because we bear the spirit (or wind/breath) of God, we live. It is this quality that animates and sanctifies otherwise lifeless flesh (see Eccles. 3:21).

The latter portion of Genesis 6 establishes the reasons for YHWH's eventual destruction of the world by flood. Verse 5 describes human beings as completely "evil." Actually, this verse emphasizes the extremity of this moral deficit by the use of the Hebrew terms *rab*, or "great," and *kōl*, or "every," to syntactically emphasize the extreme nature of humanity's evil. It is not just that they are evil, but their *great* evil is evidenced in that *every* thought framed in their mind is evil throughout *every* portion of the day.

And thus YHWH is sorry to have made them. The term *nāḥam* used here for "was sorry" suggests that God "repented" for having created humanity. The injection of pathos at the end is consistent with the anthropomorphism of the Yahwistic writer, who describes YHWH as either "grieved" or "vexed" to the heart. Here we have the first reason given for the destruction to come in the flood. This legitimating narrative suggests that humanity is wicked. It is difficult not to recognize the impact of the depravity on YHWH, who determines in 6:7 to destroy all categories of animal life and indeed all of creation because of it. The anthropocentric perspective of the author, who imagines that because of humanity's faults, all of creation must be undone, should not be lost on us. The world at large suffers due to humanity's wickedness. In the author's view, as we go, so goes the whole world; this is a message we should heed in an age of widespread oppression, corporate greed, gross income inequality, and global climate change.

Then in 6:8, with a suddenness intended to jar the reader, we are introduced to the sole exception to the rule of depravity. As in other instances in this book, at precisely the moment when the reader might expect to see YHWH's unbridled rage, we are introduced to a figure to whom YHWH will demonstrate compassion. Though it seems as if humanity has reached its fitting end, through Noah the "bearer of an alternative possibility" YHWH will offer humanity another chance (Brueggemann, 79). Over the course of the next three chapters, Noah will be revealed as a complex character who is both an exemplar of faithful behavior and a troubled father whose words will pit his sons against each other in 9:24-27.

If the reader attends carefully, there is a second legitimization for the flood given in 6:11. Now the title given to the deity is 'ĕlōhîm, or "God," and the narrator informs the reader that the earth was "corrupt . . . and . . . violen[t]." This different reasoning with a different vocabulary evidences a different source for this material. In essence, the flood story is one of the clearest examples in Genesis of its composite nature.

We see further evidence of this phenomenon as we explore chapters 7–8. The fissures in the story become apparent when the reader discerns the duplications and inconsistencies in the narrative. For example, there are two instances where the reason for God's destruction of the world are noted (vv. 5 and 11); there are multiple accounts of the number of animals taken on the ark (cf. 7:1-5 with 7:8-10); there are discrepancies about the length of time of the flood (cf. 7:12 with 7:24); there are even two different resolutions to the crisis (8:20-22; 9:11-17). To further accentuate the differences in the narratives, we can also distinguish different terms used to identify the deity in the different accounts. Suffice it to say that the actual narrative is far more complex than it appears to be at first reading.

"J" Source Flood Narrative	"P" Source Flood Narrative
• 6:5 **YHWH** saw that the inclination of hearts (minds) was evil. • 6:6 YHWH is sorry for creating humanity. • 7:1-5 YHWH says take seven pairs of clean and one of unclean animals.	• 6:11 **God** notes that earth was filled with violence and flesh was corrupt (two justifications). • 6:19 Two of every kind of animal. • 7:8-10 Two of every kind of animal (may be from an addition). • 7:11 Catastrophe caused by great deep bursting and windows of sky opening.
• 7:7 Noah and his family go into ark. • 7:12 Rains forty days and forty nights. • 7:17b Flood continues for forty days. • 8:2b-3a Rain from heaven restrained. • 8:8-12 Noah opens window and sends forth birds. • 8:20-22 Noah offers a sacrifice.	• 7:15 Noah and his family go into ark. • 7:24 Flood swells for 150 days. • 8:1-2a Fountains of deep and windows of heaven closed. • 8:14-19 Noah removes cover and sees earth dry and sends out family. • 9:6 Note the return to Priestly language from Gen. 1:27. Created in God's image. • 9:11-17 Covenant set between God and world not to cut off all flesh by waters of flood—sealed with a rainbow.

(Excerpted from Campbell and O'Brien, 211–13)

Despite the diverging details, we can discern an essential story line. The deity is enraged by the depraved behavior of human beings and for that determines to destroy the world by flood. One family will be saved from the impending disaster by means of an ark because of the deity's affection for the faultless character of its patriarch, Noah. The flood rages on the earth for a prescribed period of time, eliminating all manner of life save those beings in the ark. Once the flood subsides, the remaining humans and the deity are reconciled and a new creation begins from the redeemed remnant in the ark (8:16—9:17).

The extant combined story is a morality tale reminding human beings that our behavior matters to the deity and commending the upright and faithful behavior of Noah. It also serves to further the description of the deity, who though opposed to the deplorable actions of humans always remains ready to redeem and restore an otherwise flawed and fallen world. The act at the end of the flood account of the deity hanging the "rainbow" in the sky (9:13-16) would have been understood as the act of a warrior who hangs up his *qešet*, or "war bow," symbolizing the cessation of hostilities. Herein we find another etiology, for this serves as the origin of the rainbow in the sky.

The stories in Genesis 9:18-28 and 10 are two of the seemingly least relevant stories for contemporary Christians in all of Genesis, particularly when they are read apart. The first is the story of a familial curse that is incurred by Noah's grandson (Canaan) because one of his sons (Ham) sees his nakedness as he lies drunk and exposed in his tent and does nothing to remedy it. The problem for readers here is that the text appears to be somewhat corrupted; the one cursed is not the one who saw "the nakedness." Yet the narrative seems intent on producing a particular outcome, yielding a perpetual cursing of Canaan and his offspring. Genesis 10 presents a series of patronymics, or genealogies of generations exclusively through the paternal lines, of the three sons of Noah. On the surface, these appear to be ancient stories chronicling insignificant events that should have little relevance to contemporary audiences.

A close reading of the initial story about the cursing of Canaan with the second about the descendants of Noah's sons reveals that these narratives together provide a legitimating ideology for the ensuing biblical narratives. These two narratives together provide a biblical justification for the subsequent dispossession and oppression of the indigenous Canaanite population in Palestine by the people of Israel who, we will learn in Genesis 10, are the sons of Shem. Once this purpose is understood, these two passages take on a crucial significance in the larger biblical metanarrative, establishing the basis of relationships that will unfold between the "chosen" people and those who will be displaced.

Further exploration of Gen. 9:18-28 shows the tenuous nature of the curse. It is a curse uttered by a drunken father against the wrong offspring for an offense that is not clearly explicated, which really is void of God's sanction or any sense of moral standing. Yet the presence of the curse here offers a justification for Israel's taking of the land of Canaan from the Canaanites. Without such a story, the larger metanarrative of the Hebrew Bible would seem incomplete; this narrative offers, even if inadequately, a justification for the dislocation and oppression of the Canaanites and answers a question for the ancient audience that is as yet unasked but clearly anticipated (Sadler 2005, 26–27).

Genesis 10 has been called the "Table of Nations" and provides a series of patronymics of the sons of Noah in an order that demonstrates their increased significance in the subsequent biblical narratives. It begins with an account of the sons of Japheth, about whom little is known and who can be summed up neatly in five verses. The second son presented is Ham, who is described as the ancestor of all the great civilizations of old including the empires of Egypt, Cush (Nubia), Assyria, and Babylon among other nations of note. The descendants of these eponymous ancestors will resurface in the narrative in numerous instances in the Hebrew Bible, and this group is therefore the focus of verses 6-20. The final group presented in this chapter is the sons of Shem. Though his sons are presented in verses 21-32, this is only a precursor for another account, which will continue in 11:10-32, culminating in 11:26-32 with the introduction of Abram. Thus the genealogy of Shem becomes the dominant patronymic in the Table of Nations, establishing the familial line through which YHWH will choose to bless the world.

The narrative at the beginning of Genesis 11 represents an interpretive problem. Here, in the aftermath of the flood, we see the people of the world cooperating and working together on a major building project at Babylon. This unity is in remarkable contrast to the enmity and infighting that seem to govern other chapters (e.g., Genesis 4 and 6). Yet this unity does not seem to please YHWH. Genesis 11:6 suggests the "problem" represented in this passage. It is not sin or selfishness but the very unity and the possibility of human achievement evidenced in their common striving that drives the action in this narrative. It seems as if their actions, while not clearly "sinful," have violated YHWH's desire that they fill the earth, a desire hinted at in verses 4 and 8, or that they are getting "too big for their britches," as we might say in North Carolina. YHWH's subsequent action both protects the exclusive rights of YHWH to achieve great things and serves as a precursor for the spreading of human beings across the world. The story thus becomes a play on the name Babylon from Babel, juxtaposing it to the similar-sounding term for "confusion," *bālal*. It is also an etiology for the origins of multiple human languages and the initial Diaspora of humanity throughout the world.

In the aftermath of this story, Genesis 11 addresses the lineage of Shem with an extended patronymic that ends with the family of Abram. This narrative concludes the primordial history (Genesis 1–11) and introduces the reader to the family that will be the focal point of the subsequent narratives. With providence restored, the emphasis shifts from a general history of YHWH's interactions with all the peoples of the world to a narrative of YHWH's providence manifest in the lives of the members of a single family; from this point forward, Genesis becomes the story of YHWH's encounters with the descendants of Abram/Abraham.

▌THE TEXT IN THE INTERPRETIVE TRADITION

Genesis 6 presents a story that challenges our traditional assumptions about the nature of biblical material. Here we find details similar to texts we otherwise deem "mythological," thought to be part of the fictive imagination of a primitive pagan society. This caused considerable speculation among early interpreters (Louth, 12–126). The introduction of such unconventional mythological content has led many to dismiss the figures in 6:1-4 as having little significance "for the life of faith" (von Rad, 114). Further, Brueggemann suggests that the text itself "ill fits with the main flow of biblical faith" (Brueggemann, 71). Thus interpretation of this passage has focused on what to do with such stories.

The story of the flood has traditionally been understood as a unified narrative about God's punishment of fallen human beings for their propensity to sin. In the traditional understanding of the story, the details of the J account seem to rise to the fore, though aspects of the P account are also included. In this regard, the tradition takes from J the forty-day-and-forty-night flood caused by rain whose end is verified by the repetitive act of sending forth birds. Yet from P we note that the animals enter the ark two by two and the end of the flood is punctuated by God's rainbow, symbolizing God's promise not to destroy the world again by "the waters of a flood" (Gen. 9:11).

Why does Noah curse his son in Gen. 9:25-27? Answers to this question based on early attempts to explain this discrepancy have ranged from the act of Ham "seeing the nakedness" meaning that (1) Ham had sex with his father, uncovering the nakedness of his father; (2) Ham sexually mutilated his father; (3) Ham had sex with his mother, understood as the nakedness of his father, and produced the incestuous child Canaan; or (4) Ham simply saw his naked father and caused him shame by announcing it. These various answers are all based on potential readings that early interpreters could have had of this passage (see Sadler 2006, 390–92; McClenney-Sadler, 93–94).

What is less in dispute is the cursing of Canaan. In some respects, even if it is possible that the author's intent were to curse Ham to slavery, it is unlikely, since Ham is the ancestor of the Egyptians, the Cushites (modern Sudan), the Putim (modern Somalia), and the Libyans, as well as the great powers of Mesopotamia. The curse was likely intended for the Canaanites who, we will learn, will soon lose their land to the sons of Shem.

Perhaps one of the most significant traditions arising from this passage is the "Curse of Ham." This misappropriation combines aspects of the "Curse of Canaan" found in Gen. 9:25-27 and the Table of Nations in Genesis 10. In this regard, if Ham is cursed, then his descendants can also bear this shame. If those descendants are read to be the black Africans who descend from Ham (inasmuch as several prominent sons of Ham are indigenous to parts of northeastern Africa), then the curse can be read as a curse on Africans or "black" peoples. This is an interpretive move that originated in the 1820s and serves to undergird more than a century and a half of slavery, Jim Crow, racist, and racialist thought in the United States as it provided a theological basis for viewing black peoples (read sons of Ham) as hierarchically inferior to white peoples (read sons of Shem and Japheth) based on the Noahide curse (Haynes, 65–104).

Contrary to this interpretive move has been a tendency of Africana peoples to read the descendants of Ham in the Table of Nations as an attestation to the historic greatness of African peoples. In this regard, references to the people of Cush (Nubia), Egypt, Put (Somaliland), Libya, Babel (Babylon), and Assyria, among other great nation states in the lineage of Ham, were used to affirm that the ancestors of Africana peoples were empire-building kings. This interpretive move has fostered the notion of Africans' "stolen legacy" and served as the basis of a corrective history to the dominant Western notion of Africans as those from the "dark continent," void of history or civilization and worthy of domination by European colonial interests (Sadler 2005, 26–32; 2010, 73–74).

Traditional interpretations of Gen. 11:1-9 have suggested that the basis of YHWH's dispersion of the people was found in verse 4, in the sin of pride and their desire to build a city and make a name "for ourselves" (Heb. *lānû*). This is at best an implicit concern in the narrative, for nowhere in this passage is any clear offense explicitly stated. Yet the interpretive tradition has made this a narrative about human sin and God's punishment evidenced by the referenced peoples' subsequent inability to speak with one language.

Genesis 11:10-32 serves to clarify the lineage of Abram/Abraham, who is understood to be the "father of our faith" (see Rom. 4:16; Gal. 3:29). In this regard, this genealogy of the sons of Shem becomes more significant for interpretation than that found in Gen. 10:21-29, inasmuch as this list has immediate bearing on the origins of Abram/Abraham.

▮ THE TEXT IN CONTEMPORARY DISCUSSION

As we look at the story that begins in Genesis 6, we should note that verses 1-4 describe a very different world from the one we imagine in our scientific age, complete with encounters between heavenly beings and earthly women, which produced mythical hybrid creatures. Though these remarkable details should not distract us from the overall thrust of this narrative—and in fact the contents of these verses are probably overlooked by most readers, whose eyes hurry to the more familiar aspects of the Noah story—the initial few verses should make us suspicious about what precisely is going on in this story! Are these divine-human marriages between "sons of God" and human women the cause of the destruction of the world in the flood narrative (see v. 5)? How much attention should we pay to these aspects of the biblical canon? Should we discuss such narratives in Sunday school or biblical studies courses, and if not, why not? Does this alter our understanding of biblical material at all? We might even wonder how this material typically ascribed to Greek mythologies found its way into "the Word of God."

Further into the narrative, other concerns arise. What is the reason that the earth will be destroyed? How many times do these details occur (i.e., 6:5-7 vs. 6:11-13)? A cursory reading reveals that there do appear to be multiple accounts of certain aspects of this story. Why is this so? There are other discrepancies in this narrative too. How many animals are to go into the ark? Is the devastation caused by rain or some cosmic flooding? How long do periods of the devastation last? What are the names used for God? When we look closely, we can see a conflation of numerous details. What is the reason behind the retelling of the same narrative with slightly different details? Could this all be evidence of the composite nature of this text composed from distinct but generally compatible written sources?

In the midst of it all, we can still see a few familiar details. We see that the deity still cares for humanity, here expressed in the personhood of Noah. We also see that God continues to provide a means for redemption for God's people, here expressed in the ark. So even in the midst of the Lord's destruction of the world, we note God's persistent grace and love for humanity. If nothing else, this truly describes the nature of our God and is evident even at the outset of the first book of the Bible!

A closer examination of this tale makes readers acutely aware of the different voices that have been conflated to provide this one story. Perhaps this story, more than many others, provides a context for contemporary readers to discern the seams in the extant narrative and to understand that many biblical accounts are composed of disparate source material. As we look at such a narrative, we should wonder why the editor of this book did not do a better job of hiding its seams. We might also wonder if there were multiple flood stories that circulated among the people of ancient Israel/Judah. Further, for those aware of other flood accounts, like that found in the Gilgamesh Epic, it might be logical to consider whether that Mesopotamian narrative, fragments of which have been identified in Canaan at Megiddo, played a role in the composition history of this account.

Genesis 9:18-10 has had a distinct history of interpretation in the United States, serving as theological grounding for "racialist" thought. In this regard, the extensive use of the Curse of Ham and the Table of Nations as passages supporting slavery, segregation, and racialist thought in American political discourse should cause us to question whether the Bible is the source of racial thought. In this regard, did God intend to create three races of people corresponding to the three sons of Noah? If so, why is there no reference to differences in color, no value given to such color differences, no subsequent use of the names Shem, Ham, and Japheth to define racial groups, or any other such reference to race?

In my monograph, *Can a Cushite Change His Skin? An Examination of Race, Ethnicity, and Othering in the Hebrew Bible*, I argue that the Hebrew Bible is void of racial thought or racial hierarchies of any type. In fact, it appears that peoples whom we would identify in each of the three most commonly perceived racial types existed side by side, often functioning in alliances of mutual interdependence. Far from presenting a racialized vision of polygenesis (or differing origins) for those of different human subspecies groups, the Bible skillfully crafts its narratives of the origin of all humans. All peoples arise from a single family with a common genesis; there is no explicit attempt to define color differences as indicative of ontological differences in human types (Sadler 2005, 26–32). If there is no biblical basis for racial thought, how is it that we so often ascribe racial differences as God-given attributes?

This section ends with another interesting mythic-sounding narrative, about the Tower of Babel in Gen. 11:1-9. So, what is the sin of Babel? we might ask. Perhaps there is no sin in the way that we would perceive it. YHWH determines independent of explicit moral reasoning that the people should not achieve too much too soon. Could it be that the interjection of a moralistic reasoning into this text is alien to the original Yahwistic authors and the by-product of postbiblical theological appropriations of this text? Might the suggestion that the postflood population has actually "done something wrong" be endemic to us and absent from the original audience? More simply stated, *could we be reading moral justifications into stories where they are not present?* How do we justify such interpretive moves? Does this seem similar to the tension YHWH has with the original couple, who desire to increase in cunning by eating the forbidden fruit? Could it be that in that instance as well YHWH was keeping privileges that YHWH possessed from human beings? Could the anthropomorphic presentation of YHWH in this Yahwistic presentation of the narrative be jealously guarding certain benefits and refusing to have them manifest in humanity? What might this say about the deity that we meet in this passage and in other instances as perceived by the authors/editors of the J source?

Genesis 12–50: The Founding of a Family: The Circuitous Journey from Haran to Egypt

The ancestral saga of the people of Israel represents a significant narratological component of the larger story of Israel's origins. We should pay particular attention to the literary context in which these texts are located inasmuch as the redactors have employed them for specific purposes:

- They form a bridge between the primordial history and the exodus saga.
- They fill in the gap between where the historical credo (Deut. 26:5-9) began in Aramean territory and the arrival of the descendants of Abram/Abraham in Egypt.
- They demonstrate the surety of YHWH's word and the faithfulness of the ancestors. In spite of the passage of time, YHWH will bring to fruition the promises made to Abram/Abraham of a land populated by his descendants.
- They also demonstrate that the ancestors remain faithful to the promise, though it is never fully realized during their lives. They live as aliens in the land of promise, fully expecting that it will one day be theirs.

Theologically, the reader could determine that the way of believers in YHWH is not always an empirical account of promises realized; it is often a story of yet unfulfilled faith. An interesting dimension of the nature of the ancestors' relationship with God is that it is a relationship based on faith, for many of the promises God makes will not be fulfilled in their lifetimes. They will be left for future generations, who will have to be instructed in faith and taught about these promises so that they will know how they are to live in expectation of God's providence.

More troubling, there is a darker side to these narratives evident to contemporary audiences, who are separated from these stories by context and time. These stories serve to justify the Israelite acquisition of the land from their Canaanite (Amorite) predecessors, laying the groundwork for subsequent accounts when the descendants of Israel will appropriate "an other's" land. These texts will provide several "legitimating ideologies" justifying the taking of the land and the subsequent subjugation of the indigenous peoples. The constant promises made about the acquisition of the land tend to ignore the sentiments of the Canaanites and their interests.

As readers, we need to be critically aware of this dimension of the ancestral saga, particularly as we teach and preach from it. Perhaps we might even question as we read what such "promises" would sound like to those who will inevitably be "cursed" in order that chosen others will be "blessed." Though told from a particular perspective, how might that perspective have been deemed problematic to/by others? We might consider the role an uncritical reading of these texts has historically played in the dispossession of the Native American Indians, the Aboriginal Australians, or the black South Africans; in the enslavement of Africans in the Atlantic slave trade; and in the global colonialist activity of the Europeans in the post-Enlightenment era. Further, we might also consider the way these texts continue to undergird contemporary policies of Israel and the United States as the Israeli occupation and settlement of Palestinian lands persists in our contemporary era. Biblical interpretation is not innocuous; it is always consequential, affecting the outcomes of people in our world today, and thus interpretation should always be done with careful consideration of its impact and implications.

The following brief outline can serve to illustrate the overall structure of the ancestral saga:

12:1—25:18   Providence Heeded: Abram/Abraham the Faithful's Cycle
25:19—37:1   Providence Manipulated: Jacob/Israel the Trickster's Cycle
37:2—50:26   Providence Manifest: Joseph/Zaphenath-paneah and the Redemption Novella

Genesis 12:1—25:18: Providence Heeded: Abram/Abraham the Faithful's Cycle

■ The Text in Its Ancient Context

This narrative is one of the most significant in all of Scripture, for it serves as the basis of the relationship between Abram and YHWH. It begins where the last chapter left off with Abram in Haran. It is a narrative powerful for its simplicity. God tells Abram to go, offers no details, and Abram goes. The point of this narrative is likely to emphasize the fidelity of Abram, who will in most instances follow God's providence without pause, question, or imposition of his own will. God says do and Abram does. As we are told in verse 4, "Abram went as YHWH had spoken to him."

This call account is perhaps the exemplar for each of the call accounts that are to follow, for Abram offers neither resistance nor any hint of hesitation to the Lord's request (e.g., Exod. 3:11; Isa. 6:5; Jer. 1:6). Abram simply is said to have done what YHWH called him to do, and by so doing, the example of his fidelity is rehearsed throughout the Bible (see Romans 4; Gal. 3:6-7; James 2:21-23). Abram is called to go to a land YHWH will show him. This "land" becomes the dominant motif for blessing that will recur throughout the rest of Genesis and the majority of the Hebrew Scriptures.

This narrative is also rich because of what it shows about the nature of blessing. The Hebrew term for blessing (*brk*) occurs five times in the space of three verses, clarifying for the reader that blessing is at the heart of the narrative. Genesis 12:3 suggests that those who bless Abram will be blessed (plural) and the one who curses him will be cursed (singular). Though this interesting textual difference could be viewed as an error in the text, it may well be intentional, denoting the favor that Abram enjoys will confer greater blessing on others than cursing.

The structure of this narrative is instructive. Genesis 12:2 and 12:3 both begin by discussing the impact of the blessing on Abram and end by discussing blessings that attend to others. Abram is blessed by God, but he is not the end of this action; the end is a global blessing for "all the families of the earth." Walter Brueggemann says that "most likely the meaning of the phrase is not that Israel has a direct responsibility to do something for others, but that the life of Israel under the promise will energize and model a way for the other nations also to receive a blessing from this God" (Brueggemann, 120). Others have seen a much more active role for Abram and his descendants in God's blessing of others. For example, Gerhard von Rad suggests that "Abraham is assigned the role of a mediator of blessing in God's saving plan, for 'all the families of the earth'" (von Rad, 160). Still, others note the apparent shift in emphasis that seems a part of God's work here. So Terence Fretheim reads verse 3b as "an initially exclusive move for the sake of a maximally inclusive end. Election serves mission" (Fretheim, 424). This passage shows that God does not choose Abram to elevate him for his own sake, but to use him to be a blessing to others; though God may use an individual and even bless him, the ultimate goal involves a universal blessing that encompasses the whole world. The blessing of Abram will be the catalyst for others being blessed. The clear implication from this is that blessing is a *transitory* concept; it is intended to multiply and impact others.

We should be aware that throughout the ancestral saga, there will be several instances where the patriarchs will establish cult sites, places that were said to be sacred because a patriarch built an altar to YHWH there. This is important because the sites would likely have been known as places where people had worshiped YHWH or *ʾēl*, and their affiliation with a patriarch would give greater credibility to those sites. Sites like Shechem and Bethel would have been known as significant cult sites affiliated with subsequent worship of YHWH, and thus these narratives serve to ground the origins of worship at such sites and their significance in the experiences of prominent faithful leaders.

The latter part of this story (vv. 9-20) includes the first of three wife-sister stories (cf. Genesis 20 and 26). In each example of this type (or form) of story, the patriarch claims that his wife is actually his sister to prevent foreigners from seeing her beauty, recognizing her as the patriarch's wife, and then killing him in order to take her (see von Rad, 270). In the first two instances (Genesis 12 and 20), Abram/Abraham and Sarai/Sarah are the protagonists, and in the third it is their son Isaac and his wife Rebecca. The first of these narratives is slightly different from the other two. Here the Yahwistic author of the J source seems to be less concerned about preserving the character of the protagonists. We are left unsure at the end why Abram apparently lies to Pharaoh, telling him that Sarai is his sister, and we are left unsure if Sarai has had sexual relations with Pharaoh. What we do know, however, is that YHWH eventually intervenes, rescues Sarai from this arrangement, and Abram leaves with much greater wealth than when he arrived (Gen. 12:16; 13:2). Apparently, in addition to this strategy's saving his life, it has also served to enrich him (see also Gen. 20:13-16).

Surprisingly, neither Pharaoh nor Abimelech nor any other foreign king attempts to take the life of Abraham or Isaac because of their desire for the patriarchs' beautiful wives. Perhaps the only parallel to this story where a king takes the beautiful wife of a foreign national is when David takes Bathsheba from Uriah (2 Samuel 11). In this regard, the narrative may well have been intended as a morality tale in response to David's grievous error with the wife of Uriah the Hittite.

Genesis 13 concerns the separation of Lot from Abram, and though an understated section of the overall narrative, it becomes particularly important for the overall story. This is a story about separation. According to the account, Abram and his nephew Lot both have accumulated considerable assets and become very wealthy men. Their wealth is apparently divided between the two of them, so they need to separate their flocks to prevent the comingling of their enslaved peoples and thus to prevent infighting. Because their possessions are so great, the land is not able to support them together. In essence, great wealth causes separation, and the bonds of familial unity are threatened by the burden of distinguishing between their possessions.

This accumulation of wealth and the need to differentiate it provides a context for the separation of Lot from Abram, which serves two main purposes in the overall narrative: (1) by the physical separation of these two characters, it emphasizes that Lot will not serve as heir to Abram's promises; and (2) by Lot's taking the fertile Jordan valley and then moving further to the east, it facilitates the subsequent apportionment of the region of Canaan for Abram (Gen. 13:14-17). In these few verses, the extent of the land that YHWH promises to Abram becomes clear. This narrative also subtly foreshadows in verse 13 the troubles Lot will have in his chosen space; here we learn that the indigenous people are both *raʿ*, or "evil," and very *ḥaṭṭāʾ*, "sinful." His choice of what appears to his eyes to be the best land will prove consequential and costly, while YHWH chooses Canaan for Abram and promises to give it to him *ʿad-ʿôlām*, or "forever."

In Gen. 14:13, we have the first mention of Abram as a Hebrew. This is no familiar term with a long history of use prior to this point in the narrative, and it is most likely that there was no national or distinctively ethnic group called the "Hebrews" to which Abram belonged. Scholars have suggested that the word "Hebrew" might be related to terms like the Egyptian term *Apiru* found in the Amarna Letters or the term *Habiru* from the Cuneiform Mari Letters, which means a migrant, transient, or rebellious outsider. During the Late Bronze period (1500–1200 BCE, the period prior to the Iron-Israelite period), these groups were known to have been raiders that caused trouble for the Egyptians in Canaan (see Lemche, 95). If we accept this as the origin of the term "Hebrew," it gives us crucial insight into the way Abram was viewed by the established powers. He was a landless figure from the margins of society who threatened the current status quo and the indigenous systems of authority.

This becomes evident in the narrative, as once Lot is taken captive during a regional dispute (Gen. 14:12), Abram takes his *ḥanikim*, or "trained" men (Gen. 14:14), and raids those who have captured his nephew and rescues him, his allies, and his possessions. Abram has his own armed and trained militia of some 318 men; he is a clear threat to the established regional powers, supporting the notion that the designation "Hebrew" is a functional equivalent to the *Apiru* or *Habiru* interlopers.

Genesis 14:17-21 tells the tale of the aftermath of Abram's mission to rescue Lot. When he returns from his battle, he is said to have taken a tenth of what he captured and given it to a previously unmentioned character called King Melchizedek of Salem, identified as a Canaanite priest of *ʾēl-ʿelyôn* ("God Most High," cf. Ps. 78:35). It is unclear why Abram, who has built his own altars heretofore (implying in Gen. 12:8 and 13:4 that he made his own sacrifices) and who otherwise avoids affiliation with Canaanite religious practices, here defers to a Canaanite priest. Yet this becomes the record of the first tithe offered in Scripture.

Perhaps this story has a deeper meaning reflecting a later cultic reality for the people of Judah. If we recognize that Salem is one of the towns Jerusalem comprises and that Melchizedek's name contains within it the root *ṣdk*, the basis of the name Zadok, the subsequent priest during the time of King Solomon, perhaps we can note an etiological purpose to this account, linking the giving of the tithe to the Zadokite priesthood of Jerusalem (a group later known in the New Testament as the Sadducees) in an early account of Abram's own faithful act (see also Fretheim, 439–40). This story will have subsequent messianic significance in Psalm 110, where David—and in Hebrews 5–7, where Jesus—will be deemed priests in the "order of Melchizedek" (Ps. 110:4; Heb. 6:20).

Genesis 15 opens with a concern for Abram's lack of an heir. This problem is acute, for the basis of YHWH's promise to Abram is that his ample descendants will perpetually possess the land that he inhabits as an alien. This concern continues until Isaac is born, serving both narratological and theological ends. Narratologically, it promotes the tension in the story as a number of persons seem poised to serve the role of potential heir (Eliezer, Lot, Ishmael); but each of them is subtly disqualified in the emerging narratives. Theologically, it provides a context in which YHWH proves able to do the impossible. YHWH is challenged to provide offspring like the "stars" (15:5) to one who has had no children. In this respect, the ancestral sagas, like the primordial history, introduce us to and teach us about the nature of YHWH.

The assurance given in Gen. 15:4 that "your very own issue shall be your heir" is the basis of the subsequent Hagar narratives, for Hagar provides Abram with a child of his own issue (Genesis 16). Yet this child is conceived by Sarai's ingenuity and not by YHWH's intentionality; hence, this attempt to facilitate providence is doomed at the outset. We should note, however, that in Gen. 15:6 Abram believes in YHWH and that it is reckoned to him as "righteousness."

In this passage, we learn the high costs associated with establishing covenants. Here, as YHWH affirms the covenantal relationship with Abram and the promises of land and offspring, God has the patriarch take several animals and bifurcate them. It is between these carcasses that the covenant is "cut" (Gen. 15:10), with YHWH symbolically passing between the pieces in the smoking pot and flaming torch (Gen. 15:17). We should note from this experience that the cutting of covenants comes with the shedding of blood and with death. It is serious business, punctuated by the sacrificial loss of blood and life, calculated to serve as a reminder of the obligations that attend to this promissory agreement. There is an implied threat in the covenant that, should one of the parties violate the covenant, that same fate may well befall him (Sarna, 114–15).

We should also note the extent of this land apportioned to Abram in this passage. Not only is he promised the land of Canaan, but all the land from the Nile to the Euphrates is to belong to his descendants. In essence, this represents the extent of the Fertile Crescent, which reached into lands controlled by the great powers of Egypt and Mesopotamia. It is unlikely that the realm of Israel ever extended that far, even under the united kingdoms of David and Solomon, at the peak of their international influence. Attend also to the foreshadowing of the Hebrews in captivity for four hundred years (v. 13) and how the liberative event foretold in verse 14 will figure into the schema presented here in the acquisition of foreign lands and in the dispossession of their inhabitants.

Christians should note the sacrificial nature of cutting covenants and the way in which this narrative serves as a precursor to the crucifixion and as an interpretive lens to make sense of the death of Jesus. To fully appreciate the Christ event requires Christians to have an understanding of the sacrificial nature of the Yahwistic cultus, for it was on this framework that the early Christian community began to ponder the meaning of the tragic event of the crucifixion. As this initial covenant with Abram was sealed by the loss of life and the shedding of blood, so too Jesus' own crucifixion could be viewed as the basis of a new covenant, or a New Testament in his blood.

The problem of Abram's inheritance is temporarily solved in Genesis 16 by the birth of Ishmael to a slave woman from Egypt named Hagar. This is a morally complex narrative filled with many matters of concern about the way that Hagar is used by the combination of this matriarch and this patriarch to "fulfill" YHWH's promise. In what can best be described as a "rape," Sarai gives Hagar to her husband Abram without consulting her. The subsequent act of Abram "going in" to her without her permission seems both to be brutal and to demonstrate the gross abuses of a system that allows for slavery and the commodification of this young woman's sexuality. Hagar's will, though of no real concern to Sarai and Abram, apparently is of some consideration to the narrator, who notes that when Hagar realizes that she has been impregnated, her mistress is "belittled in her eyes" (Gen. 16:4). In this far too subtle way, the narrator suggests disapprobation for the abuse Hagar has suffered at the hands of her enslavers (Bellis, 73, 74–79). Narratives of formerly enslaved Africans in

America often contain such scenes of epiphany when an enslaved woman recognizes that she has become a sexual surrogate for her enslaving mistress and breeder for her enslaving master.

We should also note that this account contains a legitimating ideology for the Israelites' negative assessment of Ishmael's offspring. He is deemed in verse 12 a "wild ass of a man" who has enmity with various peoples, including the members of his own family. This goes a long way to framing Israel's view of the descendants of Ishmael, foreshadowing subsequent animosity between the two ethnic groups that will call Isaac and Ishmael their fathers.

Genesis 18–19 forms an important literary complex in the midst of the Genesis narratives, uniting two stories that address the treatment of strangers. Both stories, which are often taken as separate accounts, feature divine figures that come as human visitors and resident hosts that respond to the visitors in distinctive ways. The resident hosts' responses facilitate the subsequent divine disposition that they receive as well. For Abraham's actions in Genesis 18, YHWH grants Abraham the promise of a son and similarly in Genesis 19 gives Lot his life and the lives of his family, while YHWH destroys Sodom and its inhabitants as a result of their actions. Though the details of the individual narratives differ, the overall framework is similar, and for that reason, the texts should be read together as a single unit.

In the first account, Abraham sees YHWH coming to him in the guise of three men. His initial response upon seeing these strangers is to run to them and offer them the hospitality of his home, literally asking that they not pass "your servant" by (v. 3). The care of the stranger is a crucial concern, inasmuch as an alien would be vulnerable in this realm, fully dependent on the indigenous population to sustain him or her; without the assistance of residents, strangers would be exposed to the elements, have no provisions, and be subject to those who would otherwise prey on them. In its original context, Genesis 18 establishes the appropriate way to receive the stranger and uses this as a context to contrast the behavior of the people of Sodom in Genesis 19.

In that chapter, the two men who enter the town are greeted similarly by Lot, who ushers them back to his home to protect them from the violence that will be done to them if they spend the night in the square of Sodom. After they arrive at Lot's home, they are confronted by the men of Sodom, portrayed as a complete group (from the youngest to the oldest) who are uniform in their desire to "know" these visitors. In Genesis 19, we note the clear contrast between the behavior of Lot and the behavior of the men of Sodom, whom YHWH will judge at the end of the narrative.

In the ancient world, the unit Genesis 18–19 would have served as a narrative that demonstrates God's concern for the way strangers are treated. Inasmuch as the visitors in both chapters 18 and 19 are divine figures, the narrative subtly suggests that the way we treat strangers should be as divine visitors. Mistreatment of such figures could have dire consequences. That this is a concern about justice more than sexuality (see Judg. 1:7) is evident in several subsequent biblical passages, such as Isa. 1:10, which refers to the abusive officials of Jerusalem; Matt. 10:14-15 and Luke 10:10-12, which addresses the issue of towns inhospitable to Jesus' apostles; and most significantly Ezek. 16:49, which explicitly declares the "iniquity of Sodom" to be that they in their prosperity did not aid the poor.

One of the strangest stories in Genesis follows the story of destruction of Sodom in Gen. 19:30-38. It is the story of the birth of two sons to the two daughters of Lot. The narrative in many respects resembles the story of the Curse of Canaan in Gen. 9:18-27. Both stories feature an inebriated father, offending offspring, the hint of sexual impropriety, and the denigration of a subsequent foreign people. While some interpreters have suggested that the Genesis 9 account implies the birth of an illegitimate offspring to Ham through his sexual violation of his mother (i.e., producing Canaan), the story in Gen. 19:30-38 explicitly describes the eponymous ancestors of the Ammonites and Moabites born through an incestuous union between a father and his daughters (see McClenney-Sadler, 94–96) as, in the words of Randall Bailey, "incestuous bastards" (Bailey, 121–38).

As we embark on the narrative in Genesis 20, we should attend to the fact that this story has an odd beginning: "From there Abraham journeyed to the land of the Negev" (Gen. 20:1). This introduction suggests that we are continuing a story about Abraham, and fails to recognize that the most recent stories have been those about Lot and his travails. Again, this suggests that we have transitioned between sources (see von Rad, 226). As we pick up with the Elohist (E) source and its description of what will be the second wife-sister story, Abraham tells King Abimelech that Sarah is his sister and Abimelech takes her for a wife. Unlike the initial wife-sister story, in Genesis 12, the Elohist's version attends with greater care to the integrity of his characters. We are told in 20:12 that Sarah really is Abraham's sister through his father, thereby he is shown to be morally upright, having not technically lied to Abimelech. Sarah's integrity is also preserved, as verse 6 declares that God kept her unsullied by Abimelech. While the integrity of the ancestors is much less of an issue in the Yahwistic account, the Elohist clearly is concerned with these details. The matter of Sarah's purity is of particular concern in the extant combined narrative, particularly because in the next chapter she will give birth to Isaac; it is imperative that the reader know he is not the child of Abimelech, but of Abraham.

It is also noteworthy that Abraham is called a *nābî'*, or "prophet," in Gen. 20:7 of the Elohist's narrative. This is the only time this term is used for Abraham and the first time this term is used for any figure in the Hebrew Bible. Subsequently, in verse 17, Abraham also serves as an intercessor and prays for the fertility of the women in Abimelech's house in light of the intermediary role ascribed to him in verse 7. It can be discerned that the term *nābî'* in the Elohist's account attends more to intercession than proclamation (von Rad, 228). Finally, we should also note that in verse 14 Abraham is again said to have benefited materially from his deception of a foreign leader and his unorthodox use of his wife. YHWH and the angel of YHWH were divine presences in the first story (Gen. 16:7-13), unlike this account, which favors the term *ĕlōhîm*. This is evidence again of the Elohist's version, as is the retelling of the driving away of Ishmael (Gen. 21:9-21).

Genesis 21:1-7 attends to the birth of Isaac. This all-too-brief account, which Brueggemann declares is "strangely anticlimactic" (Brueggemann, 180), describes a pivotal moment in the overall narrative, as the promise of offspring born of Abraham by Sarah is finally realized in Abraham's "old age." The attempts of Abraham and Sarah to resolve their dilemma of childlessness by their own activity have proven futile in the case of Lot (Gen. 12:5), Eliezer (Gen. 15:2), and Ishmael (Genesis 16). Now all that remains is to clear the way for Isaac to be the uncontested heir, thus the story of Sarah's demand that Abraham drive Hagar and Ishmael away (Gen. 21:9-21). We should recognize the composite nature of these texts at this point: in Gen. 21:14, Ishmael is put on his mother

Hagar's shoulders along with their provisions; this is offered even though in Gen. 17:25 we learned that Ishmael was circumcised at thirteen years old! Clearly, there is a discrepancy in the sources regarding the age of Ishmael; but what is not at issue is that Ishmael, like Isaac, will be blessed to be the father of a nation (Gen. 21:13, 18) because of his descent from Abraham. As we consider the stories of Ishmael and Isaac, we should also attend to the dispossession of the firstborn, as Isaac will assume the position usually reserved for the elder son (according to primogeniture); this theme will recur throughout Genesis.

A final concern from Genesis 21 is the anachronistic reference to Philistines in the story of Abraham (also see Genesis 26 and the story of Isaac). Twice in Genesis 21 (vv. 32 and 34) Abimelech is identified as a Philistine. The Philistines, a group of people who originated in the Aegean region and who entered into Canaan from the Mediterranean Sea in the Iron I period (Katzenstein, 326–28), would not have been in the region during Abraham's lifetime. The reference to Philistines in Canaan during the time of Abraham suggests that these texts were composed far later than the period in which most scholars would imagine Abraham to have lived.

The Aqedah, or "binding," of Isaac (Gen. 22:9) is perhaps one of the most significant stories in the overall account of Abraham's life thus far. Unlike Genesis 21, where the birth of Isaac is described in a cursory way, fulfilling an important aspect of the promises given in Genesis 12, Genesis 22 spends a great deal of time addressing the threat posed to those promises by none other than God. In the course of Gen. 22:1-19, we will learn a great deal about Abraham and about God. The narrative begins with God's charge to Abraham in Gen. 22:2 to "take your son, your only son Isaac, whom you love, and go to the land of Moriah, and offer him there as a burnt offering." This command takes the reader completely by surprise inasmuch as the anticipation that has been building since our initial encounter with Abram, and which has just been resolved in Genesis 21, is now undermined a chapter later. Now it appears that we are introduced to a new set of concerns: (1) Is God a deity who requires child sacrifice? (2) Has Abraham, who has been faithful heretofore, finally received the one thing he is not willing to relinquish? and (3) How will the promises made ever be realized if Isaac is sacrificed? Each of these concerns is resolved before the end of this narrative, which ultimately shows that the divine protagonist does not require child sacrifice, that Abraham remains faithful, and that the promise through Isaac, who is perhaps a bit disturbed by the experience, is intact.

The power of this narrative is in Abraham's faithfulness. Like the story of Abram's calling in Genesis 12, Abraham here responds in utter faithfulness to God's command. The linkage between the two texts can also be seen in that they represent the only instances of the imperative phrase *lek-lĕkā* (Gen. 12:1; 22:2) in the Hebrew Bible (Sarna, 150). From his faithful *hinnēnî*, or "Here I am," in verse 1, to his faithful action to go in response to God's word in verse 3, to his reaching out his hand to take the knife in verse 10, there is no hint of hesitation, resistance, or even a second thought to God's providence. If God has determined to *nissâ*, or "test," Abraham, Abraham has determined to demonstrate his worthiness by putting all he has on the line. Abraham successfully passes the test not by fulfilling the mandate to sacrifice his son; but by his "inward intention" to do so (Sarna, 153), he is thereby proven faithful. A final note is in order about the location where God tells Abraham to offer his son. He sends him to the land of Moriah (Gen. 22:2). This seems to refer to the same place that Solomon will eventually establish the temple of YHWH in 2 Chron. 3:1, linking the eventual cult site of the people of Israel to the mountain where their own existence nearly came to a sudden end. In this regard, the offering of animals atop the Moriah altar in Jerusalem may have represented symbolic rehearsal of the averted child sacrifice of Isaac (see von Rad, 243). The story of the potential sacrifice of the firstborn at Moriah both resonates with the instruction in Exod. 13:2 that the firstborn of humanity or animals be sanctified to YHWH and is an eerie foreshadowing of both the child sacrifices that will eventually be offered in the Valley of Ben Hinnom (2 Chron. 28:1-3; 33:1-6; Jer. 7:31-32; 19:1-6; 32:35) and the sacrificial death of Jesus (Rom. 3:21-26; Eph. 5:1-2; Heb. 2:17; 9:24-28; 10:12; 1 John 2:1-2; 4:10) in the Christian canon that will take place just beyond the slope of the Mountain of Moriah. But YHWH in this narrative is not like those deities who demand the sacrifice of children; instead, YHWH is shown to be *yhwh yir'eh* (Gen. 22:14), the LORD who provides, "seeing to" the needs of faithful adherents (Brueggemann, 191).

In Gen. 23:1—25:18, the last chapters of the Abraham cycle, Sarah dies (Gen. 23:2) having secured her lineage through her son Isaac. Sarah is shown to be a powerful figure whose actions significantly influence the unfolding story of YHWH's covenantal promises. In fact, without her agency and her participation in these narratives, the story of Israel may well have been compromised. After her death, Abraham buys a field from Ephron, a Hittite, in order to bury Sarah (Gen. 23:10-20). Even in death, Sarah figures prominently, here serving as the catalyst for Abraham's purchasing the only piece of land he would ever own in Canaan (23:17-20).

In Genesis 24, we have a significant novelette describing the story of the acquisition of Rebekah as a wife for Isaac. Herein Abraham adjures his servant to swear an oath to get a wife for his son Isaac from his kin people. The oath is sworn by the servant's placing his hand beneath Abraham's thigh, and concurring before YHWH that he will not take a wife for Isaac from the Canaanites. It is interesting to see that even in this text set in ancestral times, the prejudice against the Canaanites as marital partners (a theme that recurs in Gen. 27:46—28:2) is substantial, likely reflecting the context of postsettlement Israel or postexilic Judea.

This elaborate story recalls how YHWH guides this servant to Abraham's kinfolk in Aram-Naharaim, where he meets Rebekah, a niece of Abraham, at a well (Gen. 24:1-15). Wells, like contemporary bars, or "watering holes," will recur in several narratives as places where men will encounter women and begin significant unions (see Gen. 29:1-12; Exod. 2:15-21). This context likely adds tension to the narrative in John 4, where Jesus encounters a Samaritan woman at a well. The encounter is ultimately successful as the servant returns with Rebekah to Isaac. Isaac takes her into his mother Sarah's tent and is *yinnāḥēm*, or "comforted," after his mother's passing (Gen. 24:67). From this account, we see that YHWH remains faithful to the promises made to Abraham to raise up a nation and that Isaac has found an appropriate marriage partner, consistent with the will of his father.

In Genesis 25, we come to the end of the Abraham cycle. Abraham herein takes another wife, Keturah, introducing by way of their offspring the ancestral line of many of the peoples of the Arabian Peninsula who, though they are a fulfillment of the promises made to Abraham of numerous offspring, will not participate in the promise of the land of Canaan. Also, in Gen. 25:7-11, Abraham dies at 175 years old, having never seen the fullness of YHWH's promises to him but having faithfully ensured that his son would continue his pursuit of those promises. He is buried with Sarah on his little piece of the promised land purchased from Ephron. The end of this account comes in Gen. 25:18.

▌ THE TEXT IN THE INTERPRETIVE TRADITION

The account of the first wife-sister story is a significant challenge to the general understanding of the character of Abram. In this first chapter of his narrative, just after he has shown himself to be faithful to YHWH's call, he has already attempted to manipulate the circumstances of his life by calling on Sarai to pose "less than the full truth" to the Egyptians who will encounter her. From this action, he benefits richly at his wife's expense and thus has been viewed by some interpreters as "cowardly and lacking in integrity" and "focus[ed] on self" in his engagements with Pharaoh. This account has also been viewed as a prefiguration of Israel's experience in Egypt due to details in common between the accounts as the famine, the migrations back and forth, the lead figures' intimacy with Pharaoh, and the plagues on the Egyptians, among other details (Fretheim, 428–29).

The relationship between Sarah and Hagar has been variously portrayed over the years. From the moral contrast between the spiritual Sarah as the mother of "promise" and the fleshly Hagar found in Paul's thought (Gal. 4:22-31) and in Augustine's work, to Pope Urban II's use of the contrast between the two as a basis for the Crusades, to Nachmanides' discussion of the abuse of Hagar by Sarah and Abraham, these figures have been viewed in disparate ways throughout time. Contemporary readings by feminists and womanists have been more careful to note the tenuous situation in which both women find themselves in the midst of a patriarchal world (James, 51–55).

The traditional interpretation of the Hagar stories portrays Hagar as an impertinent shrew who casts aspersions on her mistress because of Sarai's inability to conceive. Sarai and Abram are generally viewed as above reproach in their abuse of Hagar. If there is anything they have done wrong, it is that they have not waited on YHWH to act, but have tried to fulfill God's promise to them on their own. Scarcely is a word uttered about their abuse of power and violation of a seemingly unwilling young woman (see Sheridan, 41–45).

This story in Genesis 18–19 has been understood traditionally as two separate accounts, the first emphasizing YHWH's promise to Abraham and Sarah that they would bear a son (with the hint of that son's name, *yiṣḥāq*, occurring in this instance in Sarah's response to this promise). She laughs (*tiṣḥaq*), in one of several instances where etymologies for his name are offered (e.g., 17:17; 18:12-13; 21:6; 26:8). This sets the story neatly in the larger account of the unfulfilled promise of descendants to Abraham and provides a fourth potential means for an heir (first Lot, who moves away; second Eliezer, the enslaved man; and third, Ishmael, the son of the enslaved woman Hagar).

The second account, in 19:1-29, has traditionally been taken as one of the harshest indictments of homosexual behavior in Scripture. In this interpretive tradition, the homosexual urges of the men of Sodom condemn the city. The people are destroyed for this abominable behavior, which takes its name "sodomy" from this story, in a manner consistent with the expectations of Lev. 18:22 and 20:13, where such behavior is decried (Brueggemann, 163).

There have also be a considerable number of alternative readings of this passage, one most notably found in Walter Wink's short essay "Homosexuality and the Bible." Subsequent texts such as Alice Bellis and Terry Hufford's *Science, Scripture, and Homosexuality* argue that this passage is ambiguous at best as a prohibition against homosexuality and decries rape (Bellis and Hufford, 96–100). Choon-Leong Seow argues less ambiguously that the text is not about homosexuality, but about gang rape and a dangerous culture at Sodom (in Robert L. Brawley, *Biblical Ethics and Homosexuality*) as does Robert A. J. Gagnon in *The Bible and Homosexual Practice*. Each of these recent authors has given sustained attention to the essential concerns raised in this passage and considered how 19:1-29 continues to influence life in our world today.

Others have noted the interbiblical interpretive concern. For example, reading Ezek. 16:49, we note a description of the "guilt of Sodom" (cf. Isa. 1:10; 3:9; Jer. 23:14). There the actual offense has to do with the abuse of the "poor and needy," read the socially vulnerable in the midst of the community. In this regard, the actual sin of Sodomy may more fittingly be described not as homosexuality but as victimizing the socially vulnerable (Brueggemann, 165).

On the latter narrative in Gen. 19:30-38, though the tendency has been to see this account as an attempt to diminish the Moabites and the Ammonites as bastard nations from problematic unions, Brueggemann significantly notes that the authors/redactors of the text do maintain that these groups are of pure stock and that they are still deemed part of the Abrahamic family. This theological reading of the text, though unconvincing in light of the host of legitimating ideologies that denigrate "the other" in Genesis, does note the value of descent from Abram in a text so focused on this lineage (Brueggemann, 176). While not assuming that the overall perspective on the narrative is positive, Terence Fretheim notes that "even out of the worst of family situations, God can bring goodness, life, and blessing to the world" (Fretheim, 476).

Regarding the second wife-sister story, found in Genesis 20, Origen in his *Homilies on Genesis* 6.1 emphasizes that Abraham is called a "prophet" in this narrative and that he has prophetic authority to "heal" Abimelech's wife and female servants. He also allegorizes Sarah to be the personification of virtue, therefore not his wife to be held as his exclusive possession, but as his sister capable of being shared with others (Sheridan, 83–84). Brueggemann notes, following Calvin, that Abraham does not attend to God's providence as he should (178).

The binding of Isaac in Genesis 22 is a narrative with a rich history of interpretation. For example, Nahum Sarna, from a Jewish perspective, suggests that this is an opportunity for Abraham to demonstrate the fullness of his actualized faith (Sarna, 153). This notion is Christianized by Gerhard von Rad, who suggests that this is God's "temptation" of Abraham (von Rad, 239). Brueggemann notes, instead, the Christian tendency to address God's ironic "testing" and then "providing," noting the tension that resonates in the church's faith claims about crucifixion and resurrection (Brueggemann, 188–94). In each of these interpretive traditions, this striking narrative demonstrates a tension in the portrayal of God, who both makes promises and then puts them at risk. We should also note the extensive history of Christianizations of this account. Caesarius of Arles in his *Sermon* 84.2 suggests that this story is a prefiguration of the Christ event, even noting that the three days' journey is a trinitarian formula (Sheridan, 102–3). Clement of Alexandria follows a similar line of thought in his *Christ the Educator* 1.5.23 (Sheridan, 105).

▮ THE TEXT IN CONTEMPORARY DISCUSSION

As we look at these narratives in Genesis 12, we should question the perspective of the author of these texts, who never seems concerned about the fact that the giving of land to Abram means the taking of land from others. Does this suggest a bias in the authors of these texts that we should attend to as we interpret them for teaching and preaching? Whose voice is being silenced herein and to what effect? What is the lingering impact of this bias on human relations in our world today?

We might also attend to one of the subtle but not insignificant details of these stories. According to Gen. 12:5, we learn that Abram is a wealthy slaveholder who does not travel alone, but who takes an entourage with him on his journeys. What does this say about the perspective of the narrative? Who would the likely audience for such an account be? How have the voices of the impoverished, the enslaved, and the marginalized been acknowledged or ignored in these narratives? (See, e.g., Gen. 16:1-4 and note the response of Hagar to what Abram and Sarai do to her as a foreign enslaved woman in their caravansary.)

Exploring Genesis 14, we might ask why Melchizedek is recognized as such a prominent figure in subsequent narratives. Is this simply an attempt to associate Abram with conveying the tithe to the Zadokites, or does this also demonstrate the murky lines between ancient religious practices? Does Melchizedek the priest of *ʾēl-ʿelyôn* in this account function like Jethro in Exodus 18 and Balaam in Numbers 22–23 as a foreign figure who serves as an intermediary for YHWH? If so, what does this say about the assumption of the sons of Israel being the exclusive worshipers of YHWH? Could there be others who worshiped this deity before Israel? What does this suggest about our own attempts to exercise exclusive privilege in our worship of God? Does the LORD transcend the boxes that our faith tries to impose on God?

In Genesis 16, who speaks for Hagar? In this narrative, Hagar has had her voice taken from her. She has no voice in Sarai's decision to use her as a breeding implement for her husband. She has no voice in his decision to "go into her" and impregnate her. She is a female character who seeks to ensure the future of her son and herself once her position in the household of Abram is imperiled. But how have we traditionally understood her character, particularly in relationship to Sarai? Is it fair to characterize her as an "uppity" slave who has forgotten her place? Does that reading do justice to the text? It is time that we reread this narrative from the vantage point of Hagar and note that even the most faithful characters in the biblical narrative like Abram and Sarai often possess character traits that are antithetical to contemporary ethical norms.

In more recent exegesis, it has been determined that there is much more going on in the Genesis 18–19 narratives than meets the eye. The linkage of chapters 18 and 19 has been restored, and the contrast between the behavior of Abraham and Lot and the men of Sodom has been explicated. Further, recent scholarship has sought to address several other crucial concerns as well. For example, when this narrative has been compared with the account in Judges 19, it is clear that the abhorrent action is not as much the homosexual behavior (which itself would have been problematic), but the act of communal rape of the vulnerable person who has come to the community for protection. In the Judges account, we note that though the initial victim of the rape was intended to be the Levite, the actual victim is his secondary wife (concubine) who is abused and discarded. It is the offense of her attack that leads the people of Israel to destroy the Benjamites of Gibeah. Thus, in both of these accounts, the ultimate horror is not homosexuality as much as it is gang rape.

Feminist scholars have also noted the treatment of women as problematic in both the Genesis 19 and Judges 19 accounts. In these readings, the ultimate concern seems to be about preserving men from the sexual violation by other men at the expense of the women. Lot offers his daughters, who are refused by the perverse men in favor of the male outsiders. The Levite and his host offer their women to save him as a male outsider from the abuse he may face. While I concur that there does seem to be a distinctive prioritization of protecting the males, I would still suggest that the message of this unit has less to do with homosexuality and more to do with preserving the "more valuable" men in a patriarchal system from the abuse and humiliation of the act of domination that the gang rape would suggest (see Scholz, 123–26).

Perhaps the most potent message to arise from this unit is that YHWH is a God who is both merciful, as described in the negotiations with Abraham (Gen. 18:16-33), and concerned for the abuse of the vulnerable as evidenced by Genesis 19. A careful reading will demonstrate that YHWH is not acting in a moralizing manner, but demonstrating the ultimate importance of the imperative to care for the socially vulnerable; it is the violation of their rights that is the actual crime of "sodomy." Inasmuch as the strangers here are all representatives of the divine realm, perhaps the subtle message is that we should treat the socially vulnerable as if they were God in our midst. Such a message resonates with Matt. 25:31-46 and calls for a greater sensitivity toward the "least of these."

The brief narrative at the end of Genesis 19 about the sexual violation of Lot by his daughters is intentionally crafted to denigrate subsequent people groups, in this instance the Moabites and the Ammonites. In this regard, both the Genesis 9 and 19 narratives can be described as legitimating ideologies serving rhetorically to diminish the foreign "other" in the eyes of the subsequent Israelite/Judahite audience, providing a justification for their subjugation and alienation. Again, these texts pose a danger when subsequent interpreters read them uncritically. Should we adopt the perspectives of the authors/redactors of such texts because they are found in Scripture, we risk having their oppressive *Tendenz* become normalized for us. More simply stated, we need to be aware when interpreting such texts that valorize the denigration of others, for they can justify our abuse of those deemed "other" in our contexts.

The second wife-sister story, in Genesis 20, provides striking differences from the initial narrative in Genesis 12. The reader should attend carefully to the differences between these narratives and note that it is not insignificant that there is additional information given in the second narrative about Abraham's legitimate sibling relationship with Sarah and the fact that Sarah was not violated sexually by Abimelech. Why are such details requisite in this account? Why, more importantly, do we see such similar accounts in the same book? Perhaps what is most troubling of all would be, Why does it not seem that Abraham has learned anything about God's providence in the first wife-sister incident that alters his behavior in this instance? Does this suggest an artificial quality to these duplicate narratives?

The birth account of Isaac in Genesis 21 has been so long in coming that it does appear to be anticlimactic when it finally comes to pass. Perhaps this says something about the editors of the

Genesis narrative, who are more concerned that Isaac is born than they are to expend effort to discuss the birth. The true consequentiality of Isaac's birth is evident in Genesis 22, however. If the reader was not given a sense of the importance of Isaac in the account of his nativity, it is inescapable in the next chapter, as his life is put at risk by the command of God.

Reading this, one might ponder what kind of God would test a faithful follower like this? How does this experience align itself with other key narratives, like that of Job, where YHWH tests a man faithful to a fault to determine the measure of his faith? These questions can introduce the notion of theodicy, or the justice of God, for they force us to attend to the fundamental question of why it is that "good" people endure "hardships" and whether there is some divine intentionality in such tests of endurance. For Christians, the question of the relationship between the sacrifice Abraham is called to make and God's own sacrifice of his Son Jesus is one that is inevitable and requisite. In what ways does the Aqedah prefigure the crucifixion?

Genesis 24 contains an elaborate mini-novella of its own in the description of Abraham's procuring a wife for his son Isaac. Among the many questions that this passage raises are: Why is there the need to seek a wife from the same familial line? What is it about indigenous women that is deemed so wholly problematic, particularly when Abraham himself seems to marry one in the next chapter (Genesis 25)? What is the thrust of this overall narrative? Is it the faithfulness of the servant or the providence associated with his finding of Rebekah? In any case, it seems as if God is again operating behind the scenes to ensure that God's will is done and narratologically to ensure that the lineage of the promised line is pure (Gen. 24:4).

In part, the apparent concern for the familial purity (see Brueggemann, 238–40, on familial purity and syncretism) of the Abrahamic family raised in the chapter prior seems to be less of a concern for Abraham, who in Genesis 25 marries Keturah, a woman whose connection to the familial line is not clearly delineated. Through her, Abraham bears a host of children that will serve as the eponymous ancestors of many of the peoples of the Arabian Peninsula. As we look at such narratives that recount the birth of Arabian peoples through Hagar (vv. 12-18) and Keturah (vv. 1-6), we have to note that they all are descendants of Abraham, hence the fulfillment of the promise made that he would have offspring like the "dust of the earth" (Gen. 13:16) and the stars of the heavens (Gen. 15:5).

In this regard, we may wish to question why they are not vested in the promise of that land deemed holy. This is particularly troubling in relation to the children of Esau in Genesis 36, for he too is a son of Isaac, through whom the blessing was conveyed. If the reason for their removal from the promise stems from the loss of Esau's birthright (Gen. 25:29-34) and blessing (Gen. 27:30-40), then the consequences of this act of dispossession are significant indeed. Further, the effort of the authors/editors of this text to eliminate through the machinations of this literary composition all potential claimants to the promised land save those directly descended from Jacob should arouse a hermeneutic of suspicion among readers; why, we might ask, are so few of Abraham's dustlike and starlike descendants able to participate in the fulfillment of the promise? What role did the authors/editors of the narratives play in crafting a tale that serves to their advantage, and disadvantages those considered "others" in the story? What are the lingering implications of those interpretive moves that persist in our contexts? How might our uncritical appropriation of the narrative contribute to perilous assessments of human valuation of "others" and dangerous social policies toward "others" today?

Genesis 25:19—37:1: Providence Manipulated: Jacob/Israel the Trickster's Cycle

◼ THE TEXT IN ITS ANCIENT CONTEXT

In this section, Jacob is introduced as a character who will seek to manipulate YHWH's providence by attempting to control his own destiny and to manifest his own fortune. This elaborately interwoven narrative will unfold, as Brueggemann notes, based on a chiastic structure of parallel events linking Jacob's conflict with Laban to his eventual covenant with Laban, his divine encounter at Bethel to his divine encounter at Penuel, and his conflict with his brother Esau to his reconciliation with Esau as the story unfolds (Brueggemann, 213). There is an intentional balance between breaking and mending of relationships in this account as Jacob, despite his seemingly manipulative ways, eventually realizes the power of God's providence at work in his life.

This account begins with another instance of barrenness overcome by YHWH's miraculous intervention (Gen. 25:21), culminating in the story of the birth of Isaac and Rebecca's twin sons, Esau and Jacob. Esau, the elder son, is described as wild; he is characteristically masculine, a great hunter, his father's favorite (Gen. 25:28a), with a hairy body. He becomes the father of the Edomites through his union with Hittite and Ishmaelite wives (Gen. 26:34-34; 28:6-9). His twin brother, Jacob, is described as refined; he is a shepherd and is more cunning and cerebral, his mother's favorite (Gen. 25:28b), and decidedly less hairy. He will be named Israel (Gen. 32:28) and serve as the ancestor of the nation that bears his name. This story, like the previous story of Isaac and the subsequent story of Joseph, will emphasize the displacement of the firstborn in favor of a younger brother.

In this instance, the displacement of the firstborn is predicted in Gen. 25:23 and comes about by way of deception. Though Jacob is traditionally described as the deceptive "trickster" brother who takes advantage of his pathos-driven older brother (see Hiebert, 20), the narrative is actually more complex. In Gen. 25:29-34, Jacob uses Esau's intense hunger against him to secure his birthright; instead of deceiving him, he exploits the wild passions of Esau, which become his own undoing. In the second instance (Genesis 27), the deception starts with his mother Rebekah (Gen. 27:5-17), who engineers Jacob's deceit of his father Isaac and displacement of his brother's blessing. As with Sarah, the powerful matriarch's will is determinative in the fulfillment of YHWH's objective. In this regard, though Jacob alone does live up to the designation "trickster," his family's actions facilitate much of the behavior for which he has been recognized. This character trait is evident throughout the better part of the narratives describing him.

Before considering subsequent chapters in the Jacob cycle, it is necessary to consider the intervening narratives in Genesis 26. This chapter contains the third wife-sister story (Gen. 26:1-11). In this story, unlike the first two wife-sister stories, in Genesis 12 and 20, Rebekah is not taken as a wife by Abimelech the anachronistic Philistine king (von Rad, 271; see also the note on Genesis 20 above), and Isaac is not enriched by the bride price as Abram/Abraham was. The same theme of the fear of the foreign ruler and his people persists (von Rad, 270), and in this instance it is resolved by an edict from Abimelech protecting Isaac and Rebekah from harm (Gen. 26:11).

As in the other two wife-sister stories, the movement of the ancestors is toward the south; it is almost as if these accounts provide an occasion for the ancestors to move toward the south, the ultimate goal of Genesis narratives being to bring the people that will be Israel to sojourn in Egypt. In this instance, YHWH specifically tells Isaac not to go to Egypt but to another land (Gen. 26:1-3). Hence, Isaac settles in Gerar. The extant form of the entire Genesis narrative, with its three wife-sister accounts, thrice brings the readers tantalizingly close to the book's Egyptian goal, while ultimately in each instance thwarting expectations as the ancestors eventually return to the north.

The stage again is set for brotherly conflict in chapter 27 in this story of the younger son taking the privileges of inheritance typically promised to the elder son. As a result, Jacob flees from Esau and is sent by Isaac to find a wife from his mother Rebekah's family. The relationship between the brothers in this narrative is more significant than might originally be presumed, suggesting the subsequent relationship between the two peoples who will trace their lineage from these siblings. According to the legitimating ideology in Gen. 27:39-40, Esau's descendants, the Edomites, will serve the children of Israel, a relationship that is consistent with what is known about the subsequent history of these nations (see Sarna, 178; Hiebert, 21).

On the way in Genesis 28, Jacob encounters YHWH in a dream, and YHWH makes to Jacob many of the same promises previously made to Abram/Abraham of innumerable offspring, of land, of YHWH's abiding presence, and that Jacob will be a blessing to all the families of the earth (cf. Gen. 12:1-3). In response, Jacob names the place Bethel (or "House of God"), sets up a *maṣēbâ*, or standing stone-pillar sanctifying the site, and makes a vow that if YHWH cares for him and brings him safely back home in peace, YHWH will be his God (Gen. 28:10-22). In addition, Jacob promises to offer to YHWH a tithe of everything he receives, a practice that will continue among the cultic rituals of settled Israel, echoing another Abramic practice inaugurating such activity in Gen. 14:20. This is Jacob's first real engagement with God, but the story is theologically compelling, for over the course of the next several chapters, we will learn that YHWH is faithful to do all Jacob has asked. This narrative, hence, is the inaugural story of YHWH's fellowship with the eponymous ancestor of the distinctive people deemed Israel.

One theologically troubling aspect of Jacob's vow is its conditional nature. Unlike the bold action in response to the divine encounters seen in Abraham's narratives, Jacob's fidelity to YHWH in Gen. 28:20-21 is predicated on a condition that *'im*, "if," God will act, then "YHWH will be my God." Sarna suggests that Jacob really is not really "bargaining" with God, because all that Jacob wants God has already promised (Sarna, 200). Brueggemann, however, notes that "Jacob will be Jacob. Even in the solemn moment, he still sounds like a bargain-hunter. He still adds an 'if'" (Brueggemann, 248). The conditional nature of Jacob's vow seems like a further attempt of this patriarch to manipulate divine providence.

Over the next several chapters, Jacob will meet Rachel at a well and be led to his uncle Laban's house (Gen. 29:1-14), fall in love with and arrange marriage to Rachel (Gen. 29:15-20), and be tricked by his uncle to marry the "lovely" in terms of her eyes (Gen. 29:17 NRSV) or "tender eyed" (Gen. 29:17 KJV) Leah. (There is considerable disagreement on the meaning of *rakkôt* among translators of Gen. 29:21-30; see von Rad, 291; Sarna, 204; Fretheim, 553). He will eventually marry both of Laban's daughters (an arrangement wisely prohibited in Lev. 18:18) and be given the enslaved women Zilpah and Bilhah, each of whom will bear children for him. This complex arrangement unfolding over Genesis 29–30 establishes a fierce sibling rivalry between Rachel and Leah (e.g., 30:15) that will extend to the offspring of Jacob in the next generation. As Brueggemann notes, the narrative "portrays the way to the next generation as a way of conflict. The sons are born in rivalry, envy, and dispute. Undoubtedly, this presentation of the sons is a mapping of the tribes of Israel. But in the narrative itself, they are simply children yearned for, given, yet given in the midst of anguish" (Brueggemann, 253).

In Gen. 30:1-24, Jacob has children by Leah, Zilpah, Bilhah, and finally the once-barren Rachel. Eventually he has twelve sons and one daughter, who generally serve as the eponymous ancestors of the twelve tribes. The trickster Jacob resurfaces inasmuch as he strikes up a deal with Laban to take his spotted and striped sheep through "genetic manipulation" (Gen. 30:37-43), breeds spotted and striped sheep, then becomes rich in another act of deception (Gen. 31:20), and flees from Laban, who himself had determined to deceive Jacob (Gen. 30:35-36). But as in all things, God prospers Jacob, and when confronted by Laban and accused of stealing his uncle's *teraphim*, or "household gods," he attests to God's faithfulness and protection (Gen. 31:42). It is as this chapter ends that Laban proclaims the classic parting blessing, the *miṣpâ*, which is oddly Yahwistic even though arising from the pagan Laban (Gen. 31:49).

Jacob's story is one of deceit, lies, and half-truths. He is often identified as the morally ambiguous trickster, a theme not uncommon in African folklore like that of the Yoruba figure Eshu Elegba. There are a number of instances of questionable integrity in this tale:

- Jacob sells his imprudent brother Esau soup at the price of his birthright.
- Jacob deceives his father to steal his brother's blessing.
- Laban deceives Jacob, leading him to marry Leah before Rachel.
- Laban coerces Jacob to stay with him for many additional years of service.
- Laban takes the flocks that he has promised as payment to Jacob.
- Jacob manipulates Laban's flocks to produce offspring he can acquire.
- Jacob secretly flees from Laban with all he has acquired.
- Rachel deceives her father while sitting on the household gods that she has stolen from him.

Despite the tendency for deception and duplicity in the Jacob story, the narrative does not seem to impose a moralistic judgment against Jacob; instead, it almost seems that like Abram/Abraham, who twice prospers by selling his wife (Genesis 12; 20); like Tamar (Genesis 38), who will benefit from deceiving (Niditch, 41) her erring father-in-law Judah (and Judah, who caused Tamar's deceptions by his deceitful retention of his third son in Gen. 38:11); like Joseph, who will deceive his brothers and father; and like Joseph's brothers, who sell Joseph and deceive their father (Genesis 37–50), what appear to be moral flaws are often the means used in providential ways to achieve YHWH's desired will in these narratives. The trickster dimension of Jacob, not unlike the cunning sought by the original woman and man in Genesis 3, seems to be a valuable asset to facilitate the survival of God's people and the realization of YHWH's will. Brueggemann offers a poignant assessment of Jacob that aptly describes the way such character flaws are considered in the Genesis narratives.

> It is the earthy man through whom the resilient purposes of God are being worked out. The purpose of God is somehow operative in the places of scandal and deception. . . . Precisely in this doubtful character, the promise of God is being fulfilled. . . . In the midst of the ambiguities, the promise is having its way. (Brueggemann, 252)

Thus, amid the manifold manipulations in this account, God's providence continues to govern the movement of the narrative.

The reunion of Jacob and Esau is prefaced in Gen. 32:3-21 with several decisive actions. Jacob, fearing his brother will kill him, makes arrangements to offer him a portion of his wealth to appease his anger. Further, he divides his goods so that Esau will not be able to defeat him and destroy the entirety of his family should he attack. He even entreats YHWH to protect him once he hears that Esau is coming to meet him with four hundred men. Undeniably, Jacob recognizes that he has wronged his brother and has legitimate reason for concern. In a confusing amalgam of sources in Gen. 32:22-23, he is said both to have crossed the Jabbok with his family (32:22) and to have remained on one side while sending his family and possessions to the other side (32:23). The latter version in verse 23, however, provides the requisite context for what occurs next.

Jacob is alone and has a mystical encounter in the night with a "man" whose identity remains undisclosed. Who is the man? The story seems to imply that it was God (Gen. 32:28-30). But could the one with whom he wrestled have been Esau and this event served as his struggle to make his peace with his brother? Why does the man only wrestle him at night and have to let go when "day is breaking"? Might it be so his familiar face won't be recognized? Also, the question, "Why is it that you ask my name?" in Gen. 32:29 suggests Jacob might have known who he was.

Further, there are several different references to the notion of "faces" in this narrative. The first occurs in Gen. 32:20 (v. 21 in Hebrew) in reference to the presents that Jacob sends to Esau to win favor; he says in Hebrew, "I will cover his face [appease him] with the present going in front of my face [before me] and after that I will see his face, perhaps then he will lift my face [accept me]." The second is in Gen. 32:30 (v. 31 in Hebrew) in reference to his nocturnal struggle, as he says that he has seen God "face-to-face" at the place he names Peniel, "The face of God." The third is in Gen. 33:10, where he declares to Esau, "I have seen your face, [it is] like seeing the face of God."

How might this have sounded to the original audiences of this story? Could it be that Esau was Jacob's nighttime foe who, seen in the daylight, manifests the face of "God" with whom he wrestled in the shadows? Suffice it to say that there may be no clear answer to this query, save to understand the complexity of the extant narrative and the ambiguity the redactors (intentionally?) allowed to remain in the conveyed accounts.

In the midst of this nighttime struggle, Jacob has his name changed. His opponent declares in Gen. 32:28 that he will no longer be called Jacob, but Israel because he has "struggled with God and with humans and has prevailed." Though he will continue to be called Jacob throughout his narrative, the name Israel will come to define his descendants as the distinct recipients of the blessings promised to Abraham at the beginning of the ancestral saga. It will also describe their ability to prevail and persevere amid the struggles that will attend to their collective existence.

This is the first reference to the name "Israel" in all of Scripture, as the ancestor of the focal people in the Bible is herein identified. It merits attention that the name Israel is not distinctly Yahwistic and designates this people as those who follow El. El taken as a generic term can simply mean God, but during the Canaanite period this figure would have been recognized as the head God of the Canaanite pantheon (Smith, 7–10). The reverence of the deity by this name is further evidenced at the end of Genesis 33, where Jacob settles on a plot of land that he purchases from the sons of Hamor near Shechem. There he builds an altar and calls it 'ēl 'ĕlōhê yiśrā'ēl, or "El, the God of Israel" (Gen. 33:20). His settling in Shechem complicates his experience with Esau and adds a final instance of deceit to the end of the narrative. Though he says that he will return with his brother, he tells him he will soon follow him, and as his brother heads to Seir, he heads in the opposite direction, first to Succoth and then to Shechem.

The rape of Dinah in Genesis 34 is not the first abuse of women that we encounter in the Bible, nor is it the first rape that can be found on the pages of Scripture. The Genesis 16 story of Sarai's giving of her enslaved girl Hagar to Abram to serve as a surrogate womb for his offspring is reminiscent of the late-night encounters between slaveholders and enslaved women on American plantations. This sexual appropriation of an unwilling and perhaps unwitting woman as evidenced in Gen. 16:4 cannot be excused because the perpetrators are the beloved ancestors of our faith traditions. The offering of Lot's daughters in Gen. 19:8 is also an instance of abuse, as a father, based on an ethos perhaps more consistent with his era than one acceptable in our own, willingly offers his virgin daughters as sexual surrogates, alternative victims to be raped instead of YHWH's angels. Also, the account of Leah and Rachel offering Zilpah and Bilhah as spousal surrogates to Jacob should cause us to question the representation of women in these narratives. The story states that Shechem yiqqaḥ ("took"), šekkab ("laid with"), and yĕ'annehā ("oppressed/humiliated her"). Actions similar to those committed by the patriarchs and authorized by the matriarchs above are finally viewed through a disparaging lens. Here the offense seems to be a personal one, not just to Dinah, but also to the men in her life who appear to be violated by what was done to their daughter/sister. The narrator's conveying of the words and sentiments of the men while silencing Dinah betrays the focus of "his" concern. Though the abuse of a woman is finally decried, she remains silent in her suffering, and her will is unexamined as her fate rests in the hands of the men who circumscribe her life (Niditch, 40–41).

After violating Dinah, Hamor seeks to resolve the offense by marrying his son Shechem to Dinah (Gen. 34:3-4). This is a strategy of redemption that is found in the Torah. For example, Deut. 22:28-29 suggests that in such an instance of rape, the guilty man must pay a bride price, marry the woman he violated, and remain married to her for life with no possibility of divorce. In an act of deception that is reminiscent of their father, the sons of Jacob pretend to accept Shechem's offer of marriage, convince him that he and all the men of his city must be circumcised in order to intermarry with the offspring of Israel, and then slaughter the men of the city as they are recovering from their circumcisions. This act embarrasses Jacob and imperils his family, yet it seems to maintain what we will subsequently learn is YHWH's prohibition against intermarrying with Canaanites (e.g., Josh. 23:12-13, where the Israelites' possession of the land is predicated on adhering to this standard).

The final few chapters of the Jacob cycle are not uneventful. In Genesis 35, Jacob returns to Bethel, where he first encountered God when he initially fled from his father's house and his brother Esau. As part of his journey to Bethel, he ritually purifies those with him, having them rid themselves of their foreign "gods." This is perhaps the first time the verb *ṭāhar*, "purify," is used denoting a ritual purification since the flood narratives (Gen. 7:2, 8; 8:20), where the term is used in reference to ritually "clean" animals permissible for eating on the ark in the Yahwistic account, long before such practices will be put in place. Here the notion of purification is used in preparation for Jacob's reunion with God in fulfillment of his pledge to YHWH in Gen. 28:20-22 to worship and offer a tithe to this deity.

Once he arrives at Bethel (Gen. 35:6), he establishes an altar at *ʾēl bêt-ʾēl*, encounters *ʾēl-šadday*, who offers him the Priestly blessing "be fruitful and multiply" (Gen. 1:22), changes his name to Israel (again), and reiterates several of the promises to him that have previously been made to Abram of offspring and land (Gen. 35:7-12). In response, Jacob establishes another *maṣēbâ*, or standing stone-pillar, pours a libation and oil on it as an offering, and thereby consecrates the place (Gen. 35:14). At the end of this chapter, he suffers two significant losses. Genesis 35:16-21 describes the death of Rachel and her burial at Ephrath or Bethlehem, and Gen. 35:27-29 describes the death of Isaac at Hebron. Though not much is mentioned of the long-awaited reunion between father and son, the few verses at the end of Genesis 35 suggest a time when not only Jacob and Isaac were reconciled, but Jacob and Esau were as well, since these two sons of Isaac are said together to have buried their 180-year-old father.

Genesis 36, the final chapter of the Jacob cycle, turns to the descendants not of Israel (Jacob) but of Edom (Esau). Here more than in any other chapter, the relationship between the Israelites and Edomites is explicated, and the children, kings, and clans of Esau are explained in the careful, exacting style for which the Priestly writer is known. In the final chapter of this cycle, the fact that Esau is the elder brother can be correlated with the fact that Edom was known to have been settled in the region for a much longer period than Israel. This is attested by Gen. 36:31 declaring, "And these are the kings who ruled over the land of Edom before a king ruled the descendants of Israel." The relation between these two contentious peoples will unfold over the next thousand years as the offspring of each will rule side by side, will struggle against each other, and will even rule over each other. In fact, one of the final kings of Judea will be Herod the Idumean, a son of Esau (Hubner, 382–83).

Jacob as a character is one who has sought to manipulate his own destiny but who learns through trial and error to depend on YHWH's providence. In fact, God's providence works to bring both Jacob's acts of deceit and his acts of fidelity into submission to a plan he cannot hope fully to comprehend. In the end, despite the deception that characterizes Jacob's life, his fate remains firmly in YHWH's hands.

▌ The Text in the Interpretive Tradition

The story of Jacob, beginning in Genesis 25, has been variously interpreted over the years. He has been considered to be a trickster, deceptive, manipulative, cunning, and so on. Brueggemann makes an interesting claim about the nature of the overall Jacob narrative, however: "One senses that while the deception attempts to turn the blessing, in fact, the deception is only a tool for the blessing to go a way already decided upon" (Brueggemann, 230). Should this line of reasoning be followed to its logical conclusion, the Jacob presented in the narrative is often a figure that benefits through guile and apparent deceit, but the overall narrative suggests that divine providence has shaped his life just so to achieve larger purposes. He will be of benefit in greater ways than are evident initially; his trickster character is only a "tool" to achieve a predetermined end.

Hiebert offers another bit of insight regarding the reversals of primogeniture like those we see in the stories of Isaac, Jacob, and Joseph. Those who benefit from the reversals are "secondary sons, that is, by those outside the positions of power in society held by fathers and their firstborn sons." In this regard, the reversals and the trickster quality of Jacob enable him to "gain access to powers denied" to him by this birth position. So these narratives can be read as the "quest by the disenfranchised to share in the power and benefits of the family and society" (Hiebert, 21).

The story of Jacob's nocturnal wrestling match at Peniel has been variously understood. While it seems simplest just to assume that the figure with whom Jacob wrestles is his brother Esau, early Christian authors tended to presume that the figure was actually God, often prefiguring the Christ narrative (Sheridan, 218–24). More recently, Sarna determines that the figure is not Esau himself but one who must "stand for Esau" as his "alter ego" and identifies the figure as his "celestial patron" (Sarna, 404). Brueggemann conflates his assumption that the nocturnal wrestler has been YHWH with the concerns of Esau, concluding that that the stranger is "Yahweh, with shadows of Esau present" (Brueggemann, 272). It is clear that there is no interpretive unanimity regarding this passage that clarifies all the issues it raises.

The account of the rape of Dinah in Genesis 34 poses the question of who is the actual party offended by such an infraction. In this account, where Dinah is completely objectified and is not able even to express her pain, it appears that the authors/editors are more concerned with the rape as a violation of the property rights of Jacob and a source of shame for her brothers than they were about the status and well-being of Dinah (Niditch, 41; De La Torre, 288). It is in this vein that De La Torre asks why God in the text is silent about Dinah's rape and why God does not act to intervene. In part, he suggests, it is because of the male perspective of the authors. Since they do not care, it appears that God, too, does not care about what happens to Dinah (De La Torre, 292).

▌ The Text in Contemporary Discussion

As we consider the development of the stories of Abraham's offspring, it should be increasingly clear that the authors favor one familial line, while those of other lines continue to be portrayed in a less favorable light. This pattern holds true as we examine the relationship between Jacob, the father of the Israelites, and Esau, the father of the Edomites. While the theological purposes of such an act are evident, the implications for the way that subsequent readers of the narrative internalize these patterns of privileging favored groups and deprivileging "others" should be examined. While it is consistent with the goals of the author to have the reader identify with the Abrahamic, Isaacic, Jacobic protagonists and their familial lines, it is imperative that as we read we consider how these stories shape not only our understanding of the "biblical other" but also those we deem to be "other" in our own contexts today.

One cannot read the story of Jacob without considering the morally complicated portrayal of his behavior. How do we reconcile his taking advantage of his brother (Gen. 25:29-34), the deceit of his father to dispossess his brother (Gen. 27:1-29), and other such trickery with a key biblical figure on whom the unfolding narrative rests? Perhaps a more troubling issue is how to deal with the biblical perspective that God uses such human machinations to realize providential arrangements. This issue resurfaces throughout explorations of the trickster cycle.

As we explore the promises given by God to Jacob in Genesis 28, we cannot help but notice the distinctive conditional response he gives to YHWH in his vow. YHWH will be his God *if* YHWH fulfills certain conditions. This bargaining seems to run contrary to the faithful theological posture of Abraham. How is this portrayal resonant with his character in these narratives? In spite of our tendency to deem his character traits as suspect, does Jacob represent aspects of the human tendency to bargain and manipulate in our relationship with God and others?

The story of Jacob's time with Laban in Genesis 29–31 raises a plethora of questions, many of them in relation to women's concerns. How does the arrangement between Jacob and Laban serve to commodify both Rachel and Leah, thereby making them the payment for Jacob's labor (see Gen. 31:15)? To what extent are these women treated as "exploited and dispossessed slaves" by the men in the narrative (Niditch, 39). How do the sisters participate in the oppression of women by offering their enslaved women Bilhah and Zilpah as sexual surrogates and breeders for Jacob? How does the rivalry between these sisters contribute to unhealthy familial relationships among Jacob's offspring? How are readers to understand the actions of these matriarchs in light of contemporary sensibilities?

Genesis 32 presents one of the most puzzling narratives in Genesis. As Jacob has had his reunion with Laban in Genesis 31 and commemorated it with the pillar of Mizpah, he faces another conflict, that with his brother Esau. After sending flocks to appease his brother and sending his family ahead of him across the River Jabbok, Jacob wrestles with a "man" all night at Peniel, "the face of God." With whom did he wrestle? Was it with God? Was it with Esau, whose face he looks on in Genesis 33? Was it with his own conscience personified? The possibilities are rich, but ultimate clarity is elusive. Also, what role does this nocturnal encounter play in his life? If it is meant to be the moment of his transformation from trickster to faithful adherent, why then does he again deceive Esau at the period of their encounter (Gen. 33:15-17)? How does the retaliation for the rape of Dinah in Genesis 34 attest that his sons have adopted his trickster ways? Does he come to realize the consequences of deception in response to his sons' actions in Gen. 34:30?

We see these actions in Genesis 34, where in response to the rape of their sister Dinah, the sons of Jacob deceive the inhabitants of Shechem, tricking them into circumcising themselves to forge an alliance with the sons of Israel, and then slaughtering the men of the city as they lay incapacitated. Had these men lived, would their circumcisions have made them heirs of the covenant like the Idumeans conquered by John Hyrcanus (see Hubner, 383)? But far more significantly, how do we attend to a narrative that describes a brutal offense to a woman that does not allow that woman a voice in her own story? How do we respond to the proposition that the crime of rape could be atoned by having the rapist marry the woman raped? Are there advantages to such a system in an ancient context? If so, what might they be and what do they presume about the status of women in relation to men? Is this really, as Niditch notes, a dispute between two groups about the ownership of a woman and the status of men (Niditch, 41)?

Genesis 37:2-50: Providence Manifest: Joseph/Zaphenath-paneah and the Redemption Novella

▌ THE TEXT IN ITS ANCIENT CONTEXT

The final section of Genesis is the Joseph novella. This well-developed story of the life of Joseph is unlike the brief cycles that told only occasional events in lives of Abraham, Isaac, and Jacob. It is the story of a man who will suffer considerable hardship, who will be attacked and threatened with death by his brothers, who will be sold by Midianite raiders to Egyptian overlords, who will be sexually assaulted by his mistress, who will be falsely imprisoned by his master, yet who will be redeemed by God's providence in a miraculous account of divine intervention. The Joseph redemption novella unfolds in three movements:

> Joseph's conflict with his brothers (Genesis 37)
> Joseph gains favor in Egypt (Genesis 39–41)
> Joseph reunited with his brothers (Genesis 42–50)

This is a complete narrative that unfolds over the final chapters of the book with only the single significant interruption found in Genesis 38, which chronicles the Judah and Tamar story. Joseph's account, like many of the other stories in Genesis, features a disruption of primogeniture, as a younger brother will be foretold to rise to prominence over his older brothers. It will also feature sibling rivalry, reversals of fortune, deceit, and divine providence, as each of these themes contributes to the drama that unfolds in this concluding narrative of the ancestral saga.

The stage is set for brotherly conflict in Genesis 37, when the precocious younger brother Joseph is surmised to be the favorite son of his father Jacob/Israel by his older brothers. Dreams figure prominently in the narrative that weaves together classic J material with the divine insight provided by dreams often associated with E. In two dreams (Gen. 37:5-8 and Gen. 37:9-11), Joseph is given a precognition that he will eventually rule over his brothers, information he decides to share with them. This dream disclosure angers the brothers, as does the *kĕtōnet passîm*, or special garment, that Israel gives to Joseph, the son he has with Rachel in his "old age" (v. 3). In a rage resembling that of Cain in Genesis 4, the brothers hate (vv. 4, 8) and are jealous of Joseph (v. 11). Instead of luring Joseph to a field, this narrative has Jacob send him to the pastures to find his brothers, who are shepherding their flocks. When he arrives, they develop a scheme for fratricide, but convinced by their brother Reuben (vv. 21-22), they decide instead to place Joseph in a pit. At this point, the narrative is uncertain. He is removed from the pit and sold either by his brothers (vv. 25-27) according to J, or by Midianites (v. 28) according to E, to passing Ishmaelite traders. Thus begins his journey to Egypt, where he will be sold to an Egyptian court official (v. 36), a journey that will end with the entire family of the descendants of Israel in Egypt. Meanwhile, the brothers deceive Jacob, convincing him that his favorite son has died by slaughtering a goat, dipping Joseph's garment in that blood, and bewailing his demise. It should not escape notice that the trickster Jacob, known for his deceit, is now being deceived by his own children (the pomegranate does not fall far from the tree).

It is at this point that we find an odd intervening story about levirate marriage in Genesis 38. Judah, one of the sons of Jacob, has three sons: Er, Onan, and Shelah. For his oldest, he takes Tamar for a wife. Because he is "wicked," Er dies prematurely, before he can raise up offspring by himself (vv. 6-7). This places Tamar in a precarious situation, for she is now a woman who, although she is not married, cannot return as a virgin to her clan. Furthermore, she is not a mother and thus has no real standing in the patriarchal order of her deceased husband's clan (Niditch, 41–43). She is a woman in need of a remedy for her social dislocation.

According to custom, the second son of Judah, Onan, is then tasked to raise up offspring for his brother Er. He instead "goes into" (has sexual relations with) his sister-in-law, then spills his seed on the ground, and because of this, YHWH puts him to death (vv. 8-10). Ordinarily this would mean that Tamar had access to the third son, but Judah deceptively withholds Shelah for fear that he will meet the same fate as his deceased brothers. When it becomes clear that Judah has no intention of giving Shelah to Tamar, and in the aftermath of the death of Judah's wife, Tamar pretends to be a *zōnā*, or "prostitute" (Gen. 38:15), and sits at the entrance to a town Judah will pass on his way to Timnah, and waits for him to come. When he arrives and they negotiate terms (he leaves his signet, cord, and staff with her to hold until he delivers a kid to her), he "went into her" and impregnates her unwittingly, and leaves. Later, after Judah finds out that Tamar is pregnant, he prepares to have her burned as an honor killing (v. 24) only to have her offer up the items that he gave her in pledge (v. 25). Convicted, he declares that she is "more righteous than" he because he violated the terms of levirate marriage and she has cunningly strategized to ensure his family line through an appropriate kinsman (v. 26).

Though this story seems to be completely disconnected from the larger narrative, we should note that it resonates with the larger theme of familial obligation. In this instance, Judah and his son have failed to perform their responsibility to their fallen kinsman's spouse and failed to *hāqēm zera'*, or "raise up seed," for Er. Unfulfilled obligation here creates a significant interfamilial crisis imperiling both the appropriate inheritance for Er's lineage and the life and social status of Tamar. The story also has remarkable resonances with the overall narrative in which it is placed; Joseph's and Tamar's experiences with Judah can be correlated, as they both are deceived by, request a youngest son from, hide their identities from, take objects from, and are eventually reconciled to Judah (see McClenney-Sadler, 98–102). Despite the sexual intrigue engaged by Tamar, she is deemed *ṣādĕqâ*, or "righteous" (v. 26), inasmuch as she preserves the family of Judah in ways reminiscent of other female figures such as Rahab (Joshua 2 and 6) and Ruth (Ruth 3), who use their sexuality in ways that preserve the chosen family line and YHWH's divine plan (Niditch, 24–26).

If Genesis 38 introduces a compelling use of feminine sexuality, Genesis 39 demonstrates an inappropriate application of it, as Joseph is seduced by the socially potent wife of Potiphar, the captain of Pharaoh's guard, for whom he works. In response to her attempts to entice him, Joseph offers a morally compelling argument in Gen. 39:9-10 to dissuade her, noting his obligations to both Potiphar and to God. Undeterred, she continues her pursuit of this attractive young protagonist (39:6), forcing him to flee from her, leaving his clothing in her grasping hands. Her act of sexual impropriety becomes the narrative's vehicle to land Joseph in prison. His incarceration becomes an occasion for the reintroduction of YHWH to the narrative (39:21-23) and a reminder of YHWH's favor and presence in his life, assuring the reader that God's providence is still at work even amid Joseph's hardships.

Genesis 40 has Joseph as a prisoner in favor with his jailers. While incarcerated, he interprets two dreams describing the destinies of two of Pharaoh's officials imprisoned with him (Gen. 40:9-15, 16-19) and is shown to have been an accurate diviner (Gen. 40:20-22). After two years, the official for whom Joseph interpreted a dream of restoration tells Pharaoh about Joseph (Gen. 41:9-13). Pharaoh brings Joseph out of prison, confides to him his dream, and learns the fate of his nation. Joseph interprets Pharaoh's dream as foreshadowing seven years of plenty prior to seven years of famine and (shrewdly) encourages Pharaoh to appoint a man who is *nābôn weḥākām*, or "understanding and wise" (Gen. 41:33), over the land to supervise a food conservancy project to prepare for the impending famine (Gen. 41:33-36). Pharaoh, appreciating Joseph's sage counsel, appoints him over "all the land of Egypt" (v. 41), gives him unassailable authority over its people (vv. 42-44), the name Zaphenath-paneah, and Asenath daughter of Potiphera, priest of On, for a wife (v. 45). This good fortune is all attributed to the providence of God, whom Joseph commemorates in the naming of his two sons in verses 51-52. Despite the unimaginable hardships Joseph has endured, God has redeemed him and given him a place second only to Pharaoh's in Egypt.

As would any good storyteller, the narrator brings Joseph's brothers back into the story in Genesis 42. Joseph, now empowered and well-positioned, will have to attend to the needs of his family, which has treated him with hatred and disdain. Famine again serves as a reason for the Abramic clan to venture south (cf. Gen. 12:10; 26:1), this time to Egypt itself to find food. Again, the trajectory of Genesis has been leading the children of Abraham to Egypt since chapter 12, for they have to be there in order to introduce the exodus narratives. Over the course of the next few chapters, Joseph will deceive his brothers, imprison them as spies, take two of them as prisoners, and otherwise test them (Genesis 42–43). This testing culminates when he ensnares his brother Benjamin and convinces his other brothers that Benjamin must remain in Egypt as his slave; this inspires Judah to offer himself in place of Benjamin (Genesis 44). Thus, in Genesis 45, Joseph reveals himself to his brothers and assures them that all that has happened has been done by God's hand in order to preserve their lives. The initial dreams of Joseph's rule from Genesis 37 have been fulfilled as God has lifted him above his family members; but the purpose of his elevation is also clarified. It has been a result of providence; he has been elevated not for his own sake but so that they all might find salvation in their moment of distress (Gen. 45:7-8).

So Israel heads to Egypt in Genesis 46. The eponymous ancestor of the people symbolically represents the nation as it goes to sojourn in Egypt. In verses 2-5, God authorizes Jacob's migration, assuring him that this was part of God's plan, that God would remain with him, and that God would bring his family up from Egypt in the future. The journeying of the descendants of Abram is all but complete, as God has led them to Egypt as seventy souls (a fitting number forecasting the eventual number of people involved in the Egyptian translation of the Hebrew Bible into Greek—the LXX). The family, reconciled finally as Jacob sees Joseph, settles in the land of Goshen (Gen. 47:27).

One of the most interesting but oft-overlooked parts of the Joseph novella occurs in Genesis 47. After Jacob has come into Egypt, blessed Pharaoh, and settled in "Rameses" (note the anachronistic mention of this pharaoh—Gen. 47:1-12), the narrator offers a detailed description of the impact of the famine. Because of the famine, wealth becomes centralized in the hands of Pharaoh's house as Joseph takes all of the Egyptians' money, their livestock, and then their lands and their very lives in exchange for food and seed (Gen. 47:13-19). The chapter climaxes with the revelation in verse 21, where the MT has the odd reading, "he caused the people to pass to the cities," while the LXX reads that he "enslaved them." This variance in witnesses is clarified by verse 25, where the people proclaim that they will be "slaves for Pharaoh." It seems that the concept of slavery in Egypt can be attributed to Joseph, who implements a system of government that sanctioned forced labor for the entire population of Egypt. This may reflect a practice that was prevalent in the land during the annual flooding of the Nile, when agrarian life would have been halted and the displaced population would have been conscripted to work on government building projects. However it is imaged, the participation of the great patriarch Joseph in the development of the system that would subsequently imperil his own people is a crucial irony that cannot be overlooked. It is a reminder that the oppressive systems that people foster may well become the very systems that compromise the freedom of their posterity. This serves as a foreshadowing of the situation in which the descendants of Jacob will find themselves at the beginning of Exodus.

As Genesis 47 concludes, Jacob nears the end of his life. In anticipation of his death in verses 29-31, he asks Joseph to make a promise like the one Abram compelled his eldest servant to do in Gen. 24:2-4, to put his hand under his thigh and swear an oath. His desire is to be carried out of Egypt to be buried with his ancestors in Canaan; this promise is echoed in Gen. 49:29-32. Joseph brings his sons Ephraim and Manasseh to meet his father and is told by Jacob of God Almighty's promise that his descendants would possess the land of Canaan (Gen. 48:1-7). Afterward, Jacob blesses the two sons of Joseph and, as has become a recurrent theme in Genesis, reverses the primogeniture by offering the blessing of the elder son to Ephraim and the blessing of the younger to Manasseh, symbolically conveying the promises that should have gone to Manasseh to the younger Ephraim (Gen. 48:8-22).

After blessing each of his sons in Gen. 49:1-28, with a particularly meaningful blessing conveyed to the messianic line of Judah in verses 9-12, Jacob repeats his charge that his sons bury him with his ancestors in Canaan (vv. 29-32). Joseph thus leads a caravan of his family and Pharaoh's servants to the cave at Machpelah on the piece of land that Abraham purchased, and he buries his father Jacob there once he has been "gathered to [his] people" (v. 29). On their return to Egypt, the brothers, afraid of Joseph without the protection of their father, seek to preserve their lives by deceiving Joseph with a false request from Jacob that Joseph forgive them. They even volunteer themselves to Joseph as slaves (Gen. 50:18), further foreshadowing the book of Exodus. Not needing to be chided, however, Joseph again repeats the theological moral to the overall novella reflected in Gen. 45:7-8: "Though you planned evil against me, God planned it for good" (Gen. 50:20). The entire ordeal Joseph has endured is viewed through the lens of God's providence and is deemed a requisite step in the fulfillment of God's overall plan of salvation for the descendants of Israel.

As the narratives of Genesis draw to a close, God's providence is now evident to all as the deity has been revealed as the controller of the destinies of even the forlorn and forsaken and the redeemer of those who have been cast off and cast aside. God gives a wanderer like Abram the promise of a home; barren women like Sarah, Rebekah, and Rachel children; a murderer like Cain a protective mark; castaways like Hagar and Ishmael a nation; a trickster like Jacob who deceives all whom he encounters a good name; an arrogant upstart like Joseph transformed by years of suffering and humiliation the ability to forgive; and each of them one another as family members. In Genesis, the human family through its various travails of deception, jealousy, hatred, and even murder has been demonstrated to be resilient, reliable, and despite manifold fractures and failures, redeemable. Through each of the zeniths and nadirs of human existence, God's hand has been at work using each and every success and failure as a requisite part of God's larger plan.

In this regard, the Joseph novella provides the basis of a theology of hope for those desperately groping for God's hand in the midst of the overwhelming darkness that often attends human experience in a world shaped by human rebellion. As the book draws to a close in Genesis 50, it concludes with Joseph's prophetic pronouncement that "God will surely come to you, and bring you up out of this land to the land that he swore to Abraham, to Isaac, and to Jacob" (Gen. 50:24). Joseph's promise that God will take the people "up" is remarkably similar to the words that end the Hebrew Bible in 1 Chron. 36:23, predicting a time when the people will "go up" to Jerusalem. Perhaps this is not by accident. It is this confident portrayal of God's imminent return and deliverance that reminds the people to trust that YHWH, who has brought the people "thus far on the way," will lead them faithfully to the promised land. The providence that has been at work from the dawning of the world at the outset of creation to this point of the redemption of Joseph and his reconciliation with his brothers will sustain the sons of Israel no matter what obstacles they may, and soon will, face.

▌ THE TEXT IN THE INTERPRETIVE TRADITION

In his assessment of Genesis 37, De La Torre compares Joseph the dreamer to Dr. Martin Luther King Jr. and suggests that dreamers' goals are to bring in a utopian order, overcoming present oppressive paradigms and promoting a more just and equitable society (De La Torre, 302–3). Elsewhere, the author has noted the similarity between Joseph's enslavement by his brothers and the experiences of enslaved Africans, who like Venture Smith were sold by their African "brothers" (Sadler 2010, 77). Brueggemann has suggested that the narrative may be a call to the listening community to let the dream be at work, even when its outcome is less than clear (Brueggemann, 293).

The story of Tamar and Judah in Genesis 38 has been variously understood as a narrative of a woman's empowerment and cunning that secures her a place in the familial line (Niditch, 41–43); as "one of the strangest and most ethically troubling" stories in Scripture in part because Tamar in the course of her narrative is involved in "sexual intercourse with her brother-in-law (v. 8), in coitus interruptus (onanism, v. 9), in prostitution (vv. 15-16), and in sexual intercourse with her father-in-law (vv. 24-26)" (Hiebert, 23–24); and as a story meant to decry masturbation as onanism, or the sin of Onan, who spilled his semen on the ground in order to avoid impregnating his brother's wife (De La Torre, 263). This rich account describes a woman's attempt to exercise autonomy over her own life and to shape her own future when the masculine forces in society have failed her.

There is an interesting interpretative tradition to Genesis 47 in the discussion of Joseph's role in the development of slavery in Egypt. For example, Sarna reads Gen. 47:21 as though Joseph took the population from the cities, reading with a problematic MT. Other commentators, following the choice of the NIV and the NRSV favoring the witness of the Samaritan Pentateuch and the Septuagint, read verse 21 as though Joseph produced the slavery that will eventually affect his own people (see Fretheim, 655). Brueggemann notes that Joseph "played the royal game and forgot the promise" by fostering an oppressive system in Egypt that will eventually enslave his own people (Brueggemann, 358).

The stories of Joseph's reconciliation with his brothers are a fitting way to close these narratives. They are the stories that epitomize the troubled human relationships that characterize our own brokenness as people in this world. They offer the promise that even after humanity's grossest acts of injustice, threats of murder, and manifestations of hatred, forgiveness and reconciliation are still possible. Thus Hiebert concludes, "Throughout the book of Genesis, these stories of conflict and resolution hold up the values of courage and compassion over those of accusation and retaliation" (Hiebert, 23). In the end, there is the promise of restored relationships with both God and our human siblings as God's providence offers redemption to all who may have fallen on hard times along the way.

■ THE TEXT IN CONTEMPORARY DISCUSSION

We begin this final section of Genesis in chapter 37 with an account of the elevation of Joseph over his brothers. How does this narrative continue the theme of the disruption of primogeniture and the elevation of the youngest? Is there a connection with such disruption and the elevation of the youngest in this narrative with the story of the anointing of David (1 Samuel 16)? If so, what might the message of this account be? Is there an arrogance associated with Joseph at the beginning of this narrative that will be overcome at the end, and if so, how does this speak to his maturation as a character?

Genesis 38 presents an interesting narrative about levirate marriage. What benefit do you see for women under this paradigm? Who is its ultimate beneficiary, the women who are promised offspring and sustenance through marriage to a kinsman redeemer or the men who are ensured progeny and the perpetuation of land ownership? How is this narrative linked to the story of Joseph that surrounds it? Though contemporary interpreters may find the idea of levirate marriage distasteful and a remarkable imposition on both the surviving wife and the brother(s) of the deceased, what conventions for protecting the rights of young widows do we have in our society? Can we learn something from such narratives about the need to establish social systems to attend to the needs of those marginalized in our society?

There is a radical reversal of power dynamics in Genesis 39, as Joseph becomes victim to the sexual predation of Potiphar's wife. Does the presence of two narratives that explore the use of a woman's sexual prowess in the narrative offer a different perspective on the power of women in the ancient world? Are sexuality and sexual power the great equalizer for women in these narratives? How does the presence of such highly charged narratives where sexual manipulation is employed both positively and negatively serve as a challenge to traditional understandings of God's view of sex in our society?

The story of Joseph in Egypt unfolds over the next several chapters. How does Joseph's ascendancy from his nadir attest to the providence of God in his life? Though certainly a crafted narrative, what does the intervention of crises preceding the rise of Joseph say about the nature of the authors'/redactors' view of YHWH's redemptive activity? How might the message about God's providence in the Joseph novella serve as a catalyst for redemption in the lives of the oppressed and disenfranchised in our contexts?

Genesis 42–50 addresses the reconciliation between Joseph and his brothers and the fulfillment of his dream from Genesis 37. Joseph in these narratives becomes an exemplar for forgiveness and reconciliation, as he not only welcomes the brothers who have mistreated him to the sanctuary of Egypt but also assures that their needs are provided. In what way does this narrative serve as a rejoinder to that in Genesis 4 of the conflict between siblings? How could such a narrative address concepts of forgiveness between those whose transgressions have broken relationships in our contexts? What is the theology evident in these accounts of redeemed tragedies? Who is the God we meet in these accounts, and what are this God's attributes?

Perhaps the most disturbing aspect of this narrative is found in Genesis 47. Here the reader learns that as part of his national subsistence strategy for Egypt, Joseph buys the people and enslaves them to the house of Pharaoh. In essence, the narrative attributes the introduction of the corvée, or state-compelled labor, to Joseph. How does that alter our traditional understandings of Egyptian enslavement of the Hebrews? What does it say about the danger of developing oppressive paradigms that disenfranchise "others" in this world and how readily they can be turned against us? What lesson might the authors/editors want us to glean from this matter-of-fact reference to Joseph's fostering of a slavocracy in the precursor to the exodus narratives?

As we end this story, it is important to recognize whence this journey began and where it ends: from the creation of the world and the generality of a universal view of humanity to the land of Egypt and the specificity of a single man's (Israel's) family. It is clear that this focal family is the overarching concern of the authors/editors of these narratives and that these stories are told in a way that enhances their ends. How does this knowledge influence our understanding of the book of Genesis as a basis for the origins of the entire world and its people? What lessons does the reader learn about the nature of God here that can be used to apply to those outside of the purview of this family? How does this story of God's providence continue to prove useful for those in our contexts today?

Lest we forget, Genesis is a story that reaches its glorious conclusion precisely when its focal family is poised to enter slavery! It is a story the ultimate end of which is to lead its focal family to its narratological low point. But it is from this low point that its purpose is fulfilled, for without slavery there would have been no exodus; without tragic circumstances that led Joseph himself to institute systemic slavery in Egypt, his family would never have needed fully to trust YHWH, and they might never have known that their God was faithful to deliver them. As we struggle with the manifold crises that threaten to undo our collective human family, it is important to recognize that even in our darkest hours, God's providence is at work redeeming the world and providing a yet unseen path to a place of promise. This is a necessary message in an uncertain age. This is the message of Genesis.

Works Cited

Bailey, Randall C. 1995. "They're Nothing but Incestuous Bastards: Polemical Use of Sex and Sexuality in Hebrew Canon Narrative." In *Reading from This Place*. Vol. 1, *Social Context and Biblical Interpretation in the United States*, edited by Fernando Segovia and Mary Ann Tolbert, 121–38. Minneapolis: Fortress Press.

Bellis, Alice Ogden. 1994. *Helpmates, Harlots, Heroes: Women's Stories in the Hebrew Bible*. Louisville: Westminster John Knox.

Bellis, Alice Ogden, and Terry L. Hufford. 2002. *Science, Scripture, and Homosexuality*. Cleveland: Pilgrim.

Brueggemann, Walter. 1982. *Genesis*. IBC. Atlanta: John Knox.

Campbell, Antony F., and Mark A. O'Brien. 1993. *Sources of the Pentateuch: Texts, Introductions, Annotations*. Minneapolis: Fortress Press.

Dalley, Stephanie. 1989. *Myths from Mesopotamia: Creation, the Flood, Gilgamesh, and Others*. New York: Oxford University Press.

De La Torre, Miguel. 2011. *Genesis*. Belief: A Theological Commentary on the Bible. Louisville: Westminster John Knox.

Fretheim, Terence E. 1994. "Book of Genesis." In *The New Interpreter's Bible*. Vol. 1, *Genesis–Leviticus*, edited by Leander E. Keck. Nashville: Abingdon.

Gagnon, Robert A. J., 2001. *Bible and Homosexual Practice*. Nashville: Abingdon.

Haynes, Stephen. 2002. *Noah's Curse: The Biblical Justification of American Slavery*. New York: Oxford University Press.

Hiebert, Theodore. 2009. "Genesis." In *Theological Bible Commentary*, edited by Gail R. O'Day and David L. Petersen, 3–25. Louisville: Westminster John Knox.

Hubner, Ulrich. 1992. "Idumea." In *ABD* 3:382–83.

James, Elaine. 2012. "Sarah, Hagar, and Their Interpreters." In *Women's Bible Commentary*, edited by Carol A. Newsome, Sharon H. Ringe, and Jacqueline E. Lapsley, 51–55. 3rd ed. Louisville: Westminster John Knox.

Katzenstein, H. J. 1992. "Philistines." In *ABD* 5:326–28.

King, Martin Luther, Jr. 1986. "A Christmas Sermon on Peace." In *A Testament of Hope: The Essential Writings and Speeches of Martin Luther King, Jr.*, edited by James M. Washington, 253–58. San Francisco: HarperSanFrancisco.

Lemche, Niels Peter. 1992. "Hebrew." In *ABD* 3:95.

Louth, Andrew, ed. 2001. *Genesis 1–11*. Ancient Christian Commentary on Scripture, Old Testament 1. Downers Grove, IL: InterVarsity Press.

McClenney-Sadler, Madeline Gay. 2007. *Recovering the Daughter's Nakedness: A Formal Analysis of Israelite Kinship Terminology and the Internal Logic of Leviticus 18*. New York: T&T Clark.

Meyers, Carol. 1988. *Discovering Eve: Ancient Israelite Women in Context*. Oxford University Press.

Niditch, Susan. 2012. "Genesis." In *Women's Bible Commentary*, edited by Carol A. Newsome, Sharon H. Ringe, and Jacqueline E. Lapsley, 27–45. 3rd ed. Louisville: Westminster John Knox.

Rad, Gerhard von. 1972. *Genesis*. OTL. Rev. ed. Philadelphia: Westminster.

Sadler, Rodney S., Jr. 2005. *Can A Cushite Change His Skin? An Examination of Race, Ethnicity, and Othering in the Hebrew Bible*. New York: T&T Clark.

———. 2006. "Can a Cushite Change His Skin? Cushites, Racial Othering, and the Hebrew Bible." *Int* 60, no. 4:386–403.

———. 2010. "Genesis." In *The Africana Bible: Reading Israel's Scriptures from Africa and the African Diaspora*, edited by Hugh R. Page Jr., 70–79. Minneapolis: Fortress Press.

Sarna, Nahum M. 1989. *Genesis*. JPS Torah Commentary. Philadelphia: Jewish Publication Society.

Scholz, Susanne. 2012. "Judges." In *Women's Bible Commentary*, edited by Carol A. Newsome, Sharon H. Ringe, and Jacqueline E. Lapsley, 113–27. 3rd ed. Louisville: Westminster John Knox.

Seow, Choon-Leong. "Textual Orientation." In *Biblical Ethics and Homosexuality*, edited by Robert L. Brawley, 17–34. Louisville: Westminster John Knox.

Sheridan, Mark, ed. 2002. *Genesis 12–50*. Ancient Christian Commentary on Scripture, Old Testament 2. Downers Grove, IL: InterVarsity Press.

Smith, Mark S. 1990. *The Early History of God: YAHWEH and the Other Deities in Ancient Israel*. San Francisco: HarperSanFrancisco.

Turner, Bishop Henry McNeal. 1998. "Justice or Emigration." In *Lift Every Voice: African American Oratory 1787–1900*, edited by Philip S. Foner and Robert James Branham, 775–90. Tuscaloosa: University of Alabama Press.

Wink, Walter. 2005. *Homosexuality and the Bible*. Nyack, NY: Fellowship Press.

EXODUS

Thomas B. Dozeman

Introduction

Name of the Book and Location in the Canon

Exodus is the second book in the Hebrew Bible. It is one of five books that make up the Torah ("law") or Pentateuch (Greek for "five books"). The title, Exodus, derives from the Greek version of the Hebrew Bible known as the Septuagint (LXX): "Exodus from Egypt." Though the Septuagint title is the more common in English translations, in Jewish tradition, the title consists of the opening words of the book: "And these are the names." The name Exodus emphasizes Israel's departure from Egypt and their salvation from slave labor, the central event in the first half of the book, but it does not adequately describe the content of the entire book, which includes stories of Israel's initial wilderness journey as well as the revelation of the law and the tabernacle sanctuary at Mount Sinai.

The five books of Torah functioned as authoritative revelation for Jews already in the Second Temple period (516 BCE–70 CE). The combination of the five books of Genesis, Exodus, Leviticus, Numbers, and Deuteronomy suggests a close relationship among them. Upon first reading, the narrative sequence in the Torah appears to flow seamlessly. The account of creation and the ancestors (Genesis) brings the family of Jacob to Egypt, setting the stage for the liberation of the Israelites from Egypt (Exodus). The exodus from Egypt launches the nation on a wilderness journey, in which the people encounter God at the divine mountain, receive the law, and construct the sanctuary (Exodus, Leviticus, Numbers). The story concludes with Moses recounting the events from Genesis–Numbers (Deuteronomy), before he dies at the end of the book of Deuteronomy.

Authorship, Date, and Literary History

Exodus is an anthology of liturgy, law, and epic lore from many different periods of Israel's history. The author of Exodus is not explicitly stated, though tradition, including Jewish Hellenistic, rabbinic, and early Christian writings, has assigned the authorship of the book of Exodus and the entire Pentateuch to Moses. Philo, a Hellenistic Jewish author writing in the first century of the Common Era, writes in his commentary on creation, "Moses says . . . 'In the beginning God created the heaven and the earth'" (*Opif.* 26). Josephus also asserts that Moses authored the first five books (*Ag. Ap.* 1.37–40). The rabbis too state, "Moses wrote his own book" (*b. B. Bat.* 14b) and attribute to it divine origins (*b. Sanh.* 99a). Early Christian writers express a similar perspective. The apostle Paul refers to the Pentateuch as the "law of Moses" (1 Cor. 9:9). The author of the Gospel of Luke expresses the same thought, indicating the Pentateuch by simple reference to its author "Moses" (Luke 24:27), later describing it as the "law of Moses" (Luke 24:44).

The historical-critical study of the Pentateuch in the modern era has clarified that neither Moses nor any single author wrote Exodus. The identification of the anonymous authors, the time of their composition, and the method by which the literature was combined into a single narrative have dominated the interpretation of Exodus in the modern period. The central theory in the past century concerning the anonymous authorship of the book of Exodus has been the Documentary Hypothesis. It has provided biblical scholars with a model for identifying three anonymous authors in the composition of Exodus: the Yahwist (J), the Elohist (E), and the Priestly writer (P). The Yahwist and the Elohist composed their work during the monarchical period, while the Priestly author wrote during the exilic or postexilic period. The work of each author is not confined to the book of Exodus, but extends throughout the Tetrateuch (Genesis, Exodus, Leviticus, Numbers). The three authors of Exodus are evident where the same story (repetition) is told from different points of view or with different plot lines (contradiction). Examples include the two names for the mountain of God (Sinai in Exodus 19 and 24; and Horeb in Exodus 33), the two stories of the revelation of the divine name, YHWH (Exodus 3 and 6), several interpretations of the conflict at the Red Sea (Exodus 14–15), divergent law codes (Exodus 20 and Deuteronomy 5), and different accounts of the appropriate sanctuary (the tent of meeting in Exodus 33, and the tabernacle in Exodus 25–31, 35–40). These and many other repetitions confirm the existence of several anonymous authors of Exodus, with divergent views of God, community, and worship. Recent scholars, however, debate whether the Documentary Hypothesis is an adequate model for understanding the book of Exodus, preferring to distinguish simply between Priestly and non-Priestly literature, as compositions from the exilic and postexilic periods.

Historical Context

A central question in the modern interpretation of Exodus is what historical events may have given rise to the elaborate narrative of the book of Exodus. The biblical writers certainly wish to anchor the exodus from Egypt firmly in history. They date the event to the 2666th year (Exod. 12:40-41) from the creation of the world, or year 1 (Gen. 1:26-27). The construction of the tabernacle takes place in the 2667th year (Exod. 40:1-2, 17). Biblical writers state further that the Israelite period of enslavement is 430 years (Exod. 12:40-41), making their arrival in Egypt the 2236th year (Gen. 47:9). Jacob and his family settle in a specific land within Egypt, Goshen (Gen. 46:28; Exod. 8:22; 9:26), also known as the "land of Rameses" (Gen. 47:11). When the Israelites' guest status in Egypt turns into slavery, they are forced to build, according to the MT (the Masoretic text), the cities of Pithom and Rameses (Exod. 1:11; the LXX adds the city of On). During this time, moreover, the Israelite population grows from the original family of Jacob to a nation of 600,000 men (Exod. 12:37), making the total number of those leaving Egypt (including women and children) approximately 2–3 million persons, not counting the mixed multitude that accompanied them upon their leaving (Exod. 12:38).

The specific dates for the exodus, along with the careful numbering of the people, encourage a historical interpretation of the story. But the vague references to geography and the unrealistic number of the group indicate that the book of Exodus is not history. Goshen has not been clearly identified in the delta region of Egypt. Two to three million people in the Sinai desert would have overwhelmed the fragile environment. The internal problems of dating and geography further suggest that the book of Exodus is not history, but legendary literature. Research on the history of an Israelite exodus from Egypt has branched out from the book of Exodus to include the broader study of archaeology and of ancient Near Eastern literature, separating the book even further from a historical interpretation. There is no evidence that the Israelites dwelled in Egypt or that they escaped from slave labor, apart from Egyptian sources that provide information on slave laborers described as 'apiru—a term some scholars associate with the word "Hebrew" (*Egyptian Papyrus Leiden* 348).

The Israelites are identified in the Egyptian records in the Merneptah Stele, composed during the fifth year of Merneptah's rule (approx. 1208 BCE). In describing his military successes, Merneptah writes: "Canaan has been plundered into every sort of woe; Ashkelon has been overcome; Gezer has been captured. Yano'am was made nonexistent; Israel is laid waste, his seed is not" (*ANET* 378). The Egyptian writing indicates that the middle three references (Ashkelon, Gezer, and Yano'am) are cities, and that the term "Israel" refers to a people, not a city or a particular place. The Merneptah Stele indicates that an "Israelite" people could be identified in some way already in the thirteenth century BCE. But the evidence tends to argue against the exodus from Egypt, since Israel appears to be an indigenous group within Canaan who were the object of Egyptian conquest.

The story of the defeat of Pharaoh and of his army in the Red Sea is a cultic legend that spoke to an ongoing political reality in the life of Israel. Egyptian rule loomed large in Israel's life from her earliest years, and it continued throughout her political history, giving the legend of the exodus from Egypt immediacy and continuing religious significance. The ancient Israelite writers, moreover, were also familiar with Egyptian customs and practices, further underscoring the influence of Egyptian culture and politics on their life in Canaan. Egyptian language influences the book of Exodus in small details and in large events. The name "Moses" (*mosheh*), for example, derives from the Egyptian word *msi*, a common theophoric element in proper names, meaning "son." The word appears on such names as Thut*mose*, "son of Thut," or Ptah*mose*, "son of Ptah." The "bulrush" (*gome*) in which Moses is placed in Exod. 2:3 may derive from the Egyptian word "papyrus" (*g/kmy*). Even the plagues may be polemical actions against Egyptian gods, including Hapi, the god of the Nile, Osiris, the god of the dead, and Re, the sun god.

The influence of Egyptian culture on ancient Israelite writers may reach back to an experience of oppression in Egypt itself, but it need not. The reference to Pithom as one of the cities built by the

Israelites may provide historical background for dating the composition of the story of the Exodus. Donald Redford noted that the name Pithom does not appear in hieroglyphic writing as a specific reference to a town until after 600 BCE. This historical insight would place the author of Exodus in the late exilic period at the earliest (1982, Cols. 1054–58).

Structure and Contents

The book of Exodus probes two central themes concerning YHWH, the God of Israel: the character of divine power and the nature of divine presence in this world. Although the two themes are interwoven throughout the entire book, each takes prominence at different stages in the story, allowing for a loose division in the outline of the book of Exodus. The theme of divine power is explored, for the most part, in the setting of the land of Egypt (Exod. 1:1—15:21). The theme of divine presence is developed in the setting of the wilderness, as Israel journeys with God from Egypt to the promised land of Canaan (Exod. 15:22–40:38).

Exodus 1:1—15:21 narrates the conflict between YHWH and Pharaoh over the fate of Israel. It is an epic battle between kings and gods. The weapons of war are the forces of nature. YHWH summons reptiles, insects, and meteorological elements, including hail and darkness, in an initial assault on Pharaoh (Exodus 7–10). When these elements fail to persuade Pharaoh to release Israel from Egyptian slavery, the personification of death itself, described as "the destroyer," descends on the land of Egypt in the darkness of midnight, slaying all Egyptian firstborn children and animals (Exodus 11–12). Even the plague of death does not dissuade Pharaoh from continuing the conflict. During the night, he musters his army one last time and pursues the fleeing Israelites to the Red Sea (Exodus 13), where YHWH destroys him at dawn, this time using the sea itself as a weapon (Exodus 14). The hymns in Exodus 15 look back over the battlefield and confirm the power of God, praising YHWH as a warrior God who possesses power over Pharaoh and over all the forces of nature.

Exod. 15:22—40:38 describes the ways in which YHWH is able to be present with Israel in this world as they journey toward the promised land. The story is also told on an epic scale. The forces of nature change their role from providing YHWH with weapons of war to signaling the presence of God with Israel. God purifies polluted water for Israel (Exod. 15:22-27). The miracles of water from the rock (Exod. 17:1-7) and manna (Exodus 16) save Israel from starvation. Advice by Jethro, Moses' father-in-law, about worship and government (Exodus 18) provides a transition from the initial wilderness journey to the revelation of the law and the sanctuary on Mount Sinai. Exodus 19–24 describes YHWH's descent on Mount Sinai to reveal covenantal law to the Israelites. Natural forces like thunder, lightning, darkness, and fire signal the nearness of God to Israel and the danger of divine holiness. The need for cultic safeguards results in the revelation of the blueprints for the tabernacle (Exodus 25–31). Construction of the tabernacle holds promise for a divine descent from the mountain into the midst of the Israelite camp. But the process is halted when Israel worships the golden calf (Exodus 32). As a result, the story must begin anew, if it is to continue at all. God forgives Israel (Exod. 34:1-10), issues new laws for covenant renewal (Exod. 34:11-29), and commissions the building of the tabernacle (Exodus 35–40). The book of Exodus ends with YHWH finally descending from Mount Sinai and entering the completed tabernacle on New Year's Day (Exod. 40:1-2, 17), filling the sanctuary with fire and smoke (Exod. 40:34-38).

Reception History

The events in the book of Exodus have been the source of ongoing interpretation from the time of the ancient Israelites to the present. The process of interpretation begins already in the book of Exodus. The Song of Miriam (Exod. 15:21) and the theophany of God on the Mountain (Exod. 19:16-17) are likely early versions of the exodus and the revelation of YHWH on the mountain that were reinterpreted in the formation of the book of Exodus. But reinterpretation is not confined to the book of Exodus. The story of the exodus is also interpreted throughout the Hebrew Bible. The prophet Hosea, for example, interprets the exodus from Egypt as the result of prophetic leadership (Hosea 12:13). The exilic prophet Second Isaiah explores the mythical meaning of salvation from Egypt as a defeat of the sea monster (Isa. 51:9-11), while the prophet Ezekiel views Israel's wilderness journey negatively, as a time of idolatry (Ezekiel 20). The events in the book of Exodus thread their way through the entire Hebrew Bible.

The book of Exodus has also been influential in shaping the broader history of Judaism and Christianity. Jewish writers like Josephus and Philo of Alexandria reinterpreted the exodus and the life of Moses to a Hellenistic culture. Philo describes the tutoring of Moses in arithmetic and geometry by the Greeks (*Life of Moses* 1.21–23). Hecataeus of Abdera interprets the exodus as an expulsion of foreigners from Egypt to Greece, whose leader was Moses. The group founded colonies, one of which was Jerusalem (*Diodorus Siculus* 40.3.1–8.). New Testament writers explore the meaning of Jesus' ministry and passion within the framework of the exodus. Jesus is called out of Egypt (Matt. 2:15), undergoes testing in the wilderness (Luke 4:1-12), and becomes the Paschal Lamb (John 19:36), while Paul identifies the early Christians also with the wilderness generation of Israelites (1 Cor. 10:1-13). The Passover haggadah, or guide to the Passover celebration, continues to propel the events of the exodus through time, interpreting the exodus to new generations of Jewish worshipers.

The exodus also provides a resource for social criticism in contemporary biblical interpretation. Liberation theologians use the exodus as a resource for oppressed people to struggle for liberation from modern tyrants who oppress and repress them as the Pharaoh did the Hebrews. Feminists look to the exodus for models of resistance to power in such female characters as Miriam or the midwives. Postcolonialist interpreters expose the oppressive side of the exodus mythology, in which the promise of land through conquest has provided religious justification for unjust land claims throughout the colonial period to the present time.

Exodus 1:1—2:25: Divine Promise and Human Oppression

Exodus 1–2 describes the process by which the Israelites are enslaved in Egypt, setting the stage for a story of salvation as act of divine liberation. But God is absent as an active force in the life of the Israelites during their enslavement and genocide of infant males at the hands of Pharaoh.

This absence of God in Exodus 1–2 allows the biblical writers to explore the themes of power and oppression from a human perspective. The story moves quickly. Years have transpired since Joseph ruled in the land of Egypt, and the Israelites' guest status has long been forgotten. A series of vignettes provides insight into the growing alienation between the Egyptians and the Israelites, prompting a range of human responses, including fear of Pharaoh and his oppression of the Israelites, the civil disobedience of the midwives against Pharaoh's command for genocide (1:1-21), and the violence of Moses' initial attempt at liberation, when he kills an Egyptian (1:22—2:25).

Exodus 1:1-21: The Midwives and Civil Disobedience

■ THE TEXT IN ITS ANCIENT CONTEXT

The section separates into two episodes: the fertility of the Israelites in 1:1-7, which threatens Pharaoh and leads to his oppression in 1:8-21. The first episode, 1:1-7, paints a bleak picture of death and social alienation. Verse 6 recounts the death of Joseph, his brothers, and the entire generation. A similar account occurs in Judg. 2:10, where the death of Joshua's generation signifies the breakdown of tradition and memory, with the result that the generation after Joshua loses all knowledge of their past, including the salvation of God. The same meaning is likely intended in Exodus with the death of Joseph's generation. The Israelites and Pharaoh have forgotten the story of the guest status of the family of Jacob in Egypt and the role of Joseph in saving the Egyptians from starvation. Thus the book of Exodus begins without the memory of the God of the ancestors or the past social hospitality shown between the Egyptians and the Israelites. This loss of memory leads to fear and alienation. A new Pharaoh mistrusts the Israelites, who are "fruitful and prolific" (1:7). The language of fertility ties the opening of Exodus to the account of creation in Genesis 1, signaling the indirect presence of God in the story as the creator of all humans, even though YHWH, the God of Israel, is not active in Exodus 1–2.

In 1:8-21, Pharaoh and the midwives provide conflicting responses to the Israelites' fertility, responses that lead to different ethical actions. Pharaoh reacts with fear over losing power (1:9-10). To safeguard his power over Israel, Pharaoh institutes forced labor (1:11-14). But when slave labor does not curtail the birthrate of the Israelites, he secretly commands the genocide of all male babies (1:15-16). Pharaoh's fear forces him to distinguish between "his people" and "the Israelites" in order to maintain social control. Social alienation spirals out of control, leading to oppression and genocide.

The midwives Shiphrah and Puah resist the abusive power of Pharaoh though civil disobedience. Their conflict with Pharaoh is developed through a play on the motifs "to see" and "to fear," words that often sound similar in Hebrew. Pharaoh secretly instructs the midwives to kill every male Hebrew child that they "see" born on the birthstones (1:16). But the narrator tells the reader that the midwives "fear" God, prompting their civil disobedience; they allow the male babies of the Israelite women to live. The midwives' "fear of the God" is a generic description of the deity not intended to be a statement about formal religious practice but to position conscience against the tyranny of Pharaoh, thus raising the question: Will the midwives conform to the command of Pharaoh and act on what they "see," namely, the birth of Hebrew male babies condemned to death by the state? Or will they follow their conscience and act on their "fear of the God," thus letting the babies live?

The midwives follow their conscience and undertake civil disobedience. They allow the male babies to live (1:17), and they lie to account for their actions (1:18-19). When Pharaoh inquires why his order of genocide is not being executed, the midwives play on his fear, accentuating the difference between the Egyptians and the Israelites that was introduced by Pharaoh. They state: "The Hebrew women are not like the Egyptian women" (v. 19a). Then the midwives play on Pharaoh's more primordial fear, the explosive population growth of the Israelite: "[The Israelite women] are teeming with life, and before the midwife comes to them, they give birth" (author trans., v. 19b).

■ THE TEXT IN THE INTERPRETIVE TRADITION

Interpreters have struggled to discern the identity of the midwives and to evaluate the ethical implications of their civil obedience, which required not only that they oppose the power of Pharaoh but also that they lie. The interpretations vary widely, often reflecting the social and religious context of the community. The Talmud, for example, identifies the midwives as Hebrews, even equating Shiphrah with Moses' mother, Jochebed, and Puah with Miriam (*b. Sotah* 11b). The resistance of the midwives—including their lying to Pharaoh—is heroic, for they risk their lives to save the people of Israel. Writing in the Greco-Roman context, Josephus identifies the midwives as Egyptians, not Hebrews, while still interpreting their actions heroically (*Ant.* 2.206). Nehama Leibowitz underscores the universal application of the story. All humans possess the fear of God, so that even a gentile who does not act on his or her conscience against tyranny and genocide is a traitor to the most elementary obligation of a human being (1:35). But not all agree. John Calvin, for example, condemns the lying of the midwives as sin, which illustrates that all human actions—even those aimed at saving infants—contain mixed motives, requiring divine grace for purification (1950, 34–36).

■ THE TEXT IN CONTEMPORARY DISCUSSION

The interpretation of women characters like the midwives in the patriarchal world of biblical literature is an ongoing challenge for contemporary readers. Too often in biblical texts, women are stereotyped in domestic roles, where their status is tied to reproduction, usually of male characters (Fuchs, 311; Steinberg, 174–75). Feminist critics have sought to recover a more prominent role of women in the opening chapters of Exodus by shifting the focus of the identity of the midwives from ethnicity to gender in evaluating their actions. As a result, the midwives model neither the heroic action of Hebrews nor the universal conscience of all humans, but the courage of women to oppose patriarchal oppression represented by Pharaoh. The midwives, whether Hebrew or Egyptian, are tricksters who thwart the evil command of Pharaoh. Had Pharaoh known their cunning, he would have commanded all infant females to be killed (Trible 1973, 34). "Their clever response to Pharaoh is not a lie; they simply do not tell the whole truth . . . a conventional weapon of the powerless, especially women in the Old Testament" (Weems, 29). Not only are they cunning, but the midwives also embody the theme of birth in the book of Exodus. "They are the first to assist in the birth of the Israelite nation" (Setel, 30). In contemporary feminist interpretation, the resistance of the midwives is a window into the heroic role of women throughout the opening chapters of the book of Exodus. The book begins with a focus on women, including the mother and sister of Moses and the daughter of Pharaoh. They defy oppression, give life, and model wisdom. And their actions determine the outcome of events (Exum, 82).

Exodus 1:22—2:25: Identity of Moses and Human Lament

■ THE TEXT IN ITS ANCIENT CONTEXT

There is a change in perspective between Exod. 1:1-21 and 1:22—2:25. The fertility of the Israelites is a central but abstract theme in the first episode; the narrative is broad in scope, giving a panoramic perspective on the whole nation of the Israelite people. While the theme of fertility continues in Exod. 1:22—2:25, the lens narrows to a single Levitical Israelite family, telling a more intimate story of the birth of one child, Moses. The liberator of the Israelite people is born during the height of Pharaoh's oppression of the Israelites, in which all the Egyptians are called on publicly to kill the Hebrew male babies. The introduction of Moses includes the account of his birth, rescue from the Nile River, and adoption by the daughter of Pharaoh (Exod. 1:22—2:10) and two stories that probe his identity as a liberator, the act of murder in Egypt (Exod. 2:11-15a) and the rescue of Reuel's daughters in Midian (Exod. 2:15b-22).

The birth and rescue of Moses in Exod. 1:22—2:10 conforms to a common legend in the ancient Near East, in which a hero is abandoned, set adrift in water, and eventually adopted. The most striking parallel to the story of Moses is The Legend of Sargon (*ANET* 119), a Neo-Assyrian account from the eighth or seventh century BCE about the birth of Sargon the Great, who founded the dynasty of Akkad in the late third millennium. In this story, Sargon is the child of a priestess prohibited from conceiving a child. She disobeys, conceives Sargon in secret, and floats the baby on the river in a vessel of reeds. Sargon is rescued from the river and adopted by Akki, the water drawer, who raises him as a gardener, before Sargon becomes king of Akkad. The motifs of abandonment and adoption accentuate the mysterious origin of Sargon, while his humble beginnings are meant to idealize the identity of any king in Mesopotamian tradition. The ideal is that a king does not rise to power through privilege but through heroic deeds. The parallels between The Legend of Sargon and Moses' birth story include anonymous parents from the priestly class, an illegal if not illegitimate birth, a river ordeal, rescue, adoption, the protection of women, and an emphasis on the heroic deeds of Moses to establish his identity. The similarities indicate that the author of Exodus wishes to explore the identity of Moses.

The departure from the heroic pattern in the birth story of Moses provides the point of view for interpreting the theme of Moses' identity as a liberator. The expected pattern of the heroic legend is a rags-to-riches story, in which the hero progresses from the threat of death and anonymity to public leadership. The structure of Moses' birth story is inverted. Moses is indeed exalted into the family of Pharaoh, but only momentarily before he returns to the status of a hunted slave, when Pharaoh seeks his life (2:15). Many interpret the inverted structure against the backdrop of Israelite slavery and the need for Moses to become a liberator of slaves.

The identity of Moses as a liberator is explored further through his actions in the first two stories of his adult life, where acts of liberation lead to the opposite outcomes of murder (2:11-15a) and of the rescue of the oppressed (2:15b-22). The story of Moses in Exod. 2:11-15a is a tale of failed leadership. The story moves quickly. Exodus 2:11-12 narrates Moses' murder of an Egyptian. The scene is told from Moses' point of view, and the narrator identifies him as an Israelite. When venturing out one day, Moses sees the "forced labor of the Israelites (1:11; 2:11), recalling the initial act of slave labor by Pharaoh. After ensuring secrecy, Moses kills the Egyptian and buries the corpse to conceal the secret murder. Although Moses seeks to liberate Hebrews, the violent murder, performed in secret, recalls the private instructions of Pharaoh to the midwives.

Exodus 2:13-14a, told from the point of view of the Hebrews, recounts Moses' initial encounter with Israelites. Moses sees two Hebrews struggling, and he addresses one of the men with the words, "Why do you strike your fellow Hebrew?" The Hebrew questions the authority of Moses, revealing that he knows Moses is no more than a murderer: "Do you mean to kill me as you killed the Egyptian?" Whatever moral authority Moses had hoped to convey as a liberator disappears when the Hebrew slave reveals that Moses is a murderer.

Exodus 2:14b-15a concludes the tale with Moses' realization that his secret act of murder is now public information, which changes his behavior from a moral mediator for others to a fearful fugitive seeking to escape from Pharaoh. Yet, once Moses escapes from Egypt, he acts again as a liberator in the southern desert location of Midian (2:15b-22), when he rescues the daughters of Jethro, the Midianite priest, from their oppressors at the water well, who seek to drive the women away from the source of water.

The two stories of Moses' early adult life highlight different aspects of his innate ability as a liberator. In the first story, Moses sees oppression and initiated liberation by killing an Egyptian. Although intended as justice, the act is described as murder. At the water well in Midian, Moses sees another act of oppression. The words describing Moses' act of liberation in Midian emphasize life, not death. He "saves" the women (2:17). In contrast to the Hebrew man who called Moses a "killer," the daughters describe his action as a "rescue," even though they identify him as an Egyptian, not a Hebrew (2:19).

◼ THE TEXT IN THE INTERPRETIVE TRADITION

The killing of the Egyptian has prompted interpreters to discern more carefully the motive of Moses as a liberator, especially in the phrase, "he turned thus and thus." Interpreters debate whether the phrase is meant to idealize Moses as a liberator or to criticize him as a failed leader. The *Mekilta* states that the phrase indicates Moses' complete devotion to the Israelites (*Mekilta Shirata* 1.35–64). In *The Legends of the Jews*, Louis Ginzberg recounts another reading where the phrase "he turned thus and thus" indicates Moses' quest for justice. When none is forthcoming he decides to act himself, but not before consulting the angels. Only then does Moses kill the Egyptian by pronouncing the divine name (2:277–82). For Calvin, the act of "turning thus and thus" indicates hesitation on the part of Moses to risk his security in an act of divinely appointed deliverance. The hesitation is a sign of weak faith, requiring divine mercy (1950, 46–50). Philo stresses Moses' control of his emotions, his tight rein on his passions, and the power of reason guiding his actions. The killing of the Egyptian is a deliberate and just action by Moses. It is a "righteous deed," because "one who lived to destroy men should himself be destroyed" (*Mos.* 1.40–44, Philo 1954). Stephen echoes the same interpretation in Acts 7:23-29. Hebrews 11:23-28 omits the killing altogether, focusing instead on Moses' choice to give up wealth and status in order to take on the suffering of the Isra-elites. The *Midrash of the Passing of Moses* provides a more critical interpretation, stating that Moses' request not to die is denied him because of his slaying of the Egyptian (Leibowitz, 1:44–46).

▎ THE TEXT IN CONTEMPORARY DISCUSSION

Contemporary interpreters continue to reflect critically on the ambiguous nature of liberation, whether it is a force to save or to destroy. Writing from a liberationist point of view, George Pixley rightly notes that Exodus 1–2 deals with oppression and liberation. The account of Moses' killing the Egyptian is a story of social class and the coming-to-consciousness of the central character when he sees the mistreatment of a peasant slave. The episode "shows the character of Moses as a man of the upper class who sees, understands, and rejects the suffering of the people of Egypt. He thus proves to be a person whom God can trust to lead his people out of Egypt into freedom" (154–55). Gale Yee counters, however, from a postcolonial perspective, that the story of Moses' act of liberation in killing the Egyptian, and even the larger narrative of the exodus from Egypt as an event of liberation, cannot be read in isolation from the story of Israel's "conquest" of Canaan. In this case, murder as liberation can legitimate a whole range of violent acts of social and political expansion. "This double-sidedness [of liberation] should raise a red flag regarding any reading that enlists the Bible to support its cause" (231).

Exodus 3:1—7:7: The Commission of Moses

▎ THE TEXT IN ITS ANCIENT CONTEXT

This section of Exodus explores the religious experience of Moses through a series of divine encoun-ters. Twice Moses receives special revelations of his divine commission as a liberator, which repeat many similar themes in two distinct locations: Exod. 3:1—4:17 takes place in the desert at the mountain of God, when Moses stumbles on the burning bush while shepherding his animals; and Exod. 6:1—7:7 occurs in Egypt, after Moses initially fails to free the Israelite people. Exod. 4:17—5:23 links the two stories of divine revelation; it recounts the journey of Moses and his wife Zippo-rah from Midian to Egypt in order to fulfill the divine commission. This episode, however, contains a third divine encounter that moves in a very different direction from the two commissions. Rather than singling out Moses as the liberator, YHWH tries to kill either Moses or Gershom, his son, in an attack during the night, in which Zipporah, the Midianite, plays the leading role of rescuer. The three divine encounters examine the nature of special revelation and religious experience from distinct perspectives.

The two commissions of Moses single him out as a uniquely chosen liberator, while also high-lighting the special status of the Israelites as YHWH's chosen people, who are distinct from all other humans by special divine favor. God reveals the divine name YHWH to Moses (Exod. 3:6; 6:2). God acknowledges a special relationship with Moses as the God of his father (Exod. 3:6), who created a covenant with his ancestors (Exod. 6:4). God promises to be with Moses in a unique and intimate way (Exod. 3:12; 7:1), and clarifies that the commission of Moses as liberator is because YHWH also has a special relationship with Israel (Exod. 3:7-8; 6:5-8). The special revelation separates Moses from Pharaoh as God's chosen messenger (Exod. 3:9; 7:1) and the Israelite people from the Egyptians and all other nations (Exod. 3:8; 6:7-8). The two commissions provide the foundation for the development of Israelite religion in the wilderness. The central themes emphasize the character of YHWH as a compassionate liberator of the Israelites, sharing in the experience of suffering and seeking their welfare by protecting from oppression, rescuing from slavery, and giving them land.

The appearance of YHWH in the attack during the night moves in the opposite direction from the two commissions of Moses. It is not about security, divine compassion, or the ability of God to share in the suffering of the Israelites. Instead, the encounter with YHWH represents the threat of death. The literary context of the divine attack (Exod. 4:24-26) is the journey of Moses, Zipporah, and their son Gershom from the land of Midian to Egypt in order to fulfill the commission of Moses (Exod. 4:18—5:23). The section begins in a positive manner, with Jethro, the father-in-law of Moses, blessing him at the outset of the journey (Exod. 4:18-20) and with YHWH providing instructions to Moses about what he is to do upon reaching Egypt and reaffirming the special status of the Israelites as God's firstborn son (Exod. 4:21-23). But then the story takes a dark turn when the family of Moses rests for the night (Exod. 4:24-26).

The newly proclaimed kinship tie between YHWH and the Israelites as the firstborn son of God (Exod. 4:21-23) is acted out in a negative way in Exod. 4:24-26, when YHWH seeks to kill one of the male family members. It is unclear whom YHWH is attacking during the night, the son or Moses. The attack may represent YHWH's claim on the firstborn, or it may result from the absence of either Moses' or his son's circumcision. In either case, Zipporah stops the attack by circumcising her son and warding off the deity with the bloody foreskin, stating: "Truly you are a bridegroom of blood to me!" (Exod. 4:25). Zipporah likely claims some form of familial relationship with YHWH. Noteworthy in the context of the stories about the special revelation to Moses is that the Midianite Zipporah, and not Moses, performs the proper ritual to appease the deity and to protect her family. The heroic role of the midwives, who feared God more than Pharaoh, already suggested the theme of YHWH's relationship to humanity in general, even though the story of the exodus accentuates the special status of Moses and the Israelites. The story of Zipporah advances the theme beyond the midwives' general fear of God. She possesses special ritual knowledge that saves Moses from the divine attack in the wilderness and allows him to fulfill his divine commission.

◼ THE TEXT IN THE INTERPRETIVE TRADITION

Moses' three encounters with God in Exod. 3:1—7:7 have given rise to wide-ranging reflection on the nature of revelation. Interpreters have sought to identify more clearly the divine in the burning bush to provide insight into the nature of revelation within organized religious practice. The rabbis, for example, state that the divine presence in the bush is the Shekinah (*b. Sotah* 5a). Gregory of Nyssa identifies the burning bush with the Virgin Mary, explaining that just as the fire did not consume the bush so also the birth of Jesus did not alter Mary's virginity (2.37–41). Calvin equates the messenger of YHWH with Jesus and the theme of suffering with the persecuted Protestant church (1950, 1:61–62). The burning bush has also been interpreted as a resource for criticizing organized religion, especially in its claim to control revelation and religious experience. Elizabeth Barrett Browning, for example, links the burning bush with the revelation of God through nature (Browning, 265); while James Dickey equates the symbol with poetic inspiration, freed from the confines of organized religion (Dickey, 7–8). The attack of YHWH against Moses is also interpreted to reinforce institutional religious rituals. For the rabbis, the cause for the divine attack is the problem of neglecting circumcision (*b. Nedarim* 31b–32a); while for Augustine the story illustrates the danger of not baptizing infants (4.24–32).

▌THE TEXT IN CONTEMPORARY DISCUSSION

The nature of revelation, the relationship of religious experience to organized religion, and the strange role of Zipporah are continuing topics of reflection in contemporary discussion. The burning bush remains the symbol for many branches of the Reformed churches throughout the world (e.g., Reformed Churches of France, Scotland, Canada, Australia, New Zealand), while it also provides a resource for criticizing organized religion as in the Wisconsin-based nonconformist, utopian community the Burning Bush Movement. The divine attack on Moses remains a challenging text about revelation and the nature of the deity in human experience. The author of *Jubilees* already sought to overcome the problem in the earlier period of interpretation by identifying the divine being as Prince Mastema (Satan) rather than YHWH (48:1-8). Rudolf Otto moves in a different direction: he interprets the story as the paradigm of all human encounters with the divine, which he concludes always represent a premoral experience of the numinous. He likens the experience of the numinous to a deeply felt monster (Otto, 60–61). The role of Zipporah continues to demand interpretation, especially in evaluating her role as woman, wife, and a non-Israelite. Elizabeth Cady Stanton voices an early feminist critique, stating that Zipporah represents the role of all women who follow their husband's desires as secondary characters in marriage, taking an active role only when they need to rescue their husbands from danger (75–76). Recent feminist interpreters view the role of Zipporah more heroically, as a non-Israelite ritual expert who saves Moses and her son from the divine attack, thus challenging the exclusive nature of revelation in the two commissions of Moses (e.g., Meyers 2005).

Exodus 7:8—10:20: The Plagues

▌THE TEXT IN ITS ANCIENT CONTEXT

This section narrates the many plagues YHWH sends against Pharaoh and the Egyptians. The stage is set for the plagues when Pharaoh rejects Moses' demand that the people be freed to worship

YHWH in the desert (Exod. 5:1-23). Pharaoh's resistance leads to a confrontation with YHWH, not Moses. The plagues are weapons of war against Pharaoh and signs of YHWH's destructive power over the environment of Egypt. The section includes three cycles of plagues, which increase in intensity as they progress through the different elements of nature, from water (7:8—8:15), to land (8:16—9:7), and finally to air (9:8—10:20).

Cycle 1 (7:8—8:15) Nature: Water	**Cycle 2** (8:16—9:7) Nature: Land	**Cycle 3** (9:8—10:20) Nature: Air
Introduction: Aaron sea-dragon (7:8-13)	Introduction: Aaron gnats (8:16-19)	Introduction: Moses boils (9:8-12)
blood (7:14-24)	flies (8:20-32)	hail (9:13-35)
frogs (7:25—8:15)	cattle (9:1-7)	locusts (10:1-20)

In the first cycle, Aaron represents the power of YHWH over the water in the land of Egypt. Pharaoh and his magicians are the opponents. The plague of the sea monster opens the cycle. Its central theme is the transformation of Aaron's staff into the *tannin*, "sea monster." The motif of water associated with the sea monster provides the introduction to two subsequent plagues, the pollution of the Nile River into blood and the infiltration of frogs from the water onto the land. The initial confrontation results in a stalemate between YHWH and Pharaoh, since the Egyptian magicians are able to perform the same acts of power over water as Aaron: they conjure up the sea monster (7:12), turn water into blood (7:22), and bring frogs out of the Nile (8:7). Thus Pharaoh rejects YHWH's claim on the Israelite people and continues to demand their slave labor. Aaron remains the protagonist in the second cycle, where the destructive power of YHWH is redirected from the water to the land of Egypt. Aaron brings forth gnats from the "dust of the earth" (8:17), which surpasses the power of the magicians (8:18), causing them to recognize the power of God (8:19). After the gnats, flies infest the "ground" of the Egyptians, and all the Egyptian livestock of the field die. Yet Pharaoh continues to resist the claims of YHWH. In the third cycle, Moses replaces Aaron as the representative of YHWH. A plague of boils is created on humans and animals from the soot in the air (8:9), a plague so severe that the magicians are not even able to meet him (8:11). Two other airborne plagues follow the boils: a hailstorm ruins the land of Egypt (9:23), and locusts are carried into Egypt on an east wind, destroying whatever survived the hailstorm (10:13).

The description of the divine actions against the water, land, and air of Egypt underscores destructive themes in the narrative. The series of events reinforce the assault of YHWH on Egypt. The ecological disasters are described as plagues (9:3, 14) and strikes (7:27), by which YHWH smites the Egyptian environment (7:17, 7:25; 8:13; 9:15). Yet these same destructive forces are also described as wonders (7:3, 9; 11:9-10) and signs (7:3; 8:23; 10:1-2) that reveal the power and character of YHWH to Pharaoh and the Egyptians (Exod. 7:3; 8:23; 11:9-10), as well as to the Israelites (10:1-2).

▌ THE TEXT IN THE INTERPRETIVE TRADITION

The plagues receive surprisingly little interpretation in biblical tradition. They are the subjects of two psalms. Psalm 78 recounts the plagues as actions directed toward the Israelites with the aim of instilling faith in them. Psalm 105 states that the plagues are public displays of power aimed at the Egyptians. Neither psalm follows the form or sequence of the pentateuchal histories, suggesting fluidity in the tradition of the plagues. The plagues are also mentioned in a number of sermons and prayers. Moses refers to the signs performed by YHWH (Deut. 11:3; 26:8), as does Joshua (Josh. 24:5) and Ezra (Neh. 9:10). The book of *Jubilees* interprets the plagues as signs of YHWH's vengeance (48:5-8). Josephus (*Vita* 2.293) and Philo (*Mos.* 1.146), on the other hand, interpret the plagues as occasions for divine protection of the Israelites and for their instruction. In Jewish legend, the plagues parallel the cruel treatment of the Israelites (Ginzberg, 2:345–47). In the New Testament, the sermon of Stephen continues the tradition of Moses, Joshua, and Ezra, referring to the plagues as "wonders" and "signs" (Acts 7:36). The apostle Paul provides a unique midrash on Exod. 9:16 in Rom. 9:17, transforming the motif of Pharaoh's hardened heart to account for the rejection of the Jews to the mission of Jesus. Revelation 16 is more in the tradition of Psalm 105, where the plagues are public, cosmological events performed before the nations, signaling the end of time.

▌ THE TEXT IN CONTEMPORARY DISCUSSION

The ecological devastation associated with the plagues, in which the destruction of the environment is a divine weapon for saving the Israelite nation, represents a challenge to contemporary ecological theology. In his study of the roots of our contemporary ecological crisis in the Western tradition, Lynn Townsend White argues that Judeo-Christianity represents an anthropocentric religious tradition that is exploitative of the natural world (1203–7). The destruction of the Egyptian environment in the story of the exodus would appear to support his conclusion. The criticism prompted Terence Fretheim to explore anew the relationship of religion, nature, and human action in the story of the plagues. He concludes that the cycle of the plagues, with its emphasis on nature, advances a theology of creation. Central to this theology is the ancient Near Eastern belief that the morality of the king influences the well-being of creation and the fertility of the land (Frankfort, 310–12). As a result, a king who oppresses his subjects risks the ecological ruin of his country. When read from this perspective, the plagues on the land of Egypt do not represent the denigration of nature by God for the salvation of humans. Instead, they are the result of the breakdown in the moral order because of the actions of Pharaoh. Human ethics and ecology become organically related; Pharaoh's oppression not only threatens the well-being of the Israelites but also spills over to pollute the environment of Egypt. The plagues signify the undoing of creation for the Egyptians as a result of Pharaoh's exploitative actions. The breakdown of creation progresses through "every tree," "all the fruit," and "the whole land," until darkness engulfs the land of Egypt.

The intertwining of human morality and the well-being of the land remains a hallmark of the Israelite prophets. Hosea states: "Therefore the land mourns, and all who live in it languish; together with the wild animals, and the birds of the air, even the fish of the sea are perishing," because humans are acting immorally (Hosea 4:3). The prophet Amos also describes drought and even "pestilence after the manner of Egypt" (Amos 4:10) sent by YHWH as a result of immoral action. The prophet Joel too equates an invasion of locusts with divine judgment (Joel 1–2), a motif that will also appear in the plague cycle. The oracles of Hosea, Amos, and Joel indicate that human oppression has ecological consequences. It can undo creation. The same is true for the story of the plagues. The intertwining of human morality and the well-being of the Egyptian environment provides a springboard for evaluating contemporary ecological disasters, such as the Deepwater Horizon oil spill in the Gulf of Mexico or even the increase of violent storms that are tied to global warming, where exploitation goes beyond the oppression of humans to include the undoing of creation itself.

Exodus 10:21—13:16: The Exodus

■ THE TEXT IN ITS ANCIENT CONTEXT

Exodus 10:21—13:16 contains the liturgies associated with the exodus from Egypt. The plague of darkness (Exod. 10:21-29) provides the introduction to the death of the Egyptian firstborn during the night of Passover and the Feast of Unleavened Bread (Exod. 11:1—13:16). The story, building on the violent cycle of the plagues in Exod. 7:8—10:20, keeps the power of YHWH at center stage; the divine demand that Pharaoh release the Israelites for worship retains a prominent role in the events of the exodus, while the plagues also continue. The traditional interpretation of darkness and the death of the Egyptian firstborn as plagues in the Passover Haggadah, for example, underscores the continuity between the initial plagues and the events of the exodus.

But there is also intensification from the story of the plagues to the account of Passover. YHWH acts more directly against Pharaoh and the Egyptians, and as a result, the display of YHWH's power is elevated and the intercessory role of Moses recedes somewhat, especially in the death of the Egyptian firstborn. Also, YHWH's power over nature increases beyond water, land, and air to the more primordial forces of light and darkness, and life and death. The plague of darkness sets the stage for the death of the Egyptian firstborn at midnight. The Israelites, too, become active rather than passive participants in the story, as compared to their role in the previous cycle of plagues. Thus they must participate in their redemption through cultic ritual of the Passover, which protects them from YHWH's assault on the Egyptians and the death of the Egyptian firstborn children at midnight. The ritual also provides a means for the Israelites to recall and to reenact the exodus. The central question of the Passover haggadah—Why is this night different from all other nights?—interprets the events of the exodus as a development beyond the previous plague cycle.

The Passover emerges as the central liturgical event in the exodus. The blood of the paschal lamb protects the Israelites from the midnight plague of death, when YHWH strikes down all the firstborn humans in the land of Egypt (Exod. 12:29-30). Thus ritual requirements are carefully outlined, given the need to protect the Israelite firstborn from death (Exod. 12:1-20). Each Israelite family is to slaughter a one-year-old lamb and place the blood on the doorpost to ward off the divine destroyer, who will kill all of the firstborn humans in the land of Egypt during the night. Moses also instructs the elders of the Israelites about the Passover, emphasizing once again that the blood on the doorpost is a protection from the divine attack on the firstborn (Exod. 12: 21-28). And YHWH returns to the topic with further instruction to Moses, outlining who may participate in the Passover (Exod. 12:40-51).

In spite of its central role in the narrative, the Passover was not originally associated with the exodus. It may have originated in seminomadic culture, with the blood of the lamb functioning to protect against the dangers of migration, or perhaps in the monarchical period, as a ritual in the New Year festival. Whatever its origin, the linking of the Passover with the theme of protecting the firstborn from a divine attack is likely ancient, since these themes are already present in the oldest version of the rite in Exod. 12:21-23. The setting of the ritual in the land of Egypt during the events of the exodus, however, likely occurred late in the period of the monarchy, under the rule of Josiah, who is credited with instituting the Passover as a national festival (2 Kgs. 23:21-23). But even here, the Passover is not tied specifically to the exodus. In the present form of story of the exodus from Egypt, the Passover and the death of the firstborn are firmly intertwined. The use of blood to rescue a firstborn child repeats the action of Zipporah, who also used blood to ward off the attack of YHWH in Exod. 4:22-24. Later in the book of Joshua, aspects of the Passover ritual reappear in the story of Rahab, the prostitute in Jericho who rescues the spies (Joshua 2). In this story, the blood of the Passover lamb is symbolized as a red thread in the window to her home, which will protect those inside from the destruction of the city and the genocide of the residents in the Israelite attack. Like the blood of the Passover, the red thread wards off death from the collapse of the walls; it guards the inner space of Rahab's house; and it allows the family members of Rahab who remain in her house to survive the execution of the ban on the city of Jericho. The common theme in the stories of Zipporah, the Passover ritual, and Rahab is the warding off of a divine attack through blood, or in the case of Rahab, a red thread.

▮ THE TEXT IN THE INTERPRETIVE TRADITION

The Passover was a central ritual of self-identity in the Second Temple period. Ezra 6 recounts the returning exiles' observance of the Passover in Judah. But unlike the story in Exodus, in Ezra it is the Levites, rather than the individual family members, who administer Passover and slaughter the lamb. The ritual solidifies the identity of the returning exiles. The importance of the festival is further evidenced by a fifth-century-BCE letter from Jews in Elephantine, a colony in Egypt; in the letter, the senders request specific instructions about ritual observance of the Passover (Cowley, *Aramaic Papyri of the Fifth Century B.C.*, 60–65).

The observance of Passover was institutionalized during the Second Temple period into the Seder service, in which participants identify with the story of liberation from Egypt by eating the Passover lamb, unleavened bread, and bitter herbs. This event is central in the Gospel tradition as the Last Supper of Jesus and his disciples (Matthew 26; Mark 14; Luke 22; John 13–17; 19). Hellenistic Jewish authors like Philo reinterpreted the Passover from a meal that celebrates liberation to a spiritual event in which the soul is purified from physical passions (*Spec. Laws* 2.2.29). The author of *Jubilees* concentrates more narrowly on the linking of Passover and the death of the firstborn, noting that proper observance will spare the participant from death (49:15).

▌THE TEXT IN CONTEMPORARY DISCUSSION

The Passover continues to represent a ritual of liberation in contemporary interpretation. Göran Larsson, for example, describes the Passover as a celebration of relationship, renewal, and remembrance. The blood on the doorpost symbolizes "the bond between God and Israel and between every member of the people, a bond later sealed through the covenantal blood at Sinai" (82). The ritual, moreover, creates unity through time in the continued observance of the Passover haggadah as an act of remembrance of Israel's liberation from slavery (Larsson, 81–92). Other contemporary interpretations of the Passover explore the ambiguity of the ritual, focusing on the violence of the story. David Mamet's novel *Passover* is a conversation between a woman and her granddaughter while they prepare the Passover meal. The conversation models the need for intergenerational teaching of the exodus that Moses commands in the original participants. The grandmother's story extends beyond the biblical account to include her experience of pogroms, thus highlighting the continued oppression of Jews throughout Western history and the ambiguity of liberation when it is viewed as a singular event in history.

Still other contemporary writers and artists reflect on the ambiguous role of the deity in killing the Egyptian firstborn in an act of liberation for the Israelites. How could such an action on innocent children be good or liberating? William Blake's watercolor *Pestilence: Death of the Firstborn* accentuates the ambiguity of the divine slaughter of the Egyptian firstborn. In the drawing, the agent of death dominates; mothers hover over their dead children while a small angel stands in a doorway seemingly overwhelmed by the agent of death. The scene forces the reader to view the Passover as a complex ritual that gives life but also takes it away. Recent interpreters have also underscored the ambiguous and selective role of remembrance that is central to the Passover, especially as it influences the reader's view of Egypt. Regina Schwartz highlights the fluid, selective, and political role of memories: "They are forged to further some agenda even as they forge agendas" (158). Jan Assmann provides an illustration of Schwartz's general conclusion by focusing on the story of the exodus from Egypt. This story of Israelite liberation takes on a larger role in the history of interpretation, especially in the evaluation of the Egyptians in Western cultural history. Assmann concludes that the historical memory of Egypt in the Bible is reduced in Western culture to the "other," who is rejected, discarded, and abandoned (1–22, 208–12). This is symbolized strikingly in the death of the Egyptian children, who become expendable in the liberation of the Israelites from Egypt.

Exodus 13:17—15:21: Destruction of the Egyptian Army in the Red Sea

▌THE TEXT IN ITS ANCIENT CONTEXT

Exodus 13:17—15:21 recounts the Israelite flight from Egypt to the Red Sea (13:17—14:4); the pursuit of Pharaoh and his army (14:5-14); the destruction of Pharaoh and the Egyptian army in the Red Sea (14:15-31); and the celebration of the event in two songs by Moses and Israel

(15:1-18) and by Miriam and the Israelite women (15:19-21). The story of YHWH's control over the Red Sea in defeating Pharaoh and his army is influenced by liturgical motifs from ancient Near Eastern religion, where the sea represents the forces of nature at war with the god of creation. The Canaanite god of fertility, Baal, wars against the chaotic forces of sea and river, the god Yamm-Nahar (Yamm = "sea" and Nahar = "river"; *CTA* 2). The defeat of the sea god Yamm-Nahar signals the victory of order, creation, and fertility in Canaanite religion. The Babylonian god Marduk splits the sea monster Tiamat as the initial act of creation in the mythology *Enuma Elish* (*ANET* 60–99). The ancient Israelite writers know the tradition of the chaotic sea. The sea is often an opponent to God, representing chaotic forces that seek to undo creation. Isaiah 27:1 associates the sea with the sea dragon, the serpent, and Leviathan in celebrating YHWH's punishment of the sea monster. But the mythology of the sea is also historicized in Isa. 5:30 as the army of the enemy, who is compared to "the roaring of the sea." The most prominent blending of the mythological motifs of the sea and the historical enemy is the story of the exodus. Exodus 13:17—14:31 employs the mythology of the chaotic sea to describe the final conflict between YHWH and Pharaoh. YHWH dries up the sea with an east wind, recalling Baal's conflict with Yamm (14:21). At the same time, the sea is split into two walls of water, mirroring the action of Marduk against Tiamat (14:22). In both instances, the sea becomes a weapon of YHWH against Pharaoh, who represents a historicized form of chaos.

The miraculous event of salvation at the sea in Exodus is celebrated in two victory songs, the more extended version of Exod. 15:1b-18 and the shorter account in Exod. 15:21b. Both describe the power of YHWH over the sea in destroying the enemy. There is no indication that the songs were associated with Moses or Miriam in their original composition. Yet both are now thoroughly embedded in the larger narrative context. Each song has an introduction naming the singers as Moses and Miriam. The introductions function much like psalm titles, in which songs become associated with events in the life of a hero. The two songs conclude the story of the conflict between Pharaoh and YHWH: first, Moses and the Israelites sing a song to YHWH in Exod. 15:1-18, the Song of the Sea; and then Miriam and the women sing a song in Exod. 15:19-21, the Song of Miriam.

▌ THE TEXT IN THE INTERPRETIVE TRADITION

The power of YHWH to save Israel by controlling the sea remains a central theme in the biblical tradition (e.g., Ps. 77:15-20; Mic. 7:14-17). YHWH remains the primary character in the reuse of the exodus story throughout the Hebrew Bible. Isaiah 52:9-11 refers to the exodus from Egypt as the time when YHWH defeated the sea monster Rahab by drying up the sea. Isaiah 43:16 celebrates the power of God as savior and creator by describing YHWH as the one "who makes a way in the sea, / a path in the mighty waters," suggesting the imagery of the exodus. Isaiah 11:15-16 echoes the same theme, only the sea in this text is described as "the River," recalling the close association of Sea-River (Yamm-Nahar) in Canaanite mythology. In Isaiah 11, the splitting of the River results in seven channels of water (echoing the seven heads of Leviathan), rather than the two walls of water in Exodus 14. Psalm 114 also memorializes God's power over sea and river. The sea flees before the presence of God and the Jordan River turns back.

Hellenistic Jewish authors shift the focus of interpretation to idealize the human characters in the story, especially Moses. Moses is portrayed as a hero by Philo, who accentuates Moses' leadership role (*Mos.* 1.29–32). Josephus, too, underscores the faith of Moses and his courage as a leader in bringing about the exodus (*Ant.* 2.15–16). The idealization of Moses is also evident in the images at Dura-Europos, where Moses is prominent in the representations of the exodus. Gregory of Nyssa wrote the *Life of Moses* to provide the ideal of virtue and perfection in the fourth century CE. Moses is presented as a general in the Old English poem "Exodus" in the medieval Junius Manuscript. Moses continues to be the central figure in the study of the exodus into the modern period, especially in critical-biblical scholarship, which seeks to explore the social, political, and religious environment of the period of the exodus. Hugo Gressmann explored the oral traditions associated with Moses, setting the stage for a series of studies of Moses throughout the modern period (e.g., Buber; Rad; Auerbach).

▌ THE TEXT IN CONTEMPORARY DISCUSSION

Two topics confront the contemporary reader of the salvation of the Israelites at the Red Sea. The first issue is the problem of violence in the story of the salvation, especially the destruction of the Egyptian army. The text accounts for the divine destruction of the enemy with the motif of the hardening of Pharaoh's heart. This motif is developed throughout the story of the plagues to account for the increased violence on the people and the land of Egypt. The motif comes to a climax at the Red Sea, when Pharaoh leads the Egyptian army into the sea in pursuit of Israel, leading to their destruction. The exercise of divine violence on the Egyptian army, the Egyptian firstborn, or even the indigenous nations of Canaan as part of the salvation of the Israelites presents an ethical problem throughout the story of the exodus. Must the story of liberation for Israel be linked with the death of the "other"?

The second theme is the role of women in the exodus story. Feminist interpreters in the late twentieth century refocused attention on Miriam as the hero of the exodus, as compared to Moses' dominance in the history of interpretation. The central problem of the research is how to recover the tradition of Miriam and to reinterpret the relationship between the Song of the Sea (Exod. 15:1-18) and the Song of Miriam (Exod. 15:19-21). Many solutions emerge. The assumption of one line of feminist research is that patriarchal dominance in the formation of the text and in the history of interpretation has suppressed the role of Miriam in the story of the exodus. The task of feminist interpreters, therefore, is to recover the heroic role of Miriam that threatened patriarchal detractors who "tabooed her to death, seeking to bury her forever in disgrace" (Tribe 1994, 179). Her heroic role is evident in "bits and pieces of story awaiting discovery" (Trible 1994, 183). These stories include her heroic role in the birth story of Moses, where she functions as his savior (Exod. 2:1-10); her prophetic role in interpreting the exodus (Exod. 15:19-21); and the suppression of her voice in the conflict over prophetic authority (Num. 12:2-14). Ursula Rapp concludes that Miriam represents a prophetic group in the Second Temple period that lost authority over time. Some interpreters have reevaluated the literary relationship between the two songs, giving prominence to Miriam's songs in Exodus 15 (van Dijk-Hemmes, 200–206; Janzen, 187–99). Other feminist interpreters have explored anew the role of women and song in ancient Israel, emphasizing the significant role of woman as leaders in musical performance (Meyers 1994, 207–30). Still others emphasize the dynamic role of tradition as midrash, where contemporary feminist interpreters are able to influence tradition by bringing Miriam out of the shadows through imaginative reenactment with the sacred texts (Bach, 243–58).

Exodus 15:22—18:27: The Journey as a Rite of Passage

▌ THE TEXT IN ITS ANCIENT CONTEXT

The conflict between YHWH and Pharaoh in the land of Egypt (Exod. 7:8—15:18) gives way to the Israelite journey with God in the wilderness (Exod. 15:22—18:27). The central theme shifts from the exercise of divine power against Pharaoh to the presence of YHWH with Israel. The initial stories in the wilderness explore the special relationship between YHWH and Israel made evident through episodes of testing and struggle. The Israelites experience danger immediately in the wilderness in the form of poisoned water (Exod. 15:22-26), absence of food (Exod. 15:27—16:35), and lack of water (Exod. 17:1-7). In each instance, YHWH provides for the people, purifying the poisoned water, providing manna for food, and drawing water from a rock.

After the stories of testing, the narrative broadens in perspective to explore the Israelites' relationship to other nations in two stories. First, the Amalekites are identified as an enemy who attacks Israel on the journey (Exod. 17:8-16); and, second, the Midianites are presented as an ally who provides leadership in worship (Exod. 18:1-12) and in the administration of law (Exod. 18:13-27). The two perspectives toward these foreign nations are recounted in the story of King Saul in 1 Samuel 15. He wages a holy war against the Amalekites, because of their hostility to the Israelites in the wilderness journey, but he spares the Kenites (a.k.a. the Midianites) because of their hospitality. Both nations are difficult to locate in the geography of the ancient Near East, yet each is associated with the southern desert region. Moses first encounters the Midianites in the wilderness when he flees Egypt. The Amalekites are identified as descendants of Esau (Genesis 36).

The war against the Amalekites (Exod. 17:8-16) moves quickly through three scenes: attack (17:8), war (17:9-13), and remembrance for vengeance (17:14-16). The Amalekites attack the Israelites at Rephidim. The motive for the attack is not stated. The location of Amalekites in the southern desert may signify confrontation as the Israelites journey through their territory. Moses responds by calling the people to participate in war for the first time. Throughout the events of the exodus, the Israelites never participate actively in war; in fact, YHWH did not judge the people ready for war (Exod. 13:17). Now, in the wilderness, the people are commanded to wage war, with Joshua as their leader. The battle story, however, focuses on Moses, not Joshua. Moses informs Joshua that he will ascend to the summit of the hill with the staff of God. The war against the Amalekites is regulated at the summit of the hill by the action of Moses with the divine staff. When the hands of Moses and the staff are raised, Joshua prevails. When his hands are lowered, the tide of the battle turns, and the Amalekites gain the upper hand. The circumstances indicate that the power to wage war resides in the staff of God, not in Moses, and certainly not in Joshua or the Israelite warriors. The eventual inability of Moses to raise his arms underscores further that the power in the battle does not reside with him, but with God. Victory is achieved when Aaron and Hur assist Moses, providing a seat of stone and hold his arms up until the setting of the sun. The conclusion of the story is a divine speech to Moses, which turns from the present battle to the future genocide of the Amalekites. YHWH swears vengeance against the Amalekites and predicts the elimination of their memory from under heaven (Exod. 18:14). The genocide of the Amalekites is prophesied again by Balaam (Num. 24:20) and repeated by Moses to the second generation (Deut. 25:19) before YHWH commands Saul to fulfill the oath by exterminating the nation through the execution of the ban (1 Sam. 15:3).

▋ THE TEXT IN THE INTERPRETIVE TRADITION

The divine command to exterminate the Amalekites has given rise to a long tradition of interpretation. The rabbis struggled over the problem of divine justice and morality in the command for the extermination of a nation (*b. Yoma* 22b). In the second century CE, Rabbi Judah the Prince underscored Amalek's near fanatical intention to attack the Israelites to account for the divine command, traveling through five nations to achieve the goal (*Mekilta de-Rabbi Ishmael Amalek* 1). The evil intention of the Amalekites continued to be a subject of reflection in the fifteenth century. Abrabanel underscored that there was no reason for the Amalekite attack, thus accounting for their own destruction. Earlier, in the thirteenth century, Nahmanides explained that the Amalekites did not fear God after hearing about the exodus, thus prompting God to seek their destruction.

A more prominent development in the history of interpretation is the identification of the Amalekites with opponents or enemies of one sort or another through time (Feldman). In the *War Scroll* from Qumran Cave 1 (1QM), the Amalekites are identified as the Sons of Darkness, who battle against the Sons of Light (that is, the sons of Levi, Judah, and Benjamin). Philo, however, associates the Amalekites with the Phoenicians (*Mos.* 1.218); Josephus, with the residents of Petra (*Ant.* 3.39–61). The enemy was also spiritualized. The Zohar, for example, states that Amalek is Satan rather than a historical nation.

Yet the practice of identifying the Amalekites with a historical enemy continues. This is perhaps most evident in the tradition in which Haman, the evil protagonist in the book of Esther, is identified as a descendant of Agag, the king of the Amalekites (*b. Sanh.* 96b). The defeat of Jewish enemies, particularly Haman, is celebrated during the festival of Purim. A similar practice is evident in Christian tradition in a letter from Epiphanius to Jerome. Epiphanius encourages Jerome to continue his work of translation while also identifying Origen and his Alexandrian disciples as the Amalekites, who must be destroyed (*Letter 91 from Epiphanius to Jerome*). The process of identifying the enemy with the Amalekites continues throughout Western history. Beginning in the medieval period and continuing into the nineteenth century, some Jewish authorities identified the Armenians as the Amalekites. The Zohar introduces a more symbolic and supernatural interpretation of the struggle between good and evil (3.206–7; Sagi, 330–31). Christians identified Muslims as the Amalekites during the Crusades. In responding to a plea for mercy from Adolf Eichmann's wife, Itzchak Ben Zvi quoted Samuel's words in Sam. 15:33 to King Agag the Amalekite to underscore the inevitability of Eichmann's impending destruction.

▌ THE TEXT IN CONTEMPORARY DISCUSSION

Alastair Hunter states the problem of the divine curse on Amalek in contemporary discussion: "We ignore at our peril the potential for violence built into the Bible" (92–108). She notes that the Amalekites become the archetypal victims in the Pentateuch, in that the divine instruction to destroy the nation is given on several different occasions, while the circumstances of the war are never clearly stated. In spite of the lack of clarity over the conflict, the presentation of the Amalekites illustrates the rhetorical device of portraying the victim or cursed nation as the aggressor in order to justify their elimination. The result is that the Amalekites exist only to be exterminated. The literary strategy of the Bible to victimize the Amalekites as the cursed enemy has allowed later readers to empty the term of its historical meaning, so that it can be reappropriated in new ways to disenfranchise others. The result is that the word *Amalekite* becomes a cipher for the enemy, whomever it may be. As a consequence, the perpetuation of violence becomes a religious obligation, whether it be the "war on terror" or the "politics of Amalek" waged by West Bank settlers against Palestinians (Masalha, 127–31).

Exodus 19:1-19: Revelation and Covenant

▌ THE TEXT IN ITS ANCIENT CONTEXT

The wilderness journey halts in Exodus 19 when the Israelites arrive at Mount Sinai to receive the revelation of law and to enter into a covenant relationship with YHWH. The theme of covenant is introduced in the divine proposal (19:1-8), which leads to the initial revelation of law on the Mount Sinai (19:9-19). The research on the meaning of covenant in ancient Israelite religion is extensive. George Mendenhall interprets covenant through comparison to Hittite suzerainty treaties, a form of diplomatic contracts in the ancient Near East between unequal parties. The suzerainty treaty includes (1) the identification of the suzerain or lord, (2) a historical prologue listing the acts of salvation of the suzerain toward the vassal, (3) the treaty stipulations or laws required of the vassal, (4) the provisions for reading the treaty, (5) the witnesses to the treaty, and (6) the curses resulting from disobedience and the blessings arising from obedience (1955, 1–50). By way of its analogy to the political setting in the ancient Near East, the suzerainty treaty provides a framework for interpreting the covenant relationship between YHWH and the Israelites. When the form is applied to Exod. 19:3-6, the call for the Israelites to see a past action of YHWH (19:4) is identified as the historical prologue and the offer of covenant (19:5a) as the legal stipulation. The Israelites accept the divine offer and enter into covenant with YHWH.

"Covenant," according to Steven McKenzie, is the main biblical image for the distinctive relationship between the people of Israel with God (9). It signifies that the Israelites are a "chosen" or "elect" people, meaning they are special to God and thus distinct from all other people in the world. The imagery of being a chosen people emerges from the promise of reward (19:5b-6), which follows the divine offer of covenant (19:5a). If the Israelite people accept the offer of covenant (19:5a), YHWH promises that they will be a "personal possession" of God separated from the other nations.

The translation "personal possession" is from the Hebrew word *segullah*. There is debate over the meaning of this term, however. Some argue that the term conveys inherent value, best translated as "treasured property." In this case, the "chosenness" of the people arises from their distinctive character. Another interpretation, however, is that *segullah* simply describes the quality of the promised relationship between Israel and God, in which case the translation would be "personal possession." Carl Friedrich Keil and Franz Delitzsch represent the first interpretation indicating that *segulla* does "not denote property in general but valuable property" (96). The resulting meaning of the divine promise is that "although all the earth belongs to God," the Israelite people are of more value; hence they are a "treasured possession" (see NIV). Moshe Greenberg favors the second choice, noting that the Akkadian word *sikiltum*, the equivalent of Hebrew *segullah*, is an economic term designating private property regardless of its value (173). The same meaning is evident in two economically oriented texts in the Hebrew Bible, where David (1 Chron. 29:3) and the Preacher (Eccles. 2:8) refer to "private property." The second interpretation emphasizes the relationship between God and the Israelite people as a "treasured possession." In this interpretation, the special relationship between YHWH and Israel forces the people to take on a special role of service to the world as priests. The two interpretations agree that covenant designates the Israelites as a chosen people and hence special in some way from all of humans; they disagree, however, over whether the distinctiveness of the people is based on their character or on their special mission to the world.

▌ THE TEXT IN THE INTERPRETIVE TRADITION

The themes of covenant and the chosenness of Israel give rise to a long history of interpretation. In the Second Temple period, the nature of the Israelite's chosen status swings between two poles, one of which emphasizes the special quality of the people, while the other focuses instead on the ethical responsibility that accompanies election and covenant. The book of *Jubilees* describes the special status of Israel as a holy people and a holy seed, which stems from the ancestors, especially Jacob (*Jub.* 2:20, 22; 15:30-31; 16:26; 22:27; 25:18), thus emphasizing the physical descent of the people. The Qumran community followed the same line of interpretation, but they limited the interpretation of being chosen to a remnant represented by their community (1QM 14; CD 3–15). Philo also describes three categories of the "nations of the souls" to explore the nature of election and covenant: the children of the earth (sons of Adam); the offspring of virtue (sons of heaven); and the chosen race of Israel (sons of God) (*Post.* 91–92). Although these categories suggest a qualitative difference between Israel and the nations, he also emphasizes the role of wisdom in defining the different souls of the nations (*Spec. Laws* 4.180–81), thus creating a degree of ambiguity in defining what it means to be chosen of God. In the writing of the apostle Paul, the interpretation of chosenness becomes even more inclusive, since faith becomes the criterion of election (Rom. 10:4, 12-13; Gal. 3:28; 4:22-26). Thus to be chosen, according to Paul, is not tied to the inherent quality or identity of a person or a past promise to the ancestors, but to an ethical action defined as faith. This broad view of divine chosenness is accompanied with a polemic against a narrower view of covenant and election in Second Temple Judaism. Paul forms the argument by contrasting the "old covenant" of Moses, with its narrow view of the chosen people of Israel, to the "new covenant" of Jesus, in which the true Israel is chosen by faith.

The polemical nature of the debate on covenant and chosenness between emergent Christianity and Second Temple Judaism influenced subsequent interpretations in the church fathers and in rabbinic tradition. In the *Dialogue with Trypho*, Justin Martyr builds on the contrast between the old and new covenants and the implications of this distinction for understanding election and the concept of being chosen. The old covenant is the Mosaic covenant of the law, which is surpassed by the new covenant in Christ, suggesting a theology of supersession. The same line of interpretation continues in Irenaeus (*Adversus haereses* 4.5.1; 12.1–5, 13–16), Clement of Alexandria (*Stromata* 4.5.327), and even in Augustine (*Ennarationes in Psalmos* 104.7). Each emphasizes that the new covenant signifies an election based on faith and obedience, which is open to any human. The rabbinic interpretation moves in a different direction. The rabbis state that there are covenants and obligations that influence all humans, but the notion of chosenness in covenant is restricted to Jews and creates its own special sense of obligation (*'Abot* 3:14). Even with this narrower view of chosenness, the emphasis in the rabbinic interpretation remains on obligation, not privilege, although a more biological interpretation is also infrequently suggested (e.g., Judah Ha-Levi, 1086–1145 ce).

■ THE TEXT IN CONTEMPORARY DISCUSSION

The theology of covenant and chosenness presents a range of problems in contemporary discussion, where pluralism and interfaith dialogue are important values for religious health. Reuven Firestone explains: "Although God created all humanity in the divine likeness, why is one community of God's loving creatures privileged over all the others? Even with humanity's repeated failures to live up to that likeness without ongoing heavenly intervention, why would a loving God not find a way to allow all of humankind to benefit directly from engagement with the Divine?" (10). In addition to the theological problems noted by Firestone, there are also social challenges. The concept of being divinely chosen as a special people encourages superiority, while also creating the category of the "nonchosen" other, who may in turn also claim the same special, chosen status. Such competing claims create social conflict, violence, and persecution. The challenge of the biblical teaching on covenant, with its confession of being chosen by God, is finding a way to retain the experience of uniqueness that is central to religion while also allowing others to claim their own unique experience of chosenness.

Exodus 19:20—20:20: The Decalogue

■ THE TEXT IN ITS ANCIENT CONTEXT

The central content in the revelation of God at Mount Sinai is the Decalogue. Once the Israelites agree to enter into covenant with YHWH (Exod. 19:1-8), the deity descends to the summit of Mount Sinai (Exod. 19:9-19) and reveals the Decalogue to the people (Exod. 20:1-17). The title, Decalogue (also known in English as the Ten Commandments), derives from the Hebrew designation of the law code as the "ten words" used at the close of covenant renewal (Exod. 34:28) and repeated twice in the book of Deuteronomy (4:13; 10:4). The three texts share motifs that underscore the prominence of the law code. The "ten words" derive from God (Deut. 4:13). They form the basis for covenant (Exod. 34:28; Deut. 4:13), and they are written down on two tablets (Exod. 34:28; Deut. 4:13; 10:4), thus forming the core of Scripture. The Decalogue serves as a constitutional law for the Israelites, providing a foundational perspective on God and human relationships.

The authors of the book of Exodus envisioned law as representing the essence of their religion. God promises the Israelites at the outset of the wilderness journey that the revelation of law will be their source of health (Exod. 15:22-27). And the divine origin of the law is made explicit at the divine mountain. God states to Moses in Exod. 24:12: "I will give you the tablets of stone, with the law and the commandment, which I have written for their instruction." Samuel Greengus notes that the anchoring of law in religion may be unique to the legal tradition of Israel in the ancient Near East (4:243–52). The result according to Z. W. Falk is that law and spirituality become merged into one in the formation of the Hebrew Bible. He writes: "The commandments are meant not only as norms of behavior but also as objects of contemplation to lead toward the perception and love of God" (130).

▮ THE TEXT IN THE INTERPRETIVE TRADITION

The designation of the Decalogue as "ten words," written on "two tablets," provides clues to its literary structure. Yet the Hebrew Bible neither spells out the specific laws nor their organization into two sections. The ambiguity has given rise to a history of interpretation, especially concerning the number of the laws in Exod. 20:2-6 and in 20:17. In Jewish tradition, the self-revelation of God (20:2) is the first commandment. It is interpreted as a demand for faith in the deity. The prohibition against graven images (20:3-6) is the second law. The distribution of the commands on two tablets is evenly divided between 20:2-12 (five commands: self-revelation, idols, divine name, Sabbath, honor of parents) and 20:13-17 (five commands: murder, adultery, theft, false witness, coveting). The early church read the Decalogue differently. Exodus 20:2 became the prologue to the law code, with the prohibition against images the first command (20:3-6). The Roman church retained the number ten by interpreting the command against coveting (20:17) as two laws. The early church also changed the division of the law code. The first tablet was restricted to three commands (20:3-11), with seven on the second tablet (20:7-17). John Calvin provides yet another interpretation, separating 20:3-6 into two commands: exclusive worship of YHWH (v. 3) and a prohibition on idolatry (vv. 4-6). He retains the number ten by reading the command against coveting (v. 17) as one law as in Jewish tradition (1975, 2.8). Calvin also follows the Jewish division of the Decalogue, separating the law code into two tablets of five laws each (20:3-12 and 20:13-17).

The perspective on human rights in the Decalogue and its demand for singular allegiance to God echoes throughout Scripture and in ongoing Jewish and Christian tradition. The Decalogue is prominent throughout the Pentateuch. In addition to Exod. 20:1-17, the full text also occurs in Deuteronomy 5, with additional references throughout the book (Deuteronomy 4, 9, 10), including the curses for breaking the covenant in Deut. 27:15-26. The Decalogue is also central in the Priestly legislation. The version of the Decalogue in Exodus 20 indicates editing by the Priestly historian, especially in the law of Sabbath observance (Exod. 20:8-11). The result is a P (Exod. 20:1-17) and a D (Deut. 5:6-21) version of the constitutional document. The general character of the laws in the

Decalogue, such as killing, stealing, and lying, makes it difficult to trace a direct influence on other literature. Yet the influence of the Decalogue in Priestly tradition appears to go beyond Exodus 20 and likely includes the laws of holiness in Leviticus 19. The prophets also echo the Decalogue in their preaching. The book of Jeremiah lists ethical commands reminiscent of the Decalogue, warning the Israelite people not to steal, murder, commit adultery, swear falsely, or worship other gods (Jer. 7:9). Hosea includes swearing, lying, murder, stealing, and adultery as unethical actions opposed to the worship of YHWH (Hosea 4:2). The sins of Jerusalem, according to the prophet Ezekiel, include murder; contempt of parents; oppression of the alien, widow, and orphan; slander; adultery; incest; and exploitation of neighbor (Ezek. 22:1-12). The influence of the Decalogue may continue into the Psalms (e.g., Ps. 50:16-20) and perhaps also into the book of Job (Job 24:13-17), where the characterization of the wicked includes many of the laws of the Decalogue.

The influence of the Decalogue continues beyond the Hebrew Bible. It was singled out for daily prayer along with the Shema (Deut. 6:4) in Jewish worship already before the Common Era, and it continues in the liturgy of the Feast of Weeks (*m. Tamid* 4:3; 5:1). Philo of Alexandria reinforced its constitutional character, arguing that the Decalogue contained in essence all the other commands (*Decal.* 154). Direct quotation of the Decalogue is less evident in the teaching of Jesus, although he repeatedly refers to the importance of law, referring to many of the commands from the Decalogue in the Sermon on the Mount (Matthew 5–7). Jesus summarizes the essence of law as love of God above all and love of neighbor as self (e.g., Matt. 19:16-19; 22:39; Mark 10:17-20; 12:28-31). The law takes on a more polemical role in the teaching of the apostle Paul (see Gal. 3:13; 4:24). Yet he too appears to cite the Decalogue in Rom. 13:8–9, listing adultery, murder, stealing, coveting as well as "any other commandment" as actions incompatible with love.

■ THE TEXT IN CONTEMPORARY DISCUSSION

The interpretation of the Decalogue as natural law in early Christian tradition placed the law code within the world of Hellenistic ethics, where it played a role in shaping Western culture from the interpretations of Justin Martyr and Thomas Aquinas, through Luther and Calvin. The interpretation of the Decalogue as a legal resource for a just democratic society continues into the present time, as is evident in the research of Walter Harrelson and Paul Lehmann. Both authors argue that the Ten Commandments are more than religious law for believing Christians and Jews; they provide a moral foundation for our common secular society.

The Christian interpretation of the universal truth of the Decalogue for fashioning a just society has created unintended challenges in the contemporary discussion of the law code. Two problems are prominent: the first is the need to separate religion from government in order to ensure that all religions are treated equally under the law; and, second, the secular interpretation of the Decalogue as universal law about human rights threatens to misinterpret the very nature of the Ten Commandments as religious law.

First, the separation of religion and state: Increasingly, religious conservatives are wedding religion and state by arguing that the government should actively promote public morality by advancing specific religious themes and symbols in public life. The public display of the Decalogue in prominent government buildings is at the center of this debate, evident in two legal cases: *Van Orden v. Perry* challenges a large monument of the Ten Commandments in Austin, Texas; and *McCreary County v. ACLU of Kentucky* challenges the display of the Ten Commandments in two county courthouses in Kentucky. The debate is not about the religious significance of the Decalogue for Christians and Jews, but whether a secular democracy should privilege one religious symbol over other religious traditions.

Second, the interpretation of the Decalogue as religious or secular law: The Decalogue has become so central to Western culture, according to Michael Coogan, that we are in danger of blurring its religious and secular role (2). Law in the Hebrew Bible resists simple definition, but it was never intended to function outside of religion. David Daube concludes: it is clear that "the authors of the Bible saw law as part of religion" (1). Law embraces many words and metaphors in the Hebrew Bible, including Torah, judgment, statute, commandment, testimony, and covenant, but none of these of these terms is intended to separate law from religion. The dynamic and religious character of law is conveyed through metaphors of motion and speech. Law is alive, deriving from the voice of God. The words are codified in writing. Bernard Jackson cautions that ancient laws function differently than the modern Western model of law, where the legal judgments of the court are comprehensive and clearly expressed in written language available to participants in advance (70–92). Ancient legal practice was not tied exclusively to written laws, but depended on the context of a situation to resolve dispute. The less specific law or judgment created a roadway through life on which humans were able to walk. The vocabulary indicates the breadth of the subject matter, while the metaphors underscore the dynamic quality of law as a religious resource for change through time. Jewish legal interpretation employs the metaphor of walking, *halakah*, to underscore the dynamic character of religious law in ongoing tradition.

The contemporary debate over the Decalogue and its role in public life is at the center of the larger debate over the separation of all religions from government in modern democratic societies. The separation protects the rights of minority religions, while also ensuring that secular government does not subvert the majority religions by making them the basis of a national civil religion.

Exodus 20:21—23:33: The Book of the Covenant

■ THE TEXT IN ITS ANCIENT CONTEXT

The public revelation of the Decalogue (Exod. 20:1-17) is followed by the private revelation of the book of the covenant (Exod. 20:24—23:31). The name for the second law code derives from Exod. 24:7, where Moses is described as writing the law in the "book of the covenant." The laws of the book of the covenant (Exod. 21:1—23:19) are framed by an introduction (Exod. 20:21-26) and a conclusion (Exod. 23:20-33). The laws themselves divide between the *mishpatim*, or casuistic laws (Exod. 21:2—22:17), and the *debarim*, which include a variety of legal statements and divine speeches (22:18-23:1).

Slave laws are central to the book of the covenant. The initial legislation in the law code concerns debt slavery of Hebrew men and women (Exod. 21:2-11), and consists of two slave laws.

Exodus 21:2-6 focuses on the conditions of service and release of Hebrew males from debt slavery; while 21:7-11 outlines the legal rights of a Hebrew female concubine or slave-bride. The difference between the two laws is the absence of release for the female slave as compared to the male. Slave laws for non-Hebrew persons continue throughout the book of the covenant. Laws regulating slaves reappear in three other sections of the book of the covenant: the law protecting a slave from abuse (any slave hurt by an owner is given freedom as compensation for the damage, Exod. 21:26-27), the property rights of a slave master (if a slave is gored by another person's ox, the slave owner must be compensated for the damaged property, Exod. 21:32), and the law of Sabbath rest for slaves (Exod. 23:10-12). The repetition between the Sabbath release of debt slaves (Exod. 21:2-11) and the law of Sabbath rest for slaves is striking (Exod. 23:10-12), suggesting literary design in the composition of the book of the covenant. More recent studies have identified additional structures in the distribution of the slave laws in the book of the covenant (Dohmen, Exodus 19–40, 150). The slave laws organize Exod. 21:2-27: the laws of release (Exod. 21:2-11 and 26-27) form the outer frame, with the law on the assault of slaves (Exod. 21:20-21) at the center. The protection of debt slaves (Exod. 21:2-11) and the protection of the resident alien and poor (Exod. 22:21-25) may also frame the first half of the book of the covenant. The psychological identification with the resident alien from the Israelite experience of slavery in Egypt (Exod. 23:9) certainly reinforces the emphasis on protecting slaves.

The slave laws in the ancient Near East provide a broader vantage point for interpreting the role of the slave laws in the structure of the book of the covenant. The frequent comparison to Mesopotamian law in the exegesis of Exod. 21:2-11 indicates the common culture of the legal tradition regulating slavery in the ancient Near East. In addition to the slave laws from Nuzi, the topic is also included in the Laws of Eshnunna, the Laws of Lipit-Ishtar, the Hittite Laws, the Middle Assyrian Laws, the Neo-Babylonian Laws, and, perhaps most significantly, the Laws of Hammurabi (LH), where the laws regarding male and female slaves are also not confined to any one section but appear throughout the law code under a variety of topics. A central presupposition is that slaves are property requiring a series of laws on property damage (any free person damaging a slave must pay compensation, LH 199, see also 213–214, 231), warranty (an epileptic attack within one month of purchase negates the sale of a slave, LH 278), resale (LH 118–19), insurance against improper health care (a surgeon who kills a slave in operation must repay the owner, LH 219, see also 223), theft (LH 7), and workplace compensation (a slave owner is owed one-third *mina* for any slave gored by an ox, LH 252).

Other laws regulate the behavior of slaves, stating the punishment for aiding a slave in an escape (LH 15–20) or in assisting with the removal of a slave brand (LH 226–27). Still other laws address the circumstances by which a person might move between the different social classes from free to slave (debt slavery, LH 117–19) or from slave to free (the laws of redemption, LH 32, 116–19). The laws regulating marriage also address the change of status between free persons and slaves (LH 144, 146–47, 175–76). The slave laws may also play a role in the structure of the Laws of Hammurabi, similar to the book of the covenant, inaugurating a sequence of themes including slavery, bodily injury, commercial law, and family law.

Muhammad Dandamayev summarizes the prominence of slavery in the ancient Near East: The "institution of slavery had a profound influence on the social structure, ideology, law, social psychology, morals and ethics of the various cultures of the Ancient Near East" (6:61). Ancient society was structured in three levels: independent free persons (landowners and craftsmen), semi-independent serfs (laborers for the palace or temple who might also own property), and slaves (human property or chattel). The slave class, according to Boecker, was an "essential factor in the economy" of the ancient world (77–78).

■ THE TEXT IN THE INTERPRETIVE TRADITION

The interpretation of slave laws in the book of the covenant was central in the nineteenth-century debates over slavery in North America. The Episcopal bishop of Vermont John Henry Hopkins defended slavery based on the clear defense of the practice throughout biblical literature. The slave laws in the book of the covenant played an important role in the debate. Advocates for slavery, like Hopkins, cited Exod. 21:2-11 as evidence for the justification of debt slavery; the laws clarified that slavery is sanctioned by God and incorporated into the national constitution of ancient Israel. Albert Barnes represents nineteenth-century interpreters who opposed slavery. He suggests that the starting point for rejecting the biblical teaching on slavery was to deny the authority of the literal meaning of the laws of slavery, as in Exod. 21:2-11, and to qualify the laws by placing them in an ancient setting. For example, slavery was defined as a form of kidnapping, which is forbidden in Exod. 21:16, thus setting the laws of slavery and kidnapping in opposition. The historical context of the slave laws also allowed for the clarification of the contrast between the ancient practice and the nineteenth century. Barnes, for example, noted that the law of debt slavery in Exod. 21:2-11 is a voluntary action that functions as security against poverty, as opposed to the system of slavery in North America, which was based on chattel slavery for economic profit. The law against striking a slave in Exod. 21:20-21 indicated to some antislavery interpreters that ancient Israelite slavery was actually a benevolent institution aimed at the poor, which has nothing in common with modern chattel slavery. The proslavery advocates responded to these arguments by advocating a literal interpretation of the Bible. The literalist interpretation of slavery in the Bible is illustrated by Governor Hammond, who wrote: "But when I show them (the anti-slavery interpreters) that to hold 'bondmen forever' is ordained by God, they deny the Bible, and set up in its place a law of their own making" (quoted in Swartley, 50).

■ THE TEXT IN CONTEMPORARY DISCUSSION

The contemporary discussion of the slave laws in the book of the covenant focuses in particular on the law of the female slave in Exod. 21:7-11. This law describes the sale of a daughter into slavery as a concubine or slave-bride. In this law, the daughter is a commodity, owned by her father. Her economic value is tied to her sexuality. The economic transaction changes the status of the girl from daughter to slave, who becomes the property of the purchaser. The law clarifies further that the master/purchaser may pass his slave-bride on to his son, should he find any fault or displeasure in her.

The emphasis in contemporary discussion of the slave laws is how closely the law of the female slave, as a sexual commodity, mirrors the vast business in human trafficking, where girls are bought and sold in a global marketplace of slavery. Jonathan Tran writes of this practice: "Slavery may be one of the most representative consequences of global capitalism. In the same way that chattel slavery epitomized the period of colonization, so contemporary human trafficking epitomizes the political, economic and social realities of the world in which we find ourselves" (22). As in the biblical law of the slave-bride, the girls in the trafficking business are sexual commodities for males. The United Nations has concluded that the more common form of human trafficking is sexual exploitation (79 percent), followed by forced labor (18 percent). The result is a multimillion dollar industry in which daughters (young virgin girls) are bought in one country for $300 and sold in another for $20,000. In the United States alone, between 100,000 and 300,000 children are yearly being trafficked in the sex industry. The profit in the slave trade of human trafficking is estimated at thirty-two billion dollars, six billion more than the profit of Apple in 2011.

Exodus 24:1—31:18: Sabbath and the Revelation of the Tabernacle

■ The Text in Its Ancient Context

This section describes the ascent of Moses to the summit of Mount Sinai (Exod. 24:1-18) to receive the architectural plans for the tabernacle (Exod. 25:1—31:11). The revelation of the tabernacle will allow Moses to build a copy of God's heavenly home on earth, so that YHWH might dwell with the Israelites (Exod. 25:8-9). The building of the tabernacle creates a sanctuary, or holy place on earth, which, when coupled with holy time in the law of Sabbath (Exod. 31:12-17), will allow for Israel to commune with God through the experience of rest from work on Sabbath. The sequence of temple building and rest is a common motif in ancient Near Eastern religion. Gods rest after they construct their temples (Hurowitz, 330–31). Nabonidus prays to Shamash, calling Ebabaar the "residence of your rest." Also, Enlil and Ea "dwell on a restful dais in a pure dwelling." The relationship of temple building and the god's rest likely influenced the biblical author, but the focus shifts in the construction of the tabernacle from the rest of the deity to that of the people. The result is the emphasis on Sabbath as a day of human rest from work in the profane world.

The origin of Sabbath observance has been extensively researched without firm conclusions. Sabbath observance may be Babylonian in origin (*sab/pattum*), in which case Sabbath is not a weekly day, but perhaps the day of the full moon. Sabbath does occur in ancient Israel along with reference to the full moon (Isa. 1:10-14; Hosea 2:11-15; Amos 8:4-7). Sabbath is mentioned in the story of the prophet Elisha (2 Kgs. 4:23). King Ahaz of Judah is described as dismantling a Sabbath canopy in the temple in the late eighth century. And the Sabbath command appears in the cultic laws of Exod. 23:10-12. The authorship of each of these texts is debated, yet the distribution suggests the observance of some form of Sabbath in the monarchical period, although its centrality in that period of time is not clear. Sabbath observance takes a more prominent role in the exilic and postexilic prophetic literature. Late Jeremiah tradition (Jer. 17:19-27), the exilic prophet Ezekiel (20:8-26;

46:1-12), and postexilic literature in the book of Isaiah (56:2, 6; 58:13; 66:23) forbid work on the Sabbath. The observance of Sabbath also concludes the postexilic book of Nehemiah (13:15-22).

The observance of Sabbath emerges as a central law in the design of the Priestly literature. The foundation for Sabbath observance is established in creation (Gen. 2:1-3). The ideal rhythm of creation is six days of work punctuated by one day of rest. It is lost with the flood and only reappears gradually in the wilderness journey. Sabbath first appears in the cycle of manna (Exod. 16:22-26); it is established as a law in the Decalogue (Exod. 20:8-11); and the penalty for violating the law is outlined after the construction of the tabernacle (Exod. 21:12-17). The law of Sabbath in the Decalogue is humanitarian; it is a day of rest for all humans, slave and free, as well as animals. The rationale derives from creation, when God rested after the six days of creation (Exod. 20:11). The seventh day of rest would be Saturday, not Sunday. Violation of the humanitarian law, however, carries the death penalty: Exod. 31:12-17 states that Sabbath is an eternal covenant and that the violating of the law would require the execution of the offender.

■ THE TEXT IN THE INTERPRETIVE TRADITION

Sabbath observance is central in Jewish tradition. Sabbath begins at sundown on Friday evening and continues until Saturday evening. Sabbath is observed in the home with a dinner, which begins with the kiddush over wine and blessings over the bread. Sabbath commemorates both creation and the redemption of the Jewish people from Egypt, and it provides a glimpse into the messianic age. It is a time for study and reflection. The Talmud lists thirty-nine activities that are forbidden on Sabbath, including agricultural work, baking, housework, extensive writing, and making fires (*m. Shabbat* 7:2). The prohibitions against work are interpreted in distinct ways. For example, Orthodox Jews refrain from all thirty-nine prohibitions; they may forbid turning on electrical items or driving an automobile, although there may be modifications to the restrictions. Reform Judaism allows for more individual choice with regard to Sabbath practice.

Sabbath observance is equally important in Christian tradition. Jesus observed the Sabbath, even though he argued with Jewish leaders about the appropriate restrictions (Matt. 12:1-12; John 5:1-18). The early disciples also observed the Jewish Sabbath (Luke 23; Acts 3; 5; 13; 18). But eventually, sometime between the second to the fourth centuries CE, Christians began to worship on Sunday rather than Saturday, thus designating the first day of the week as the "Lord's Day." The emperor Constantine made the shift in the Christian "day of rest" official with an edict in 321 CE: "All judges and city people and the craftsmen shall rest upon the venerable day of the sun" (Ayer, 1913, 284–85). The edict also indicates that agricultural work is not forbidden, thus introducing a debate in Christian tradition not only over the proper day for Sabbath, but also about restricted activity. Yet, already in the fourth century CE, the church father Augustine spiritualized the Sabbath commandment, allowing for all types of work. Aquinas, however, interpreted the Sabbath command to be in effect for all Christians because it represented moral law. In the Reformation, Calvin and Luther abolished the religious authority of the Sabbath law, but they followed Aquinas in retaining the law of Sabbath on moral grounds. The Westminster Confession demands the cessation of work on the Sunday as well as all thoughts about work (chap. 21, sections 7–8). The Puritans and other seventeenth-century Calvinists emphasized the strict observance of the Sabbath command even further, introducing a Sunday sabbatarianism. In the nineteenth century CE, Seventh-day Adventists retained the seventh day (Saturday) as the day of rest, marking its duration from sunset to sunset. Seventh-day Adventists forbid work, except in times of need to alleviate suffering.

▎ THE TEXT IN CONTEMPORARY DISCUSSION

Contemporary discussion of Sabbath has moved in a very different direction from the traditional concerns about the proper day or the approved activities. The most pressing concern in current reflection on Sabbath is the frantic pace of work and cultural lifestyle of modern society, as well as growing economic injustice in the global economy. In 1998, Pope John Paul II addressed the problem of the frantic lifestyle of modern society in the apostolic letter *Dies Domini*. He cautioned Catholics to resist the "weekend" mentality that has come to dominate modern culture by keeping the Lord's Day holy. Other modern authors expand on the same problem of our fast-paced, work-oriented culture. Wayne Muller, for example, bemoans the relentless emphasis on success and productivity, which deprive contemporary humans from any life rhythm or time for reflection (Muller, 1–12). Abraham Heschel deepens the same perspective, arguing that Sabbath is not an interlude between work, but the climax of living (Heschel, 101). The contemporary discussion moves even further away from the past concern about time and orthodox observance by tying Sabbath to the problems of social justice in the global economy. Richard Lowery argues that Sabbath is about recovering proportion, social solidarity, and economic justice in the global marketplace (Lowery, 1–6). The emphasis on economic justice returns to the central theme of Sabbath law in the Decalogue and in the Jubilee laws (Leviticus 25).

Exodus 32–33: The Golden Calf and the Mediation of Moses

▎ THE TEXT IN ITS ANCIENT CONTEXT

This section describes the construction of the golden calf (Exod. 32:1-6), while Moses is away from the people receiving the tablets of the law at the summit of Mount Sinai. The calf represents the people's request that Aaron make gods for them to replace Moses, because they "do not know what has become of him" (Exod. 32:1). The story moves quickly, recounting the divine rage over the golden calf (Exod. 32:7-14); the destruction of the calf by Moses and the purging of the people by the Levites (Exod. 32:15-29); and the intercession of Moses for the renewed presence of YHWH (Exod. 32:30—33:23).

The construction of the golden calf in Exodus 32 represents Israel's rejection of the covenant, which Moses describes as a "great sin" (Exod. 32:30). But it is difficult to interpret the content of the sin. The golden calf certainly represents the sin of idolatry, since it breaks the second commandment of the Decalogue. The statement of the people, identifying the calf with God, confirms this meaning: "These are your gods, Israel, who brought you out of the land of Egypt" (Exod. 32:4). But the sin of idolatry can be interpreted further. Rabbinic (*m. Abot* 5:18) and New Testament (2 Pet. 2:15) interpreters state that idolatry is more than imaging God in a forbidden manner; it is also a form of human greed—the desire to possess and to control God. This deeper meaning of idolatry is clarified in the parallel account of the golden calf story that takes place during the rise to power of the first northern king, Jeroboam I (1 Kgs. 12:31-32). Jeroboam tries to legitimate his rule by means of religion. To this end, he builds two golden calves and, like Israel in the wilderness, identifies them with God: "Here are your gods, Israel, who brought you up out of the land of Egypt" (1 Kgs. 12:28).

The episode of Israel in the wilderness and that of Jeroboam I are closely related. They provide commentary on each other, clarifying how the golden calf in each story is not only a religious sin but also a political transgression about controlling God through government. The "golden calves" of Jeroboam I represent the apostasy of all monarchs throughout the Deuteronomistic History who sought to justify their rule by anchoring political power in religion. Jeroboam I is guilty of this when he ties his rule with the worship of the golden calves at Bethel and Dan (2 Kgs. 10:29). The biblical authors judge the equation of political power and religion as the sin that leads to the destruction of monarchs (2 Kgs. 17:7-23). The Deuteronomistic History provides a backdrop for interpreting the idolatry of the golden calf in Exodus 32 as a political and religious allegory about the inherent conflict between YHWH and kings. The intrabiblical quotation between Aaron (and the Israelites) and Jeroboam signals that, on one level, the golden calf in the wilderness is the taproot, which will inevitably lead to the political idolatry associated with monarchy in the promised land. In this case, the content of the idolatry is not only imaging God but also worshiping the power of the king over YHWH.

■ THE TEXT IN THE INTERPRETIVE TRADITION

The story of the golden calf is the nearest equivalent to the concept of original sin in postbiblical Jewish literature (Aberbach and Smolar). All subsequent misfortunes that have befallen the Jewish people go back in part to the sin of the calf (*b. Sanh.* 102A). Given the gravity of the sin and its immediacy after the experience of revelation, the rabbis reflected on how the construction of the golden calf was even possible. Solutions include the identification of the guilty party as the "mixed multitude" (Exod. 12:38), who accompanied Israel out of the Egypt, along with the Egyptian magicians Yanos and Yambros (*b. Shab.* 89A). Another possibility was that Moses was late in descending the mountain. The action of Aaron in making the calf also requires explanation; his action may have arisen from fear (pseudo-Philo), perhaps was intensified from the murder of Hur (*Rab. Lev.* 10:3). He may not even have fashioned the calf (*b. Sanh.* 102:2). This is also the conclusion of the Qur'an, where Aaron also does not build the golden calf (sura 20). Instead, a person named Samiri builds the calf, while Aaron warns the people not to worship it.

Early Christian interpreters interpret the golden calf story polemically to illustrate that the Jews had rejected God. The speech of Stephen in Acts employs the story of the golden calf to confirm the Israelite rejection of Moses and God's rejection of Israel (Acts 7:38-43). The idolatry of the golden calf also explained why the Jews lost the covenant (*Epistle of Barnabas* 4.5–9). The polemical reading continues in the church fathers. Ephrem the Syrian interprets Israel's worship of the golden calf as a sign of their permanent impurity (Nat. 14.19).

▮ THE TEXT IN CONTEMPORARY DISCUSSION

The modern period contains a more political and economic interpretation of the golden calf that is also rooted in the critique of monarchy, which is at the heart of the original story. Benjamin Franklin, for example, identified the anti-Federalists opposing the Constitution to be like the Israelites, who worshiped the golden calf and wished to return to Egypt. The political and economic interpretation of the golden calf has continued into the twentieth century. Dietrich Bonheoffer employed the story of the golden calf in critically evaluating the antisemitic policies of Hitler and the complacency of the German church by contrasting the church of Moses, a church committed to the prophetic word, with the church of Aaron, a worldly church that makes its own gods (Bonhoeffer, 243–48). The political and economic reading of the golden calf is extended in the contemporary social context to signify the decadence of excessive wealth. The golden calf is likened to the Wall Street bull. Donna Schaper, for example, describes carrying a golden calf named "Greed" in the Occupy Wall Street movement as signifying the social and economic decadence in the global economy, which points to a contemporary false god.

Exodus 34: Covenantal Renewal

▮ THE TEXT IN ITS ANCIENT CONTEXT

After Israel breaks the covenant in the construction and worship of the golden calf (Exodus 32), the successful mediation of Moses (Exodus 33) leads to covenant renewal and the divine promise of land (Exodus 34). Exodus 34 is divided between a new revelation to Moses (34:1-9), which takes place this time in a cave on the divine mountain, and a new law code (34:10-28). The new revelation to Moses emphasizes the quality of divine grace: YHWH is a "God merciful and gracious, slow to anger, and abounding in steadfast love and faithfulness, keeping steadfast love for the thousandth generation" (34:6-7). Divine grace is the basis on which Moses requests forgiveness: "pardon our iniquity and our sin and take us for your inheritance" (34:9). The use of the word "to inherit" introduces the theme of the promised land, since the word is associated with the promise of land throughout the Pentateuch. The Song of the Sea, for example, identifies the inheritance of God with the divine temple in the midst of the land (Exod. 15:17). The epilogue to the book of the covenant also equates inheritance with the land: "Little by little I will drive them out from before you, until you have increased and possess the land (Exod. 23:30). And during the crisis of the golden calf, Moses reminds God of the divine promise to the ancestors: "all this land that I have promised I will give to your descendants, and they shall inherit it forever" (Exod. 32:13).

The divine promise of land requires a violent conquest of indigenous people. YHWH promises to drive out the residents of the land, identified as Canaanites, Perizzites, Hivites, and Jebusites (Exod. 34:11). Once the indigenous people are conquered, the Israelites are also not allowed to interact with them in any way, either through shared worship or through intermarriage (Exod. 34:12-16). The demand for exclusive loyalty to YHWH provides insight into the theological motivation. The identity of the Israelites, as people who are not indigenous to the land of Canaan, fuels the theological demand that the Israelite nation be culturally and religiously separate from other nations in the land of Canaan and from their religious traditions. The exclusive vision of life in the land achieved through invasion is not the only perspective in the Hebrew Bible; it contrasts, for example, to the portrait of the patriarchs in Genesis who are indigenous to the land and make covenant with their neighbors. Sperling characterizes the biblical conquest tradition as a political allegory to support the utopian goal of religious exclusion. The theme of exclusivity arose in the first section of the epilogue to the book of the covenant (Exod. 23:20-26), when God demands that the Israelite people not worship indigenous gods, focusing in particular on the destruction of their cultic objects (Exod. 23:24). In the same context, God also forbids all covenants with foreign gods (Exod. 23:32). The separate commands reinforce the first two commandments of the Decalogue, which also demand that the Israelites serve no other gods than YHWH (Exod. 20:3 = 23:32) and that they refrain from the worship of idols (Exod. 20:4-6 = 23:24-25). Thus the law of covenant renewal reinforces the earlier law codes, which state that faithful obedience to covenant and the realization of the promised land requires the conquest of the indigenous nations.

▌ THE TEXT IN THE INTERPRETIVE TRADITION

The themes of the promised land and conquest have undergone a wide range of interpretation. The church fathers turned the themes inward through the method of typology. Origen, for example, interprets the conquest of the indigenous nations as spiritual warfare against the "violent impulses of anger and rage" in Christians, which the believer must expel from the "land of promise" (*Hom. Josh.* 1.5–6). He explains: "Within us are the Canaanites; within us are the Perizzites; here are the Jebusites." The promised land is "the land about which the Lord says, 'Blessed are the meek, who will possess the land as their inheritance" (*Hom. Josh.* 2.2).

In the modern period, most interpreters have rejected the typological hermeneutic of the church fathers, favoring instead a more literal reading of the text. As a consequence, the conquest of the indigenous nations and the realization of the promised land take on political meaning, especially under the influence of nationalism and colonization. The pilgrims identified themselves as the new Israel, a chosen people entering the promised land. Thomas Jefferson employed biblical imagery of the promised land in his second inaugural address, calling for help upon the "Being, in whose hands we are, who led our fathers, as Israel of old, from their native land and planted them in a country flowing with all the necessities and comforts of life" (quoted in Cherry, 65). The influence of the theme of the promised land coupled with a sense of Manifest Destiny in colonization goes beyond North America to include the Afrikaners, who understood themselves as God's chosen people and South Africa as the promised land, and more recently in the rise of the modern state of Israel, with the dispute over land with the indigenous Palestinians (Akenson, 76–77, 319–22).

▌ THE TEXT IN CONTEMPORARY DISCUSSION

The contemporary discussion centers on the violence of the theme of conquest as a method for achieving the promised land, especially in the postcolonial, multicultural setting of the twenty-first century. Robert Allen Warrior, a member of the Osage Nation of American Indians, argues that liberation is too often narrowly defined from the perspective of Israelites who function as invaders. He counters that any contemporary discussion of achieving a liberated life in the promised land must begin with the Canaanites, not the Israelites. In the story of the exodus, the Canaanites only have status "as the people that Yahweh removes from the land in order to bring the chosen people" (239). The rights of the indigenous people are overlooked. This is a problem not simply of hermeneutics but also of social history. The conquest of the indigenous nations has worked its way into Americans' consciousness and ideology, sanctifying colonialism as Manifest Destiny. Warrior questions whether "Native Americans and other indigenous people dare trust the same god in their struggle for justice" (Warrior, 240). Musa Dube probes the same hermeneutical problem from the perspective of an indigenous African, who stands outside of the Afrikaner myth of being chosen (Dube, 3–7). Writing from a Palestinian perspective, Edward Said judges the use of the exodus-conquest myth in the rise of the modern state of Israel as an instance of blaming the victim (Said, 161–78); the Palestinian priest Naim Ateek declares that the use of the conquest myth in Joshua to accord "the primary claim over the land to Jews" is an abuse of the Bible (Ateek, 227–28). The historical conflicts drive home the conclusion that the themes of the promised land can inspire liberation and legitimate oppression (Yee 2010).

Exodus 35–40: Building the Tabernacle

■ THE TEXT IN ITS ANCIENT CONTEXT

The building of the tabernacle concludes the literature in the book of Exodus (chaps. 35–40). The final episode recounts how the heavenly vision of the temple that Moses receives on Mount Sinai becomes an earthly reality, allowing God to dwell on earth in the midst of the people of God (Exod. 40:34-38). The construction separates into four parts: the building materials are presented as a freewill offering by the people (35:4-29); the builders, Bezalel and Oholiab, are identified (35:30—36:7); the construction of the tabernacle sanctuary and its furnishings is completed (36:8—38:20); and there is a census and a tax levy to support the tabernacle cult (38:21-31). Once completed, the deity descends into the sanctuary (40:34-38).

The process of building (Exodus 35–40) repeats the earlier divine revelation to Moses (Exodus 25–31), where the theological signification of the tabernacle is stated in Exod. 25:1-9. God commands Moses in Exod. 25:8 to make a sanctuary (*miqdash*). The word "sanctuary" underscores the quality of the building as holy space, deriving from the root "to be holy" (*qadash*). The conclusion to the Song of the Sea (Exod. 15:17) also describes YHWH's temple as a sanctuary constructed by God, not humans. God further describes the tabernacle and its furnishings in Exod. 25:9 as a "pattern" (*tabnit*) "shown" (*mar'eh*) to Moses on Mount Sinai. The meaning of the text is difficult. The word *tabnit* translates as "form, structure, or shape," while *mar'eh* indicates a "vision" or even the "form" of an object. A *tabnit* describes blueprints for the Jerusalem temple (1 Chron. 28:11), and it may even describe the replica of the temple (1 Chron. 28:19). In Num. 8:4, YHWH shows Moses a form or perhaps a copy (*mar'eh*) of the lampstand. The language suggests that the tabernacle is a copy of the heavenly dwelling of God. The purpose of the revelation is to instruct Moses in the building process, with the goal of allowing God to dwell on earth with Israel in a holy place (Exod. 25:8).

The symbolism of the temple as a copy of God's heavenly home creates a web of related themes from ancient Near Eastern religion, which influence the interpretation of the tabernacle sanctuary. The ability of temples to link heaven and earth is symbolized through the mythology of the cosmic mountain. The cosmic mountain represents the meeting place between heaven and earth, and hence the residency of God within the temple. The Canaanite god Baal, for example, invades the created world by taking up residency in his temple on Mount Zaphon. The same is true with YHWH. The Jerusalem temple is located on Mount Zion, which the psalmist describes as the highest of all mountains, because it is the place where YHWH is enthroned and has "shown himself a sure defense" (Ps. 48:3). The book of Exodus ends with the same mythology of the temple and the cosmic mountain, when YHWH takes up residency in the tabernacle at Mount Sinai, providing a holy place, a sanctuary (*miqdash*), that replicates the heavenly temple, thus allowing God to dwell on earth.

■ THE TEXT IN THE INTERPRETIVE TRADITION

The history of interpretation builds on the understanding of the tabernacle as sacred space. Ancient readers used the details of the tabernacle as a means for symbolic interpretation. The author of *1 Enoch*, for example, describes the details of the sanctuary in a vision (14:1-25). The vision includes not only the house but also a foundation of crystal, a ceiling of stars, cherubim, and a fiery throne. Philo identifies the tabernacle with the universe, in which the building represented the spiritual world, while the courtyard is the material; the colors represent the elements of nature, and so forth (*Mos.* 2.15–26). The author of Hebrews reinterprets the tabernacle to describe Christ as the new high priest, who enters the holy of holies and mediates for humans (Hebrews 8). Origen also interprets the sacred space of the tabernacle to reveal the mystery of Christ and the relationship of Christ to the church. He extends the symbolic interpretation further to correlate the metals in the tabernacle with Christian virtues: gold is faith; silver is the word; and bronze is patience (*Hom. Exod.* 9.3). The English Bede wrote an entire commentary on the tabernacle in the eighth century CE. His interpretation relates the tabernacle to the church, the role of the gospel in the world, the proper interpretation of Scripture, and the role of church leaders (*Commentary on the Tabernacle*). The rabbis moved in a different direction, interpreting the tabernacle in relationship to Torah. The revelation of the tabernacle represents the climax in the revelation of the Torah, which is evident in the central place of the ark (*Exod. Rab.* 34.2).

The modern period shifted the focus from the symbolic meaning of the tabernacle to a literal interpretation within the framework of the history of composition. Julius Wellhausen, for example, concluded that the tabernacle never existed, but was a literary fantasy that sought to reinterpret the temple of Solomon. Other interpreters sought to compare the tabernacle with different tents of worship in the ancient world to provide historical background to the literature. Possible comparative material includes the Bedouin worship tents, or *qubbah*; Persian royal tents that functioned as movable palaces; and Egyptian funeral tents (see Homan).

■ THE TEXT IN CONTEMPORARY DISCUSSION

The rise of secularism in contemporary culture challenges the religious meaning of the tabernacle as sacred space. Modernity has not only called into question the role of religion in human experience but also contested the power of sacred space as a resource for channeling the divine presence. As a result, contemporary discussion of the tabernacle is far removed from the ancient symbolic interpretations of the architecture and furnishings, which assumed the power of sacred space. The contemporary questions are whether the sacred is a reality as opposed to profane space and what ritual processes might allow a human to enter the world of the sacred.

Mircea Eliade explores the problem, characterizing the separation between the sacred and the profane as "two modes of being in the world" that give rise to two different qualities of experience. He employs the metaphor of geometry to describe the similarity of experience in the profane or secular world, since geometrical space can be cut and delimited in any direction without qualitative differentiation. Profane experience, like geometry, is "homogeneous space." The sacred, he contends, is a different mode of experience altogether from the homogeneous space of the profane world (Eliade, 14). Arnold van Gennep argues further that the process of leaving the secular world and entering the sacred requires careful rituals of the separation. The rite of passage requires separation from the secular world; the state of transition (or liminality), which opens one to the reality of the sacred; and eventually reincorporation in the profane world, which is now reoriented (15–25).

Works Cited

Ayer, Joseph Cullen. 1913. *A Source Book for Ancient Church History.* New York: Charles Scribner's Sons.

Aberbach, Moshe, and Leivy Smolar. 1968. "The Golden Calf Episode in Postbiblical Literature." *HUCA* 39:91–116.

Akenson, Donald Harman. 1992. *God's Peoples: Covenant and Land in South Africa, Israel, and Ulster.* Ithaca, NY: Cornell University Press.

Assmann, Jan. 1997. *Moses the Egyptian: The Memory of Egypt in Western Monotheism.* Cambridge, MA: Harvard University Press.

Ateek, Naim S. 2006. "A Palestinian Perspective: Biblical Perspectives on the Land." In Sugirtharajah, *Voices from the Margin,* 227–34.

Augustine. 1956. *On Baptism, against the Donatists.* In vol. 4 of *NPNF¹, The Anti-Manichean Writings, the Anti-Donatist Writings.* Translated by J. R. King.

Auerbach, Elias. 1975. *Moses.* Detroit: Wayne State University Press.

Bach, Alice. 1994. "With a Song in Her Heart: Listening to Scholars Listening for Miriam." In *A Feminist Companion to Exodus to Deuteronomy,* edited by Athalya Brenner, 243–58. Sheffield: Sheffield Academic Press.

Blake, William. 1805. *Pestilence: Death of the First Born.* Boston: Museum of Fine Arts.

Bloom, Harold, ed. 1987. *Exodus: Modern Critical Interpretations.* New York: Chelsea House.

Boecker, H. J. 1980. *Law and the Administration of Justice in the Old Testament and Ancient East.* Translated by J. Moiser. Minneapolis: Augsburg.

Bonhoeffer, Dietrich. 1965. *No Rusty Swords: Letters, Lectures and Notes, 1928–1936.* Vol. 1. Edited by Edwin H. Robertson. Translated by Edwin H. Robertson and John Bowden. New York: Harper & Row.

Brenner, Athalya. 1994a. "An Afterword: The Decalogue—Am I an Addressee?" In Brenner, *A Feminist Companion to Exodus to Deuteronomy*, 255–58.

———, ed. 1994b. *A Feminist Companion to Exodus to Deuteronomy.* Sheffield: Sheffield Academic Press.

Browning, Elizabeth Barrett. 1996. *Aurora Leigh: Authoritative Text, Backgrounds and Contexts, Criticism.* Edited by M. Reynolds. New York: W. W. Norton.

Buber, Martin. 1946. *Moses.* Oxford: Oxford University Press.

Calvin, John. 1950. *The Four Last Books of Moses Arranged in the Form of a Harmony.* Vol. 1. Translated by C. W. Bingham. Grand Rapids: Eerdmans.

———. 1975. *Institutes of the Christian Religion: 1536 Edition.* Translated by Ford Lewis Battles. Grand Rapids: Eerdmans.

Cherry, Conrad, ed. 1971. *God's New Israel: Religious Interpretation of American Destiny.* Chapel Hill: University of North Carolina Press.

Childs, Brevard S. 1974. *The Book of Exodus: A Critical, Theological Commentary.* OTL. Louisville: Westminster John Knox.

Coogan, Michael D. 1999. "The Ten Commandments on the Wall." *BRev* 15:2.

Cowley, A. 1923. *Aramaic Papyri of the Fifth Century B.C.* Oxford: Oxford University Press.

Dandamayev, Muhammad A. 1992. "Slavery." In *The Anchor Yale Bible Dictionary*, ed. David Noel Freedman, 6:58–65. New Haven: Yale University Press.

Daube, David. 1947. *Studies in Biblical Law.* Cambridge: Cambridge University Press.

Dickey, James. 1968. "The Son, the Cave, and the Burning Bush." In *The Young American Poets: A Big Table Book*, edited by P. Carroll. Chicago: Follett.

Dijk-Hemmes, Fokkelien van. 1994. "Some Recent Views on the Presentation of the Song of Miriam." In Brenner, *A Feminist Companion to Exodus to Deuteronomy*, 200–206.

Dohmen, C. 2004. *Exodus 19–40.* Herders Theologischer Kommentar zum Alten Testament. Freiburg: Herder.

Dozeman, Thomas B. 2010a. *Exodus.* Eerdmans Critical Commentary. Grand Rapids: Eerdmans.

———, ed. 2010b. *Methods for Exodus.* Methods in Biblical Interpretation. Cambridge: Cambridge University Press.

Dube, Musa W. 2000. *Postcolonial Feminist Interpretation of the Bible.* St. Louis: Chalice.

Eliade, M. 1959. *The Sacred and the Profane.* New York: Harper & Row.

Exum, J. Cheryl. 1983. "'You Shall Let Every Daughter Live': A Study of Exodus 1:8—2:10." *Semeia* 28:63–82.

Falk, Z. W. 1990. "Spirituality and Jewish Law." In *Religion and Law: Biblical Judaic and Islamic Perspectives*, edited by E. B. Firmage et al., 127–38. Winona Lake, IN: Eisenbrauns.

Feldman, Louis H. 2004. *"Remember Amalek!" Vengeance, Zealotry and Group Destruction in the Bible According to Philo, Pseudo-Philo, and Josephus.* HUCM. Cincinnati: Hebrew Union Press.

Fernandez, Eleazer S. 2006. "Exodus-toward-Egypt: Filipino-Americans' Struggle to Realize the Promised Land." In Sugirtharajah, *Voices from the Margin*, 242–57.

Firestone, Reuven. 2008. *Who Are the Real Chosen People? The Meaning of Chosenness in Judaism, Christianity and Islam.* Center for Religious Inquiry. Woodstock, VT: Skylight Paths.

Frankfort, H. 1978. *Kingship and the Gods.* Chicago: University of Chicago Press.

Fretheim, Terence. 1991. "The Plagues as Ecological Signs of Historical Disaster." *JBL* 110:385–96.

Fuchs, Esther. 2000. "A Jewish-Feminist Reading of Exodus 1–2." In *Jews, Christians, and The Theology of the Hebrew Scriptures*, edited by A. Ogden Bellis and Joel S. Kaminsky, 307–26. Symposium 8. Atlanta: Society of Biblical Literature.

Gennep, Arnold van. 1909. *The Rites of Passage.* London: Routledge and Kegan Paul.

Ginzberg, Louis. 1909–1938. *The Legends of the Jews.* 7 Vols. Philadelphia: Jewish Publication Society.

Graetz, Naomi. 1994. "Did Miriam Talk Too Much?" In Brenner, *A Feminist Companion to Exodus to Deuteronomy*, 231–42.

Greenberg, Moshe. 1951. "Hebrew *segulla*: Akkadian *sikiltu*." *JAOS* 71:172–74.

Greengus, Samuel. 1992. "Law." In *Anchor Yale Bible Dictionary*, edited by David Noel Freedman, 4:243–52. New Haven: Yale University Press.

Gregory of Nyssa. 1978. *The Life of Moses.* Translated by Abraham J. Malherbe and Everett Ferguson. Classics of Western Spirituality. New York: Paulist Press.

Gressmann, Hugo. 1913. *Mose und seine Zeit: Ein Kommentar zu den Mose-Sagen.* FRLANT 1. Göttingen: Vandenhoeck & Ruprecht.

Harrelson, W. 1980. *The Ten Commandments and Human Rights.* OBT. Philadelphia: Fortress.

Herdner A., editor. 1963. *Corpus des tablettes en cuneiforms alphabétiques découvertes à Ras-Shamra-Ugarit de 1929 à 1939.* Paris: Mission des Ras-Shamra 10.

Heschel, Abraham Joshua. 1951. *The Sabbath.* New York: Farrar, Straus & Giroux.

Homan, Michael M. 2002. *To Your Tents, O Israel! The Terminology, Function, Form, and Symbolism of Tents in the Hebrew Bible and the Ancient Near East.* Culture and History of the Ancient Near East 12. Leiden: Brill.

Hunter, Alastair G. 2003. "(De)nominating Amalek, Racial Stereotyping." In *Sanctified Aggression: Legacies of Biblical and Post Biblical Vocabularies of Violence*, edited by Jonneke Bekkenkamp and Yvonne Sherwood, 92–108. New York: T&T Clark.

Hurowitz, V. 1992. *I Have Built You an Exalted House: Temple Building in the Bible in Light of Mesopotamian and Northwest Semitic Writing.* JSOTSup 115. Sheffield: JSOT Press.

Jackson, Bernard S. 2000. *Studies in the Semiotics of Biblical Law.* JSOTSup 314. Sheffield: Sheffield Academic Press.

Janzen, J. Gerald. 1994. "Song of Moses, Song of Miriam: Who Is Seconding Whom?" In Brenner, *A Feminist Companion to Exodus to Deuteronomy*, 187–99. Sheffield: Sheffield Academic Press.

Keil, C. F., and F. Delitzsch. 1981. *Commentary on the Old Testament.* Vol. 1. Grand Rapids: Eerdmans.

Kirk-Duggan, Cheryl A. 2006. "Let My People Go! Threads of Exodus in African American Narratives." In Sugirtharajah, *Voices from the Margin*, 258–78.

Larsson, Göran. 1999. *Bound for Freedom: The Book of Exodus in Jewish and Christian Traditions.* Peabody, MA: Hendrickson.

Lehmann, Paul L. 1994. *The Decalogue and a Human Future: The Meaning of the Commandments for Making and Keeping Human Life Human.* Grand Rapids: Eerdmans.

Leibowitz, Nehama. 1981. *Studies in Shemot: The Book of Exodus.* Translated by A. Newman. 2 vols. 1976. Reprint, Jerusalem: World Zionist Organization.

Lowery, Richard H. 2000. *Sabbath and Jubilee.* Understanding Biblical Themes. St. Louis: Chalice.

Mamet, David. 1996. *Passover.* New York: St. Martin's.

Masalha, Nur. 2000. *Imperial Israel and the Palestinians: The Politics of Expansion.* London: Pluto.

McKenzie, Steven L. 2000. *Covenant.* Understanding Biblical Themes. St. Louis: Chalice.

Mendenhall, George. E. 1955. *Law and Covenant in Israel and the Ancient Near East*. Pittsburgh: The Biblical Colloquium.

Meyers, Carol. 1994. "Miriam the Musician." In Brenner, *A Feminist Companion to Exodus to Deuteronomy*, 207–30. Sheffield: Sheffield Academic Press.

———. 2005. *Exodus*. New Cambridge Bible Commentary. Cambridge: Cambridge University Press.

Muller, Wayne. 1999. *Sabbath: Finding Rest, Renewal, and Delight in Our Busy Lives*. New York: Bantam.

Origen. 2002. *Homilies on Joshua*, edited by Cynthia White. Translated by Barbara J. Bruce. *The Fathers of the Church*. Washington, DC: Catholic University of America Press.

Otto, Rudolf. 1958. *The Idea of the Holy: An Inquiry into the Non-Rational Factor in the Idea of the Divine and its Relation to the Rational*. Translated by J. W. Harvey. 2nd ed. 1923. Reprint, London: Oxford.

Philo. 1929. *On the Creation: Allegorical Interpretation of Genesis 2 and 3*. Translated by F. H. Colson and G. H. Whitaker. Loeb Classical Library. Cambridge, MA: Harvard University Press.

———. 1954. *Moses I. and II*. Translated by F. H. Colson. Loeb Classical Library. Cambridge, MA: Harvard University Press.

Pixley, George V. 1987. *On Exodus: A Liberation Perspective*. Maryknoll, NY: Orbis.

———. 2010. "Liberation Criticism." In Dozeman, *Methods for Exodus*, 131–62.

Pixley, George V., and Clodovis Boff. 2006. "A Latin American Perspective: The Option for the Poor in the Old Testament." In Sugirtharajah, *Voices from the Margin*, 207–16.

Pritchard, J. B., ed. 1969. *Ancient Near Eastern Texts Relating to the Old Testament*. 3rd ed. Princeton: Princeton University Press.

Propp, William. 1999. *Exodus 1–18*. AYB. New Haven: Yale University Press.

———. 2006. *Exodus 19–40*. AYB. New Haven: Yale University Press.

Rad, Gerhard von. 1959. *Moses*. 2nd ed. World Christian Books 32. New York: Association Press.

Rapp, Ursula. 2002. *Mirjam: Eine feministisch-rhetorische Lektüre der Mirjamtexte in der hebräischen Bibel*. Berlin: de Gruyter.

Redford, D. B. 1992. *Egypt, Canaan, and Israel in Ancient Times*. Princeton: Princeton University Press.

———. 1982. "Pithom." In *Lexicon der Ägyptologie*, edited by W. Helck and W. Westerdorf. Wiesbaden: Harrasowitz. Cols. 1054–58.

Sagi, Avi. 1994. "The Punishment of Amalek in Jewish Tradition: Coping with the Moral Problem." *HTR* 87:323–46.

Said, Edward W. 1988. "Michael Walzer's Exodus and Revolution: A Canaanite Reading." In *Blaming the Victims: Spurious Scholarship and the Palestinian Question*, edited by Edward W. Said and Christopher Hitchens, 161–78. London: Verso, 1988.

Schaper, Donna. 2011. "Occupy Wall Street, The Golden Calf and the New Ideology." *Huffington Post*. http://www.huffingtonpost.com/donna-schaper/occupy-wall-street-the-go_b_1004946.html. October 11.

Schwartz, Regina M. 1997. *The Curse of Cain: The Violent Legacy of Monotheism*. Chicago: University of Chicago Press.

Setel, D. O'Donnell. 1992. "Exodus." In *The Women's Bible Commentary*, edited by C. A. Newsom and S. H. Ringe, 26–35. Louisville: Westminster John Knox.

Sperling, S. David. 1998. *The Original Torah: The Political Intention of the Bible's Writers*. New York: New York University Press.

Stanton, Elizabeth Cady. 1993. *The Woman's Bible*. Evanston, IL: Northwestern University Press.

Steinberg, Naomi. 2010. "Feminist Criticism." In Dozeman, *Methods for Exodus*, 163–92.

Sugirtharajah, R. S., ed. *Voices from the Margin: Interpreting the Bible in the Third World*. Maryknoll, NY: Orbis.

Swartley, Willard M. 1983. *Slavery, Sabbath, War, and Women: Case Issues in Biblical Interpretation*. Scottdale, PA: Herald.

Tran, Jonathan. 2007. "Sold into Slavery." *Christian Century* 124, no. 24:22–26.

Trible, Phyllis. 1973. "Depatriarchalizing in Biblical Interpretation." *JAAR* 41:34–45.

———. 1994. "Bringing Miriam out of the Shadows." In Brenner, *A Feminist Companion to Exodus to Deuteronomy*, 166–86.

Warrior, Robert Allen. 2006. "A Native American Perspective: Canaanites, Cowboys, and Indians." In Sugirtharajah, *Voices from the Margin*, 235–41.

Weems, Renita J. 1992. "The Hebrew Women Are Not Like the Egyptian Women: The Ideology of Race, Gender and Sexual Reproduction in Exodus 1." *Semeia* 59:25–34.

Wellhausen, Julius. 1957. *Prolegomena to the History of Ancient Israel*. Translated by J. Sutherland Black and Allan Menzies. 1883. Reprint, New York: Meridian.

White, Lynn Townsend Jr. 1967. "The Historical Roots of Our Ecologic Crisis." *Science* 155:1203–7.

Yee, Gale A. 2010. "Postcolonial Biblical Criticism." In Dozeman, *Methods for Exodus*, 193–233.

LEVITICUS

Robert Kugler

Introduction

A book addressing sacrificial practices, the manner of selecting priests, the relative degrees of purity in animals and humans, and other topics related to ritual practice, Leviticus has come in for more than its fair share of neglect. Compelling narratives like those found in Genesis and Exodus are virtually absent in Leviticus, and its theological significance is difficult to recognize, at least on a casual reading. By comparison with its predecessors in the Torah, Leviticus hardly inspires a reader's rapturous attention.

Worse yet, when Leviticus has received attention, it has often been rather unwelcome. Some early Protestant historical critics used the book's focus on ritual practice to license grossly inappropriate caricatures of Judaism, ancient and contemporary, as lacking in theological depth and reduced to "mere" ritual practice. In more recent years, select passages in the book have also featured prominently in often irrational and emotionally charged debates regarding homosexuality.

Yet for all the obstacles that have been set against Leviticus, it has managed to win a thoughtful readership that has endured for centuries, a readership that points time and again to the considerable theological gravitas the book does in fact possess. From the people of the Dead Sea Scrolls to the great exegetes of rabbinic Judaism, from the earliest Christian communities to the "new evangelicals" of today, from scholars in the school traditions of the ancient world to contemporary cultural anthropologists—Leviticus has elicited a rich history of interpretation and analysis by generations of readers.

The survey of the book's contents that plays a role in the following commentary does confirm, though, that Leviticus is concerned above all with ritual practice. Chapters 1–7 are about sacrifice, chapters 8–10 deal with the priestly selection and ordination, chapters 11–15 are about ensuring the laity's purity for the cult, chapter 16 sets out the annual rite for purifying Israel for the cult, and chapters 17–26 reflect on the consequences of all Israel being made holy given God's presence in the sanctuary. Even chapter 27, an otherwise unrelated appendix, gets in on the act, addressing the redemption of sacred vows made to God. There can be no denying it: Leviticus *is* consumed with rules and regulations governing ritual practice. How, then, can we account for the theological depth generations of interpreters have discovered?

One way to answer that question is to contextualize Leviticus in its larger literary and historical setting, as a key component of the Priestly writer's contribution to the Torah. From the earliest days of the Documentary Hypothesis, Leviticus was assigned to a late exilic or early postexilic Priestly work (abbreviated as P). Many share Martin Noth's early judgment that only Leviticus 8–10 was integral to P as the logical continuation of the narrative that leaves off in Exodus 40, and that the rest of Leviticus, especially the so-called Holiness Code in chapters 17–26, amounted to later additions to this "narrative kernel" of the book (Noth, 13-15; cf. Campbell and O'Brien; Grabbe, 16–19). There is, however, significant dissent from this broad consensus, and this commentary joins that chorus of voices. On this reading, at least Leviticus 1–16 as a whole was integral to P from its inception (e.g., Nihan). As for Leviticus 17–26, the Holiness Code, this commentary joins with those who treat it as an addition to P that aimed to critique P from within (see Milgrom; Knohl).

What date do we assign to P and to Leviticus 1–16, and to the Holiness Code as a later supplement? In spite of valiant attempts by some to place P, Leviticus 1–16, and the Holiness Code in the First Temple period (e.g., Milgrom; Knohl), the weight of the evidence favors a late exilic or early postexilic date for all three (Noth; Nihan), even if some of the specific cultic instructions and priestly ordinances found especially in Leviticus may go back to the First Temple and its practices (see further Grabbe, 13–16).

As for the purpose of P in Second Temple Judea, and of Leviticus in particular, much seems obvious. Constructing a new temple, restarting the cult, establishing a legitimate priesthood, setting purity boundaries for laity vis-à-vis the sacred site—these were sure to be complicated and contested matters among the Judeans who returned to Judea under Persian rule with imperial authorization to do these things; without clear direction, chaotic conflict to control the cult could have reigned supreme. The Priestly work, an account of God's word on these topics to Moses and Aaron in hoary antiquity, settled matters and assured order where there might have been chaos. Leviticus played a key role in achieving this purpose.

Additionally, even though Persia had authorized Judeans to control Judea and manage its temple economy, they faced serious challenges to achieving that purpose. They were just one minority ethnic group in the midst of a veritable hegemonic pluralism of ethnic groups that had taken up residence in the land during the period of Babylonian control. The fields they were to make productive had been sorely abused and neglected in the generations since their forefathers were deported, the temple they were supposed to operate was little more than an open-air altar in the midst of a shambles, and the public infrastructure necessary to support this temple-based economy was nonexistent. Where communal and cosmic order was required to achieve the Persian mandate, there was only chaos; where abundant life was the goal, foreboding death and decay threatened. In response to this, P offered a narrative and ritual-legal prescription for cosmic and communal order and life, and in achieving this purpose, Leviticus also played an important role.

Last, the Priestly tradents were also acutely aware of the fact that not all Judeans were able to live in the land and contribute to its restoration. How should they maintain their Judean identity without that opportunity? This, too, received an answer from the Priestly writers, parts of which appear in Leviticus (esp. chapter 16, the Day of Atonement).

There is little surprise in the general shape of the interpretive tradition that Leviticus engendered, considering the book's focus on ritual, priesthood, and purity, and the character of some of its best-known passages in contemporary thought. The people of the Dead Sea Scrolls, concerned with the Jerusalem temple, its priestly leadership, and its purity or impurity, produced a substantial body of literature that engages with norms laid out in Leviticus. Early rabbinic Judaism, committed in its own way to continued speculation about the temple and priestly matters, was also intensely occupied with Leviticus. The Mishnah, a work dated to around 200 CE, is predicated on the existence of the Jerusalem temple, and as such invokes Leviticus, even if it is often oblique in doing so. *Sifra*, "the Book," is a priest's handbook based on Leviticus, also datable to around 200 CE. And *Leviticus Rabbah*, datable to the fifth century CE and one of the oldest midrashim, is a "homiletical midrash" on Leviticus passages. To be sure, as Christian traditions began to dominate in the production of new interpretive traditions, Leviticus receded a bit from prominence as a focal point for exegetical and hermeneutical interest, but even then it continued to draw interpretive comment and interest, and key passages were often deployed to support and interpret central Christian claims (see, e.g., Rom. 3:25, on Jesus as a "sacrifice of atonement"; cf. Heb. 9:1-14).

To say, however, that Leviticus comes in for a great deal of attention in contemporary discussion apart from the community of scholars devoted to critical study of the Scriptures and/or to tracing Jewish and Christian origins would be disingenuous at best. To be sure, many take great interest in passages thought to legitimate their condemnation of homosexuality (see further on Lev. 18:22; 20:13), but beyond that, vigorous engagement with Leviticus like that which one sees with the well-known stories of Genesis and Exodus is scarce. Perhaps, though, as a result of gaining greater acquaintance with this rich book of the Bible, through this commentary readers will be encouraged to bring it more fully into their own, contemporary imagination and discourse, especially its capacity to address the human experience of chaos and death with such a powerful vision of life and order, authored by God in the words of Moses and Aaron.

Leviticus 1–7

Chapters 1–7, the first large unit of text in Leviticus, can be divided into two subunits: Lev. 1:1—6:7 is a "layperson's manual" for how offerings are to be made, and 6:8—7:38 amounts to a "priest's manual" for making those sacrifices. For the sake of brevity, the corresponding portions of the two subunits are addressed together in the following commentary.

Many commentators observe that Leviticus 1–7 is discordant with the narrative thread that left off at the end of Exodus and that a narrative transition from the latter point to Leviticus 8 is easier to make. That observation supports the theories of compositional disunity described above. Yet coming on the heels of the sanctuary's completion in Exodus 40, instructions for its chief use, in fact, seem to be the natural next step in a larger narrative intended to ground the Second Temple and its operation in the authority of Mosaic instructions received directly from God. Thus skepticism about the place of Leviticus 1–7 in the "first draft" of the Priestly work is unwarranted.

This seems all the more true when we consider the way Leviticus 1–7 functions in P as a whole. Among the concerns of the postexilic Judean community the P tradents surely had to address was how the sacrifices should be offered in the restored temple. We know from a variety of sources (e.g., Ezra, Haggai) that the temple site was in ruins when the people returned from exile; yet they were authorized—indeed, required—by their Persian overlords to rebuild the temple and renew the cult. Haggai, among others, makes it clear that the temple was rebuilt, but we also know from the same prophet and from his contemporary Zechariah that there were disputes about how the new temple was to operate. By whose rules and regulations should the rites be performed in the new temple? Leviticus 1–7, the rubrics for sacrifice in God's sanctuary given by God to Moses in the wilderness, supplied an answer to the question of *what* rules and regulations should prevail. As we shall see, Leviticus 8–10 answered in turn the question of who should administer those rules and regulations.

Leviticus 1:1-17; 6:8-13 (Heb., 6:1-6): A Manual for Sacrifice

▮ THE TEXT IN ITS ANCIENT CONTEXT

Chapter 1 addresses the burnt or whole offering, which entails immolating the useful parts of the sacrificial animal. Verses 1-17 then address the sacrifice of cattle, goats and sheep, and birds as whole offerings. Leviticus 6:8-13 covers in some detail the manner in which the priests are to do the work of making this sacrifice.

While the purpose of the whole burnt offering in Israel could vary (e.g., dedication of a new altar or sacred site [Exod. 24:5], thanksgiving [Gen. 8:20], penance for sin [Judg. 20:26]; see Budd, 43), from the perspective of this chapter, its chief function is to make a pleasing odor for God (1:9, 13, 17). Thus its meaning is perhaps best understood as an extraordinary gift to God, a *whole* burnt offering (save the hide, which is set aside for the priest; see 7:8) that is meant above all to powerfully draw God's attention to the worshiper.

From the perspective of P as a whole, this offering, the first to be explained, makes it emphatically clear that sacrifice is above all else to ensure a line of communication between God and people, with the altar priest serving as the human mediator in that exchange. Other functions for sacrifice are secondary to this one. This is hardly surprising in postexilic Judea, a time and place fraught with serious challenges to the people's ability to remain faithful to their traditions. Judeans needed a reliable means of remaining tied to their God living under conditions that so threatened to undo their commitment to the Yahwistic tradition they were called to uphold. The whole burnt offering signals the Priestly interest in serving that interest above all others (see Levine, 22–27).

▮ THE TEXT IN THE INTERPRETIVE TRADITION

The guidelines for sacrificing a whole burnt offering appear to have been particularly interesting to early Jewish commentators, perhaps because the sacrifice is devoted so completely to the overarching purpose of bringing God's attention to the one making the offering. It is not surprising, then, that among those who disagreed with the ways of the ruling priestly class in the Second Temple, rewriting Leviticus 1 was a popular strategy for doing so. A prime example of this is the revisionist reading of Lev. 1:8-9, 12-13 in 4Q214 2:3-7 (cf. 1Q21 45; 4Q214b 2-3 8), a fragment of *Aramaic Levi*, a third-century-BCE reworking of the life story of Levi that portrays him as the *first* and *most legitimate* recipient of priestly instructions. These are slightly different from those later given to Moses. There can be no mistaking the purpose in such a "rewriting" of Leviticus 1: given to the progenitor of all of Israel's priests, *these* norms for making a whole burnt offering were superior to those of the Aaronites, mere descendants of the original, truest priestly servant of God, Levi.

■ THE TEXT IN CONTEMPORARY DISCUSSION

The sacrifice addressed by Leviticus 1 has featured obliquely in modern public discourse about the World War II Nazi murder of Jews. Since the 1960s, the word for the sacrifice detailed in this chapter in the Greek translation of the Jewish Scriptures, *holokautoma*, has been used to refer to the Nazi destruction of the European Jewish communities, the Holocaust. Many find the use of the word in this way troubling, and not just because of the difficulty of associating a sacrifice to God with the Nazi act of genocide. Some within the Jewish community view it as an inappropriate term for the Jewish experience because its original use was to denominate *Greek* sacrificial practices, while others object to its use because they think it *too* Jewish-centric, potentially leading people to overlook the death-dealing violence the Nazis did to non-Jews as well, including people of color, Romani, gay and lesbian people, political opponents, physically disabled persons, and others. A widely used alternative to "Holocaust" used among Jews include *HaShoah*, Hebrew for "the Catastrophe" (on the history of the use of the term, see Petrie).

Leviticus 2:1-16; 6:14-23 (Heb., 6:7-16): Grain Offerings

■ THE TEXT IN ITS ANCIENT CONTEXT

According to Lev. 2:1-16, the cereal offering, or grain offering, is an offering of uncooked or cooked "choice flour" (Heb., *sōlet*) mixed with oil and frankincense, from which the priest takes a portion for himself. The offering should contain no leaven, nor should honey be mixed with it, but it must be salted. If you bring a firstfruits offering of grain, it may also serve as a grain offering and should conform to the norms laid out here. The instructions to the priests and the high priest for making their respective cereal offerings are in 6:14-23. A handful of grain is to be offered to God, and the rest of the offering may be eaten by the priests and their male children or the high priest in the courtyard of the tent of meeting, a holy place, as they are holy.

The occasions for making grain offerings are not easy to discern from the wider evidence, let alone from the present chapter. To be sure, though, it is, like so many other offerings, first about getting God's attention and pleasing God in a general sense. It also seems to be an offering that commonly accompanies whole burnt offerings (e.g., Lev. 23:12-13; Num. 8:8; Judg. 13:19), and its natural role in the firstfruits offerings is evident.

▌THE TEXT IN THE INTERPRETIVE TRADITION

In a midrash that typifies the work's interpretive method, *Leviticus Rabbah* 3:1 begins with a quotation of Lev. 2:1-2 and immediately follows that with a quotation of Eccles. 4:6, linking the verses through their shared use of the word "handful." After a typically long and involved exploration of the idea behind the phrase "Better is a handful of quietness" in Eccles. 4:6, the midrashist concludes by saying that the best understanding of the relationship between the two passages associated by catchword is that Qoheleth exalts the handful of grain that a *poor person's offering* amounts to according to Lev. 2:1-2 over the incense of spices brought by the whole community (Lev. 16:12; Neusner, 168–80).

▌THE TEXT IN CONTEMPORARY DISCUSSION

A contribution can be made to the emerging subdiscipline of ecological hermeneutics by reading this sacrifice within the larger Priestly tradition. It was the Priestly writer who established the fruit of the earth as God's food gift to humanity according to Gen. 1:29-30. That this Priestly chapter places grain among those fruits that should in turn serve as a food gift to God can be used to suggest a driving logic for giving attention to special care for the earth: the one and the same fruit of the earth that sustains humanity honors its Creator; and as such, human stewardship over creation, granted also by God through the rhetoric of the Priestly writer in Gen. 1:26-28, should be exercised with special reverence.

Leviticus 3:1-17; 7:11-38: The Well-Being Offerings

▌THE TEXT IN ITS ANCIENT CONTEXT

Leviticus 3 deals with the well-being offering, addressing in succession the details of making one with cattle, sheep, and goats, and concluding with the prohibition on consuming the blood and fat of the offering. The suet on the entrails, the two kidneys and the suet on them, and the caudate lobe of the liver are to be burned whole as an offering to God, and the rest of the sacrificial animal may be consumed by the offerer. Leviticus 7:11-36 gives the administrative requirements of the well-being offering, a more elaborate declaration against eating fat or blood, and an explanation of the prebends from the well-being offering for the priests. Verses 37-38 serve as the capstone to the entire sacrificial legislation in chapters 1–7.

The purposes of the well-being offering would seem to cluster around familial observances associated with thanksgiving (see Lev. 7:11-18), although public events are also associated with it (e.g., Saul's elevation to king in 1 Sam. 11:15; the restoration of the altar in 2 Chron. 33:16). As for its meaning, the use of the term "peace" in naming it is suggestive, as are the occasions on which it is used; it connotes a restoration of balance between God and those who make the sacrifice, a balance that may have been undone both by negative events (the desecration of an altar) or positive ones (a blessed event happens to a family). This understanding of the sacrifice in light of the larger Priestly prescription for cosmic, communal, and cultic order in the face of the chaos of postexilic Judea is enlightening. Inasmuch as the peace offering provides a cultic avenue to bringing balance and order to situations that have become disordered and imbalanced, it extends the power of sacrifice to meet the existential needs of Judeans living in the difficult conditions of early Persian-period Judea.

▌THE TEXT IN THE INTERPRETIVE TRADITION

A particularly notable aspect of this passage is the stress it places on assigning the offering's blood and fat to God and to God alone. The emphasis features in the interpretive tradition in various ways, but most charmingly in the prayer of R. Sheshet in *b. Ber.* 17a. In the absence of a temple in which to make offerings of blood and fat to God to render oneself acceptable to God, he pleads that the fat and blood he loses by fasting might be counted as such instead (Milgrom 1991, 214)!

On a relatively more mundane level, in 1QapGen 11:17 (*Genesis Apocryphon*) the prohibition against eating blood issued to Noah after the flood (when permission to eat animal flesh was granted) surprisingly echoes more closely Lev. 3:17 than the actual source text for the command, Gen. 9:4.

▌THE TEXT IN CONTEMPORARY DISCUSSION

A notable instance of contemporizing this passage was provided by a reflection on the act of giving blood in New York City in the wake of 9/11. Laura Duhan Kaplan entertains the notion that Lev. 3:1-17 is the best analogy in the sacrificial legislation for giving blood after the horror of that day, but opts instead for the sin offering of 4:1—5:13 (to which we will return below), arguing that the celebratory potential of the sacrifice in Lev. 3:1-17 disqualifies it in spite of its emphasis on restoring balance through the gift of blood to God. Kaplan may be right in a specific sense, but her general point—that giving blood for those who need its life-giving qualities is in unrecognized ways analogous to sacrifices that render life force to God—is worth taking note of in regard to the blood-focused legislation for this sacrifice and the disposition of its yield.

Leviticus 4:1—5:13; 6:24-30: The Purification Offerings

▌THE TEXT IN ITS ANCIENT CONTEXT

Leviticus 4:1-35 elaborates the purification offering to be made in the event of sanctuary-polluting, unintentional violations of God's prohibitive commandments. It begins with the case of the anointed or high priest who sins unintentionally, and continues with provisions for sacrifice after the unwitting violation of a prohibitive commandment by the whole congregation. In these two cases the offering is to be a bull. In the case of the ruler the offering is to be a male goat, and an ordinary person brings a female goat, although in both cases the goat may also be replaced with a sheep. The chapter concludes with the declaration that making a "sin" offering on the terms laid out in the preceding verses relieves the offerer of guilt. Leviticus 5:1-13 then stipulates some specific instances that require sin offerings. Leviticus 6:24-30 gives the priests instructions for making the offering, providing an unusually significant amount of detail.

Jacob Milgrom argues persuasively that this sacrifice is not about setting a sinner right with God, as one might assume, but repairing the holiness of the sanctuary that was harmed by the sinner's deeds—thus the designation of it as a "purification offering." Citing ancient Near Eastern parallels where the concern is to guard the sanctity of a sanctuary against demonic forces, Milgrom argues that among the Israelites the demonic was replaced by the human actor; the deeds of the Israelites were what endangered the sanctity of the sanctuary and threatened to drive God away from it (Milgrom 2004, 31–33).

Here too the significance of this sacrifice within the framework of the Priestly proposal for postexilic Judea is transparent, especially in light of Milgrom's reading of the offering's significance. With a poignancy mostly overlooked by commentators on the Priestly literature, the sacrifice provides a vital avenue for the people of God to readily acknowledge and ensure the integrity of their dependence on God's presence for them in the restored temple. This must have been a powerful reassurance for them in the challenging world of postexilic Judea.

▌ THE TEXT IN THE INTERPRETIVE TRADITION

Leviticus Rabbah 5:1-3 weaves a remarkable discourse together by juxtaposing Lev. 4:3 and Job 34:29-30. The former verse charges the anointed priest with making a purification offering if he sinned unwittingly, and the latter states,

> When he is quiet, who can condemn?
>> When he hides his face, who can behold him,
>>> whether it be a nation or an individual?—
> so that the godless should not reign,
>> or those who ensnare the people.

As Jacob Neusner points out in his commentary on the *Rabbah* passage, the long, involved discourse amounts finally to making clear that before God the anointed priest and the lay community are the same in terms of the magnitude of their sin and in the consequences of their sin for purification *and* suffering, such as when God seems hidden from the people. In this the midrashist demonstrates the *Rabbah*'s great virtue—drawing out a theological significance intrinsic to the Leviticus text, but not so easily evident without such illumination (Neusner, 192–98).

▌ THE TEXT IN CONTEMPORARY DISCUSSION

Jacob Milgrom offers a remarkable contemporizing reading of the purification offering. Reminding readers of his view that the offering is about ensuring that the sanctuary is repaired from the violence done to it by human sin so that God would not flee creation before the magnitude of human immorality, he asks what the priests would see in today's world. He replies to his own question with a litany of the environmental, economic, military, and political injustices and offenses committed by others, which we observe, yet do little to stop and even less to repair the damage they do. To this he imagines the priests would cry out, "How long . . . before God abandon's God's earthly sanctuary?" (Milgrom 2004, 33).

Leviticus 5:14—6:7; 7:1-10: The Reparation Offerings

■ THE TEXT IN ITS ANCIENT CONTEXT

This section of text elaborates the sacrifice to be made in reparation for individual unintentional sins that desecrate, that have the impact of "affecting only its committer" (Milgrom 2004, 51). If one has desecrated any of the sanctified things of the Lord, a ram convertible to "silver by the sanctuary shekel" one-fifth of the value of the thing desecrated is due (5:14-16). If one has sinned without knowing it—a possibility that likely occurred to people when they were suddenly experiencing inexplicably difficult life circumstances—a guilt offering of a ram makes the atoning sacrifice (5:17-19). Leviticus 5:20-26 (Heb., 6:1-7) enumerates some specific sins for which a reparation offering may be made (deceiving someone in a deposit or pledge, robbery, fraud, and finding and not reporting a lost object) and prescribes reparation—acknowledging guilt, paying the injured person 120 percent of the value lost, and bringing to the priests a ram for the atoning sacrifice. Leviticus 7:1-10 directs the priest to perform essentially the same ritual for this sacrifice as the one performed for a purification offering.

Given the evidence that reparation for damages done was practiced more widely in the ancient Near Eastern world as a means of placating the gods offended by one's bad act, it seems likely that this particular sacrifice, attested only in P and similarly late texts (e.g., Ezek. 40:39), was a Priestly development that merged the wider practice of reparations to appease the gods with an atoning sacrifice by Israel's priests to set the sinner right with the Lord. Milgrom further argues that the offering process as a whole is the Priestly legist's invention whereby *intentional* sins are converted by acknowledgment and repentance to unintentional sins that can then be atoned for through the sacrifice of the ram (Milgrom 2004). Once more, we see the great concern of the Priestly tradition for the existential needs of the people of Judea.

■ THE TEXT IN THE INTERPRETIVE TRADITION

The document *m. Seqal.* 6.6 answers the interesting question raised by the deposit of monetary reparations by the persons bringing a reparation sacrifice, "What comes of the proceeds of such ritual deposits?" Although the argument is more complex, the Mishnah boils down to a single proof text, 2 Kgs. 12:6, "The money from the guilt offerings and the money from the sin offerings was not brought into the house of the Lord; it belonged to the priests." And how could this be done without unduly enriching the priests? The answer the Mishnah provides is that they used it to purchase whole burnt offerings for the altar, all of which were dedicated to the Lord (save the hide, which was the priests' prebend).

■ THE TEXT IN CONTEMPORARY DISCUSSION

The reparation sacrifice offers a fascinating window on the difference between the norms accepted by the ancient legists who lived in the light of their election by the God of Israel and recent historical and contemporary attitudes toward reparations payable to those who have been unjustly wronged by another's sinful act. Taking the case of Japanese Americans interned or relocated during

World War II as a result of Franklin Delano Roosevelt's Executive Order 9066 of February 1942 (which established "exclusion zones" and set in motion a cascade of other public proclamations that facilitated the internment and relocation process), we can see the contrast in stark detail. The Priestly writers treated the act damaging the neighbor as a violation against God that was then in the transgressor's best interest to repent of and repair as speedily as humanly possible, and they pre-scribed the means for doing so at a level more generous than the damage done. By contrast, getting compensation for the Japanese Americans who lost livelihoods, land, and even families as a result of EO 9066 took nearly five decades to accomplish, and produced a paltry $20,000 in compensation for each internee. Reparations were neither speedy nor generous. One wonders how the process might have gone if much attention had been paid to the example of Leviticus.

Leviticus 8–10

Following the legislation on sacrificial practices, the narrative thread left off in Exodus 40 resumes with the account of the ordination of the sons of Aaron to the altar priesthood (chapters 8–9) and the story of the sin and destruction of two of Aaron's sons, Nadab and Abihu (chapter 10).

As noted above, many assume that since these chapters resume the narrative that was sus-pended in Exodus 40, Leviticus 1–7 must have been belatedly introduced into a continuous P nar-rative. However, Christophe Nihan argues that in fact the sacrificial legislation in Leviticus 1–7 is the prerequisite for the priestly inauguration of the cult in chapter 9, which follows the ordination narrative in chapter 8, and thus as a consequence it makes little literary sense to regard chapters 1–7 as a late insertion. Nihan's argument is fortified by the observation that the shift in focus to priests fits what might be a broader pattern of literary structuring employed by the Priestly writer. Exodus 25–31; 35–40 focuses on establishing the space within which priests and laity share in cultic activ-ity; Leviticus 1–7 focuses on the life-sustaining, community-mending cultic activities of the laity in that sanctuary space (aided by the priests); and now the focus shifts to ensuring that the priests who staff the cultic space and carry out the cultic rites for the laity are prepared for their duties. This threefold structure places the lay community and its existential needs at the center, treating the creation of a space for meeting those needs and the personnel required to assist in that as adjuncts to the central concern of the Priestly writer, the good of the Judeans forming community in postexilic Judea.

Leviticus 8:1—9:24: Ordained and Set Apart

■ THE TEXT IN ITS ANCIENT CONTEXT

Chapter 8 addresses the ordination of the priests. God commands Moses to take Aaron and his sons the priestly vestments, a bull for a sin offering, two rams, and a basket of unleavened bread to the entrance of the tent of meeting and to assemble the people there. Then Moses cleanses and vests Aaron and his sons, and makes the sin offering of the bull and the ram of the burnt offering. The ordination sacrifice of the second ram follows, a rite that includes touching the blood of the ram to the lobe of each priest's right ear, the thumb of his right hand, and the big toe of his right foot. The chapter then dictates the use of the offerings and prescribes a seven-day waiting period within the entrance of the tent of meeting for Aaron and his sons to complete their ordination. Chapter 9 then inaugurates the cult, with Aaron and his sons performing sacrifices on the eighth day, which include sin and burnt offerings for Aaron and his sons and sin, whole burnt, grain, and well-being offerings for the people. The chapter concludes with a priestly blessing to draw the eighth-day celebration to a close, followed by a theophany whereby the fiery presence of God consumes the whole burnt offering and the fat on the altar.

Relying on the cultural-anthropological notions of liminal states and rites of passage explains how the ordination rite in chapter 8 works in the Priestly agenda. The containment of Aaron and his sons in the sacred space during the ordination rite signals the liminal state between profane and holy status that Aaron and his sons enter into and the transformation they undergo to be set apart for the people's service. Further, smearing the blood of the sacrifice on their body parts intensifies the character of the moment as a rite of passage, joining them in a graphic and dangerous way to the sacrifice as something dedicated completely to God, even unto loss of life, but also for the purpose of giving life to those who make the offering (see by contrast Milgrom 2004, 85–86, who argues that the daubing accomplishes purgation). In this way, the Priestly tradents deploy imagery that signals the lengths and depths to which priests and God will go in partnership together to ensure the integrity of the people's relationship to God. Again, this was a powerful theological message for the people of Judea in the challenging context of the early Persian period.

The Priestly writer underscores this point with the next chapter. Having been set apart for their mediating service between God and people, Aaron and his sons immediately set about doing what they were ordained to do, making the sacrifices that connect God and people. And as if to drive home the point that this is to ensure the presence of God to the people, in 9:4 Moses instructs Aaron to tell the people that in the doing of these sacrifices, "the LORD will appear to you," and God does indeed appear, as fire that consumes the proceeds of the sacrifice (9:24). In the Priestly work, that sort of theophany had taken place once before, as the evidence of God's presence on Sinai (Exod. 24:17). The point is clear: by virtue of the mediating role of the priests, who deliver the people's offerings to God, God is immediate and present to the people in the sanctuary. Here we have yet another assurance from the Priestly tradents for the people living in Persian-period Judea.

◼ THE TEXT IN THE INTERPRETIVE TRADITION

Leviticus Rabbah 10:1-4 provides a remarkable reading of Lev. 8:1-3, tackling the problem that Aaron acquiesced to the people's desire to worship an alternative god in Exodus 32. At the beginning of the first unit, the *Rabbah* cites Lev. 8:1-3, with its mention of anointing, and Ps. 45:7, which declares that God has anointed the addressee of the psalm over his fellows because he loves righteousness and hates wickedness. The section in *Lev. Rab.* 10:1-2 then provides a series of proof texts for the notion that those who are anointed are oriented to God's service no matter the circumstances; 10:3 follows by quoting in succession Ps. 45:7 and Exod. 32:1, implicitly posing at last the question the passage has been driving at: How could Aaron, God's anointed, have led the rebellion in Exodus 32? The following pastiche of quotes and an account of a folktale confirm what 10:1-2 established, that God's anointed are tireless in their service to God; and just so, Aaron was tireless in creating the golden calf for the people, "taking upon himself the sin they would have committed had he not made the sacrifice of his own sin." Wonderfully, what one finds at the heart of this exegesis is the evidence of the rabbinic commentators' conscious appreciation of the P tradition's aim of affirming the dedication of the Aaronites in telling the story of the ordination in the first place.

Turning to the offerings made for the people by Aaron and his sons, their reaction in 9:24 to the appearance of the Lord is that they "shouted and fell on their faces." In what could be seen as another example of later exegesis underscoring the joyously awesome nature of this event for the people, the *Temple Scroll* from Qumran gives its own version of that ceremony in column 17, lines 1–5. The interpreter read the ambiguous "shouted and fell on their faces" in Lev. 9:24 as one unequivocal action, rendering it as "the people *rejoiced*."

■ THE TEXT IN CONTEMPORARY DISCUSSION

The Priestly writer's notion that ordination is a rite of passage that moves its recipient across a boundary on either side of which are two different ontological states is not common in religion in the contemporary West. The Christian communities that do treat the rite of ordination as sacramental in character (e.g., Roman Catholic, Anglican, Orthodox), struggle to make the rite communicate that significance to their recipients, let alone those who witness the rite. Recognizing the absence of awe in setting apart of a man or woman to the dedicated service of God makes one wonder if this is not testimony to the accuracy of Max Weber's gloomy confidence that Western society is doomed to go ever further down the road of rationalization and disenchantment.

Yet among those Christian communities where a fully developed liturgical rite of ordination is carried out, the eucharistic meal follows, a clear and appropriate echo of the celebration of the sacrifices by Aaron and his sons for all of Israel. In this, at least, the ordination rite in some of its modern, Christian forms does gesture toward the profound significance of assigning to a member of one's larger community the burden and privilege of mediating between God and people.

Leviticus 10:1-20: Aaron's Sons, Nadab and Abihu

■ THE TEXT IN ITS ANCIENT CONTEXT

This chapter begins with the tale of Nadab and Abihu offering of "strange" or "unauthorized" fire (incense), their death by fire as a consequence, and the disposal of their bodies. A series of priestly precautions, rights, and duties follows, prohibiting Aaron and his sons from partaking in strong drink before serving in the sanctuary, instructing them to differentiate for the people between the common and the sacred (*ḥōl* and *qōdeš*) and teaching the people of Israel all the statutes given through Moses. Further, their eating of grain offering is restricted to holy space (next to the altar), while the consumption of the "elevation offering" is allowed in any clean place. The chapter closes with Moses' complaint to Aaron and his sons that they acted improperly because they burned the sin offering rather than eating it, and Aaron's reply that it would have been inappropriate for him to consume the most holy sacrifice given the things that "have befallen" him.

This odd story is yet another piece of the picture puzzle the Priestly writer promotes for postexilic Judeans under Persian rule. Some suggest that private offerings of incense may have been seen as low-cost alternatives to sacrifice, a means of making contact with God without the mediation of a priest. Such behavior might have been implied by Nadab and Abihu's actions. If so, this story makes clear that even the priests were subject to the negative consequences of sidestepping the new system of sacrifice and offerings. Maintaining an ordered cult for *all* the people transcended even the rights of the newly ordained priests.

■ THE TEXT IN THE INTERPRETIVE TRADITION

The deaths of Nadab and Abihu have long troubled commentators because they seem so pointless. One sophisticated example of solving that difficulty comes from Philo, who asserts that in fact the brothers were so zealous in their piety that their expression of it transcended the earthly realm and approached the heavenly, and they were thus swept up into heaven as a sacrifice to God through immolation (*Dreams* 2.67). Other interpreters, particularly among early and medieval Christian readers, were more inclined to assume Nadab and Abihu's culpability for some error, using them as examples of the fate that awaits priests who are misdirected in their zeal (Bede, *On the Tabernacle*) or people who abuse the church's sacrament of baptism (Cyprian, *The Baptismal Controversy*; both cited in Lienhard, 175).

■ THE TEXT IN CONTEMPORARY DISCUSSION

In a provocative treatment of Leviticus 10:1—11:47, Tamar Kaminkowski picks up Philo's interpretation to argue that he was on the right track in discerning what actually lay behind the story. Indeed, she suggests that the earliest version of the story was a homoerotic account of two men who, having experienced the intensity of the ordination rite, were stirred to seek complete union with the male God into whose service they had been ordained, and so they approached God with zeal to seek deeper intimacy with God. On this reading, God responded *positively* by meeting "them in a passion, taking them in completely." She points to God's declaration in 10:3 that "through those who are near me I will show myself holy" as support for her positive reading of the incident, but she also acknowledges that the remainder of the narrative suppresses the exalted nature of the encounter, placing boundaries around the memory of the encounter, lest all Israel also be so consumed by seeking intimacy with God (Kaminkowski, 135–39).

Leviticus 11–15

These chapters turn attention from the priests to the laity and the sort of purity they must maintain to enjoy the benefits of communion with God made possible by the construction of the sanctuary (Exodus 25–31; 25–40), the pronouncement of the rubrics for making sacrifice (Leviticus 1–7), and the establishment of the altar priesthood (Leviticus 8–9); their purity in contact with the sanctuary is also necessary to prevent them from experiencing the fate that befell Nadab and Abihu (Leviticus 10).

The chapters address what at first seem to be the only loosely related topics of the categories of creatures that are clean and unclean to human beings (chapter 11), the purification for a woman after childbirth (chapter 12), the diagnosis of and purification procedures for skin disease and contaminated garments and buildings (chapters 13–14), and the diagnosis of impurity resulting from genital discharges and modes of purification from them (chapter 15). Yet close reading of this "purity manual" indicates that these chapters expand in significant and sophisticated ways the theological argument the Priestly writer makes throughout Leviticus regarding the sustaining life that God grants to Judea in its postexilic context through the cult, the priesthood, and boundaries for the pure and the impure, the sacred and the profane. Indeed, this textual unit provides something of a hermeneutical key to the rest of Leviticus and the Priestly tradition as a whole: it focuses attention squarely on God's desire that the people of Israel, living in the complex context of Persian-period Judea, have order and life where there might otherwise be chaos and death.

Leviticus 11:1-47: Clean and Unclean Animals and Foods

▋ THE TEXT IN ITS ANCIENT CONTEXT

A lengthy discourse that classifies animals that are clean and unclean for human consumption—as well as in some cases for mere touch—this chapter is one of the best known in Leviticus. It declares land animals that are divided-hoofed or cleft-footed and also chew the cud clean, but those that are one of these but not the other unclean, and any of the latter group found dead are declared unclean. It designates water creatures that have fins and scales as clean, and all others as unfit for consumption, and unclean to the touch in carcass form. It provides a list of flying creatures that are unclean, declares winged insects to be unclean, except those that also hop, and addresses further kinds of animals encountered in carcass form that make one unclean by contact, including the carcasses of all land animals that go on four paws. It addresses the impurity of eight kinds of creatures that "swarm" upon the earth and ways they can transmit their impurity, and it extends the standard of impurity even to animals that are clean to Israel, but are encountered in carcass form. It returns to concern for swarming creatures, declaring *all* such creatures to be unclean, and justifies the prohibition on the basis of all Israel's holiness before God. It closes with the declaration that all these regulations are *torah*.

The boundless speculations regarding the rationale behind this chapter's seemingly whimsical classification of animals aside, some things are clear regarding Leviticus 11 in the larger Priestly agenda. First, drawing such strong distinctions between clean and unclean animals has the symbolic power to evoke ideas of order and chaos, life and death. Second, one clear rationale in the chapter reinforces the latter point—animals encountered in carcass form, clean or unclean in living form, are unclean—suggesting that the heart of the matter is an opposition between life and death. And third, the purpose in making these distinctions is to ensure that the people of Israel, when they do incur the impurity that contact with loss of life brings on them, do not pollute the sanctuary, the locus of their life-sustaining contact with their God (but see also Milgrom 2004, 104, for the theory that the dietary laws reflect "an ethical guide—a system whereby people will not be brutalized by killing animals for their flesh").

∎ The Text in the Interpretive Tradition

It should not surprise that the challenging nature of Leviticus 11 ensured that broadly allegorical readings would dominate much of its interpretive career. To mention but a few, *Leviticus Rabbah* 13.5 equates the nations that had been hostile to Israel with unclean animals, delivering condemnation by association with the camel, rock badger, hare, and pig to Babylonia, Media, Greece, and Rome (Neusner, 296–305), and among Christians, Clement of Alexandria identifies the clean animals with just persons who look for spiritual nourishment (*Christ the Educator* 3.11.76), and Novatian matches traditional vices with the unclean animals (Novatian, *Jewish Foods* 3.13–23; Lienhard, 176–77).

∎ The Text in Contemporary Discussion

It should come as no surprise that even though the dietary laws in Leviticus 11 were likely symbolic pointers to larger issues, many modern readers find in them practical advice for contemporary dietary practices. Such contemporary appropriations range from thoughtful reflections on food consumption and human health that use the thought world of Leviticus 11 as a departure point, to literalist readings of the text that seek to explain how the rulings might be implemented by "Bible believing Christians," to opportunistic hucksters who use the Bible to legitimate "God's diet" that ensures weight loss! A visit to the "Food and Diet" section of most any bookstore provides abundant evidence of this recurring trend in the "interpretation" of Leviticus 11.

Leviticus 12:1-8: Purity and Childbirth

∎ The Text in Its Ancient Context

Chapter 12 turns to the impact of childbirth on a woman's purity. A woman who gives birth to a male is ceremonially unclean for seven days, and for another thirty-three days of purification, during which she should not come into contact with holy things or the sanctuary; the time of impurity doubles for the birth of a daughter. At the conclusion of the woman's period of purification, sacrifice is required.

The crux in this chapter is the difference in the time of impurity between a male or female child's birth. Although there is much debate and vivid speculation as to why this is so (see, e.g., Whitekettle), that it has to do with the same theme announced in chapter 11—that loss of life, death, is the most impure-making condition possible—seems like the most plausible explanation of the difference. As a woman in childbirth endures the loss of life force, blood, in delivering a child—and is thereby the site of a great contest between life and death, between order and chaos—all the more so is she made impure when she brings a daughter into the world, who will also likely give birth in time. Likewise, she will experience menses as does her mother, another impurity-inducing loss of life force (see Leviticus 15). Thus the doubled time of impurity is unsurprising, especially given the Priestly tradents' intense interest in creating a world where the contaminating threat of death and the loss of life force is kept far removed from the sanctuary.

▪ THE TEXT IN THE INTERPRETIVE TRADITION

Jubilees, a Jewish pseudepigraphic work from second-century-BCE Judea, rewrites Genesis 1 to Exodus 14. Among its various purposes was to provide origin stories for legal norms given to Moses at Sinai in the narratives that extend from creation to the escape from Egypt. In doing this, *Jubilees* gets in on the effort to make sense of the double period of purification for a woman who bears a daughter. *Jubilees* 3 explains that God required Adam to wait a week and thirty-three more days before entering Eden, and because she came from Adam, Eve was compelled to wait twice that period before she could enter.

▪ THE TEXT IN CONTEMPORARY DISCUSSION

Remarkably, there are modern Christian rites that depend on Leviticus 12, although they are now mostly abandoned. One is (or better, was) the practice among Anglicans and Roman Catholics of "churching" (welcoming back into the communion) a postpartum woman at the relevant time. Interestingly, at least in the Anglican Communion, instead of altogether abandoning the outdated and objectionable rite of "churching" prescribed by the 1662 Book of Common Prayer, it has been replaced in the 1979 Book of Common Prayer by the "Thanksgiving for the Birth or Adoption of a Child," a rite that welcomes the newborn and her parents into the community of faith *as soon as the family desires* (for other examples, see further Schearing).

Leviticus 13:1—14:57: Impurity through Skin Eruptions

▪ THE TEXT IN ITS ANCIENT CONTEXT

This long section deals with what is often referred to as "leprosy," translating the Hebrew word *ṣārāʿat*. But since the word refers to the "disease" in garments and buildings as well, the term is hardly apposite. An alternative approach might be to speak of "consequential eruptions" of the skin inasmuch as the breaking of boundaries that contain human life force seems to be at issue here, as was the case in chapter 12. On this reading, chapter 13 addresses how the priests identify consequential skin eruptions—ones that break the skin and have the potential for loss of blood, life force—and prescribe ways of dealing with them as instances of impurity. The same sort of reasoning about what is a consequential eruption and one that is not seems to be at work in sections that address boils as another form or skin disease, burns, eruptions on the head and in the beard, rashes and blisters, and balding heads. Anyone deemed impure by the priests must live alone, wear torn clothes, cover the upper lip, and cry out in warning to all who encounter him or her, "Unclean! Unclean!" The chapter concludes with a long passage that applies the same rules for determining the significance of eruptions and blemishes in garments.

Chapter 14 lays out the elaborate rite of purification that someone who has suffered from a consequential eruption of their skin must perform, followed by provisions for the poor who cannot afford the offering of the goods normally required for purification. The chapter also addresses the diagnosis and purification of walls in dwellings made impure by "consequential eruptions," probably of mildew.

Understanding this involved treatment of various sorts of "skin" diseases within the framework of the Priestly agenda in postexilic Judea helps one appreciate what might otherwise seem like some of the strangest material in Leviticus. First, recall the concern of the Priestly tradents to assure recipients that the hegemonic pluralism of postexilic Judea would not overwhelm their own communal order with chaos. Next, consider the fact that in many ancient (and contemporary) cultures the human body serves as a metaphor for one's community (Douglas 1966). Then envision how an elaborate system of purity and impurity measures meant to contain and limit instances of skin disease, losses of life force from the human body, might have functioned in the imagination of those postexilic Judeans. On this reading, these chapters were likely intended to inspire the Judeans of Persian-period Judea to share in the responsibility of guarding the boundaries that preserved the integrity of their community, and allusively instructed them on how to do so.

▌▌THE TEXT IN THE INTERPRETIVE TRADITION

Given the foregoing analysis, it is not surprising that the Dead Sea Scrolls community—a sectarian Judean group that flourished around the turn of the eras—seems to have been particularly adept at deploying some of the legislative norms of Leviticus 13–14 in their own communal organization. For example, according to 1QS 3:5-6, the would-be member of the community who refuses the offer of inclusion in the fellowship is to be shunned and is referred to by the community membership as "Unclean! Unclean!" all the days of his life. The imprecation is a clear use of Lev. 13:45-46, a way of bringing to mind the "scriptural" manual on ensuring that bodily (read: communal) boundaries are observed so as to guard the purity of the body (read: community). This is a remarkable case of using language that mused about bodily boundary disruption as a way of speaking metaphorically of the human community to address directly the disruption of the human community.

▌▌THE TEXT IN CONTEMPORARY DISCUSSION

A survey of homiletical attempts, online and otherwise, to contend with this difficult material is routinely disappointing. On the side of escaping the text's difficulty by occupying oneself with historical observations, discussions of the appropriate terminology for "leprosy" abound; and on the side of reading allegorically or the like are the numerous attempts to make the skin disease discussed in the text a metonym for alienating sin in contemporary human conduct. Neither approach serves much homiletical good, and both show little regard for the text's capacity for depth of meaning. Perhaps a more useful approach would begin by acknowledging how profoundly disturbing this text really is, precisely in the effect the restrictions of the skin-diseased would have had in the ancient Mediterranean world (esp. 13:46). There your identity was constituted by your connections with others; alone, you had no discernible identity. In this light, the insistence that the skin-diseased person afflicted with consequential eruptions remain completely apart—that he or she dwell utterly alone (Heb., *bdd*)—is shocking. A sermon worth listening to would be one that wrestles with this difficulty and asks where in contemporary life and society similar dilemmas appear in our midst— and how we might respond.

Leviticus 15:1-33: Discharge of Life Fluids

■ THE TEXT IN ITS ANCIENT CONTEXT

Leviticus 15 concerns genital discharges of various types and degrees of severity. A man with a "flow" from his penis is impure, as is anyone who comes into contact with him or with an object he has polluted. To become pure again, the man with the flow must wait, wash, and make a sacrifice after the flow ceases. The discharge of semen in intercourse is a less severe instance of impurity, requiring only that the man and woman wash and wait until evening to be ritually pure again. Likewise, ordinary menses, though making a woman impure for seven days, is clean again after simply washing and waiting until evening, as is a man who lay with her during menses. By contrast, a woman's abnormal bleeding—presumably menses out of cycle and other conditions that cause vaginal bleeding—requires her to wait the usual seven days, wash and wait until evening on the last day, and like the man with a nonprocreative penile discharge, make an offering to be fully restored to ritual purity. The chapter concludes with the rationale for regulating so closely the variety of potential genital discharges: polluting the tabernacle through one's impurity could be deadly.

Little needs to be said about the role of this chapter in the Priestly agenda—what was already said about the concern to regulate consequential eruptions of the skin applies a fortiori to genital discharges as they are equally losses of life force, if not more so. Any loss of life force is defiling, out of the ordinary losses are most concerning (requiring sacrifice at the end of the purification process), all of them are symbolic of the potential decline of the community itself, and all of them are dangerous to their bearers vis-à-vis the holiness of the sanctuary and potentially damaging to the integrity of the sanctuary as well.

■ THE TEXT IN THE INTERPRETIVE TRADITION

The Qumran community's treatment of Leviticus 15 is an interesting reminder of the surprising diversity we find in the legal writings of that group, which is nonetheless tempered by their shared tendency to intensify the legal norms of Leviticus. For example, the *Temple Scroll*, 4Q274, and 4Q277 address the impurity of a man with a genital discharge; all three extend and intensify the requirements in Leviticus 15, safeguarding him and others from the consequences of his impurity. Yet while 4Q274 and the *Temple Scroll* quarantine the man with the discharge away from the clean and unclean, the concern in 4Q277 that he wash his hands lest the things he touch pollute others who are clean indicates that it does not require quarantine.

■ THE TEXT IN CONTEMPORARY DISCUSSION

The late Dame Mary Douglas (1921–2007), one of the twentieth century's most significant anthropologists, shaped a great deal of the contemporary understanding of Leviticus 11–15. Her 1966 book *Purity and Danger* already addressed the dietary laws in Leviticus 11, and suggested that the regulations were not explicable on some hygienic basis, but were symbolic of larger concerns for boundary maintenance (and thus unclean animals were ones that did not fit established categories—they were boundary violators). Even though Douglas later adjusted her argument regarding chapter 11 in particular (suggesting that the aim was rather to map the human body and what it can receive for sustenance to the sacrificial altar; Douglas 2001), this 1966 reading was and remains influential in how people read the purity laws of Leviticus 11–15 as a whole, something evident even in this commentary's approach to this central section of Leviticus.

Leviticus 16:1-34: The Day of Atonement

This chapter is a distinct unit within Leviticus, addressing the procedures for observing the Day of Atonement. Some assume that it originally followed Leviticus 10 because it begins with the announcement that the Lord spoke to Moses after the death of Aaron's two sons, which arguably overlooks everything between the end of chapter 10 and 16. There is also a thematic coherence between the former episode and the rite described in chapter 16, as both relate in some way to ensuring the sanctity of the sanctuary. That said, chapter 16 has its own concerns that transcend the Nadab and Abihu incident, as well as the material that intervenes between that episode and the present chapter: its focus is on the rite by which the high priest ensures all Israel, everywhere, is reconciled to God on an annual basis. In that sense, it can be argued that it was the appropriate conclusion to the trajectory the P tradents constructed beginning with Exodus 25, ensuring as it does that *all* Judeans anywhere in the world would benefit from the temple cult's purpose in connecting them inextricably to their God.

▌ THE TEXT IN ITS ANCIENT CONTEXT

After recalling the Nadab and Abihu incident, the narrator records God's speech to Moses, warning him that Aaron should not approach the ark of the covenant willy-nilly, lest he die from contact with God's presence. Instead, he should prepare for such an encounter by clothing himself in appropriate garments, and by bringing a young bull for a sin offering and a ram for a burnt offering, as well as two male goats for a sin offering and ram for a burnt offering for the people. The bull is a sin offering for Aaron, and one goat is the people's sin offering, while the other goat is the animal to be sent into the wilderness alive "for Azazel." Aaron confesses the people's iniquity over the goat and sends it into the wilderness by a person designated for the task. Then he washes and changes into his ordinary vestments and makes the burnt offerings of the two rams to atone for himself and Israel, and he turns the fat of the sin offering into smoke on the altar. The one who set the goat for Azazel free washes and returns to the camp, and another person takes the remains of the bull and goat of the sin offerings outside the camp to be burned, after which he washes and returns to the camp. The chapter declares this an annual observance set for the tenth day of the seventh month, a day of fasting and rest from work for all of Israel; the rite should be performed by the high priest as an act of atonement for the tent of meeting, the altar, the priests, and the people altogether.

▌ THE TEXT IN THE INTERPRETIVE TRADITION

The interpretive history of Leviticus 16 is understandably rich; the powerful encounter between God and humanity that the Day of Atonement ceremony creates was and is an irresistible topic for Jews and Christians alike. We already see echoes of the rite in the penitential prayers of Ezra 9 and Nehemiah 9 (Bautch). Its observance played a central role in the life of the Qumran community (Gilders), and its abiding significance even after the destruction of the Second Temple is evident in the rich tradition of Jewish and Christian remakings of it for new uses (Stöckl). At the center of this vast interpretive tradition is the goal of invoking and keeping alive the rite's capacity to bring humanity into intense contact with a God who intends to repair all of creation (e.g., Rom. 3:25).

The mysterious character Azazel has also attracted considerable attention in the interpretive history of Leviticus 16 (see, e.g., *1 Enoch* 8:1-3; 10:8, where he is one of the "fallen angels" of Gen. 6:1-4). One of the most important moments in that history came in its earliest stages. The Septuagint (Lev. 16:8 LXX) renders the Hebrew of Azazel with the Greek *apopompaios*, "sent away," so that Aaron casts lots to determine one goat for the Lord and another "to be sent off." The translation of the three further occurrences of the name in 16:10, 26, follow suit, more or less, effectively erasing the existence of Azazel as a separate being, and replacing him with the concept of the "go-away goat," or the "scapegoat," which itself has had a long interpretive afterlife.

▮ THE TEXT IN CONTEMPORARY DISCUSSION

Surely the Day of Atonement (*Yom Kippur*, the conclusion of the "Days of Awe") competes closely with the feast of Passover for the distinction of being the most widely observed moment in the yearly Jewish liturgical calendar. Apart from the obvious exception of temple sacrifice, all the other requirements of the rite declared in 16:29-34 are kept, and to this have been added other observances related to the day's focus (e.g., *Teshuva*, confession of sins; *Avodah*, recalling the temple sacrifice). Notably, this relatively intense commitment among secular and religious Jews around the world to observing Yom Kippur is in the spirit of the Priestly tradition's likely aim in legislating it. In the Persian period, many Judeans lived in Diaspora, and the ritual acts of the high priest were intended, among other things, to release the sins of all Judeans, everywhere. In its modern form, a sort of democratization of its observance upholds that key focus of the Day of Atonement in Leviticus 16.

Leviticus 17–26

Leviticus 17–26 is commonly called the "Holiness Code" because of the insistence in key passages that the people of Israel be as holy as their God. While the command to be holy appears relatively infrequently (e.g., 19:1-2; 20:7), the title is nonetheless appropriate: the driving interest of these chapters is to address the consequences that come from a different sort of democratization, in this case of the quality of holiness among the people of Israel.

The relationship between the Holiness Code (abbreviated as H) and the rest of the Priestly work, within which it is situated, is a matter of ongoing dispute. Some argue that it was a law code the Priestly tradents knew and appreciated and that they felt comfortable integrating into their larger contribution. Others view it as a friendly amendment to P created by a "priestly" writer interested in bringing Deuteronomic law into alignment with P interests. Still others hold that it is of such a different character, especially in its view of holiness, that it cannot have been embraced by the Priestly tradents but should instead be treated as a critical response to the P material. Among those who take the latter view, there is further division; some treat P and H as First Temple tradents, and others hold to the view that they are Second Temple, postexilic thinkers and writers. (For a full history of scholarship, see Nihan, 4–11.)

This commentary assigns H a post-P, postexilic date, and understands it to have been composed as a literary supplement that offered a critical contrast with the Priestly work. It did this by positing the democratization of holiness and then imagining the consequences for the cult, the priests, and the laity.

Why a thinker might have felt this necessary in Persian-period Judea is easily surmised from the literary evidence that the priests had come to abuse their privileges, and the laity may also have engaged in practices that undercut the justice of the postexilic community. Malachi condemns the priests for replacing pure offerings with blemished beasts from the temple flocks (Mal. 1:7-8) and the laity for bringing similarly unacceptable offerings in the first place (1:13-14). And it is perhaps both groups that Malachi condemns with his withering attack on the infidelity of the people to their God and husbands to their wives, a pairing that may have had to do with the worship of foreign gods and goddesses (perhaps even through cultic intercourse; 2:10-16). And Third Isaiah rails in myriad ways against the priests in particular, but also the economic and power elite for the abuses that inflicted injustice on the nonelite, even calling Israel's "sentinels" and "shepherds" by a most vile name in antiquity, "Dogs!" (Isa. 56:10-11). It is not hard to imagine how these things happened: the priests, enriched by the offerings of the laity, welcomed every opportunity to receive them, and the laity, hoping to benefit from unjust dealings and the occasional worship of other gods, were only too happy to oblige as they sought restoration to God's good graces through sacrificial offerings.

In envisioning a world where the holiness that the Priestly tradition confined to the temple and priests extends to all of Israel—a world where all experience was holy—the Holiness Code offers a powerful thought experiment. What would be the consequences in a world imbued with holiness for the priests and the people if they lived as Malachi and Third Isaiah suggest? As the following commentary suggests, the Holiness Code systematically considers that possibility, and in so doing might well have called the people and their leaders to account for their death-dealing, chaos-engendering abuse of a system meant to give order and life.

Leviticus 17:1-16: Blood Is Life

▌ THE TEXT IN ITS ANCIENT CONTEXT

Like the other law codes in the Torah, this one begins by addressing sacrifice (cf. Exod. 20:22-26; Deuteronomy 12). But H is truly radical, declaring that any slaughter of a beast must be recognized as a holy act—a sacrifice—through the priest's sacralization of it at the sanctuary's entrance by splashing its blood on the altar placed there and burning some of its fat as a pleasing odor to God; failure to do this results in being "cut off from the people." The chapter further prohibits any human consumption of the blood of the sacrifice and declares that any blood shed in the act of hunting for food must be poured on the ground and covered with earth, and that eating an animal found dead merely makes one unclean, a condition remedied by washing and waiting until evening.

The potential impact of this legislation on priestly prebends is highly suggestive of the Holiness Code's larger agenda. By sacralizing the death of *any* animal, H significantly expanded the opportunities for laypersons to get God's attention through sacrifice and at the same time potentially threatened the supply of prebends to the priests in the temple. The consequence of making all of Israel's experience holy, at least with respect to sacrifice, is to undercut the benefits of the sacrificial system to the priests and increase its capacity to serve the laity. There could hardly have been a better way to suggest the powerful consequences for the priests if holiness, which it was their responsibility to guard and protect, were to escape its boundaries and make all experience holy.

▌THE TEXT IN THE INTERPRETIVE TRADITION

The obvious difficulties of implementing the legislation proposed in Leviticus 17 not only speaks in favor of H having been largely a "thought experiment," a sort of utopian critique of P, but also provoked its share of imaginative reworking by later interpreters who did not see it as such, but as a proposal for actual practice. Column 52 of the *Temple Scroll* from Qumran is an example of this response. It engages in a complex "exegesis" of the chapter that first confirms the ruling in Leviticus 17, but also restricts it by saying that it applies only to those within three days' walk from the temple and that any proceeds from the slaughter-become-sacrifice due the offerer must be consumed at the temple. But then the scroll immediately adds that a *blemished* clean animal may be slaughtered in a profane way and its flesh consumed without the trouble of a trip to the temple at so little a distance as four miles from the sanctuary (52:13-18). Here we encounter a legist who was looking for—and found—a loophole in the Holiness Code law that that would have made it doable, even if still onerous.

Providing a sharp contrast to interpreters of different backgrounds, John Chrysostom ignores the sacrificial impracticalities of Leviticus 17. Instead, he focuses on the heightened concern for the blood of the beast in the chapter to argue that this points to what distinguishes humans from animals—the animal's blood carries its soul (thus the intense concern to treat it with enormous respect), but the human soul is incorporeal and transcends the body (*Homilies on Genesis* 13.10; cited by Lienhard, 186).

▌THE TEXT IN CONTEMPORARY DISCUSSION

Interestingly, it was not only in antiquity that the (probably) utopian vision of the H legist was nonetheless treated as a requirement for real practice; at least in one respect, the laws of *kashrut* through the ages reflect respect for the chapter as well. Leviticus 17:10-14 is taken to require that in preparing meat from animals for food, the greatest amount of blood is drained away as possible, something accomplished through soaking meat in water and then salting it and letting it sit before cooking. Today much of that work is done by meat packers so that kosher meat can be purchased, already prepared for the consumer.

Leviticus 18:1—20:27: Being Holy People

■ THE TEXT IN ITS ANCIENT CONTEXT

Leviticus 18–20 is perhaps best characterized as a collection of prohibitions and admonitions for laypeople who have been declared holy by their holy God. Leviticus 18 focuses almost exclusively on forbidden sexual relations, declaring that even though the people of Canaan may have indulged in these relations, the people of Israel should not. The prohibitions include sexual relations with women in a man's extended family, with a woman in menstrual uncleanness, with a kinsman's wife, with another male, and between a woman and an animal; additionally, Israelites are forbidden to give their offspring to Molech. The rationale for forbidding these things is that Canaanites did all of them and defiled the land, and if Israel were to follow their example, they would defile the land and be cast out too, and cut off from their people in the bargain.

Chapter 19 follows this set of prohibitions with a more disparate collection of prohibitions and admonitions controlled by the opening declaration, "The LORD spoke to Moses saying: 'Speak to all the congregation of the people of Israel and say to them: You shall be holy, for I the LORD your God am holy.'" An expanded Decalogue of sorts follows, reflecting on the consequences of being declared holy by God, and the chapter concludes with a potpourri of specific regulations dealing with everything from prohibitions on mixing kinds of animals, seeds, and thread types in garments to how a man may trim his beard.

Chapter 20 then recalls many of the offenses already detailed in chapters 18–19 and assigns to them (somewhat vague) penalties, and concludes with general exhortations to keep God's statutes and commandments to be worthy of the land and avoid expulsion from it.

Within the broader agenda of the Holiness Code, this long text unit functions to indict and challenge the laity, just as chapter 17 did the priesthood. It is useful to take the prohibition of various sexual unions in chapter 18 as an example. The range of possibilities as to why such behaviors might have been a concern remains much under discussion, yet some basic options can be surmised: in a male-dominated culture, sexual victimization of weaker parties (women in one's household, men in subservient positions) may have been an ongoing problem, and a practice perpetrators thought they could be "excused" from through the sacrificial system the P tradents offered (see especially the possibility of converting intentional sins into unintentional ones in 5:14—6:7); it is also possible that these were sex acts that could count as worship of fertility gods and goddesses, and could also have been viewed by their perpetrators as remediable under the Priestly system. Assuming something like one of these scenarios (or other possibilities scholarship has conjured to explain this passage), the Holiness tradents offer a stark portrait of the consequences for committing these sins against the weaker members of one's wider community, if all experience were holy: offenders would not be able to make sacrifice and be restored, but would instead be "cut off" from the community, a penalty that may have involved death administered by the community, but was more likely thought to be a consequence that God brought upon the sinner (Milgrom 1991, 457–60)—in any case, it was sin with grave consequences that could not be avoided through the sacrifices prescribed by the P legislation.

■ THE TEXT IN THE INTERPRETIVE TRADITION

The simple declaration in Lev. 18:5 that by keeping and doing God's statutes and ordinances "one shall live" is often missed in the contemporary fascination with the sexual-misconduct legislation in the rest of the chapter; yet it was this verse that had the richer interpretive history in antiquity. One example of that interpretive vein is evident in the *Damascus Document* (CD), a key work from the Qumran community. CD 3.12–20 opens with the declaration that a select group that had kept God's revealed commandments received a further revelation of deeper secrets having to do with calendrical observances and "the testimonies of his righteousness and the truth of his ways, and the desires of his will *which one must do so that he will live by them* (Lev. 18:5)" (3.15–16). The passage continues to make clear that if this select group keeps these norms, they will not just have life, but life eternal. The sectarian author, in short, has claimed the promise of Lev. 18:5 for the special way of life to which his community was committed.

In sharp contrast to this is the way Paul puts Lev. 18:5 in complex tension with other "proof texts" from the Hebrew Bible (including, among others, Hab. 2:4) in Gal. 3:10-14, essentially arguing for the negation of its effect for believers (Martyn 1997, 307–36). Just as the Qumran covenanters thought it a powerful verse for making their claims to superior law keeping, Paul saw it necessary to negate it through complex rhetorical argumentation. There can hardly be better evidence for the degree of influence this one verse in Leviticus exerted over the ancient Jewish and Christian imagination.

■ THE TEXT IN CONTEMPORARY DISCUSSION

While Lev. 18:5 fascinated ancient interpreters, the two prohibitions of intercourse between males in Lev. 18:22; 20:13 are what fascinate contemporary audiences, for good or for ill. And no amount of reasoning from a historical-critical perspective that the passages are not about homosexuality, but rather the sexual victimization of a weaker party by a stronger party, seems to call a halt to the vehement use of both verses by parties on all sides of the debate (for one of those sensible historical-critical discussions, see Wright Knust, 147–50). For that reason, perhaps the best way to approach the contemporary debate is through reading reasonable attempts to survey the breadth of actual uses of the passages in Leviticus in discussing homosexuality today (see, e.g., Stahlberg). The result is a dizzying array of readings, many of which speak more to the horizons of the interpreters than of the texts—which may be as much a lesson about interpretation in general as it is about how these simple texts play out in volatile debates.

Leviticus 21:1—22:33: Priestly Holiness and Offerings

■ THE TEXT IN ITS ANCIENT CONTEXT

This long section addresses the consequences of holiness for the priesthood and for the offerings of Israel. Leviticus 21 makes (remarkably strong) prescriptions regarding all priests: because they are holy to God and make God's offerings, they should only have limited contact with the dead; they should not mar their bodies or cut away facial or cranial hair unnecessarily; and they should not marry women who are unclean by prostitution, divorce, or other defilement. Laypeople should treat them with the respect owed to the sanctified, and their daughters who profane their line by acts of prostitution should be executed by fire. The chapter further lays out the standards to which the anointed (high) priest is held: he should not make a mess of his hair, tear his garments, have any contact with the dead, or even go outside of the sanctuary lest he defile it, and he can only marry a virgin of his own kin. The rest of the chapter then lists a range of physical blemishes that would disqualify someone of the priestly line from service in the sanctuary, allowing them nonetheless access to the proceeds of the offerings. Leviticus 22 then commands that priests who have somehow incurred any kind of impurity may not approach the sanctified foodstuffs provided to the priests through the people's offerings, and decrees that no layperson may eat of the sacred portions (excepting only those who are of the priest's household by purchase, or by birth and still within the household). Additional detail is added to the general claim that a layperson's animal offering must be without blemish, naming a broad range of circumstances that can render a beast unfit, and there are instructions on how a newly born animal may be offered as a sacrifice. The section closes with another passage remarking on God's holiness as the motivation for keeping the commandments laid out in the preceding section.

Within the framework and agenda of the Holiness Code as a whole, this section seems intended to point out the consequences of intensifying God's holiness in Israel for the priests and the things they deal with. And just as the legislation for the laity in the preceding section makes clear that the chief significance of making all experience holy is to render things possible under the Priestly system impossible—at least without serious consequences coming to bear—the same holds true here. Priests who might have qualified for service and all of its benefits in the Priestly world—and certainly did, if we are to believe the level of corruption that Malachi and Third Isaiah identified—would be summarily dismissed from contact with the sacred offerings and precincts under the Holiness Code's stipulations. Similarly, the rules on how prebends might be handled were more limiting, as were the norms for everything from whom a priest might marry to how he might groom himself. On the reading of the Holiness Code promoted in this commentary, at least, this section is thus a wily indictment of the priestly abuses which might have been allowed by the Priestly perspective achieved precisely by taking with utmost seriousness the P tradition's own view that the priests, the sanctified offerings of Israel, and the space they worked in were the locus of God's holiness.

▌ THE TEXT IN THE INTERPRETIVE TRADITION

Because of the Qumran community's intense interest in the purity (or better, impurity) of the priesthood and temple practice in Jerusalem and in creating their own alternatives to those, portions of this passage in Leviticus were frequently commented on by the Essene tradents. Two examples from 4QMMT, a legal document that lays out a number of the group's (early?) legal positions, demonstrate this.

The first instance involves a reading of Lev. 22:28, which prohibits slaughtering an offspring with its parent on the same day. 4QMMT B 36–38 seems to rely on an expansive reading of that rule in answering the question of what one does if an animal brought for sacrifice proves to be pregnant: the text seems to read the "slaughter" of Leviticus as "sacrifice" and "parent" and "offspring" as "mother" and "fetus" to decree that both may not be counted as an offering to God. The second instance is 4QMMT B 75–82, a much-discussed passage, that in any case agrees with and seems to intensify the sharp limitations on who might be acceptable as a wife for a priest (Lev. 21:7, 14).

Interestingly, the Essene use of this section of Leviticus grows out of the same sort of concerns this commentary assumes provoked the author(s) of the Holiness Code to create their utopian, corrective, critical vision of what the Priestly work wrought. The Essenes, however, distinguished themselves sharply from the Holiness school, using H's extension of holiness to all Israel and all of its experience not merely as a utopian corrective but also as a guide for rules they wanted to be implemented in real time, in the real world.

◼ The Text in Contemporary Discussion

In a somewhat embarrassing contemporary use of the same regulations regarding priests and marriage in Leviticus 21, one does not have to search far on the Internet to discover American right-wing fundamentalist readers of the Bible who cite Lev. 21:13 (in a selective and decidedly nonliteralist way!) to argue that the prohibition on married clergy in the Roman Catholic communion is antibiblical. And searching just a little further turns up those among the latter group who will go so far as to suggest, ignorantly, that the sex abuse scandals that plagued Catholicism in recent decades would have been avoided if only marriage had been permitted. That it is difficult to find much from this portion of Leviticus in contemporary discussion may say more about the sensible allergy to getting caught up in such nonsense than about the availability of this section of text for thoughtful reflections on contemporary pastoral and priestly leadership across Christian and Jewish denominations.

Leviticus 23:1-44: Feasts and Sacred Observances

◼ The Text in Its Ancient Context

Alongside Num. 28:1—29:40, this chapter offers P's calendar of feasts and sacred observances. After an introductory passage in verses 1-2, verse 3 declares the Sabbath. Then verse 4 gives a typical Holiness Code title to all that remains: "These are the appointed festivals of the Lord, the *holy* convocations, which you shall celebrate at the time appointed for them." Passover is addressed in verses 5-8, verses 9-14 address the offering of the firstfruits, verses 15-22 the Feast of Weeks, verses 23-25 the Feast of Trumpets, verses 26-32 the Day of Atonement, and verses 33-44 the Feast of Booths (Sukkoth; see below). Here too a recurring feature is reference to holiness as a feature of the feasts and/or a motivation for them. And by now, the role of a text like this within the Holiness Code's larger agenda should be relatively predictable. In this case, the concern is to extend the imagined world as imbued with holiness to the concept of time itself.

◼ The Text in the Interpretive Tradition

It almost goes without saying that the calendar laws articulated in this chapter, in spite of featuring in a work that was likely utopian in its original vision, had great impact on later Jewish and

Christian liturgical calendars, both in terms of the timing of major observances and on the way in which observances were carried out.

More interesting, though, were the ways in which some interpreters sought to spiritualize or moralize the temporal legislation in chapter 23. A parade example comes from Augustine, who instructed his congregants in a sermon on the true meaning of the admonition in Lev. 23:3 not to perform any "servile work" on the Sabbath. He argued that observing the Sabbath in that sense is to resist sin, as sin is servile work (*Homily* 270; cited in Lienhard, 193–94).

▌ THE TEXT IN CONTEMPORARY DISCUSSION

The calendar of major observances laid out in Leviticus 23 continues to shape modern Jewish practice, and in a time when many religionists in America are working to revive their traditions, various of the customs in Leviticus 23 that may have gone by the wayside in the past are being observed with renewed vigor in contemporary Jewish life. One visible example on many college campuses across America every fall is the observance of Sukkoth by Hillel groups, who construct in a public, open space and use according to rabbinic teaching a *sukkah* ("booth").

Leviticus 24:1-23: Temple Observances and Blasphemy Punishment

▌ THE TEXT IN ITS ANCIENT CONTEXT

This chapter, seemingly out of context, addresses two vaguely related "temple" topics, the maintenance of an eternally burning lamp inside the sanctuary and the provision of the "sanctuary bread" consumed on a regular basis by the Aaronites as their "perpetual due," and the tale of a blasphemer that forms an inclusio around a list of communal crimes and their punishments. The chapter closes with the declaration that Israel should have a common law for the alien and the citizen.

▌ THE TEXT IN THE INTERPRETIVE TRADITION

Early Christian interpreters were understandably drawn to the twelve loaves stipulated in Lev. 24:5-9, evoking so easily thoughts of the dozen apostles and the Eucharist. In the (rather unwelcome) spirit of supersessionism, Cyril of Jerusalem argues that the bread and cup of the Eucharist bring the "Old Covenant" reflected in this passage to an absolute end and replace it with the "New Covenant" (*Catechetical Lecture* 4.5; cited in Lienhard, 196). More imaginative is Bede's suggestion that this foretells the twelve baskets of bread fragments the twelve apostles gather from the five loaves they distributed to the hungry, and that this story refers to the "sacraments of the Scriptures," which the multitudes could not receive, but which the "apostles" and "apostolic men" (read: ecclesiastical elites) could take in (*On the Tabernacle* 1.7; cited in Lienhard, 196).

▌ THE TEXT IN CONTEMPORARY DISCUSSION

"Diaspora studies" is a vibrant new field in the academy. Leviticus 24:22 surely has something to contribute to those who study populations in diaspora, seeking to make their way in legal systems that are alien to them along with just about everything else they experience. What would it mean to take seriously the verse's admonition that there be *one law* for the alien and the citizen? In its

Holiness Code context, it seems certain to have been a stipulation meant to critique a system in which that was not the case, and presumably the alien was experiencing injustice as a consequence. In a globalized world, does this same, implicit critique hold true? Or have circumstances become such that a country's legal systems need to become more pluralistic, more flexible to take into account the norms and customs of guest people? This is surely the issue in several European countries and America today as judicial systems and legislation seek to be responsive to the needs of guest peoples, and in some instances seek the opposite, to require guest populations to conform to local law and custom. Applying Lev. 24:22 to today's context, in fact, presents interesting questions of justice, though far removed perhaps from those the text originally might have sought to address.

Leviticus 25:1-55: Sabbatical and Jubilee Years

▌ THE TEXT IN ITS ANCIENT CONTEXT

In this long chapter, the Holiness Code gives the rules for observing the Sabbatical and Jubilee Years, the rationale for their observance, and the specifics of implementing the general guidelines for both observances. Every seventh year is a Sabbatical Year, a year of rest for the land; and every fiftieth year is a Jubilee Year, in which land sold to others reverts to the original owners, and Israelites in servitude to others are freed to return to their own homes and families. The chapter offers further instruction on how to execute redemption of property in the Jubilee and how Israel should treat its own poor and impoverished resident aliens, particularly when their poverty leads to indentured servitude (which can be resolved by redemption).

This chapter surely originally followed Leviticus 23 and as such continued the utopian legislation to sanctify all of Israel's experience, including its time. And it is this chapter in particular that suggests the utopian nature of the Holiness Code. As lofty as the ideal is of giving the land and indentured servants rest from their respective labors and of returning land purchased to sellers at regular intervals in time, these were very likely stipulations few if any observed, and may even not have been intended as such by the H tradent. It was perhaps enough for this writer to make clear again the consequences of taking seriously God's intentions for Israel and its resources; if God's holiness were extended to *all* of Israel's time, *all things* would be required to experience their rest in ways no one could have otherwise ever imagined.

▌ THE TEXT IN THE INTERPRETIVE TRADITION

The Jewish interpretive tradition that builds on this chapter's Sabbatical and Jubilee legislation is enormously rich. Elements of the *Enoch* traditions hearken to it, its echoes are present in the Jesus traditions, and of course, the Jewish pseudepigraphon *Jubilees* relies on its basic principles. It is remarkable, then, that the Dead Sea Scrolls were actually able to enrich our database in this regard. 4Q226, a document that looks to have been a Hebrew text resembling *Jubilees* (thus its moniker, 4QPseudo-Jubilees) seems to recall the exodus much as it is narrated in *Jubilees* 48. However, this fragment echoes the otherwise singular instance of marking a Jubilee as "holy" in Lev. 25:12. The author of the *Jubilees* narrative, it seems, sought to "out-holy" the Holiness Code, designating the Jubilee related to the exodus as transcending even the "ordinary holiness" of an ordinary Jubilee.

■ THE TEXT IN CONTEMPORARY DISCUSSION

While the "Jubilee Year" is not recognized in modern Judaism, since 1300 CE the Christian church has marked its passage and the tradition survives in modern Roman Catholicism. The last observance of it was from Christmas Eve 1999 to Epiphany (January 6) 2001, under the leadership of John Paul II. Echoing the merciful aspects of the biblical Jubilee, the pope marked the beginning of the year by opening the *porta sancta*, the "holy door," to St. Peter's Basilica, which is unsealed only in the Jubilee Year to signal the opening of the portals of grace to the whole church.

Leviticus 26:1—27:34: Blessing and Curse, Vow and Offering

■ THE TEXT IN ITS ANCIENT CONTEXT

Chapter 26 completes the Holiness Code, and as such performs a typical purpose, offering blessing and curses on those who keep or do not keep the statutes and ordinances contained in the rest of the code. Roughly the first third of the chapter describes the blessings that flow from obedience to the triple commandment to avoid idolatry, to keep the Sabbath, and to honor the sanctuary. Nearly the remaining two-thirds rehearse the deepening crisis God would bring on Israel in the land if it were not to obey, culminating in the people's expulsion from the land and the land's Sabbath rest from their affliction of it. The chapter draws to a close by offering the possibility that even if Israel is driven from the land by its own sin, if Israel calls on the Lord again from its exile, God will not spurn them but will remember them and the covenant with their ancestors.

This is surely the closing chapter of the Holiness Code. As such, it admirably achieves the purpose of drawing to a resounding conclusion the argument for a utopian vision makes vis-à-vis the reality it critiques. It states clearly the consequences of living *as though* God's holiness filled every aspect of Israel's experience—what this utopian visionary commends to his audience as the remedy for the abuses of the Priestly system—and it paints a picture of the fulfillment of Israel's destiny as God's people prosperous and at peace in the land God promised. With equal clarity, it lays out the consequences of living *as though* God's holiness could be disregarded at every turn—the loss of the promise, of peace, of prosperity, and of the land itself.

Clearly an appendix to Leviticus as a whole, chapter 27 gives guidelines for redeeming vows of persons (vv. 1-8), animals (vv. 9-13), buildings (vv. 14-15), land (vv. 16-25), firstlings (vv. 26-27), other things devoted to the Lord (vv. 28-29), and tithes (vv. 30-33); verse 34 indicates that the preceding regulations were given to Moses by God for the people of Israel on Sinai.

■ THE TEXT IN THE INTERPRETIVE TRADITION

The last word in the interpretation of Leviticus goes to Augustine, who in alluding to Lev. 26:12, "I will be your God," writes: "God will be the source of every satisfaction, more than any heart can rightly crave, more than life and health, food and wealth, glory and honor, peace and good—so that God, as St. Paul said, 'may be all in all' (1 Cor. 15:28). He will be the consummation of all our desiring—the object of our unending vision, of our unlessening love, of our eternal praise. And in this gift of vision, this response of love, this paean of praise, all alike will share, as all will share in everlasting life" (*City of God* 22.30; cited in Lienhard, 204).

◼ THE TEXT IN CONTEMPORARY DISCUSSION

Just so, in contemporary reflection on Leviticus, it is chapter 26 that most evokes soaring theological sentiments, and for good reason. Beginning with blessings for the covenant keepers and continuing with curses for those who fail by the covenant's standards, the chapter nonetheless returns to the theme of God's blessing for those who seek a connection with God, even from the circumstances of sin and rebellion. As John Goldingay remarks in a discussion of "Old Testament answers" to "key questions for Christians," Lev. 26:42, 44-45 makes clear that God is not constrained by the covenant from "taking action on the people's behalf" even "in the context of their wrongdoing"; indeed, it is God's being "mindful of the covenant" (123) that ensures such graciousness even for a wayward creation.

Works Cited

Bautch, Richard. 2012. "The Formulary of Atonement (Lev 16:12) in Penitential Prayers in the Second Temple Period." In *The Day of Atonement: Its Interpretation in Early Jewish and Christian Interpretations*, edited by Thomas Hieke and Tobias Nicklas, 33–45. Leiden: Brill.

Budd, Philip. 1996. *Leviticus: Based on the New Revised Standard Version*. NCB. Grand Rapids: Eerdmans.

Campbell, Antony, and Mark O'Brien. 1993. *Sources of the Pentateuch*. Minneapolis: Fortress Press.

Douglas, Mary. 1966. *Purity and Danger*. Oxford: Routledge and Kegan Paul.

———. 2001. *Leviticus as Literature*. Oxford: Oxford University Press.

Gilders, William. 2012. "The Day of Atonement in the Dead Sea Scrolls." In *The Day of Atonement: Its Interpretation in Early Jewish and Christian Interpretations*, edited by Thomas Hieke and Tobias Nicklas, 63–73. Leiden: Brill.

Goldingay, John. 2010. *Key Questions about Christian Faith: Old Testament Answers*. Grand Rapids: Baker Academic.

Grabbe, Lester. 1997. *Leviticus*. OTG. Sheffield: Sheffield Academic.

Kaminkowski, Tamar. 2009. "Nadav and Avihu and Dietary Laws: A Case of Action and Reaction *Parashat Shemini* (Leviticus 9:1–11:47)." In *Torah Queeries: Weekly Commentaries on the Hebrew Bible*, edited by Gregg Drinkwater, Joshua Lesser, David Shneer, and Judith Plaskow, 135–39. New York: New York University Press.

Kaplan, Laura Duhan. 2001. "The Blood of Life: Priestly Sacrifice and September 11." *The Maqom Journal for Studies in Rabbinic Literature* 2, n.p. http://www.maqom.com/journal/paper3.pdf.

Knohl, Israel. 1995. *The Sanctuary of Silence: The Priestly Torah and the Holiness School*. Minneapolis: Fortress Press.

Levine, Baruch 1974. *In the Presence of the Lord: A Study of Cult and Some Cultic Terms in Ancient Israel*. Leiden: Brill.

Lienhard, Joseph T., ed. 2001. *Exodus, Leviticus, Numbers, Deuteronomy*. Ancient Christian Commentary on Scripture, Old Testament 3. Downers Grove, IL: InterVarsity Press.

Martyn, J. Louis. 1997. *Galatians: A New Translation with Introduction and Commentary*. AB. New York: Doubleday.

Milgrom, Jacob. 1991. *Leviticus 1–16: A New Translation with Introduction and Commentary*. AB. New York: Doubleday.

———. 2000. *Leviticus 17–22: A New Translation with Introduction and Commentary*. AB. New York: Doubleday.

———. 2004. *Leviticus*. CC. Minneapolis: Fortress Press.

Neusner, Jacob, trans. and ed. 1986. *Judaism and Scripture: The Evidence of Leviticus Rabbah*. Chicago: University of Chicago Press.

Nihan, Christophe. 2007. *From Priestly Torah to Pentateuch: A Study in the Composition of the Book of Leviticus*. Tübingen: Mohr Siebeck.

Noth, Martin. 1965. *Leviticus: A Commentary*. OTL. Louisville: Westminster John Knox.

Petrie, Jon. 2000. "The Secular Word HOLOCAUST: Scholarly Myths, History and 20th Century Meanings." *Journal of Genocide Research* 2:31–63.

Schearing, Linda. 2003. "Double Time . . . Double Trouble? Gender, Sin, and Leviticus 12." In *The Book of Leviticus: Composition and Reception*, edited by Robert Kugler and Rolf Rendtorff, with the assistance of Sarah Smith Bartel, 429–50. Leiden: Brill.

Stahlberg, Lesleigh Cushing. 2008. "Modern Day Moabites: The Bible and the Debate About Same-Sex Marriage." *BibInt* 16:442–75.

Stöckl Ben Ezra, D. 2003. *The Impact of Yom Kippur on Early Christianity*. Tübingen: Mohr Siebeck.

Weber, Max. 1976. *The Protestant Ethic and the Spirit of Capitalism*. 2nd ed. Sydney: George Allen & Unwin.

Whitekettle, Richard. 1996. "Levitical Thought and the Female Reproductive Cycle: Wombs, Wellsprings, and the Primeval World." *VT* 46:376–91.

Wright Knust, Jennifer. 2011. *Unprotected Texts: The Bible's Surprising Contradictions about Sex and Desire*. San Francisco: HarperOne.

Yang Murray, Alice. 2008. *Historical Memories of the Japanese American Internment and Struggles for Redress*. Stanford: Stanford University Press.

NUMBERS

Karl N. Jacobson

Introduction

"Numbers," or "In the Wilderness" as it is called in the Hebrew Bible, is the story of the nation of Israel from its first encounter with God at Mount Sinai (see Lev. 27:34), to the final instructions given by God to Moses on the plains of Moab at the banks of the Jordan opposite Jericho: the "beachhead" of Israel's entry into the promised land (see Joshua 2). "Numbers" is an appropriate title for the work in the sense that Israel is counted in its entirety (both the eleven lay tribes and the Levites) not only once, but twice. "In the Wilderness" is equally fitting—and perhaps more so—in that the bulk of the book's material takes place in this particular physical landscape. What's more, "in the wilderness" serves as a "spiritual geography" (Olson 1996, 2), and so the book is and has been readily accessible to successive generations of readers.

There is in Numbers great variety of literary genre; there is prose (Numbers 11) and poetry (6:24-26), narrative (20), law (29), censuses (1–3; 26), and itineraries (33:1-49). In addition, there are various markers or transition points in the story. These markers are chronological (1:1, "on the first day of the second month, in the second year"; 10:11, "in the second year, in the second month, on the twentieth day"; 33:38, "in the fortieth year . . . on the first day of the fifth month"); geographical (1:1 "after they had come out of the land of Egypt"; 12:1, "While they were at Hazeroth"; 13:3, "So Moses sent them from the wilderness of Paran"; 21:11, "They set out from Oboth, and camped at Iye-abarim, in the wilderness bordering Moab"); and generational (14:22; 26:24; 32:11; 33:1). Such literary diversity, and the attendant difficulties of identifying a clear flow to the book, has resulted in no clear consensus as to how best to understand the order or structure of the material, as well as a range of disciplinary approaches to understanding the book (Childs, 195; Olson 1997, 2–3; Milgrom, xiii). A great deal of intertextual interpretation takes place in conversation with Numbers, both in the Hebrew Bible and the New Testament. Numbers shows literary connectedness (both influence and dependence) with Exodus, Leviticus, Deuteronomy, and Joshua (Milgrom,

211

xxi), as well as Chronicles and Psalms (Dozeman, 214). The question of the "direction" of influence is muddy at best, as Milgrom notes: "the pericopes of Numbers are not, in the main, unitary compositions but are composites of or contain insertions from other sources. Some of these sources are old poems, narratives in Exodus, and cultic material from Leviticus. Conversely, Numbers material can be shown to have influenced the composition of Exodus and Deuteronomy" (xxi). In the New Testament, there are several examples of reinterpretation of Numbers: In Matthew (5:33-37), Jesus alludes to Numbers 30, rejecting outright the laws on making vows; in John (3:14-15), the story of the bronze serpent is reinterpreted as a sign for Jesus, who saves not from the immediate threat of physical death, but brings life through death; and Paul (1 Cor. 10:11) refers to this same incident as an example for the believer, to keep from evil and complaint.

This intertextuality is characteristic of the book of Numbers itself as well. As will be shown below, the book of Numbers is structured (however imperfectly) around parallel panels of material. The stories and census lists, as well as patterns of legal and votive materials, once established are revisited within the book. Numbers 32:6-15 is a response to two tribes asking for their allotment of territory to be outside of the promised land. Numbers 32 recalls a story from Num. 13:25—14:25 to make response, exhorting the Reubenites and the Gadites to remain faithful, and to continue to follow after the Lord. This distinctive intertextuality *within* the book is central to how Numbers functions literarily.

For the purposes of this essay, both in terms of the layout of the following commentary, and in an attempt to navigate the literary function of the material, the work of Dennis Olson will be used (Olson 1996, 5–6). The structure and flow of Numbers is best seen as a series of parallel episodes or panels that centers the experience of a people wandering in the wilderness, a wilderness both literal and figurative. In this commentary, these parallel episodes will be treated in tandem. There are four major parallel sections in the book of Numbers, and one stand-alone section. The format of these parallels is as follows:

1. The Numbering of Israel: Tribes and Levites (1–4 / 26)
2. Women, Vows, Offerings, and Passover (5–9 / 27–30)
3. Complaint, Jealousy, and Restoration (10–21 / 32–35)
4. A. The Balaam Cycle (22–24)
5. War against Midian (25 / 31)

The reader of Numbers is called to join in the transition from the generation that complained, doubted, and died to the generation born out of the wilderness, trusted in their God, and was settled in the promised land, to live.

Finally, let us return to the title of the book, as it is critical to understanding the theological significance of the work as a whole: In the Wilderness (*bĕmidbar*). Order in, through, and out of chaos is an important lens through which to view the varied literature of Numbers, the various interpretations it has enjoyed, and the applications it may find. The operative theological and religious modus operandi of the book is, in keeping with the first book of the Pentateuch, one of creation. In the locale of "the wilderness," and thus in the book of Numbers, the nation of Israel, its religious and social structure, its worship and laws, are created by God. It is out of the wilderness of wandering that the nation of Israel is made. Commenting on the story of the bronze serpent, Martin Luther noted that this is the creative, life-giving power that is attested to in Numbers.

> The serpent which Moses raised up in the desert (Num. 21:9) did not make alive through its inherent character (for it was made of bronze, just as we could form a serpent from bronze now); but the Word which was added to that brazen serpent was life-giving because God commanded the serpent to be set up, and added the Word (Num. 21:8): "Whoever looks at it will be healed." This Word you do not have if you form a serpent from bronze today. Moreover, the reason for the healing lay not in looking at it but in the command from God that they should look at the serpent and in the promise of deliverance. (*LW* 1:227)

The book of Numbers is, at its core, a theological argument; an argument for life ordered by God, among a people marshaled by God, in a land (read: Land) created for this people by the promise of God.

Numbers 1:1—4:49; 26:1-65: The Numbering of Israel, Tribes, and Levites

▌ THE TEXT IN ITS ANCIENT CONTEXT

The book of Numbers opens with four chapters dedicated to a "census of the whole congregation of Israelites" (1:2a). The census of Israel is literally a "counting of the heads" (*śĕʾû ʾet-rōš*). The recurring verb in Numbers 1 is *pāqad*, "to number, allocate, or muster"; *muster*, as in a military ordering, a point to which we return below. *Pāqad* is used twenty-one times in the first chapter of Numbers, in the introduction to the census (1:1-19), in the "enrolling" of each of the tribes (including the two "tribes" of Joseph's sons Ephraim and Manasseh; 1:20-43) in the census, and in the summary of the census (1:44-54). The Levites alone are not to be counted (1:49-50), until they are counted in a different kind of census that is not martial but clerical.

In addition to the Levites, it must be noted that this census is not of the whole congregation; rather, it is of all the men of the eleven tribes of Israel (excluding the twelfth tribe, the tribe of Levi) who are of fighting age: "in their clans, by ancestral houses, according to the number of names, every male individually; from twenty years old and upward, everyone in Israel able to go to war" (1:2b-3). In the lists of each of the tribes, the enlistment age is twenty (cf. 2 Chron. 25:5 and the census taken by Amaziah). As each of the tribes is enrolled, the phrase "everyone able to go to war" (*kōl yōṣēʾ ṣābāʾ*) occurs; fourteen times total. The phrase *yōṣēʾ ṣābāʾ* literally means "to go forth as a host." This phrase is striking in that it connects the tribes of Israel to one of the central epithets of the God of ancient Israel, *ʾădōnāy ṣĕbāʾōt*, "YHWH of Hosts." While the title never occurs in the book of Numbers (or anywhere in the Pentateuch), through this phrase YHWH is understood as the divine King who goes into battle before the hosts not just of heaven but also of the people of Israel (cf. Ps. 24:10); and the people of Israel are to be understood as God's host.

As the "able-bodied" men of the eleven tribes are counted ("enrolled," NRSV), they are in fact being enlisted and mustered. While there may be some discomfiture for certain modern readers with the military language employed here in Numbers, and the emphasis it places on the conquest model of the settlement of the promised land, it cannot be denied. The repeated phrase (always bridging the end of one verse and the beginning of another) is *kōl yōṣē' ṣābā' pĕqūdêhem* (see, e.g., 1:20-21, 22-23, 24-25, 26-27, 28-29, 30-31, 32-33), and is perhaps best translated "all those able to go to war, those mustered." Thus the census list here in the book of Numbers is not a numbering of the people of Israel; it is the marshaling of Israel in the wilderness in preparation for the conquest of the promised land.

The transition from the census of the fighting men of Israel to the prelude to the appointment of the Levites to service in the tabernacle (1:48-51, anticipating 3:14-39) is marked by a confluence of identical terminology. The language of marshaling and census is used both to prohibit the Levitical census and to define their appointment in successive verses. Numbers 1:49 declares: "Only the tribe of Levi you shall not enroll [*tipqōd*], and you shall not take a census [*wĕ'et-rōšām lō' tiśśā'*] of them with the other Israelites." Linguistically, it may be that there is a distinction here, as Milgrom finds (10), between the numbering of individuals and sum totals, but this does nothing to explain why the same terms are employed both in prescription and prohibition. In Num. 1:50, the central term for the enrollment of Israel is employed again, this time in an affirmative sense for the appointment of the Levites to serve in the tabernacle, "Rather, you shall appoint [*hapqēd*] the Levites over the tabernacle of the covenant." Textually, there is rather abrupt movement—using the same terminology—from the prohibition of counting the Levites, to the appointment of the Levites to a particular role in the religious—and military—life of Israel.

The prohibiting language parallels the prescriptive language in Num. 1:2-3, "Take a census [*śĕ'û 'et-rōš*] of the whole congregation of Israelites.... You and Aaron shall enroll [*tipqĕdû*] them." From a literary perspective, the function of the balancing of directive and prohibition may be inclusion, setting the marshaling of Israel—by Israel's prophet and priest—within the context of Israel's religious identity. Later in Numbers (31:6) it is the high priest who leads the hosts of Israel to war, preceded not by the instruments of war, but the "holy instruments" (Niditch, 52). The ordering of the encampment, with the tabernacle in the center and the hosts of Israel encamped around it, facing the tent of meeting (2:1-34), which follows the military census, matches the inclusio nicely.

The census of the Levites that follows in two parts (3:14-39 and 4:34-49) is carried out "according to the word of the Lord"—*'al-pî yhwh*, 3:16, 29, 51; 4:37, 41, 45, 49. The emphasis in this particular census is that it is the Lord who does the counting (Milgrom, 19).

At the end of chapter 4, following the enrollment of the subclans of the tribe of Levi, the Kohathites, the Gershonites, and the Merarites, there is an abrupt shift in the narrative flow, in the genre of the text, to legal material. This shift not only marks a break in the sense units of the book but also highlights the impetus of the census lists in chapters 1–4, which orders the people of Israel, gives them vocational and spiritual direction. Chapters 5 and following move to ordering the relational life of the newly ordered community, to which we will turn below.

The parallel panel in 26:1-65 relates the second census in Numbers, the census of the new generation that will succeed in the conquest of the promised land, where the former generation failed. As in the first census, the second is a census of "everyone in Israel able to go to war" (*kōl-yōṣē' ṣābā' bĕyiśrā'ēl*). This, again, is the military enlisting of the people. This second account is terse compared to the first, and the emphasis is on the transition to the new generation. Numbers 26:64 sets up the enrollment of the new generation in contrast with the fate of the old: "Among those there was not one of those enrolled by Moses and Aaron the priest, who had enrolled the Israelites in the wilderness of Sinai" (cf. Numbers 1; 14; 26). Milgrom characterizes Num. 26:63-65 as a "postscript" (227), while Olson sees these verses as sounding "the theme of the whole book. . . . This text provides a programmatic summary of the structure of Numbers. The second census list is both a sign of completed judgment on the first generation and a sign of God's promise for a new generation" (1996, 163).

■ THE TEXT IN THE INTERPRETIVE TRADITION

One of the thornier issues raised by the censuses, specifically in the second census in Numbers 26, is in the allotment of tribal territory. As Jewish commentators from Rashi, to Ramban (Rabbi Moshe ben Nahman), to Abravanel have wrestled with (for a detailed discussion, see Milgrom, 227–28, and Excursus 62), there seem to be two competing means of deciding on the allotment of land to the tribes. The first is according to tribal size (26:54); the second, by lot (26:56). Solutions to the problem of which means was preeminent are legion. Milgrom rightly points out that the simplest solution is based on "the basic principle of apportioning the land according to tribal clan size (26:53-54, with Ramban), qualified by the secondary principle that, initially, the location of the tribal and clan territory should be determined by lot (26:55-56, with Abravanel)" (Milgrom, 482). Rashi, however, concluded that God saw to it that the lot fell a certain way, so that the drawn lots were in accordance with tribal sizes and needs. Thus the use of lots was understood as a means of gauging the divine will. As is seen subsequently in Numbers (34:13; 36:2-3) and elsewhere in the Bible (Josh. 14:1-2; 18:1-10), the lot was the primary means of allocating tribal inheritances.

Regardless of the motivation behind the pairing of lot and need-based allocation, this, once again, seems to be a matter of ordering the people. The divine goal, it would appear, is to afford a balance between need and fairness. God's ordering is, therefore, along both lines.

■ THE TEXT IN CONTEMPORARY DISCUSSION

The census lists of Numbers 1–4; 26, serve to emphasize a dialectic of wrath and promise. The intent is to order the people, to marshal them so that they might occupy the promised land. The intervening narrative reports that this ordering of the people was disordered by their lack of trust in God's work (see the story of the spies and their report in 13:17—14:25). For the present reader of Numbers, this is the tension to which the book speaks. In recent generations, the move to allegorical interpretation has often been either deemphasized, or rejected outright. There is, however, a sense in which the wilderness allegory is a central one: not merely because it makes sense to the present-day reader of Numbers but also because this is how Numbers is most clearly employed in the Scriptures themselves.

It was noted above that census lists of Numbers 1–4 are meant to order, organize, galvanize, and motivate the people. And in Numbers 26, the second census sees the intention realized; Israel is reordered, reorganized, regalvanized, and this time to full effect.

Exploring the tale of Israel between the wildernesses of Sinai and Moab may well resonate with any number of similar tensions today. In the midst of the "wildernesses" of our time—the wildernesses of loss, of mistrust, of human-on-human crime, of religious pluralism, of searching for genuine, life-changing faith in an increasingly complicated and wild world—the story of Israel "in the wilderness" is potentially meaningful. The struggles that believing people face, in their daily living as individuals and in their lives as a part of community, can be made sense of "in the wilderness."

And therefore the vocations of believing people—of people who not only trust God's ordering of their world but who also see themselves as a part of God's chosen people—may be fruitfully explored and informed through an interaction with Numbers. To what is God mustering us, as parents and children, spouses and siblings—in the communities of our families, faced with brokenness and loss; as employees and bosses, as citizens of our home nations and of the world—when we are faced with the ethical and moral ambiguities of our decisions; as members of religious communities adrift in a world of rich diversity and competing truth-claims? We are, all of us, very much "in the wilderness," as we live and move and have our being. To what is God calling us who read Numbers and seek to answer God's mustering-call? The answers may well be different—perhaps markedly so—depending on who and where we are.

The census lists of Numbers 1–4 and 26—at first blush either uninteresting or confusing, much like the genealogies that begin the Gospel of Matthew—offer the setting through which the rest of the book is understandable. It is believed by many that God speaks order into human community, and that this ordering is trustworthy. Those who are unable or unwilling to trust it, according to Numbers, will not see the promises of God come to fruition; perhaps their children will.

Numbers 5:1—9:23; 27:1—30:16: Women, Vows, Offerings, and Passover

▌ THE TEXT IN ITS ANCIENT CONTEXT

Numbers 5 marks the first major shift in terms of genre in the book. Following the ordering of the tribes into martial units, the text moves abruptly not to the march, or to battle, but to legal questions of purity, fidelity, and worship. This shift may strike the reader as disjointed, but what is happening in the narrative flow—which if understood correctly is actually quite smooth—is the ordering of daily life in the encampment, the next step in the forming up of Israel.

Numbers 5 is made up of three sections addressing, respectively, different challenges to the community. First, Num. 5:1-3 addresses unclean persons, whether through disease or contact with the dead. Any person who is unclean, and therefore a danger to the wider community, is to be put outside the encampment. This expulsion is not, however, to be taken as permanent. Providing the unclean have been cleansed, they can be restored to the community (cf. Leviticus 13–14 regarding leprosy, and Num. 19:11-22 regarding those who have touched the dead).

Second, Num. 5:4-10 is about broken vows, which are characterized as "breaking faith with the LORD" (*lim'ōl ma'al byhwh*, 5:6). This brief passage acknowledges that human community is threatened by transgression whenever "a man or a woman wrongs another." Here transgressions against one's fellow human beings are equated with breaking faith with God (a not uncommon move in Leviticus; see 5:15, 21), which is reminiscent of the exhortation in Genesis 9 against murder.

> Whoever sheds the blood of a human,
>   by a human shall that person's blood be shed;
> for in his own image
>   God made humankind. (Gen. 9:6)

Because human beings are made in God's image, to wrong another is to wrong God, and therefore to jeopardize the community. Here again there is hope, or means provided by which the community can be restored even after such wrongdoing, through restitution not only to the individual wronged (5:7) but also to the community in his or her stead, either the next of kin in the case of death, or the community as a whole (5:8-11).

Finally, in the longest section, 5:11-31, the dangers of adultery are addressed. The case law concerning suspected adultery includes a ritualistic trial by water to ascertain guilt or innocence in the case of a woman accused of unfaithfulness.

What is striking is that in each case these legal matters address both men and women, a remarkably egalitarian stance within the larger biblical corpus (see 5:3, 5, 29-30; cf. Exod. 21:28-29; Lev. 13:29, 38; Deut. 17:2-7). At stake is "disruption of human relationships" (Olson 1996, 39), and this includes every human being, both male and female.

Following legal matters, the narrative moves on to matters of vows and offerings, enumerating key elements of the nation's relationship with God. Olson, addressing the second of the parallel panels (Numbers 28–29), notes that the pattern of offerings leading up to the celebration of the Passover, which orders the Israelite people and their relationship with God, is wrought through "a systematic program of offerings and sacrifices that mark important boundaries of time" (Olson 1997, 237). As with the clerical numbering of the Levites, the vow of the Nazirite and the series of offerings by the leaders of the people (7:1-83) are set up, and apart, for a purpose: "The structure of time and temporal boundaries that stands behind these offerings and sacrifices regularly reminds the Israelites of their status as God's holy people and sustains the order of the community's social and religious life against the forces of chaos" (Olson 1997, 237). Through law, ritual setting apart, and ritual observance, the young nation is stabilized.

The parallel panel of Num. 27:1—30:16 includes, again, a treatment on vows, offerings, and the celebration of Passover. It also includes a striking passage on the place of women, this time having to do with inheritance. The case of the daughters of Zelophehad, a member of the tribe of Manasseh who died without a male heir, sets a precedent for female inheritance in Israel. The case is remarkable as a whole, as it includes women speaking in the assembly in the Tent of Meeting, that they argue for women's inheritance, and that each of these women is named—Mahlah, Noah, Hoglah, Milcah, and Tirzah (Nowell, 115). As is the case with the laws concerning levirate marriage (see Deuteronomy 25), the inheritance practices endorsed here—which do not go unchallenged (Numbers 36) but which do stand—serve as a protection and provision for the women of Israel. While it may not seem obvious even to the critical eye, this case law precedence regarding inheritance parallels the case law and trial by ordeal of 5:11-31. In both cases, provision is made so that a woman cannot be excluded from the community, in terms of either her place as a daughter or her rights in relationship to her spouse. Numbers 5:1—9:23; 27:1—30:16 is, in largest part, aimed at the ordering of Israel's internal relationships in terms of its relationship with God. This matter is about order in, and the preservation of, God's chosen people.

▐ THE TEXT IN THE INTERPRETIVE TRADITION

Much in these parallel passages has been the cause of interpretive and applicative struggle. There is, perhaps, no more difficult text in the book of Numbers than the case of suspected adultery. Olson articulates accurately the tension this story raises. On the one hand, the woman, when accused, has no choice but to undergo the ordeal, drinking bitter water made dangerous by dust taken from the sanctuary floor and the infusion of an inky curse to see whether she is in fact guilty. The history of interpretation of this text—or, if Olson is correct, the history of attempted "softer interpretation," that is, of making the text palatable—is rich (see his survey in Olson 1996, 36–39). What seems often to be overlooked is the conditional nature of the ordeal. Irene Nowell (29) suggests that the accused woman must respond to a curse that presumes her guilt (see Num. 5:21-22) with "Amen, amen!" Olson seems to prioritize the assumption of guilt, while allowing for some potential for innocence: "Much of the legal case seems to assume the woman's guilt, although the possibility of her innocence is acknowledged in 5:14 and 5:30" (36).

Olson further represents a significant majority of interpreters of this text when he states that it is "highly disturbing," reflecting "cultural mores that most readers would find unacceptable today," and that it "seems extremely repulsive and degrading to women." These criticisms of the text cannot be dismissed out of hand, for they are correct insofar as modern culture would demand far more equality than this text is able to engender. However, the modern reader ought to be careful not to react so strongly that the conditional nature of trial, and therefore the protection that it is—to some degree at least—affording the accused woman, is overlooked. In 5:19-20, conditional clauses clearly differentiate the two possibilities: if the woman is innocent, she will be immune; and if she is guilty, she will succumb to the holy water. The conditional nature of the ordeal is, at the very least, an attempt to protect the woman from an unfounded accusation. She cannot simply be put aside without proof or trial. While it must be made clear that this standard falls short of what we would practice today (one hopes)—and indeed, there seems to be no fallout for the man who has accused his wife falsely—it was an attempt, a beginning of sorts, at protecting the women of Israel. And as Geoffrey Hartman notes, "We are often returned by the Jewish Bible to a realistic transaction that indicates how human rights are not a given, but are established by grant and negotiation" (41). Numbers 5:11-31 can be helpfully read through the lens of an early attempt, or early evidence of a community of people, shaped by their relationship with God, creating space for a trial mediated by a vow to their God.

Similarly, the matter of the order of inheritance raised in Numbers was taken up in the early Jewish practice. In *Baba Batra* 8:1-3 (376–77), the question of inheritance was applied critically:

> This is the order of inheritance: *If a man die and have no son, then ye shall cause his inheritance to pass unto his daughter* (Num. 27:8)—the son precedes the daughter, and all the son's offspring precede the daughter; the daughter precedes the brothers (of the deceased) and the daughter's offspring precede the brothers. (367)

And again,

> The daughters of Zelophehad took three portions of the inheritance: the portion of their father who was of them that came out of Egypt, and his portion among his brethren from the property of Hepher, who also, in that he was the firstborn, received a double share. The son and the daughter are alike concerning inheritance. (367–77)

Each of these cases, that of the daughters of Zelophehad and the trial by ordeal of the suspected adulteress, have been critical but sensitive matters that readers and interpreters of the book of Numbers have taken up.

◼ THE TEXT IN CONTEMPORARY DISCUSSION

No modern reader with any sensitivity to the treatment of women can be comfortable with simply accepting and applying Num. 5:11-31. This intricate case law concerning the dangers both of adultery and of jealousy is not the kind of casuistic text that we should appropriate as our own and apply. However, if the modern reader can explore this text's implications without merely applying it simplistically, then Num. 5:11-31 may still have something to teach us. Following closely the admonition that to wrong another is to transgress against God (5:6), this text explores the real dangers posed by broken faithfulness in human relationship. Numbers 5:11-31 takes these dangers seriously and works, in at least a limited fashion, to allow for a testing of faithfulness against jealousy. If, with Genesis, we hold that both men and women bear the divine image, then the intent of this text appears to be to hold the relationship between man and woman—between wife and husband—in close care. Such a text, difficult as it may be, which works to establish safer grounds for the evaluation of guilt or innocence, should be honored for what it is, limits and all.

Our modern world is no less troubled by the dangers inherent in adultery, in divorce, and in the harm to and even destruction of families, than was wilderness-bound Israel. In fact, considering divorce rates, and the expanding understanding of what marriage is and for whom it is available, the intersection of faithfulness, jealousy, and human brokenness is all the more dangerous and dear. While modern communities will not apply Numbers 5 directly, we do well to be mindful of the power that human love and human relationships have in—and on—human communities, and to consider the admonition that closes out the chapter, that all such relationships should be "set before the LORD" (5:30).

One final note. The first panel of this sense unit in our parallel, intertextual reading of Numbers is anchored by the first of several poetic fragments that stand out in Numbers. In 6:22-27, we find the priestly blessing, in which the people of Israel is claimed and blessed by God:

> The LORD bless you and keep you;
> the LORD make his face to shine upon you, and be gracious to you;
> the LORD lift up his countenance upon you, and give you peace.

This blessing is described as a sort of "nameplating" of Israel, for by the blessing, "they shall put my [the LORD's] name on the Israelites" (6:27). This is, in a basic and fundamental sense, an invocation, the calling on the name of God, a claiming of the divine name that serves to establish and shape the identity of the people in all they do. In terms of the internal relationships of the people, this blessing and naming of Israel as God's hearkens back to the closing verses of Numbers 4, in which the Levites are enrolled (marshaled) "according to the commandment of the LORD" (4:37, 41, 45, 49). For the present reader of Numbers, for communities of believers, this blessing, naming, and claiming is not only an anchor for communal living but also a lens through which to view the world—the wilderness world in which we live, and the promised world toward which we move.

Numbers 10:1—21:35; 32:1—35:34: Complaint, Jealousy, and Restoration

▌ THE TEXT IN ITS ANCIENT CONTEXT

At the end of the last sense unit (9:15-23), the narrative of Numbers brings its version of Israel's travelogue even with the ending of the book of Exodus (40:34-38). Although the details and terminology clearly show divergence, reflecting differing literary traditions, Num. 9:15-23 appears to be an extension or extrapolation of Exodus, enumerating the same stages of travel, and a similar pattern to Israel's sojourning:

1. The glory of the LORD was on the tent of meeting (ʾōhel môʿēd, Exod. 40:34), and/or tabernacle (hammiškān, Exod. 40:34; Num. 9:15), or tent of the covenant (ʾōhel hāʿēdūt, Num. 9:15).
2. When the glory of the LORD, a cloud by day and fire by night (Exod. 40:38; Num. 9:15, 16), lifted, the people would set out on the next stage (Exod. 40:36; Num. 9:17).
3. At times the cloud/fire would remain over the tabernacle, and the people would remain encamped (Exod. 40:37; Num. 9:18-23).

Exodus relates this pattern in a scant five verses, while Numbers does so in almost twice that; this is because Numbers is more concerned with the length of time that Israel might stay encamped, allowing for a time variance of "two days, or a month, or longer" (9:22).

Having arrived at the same relative point in the story of Israel's journey from Egypt, Numbers then departs drastically from the Exodus tradition. In Exodus, the people complain, asking for water and food, prior to their arrival at Sinai (Exodus 17). In Numbers, the complaining begins after the people have departed Sinai (Numbers 11). This marked difference—shifting the complaining vis-à-vis the locus of Sinai—serves to highlight a key difference in the Numbers complaint account. As Olson (1996, 61) has noted, the complaints of Israel are, in the book of Exodus, "treated as legitimate needs: the people need water (Exod. 15:22-26), the people need food (Exodus 16), and the people again need water (Exod. 17:1-7). In each case God takes the complaints seriously and fulfills the needs of the Israelites." But in Numbers, the complaints are portrayed as signs of Israel's lack of trust, a prelude of sorts to the episode of the spies sent into the promised land, which follows shortly (13:25—14:12). The initial response of God to the complaining of the Israelites is not provision, but pyrotechnics, "Then the fire of the LORD burned against them, and consumed some outlying part of the camp" (11:2).

Over the course of Numbers 11–21 we find several parallel complaints, often different in articulation, but representative of a single fundamental issue: mistrust of God and God's chosen leaders. At key points in the recurring pattern of mistrust or jealousy, God responds to the people's complaining in varied ways. The litany of complaints is as follows:

Numbers   11   complaint about manna and meat; a question of trust

            12   complaint about Moses' leadership; Aaron and Miriam's jealousy

            13–14   complaint about the promised land; a question of trust

            16   complaint about Moses' leadership; Korah's rebellion

            20   complaint about water; a question of trust

            21   complaint about food and water; summary of Israel's lack of trust

The first complaint is to and against Moses because the people are hungry. They complain about the manna (11:4-6). But the people want meat. God's response is to "come down and talk," first to talk to Moses (11:17) and again to empower the elders appointed to help Moses manage this "rabble" (11:25). When God comes down to speak to Moses, Moses is told to tell the Israelites that they will have more meat than they can handle, so much that it will "come out of your nostrils and become loathsome to you" (11:20). Israel's ungracious complaining is met with provision that becomes punishment: as Num. 11:33 puts it, "while the meat was still between their teeth, before it was consumed, the anger of the Lord was kindled against the people, and the Lord struck the people with a very great plague." Unlike in Exodus, God's provision is tinged with threat, danger.

Aaron and Miriam also raise a complaint against Moses, angered (supposedly) by their brother's Cushite wife (12:1). It is unclear what is meant by the phrase *ha'iššâ hakkūšît*. The only wife of Moses of whom the Bible otherwise speaks is Zipporah, who is a Midianite, not Cushite. Milgrom (93) suggests correctly that settling the question is irrelevant, because the real reason for the complaint is that Aaron and Miriam are feeling marginalized: "Has the Lord spoken only through Moses? Has he not spoken through us also?" (12:2). As Micah 6:4 relates, the tradition maintains to some degree the shared leadership of Moses and his siblings. But here their complaint suggests that their influence—among the people? with Moses?—is flagging. As with the complaint about food, "the Lord came down . . . and called" out to Aaron and Miriam, putting them in their place:

And he said, "Hear my words:

When there are prophets among you,
     I the Lord make myself known to them in visions [*bammar'â*];
     I speak to them in dreams [*baḥălôm*].
Not so with my servant Moses;
     he is entrusted with all my house.
With him I speak face to face—clearly, not in riddles;
     and he beholds the form of the Lord." (Num. 12:6-8)

Moses is the prophet extraordinaire, no mere dreamer (*ḥălōmôt*) or seer (*rō'eh*), but the prophet to whom God comes down to speak with directly.

These complaints—against Moses because of the food and because of his pride of place in leadership—serve in part as a prelude to the response of the people to the report of the spies who are sent into Canaan. Representatives of each tribe are sent, under the direction of Joshua, to survey the promised land (13:1-24). The report is that the land is good, flowing with "milk and honey" (13:27), but that it is occupied by the Nephilim (13:33), the "heroes that were of old, warriors of renown" (see Gen. 6:4). The conclusion of the people is that they cannot possibly take the promised land (13:32). They have, it seems, forgotten what their God did both in Egypt and in their own encampment. And so again, and for a third time, the Israelites complain. In response to this renewed complaint, God concludes that this people, faithless again, are unworthy to bear the name of God and to be so blessed; Moses—and his offspring—will take their place. For this third complaint, the people will receive the ultimate punishment, the withdrawal of God's promise.

But Moses intercedes for them. And what is striking about his intercession is that he remembers, and reminds God, of what the Israelites have apparently forgotten, what God did in Egypt (see 14:14, 16) and the promise that ought to be Israel's because of who God is; as God said,

> The Lord is slow to anger,
> and abounding in steadfast love,
> forgiving iniquity and transgression,
> but by no means clearing the guilty,
> visiting the iniquity of the parents
> upon the children
> to the third and the fourth generation. (14:18; cf. Exod. 34:6-7)

And it is here that one of the core statements of Deuteronomy (5:1-3) in comparison is, on the surface, observably false. YHWH, reminded of the divine character, does forgive, but does not clear the guilt of this faithless generation, almost none of whom will see the promised land (14:20-25). This generation, which fails in its attempt to enter the promised land (14:26-45), will be effaced by the generation to come, which follows more closely, trusts more fully, and is rewarded with the inheritance of Canaan and the Transjordan (32:1—34:20).

Following Moses' intercession, the narrative once again shifts quite drastically, returning to two matters of ritual practice. First, offerings are again prescribed and outlined. These offerings pertain primarily to the promised land, and do seem somewhat out of place, although there are numerous connections to the preceding chapters (11–14) as Olson has outlined (1996, 97–99). Those connections notwithstanding, it seems clear the movement to ritual action and—more importantly—dress serves the purpose in the narrative of turning the people's attention away from their complaining and back to God. The movement forces the Israelites, and the reader, to remember what God has done.

In Numbers 16 there is, again, a challenge to the leadership of Moses, this time by Korah, Dathan, and Abiram. Korah accuses Moses of going too far, of elevating himself above the people, all of whom are holy (16:3). The complaints of Dathan and Abiram echo the complaints of the manna incident indicting Moses as a failure: "it is clear that you have not brought us into a land flowing with milk and honey" (16:13-14). And once again, God answers, the earth opening up and swallowing the households of Korah, Dathan, and Abiram, and fire consuming 250 others. What follows, in Numbers 17–19, is the elevation of the Aaronic priesthood and the reestablishment of the order God put in place in Numbers 1–4; 26.

The final episodes of complaint, in chapters 20–21, serve to summarize Israel's lack of trust in God's provision. In these successive episodes, the people complain about water, then about food and water: "The people spoke against God and against Moses, 'Why have you brought us up out of Egypt to die in the wilderness? For there is no food and no water, and we detest this miserable food'" (21:5). God's response this last time is to send "fiery serpents," poisonous snakes, into the camp; the people are bitten and die. Only when Moses makes a serpent of bronze (*nĕḥaš nĕḥōšet*)—a play on words in Hebrew similar to assonance, in which the two words sound very much alike—and the peoples' eyes are drawn to it are they then drawn back to God; seeing it they remember and live.

The pattern of complaint, punishment (or struggle, see Num. 14:26-45; 20:14-21), and restoration that shapes this largest portion of Numbers is a familiar motif in the Hebrew Bible (cf., e.g., the pattern in Judges). The back-and-forth movement in these chapters sets the table for the cleansing of Israel, for the new generation to be born and begin to grow in faith and trust even as the old generation wanes. The end of this section (10–21) sounds the first positive note in Israel's attempt to conquer the promised land, with the victories over the Amorites (21:21-32) and Bashan (21:33-35). These notes echo resoundingly in Numbers 32–35, in which Israel's conquests become decisive, and they at last reach the end of their journey.

▌ The Text in the Interpretive Tradition

The book of Numbers itself—interpreting the tradition within the tradition—picks up this transition, and in chapters 32–35 revisits and summarizes the journey from Egypt (in chapter 33)—a journey that is martial in nature, the people going out "in military formation" (*lĕṣibʾōtām*), that is, as a host to war—then next charts the boundaries of the land (34), and lays out the cities in which the Levites will live. The end of chapter 35 (vv. 16-34) returns once more to case law. This is, yet again, an apparently strange transition in the narrative, but takes seriously the strains and perhaps the proclivities of a people schooled in war, trying to live in peace.

The incident of the bronze serpent is taken up in the biblical text in a couple of places. It reappears first in the story of Hezekiah's reforms (2 Kings 18), when the king destroys the *nĕḥuštān*, the "bronzed thing," because it had become an object of worship for Israel. In the New Testament, the serpent in the wilderness becomes an allegory for the crucifixion of Jesus who, like the serpent in the wilderness, will be lifted up (John 3:11-15). In the case of Jesus, it is not simply seeing the crucified Christ that brings life, but believing in him. The parallel is striking, that life out of death—whether deliverance in this life or eternal life after death—comes from turning away from complaining (or in the case of Nicodemus, questioning and doubting) and being reoriented to God.

These incidents of complaining are taken up in the New Testament as well, in 1 Cor. 10:1-21, in which Paul draws on Israel's story to exhort his listeners to avoid the dangers of idolatry. The purpose, according to Paul, of retelling Israel's story—a relatively common move in Acts in particular, see Acts 2:14-36; 7:1-53; 13:16-43—is to "serve as an example, and they were written down to instruct us" (1 Cor. 10:11).

One of the most striking features of this sense unit is found in the complaint Moses makes to God. In Num. 10:15, Moses employs the extended metaphor of motherhood. He argues with God, asking, "Did I conceive this people? Did I give birth to them that you should say to me, 'Carry them in your bosom, as a nurse carries a sucking child,' to the land that you promised on oath to their ancestors?" (Num. 11:12).

The feminine metaphor, which *Targum Onqelos* 11:12 rejects, altering the expression "Did I give birth to them" to "Am I the father of," is fitting, according to Ramban, because "it is the mother who suffers the pains of rearing children" (Milgrom, 85). But the maternal metaphor Moses uses for himself and his leadership of the people is, in verse 15, taken a step further still. When Moses turns his accusation directly and aggressively to God, he says, "If this is the way you are going to treat me, put me to death at once." What is striking is that the pronoun Moses uses when addressing God in this verse is feminine (*'at*). Moses addresses God literally as Israel's mother. As Nowell puts it, "Moses points out that he is not their mother; God is! God conceived them and gave them birth, so why does Moses have to nurse them?" (Nowell, 50).

As Nowell observes, it may be shocking to some readers to imagine God as mother rather than father—to others it may be refreshing!—but the address fits the metaphor perfectly. Moses is tired of playing wet nurse to a whining Israel, and wants the people's Mother to get back into the picture.

▮ THE TEXT IN CONTEMPORARY DISCUSSION

While there are a number of elements of this major section that will have implications for the modern reader or community—from jealousy and sinful challenging of leadership, to the dangers of idolatry in personal and ritual religious practice, to the dangers of lives shaped both overtly and subtly by violence—there are two particular aspects of Numbers 10–21 and 32–35 that are particularly ripe for contemporary discussion and interpretation.

The complaint accounts of Numbers show a sharp departure not just from the comparative account in Exodus but also from a broad biblical tradition that takes complaint seriously. While this probably reflects the predominant pattern in many Christian religious communities—where music is for praising, prayers are for thanking, and crying out bitterly to God is frowned on—for many readers this may be the most difficult aspect of the book as a whole. The complaint that is so central to the prayers for help or lament in the Psalms, and the complaint of Job, which God calls true and faithful speech (Job 40:7), seems to be stifled in Numbers. This is problematic. As Hartman concludes, the situation in which Israel finds itself—wandering in the wilderness, lost between the relative "bounty" of Egypt, "the cucumbers, the melons, the leeks, the onions, and the garlic" (Num. 11:5), and the promise of Canaan, of "milk and honey . . . an inheritance of fields and vineyards" (Num. 16:14)—does not allow much room for Israel to trust; complaint may be the only outlet. "Starvation does not breed trust. It is a reasonable cry that is heard, of men afraid not only for themselves but also for their families. They recall the Promise made to them and, instead of its realization, see the opposite: decimation or even destruction, rather than increased numbers in a land of their own" (Hartman, 47). But is their complaint truly legitimate? One may well wonder if what Numbers is doing is outlining the kind of complaining that is neither true nor faithful.

The tension in these stories of complaint is critical: the people have been freed from slavery, met by God, ordered, mustered, and led to the promised land. And in the face of all of this, they are not satisfied, and will not trust. The modern reader does well at this point to follow Paul's lead and take from these stories of complaint a warning, and a lead. What is enough for us? Enough education, enough wealth, influence, family, and health? What challenge, be it professional, familial, political, is so great that the God "who brought you out of the land of Egypt, to be your God: I am the LORD your God" (Num. 15:41) cannot be your God even now? The kind of baseless, faithless complaining that the Israelites do—at least according to Numbers—is to be resisted, and these stories are best read with an eye to learning from them; they may be, for any reader, metaphorical fringes on the corners of our garments, so that when one reads it, "when you see it, you will remember all the commandments of the LORD and do them, and not follow the lust of your own heart and your own eyes" (Num. 15:39).

And perhaps most importantly—as has already been noted—Numbers reveals what may seem a surprisingly progressive stance toward women and an equally surprisingly flexible theological imagination. The Bible is by no means replete with feminine imagery for God. It is, however, much more comfortable with that kind of imagery than the religious communities have been in the generations since these stories were written. There are other examples of such imagination employed in theological construction, from Isaiah's depiction of God's love for Israel in terms of a mother's love (Isa. 49:15), to the psalmist comparing herself to a weaned child to God's weaning mother (Ps. 131:2), to Jesus longing to gather the people to himself like a mother hen gathers her brood (Matt. 23:37; Luke 13:34). Moses' use of the feminine metaphor, paired as it is with a feminine pronoun used in direct discourse to God, is remarkable in several ways.

Neither metaphor nor pronoun is used ironically, or negatively, but they serve to deftly illustrate both the nature of God's relationship to and care for the people of Israel, as well as to illustrate the nature of the leadership role. In a world in which theological imagination has, for a long time, been predominantly masculine, Moses' use of feminine imagery is refreshing and freeing. This ancient text can empower the theology of a new generation in both directions, in thinking about the nature of the divine and in reflecting on the struggles of believing leaders—in both religious and secular settings.

Numbers 22:1—24:25: The Balaam Cycle

▮ THE TEXT IN ITS ANCIENT CONTEXT

One of the few stories from Numbers that is more or less well known, the story of the prophet Balaam, is the only stand-alone narrative within the book. After Israel's victory over the Amorites (Num. 21:21-32), their neighbors, the Moabites, are in fear of Israel, this horde that "has come out of Egypt" (Num. 22:5). Balak, king of Moab, sends to the prophet Balaam, asking him to curse Israel on Moab's behalf.

Three times Balak asks for a curse, and six times Balaam responds in a telling manner. Balaam emphasizes, at every turn, that as a prophet of the LORD he can speak only the words the LORD gives him to speak.

22:8   "I will bring back word to you, just as the LORD speaks to me."

22:18   "Although Balak were to give me his house full of silver and gold, I could not go beyond the command of the LORD my God, to do less or more."

23:3   "Perhaps the LORD will come to meet me. Whatever he shows me I will tell you."

23:12   "Must I not take care to say what the LORD puts into my mouth?"

23:26   Balaam answered Balak, "Did I not tell you, 'Whatever the LORD says, that is what I must do?'"

Finally, at the close of the exchanges between Balak and Balaam, in response to Balak's desperate anger, Balaam replies to Balak, "Did I not tell your messengers whom you sent to me, 'If Balak should give me his house full of silver and gold, I would not be able to go beyond the word of the LORD, to do either good or bad of my own will; what the LORD says, that is what I will say'?" (24:12-13).

The emphasis here is both on the LORD's control of the situation—the bellwether theme of the trust-faithlessness dialectic of Numbers—and on Balaam as a true prophet. Balaam's insistence that he can say only what God gives him to say is in keeping with the standard by which later prophets will be evaluated, according to the Deuteronomic principle:

I will raise up for them a prophet like you from among their own people; I will put my words in the mouth of the prophet, who shall speak to them everything that I command. Anyone who does not heed the words that the prophet shall speak in my name, I myself will hold accountable. But any prophet who speaks in the name of other gods, or who presumes to speak in my name a word that I have not commanded the prophet to speak—that prophet shall die. (Deut. 18:18-20)

It is interesting that we find in Balaam a non-Israelite Yahwist—not unlike Jethro the Midianite (or Hebob in Num. 10:29; Exodus 18)—who is portrayed in this story in an entirely positive light. And it is beyond question that Balaam is, in fact, a prophet of YHWH, as he says for himself in 22:18, "I could not go beyond the command of the LORD my God, to do less or more."

As Michael Barre notes, "In Numbers 22–24 he never wavers from his resolve to report only what God has communicate to him, whether for good or ill, and whether it pleases the king or not. Balaam is portrayed as a man of integrity, a seer completely open to the divine message, whatever it might be" (Barre, 259).

In the broadest terms, this story fits into the larger narrative of Numbers perfectly, serving to demonstrate both to Israel—in the face of its doubt, lack of confidence, and forgetfulness—and to Israel's new neighbors that it is God who is in control. Even down to the prophetic voice of an ass.

▌ THE TEXT IN THE INTERPRETIVE TRADITION

As has already been seen, the book of Numbers frequently reengages the tradition, repeating, reiterating, and reinterpreting stories it has already told. This appears to be true of the Balaam cycle in two ways.

First, Numbers portrays Balaam as a prophet of YHWH (the LORD), and it does so methodically. And then, rather strangely, the book returns to the Balaam cycle in chapter 31, altering what is an otherwise positive portrayal of this non-Israelite Yahwist, connecting him explicitly to the apostasy of Israel and its sin in the matter of the Baal of Peor (see Numbers 25; 31:16). According to Num. 31:8, 16, Balaam is killed—slain by the Israelites during the Midian campaign—presumably because he influenced a number of Midianite women to make "the Israelites act treacherously against the LORD in the affair of Peor" (31:16). The shift in the portrayal is difficult to follow, from staunch Yahwist to idolater. It should be noted that almost every other reference to Balaam in the Bible, Hebrew and New Testaments alike, is negative. In Josh. 24:9-10, God is made to say of Balaam, "I would not listen" to him, and the same again in Deut. 23:4-7, while in 2 Pet. 2:15 the "way of Balaam" is described as loving gain and speaking in God's name to get it, for which he is punished; finally, in Rev. 2:14, "the Balaam stories in Numbers 22–24 and the Baal Peor incident in Numbers 25 are combined in such a way that it is Balaam who induces Balak to harm Israel by enticing them to partake of pagan practices" (Barre, 255). It seems likely that the shift in the way Balaam is portrayed in Numbers 31 reflects the wider biblical tradition (of the Hebrew Bible that is), while incorporating the Balaam cycle—its own discrete narrative—into its narrative largely as is.

The second example of intratextual influence in the story of Balaam and his mule is a strange one, and creates an odd disjunction within the narrative. Prior to the first oracle and after the second invitation, Balaam first tells the king no, and then, having heard from God in a dream, "Balaam got up in the morning, saddled his donkey, and went with the officials of Moab" (22:21). It is likely that this was, at one point, an intermediate ending to the story. Another Balaam tradition (perhaps from the early stages of the reimagination of the prophet's character and identity) then picks up in 22:22, where we find God suddenly angry with Balaam that he is going to Moab, even though God told Balaam to do so. The incongruity is marked.

What follows is the best-known part of Balaam's story, where God speaks to the prophet through his donkey. Traditional interpretation has echoed with the ironic humor of the exchange.

Martin Luther loved the story of Balaam and his mule so much that he used the image several times in his writing:

> If God spoke then through an ass against a prophet, why should he not be able even now to speak through a righteous man against the pope? (*LW* 44:136)

> God once spoke through the mouth of an ass [Num. 22:28]; therefore, no man is to be despised, however humble he may be. (*LW* 45:121)

> In ancient times God actually spoke through an ass against the prophet who was riding it [Num. 22:28]. Would to God that we were worthy to have such doctors given to us. (*LW* 44:205)

■ THE TEXT IN CONTEMPORARY DISCUSSION

Who speaks for God? And when God is spoken for, what is at stake? The stories of Balaam and his oracles provide an important framework for thinking about addressing social, political, and personal issues in theological terms. The prophet—and so the preacher, the disciple, churchgoer—speaks only what God gives her to speak. So what are the implications of speaking theologically, of speaking in the wildernesses in which the reader of Numbers wanders, in God's terms?

First, Balaam's stories suggest caution in this regard. God's word is God's and not ours in a fundamental sense. A modern Balaam should be as careful as the early Balaam to listen to what God says—through Scripture, prayer, and the mouths of others—and be careful not to speak words that are simply pleasing either to the listener or the speaker. God's word, whether curse or blessing, whether encouragement or challenge, is not for sale or for manipulation to our own ends.

Second, it is important to note that Balaam is, in certain very important ways, an outsider; he is not an Israelite, and he is not one who came out of Egypt. Yet God speaks with him, appears to him, and uses him. If we think of ourselves as the insiders, then we ought to be mindful that God can work and speak through others who are not like us, living in the same place or way as we do, with the same struggles, and that through others such as these God can bless God's people.

Finally, following Luther's laughing takeaway from the story, the modern reader might dare to be bold. If God will speak through an outsider, and yes even through an ass, then God can speak through anyone. While Balaam did not add to or determine what God's word would be, he spoke that word boldly, both in his responses to a king and in his blessing of God's people. Balaam withstood the ire of a king, holding to the power and importance of God's will. And Balaam, seeing that it pleased the LORD to bless Israel, did not look for omens or visions or signs, but "set his face toward the wilderness," and spoke God's blessing. If Balaam's story holds any truth, it lies in this: God's word does not return empty, but accomplishes its purpose (Isa. 55:11). Numbers echoes this basic biblical claim, exerting it on any who would read it.

Numbers 25:1-18; 31:1-34: War against Midian

▌ THE TEXT IN ITS ANCIENT CONTEXT

The story of Israel's apostasy at Peor is the wilderness generation's final failure. It is paired here with the victory over the Midianites, the final step in securing the promised land. The narrative is relatively sparse, stating only that the people "yoked itself" (*yiṣṣāmed*) to the Baal (a word that in this case simply means "lord" or local god) of Peor. This was done when Israel intermarried with the people of Moab and Midian and defiled themselves not through their sexual relations or intermarrying but through the attendant religious mingling. The people attended sacrifices and ate from the offerings made to another God.

As has been frequently observed (see Olson 1996, 153–54; Grossman, 59–61), Israel's apostasy with the Baal of Peor is likened to the incident of the golden calf in Exodus 32. There are numerous parallels, but the most striking aspect of a comparison of Numbers 25 with Exodus 32 is the sense that the practices described—at least in their original settings—are not what are objectionable; rather, it is the object of devotion that is a problem. In Exodus 32, it is not the nature of Israel's worship that is problematic but that they have made an idol—a false image of the true God. The transgression in Numbers 25 is more serious and, if it builds to some degree on Exodus 32, amplifies Israel's guilt; again, not because their worship practices are wicked in and of themselves, but because they worship an idol—an image of a false god. There is no sense whatsoever in the original narrative that eating, drinking, and rising up to revel are a problem, nor that their worship is explicitly sexual in nature (contra Grossman, 59; see Nowell, 105). What is stunning in Numbers 25 is that Israel, moving far beyond complaint and mistrust of YHWH, has turned for the first time, and fully, to the worship of another god. And once again, God punishes Israel, this time sending a plague that fulfills the judgment pronounced in Num. 14:23.

This is the final failing of the untrusting generation that will not enter the promised land. As Olson notes, "The story of Israel's worship of an alien god in Numbers 25 brings to an end the life of the first generation of Israelites who came out of Egypt. The twenty-four thousand Israelites who died in the plague of 25:9 are presumably the last remnants of the old generation. They have left the stage to make room for a new generation who will again stand on the edge of the promised land" (1996, 156).

One of the difficulties in Numbers 25 is that there appears again to be a conjoining of two different narratives. Verses 1-5 report the difficulties caused by Moabite women. This vignette could stand alone, but to it has been added the incident of a Midianite woman being "brought home to meet the parents" in 25:6-9. What this blending of stories serves to do is point to the war against Midian in Numbers 31, providing the reason and the motivation for the extermination of the Midianites, on whom the Israelites are seeking vengeance. The implications of the cultural and religious intermingling, brought about through marriage, are presented as fraught with danger; and in the case of the Baal of Peor incident, with disaster and mass death. Only through the intercession of Phineas does the plague—God's judgment on Israel—stop short of spilling over from one generation to the next.

■ THE TEXT IN THE INTERPRETIVE TRADITION

The incident of the Baal of Peor has a lasting effect in the biblical text. In the historical Psalm 106, which was likely used as a form of liturgical remembrance and instruction, this part of the story is recalled graphically,

> Then they attached themselves to the Baal of Peor,
>   and ate sacrifices offered to the dead. (Ps. 106:28)

Meat offered to idols is the danger. In Joshua (22:10-20), the incident is recalled as a part of a conflict after the tribes that had settled in the Transjordan build an altar; the tribes that have settled in Canaan, with worship "centralized" at Shiloh, fear that the altar will be a place of false worship again. This may also reflect a later tradition, centered on the temple in Jerusalem, and be reading back into earlier narrative tradition a distinctively Jerusalemite concern. Finally, in Deut. 4:1-4, Peor is an illustration of what happens when anything is added or taken away from the commandments of God.

As Susan Niditch has observed, there are serious questions and concerns raised by the just war themes brought together in Numbers 25 and 31, not least of which is the role the women play first as "sensuous and evil enticers, embodiments of the wrong way" (45), but also as booty. "Their presence marks the passage into war and the exodus from it; they are marginal, border figures, central in the events around them, and yet they are usually nameless, voiceless items of exchange and symbols of transition" (44). On the one hand, these foreign women are seen as dangerous. On the other, they are the spoils of war, and central to new life in Canaan.

The connection between these two chapters, bringing together the motivations for Israel's holy war of conquest and the danger of intermarriage, of idolatry, syncretism, and more, serve as a sort of prelude to the issues that will define the rest of the biblical narrative that follows in the so-called historical books. Israel's life in the promised land will be marked by this same tension.

◼ THE TEXT IN CONTEMPORARY DISCUSSION

These two chapters present—in a rather stark and pressing way—a reality that not only remains a part of global reality, but is also, if anything, greatly intensified and far more pressing today than it was in the days described in Numbers: the reality of pluralism. Racial, social, and religious intermingling brings many advantages, including opportunities for growth and learning; but pluralism also can bring struggle and tension. This was the promised-land reality for the people of Israel, and it is the reality of life in a shrinking global community as well.

In the aftermath of dealing with false worship and idolatry in the face of interracial marriage and shared life—the aftermath of slaughter and destruction—the officers of Israel bring an offering to God saying, "we have brought the LORD's offering, what each of us found, articles of gold, armlets and bracelets, signet rings, earrings, and pendants, to make atonement for ourselves before the LORD" (Num. 31:50). The key phrase here is "to make atonement for ourselves," but for what are they making atonement? Niditch has captured the struggle revealed in this move beautifully.

> In Numbers 31, as in the ban texts, war on some level is ritual, and yet war in Numbers 31 is not cleansing or whole-making in the spirit of extirpation of wayward Israelite cities in Deuteronomy 13 or the ban texts demanding erasure of the idolaters from the land. Doubts have crept in about the whole enterprise, for in killing one becomes part of the abomination, the enemy one seeks to eliminate. . . . Is it in recognition of this ambivalence that the commanders are pictured to offer up what each has found among the personal effects of the dead enemies . . . , "to make atonement for ourselves before the Lord"? For what do they atone? Is it for sins in general, is it finally to close the matter of Baal Peor (Olson, 88), or is it to atone for the defilement of bringing death to human beings (Wenham: 212; de Vaulz: 359)?

These are the questions, the tensions, the realities of life in the wilderness, both the wilderness of Sinai and Moab, and the wilderness of human sin—on interpersonal and intercontinental levels.

Numbers raises a series of questions: questions of trust in God, questions of fidelity and true worship, questions of life and death; questions that are meant, in the end, to reorient the reader, to remind her or him both of what God has done in this people's past and to declare that God and God's Word will have the final say.

Works Cited

Barre, Michael L. 1997. "The Portrait of Balaam in Numbers 22–24." *Int* 51, no. 3:254–66.
Childs, Brevard S. 1979. *Introduction to the Old Testament as Scripture*. Minneapolis: Fortress Press.

Danby, Herbert. 1933. *The Mishnah*. Oxford: Oxford University Press.

Dozeman, T. B. 1999. "Numbers." In *Dictionary of Biblical Interpretation*, edited by John H. Hayes, 2:214–18. Nashville: Abingdon.

Grossman, Jonathan. 2007. "Divine Command and Human Initiative: A Literary View on Numbers 25-31." *Biblical Interpretation*, no. 15:54-79.

Hartman, Geoffrey H. 1987. "Numbers: The Realism of Numbers, the Magic of Numbers." In *Congregation: Contemporary Writers Read the Jewish Bible*, edited by David Rosenberg, 39–50. New York: Harcourt Brace Jovanovich.

Levine, Baruch A. 2000. *Numbers 21–36*. AYB. New Haven: Yale University Press.

Milgrom, Jacob. 1989. *Numbers*. JPS Commentary. New York: Jewish Publication Society.

Niditch, Susan. 1993. "War, Women, and Defilement in Numbers 31." *Semeia* 61, no. 1:39–57.

Nowell, Irene. 2010. *Numbers*. New Collegeville Bible Commentary. Collegeville, MN: Liturgical Press.

Olson, Dennis T. 1996. *Numbers*. IBC. Louisville: John Knox.

———. 1997. "Negotiating Boundaries: The Old and New Generations and the Theology of Numbers." *Int* 51, no. 3:229–40.

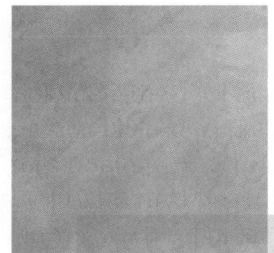

DEUTERONOMY

Harold V. Bennett

Introduction

Deuteronomy, traditionally known as the fifth book of Moses, occupies a very important place in current discussions about the life and faith of ancient Israel. The title of the book comes from the Greek *Deuteronomion,* meaning "the second law." The title of the book in Hebrew is *'elleh haddebarim* ("These are the words") or, more simply, *debarim* ("words"; see 1:1) which comes from the opening words of the manuscript. Those who explore the book of Deuteronomy may get the impression that it is a single, unified speech of Moses, which he delivered to Israel as they prepared to enter the promised land and receive the fulfillment of YHWH's promises to Abraham, the theological progenitor of those who comprised biblical Israel.

While Deuteronomy appears as a single oration delivered in one instance, four pieces of evidence justify raising questions about whether that is true: (1) Multiple superscriptions are present, for example, Deut. 1:1-5; 4:44–49; 29:1; and 33:1; (2) accounts in which Moses appear are written in the third-person singular—as though someone were talking to us about Moses; (3) duplications and inconsistencies are present in the laws in Deuteronomy 12–26; and (4) a report about the death of Moses appears at the end of the book (Deut. 34:1-8). Critical scholarship argues that a movement composed of scribes, priests, and prophets collected and brought together the individual speeches, cultic traditions, legislation, and narratives that constitute Deuteronomy, and that this movement, which began its work in the South in the latter part of the seventh century BCE, completed its project during the sixth century BCE (A. D. H. Mayes 1991, 34–55; Alexander Rofé 2002, 4–9; Moshe Weinfeld 1992, 1–9; and Richard Nelson 2002, 6–9).

Points of contact are present between the present structure of Deuteronomy and treaties between suzerains and vassals in the ancient Near East. Moreover, the book of Deuteronomy employs a distinctive language and phraseology. It also advocates for a particular ideology. This point of view serves as the basis for the distinct historiography that appears in Joshua, Judges, 1–2 Samuel, and 1–2 Kings. What is more, the theological and moral ideas that appear in Deuteronomy serve as the backdrop for action against ethnic groups, social classes, and religious communities. Moreover, political and religious leadership gets prescribed, proscribed, and appraised. This essay focuses on Deuteronomy as a whole, the Deuteronomic program in biblical Israel, and the distinct ways the book has been understood. It also calls attention to the significance of Deuteronomy for theological, philosophical, social, and ethical conversations today. Unless otherwise noted, the translations of Deuteronomy, which appear in the following article, are those of the author.

Deuteronomy 1:6—4:43: Setting the Stage for the Covenant

▌ THE TEXT IN ITS ANCIENT CONTEXT

Deuteronomy 1:6–4:43 gives an account of Israel's journey from Horeb to Moab, and important differences appear in its narrative. Horeb, not Sinai, is the name for the site from which the journey commenced and the name of the mountain where Moses received the revelation from YHWH. This section contains the account of Moses' appointing officials to help with governance in the Israelite community. The version of this event in Exodus 18 introduces Moses' father-in-law into this event, and it suggests that Moses himself identified the men who would serve as leaders among the people. Deuteronomy 1:6—4:43 neither mentions Moses' father-in-law nor places the onus for identifying the men that will act as judges on the shoulders of Moses. In the account of Deuteronomy, the people choose these officials.

Deuteronomy 2:26—3:17 introduces the theme of sacred war (*herem*), namely, the practice of slaughtering opponents in combat, destroying their property and livestock, and razing their cities. The concept of holy war describes the way the redactor viewed the conflict with Sihon king of Heshbon and Og king of Bashan. The redactor of Deuteronomy will introduce this campaign throughout the narrative, for the traditions about the destruction of Sihon and Og play a major role in the moral thought of the Deuteronomic program. Key motifs and metaphors in Deut. 1:6—4:43 are also present in Judges, 1–2 Kings, Hosea, Jeremiah, and in the literature of early Christianity. The key motifs and metaphors are as follows: The charge to exterminate entire groups of people (Deut. 2:26—3:11); the demand to embrace the worship of YHWH (Deut. 4:1-14); the command to abjure idolatry (Deut. 4:15-20); the metaphor that YHWH is a consuming fire (Deut. 4:21-24); and the indication that banishment from the land will be the punishment for apostasy (Deut. 4:25-31).

▌ THE TEXT IN THE INTERPRETIVE TRADITION

Several key thinkers in the history of Christianity adopted the idea that YHWH is a consuming fire. Origen (184–253 CE) contends that this metaphor best explains God's dealings with sins and human imperfections. According to Origen, the presence of God as fire cleanses the believer for the sake of purity. Ambrose (340–397 CE) proffers that just as illumination is a feature of fire, so God is a consuming fire (Lienhard 2001, 278). Spinoza uses the language of God as fire to argue for the use of allegorical hermeneutics in interpreting the Hebrew Bible (Spinoza 2001, 86–104).

■ THE TEXT IN CONTEMPORARY DISCUSSION

How should one speak about God? Which metaphors are apropos? What evidence should inform our beliefs about the nature of God? Which metaphors do Deut. 1:6—4:43 support? Undoubtedly, the battle reports in Deut. 1:6—4:43 call attention to beliefs about the moral fiber of God (Craigie 1978, 9–19; Niditch 1993, 3–27; Copan 2011, 158–97; Seibert 2009, 24–26). Deuteronomy 2:26—3:11 recounts the killing of women, children, and other noncombatants, and it places the onus for this act of violence on the shoulders of Sihon. Yet one cannot help but be bothered by this story. At the center of this troubling report is Deut. 2:30, which reads: "YHWH, your God hardened [*qāšâ*] his spirit and toughened [*'āmēṣ*] his heart." Thus YHWH instilled obstinacy in Sihon, and this stubbornness led to his death and to the massacre of a large segment of human beings. If one allows this text to inform the attributes and designations he or she uses for the Holy, then Deut. 2:30 elicits questions about the character of God, for it invites discussion about how the moral agent on the present scene should speak about the moral attributes of the deity. As it was mentioned above, Paul Copan 2011 and Eric Seibert 2012 help to describe the backdrop against which to discuss this issue. Copan frames the discussion by asking: "Is God a moral monster?" Seibert also contends that disconcerting notions about God are in the Hebrew Bible. Both thinkers draw attention to the brutality and hawkish nature believed to comprise the deity in the Deuteronomic traditions; therefore, investigations into beliefs about the moral attributes of God receive treatment in popular literature as well as in standard discussions in the philosophy of religion (Peterson et al. 2013, 135–56).

Deuteronomy 5:1—6:19: Faithfulness to YHWH

■ THE TEXT IN ITS ANCIENT CONTEXT

Deuteronomy 5:1-5 narrates the specific obligations of the covenant between YHWH and Israel. Since the group of liberated slaves with whom YHWH cut a covenant at Horeb/Sinai was not present as Israel *entered* the promised land, the redactors of Deut. 5:1-5 inserted Deut. 5:3 into the record. It says: "YHWH our God did not cut this covenant with our fathers, but with all of us who are here today." By adding the aforementioned statement, Deut. 5:1-5 suggests that the group standing in the plains of Moab, preparing to enter the land, consists of the ones with whom YHWH cut this particular covenant (Weinfeld 1991, 237–38). Moreover, Deut. 5:1—6:19 indicates that the people saw "fire" on the mountain and that YHWH spoke to them from the midst of the fire, but that Moses translated the voice of YHWH to them.

Deuteronomy 5:1—6:19 contains two important texts for understanding orthodox Yahwism in biblical Israel. The Decalogue, on the one hand, appears in Deut. 5:7-21. Walter Harrelson points out that various ways for numbering the commandments in Deut. 5:6-21 are present (Harrelson 1985, 45–48). At the center of this problem is whether to list the verse that contains the self-introduction of YHWH and the deliverance from Egypt as a commandment as well as whether to combine into a single commandment the prohibitions against worshiping other deities and idolatry. It is noteworthy that its treatment of the commandment to observe the Sabbath, or day of rest, possesses a noticeable difference from the commandments to observe the Sabbath in Exod. 20:8. The commandment to observe the Sabbath in Deut. 5:12-15 contends that persons should observe the day of rest *because they were no longer slaves in Egypt*, but the legislation to observe the Sabbath in Exod. 20:8 instructs the moral agent to respect the Sabbath *because the deity completed creation in six days and rested on the seventh day*. The commandment in Deuteronomy has a ring of justice, focusing on using the Sabbath to treat even slaves with compassion (since the Israelites were once slaves themselves), while the Exodus version focuses on establishing the Sabbath as day when work and other activities cease.

The Shema, on the other hand, appears in Deut. 6:4-19. It reads: "Hear, Israel, YHWH our God: YHWH is one." The Shema acquires its name from the Hebrew term *šĕma'*, which means "hear" or "listen." The Shema articulates sole monotheism, a tenet that is critical for understanding the theological precommitments of the group that was responsible for codifying the traditions that appear in Deuteronomy. One can argue that prior to the Babylonian period, monolatry or henotheism was the ascendant religious ideal in Israel. During the Babylonian period but before the Persian period, monotheism and the notion of exclusive loyalty to YHWH became the ascendant religious ideology in the decimated community of Israel.

■ THE TEXT IN THE INTERPRETIVE TRADITION

The sentences that comprise the Ten Commandments have been understood in a variety of ways. For the sake of manageability, the following section will cast light on the commandment to observe the Sabbath. In short, this legislation has often been interpreted to mean avoiding or not performing physical labor on the seventh day. Rabbinic exegesis cites thirty-nine categories of work that are forbidden on the Sabbath (*m. Ñabb.* 7:1-4). Jesus, however, permits work on the Sabbath day (Matt. 12:1-8; Mark 2:23-28; and Luke 6:1-5). It is noteworthy that the Qur'an, on the one hand, advocates for observing the Sabbath, but it is silent on how to observe it (Qur'an 4:154). In short, it does not command Muslims to abstain from work on the seventh day. What is more, the Qur'an does not advocate that the deity needs rest from work (Qur'an 2:255). Augustine (354–430 CE) interpreted the biblical commandment to rest on the Sabbath to mean that people should regularly involve themselves in moments of tranquility. For him, the commandment to observe the Sabbath is an invitation for the spirit of a person to take a break and to rest in God (Lienhard 2001, 104).

■ THE TEXT IN CONTEMPORARY DISCUSSION

Deuteronomy 5:1—6:19 contains the Ten Commandments, a set of sentences that are perhaps the most well-known norms for decision making in the West. These regulations claim to have their origin in YHWH. The belief that the deity bequeathed these moral principles to humankind opens the door for an exciting conversation in metaethics. That is to say, as one attempts to delineate those issues, conditions, or phenomena that must be present for a meaningful morality to exist, he or she must account for the origin of morality. Deuteronomy 5:1—6:19 assumes the existence of God, and that ethical truth proceeds from God. This way of talking about the source of moral truth has it benefits. The reality, however, is that we live in a postmodern world. Concomitant with postmodernity is the skeptical point of view that truth does not exist, or if it does, is unknowable. This line of thinking leaves the door ajar for arguing whether the existence of

God is a necessary condition for the presence of systems for good decision making (Nielsen 1990, 70–112). The Ten Commandments invite the present-day believer in God to formulate a theory about morality that accounts for the origin and presence of justifiable moral ideas about the good life, happiness, moral responsibility, and meaningful human existence against the backdrop of a postmodern worldview.

Deuteronomy 6:20-25: Passing on the Sacred Traditions

▌ THE TEXT IN ITS ANCIENT CONTEXT

Deuteronomy 6:20-25 envisions parents, male and female, educating their children about the significance of the distinct stipulations that define the agreement between YHWH and the group that stands on the brink of possessing the land. Salient among the terms in this passage is the word "testimonies" (*'ēdōt*). This term also appears in Deut. 4:45 and 6:17, and it receives frequent usage in Psalm 119. One expects this term to denote a statement or account that a witness gives about his or her personal experience regarding a specific event. Nelson and Mayes support this understanding of *'ēdōt*, but they advocate for a report that accentuates the tradition about the law-giving at Horeb. These scholars maintain that the phrase "testimonies, statutes, and judgments" is a direct reference to the Ten Commandments, and that the placement of these terms into a single literary formula is characteristic of the Deuteronomic narratival tradition (Nelson 2002, 72; Mayes 1991, 159–60). What is more, the storyteller uses language and concepts, for example, "great and evil wonders," to compel the children to appreciate that YHWH acted on their behalf, and that YHWH perpetrated a series of "amazing and extraordinary deeds" against Pharaoh and Egypt. Thus the tradition about the rescue from bondage in Egypt is a major piece in the catechizing of Israelite children.

▌ THE TEXT IN THE INTERPRETIVE TRADITION

The tradition about the deliverance of the Hebrew slaves from bondage in Egypt contains symbols and motifs that are central to liberation theology, ethics, and biblical exegesis and hermeneutics. These themes and their symbols are the following: (1) a source of power, domination, and exploitation in a social order (Pharaoh); (2) a milieu saturated with injustice and dehumanization (the presence and variety of slavery in Egypt); (3) an oppressed social class (Hebrew slaves); (4) a liberator deity who sides with the weakest in society (YHWH and the plague stories); and (5) an ongoing desire and struggle for freedom from dehumanization (the Sea of Reeds and wilderness wanderings stories). Persons of African descent, in the African Diaspora, and persons from other groups that exist on the periphery of the socioeconomic and political structures in the West find parallels between their plight and struggle for freedom and the plight and existential situation of Israel prior to its emancipation from subjugation in Egypt. Liberation theologians, ethicists, and biblical scholars take the tradition about the exodus from Egypt to mean that YHWH identifies with the weak and most defenseless in society, and that YHWH acts in ways that seek to ameliorate the conditions of the poor and those who suffer exploitation at the hands of the powerful (Gutiérrez 1999, 29–46; Hopkins 1999, 42–43).

▰The Text in Contemporary Discussion

The exodus from Egypt is an important event in the lore of ancient Israel. Chief among the sequence of events that freed the Hebrew slaves from captivity was the death of the firstborn of the Egyptians; therefore, the death of human beings who might have had nothing to do with the cruelty toward the Hebrews was one of the great and evil wonders of YHWH, and the Deuteronomic narratival tradition demands that Israelites pass on this story to their children; but it proceeds without any attempt to appreciate the very important and problematic implications of this claim.

The present reader is compelled, therefore, to assess the philosophy of education implied in Deuteronomy 6:20-25. The research of Paulo Freire helps to cast light on this issue. In his classic book *The Pedagogy of the Oppressed*, Freire contends that human beings should strive for the humanization of all peoples, and that the recognition of the inherent dignity of all human beings entails that one denounce social conventions, ideas, structures, and other phenomena that exploit and degrade people. Education is a critical element in this process. Thus one goal of the education of children on the current scene should be to enable them to analyze and evaluate in a dispassionate manner traditions and other cultural phenomena they have received from their ancestors (Freire 2005, 43–87).

Deuteronomy 7:1-26: Conquest and Election

▰The Text in Its Ancient Context

Deuteronomy 7:1-26 casts light on the notion of election, a fundamental issue in Deuteronomic legislation. The notion and language of election finds its clearest expression in Deut. 7:6, for this verse says that YHWH chose (*bāḥar*) Israel to be a *sĕgullâ* (a collection of prized jewels). Deuteronomy 7:7 seeks to limit any pride or arrogance that might arise in the community regarding its being chosen by YHWH, by pointing out that it was simply the deity's love (*'ahăbâ*) and the deity's loyalty to the promise made to the ancestors of Israel that accounts for its being selected by YHWH to be in this exclusive relationship. It was a favor that a superior showed to an inferior.

Deuteronomy 7:1-26 tells Israel that because it is in a special relationship with YHWH, there are obligations that accompany this arrangement. Salient among these responsibilities are the following: (1) Israel is to annihilate the inhabitants of the land that lived there prior to their entry (Deut. 7:2, 16, 24); (2) Israel is to eradicate the cults of these people (Deut. 7:5); (3) Israel is not to practice exogamy (i.e., marriage outside their own people) (Deut. 7:3); and (4) Israel is to obey YHWH (Deut. 7:12). The instructions to massacre and expunge the cultures of the Hittites, Girgashites, Amorites, Canaanites, Perizzites, Hivites, and Jebusites from the promised land receive reiteration throughout this chapter. Obviously, the biblical community did not carry out the total destruction of these peoples when they entered the promised land because the Jebusites were around in the time of David. Rather, the narrative introduces the claim that the Israelites are to destroy seven nations. Mayes and Nelson suggest that the usage of the number seven is a rhetorical and ideological device to indicate completeness or total destruction of these social groups (Mayes 1991, 182–83; Nelson 2002, 99). One cannot help but to notice that Deut. 7:1-26 is replete with terms that denote horrific acts of violence to entire groups of people, and protecting and reverencing the YHWH cult is the justification offered for these types of behaviors by the Israelites.

■ THE TEXT IN THE INTERPRETIVE TRADITION

This notion of Israel's election appears throughout the classical prophets. Amos 3:1-2 contends that the deity has chosen Israel, and that discipline at the hand of the deity is concomitant with this status. Hosea 11:1 links deliverance from bondage in Egypt to being elected by the deity. Isaiah 42:5-9 implies that because the deity chose Israel, it is to serve as a witness to the nations elsewhere in the world about the power of YHWH. These schools of thought agree that YHWH has chosen Israel, namely, the sociopolitical entity that traces its ancestry back to Abraham through Isaac.

The tradition about YHWH choosing Israel received treatment in the theological program of Paul. In Romans 9–11, Paul contends that Israel is not a biological, genetic classification; it is a religious category. Israel and those whom the deity has chosen are those persons who accept salvation as offered through Jesus. The writer of Ephesians contends that the elect were the believers in Christ whom the deity handpicked before the foundation of the world (Eph. 1:3-14). Camps in Christendom, therefore, advocate for the position that descent from Abraham through Isaac is unnecessary for inclusion in Israel, the elect of God.

■ THE TEXT IN CONTEMPORARY DISCUSSION

Deuteronomy 7:1-26 raises two important issues for consideration. One issue is whether peaceful strategies should be the method for addressing religious diversity on the local or international scenes. Given the supposed humanitarianism of Deuteronomy, it is odd that Deut. 7:1-26 prescribes the complete separation from or annihilation of entire groups of people who ascribe to faith traditions that are different from Israel's faith tradition. Perhaps Deut. 7:1-26 is inviting the theological agent to reject the approach that Israel utilized and to frame a paradigm that respects religious, philosophical, and cultural difference, while at the same time permitting people to inhabit a common spatiality and realize the beloved community.

While the text contends that YHWH "handpicked" Israel, debate is widespread about how one appropriates this theme of election. For the sake of manageability, the following comments cite three of these difficulties: (1) Who is Israel? That is to say, is "Israel" a social, political, or theological designation? Does this designation refer to a group of people that descended from "Jacob"? It is noteworthy that the notion of "Israel" as a political entity changed during the history of Israel. (2) Is Israel in these regulations synonymous with the sociopolitical entity called Israel, that country, which is located in the Middle East, on the southeastern coast of the Mediterranean Sea? (3) Does election mean that Israel receives a set of special favors, or does it mean that as a community it has been assigned a group of distinctive humanitarian responsibilities?

Deuteronomy 8:1—9:6: Not on Your Own

■ THE TEXT IN ITS ANCIENT CONTEXT

Deuteronomy 8:1—9:6 reiterates the theme of the undeserved goodness of YHWH. This motif appeared in Deut. 6:10-15, citing the provision of food, clothes, and good health as Israel made its trek to the promised land. Deuteronomy 8:1—9:6 mentions the fruitfulness of the bovine herds that Israel owns, and the fecundity of the land in which the Israelite people will live. It also contends that abundance and fertility are signs of the unearned compassion of the deity toward Israel. Deuteronomy 8:1—9:6, however, introduces one caveat: Israel must bear in mind that when it begins to enjoy the bounty of the land, it should remember that it was the generosity of YHWH that made this "good life" possible.

■ THE TEXT IN THE INTERPRETIVE TRADITION

In the tradition about the temptation of Jesus, the Synoptic Gospels report that Jesus drew on Deut. 8:1—9:6 and took it to mean that there are other items that give human life its vitality and importance, namely, possessing faith in God and ensuring that one's innermost being is in right standing with God (Matt. 4:4; Luke 4:4). Clement of Alexandria (150–215 ce) casts a different light on Deut. 8:1—9:6, by talking about this story against the backdrop of the virtuous person. His reading of this passage brings into play the view that the truly righteous person, that is, the moral agent who is in right relationship with God, will never be in a permanent condition of involuntary physical neediness. Ambrose introduces into the marketplace of ideas an alternative reading of Deut. 8:1—9:6, saying that this passage teaches against self-sufficiency. Ambrose argues that this speech warns against confiding totally in one's strength, and he directs individuals not to overestimate their own ability to provide for themselves. According to Ambrose, accepting that God is the source of sustenance undermines pride and other vices that ground themselves in hubris (Lienhard 2001, 289).

■ THE TEXT IN CONTEMPORARY DISCUSSION

Deuteronomy 8:1—9:6 invites the community to recognize the source of life and success. This passage states that YHWH ensured the safety and well-being of Israel, and that the community should remain aware that YHWH is the staple of life. Israel must not forget YHWH. The question naturally arises: How do persons on the current scene forget about God? While several answers to this question vie for our attention, the response that receives the most support, in light of Deut. 8:1—9:6, is ingratitude. The text encourages people to demonstrate gratefulness daily to God for life, health, and strength. In doing so, people can face life with a degree of optimism regardless of their circumstances.

Deuteronomy 9:7—10:22: Rebellion against YHWH

■ THE TEXT IN ITS ANCIENT CONTEXT

Deuteronomy 9:7—10:22 recounts three episodes in the plight of Israel. It retells the story of Moses ascending Horeb to receive the commandments from YHWH. It rehearses the incident involving the making of the golden image, and describes Moses' breaking of the tablets, which contained the "Ten Words." While elements in the narrative about Moses' ascending the mountain, the making of the idol, and his shattering of the tablets correspond with parts in the accounts about these same events that appear elsewhere in the Pentateuch, noticeable inconsistencies are present. While *Horeb* in Deuteronomy refers to the name of the mountain where Moses received the law, *Sinai* denotes this site in the account in Exod. 24:12-18. Moreover, the version in Deuteronomy mentions that Moses fasted forty days and forty nights; however, Exod. 24:12-18 says nothing about Moses fasting while he was on the mount. Deuteronomy 9:7—10:22 suggests that Moses made the trek to the mountain by himself, but Exod. 24:12-18 indicates that Joshua accompanied Moses on his trek to the mountain. The narrative in Deuteronomy also omits the account, included in Exodus 32, of the Levites killing thousands of Israelites and the use of this incident to justify the Levites being set apart for the service of YHWH.

▋ THE TEXT IN THE INTERPRETIVE TRADITION

The wilderness-period motif played a key role in the prophecies of Jeremiah, Hosea, and Ezekiel. Jeremiah and Hosea, however, interpret the wilderness-period motif differently from its articulation in Deut. 9:7—10:22. Jeremiah and Hosea take the wilderness period to indicate that moment in Israel's history when it was loyal and faithful to YHWH (Jer. 2:2; Hosea 2:14). Yet, Ezekiel agrees with the Deuteronomic program and contends that the wilderness period was when Israel showed her obstinacy toward YHWH (see Ezek. 20:13). The author of Hebrews understands the wilderness experience typologically; it is to be thought of as a *method for understanding an event* in the history of Israel. Hebrews 3 takes the wilderness motif to represent obduracy and the way a person can respond to the voice of the deity. The theology in Hebrews urges the audience not to repeat the wilderness experience in regard to its response to God. The audience is told to accept, not to resist, God's invitations for fellowship.

▋ THE TEXT IN CONTEMPORARY DISCUSSION

Resisting the will of the Holy and frequently rebelling against God are common themes in the Deuteronomic literature, and the notion of this resisting the deity is a commonplace in the religious traditions of the world commonly referred to as Western religions: Christianity, Judaism, and Islam. Each believes in different ways that this issue is a fundamental feature of the human condition, and each offers strategies for managing and perhaps ultimately correcting this problem. Christianity emphasizes the notion of sin, and in some ways maintains that rebellion against God is one of the ways that this problem perennially demonstrates itself. Christianity therefore advocates for its adherents to perform ongoing self-inventories to guard against standing in mutiny against God.

Deuteronomy 11:1-32: YHWH Delivers

▋ THE TEXT IN ITS ANCIENT CONTEXT

Deuteronomy 11:1-32 admonishes the people to love and remember the deeds of YHWH, and to honor the statutes and regulations of YHWH. In citing some of the deeds of YHWH, this passage introduces the account of the Israelite deliverance and escape through the sea. It also mentions the incident when YHWH opened the ground, and it swallowed Dathan and Abiram. Numbers 16 gives the reader another account of this story. In fact, the version in Numbers 16 provides more detail, in that it identifies the principals in the story and some of the issues that spawned the event. Deuteronomy 11:1-32 closes out this section of the book by contending that a nexus exists between obedience and prosperity, and that a correlation is present between disobedience and misfortune. In classic Deuteronomic fashion, Deut. 11:1-32 invites the Israelite community to understand that because YHWH delivered them from servitude in Egypt, it owes its allegiance to YHWH. Thus, once they cross the Jordan, they are commanded to call down the blessings from Mt. Gerizim and to invoke the curses from Mt. Ebal.

▌ THE TEXT IN THE INTERPRETIVE TRADITION

It is noteworthy that the motif of the deliverance at the sea resurfaces in different hermeneutical traditions. The Hebrew text of Deut. 11:4 uses the term *yam-sûph* ("sea of reeds") to denote this body of water, while the translators of the Septuagint use the term "Red Sea" (*thalassēs tēs erythras*). A Negro spiritual says in the chorus, "Moses don't you weep, and Martha don't you mourn. Pharaoh's army drowned at the Red Sea, so Moses don't you weep, and Martha don't you mourn." Different terms for the body of water through which the people escaped appear in the lore of ancient Israel. Regardless of the terms used, the theme persists: YHWH delivers.

While Deut. 11:1-32 talks about liberation, it cites Dathan and Abiram, men who played critical roles in a mutiny in the wilderness; it excludes Korah from its rendition of its account of this episode. Jeffrey Tigay contends that two rebellions occurred. Dathan and Abiram were the principal actors in one revolt, and Korah was the leading figure in another, separate rebellion. He then argues that the account in Deut. 11:1-32 reports the uprising led by Dathan and Abiram, and represents a stage in the interpretive history of the story prior to the combination of the accounts (Tigay 1996, 111).

▌ THE TEXT IN CONTEMPORARY DISCUSSION

The theme of deliverance is central to the narrative in Deut. 11:1-32. This idea appears frequently in Pentecostal and charismatic pneumatologies. While Deut. 11:1-32 implies that deliverance is liberation from a socioeconomic and political predicament, these religious groups link deliverance to freedom from personal moral bankruptcies such as lying, drinking, illicit sexual activities, stealing, and other private vices. In other words, private morality and individual psychological phobias are the backdrop against which Pentecostals and Charismatics discuss deliverance. Thus they also take deliverance to mean freedom from fear, uncertainty, hopelessness, despair, faithlessness, and other psychological phenomena.

Deuteronomy 12:1-32: Only One Place to Worship YHWH

▌ THE TEXT IN ITS ANCIENT CONTEXT

Deuteronomy 12:1-32 directs the Israelite colonizers to destroy the cults of the inhabitants of the promised land. One cannot help but contrast these injunctions with the codes in Deut. 7:1-26.

Conspicuous, however, are some inconsistencies between Deut. 7:1-26 and Deut. 12:1-32. While Deut. 12:1-32 uses the term *gôyîm* to refer to the residents of Canaan, Deut. 7:1-26 specifies that Hittites, Girgashites, Amorites, Perizzites, Hivites, Jebusites, and Canaanites are the occupants of the land. Given the difficulties one encounters when attempting to account for the presence of these groups in Syria-Palestine at the end of the Late Bronze Age, the placement of these peoples in a single list is likely a stylistic device and theological maneuver of the redactor (see the section above on Deut. 6:20-25).

Deuteronomy 12:4-14, 26-28 builds a framework for understanding the proper altar for sacrifice in the Deuteronomic program. It is important to note that the placement of regulations having to do with altars appears at the start of the Covenant and Holiness Codes. It has been argued that this placement at the start of the Deuteronomic Code is consistent with the practice of beginning law codes with stipulations regarding the altar (see Nelson 2002, 146). Deuteronomy 12:4-14, 26-28, instructs the people of Israel to present their offerings at a single site. This ideology emerges from the chosen place theology and its concomitant phrase "the place that YHWH your God will choose," which are widespread in the Deuteronomic program (see Weinfeld 1992, 324–26). While it is probable that the origins of this philosophy lie in the North, the Deuteronomic redactor applied this ideology to sites in the South. The Jerusalem temple became the legitimate site for celebrating festivals, worshiping YHWH, fulfilling vows, presenting tithes, and encountering the power of YHWH (e.g., Deut. 12:17-19; 14:22-27; 16:1-17; 26:1-11).

Deuteronomy 12:15-16, 20-25, provides guidelines for the slaughter of animals for food and directions for the disposal of their blood. Members of Israel were allowed to kill and consume these animals in their local villages. This regulation may have been the Deuteronomic response to the demand that if the killing of animals for food was in fact sacrifice, and that this cultic act could occur only at the Jerusalem temple; traveling to this site to kill animals for food might have been too impracticable (Mayes 1991, 225–27; Nelson 2002, 146–47). The only stipulation is that the blood is to be poured out (*šāpak*) on the ground. Points of contact are present between Deut. 12:15-16, 20-25, and Deut. 15:19-23. Both regulations deal with the slaughter and consumption of animals. It is noteworthy, however, that Deut. 15:19-23 indicates that the Israelite community is to protect firstlings, which are to be offered at the central sanctuary. These animals are not to be involved in the plowing of fields or in the carrying of cargo. The firstlings of the sheep are not to be sheared. Animals that possess a flaw are not to be sacrificed to YHWH; these animals are to be slaughtered and consumed in the local villages. Consistent with Deut. 12:16 and, because the blood is the sole possession of YHWH, the blood of the slaughtered animals must be disposed of properly.

▌▌ THE TEXT IN THE INTERPRETIVE TRADITION

Deuteronomy 12:4-14, 26-28 instructs the people of Israel to present their offerings at an authorized site. These regulations limit the sites where persons in the community may perform their cultic activities. The people are told that there is one place where they are authorized to worship. Perhaps this regulation alludes to a single corporate sanctuary in each of the tribal areas, or to just one shrine for the entire community. The ambiguity of this regulation clears space for arguing for the existence of as many shrines dedicated to YHWH as there were "tribes" in the Israelite community, or it allows one to contend that there was one and only one shrine for members of the YHWH cult to worship and carry out their religious duties and activities.

Single-sanctuary language appears in Deuteronomy 12, and one cannot help but conclude that this law had serious effects in Israel. Josephus links the requirement for a single sanctuary in Israel to monotheism. He argues that the presence of many sites for worship supported the claim that many deities were present in Israel. Maimonides argued that Deuteronomy 12 is to be understood as an attempt by YHWH to limit the role of sacrifice in worship and to maximize the role of prayer in religiosity. Abravanel, a fifteenth-century Jewish scholar, understood Deuteronomy 12 as an attempt to prevent Israelites from killing animals in the wilderness and offering sacrifices to demons (Tigay 1996, 460–64).

■ The Text in Contemporary Discussion

Deuteronomy 12:1-32 demands that only the YHWH-alone cult was to be permitted to exist in the promised land. According to the Deuteronomic agenda, if these cults were allowed to remain, their presence would jeopardize the existence of the YHWH-alone cult. What is the reader on the present scene to make of the Deuteronomic proclivity for religious intolerance? Through the Internet, Facebook, and other forms of social media, persons have access to a plethora of information about religions and competing faith traditions. The Deuteronomic agenda, then, invites people for whom religion is a key force in life to frame a paradigm for how they should respond to the presence of different, conflicting faith communities and various belief systems on the global landscape.

Several options for addressing the issue of religious tolerance vie for our attention. Persons can opt for pluralism, the belief that multiple religions contain equal soteriological and ethical truth; exclusivism, the position that one and only one faith tradition is acceptable and efficacious; or inclusivism, the view that while a degree of truth and soteriological efficaciousness is present in many religions, one religious tradition is supreme. In light of globalization and the presence of competing diverse faith traditions in a common socio-spatiality, the moral and theological behavior in Deut. 12:1-32 puts the issue of religious tolerance into play.

Deuteronomy 13:1-18: Backsliding

■ The Text in Its Ancient Context

Deuteronomy 13:1-18 identifies four possible sources with whom the temptation to abandon the worship of YHWH could originate. This literary unit suggests that prophets (Deut. 13:1-5), family members and close friends (Deut. 13:6-11), and anonymous wicked persons in the general population of a city (Deut. 13:12-18) are possible initiators of infidelity to YHWH. According to Deut. 13:1-5, the enticement by the prophet to serve deities other than YHWH is the indication that YHWH has not endorsed this person: this individual is a false prophet. Since the predictions of false prophets can happen, this makes the false prophets credible. The speaker in this passage tells the people not to be swayed by the signs and wonders that the prophet or dreamer of dreams performs. The effort to persuade people to abandon the worship of YHWH is treason, and Deut. 13:1-5 prescribes the death penalty for the false prophet.

Deuteronomy 13:6-11 draws attention to family members, friends, and other close relationships that might instigate serving deities other than YHWH. This literary unit, therefore, warns that each member of the biblical community should be on guard for covert invitations from their closest relatives to abandon the worship of YHWH. It is noteworthy that these types of enticements come from persons who might have tremendous emotional influence in the lives of their loved ones, and that the attempt to lure an Israelite away from devotion to YHWH is a capital offense. One also cannot help but notice that Deut. 13:10 prescribes death by stoning as punishment for this crime. One cannot help but to notice that points of contact are present between the scene depicted in this case and that of a public lynching. Weinfeld and Mayes argues against the "public lynching scenario" by claiming that the text calls for a trial, and that if the alleged provocateur is found guilty, the Israelite who witnessed the crime should throw the first stone and the entire community is to join in after him in the stoning of the instigator; consequently, the entire community participates in administering the death penalty. Mayes is careful to point out that Deut. 13:10 is one of the few passages in the Hebrew Bible that prescribe death by stoning for certain offenses in the biblical community (Weinfeld 1992, 95; Mayes 1991 234–35).

Deuteronomy 13:12-18 deals with the fate of entire cities or social groups that have succumbed to the temptation to embrace the worship of deities other than YHWH. Deuteronomy 13:13 suggests that "men, the sons of Belial," instigated the infidelity. Peter Craigie attempts to cast light on the meaning or identity of these "men, the sons of Belial," by translating this phrase as "wicked men" (Craigie 1976, 226). Mayes translates this phrase as "base fellows" (Mayes 1991, 236). While the term "Belial" is not widespread in the Hebrew Bible, Craigie (1976) and Mayes (1991) link this phrase to the notion of moral and theological corruption. Thus, when "Belial" appears in this appositional phrase in Deut. 13:13, it seems fair to claim that the phrase denotes immoral and apostate individuals who lured an entire city into infidelity to YHWH. After the suspicion of treason against YHWH has been verified by some judicial proceeding, the inhabitants of the city are to be killed, the livestock in the city are to be slaughtered, and the city is to be destroyed by fire and never rebuilt.

▮ THE TEXT IN THE INTERPRETIVE TRADITION

Vincent of Lérins suggested that from time to time, teachers who stray from the truth arise. He argued, however, that these are moments when the Christian should invoke principles and concepts in Deuteronomy 13 to demonstrate his or her commitment to the deity. Chief among these ideas are that the believer should love God with all of his or her heart and soul (Deut. 13:3); cleave to God (Deut. 13:5); and obey the voice of God (Deut. 13:18). The Deuteronomic program instructs Israel to withstand the temptation to abandon YHWH. YHWH alone is God. YHWH is to be worshiped. Vincent, therefore, builds on this theological legacy by contending that the true Catholic loves God with all of his or her being (see Lienhard 2001, 296).

■ THE TEXT IN CONTEMPORARY DISCUSSION

Death, as the punishment for instigators of apostasy, was a major feature of the Deuteronomic program. Deuteronomy 13:12-18 does not consider a response that would position the people to reexamine their decisions and decide the truth of the competing religious claim that confronts them. If a faith community on the present scene senses that unbelief is gaining ground in its ranks or that something is awry with the theological or philosophical views of one of its member communities, then taking actions that seek to correct those perspectives, while simultaneously humanizing the constituents, may be the appropriate choice. Creating an environment for groups in the community to explore the veracity of faith claims to which they are supposed to adhere, not a climate that demands the execution of the alleged nonconformist group or a milieu that mandates blind obedience to religious doctrine from collections of conscious individuals, should be the prescribed strategy for dealing with people who seek to adjudicate the various sides of a theological issue. In *When Religion Becomes Evil*, Charles Kimball cites features of dangerous religiosity and invites the reader to consider problems that arise when faith communities use force to coerce people into accepting a specific religious ideology. To avoid many of the crises that Kimball articulates, a critical assessment of the handling of apostasy in Deuteronomic theology and moral philosophy is essential for individuals for whom the Hebrew Bible is normative for faith and praxis.

Deuteronomy 14:1-21: Mourning Rites and the Diet of a Holy People

■ THE TEXT IN ITS ANCIENT CONTEXT

Deuteronomy 14:1-21 contains two subgroups of moral injunctions. Regulations treating mourning rites, on the one hand, appear in Deut. 14:1-2. An injunction of this type also appears in Lev. 19:28. Juxtaposing these regulations reveals the following similarities and differences: (1) Both Deut. 14:1-2 and Lev. 19:28 ban two and only two moral actions; (2) both laws indicate that making incisions in one's flesh for the dead is unacceptable; (3) Lev. 19:28 forbids placing writings or marks on the body for the dead; and (4) Deut. 14:1-2 disallows removing part of one's eyebrows for the dead. The common denominator between these laws is the ban on lacerating one's body in response to the death of another person, and the difference between them is that one bans tattooing the body for the dead while the other law prohibits shaving off part of one's eyebrow for the deceased. While Lev. 19:28 limits its prohibitions against participation in certain mourning rites to priests, Deut. 14:1-2 extends this prohibition to include the laity.

Archaeological finds from Ras Shamra have bequeathed to us a body of texts that contributes to our understanding of the Canaanite pantheon. The mythological texts that come to us from this city cite a plethora of deities, for example, El, Baal, Dagon, Yamm, Mot, and Anat, and these texts suggest that these mythological figures played key roles in the lore of subgroups who inhabited Canaan during the Late Bronze Age. Moreover, many of these peoples believed they existed in a special covenantal relationship with their deity (Craigie 1983, 62–66; Miller 2000, 1–45). Therefore, it comes as no surprise that the individual or school that determined the Deuteronomic agenda sought to impress on the people of Israel that they belonged to YHWH, that they were a *sĕgullâ*, and that this privileged relationship with YHWH should exhibit itself in ways that differentiated the Israelites from their neighbors.

Placing deep cuts in one's flesh and cutting bald spots in one's hair for the deceased were practices associated with the cults of other gods; therefore, Nelson (2002) suggests that Deut. 14:1-2 could refer to demonstrating grief for the death of a person or to expressing extreme sorrow in the cults of other deities (Nelson 2002, 179). He, therefore, leaves the door ajar for claiming that this ritual bans mourning practices in cults for people who have died or for mourning the death of a deity. Mayes (1991) steps into this gap by interpreting "dead" in this passage to refer to humans or a god; consequently, he suggests that this regulation is a response to mourning practices in the Baal cult. Thus he interprets this regulation to identify another type of apostasy, namely, that involvement in mourning rituals linked to any other deity counts as abandoning the YHWH cult (Mayes 1991, 238–39).

■ THE TEXT IN THE INTERPRETIVE TRADITION

Regulations treating diet, on the other hand, appear in Deut. 14:3-21. The codes in Deut. 14:3-21 deal with the consumption of land animals (Deut. 14:4-8), water creatures (Deut. 14:9-10), fowl (Deut. 14:11-19), and insects (Deut. 14:20), and these laws place no restrictions on those vegetables, plants, and fruits that the people of Israel may eat. The Deuteronomic program adopts the principles of clean (*ṭāhôr*) and unclean (*ṭāmēʾ*) to classify animals; animals that are categorized as "clean" are fit for consumption, and fauna that are classified as "unclean" are unfit for consumption. A competing set of codes regulating the consumption of animals appears in Lev. 11:2-23, and a significant difference between these codes is present. While the regulations in Lev. 11:2-23 give detailed attention to citing those animals that Israel may not eat, Deut. 14:4-8 cites those animals that the people are permitted to consume.

While the dietary ordinance in Deut. 14:3-21 instructs the people to eat clean animals, one cannot help but notice that this law does not articulate the criteria that inform its ideas about "cleanliness and uncleanliness." Considerable difference of opinion is present among scholars over why animals are classified as either clean or unclean and about how the reader should interpret these regulations on fauna in the biblical legal corpora. Critical scholarship on the HB identifies four organizing principles or frameworks for classifying the fauna and for understanding the arrangement of the dietary stipulations in Deut. 14:3-21. The gist of the positions is as follows: (1) The hygienic construct proffers that in the worldview of biblical Israel, the flesh of certain fauna was unhealthy and carried disease and thus it was unfit to eat; (2) the cultic framework contends that those animals that are cited as unclean were fauna that were linked to the cults of the people who inhabited Syria-Palestine with biblical Israel; (3) the subjective construct proffers that YHWH decided the issue and that is the end of it; and (4) the ethical/representational framework argues that these regulations are symbolic of a higher moral principle, namely, the belief that Israelites must respect life as they seek to satisfy their appetite for protein (Ross 2002, 251–52; Milgrom 2004, 102–15; Houston 2003, 142–61).

◼ THE TEXT IN CONTEMPORARY DISCUSSION

A model for interpreting biblical law that is informed by critical legal studies clears space for arguing that those codes regarding edible fauna in the Hebrew Bible worked to the disadvantage of certain social divisions in ancient Israelite society (Bennett 2002, 12–21; Knight 2011, 1–86). Two issues naturally arise: which social subdivision in the biblical community was affected adversely by these codes, and how did they affect this social class? A plausible response to the question might be the following: While the goal of Deut. 14:3-21 might have been to place limits on the diet of members in Israel, these codes placed hardships on "the have-nots," that is, the largest and most diverse social class in the community. Mark Sneed (1991) offers a collection of essays that point out that biblical scholars have used a plethora of terms and systems for arranging and discussing the demographics of Israelite society subsequent to the appearance of the monarchy. He contends that while a plethora of terms are present for delineating the social subdivisions in Israel, the consensus of social-scientific research on ancient Israel contends that at least two major socioeconomic classes were perennial features of ancient Israelite society during the Late Iron Age I and Iron Age II. One subdivision possessed wealth and political power (the haves), and the other subdivision was without wealth and political power (the have-nots). Slaves, widows, free peasants, orphans, sharecroppers, and perhaps other vulnerable groups constituted the have-nots (Sneed 1991, 54). This social class daily eked out their existence and lived at the mercy of urban elites, priests, and creditors. Absent from this social class were the concomitants of wealth, that is, a wide choice of food options and the means to obtain whatever they wanted to consume. It therefore stands to reason that while the have-nots might have viewed certain fauna as clean or unclean, it is highly improbable that the groups comprising this category had the luxury of refusing to eat certain meats to the degree that was present among the haves. Hungry stomachs know no morality when it comes to food; while the have-nots in Israel might have demonstrated some allegiance to religious codes, it stands to reason that these people would be more concerned with putting an end to their daily hunger problems than they would be concerned with being ethical and theologically correct or even nutritious when it comes to diet. They just wanted their children to be fed and the pain in their empty stomachs to subside. Chances are that the have-nots, the majority of Israelites, were compelled more often to consider eating "unclean animals," however reluctantly, in order to survive.

Consequently, Deut. 14:3-21 invites the reader to consider the role that this legislation played in a fundamental issue of social justice, namely, whether laws in the Hebrew Bible contributed to the problem of hunger in Israel. When read through a lens shaped by current sociological studies of law and the conversation on demographics in ancient Israel, Deut. 14:3-21 appears to provoke circumstances that those who lived at the mercy of urban elites, priests, and creditors might not have been able to navigate.

Deuteronomy 14:22-29: Tithes

▌ THE TEXT IN ITS ANCIENT CONTEXT

Deuteronomy 14:22-29 deals with tithes in the biblical communities. According to these legal traditions, the tithe (*ma'ăśēr*) is one-tenth of grains, wine, oil, cattle, and sheep. Genesis 14:18-20, on the one hand, cites Abram and links him to this practice of paying tithes, for Abram gives tithes to Melchizedek. While Gen. 28:18-22 and 35:1-14, on the other hand, link the practice of tithing in ancient Israel to Jacob, these traditions in which he appears never provide the textual basis for concluding that Jacob fulfilled his vow to give tithes to the deity. First Samuel 8:10-18 also casts light on tithing in ancient Israel. This narrative recounts Samuel's speech to those elites who request transitioning from a loose, acephalous configuration of tribes to a single, political entity headed by a monarch. In his response to them, Samuel tells these leaders that the crown will exact one-tenth of their produce and flocks, and that it will use them to fund its operation. This passage, therefore, provides a basis for arguing that tithes were a major element in the fiscal system that supported the royal bureaucracy in ancient Israel.

H. Jagersma (1981) and Marty Stevens (2006) situate the conversation about tithes in ancient Israel in the larger discussion on tithes in the ancient Near East. The former cites textual data from Mesopotamia and indicates that the custom of paying tithes was present in the third dynasty of Ur. The latter cites data from Mesopotamia and Egypt and points out that tithes and taxes were key elements in systems for the upkeep of the temple and for funding the programs of the crown. According to Stevens, the term *ešrû*, a term that denotes a tenth of one's income, appears in the Mesopotamian data. Stevens also calls attention to data from the Old Babylonian period and shows that people were obligated to give one-tenth of their crops and orchards to the cult and royal administration. He points out that the term *miksu* appears in the data from the Old Babylonian period, and that this term denoted income received by the state and temple. The data also suggest that the payment of tithes was one element in the exacting of revenue from crops and herds from the general population in ancient Southwest Asia. This income was for temples and for the king. The custom of paying tithes appears in Israelite society, but how it made its way there may be forever lost to us.

▌ THE TEXT IN THE INTERPRETIVE TRADITION

Two traditions about tithes appear in Deut. 14:22-29, and these regulations stand in stark contrast to the law on tithes in Deut. 12:2-7. The ordinances governing tithes in Deut. 12:2-7 are silent on how frequently the tithes should be brought to the site that YHWH chooses. Deuteronomy 14:22 opens with the command "you will set aside tithe of all the increase of your seed that the field brings forth each year." What is more, Deut. 14:23 directs Israel to present the tithes in the place where YHWH's name is present, that is, "in the place where YHWH has put YHWH's name." This centralization formula forbids the consumption of these tithes in local villages. It is worth noting that Deut. 14:22-27 makes a concession: if the person who desires to present tithes resides a great distance from the central sanctuary, the regulation allows for the presenter to exchange for money produce, animals, or other items, and make the trek to the place where the name of YHWH is present. Once he or she arrives at the central shrine, he or she is to purchase food and drink and consume it there. Thus the annual tithe is the focus of Deut. 14:22-27.

Deuteronomy 14:28-29 directs the biblical community to offer tithes "every three years," but this piece of legislation instructs the biblical community to store the tithes "in their villages." Deuteronomy 14:28-29 reminds the biblical community to share their tithes with the widow (*'almānâ*), stranger (*gēr*), fatherless (*yātôm*), and Levites. It is argued that the widow, stranger, and orphan appear together in a single literary formula because they share minimally two social features: (1) The individuals in this social group are bereft of a masculine protector; and (2) the persons in this social group are vulnerable and are at the mercy of priests, urban elites, land owners, creditors, and other exploiters in Israel (Bennett 2002, 55–56). Thus the regulations on tithes instruct the community to share tithes with these people on a regular basis.

These regulations on tithes in Deut. 14:22-29 are very different from the regulations governing tithes in Lev. 27:30-33 and Num. 18:21-32. Leviticus 27:30-33, on the one hand, contends that the tithes are holy to YHWH, meaning that these items belong to the priests. The passage indicates that if one fails to present the complete 10 percent of the tithes to the priest, he is penalized, and must increase the amount of his tithes by 20 percent the next time he presents them. Numbers 18:21-32, on the other hand, stipulates that the tithes are for the support of the Levites and their households in lieu of their not having any inheritance in Israel. This passage, however, adds an additional element to the regulation on tithes: the Levites are instructed to share 10 percent of their tithes with the priests.

Deuteronomy 14:22-29 suggests that the payment of tithes was an important feature of the religious and economic milieu in biblical Israel. The evidence on tithes in the Deuteronomic program and on tithes in the program advanced by priests suggests that there were, minimally, three traditions about obligatory tithing in Israel: (1) There was the annual tithe that was to be presented and eaten at the central sanctuary by the presenter, his family, and the cultic official; (2) there was the annual tithe that was to be presented at the cultic site and was the sole property of the Levites; and (3) there was the triennial tithe that was stored in the local village and was to be shared with the vulnerable in Israelite society. Moreover, 1 Samuel 8 supports the claim that tithes were one element in the material endowment of the monarchy.

■ THE TEXT IN CONTEMPORARY DISCUSSION

Deuteronomy 14:22-27 identifies those items that are subject to tithes, and this regulation provides guidelines on the consumption and distribution of these items in Israel. Deuteronomy 14:22-27 regulates the annual tithe, and Deut. 14:28-29 regulates the collection and distribution of the triennial tithes. What gives these codes relevance for today is the ethic that informs them. In short, these codes are of significance for the current conversation on social justice. Deuteronomy 14:22-29 provides at a minimum temporary economic relief to vulnerable groups. That is to say, these regulations provided these persons with food and other items that they needed to live. Providing temporary, immediate aid to the vulnerable is one of those actions that Islam, Judaism, and Christianity find praiseworthy.

Deuteronomy 15:1-18: Indebtedness and Slavery between Israelites

▌ THE TEXT IN ITS ANCIENT CONTEXT

Deuteronomy 15:1-18 contains two distinct regulations. The common denominator between these legal injunctions is a response to socioeconomic conditions and problems, which proceeded from poverty and debt. Deuteronomy 15:1-11, on the one hand, demands the forgiveness of loans; Deut. 15:12-18, on the other hand, regulates behavior towards persons who have become slaves as a result of personal debt or as a consequence of the loans or debt of someone else. Both pieces of legislation command creditors and enslavers to extend mercy, and these legal injunctions specify that every seven years debts should be canceled and slaves should be given their freedom.

Jeffries Hamilton (1992) aids in delineating a cross-cultural backdrop against which to discuss the regulations on forgiveness of debt and the manumission of slaves that appear in Deut. 15:1-18. Hamilton also cites data from the third dynasty of Ur and from other cultures in Mesopotamia. According to him, *mīšarum* decrees demanded clemency in the form of the forgiveness of individual debts and the forgiveness of selected taxes owed by individuals to the state, and some *mīšarum* decrees demanded the release of slaves. He further indicates that monarchs issued these proclamations, and that these legislations were frequently concomitant with the ascendency of a new king. Hamilton notes that the Mesopotamian evidence attests also to the *andurārum* proclamations. However, he points out, there is considerable difficulty in interpreting the texts where the *andurārum* edicts are present. They provide inconclusive evidence about the direct object of the *andurārum*; therefore, whether the *andurārum* act refers to the release of slaves or to the freeing of someone from some other debtor obligation remains open to debate. Thus, while the cross-cultural parallels in the ancient world are sometimes ambiguous, the larger discussion on social justice in the ancient world nevertheless provides a helpful context for considering the individual stipulations in Deut. 15:1-18.

▌ THE TEXT IN THE INTERPRETIVE TRADITION

The legal injunction in Deut. 15:1-11 instructs creditors in Israelite society to discontinue attempts to collect monies owed to them by their debtors. The translation "remission of debts" appears in English translations of Deut. 15:1-11. The term in biblical Hebrew is *šĕmiṭṭâ* (the act of letting something drop) and the LXX uses the Greek term *aphesis* (the act of discharging something). The general sense of this piece of legislation, then, is to "drop from the books" or "to give a debtor a zero balance for arrears incurred over the past seven years." Mayes contends that the law of release that appears in Deut. 15:1-11 circulated first as a legal sanction governing the use of the land, and that the Deuteronomic program reappropriates a legal injunction that demanded that farmers allow the land to rest by reapplying this code to the forgiveness of loans (Mayes 1991, 246–49). Craigie (1976) argues that *šĕmiṭṭâ* codes call for a suspension of any attempts to collect debts in the seventh year (Craigie 1976, 236–37). Mayes, then, disagrees with Craigie by rejecting the notion that Deut. 15:1-11 calls for only temporary relief or for only a brief suspension of attempts to collect monies owed by the poor. In doing so, Mayes contends that Deut. 15:1-11 calls for the permanent forgiveness of arrearage by creditors. Because of its demand to show kindness to remit debts, Deut. 15:1-11 often appears among those regulations that attest to the humanitarian ethos in the book of Deuteronomy.

Points of contact are present between the legal injunction in Deut. 15:12-18 and the regulations in Exod. 21:2-6 and Lev. 25:39-46. These traditions deal with the release of slaves who are Hebrew. It has been a commonplace in Hebrew Bible studies to contend that the collection of laws in Deuteronomy 12–26 is a redaction of the legal traditions in Exodus 21–23. Bernard Levinson, however, invites us to consider the implications of this presupposition. Central to his argument is the claim that the ideology in the laws in Deuteronomy 12–26 neither depends entirely on the ethos of legislations in Exodus 21–23. He therefore leaves the door ajar for arguing that another social, political, and theological agenda sculpted those legal injunctions, which are present in Deuteronomy 12–26 (Levinson 1997, 1–22).

Juxtaposing Exod. 21:2-6 and Deut. 15:12-18, therefore, is a fruitful enterprise. The law on the manumission of Hebrew slaves in Deut. 15:12-18 contains several innovations. (1) This piece of legislation includes treatment of the Hebrew female slave with the treatment of the Hebrew male slave (Deut. 15:12); (2) this law demands that the enslaver give the slave provisions and other commodities when he liberates the slave (Deut. 15:13-14); (3) this legal injunction contains no directions about what to do if the Hebrew male slave marries; (4) this code is silent about the fate of any children born to the Hebrew male slave while he is enslaved; and (5) this regulation adds a motive clause to this revised law on the liberation of slaves in Israel (Deut. 15:15). The inconsistencies in this piece of legislation compared with the Exodus laws fit with innovations that appear elsewhere in the Deuteronomic collection of laws that deal with the vulnerable in Israelite society by instructing the reader to develop sensitivities to the plight of the less fortunate.

■ THE TEXT IN CONTEMPORARY DISCUSSION

Deuteronomy 15:1-18 invites the community to explore ways to improve the economic conditions of persons who exist on the margins. This subgroup of legislation advocates for the forgiveness of debts and for the manumission of Hebrew slaves. The question arises, however, whether these regulations are in support of all persons who exist on the fringes of society or support primarily the improvement of conditions for the Hebrew poor. Be mindful that these laws advocate the forgiveness of the debts for Israelite kinsmen and for the release of Hebrew/Israelite slaves only after seven years.

Deuteronomy 15:1-18, therefore, sanctions retaining the debts of the non-Israelite poor, and institutionalizes the ownership of human beings in society. By formulating laws that indicate that the enslavement of certain groups by Israelites is acceptable, this code provides a basis for arguing that enslavement of certain races is just. Deuteronomy 15:1-18 ensures that a subgroup of human beings who may be in need of financial support or economic relief might not receive it.

Deuteronomy 15:1-18 foreshadows the socioeconomic and political theology and policies that informed notions about the enslavement of Africans in the antebellum South. It is unfortunate that Deuteronomy uses religion to shape social conventions that legitimize the perpetual exploitation of certain ethnic groups.

Deuteronomy 16:1-16: Major Cultic Celebrations

■ THE TEXT IN ITS ANCIENT CONTEXT

Deuteronomy 16:1-16 delineates three cultic celebrations. These festivals are Passover (Deut. 16:1-8), the Feast of Weeks (Deut. 16:9-12), and the Festival of Booths (Deut. 16:13-16). Deuteronomy 16:17 lists the required festivals in a single independent clause; and Exod. 23:14-19 also lists these festivals together. Competing passages that treat festivals appear elsewhere in the legal corpora in the Hebrew Bible. These passages are Exod. 34:18-26; Leviticus 23; and Num. 9:1-14; 28:1—29:40. It is important to note that the previously mentioned texts are not the only regulations that deal with major cultic celebrations in the ancient biblical communities.

Inconsistencies are present among the regulations that govern the festival calendar in Deut. 16:1-17 and those found elsewhere in the Hebrew Bible. It has been argued that the code governing the Feast of Passover in Deut. 16:1-8 combines two independent cultic celebrations, namely, the Festival of Unleavened Bread (maṣâ) and Passover (pesaḥ) (Mayes 1991, 254–55). Duane Christensen (2001) cites three salient positions present in scholarship, which seek to adjudicate this literary feature of Deut. 16:1-8. These theories are the following: (1) The tradition concerning the Feast of Unleavened Bread was added to an extant tradition on the Festival of Passover; (2) a tradition concerning the Festival of Passover was added to an extant tradition dealing with the Feast of Unleavened Bread; (3) the Feasts of Unleavened Bread and Passover existed concurrently without referencing each other (Christensen 2001, 331). When one juxtaposes Deut. 16:1-8 with Exod. 12:21-28, one notices that the regulation governing pesaḥ in Deut. 16:1-8 removes the Passover celebration from the home of families and mandates that households celebrate the Passover at a central location in Israel, namely, the site YHWH chooses. This difference casts light on the Deuteronomic agenda of removing the celebration of major cultic festivals from local homes and relocating them to the central site, which placed control of key resources there and created opportunities for the YHWH-alone cult to promulgate its key tenets to persons in Israelite society.

■ THE TEXT IN THE INTERPRETIVE TRADITION

Scholarship that proceeds from the Jewish tradition on Deut. 16:1-8 contends that it is better to translate pesaḥ as the "protective sacrifice." Tigay (1996) contends that this naming of the sacrifice commemorates the fact that YHWH spared the eldest children of the Israelite households (Tigay 1996, 153). He also draws attention to the fact that the regulation on pesaḥ in Exod. 12:21-28 limits sacrifices to sheep and goats, while Deut. 16:1-8 includes bovine animals among those items that can be consumed in the festival that recollects the protective sacrifice in Egypt. Jesus, in the Synoptic tradition (Luke 22:14-23), expresses an eagerness to consume the Passover meal, or protective sacrifice, with his disciples. Jesus takes this ritual to mean that the moment for a second act of deliverance is imminent. In fact, the author of Luke links the tradition about the protective meal in Egypt with the tradition of the death of Jesus and the shedding of his blood to establish a new covenant and deliver those persons who were held captive by the power of Satan and evil.

■ THE TEXT IN CONTEMPORARY DISCUSSION

The tradition about the Passover, or the protective meal, receives wide currency in Christian theology. As mentioned above, it becomes the backdrop against which many discuss and interpret the death of Jesus. In fact, this ancient tradition provides the symbolism for linking the two Testaments in the Christian canon. That is to say, the blood of the Passover sacrifice in the First Testament was seen as that which protected and delivered Israel from the death angel in Egypt. The blood of Jesus in the Second Testament was seen as that which delivers people from their sin and positions the faithful to triumph over the powers of evil (Rev. 12:11). What is more, the tradition about the protective meal informs Easter, which is a central time of the year for Christians worldwide.

Deuteronomy 16:18—17:20: Ethical Leadership

■ THE TEXT IN ITS ANCIENT CONTEXT

Ensuring that ethical leadership is present in the Israelite community is the focus of Deut. 16:18—17:20. To this end, this section prescribes behavior for persons in the judiciary who are responsible for settling disputes among Israelites, and it prescribes what counts as acceptable conduct for the monarch. Deuteronomy 16:18—17:13, therefore, deals minimally with four items: (1) It identifies the group on whom the onus rests for selecting the persons who will carry out justice (*mišpāṭ*); (2) it points out who had the specific responsibility of administering *mišpāṭ*; (3) it identifies the site for the administration of *mišpāṭ*; and (4) it indicates the principle that should govern the resolution of controversies. Deuteronomy 17:14-20 provides insight into what is expected of the king, and it treats this issue by delineating primarily an assortment of actions that he should avoid.

In reference to the pursuit of *mišpāṭ*, Deut. 16:18a directs Israel to abet the pursuit of justice. It instructs them to appoint persons from their communities to assume responsibility for settling disagreements. While the text is silent on the process of selection, it is noteworthy that the people, not a prophet, priest, or monarch, are to select these persons.

Judges (*šōpĕṭîm*) and officers (*šōṭĕrîm*) are to be appointed, and they are charged with responsibility for solving disputes in the community. While Deut. 1:15-18 indicates that the leaders of tribes were judges, Deut. 16:18a does not specify the social group from which the *šōpĕṭîm* and *šōṭĕrîm* come; perhaps these judges and officers were heads of tribes, persons of affluence, priests, prophets, or aged persons. Scholarship on these legislations proposes that villages selected chiefs from amongst the prominent elders, and that these village chiefs became judges (Tigay 1996, 160;

Christensen 2001, 363). Perhaps, there might have been a special class of persons trained in adjudication in ancient Israelite society.

Deuteronomy 16:18 directs Israel to appoint *šōpĕṭîm* and *šōṭĕrîm* in their "gates." This text casts light on the location in the local village where *šōpĕṭîm* and *šōṭĕrîm* heard cases, namely, at the local "gate." The local city gate was the site for the administration of justice. It contained compartments, and these spaces were often the site for small gatherings, official public activities, the transaction of business deals, and that from time to time, the gate was the location where prophets sought to bring the word of YHWH to Israel (Drinkard 2007, 523; Ruth 4:1-11; Amos 5:10-17).

The phrase *mišpāṭ-ṣedeq* appears in Deut. 16:18b. In English translations, one can render it "righteous judgment." Deuteronomy 16:20a contains the wording *ṣedeq ṣedeq tirdōp* ("righteousness and righteousness only you shall pursue"). The admonition to do what is right, honest, and fair implies that *šōpĕṭîm* and *šōṭĕrîm* were responsible for providing a neutral, impartial conflict-resolution process in Israelite society. The *šōpĕṭîm* and *šōṭĕrîm* were to avoid favoritism: they were to assess facts, resolving disputes based on a careful weighing of the evidence, not on friendship, relationship, or the promise of personal gain. In the words of Deut. 16:20a: righteousness and righteousness alone you shall pursue!

Deuteronomy 17:2-7 discusses the role of adequate, dependable evidence in the pursuit of *mišpāṭ*. The passage brings into play the possibility that gossip is spreading through the community, and the report is that a man and his wife have been engaged in the worship of foreign deities. Deuteronomy 17:4 directs the judge or the officer to investigate the case. As he hears the report, the judge or the officer is to ensure that sufficient evidence is present for a conviction, because Deut. 17:6 indicates that the judge or officer cannot base his decision on the testimony or evidence presented by one and only one witness. A verdict of guilty has to be based on reliable, sound evidence. This type of judicial process positions judges and officers to be objective adjudicators of issues in the biblical communities.

Deuteronomy 17:8-13 attempts to ensure justice in Israel by providing guidelines for adjudicating a series of issues that might be too hard to be resolved in the local tribunal. Deuteronomy 17:8 contains the following terms: *dām* ("blood"), *dîn* ("a disagreement requiring resolution"), and *negaʿ* ("wound"). Christensen (2001) contends that these terms pertain, respectively, to issues of homicide, civil offenses, and disputes involving physical injury (Christensen 2001, 374–75). Perhaps the evidence is inconclusive or insufficient. Yet the litigants are instructed to carry the matter to the central sanctuary and allow the priest (*kōhēn*) or judge (*šōpēṭ*) who is present at that site to adjudicate the issue. Deuteronomy 17:12 indicates that verdicts issued at the central sanctuary are irrevocable, and that the death penalty can be applied to the individual or group who decides to disobey these rulings.

In reference to the king, Deut. 17:14-20 permits the community to move from a decentralized, acephalous society to a form of sociopolitical organization that is centralized and has a figure over it. Deuteronomy 17:15 allows the community to appoint a king (*melek*) over it; however, the king must be one whom YHWH chooses and approves. The rest of the passage specifies a legitimate king, and it identifies those actions the king must avoid and embrace. The legitimate king must not be a foreigner (*nokrî*); he must be from one of the tribes that constitute Israel. Chief among the actions the king must avoid is the amassing of horses for himself (Deut. 17:16). Perhaps assembling such a large number of horses was for military usage or for prestige. The king is told not to form a harem (Deut. 17:17). It is probable that this code prohibited entering marriages with foreign women. These marriages were concomitant with political alliances; therefore, the prohibition on entering marriages with many foreign women was an attempt to keep the Israelite monarch from entering polity coalitions with many of the nations in the ancient Near East. The king is also banned from the stockpiling of silver and gold for himself. He is to avoid greed and must not become an object of worship in Israel. Deuteronomy 17:18-20 instructs the king to keep a copy of this code, and to read it frequently to remind himself of the duties of a legitimate king.

◼ The Text in the Interpretive Tradition

Deuteronomy 16:18—17:13 develops the circumstance that received treatment in Deut. 1:13-17, namely, the conversation about judiciary decorum in ancient Israel (Tigay 1996, 160). While the judicial system established in Deut. 1:13-17 worked while the people were en route to the promised land, this system for the administration of justice became problematic. Thus Deut. 16:18—17:13 adjusts to the need for justice in the promised land by instructing the people to select magistrates. The Israelite community, then, might have assigned village chiefs to the position of judges and included cultic officials in this group, which was responsible for the adjudication of conflicts among members and social groups in Israel. Yet the persons responsible for solving disagreements in the community were instructed not to take bribes and to ensure that righteous decision making prevailed in regard to settling disputes.

Caesarius of Arles casts light on the passages treating judges and the pursuit of *mišpāṭ* in the legal codes in Deuteronomy. He takes these regulations to teach that in the acceptance of bribes, the judge or priest may have obtained some profit or income. The income, however, cost them something of far greater value—their conscience. Caesarius of Arles, then, takes these codes to mean that the inner voice of right is that to which one should adhere, regardless of the financial profit he or she might receive (Lienhard 2001, 301–2).

What is more, the position on monarchy in Deut. 17:14-20 contrasts with the tradition about monarchy in subgroups of texts in the Deuteronomistic History (DtrH). That is to say, evidence is present in DtrH that subgroups in Israel were hostile to the notion of a centralized government headed by a king. These texts are the following: (1) 1 Sam. 8:1-22; (2) 1 Sam. 10:17-27; and (3) 1 Sam. 12:1-15. In the Deuteronomy passage, YHWH supports the establishment of a monarchy, but in the 1 Samuel passages, YHWH does not.

◼ The Text in Contemporary Discussion

Deuteronomy 16:18—17:20 provokes us to ensure that ethical leadership is in our judiciary, government, and religious communities. This conversation invites the critic to identify those principles that inform decision making and legal judgments by individuals and groups in key legal, political, and religious offices in our communities. This conversation also necessitates exploring the possibilities that particular agendas are in play regarding the rendering of judicial decisions, the formation of policies, and the sculpting of theological claims. Recent cases dealing with racial profiling; clergy sexual misconduct; and the misuse of religion to acquire money, status, and property invite modern-day thinkers to practice what critical theorists call a *hermeneutic of suspicion* when it comes to viewing magistrates and other persons in leadership positions.

Deuteronomy 18:1-8: Payment of Priests

■ THE TEXT IN ITS ANCIENT CONTEXT

Deuteronomy 18:1-8 deals with the remuneration of cultic officials in the community. Notably, this code presents a different point of view about who can preside over the sacrifices and sacred rituals and direct matters in the cultus. Deuteronomy 18:1 uses asyndeton: it omits the use of conjunctions from a series of clauses that are in sequence; therefore it reads: "the priests, the Levites, the entire tribe of Levi." This syntactic maneuver suggests that all the personnel in the Israelite cultus were of equal rank. According to Deut. 18:1, all males from the tribe of Levi are priests and have no inheritance in Israel. The Priestly tradition, for example, Num. 3:5-10, avers that a tiered system governing responsibilities and personal remuneration constituted the Israelite cultus. According to the Priestly tradition, the priests were the sons of Aaron, and they presided over the sacrifices, officiated at the sacred rituals, and adjudicated matters of ceremonial cleanliness. Numbers 3:5-10 relegates other men who constituted the tribe of Levi to positions of servitude to the priests, the sons of Aaron. What is more, Num. 18:25-32 directs the Levites to give the priests a portion of the compensation they received from working in the cult. Deuteronomy 18:2-8, however, permits all Levites to serve at the central shrine, and it prescribes that they should receive economic support from the rituals and sacrifices over which they preside. Deuteronomy 18:1-8 does not direct the Levites to share their income with any other personnel in the Israelite cultus.

■ THE TEXT IN THE INTERPRETIVE TRADITION

The notion about the support of Levites in the Israelite cultus informs notions about the remuneration of clergy in the early church. Paul, however, writes: "Do you not know that those who are employed in the temple service get their food from the temple, and those who serve at the altar share in what is sacrificed on the altar? In the same way, the Lord commanded that those who proclaim the gospel should get their living by the gospel" (1 Cor. 9:13-14 NRSV). Paul takes the tradition about the method for the support of personnel in the Israelite cult to mean that ministers in the early Jesus movement are entitled to the resources of a subgroup in the community because congregations should support those clergy from whom they received services.

First Timothy links the notion of the remuneration of cultic officials in Deuteronomy to the material endowment of ministers in the early church. While 1 Timothy does not cite Deut. 18:1-8, the author establishes a line of thought and connects it with the economic philosophy expressed in Deut. 18:1-8. The author writes: "for the scripture says: 'You shall not muzzle an ox while it is treading out the grain,' and, 'The laborer deserves to be paid'" (1 Tim. 5:18 NRSV). The person responsible for this epistle cites Deut. 25:4 and uses it to advocate for clergy receiving compensation for the work they performed in the promulgation of the gospel. Key persons in the history of early Christianity grounded notions about the payment of clergy in notions about the compensation of cultic officials in Deut. 18:1-8.

■THE TEXT IN CONTEMPORARY DISCUSSION

Deuteronomy 18:1-8 indicates that the material support of priests should come from the services they provide at the central sanctuary. This system for compensating priests raises the current question about the remuneration of clergy, and, as it is to be expected, considerable difference of opinion about compensation and benefits for clergy is present today. Several items receive treatment in this conversation. Chief among these issues are the following: the method for arriving at equitable compensation; the amount of compensation the minister will receive; services for which the minister will receive compensation; and the particular system the institution will use to pay the minister. Some congregations adhere to a specific set of salary guidelines that have been determined and approved by a larger authority, while some congregations are autonomous and decide for themselves the compensation they are going to provide to clergy who serve them. The implication of Deut. 18:1-8, however, is that economic support should come from the services ministers provide to congregations and to the community.

Deuteronomy 18:9-22: The Prophet Like Moses

■THE TEXT IN ITS ANCIENT CONTEXT

Deuteronomy 18:9-22 contends that YHWH uses a human to communicate with the people. The text calls this individual a prophet (*nābîʾ*); this code emphasizes that this person will emerge from within Israel, and Deut. 18:15 points out that he will resemble Moses. Chief among this point of contact between Moses and this envisaged person is that of being the mediator between the deity and the people, and that of being the spokesperson on behalf of the deity to the people. The fact that the prophet, not the priest, is the intermediary between YHWH and the people is a significant feature of the Deuteronomic program. Elsewhere, in other parts of the Hebrew Bible that reflect the ideology in the Deuteronomic code, the prophet carries messages from YHWH to the king and to other individuals in the community. Deuteronomy 18:9-22, therefore, orders the people to obey this prophet, and not to engage diviners, soothsayers, witches, or other types of persons who play key roles in the cultic practices of those non-Israelite nations that inhabit Syria-Palestine with biblical Israel.

■THE TEXT IN THE INTERPRETIVE TRADITION

The Hebrew Bible identifies people and events that are important for understanding Judaism, Christianity, and Islam. While it is possible to mention quite a few individuals and circumstances, no one in these literary traditions is as important as Moses. What is more, Judaism, Christianity, and Islam contain different ways of reading, discussing, and appropriating texts where Moses is present. These religious traditions apply different hermeneutical lenses to Deut. 18:9-22, and especially to the words of Moses in Deut. 18:15: "YHWH will raise a prophet, from your brothers, who is like me." Camps in Judaism contend that Elijah is that prophet about whom Deut. 18:15 speaks. Instances of this hermeneutical move are found in Mal. 4:4-6 [3:22-24 MT] and Sir. 48:1-11. Camps in the early Christian community saw Jesus as this new Moses, and this connection becomes the backdrop against which to discuss the Gospel according to Matthew. What is more, Muslim communities took the claim that the deity would raise a prophet *like Moses* from among the brothers in the community to refer to the prophet Mohammad (Phipps 1996, 102).

■ THE TEXT IN CONTEMPORARY DISCUSSION

"A prophet like me" is a significant phrase in Deut. 18:9-22. This expression leaves open the possibility that a person who has a link to the divine will appear, and that this person will resemble Moses in some form or fashion. The fact that competing interpretations of this person are present in Judaism, Christianity, and Islam brings into play the crux of the problem, namely, delineating those criteria that must be satisfied for a person to be "a prophet like Moses." Since Deut. 18:15 is silent about these measurements, this has left the door ajar for believing that a person may arise in the modern world and, in the custom of the *nābî'*, deliver a message that speaks in a redemptive way to the theological, ethical, and socioeconomic predicaments of people. Marcus Garvey (1887–1940) immediately comes to mind as an example (see Erskine 2005, 116–68).

Deuteronomy 19:1-14: Manslaughter

■ THE TEXT IN ITS ANCIENT CONTEXT

Deuteronomy 19:1-14 prescribes the response to inadvertent homicide in the Israelite community by identifying six additional places of safety to which one who is guilty of a fortuitous homicide of another Israelite (*rēʿēhû*). This legislation introduces the avenger of blood (*gōʾēl haddām*). Scholars have competing views about the identity of this person: the avenger of blood was the male next of kin who bears the moral responsibility of retaliating against the perpetrator for the killing of his family member (Tigay 1996, 181). The avenger of blood was thought to be an appointed official, whose assignment it was to retrieve the perpetrator from the city of refuge and to administer the death penalty (Mayes 1991, 286–87). Regardless of the identity of this person, Deut. 19:6 attempts to prevent the avenger of blood from acting out of pure emotion; this code seeks to undermine decision making about culpability without getting the facts about the homicide. If neither malice nor premeditation played a part in the homicide, then the perpetrator is without blame. The asylum is for the innocent party, not for the guilty party.

Thematic points of contact exist between Deut. 19:1-14 and other regulations in the Hebrew Bible that deal with the unintentional killing of another Israelite. Deuteronomy 19:1-14 is similar to Exod. 21:12-14. Both codes deal with the loss of life. While Exod. 21:12-14 legislates behavior in the case of inadvertent homicide, it does not mention the setting aside of cities for protection of the supposed killer until the situation is resolved; rather, it indicates that a single place is set aside for asylum for the perpetrator. Similar to Deut. 19:1-14, Deut. 4:41-43 lists cities to which persons guilty of an unplanned homicide may escape. DtrH designates a place of safety for supposed criminals. This site is the altar in the sanctuary, for the fugitive is allowed to grab hold of the horns of the altar, and while he is holding to the horns of the altar, the supposed criminal is granted mercy (see 1 Kgs. 1:49-53). The fact that 1 Kgs. 1:49-53 predates the construction of the Jerusalem temple raises questions about the role that these cities, that is, places of safety, played in the case of a chance homicide. In its handling of the case, Deut. 19:1-14 attempts to avert the intentional killing of an innocent Israelite by the *gōʾēl haddām*. Seen through this lens, Deut. 19:1-14 seeks to protect the lives of Israelites, not simply to exculpate one who is responsible for the death of another Israelite. Protecting the lives of innocent Israelites is also a major feature of Num. 35:6-34 and Josh. 20:1-9, for these texts identify asylums for Israelites accused of manslaughter.

■ THE TEXT IN THE INTERPRETIVE TRADITION

Gregory the Great (540–604 CE) takes an interesting hermeneutical approach to Deut. 19:1-14. He views this passage through the lens of counseling, that is, through ensuring self-discipline while caring for the souls of human beings. He therefore likens the forest in Deut. 19:1-14 to the shortcomings of human beings. He associates the cutting of wood with making an effort to address the shortcomings of other humans. He connects the ax head to the notion of chastising someone. Gregory then contends that the ax head slips off the handle when moral and spiritual correction contravenes appropriate boundaries. Thus "an accidental killing" occurs when a person abandons or loses self-control when she or he is rebuking another person and delivers a form of correction that is extremely brutal and insensitive, which brings about the emotional and psychological devastation of another human being. He therefore urges people to practice self-control when seeking to correct other moral agents (Lienhard 2001, 305).

■ THE TEXT IN CONTEMPORARY DISCUSSION

While Deut. 19:1-14 deals with the murder-versus-manslaughter distinction in homicide cases, it invites us to ensure that persons accused of crimes are given opportunity to defend themselves. This becomes a very important issue given the fact that emotion, relationships, and assumed moral obligation inform decision making and conclusions about culpability. The person or entity who is responsible for the administration of justice should practice self-control and strive to demonstrate conclusively, in an unbiased way, that a crime has been committed.

Deuteronomy 19:15-21: Suspect Evidence in Tribunals

■ THE TEXT IN ITS ANCIENT CONTEXT

While Deut. 16:18—17:13 mandates multiple attestation for capital cases only, Deut. 19:15-21 requires accurate evidence to sustain a conviction in any matter that warrants adjudication. In its attempt to ensure *mišpāṭ*, Deut. 19:15-21 requires the presence of three items: (1) reliable evidence

(Deut. 19:15-16, 18b-19); (2) responsible leadership (Deut. 19:17); and (3) good judgment on the part of the magistrates (19:18a). Deuteronomy 19:17-18a indicates that the judges (*haššōpetîm*) and priests (*hakkōhănîm*) are responsible for supervising the administration of justice. Deuteronomy 19:18a instructs these persons to undertake a painstaking, meticulous investigation (*hêtēb*). If it is discovered that a witness presents misleading information, then the magistrates are directed to impose on the false witness the punishment that would have befallen the accused. In its attempt to impose the penalty on the false witness, Deut. 19:21 specifies that the judge apply the *lex talionis*, the law of retaliation in ancient Israel. Exodus 21:22-25 and Lev. 24:17-21 provide additional attestation of the *lex talionis*. In each of the passages that cite this custom, the goal is to control the impulse to get revenge by placing limitations on punishment or compensation for wrongdoing; thus the reprisal or penalty for the false witness in Deut. 19:21 should be specific and should be in proportion to the crime.

▌ THE TEXT IN THE INTERPRETIVE TRADITION

Flavius Josephus takes this code to mean that a minimum of two good witnesses is required for a conviction in any legitimate tribunal. According to Josephus, a reputable witness is male and is of virtuous character. He expands this legal tradition to include prohibitions against the testimonies of women and slaves being admissible in a court proceeding. At the heart of Josephus's problem with women is the belief that women are frivolous. He believes that slaves cannot provide good testimony because of their shameful, immoral being. What is more, Josephus works with the assumption that the prospect of freedom or punishment might influence the testimony of servants (*Ant.* 4:15).

▌ THE TEXT IN CONTEMPORARY DISCUSSION

Deuteronomy 19:15-21 advocates for truth-telling when reporting or reconstructing an event: it demands faithful witnesses. This code even requires punishment for the person who misrepresents an event or issue. This code, then, brings into play the importance of getting the story right. This type of thing is very much a concern not only in legal disputes but also in the business of reporting the news, and in reconstructions of history, for one can examine books about the history of the United States and notice that the story of blacks and other minorities fails to appear. Critical theorizing about history-writing invites us to raise the question about *whose story is being told*. We must raise the question: Is history-writing propaganda, or is it a trustworthy attempt to reconstruct a previous event or period? What is more, this business of accurate reporting is a real issue, given the ability to spread misinformation quickly through modern technology, particularly social media. With just a few keystrokes, someone can misrepresent a situation, and in seconds, this lie can be all over the world, doing enormous damage to a person's reputation. Truth-telling, the gist of Deut. 19:15-21, is critical.

Deuteronomy 20:1-20: The Conduct of War

▌ THE TEXT IN ITS ANCIENT CONTEXT

Two subgroups of regulations appear in Deut. 20:1-20. Verses 2-9 deals with gearing up for combat. In this regulation, the priests exhort the men not to fear the enemy, regardless of the size and strength of the enemy's infantry and cavalry, because YHWH is fighting this battle for Israel and will effect victory (*lĕhôšîaʿ*) on their behalf (Deut. 20:1-4). What is more, the officers (*šōṭĕrîm*) are told to strengthen the quality of the force in combat by weeding out the weak links; therefore, they identify three categories of men who are exempt from combat. Men who have planted a vineyard but have not eaten from it; men who have built a house but have not inhabited it; and men who have recently got engaged but have not consummated the marriage are excused from military service (Deut. 20:5-9). What is more, men who are scared to death are simply told to go home to avoid spreading timidity to the rest of the men who are preparing to attack a city and engage the enemy in combat.

Deuteronomy 20:10-20 details the method of warfare. The code assumes that Israel is on the offensive, for it says, "when you draw near" (*kî-tiqrab*). Deuteronomy 20:11-15 sets out policies for dealing with cities that are not within the borders of the Israelite community. This piece of legislation instructs Israel first to see if the people are unwilling to fight and are willing to surrender the city. If so, then Israel is to enslave the inhabitants of the city (*yihyû lĕkā lāmas*). If the inhabitants of the city decide to fight for their lives and defend their property, then Israel must attack and kill all the adult males of the city. While Israel may pillage the city, they are told to spare the women, infants, and the large cattle. Deuteronomy 20:16-20 sets out the policy for dealing with non-Israelite cities that are within the borders of Israel's land. In short, Israel is instructed to annihilate them. The Girgashites are missing from this list of peoples (see Deut. 7:1). This piece of legislation, however, tells Israel that while she is waging war she is not to kill the trees that bear fruit.

▋ THE TEXT IN THE INTERPRETIVE TRADITION

Deuteronomy 20:1-20 has received considerable discussion among different groups. In Excursus 18, Tigay (1996) provides insight into Jewish views about this law on warfare. Citing M. Greenberg, he contends that the rabbis recognized the harshness of this code and, aligning themselves with a humanitarian ethic at odds with the moral ideas about the treatment of the Canaanites expressed in this regulation, rejected it. According to Tigay, Maimonides argued that this code represents an offer of surrender to all groups, not just to the Canaanites (Tigay 1996, 470–72).

Clement of Alexandria also reads this piece of legislation from a humanitarian perspective. He argues that it is merciful in that it exempts unfocused men from combat. For Clement, the fact that men who would be unenthusiastic about fighting in a war are to be excused from combat is a good example of compassion in the Deuteronomic regulations (Lienhard 2001, 307).

▋ THE TEXT IN CONTEMPORARY DISCUSSION

Deuteronomy 20:1-20 provides a divine sanction for the annihilation of the Canaanites. This bifurcation provides the theological basis for seeing one group as the people of God and all other people as not being the people of God. God is on one side and fighting against the other. This type of thinking provides theological justification for crusades, jihads, and other types of religious wars. What is more, seeing one group as good and another group as evil creates an ideology that spawns all types of atrocities toward other human beings. In light of the conversation surrounding terrorism and Christian-Muslim relations on the modern scene, the theological and moral ideology promulgated by Deut. 20:1-20 warrants sustained conversation.

Deuteronomy 21:1-9: Unsolved Homicide

■ THE TEXT IN ITS ANCIENT CONTEXT

Deuteronomy 21:1-9 casts light on the handling of an unsolved homicide. The Hebrew term that appears as "body" in English translations of Deut. 21:1a is *ḥālāl*. The usage of this term suggests that some type of puncture wound contributed to the death of the person. A thematic similarity is present between this regulation and a law governing the commission of a homicide during a robbery in the Code of Hammurabi. In both instances, the notion of corporate culpability is in question. The law in the Code of Hammurabi calls for the city in which a homicide during a robbery occurred to incur the responsibility for the death of the person (Roth 1997, 85). Deuteronomy 21:1-9 links guilt for the homicide to the nearest city where the corpse was discovered. Whereas the Code of Hammurabi directs the city and its political leader to pay a fine, Deut. 21:1-9 requires the elders of the city nearest to the site where the body was discovered to bring a cow down to a place of flowing water, break her neck (*ʿōrep*), wash their hands over the cow, declare the noncomplicity of the city in the homicide, and ask YHWH not to hold the city responsible for the death of a fellow Israelite.

■ THE TEXT IN THE INTERPRETIVE TRADITION

Deuteronomy 21:1-9 deals with bloodguilt. This regulation contains an array of perplexing actions associated with breaking the neck of a heifer. Tigay (1997) indicates that rabbinic exegesis grouped this command with the goat sent to Azazel and the regulation on the red heifer, and that the rabbis contended that these three regulations are simply hard to understand. What is more, Tigay contends that due to the widespread, conspicuous practice of homicide, rabbis put an end to the carrying out of this ritual in the first century CE (Tigay 1997, 473).

■ THE TEXT IN CONTEMPORARY DISCUSSION

Deuteronomy 21:1-9 invites leaders to consider the importance of ensuring that they are not complicit in wrongdoing. This regulation seeks to hold someone accountable for the loss of life, and it suggests that persons in leadership should be the first ones to affirm their innocence in the matter. Political leaders should work to guarantee that their policies do not victimize people. Religious leaders make sure the theologies, moral theories, and social programs they advance neither prevent individuals from actualizing the human potential nor contribute to the dehumanization of particular religious, ethnic, economic, or religious groups. Remember, the regulation on bloodguilt demands that leaders set the moral example of not taking part in criminal behavior and of respecting life.

Deuteronomy 21:10—25:19: Laws on Marriage, Family, and Miscellaneous Subjects

▌The Text in Its Ancient Context

Deuteronomy 21:10—25:19 governs a host of unconnected subjects. Deuteronomy 21:10-14 treats the duty of Israelite men to women they have captured in combat and subsequently married. While Deut. 21:10-14 permits exogamy, Deut. 7:3 prohibits it. This regulation instructs Israelite men to allow these women to mourn for one month. Once the month passes, he may have sex with the woman. If for some reason the male is not pleased with the woman (*'im-lō' ḥāpaṣtā*), he has the option of allowing her to leave. He, however, cannot sell her for money or into slavery. Deuteronomy 21:10-14 is the first of three codes on marriage in Deuteronomy 12–26. These other codes are 22:13-30 and 24:1-4. The fact that three codes governing marriage appear at different places in the Deuteronomic code supports claims that Deuteronomy 12–26 is a collection of legislations that come from different periods and sociopolitical conditions in the history of Israel.

Deuteronomy 21:15-17 provides guidelines on duties owed to the son of the hated wife (*ḥāśśĕnû'â*). The text specifies that if a man has two wives, the firstborn male child of the father receives the majority of the possessions of his father regardless of how his father felt about his mother. This law privileges the firstborn of the union between Israelite men and mainly Israelite women, not the firstborn of any woman that an Israelite man might marry, for a woman could have had children from a previous relationship, for example, women taken captive in war. This regulation works to ensure that property remains in the Israelite community.

Deuteronomy 21:18-21 specifies a procedure for the treatment of an unruly child. This regulation says that if a man has an insolent child (*bēn sôrēr*), he and his wife are to grab the child (*tāpśû bô*) and take him to the elders of the city and declare openly that the child is unruly. Deuteronomy 21:21 authorizes the men of the city to execute the child. By doing this, the men of the city send a message that disrespect for parents will not be tolerated. Parents, therefore, had to watch the village elders kill their son. It stands to reason that this incident casts an extremely negative shadow on the parents, for one cannot help but wonder what in the upbringing of the child could have culminated in this disrespectful behavior.

Deuteronomy 21:22—22:12 is another group of various regulations. This assortment of laws deals with the treatment of a corpse that has been hung (*tālâ*) on a tree (Deut. 21:22-23); the duty of one Israelite to another Israelite in regard to wandering livestock (Deut. 21:1-4); the practice of cross-dressing (Deut. 22:5); the extinction of animal species (Deut. 22:6-7); the avoidance of culpability for homicide (Deut. 22:8); and the promotion of harmony in society (Deut. 22:9-12). While the codes on the promotion of harmony in society argue against mixing certain practices or items (e.g., different kinds of seed, animals of unequal strength, and different fabrics), there appears to be no logical or thematic points of contacts between these legislations, which treat animals that have wandered off, transvestitism, and bloodguilt in Israel.

Deuteronomy 22:13-30 deals with sex and marriage in ancient Israel. (1) Deuteronomy 22:13-21 indicates that a man has the option of imposing the death penalty on a young girl (*hanna'ar*) whom he has married and suspects has had intercourse with another man prior to their marriage. The parents of the young girl have the responsibility of refuting the charges, by presenting evidence of the young girl's virginity (*bĕtûlê hanna'ar*). Tikva Frymer-Kensky argues that the tokens of virginity were the blood-stained cloths from the bride's last menstrual cycle, thus proving that the bride was not pregnant (Frymer-Kensky 1992, 57). If the charge of unchastity is unsubstantiated, the complainant shall pay the father one hundred pieces of silver, and the accuser forfeits the right to divorce her. (2) Deuteronomy 22:22 prescribes the death penalty for a married woman who has sex with a man who is not her husband. It may be inferred from this piece of legislation that adultery is a voluntary sexual relationship of a married or engaged woman with a man to whom she is neither engaged nor married. (3) Deuteronomy 22:23-29 prescribes the death penalty for both the man and the woman in the case of a young girl who is a virgin and engaged, and who has been raped in the city. This regulation implies that the girl did not seek to prevent the rape. If the rape happens in the field, only the man shall be executed, for it is implied that the girl attempted to prevent the rape. According to Deut. 22:28-29, if a young girl, who is a virgin but is not engaged is raped, the rapist has to pay the victim's father fifty shekels of silver and marry the victim. He can never divorce her. (4) Deuteronomy 22:30 prohibits a woman from having sex with her son-in-law. No penalty is prescribed for this action.

Deuteronomy 23:1-8 denies the following people membership in the congregation of YHWH (*qāhāl yhwh*), that gathering of fully enfranchised Israelite males who are members of the YHWH-alone cult: (1) men with damaged sexual organs (23:1) and (2) the *mamzēr*, or bastard (23:2). There has been considerable discussion regarding the identity of the *mamzēr*; several options vie for our attention. Rabbi Akiba says a *mamzēr* is a person who is the offspring of a sexual relationship between near relatives that Israelite law prohibits. Rabbi Joshua says that a *mamzēr* is the offspring of any sexual relationship that was punishable by death in Israelite law. Thus the offspring of incest, an adulterous relationship, or a liaison with a person who is one of those ethnic groups with whom Israelites are forbidden to intermarry would be considered a *mamzēr* (m. *Yebam*. 4:13). Be mindful that a *mamzēr* is not simply a child who is born out of wedlock.

Deuteronomy 23:1-8 also denies the Ammonite or Moabite membership in the *qāhāl yhwh*, a cultic term for the assembly of fully enfranchised Israelite male citizens, which served as a pool from which men were taken for military service in the community. This gathering of adult males met to conduct large-scale political transactions, such as inaugurating a new monarch (Tigay 1996, 209–10; Mayes 1991, 315). Since the *qāhāl yhwh* is a religio-political designation, those persons who are excluded from membership in it are individuals who are deemed unacceptable by those principles that were consistent with the YHWH-alone cult and its political program.

Deuteronomy 23:9-14 regulates cleanliness in the army camp (*mahăneh*), that is, a gathering of Israelite men in the field and preparing for battle. This regulation prescribes purity on the part of the individual and the group. Reaching this level of hygiene requires that the soldiers in the camp expel for a short period men who have ejaculated during a dream, and that they readmit these individuals to the camp once they have cleansed themselves. Deuteronomy 23:9-14 also prescribes the designation of a site outside of the camp for the members to relieve themselves of human waste. Deuteronomy 23:14 requires the military camp to maintain a strict level of sanitation because

YHWH is walking around in the midst of the camp (*mithalēk běqereb maḥăneka*). If the military camp is polluted, it might provoke YHWH to abandon it, and the absence of YHWH from the camp guarantees Israel's defeat in combat. It is argued that these rules for cleanliness governed the gatherings of Israelite men during sacred pilgrimages, when the community reenacted its beliefs about YHWH and holy war (Christensen 2002, 543–44).

Deuteronomy 23:15-25 is another collection of miscellaneous legal traditions. These laws deal with slavery (Deut. 23:15-16), prostitution (Deut. 23:17-18), exacting interest on loans (Deut. 23:19-20), fulfilling vows (Deut. 23:21-23), and handling hunger while traveling (Deut. 23:24-25). Regulations on several of these subjects appear earlier in the Deuteronomic code. Both Deut. 23:15-16 and Deut. 15:12-17 deal with slavery. Deuteronomy 15:12-17 places no limits on the length of time an Israelite may enslave a non-Israelite, and Deut. 23:15-16 instructs Israel to become a safe haven for runaway slaves. The Code of Hammurabi prescribes the death penalty for providing asylum from capture to fugitive slaves (Roth 1997, 84). Since the general term for slave (*'ebed*) is in Deut. 23:15-17 and, since Deut. 15:12-17 required Israelites to release Hebrew slaves every seven years, it is probable that this code refers to persons who were Hebrews. Deuteronomy 23:17-18 prohibits Israelites from becoming temple prostitutes or from engaging in prostitution in general. The terms in Hebrew, which are at the center of this controversy, are *qādeš* ("male prostitute") and *qĕdešâ* ("female prostitute"). It has been argued that these terms, on the one hand, denote prostitution associated with festivals, rituals, vows, and other religious activities (Craigie 1976, 301–2), and that these terms, on the other hand, refer to prostitution in general (Tigay 1996, 215–16). What is more, this code leaves unanswered whether these prostitutes engaged in heterosexual or homosexual activity. What is clear, however, is that this law forbids accepting money for the payment of vows that comes from prostitution, regardless of the gender of the prostitute, for terms that denote both genders are in Deut. 23:19 (*zônâ*, a female prostitute, and *keleb*, a male prostitute).

Deuteronomy 23:19-20 regulates interest on loans to Israelites. The code states its position firmly by using the absolute negative particle "never" (*lō'*). This piece of legislation says never, ever charge your brother (*'āḥîkā*) interest on anything you give him. In the tradition of the Deuteronomic program, the Israelite is allowed to lend to the foreigner (*nokrî*), and he may assess as much interest to the food, money, and anything else loaned to this type of person as he desires. Clearly, membership in the community has its obligations, namely, to assist any brother who is in need and not to exacerbate his situation.

Deuteronomy 23:21-25 deals with the making of vows and travelers obtaining sustenance while they are en route to their destination. Deuteronomy 23:21-23 advises against making promises recklessly to YHWH. It encourages the moral agent to think about what is at stake when pledging to do something for YHWH and then failing to carry out the agreement. Deuteronomy 23:21-23 indicates that it is better for a person not to make a promise than it is to make one and then fail to do what one has said. No verse on the making of vows appears in the Covenant Code, and the fact that theological and philosophical points of contact are present between Eccles. 5:4-6 and Deut. 23:21-23 might be an instance of the influence of the wisdom traditions on the Deuteronomic school of thought (Mayes 1991, 321; Christensen 2002, 218).

Deuteronomy 23:24-25 regulates the amount of food one Israelite can consume from his neighbor's field while he is traveling. Traveling Israelites can eat as much as they want, but they are not allowed to package any of the food and take it with them. The traveler must recognize the property rights of the owner of the field (Craigie 1976, 321; Tigay 1996, 219).

Deuteronomy 24:1-4 deals with the issue of whether remarriage to a previous spouse after divorce from a former spouse is permissible. This regulation specifies that once a woman has been sent out of the house of her first husband and remarries and her second husband dies or hates her and sends her out of his house, the first husband is not permitted to remarry her. It is possible that this proscription prevents the first husband from gaining control of any property his former wife might have acquired from a previous remarriage (Frymer-Kensky 1992, 60). The law cites "not finding grace in the eyes of her husband" (*'im-lō' timṣa'-ḥēn*) and the presence of a "flaw" (*'erwat dābār*) as grounds for divorce, and the meaning of these phrases remained at the center of considerable controversy in ancient Israelite moral philosophizing. In Deuteronomy, divorce is the prerogative of the husband. In the Code of Hammurabi, a woman is permitted to leave her husband (Roth 1997, 107–8).

Deuteronomy 24:5—25:19 is another large block of laws that treats different subjects. Deuteronomy 24:5 exempts a newly married man from combat or from any duty linked to military service. This regulation contrasts with Deut. 20:7, which exempts a man that is engaged and has not consummated the marriage from combat or from any duty linked to military service.

Deuteronomy 24:6 sets limits on what can serve as collateral for loans by prohibiting lenders from taking possession of those essential items that borrowers would need to survive. The creditor is banned from seizing the millstones (*rēḥîm*) or the upper millstone (*rekeb*) from a borrower. These items were used to crush or grind grain so that it could become flour and be used in the making of bread. Without these items, the debtor might not have the ability to produce the main element in his or her daily diet (Christensen 2002, 572–73). Perhaps taking millstones or at least one of them from debtors was a commonplace in Israel, and Deut. 24:6 attempted to end this practice.

Deuteronomy 24:7 bans the kidnapping and selling of Israelites into slavery. This regulation says nothing about stealing or selling non-Israelites into slavery. Moreover, Deut. 24:7 conflicts with Deut. 15:12-18, for Deut. 15:12-18 permits the enslavement of Israelites. Deuteronomy 24:7, however, shares a socio-ethical point with Deut. 15:12-18, for as it has been noted, neither piece of legislation offers protection to all types of human beings. Note should be taken that Deut. 15:12-18 permits the perpetual enslavement of persons who are not Israelites, and that Deut. 24:7 assigns neither a penalty nor a consequence to either stealing or enslaving a person who is not an Israelite.

Deuteronomy 24:8-9 directs people in the community to pay attention to any possible skin infection. This code uses the term *ṣāra'at*, which is widely translated in most English versions as leprosy. The Hebrew term *ṣāra'at*, however, could denote a spectrum of skin diseases. The Israelites are admonished to deal immediately with any intimation that *ṣāra'at* is present by consulting the priests and following the treatment they prescribe.

Deuteronomy 24:10-15 defends the dignity of the poor. Deuteronomy 24:10-13 reminds creditors to practice self-control by not going into the house of a debtor to seize collateral for a loan. If a garment is used to guarantee the loan, the creditor is required to remain outside the debtor's house and allow the debtor to exit the house and surrender his garment. The creditor is reminded to return the garment before sunset so that the debtor will have covering for warmth at night. Deuteronomy 24:14-15 requires employers to pay the poor and economically vulnerable by the end of the day for the work they have provided. Payment should be made to both the Israelite worker and to the stranger (*gēr*) who works. This code cites fear of retribution from YHWH as the reason employers should pay these types of people before sunset.

Deuteronomy 24:16 deals with personal accountability. It specifies that parents should not be penalized for the behavior of their children, and that children should not be punished for the actions of their parents. At the center of this regulation is the assumption that a moral agent should be punished for his or her own actions. Points of contact are present between this legislation and the speech on personal accountability in Ezek. 18:1-32. One cannot help but notice that this notion of personal accountability does not apply to Ammonites, Moabites, or Amalekites, for the descendants of these groups are punished for the actions of their ancestors (Deut. 23:3-6).

Deuteronomy 24:17-21 prescribes social justice for the stranger (*gēr*), the fatherless (*yātôm*), and the widow ('*almānâ*). These types of persons appear in lists throughout Deuteronomy (Deut.14:22-29; 16:9-12, 13-15; 24:17-18, 19-22; and 26:12-15). According to these regulations, the stranger and the fatherless person should receive fair treatment in trials. The stranger, fatherless, and widow are entitled to gleanings in the field, and the prohibition is present against seizing the garment of a widow as collateral for a loan. This piece of legislation reminds one of Deut. 24:10-13.

Deuteronomy 25:1-3 places limitations on the number of lashes a judge may prescribe as punishment for a specific offense. This code argues that the magistrate may rule that the guilty party receives no more than forty lashes, because applying forty-one lashes to a human being is abusive and undermines the dignity of a human being. This seems quite odd in light of the fact that Deut. 25:1-3 demands that the guilty party receives a beating in public.

Deuteronomy 25:5-10 casts light on the institution of the *yābām*, that is, the responsibility of the brother-in-law. This custom requires that if a man dies without a male heir, the eldest living brother of the deceased has a moral obligation to marry the wife of the deceased and to impregnate her. According to Jewish tradition, a widow had to wait three months before she could enter a marriage with the eldest brother of her deceased husband (*m. Yebam.* 4:10). Deuteronomy 25:7 specifies the procedure to follow if the brother-in-law refuses to carry out the institution of the *yābām*. This institution is the backdrop against which to understand the Ruth-Boaz account in Ruth 4. Perhaps the goal of the codes in Deut. 25:5-10 was not to ensure male heirs as much as it was to ensure that property remained in the family (Mayes 1991, 328).

Deuteronomy 25:11-12 also seeks to ensure that families do not become extinct. It indicates that if two men are fighting, and the wife of one of the men in the altercation grabs the penis of the man with whom her husband is fighting, the magistrate is to amputate the hand of the woman. By demanding the maiming of the woman who grabs the sexual organ of the male, perhaps the goal of this regulation is to protect the ability of men to procreate so that sons can be born.

Deuteronomy 25:13-17 prescribes economic justice in Israel. It directs persons to use fair and equal standards in issues of commerce. Merchants are required to use the same type of weights when selling, buying, and exchanging goods. In other words, merchants are not to use one unit of measurement when they are selling goods and another unit for weight when buying goods. Fraudulent activity in commerce is to be avoided. Deuteronomy 25:16 contends that dishonest merchants are an abomination to YHWH.

▊ THE TEXT IN THE INTERPRETIVE TRADITION

Subgroups of distinct legislations are present in Deut. 21:10—25:19. Present amongst these codes are laws on divorce. Due to the relevance of this issue, this section will discuss the laws on divorce. Codes on divorce in Deut. 21:10—25:19 (i.e., Deut. 21:10-14; 22:13-21, 28-29; 24:1-4) have an extensive history of conversation. Matthew 19:3-9 and Mark 10:2-12 suggest that divorce was at the center of considerable debate in Judaism during the time of Jesus. In both accounts, the Pharisees raise different issues about this subject. In Mark 10:2-12, the Pharisees ask about the legality of divorce. In Matt. 19:3-9, the issue is the reason a husband divorces his wife. Matthew 19:3-9 brings Deut. 24:1-4 into play, for it permits a husband to end the marriage if he dislikes or finds some flaw in his wife. According to the account in Matthew, Jesus declares that only sexual immorality (*porneia*) on the part of the woman is grounds for divorce.

Rabbinical schools often differed over the meaning of the "not finding favor" clause in Deut. 24:1. The school of Rabbi Shammai interpreted this clause to refer to sexual immorality on the part of the wife. The school of Rabbi Hillel argued that the "not finding favor" clause in Deut. 24:1 permits the ruining of a meal by a wife to suffice for divorce. Rabbi Akiba contends that the "not finding favor" clause in Deut. 24:1 means that finding a wife more beautiful than one's current wife is grounds for divorce (*m. Git.* 9:10). According to the account in Matthew, Jesus sides with the school of Rabbi Shammai on the meaning of the "not finding favor" clause in Deut. 24:1.

Augustine takes Deut. 24:1-4 to mean that husbands ought not be too quick to end their marriages. He contends that this is the reason Deut. 24:1-4 requires the husband to draft a bill of divorce. By drafting this document, the husband will have time to consider the situation. Thus, this piece of legislation is a tool designed to curb eagerness to dissolve the union and to provoke introspection on behalf of the husband regarding his marriage (Lienhard 2001, 315–16).

▊ THE TEXT IN CONTEMPORARY DISCUSSION

Marriage is a key institution in our society. Current reports suggest that between 40 and 50 percent of first-time marriages will end in divorce. This statistic is important because it is highly probable that divorce works to the detriment of children, and that ending marriages contributes to socioeconomic problems for society. Deuteronomy 24:1-4, then, invites us to explore the role husbands can play in reducing the divorce rate. At the center of this claim is the fact that Deut. 24:1 places the onus for initiating divorce on the husband, for it states that if he notices a "fault" in his wife, he has grounds for terminating the marriage. It is virtually impossible to imagine a wife (or a husband) who has no shortcomings. Husbands can adopt an ethos that promotes compassion and forgiveness toward their wives and thus strengthen marriage.

Deuteronomy 26:1-19: Two Liturgies, One Site

▌ THE TEXT IN ITS ANCIENT CONTEXT

Deuteronomy 26:1-15 contains guidelines for two ceremonies. Verses 1-11 delineate the procedure for offering the firstfruit (*re'šît*, Deut. 26:1-11). The code directs the presenter to place these items in a basket and to carry the basket to the central sanctuary. Once there, the basket will be given to the priest and placed in front of the altar. Included in this ritual is a declaration that reviews key events in the history of Israel. According to this speech, Jacob was a wandering or perishing Aramean (*'ărāmî 'ōbēd*) who went down into Egypt and whose people increased numerically and experienced oppression at the hand of Pharaoh and deliverance by YHWH (Deut. 26:5-9). Gerhard von Rad argues that this recitation is a very old declaration of faith from the lore of ancient Israel. G. E. Wright refers to the contents of this credo as the "mighty acts of God" (Christensen 2002, 632). This celebration closes by the presenter declaring that he brought the firstfruits from the land the deity gave to him (*hā'ădāmâ 'ăšer-nātattâ lî*).

Deuteronomy 26:12-15 regulates the triennial tithes, and Deut. 26:16-19 contains an admonition to remain faithful to YHWH. Deuteronomy 26:12-15 reminds Israel to share these tithes with the widow, stranger, fatherless, and Levites. Deuteronomy 26:12b specifies that the local villages are to be the venues for the distribution and consumption of the triennial tithes. Similar to the ritual for the presentation of the firstfruits, a declaration accompanies the presentation of the triennial tithes. It is conspicuous that no declaration accompanies the presentation of the triennial tithes in Deut. 14:28-29. Perhaps the addition of a speech to the presentation of the triennial tithe in Deut. 26:12-15 occurred at a later stage in the formation of the book of Deuteronomy (Merendino 1969, 371–72).

▌ THE TEXT IN THE INTERPRETIVE TRADITION

The rabbis reflected on the meaning of Deut. 26:12-15, and attention to their musings reveals the following tenets: (1) Portions of the seven kinds, namely, wheat, barley, grapes, fig trees, pomegranates, olive trees, and honey, constituted the firstfruit offering; (2) there are people who can present firstfruits and make the public declaration; (3) there are people who can present firstfruits and not make the public declaration; (4) there are people who can neither present firstfruits nor make the public declaration; (5) firstfruits should be brought to the central sanctuary between Pentecost and the Festival of Booths, which is between late spring/early summer and early fall (*m. Bik.* 1:1-10). Deut. 26:13 directs the presenter to perform this ritual *in the presence of the deity*, and elsewhere in Deuteronomy, where this phrase appears, it denotes the official sanctuary. While depositing and allocating the poor-tithe occurred in the local villages, it is probable that the Jerusalem temple is the site for the ritual accompanying the poor-tithe, that is, the tithe in the third year (Mayes 1991, 336).

▌ THE TEXT IN CONTEMPORARY DISCUSSION

Deuteronomy 26:12-15 points out that a class of oppressed social groups constituted Israelite society. While this piece of legislation identifies members of this socioeconomic category, the reader must keep in mind that others in ancient Israelite society constituted this class. Once the poor-tithe had been allocated and consumed, these types of persons returned to eking out their existence with virtually no one to help them. This circumstance, then, placed them at the mercy of creditors and other nefarious types of persons in ancient Israel.

Deuteronomy 26:12-15, then, invites the present reader to make the following claim: the onus rests on someone or some entity to work to improve permanently the circumstance of the vulnerable in society. Oppression works against the chances of human beings developing self-respect and becoming self-determining moral subjects. This passage invites social institutions, namely religious organizations, to do more than provide temporary relief to the oppressed: it invites them to formulate strategies and adopt legislations that seek to remove the causes of oppression in society. Thus these texts challenge those religious communities for whom the Hebrew Bible is normative for faith and praxis to take seriously its duty to effect social justice among some of the most distressed individuals in our communities.

Deuteronomy 27:1—28:68: Blessings and Cursings

■ THE TEXT IN ITS ANCIENT CONTEXT

Form criticism suggests that Deuteronomy contains the following elements: (1) Historical introduction(s) (Deut. 1:1—11:32); (2) stipulations of the agreement (Deut. 12:1—26:19); (3) citation of blessings and punishments for keeping or violating the covenant (Deut. 27:1—28:68); and (4) miscellaneous materials (Deut. 29:1—34:12). The following are major features of Hittite treaties: (1) The self-identification of the suzerain; (2) the historical recapitulation, in which the suzerain cites mercies shown to the vassal; (3) the stipulations of the agreement; (4) reiteration of the need for frequent rehearsal or review of the covenant; and (5) a curse and blessing for either violating or keeping the covenant. Although fragmentary, the data suggest Assyrian treaties contained the following elements: (1) Lists of witnesses; (2) the stipulations of the agreement; and (3) curses for violating the covenant (Mayes 1991, 32). Therefore, it is widely accepted that treaty traditions in the ancient Near East are the backdrop against which to discuss the present structure of Deuteronomy (Weinfeld 1992, 146–57).

Hittite and Assyrian treaties contain concluding sections that cite curses for violating the agreement. Deuteronomy 27:1—28:68 contains a series of curses and blessings. It appears to have been appended to Deuteronomy 12–26 by the redactor, for this narrative connects with the account that ended abruptly in Deut. 11:29-32. The presence of these series of curses and blessings ensures that the pattern of the final form of Deuteronomy more closely resembles that of treaty traditions in the ancient Near East.

■ THE TEXT IN THE INTERPRETIVE TRADITION

Moses and the elders instruct the people to erect stones, cover them with plaster, and write this teaching (*hattôrâ hazzô't*) on them (Deut. 27:1-8). While the text is silent on the specifics of "this teaching," contemporary Jewish scholarship on this verse suggests that "this teaching" denotes the regulations in Deuteronomy 12–26 (Tigay 1996, 248). What is more, rabbinic exegesis of this passage claims that the Israelite community wrote the contents of "this teaching" in seventy languages on the stones (*m. Sotah* 7:5).

Deuteronomy 27:4-5 instructs the community to construct an altar on Mt. Ebal, where the Levites, with six of the tribes that composed Israel, cite twelve morally and theologically reprehensible behaviors. The Levites also declare a malediction (*'ārar*), a divinely established, permanent condition of disaster, trouble, suffering, and pain in the lives of those who perpetrate them (Deut. 27:15-26; 28:16-68). Deut. 27:15-26 refers to twelve actions that are surreptitious but known by YHWH; consequently, YHWH will punish those who commit these offenses (Tigay 1996, 251–57). The text indicates that YHWH will use a nation from afar (*gôy mērāḥôq*) to punish Israel. The identity of the nation from afar (*gôy mērāḥôq*) spoken of in Deut. 28:47-68 that will subjugate Israel is unknown. In light of the calamities that befell Israel in 722 BCE and 586 BCE, Assyria and Babylon are often cited as this nation from afar (Tigay 1996, 269).

Deuteronomy 27:12 and 28:1-14 indicate that six of the other larger kinship subgroups that constitute Israel should stand on Mt. Gerizim and invoke a blessing (*bārak*), a divinely established, permanent condition of favor, happiness, health, fecundity, and peace in the lives of those who obey the contents of this teaching. Basil the Great (329–379 CE), one of the three Cappadocians fathers, applies an allegorical reading to this text by associating the basket in Deut. 28:5 with the soul, and argues that if the soul gets developed, it can be prosperous, that is, filled with good things. According to Basil, it must be nurtured and refreshed by heavenly waters (Lienhard 2001, 321). Current Pentecostal biblical scholarship would argue that growth of the soul comes from allowing the Spirit of God to nurture one's soul (Warrington 2008, 46–48).

■ THE TEXT IN CONTEMPORARY DISCUSSION

Deuteronomy 27:15-26 lists twelve evil curses. These maledictions condemn seedy actions that are perpetrated in secret or without an audience. Since these deeds are carried out in private, it is easy for one to think that these actions are less dangerous than those moral actions that are noticeable by all and are easily detectable. Deuteronomic moral thought invites us to consider that furtive wicked deeds are a detriment to the community. Thematic similarities are present between key assumptions about the moral agent that inform Deut. 27:15-26 and the account about the Ring of Gyges in book 2 of Plato's *Republic*. Both of these accounts bring into play the tenet that clandestine actions reveal the true character and real moral qualities of a moral agent. Actions done in secret neither hide our character nor obfuscate those values that underlie them: they reveal them.

Deuteronomy 29:1—30:20: Moses Speaks

■ THE TEXT IN ITS ANCIENT CONTEXT

Deuteronomy 29–30 contains another sermon by Moses. In these chapters, Israel is standing on the brink of entering the promised land, and Moses once again rehearses the deeds of YHWH in the life of Israel. The most conspicuous of these actions is the tradition of YHWH's rescuing an oppressed group of slaves from bondage in Egypt, the nucleus of biblical Israel, and of YHWH's entering a formal relationship with this group at Horeb. Moses admonishes Israel to abide by this covenant. He cites Sodom, Gomorrah, Admah, and Zeboiim, and contends that the fate of these cities is what lies on the horizon if Israel violates the agreement YHWH has made with them. These chapters, therefore, continue that type of thinking that is widespread in Deuteronomic thought by making obedience to the law a necessary condition for well-being, fecundity, peace, and good fortune. Speeches of Moses introduce and are appended to the large block of law and curses and blessings in Deuteronomy 12–28. These orations "bookend" the nucleus of the book.

▋ THE TEXT IN THE INTERPRETIVE TRADITION

Deuteronomy 29–30 reviews the journey of the Israelites from Horeb to Moab. What is more, this account revels in the defeat of Sihon and Og, two monarchs whom the Israelites engaged in combat on their way to the promised land. These chapters mention both Horeb and Moab, indicating that YHWH made covenants with Israel in both of these locations. The speech concludes with Moses admonishing the people to be faithful to YHWH by choosing life over death. It is argued that Deuteronomy 29–30 contains the concluding charge of the book (Craigie 1976, 356).

Deut. 29:14 contains a very interesting phrase. It says that the covenant was with those who are not here with us today (*'ăšer 'ênennû pōh 'immānû*). This wording attracts attention, because elsewhere in Deuteronomy the narrator says that covenants were made at Horeb (Deut. 1:6) and at Moab (Deut. 1:5; 29:1). Since the people with whom YHWH cut a covenant at Horeb died in the wilderness, Deut. 5:2 implies that YHWH was cutting a covenant with those who were present at Moab. Now, Deut. 29:14 talks about YHWH cutting a covenant *with those who are not present*. About whom is the text speaking? Rabbinic exegesis contends that those "not present" in Deut. 29:14 refers to the souls of future generations of Jews. YHWH is cutting a covenant with those who are present at Moab as well as with those Jews who are forthcoming (Tigay 1996, 278).

The notion of YHWH cutting a covenant with Jews was a source of discussion in the early Christian community. The author of the epistle to the Hebrews says: "In speaking of 'a new covenant,' he has made the first one obsolete" (Heb. 8:13 NRSV). He also introduces Jer. 31:31-34 into the discussion of soteriology and Christology, arguing that the work of Jesus has brought into play a new, different mechanism for people to maintain a relationship with God. This covenant is not tied to the ongoing offering of animal sacrifices for atonement, but is linked to the act of accepting by faith the salvific atoning work of Jesus. For the writer of Hebrews, the first covenant, the one that was instituted at Horeb/Sinai and Moab, has been superseded by the covenant through Jesus.

▋ THE TEXT IN CONTEMPORARY DISCUSSION

The "prosperity gospel" is present in many religious communities. This type of theology argues that good health, money, power, cars, and temporal success are how a right relationship with God is measured. In fact, it has become quite fashionable in many Christian circles to claim that obtaining possessions, capital, affluence, power, physical well-being, and good fortune is the entitlement of a person who is in good standing with God, via Jesus. At the center of this phenomenon is a type of preaching, teaching, and exposition of the Bible that reads the text through the lens of prosperity, perhaps through the lens of Deut. 30:15. This trend in theologizing brings into play a host of interpretive and theological issues, chief of which is an approach to biblical hermeneutics that embraces one, single idea or principle as the key criterion for understanding the Bible. In the case at hand, enjoying great wealth, success, and good fortune in this world is the theme that unites all of Scripture. While portions of the Bible speak about prosperity, a close look at prophecies in Amos, Jeremiah, and Micah reveals that a host of other principles are also present. Perhaps the reader should be wary of all forms of hermeneutical monism and embrace a framework for reading the Bible that affirms the texts' diversity of thought surrounding the moral life.

Deuteronomy 31:1—34:12: Concluding Matters

◼ THE TEXT IN ITS ANCIENT CONTEXT

Deuteronomy 31–34 casts light on several important speeches, deeds, and events in the final days of Moses: (1) The transfer of leadership to Joshua (Deut. 31:7-8, 14-15, 23; 34:9). Traditions that anticipate this event appear in Deut. 1:38 and 3:28. Moreover, Num. 27:12-23 contains an alternative account of Joshua's appointment as the next leader of Israel. (2) The command to read the law every seven years during the Festival of Booths/Tabernacles (Deut. 31:9-13). (3) The construction of a poem, the Song of Moses, which speaks about Israel's inclination toward apostasy and the proclivity of YHWH to punish Israel for her unfaithfulness (Deut. 32:1-43). A poem by this title appears in Exod. 15:1-21, but it celebrates the deliverance of Israel from slavery in Egypt. (4) Moses' blessing of the tribes of Israel (Deut. 33:1-29). Genesis 49:1-28 preserves the traditions that Jacob uttered when he blessed those twelve tribes that afterward would constitute Israel. (5) The death and eulogy of Moses (Deut. 34:1-12). Deuteronomy 31–34 reflects the essence of the Deuteronomic program, namely, that observing the laws of YHWH and commitment to the exclusive worship of YHWH bring prosperity.

◼ THE TEXT IN THE INTERPRETIVE TRADITION

Because the Song of Moses (Deut. 32:1-43) contains several individual literary units that imply moral and theological ideas, it has been the object of considerable reflection among the early church fathers. John Cassian (360–435 CE) took Deut. 32:7 to mean that individuals should take advantage of the wisdom of the elders and, when possible, they should confer with church leaders when unsure about decisions regarding ethical and theological matters. John Chrysostom (347–407 CE) took Deut. 32:15 to mean that the moral agent should guard against the dangers of abundance, for according to Deut. 32:15, bounty often leads to ungratefulness and to a set of other behaviors that cause one to ignore his or her need for God (Lienhard 2001, 332–34).

◼ THE TEXT IN CONTEMPORARY DISCUSSION

Israel was in transition: it was on the brink of entering the promised land, and Moses had taken them as far as he could take them. However, he understands that if the community does reach the promised land, they will not reach it under his leadership. The Song of Moses provides a paradigm for transitioning leadership in religious organizations. It invites leaders to appreciate several items: (1) Leaders need to recognize that their time for supervising and providing leadership to a community will expire; (2) leaders can be gracious to individuals in the organization when they depart; (3) leaders can depart and pass on some insight into what they foresee will be challenges for the success of the organization; and (4) leaders can find public ways to support their successors before they depart. Leaders can finish strong.

Works Cited

Bennett, Harold. 2002. *Injustice Made Legal*. Grand Rapids: Eerdmans.

Christensen, Duane L. 2001. *Deuteronomy 1:1—21:9*. Nashville: Thomas Nelson.

————. 2002. *Deuteronomy 21:10—34:12*. Nashville: Thomas Nelson.

Copan, Paul. 2011. *Is God a Moral Monster? Making Sense of the Old Testament God*. Grand Rapids: Baker Books.

Craigie, Peter C. 1976. *Deuteronomy*. Grand Rapids: Eerdmans.

————. 1983. *Ugarit and the Old Testament*. Grand Rapids: Eerdmans.

Danby, Herbert, trans. 2011. *The Mishnah: Translated from the Hebrew with Introduction and Brief Explanatory Notes*. Peabody, MA: Hendrickson.

Drinkard, Joel, E. 2007. "Gates in the Old Testament." In *The New Interpreters' Dictionary of the Bible*. Volume 2. Edited by Katherine Doob Sakenfeld. Nashville: Abingdon Press.

Erskine, Noel Leo. 2005. *From Garvey to Marley: Rastafari Theology*. Gainesville: University of Florida Press.

Freire, Paulo. 2005. *Pedagogy of the Oppressed*. Translated by Myra Bergman Ramos. New York: Continuum.

Frymer-Kensky, Tikva. 1992. "Deuteronomy." In *The Women's Bible Commentary*. Edited by Carol A. Newsom and Sharon H. Ringe. Louisville: Westminster John Knox.

Gutiérrez, Gustavo. 1999. *A Theology of Liberation*. Translated and Edited by Sister Caridad Inda and John Eagleson. Maryknoll, NY: Orbis.

Hamilton, Jeffries M. 1992. *Social Justice and Deuteronomy: The Case of Deuteronomy 15*. Atlanta: Scholars Press.

Harrelson. Walter J. 1985. *The Ten Commandments and Human Rights*. Philadelphia: Fortress Press.

Hopkins, Dwight N. 1999. *Introducing Black Theology of Liberation*. Maryknoll, NY: Orbis.

Houston, Walter J. 2003. "Towards an Integrated Reading of the Dietary Laws of Leviticus." In *The Book of Leviticus*. Edited by Rolf Rendtorff and Robert A. Kugler. Atlanta: Society of Biblical Literature.

Josephus, Flavius. 1985. "The Antiquities of the Jews." In *Josephus: Complete Works*. Translated by William Whiston. Grand Rapids: Kregel.

Kimball, Charles. 2008. *When Religion Becomes Evil*. San Francisco: HarperOne.

Knight, Douglas A. 2011. *Law, Power, and Justice in Ancient Israel*. Louisville: Westminster John Knox.

Levinson, Bernard M. 1997. *Deuteronomy and the Hermeneutics of Legal Innovation*. New York: Oxford University Press.

Lienhard, Joseph T., ed. 2001. *Exodus, Leviticus, Numbers, Deuteronomy*. Ancient Christian Commentary on Scripture, Old Testament 3. Downers Grove, IL: InterVarsity Press.

Mayes, A. D. H. 1991. *Deuteronomy*. NCB. Grand Rapids: Eerdmans.

Merendino, Rosario P. 1969. *Das Deuteronomische Gesetz*. Bonn: Peter Hanstein.

Milgrom, Jacob. 2004. *Leviticus*. CC. Minneapolis: Fortress Press.

Miller, Patrick D. 2000. *The Religion of Ancient Israel.* Louisville: Westminster John Knox.

Nelson, Richard. 2002. *Deuteronomy.* OTL. Louisville: Westminster John Knox.

Niditch, Susan. 1993. *War in the Hebrew Bible: A Study in the Ethics of Violence.* New York: Oxford University Press.

Nielsen, Kai. 1990. *Ethics without God.* Amherst, NY: Prometheus.

Peterson, Michael, William Hasker, Bruce Reichenbach, and David Basinger. 2012. *Reason and Religious Belief: An Introduction to the Philosophy of Religion.* New York: Oxford University Press.

Phipps, William E. 1996. *Muhammad and Jesus: A Comparison of the Prophets and Their Teachings.* New York: Continuum.

Rofé, Alexander. 2002. *Deuteronomy: Issues and Interpretation.* OTS. London: T&T Clark.

Ross, Allen. 2002. *Holiness to the Lord.* Grand Rapids: Baker Academic.

Roth, Martha T. 1997. *Law Collections from Mesopotamia and Asia Minor.* Atlanta: Scholars Press.

Seibert, Eric A. 2009. *Disturbing Divine Behavior: Troubling Old Testament Images of God.* Minneapolis: Fortress Press.

Sneed, Mark. 1999. *Concepts of Class in Ancient Israel.* Atlanta: Scholars Press.

Spinoza, Baruch. 2001. *Theological Political Treatise.* Translated by Samuel Shirley. Indianapolis: Hackett.

Stevens, Marty. 2006. *Temples, Tithes, and Taxes: The Temple and the Economic Life of Ancient Israel.* Peabody, MA: Hendrickson.

Tigay, Jeffrey H. 1996. *Deuteronomy.* Philadelphia: Jewish Publication Society.

Warrington, Keith. 2008. *Pentecostal Theology: A Theology of Encounter.* London: T&T Clark.

Weinfeld, Moshe. 1991. *Deuteronomy 1-11.* AB. New York: Doubleday.

———. 1992. *Deuteronomy and the Deuteronomic School.* Winona Lake, IN: Eisenbrauns.

THEMES AND PERSPECTIVES IN THE HISTORICAL WRITINGS

Norman K. Gottwald

Introduction

The so-called historical books of the Hebrew Bible provide a sweeping view of ancient Israel in the period from circa 1225 BCE to circa 400 BCE. These books form a continuous series in the Christian canon, extending from Joshua through Judges, 1–2 Samuel, 1–2 Kings, 1–2 Chronicles, Ezra-Nehemiah, and concluding with Esther. In the Jewish canon, Joshua through Kings are called the Former Prophets, 1–2 Chronicles and Nehemiah are included in the Writings, as is Esther, which is grouped with four other shorter books connected with Jewish festivals (the Megilloth). Joshua through Kings are probably named Former Prophets because they contain traditions about prophets who preceded Hosea (the first book listed in the Latter Prophets, also known as the Writing Prophets), and there is major attention to the prophets Elijah and Elisha in 1–2 Kings.

The flow of Israelite life begins with Joshua's conquest of Canaan and continues with the leadership of "judges" before recounting the fortunes of the united and divided kingdoms in 1–2 Samuel and 1–2 Kings. Interestingly, 1–2 Chronicles covers in part the same ground as Kings but does so by repeating much of Samuel-Kings, to which it adds traditions of its own, producing a decidedly more religious view of the monarchy than the former. Oddly, the period of the exile is omitted and the story line jumps to the postexilic return to Palestine (Ezra-Nehemiah) and ends with the outlier short story about a Jewess who rises to the status of queen of Persia (Esther).

Authorship and Date

The author or authors of the historical books are unknown, and in this respect they differ from the works of Herodotus and Thucydides of Greece, widely regarded as the first historians in the

Western world, who composed roughly at the same time as Joshua-Kings. The Greek histories are clearly written by identifiable individuals. By contrast, with an unknown author and a division into six books that differ greatly in design and style, the books of Joshua, Judges, 1–2 Samuel, and 1–2 Kings might easily be judged to constitute three separate books. The transition from Joshua to Judges and from Judges to 1 Samuel is abrupt, whereas the four volumes of Samuel and Kings flow seamlessly into one another. Chronicles stands apart as a briefer reinterpretation and supplement to the longer work.

Nonetheless, in Joshua-Kings, there is a continuity of viewpoint expressed in a common language at key junctures in all six books, demonstrating that the overall composition is the work of a single hand, or of a company of like minds. This unknown author, or joint authors, has been given the clumsy moniker of "the Deuteronomist" (hereafter as Dtr) because these historical books share a common vocabulary, style, and theology with the book of Deuteronomy. In fact, the book of Deuteronomy is the actual introduction for Dtr, even though it has been separated from the historical books and is counted as the last book of the Law in Jewish and Christian canons. For this reason, Joshua to Kings has been described as the Deuteronomistic History (hereafter as DH).

Apart from the common language and theology spanning the six volumes of DH, the contents of these historical books are sufficiently different that they pose the question: Is Dtr an author or an editor-compiler? We make the best sense of the literary data if we understand Dtr as both editor-compiler and author. Clearly DH has been composed of varied traditions differing greatly in genre and often reaching back in time, so that they constitute a veritable depth-dimensional anthology of Israel's historical and cultural memories. Consequently, the loosely connected stories of the judges read very differently from the smoothly rendered narratives about Samuel, Saul, and David, and the accounts of the so-called conquest of Canaan are far less likely to give us material for a history of Israel than information from Kings on the divided kingdoms of Israel and Judah. It almost goes without saying that a poem like the Song of Deborah (Judges 5) needs to be approached with quite another sensibility and mind-set than the tribal allotments. In short, scattered sources of varying age and provenance have been assembled and edited to form the contents of Dtr (the editor-compiler function) and stamped with an emphatic, even dogmatic, explanation of why Israel's history transpired as it did (the author function).

Likewise, Chronicles lacks an authorial identity, and the author is called simply the Chronicler (hereafter Chr). His compositional practices differ from those of Dtr in that there is a single, well-known primary source in 1–2 Chronicles, namely, the books of Samuel-Kings, which serve as the backbone of the work. In this dependence on a single published source, Chr operates in much the same manner as the New Testament Gospels of Matthew and Luke, whose authors employ Mark as the ground plan of their Gospels. The unique materials in 1–2 Chronicles include long genealogies that preface a glowing, almost rapturous account of David and his dynasty. These books have a compelling interest in the glorious dynasty of David, especially the religious practices in the temple prepared by David and built by his son Solomon. The names of priests and musicians who minister at the temple are recited. The northern kings are ignored except at points where they interact with the Davidic dynasty. Nonetheless, surprisingly, Chr issues an invitation for the apostate northern tribes to rejoin Judah, submit to the Davidic dynasty, and adhere to worship at the Jerusalem temple.

The date of the historical books is as uncertain as the identity of their author(s). Nevertheless, some clues to date appear within the documents. The narratives in DH and Chronicles stop abruptly with the fall of Jerusalem and the deportation of its upper class to Babylonia (the so-called exile). The sole exceptions are a reference by Dtr to the favor shown by a Babylonian ruler to the captive king Jehoiachin (2 Kgs. 25:27-30) and by Chr's inclusion of the proclamation of Cyrus the Persian in 538 BCE to return the deportees to Jerusalem and to rebuild the temple (2 Chron. 36:22-23). As a result, the critical fifty years between the eclipse of the political and religious sovereignty of Judah (586 BCE) and the proclaimed restoration of Judah as a province of the Persian Empire (538 BCE) are virtually a blank slate in the biblical historical record. It also means that the terminal stage in the composition of Joshua-Kings was later than the favor shown Jehoiachin in 561 BCE. Likewise, the finished composition of 1–2 Chronicles was later than the proclamation of Cyrus in 538 BCE. However, it is persuasively argued by some scholars that Joshua-Kings went through two editions, the first during the reign of King Josiah (640–609 BCE), celebrating a sweeping religious reform, and the final edition explaining why the kingdom of Judah was totally destroyed in spite of its promising future under Josiah. As a consequence, DH contains both the promise to David of an eternal dynasty and the nullification of that promise by the destruction of state and temple and the decimation of Judah's religious and political leadership. Chronicles softens the blow of exile by symbolizing exilic Judah as a land enjoying a Sabbath rest for seventy years, and little is made of the eclipse of the Davidic dynasty.

The books of Ezra and Nehemiah present yet a different picture. Past scholarship commonly understood Chr to be the author of these two books, but that attribution is now generally denied on stylistic and ideological grounds. The books tell of a period in the history of restored Judah, dated in the fifth century BCE, when the priest Ezra headed a sizable group of deportees returning to Judah and the layman Nehemiah served as governor of the province of Judah under Persian imperial rule. The two leaders are presented as contemporaries, but a close study of the disordered narrative suggests that Nehemiah came first and laid the foundation for the political and economic restoration of Judah that Ezra subsequently capitalized on in securing commitment of the populace to reforms that purify religious belief and practice. The sources of Ezra-Nehemiah include actual or allegedly Persian political documents, lists of returnees, and portions of first-person memoirs by Nehemiah and Ezra.

In contrast, Esther is a piece of historical fantasy telling how a young Judahite woman became queen of the Persian Empire and saved her people from a plot to annihilate them. The story reflects the known practice of Judahites serving at times in foreign administrations, but its descriptions of the Persian royal court and empire are distorted and exaggerated. It features a lurid account of how the table is turned on those who plan to massacre all Judahites in the kingdom, with the result that the nefarious plotters are visited with the fate that they intended for Esther's people. The book is connected to the festival of Purim, a late Jewish holiday of unknown origin. The intense hatred exhibited between Jews and gentiles appears to reflect the late Hasmonean dynasty, when Judah was briefly independent and a power-wielding player in Palestinian politics that pitted Jews against Hellenists, and even traditional Jews against Hellenized Jews. Esther is likely the latest book included in the Hebrew Bible, written between 180 and 80 BCE.

Clues to Reading the Historical Books

When we pick up a work of nonfiction, we often scan the introduction and conclusion in order to orient ourselves to the content, often to decide whether we want to read the whole book. The biblical historical books give us little such help. They plunge into their stories immediately, Dtr with "after the death of Moses," and Chr with the genealogy of David, who is unspecified until the end of its catalog of names, "Adam, Seth, Enosh . . ." The conclusions trail off with Dtr's "a regular allowance was given him [King Jehoiachin in Babylonian captivity] by the king [Evil-merodach, king of Babylon], every day a portion, as long as he lived," and Chr ends with the voice of Cyrus, king of Persia, speaking to the captive Judahites: "Whoever is among you of all his people, may the LORD his God be with him. Let him go up." Even the opening line of Deuteronomy, which is the first book of Dtr, is terse, "These are the words that Moses spoke to all Israel beyond the Jordan." Chr does not even offer a prefatory sentence but plunges into the story with a lengthy genealogy running from the first human to King David. In short, we must read some distance into the historical books, certainly beyond a speech by Moses (in Deuteronomy) or the alleged ancestry of David (in Chronicles), to get a sense of what they are about. Similarly, Nehemiah and Ezra require guidance to unravel the order of events in the two books, since they provide neither preface nor concluding summary.

Because the historical books are normally read individually according to the interests that scholars and ordinary readers bring to the biblical text, it is easy to overlook the great differences among them. For one thing, with the exception of Ezra and Nehemiah, the principal characters receive unequal space. A long narrative in DH recounting the reigns of Saul, David, and Solomon is spread over two and a half books, namely, 1 Sam. 1:1—1 Kgs. 11:43. This account of the first three kings of Israel is a developed narrative, with plot, connected episodes, and vivid characters, whereas Joshua, Judges, and the remainder of post-Solomonic kings (1 Kings 12—2 Kings 17) are described by single stories, clusters of stories, or excerpts from royal archives, either unconnected or only loosely connected. As the kingdom of Judah nears its end, however, Dtr provides a more integral narrative from Hezekiah to Zedekiah (2 Kgs. 18–25). Some of the sources of Dtr are cited in the text: the Book of Jashar (Josh. 10:15; 2 Sam. 1:18); the Book of the Acts of Solomon (1 Kgs. 11:41); the Book of the Acts of the Kings of Israel (beginning with 1 Kgs. 14:9, et passim); the Book of the Acts of the Kings of Judah (1 Kgs. 14:29, et passim). The poems of Hannah, David, and Deborah may derive from liturgical usage. Accordingly, the known and likely pre-Dtr writings are clusters of written, possibly oral, traditions, recounting the activities of a colorful cast of characters both political and religious.

Thus the first three kings of Israel receive as much press as all the remaining kings of Israel and Judah! Most of the kings are treated in brief cameos, with the fullest attention given to Jeroboam I, Ahab, Jehu, Jehoshaphat, Jehoash, Hezekiah, and Josiah, as well as extended legends about the prophets Elijah and Elisha, who interact critically, and less often supportively, with the northern house of Omri. Most of the monarchs are presented hurriedly, with the briefest of comments on their reigns. Unmistakably, David is the prime personage for Dtr, and even more so for Chr. All the action and energy in Joshua and Judges points toward the coming house of David, but after

Solomon, the dynasty of David is in decline and is finally extinguished by the Neo-Babylonians. Dtr presents David as the acme of royal popularity, piety, and virtue (in spite of his glaring shortcomings). Solomon receives great wisdom, but squanders the political unity of the kingdom achieved by David. In short, the reader must approach DH aware of the literary habits and notions about "history" typical of ancient Israelite narration of past events, as they impinge on and give shape to the present time of the author.

Sources and Composition

Dtr employs several structural and rhetorical devices that underscore the leading themes and signal the important stages and turning points in the story. Attention to these compositional features enhances appreciation of the challenges Dtr faced in composing his lengthy history from seemingly incompatible materials. Dtr not only unifies his work with transitions that link era to era but also employs several devices to link individual texts within each segment of history and spanning two or more segments. These thematic and rhetorical devices are editorial maneuvers that show DH to be a single document, forged from many documents and oral traditions and sprinkled with editorial comments and connections that show a consistent religious ideology. The architecture of this literary tour de force, like centuries-old cathedrals, is in no way diminished if, as seems likely, it has been worked on by several editors with shared understandings.

Grand Design

It is fairly easy to identify the principal theme of Dtr as the momentous clash between two versions of the Israelite story: the conditional terms of the Mosaic covenant and the unconditional terms of the Davidic covenant. The more challenging task is to bring to light the literary means by which that clash is represented. What makes the movement from Joshua to Kings so engaging is that we see at each point in the history a clash between the two covenants, but in different guises and with a constantly changing cast of characters. Assuming that Dtr aimed to show how the two covenants played out through the centuries after Moses, the big challenge was to decide what sources to use, how to arrange them, and how to link the sources into a continuous story from Joshua to the collapse of the two kingdoms.

Dtr had in hand several blocks of material, each dealing with a segment of that long history: taking of the land of Canaan; judges arising in a tribal system; the united kingdom under three successive kings, Saul, David, and Solomon; splitting into two states, one in the north (Israel) and one in the south (Judah), followed by the sequence of the kings in each monarchy and the loss of independence for both. It is crucial to realize that Dtr was not writing six books but one segmented history only later divided into six books within the canon. The four segments of Dtr's work are sewn together with transitional links:

Era of the Occupation of Canaan
with a link to the era of judges: Joshua's death and burial (Josh. 24:29-33)
repeated in the introduction to the judges (Judg. 2:6-10)

Era of the Judges

with a link to the united kingdom: annual festivals at Shiloh provide the setting for the last episode about judges (Judg. 21:16-23) and the first episode about the United Kingdom (1 Samuel 1)

Era of the United Kingdom

with a link to the divided kingdoms: episodes of Jeroboam and Ahijah before the death of Solomon (1 Kgs. 11:26-31) and after the death of Solomon (1 Kgs. 12:15)

Era of the Divided Kingdoms

ends with destruction of the two kingdoms, deportation of Judahite officials to Babylon, and an open-ended note about the favor shown to captive King Zedekiah by a Neo-Babylonian ruler.

The era of the united kingdom is told in a continuous narrative, by far the most cohesive segment of Dtr. In fact, many interpreters have treated the so-called Court History of David as an eyewitness account, so vividly and artfully is it fashioned (2 Samuel 9–20; 1 Kings 1–2). However, the sources for the other eras were not as cohesive, so that Dtr had to find a way of shaping them into an ongoing narrative. With the era of Joshua, the stories and lists are framed by his introductory and farewell speeches. With the era of the judges, Dtr linked episodes by means of an artificial cyclical framework with a repeated pattern: Israel does evil by abandoning the covenant, YHWH punishes the people by oppression at the hand of enemies, the oppressed Israelites cry out for deliverance from oppression, YHWH rescues the Israelites by raising up a military judge, and at the death of the judge the Israelites revert to their evil ways. Then the identical cycle is repeated several times. For the final phase of his history, Dtr tells the story of the divided kingdoms by drawing information about each king from royal archives, and using a formula that includes length of the reign and a verdict of good or bad on the king's performance. Dtr inserts into this scheme a cycle of stories about the northern prophets Elijah and Elisha, largely folk traditions that venerate them as YHWH loyalists and defenders of the people.

Programmatic Texts

Lacking introduction and conclusion, the dominant themes of Dtr have to be ferreted out in the course of its narrative. Set in motion by Moses' command to observe the law (Deuteronomy 1–4), interpretive passages at strategic points throughout the history describe and explain how the unfolding course of events is shaped by Israel's failure to adhere to that law. Counting Deuteronomy as the fountainhead and pacesetter for the historical books, these programmatic texts are presented in the form of speeches and prayers by the leaders of Israel and discourses or notations by the author. Among the most important of these programmatic texts are the following:

Parting speech of Moses (Deuteronomy 29–30)
Inaugural speech of Joshua (Josh. 1:10-15)
Speech of God introducing the covenant (Josh. 24:1-13)
Speech of Joshua at the making of the covenant (Josh. 24:14-28)

Discourses on the Judges (Judg. 2:6—3:6; 10:10-16)
Speech of Samuel about kingship (1 Samuel 8)
Parting speech of Samuel (1 Samuel 12)
Speech of Nathan and prayer of David (2 Sam. 7:4-29)
Blessing of the temple, prayer, and speech of Solomon (1 Kgs. 8:14-61)
Speech of God to Solomon (1 Kgs. 9:1-9)
Speech of Ahijah to Jeroboam (1 Kgs. 11:29-40)
Message of the Assyrian general to Hezekiah (2 Kgs. 18:19-25; 19:8-13)
Speech of the Assyrian general to the Jerusalemites (2 Kgs. 18:28-35)
Discourse on the fall of the northern kingdom [Israel] (2 Kgs. 17:7-23, 34-40),
Discourse and speech on the fall of the southern kingdom [Judah] (2 Kgs. 21:2-16)

When these pivotal texts are read together, it becomes abundantly clear that the central motifs in DH are the binding law of Moses and the promise of an everlasting dynasty to David. While both themes are of immense importance, they stand in radical contradiction to one another. This series of texts is as close as Dtr comes to explicitly disclosing his own interpretation of the story he composes. In the end, obedience to the law trumps the promise to David. The stunning consequence is that the dynasty of David is cut off with the fall of Jerusalem. Nevertheless, the outcome of the conflict between the law of Moses and the dynasty of David is so skillfully delayed by Dtr that the reader is kept in suspense until the final years of the kingdom of Judah.

Lists of Names

While the programmatic texts of Dtr give a measure of coherence to the history, there is another type of text favored by Dtr that militates against narrative coherence, at least for today's reader. Contemporary readers are easily intimidated by the lists of the names of persons and places that disturb, even interrupt, the narrative flow, most grievously so in Chr. These personal names are identified as ancestors, officials, and priests with specified duties and privileges, or deported leaders. The named places are variously tribal regions, monarchic territories, or political and religious sites. In DH, these recitals of the names of people and places occur frequently and at times bridge the gaps between narrated events:

Conquered and unconquered kings and territories in Canaan (Josh. 12:1—13:6; 23:1-13)
Land allotments of the tribes (Josh. 13:6b—19:51)
Minor judges (Judg. 10:1-5; 12:7-13)
David's officials (2 Sam. 8:15-18)
David's mighty warriors and bodyguards (1 Sam. 23:8-39)
Solomon's officials (1 Kgs. 4:1-19)
Details of Solomon's palace and temple (2 Kgs. 6–8)
Ahaz's alteration of temple worship (2 Kgs. 16:15-18)
Assyrian deportation of Israelites replaced by foreign captives (2 Kgs. 17:6, 24)

Foreign gods accepted by Samaritans (2 Kgs. 17:29-31)
Officials of Judah deported to Babylon (2 Kgs. 24:10-17; 25:11, 18-21)

Some of these are lists in freestanding form, while others have been more or less integrated into the narrative. In a modern history, much of this sort of information would be relegated to footnotes or appendixes. Nevertheless, some of these narrative "asides" preserve informative details of historical value, especially the data from state archives. In 1–2 Chronicles, in addition to the lists, the author also attaches names to each of the many sources he cites. Some of these sources, if not all, seem to be modeled on the less frequent naming of sources in DH:

In 1 Chronicles (samples)
Lineage of David and the tribal heads (1–9)
David's mighty men (11)
David's Levitical musicians (15:16-24)
Priests and officials in court of David (24–27)

In 2 Chronicles (samples)
Solomon's building projects and chief officers (8:1-10)
Solomon's riches (9:13-28)
Rehoboam's fortified cities (11:5-12)
Jehoshaphat's princes and Levites' instruction of people in the law (17:7-9)
Levites cleanse the temple and restore the utensils Ahaz discarded (29:12-19)
Officers collect offerings for the temple (31:11-15)
Workmen repair and restore the temple (34:8-13)

The books of Ezra-Nehemiah give census-like lists of names that seek both to describe and to authenticate the return of the exiles to Judah. The whole assembly of returnees is said to consist of 42,360 priests and laity, plus 7,337 of their servants (Ezra 1–2). Of course, these figures cannot be verified, but they are strikingly less than the hundreds of thousands elsewhere in DH. Furthermore, the rebuilders of the walls of Jerusalem are identified by name and the section of the wall they worked on (Nehemiah 3).

The effect of these lists is to break the momentum of the story line, or at least to slow it down dramatically, especially so if the reader pauses to dwell on the names listed. Truth be told, these lists contribute to the impression that DH is a miscellany of traditions held together by a chronology of questionable merit. Since most of the lists appear to be collected by Dtr and Chr, rather than composed by them, their original life settings are a matter of conjecture. Many were excerpted from governmental or temple documents. It is debated as to whether the name lists actually belonged to the historical settings to which Dtr and Chr assign them or rather were derived from later historical contexts and reassigned to Joshua, David, Solomon, or a later king. One thing seems abundantly clear: both author and original readers found delight in punctuating narrative texts with lists of this sort. It is conceivable that it was a matter of pride that the narrator could confidently produce such details to embellish and authenticate the narrative.

Chronological Schemes

For long stretches of DH, there are no temporal indicators, but at certain points the narrative is punctuated, even organized, by temporal considerations. These markers are often simply given in round numbers. The most elaborate temporal scheme in round numbers is the forty-year periods of rest secured by several judges who delivered Israel from foreign oppressors (Othniel, Deborah, Gideon, and Samson, with an eighty-year [2 × 40] rest for the land secured by Ehud). Forty years seems to be an idiom for "a very long time," also claimed as the length of rule by both David and Solomon. This amplitude of time is contrasted with the ill-fated Saul, whose reign of two years is cited in a broken text (1 Sam. 13:1), which speaks for his failure as king, even though he is estimated to have ruled for as much as twenty years. On the other hand, the so-called minor judges are assigned periods of office in an irregular pattern along a spectrum from six years (Jephthah), to seven (Ibzan), eight (Abadon), ten (Elon), twenty-two (Jair), and twenty-three years (Tola). It is not always clear whether the specified years were already in Dtr's sources or were introduced by him.

When Dtr reaches the divided kingdoms, instead of rounded numbers, we encounter precisely calibrated periods of time for the reigns of all the kings of north and south. Dtr informs us that this chronological information is derived from the royal annals of Israel and Judah. The reigns in the two kingdoms are staggered, switching back and forth in an ingenious method that confuses readers, because the account does not move forward in a straight line but doubles back to catch up on events that occurred earlier in the other kingdom. This method is a way of emphasizing the point that the two kingdoms have a common religious heritage, enduring even when they are political enemies.

There is no reason to doubt the authenticity of the records, especially since at the points where events in Kings are also recounted in extrabiblical texts, the biblical numbers are accurate enough in terms of an absolute chronology. The split into two kingdoms can be dated to 930 BCE, plus or minus no more than ten years, and narrowing to a one-year difference for the fall of the northern kingdom in 722–721 BCE and the destruction of Judah in 587–586 BCE. This of course is not to claim that everything Dtr says about particular kings is factual or that the court records praised or maligned kings as Dtr does. It does, however, strengthen the hypothesis that kings with the biblical names did rule in north and south within the time spans indicated, and that claims Dtr makes about what happened during their reigns must be given serious consideration, which is not the same as validating Dtr's interpretations of events.

Confounded by the early death of Josiah and the subsequent collapse of Judah so soon after the sweeping reforms of Josiah, Dtr resorts to blaming the decline and fall of Judah on Manasseh, "because of all the provocations with which Manasseh had provoked [the LORD]" (2 Kgs. 23:25-27). This is strange since Manasseh preceded Josiah, whose reforms proceed on the assumption that the heartfelt repentance and zealous reforming program of Josiah totally reversed the apostate policies of Manasseh his predecessor. Adding to the confusion is the promise to Josiah that "you shall be gathered to your grave in peace" (2 Kgs. 22:20), an assurance immediately shattered by Josiah's untimely death (2 Kgs. 23:29-30). Even more anomalous is the report by Chr that when Josiah sallied forth to confront Neco, the pharaoh advised him not to attack his Egyptian forces. Speaking in the unexpected role of a prophet, the pharaoh warns Josiah, "Cease opposing God, who is with me [Neco], so that he will not destroy you [Josiah]. . . . He did not listen to the words of Neco from the mouth of God" (2 Chron. 35:20-24). This jumbling of events, both propitious and ominous, represents groping attempts by Dtr and Chr to find causal relationships between Judah's apostate past, its sudden radical renewal, and its precipitous decline and downfall after the reign of Josiah.

Predictions/Commands and Their Fulfillment

Dtr pictures the word of God as often delivered by prophets who predict future events that unfailingly occur or who issue peremptory commands not to be questioned. Even before prophets begin to appear at the dawn of monarchy, Joshua utters an oath declaring that anyone who even starts to rebuild Jericho will do so "at the cost" of his older and younger sons (Josh. 6:26), and this curse is activated during the reign of Ahab, when Hillel of Bethel loses both of his sons upon laying the foundation stone and erecting the gates of Jericho (1 Kgs. 16:33-34). Ahijah prophesies the split into two kingdoms and later announces that the house of Jeroboam will be wiped out because of his idolatry (1 Kgs. 11:29-31; 12:12-5; 14:17-18; 15:29). When an old prophet of Bethel discovers a second prophet has lied, he announces that the lying prophet will not be buried in his family tomb, which proves to be the case after he is killed by a lion (1 Kgs. 13:20-32).

Shemaiah, by the word of the Lord, forbids Rehoboam to try to quell the rebellion of the north: "You shall not go up or fight against your kindred the people of Israel," so Rehoboam doesn't (1 Kgs. 12:22-24). Jehu ben Hanani announces the overthrow of the house of Baasha (16:1-4, 7). Elijah declares a three-year drought in the land (1 Kgs. 17:1) and ends it by defeating the prophets of Baal (1 Kgs. 18:1, 45). Elijah specifies that Ahab will die in Jezreel, the very place where he seized Naboth's vineyard, and he does (1 Kgs. 21:17-19; 22:37-38).

The most awesome of these predictions is made by an unnamed "man of God" who not only declares that the altar at Bethel where Jeroboam worships will be destroyed, but actually names Josiah as the future king who will destroy the profane altar (1 Kgs. 13:1-2). In this instance, the prophet is described as foreseeing an action by a ruler who will not ascend the throne until nearly three hundred years later and will indeed destroy the altar at Bethel as prophesied (2 Kgs. 23:15-20). Isaiah, on hearing that God will spare the life of Hezekiah, declares that the sick king will be healed and add fifteen years to his life (2 Kgs. 20:1-7). Sometimes the prophet not only announces what is to come but also serves as the agent of fulfillment, as when Elisha incites Jehu to overthrow the house of Ahab because of the wickedness of Jezebel, the Baal-worshiping queen, who killed the prophets of God (1 Kgs. 9:1-3, 6-10). And Isaiah becomes the agent for Hezekiah to live on by applying a poultice of figs to the king's boil (2 Kgs. 20:7).

These close engagements of prophets in the unfolding history emphasize that God determines the course of events in response to Israel's fitful commitment to the covenant with YHWH. The prophetic words and actions underscore the thoroughly religious evaluation of the history of the two kingdoms. The literary effect of these prophetic interventions is to move the story forward, to compensate as it were for the interrupting name lists and to give implementation to the programmatic texts. In this way, God's guidance of the history is implemented through persons who are active in the story, but whose authority is independent of the established political and religious leadership, and who as "outsiders" are able to anticipate the outcome of Israel's adherence to or violation of its covenant with God.

Book by Book

One searching for a plot in DH might summarize it on this order: It is the story of a tribal people in covenant with God who, after long bondage, acquire a homeland with great effort in the face of opposition from outside and conflicts within, and who transition from tribal life to a monarchic form of government that, in spite of its pomp and prosperity, splits into two states. Increasingly, these states are dominated by foreign powers, against whom they rebel and are defeated, their leadership deported, and their political and religious independence lost. This downfall of the kingdoms is repeatedly explained as the punishment of God for the people's abandonment of the covenant.

Summarized in this manner, however, the story feels abstract and colorless, lacking the vivid force of the stories about judges, kings, priests, and prophets—brilliant narratives that have earned the praise of Jewish, Christian, and secular readers. Moreover, such a plot summary fails to capture the overarching tension between adhering to or departing from prescribed religious practice that Dtr asserts to be the determining factor in Israel's history. It is a "tragic" tale, but a course self-chosen by the people who nevertheless should have known better, having been warned of the consequences of disobeying the law of Moses (Deuteronomy 27–28). So one of the abiding attractions of DH consists in the way it introduces its readers to religious and political leaders around whom political and religious forces swirl with an uncertain outcome: led by such leaders, will this people live on or die off?

A more detailed book-by-book account of Joshua through Kings reveals the events of Israel's past that Dtr counts as of importance in understanding how and why its initial achievements are cut short by the demise of the kingdoms of Israel and Judah.

Book of Joshua

The book of Joshua is the first chapter in the centuries-long story Dtr records. It begins with Moses handing off leadership of Israel to Joshua with the charge to conquer the land of Canaan. This follows directly on the final verses of Deuteronomy. The significance of Deuteronomy for understanding Dtr is that it presents a body of laws incumbent on Israel to observe (Deuteronomy 12–26), and it is precisely by these laws that Dtr passes judgment on the priests, prophets, and kings of Israel. He gives each of them a "thumbs up" or a "thumbs down" depending on whether or not they have complied with the laws.

To be sure, Joshua purports to be obeying the laws, but he himself fails to fully obey the divine command to annihilate all the inhabitants of Canaan. Joshua aggressively attacks Jericho, Ai, and

Hazor, but he exempts Rahab (Joshua 2; 6:22-25) and the Gibeonite cities (Joshua 9; 10:1-6) from destruction, even though the latter have tricked Joshua into entering a treaty with them. So, although the laws are to be kept in their totality on pain of death (Deuteronomy 28), the first generation after Moses is already knowingly breaking them. Israelites have joined Canaanites in marriage and in worship, which is tantamount to breaking faith with the God of Israel. Much as Joshua has tried to conquer the entire promised land, large parts of Canaan and Transjordan remain unconquered. The stated reason for this failure is that the conquerors have broken divine commands and must accept partial victory as their punishment. However, a bit later in DH, a different reason is given for the continued resistance of Canaanites: they are allowed to stay on in the land in order to train Israel in the arts of war (Judg. 3:1-2).

Book of Judges

The most striking feature of the book of Judges is the dramatic change in the protagonist of the story. In Joshua, as throughout the Torah, the subject of the story is a united people, Israel, under the leadership of Joshua, in continuity with the united people under Moses. Suddenly in the stories of Judges, the single entity Israel breaks into its tribal components who act alone or in combinations as they choose. The largest of these intertribal actions is celebrated in the Song of Deborah, where six tribes fight together and four tribes are condemned for failing to show up for battle (Judges 5). This presupposes that Israel consists of tribal units that ought to act in unison but may not do so. In the other episodes in Judges, the actors are single tribes, or at most two or three together, with charismatic military leaders who arise from time to time: Othniel, Ehud, Deborah, Gideon, Jephthah, and Samson. Dtr presents these leaders of the moment as the best Israel can muster to carry on the work of Moses and Joshua, yet most of them show no knowledge of the Mosaic law by which Dtr judges them!

Only in the last episode of the book are all the tribes united, save one, to punish the tribe of Benjamin because it is held responsible for the rape and murder of a Levite's concubine (Judges 19–21). The book ends with a detailed account of this horrific crime, which the narrator insists demands a king, who would presumably prevent such deplorable behavior (21:25). It appears that Dtr wants to conceive of Israel as a unity, but is pressured by his sources into drawing the picture of a seriously fragmented people who repeatedly breach the law of Moses. Only the long-suffering lenience of YHWH allows the story of Israel to continue. The last word of Judges, "In those days there was no king in Israel; every man [tribe?] did what was right in his [its?] own eyes (21:25)," clearly anticipates the kingdom of David, as it also embraces the implicit understanding that the deeds condemned in the book are not only divisive of community but also stand in blatant violation of the law. However, which deeds are condemned? Only those of the Gibeonites, or also of Micah and the Danites (Judges 17–18), as well as the idolatry that leads to the cycles of oppression and deliverance? What about the behavior of the judges who deliver Israel but also engage in actions inimical to the laws? Abimelech, the would-be king, dies in retribution for the murder of his brothers, and the Shechemites who follow him perish as the just punishment for their folly (Judg. 9:56-57), but there is no claim that he is a judge, even a lapsed judge.

Books of Samuel and Kings: The United Kingdom

The history of the united kingdom of David and Solomon is told in one long stretch in 1–2 Samuel and 1 Kings 1–11. Dtr accords so much space to telling the story of the establishment of the monarchy in part because his sources were especially abundant for this era, but also because he wants to describe the historical roots of the Davidic dynasty and the Jerusalem temple, the two institutions that rival the law of Moses in importance, which are not necessarily in conflict, but become so as the post-Solomonic rulers undermine the moral foundations of dynasty and temple. Extended attention is given to tracing the rise of David to the kingship, with the intention to exonerate him of all suspicions that he conspired against Saul. The reported decline of Saul is intertwined with the ascent of David as his rival and eventual successor. Once established on the throne, serious conflicts erupt within David's family following his murder of Uriah in order to acquire Bathsheba as wife. These family conflicts are intertwined with his struggle to retain the throne against rebellions, one being led by his own son, Absalom. Although David is rebuked by Nathan the prophet, and David even "repents" of the Bathsheba affair, he is not required to give her up (2 Sam. 12:1-25), and it is Bathsheba's cunning advocacy that secures the throne for her son Solomon (1 Kgs. 1:11-21, 28-31).

The achievements of David as king, beyond his military successes against the Philistines and Transjordanian kings, are lightly touched on. His rule over his subjects is pictured as being much less onerous than that of Solomon. David aspires to build a permanent temple for YHWH in Jerusalem, but is prevented from doing so by the prophet Nathan, who declares God's extreme displeasure with "a man of blood" honoring the deity in this fashion (2 Samuel 7). David proves very indulgent of his adult sons and seems to have been lax in his duties as chief justice in the system of criminal law. All in all, David is portrayed as remarkably human in showing his failings as well as his accomplishments. The David described here is far from the paragon of virtue and piety elsewhere venerated as preeminent psalmist (2 Sam. 23:1) and the very model of the messianic ruler to come (Isa. 9:1-7; 11:1-9). Solomon becomes successor to David after a bitter dynastic fight in which he forcibly suppresses a powerful faction backing his brother Adonijah.

Opening his reign with an iron fist, Solomon is emboldened to launch an ambitious program to increase the wealth and extend the power of his kingdom. His basic resources were heavy taxation on the agricultural surpluses of his peasant subjects, supplemented by income from tolls on caravans in transit, as well as shrewd commercial deals as middle man for the arms sales of Anatolian horses and Egyptian chariots to other states. In order to secure his booming economic empire, Solomon reaches for military superiority by building massive fortifications and equipping large chariot forces. With his newfound wealth, he builds the temple in Jerusalem that his father had been forbidden to build, along with a palace that greatly exceeds the temple in size. This temple would have been little more than a royal chapel rather than the national shrine that Dtr anachronistically envisions as the sole legitimate place of worship in Israel.

To facilitate state administration, Solomon redistricts his kingdom and appoints officials in each of the new districts, centralizing his command structure to secure delivery of taxes and to forestall rebellion against his regime, such as the rebellions David had to put down (1 Kgs. 4:1-28). In short, Solomon is pictured as hugely successful in securing a luxurious and privileged life for a small upper class in government and trade, but only with contradictory policies that threaten agricultural production by pulling peasants off the land to form labor battalions for his pet building projects (5:13-18; 9:10-21). He overspends to the point that he has to pay off a debt to the king of Tyre by surrendering a sizable area of his kingdom (1 Kgs. 9:10-14).

One would think that the enhancement of the power and wealth of his kingdom would have secured Solomon the unalloyed approval of Dtr. This, however, is not the case. It is true that the king's successes are attributed to wisdom bestowed on him by God (1 Kgs. 3:3-28; 4:29-34). Moreover, the lavish adornment of the temple and its appointments and the pomp of its dedication are reported in great detail, because for Dtr the building of the temple is Solomon's principal achievement (1 Kings 5–6; 7:9-51). In fact, Dtr insists that this Jerusalem temple is the sole site where YHWH worship can henceforth be carried out, and it becomes the litmus test by which Dtr judges all later kings: Did they or did they not restrict worship to Jerusalem? In glaring contrast to his noble start, Solomon eventually falls into idolatry by adopting the gods of the many wives he has acquired in diplomatic alliances with other countries (1 Kgs. 11:1-13)

A further contradiction arises when it becomes evident that Jeroboam, the leader of the northern labor battalions, rebels against Solomon, not because of idolatry in the narrow religious sense, but because of the heavy social and economic burdens Solomon's policy of forced labor has imposed on the north (1 Kgs. 11:27; 12:1-20). To further complicate Dtr's account, the split of the kingdom approved as divine punishment on Solomon automatically consigns all northern worship of YHWH to idolatry, since the northerners no longer recognize the religious legitimacy of the Davidic dynasty in Jerusalem and will henceforth have nothing to do with worship in what has now become a foreign state (12:25-33). In effect, Jeroboam is damned if he does separate from Judah and damned if he doesn't!

Book of Kings: The Two Kingdoms

It is axiomatic for Dtr that Solomon built a temple intended to be the sole place of worship in his kingdom and in the reigns of all his successors. In his account of the two kingdoms, Dtr holds fast to this prohibition of worship at any other site than the Jerusalem temple. This immediately means that any and all worship practiced in the northern kingdom is condemned by Dtr, even though the northern prophets (Elijah and Elisha and later Hosea), while lambasting their rulers for infidelity to YHWH, do not include failure to worship at Jerusalem as one of these infractions. It also means that every subsequent ruler in Judah is judged by a religious requirement that did not come into force until centuries later under Kings Hezekiah and Josiah. Consequently, even when Dtr has some good things to say about particular kings, he counts their rule as a failure if they allow worship at any other place in the kingdom (characteristically, "on the high places" of false worship).

In spite of this grossly contradictory and flagrantly anachronistic religious criterion that Dtr has applied to the post-Solomonic rulers of both kingdoms, his account provides a considerable body of information about social, political, and religious conditions. Much of this information appears to have been drawn from court documents cited as "the Book of the Records of the Kings of Israel," paired with a similar source for the kings of Judah. Where the chronology of the royal reigns intersects with events also reported by Assyrian and Babylonian texts, its dates are confirmed. There is also information about religious developments in both kingdoms, which disclose practices outlawed by Deuteronomy. In addition, there is a sizable body of traditions about the northern prophets Elijah and Elisha, who worship apart from Jerusalem without Dtr's censure. These inconsistencies in the criteria in the historical books for valid worship are indicative of a document that tells us the views of Dtr and his several sources without much of an attempt to reconcile them.

Instead of recounting the two histories one after the other, or interweaving their fortunes so as to emphasize certain phases or aspects of the two histories, Dtr treats political events in Israel and Judah in self-contained literary panels devoted to each ruler. Moreover, the sequence of these panels switches back and forth between north and south. The result is a staggered recital of the two kingdom histories, entailing some repetitions and a certain amount of chronological "backtracking." Into this synchronic framework are inserted annalistic accounts of diplomatic maneuvers, battles, political coups and purges, deeds of prophets, and religious reforms. Chronicles follows the same regnal formulas for Judah as does 1–2 Kings but lacks the latter's synchronisms, since it does not recount the full history of the north but only episodes involving Judah.

Ingenious as is this interweaving of the northern and southern histories, it fails to give a balanced, coherent account, broken as it is into brief glimpses of the reigns of a majority of the kings, but alternating with fuller accounts of others. This creates a pronounced disproportion in coverage, such that we have in effect two styles of presentation, one consisting of little more than a chronicling of events and the other going into greater detail about rulers who initiated religious reforms centered on the Jerusalem temple (Jehoash, Hezekiah, Josiah) or who interacted with prophets (Ahab, Hezekiah), while saying surprisingly little about kings whom we otherwise know or suspect to have been major political figures (Omri, Jeroboam II, Manasseh).

Why did Dtr resort to such a tortuous manner of recounting the histories of the two kingdoms? He did so, it seems, in order to underscore his belief that the history of the two kingdoms was actually the history of one people with a common religion. Politically, there were two kingdoms, but they spoke the same language, shared the same culture, and practiced the same religion, albeit in regional variations. Following the acclaimed reigns of David and Solomon, the rulers of the two kingdoms, with a few exceptions, are described as a sorry lot, unacceptable to YHWH because of the political corruption, social injustice, and religious apostasy they practiced or permitted. The exceptions are Hezekiah and Josiah, who undertook religious reforms that cleansed the Jerusalem temple of foreign accretions and reestablished it as the sole legitimate place of worship. The reforms of Josiah so closely correspond to the religious demands of Deuteronomy that the book on which Josiah is said to have based his actions is generally taken to be Deuteronomy or some version thereof. The reforms of Hezekiah manage to spare Jerusalem from destruction by the Assyrians, but in spite of Josiah's laudable, more extensive reforms, they do not prevent Josiah from execution by the Egyptians or the eventual destruction of Jerusalem and its temple by the Neo-Babylonians. These political catastrophes following earnest reforms are so troubling to Dtr that he explains them as due to the evil deeds of King Manasseh, which outweigh the reformers' achievements.

Fact-Checking the Historical Books

Are the "historical books" an accurate account of the early history of Israel? Yes and no.

No, in the sense that they are not word-for-word transcripts of events that occurred long ago, and they misjudge the time when worship at the Jerusalem temple was mandated as the sole place of worship for all Israelites. The events recorded and the time and place of those doing the recording are so far removed from one another—often by many centuries—that the very capacity of Dtr and Chr to know the past in great detail is thrown into doubt, and the sources at their disposal lack no more than scraps of eyewitness testimony. The sources they depended on mostly showed so little interest in doing history as we know it that we do them an injustice to measure them against the practices of present-day historiography.

Both "historians" certainly had an urgent reason for writing as they did. Their overwhelming concern was to describe the past as best they could in order to lay a foundation for rebuilding a new "Israelite/Judahite" community after the destruction of Jerusalem. They differ, however, in what they conceive that "foundation" to be. Writing after the temple is rebuilt, Chr asserts that the future of Israel lies in faithful worship at the restored temple led by priests and Levites according to the arrangement prescribed by David and Solomon. Writing before the restoration of Judah, Dtr has in mind that the society prescribed in the book of Deuteronomy should be the basis of the restored community. However, Deuteronomy's laws had been so infrequently observed in the history that it seemed unthinkable for Dtr to anticipate an independent Judah. That would require the dubious return of the dynasty of David, not to mention permission and support from the imperial overlord, Neo-Babylonia or Persia. He is so deeply uncertain about Israel's future that he can offer no more than the hint of the future by relating the favor accorded to the captive king of Judah by the Neo-Babylonian king. Concerning the condition of the survivors of the fall of the northern kingdom, Dtr and Chr seem to have no knowledge and little historical interest.

Yes, Dtr writes a trustworthy "history," provided we allow a fairly broad conception of history-writing and correct for anachronisms. However, when Chr introduces material not in Dtr, it is of uncertain worth. The genre in which Dtr and Chr have cast their narratives is sometimes called "history-like tradition." In short, they are works of the historical imagination, employing the sources at hand but shaped by the imaginative vision of the writer. Dtr presents an amazing array of portraits of the past, some being better anchored historically than others. Chr presents a monochromatic view of the past, single-mindedly focused on the ascent and triumph of David and erection of the temple by Solomon, with no more than a glance at other aspects of Israel's past. Chr's account is narrowly and unrelentingly religious, with no interest in Joshua, Judges, or events in the life of David before he ascends the throne.

In assessing the accuracy of Dtr, it is essential to understand his mind-set. Dtr is primarily interested in the religion of ancient Israel. He traces the fortune of the belief and practice of Yahwism, reaching heights under David, Solomon, Hezekiah, and Josiah but lapsing into idolatry and prohibited behavior for long stretches of time under judges and kings. Sadly, a majority of the populace of both kingdoms has abandoned the cult of YHWH or clings to corrupt forms of worship. In Dtr's view, God has tolerated this faithlessness and corruption for centuries. In exasperation, God finally abandons both kingdoms and delivers them to conquest by the Assyrian Empire and the Neo-Babylonian Empire. Over the centuries, the erring people of Israel and Judah have become so apostate that God delivers both kingdoms into the hands of the great empires, who not only defeat them militarily but destroy their political and religious institutions as well, leaving them bereft of resources to rebuild community. The troubled and agitated mind-set of Dtr is preoccupied with this tale of the cataclysmic end of both kingdoms.

As he writes, Dtr knows that these terrible events have left the people in despair. YHWH has warned Israel through Moses and subsequent leaders that it risks annihilation if it abandons exclusive worship of the deity. The defecting populace has no excuse, but they have come to overly rely on the promise to David of an eternal kingdom. Surely, out of his love for David, God will not break his promise and the line of David will continue to give the people confidence in God's forbearance and shelter from foreign aggressors. Surely, they reasoned, God would not cut off the dynasty of David or permit desecration of the holy sanctuary. But Dtr, the leaders, and the people were wrong. So, even though it is difficult to establish the facticity of many of the details in these history-like traditions, the overriding "fact" is the threatened demise of stateless Israel, which the author is seeking to forestall by telling the amazing story of the people through multiple generations.

Three Zones of Political Economy

Dtr and Chr focus on the political and religious histories of Israel, but give far less attention to the social and economic facets of life in the periods they cover. To get a more fully rounded picture of the terrain Dtr covers, we must shift our inquiry into an entirely different register by calling on the social sciences to help us grasp the society-wide context *in* which and *about* which Dtr and Chr wrote.

Political economy is the way goods are produced and distributed in a society under prevailing forms of social and political power. When analyzed, this process yields an answer to a key question about any society: *Who* gets what, *how* do they get it, and, if possible, *why* do they get what they do get? In its long history, ancient Israel passed through three zones or modes of production (hereafter MP).

1. The Communitarian Tribal MP (reflected in Joshua and Judges and evident in some of the tribal rosters in 1 Chronicles)
2. The Native Tributary MP (1–2 Samuel; 1 Kings as far as 2 Kgs. 23:30 // 1 Chron. 10:1—2 Chron. 35:16)
3. The Imperial Tributary MP (2 Kgs. 23:31—25:30 // 2 Chron. 35:20—36:23)

Now, for ancient Israel, the primary production of the necessities of life—namely, the agrarian and pastoral yields of grains, fruits, olives, milk, wine, and occasional meat—continued more or less the same over its entire history. What marked the difference between these modes is the allotment of what is produced. In the Communitarian (or Household) MP the people who produce are those who garner their product directly without payment to or permission of third parties. In the Native Tributary MP, what is produced is subject to onerous loans, taxation, and forced labor imposed by a central government and an elite class, and the remainder is allotted to the producers. In the Imperial

Tributary MP, what is produced is "taken off the top" by the imperial elite, secondly by the native elite, and finally the remainder of the product, such as it is, is allotted to the producers.

The Communitarian MP

Early Israel was born as an anti-imperial resistance movement that broke away from Egyptian and Canaanite dominion to become a self-governing community of free peasants who emerged in the central highlands of Palestine toward the close of the thirteenth century BCE. Israelite subsistence lay in the cultivation of crops that they enjoyed, freed from the double taxation of tribute in kind to nearby city-states and to the Egyptian Empire. Instead of their surplus production being taken to support national or imperial elites, as was the case among peoples living around them, it was directly consumed or bartered or shared in a system of mutual aid characterizing the Communitarian MP. Israelites controlled their own lives, labor, and produce with an enhanced sense of dignity and self-worth. Loans in kind to assist impoverished farmers were offered without interest. Owing to difficult growing conditions, theirs was not an easy life, but it compared favorably with peasants subject to state and empire.

The marks of the Communitarian MP are everywhere exhibited in the first Israelite MP. Their society is without centralized government. They are a loose association of tribes with common interests in livelihood, domestic peace, defense, and religion. Tribal elders in consultation decided on major issues within the tribe, and deliberated on external matters that affected the whole tribe, such as joining other tribes in self-defense. There was room for charismatic leaders (so-called judges) to rally the tribes to battle. A covenant linked the tribes in worship to YHWH, but other forms of religion were practiced, probably viewed in many cases as manifestations of YHWH or at least permitted, since YHWH was not believed to be the only deity—just the most powerful as well as the special god of the Israelites.

The antipathy of early Israelites to centralized political structures is dramatically highlighted by their repeated mockery of the brutality, incompetence, and misrule of kings, expressed in narratives about the king of Jericho (Josh. 2:1-4), the Canaanite ruler Adonizedek (Judg. 1:5-7), the Moabite king Eglon (Judg. 3:5-25), and the rise and fall of Abimelech, who aspired to kingship in Israel (Judges 9). The crowning blow against the arrogance and self-inflation of rulers is brilliantly etched in Jotham's fable about the "trees" that set out to anoint a king over themselves. Three trees are invited in succession to become king: the olive tree, the fig tree, and the grapevine. All three scornfully reject the offer because they do not want to abandon their socioeconomic role as providers of Israel with food and drink. However, the nonproductive bramble readily agrees to serve as king and ludicrously offers refuge to the trees in its shade, which of course the scraggly bramble does not possess (Judg. 9:7-15). The patent lesson of this satirical fable declares that kings are socially and economically worse than useless, since they make false promises to their subjects and in the end bring destruction on those who rely on them. The military leader Gideon is said to have erred in making an image for worship, but he is credited with refusing to accept the role of king that some of his troops propose. As he succinctly puts it, "I will not rule over you, and my son will not rule over you; YHWH will rule over you" (8:23).

The fragile unity of the tribes is illustrated by six tribes responding to the muster of troops for a major battle against Canaanite kings (Judges 4–5). When four tribes are condemned for not responding, the only sanction that can be imposed on the offending tribes is a religious curse. Using primitive weapons and guerrilla tactics, and with the help of a flash flood, the tribes achieve victory by immobilizing the Canaanite chariots. The victory is attributed to YHWH, but the agency is credited to the peasant warriors of Israel. So it is throughout the Hebrew Bible that the acts of God claimed to guide Israel's history are nearly always enacted by humans.

The Native Tributary MP

There is a great gulf in social organization between "the regulated anarchy" of tribes without rulers and the hierarchic state organization that restructures society with priorities, powers, and values that befit the rule of elites who consume what the lower classes produce. Tribes do not "evolve" into states. In fact, they resist the state as both unnecessary and invasive. Always some factors "push" the tribe toward statehood. By far the primary pressure arises from states that threaten to overwhelm tribes and incorporate them into the invasive state, even when such a manufactured political status is cast as a vassal state. In our time, this has been the reality of the so-called third world, where tribe after tribe has fallen under the control of invasive states eager to build empires on the contention that "might makes right." But the pressure from outside is often preceded or accompanied by internal forces of two kinds: weak or corrupt leadership from within the tribe or collaboration of some tribesmen who encourage or hasten state control, often because they are rewarded by the enemy state.

In early Israel, the tribes resisted the Philistines, a powerful league of city-states eager to turn the Israelite highlands into a "breadbasket" to deliver the cereals that were in short supply in the Philistine coastal plain. Samuel, a priest and seer—and in many ways the last of the judges—managed to keep the Philistines at bay for some time. But, as the situation darkened, the cry went up for a warrior-king who would overcome the Philistines and secure domestic tranquility.

With their tunnel vision, most tribesmen did not realize what else went with kingship. Samuel warns them that along with the military strength of kingship come transformations of society so far-reaching that they spell the loss of tribal life and the Communitarian MP, precisely the social and economic institutions that most Israelites cherish, even the very folk now demanding a king. "You shall be his [the king's] slaves" (1 Sam. 8:17). In short, these measures taken together strike at the integrity and viability of village life, where at least 85 to 95 percent of Israelites continued to live.

Samuel's warning rejected, Israel set forth on the road to statehood. The first three kings were assertive leaders, each of them taking steps to introduce and tighten the structures of state rule, precisely as Samuel had predicted. Saul operates as "a glorified judge," who lacks most of the powers that a king exercises while he seeks in vain to secure a dynasty. David operates as a crafty chieftain who holds the loyalty of the tribes for a time, long enough to make Jerusalem his state capital, lay down the rudiments of state organization, and begin a long-lived dynasty. Solomon increases the powers of state by introducing systematic taxation and forced labor, lives extravagantly, connects diplomatically with other states, builds the elegant temple. His displays of wealth and power backfire on him as he runs into debt and pushes his forced labor battalions until they rebel, and the northern tribes withdraw from his rule altogether, forsaking Judah and Jerusalem to found their own state. This new state eventually falls prey to the same Tributary MP against which it has revolted, replacing Solomon with the autocratic house of Omri and subsequent kings. Kingship, centralized rule, was anathema to the tribes, even when they were compelled to come to terms with the state. It is perhaps more correct to say that the sentiment of many tribesmen was to adopt the state, while others abhorred adoption or submission to statehood. Israelite attitudes toward the state continued to reflect this ambivalence.

The Imperial Tributary MP

At the level of the production of goods, the Imperial Tributary MP sustains the same shape it took under the Native Tributary MP, but the distribution of agrarian wealth escalates, flowing to the upper class as it weakens the cultivators and herdsmen who produce what wealth the nation possesses. It was characteristic of the empires to retain the mode of production of the conquered and to retain some of the former royal staff to supervise the producing class below them, and even on occasion appoint a puppet "king." Empires tended to have two stages in the absorption of foreign lands. At first, the conquered states, still intact, were given the status of "vassal kingdoms." The former ruler may have been retained as administrator if judged to be loyal and competent. Hezekiah and Manasseh apparently held this status when the Assyrians overpowered Judah and ruled until Josiah broke free as the Assyrian Empire declined. In the second phase, vassal states were turned into provinces of the empire and governed by imperial appointments. In some cases, the officers of vassal states were deported, this being the case with Judah. On occasion, whole populations were deported and replaced with captives transferred from abroad, as was the fate of Israel, the northern kingdom.

It is the conviction of Dtr and Chr that obeying or disobeying the law of Moses determines the course of Israel's history. Granted that a people's religion may be an important factor in its corporate life, nonetheless the biblical account is a gross simplification. It ignores, downplays, or does not recognize the interplay of economic, social, and political factors that shape the context of Israel's religion. Simply put, the course of Israel's experience from tribal life to statehood, and on to eventual extinction by more powerful states, was much the same course followed by other small states in the ancient Near East. Even had Israel and Judah kept the law of Moses in its entirety, it is not likely that either kingdom would have been able to withstand the juggernauts of Assyria, Neo-Babylonia, and Persia or the depredations of their ruling elite.

What *is* different about Israel is that it preserved an extensive national literature that contains abundant indications of the trajectory from tribal life through independent statehood to foreign domination. For instance, we may safely say that nearby Moabite, Ammonite, and Edomite states took shape as stateless societies that practiced the Communitarian MP, and then advanced to kingship and the Native Tributary MP before being extinguished by the Assyrian Empire in much the same way that Israel was conquered. Also, it is known that these peoples worshiped national deities thought to control their destinies, much as Israel conceived of YHWH's role amid his people Israel.

We tend to treat Israel's history as distinctive and its religion as superior to other religions, over-looking Israel's immersion in ancient Near Eastern culture, because the religion of ancient Israel developed without a break into rabbinic Judaism and Christianity. In short, Dtr's and Chr's views on the history and the religion of ancient Israel have been "saved" by their canonization as Scripture, not because they are adequate sociohistorical accounts. The point is that just as the religion of other small states was interwoven with their economy, society, and politics, so exactly was the religion of ancient Israel bound up with its economic production, social structure, and political order. In this way, judicious use of the social sciences can facilitate our understanding of the origins of the religions we practice. Because the secular and religious dimensions are so closely related, we shall misconstrue the religion by isolating it from all the other aspects of life. Quite the contrary, if we are to see the religion of ancient Israel in the depth and detail that its impact on our lives categorically merits, we must come to terms with how it has been shaped by the enduring structural effects of political centralization, social stratification, shifts in land tenure, and the transformation wrought by international trade, diplomacy, and warfare. In brief, in ancient Israel, materiality and spirituality are not only joined but also inextricably intertwined.

The Historical Books over the Centuries

The historical books have undergone (one is inclined to say "suffered") the same range of interpretation as the rest of the Bible. In what sense are they true? Do they tell us what to do? Some say no and some say yes.

Literalists, on the one hand, say that every (or nearly every) word of the historical books is accurate. If the biblical text says that the sun stood still at Gibeon, the sun certainly did stand still (Joshua 10). If 1 Kings reports that Solomon spoke 3,000 proverbs, wrote 1,005 songs (4:13) and had 1,000 wives and concubines (11:3), those are the exact numbers, no more and no less. When 2 Kings reports that an angel of the Lord killed 185,000 Assyrian soldiers in one night, both the angelic agency of the slaughter and the huge number of casualties are accepted without question (2 Kgs. 19:35).

Nonliteralists, on the other hand, view the sun standing still as symbolizing the determination of Joshua's troops, with the help of the heavens, to finish off the Canaanites in short order. The writer, overawed by the grandeur of Solomon's reign, piles up claims about the volume of his productivity in sealing diplomatic marriages and in creating proverbs and songs. The huge number of Assyrians slain by the messenger of God dramatically underscores the miraculous delivery of Jerusalem from Sennacherib's tightening siege.

Thus, for some readers, the words of the Bible, spoken by the mouth of deity, are the very Word of God, while others, without prejudice to their religious value, believe that the Bible is subject to the same rules and practices of interpretation as all other books. Flowing from these differing hermeneutics, readers reach divergent conclusions regarding the applicability of biblical texts in today's world. Are the historical books a proper source for Jewish and Christian ethics? If so, in what sense and with what consequences?

For example, Joshua's murder of all Canaanites and the seizure of their land has been "a bone in the throat" of innumerable readers, while others relish it. Is it simply a recital of past events or does it in some way reinforce, even legitimate, the aggressive policies and practices of nations today? All we need to do is cite the brutal record of Western colonialism, in the course of which "inferior" peoples have been plundered, their land seized, and literally millions on millions of them have been killed without compunction. Other similar instances are worldwide: the treatment of Native Americans by transplanted Europeans; the dispossession of South Africans by British and Boer settlers; the murder of Chinese by Japanese invaders; the murder of Jews, gypsies, and homosexuals by Germans; and we could continue the litany. Moreover, some Jews and Christians consider Joshua's taking over Canaan as outright biblical support for the state of Israel's occupation and settlement of Palestinian land, regardless of international rules of warfare to the contrary. All these atrocities are justified by the right of nations to wage war, the policy of "might makes right," and the dehumanization of whole populations.

Do nations commit these atrocities because they have been motivated by reading Joshua? No, the will to colonize was already there, but in the eyes of many Jews and Christians, Joshua's deeds excuse their own nation's aggression by giving it religious sanction. It does not greatly help to argue historically that the first Israelites were actually themselves native to Canaan and that such killing as occurred was directed chiefly against city-state rulers and officials, not the general population. It matters little to most readers that the Israelites were colonists under attack by colonial Egypt and their Palestinian allies, since most readers know only the Joshua account as fantasized by Dtr. However, Joshua aside, the other historical books teem with violence, and it would be an impossible task to eliminate all violence-laden texts. If we did, it would be something like Jefferson's shortened Bible!

Yet another questionable use of the Bible is to cast an aura of authority and invincibility around rulers in Christendom, ever since Christianity became the official religion of the Roman Empire. The key text in the historical books is 2 Samuel 7, which promises David an everlasting dynasty, a promise brilliantly confirmed by the wealth and power of his son Solomon. Since it is in the nature of political leadership to hold on to power as long as possible, this assurance of divine appointment and longevity of the head of state has been tempting consolation to rulers and a warning against rebellion by those ruled. Ever since Christianity was adopted as the official religion of the Roman Empire, heads of state have happily laid claim to similar divine endorsement. "The divine right of kings" has been the bulwark against any who would threaten the emperor, king, or prince of the moment. Of course, little attention has been given to the caveat buried in the Davidic promise, "when he commits iniquity, I will chasten him with the rod of men" (7:14 RSV), much less to the unholy conduct of a succession of kings following Solomon who are roundly criticized by Dtr as well as by the Latter Prophets. It is not surprising that postbiblical monarchs and their ecclesiastical minions have failed to follow the whole narrative of kingship throughout the historical books. Of course, as monarchy has waned and democracy has prospered, appeal to the Davidic promise is largely an empty gesture, even if retained ceremonially with the trappings of religious sanctity. Nonetheless, it is arguable that the substance of the promise has transmogrified into its secular equivalent by claiming the unshakable foundation of the state, any state, through all changes in its leadership, even when corrupt or incompetent.

Nevertheless, while the present heads of state and their regimes bask in the confidence that God will uphold their power, there are others who go beyond 2 Samuel 7 to read all of the historical books and prophets and, in doing so, notice how the majority of rulers have broken faith with the lofty terms of their installation, so seriously that the line of David falls, along with all the political, social, and religious institutions of Judah. Some of these contemporary readers are severe critics of the conduct of their own state, which is allegedly securing justice at home and peace abroad. In fact, some of the political critics have turned the Davidic promise on its head by affirming the right of rebellion against unjust rule, citing the rebellions of Absalom and Shebah against David, Jeroboam against Solomon, and Jehu against the House of Omri. Indeed, in the historical books, Dtr provides numerous examples both of kings worthy of support and those deserving of severe criticism, even death.

Taking the historical books in their wider biblical context, we see that the legacy of ancient Israel provides no distinctive politics and no template for translating culture and religion into viable social programs and polities. The historical books have been mined not only in support of the divine right of kings (or of any autocratic rulers) but also in support of the countervailing right of revolt against unjust authorities. Additionally, the historical books have been used to give support to a wide spectrum of political systems, such as covenanted commonwealths, liberal democracy, nationalism, capitalism, anarchy, and socialism. This search for a biblical warrant for particular political systems is due in part to the scriptural and cultural authority vested in the Hebrew Bible, repeatedly tempting proponents of sociopolitical systems to claim biblical legitimation. This problematic basing of politics on biblical warrants is further encouraged by the unsystematic and unreconciled political structures, practices, and values expressed in the Hebrew Bible, containing elements thought to have affinities with one or another modern political system. The best governance and social order are the province of history, social ethics, and political science, not the historical books of the Hebrew Bible.

Works Referenced

Berrigan, Daniel. 2008. *The Kings and Their Gods: The Pathology of Power*. Grand Rapids: Eerdmans.

Gottwald, Norman. 2001. *The Politics of Ancient Israel*. Louisville: Westminster John Knox.

Grabbe, Lester L., ed. 2005. *Good Kings and Bad Kings*. New York: T&T Clark.

Hawk, Daniel L. 2010. *Joshua in 3-D: A Commentary on Biblical Conquest and Manifest Destiny*. Eugene, OR: Cascade.

Horsley, Richard, ed. 2008. *In the Shadow of Empire: Reclaiming the Bible as a History of Faithful Resistance*. Louisville: Westminster John Knox.

Jobling, David. 1998. *1 Samuel*. Berit Olam. Collegeville, MN: Liturgical Press.

Lasine, Stewart. 2001. *Knowing Kings: Knowledge, Power, and Narcissism*. Atlanta: Society of Biblical Literature.

Polzin, Robert. 1993. *David and the Deuteronomist: 2 Samuel*. Bloomington: Indiana University Press.

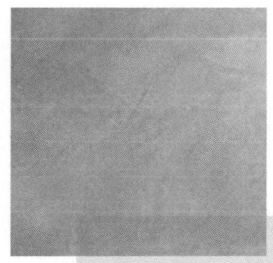

JOSHUA

Pekka M. A. Pitkänen

Introduction

The book of Joshua, following on the narrative of the Pentateuch, describes how the Israelite people, having been liberated from slavery in Egypt and made a covenant with YHWH at Horeb in the wilderness of Sinai and at the plains of Moab, now move on to conquer and settle the land of Canaan. Joshua 1–5 describes the crossing of the River Jordan, and 6–12 portrays the main Israelite conquest. Joshua 13–21 then describes the allotment of the land, with some short, conquest-related interludes. Joshua 22–24 describes a number of events after Israel has settled, with Joshua in chapters 23–24 exhorting the Israelites to follow YHWH, just before his death. Hendrik Koorevaar succinctly describes this four-partite division as follows: 1:1—5:12 *avar* ("cross"), 5:13—12:24 *laqah* ("take"), 13:1—21:45 *halaq* ("divide"), and 22:1—24:33 *avad* ("serve") (Koorevaar, 283).

As Joshua 1–9 and 13–24 ultimately describe just a few events, the book of Joshua really appears to be about the allotment and settlement of the land in a larger context and over a longer period of time. This is mostly achieved by war, but also relatively peacefully in parts (e.g., 17:12-13), and large swathes of land are still classified as unconquered (esp. 13:1-7). The book's literary style has affinities with other extant ancient Near Eastern conquest accounts (see esp. Younger). A number of comments interspersed throughout the book imply a date of writing already at least somewhat removed from the time of the events portrayed (e.g., 6:25; 7:26; 13:13; 15:63).

The Masoretic text (MT) of Joshua differs from that of the Septuagint (LXX) to some extent, but not radically. The main divergences are found in connection with 5:2-9 (circumcision at Gilgal), 6:1-15 (the circling of Jericho), the placement of 8:30-35 (Ebal incident) and 20:1-6 (establishment of the towns of refuge), and there are a few extra verses at the end of the book in Greek. There is also variation between the MT and LXX in the town and boundary lists of Joshua 13–21. For simplicity, this commentary will mostly follow the MT, noting some of the main divergences and some possible implications (for more detailed treatments, see, e.g., Butler; Nelson; Meer; Tov).

The book of Joshua incorporates various sources, such as the poem in 10:12-13 (note the Book of Yashar mentioned in the verse) and the town and territorial lists in chapters 11–21. In the larger context, since the birth of modern biblical criticism, the book of Joshua was generally seen as part of the Hexateuch (Genesis–Joshua), with Joshua completing the story of Israel from creation to conquest. However, since the publication of Martin Noth's *Deuteronomistic History* in 1943 (for the ET, see Noth 1991), Joshua has generally been seen as part of the Deuteronomistic History, which spans from Deuteronomy to 2 Kings, incorporating earlier sources into a Deuteronomistic frame-work and then also some post-Deuteronomistic Priestly additions. Recently, a number of scholars have rejected the idea of a Deuteronomistic History and essentially returned to the Hexateuch theory (see, e.g., Westermann; Carr; Otto 2000; 2012; Dozeman, Römer, and Schmid), and this basic concept is followed here (see also Pitkänen 2010, 2013a).

It is recognized that Joshua and Deuteronomy are closely connected. As modern biblical criti-cism has generally dated Deuteronomy to the seventh century BCE (see, e.g., Otto 2012, 62–230), Joshua, too, has been dated to the same time, even though it is seen to have possibly incorporated earlier traditions (see Noort). With the rise of the discipline of archaeology, scholars since the latter part of the nineteenth century (see, e.g., Moorey; cf. Levy for the present status) have generally viewed events described in the Bible from the period of the judges on as reflecting actual history, but events earlier than that became suspect. In addition, some recent, more "radical," or minimalist, scholars have argued that biblical Israel is a scholarly construct from the Persian period (see, e.g., Lemche; T. L. Thompson) and that nothing can really be known about preexilic Israel based on biblical documents. Historically, there have been three main models for the Israelite conquest and settlement (see Dever for a summary). First, the conquest model argued for the general veracity of the biblical record, even though it moved the date of the conquest from the thirteenth century to the fifteenth century implied by the biblical chronology. Second, the peaceful infiltration model suggested that the Israelites were nomads who peacefully immigrated to the land from outside. Third, the peasant's revolt model proposed that the Israelites were Canaanites who revolted against the existing socioeconomic structure and withdrew to the highlands to form a new society. All three of these models have been subjected to criticism. Most recently, the indigenous origins of the Isra-elites has often been held (see, e.g., Dever), with some allowance for an external influx of people as well (e.g., Faust). In terms of diversity of opinion, presently the so-called maximalists tend to date the book early and to see it largely as reflecting actual history, with a modified form of the original conquest model that does not exclude peaceful immigration and assimilation (e.g., Kitchen; Pit-känen 2010; 2013a). Proponents of more mainstream approaches lean toward peaceful immigration and Canaanite origins (see, e.g., Miller and Hayes; Dever). The minimalists, for whom the history of ancient Israel is largely postexilic fiction, again go with the peaceful transformation models, mostly based on the indigenous origins of the Israelites (see, e.g., Liverani; T. L. Thompson).

The view taken in this essay, on which readers are invited to reflect critically, is that an external group of Semites escaped from slavery in Egypt (see Hoffmeier 1997; 2005) and brought with it memories of its founding fathers the patriarchs and a belief in YHWH. This group then somehow gained a foothold and overall control of the Canaanite highlands and subsequently reproduced and assimilated indigenous and possibly other exogenous elements to form Israel (see Pitkänen

2010; 2013a). Arguably, the archaeological evidence can be seen to support the possibility of such an idea, even when it is not easy to verify a number of the related details directly. The change from the Late Bronze culture to the Iron Age hill country culture happened first in the central highlands and expanded on from there over the next two to three hundred years (e.g., Finkelstein, 324–30; Junkkaala, esp. 308–9). Much of this process was peaceful, but some violence could easily have been involved. A process of that type can be compared with processes known from the more modern world that have recently been labeled and analyzed as settler colonialism (see Veracini 2010; Day; see Pitkänen 2013a for considerations of how modern settler-colonial theory can be applied to the ancient world). Settler-colonial societies are "autonomous collectives that claim both a special sovereign charge and a regenerative capacity" (Veracini 2010, 3–4). Settlers are founders of political orders who carry their sovereignty with them, as opposed to migrants, who are suppliants seeking to fit into an established political order (Veracini 2010, 3). As David Day suggests, a related "process of supplanting" involves three often overlapping stages: Establishing a legal or de jure claim to the land; making a claim of effective or de facto proprietorship; and setting a claim of moral proprietorship over the territory (Day 2008, 7–8). In a broad sweep and keeping in mind that the Late Bronze Canaanite societies somehow became Israelite, in Genesis–Joshua, the patriarchal promises reflect the first claim, the conquest and settlement the second, and recourse to Yahwism as an exclusive ideology, together with the constitution of the new Yahwistic society, the third, moral claim (see, e.g., Deuteronomy 7 in contrast to the previous inhabitants). Settler colonialism aims to effect a dissolution of native societies and erect a new society on an expropriated land base (see Wolfe, esp. 103), with the eliminatory aim typically involving a "genocidal imperative" (see Day, 176–97), but not limited to it (see esp. Veracini 2010, 16–52). For the ancient Israelites, this genocidal imperative is reflected in the concept of *herem*, though one must keep in mind that it has a wider scope, encompassing objects also in cultic use (e.g., Lev. 27:28; Num. 18:14).

Arguably, then, the main problems for interpreting Joshua in today's contexts relate to the violence portrayed in the book. This problem has much to do with the book's relation to actual history. While reading the book as a mythical narrative of a distant past would undoubtedly reduce the problem of its apparently violent character (see, e.g., Earl), at the same time, denial of the problems can also be compared with disavowal, cognitive dissonance, and screen memories identified in modern settler-colonial studies (see Veracini 2010, 95–116). These reactions try to deal with trauma that results from seeing violence committed by one's own community (see ibid.). From an explicitly theological angle, as Eryl Davies points out, there are five main possible responses to acknowledging the violent and hence problematic character of the book. In the so-called evolutionary approach, the text represents primitive thinking that has now been superseded. The cultural relativists' approach sees the text in terms of an ancient and therefore different culture and therefore less relevant for moderns. Canonical approaches in practice exclude the text from the canon. The paradigmatic approach extracts acceptable general principles from the texts. Finally, the reader-response approach accepts the problematic nature of the texts and tries to respond to them accordingly (Davies).

This commentary is broadly in agreement with a reader-response approach, which does not seek to disavow the violence. Such an approach, in fact, builds on an already-existing biblical mode of questioning God and his actions, for example, by the book of Job and a number of the Psalms (cf., e.g., M. E. W. Thompson 2011), without necessarily jettisoning belief in him. The apostle Paul also touches on this issue in Romans 9, though without questioning God. Finally, we do well to remember that the ostensible promotion of violence in the Bible is not confined to Genesis–Joshua; other examples include the imprecatory psalms and the book of Revelation. The book of Joshua, then, encourages Christians to reflect on theodicy and the role of violence in human history as a whole, seen from the perspective of salvation history and, importantly for Christians, the first-century Christ event. Politically, a reader-response approach is generally in line with postcolonial approaches. Any material in the book that can be read theologically in a reasonably straightforward and "nonproblematic" way as reflecting courage, trust in YHWH, and so on must arguably be read against the backdrop of postcolonial readings.

Joshua 1–5: Transitions and Memory

■ THE TEXT IN ITS ANCIENT CONTEXT

The beginning of the book of Joshua describes a people in transition. Israel is at the plains of Moab, and their great leader Moses has just died. Joshua takes on the leadership, and people move over into the promised land in preparation of the conquest. Joshua 1 describes how Joshua receives his orders from YHWH himself (1:1-9) and then commands the rest of the people (1:10-18). Importantly, the Transjordanians who settled East of Jordan (Numbers 32) are required to help the rest of the people in their conquest of Cisjordan (land west of the Jordan River), which they again commit to do (1:12-18). Joshua 2 describes the reconnaissance of Jericho, in preparation of its conquest, which is related in chapter 6. Joshua 3 and 4 describe the crossing of the Jordan and setting camp at Gilgal, mirroring the wider Hexateuchal narrative of the crossing of the Sea of Reeds in Exodus 14. In Joshua 5, after a note about the worry of the indigenous peoples concerning Israel's entrance (5:1), the Israelites are circumcised (5:2-9; cf. Genesis 17; Exod. 12:43-48) and subsequently celebrate the Passover (5:10-12; cf. Exodus 12). Joshua then meets a commander of the army of YHWH (5:13-15; cf. Exod. 3, incl. v. 5).

For Noth, Joshua 1 as a whole should be seen in the context of the wider Deuteronomistic History (Noth 1953, 27). However, while it is true that Deuteronomic ideology is prominent in the chapter, such ideology is also tied to broader ancient Near Eastern ideologies. YHWH's reassurances in Josh. 1:5-6 in a Deuteronomistic style can be compared with the Zakkur stele (e.g., lines 11–15: "But I lifted my hands to Baalshamayn, and Baalshamay[n] answered me, [and] Baalshamayn [spoke] to me [thr]ough seers and through visionaries, [and] Baalshamayn [said], 'F[e]ar not, for I have made [you] king, [and I who will st]and with [you], and I will deliver you from all [these kings who] have forced a siege against you!'"; see Nissinen, 204–6). In Joshua 1, and the book as a whole, Joshua can in some respects be seen to reflect a royal figure (Nelson, 29), with links with Josiah suggested (Nelson, 29); however, there is no royal succession with Joshua, and the names Joshua and Josiah appear to derive from different Hebrew verbal roots.

Previous academic discussion on chapter 2 has mainly centered on its provenance, purpose, and literary prehistory, including sources (Noort, 131, 135–43). Commentators have generally thought in essence that the story of Rahab was originally self-standing and that the author only later picked it up and tied it to its present context of the conquest of Jericho (Noort, 131–32; cf. Noth 1953, 29; Nelson, 41). Such a conclusion is not necessary, however. Biblical parallels to the chapter include Judges 1:23-26 and Genesis 19:1-23. Such parallels extend beyond the Bible (Noort, 132). The story as a whole has generally been seen as etiological, giving a rationale for the existence of the family of Rahab in the midst of Israel (Noort, 131), thus accounting for the story's inclusion. The spying motif can also be compared to other accounts of spying in the Israelite conquest tradition (see Nelson, 45).

The literary form of Joshua 3–4 has been subject to much discussion. Above all, the narrative appears to be uneven, and the text seems to present a number of inconsistencies, even contradictions (see Nelson, 55, 65 for details). However, if it had an oral existence or was meant to be read to audiences, one can read the material as having a purposeful structure and as having been constructed fairly well (see Pitkänen 2010, 129–32). The material has often been seen as stemming from a cult center at Gilgal (see Noth 1953, 11–12), which appears to have had an important role in Israelite history. That there was a sanctuary of some kind at Gilgal seems warranted, but fuller details are unknown, including that the site has not been identified. In any case, in the book of Joshua, the stones set up there serve as a memorial and as a sign for the future generations.

The similarities between the crossing of the Jordan and the crossing of the Sea of Reeds in the book of Exodus are significant (see Ottosson, 79) in the overall Hexateuchal narrative. The crossing of the Sea of Reeds starts the period of wilderness wanderings, and the crossing of Jordan ends it. Both stories also involve a miraculous dividing of the waters. The related children's questions in the chapter (4:6-8, 21-24; cf. Josh. 22:24-28) are paralleled with Deut. 6:20-25. The cultic procession of the ark, with YHWH's presence at the ark, is reminiscent of Priestly material in Numbers (similarly also Ottosson, 54).

As with Joshua 3–4, the link to what has happened before Joshua's time is strong in chapter 5. Joshua 5:1 certainly links back to Deuteronomy's promises about a fear that will fall on Israel's opponents (Deut. 2:25; 11:25). Joshua 5:2-9 explicitly links back to Egypt and the wilderness, as does the reference to manna in verses 10-12. The story about the commander of YHWH's army reminds one of Exod. 3:1-5 (cf. esp. Josh. 5:15 with Exod. 3:5). Importantly, the appearance of the commander is in line with ancient Near Eastern motifs of gods fighting with the troops as a divine vanguard (see Mann, 40–41). Chapter 5 also contains two etiological comments, on Gilgal (v. 9), and, even if not stated completely explicitly, on the Hill of Foreskins (v. 3). The MT and LXX of 5:2-9 differ, primarily in the clarification that unleavened bread was eaten on the day following the start of Passover, which is included only in the MT. This brings it in line with Lev. 23:4-8, whereas the LXX suggests eating unleavened bread on the eve of the Passover, more in line with Deut. 16:1-8 (see Nelson, 72–73, 78–80).

▮ THE TEXT IN THE INTERPRETIVE TRADITION

The beginning of the book of Joshua opens the story from the perspective of salvation history. This salvation history is referred to in Stephen's speech in Acts 7, which also refers to Joshua (v. 45).

Hebrews 4:8 implies that the rest achieved in the time of Joshua was not a true rest, suggesting that such a rest is achieved in Jesus under the new covenant. Hebrews 11:31 and James 2:25-26 praise the faith of Rahab as exemplary in her welcoming the spies, with the latter passage also drawing out a spiritualized lesson for salvation.

Patristic and later Christian commentators continued along similar lines, considering themes of transition and spiritual rest and spiritual battle instead of physical battle (see description in Earl, 111–15). As for Rahab, commentators have asked how her deception should be viewed and also how she relates to *herem* (Earl, 116). Postcolonial literature sees her as a traitor instead of a hero (see Earl, 48). As for *herem*, Rahab's example, in contrast to Achan, transfers her into an "insider," which saves her from death, whereas Achan becomes an "outsider" through his transgression and is thus destroyed (Hawk 2000, 20 and passim; cf. Hawk 2010, 79 and passim).

Crossing the Jordan in Joshua 3–4 can easily be equated with new life, and indeed, Gregory of Nyssa links the story with baptism (Earl, 122–23), even if the connection relates much to the symbolism of the Jordan in the biblical tradition otherwise. In Joshua 5, the fullness of new life begins to manifest itself, with the gifts of the new land instead of the manna that was eaten in the wilderness (Earl, 126, referring to Brueggemann). Origen also saw the wilderness as representing the present Christian life under instruction of the word of God, which is equated with manna, and the implication of the promised land representing the hereafter (Earl, 126–27). In a preliminary sense, with the physical being spiritualized, early Christian commentators did not give much attention to the problem of violence in the book, but it is also true that a fair bit in these chapters can be interpreted in such a spiritualized way.

■THE TEXT IN CONTEMPORARY DISCUSSION

The considerations in the section directly above are entirely valid for modern Christian communities. Here attention will be drawn to a few further aspects of possible contemporary reflection.

In all life, humans often experience change, in leadership and in other areas, and people may have to "cross the river" to new things. Such situations are often a time of uncertainty, sometimes even great uncertainty. But they can also be a time of new beginnings. At these times, Christians can think of the words of YHWH to "be strong and courageous" (1:6-7, 9), especially when they are taking a leadership position; but, equally, Christians can also trust in God for the future, even under new leaders. Trust in God and in God's presence is an important consolation and comfort, even in the tightest of situations.

Joshua 1 (esp. 1:18) raises an interesting dilemma in a wider context. How should a Christian react to a war (or comparable societal actions) that he or she does not approve of? For example, one might be a member of a society that moves to invade the lands of another society. In such situations, the resulting ethical dilemma can be a vexing one, and refusing national service for reasons of pacifism can already in itself bring a great stigma in societies that have a general draft. The effects of this stigma have affected and continue to affect Christians who also rely on their surrounding societal structures for their life and survival.

The ark of the covenant features prominently in Joshua 3–4 as the locus of YHWH's presence. In the Priestly material of Genesis–Joshua, it belongs in the tent of meeting, where it is housed and where YHWH dwells in the midst of his people; and in Deuteronomy, people are required to assemble in YHWH's presence three times a year and make sacrifices only there (Deuteronomy 12, 16). In contrast, for Christians, an ark or a temple (see the tabernacle in Josh. 18:1; see also 22:9-34) is no longer necessary as a place of God's presence. Their bodies are now the temple of God (1 Cor. 3:16; 2 Cor. 6:16). Of course, attending church with other people is a partaking of the body of Christ, and this has a special significance. But the concepts of holy objects and holy places are now less important in themselves. While most people would feel something special about a building that has been dedicated to God, fundamentally, the place of worship is no longer crucial from the standpoint of Christianity, and this may help in the Western context when people see worship buildings sold and converted into the "secular" realm.

One of the emphases of Joshua 3–4 is the remembrance throughout the generations of the crossing the Jordan. As for Christians, they also have items for remembering God. Many people have crucifixes hung on the walls in their homes, or they wear them as pendants. Catholic and Orthodox believers have traditionally used icons, or images of Christ and the saints. Some Protestants in particular have objected to such pictorial representations, worrying that they might become objects of worship. Here the issues are surprisingly similar to Joshua 3–4 and the use of standing stones. The stones are to serve as memorials, but in the ancient world, people also frequently made such stones objects of worship. Perhaps it can be said that Christians can also be encouraged to use memorials, as long as they do not elevate them to a status where they become objects of worship. Along these lines, Christians may also travel to holy places and consider church buildings as inspirational objects, but really only so that seeing such places might help them remember the great deeds of God.

Chapter 5 looks to the past (5:4-7), to the present (5:8-11), and into the future (5:12-15). Transition from old to new usually involves both looking back at old things and seeing the changes that are taking place and are likely to take place with the transition. For a people of faith, this may involve meditating on the great deeds of God for them, and remembering in faith God's guiding hand and presence in preparation for things to come. And, just as YHWH fought for Israel, Christians can trust God's presence in times of need, even if one should not expect that this will involve physical violence.

Joshua 6–9: Insiders and Outsiders

■ THE TEXT IN ITS ANCIENT CONTEXT

Joshua 6–9 describes a number of events taking place at the initial stages of the conquest. Joshua 6 describes the conquest of Jericho, in conclusion to the story in chapter 2. Joshua 7–8 describes the conquest of Ai. Joshua 8:30-35 describes the building of an altar on Mount Ebal. Joshua 9 describes the Gibeonite deception, and as a result the Gibeonites make a covenant with the Israelites that protects them against extermination based on the concept of *herem*.

The literary form of Joshua 6 resembles a Ugaritic entry ritual (Pitkänen 2010, 158), suggesting that the account does not necessarily need to be taken in a literal manner in all its details, also considering that, according to the narrative, it is the first locality in Canaan to be conquered (Pit-känen 2010, 162–69). Nevertheless, allowing that the story is being creatively retold, a conquest of a modest Late Bronze Age town is historically possible. The conquest of Ai, however, is extremely difficult to verify archaeologically (Pitkänen 2010, 182–84), and its historicity must be left open. The Ai narrative has parallels with Judges 20 and 1 Samuel 14–15. The building of an altar on Mount Ebal in Josh. 8:30-35, which is placed slightly differently in certain manuscripts, is tied to Deuteronomy 27 and can also be compared with the altars built by the patriarchs in Genesis, including those by Abraham at Shechem in Genesis 12. The Gibeonite treaty is mentioned in 2 Sam. 21:1-14, and Gibeon acts as a cultic center in the time of Solomon (1 Kings 3:4; cf. 1 Chron. 16:39; 21:29). The archaeological data from Gibeon is somewhat equivocal in terms of the question of the potential historicity of the related events in Joshua (Pitkänen 2010, 214–16).

An important issue in these chapters is the question of insiders versus outsiders, a theme pointed out most notably by L. Daniel Hawk (2000; 2010). The basic idea of the book of Joshua is that those outside the Israelite community may in certain circumstances become members of the community (Rahab in Joshua 6, Gibeonites in Joshua 9). Conversely, those not following YHWH can be excluded from the community and may even fall under *herem* (Achan in Joshua 7). Again, subjecting these issues to a postcolonial analysis can help elucidate the text. We may first note the complexity of colonial situations. As Maria Aubet summarizes, "Colonialism cannot be studied only from the dominator's point of view nor only from that of the dominated," as has often been the case until now, "because the relationship between domination and resistance changes in the course of a colonial situation" (2013, 76). "The colonised do not form a homogenous group; some are dominant over others and there are internal conflicts, so it is necessary to contextualise the colonial process" (Aubet, 76, quoting Gledhill). A dichotomy between the dominators and the dominated "in fact masks highly complex practices of interaction" (Aubet, 76).

Anthropologists and archaeologists "have started to study the mixed character of some colonial situations, that on occasion actually constitute new and hybrid cultural entities" (Aubet, 77). These comments apply to Rahab and Gibeon in that her relationship to Israel is complex, both before and after their encounter with the Israelites. In addition, one may note here the basic tripartite settler-colonial dynamic between the settler collective and indigenous and exogenous others in settler-colonial situations (Veracini 2010, 20–32). While indigenous others are a threat to the existence and legitimacy of the settler collective, there can be a selective inclusion of exogenous others, as there is the possibility of collaboration (Veracini 2010, 26). However, there can also be undesirable exogenous others who may be subject to deportation or segregation (Veracini 2010, 27), and abject others who are permanently excluded from the settler collective and have lost their indigenous or exogenous status. In the case of ancient Israel, the Israelite *qahal/edah* corresponds to the settler collective (Josh. 8:30-35; 22:9-34). The Canaanites who—according to the Israelite view—are to be destroyed (Deuteronomy 7) are the indigenous others. The *ger* are the exogenous others (e.g., Exod. 12:38 [mixed multitude]; Josh. 8:33). Abject others might include people who have been subject to the *karat* punishment of being cut off from the people (e.g., Lev. 7:20-27; 17:4-14; 18:29). As Lorenzo Veracini suggests, a "successful" settler society "is managing the orderly and progressive emptying of the indigenous and exogenous others segments of the population economy and has permanently separated from the abject others" (Veracini 2010, 28; see also Deut. 23:1-8).

We can now see what is happening with Rahab, Achan, and the Gibeonites. Rahab is transferred away, defining *transfer* as "cleansing" the settler body polity of its indigenous and exogenous alterities, whether by violence or by some more subtle conceptual means from the indigenous other category, and she is no longer under *herem*, a transfer by killing. As to her new status, it is unclear whether she is considered as part of the *qahal* or as equivalent to a *ger* ("resident alien"), at least initially. As for Achan, whose desire of prestige goods was typical of those belonging to ancient societies, if not also modern ones (Aubet 2013, incl. 98–99), he is transferred away from the Israelite collective by execution, which is close to the *karat* command, but apparently not the same.

As for the Gibeonites, they are transferred away from being Canaanites under *herem* into a servant class (see also 2 Samuel 21), which, however, is closely connected with Israelite worship (1 Samuel 7, where the ark is at Kiriath Jearim, a Gibeonite town). Later on, the Gibeonites seem to be considered as Israelite; this generally seems to be achieved by a transfer of assimilation by incorporating them into Israelite genealogies (1 Chron. 2:50-52; Neh. 7:25-30), as is done with Caleb at an early stage, at least in the narrative world (Num. 13:6; 32:12; Josh. 14:6-14; 15:13). At the same time, the responses to Rahab and the Gibeonites can also be considered as "unintended consequences" of colonialism (Dietler, 18).

Similar processes of incorporation into a genealogy can be detected in the Iron Age Aegean world, probably dating back to the Late Bronze Age (Finkelberg, 24–41) and in the more modern world (Horowitz, 78). The "transfers" of Rahab, Achan, and the Gibeonites therefore represent the larger number of transfers happening in early Israel according to the biblical texts. In these transfers, the Israelite society of settlers is expanding its scope and influence under a complex dynamic between the Israelite society and the natives. This process takes centuries and in many ways can be seen to have been completed by the postexilic time (e.g., 1 Chron. 2:50-53; Ezra 2:25; Neh. 7:25, 29; vs. Josh. 9:17).

The building of the altar on Mount Ebal is tied with the Israelites' staking a legal claim to the land. It can be compared with the practices of the modern English, Spanish, Portuguese, Dutch, and French colonialists. For example, Columbus erected in "every harbour which his ships entered and on every suitable promontory 'a very large cross in the most appropriate spot'" (Day, 13). Or Vasco Balboa, when reaching the Pacific Ocean in the Americas, ordered his escorts to kneel and sing the *Te Deum* and then waded in the waters of the sea, claiming in the name of his king all the lands whose shores would be washed by this sea. The Portuguese typically erected a *padrão*, or stone pillar topped with a cross, together with an inscription, to mark their discoveries and accompanying claims, and providing markers for navigation on sea routes for the future. Tasman, the Dutch explorer, erected a flagpole in the southern Australian island that came to bear his name "as a memorial for those who shall come after us, and for the natives of this country" (Day, 18). On the main island of New Zealand, Cook erected a cairn, inside which he placed some coins and musket balls (Day, 22). The Israelite ceremony in Joshua then harks back to the actions of the patriarchs in Genesis. Especially Abraham, who is described as building his first altar at Shechem (esp. Gen. 12:6-7), which is in the vicinity of Mount Ebal (Deut. 11:30; see Moreh in this verse and Gen. 12:6).

◼ THE TEXT IN THE INTERPRETIVE TRADITION

As indicated above, many of the indigenous peoples were sooner or later integrated into ancient Israelite society. In the New Testament, the scope of ancient Israel is explicitly extended to include all nations of the world (Acts 2; 10–11; Galatians) as the new Israel (Romans 11). Only faith in Christ, not any national association, is required. Yet a type of insider-versus-outsider distinction still remains in the New Testament, but it centers on faith and on no other characteristic. There is to be no real difference in status among those belonging to the Christian community (Gal. 3:28).

Origen spiritualized the destruction of Jericho into an idea of the destruction of evil (Earl, 135). A main point of the Achan narrative is that one must follow YHWH's instructions, and it is particularly emphasized that one should not violate what has been devoted to him. However, in terms of the Christian community, whereas Achan had to die, Christians do not need to, as Jesus has borne their transgressions. In this respect, it is true that Ananias and Sapphira died because of their attempted deception against God (Acts 5:1-11), but this seems to be somewhat of an extraordinary exception. It is perhaps true that God also chastises God's children, but this can be understood to be for developmental purposes, and the nuance is different from that in Joshua. Christians are not to have a spirit of fear but of sonship (Rom. 8:15). Achan has been seen as a type who confessed his or her sin, even if Achan himself did not seem to benefit from such confession (Earl, 144–45). Emphasis on the law in 8:30-35 has been seen as pointing to Christ (Earl, 146).

◼ THE TEXT IN CONTEMPORARY DISCUSSION

In actual practice, churches and other human communities do set rules, whether implicitly or explicitly, of who is an "insider" and who is to be an "outsider." Issues such as race, wealth and social status, religion, and sexual orientation may be determining factors. Even dressing differently from others can be a reason for exclusion. For example, a church consisting of middle-aged, middle-class people might find it difficult if a "goth" were suddenly to sit in the pews. Similarly, while present human rights legislation speaks for diversity and inclusion in wider society, there is still work to be done. One area is integrating foreigners and people of different ethnic origin and religion into societies as equal participants. The situation can be fairly good in this respect in Britain and in many ways in the United States and Australia, to a degree, but can presently be problematic in certain countries in continental Europe, Russia, and Asia, not to mention Israel—at least in terms of practical life, if not in a legislative sense. As for women, despite feminism, there are still many areas where their rights and equality need further work. LGBT rights is a further issue to reflect on, both at a societal and church level; debates are currently taking place as to what extent they should be considered equal in churches.

Today's settler-colonial societies have provided and continue to provide special challenges (Veracini 2010, 95–116). For example, in American history, the original settler collective consisted only of whites, with blacks as slaves, essentially abject others, and with newly entering whites and Asians as exogenous others, though with a better status for whites. In time, the settler collective has uplifted the status of the blacks and Asians. It nevertheless still sees Native Americans as indigenous others, having transferred them by killing, displacement, and forced or voluntary assimilation (see Stannard; see Hawk 2010 for a number of parallels between the book of Joshua and the North American conquest). The natives living in reservations are still oppressed. Even today, a person coming from outside who commits a crime in reservation territory cannot be tried by the Native Americans, and in practice, US law enforcement is tardy in pursuing such cases. It is no wonder that Native Americans are still experiencing a continued terrible trauma of the past (Tinker 2004; 2008). Other indigenous peoples around the world still experience similar traumas. For them, the issue is not so much inclusion to the new society but regaining their past freedom, land, and property. Decolonization would include such issues as an apology by the colonizer and restitution of land, property, and dignity to the victims, but this has proven extremely difficult in settler-colonial situations, such as with the United States, Australia, and New Zealand (see also Veracini 2010, 95–116).

In South Africa, with the whites never constituting a majority of the population, after a period of apartheid, blacks have regained power. In modern Israel, a settler-colonial process against the indigenous Palestinians continues unabated (Veracini 2006). The recent UN Declaration of the Rights of Indigenous Peoples (2007) is a step in the right direction in the global context, but much work remains to be done.

Joshua 10–12: Conquest and Genocide

▌ THE TEXT IN ITS ANCIENT CONTEXT

Joshua 10–12 describes the main conquests Joshua and the Israelites achieve in Canaan. In Joshua 10, the Israelites defeat a southern coalition of indigenous forces, and in chapter 11 they overcome a northern coalition led by the king of Hazor. Joshua 12 summarizes these and other conquests, together with conquests already previously achieved by the Israelites, including in Transjordan, as described in Numbers and Deuteronomy.

Joshua 10 follows on from the story of the Gibeonites. The southern coalition attacks Gibeon on hearing about their treaty with the Israelites. The Gibeonites call for the help of the Israelites, who respond and then achieve victory aided by a miraculous hailstorm and celestial portents (10:11-13). The kings of the coalition are then executed in verses 16-28. From here, Joshua attacks further towns in the South. In Joshua 11, the scope widens toward the north, which then leads to a yet fuller scope in chapter 12. At this point in the narrative of Joshua, what had started at the crossing of the Jordan and the conquest of Jericho and Ai now branches out to cover the whole land, to be followed by the allotment of the land in Joshua 13–19. While one can see the author's logic in framing Joshua as part of the wider Genesis–Joshua narrative, in which the Israelites move in from Egypt and the wilderness, the narrative should be seen as at least a partially artificial creation. There could have been a unified campaign by a leader of a main exodus group, but in reality it is more likely that a number of conflicts with locals occurring at various times have been telescoped together into a narrative and attributed to Joshua as the military leader par excellence of the Israelites (see 12:7, which mentions Joshua *and* the Israelites). A number of these battles and conquests can be difficult to verify archaeologically. For example, 11:14 suggests that Joshua and the Israelites did not normally burn the conquered towns. If so, and if towns were not demolished otherwise, few traces would be likely to have been left in the archaeological record (cf. 24:13; Deut. 6:10-11).

In Josh. 10:11, a hailstorm caused by YHWH settles the score for the Israelites. Hailstorms are not uncommon in Israel, especially between October and May. The size of hail can be considerable and can cause damage (Pitkänen 2010, 224). In terms of the Joshua narrative, above all, the timing is providential. The storm is sent by YHWH to help the fighting Israelites. It should also be noted that no Israelites are reported to have been harmed, even though the point may simply be that, even if there were Israelite injuries, as a whole, the storm resulted in an advantage to the *Israelites*. That in itself could already be seen as a miracle.

A bigger miracle is then described in Josh. 10:12-14. The heavenly bodies stop their travel in the sky until the Israelites are victorious. Understood according to a modern scientific worldview, the implication is that the earth's rotation slowed or stopped altogether. This would of course be stupendously miraculous, and many commentators have accordingly sought to explain the comments in some other way. Joseph Blenkinsopp suggests that the narrative references local understandings of the sun and the moon as deities, which should be seen to be under YHWH's control during the battle. Whether or not this was the case, it is true that the sun and moon were considered divine throughout the ancient Near East at the time (Blenkinsopp, 44–50). However, it appears that the Israelites were not to think in this way, or at least not worship these deities (Deut. 4:19).

In the context of this passage, then, it cannot be said with confidence whether any divine implications are intended. Richard Hess has summarized other attempts to solve the meaning of the passage, including an eclipse and an interpretation of the position of the constellations as an omen, but he notes that none of the suggested solutions is "entirely satisfactory" (197–99; cf. Younger, 211–20). Richard Nelson (145) suggests that "these two heavenly bodies were being called upon to stand frozen or fixed, or perhaps silent, in stunned reaction to an awe-inspiring victory," and the (apparently Deuteronomic) redactor then directed the speech through the accompanying prose section "*away* from sun and moon and towards Yahweh." Whatever one thinks about the matter, the narrative itself states that what happened was something very special and something that has never happened before or since the time of Joshua (10:14). The occurrence of the miracle is also attested in the "book of the righteous" (*sefer hayyashar*), and the writer here appears to call on the book in support of the authenticity of what he is saying, as a kind of ancient footnote (cf. 2 Sam. 1:18; possibly 1 Kgs. 8:53 LXX).

■ The Text in the Interpretive Tradition

There is little reference to the conquests in Joshua 10–12 throughout the rest of the Bible. Until the rise of postcolonial analysis, subsequent commentators appear to have had little problem with the violence portrayed in these chapters. The following comments from John Calvin are instructive (1854, on Josh. 10:40).

> Here the divine authority is again interposed in order completely to acquit Joshua of any charge of cruelty. Had he proceeded of his own accord to commit an indiscriminate massacre of women and children, no excuse could have exculpated him from the guilt of detestable cruelty, cruelty surpassing anything of which we read as having been perpetrated by savage tribes scarcely raised above the level of the brutes. But that at which all would otherwise be justly horrified, it becomes

them to embrace with reverence, as proceeding from God. Clemency is justly praised as one of the principal virtues; but it is the clemency of those who moderate their wrath when they have been injured, and when they would have been justified, as individuals, in shedding blood. But as God had destined the swords of his people for the slaughter of the Amorites, Joshua could do nothing else than obey his command.

Similarly, the New England Puritans could see the destruction of the indigenous peoples as a result of divine providence (see Guyatt, 178) that was tied to their identification with the Israelite foundation story (see Waswo). The text allowed Cotton Mather to say in a 1674 sermon at the eve of a (brutal) war with Metacom and the Wampanoag Indians (quoted in Guyatt, 48),

> The Lord will not as yet destroy this place: Our fathers have built Sanctuaries for his Name therein, and therefore he will not destroy us. The Planting of these Heavens, and the laying the Foundations of the Earth, is one of the Wonders of this last Age. . . . God hath called out a people, even out of all parts of a Nation, which he hath also had a great favour towards, and hath brought them by a mighty hand, and an out-stretched arm, over a [sic] greater than the Red Sea, and here hath he planted them, and hath caused them to grow up as it were into a little Nation; And shall we think that this is to destroy them within forty and fifty years.

Presumably Joshua could have expounded a similar message to his troops before the battle with the southern coalition, or any other battles with the indigenous peoples. While the Puritans were slightly different in that they also had a missionary inclination toward the natives, the genocidal disposition prevailed as a whole, as can be seen in the extent of native dispossession on the North American continent since then. Broadly similar stories apply to Australia and parts of South Africa. While there were those among Christians who spoke against the Western genocidal colonial advance (e.g., Bartolomé de las Casas), their arguments could not stop the colonial tide. In addition, many Zionists, including the first prime minister of Israel, David Ben-Gurion, looked back at the stories of Joshua as legitimation for the Zionist project of conquest and dispossession of the Palestinians, even if this has been dampened by the relatively recent challenges against the historicity of the biblical narrative (Sand 2010, 74–75).

■ THE TEXT IN CONTEMPORARY DISCUSSION

The main problem for modern readings of Joshua 10–12 is that the material attests a genocide ideology. While it is not always entirely easy to define genocide, we may reproduce the UN definition of genocide here as an indicative statement.

> In the present Convention, genocide means any of the following acts committed with intent to destroy, in whole or in part, a national, ethnic, racial or religious group, as such:
>
> (a) Killing members of the group;
> (b) Causing serious bodily or mental harm to members of the group;
> (c) Deliberately inflicting on the group conditions of life calculated to bring about its physical destruction in whole or in part;
> (d) Imposing measures intended to prevent births within the group;
> (e) Forcibly transferring children of the group to another group.

We can see that items (a) through (c) are clearly attested in Joshua. Items (d) and (e) do not seem to apply, even though the Israelites themselves are described as suffering something like (d) and (e) in Egypt (Exod. 1:15). These examples show the role of power in genocide. The relative power portrayed is what changes the Israelites from victims to perpetrators. In Egypt, they are the weaker party and thus become the victims of the Egyptians. In Canaan, they are, or at least aspire to be, the stronger party and wish to found a perfect society, into which the Canaanites do not fit. Thus the Israelites intend and partially implement genocidal policies. This does not all go according to plan, as Judges shows the Israelites intermixing with the indigenes. However, battles and killing are only an aspect of the actual settler-colonial process. There are other, more subtle ways to achieve control over the area, such as assimilation (see comments on Joshua 6–9). Of course, with the lack of modern communications and possibly largely oral nature of early Israel, together with the question of the dating of the biblical materials, it is unlikely that the Israelites had the effective organization that would have enabled them to carry out the orders of the Yahwistic purists in Deuteronomy 7 (see Judg. 2:6-13).

In this vein, modern communities may ask how to deal with those who do not fit with their plans, which ties in with the question of exclusivity. History shows how—time and again—a desire for uniformity, or the desires of one particular interest group followed at the expense of others, can lead to violence and genocide. Therefore, it is of vital importance for today's individuals, groups, and societies to acknowledge pluralism not only at the innersocietal level but also at the intergroup and intersocietal level. So, for example, powerful societies like the United States or the West in general, or powerful groups within them, should reflect on whose interests are being promoted in international economics and politics: those of merely their own, or those of humanity at large?

Joshua 13–19: Settler-Colonial Advance

▮ THE TEXT IN ITS ANCIENT CONTEXT

Joshua 13–19 describes the allotment of land to the tribes of Israel. Together with chapters 20–21, the allotments make provision for everyone in the land of Canaan. These chapters begin a new, distinctive section in the book. Focus shifts away from conquest to allotments and settlement, to be continued with exhortation for a life according to the commands of YHWH in Joshua 23–24 in particular. Chapters 14–19 form a chiastic structure, as pointed out by Koorevaar (289).

a	14:6-15	Beginning: Caleb's inheritance
b	15:1—17:18	The lot for Judah and Joseph
c	18:1-10	The tent of meeting taken to Shiloh and the apportioning of the land
b'	18:11—19:48	The lot for seven remaining tribes
a'	19:49-51	Ending: Joshua's inheritance

In addition, Joshua 13, a passage that relates to the Transjordanian tribes, can probably be matched with the towns of refuge and the Levitical towns in chapters 20–21. These pertain to groups that have in some way a special status in Israel. The link, however, is perhaps somewhat more tenuous than with 14:6—19:51. The Greek text differs in a number of details for the boundary and town lists.

The above shows that the setting up of the tent of meeting at Shiloh and the apportioning of the land stands at the center of the allotments. This structure fits with the importance of the tent of meeting as the place where YHWH dwells in the midst of the people of Israel, perfectly in line with Priestly theology, including that of the Holiness Code (Exodus 25–40; Lev. 26:11). YHWH's dwelling in the tent amid the people is also broadly in line with Deuteronomistic theology, which is the primary framework of Joshua. Thus, together with the chapters as a whole, Priestly material has been incorporated into a Deuteronomistic framework.

In relation to the centrality of the concept of land here and throughout Genesis–Joshua (including the Holiness Code and Deuteronomy), again, we may make a comparison with settler-colonial studies. According to Patrick Wolfe (130n71): "settler colonialism has . . . two principal aspects—not only the removal of native society, but also its concomitant replacement with settler institutions. This latter, positive aspect involves the establishment and legitimation of civil hegemony." And, "eliminatory strategies all reflect the centrality of the land, which is not merely the component of settler society but its basic precondition" (Wolfe, 103).

There has been enormous discussion about the boundary and town lists in the past (see Pitkänen 2010, 252–53 for a summary). Even today, there is no agreement about their dating. However, it seems safe to suggest that Judah's town list dates from the late monarchy. Also, the boundary lists are more detailed for Judah and Benjamin, the two main tribes of the southern kingdom. At the same time, we know from Hittite treaties that boundary and town lists were in use already in the second millennium BCE. So it is entirely possible that, whatever way they were then incorporated into the book and possibly edited after their initial incorporation, the Israelite materials originate from an earlier time than their final form.

Joshua 14:6-15 and 19:49-51 and the emphasis on Caleb and Joshua tie back to the narrative in Numbers 13–14, in which the Israelites spy the land before their actual entrance into it. All the spies except Caleb and Joshua, representatives of the tribes of Judah and Joseph, bring back a bad report. These tribes, then, are portrayed as leading tribes here in Joshua. Joshua himself becomes the leader of the Israelites, and Caleb is given Hebron, an important town in the Israelite tradition, as it serves as both a town of refuge (Josh. 20:7) and a priestly town for the Aaronides (Josh. 21:11). It is also the town from where David rules initially, before the move to Jerusalem (2 Sam. 5:1-4). In addition, it is an important town in the patriarchal narratives and is the place where most of the patriarchs were buried (Gen. 13:18; 23; 49:31; 50:13; but cf. Gen. 35:19-20 for Rachel and Josh. 24:32 for Joseph). Thus, arguably, the North and the South are also represented by Shiloh and Hebron in Joshua 13–19 and in 20–21.

As already indicated, these chapters reflect a more peaceful process than that in Joshua 1–12, even though they also portray conquests, for example, with Caleb. In this respect, these chapters are more in line with Judges 1. They are also in line with how typical settlement processes work. As in early America—among other cases—such processes may include periods of apparently peaceful coexistence, and then extensions of the process of settlement that may include further fighting, killing, and expulsion (see Josh. 13:1-7; 15:63; 16:10; 17:12-18; 18:5-7; 19:47; Exod. 23:20-30), and may also include assimilation, or attempts to assimilate, indigenous peoples (see, e.g., Kakel; cf. Veracini 2010, esp. 16–52, which lists twenty-six different ways to "purge" a settler collective of indigenous elements).

In addition, visions of territory may include areas that have not yet been conquered (see Kakel, 130 for *two* differing visions of territory in Germany during the Second World War), and this seems to be the case with Joshua also (13:1-6). In Joshua 13–19, a settler-colonial "structure" (rather than an event; see Wolfe) has been put in place in which the Israelite polity is set to expand, and this actually seems to mirror what happened during Iron Age I, as archaeological evidence indicates that the Israelite settlement and control started from the central, eastern, and northern highlands and expanded out from there, to include lowlands in the later course of Israel's history (Finkelstein, 324–30; cf. Junkkaala, 308–9). Eventually, by the time the Israelite state(s) itself was conquered by the Assyrians and Babylonians, indigenous peoples had been assimilated into the Israelite community (1 Chron. 2:50-53; Ezra 2:25; Neh. 7:25, 29; vs. Josh. 9:17), and Solomon is said to have incorporated non-Israelites as slaves at the early stages of the ancient Israelite monarchy (1 Kgs. 9:20-23). The daughters of Zelophehad may actually represent one group of indigenous peoples that had been assimilated early and incorporated in the Israelite genealogies, as many of their names correspond with localities in Samaria (Josh. 17:3-4; cf. Numbers 36).

■ THE TEXT IN THE INTERPRETIVE TRADITION

Stephen's speech in Acts 7:45 refers to the tabernacle and the taking of the land from the indigenes as part of the salvation history described, which can be compared with the allotment of the land and the setting up of the tabernacle at Shiloh in Joshua 13–19 in particular. The passage exhibits no criticism of the process of dispossession, and, again, it is only postcolonial criticism that really has started to ask questions about the legitimacy of what is depicted here. That said, the apostle Paul touches on the matter in Rom. 9:6-24. Paul acknowledges the problem of theodicy but nevertheless puts it aside under the explanation that it is a mystery of God that humans cannot understand.

At the same time, the Old Testament describes how the focus of Josiah's reform on the destruction of non-Yahwistic religious objects and any killing is marginal (as pointed out by Moberly), and the book of Ezra only advocates separation from the people of the land (Ezra 9–10), not the extermination of those peoples. Also, according to 1 Kgs. 9:20-21, while the destruction of non-Israelites should have taken place during the time of the conquest, such an attitude did not prevail any more during the time of Solomon. Thus one can suggest that the destruction of the Canaanites during the early history of Joshua was part of a unique situation as part of God's plan of salvation that is not to be repeated otherwise, which is how many recent commentators have tended to approach the subject. Some also see the violence that is portrayed as ultimately mythical (e.g., Earl), or only as a story (see Docker, 113–29). And yet, as also pointed out in the previous sense unit, settler-colonial processes have repeated themselves in world history and have sometimes been at least partially legitimated by recourse to the ancient Israelite conquest and settlement story through an identification with the conquering Israelites. This is unfortunate, as the concept of the promised land has been spiritualized in the New Testament, referring there to the eternal life for which Christians wait. It is true, too, though, that Origen did spiritualize the extermination of the Canaanites into the mortification of the flesh (see Earl, 166). And, more broadly, it was typical for the church fathers to interpret chapters 13–19 typologically and spiritually, with the new land signifying new Christian life (see Franke, 71–87).

◼ THE TEXT IN CONTEMPORARY DISCUSSION

Recent postcolonial analysis has been critical of the overall ancient Israelite colonial and settler-colonial expansion into the highlands as described by Joshua 13–19, viewing it as a form of exploitation in an intercultural and intersocietal context where a stronger party dominates a weaker party and exploits that party for their own benefit (see Osterhammel, 15–22). Historically, texts have often drawn attention to exploitation by the powerful within society (e.g., Laws of Hammurabi; Deuteronomy and the widow, orphan, and alien; the Gospels). It is thus now time to draw increasing attention to intersocietal and international oppression and exploitation. The New Testament can be seen to support this.

According to the New Testament, greed is idolatry (Eph. 5:5; Col. 3:5). In the Old Testament, the second part of the Decalogue already also speaks against greed (Exod. 20:13-17; Deut. 5:17-21) after an explicit warning against idolatry. The New Testament extends the older covenant, which originally applied to the Israelite nation only, to apply to people from all nations instead of only one, and thus to international politics also. Especially those nations and people that are politically and financially powerful should thus reflect on their dispositions and actions so that the interests of humanity as a whole are served and not just those of one powerful interest group.

In light of the above, we can say that oppression and greed in these contexts is idolatry and should be avoided at all costs. While the explicit era of colonialism is now largely over, neocolonialism is still a reality in many parts of the world. Neocolonialism still includes occasional conquests—and even at least partial genocide—by powerful nations to exploit raw materials, such as the conquest of Iraq by the United States in 2003. However, exploitation by powerful multinational companies and financial institutions in the interest of excessive capitalism should also be included in this category, and the banking crisis of 2007–2008 and beyond has demonstrated that exploitation is not limited to non-Western peoples.

In terms of settler colonialism, the recent UN Declaration on the Rights of Indigenous Peoples (2007) is a step in the right direction for recognizing the rights of the weaker peoples. However, constant vigilance is still needed, especially in acknowledging the right of these peoples to determine their own destiny. In addition, those societies that have oppressed and in many ways destroyed and taken land from indigenes should acknowledge what they have done and offer restitution to those indigenous people that have survived their onslaughts. This is an issue for humanity as a whole, and settler-colonial studies has shown how resistant settler-colonial societies are to this and other related types of decolonization (Veracini 2010, 95–116).

There are also societies that continue their assault on indigenous peoples, sometimes under the full gaze of the world. These include powerful nations such as the United States and the modern state of Israel. In the United States, most of the settler-colonial process was completed by the second half of the nineteenth century, but the Native American communities still live in often destitute situations (Tinker 2004; 2008). In modern Israel, the settler-colonial process of taking land from the indigenous Palestinians that started some one hundred years ago is currently in full swing (see Veracini 2006). In this case, some modern Israelis may legitimate their actions by recourse to the ancient biblical texts, including Joshua. From an ideological perspective, except for Jewish Zionism, Christian popular eschatology has caused many Christians to support Israel (see Sand 2012, esp. 119–253, for the history of Zionism). As part of this, those who take a so-called dispensationalist premillennial view on the Scriptures (see Clouse for a basic exposition; and Court, 123–24 for its origins in nineteenth-century America) argue that Israel should still be considered as a literal concept, that the return of the Israeli(te)s to Palestine is foretold in the Bible, and even that the temple will be rebuilt in Israel, if only to administer sacrifices that serve as memorial for Jesus. However, the dispensationalist view is by no means the only one available.

So-called historical premillenialists, amillenialists, and probably postmillennialists all see, in the light of the New Testament, the promises to Israel as now applying to the church (Romans 9), even if the "literal" Israel still has some kind of role (for the basic positions, see Clouse; for a historical dimension to millennial movements, see Court). In this light, there is no need to interpret biblical material as foretelling a literal return of the Jews to Israel (the concept of Jews as more than ideological heirs—i.e., rather as descendants of converts than physical descendants of the ancient Israelites—has also been challenged; see esp. Sand 2009; cf. Sand 2012). Therefore, prophecies about Israel's return to the land can be received metaphorically (see Chapman). Interestingly, before Zionism's nineteenth-century rise—having been connected with the rise of European nationalism (Sand 2012)—Jews largely thought that they should not "go up the wall," that is, collectively migrate to the land. This view was based on a passage in *Ketubot* 13:11 in the Talmud. (There were also two other injunctions in the talmudic passage, that Israel should not rebel against the nations and that the idolaters, that is, the nations of the world, should not oppress Israel too much; see Sand 2012, 106–7.) Through this lens, we can see a strong argument for the support of Palestinians, who are losing their land to Israeli policies.

Joshua 20–22: YHWH's People—Unity, Right Worship, Justice, and Provision for All

▮ THE TEXT IN ITS ANCIENT CONTEXT

Joshua follows on the great Deuteronomic vision of unity, right worship, justice, and provision for all in the land YHWH has promised to Israel's forefathers. There is unity in conquest, in that the Transjordanians take part in it rather than staying east of the Jordan (1:6-9; 3-4; 22:1-8). Joshua's altar at Mount Ebal (8:30-35) attests unity in worship in the promised land, as does the memorial altar in Transjordan (22:9-34), even if there are initial suspicions that the Transjordanian altar had been built in order to provide an alternative place of worship to that at Shiloh. After land has been allotted to the Israelite tribes (13–19), the institution of Levitical towns (21) helps take care of cultic functionaries; and the institution of towns of refuge (20) that cover the land as a whole, both east and west of the Jordan, helps to protect a person who has committed accidental manslaughter. The Greek text of Joshua 20 differs from the MT in that, for example, 20:4-6 is missing in LXX B. The Greek text also differs somewhat from the MT in the list of towns in Joshua 21.

The system of blood avenging seems to be attested in the ancient Near East, and already well into the second millennium. The victim's family generally had a chance to choose between killing the offender or to receive "blood money" in compensation (see Barmash, 20–70). The vassal treaties of Esarhaddon directly mention that, "just as a stag is overtaken and killed, so may the avenger overtake and kill you, your sons and daughters" (Barmash, 54). Also, cuneiform legal material stipulates for capital punishments in case of homicides (e.g., Barmash, 168–70). We may conclude from this that the system of towns of refuge had its grounding in ancient Near Eastern law and practice, but appears to have a specifically Israelite slant in the book of Joshua. In the present form of the text, the towns have been set up roughly evenly across the Israelite territory (comments by Zvi, 97–98 notwithstanding). This would enable one equally easy access to a town of refuge throughout the land (as observed by Barmash, 85; see also Boling and Wright, 447, for a rough map). The relationship of Joshua 20 to Exod. 21:12-14; Num. 35:6, 9-34; and Deut. 4:41-43; 19:1-3, which also deal with cases of accidental manslaughter, is a much-discussed issue (see Barmash, passim). For our purposes here, we may note that Joshua 20 seems to be based on both Deuteronomic and Priestly materials (Pitkänen 2010, 334–36; Barmash). The actual implementation of the towns of refuge as described in Joshua would suggest that this part of the Israelite legal provision was intended as realistic rather than theoretical, at least in the narrative world.

Apart from their first mention in Lev. 25:32-34 as something known, the Levitical towns are first "properly" introduced in Num. 35:1-8 in the canonical context (and order), and the passage here in the book of Joshua provides a fulfillment of the stipulations in Numbers. The Levitical towns are not directly mentioned in Deuteronomy proper. The legislation regarding the towns in Lev. 25:32-34 is in agreement with the corresponding legislation in Numbers and Joshua. Apart from Joshua 21, another list of the towns is provided in 1 Chron. 6:54-81 (Hebrew 6:39-66). The lists in Joshua and Chronicles differ somewhat, as do the Hebrew and Greek versions of Joshua 21. Much discussion has surrounded the Levitical towns (Kallai 1986; 2010; Hutton). By and large, they have been dated from the early monarchy to the postexilic period. Much of the discussion has also centered on the question of whether the system should be seen as programmatic (or idealistic, even "utopian") or as based on some actual historical reality during the history of Israel. The concept does, however, have parallels with land and town grants and property sales in second-millennium-BCE Ugarit and Alalakh (see Pitkänen 2010, 342).

Joshua 21:43-45 suggests that Israel achieved rest in the promised land during the time of Joshua, after the allotment of the tribal land. Commentators have often pointed out that this seems to contradict the rest of the book, which portrays fighting and incomplete settlement. However, recourse to settler-colonial studies can again help. Settler-colonial societies generally wish to "disavow" their violent origins. According to Veracini, as one part of such processes, "An anxious reaction to disconcerting and disorienting developments produces a drive to think about a pacified world that can only be achieved via voluntary displacement" (2010, 89). Also, while "settlers are natural men engaged in building a settled life in an ahistorical locale, recurring representations of settler original idylls insist on an immaculate foundational setting devoid of disturbing indigenous (or exogenous) others" (2010, 88). The contradictions in the book of Joshua can thus be understood in psychological terms. The cognitive dissonance between founding violence and desired idyllic peace is a contradiction that the author of Joshua was not able to completely resolve, and neither can the readers of the book. As Veracini (2010, 89) notes in terms of settler-colonial situations, "Ultimately, the fact that these images coexist with ongoing (explicit, latent, or intermittently surfacing) apprehension may actually suggest the activation of a splitting of the ego-like process, where two antithetical psychical attitudes coexist side by side without communicating, one taking reality into consideration, the other disavowing it."

Joshua 22 describes how the Transjordanians, having assisted their brothers in the conquest, are sent home (22:1-8; a passage in Deuteronomistic style) and how they then build an altar in the Transjordanian territory (22:9-34, a passage in Priestly style, with a plotline similar to Numbers 32). After achieving rest, sacrifices are to be made only at the central sanctuary (22:19, 23, 27; cf. Deut. 12:10-11). The Transjordanians explain to the representatives of the Western tribes that the altar is to only serve as a monument, and a civil war over the cultic matter is averted (22:26, 28, 33).

◼ THE TEXT IN THE INTERPRETIVE TRADITION

The application of the institution of towns of refuge does not receive a lot of discussion in other parts of the Old Testament. The flights of Joab and Adonijah to the tent of YHWH (1 Kgs. 1:50-53; 2:28-34) have often been seen as related to the matter but in reality are more likely based on political asylum (Barmash, 72–80). The concept does not carry over to the New Testament except for its general principle of justice. In modern democratic societies, perhaps the idea of a trial by jury can be taken as a safeguard against unreasonable response to capital cases.

The Levitical towns are also not mentioned in the New Testament. However, their basic principle of taking care of cultic functionaries carries over quite strongly in the New Testament. Jesus was supported financially by a number of people (Luke 8:2-3), and Paul states it as the right of a church worker to be supported financially (1 Cor. 9:7-10), also referring back to the cultic system of the Old Testament (1 Cor. 9:13-14), and surely the system of Levitical towns is at least implicitly included here. Paul himself, however, relinquishes that right (1 Cor. 9:15) and supports himself through his own means, apparently by his tentmaking skills (Acts 18:1-3).

Hebrews 4 speaks about rest for God's people. According to the chapter, the rest achieved by Joshua was not yet a real rest (4:8), and the author quotes Psalm 95 in support, especially 95:7-8. That is, had Joshua already been given that rest, the psalm would not have spoken of yet another day, as per 95:7-8, 11. On a broader canvas, certainly, the later history of Israel showed that the nation was not able to follow YHWH and ultimately fell to the Assyrians and the Babylonians, only to be restored partially in the postexilic and intertestamental times. Instead, for the writer of Hebrews, the rest to be achieved by Christians is the real rest (4:9-11), and apparently eternal life is its ultimate realization (4:11), emphasizing the "already and not yet" thematic typical of the New

Testament. Interestingly, Joshua's rest is also compared to and at least partially equated with the Sabbath rest in the Hebrews passage, another Old Testament concept that relates to the founding stories of the Israelite nation.

Questions about the right way to worship YHWH permeate the New Testament. Jesus' ministry challenged established practices, and this was the main reason for his crucifixion. The new Christian worship continued to define its ways of worship against internal challenges (e.g., 1 Chronicles 11–14) and external threats, such as those coming from the Jewish community (Acts 8:1-3; 21:27—26:32; Galatians) and gentile community (Acts 16:16-40; 19:23-41). Both the Roman persecutions of Christians and the various factions and churches within Christianity, including those resulting from the Reformation, demonstrate the continuing importance of religious matters and the right worship of God.

The early church fathers again spiritualized the cities of refuge and the Levitical towns. Jesus is the high priest in a city of refuge (Ambrose), and the lots were drawn in order, referring to the orderliness of the resurrection and also the orderliness of the heavenly power (Origen; see Franke, 88–90). The dismissal of the two and a half tribes indicates the mystery of the fullness of the nations, and the Transjordanian altar is a type of the true altar that is with Jesus (Origen; see Franke, 91–92).

▌ THE TEXT IN CONTEMPORARY DISCUSSION

As with the ideal presented in Joshua, today's communities should strive to provide the best possible environments and institutions in order for people to flourish and so that justice and provision might be available for all. One should also ask what the role of religion should be in society. In the Old Testament, religion was part of the society, much in line with other societies of the time. Judaism, however, was not a dominant religion in Roman society, even though it was a religion with some special privileges from the state. Christianity diverged from Judaism in the Roman Empire, was initially persecuted, and then became an accepted religion and shortly thereafter in the fifth century the only allowed religion. The concept of Christendom was carried over in Europe by the successors of the Roman Empire, and Christendom's hold started to weaken only after the Enlightenment. In most countries outside the West, however, churches have usually not been connected with political power. The history of colonialism has shown the abuses that can take place when Christianity allies itself with political power.

Perhaps the way forward for Christians is to continue acting as leaven (see Matt. 13:33) and lobby political powers (some Christians may themselves be in high positions in society) in order to achieve both societal and intersocietal justice and provision for all. In this, they can ally themselves with secular organizations that have similar goals. For example, the great social movements of the nineteenth and twentieth centuries that achieved universal health care for those who would not be able to have it otherwise should be seen as one good example of the types of programs that Christians can advocate in wider society. In the international context, Christians can lobby for such issues as political and economic justice, as well as equality for weaker nations and the rights of indigenous peoples. As one specific example, Western Christians can work toward moving past the continuing disavowal of the recognition of the rights of indigenous peoples in such countries as the United

States, Canada, Australia, and New Zealand. With the expansion of the new covenant to include all peoples, the welfare of all of humankind should be considered, and not only that of one nation or interest group. Care for the environment and for the creation of God as a whole can also be included in this category.

In terms of the Christian church, the end of Christendom in the West and the lessening or withdrawal of state support from the church in Europe is changing the role of how those in Christian ministry should be supported. These texts from Joshua can be used to encourage people to offer freely from their own in order to support churches. Perhaps the principle of the Old Testament tithe is no more directly applicable, but it can provide a good, broad guideline in a number of cases. It is important that churches trust in the provision of YHWH and not seek to present their message in a "market-oriented" manner, as is the case with the so-called success theology, or the "prosperity gospel."

The spirit of unity promoted in Joshua 20–22 could speak to religious communities that struggle with worship styles. While working to find their right way of worship, they might do well to recognize diversity of opinion and peacefully seek to resolve their differences, rather than heading toward schism. This may be of particular use for faith communities that struggle with contemporary-traditional divides.

Joshua 23–24: Looking into the Future

■ THE TEXT IN ITS ANCIENT CONTEXT

As with the beginning of the book of Joshua, the last two chapters describe a people in transition. Joshua is about to die, and the people are again in a situation where they have to manage on their own, without their great leader. The two chapters constitute a kind of "double ending" for the book. Broadly speaking, Joshua 23 is more concerned with Deuteronomistic themes, and chapter 24 more with overall Hexateuchal themes. However, the fact that the book of Joshua as a whole already mirrors Genesis–Joshua, and that Joshua 24 is presented in an overall Deuteronomistic style, speaks against an easy detachment of this chapter from the rest of the book.

The structure of Joshua 23, while slightly difficult to delimit, can be described as follows (partly based on Nelson, 256).

> Joshua summons Israel in his old age (23:1-2a)
> Joshua's speech (2b-16)
> Joshua's note about his old age (2b)
> Review: YHWH's victory and land allotment (3-5)
>> YHWH's faithfulness (3)
>> Overview of conquest and settlement thus far, and promise of driving out remaining
>> nations in the future (4-5)
> Exhortation to follow the law of Moses and not to join with the remaining nations and their
> gods (6-8)
> Review: YHWH's victorious fighting for Israel (9-10)

Exhortation to love YHWH and conditional threat in regard to alien nations, with special mention against intermarrying (11-13)
Joshua's note about his impending death (14a)
Review: fulfillment of all of YHWH's promises (14b)
Conditional threat about covenant violation (15-16)

Nelson helpfully notes the increasing severity in the threats as the chapter progresses—see 23:6-8, 13 and 15-16 (Nelson, 256). The word "peoples" is used six times (23:3-4, 7, 9, 12-13.) The expression "good land" is important at the end of the passage (see Nelson, 256–57). In other words, the chapter uses a strategy of rhetorical persuasion.

The structure of Joshua 24:1-28 can be described as follows:

The covenant renewal at Shechem (24:1-28)
    Joshua assembles Israel at Shechem (1)
    Joshua's first speech: YHWH's message (2-16)
        Historical recital (2-13)
            Call of Abraham (2-3)
            Isaac, Jacob, Esau, and going down to Egypt (4)
            Moses and Aaron and the exodus (5)
            Miracle at the Sea of Reeds (6-7a)
            Wilderness wanderings (7b)
            The conquest of Transjordan (8)
            Balaam incident (9-10)
        Conquest of Canaan with YHWH's help (11-13)
        Exhortation to serve YHWH (14-15)
    Response by the people (16-18)
        Denial that the people will serve other gods (16)
        Acknowledgment of YHWH's work (17-18a)
        Promise to serve YHWH (18b)
    Joshua's second speech (19-20)
        People cannot serve YHWH (19a)
        Threat of punishment (19b-20)
    Response by the people promising to serve YHWH (21)
    Joshua's response, making people witnesses (22a)
    Response by the people, acknowledging that they are witnesses (22b)
    Joshua's exhortation to put away foreign gods (23)
    Response by the people, promising to serve YHWH (24)
    Summary about making a covenant (25)
    Joshua writes the words of the covenant in a book of the law of God (26a)
    The stone of witness (26b-27)
        Setting up the stone (26b)
        Joshua's summary about the role of the stone (27)
    Joshua sends the people back to their homes (28)

The overall purpose of verses 1-28 strengthen Joshua's overall rhetoric in exhorting the Israelites to follow YHWH exclusively. The forming of a covenant (see Koopmans for this aspect, including comparisons with ancient Near Eastern treaty formats; but note also the *misharum* acts in Babylonia, which were basically minor legal edicts addressing specific situations, meant to be understood as additions to existing legal or legal-related practice), examples from past history, and various exhortations throughout serve to reinforce this objective. As Nelson notes, repetition serves to "impel the reader to go along with the assembled Israel and to concur with the text's agenda" (268). The means of pleading, setting an example, and using accusatory speech are part of the rhetorical means of persuasion in 24:14-21 (Pitkänen 2010, 396).

The location of the covenant ceremony and of charging the people to remove all foreign gods and consider YHWH only heightens the symbolism of the occasion, as this is *the* place (24:25-26) where Jacob, the grand patriarch of Israel *in actuality* threw away *his* foreign gods (Gen. 35:1-5). Thus the whole point of the ceremony in this chapter is to emphasize total commitment to YHWH, a decisive point of no return in the life of the new Israel in the land of their forefathers, where they have now returned after a long absence. Just as Jacob was to purify himself of foreign gods after his stay away in Paddan Aram and YHWH's gracious granting of return and prosperity to him (Genesis 35), so is Israel to do also. Of course, the reader (or hearer) of the book of Joshua is expected to take note accordingly. Chapters 23–24 are generally in line with the idea that religiopolitical ideology is often driven by political elites, even if it can be helped by popular support or even partially also driven by it (see Kakel, 213–14). Religious diversity in ancient, preexilic Israel is confirmed by known archaeological evidence, and it would appear that the idea that the people followed YHWH in the time of Joshua should be seen as a more or less idealized concept (see the comments on 21:43-45 in the Joshua 20–22 sense unit).

Joshua 24:28-33, which is followed by a few lines of extra material in Greek manuscripts, describes the death and burials of Joshua and Eleazar, together with the burial of Joseph's bones, tying the material explicitly to Genesis. The additions in the Greek attest connection with the book of Judges, and such a connection must have been done at a suitable time, as Judges in its present form follows on from the book of Joshua relatively seamlessly. This is true even when Judges, at least arguably, is clearly a separate book (even though, for Noth and those following him, both Joshua and Judges are part of a unified historical work of a Deuteronomistic History).

■ THE TEXT IN THE INTERPRETIVE TRADITION

The Bible itself shows that the ideology of following YHWH as advocated by Joshua 23 and 24 did not fare well in the wider societal setting. This is the overall conclusion of the writer(s) of 1–2 Kings (e.g., 2 Kgs. 23:26-27; cf. Ps. 78:56-64) and many of the Old Testament prophets, and of course the Pentateuch shows that the Israelites already did not follow YHWH wholeheartedly in the wilderness from Exodus on either (see also Ps. 78:8-57).

The New Testament, of course, exhorts Christians to follow God wholeheartedly. The concept is so pervasive that hardly any additional commentary is required on the principle itself. And yet, the question of what is the right way to follow God is equally alive in the New Testament. The New

Testament includes many descriptions about internal debates already at the time of the first apostles. Even the apostles themselves could be of differing opinion (Acts 6:1-15; 15:36-40) and could also rebuke each other in case of perceived inappropriate practice (Gal. 2:11-14; cf. 1 Cor. 11:18; 1 Thess. 5:21). Of course, Christian history shows many debates about what is the right way to follow YHWH, as attested by the great church councils of the first few centuries of the Common Era and by the Reformation in Europe.

The early church fathers generally understood chapters 23–24 less typologically than usual with the book of Joshua (see Franke, 93–98), probably simply because these chapters lend themselves more easily to a straightforward theological interpretation from a post–New Testament perspective. But Cyprian saw the stone of witness in Joshua 24:26-27 as Christ (Franke, 97). Interestingly, Jerome assumed that Joshua had no children and was not married since they are not mentioned, and thus argued for celibacy as a better status than marriage (see Franke, 97–98). Jerome also suggested that the fact that there is no mention of the Israelites' grieving Joshua (as they did with the death of Moses) symbolizes our not needing to grieve in the face of death, since we have put on Christ (see Franke, 98).

∎THE TEXT IN CONTEMPORARY DISCUSSION

Christians, when thinking about their covenant ("treaty") with God, can also reflect on their past history with God. Such history consists of YHWH's acts through history as expressed in the Bible (both the Old and the New Testaments), in church history, and in remembrance of YHWH's acts in their personal lives (and also in the lives of others they may know [about] in their communities). Such memory and understanding serves as a vital basis for one's faith. If one wishes, one may also write down one's experiences in a book and arrange for some kind of object (e.g., some like to wear a crucifix) to commemorate such events and experiences. Christians may also reflect on other aspects of the (new) treaty that was established through the sacrifice of Christ on the cross. They may draw attention to Joshua's call to his hearers to choose between YHWH and other gods. This call to follow YHWH is also reflected in Jesus' call to "follow me!"

However, for Christians in a post-Christendom and postcolonial world, this exhortation to follow ought to be tempered by a caution against desiring a form of political power tied to religion, and it ought not include any violent inclination toward those who think differently, even when differences of opinion and their testing are appropriate (see 1 Cor. 11:18; 1 Thess. 5:21). In addition, in general, Christians are exhorted to reflect humbly on the role of violence in the development and history of their own religion and its relation to questions of theodicy, rather than disavowing that violence (see Davies, 120–47). In an eschatological sense, while portions of the Gospels and the book of Revelation may be viewed as predicting eschatological violence, Christians should refrain from being instigators of such violence. And, while in some cases the attainment of justice and protection of others would seem to require the use of violence, one should always consider its use as the last resort after all other possible means have been exhausted.

A related issue in following YHWH is the question of what one should do when life does not seem happy or worth living even when one is following YHWH wholeheartedly (e.g., the book of

Job). One may be struggling to earn a living, be ill or grieving, or persecuted because of one's faith. Such situations can often also make one reflect on the concept of theodicy. As with the question of violence, it may not be that a rational theodicy of the Old Testament—and often not one of the New Testament either—seems attainable. Instead, when thinking of the past, present, and the future, the only option for Christians is often to make an existential leap of faith, trusting in God and God's goodness, that everything will ultimately go well with those who do so, exactly whatever this "going well" may entail (see M. E. W. Thompson 2011).

Works Cited

Aubet, M. E. 2013. *Commerce and Colonization in the Ancient Near East.* Cambridge: Cambridge University Press (Spanish original 2007).

Barmash, Pamela. 2005. *Homicide in the Biblical World.* Cambridge: Cambridge University Press.

Blenkinsopp, Joseph. 1972. *Gibeon and Israel: The Role of Gibeon and the Gibeonites in the Political and Religious History of Early Israel.* Cambridge: Cambridge University Press.

Boling, R. G., and G. E. Wright. 1982. *Joshua: A New Translation with Introduction and Commentary.* AB. Garden City, NY: Doubleday.

Butler, T. 1983. *Joshua.* WBC. Waco, TX: Word.

Calvin, John. 1854. *Commentaries on the Book of Joshua.* Translated by Henry Beveridge. Edinburgh: Calvin Translation Society (Original 1564).

Carr, David M. 2011. *The Formation of the Hebrew Bible: A New Reconstruction.* New York: Oxford University Press.

Chapman, C. 2005. "God's Covenant—God's Land?" In *The God of Covenant,* edited by Alistair I. Wilson and Jamie A. Grant, 221–56. Leicester, UK: Inter-Varsity Press.

Clouse, R. D., ed. 1977. *The Meaning of the Millennium: Four Views.* Downers Grove, IL: InterVarsity Press.

Court, J. M. 2008. *Approaching the Apocalypse: A Short History of Christian Millenarianism.* London: I. B. Tauris.

Davies, E. W. 2010. *The Immoral Bible: Approaches to Biblical Ethics.* New York: T&T Clark.

Day, D. 2008. *Conquest: How Societies Overwhelm Others.* Oxford: Oxford University Press.

Dever, W. G. 2003. *Who Were the Early Israelites and Where Did They Come From?* Grand Rapids: Eerdmans.

Dietler, M. 2010. *Archaeologies of Colonialism: Consumption, Entanglement and Violence in Ancient Mediterranean France.* Berkeley: University of California Press.

Docker, J. 2008. *The Origins of Violence: Religion, History and Genocide.* London: Pluto.

Dozeman, Thomas B., Thomas Römer, and Konrad Schmid, eds. 2011. *Pentateuch, Hexateuch, or Enneateuch? Identifying Literary Works in Genesis through Kings.* Ancient Israel and Its Literature 8. Atlanta: Society of Biblical Literature.

Dozeman, Thomas B., and Konrad Schmid, eds. 2006. *A Farewell to the Yahwist? The Composition of the Pentateuch in Recent European Interpretation.* SBLSymS 34. Atlanta: Society of Biblical Literature.

Earl, D. S. 2010. *Reading Joshua as Christian Scripture.* PhD diss., Durham University. Available at *Durham E-Theses Online*: http://etheses.dur.ac.uk/2267/ (also published in slightly revised form as *Reading Joshua as Christian Scripture.* Journal of Theological Interpretation Supplement 2. Winona Lake, IN: Eisenbrauns, 2010).

Faust, A. 2006. *Israel's Ethnogenesis: Settlement, Interaction, Expansion and Resistance.* London: Equinox.

Finkelberg, M. 2005. *Greeks and Pre-Greeks: Aegean Prehistory and Greek Heroic Tradition.* Cambridge: Cambridge University Press.

Finkelstein, I. 1988. *The Archaeology of the Israelite Settlement*. Jerusalem: Israel Exploration Society.

Franke, J. R., ed. 2005. *Joshua, Judges, Ruth, 1–2 Samuel*. In Ancient Christian Commentary on Scripture, Old Testament 4. Downers Grove, IL: InterVarsity Press.

Fritz, V. 1994. *Das Buch Josua*. HAT I/7. Tübingen: J. C. B. Mohr.

Guyatt, N. 2007. *Providence and the Invention of the United States, 1607–1876*. Cambridge: Cambridge University Press.

Hawk, L. D. 2000. *Joshua*. Berit Olam. Collegeville, MN: Liturgical Press.

———. 2010. *Joshua in 3D: A Commentary on Biblical Conquest and Manifest Destiny*. Eugene, OR: Cascade.

Hess, R. S. 1996. *Joshua: An Introduction and Commentary*. TOTC. Leicester, UK: Inter-Varsity Press.

Hoffmeier, J. K. 1997. *Israel in Egypt: The Evidence for the Authenticity of the Exodus Tradition*. Oxford: Oxford University Press.

———. 2005. *Ancient Israel in Sinai: The Evidence for the Authenticity of the Wilderness Traditions*. Oxford: Oxford University Press.

Horowitz, D. 2000. *Ethnic Groups in Conflict*. Berkeley: University of California Press, 1985. Reprint.

Hutton, J. 2011. "The Levitical Diaspora (II): Modern Perspectives on the Levitical Cities Lists (A Review of Opinions)." In *Levites and Priests in Biblical History and Tradition*, edited by Mark Leuchter and Jeremy Hutton, 45–82. Ancient Israel and Its Literature 9. Atlanta: Society of Biblical Literature.

Junkkaala, E. 2006. *Three Conquests of Canaan: A Comparative Study of Two Egyptian Military Campaigns and Joshua 10–12 in the Light of Recent Archaeological Evidence*. Turku: Åbo Akademi University Press. https://oa.doria.fi/handle/10024/4162.

Kakel, C. P. 2011. *The American West and the Nazi East: A Comparative and Interpretive Perspective*. Basingstoke, UK: Palgrave Macmillan.

Kallai, Z. 1986. *Historical Geography of the Bible: The Tribal Territories of Israel*. Jerusalem: Magnes Press; Leiden: Brill.

———. 2010. *Studies in Biblical Historiography and Geography: Collection of Studies*. BEATAJ 56. Frankfurt am Main: Peter Lang.

Kitchen, K. 2003. *On the Reliability of the Old Testament*. Grand Rapids: Eerdmans.

Knauf, E. A. 2008. *Josua*. ZBK 6. Zürich: Theologischer.

Koopmans, W. T. 1990. *Joshua 24 as Poetic Narrative*. JSOTSup 93. Sheffield: Sheffield Academic Press.

Koorevaar, H. J. 1990. *De Opbouw van het Boek Jozua*. Heverlee: Centrum voor Bijbelse Vorming Belgie v.z.w. (Dutch, with an English summary).

Lemche, N. P. 1998. *The Israelites in History and Tradition*. Louisville: Westminster John Knox.

Levene, M. 2005. *Genocide in the Age of the Nation State*. Vol. 1, *The Meaning of Genocide*. London: I. B. Tauris.

Levy, T. E., ed. 2010. *Historical Biblical Archaeology and the Future: The New Pragmatism*. London: Equinox.

Liverani, M. 2005. *Israel's History and the History of Israel*. London: Equinox (Italian original, 2003).

Mann, T. W. 1977. *Divine Presence and Guidance in Israelite Traditions: The Typology of Exaltation*. Baltimore: Johns Hopkins University Press.

Meer, M. N. van der. 2004. *Formation and Reformulation: The Redaction of the Book of Joshua in the Light of the Oldest Textual Witnesses*. VTSup 102. Leiden: Brill.

Miller, J. M., and J. H. Hayes. 2006. *History of Ancient Israel and Judah*. 2nd ed. London: SCM.

Moberly, R.W.L. 1999. "Toward an Interpretation of the Shema," in *Theological Exegesis: Essays in Honor of Brevard S. Childs*, ed. by C. Seitz and K. Greene-McCreight. Grand Rapids: Eerdmans.

Moorey, P. R. S. 1991. *A Century of Biblical Archaeology*. Cambridge: Lutterworth.

Nelson, R. D. 1997. *Joshua*. OTL. Louisville: Westminster John Knox.

Nissinen, M. 2003. *Prophets and Prophecy in the Ancient Near East*, with contributions by C. L. Seow and Robert K. Ritner. SBLWAW 12. Atlanta: Society of Biblical Literature.

Noort, E. 1998. *Das Buch Josua: Forschungsgeschichte und Problemfelder*. Darmstadt: Wissenschaftliche Buchgesellschaft.

Noth, M. 1953. *Das Buch Josua*. 7th ed. HAT, series 1. Tübingen: Mohr Siebeck.

———. 1991. *The Deuteronomistic History*. 2nd ed. JSOTSup 15. Sheffield: Sheffield Academic (German original: *Überlieferungsgeschichtliche Studien*. Vol. 1. Halle: M. Niemeyer, 1943).

Osterhammel, J. 2005. *Colonialism: A Theoretical Overview*. Translated by Shelley L. Frisch. 2nd ed. Princeton: Markus Wiener.

Otto, E. 2000. *Das Deuteronomium im Pentateuch und Hexateuch: Studien zur Literaturgeschichte von Pentateuch und Hexateuch im Lichte des Deuteronomiumrahmens*. FAT 30. Tübingen: Mohr Siebeck.

———. 2012. *Deuteronomium 1,1–4,43*. HTKAT. Freiburg: Herder.

Ottosson, M. 1991. *Josuaboken: En programskrift för davidisk restauration*. Acta Universitatis Uppsaliensis, Studia Biblica Uppsaliensia 1. Stockholm: Almqvist & Wiksell.

Pitkänen, P. M. A. 2010. *Joshua*. AOTC 6, Leicester, UK: Inter-Varsity Press.

———. 2013a. "Pentateuch-Joshua: A Settler-Colonial Document of a Supplanting Society." *Settler Colonial Studies*.

———. 2013b. "Ancient Israel and Settler Colonialism." *Settler Colonial Studies* 4, no. 1.

Sand, S. 2009. *The Invention of the Jewish People*. London: Verso.

———. 2012. *The Invention of the Land of Israel*. London: Verso.

Stannard, D. E. 1992. *American Holocaust: Columbus and the Conquest of the New World*. Oxford: Oxford University Press.

Thompson, M. E. W. 2011. *Where Is the God of Justice? The Old Testament and Suffering*. Eugene, OR: Pickwick.

Thompson, T. L. 1992. *Early History of the Israelite People: From the Written and Archaeological Sources*. Leiden: Brill.

Tinker, G. E. 2004. *Spirit and Resistance: Political Theology and American Indian Liberation*. Minneapolis: Fortress Press.

———. 2008. *American Indian Liberation: A Theology of Sovereignty*. Maryknoll, NY: Orbis.

Tov, E. 2012. *Textual Criticism of the Hebrew Bible*. 3rd ed. Minneapolis: Fortress Press.

Veracini, L. 2006. *Israel and Settler Society*. London: Pluto.

———. 2010. *Settler Colonialism: A Theoretical Overview*. New York: Palgrave Macmillan.

Waswo, R. 1997. *From Virgil to Vietnam: The Founding Legend of Western Civilization*. Hanover, NH: Wesleyan University Press.

Westermann, C. 1994. *Die Geschichtsbücher des Alten Testaments: Gab es ein deuteronomistisches Geschichtswerk?* ("The Historical Books of the Old Testament: Was There a Deuteronomistic History?"). Gütersloh: Chr. Kaiser/Gütersloher.

Wolfe, P. 2008. "Structure and Event: Settler Colonialism, Time and the Question of Genocide." In *Empire, Colony, Genocide: Conquest, Occupation and Subaltern Resistance in World History*, edited by D. Moses, 102–32. New York: Bergahn.

Younger, K. L 1990. *Ancient Conquest Accounts: A Study in Ancient Near Eastern and Biblical History Writing*. JSOTSup 98. Sheffield: Sheffield Academic Press.

Zvi, E. ben. 1992. "The List of the Levitical Cities." *JSOT* 54:77–106.

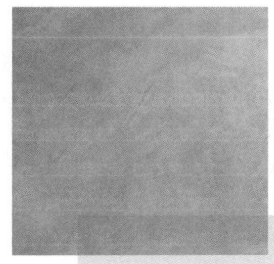

JUDGES

Victor H. Matthews

Introduction

Since the time of Martin Noth, the book of Judges has been included by scholars in the Deuteronomistic redaction (Deuteronomy–2 Kings). However, portions of the book, especially chapters 1 and 17–21, do not readily fit the theological pattern of obedience/success and disobedience/punishment (Greenspahn, 389–95). Like the book of Job, the book of Judges is characterized by a sandwich structure. The introductory materials in 1:1—3:6 and the judge-less narratives in 17–21 envelop the collected tales of the judges as they are presented within the context of the framework cycle (compare Genesis 1 and Exod. 7:14—12:32 for similar literary frameworks). In this middle portion of the book, a succession of individuals, both male and female, are portrayed in a variety of contexts. Each (excluding the minor judges, who function simply as literary pauses between the tales of major figures), however, must deal with a crisis precipitated by Israelite apostasy.

Interspersed within the narratives are small vignettes, often depicting physical humor, that point to individual heroes operating in a time when violence is common. For instance, the stories of Caleb and Othniel (Judg. 1:11-21) set the stage for later, more developed episodes like those of Gideon and Samson (Judges 6–8 and 13–16). Perhaps they serve as oral reminders of the body of tales in the storyteller's repertoire or a way to portray aspects of life and the difficult land the Israelites have come to inhabit. In sum, the stage is set for future tensions with neighboring peoples that appear more graphically in the framework-bound stories in Judges 3–16.

In what appears to be an addendum to the book of Judges, the last five chapters are remarkable for their gross violations of the covenant with God and for their gratuitous violence and are therefore a fit conclusion to a text that shows the Israelites to be their own worst enemy (McCann, 117). They are reminiscent of the unsettling events recounted in the fourteenth-century-BCE Egyptian El Amarna tablets that describe Canaan as filled with lawlessness men (ʿapiru) and political opportunists.

Even though the conclusion to Judges does not follow the structure of chapters 3–16 and does not include the activities of a judge, it achieves the goal of showing that social, religious, and political chaos are prone to exist in the absence of a central government and a king (Judg. 21:25). That is not to say that they are entirely promonarchy. After all, the Deuteronomistic Historian is a politico-religious voice that generally promotes the house of David. It is therefore not surprising to find in these final chapters some poorly disguised political polemics (Leuchter, 438). Thus the house of Saul is tied to the setting (Gibeah) and atrocities in the story of the Levite's concubine (cf. 1 Sam. 11:4-7 and Judg. 19:22-30), and Jeroboam's placement of a golden calf and shrine in Dan (1 Kgs. 12:28-30) finds it origins in the story of Micah's idol (Judg. 18:27-31).

It is still unclear how the Israelite tribes entered Canaan and coalesced into an identifiable people (Niditch, 6–8). Archaeological evidence indicates a large number of new settlements in the central hill country after 1200 BCE, but they may be tied to the collapse of the Canaanite city-states after the sea people's invasion or to a synthesis of refugees and new peoples. Judges, with its stories that range from a set of ancient "battle-story accounts" (Younger) to a theodicy of the Israelites' failure to conquer the promised land, diverges from the triumphalist conquest account found in Joshua. Its narratives present a mix of victory and defeat, with the Israelite tribes continually falling short of their obligations under the covenant and then "crying out" for divine assistance. In fact, the accounts are closer in tone to the ninth-century-BCE Moabite inscription of King Mesha, with its acceptance of divine wrath of their god Chemosh (see Judg. 2:14; 11:24), and a subsequent return of divine grace that leads to military victory and an end to oppression (compare 2 Kings 3).

When stories are so "over the top" in their depiction of characters and their antisocial activities, modern audiences come to see them as either satire or as a gross form of comedy. Who could believe anyone or any group could possibly do the things described in these final chapters in Judges? And yet, news reports are filled today with incredible statements or violent acts in the name of religious piety. Mass murders, rape, and mayhem are a part of civil wars around the world. It may be that shock literature such as this in Judges or portrayals of the dark side of human nature are necessary to make the point that it takes more than identifying a problem to cure it. Conscious intent to work with and ease the pain of those who have been broken in spirit and body is needed far more than taking revenge on the culprits. When everyone does what is "right in their own eyes" (Judg. 21:25), there is no justice except by force; and there is no peace when self-interest overrides the well-being of the community.

Judges 1:1—3:6 Introductory Narrative

Post-Joshua Conquest Attempts (Judges 1:1—2:10)

▮ THE TEXT IN ITS ANCIENT CONTEXT

There are two distinct beginnings to Judges, although both reference the end of Joshua's life and career (1:1 and 2:6-10). The first, stating "Judah is to go up" first to fight against the Canaanites provides justification (linked to later political realities) for the emergence of the tribe of Judah as one of the two most important tribes in Israel's later history (1:2). The second introductory passage begins with a divinely heralded proclamation of the Israelites' failure to obey the covenant. Therefore, they will be unable to drive out the Canaanites (2:1-6), who will subsequently become a test of Israel's faithfulness and a means of sharpening their skills in war (3:4).

Despite Judah's initial success, more realistic references to differences in material culture (i.e., use of more sophisticated weapons) are injected into the text that explain why the tribes are bottled up in the hill country (1:19). The Joseph tribes (Manasseh and Ephraim) do achieve mixed success, but the rest of the tribes are listed in a litany of failures in other areas of the land (1:21-36). This section also includes the ironic fate of King Adoni-bezek (Judg. 1:5-7), who suffers the same mutilation as the seventy kings he had defeated. It serves as a reminder that the proud, Canaanite or Israelite, can also fall. His scuttling about under the table without thumbs or big toes punctuates the rough humor of a frontier society often quick to laugh at the misfortunes of a former oppressor.

▌ The Text in the Interpretive Tradition

The third-fourth-century Christian historian Eusebius of Caesarea traces Judah's emerging prominence among the tribes (1:1-10) as an indicator of the tribe's future role in producing leaders like David, Zerubbabel, and ultimately Jesus. Another church father, Jerome, the translator of the Vulgate, sees the reference to the tears shed by the disobedient Israelites at Bochim (Judg. 2:1-5) as an allegory for the "vale of tears" imposed on all humankind after their expulsion from Eden. In this way, humanity had the opportunity to wrestle with vice and obtain merit through its righteous labor.

▌ The Text in Contemporary Discussion

These narratives represent the struggles faced by pioneers in their effort to exploit the resources of the land while fighting to maintain their hold over the land and its resources in order to survive. It is, of course, possible for North American audiences to identify with the settlers as part of their own pioneering history. The push to conquer or eliminate the indigenous population from territory assumed to be given to the settlers as their Manifest Destiny is also familiar.

It is also apparent that these shocking tales contain little that is uplifting or admirable. However, when seen in the light of how oppressed or marginalized people depict themselves, Judges emerges in its original context as a way of coping with oppression. These first two chapters make it clear that obtaining ownership of the land will not be an easy task. The pluralistic and polytheistic environment in which the settlers find themselves becomes a major stumbling block. At the same time, these chapters demonstrate that people do not live in a social vacuum and that hard choices must be made continually. Interestingly, the Israelite tribes in these introductory chapters do not adequately recognize cause and effect. They simply know that they have either succeeded or failed, and occasionally they acknowledge the role of God in this process. It is their unsteady relationship with Yahweh that is highlighted in these texts. The stories show God's persistence in upholding the covenantal agreement in the face of a "stiff-necked" and disobedient people. They also demonstrate that the benighted Israelites do keep crying out for relief, a sign that they have not abandoned their hope in Yahweh.

Disobedience, the Judges Cycle, and Testing (Judges 2:11—3:6)

∎ THE TEXT IN ITS ANCIENT CONTEXT

In a tightly reasoned theodicy, the Deuteronomic editors of the Judges material lay out a clearly defined cycle of disobedience, divinely sanctioned oppression by neighboring peoples, divine redemption (rising up of a judge), and a return to disobedience. A more explicit tone of repentance by the Israelites is injected in the actual accounts of the judges (3:9), but in this initial version they are simply described as being "in distress" (2:15). A similar pattern is reprised in the prophetic materials in which God responds to idolatrous behavior with foreign invasions, drought, and plague, and then raises up prophets to call on the people (usually just a righteous remnant) to return to proper compliance with the covenant (see Jer. 26:4-6; Hag. 1:2-11). However, in Judges the cycle also functions as a sort of literary glue holding together a disparate collection of narratives.

The use of a collective "Israelites" (*bᵉnê yíśrāᵉēl*) throughout the book (sixty-one times) might be compared to the hieroglyphic determinative for a people attached to the ethnic name Israel in the Egyptian Merneptah Stela (1208 BCE), at least in the sense of assigning collective guilt. However, there is no real effort at chronological progression in these stories, and their settings never encompass all of the Israelite tribal allotments. It is enough to say that disobedience to the stipulations of the covenant, and in particular idolatry (2:19), provides sufficient justification for divine anger and action.

The injection of a divinely appointed hero/champion is an interesting story element and does seem to preshadow the introduction of the earliest anointed kings (Saul and David) when the monarchy is established (see Nathan's reference to the judges period in 2 Sam. 7:11). Of course, the hero archetype is as old as the third- and second-millennium-BCE Gilgamesh legends of ancient Mesopotamia. These figures are often aided by deities and demonstrate greater than human abilities. Where the archetype differs in the biblical account is in the stated purpose for the judge's appearance. Each is to function as a temporary deliverer whose job is to remove the current form of oppression inflicted on the Israelites. While some do display feats of strength, skill, and courage, they are different enough in their methods and character to escape too much stereotyping.

God's response to the recurrence of disobedient behavior following the death of each judge is to set aside divine protection so that the indigenous inhabitants of Canaan remain in the land (Judg. 2:20-23). Conflict with these enemy nations functions as a live classroom for the Israelites to learn the arts of war while testing their allegiance to the covenant (3:1-4). Unfortunately, the presence of these foreign peoples simply entices the Israelites to intermarry with them and to worship their gods (3:5-6)—a socio-theological situation that provides the spark to begin the cycle and the raising of the first judge, Othniel.

∎ THE TEXT IN THE INTERPRETIVE TRADITION

In his recounting of the Judges narrative, Josephus cites the Israelites' refusal to fight against the Canaanites, preferring to indulge themselves with luxuries obtained from their cultivation of the land (*Ant.* 5.132–35). He then demonstrates their corruption by appending the stories of the Levite's concubine (Judges 19–21) and the migration of the tribe of Dan (Judges 17–18). The church fathers drew comparisons between unbelievers in the time of Christ and those who bent the knee to Baal (Origen—third century), and saw the testing of the Israelites (Judg. 3:1-4) by the nations left in the land as part of God's plan to teach humility (John Cassian—fifth century) and to develop perfection through trial (Isaac of Nineveh—sixth century).

∎ THE TEXT IN CONTEMPORARY DISCUSSION

It is tempting to see these introductory sections of the book of Judges as part of the "apology" of David and thus a political treatise arguing for the establishment of the monarchy as an alternative to anarchy. But that sets aside the Deuteronomistic Historian's focus on the need for religious fidelity (Block 1988, 46). At the heart of these stories is the temptation faced by the Israelites to assimilate to a wider culture and to set aside allegiance to their tribal god and what may be considered less sophisticated customs. In a pluralistic society (then and now), it is easy to lose focus on what really matters and be drawn to the dominant culture or the latest craze or religious movement. Is it possible to say that we are "tested" by God in our own society, as the Deuteronomist believed the Israelites were tested in theirs? A complementary issue has to do with human recidivism and divine patience. A divine patron who saves once is not remarkable, but one who repeatedly forgives is. The Judges cycle does not end with just a single revolution of its elements. God is shown to be patient and willing, after getting the people's attention through very harsh measures, to provide them yet another chance; and that is indeed remarkable and worth taking seriously.

Judges 3:7—16:31 Collected Tales

∎ THE TEXT IN ITS ANCIENT CONTEXT

What becomes quite evident after the judgeship of Othniel is that a literary framework provides a narrative vehicle to highlight the personal flaws of each successive judge, ultimately overshadowing their accomplishments. While Othniel succeeds with the help of God's infusing spirit and without any comment beyond his total success, other judges will not be as successful. There is always something about their character (tricksters like Ehud and Gideon) or the degree to which they can call on the allegiance of other tribes (Deborah and Jephthah) that suggests matters are just not quite right. In the end, the last of these divinely appointed figures (Samson) is portrayed as an utterly self-centered, self-indulgent womanizer, and much closer to the stereotypical ancient hero typified by Gilgamesh or Hercules.

Perhaps this downward progression is part of a larger editorial plan designed to set up the audience for the political statements in 18:1 and 21:25 that blame a lawless society on the lack of a king to rule the tribes. However, that may be too narrow a view given a similar pattern of stubborn disobedience to God's commands found elsewhere in the Deuteronomistic History (see 2 Kgs. 17:7-20) and in the Psalms (78; 81) and in the Prophets (Jeremiah 5; Hosea 4; Zech. 7:8-14). The judges, like the kings in a later period, have to deal with real-world situations and yet will also have to work within a structure in which they are the servants of a god. The mixture of secular situations and crises, and divine assistance/interference is a favorite device of ancient authors. (The Sumerian sage Adapa, for example, is offered the "bread of life" by the gods, but is counseled by his patron deity Ea to refuse to eat, and thus loses the chance for personal immortality.)

▌ THE TEXT IN THE INTERPRETIVE TRADITION

The need for humility and the expunging of a prideful and destructive spirit were self-evident to the church fathers, who used the text of the book of Judges to call on Christians to recognize God's active concern in current difficulties. Just as the Israelites were handed over to enemy nations because of their wickedness, those who call on God in repentance can expect that they will be lifted up by "throngs of archangels" and restored to their inheritance of salvation (Origen; cf. Eph. 2:1-2). In that way, it is possible to interpret the succession of judges as divine deliverers, brought to the people because of the Israelites' tendency to become "tepid" in their faith and thus need more than a single lesson in humility (Cassian).

▌ THE TEXT IN CONTEMPORARY DISCUSSION

Among the questions that can be asked about these texts is how they relate to our perception of leadership today, and whether it makes a difference if the Bible does not present the judges as perfect heroes. Given the fact that some of today's leaders are shown to be flawed and unethical in their dealings with their constituents and others, does the book of Judges simply excuse such behavior as "simply human"? Are the obvious narrative cues and a host of incidents that contain social gaffes to be taken as social criticism or humor? To be sure, modern literature is filled with these types of characters, and it is almost a comfort to be introduced to less-than-perfect protagonists with whom it is possible to identify. There is also a clear sense in these stories of divine redemption apart from the merit of those to be redeemed. Biblical characters are thus released from the unreasonable expectation that they must always be perfect role models.

Othniel (Judges 3:7-11)

▌ THE TEXT IN ITS ANCIENT CONTEXT

The story of the first judge, while it sets a precedent , tells little more than the fact that Othniel of the tribe of Judah "went out to war" and with God's help defeated King Cushan-Rishathaim, most likely a king of Edom (Sadler, 812–13; Judg. 3:10). Such a bare-bones account of the unvarnished steps of the cycle format may have been intended to set the proper tone for the behavior of judges. It does resemble the initial presentation of Abram, who answers God's call to immigrate without question (Gen. 12:1-4), and shows unquestioning loyalty to God's command through his willingness to sacrifice his long-desired son Isaac (Gen. 22:1-19). However, it would be impractical to think that the storyteller would choose to present every other judge in the same shorthand manner. In fact, the editors do not, resorting instead to the Deuteronomist's theme of social and religious disintegration.

Curiously, there is a similar story in Judg. 1:11-15 in which Othniel successfully, and without any narrative elaboration, captures the city of Kiriath-sepher. More interesting here is the interchange between Othniel's new wife Achsah and her father Caleb. It provides a human-interest story that includes a tone of barely disguised, disrespectful dissatisfaction over the dry dowry lands provided as part of her wedding contract. Caleb's quiet acquiescence to Achsah's request for springs to water their given section of the Negev acknowledges that she is in the right (1:14-16; compare Judah in Gen. 38:25-26).

■ THE TEXT IN THE INTERPRETIVE TRADITION

Both Josephus (*Ant.* 5.182–83) and his first-century contemporary Pseudo-Philo (*L.A.B.* 26–28) have recounted Othniel's story, ascribing his accomplishments to his father Kenaz/Cenaz. Josephus focuses more on the political crimes of the Israelites rather than their covenantal failures as the cause for the crisis that leads to God's revealing to Kenaz what he must do. Pseudo-Philo grants Kenaz a larger role than in either the Bible or in Josephus, expanding his leadership efforts to include interrogating sinners and punishing those who question his authority (Begg, 334–35).

■ THE TEXT IN CONTEMPORARY DISCUSSION

The editors of Judges have created a sliding scale of effectiveness in their portrayal of the deliverers, which requires the first judge to be an unsullied paragon and the last to exhibit total self-interest and disregard for the needs of the community. Modern society publicly sets a high standard of ethical leadership for its officials, but few actually measure up to that ideal. The twenty-four-hour news cycle and the ability to delve into every aspect of a leader's life put extreme pressure on them and sometimes leads them to make foolish decisions. The pattern of decline in Judges does allow for a more realistic view of leadership while warning society against letting bravado and demagoguery replace substance. Many would appreciate a conscientious public servant like Othniel, but we often settle for someone who simply gets things done.

Ehud (Judges 3:12-30) and Shamgar (Judges 3:31)

■ THE TEXT IN ITS ANCIENT CONTEXT

The second judge, Ehud, is a successful leader, and he serves in that capacity for eighty years, longer than any other judge/deliverer. His narrative also begins the downward spiral that will take the judges from the pinnacle represented by Othniel to the lawless egotism of Samson. In many ways, these stories echo the character types among Homer's heroes in their struggle before Troy. Some, like Achilles, are able to achieve remarkable feats of strength, usually with the assistance of a patron deity; some are trickster figures (Odysseus); and some are willing to make incredible bargains with the gods to gain a victory (Agamemnon). Ehud falls into the trickster category, a favorite character in Israelite tradition (cf. Jacob).

Ehud's tale begins with an indictment of the Israelites for their unfaithfulness (3:12). An affronted God then allows an alliance of traditional foes led by Eglon, king of Moab, to take possession of portions of the land for eighteen years (3:13-14). The audience is then provided with a series of narrative cues and puns. Ehud is a Benjamite (Saul's tribe; 1 Sam. 9:1-2), and the seat of power chosen by Eglon is the "city of Palms" (probably Jericho), a reference to the partial dismantling of Joshua's conquests (Joshua 6). The fact that Ehud is left-handed, possibly ambidextrous

(3:15), and carries a specially designed dagger on his right thigh (3:16) foreshadows Ehud's means of assassinating Eglon. The play on Ehud's name ("Where is majesty?") and Eglon's name ("calf" or "bull") plays into the contest-between-gods motif in which Yahweh challenges the power of Baal, who is often represented as a bull or astride a bull (Keel and Uehlinger, 144–46; see 1 Kings 18). For comic-relief purposes, it is possible that a phonetic pun on Eglon's name may be stretched to include the "round" nature of the king's ample belly fat (3:17b, 22; Butler, 69).

Ehud's trickster nature emerges in his fabrication of a sleek, double-edged dagger, which he hides under his right thigh. A right-handed man would normally draw from his left side, and it is not surprising the guards miss the weapon when they search his person (cf. Joab's assassination of Amasa in 2 Sam. 20:9-10). Extending the trickster theme, Ehud first tempts Eglon's cupidity with the promise of a "secret message" (3:19), and then expands this to a "message from God" (3:20) in order to get the king alone. Given the opportunity, Ehud thrusts his dagger into Eglon's belly and the fat completely envelops the blade (3:21-22). In what may be the first "locked-room mystery," Ehud foils any likelihood of quick discovery of the king's body by locking them both into Eglon's private toilet and escaping through the opening to the cesspit (3:23-26; Halpern, 43–46). The victory over the leaderless Moabites, completing the narrative framework, is almost an anticlimax (3:27-30).

Susan Niditch (57–58) compares Eglon's murder to the emasculation of enemy soldiers in the *Iliad* and to the surprising narrative shift when Jael's tent peg penetrates Sisera's skull (Judg. 4:21). Certainly, that does fit into the type scene of an unlikely victory against great odds (see David and Goliath in 1 Sam. 17:31-54).

The single verse describing the exploits of Shamgar ben Anath (3:31) serves, like the listing of other minor judges (10:1-5; 12:8-15), as a literary interlude separating the tales of the major figures. Since his name includes the name of a Canaanite goddess, it is unlikely that Shamgar is an Israelite. However, because he is able to slay six hundred Philistines with a weapon generally used to herd cattle, he fits into Israelite tradition as a heroic ally (like Jael the Kenite in Judg. 4:17-22).

◼ THE TEXT IN THE INTERPRETIVE TRADITION

The church fathers seem to have been impressed with Ehud's ambidextrous abilities. However, because the left hand is often associated with "unfortunate" purpose or occurrence, they style the ability to use both hands for righteous purposes a divine gift that guides him to proper uses and "turns both into a right hand" (Cassian). Jerome also refers to Ehud as having "two right hands" because he was "a just man." Origen, who appears to be enthused by Ehud's story, labels his actions as a "praiseworthy deception," a remark that reinforces the view that many acts are justified if they are done in battle for God and the right. Later thinkers had mixed views of Ehud's assassination of King Eglon. Voltaire (*Philosophical Dictionary*, 1764) decried regicide as a sign of fanaticism, while John Milton used Ehud's example to justify the regicide of King Charles I in England (Gunn, 38–39, 45).

◼ THE TEXT IN CONTEMPORARY DISCUSSION

In current political discourse, there is a fine line between the recording of freedom fighting that includes acts of extreme violence for a just cause, and criminally minded insurgents, whose fanatical and bloody deeds are decried by other nations and by their victims. Since stories are composed for particular audiences, it is unlikely that all will share the same viewpoint on the matter any more than the Moabites would have appreciated Ehud's heroics. In modern parlance, it remains to be seen, for instance, how suicide bombers and political assassins will be viewed in the future, both within their own social context and by outsiders. Perhaps it is possible to laud Ehud's desperate act as a model of bravery for a subject people. However, because the story contains raw details and comic asides, it is difficult, as Heb. 11:32 seems to indicate, to include it in the litany of heroes of the faith.

Deborah (Judges 4–5)

■ THE TEXT IN ITS ANCIENT CONTEXT

There are a number of remarkable aspects to the dually presented story of Deborah. The narrative version in Judges 4 helps to fill some of the gaps left in the "song" in Judges 5, which concentrates more on the theme of blessings and curses (Butler, 133). The most obvious point is that Deborah is the only female judge ("a mother in Israel," 5:7), the only figure in the book to be given the label of "prophetess," and the only person to actually participate in legal mediation (4:4-5). Her role as prophet places her in company with Moses' sister Miriam (Exod. 15:20) and Huldah in Josiah's time (2 Kgs. 22:14). As an arbitrator of the law, Deborah, unlike Samuel who worked a circuit of sites (1 Sam. 7:16-17), has a recognized location in the Ephraimite hill country beneath a palm tree where the people come for justice. From her seat of authority, Deborah summons the Naphtali war chief Barak and exercises her prophetic office to call on him in God's name to lead his men against the Canaanite general Sisera at Mount Tabor (4:6-7; cf. Samuel in 1 Sam. 15:1-3).

While Barak's request that Deborah accompany his army suggests a lack of faith on his part (cf. Saul in 1 Sam. 13:8-10), it was not unusual for an army to include prophets as an intermediary for divine presence (see Elisha in 2 Kgs. 3:9-20). In this case, Barak's reluctance becomes a narrative catalyst for gender reversal, substituting a female champion whose "hand" would bring the ultimate victory (4:9). The battle in which Sisera's forces are defeated is barely mentioned (4:12-16), although the "song" in Judg. 5:19-23 does contain elements of the divine warrior's intervention ("mountains quaked," 5:5; "stars fought from heaven," 5:20). More important is the praise for the faithful tribes who joined the campaign (4:10; 5:13-15a, 18) and the sarcastic remarks made against those who stayed away (5:15b-17). In this chaotic period, it will take more than the call of a prophet and her war chief to unite the tribes in a common cause (cf. Saul in 1 Sam. 11:5-7). Deborah's only fault, then, is an inability to unite the people.

Of central interest here is the role of the Kenite woman Jael, who is called "most blessed of women" (5:24) while performing horrific acts that would under normal circumstances violate hospitality protocols (Matthews, 66–74). Serving as a narrative surprise, it is Jael's "hand" rather than Deborah's that will dispose of Sisera and the Canaanite threat (4:17-22; 5:24-27). Demonstrating that this is a world without the normal social constraints, Jael takes on the male role by playing host, inviting Sisera chaperoned into her tent, and then playing the vengeful angel (perhaps echoing God's angel in 5:23) by driving a tent peg through his skull (a sexual innuendo that would not have been lost on the ancient audience).

The "song" then supplies a poignant and stinging satire comparing Jael's heroic act to the greedy anticipation of Sisera's mother, who looks in vain for the plunder she expects will accompany the return of her son (5:28-31). For a people so often oppressed by their more powerful neighbors, there is great satisfaction found in the ability to say "so perish all your enemies" (5:31).

■ THE TEXT IN THE INTERPRETIVE TRADITION

There is much praise in the church fathers for Deborah, the "mother" who provides prudent advice, exhorts Barak to victory, and saves the nation by directing men to do their duty (Chrysostom). Jael the Kenite becomes for Ambrose the model of the righteous gentile, who is quicker than the Jews in accepting the doctrines of the church. Origen agrees by saying Jael, the foreigner, "symbolizes the church, which was assembled from foreign nations" (Franke, 117). Artistic representations of Jael's act range from a graphically pinned Sisera to more subtle depictions (Gunn, 78). While ancient and medieval commentators subordinate the role and accomplishments of women in the bible, in the nineteenth century Elizabeth Cady Stanton (*The Women's Bible*) hails Deborah's self-reliance and heroic virtues as "worthy of their imitation," and demonstrating women's ability to take a more active role in society. However, she is more reserved in her treatment of Jael, noting the Kenite must have at least "imagined herself" called by God to commit an otherwise fiendish act (Gunn, 64–65, 83).

■ THE TEXT IN CONTEMPORARY DISCUSSION

There is an interesting mixture in this tale of decisive purpose, prophetic anticipation of divine intervention in warfare, and personal triumph made possible by taking incredible risks. For once in Judges, it is possible to identify with women who are positive role models. Deborah can easily be compared to other powerful female figures (cf. Abigail in 1 Sam. 25:2-42) whose actions drive the narrative and who often overshadow their husbands, just as Deborah overshadows Barak. However, even the celebration of her as a "mother" in Israel, usually a nurturing, life-giving role, is used by the narrator to remind us that rape and the exploitation of women is a factor in the male ideology of war (Judg. 5:30; Exum, 73–74).

Jael may be more difficult for modern audiences. Her remarkable fortitude and courage is matched by her bloody-handedness. Is she to be compared to women today who are used as suicide bombers to kill crowds of people? Is her encounter with Sisera an example of collateral damage in wartime, or just another instance of the blasé attitude about the rape of women in a war zone (see Sisera's mother's musing in 5:28-30)? While the editors' narrative shell enclosing Sisera's encounter with Jael is built around how God uses unlikely vehicles to achieve victory, there is also an internal drama centered on Jael's choices. She is engaging in risk calculation designed to uphold the honor of her household and to preserve her body from the potential of rape and death at Sisera's hands. Does that, then, justify her deception and Sisera's murder? Can today's "castle doctrine" apply here, allowing her, like us, to protect herself against an unfriendly invader?

Gideon (Judges 6–8)

■ THE TEXT IN ITS ANCIENT CONTEXT

Despite the heavy-handed oppression of the Midianites (Judg. 6:1-6), Gideon is the only judge who actively campaigns against his own appointment. In that sense, his call narrative is similar to that of Moses (Exod. 3:7—4:17), Isaiah (Isa. 6:5-8), and Jeremiah (Jer. 1:4-10; Habel, 287–305). Like these reluctant prophets, Gideon shows his temerity by claiming to be too insignificant (Judg. 6:15), and prior to battle with the Midianite coalition he twice requests that God provide an oracular sign that Gideon will be able to deliver Israel (Judg. 6:36-40). The comparison breaks down, however, because Gideon never manages the ability to truly trust God or to grow into his potential as a leader (Butler, 199–200).

Intertwined with Gideon's vacillating allegiance to God's command and his own desire to gain fame for himself is another theme, the contest between Yahweh and Baal for worshipers (Bluedorn, 69). Both themes appear when Gideon is required to tear down the Baal altar that his father had built in their village (Judg. 6:25-27). Lacking the courage to perform this ritually cleansing act, Gideon dismantles the altar in the dark of night and then only escapes the wrath of the villagers when his father asserts that it is up to Baal to take vengeance, if the Canaanite god can (Judg. 6:28-31). There is a clear parallel here to Elijah's challenge of Baal's divinity on Mount Carmel (1 Kgs. 18:21), but again Gideon is in the shadows. He benefits from his actions, but he is not the one to assert Yahweh's preeminence.

In a similar manner, the battle narrative against the Midianite host contains an element of resignation on God's part about the people's and Gideon's trust. Almost with a divine shrug of the shoulders, it becomes necessary to radically diminish the size of Gideon's army so that the victory can only be attributed to God's intervention (compare the fight against the Amalekites in Exod. 17:8-13). Thus only three hundred men, all of whom have shown their lack of vigilance by lapping up water from a stream (Judg. 7:4-7), are mustered for a night attack. Still Gideon has doubts, and once again God gives him the chance to pluck up his courage by a secret foray into the enemy camp, where he hears a dream interpreted (Judg. 7:9-15). What is remarkable is that Gideon's battle call, "For the Lord and for Gideon," allows him to share credit with God, a strategy Shakespeare echoes in *Henry IV*: "God for Harry, England, and Saint George!" (act 3, scene 1). Moses was denied the promised land for a similar lack of faith when he gave himself more credit than God for providing water in the wilderness (Num. 20:7-12). Gideon's action, however, is in tune with the growing egotistic tendencies of the judges.

His initial battle is won using trumpet blasts (compare the "battle" of Jericho in Josh. 6:15-16) and nocturnal brandishing of torches that frighten the enemy (Judg. 7:19-22). Gideon's hurled torches and smashed pots may have evoked the fear of divine lightning strikes or might associate him with shamanistic abilities to call down a fiery torrent (see Elijah's acts in 1 Kgs. 18:36-38) like Apollodorus's description of Salmoneus, who attempts to imitate Zeus (Brown, 385–86). Whatever the case, the aftermath is a chase to round up the enemy leaders.

Two facets of the narrative stand out here. First is the shrewd diplomatic speech employed to mollify the Ephraimites, who had entered the fray late and were angry that they did not share in the loot (Judg. 8:1-3). Gideon distinguishes himself, using flattery to prevent conflict between tribes. That magnanimity is not extended to the towns of Succoth and Penuel, who were reluctant to trust the Israelites' ability to achieve total victory. Gideon therefore takes heavy vengeance on those who had refused to assist his men (Judg. 8:4-21). His savage treatment of the elders and the enemy chiefs shows no hint of forgiveness and serves to enhance his role as a commander, who is to be feared by all who oppose him (Judg. 8:16-21).

At the height of his popularity, Gideon refuses the offer of hereditary kingship, saying that the people will be ruled by God alone (Judg. 8:22-23). However, he spoils what could have distinguished him as a servant-leader by presenting the people with an ephod made from the spoil taken from the Midianites (8:24-27). This trophy, a memorial to Gideon's successes, later becomes a cult object, drawing the people away from Yahweh after Gideon's death (8:33-34). In the end, Gideon earns a sad epitaph, in that the people exhibit no loyalty to either God or him. It foreshadows the editorial comments about the kings of Israel, who continue the "sins of Jeroboam" and "caused Israel to sin" (1 Kgs. 22:52-53; 2 Kgs. 13:2).

The Text in the Interpretive Tradition

Setting aside any concern over the existence of a Baal altar in Gideon's village, Ambrose focuses on the analogy between Gideon's sacrifice of a bull (making an end to all gentile sacrifices) and Jesus' crucifixion as the true offering for the people's redemption. In like manner, the church fathers pass over Gideon's lack of faith in asking for a sign and instead see the dew (Judg. 6:36-40) as the divine word sent down from heaven (Ambrose), Christ as the "sweetness of the dew" (Augustine), and the fleece as Mary, who in her conception of the Lord "absorbed him with her own body" (Maximus of Turin, fifth-century bishop in Franke 127). Gregory the Great (sixth-century pope) styles Gideon's army as "glittering martyrs, who willingly exposed their bodies to their opponents' swords" (Franke, 131–32).

The Text in Contemporary Discussion

What kind of role model can Gideon the reluctant judge be for modern audiences? The degree of divine hand-holding necessary to get him in motion throughout his career may be taken as either indecisiveness or dependence. Some leaders today justify their inaction by constantly seeking out new polling data or going on endless fact-finding excursions. Are today's leaders turning a blind eye to "Baal's altar" in their town square while decrying the community's failure to erect a monument to the Ten Commandments? Do we prefer flashy, if temporary, victories or vengeful attacks to seeking out the causes of cultural differences and discontent? While Gideon was a successful general, with God's assistance, he did not pave the way to stable leadership, and he left a legacy of idolatry and divided loyalties. For modern audiences, that may raise the question of how leaders should be chosen and what long-term expectations we have for their accomplishments.

Abimelech (Judges 9) and the First Minor Judges Interlude (Judges 10:1-5)

▮ THE TEXT IN ITS ANCIENT CONTEXT

The contrast between Gideon's refusal to accept the kingship (Judg. 8:22-23) and the striving by his son Abimelech to obtain that office is symptomatic of a society that desires stability but is not yet ready for the full implications of centralized government (Amit, 111). Plus, the association with Shechem may be another Deuteronomic, political polemic against northern-based leaders (Schneider, 136). Other interesting facets of this narrative include the importance placed on kinship in elevating Abimelech (Judg. 9:2-3) and the extensive use of direct speech (Judg. 9:2, 16-20, 28-29, 31-33) and dialogue (9:36-38) at crucial points in the political drama, drawing the audience more closely into the action.

What is bloodily begun when Abimelech murders his seventy brothers (Judg. 9:5; cf. Saul's slaughter of eighty-five priests at Nob) ends with Abimelech's bloody demise (9:54). Between these two events is a frenzy of activity resulting from a change of heart by the "Lords of Shechem," who had originally supported Abimelech's rise to kingship. They make the roads unsafe, robbing travelers (9:25), and support Gaal (9:26-29). Gaal's challenge, "Who is Abimelech?" (9:28), calls his legitimacy into question (cf. Nabal, who defames David's right to the throne, saying, "Who is David?"; 1 Sam. 25:10). His brief venture into Shechem's vacillating politics concludes with many of his supporters killed, the city captured, and its ruins "sowed with salt" (cf. eighth-century Aramaic vassal-treaty of Sefire's curse imposed on covenant-breakers, "Hadad will sow salt thereon"; Fensham, 49). Abimelech's escalating rampage finally comes to a conclusion when he is struck by a millstone thrown by a woman from the walls of Thebez (Judg. 9:53). Rather than die at her hands (like Sisera in 4:21), he orders his armor bearer to slay him (9:54). Abimelech's mistake of going too near the wall becomes a military maxim cited by Joab when he sends David a report that Uriah the Hittite has been slain (2 Sam. 11:20-21).

Embedded in the narrative is a fable recited by Jotham, the only surviving son of Gideon (Judg. 9:7-15). His fable is a political metaphor cautioning the "Lords of Shechem" to consider the type of ruler they have chosen for themselves, which will likely "backfire" on them (Butler, 241–42). The comical selection process and the subsequent curse predicting a fiery ending to these events matches the tone of the overall narrative (9:56-57).

Abimelech's death forms a bridge to two minor judges, Tola and Jair. The only information contained here (Judg. 10:1-5) is the number of years they served as a judge and in Jair's case the symmetry of thirty sons, thirty donkeys, and thirty towns. These brief remarks may be based on an annalistic style more typical in the monarchy period (cf. 2 Kgs. 17:1-2). While they may have served as local leaders, the lack of a formal call from God diminishes their importance except as representatives of a brief period of stability between two violence-prone judges, Abimelech and Jephthah (Block 1999, 337).

▮ THE TEXT IN THE INTERPRETIVE TRADITION

The church fathers had to stretch to find anything uplifting in the tale of Abimelech. Augustine chose to defend the value of fables to achieve understanding through metaphor, and Methodius, a fourth-century bishop of Olympus, sees Jotham's parable as a prediction of the future reign of chastity, viewing the story of trees meeting to appoint a king as a representation of humble penitents who approach God asking to be governed by his pity and compassion.

◼ THE TEXT IN CONTEMPORARY DISCUSSION

Considering the problems created throughout history by persons whose ambitions have led them to take power by violence, Abimelech's story does not sound all that unusual to modern audiences. The damage to lives and property caused by political purges, wars of conquest and retribution, and the brutalizing of society can be ascribed to poor political choices and rampant ambition (e.g., Hitler's rise to power first through constitutional means and then by force and fiat). The question is always how long societies that accept high levels of everyday violence can last. And, is there a higher dictum to question and if necessary remove leaders who foster tyranny?

Jephthah (Judges 10:6—12:7) and the Second Minor Judges Interlude (Judges 12:8-15)

◼ THE TEXT IN ITS ANCIENT CONTEXT

Jephthah's narrative is sandwiched between two lists of minor judges (Judg. 10:1-5; 12:8-15). Both lists recount individual leaders who are apparently quite prosperous and, more importantly, have numerous progeny. That alone provides a marked contrast with both Abimelech and Jephthah, who spent their lives in continual conflict and died childless.

Before Jephthah is introduced, the editors provide an extended review of the Israelites' apostasy comparable to Judg. 2:1-5, 11-23 (10:6-18; Block 1999, 344). The Ammonite oppression leads to a beseeching cry for deliverance by the Israelites. Before God relents, there is a caustic retort that the Israelites should turn to the gods they had chosen to deliver them (compare Joash's challenge to Baal in 6:31). Only after the Israelites cleanse themselves of their foreign worship can the search begin for someone to lead them in battle (10:17-18; cf. 1:2; 20:18).

What follows is a strange pedigree for a judge. Jephthah is an illegitimate son whose brothers have expelled him from his father's household. Operating as a bandit chief out of the Gileadite city of Tob (11:1-3), his experience compares with David's outlaw period (1 Sam. 22:1-2) and with the fifteenth-century-BCE king of Alalakh, Idrimi, who spent years living with the outcasts of society before regaining his throne (*ANET* 557–58). His outsider status and experience as a seasoned military leader make him a good choice as deliverer, and aids his negotiations aimed at being recognized as their legitimate leader (Judg. 11:6-10). Unlike Gideon, Jephthah is not a reluctant leader, but it is only when he is filled with God's spirit that it is made clear he has divine sanction as a judge (11:29).

Before the conflict begins, there is an interesting diplomatic exchange between Jephthah and the Ammonites (11:12-28). Using the ancient Near Eastern lawsuit form (O'Connell, 195), his messenger recites the Israelites' preconquest narrative of their dealings with the peoples of Transjordan (see Num. 21:21-31 and Numbers 22) while discounting Ammonite claims. Unable to find a diplomatic solution (cf. the failure to appease the Ephraimites in Judg.12:1-6), Jephthah attempts to negotiate with God to obtain a victory. He takes a rash vow promising to sacrifice the first member of his household to greet him after the battle (11:30-31). Some commentators have attempted to compare Jephthah's sacrificial offer to the classical story of Agamemnon's vow to sacrifice his daughter Iphigenia, but there are too many variations to make this conclusive (Marcus, 40–43). More important is the parallel to Saul's rash oath to execute anyone who eats during a battle with the Philistines (1 Sam. 14:24-45).

Jephthah does gain his victory, but it precipitates a poignant scene when his daughter rushes out to celebrate and he realizes he has condemned her to death. She demonstrates a stronger spirit than her father by insisting he must carry through rather than become an oath-breaker (Judg. 11:34-40). Thus Jephthah wins his battle and loses the chance to continue his line. Jephthah's final episode is equally tragic. Although he is victorious over the greedy Ephraimites, his dialectal strategy of demanding that each man crossing the fords of the Jordan River pronounce the word *shibboleth* costs the Israelites a staggering toll of 42,000 lives (12:1-6).

▌ THE TEXT IN THE INTERPRETIVE TRADITION

Most interpreters focus on Jephthah's vow and whether he actually sacrificed his daughter. Luther considers the text to be ambiguous, and Augustine argues against the possibility that an animal was meant. The *Midrash Tanḥuma* attempts to excuse Jephthah on the grounds that he was ignorant of the law allowing the substitution of payment for a human vowed to be sacrificed (Lev. 27:1-8; Marcus, 47). Josephus blames the daughter for "rushing out" to meet Jephthah and thus causing her father such distress (*Ant.* 5.265), but later interpreters see her in a more sympathetic light. Peter Abelard (twelfth century) considers her embracing of a sacrificial death a model for monastic women devoted to God, and Lord Byron (1814) portrays her as a cheerful martyr who wins her father's freedom from his vow (Stewart, 133–37).

▌ THE TEXT IN CONTEMPORARY DISCUSSION

The narrator of the story of Jephthah's unnamed daughter emphasizes her adherence to legal principles and her self-sacrifice (Judg. 11:37-40). However, that only serves the interests of the male-dominated society that approves her brave action while not questioning why God did not stop the sacrifice as in Gen. 22:10-12 (Exum, 74–77). Are children to be abused or used in this way when their parents make foolish choices or are governed by their own mental pathologies? Are they expendable resources, too weak to prevent becoming victims of their parents or other adults? The irony is that Jephthah must live on childless and be labeled as a fool, while his daughter's memory lives on among her more compassionate female friends (Judg. 11:39-40).

Samson (Judges 13–16)

▌ THE TEXT IN ITS ANCIENT CONTEXT

With a brief tip of the hat to the Judges structure (citing disobedience as the cause for Philistine oppression—Judg. 13:1), Samson's saga is launched with a remarkable birth narrative (cf. Moses in Exod. 2:1-10 and Samuel in 1 Samuel 1). The theophany and annunciation instruct Samson's parents three times to maintain a strict Nazirite discipline (Num. 6:1-8) while his mother is pregnant (Judg.

13:2-14; cf. Luke 1:8-15). That holy discipline imposed on mother and son (Bal, 200) becomes the ironic foil to Samson's decidedly un-Nazirite lifestyle. There is also an interesting dynamic between Manoah and his unnamed wife. The angel appears to her first, and she recognizes the messenger as a "man of God" with an angelic appearance (13:3-6). Manoah cannot simply accept her word and entreats God for further instructions. Lacking true perception (13:16), he is shocked to discover they have been in the presence of the divine and responds with frightened awe (13:22; cf. Jacob in Gen. 28:16-17), and has to be comforted by his wife's logic (13:23). The interplay between the sexes will become a subtheme in the stories, as Samson is entrapped by his dealings with a series of women throughout his life.

There is a curious juxtaposition between Samson's potential to accomplish great things (regular infusion of God's spirit: Judg. 13:25; 14:6, 19; 15:14) and his carnal appetite, which continually draws him into the company of dangerous, foreign women (14:2; 16:1, 4). His dual character plays into the hero archetype, which places him in the company of other flawed strong men whose superhuman passions include feats of courage and strength and the need to demonstrate their virility with women (Gilgamesh and Hercules).

Contests and trickery also play heavily in these tales (Niditch, 153–54). The riddle game during his marriage feast is fraught with cultural conflict and ends with Samson being deceived by his Philistine wife and his slaughter of thirty Philistines to pay off his debt (14:12-19). In a similar manner, Samson's taunting the Philistines by burning their fields leads to confrontation and slaughter (14:3-8) while demonstrating that he is merely acting alone without any consultation with tribal leaders (Wong, 178). The frightened elders of Judah are caught in the middle since they are under Philistine control and must turn him over to their masters (14:9-13). Samson plays both sides, using this opportunity to obtain a nonaggression pact with the Judahites and then breaking his bonds and killing a thousand Philistines with a donkey's jawbone (14:12-16; cf. the surprise encounter at Gaza's gate in 16:1-3). Like Ehud's deception (3:21-22) and Jael's slaying of Sisera (4:21), these bloody episodes appeal to the partisan, ancient Israelite audience and also provide some comic relief.

The final contest centers on Samson's relationship with Delilah, the Philistines' spy (16:4-21). Paid to discover the source of his strength, Delilah plays a fourfold game, cajoling and pleading with her lover and repeatedly frustrating the Philistines waiting in her back room to pounce on what they hope is a helpless victim. Samson appears to be enjoying both the game and Delilah's growing anger. But like his first wife, who also nagged him incessantly (14:17; Ackerman, 232), Delilah's repeated pleas for him to demonstrate his love by revealing his secret wears Samson down and he tells her the truth (16:16-17). It is not clear why Delilah believes him this time, although some structured folktales do have a limit on the number of times a deception can be spoken (Matthews, 160).

At the height of Samson's despair over his capture and blinding, the storyteller injects the seed for ultimate revenge and reversal: his hair begins to grow back (16:22). The Philistines' decision to display a potentially dangerous captive for their entertainment (16:23-25) is a match for Samson's own hubris when he does not mention God in his victory hymn (15:16; Crenshaw, 36). The text does not contain a direct answer from God to Samson's petition (16:18; cf. the etiological vignette in 15:18-19). Perhaps the regrown hair gave him the strength to pull down the Philistine temple, killing the celebrants and him in the bargain (16:28-30). Or, he may have been an unwitting participant in another contest between gods that gives Yahweh a victory over Dagon (cf. 1 Sam. 5:1-5). Samson's career had begun with such hope, but ends with a destructive gesture and a simple epitaph noting he was buried in his father's tomb (16:31). His story serves as a fitting metaphor for Israel's unfaithfulness and self-centered behavior.

▌ THE TEXT IN THE INTERPRETIVE TRADITION

Most commentators have taken a more positive view of Samson's exploits. Pope Gregory the Great and the sixth-century bishop Caesarius of Arles even see his carrying away of the gates of Gaza (16:3) as a metaphor for Christ's breaking the gates of death and freeing the righteous souls from limbo. They are less kind to the women in his life, whose roles as temptresses or harlots lead Samson astray. Ambrose labels Delilah a prostitute and cautions that men should avoid marriages with those "outside the faith." Milton (*Samson Agonistes*) first portrays Delilah as a penitent, asking for forgiveness and offering to care for the blind Samson, but when he spurns her she becomes the spiteful Philistine attempting to sting him with verbal abuse. Modern film (Cecile B. DeMille's *Samson and Delilah*) romanticizes their relationship without offering much in the way of character development.

▌ THE TEXT IN CONTEMPORARY DISCUSSION

Samson is neither an unredeemable character nor a fictionalized figure drawn from various folklore strands. His reckless enthusiasms for women, adventure, and violence provide the ancient and modern audience with the consequences of the destructive actions of fools and a contrast with the wise, thinking person, who can be instructed (cf. Prov. 11:29-31; 14:16-17; Greene, 54). Similarly, the women in his life are not just sources of temptation. They often become victims of Samson's appetites, being used and then cast away. Even the self-sufficient Delilah, who apparently makes her living without the benefit of a husband (Fewell, 73–74), serves as Samson's unwitting, comedic foil until he plays the gambit once too often. Seemingly, the outlandish behavior by caped superheroes (Superman, Batman) seems excusable when hope emerges in the form of a champion. However, it is always dangerous to put too much confidence in them to change the world.

Judges 17–21 Anarchy (Tales without Judges)

Micah, the Levite, and the Migration of Dan (Judges 17–18)

▌ THE TEXT IN ITS ANCIENT CONTEXT

The Deuteronomic editors of the story of Micah's idol create a "morality play" focused on lawbreaking and indifference to covenant obligations in a time before the rule of kings (Mueller, 76–82). The tale begins with Micah's dishonorable theft of silver from his mother and his fearful return of the hoard to avoid a curse (17:2-3a; Amit, 324). She in turn "consecrates" the silver to the Lord so that it can be cast into an idol (17:3b). Like Aaron (Exod. 32:4) and King Jeroboam (1 Kgs. 12:28), neither Micah nor his mother can discern the difference between idols and Yahweh (McCann, 121). These three violations of the Decalogue (Exod. 20:4-5, 12, 15) provide the backdrop to Micah's creation of a house shrine for his newly minted cultic objects, including an ephod and *těrāphîm* (cf. Gen. 31:19; 2 Kgs. 23:24). Providing yet another insight into religious practices in the village context, Micah initially installs one of his sons as the priest (17:4-5). However, that will change when an itinerant Levite from Bethlehem arrives in search of his own "place," something not unusual prior to the establishment of the central shrine. Micah is quick to hire him to raise the social and cultic value of his shrine, and the Levite apparently has no qualms about serving before idols (Judg. 17:10; Niditch, 182).

Micah's prideful attitude in acquiring a Levite for his household takes an ironic turn in the next scene, when the scouts from the tribe of Dan stop at his house and encounter the household's live-in Levite. They ask for an oracle on the success of their mission to locate a new territory for their tribe (a further sign of Israel's political decline; Butler, 389). The Levite obliges with an ambiguous benediction, "Go in peace," noting that their efforts are "under the eye of the Lord," but not suggesting they have divine sanction (18:4-6; Schneider, 237). Once the scouts complete their mission by spying out the vulnerable northern city of Laish (Butler, 394), they return to Micah's house. Just as they later forcefully capture Laish and its lands, the Danites take the opportunity to steal Micah's sacred objects (violating Deut. 7:25), and they hire away his Levite. The Levite makes the best of the situation (Mueller, 71), matching Micah's avaricious nature and readily accepting the Danites' offer to become the "priest to a tribe and clan" (18:14-20).

The source of Micah's pride and boasting thus vanishes with these marauders (Judg. 17:13). Adding to the irony and the level of covenant disobedience is the creation of a tribal worship center at Laish (renamed Dan), with Jonathan son of Gershom, son of Moses, and his sons serving as priests for the tribe of Dan and its ill-begotten idols (18:30). Tying the Mosaic priestly line to what the Judeans would consider an illegitimate shrine serves as the editors' justification for Israel's destruction by the Assyrians in 721 BCE (Niditch, 184). It also reiterates the Deuteronomic polemic against the northern kingdom's shrines at Dan and Bethel and its priests (1 Kgs. 12:29).

▌ THE TEXT IN THE INTERPRETIVE TRADITION

Some rabbinic sources (midrash *Tanhuma, Yelammedenu* 1:100) tie Micah to the exodus story and especially to Aaron's construction of the golden calf (Exod. 32:4). Chapter 24 of the midrash *Exodus Rabbah* contends that Micah's idol was created in Egypt and passed with the Israelites over the Red Sea. The *Babylonian Talmud Sanhedrin* 103b, however, says only the metals crossed the sea and were later cast into an idol. Protestant commentators, including Milton, use Micah's idol as part of their polemic against the veneration of images in the Roman Catholic Church (Gunn, 234–35).

▌ THE TEXT IN CONTEMPORARY DISCUSSION

One of the admonitions included in police investigations is "follow the money." If the audience follows the silver in Micah's story, it is possible to see how the covetous desire (Exod. 20:17) for this precious metal becomes the catalyst for crime and covenant-breaking. Micah's tale is not just about idolatry or the unfaithfulness of itinerant Levites or the migration of the tribe of Dan. From a single act of theft comes dishonor to one's parent, the casting of idols, suborning of a Levite to serve in a house shrine dedicated to cultic images and the personal pride of the owner, and then theft on a grander scale and the transference of the crime of idolatry from a single household to an entire tribe. The narrative provides a warning to modern hedge fund managers and investors (foundations and individuals) to beware of the corrupting influence of ill-gotten riches at the expense of the public and the economy.

Levite's concubine and civil war (Judges 19–21)

∎ THE TEXT IN ITS ANCIENT CONTEXT

The editors of the final set of episodes in Judges recast the story of Lot in Sodom (Genesis 19; Lasine) using an unnamed Levite and his concubine as the narrative catalyst for a horrific tragedy. The Levite is presented as a failed husband (19:2), a traveler who exercises poor judgment (19:11-14), an ungrateful guest (19:16-20), and a coward who sacrifices the life of his concubine to preserve himself from a mob of lawless men in Gibeah (19:22-25). Hospitality protocols are turned upside down throughout the narrative (Matthews, 181–88). When the long night is over, the Levite shows no concern for his concubine's brutal gang rape, not even crying out after finding her body lying on his host's doorstep (19:27-28; Yee, 154–56). Instead, he bundles her onto his donkey, and when he arrives home he gruesomely carves her body into twelve pieces (cf. Saul's butchering his oxen in 1 Sam. 11:7). Then the Levite sends these grisly items "throughout all the territory of Israel" with the inflammatory message "Has such a thing ever happened? . . . Consider it, take counsel, and speak out" (19:29-30).

Without questioning the Levite's claims, all of the Israelite tribes gather at Mizpah, creating the only instance in the book when they are all gathered together (20:1; cf. 1 Sam. 7:5-7; 10:17). The Levite uses this opportunity to condemn Gibeah and the tribe of Benjamin while painting himself as a helpless victim. Similarly, the Benjaminites, when asked to "hand over those scoundrels in Gibeah" in order to "purge the evil from Israel" (20:13; cf. the stoning of Achan's household in Josh. 7:16-26), absolutely refuse to comply and proceed to gather their own army (20:14-15). There is a mad dash to judgment and intemperate action on both sides. The result is a series of three battles, none of which need have occurred if wiser and cooler heads had intervened (cf. the negotiations in Josh. 22:10-34).

Two military defeats lead to the sole appearance in Judges of the ark of the covenant and a cameo appearance by Phinehas, a contemporary of Joshua, as the Levite in charge (see Num. 25:7-11; 31:1-12; Josh. 22:13-34). However, the Israelites' desperation and the editors' efforts to draw the combatants back to proper cultic procedures require the tribes to seek God's help through proper channels (Judg. 20:19-25; cf. Num. 14:39-45; Butler, 445–47). Duly chastised, they receive not only the command to "Go up" but also the divine assurance that this time "I will give them into your hand" (cf. Josh. 7:8-9).

In the end, the tribe of Benjamin is decimated and is only able to survive through an artful avoidance of the stipulations of the tribal oath and the capture of women from Jabesh-gilead and Shiloh (Judges 21). These female captives, unable to protect themselves from the desperate Benjaminites who pursue them, form an inclusio with the Levite's concubine, whose rape served as the cause célèbre for this destructive civil war (Keefe, 85–86).

THE TEXT IN THE INTERPRETIVE TRADITION

Josephus, explaining why Israel needed to call on God for deliverers, places the Levite's concubine incident prior to the rise of individual judges rather than after that sequence had begun (*Ant.* 5.2.8). The church fathers are less condemning of the Levite than modern commentators. The fourth-century bishop of Alexandria Athanasius merely describes this crime against the Levite's concubine as an affront to her husband, and then points to her death as a small thing compared to the atrocities committed against the church. Milton saw the rape as a sign of civil unrest that could not go unpunished. However, the seventeenth-century cleric Robert Gomersall, facing the prospect of civil war and political chaos in England, argued against the type of inflammatory political rhetoric used by the Levite to stir up intemperate violence (Gunn, 260–61).

THE TEXT IN CONTEMPORARY DISCUSSION

Contemporary readings of this text have most often centered on the theme of sexual violence against women and spousal abuse. Rape, damaging to the psyche as well as the body, must be addressed openly without transforming the victim into a harlot who provoked the attack. Perhaps by using this story as a pedagogical tool, it will be possible to strengthen the ability to confront the crime and its consequences publicly (Scholz, 7). Also contained here is an argument for mediation rather than unthinking, precipitate action (see Prov. 15:18). A reasoned approach that avoids the self-serving, shallow arguments of demagoguery can lead to reconciliation and a cooling of tempers (Prov. 7:27). Plus, a husband who sees his wife as an equal rather than as a sex object or as a trophy to his success is less likely to cause her to be harmed by inaction or inattention.

Works Cited

Ackerman, Susan. 1998. *Warrior, Dancer, Seductress, Queen: Women in Judges and Biblical Israel*. New York: Doubleday.

Amit, Yairah. 1999. *The Book of Judges: The Art of Editing*. Leiden: Brill.

Bal, Mieke. 1988. *Death and Dissymmetry: The Politics of Coherence in the Book of Judges*. Chicago: University of Chicago Press.

Begg, Christopher. 2006. "Israel's First Judge According to Josephus." *NedTT* 60:329–36.

Block, Daniel I. 1988. "The Period of the Judges: Religious Disintegration under Tribal Rule." In *Israel's Apostasy and Restoration: Essays in Honor of Roland K. Harrison*, edited by Avraham Gileadi, 39–57. Grand Rapids: Baker.

———. 1999. *Judges, Ruth*. NAC 6. Nashville: Broadman & Holman.

Bluedorn, Wolfgang. 2001. *Yahweh versus Baalism: A Theological Reading of the Gideon Abimelech Narrative.* JSOTSup 329. Sheffield: Sheffield Academic Press.

Brown, John P. 1981. "The Mediterranean Seer and Shamanism." *ZAW* 93:374–400.

Butler, Trent. 2009. *Judges.* WBC. Nashville: Thomas Nelson.

Crenshaw, James L. 1978. *Samson: A Secret Betrayed, a Vow Ignored.* Macon, GA: Mercer University Press.

Exum, J. Cheryl. 2007. "Feminist Criticism: Whose Interests Are Being Served?" In *Judges and Method: New Approaches in Biblical Studies,* edited by Gale A. Yee, 65–89. 2nd ed. Minneapolis: Fortress Press.

Fensham, F. Charles. 1962. "Salt as Curse in the Old Testament and the Ancient Near East." *BA* 25:48–50.

Fewell, Dana N. 1987. "Feminist Reading of the Hebrew Bible: Affirmation, Resistance, and Transformation." *JSOT* 39:77–87.

John R. Franke, ed. 2005. *Joshua, Judges, Ruth, 1-2 Samuel.* Downers Grove, IL: InterVarsity.

Greene, Mark. 1991. "Enigma Variations: Aspects of the Samson Story, Judges 13-16." *VE* 21:53–79.

Greenspahn, Frederick E. 1986. "The Theology of the Framework of Judges." *VT* 36:385–96.

Gunn, David M. 2005. *Judges.* Malden, MA: Blackwell.

Halpern, Baruch. 1988. *The First Historians: The Hebrew Bible and History.* San Francisco: Harper & Row.

Keefe, Alice A. 1993. "Rapes of Women/Wars of Men." *Semeia* 61:79–97.

Keel, Othmar, and Christoph Uehlinger. 1998. *Gods, Goddesses, and Images of God in Ancient Israel.* Minneapolis: Fortress Press.

Lasine, Stuart. 1984. "Guest and Host in Judges 19: Lot's Hospitality in an Inverted World." *JSOT* 29:37–59.

Leuchter, Mark. 2007. "'Now There Was a [Certain] Man': Compositional Chronology in Judges–1 Samuel." *CBQ* 69:429–39.

Marcus, David. 1986. *Jephthah and His Vow.* Lubbock: Texas Tech Press.

Matthews, Victor H. 2004. *Judges and Ruth.* New Cambridge Bible Commentary Cambridge: Cambridge University Press.

McCann, J. Clinton. 2002. *Judges.* IBC. Louisville: Westminster John Knox.

Mueller, E. Aydeet. 2001. *The Micah Story: A Morality Tale in the Book of Judges.* New York: Peter Lang.

Niditch, Susan. 2008. *Judges.* Louisville: Westminster John Knox.

Noth, Martin. 1981. *Deuteronomistic History.* JSOTSup 15. Sheffield: Sheffield Academic Press. [2nd ed. first published in 1957]

Redditt, Paul L. 2007. "Themes in Haggai–Zechariah–Malachi." *Int* 61, no. 2:184–97.

Sadler, Rodney S., Jr. 2006. "Cushan-Rishathaim." *New Interpreter's Dictionary of the Bible,* 1:812–13. Nashville: Abingdon.

Schneider, Tammi J. 2000. *Judges.* Berit Olam. Collegeville, MN: Liturgical Press.

Scholz, Susanne. 2010. *Sacred Witness: Rape in the Hebrew Bible.* Minneapolis: Fortress Press.

Stewart, Anne W. 2012. "Jephthah's Daughter and Her Interpreters." In *Women's Bible Commentary,* edited by Carol A. Newson et al., 133–37. 3rd ed. Louisville: Westminster John Knox.

Wong, Gregory T. K. 2006. *Compositional Strategy of the Book of Judges: An Inductive, Rhetorical Study.* Leiden: Brill.

Yee, Gale. 2007. "Ideological Criticism: Judges 17–21 and the Dismembered Body." In *Judges and Method: New Approaches in Biblical Studies,* edited by Gale Yee, 138–60. 2nd ed. Minneapolis: Fortress Press.

Younger, K. Lawson, Jr. 1994. "Judges 1 in Its Near Eastern Context." In *Faith, Tradition, and History: Old Testament Historiography in Its Near Eastern Context,* edited by Alan R. Millard et al., 207–27. Winona Lake, IN: Eisenbrauns.

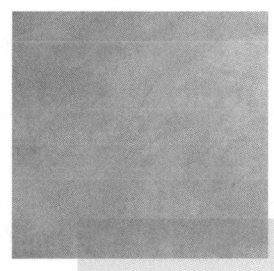

RUTH

Gale A. Yee

Introduction

In the Christian Old Testament, the book of Ruth is located after the book of Judges and before 1 Samuel, most likely because it is set during the time of the judges (Ruth 1:1), but before King David comes on the scene in 1 Samuel. In the Tanak, the Jewish Bible, the book is found in its third canonical section, known as the Writings, and is part of the five Megillot (Scrolls) that are read at different times during the Jewish liturgical calendar. Ruth is read during the feast of Shavuot (Feast of Weeks), fifty days after the feast of Passover.

The book narrates the story of Ruth, a foreign woman from Moab who journeys with her widowed mother-in-law Naomi to Judah, where she meets her future husband Boaz and becomes the ancestress of the great King David. The book was written either as an apology for the Moabite ancestry of David (c. tenth century BCE) or during the time of Ezra and Nehemiah (fifth century BCE), when intermarriages between Judeans and the indigenous peoples of Yehud (Judah) became an acute concern. Although often read as a tender love story between a man and woman, the book covers a greater range of social relationships: husband/wife, mother/son, mother-in-law/daughter-in-law, owner/overseer/laborers, resident/foreigner, native/immigrant, and so forth. How one reads Ruth depends on one's context and social location. For example, readers in cultures such as China, where mother-in-law/daughter-in-law relations are quite conflicted, will have different readings of the book of Ruth than those in which this relationship is more harmonious.

The book of Ruth has a rich interpretive history (Koosed), especially in music (Leneman). For an imaginative retelling of the Ruth, Orpah, and Naomi story that takes into account the various interpretations of biblical scholarship, see Brenner 2005.

Ruth 1:1-22: To Moab and Back

▌ THE TEXT IN ITS ANCIENT CONTEXT

The book of Ruth begins with a spare report of the who, what, where, when, and why. During the time of the judges, a famine in the land compels Elimelech from Bethlehem to take his wife Naomi and two sons, Mahlon and Chilion, to live in Moab, where the sons marry Moabite women. After ten years Elimelech and his two sons die, leaving Naomi with her two daughters-in-law, Ruth and Orpah. Hearing that Judah has become fertile again, Naomi decides to return to Bethlehem. She encourages her daughters-in-law to return to their "mother's house." Although Orpah leaves, Ruth declares her desire to remain with Naomi. Both return as widows to Bethlehem during the barley harvest.

The Genesis ancestral narratives record several migrations to foreign lands because of famine (12:10; 26:1; 41:57; 42–43). Elimelech's family thus become strangers in a strange land, just as Ruth will become a foreigner in Judah as the story progresses. The choice to emigrate to Moab would have provoked negative associations in the implied reader. According to Gen. 19:37, its people can be traced back to an incestuous relationship between Lot and one of his daughters. Because of their incestuous origins, no Moabite shall be admitted to the assembly of the LORD (Deut. 23:3-4).

Although the preferred marriage in Israel was within one's family lineage and ethnic group (known as endogamy), Mahlon and Chilion espoused Moabite women. Marriages with foreign women were often disparaged in Israel, because they were thought to lead to idolatry (1 Kgs. 11; 18). Moabite women were especially censured for using their sexuality to lead Israel astray (Num. 25:1-5). During the Persian period, the marital policies of Ezra and Nehemiah condemned intermarriage with foreign women (Ezra 9–10; Neh. 13:23-31). Some scholars think that the book of Ruth was written to counteract their strict interdictions, by highlighting a Moabite female convert to Israel, one who will be the ancestress to King David.

In 1:11-13, Naomi declares that she can no longer bear sons because of her age, and even if she could have sons, it would be foolish for her daughters-in-law to wait for them to grow up. These verses have been used to support the idea that the marriage between Ruth and Boaz was a levirate union, in which a levir, the closest male relative of a deceased husband, was duty-bound to marry the widow (Deut. 25:5-10). Naomi's main point, however, is that she is just too old to give birth to sons for Ruth and Orpah. She does not mention the possibility of levirs in Judah, who would be obliged to marry them as widows. This lack of disclosure is significant, raising questions about Naomi's motives for wanting her daughters-in-law to return to Moab.

The Hebrew verb used to describe Ruth "clinging" to Naomi in 1:14 is the same one used in Gen. 2:24 to describe a man "clinging" to his wife in marriage and becoming "one flesh" with her. Ruth declares her commitment in a well-known speech that culminates in her desire to die and be buried in the same land as Naomi (1:16-17). Although most scholars interpret these verses as a literary expression of fidelity, others suggest that they may refer to a contractual relationship in which Ruth works for Naomi in some capacity in Judah (Brenner in Brenner 1999; Yee).

◼ THE TEXT IN THE INTERPRETIVE TRADITION

Even though there is no value judgment in the biblical text on Elimelech's migration to Moab, some rabbis have argued that Elimelech was a wealthy man who could have fed the whole country with food for ten years. However, he fled to Moab instead of helping the poor out of his own bounty and was justly punished (*Ruth Rabbah* 1:4; Rashi). While the text does not disparage the intermarriage between Elimelech's sons and Moabite women, the Targum on Ruth 1:4 says that they died because "they transgressed the decree of the Word of the LORD and took unto themselves foreign wives, of the daughters of Moab." Orpah herself is raped by "a hundred heathen" on the night when she separates from Naomi. She is also identified as the mother of the Philistine Goliath (*Ruth Rabbah* 2:20).

One of the main interpretive difficulties that confronted the rabbis was in dealing with a Moabite woman who, because of her ethnicity, was forbidden to enter the assembly of the LORD (Deut. 23:3), yet became a praiseworthy character and ancestor of King David. To explain these incongruities, the Targum on Ruth 1:4 and *Ruth Rabbah* 2:9 describe Ruth as the daughter of Eglon, king of Moab (see Judg. 3:12). David's line thus has royal blood on both paternal and maternal sides. Turning her back on Moab and embracing the God of Israel, Ruth becomes the exemplar of the perfect convert (see Targum on Ruth 1:16; 2:16, 11; 3:10), teaching Israel the true meaning of *hesed* ("loving-kindness": *Ruth Rabbah* 2:14).

Philip Hermogenes Calderon's painting *Ruth and Naomi* (1902) interprets their relationship homoerotically, by depicting a very feminine-looking Ruth passionately embracing a masculine-looking Naomi. The 1960 celluloid adaptation *The Story of Ruth* creates a backstory of Ruth as a Moabite princess who was sold by her parents to be raised in the temple of Chemosh.

◼ THE TEXT IN CONTEMPORARY DISCUSSION

Ruth's heartfelt speech to Naomi in 1:16-17 has become a popular reading in heterosexual Christian wedding services. Furthermore, because two women are involved in this intimate relationship, these verses have also been adopted in same-gender blessing and marriage ceremonies. In the movie *Fried Green Tomatoes*, the character Ruth sends her female "friend" the text of Ruth 1:16 to inform her of her desire to leave her abusive husband and live with her.

Even though the relationship between mother-in-law and daughter-in-law in the book seems to be amiable and collaborative, in Western cultures these relations can be strained, and in some Asian cultures, downright oppressive. Care must be taken in imposing Ruth and Naomi's relationship on present-day relations between mothers and daughters-in-law in exploitative ways.

Migration to foreign lands because of famine, drought, and poverty still occurs in many parts of the world today. The book of Ruth presents a positive picture of assimilation in the intermarriage between Judeans and Moabites and the devotion between mothers-in-law and daughters-in-law. Nevertheless, we must recognize that migrants often face intolerance and great hostility from the host country as they try to assimilate into new surroundings and cultures, and partake of their resources.

Ruth 2:1-23: In the Fields by Day

▌THE TEXT IN ITS ANCIENT CONTEXT

Chapter 2 opens with the detail that Naomi had a prominent wealthy kinsman on her husband's side whose name was Boaz, leading the reader to suspect that this character will play a major role in the coming narrative. Gleaning the land's leftovers was an institutionalized social practice to provide for the most vulnerable and impoverished in the community: the alien, orphan, and widow (Lev. 19:9-10; 23:22; Deut. 24:19). Entitled to glean as both a foreigner and a widow, Ruth obtains Naomi's consent to glean in the fields with the express purpose of finding a patron of some sort who will look favorably on her (2:2). And "as luck would have it" (JPS), Ruth ends up gleaning in the field belonging to the self-same Boaz, who takes notice of her and finds out from his overseer that she is the Moabite who returned with Naomi (2:3-6). Boaz tells Ruth not to glean in anyone else's field, but to keep close to his young women and to where they reap. He orders his men not to "bother" her, perhaps because female reapers were targets of sexual harassment, and instructs Ruth to drink water from the vessels the men have drawn (2:8-9).

Ruth prostrates herself before Boaz, wondering why she has "found favor" in his sight despite being a foreigner, recalling 2:2, where she hopes to encounter someone "in whose sight I may find favor." Boaz responds that he has heard of what she has done in leaving her native land and family to come with her mother-in-law to a strange land and people. He prays that the God of Israel, under whose wings Ruth finds refuge, will reward Ruth for her all her deeds (2:10-12). These divine maternal wings (*kanap*, see Deut. 32:11; Ps. 17:7-9; 36:6-8; Matt. 23:37) will have a human male complement in 3:9, when Ruth asks Boaz to spread his protective cloak (*kanap*) over her as her next of kin.

When Ruth returns home with a large stash of barley, an astounded Naomi asks where she gleaned and invokes a blessing on the man who took notice of Ruth. Upon discovering that Ruth's patron is Boaz, she tells Ruth that this man is a near relation, more precisely, a *go'el*, one with the right to redeem. Redemption in the Bible refers to the responsibility to assist impoverished relatives during times of hardship (Eskenazi, liii–liv). Because Naomi did not tell Ruth that there was a close male redeemer in Bethlehem and did not warn her about the dangers women faced in the fields during harvest, some interpreters think that Naomi was ambivalent about Ruth's welfare (Eskenazi, 29; Sakenfeld, 38–39; Nielsen, 64). In any case, Ruth continues to live with her mother-in-law and glean in Boaz's field, close to his young women until the end of the barley and wheat harvest (2:19-23).

▌THE TEXT IN THE INTERPRETIVE TRADITION

Why does Ruth catch Boaz's eye? Although the biblical text does not describe Ruth's appearance, later rabbis comment that Ruth was beautiful, modest, less greedy, and did not flirt with the reapers, compared to the other women in the field (Ibn Ezra, *Ruth Rabbah* 4.6; Rashi). The Targum to Ruth expands on Boaz's speech in 2:11 with the details that God's prohibition of Moabites entering the assembly of God affected only the men, not the women, and that Boaz had received a prophecy that kings and prophets will be Ruth's descendants because of the kindness she has shown to her mother-in-law.

Perhaps the most famous literary reference to Ruth gleaning in the fields is in John Keats's "Ode to a Nightingale," where the nightingale's song that Keats hears is "the selfsame song that found a path / through the sad heart of Ruth when, sick for home, / She stood in tears amid the alien corn" (65–67).

◼ THE TEXT IN CONTEMPORARY DISCUSSION

U.S. agriculture depends greatly on immigrant menial laborers, many of whom enter the country illegally. They are subject to poor working conditions, lack of medical benefits, sexual harassment, and the threat of deportation. Some feminists have interpreted Ruth from the perspective of migrant foreign workers and their lower-class status in their host country (Brenner in Brenner 1999; Yee).

The ancient biblical practice of gleaning still continues today, causing us to reflect on those who must resort to gleaning in our world in order to survive: the global poor and destitute. One major area of food waste in the United States is in fields where crops that do not meet top quality standards are left to rot on the fields or to be plowed under. Some 96 billion pounds of food are wasted each year, according to some statistics. A number of humanitarian organizations, such as the Society of St. Andrew, coordinate thousands of volunteers from many different social groups to glean the fields to deliver food to the hungry. Gleaning not only occurs in agricultural fields but also appears in the heartrending face of urban dumpster diving, as depicted in Agnès Varda's 2001 documentary *The Gleaners and I*.

Ruth 3:1-18: In the Fields at Night

◼ THE TEXT IN ITS ANCIENT CONTEXT

According to 2:23, the grain harvests are coming to an end, and so with them is Ruth and Naomi's economic livelihood. Naomi therefore suggests a daring plan to secure financial security for Ruth and, implicitly, for herself. Her instructions that Ruth wash, anoint herself, and don her best clothes can signify the end to Ruth's period of mourning (2 Sam. 12:20, a preparation for a wedding celebration (Ezek. 16:9-10), or even sexual seduction (Jth. 10:3-4). Ruth is then supposed to go down to the threshing floor secretly, mark where Boaz lies down after eating and drinking, and in an audacious act, uncover his feet and lie down (3:3-4).

The whole encounter between Ruth and Boaz is filled with sexual innuendo and ambiguity (3:6-16). The meeting occurs at night, the favorite time of many carnal assignations. The threshing floor is associated with illicit sexuality (see Hosea 9:10). Although it can simply mean to "lie down" to sleep, the verb *shkb* can also imply sexual intercourse (Gen. 19:33-35). Its eight occurrences in this chapter highlight the eroticism of the scene (v. 4, three times; v. 7, twice; vv. 8, 13-14). Ruth is instructed to *uncover* Boaz's *feet* and "lie down" (3:4, 7). The verb "uncover" (*glh*) evokes unlawful sexual intercourse (Lev. 18:6-18; Deut. 27:20); "feet" can refer to genitalia (Isa. 6:2; 7:20). Nevertheless, the text is completely silent about whether Ruth and Boaz actually had sexual intercourse that night, leaving it to the imaginations of many of readers and interpreters.

When Boaz awakens at midnight and blurts out "Who are you?" the woman lying at his "feet" informs him of her identity and bids him to spread his cloak (*kanap*) over her, because he is a *go'el*, a redeeming kinsman (3:8-9, JPS translation). Just as Boaz evokes God's blessing on Ruth, under whose wings (*kanapim*) she has come for refuge (2:12), so now Ruth requests the same patronage from Boaz. Because *kanap* as a "cloak" or "skirt" is spread over a woman who will become one's wife (cf. Ezek. 16:8), one can also say that Ruth is proposing marriage to Boaz, as well as asking for his protection.

Boaz responds by blessing Ruth, praising her for her acts of *hesed* (meaning "loyalty" in this instance), the first by accompanying her mother-in-law to Judah, and the second by choosing him as *go'el* over younger men, whether rich or poor. Ruth picks someone within Elimelech's line when she doesn't have to, thus reinforcing her kinship with Naomi. Boaz agrees to do what Ruth asks, but points out that there is "another kinsman more closely related" than he. If this kinsman will not agree to be a redeemer-kin for Ruth, Boaz will do so on her behalf (3:10-13).

Ruth remains the rest of the night "lying at his feet until dawn," leaving the reader to speculate what might have happened between the two during that interval. That Ruth's nocturnal appearance at the threshing floor was unconventional and perhaps even scandalous is evident when Boaz says, "It must not be known that the woman came to the threshing floor" (3:14). Boaz gives Ruth a significant supply of grain, which she carries back to Naomi. After relaying to Naomi what Boaz has done for her, she explains the gift of grain as Boaz's intention that Ruth not return to her mother-in-law empty-handed, even though this detail is not recorded in their interchange. This is the last time Ruth speaks in the book. Her fate now rests with the man who "will settle the matter today" (3:16-18).

▌ THE TEXT IN THE INTERPRETIVE TRADITION

Rashi has Ruth questioning Naomi's orders: "'If I go down all dressed up, anyone who meets me and sees me will think I am a harlot.' Therefore she went down in the first place to the threshing-floor and afterwards adorned herself as her mother-in-law had instructed" (Beattie, 107). To settle the problem of Ruth's uncovering Boaz's "feet," Salmon ben Yeroham says that Ruth really uncovers her face, which was covered to conceal her identity as she went through the threshing floor (Beattie, 47). The rabbis are thus at pains to exclude any possibility that Ruth and Boaz had sex that night. Commenting on 3:7, they highlight that when Boaz was "in a contented mood" (lit. "his heart was good"), "he occupied himself with the words of the Torah," and that he was looking for a wife (*Ruth Rabbah* 5:15), and that he "blessed the name of the Lord" (Targum on Ruth). According to the Targum on Ruth 3:8, when Boaz sees Ruth sleeping at his feet, he "subdues his evil inclination" and resists drawing closer to her, like Joseph who refused to sleep with Potiphar's wife, and Paltiel who put a knife between himself and Saul's daughter Michal. *Ruth Rabbah* 7:1 also highlights Boaz's virtue in not giving in to sexual temptation.

Several artists render Ruth sleeping at Boaz's feet literally: for example, an anonymous illustrator in the Wenzel Bible (Codex 2760); James Tissot, *Ruth and Boaz* (1900); and Marc Chagall, *Ruth at the Feet of Boaz* (1960).

■ THE TEXT IN CONTEMPORARY DISCUSSION

While the biblical text is circumspect about the matter, many Western readers in the twenty-first century most likely will have no problem imagining Ruth and Boaz having sex on the threshing floor that fateful night. Explicit sexuality can be found in many aspects of Western culture, such as film, television, advertising, books, and so forth. However, this was not the case in ancient Israel and is not for a good part of today's world where sexual expression among the genders is strictly enforced and can have insidious undersides. We must never forget the desperate circumstances of poverty that compelled Naomi and Ruth to transgress the norms of their culture to carry out such a scandalous plan. Ruth, as a poor foreign woman, already a target for sexual harassment, secretly approaching an important landowner in the middle of the night, had the most to lose. For many destitute women today, marriage or concubinage to a wealthy man are their only sure routes out of poverty. Others must resort to or be forced to selling their bodies to men who sexually exploit them. While the book of Ruth ends "happily," it could have ended in humiliation, rejection, and sexual exploitation, which many impoverished women experience today in order to survive (Sakenfeld 2002).

Ruth 4:1-21: At the City Gate

■ THE TEXT IN ITS ANCIENT CONTEXT

In this chapter, Boaz cleverly maneuvers this nearer kinsman to decline his role as redeemer-kin for Ruth before the elders at the city gate. Precisely *how* Boaz negotiates the transaction is problematic. In the first place, Boaz tells the nearer kinsman that Naomi is selling a parcel of land that belonged to Elimelech. The land redemption laws in Lev. 25:25-28 specify that the next-of-kin (*go'el*) must buy the land of an impoverished "brother" to prevent its leaving the family lineage. However, why wasn't Naomi's piece of land mentioned earlier? Its economic value would have saved Ruth from the backbreaking work of gleaning. Second, why wasn't this nearer-kinsman mentioned earlier as a possible redeemer-kin for Naomi and Ruth? Was he simply a literary functionary brought in to create suspense in the "romantic" story of Ruth and Boaz? Third, although many interpret Boaz's coupling of land redemption with the obligation of a levir to marry the widow of the dead man (Deut. 25:5-10), the redemption of land does not require marriage with the widow of the deceased kinsman. These are two separate issues. Furthermore, the ritual of the sandal described in Deut. 25:9 is enacted between the rejected widow against the man who refused to be her levir, humiliating him by spitting in his face. The ritual in Ruth 4:7 is a more understated legal transaction between Boaz and the nearer-kinsman. Ruth plays no part in the negotiations.

Despite these and other difficulties, Boaz successfully declares before the elders and all the people that he has acquired the piece of land that belonged to Naomi's dead husband and sons (4:9) and has also acquired Ruth the Moabite as wife, in order to maintain the dead man's name on his inheritance (4:10). The elders and the people acknowledge the legality of the proceedings as Boaz's witnesses, blessing Ruth with the fertility of Rachel and Leah (the mothers of the tribes of Israel). The people's blessing concludes ironically with references to the house of Perez, whom Tamar bore to Judah (4:11-12). Tamar was a widow who disguised herself as a prostitute to seduce her father-in-law Judah, who had refused his levirate obligations by withholding her marriage with his surviving son (Genesis 38). Both Ruth and Tamar are widows. Both use socially unorthodox means to form an alliance with older men who will secure their economic and social future.

Although the "Moabite" designation is dropped from Ruth when she marries Boaz and conceives a son (4:13), one cannot presume that Ruth has been completely assimilated into the Judean community. She actually disappears from the story at this point, and the narrative turns to Naomi. The women bless God, who has provided Naomi with a redeemer-kin (*go'el*). Without naming Ruth, they praise the daughter-in-law who loves Naomi and is worth more to her than seven sons. It is significant to note that this praise of Ruth by the women appears only after she gives birth to a son (4:14-15). These women did not acknowledge Ruth when she returned with Naomi from Moab (2:19). It is Naomi, not Ruth, who becomes the child's nurse, and it is the local women, not Ruth, who names the child "Obed" (4:16-17). The book ends with the genealogy of Perez, concluding with Obed of Jesse, and Jesse of David. Although not specified as such, Ruth becomes the great-grandmother of King David.

▌ THE TEXT IN THE INTERPRETIVE TRADITION

The unnamed redeemer-kin in 3:13 and 4:1-6 is given the name Tob in rabbinic literature, where he is sometimes described as the uncle of Mahlon and Chilion, while Boaz is the son of another uncle, and thus cousin to Elimelech's sons. As an uncle, Tob takes precedence over Boaz in inheritance and redemption. Other rabbis argue that Tob and Boaz were brothers, but since Tob was older, he took precedence. Some rabbis speculate that Tob refuses to marry Ruth because he was poor and had his own children to support, and could not be saddled with another wife. Another view has Tob's wife threatening divorce if he takes another spouse (Beattie, 79–82). The Targum to Ruth 4:7-8 has Boaz taking off his right glove to seal the transaction. In the biblical text, the object of exchange is a sandal, not a glove, and it is unclear who removes it.

Matthew 1:5 places Boaz, Ruth, and Obed into Jesus' genealogy. Ruth joins four other women in the ancestral list: Tamar (Genesis 38), Rahab (Joshua 2), the wife of Uriah (Bathsheba, 2 Samuel 11), and Mary the mother of Jesus. Why these women? Perhaps because there is a whiff of sexual unconventionality surrounding these women. Tamar disguises herself as a hooker by the side of the road to seduce her father-in-law to fulfill his levirate obligations. Rahab actually is a prostitute. Bathsheba commits adultery with David, Mary is a pregnant unwed teenager, and Ruth places herself in a compromising position on the threshing floor with Boaz.

▌ THE TEXT IN CONTEMPORARY DISCUSSION

In contrast to the Disney princess Snow White, who waits longingly for her prince to come, women in Western societies usually do not have to marry in order to become financially secure. They can acquire upper levels of education in order to make a living for themselves. They can inherit their family's resources. They usually do not operate under the social and sexual strictures that prohibited certain gender relations in ancient Israel. However, the story of Ruth supports attitudes regarding female dependence on men and the social necessity to marry in order to live in a financially safe environment. Naomi could not inherit the land owned by her husband, which had to be purchased by a male "redeemer." The Cinderella story of finding and seducing a rich man who will become her patron is often the hope of many impoverished women today in the third world. Their hopes are usually dashed when confronted with realities of sexual exploitation and human trafficking (http://facts.randomhistory.com/human-trafficking-facts.html). Although Ruth's story ends "happily" in that she "gets her guy" in the end and becomes upwardly mobile, this is not the case for many poor women today, thousands of years later, whose stories often end quite tragically.

Works Cited

Beattie, D. R. G. 1977. *Jewish Exegesis of the Book of Ruth*. JSOTSup 2. Sheffield: JSOT Press.

Brenner, Athalya, ed. 1999. *Ruth and Esther: A Feminist Companion to the Bible*. 2nd Series. Sheffield: Sheffield Academic Press.

———. 2005. *I Am . . . Biblical Women Tell Their Own Stories*. Minneapolis: Fortress.

Bush, Frederic W. 1996. *Ruth, Esther*. WBC 9. Waco, TX: Word.

Eskenazi, Tamara Cohn, and Tikva Frymer-Kensky. 2011. *Ruth: The Traditional Hebrew Text with the New JPS Translation and Commentary*. Philadelphia: Jewish Publication Society. [Cited as Eskenazi]

Koosed, Jennifer L. 2011. *Gleaning Ruth: A Biblical Heroine and Her Afterlives*. Columbia: University of South Carolina Press.

Leneman, Helen. 2007. *The Performed Bible: The Story of Ruth in Opera and Oratorio*. Sheffield: Sheffield Phoenix Press.

Matthews, Victor H. 2004. *Judges and Ruth*. NCBC. Cambridge: Cambridge University Press.

Nielsen, Kirsten. 1997. *Ruth: A Commentary*. Translated by Edward Broadbridge. OTL. Louisville: Westminster John Knox.

Sakenfeld, Katherine Doob. 1999. *Ruth*. IBC. Louisville: John Knox.

———. 2002. "At the Threshing Floor: Sex, Reader Response, and a Hermeneutic of Survival." *OTE* 15:164–78.

Yee, Gale A. 2009. "'She Stood in Tears Amid the Alien Corn': Ruth, the Perpetual Foreigner and Model Minority." In *They Were All Together in One Place: Toward Minority Biblical Criticism*, edited by Randall C. Bailey, Tat-siong Benny Liew, and Fernando F. Segovia, 119–40. Atlanta: Society of Biblical Literature.

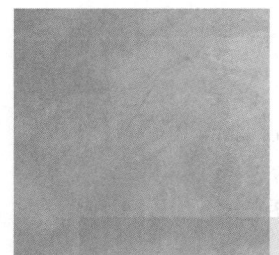

1 AND 2 SAMUEL

Hugh S. Pyper

Introduction

The books of Samuel are treated in the Hebrew tradition as a single work. The division into two may well be a practical consequence of the conventional size of a scroll, and the death of Saul provided a convenient and appropriate breakpoint. These books cover the careers of the first two kings of Israel—Saul and David—and give an account of the reasons why this new institution arose in Israel and its effects. The Masoretic Hebrew text of the books has its problems, which are often explicable if reference is made to the different readings in the Dead Sea Scrolls and in the Greek translations, especially the so-called Lucianic tradition.

Critical scholarship on the text has been troubled by duplications of stories and inconsistent attitudes to the monarchy. This has been explained by postulating the combination of pro- and antimonarchic sources, either from different eras or perhaps originating in different circumstances. It has also been postulated that the text collects a number of originally separate works. Those identified include the Ark Narrative (4:1 to 7:1), concentrating on the history of the ark of the covenant; the History of David's Rise (16–31); and the Succession Narrative (2 Samuel 9–20; 1 Kings 1–2). In addition, the books of Samuel now form part of the great sweep of historical narrative that runs from Genesis to 2 Kings and are also included in the scholarly construct of the Deuteronomistic History, which includes Joshua, Judges, and the books of Kings. Such passages as 2 Samuel 12 do seem to accord with the language and theological concerns of the writers of Deuteronomy.

Without denying that there may be a complex history of accumulation and editorial revision behind the present form of these books, at some point the texts we have were accepted by some readers as at least an adequate representation of what they and their traditions had to say on the matters of David's kingship and its role in Israel's history. What may trouble some readers as inconsistency, both stylistically and ideologically, can also be seen as an acknowledgment of the complexity and messiness of human nature and human history, due to the residuum of the unknowable and unpredictable in any human transaction.

Literary scholars, most notably Robert Alter, have held up the characterization of David in these texts as an astonishingly rounded and subtle treatment of an endlessly fascinating and elusive personality. Indeed, he has been called the model of the ambiguity of what it is to be human (Frontain and Wojcik, 5). Rather than offering a simple stereotype of the hero and king, the books of Samuel present several Davids, public and private: father, son, lover, outlaw, and king. In the interplay of these Davids with each other and the other characters, there is a fascinating possibility for exploring the limits of these markers of identity.

Of course, there is a danger of over-reading here. Accidental and unintended juxtapositions may be just that, rather than precursors of modern and postmodern literary effects. Yet one thing is clear from reading these books. Those who handed on these traditions tell stories the whole point of which depends on the subtle ways in which language and power are related and the way history and story can be manipulated and reread in order to provoke particular responses from an audience. Time and again, it is David's ability to access, process, and manipulate the flow of information within the text that gives him his advantage; his failures occur when he is distracted or outwitted in this deadly game. It is surely not inappropriate to imagine that storytellers and writers who show their characters using and responding to complex communicative strategies would themselves be capable of using such strategies in their own work.

The message of works such as the books of Samuel resides, then, not so much in explicit accounts of actions, speech, and intention, but in the structure of the language, syntax, and narrative conventions that go together to make up this extraordinary work. The effort to match intention and effect is shown to be constantly thwarted. Speech and actions have unintended and unforeseen consequences. This implies that the attempt to reverse the process and deduce intentions from results is even more subject to error and misunderstanding (Frontain and Wojcik, 10).

Hence the importance of the promise and the oath, its divinely sanctioned refinement, in the narrative structure of Samuel 1and 2 (Pyper, 131–55). Promises in the books of Samuel seem to bridge the gap between intention and action by invoking the divine but then compound it when they are broken or reinterpreted. Oaths are only necessary because plain statements do not bind people to a course of action.

This also emphasizes the paradoxical vulnerability of masculinity as a social category. Just as the spoken word always risks misinterpretation by its hearers, so the male has to entrust his seed to a woman, with no guarantee that a son will be forthcoming, or that any child will be his. The gap between intention and achievement that bedevils speech is structurally equivalent to the one between intercourse and childbirth.

Death and succession go together. It is because of death that a successor becomes necessary. This essential heir is also the paradoxical reminder of the inevitability of death and may in fact become the embodiment of that threat to the father. Death, however, is the ultimate downfall of human intention. No one can live forever simply by intending to. Human beings can bring about death, but cannot reverse it; they may bring death inadvertently or fail to do so when they try to.

This paradox is heightened when the political continuity of a community is tied to biological succession, as is the case in a hereditary monarchy. The books of Samuel explore the consequences of the move to a dynastic system in Israel. Questions as to how communities and individuals interact to preserve identity through time are at the heart of their concerns. If we take it that the form we now have of these texts is a product of a time no earlier than the latest incidents they relate, those who are transmitting them know also that the story of the monarchy ends in the defeat and destruction of the Davidic kingdom. They tell these stories to audiences that know the promises of peace and stability have proven to be untrue. How is this to be explained? What lessons can be learned from the past so that a meaning that has relevance to their present situation can be found?

These books also describe a crucial transition in the understanding of Israel as a political entity in the context of the conflicting power claims of the ancient Levant. They describe it, however, for the benefit of communities that are wrestling with the need to understand what Israel is in their own very different situation of defeat and the continued influence of powerful imperial forces. The model of communal identity put forward here has had persisting effects on the models of nationhood that shaped modern Europe and the ideology of colonial expansion, and in turn the complex issues around identity that underlie the struggle for independence from colonial rule (Hastings). The utopian dream of an independent and homogenous Israel united under one king and one God is presented and critiqued in the book in ways that can still inform and unsettle current political arguments.

For modern readers, they raise difficult questions about how identity is to be understood and how differences between genders, generations, and ethnic groups are to be dealt with. Although the cultural assumptions may not be ours and we need always to guard against importing our questions and our answers into ancient texts with different concerns, staying alert to the way in which these texts display the interchange of information and identity as the political and social systems of Israel develop and change can illuminate present dilemmas, often as cautionary tales.

1 Samuel 1–3: Samuel and the Promise to Eli

▮ THE TEXT IN ITS ANCIENT CONTEXT

The first three chapters of the books of Samuel act as a prologue to the story of Israel and its kings up to the destruction of the temple, as told in Samuel and Kings. In many ways, they also foreshadow the key themes and dilemmas with which this longer history has to deal.

The extrabiblical evidence for the rise and fall of the Davidic kingdom is surprisingly scant as the archaeology of this period is contested and no accounts exist in other ancient literatures of the time. However, the period they cover marks a time when the two great powers of Egypt and Babylon—which lay to the south and the north of the area where these stories are set—were both undergoing internal convulsions. This left an unusual space for the various peoples of Palestine and Syria to assert their independence and indulge in local battles for supremacy. For the ancient reader, these books are one attempt to explain how and why the promises Israel saw as its heritage turned out so differently from what had been expected. A community that has experienced exile, the destruction of the temple, and the effective end to the Davidic monarchy needs to understand why this does not mean that the God whom the tradition says made promises of protection and enduring sovereignty has failed.

Read in sequel to the book of Judges, 1 Samuel 1 could easily be the birth story of the next judge. The repeated use of the verb "ask" in this story, which resembles the name "Saul" in Hebrew, has led to scholarly debate as to whether this was originally the birth story of Saul (McCarter 1980). Strikingly, neither Saul nor David has such a birth story in Samuel. The familiar story of a childless woman bearing a son through God's intervention has some twists, however. It is Hannah who takes the initiative in praying for a son, and the reassurance she needs is given by the priest Eli in the temple at Shiloh, rather than by a mysterious messenger. There is a further twist when Hannah vows to dedicate her son to God for life and in her song of praise.

A key theme that runs throughout Samuel and Kings is introduced in the discussion of the failures of Eli's sons. They are the presumptive heirs to hereditary priesthood of Eli, but their conduct is unacceptable. The narrative tensions develop around vows and their fulfillment, and around the related theme of the hereditary principle. A man of God comes to Eli and announces that despite God's much earlier promise that Eli and his family would be priests before him forever, now his sons are to be killed and a new order will come into force. This introduces a worrying principle into the narrative. God may rescind the promises he has made, even of an eternal priesthood. The unsatisfactory actions of sons may mean that a promised destiny is not fulfilled. Eli seems to have little influence over his sons but has less over the divine promise. As a model of the future prospects for kingship in Israel, this is sobering.

In another foreshadowing of the later story, Samuel has already entered the story as the one who will supplant Eli's sons as his successor, combining the roles of priest, prophet, and judge in an unprecedented synthesis. The young Samuel is inspired by the Lord to make this clear to Eli, whose response is the faithful acceptance of his fate. A pattern has been set, of sons who cannot be trusted, of promises, even divine ones, that turn out to be provisional or to have unlooked-for consequences, and of the rise of an unexpected successor.

▌ The Text in the Interpretive Tradition

The interpretative tradition has focused on the incident of Samuel's call and the rejection of Eli. For writers such as John Cassian and Basil the Great, it is a story that resonates with the issue of how and why God chooses people; in discussions of election, Samuel can be an important example (Franke). He is set aside from childhood, and the story does not argue that any particular gifts on his part set him aside. Eli as the representative of a failing priestly dynasty does, however, have the wisdom to understand that his own role in the story is to bow out graciously, giving what wisdom he can to Samuel.

▌ The Text in Contemporary Discussion

For readers such as Donna Nolan Fewell and David Gunn (1993), the role of Hannah in this story has become a focus for attention. Her initiative and, particularly, the potentially revolutionary content of her song mean that she can speak for women who challenge any system that attempts to subjugate them. It resonates with the Magnificat in Luke 1:46-55 in its repeated praise of God as the one who reverses status, exalting the weak and humbling those with riches and power. Her song continues to be a challenge today, especially as the systems of power and privilege are constantly threatened in the story to follow, but often reestablish themselves in a new guise. Quite how radical a true expression of Hannah's sentiments would be is a continuing point of debate as the relationship between belief and political structures is negotiated.

1 Samuel 4–6: The Ark at Large

▌The Text in Its Ancient Context

In 1 Samuel 4–6, our attention is turned outward to the international and political environment of Samuel's new status in Israel. In a manner that becomes familiar through its repetition in the book of Judges, the test for the new political order is a Philistine invasion. Israel is reduced to playing its trump card when it brings the ark of the Lord into the camp, only for this to have the opposite effect of what was intended; the Philistines rally and capture the ark.

Scholars have speculated that a so-called Ark Narrative once formed part of an independently circulated cycle of stories (Gordon). This may be so, but one of the points of the books of Samuel is to account for the bringing together of the Davidic king and YHWH's temple in Jerusalem and to illuminate the tensions to which this juxtaposition gives rise. In these early chapters, neither the future king nor the ark—as the nearest thing to a physical embodiment of YHWH—are in Jerusalem, and the separate—and sometimes apparently random—stories of the ark and the king are juxtaposed rather than linked. How these two stories come to run together without becoming inseparable is the point of the narrative. In the end, the fate of the kings and the fate of YHWH will be very different. The human institution fails and is transformed, while YHWH's position continues undiminished despite the fate of the ark, at least within the ideology of the texts.

Even at this point in the story, what in an ancient context might seem to be the defeat of Israel's God turns out to be quite the opposite. In a series of comic accidents, the Philistine god Dagon is overthrown and the people are plagued with mice and hemorrhoids. The trouble is, however, that no one seems to be able to control the ark, and the story evolves into a sort of hot-potato game as various communities try to get rid of it until it finally comes to rest in Kiriath-jearim. There it waits until much later in the story when David is in a position to bring the ark into the orbit of his growing power.

▌The Text in the Interpretive Tradition

This story of the ark has led to a rich allegorical series of interpretations. As the sign of God's earthly presence with Israel, Christian interpreters tied it to the incarnation of Christ (so, for instance, Bede) or to Mary as the vehicle of that incarnation (Jeffrey). In less concrete terms, it becomes a focus for meditation on the reconciling work of God in Christ, drawing on the understanding of the ark as God's mercy seat. Again, it is the point of encounter. Typically, the history of interpretation comes late to recognizing the satirical bent of the tales.

▌THE TEXT IN CONTEMPORARY DISCUSSION

Theologically, these stories, which have a strong resemblance to folktales, remind the modern reader that these texts are well aware of the uncanniness and the unpredictability of the God they bear witness to. This story is as near as the Bible comes to comic writing. Its message is a serious one for modern readers. Whatever is powerful is also dangerous; whatever can protect us can also be a threat. Any tendency to treat God as a possession or, indeed, to use him as a weapon or as a threat against others is likely to have consequences that no one will enjoy. The unpredictability, allure, and danger of what is, after all, a wooden box on an oxcart, reminds readers that none of the human characters is in control of the story. Those in contemporary political discourse who claim divine support for their policies might well remember this. Humor and irony are appropriate in discussing God's dealings with humanity. The downside of this is that the opponents of God and of Israel are at times depicted as caricatures and figures of fun in a way that can, if unchecked, seem to justify a stereotypical response that risks forgetting their humanity. How biblical texts portray those who are alien and the proper response to them is a complex question. We do need to note the moments when the Philistines show unexpected courage and those when the people of Israel react through fear or prejudice.

1 Samuel 7–8: Samuel and His Sons: The Case for a King

▌THE TEXT IN ITS ANCIENT CONTEXT

First Samuel 7 shows that Samuel has succeeded in the way that counts for a judge. Under his leadership, the Philistines are defeated. He does this, however, not by military power, but by exercising his priestly office and offering a sacrifice. Now, once more, there is a problem of succession. Samuel is in the same situation as Eli. His sons are worthless, yet, despite this, he names them as his successors. At this, the people protest and ask for a king "like other nations" (8:4).

Samuel takes his resentment at this to God, who agrees to the demand, but with a warning. The warning in 8:8-18 is Samuel's, however, not God's. This passage is often read as reflecting a later Deuteronomistic view of the inevitable failure of the monarchy and as being a definitive statement of the antimonarchical trend in these texts. Read in context, however, is it quite the condemnation that Samuel seems to think? After all, what he warns the people is that the king they are seeking will organize the army, give their sons a proper military training, and even find occupations in his palace for their daughters. After the years of uncertainty and chaos that are depicted in the book of Judges, when Israel had no clear leader or any mechanism for appointing one until they had suffered defeat, this is surely just what the people are asking for. Samuel is no longer able to lead them, and his sons offer no prospect of being able to provide stability.

■ THE TEXT IN THE INTERPRETIVE TRADITION

Traditionally, this reading has led to a suspicion of kingship that has not always helped relationships between the church and the state. In response to the Geneva Bible's questioning of royal legitimacy in the footnotes to passages such as this, based on its endorsement of the Calvinist position that the people have the right to depose a tyrannous ruler, King James decreed that the new version of the Bible produced under his sponsorship should have no footnotes.

■ THE TEXT IN CONTEMPORARY DISCUSSION

In a contemporary reading, we can recognize the same questioning of what constitutes legitimate power in the complex politics of identity that surrounds the call for independence among former colonies, which has led to the establishment of current political boundaries around the world. These issues are the topic of postcolonial studies. A key topic in such studies is the role of mimicry: the way in which the colonized take on the customs and institutions of the colonizer. Paradoxically, a colonized group can only be taken seriously if it shows itself to meet the colonizers' criteria for nationhood. Here, the people of Israel encapsulate the paradox in a phrase. To maintain their distinctive identity, they need to become "like the other nations." In particular, they need a king who will provide both a point of union and a continuity of leadership not available under the judges and who will be recognized by their enemies as a legitimate leader. The kind of decisive leadership and economic coordination of society that Samuel warns the people to expect from their king may actually be exactly what they feel they have been missing.

These texts give us an insight into the paradox that by seeking to establish the distinctiveness of our identity, we almost always have to reformulate and even compromise it. Whose criteria do we use? Religious groups fall prey to the same paradoxes as nation states. It also reminds us that any claim, even from a recognized authority, to speak in the name of God needs to be examined.

1 Samuel 9–13: Samuel and the Promise to Saul

■ THE TEXT IN ITS ANCIENT CONTEXT

First Samuel 9 begins by introducing a new character who literally stands out in contrast to the rest of Israel: Saul, son of Kish. He arrives full-grown in the story, with no birth narrative. In fact, the obscurity of his ancestry is made a point. In the wake of 1 Samuel 8, the question—Is this character the new king?—comes to mind, but clearly nothing can happen unless Saul comes to Samuel's attention. In a story that almost seems to parody the way narratives need to get their protagonists to meet, Saul finds Samuel by accident as he seeks his uncle's lost asses and is directed to a seer whose words always come true. Samuel anoints him as ruler of Israel (note, however, that the word "king" is never mentioned at this juncture), an unprecedented act in Israel's story. There follows a promise, but only in the Greek translation. The Hebrew text does not specify what being a "ruler" entails.

Samuel does tell Saul of a sign that will show he has God's favor. This is an encounter with a band of prophets that throws him into a trance. In itself an intriguing glimpse into the prophetic culture as the writer understood it, this story leaves some doubt as to whether Saul's experience is seen as creditable.

The narrative recounts two further episodes where Saul is in fact declared king, rather than ruler, although it is the people and the narrator who use the word, not Samuel. In addition to prophetic anointment (10:1), he must be seen to be God's chosen by lot (10:21) and he must be acclaimed as king by the people (10:24). Again, this may represent the combination of different traditions, but it also emphasizes the fact that Saul's role is a new one. He is no one's successor but at the same time embodies a number of leadership roles, and then demonstrates his fitness for office through a military victory over the Philistines (11:11-15). Even so, his rule is challenged from the outset, and no sooner is he acclaimed than Samuel is given a speech—markedly Deuteronomistic in tone—that makes no bones about the fact that the kingship shows the people's wickedness. Not long after that, Saul takes it upon himself to undertake a sacrifice in the absence of Samuel. On his arrival, Samuel tells Saul that he has broken a divine command, although it is not easy to see from the text just what specific command is meant here (13:13). It is only at that point that we learn of a potential promise to Saul that has now been rescinded. He would have been promised an eternal kingdom, but now his kingdom is already superseded. Another has already been appointed ruler in his stead, although the reader is in the dark as to who this is.

In addition, the final verses of 1 Samuel 13 show that by this stage the vaunted independence of Israel is rather hollow. The nation may have a king, but it is still harried by Philistine invasion and indeed seems to be entirely dependent on the Philistines for any ironwork, as Israel is forbidden to have blacksmiths.

▌ THE TEXT IN THE INTERPRETIVE TRADITION

Saul is mentioned only once in the New Testament, but at a crucial moment in the book of Acts, where his namesake, Saul, becomes known as Paul. In Acts 13:21, Saul is mentioned as the first king, but as one supplanted by David. Here Saul becomes the example that explains how those who are legitimately chosen by God can be replaced. Paul's speech is part of his argument that the rise of the new Israel of the church does not mean that the chosen status of Israel is to be questioned. Saul is legitimately king, even if his kingship passes to David.

▌ THE TEXT IN CONTEMPORARY DISCUSSION

To modern eyes, Saul may seem a tragic figure (Exum). He resembles a number of modern leaders whose military prowess and charisma in their struggles for national independence did not equip them to deal with the infighting and political maneuvering that ensued once independence was won, and whose responses typically become increasingly arbitrary and dictatorial. Plucked unwillingly from obscurity, he carries out his key responsibility, to lead the people to military victory, with notable success. However, his status remains undefined and his kingship depends on the assent of the people and the continued support of God. He is then placed in the dilemma of risking loss of loyalty among the people because of the unrest caused by Samuel's failure to come when he had promised. He makes his decision, only to find that he has lost everything and faces an unknown rival who is destined to supplant him. Given Samuel's attitude to the kingship, what is his role in the whole story? How is Saul to know what God's commands are and what comes from Samuel himself? The real crisis of his story is that he loses all communication with God, which is a personal and political disaster. This is something that may speak to rulers of Egypt, Tunisia, and other countries that have experienced upheaval during and after the "Arab Spring."

1 Samuel 14: Saul and His Son

▮ THE TEXT IN ITS ANCIENT CONTEXT

We now encounter Saul's son Jonathan. His appearance in the story may remind us that we have been told nothing up to now of Saul's domestic life. Jonathan simply arrives in the story as a fully grown warrior. Given the move in these narratives toward hereditary succession, at this point in the narrative the question might arise, Is this the already-designated successor to Saul?

What follows is another story that revolves around an oath. One small detail sets up the unfolding disaster that will eventually destroy Saul's household. Jonathan goes out to fight the Philistines with just his armor-bearer, "but he did not tell his father" (14:1).

This lack of information becomes crucial. Throughout the books of Samuel, the importance for a ruler to control and master the flow of information in his court and kingdom is a recurrent theme. Because of Jonathan's omission, Saul has to find out who it is that is missing from the army, has managed to storm the Philistine garrison, and has caused the panic that leads to a full-scale Philistine retreat. We then learn that Saul commits what the Greek text describes as a "very rash act" (14:24). He swears an oath that no one is to eat anything before evening. Jonathan, who has not heard the oath, eats some honey. Things begin to go wrong quickly, culminating in YHWH's refusal to answer Saul's question as to whether he should attack the Philistines. Another vital channel of communication seems to be severed.

Saul's response is to declare that whoever has sinned shall die, even if it is Jonathan. Traditionally, this is seen as yet another rash oath. Yet Saul knew that the only people who were not around when he proclaimed his first oath about the fast were Jonathan and his armor-bearer. Is this second oath an innocent piece of folly, or is it made with that knowledge in mind?

When Jonathan returns, he is subjected to the lot but already seems to have been singled out by Saul. Jonathan owns up to his deed when the lot falls on him and is condemned to die until a unique event in the Hebrew Bible occurs. The people counter Saul's oath by a directly opposing oath, both invoking the name of YHWH, and thereby save Jonathan, but at the expense of the credibility and prestige of Saul (14:44). He is the only character in the Hebrew Bible who makes an oath in YHWH's name that is not fulfilled. This outcome also reinforces the growing separation and indeed hostility between Saul and YHWH. Yet despite all this, Saul continues to be a successful war leader, and we are finally told further details of his family. He has several sons and therefore several potential successors. His cousin is now serving as his general.

▌ THE TEXT IN THE INTERPRETIVE TRADITION

In rabbinical discussion, this text stands with the story of Jephthah in Judges 11, where another child is put in mortal danger because of the unthinking oath sworn by her father. The warnings against oaths in the Hebrew Bible and the New Testament prohibitions of oaths (Matt. 5:33-36; James 5:12) are defended in later Christian writings with reference to these episodes. Saul's reputation is further besmirched in the tradition by these words. This is tempered by the interest in later Christian writers, including Tertullian and Bede, in the discipline of fasting. In that context, Saul's imposition of punishment for a breach of the rules of fasting without fear or favor is viewed favorably (Franke).

▌ THE TEXT IN CONTEMPORARY DISCUSSION

This story can certainly stand as a warning against rash oaths, but there seems to be something deeper at work here that is a recurrent theme in biblical texts, with troubling repercussions for modern readers. It concerns the dynamics of the relationship between fathers and sons in the ancient world. On the one hand, a son is essential to ensure that the memory and legacy of the father are maintained, but on the other hand, he is a potential rival.

This tension is heightened when it comes to a royal family. Why would a royal son and heir wait for his father to die in order to succeed? A similar fear has prevented many contemporary dictators from nominating a successor until too late, resulting in the collapse of their regime on their death. The fate of Yugoslavia after Josip Broz Tito's death is one example among many.

Jonathan's military success and independence suggest that the day may come when he can supplant his father. Is Saul's oath, consciously or unconsciously, an expression of what in psychoanalytic terms could be a "Laius complex"? This is named after the father of Oedipus, who exposed his infant son in response to a prophecy, later fulfilled as we know, that his son would kill him. This will not be the only time Saul makes an attempt on his son's life.

1 Samuel 15: Saul's Broken Promise

▌ THE TEXT IN ITS ANCIENT CONTEXT

There is an odd disconnection between the preceding chapters and 1 Samuel 15. Samuel reappears and this time seems to be about to anoint Saul as king, yet he has already declared that God's favor has passed to his successor. The episode suggests that, after all that has happened, Saul is not yet king. It is also the first time Samuel has brought himself to utter the word in Saul's presence (15:1). This renewal of Saul's kingship, if we read it in this way, brings with it a new test. Saul must eradicate the Amalekites in revenge for their ancient insult against Israel. Not only are the people to be killed, including the infants, but their livestock—even including the donkeys—are also to be wiped out, in accordance with the biblical law related to holy war.

Saul then takes it on himself to warn the Kenites, traditional allies of Israel, to leave the city. Saul and his army then carry out their task, but spare the Amalekite king and the best of the livestock, destroying "all that was despised and worthless" (15:9), a category presumably including the Amalekite women and children. Samuel, once more absent at a crucial juncture, returns, having heard directly from YHWH that he has repented of making Saul king because of his failure to obey divine commands (15:10). The prophet confronts Saul with the fact that he can hear the sounds of animals, and Saul explains that he has spared them in order to offer sacrifice to God.

Samuel rejoins that obedience is better than sacrifice, provoking Saul to a plea for forgiveness and for a restoration of the crucial communication between him and God. This Samuel refuses, which leads to a scene where Samuel expressly denies that "the Glory of Israel" can repent, despite the fact that he has earlier had an explicit message from God that he has indeed repented (15:29). This disparity is highlighted by the end of the chapter, where Saul and Samuel part for good, thus removing Saul's only remaining connection to God. We are left with a picture of the three in their separate spheres; Saul in Gibeah, Samuel in Ramah, grieving over Saul, and YHWH, explicitly sorry that he made Saul king.

■ THE TEXT IN THE INTERPRETIVE TRADITION

This passage raises for the interpretive tradition some complex moral dilemmas and philosophical quandaries. Obedience may be better than sacrifice, but are there commands that ought not to be obeyed? The problem is compounded in this case because the command is represented as the command of a God who can repent of his previous decisions. For patristic commentators such as Tertullian and Augustine, the implication that God might have been in error is inconceivable, and they explain at length why any language that seems to impute such human qualities to God is to be interpreted allegorically (Franke, 258). This complicates the sort of argument that would defend such genocide on the grounds that whatever God commands is by definition good. If God can change his mind, then what is good today may be bad tomorrow.

■ THE TEXT IN CONTEMPORARY DISCUSSION

Using this story and its cognates in the Bible as any sort of guide to contemporary political action poses acute difficulties. We have to rely on the authority of a human interpreter to find out what God's will may be. Can that ever be certain enough to justify such blind obedience? Can it ever involve the demand for complete annihilation of a people? In our contemporary context, where acts of terrorism and the use of overwhelming violence in response to these have both been justified by appealing to divine judgment, these stories have a troubling relevance.

Some glimmer of redemption of this text comes from the fact that, by the end of this chapter, apparently all the Amalekites, including the king, have been eradicated. Yet throughout the rest of Samuel, Amalekites continue to turn up, often in quite influential roles in the text. The text does not support its own claim of total annihilation. Do the writers know that such rhetorical claims are almost impossible to achieve and that they say more about the needs and anxieties of the text's writers many hundred years later than they do about God's actions in the context of Saul's reign?

1 Samuel 16: Samuel and the Promise to David

▊ The Text in Its Ancient Context

First Samuel 16 begins with God's rather peremptory call to Samuel to stop grieving for Saul and to find the new king from the family of Jesse in Bethlehem. This begins a block of material running from 1 Samuel 16 to 2 Sam. 1:27, which has been called "the History of David's Rise." In this case, there is no ambiguity about the use of the word "king." Samuel rather unexpectedly hesitates for fear of what Saul will do to him, not having shown much fear of him before (16:2). Once in Bethlehem, he inspects all the sons who attend the sacrifice to which he invites them. At first, he is impressed by the physical appearance of the oldest son, in the way that Saul was impressive, but is told only to pay attention to the heart. All the sons prove not to be the chosen one, so Samuel asks if there is another, even younger son and is told that there is, but that he is out tending sheep. This reflects the common folktale motif of the successful younger son.

When David finally arrives, he ironically turns out to be good-looking as well. Samuel anoints him, and the spirit descends on him. We are then transported back to Saul's dwelling, where an evil spirit replaces the spirit of YHWH (16:14). He calls for a musician to be found to dispel the effects, and David is recommended in glowing terms as both a skilled player and a mighty warrior (16:18). David is thus installed in the royal entourage.

▊ The Text in the Interpretive Tradition

In the tradition of interpretation, David's lowly status as shepherd boy and his obscure origins give a particular focus to the metaphor of the shepherd in the subsequent history of interpretation. His musical skills are also at the heart of both Jewish and Christian understandings of the use of music in worship. This also is linked to his association with the Psalms and with the inauguration of the temple services in Chronicles. His role in the liturgy is a large part of his enduring significance in the spiritual life of the communities that look to these works as part of their heritage.

▊ The Text in Contemporary Discussion

Modern interpreters may see here a common trope of the poor boy made good in many folktales. David is not the third son, or the seventh, as is often the case in such tales, but the eighth: a status pointing to both his marginality and his exceptionality. The role of music in alleviating Saul's suffering is also intriguing, foreshadowing much modern research on music as therapy.

The instruction to Samuel not to look at the outward appearance to judge who is the man fit to take on the kingship but to look at the heart is often held up as an example to condemn superficial judgments. The story, however, may complicate what is being meant. What exactly is it that Samuel sees in David's heart? Does he see the qualities that will lead to David's downfall as well as those that will allow him to rise to the kingship in the first place? The narrator of Samuel almost never gives us a glimpse into David's inner thoughts and motivations, although other characters are laid open to us at times. It is this that gives him his core of mystery, which is both alluring and at times disturbing and which has made him a character that different generations have been able to rewrite to fit their notions of what kingship might be (Josipovici).

1 Samuel 17–20: David, Saul, and Jonathan: The Transfer of the Promise

■ THE TEXT IN ITS ANCIENT CONTEXT

What follows in 1 Samuel 17 is one of the few cases in the Bible where seemingly discrepant elements in the Hebrew traditions of the story correspond to the fact that the Greek translations omit sections of the narrative and thereby read more coherently. The story of David and Goliath is so well known that the discrepancies get overlooked. At the beginning of 1 Samuel 17, David seems to be once again living in Bethlehem and is visiting his brothers on the battlefield with the Philistines, in a very inferior position. His questions and his brothers' responses do not square easily with the picture of the celebrated warrior introduced to Saul in the previous chapter. Indeed, the way in which they dismiss him seems to show that he has caused tension in his own family previously by his precocious self-confidence.

There seem to be at least two stories combined, one in which David is already Saul's squire and a respected warrior and one in which his first encounter with Saul is when he is brought to him because of his brash boasts about dealing with Goliath. First Samuel 17:13 seems to imply that he needs introducing to the reader, and Saul shows no knowledge of him when he is brought to him; the Greek versions omit much of this material (McCarter 1980, 306–9).

The felling of Goliath is a key moment. Goliath's height recalls the stories of giants in Num. 13:32-33 and Deut. 2:10-11, but also harks back to the description of Saul in 1 Sam. 9:2. Yet, what is stopping Saul and Jonathan, who elsewhere have shown both skill and courage as leaders of Israel, from taking on this challenge? In David, a new champion emerges who wins by cunning and skill rather than by strength or force of numbers. When the victorious David is brought to Saul, he asks a strange question: "Whose son are you?" (17:58). Again, this seems incongruous, given that in 16:19 Saul had dealt with Jesse himself. Historical criticism may explain this as an effect of the editing together of different accounts. However, that does not explain why such an obvious discrepancy has been left in the text. Another way of dealing with this text is to concentrate on the effect of this puzzling question. It highlights the key question of succession and the future of the kingship. The next king should be Saul's son. In the following chapters, David not only takes on the role of Saul's son and successor but also founds his own dynasty.

The celebrity of this story and its message that the plucky underdog can, with God's help, overcome the most intimidating and dangerous enemies has led to David and Goliath becoming part of a cliché. This story of victory against the odds may, however, be less clear-cut than it seems. In ancient warfare, the tactical advantage of the agile sling-bearer against an infantryman weighed down with heavy armor was clear.

However it happens, by the end of 1 Samuel 17, David has undoubtedly come to Saul's attention. We know, though most of the characters do not, that David has already been chosen as Saul's replacement. The next section can be read as a remarkable narrative achievement in that David, the chosen successor, exchanges roles with Jonathan, the presumed heir to Saul, in a way that means he can be at the same time the first Davidic king, but not the first king. Jonathan's soul is bound to David's at their first meeting, and he clothes David in his own princely garments and gives him his weapons (18:1-2). Saul also takes him into his own house and sets him over the army. Saul becomes a surrogate father to him. This also brings into play once more the Laius complex, the father's fear of the son who will supplant him and who is the reminder of his own mortality. The song the women sing that compares Saul unfavorably to the new young hero bespeaks a threat to Saul's position (18:7).

Problems quickly arise, which will repeat throughout the rest of the books of Samuel. Kingship is linked to military prowess. Almost inevitably, a successful king's territory and army will expand to the point where no one man can lead it. Yet appointing a general means risking the possibility that he will outdo the king in gaining victories, thus becoming a rival, just as Jonathan had been.

David's popularity rises, and Saul sees a threat to his position. In a dark reversal, the Philistine enemies become a potential solution to this problem if David can be induced into foolhardy attacks against them. Saul also uses his daughters to set up traps for David using the promise of marriage as bait in a way familiar from folktales around the world.

What Saul does not reckon with is his children's loyalty to David, which allows his rival to escape a series of plots against his life. Both his daughter Michal and Jonathan relay Saul's plans to David and enable him to evade their father (19:11-17; 20:35-42). In this situation, Saul may have the political power, but David has the crucial advantage when it comes to information. Through Jonathan, David can learn what Saul is doing and interpret it more astutely than Jonathan himself. Saul's anger against David extends thereafter to Jonathan, cementing the bond between the two younger men. Jonathan becomes the target of his father's spear as David had before him (18:10; 20:33). Both are united against "the enemies of David" (20:16), chief among whom is Jonathan's own father, Saul.

▊ The Text in the Interpretive Tradition

Jonathan's relationship with David becomes a model for later writers to discuss the nature of friendship, often drawing on Greek models (Harding). Either the two are seen as an example of equal friendship, one soul in two bodies, or else they are seen as corresponding to the model of the friendship between an older mentor and the lad of promise. Insofar as David is seen as a type of Christ, Jonathan can be seen as the archetypal believer, content to renounce his own power and privilege in devotion to the church.

▊ The Text in Contemporary Discussion

The stories of David and Jonathan have been at the heart of recent discussions over biblical attitudes to same-sex relationships. The devotion of Jonathan to David is clear, but there is no unambiguous evidence as to whether this had a sexual component; the text will bear rather different interpretations (Harding). As is often the case in trying to answer contemporary questions from an ancient text, we risk applying alien categories to the ancient world. A good way of detecting this is to ask, Could I ask that question in Biblical Hebrew? If the answer is no, that should alert us to the possibility that our categories may be inappropriate. In any case, the word translated "love" in Hebrew is used in the contexts of covenant loyalty. David is never the subject of the verb in the books of Samuel; he is the one who is loved.

1 Samuel 20–23: Saul against David

▌THE TEXT IN ITS ANCIENT CONTEXT

David is now a hunted man, and the next section depicts the lengths to which he will go to protect himself from Saul. Indeed, he becomes so implicated with the traditional enemies of Israel that the text has to go to improbable lengths to assure us that he was always at heart working in Israel's interests. Is this a later attempt to whitewash a murky series of tales? In any case, it resembles those in other cultures, such as the English tale of Robin Hood, featuring an outlaw who is really on the side of the oppressed and of justice.

David first flees to the temple at Nob (21:1). This is the first time we have seen David in the context of a temple and dealing with the priesthood. He asks for bread, but there is only holy bread available, hedged about with conditions. David claims to be on a secret mission from the king, but that does not convince the priest, Ahimelech. David declares that his men have obviously not been in contact with women, as they are on campaign (21:5), a declaration that will come to be ironic in the context of his later dealings with Uriah the Hittite (2 Samuel 11). Thus reassured, but also under duress, the priest allows him and his men to eat the bread.

David regains Goliath's sword (1 Sam. 21:9), although he is seen by one of Saul's servants, and then seeks refuge with the king of Gath, Goliath's own city, of all places. His reputation has gone before him, however, and only feigning madness saves the day. He then escapes to a cave, where he assembles the equivalent of Robin Hood's band of merry men from the marginalized people of Saul's kingdom, including his own brothers (22:1-2). Saul's servant, however, tells the king of David's doings at Nob, which leads Saul to order the slaughter of all the priests. David then moves to Keilah, where he is warned by YHWH that he will be given up to Saul.

Significantly, David now has the access to divine guidance that Saul has lost. The stories proceed through a series of near misses where the flow of information is all-important. David is informed against, but he always seems to be one step ahead through his own sources of information, crucially including divine guidance through his consultation of the ephod.

Toward the end of these stories, Jonathan and David meet again at Horesh (23:16-18). Jonathan for the first time explicitly states that David will succeed Saul as king, with Jonathan second in command. They make a covenant together once more, and David's position seems to be settled.

▌THE TEXT IN THE INTERPRETIVE TRADITION

The incident of David's eating the bread from the altar is recalled by Jesus in Mark 2:26 as part of his justification to the Pharisees for his disciples' act of plucking grain on the Sabbath. This has taken on a particular significance for subsequent interpreters in arguments over the authority of the Gospel. Jesus is represented as referring to Abiathar as high priest rather than Ahimelech as in 2 Samuel 21. Is Jesus mistaken? Is Mark mistaken? In order to avoid either conclusion, there is a body of literature that seeks to account for this difference with varied degrees of ingenuity. This may seem a rather small detail, but it has become a test case for belief in the historical reliability of the Gospels for certain groups. Others argue that the truths of the Christian message do not stand or fall by such textual details, and asserting that they do misconstrues the nature of these texts and the way in which the fallibility of communication is part and parcel not only of their message but also of their construction.

▌THE TEXT IN CONTEMPORARY DISCUSSION

For the contemporary reader, the connections between religious institutions, political authority, and the control of information in this story has resonances with doubts about the implications for various political systems of the growth of surveillance, coupled with the possibilities for all sorts of groups, official and unofficial, to tap into supposedly confidential information. It is a useful reminder that, although the technology is vastly different, the moral issues around secrecy, spying, and disclosure were also of concern in the ancient world. Second Samuel 20–23 also raises issues as to whether the religious establishment and its rules should stand aloof from politics. Ahimelech is in an invidious position. Is his loyalty to David, to Saul, or to God? How is he to work out the alliances between them? Is complying with David's wishes going to please or offend either Saul or God? As so often, there is no clear answer in this complex situation. The story leaves us with a heightened awareness of the issues at stake, however.

1 Samuel 24–26: Saul, Nabal, and David

▌THE TEXT IN ITS ANCIENT CONTEXT

First Samuel 24–26 forms an intriguing unit. The two outer chapters bear striking similarities, to the extent that they look like two versions of one underlying story. Between them is the apparently unrelated story of Nabal, the inhospitable rich man. Yet, read as a unit, these three stories shed light on each other.

In 1 Samuel 24 and 26, the basic premise is that Saul is in pursuit of David in the wilderness. David, by luck or cunning, is able to approach the unsuspecting Saul and take away part of his possessions. David then, brandishing his trophy, appears to Saul and his army (24:11; 26:16), allowing David to make the double point that he has had Saul at his mercy, but that he has chosen not to kill Saul because he is YHWH's anointed. As David is the new anointed leader, we might suggest that this is a good general principle for him to establish. Saul's response in both cases is, surprisingly, to acknowledge David's moral superiority. Nevertheless, his apparent acceptance of David's position proves to be short-lived.

There are significant differences in the stories and their results, however. In the first story in 1 Samuel 24, David cuts off Saul's robe as he is relieving himself. This harks back to the episode where Saul, clutching at Samuel's robe in despair, tears it, which Samuel interprets as a sign that the kingdom will be torn from his grasp (1 Sam. 15:27). Saul acknowledges explicitly that David will be king and in return exacts an oath from him that he will not wipe out Saul's name from Israel (24:19-20). This seems to be an acceptance by Saul that his line will go into decline.

In the second version of this encounter, in 1 Samuel 26, David takes Saul's water jar and spear—perhaps the very one hurled at David's own head in 19:10—from the midst of the army. David then reproaches Abner, Saul's general (and cousin), for not protecting the king (26:13-16). Intriguingly, this time Saul addresses David explicitly as his son (26:17), but makes no mention of his kingship, simply making a general statement that David will succeed in many things. After the apparent reconciliation of 1 Samuel 24, this is quite a contrast. David's reaction in 1 Samuel 27 is to see the lack of any specific pledge as the final confirmation that Saul will not rest until David is dead.

In between these two tellings, in 1 Samuel 25, is the story of Nabal, the man whose behavior is, at least from David's point of view, summed up by his name, which means "fool." In response to a request from David for food for his men, albeit with an implicit threat in his reminder that Nabal's wealth had remained untouched despite the presence of his band, Nabal dismisses David and his pretentions with scorn (25:10). David angrily orders armed reprisals but is forestalled by Abigail, Nabal's beautiful wife, who urges him not to incur the guilt of a rash blood revenge (25:24-31). In contrast to Nabal's characterization of David as a resentful ex-servant, she describes him as fighting the Lord's battles. David is mollified and accepts her gifts (25:35). She returns to the feasting Nabal and next morning tells him the news, which kills him. David is then free to marry Abigail himself.

In context, Nabal is a kind of surrogate Saul (Gordon). Here David is on the point of exacting satisfaction for an insult, which is much less dangerous to him than Saul's threats. Just as he has protected Nabal's herdsmen from attack, he has done more than any to preserve Saul's kingdom from Philistine attack. Saul in chapter 24 speaks in the conciliatory tones of an Abigail, but in 1 Samuel 26, his true feelings, which are much closer to Nabal's, seem to come to the fore. Yet the story of Nabal shows that restraint on the part of David leads to the outcome that favors him in the end while enabling him to avoid the charge that he is guilty of an inappropriate blood revenge. That would provoke a counteraction that would end in a general massacre, either of Nabal's men on one hand or of Saul's army on the other. A pattern that has already been set but that will recur throughout David's career is exemplified here. Anyone who is an obstacle to David tends to die unexpectedly and often violently, but in a way that allows David an alibi which, at least on the face of it, removes the suspicion of guilt from him.

▌ THE TEXT IN THE INTERPRETIVE TRADITION

Abigail is seen by early Christian interpreters such as Ambrose and John Cassian as exemplifying the virtues of wisdom, particularly in her skill both in her speech and in knowing when to keep silent (Franke, 310). As a particularly favored wife of David, who is often identified with Christ, she can also come to represent the church. As a type of the convert, she sees David's worth and throws in her lot with him. However, both the fact that she is still married and the fact of David's conduct have meant that this interpretation has some difficulties. That aside, she is an exemplar of the complex relationship between human initiative and divine purposes. By acting prudently to forestall a possible sin by David, she furthers God's purposes.

◼ THE TEXT IN CONTEMPORARY DISCUSSION

These stories show once again the psychological complexity of the books of Samuel. The inclusion of the story of Nabal can be read as an intriguing narrative device to reveal more than one side of David's character and to show the possibility of another response on his part to Saul. The respect he shows to Saul, and the respect he gains from Saul, may seem to point to the power of restraint to settle situations, but we would do well not to be carried away by the lofty sentiments of either Saul or David. Saul's words, however sincere, do not stop him from pursuing David. David's professed loyalty to the king, again whether sincere or not, turns to his advantage and sets a precedent for the treatment of the king that is to his benefit. The rapprochement between former enemies exemplified by such contemporary cases as the meeting between Egyptian president Anwar Sadat and the Israeli prime minister Menachem Begin in the late 1970s is essential at some stage if a protracted conflict is to find any resolution, but this story shows that overidealizing such a situation is rarely wise.

1 Samuel 27–28: Samuel and Saul's Final Meeting

◼ THE TEXT IN ITS ANCIENT CONTEXT

The result of the potential rapprochement between Saul and David is that David once again flees to the heartland of Saul's—and Israel's—enemies: the court of Achish, the king of Gath, the city of Goliath. He takes six hundred men and his wives to Gath and asks Achish for a city (27:5). He is given Ziklag. This seems extraordinary. The anointed king of Israel is installed as a vassal of the king of Gath, now allied with the enemy whose defeat gained him his fame.

It is also clear that Achish, for one, has taken David's final break with Saul to mean that he has also broken with Israel. The chapter explains how David practices an effective deception in this regard. He tells Achish that he is raiding Israel and its allies while in fact attacking other Philistine cities (27:10). He takes the precaution of following the practice that Samuel urged on Saul by massacring entire populations so as to leave no witnesses as to what had occurred. Note that the Amalekites, whom Saul supposedly wiped out, are among those mentioned. Again, David shows his adeptness at manipulating information. Achish takes this as meaning that David has burned his bridges with Israel (27:12). The arrangement works well until Achish decides that David will become his bodyguard and that he and his men will join Achish in a campaign against Israel at Shunem. This presents David with quite a dilemma. How will he maintain his double game?

The story then switches back to Saul. He is confronted by this powerful Philistine force and is now intimidated, in contrast to his younger self. He desperately seeks God's guidance, but fails to find any means of learning God's will in the matter (28:6). Samuel, who was one certain means of accessing God, has died. Saul resorts to seeking out a medium at Endor to summon Samuel's spirit even though he has himself ordered the expulsion of all practitioners of divination (28:7).

The encounter at Endor is an extraordinary passage. The Hebrew Bible contains repeated injunctions against those who have any dealings with the dead. Other ancient cultures in the region have no doubt that the dead have continued importance for the living and expend considerable resources placating them and consulting their wishes. Israel's traditions do not deny the possibility of such contacts, but forbid them (Lev. 20:6).

Saul, in stark contrast to David, is starved of information and sees no alternative but to break this taboo. Samuel indeed responds to the woman's summons and, ironically, simply confirms what Saul has already been told, rendering the consultation pointless. The kingdom has been given to David because of Saul's failure to carry out YHWH's instructions to annihilate Amalek. Saul collapses, partly because he has not eaten, which brings to mind his earlier rash injunction to his army in 1 Samuel 14. He initially refuses the woman's offer of food but relents, and she feeds both him and his men generously (28:22-25).

▌THE TEXT IN THE INTERPRETIVE TRADITION

This passage has, not unnaturally, been a source of a great deal of theological speculation on the nature of life after death and of the relation between the holy prophet Samuel and the abhorrent practices of witchcraft. Augustine and Tertullian both puzzle over this. King James VI of Scotland in his *Daemonology*, a dialogue on the reality of witchcraft, is one of those who uses this story to argue that witchcraft is a reality, not simply an illusion. In his case, this is used to justify his campaign to extirpate witches from his newly united kingdom, with appalling results for the next century.

What is it of Samuel that survives, and from what state has he been recalled? The text itself is not particularly interested in these details. It may well be that the ancient audience would have been familiar with the practices and beliefs of mediums. In any case, for the purposes of the story, an entirely consistent metaphysical account of the realm of the dead is not required. This story is also a source in the tradition for reinforcing the ban on witchcraft and for aligning witchcraft with necromancy. The effect of this on the sad history of witchcraft trials, such as the 1692 trials in Salem Village, Massachusetts, is well documented.

▌THE TEXT IN CONTEMPORARY DISCUSSION

Feminist commentators, in contrast to those who condemn the medium at Endor, have noted the surprisingly sympathetic treatment the text gives her (Frymer-Kensky 2002, 310). She shows genuine concern for the king, whose decrees have threatened her and her colleagues with banishment and death, providing him with food and with comfort. She represents a strand of female expertise and spirituality in ancient Israel that is otherwise suppressed. The books of Samuel, after all, are not written in order to give us an anthropological and sociological account of ancient Israel's religious practices. They have a clear ideology of their own. Yet we get glimpses in such passages of a religious situation in ancient Israel that is much more complex, and much more in line with wider cultural practices, than the texts are comfortable with. This could well enter into discussions pertaining to the persecution of those whose religious conventions do not represent a society's norm.

1 Samuel 29–31: Saul and Jonathan United in Death

■ THE TEXT IN ITS ANCIENT CONTEXT

Chapters 29–31 of 1 Samuel bring Saul's story to a close and explain David's part in his death—or, rather, his alibi. After all, no one, on the face of it, stands to gain more by Saul's death, and David is now allied, in appearance at least, with Saul's enemies. We go back to the mustering of the Philistine forces. The army of Achish joins those of their fellow Philistine lords, and David and his men are obliged to follow on.

The song of the women about David's prowess compared to Saul's, which has followed David and has haunted Saul, now gives him an unexpected excuse. The other Philistine kings are highly suspicious of David and quote this song, pointing out to Achish that the coming battle gives David a good opportunity and motive for treachery against his new allies (29:5). By turning against them, he might hope to restore his damaged reputation in Israel. Achish defends David's record as a loyal servant but orders him to remain behind. David protests against the injustice of the accusation from the Philistine lords, and Achish repeats his high opinion of him, but again insists that David and his men part company with the Philistine army (29:9). The irony of Israel's hero pretending to be offended by the suggestion that he should be left behind in a Philistine assault on Israel is almost labored in this chapter. The upshot is that David goes back to Philistia while the Philistines go up to Jezreel (29:11).

On their return, David and his men discover that the Amalekites, who seem once more to have survived complete annihilation, have taken advantage of David's absence to subject his city, Ziklag, to the kind of destruction they themselves have suffered (30:1-2). Rather than slaughter all the inhabitants, as David would have done, however, they have captured and taken away the women and children. David's leadership is threatened as the people blame him for this catastrophe, but he takes swift action, with the Lord's support, to pursue the raiding party (30:10). An abandoned Egyptian slave directs them to the Amalekite camp, and they mount a successful rescue, killing all the Amalekites except for four hundred who escape on camels. On their return, the victorious party comes across those of their number who were too exhausted to follow them all the way, and a dispute arises as to whether they should share in the plunder (30:21-25). David makes it plain that the spoils are to be divided equally. He also begins the process of mending bridges with the people of Judah by sending them a portion of the spoil as well.

While this has been going on, the Philistine attack is continuing. Saul's sons are killed, including Jonathan, and Saul himself is surrounded (31:3). In extremis, he asks his armor-bearer to kill him so that he at least will not suffer the disgrace of being killed by the uncircumcised Philistines. The armor-bearer refuses, so Saul falls on his own sword. The news of his death leads to a wholesale flight by Israel, leaving the Philistines in occupation of the land (31:7). Saul's story is not yet finished. His body is found, his head cut off, and his body displayed on the wall of Beth-shan (31:10). Hearing of this, the people of Jabesh-gilead, the city Saul defended against Nahash as the first act of his leadership, make the journey to Beth-shan, rescue the bodies of Saul and his sons, and then burn and bury them with appropriate mourning.

▌The Text in the Interpretive Tradition

In marked contrast to the praise by many philosophers in the Greco-Roman world of the hero who shows mastery of his emotions and of his fate by taking his own life rather than face disgrace, the biblical tradition has been read as condemning any such act as a final rejection of God. Augustine is the most influential of the church fathers to write on the subject, and his views have shaped those of both Catholic and Protestant commentators in succeeding centuries (Augustine 1972). Rather than being seen as the final flaring of nobility for a tragic hero, Saul's suicide confirms his rejection by God. The text, be it noted, simply reports Saul's actions, offering no judgment.

▌The Text in Contemporary Discussion

For the modern reader, there is a poignancy in Saul's desperation to maintain his relationship with God, which simply becomes yet another occasion for his inevitable fate to be reinforced. There is an uncomfortable message here about the possibility of coming to a point of no return in this relationship. Saul's culpability here is not easy to assess. After all, once he has become subject to the attentions of an evil spirit "from YHWH," is he morally responsible for his own actions anymore? If God is the source of the rebellion against himself, it is difficult to condemn Saul unequivocally. One message of the books of Samuel is that human judgment of others is deeply flawed. Achish and Saul both misjudge David, but he too is capable of misjudgment. The best result may be a due humility in judging others.

2 Samuel 1: The Amalekite Deception: A Pattern Set

▌The Text in Its Ancient Context

Saul's death marks the transition to the second book of Samuel. The first chapter of 2 Samuel is typical of the ever-growing complexity of the book as David begins his rule. It begins with an extended incident that puts under the microscope the ability of the new king to assess and respond to information and to deal with the complex rivalries and loyalties of the various factions within the kingdom.

David is at Ziklag when a dirty and disheveled messenger arrives who does obeisance to David, the first person who has offered him such royal recognition (1:2). In answer to David's questions, the messenger reveals that he has escaped from the battle but that Saul and Jonathan are dead. Asked how he knows, he says that he came across the wounded Saul and, at his pleading, delivered a mercy blow. Picking up Saul's crown and armlet, he has brought them to David.

For the reader, this is, intriguingly, not the story we have just been reading in 1 Samuel 31. This messenger, who describes himself as an Amalekite, does not appear in that chapter; Saul killed himself (1 Sam. 31:4). Is this simply a contradiction caused by editing together different versions, or should we take seriously the fact that the earlier version has the authority of the narrator, whereas we only have the word of the Amalekite in 2 Samuel 1? Has he simply robbed the body of the dead king, seeking to curry favor with his successor?

Be that as it may, the king's first reaction is to order mourning for Jonathan and Saul (1:18). For all the enmity between them, the honor due to a dead king must be paid. David then questions the young man again and has him executed, not directly for killing the king, but for entertaining the idea of killing him (1:10). Very cunningly, David's judgment does not depend on deciding between the narrator's account of Saul's death in 1 Samuel 30 and the young man's version. His words, not his deeds, condemn him. Drastic as this is, it makes a clear point to anyone who might have problems with David's own rule.

We might also note that any other secrets the young man had have now died with him. More suspicious readers have even wondered if David engineered this whole scenario, as it all falls out remarkably well for him (McKenzie, 109). Saul and Jonathan, his key rivals, are dead, yet he is able to present himself as their chief mourner so as to begin to build bridges with his erstwhile opponents in Israel. He is also able to show the firmness of his rule and to reinforce the message that the person of the anointed king, no matter what he has done, is sacrosanct.

The last part of the chapter is taken up with a funeral lament for Saul and Jonathan (1:19-27). It is powerful and moving and yet distinctly at odds with the story we have read in the last few chapters. The elegy depicts Saul and Jonathan as "not divided." This ignores the accounts of their quarrels over David, not to mention Saul's attempts to kill his own son. David's lament for Jonathan, which stresses that his love was greater than the love of women, is a resonant line (1:26). Once again, though, we should note that there is no mention of David's love for Jonathan.

For all the emotional weight of this lament, the text could hardly be clearer that David is not simply giving vent to his private feelings but is making a public statement, one he orders to be taught to the people and recorded in the book of Jasher. Under the gaze of his people, he needs to reinforce the respect due to Israel's kings and to make it clear that the claims of the Saulide dynasty have ended in the regrettable death of Jonathan. As happens so often in 2 Samuel, David is not only the beneficiary of the deaths of his rivals but also in the position to lead the mourning and to condemn their killers. He is also, as we have seen, a master at using language through all the channels of communication at his command to turn events to his own advantage.

▌ The Text in the Interpretive Tradition

In the history of interpretation, the lament for Saul and Jonathan has redounded to David's credit, being a sign of his prowess as a poet and musician and of his generosity of spirit. Many of its phrases have passed into the poetry of subsequent languages, and it remains a moving if enigmatic work, as evidenced by the variety of English translations. As such, it becomes part of the defense of religious poetry as a genre by Jerome and by Protestant writers after the Reformation (Jeffrey, 184).

■ THE TEXT IN CONTEMPORARY DISCUSSION

For modern readers, this chapter raises complex questions about David's motivations and the way in which the manipulation of perceptions about a ruler is a key part of any political system. Everything David is represented as doing here is part of a public display, and the reaction of his audience, first his own loyal followers and second the wider people of Israel, is firmly in view at all times. An attentive reading makes it hard to escape the conclusion that the text exposes in a sophisticated way some of the hidden workings of any political system. The release of state secrets after a period of embargo in the modern world often reveals that governments, even in democracies, have been routinely engaged in covert operations that were denied at the time.

2 Samuel 2: David at Hebron

■ THE TEXT IN ITS ANCIENT CONTEXT

David now begins to make his move to establish his rule in Judah, anchoring his claim to the kingship of Israel in the loyalty of his own tribe. He needs divine advice to work out his plan of action and is told that he should begin from Hebron. There the people anoint him as king of Judah. David is told that the people of Jabesh-gilead buried Saul and quickly sends a message of appreciation (2:5). This is necessary, because his claim to power is by no means unopposed. Abner, Saul's cousin and general, whom David had taunted, is sponsoring and protecting an alternative candidate, Saul's son Ishbaal, who is made king over all of Israel at Mahanaim. For seven and a half years, David is acknowledged as king only in Judah.

For reasons that are not made clear, this situation is destabilized by a contest between David's men and Abner's, drawn from Saul's tribe, Benjamin. David is not present, but is represented by his equivalent to Abner, his nephew Joab (2:12). In an oddly choreographic moment, the twelve champions from each side kill each other seemingly simultaneously and a fierce battle ensues. Abner is pursued by Joab's brother Asahel and is killed as he refuses to give up the chase (2:23). Joab and his remaining brother Abishai take up the pursuit until there is a standoff in which Abner asks how long this pursuit should last (2:26). Joab and Abishai break off their pursuit, but the damage has been done. Blood has been spilled on both sides. The Benjamites have lost 360 men, whereas Abner's men have only lost nineteen, but the loss of Asahel means that a potential cycle of vengeance is poised to restart at any moment.

■ THE TEXT IN THE INTERPRETIVE TRADITION

The continued success of the Saulides is one of the many aspects of this transition period between the two kings. It is completely passed over by the books of Chronicles. There, the transition from Saul's death to David's reign over all is accomplished by immediate general acclaim (1 Chron. 10:13—11:3). The tendency for the tradition to elevate David above the realpolitik of the books of Samuel clearly has begun early, which makes the depiction of David in Samuel all the more remarkable.

THE TEXT IN CONTEMPORARY DISCUSSION

The modern reader is able, however, to see that the books of Samuel offer a picture of David that glosses over or explains away a number of potentially damaging incidents and decisions. How suspicious should we be of the books of Samuel as themselves products of royalist propaganda, or can we detect in them a hidden rhetoric of resistance that at various points in the history of these texts has been necessarily concealed? The most powerful message of this sort of biblical book, after all, may not be in what it explicitly states but the way in which it hints at the complex nature and motivations of any account of a national and political history. These dynamics are explored in a masterly way in Stefan Heym's novel *The King David Report*, which recounts the way in which Solomon ensures that the history of his father is written in such a way as to make his own succession inevitable. Heym, however, was writing under the Communist government of East Germany. Under the guise of a critique of the Bible, which suited the political censors, he was able to write a devastating attack on the manipulation of history by any oppressive regime, including the East German government.

2 Samuel 3–5: David and Saul's Successors

THE TEXT IN ITS ANCIENT CONTEXT

In 2 Samuel 3, this incident proves to be the beginning of a long war for ascendancy between David and the descendants of Saul. In the meantime, we learn David has been fathering sons (3:2-5). This sets the conditions for a whole series of potential future conflicts between him, his sons, and his followers as the succession to the kingdom becomes an issue. At this point, however, David's own kingship over Israel is still far from established.

In Ishbaal's court, things are becoming complicated as well. Ishbaal accuses Abner of dalliance with one of his father's concubines, Rizpah, an act that could be construed as a bid for power on Abner's part and a claim to succession in his own right (3:7). Abner, who after all seems to have been the moving force behind Ishbaal's reign, is outraged and threatens to throw his weight behind David. In fact, he enters into negotiations with David, restores to him his former wife Michal, and communicates with the elders of Israel and Benjamin confirming that David is indeed the Lord's chosen ruler. This seems to imply that Abner and the elders have already been contemplating switching their loyalty from Ishbaal.

David then meets with Abner, and all seems to be arranged for Abner to deliver the loyalty of Israel to David (3:20-21). Joab learns of this and berates David for failing to realize that Abner is looking to his own advantage through learning David's plans (3:24-25). Is David this time the one who is on the receiving end of a political deception, or is Joab blinded by his personal vendetta against Abner? Joab solves the problem in a characteristically direct way. He arranges for Abner to be called back, without David's knowledge, and stabs him to death.

David is furious and curses Joab's household. He organizes a public funeral for Abner and himself offers a lament over Abner (3:33-34). As in the case of Saul, however, the narrative itself is clear that this mourning has an explicitly political purpose. All Israel is convinced that

David had no hand in Abner's murder, and David goes out of his way to praise Abner as a great man (3:37-38).

Once again, David has turned a situation to his own good. Abner—a much more formidable foe than the puppet Ishbaal—is dead, but the disastrous rift that the murder of Abner could have caused between David and Ishbaal's followers has been averted. Joab has conveniently taken the blame, and David has managed to establish an important precedent for any future problems (3:19). If things get out of hand, he can point to the distance between himself and Joab's actions even if they in fact benefit him. He has achieved what in political parlance would be called "deniability," an asset to any leader.

Ishbaal, not unnaturally, takes alarm at the loss of his mentor. In a rather piecemeal way, which may mirror the apparent disarray of Ishbaal's kingdom, the story proceeds. We are told that Ishbaal has two Benjamite raiders. Apparently inconsequentially, we then learn that Saul has another grandson, Jonathan's son, whom the text calls "Mephibosheth," a name that contains an element meaning "shame" (4:4). Chronicles preserves this name as Merib-baal (1 Chron. 8:34; 9:40), which seems more plausible and is in line with his uncle Ishbaal's name, although it carries the same problematic echo of the divine name Baal. The information that he is lame is introduced in a way that suggests this will become a significant plot element, but we hear no more of him at this juncture.

The two raiders kill Ishbaal in his own house, cut off his head, and bring it to David at Hebron (4:8). The reader may be struck by the similarity to the actions of the unnamed Amalekite in 2 Samuel 1, and this is confirmed when David makes explicit mention of the analogy as he condemns the two to death (4:9-11). Like the Amalekite, they had presumed that David would be pleased at the death of his rival. Like him, they learn how wrong that assumption was. They are killed, mutilated, and their bodies hung up.

At long last, in 2 Samuel 5, David is anointed king of all Israel after all the tribes come and declare their belief in him (5:1-3). His first act is to conquer the Jebusite stronghold of Zion (5:7). Politically, this is an astute move. Rather than elevate the Judahite capital of Hebron to the new seat of kingship or risk alienating his Judahite following by moving to an Israelite city, David marks a new beginning by establishing a new center for Israel. The rather odd byplay over David's apparent hostility to "the lame and the blind" remains mysterious (5:6-8), although the reminiscence of the lameness of Mephibosheth is clear (4:4). Zion is renamed the "City of David" (5:7), and David's international reputation is indicated by the fact that the king of Tyre sends him the materials and the craftsmen to build himself a house (5:11). More children are born to David in Jerusalem: twelve in all. The old enemy, the Philistines, make one final attempt to disrupt David's kingdom, but David defeats their army not once but twice (5:20, 25), the second time with the eerie aid of the Lord's army, signaled by the sound of marching in the treetops.

A pattern, however, has repeated itself. David's rival has met with his end in circumstances that, at least to the public eye, exonerate him from any possible blame. Any story to the contrary again has died with the perpetrators. David has succeeded in gaining the united acclaim of the people of Israel, but there are undercurrents of unsettled scores, potential rivalries, and stories that clearly admit of more than one interpretation. The rhetoric of kinship contains contradictions that can be managed but not eliminated.

∎ The Text in the Interpretive Tradition

Ambrose of Milan speaks for many in the subsequent tradition who take David's integrity and piety as expressed in passages such as his mourning for Abner entirely at face value and hold him up as a model of conduct (Franke). It is incidents such as this that explain why God is prepared to forgive the sins of David and his sons, on this reading. Marcion, in his attack on the Old Testament, makes a point of the contrast between David's rejection of the blind and Jesus' healings to argue that Jesus is not David's son. This point is refuted by Tertullian, who finds the contrast in the faithfulness of the blind in the New Testament (Franke).

∎ The Text in Contemporary Discussion

For the modern reader, the books of Samuel are full of insights into these dynamics that can occur in any human organization: a school, a company, or a church, as much as in a kingdom. Once any organization grows beyond a certain size, its leader can no longer personally supervise every detail and so he or she needs trusted deputies. As we have seen, however, in David's own case, that deputy may begin to accrue the credit that the king depends on for his own popular success. Furthermore, there is a dangerous game to be played in relying on the loyal deputy to carry out the dirty work so as to leave the leader above suspicion. Inevitably, the deputy has knowledge that the leader cannot afford to make public. If relations become strained, this becomes a serious potential threat.

2 Samuel 6: The Ark Contained

∎ The Text in Its Ancient Context

Having disappeared from the narrative for many chapters, the ark of YHWH reappears as the topic of 2 Samuel 6. David leads a great procession of people down to the ark's resting place in order to retrieve it and bring it up to his new capital. A new cart is provided to move it, and as it travels David and the whole troupe dance and play musical instruments (6:5). Not all goes according to plan, however, and Uzzah, one of the drivers, is struck dead when he takes hold of the ark to steady it (6:7). The narrative strikingly tells us that David is both "angry" with God and "frightened" of him (6:8-9). This is something he cannot manage, and the presence of the ark in the royal city begins to seem a potential threat as well as an asset. The ark is left with a non-Israelite, indeed possibly a native of Achish's city of Gath, to see what will transpire. Its caretakers prosper, so David takes this as a good omen (6:11). In an even more elaborately choreographed procession, he and the people bring the ark to Jerusalem, sacrificing animals every six paces. David, wearing the priestly garment called the ephod, dances with all his might before it. Michal, Saul's daughter, watches him from the window and despises him (6:16).

The ark is brought to a tent, reminiscent of the tabernacle of the exodus stories, and David offers sacrifices, blesses the people, and distributes food to them, again carrying out typically priestly functions (6:17-19). He has succeeded in bringing into his own camp a potential source of division in his kingdom by avoiding any possibility that the ark and its attendant priesthood should become an alternative focus of the people's loyalty. He has also paved the way for his new capital to become the new center of Israel's religious life, trumping the claims of the ancient shrines such as Shiloh and Bethel.

One person is less impressed, his wife Michal, who scolds him for uncovering himself in the eyes of the people (6:20). His retort is stinging. The God before whom he danced is the one who decreed that he would supplant her father. She might not be pleased, but, as ever, David's concern is with his image among the people at large. If they honor him, his own sense of self-abasement counts for nothing. A brief phrase seals both Michal's fate and that of the Saulide dynasty. Michal bore no children; should any son of David succeed him, that son will not be a grandson of Saul (6:23).

▮▮ THE TEXT IN THE INTERPRETIVE TRADITION

In the tradition, the coming of the ark into Jerusalem represents God's endorsement of the temple on Mount Zion. For early Christian writers such as Maximus of Turin, the ark, as the place where the Word was housed, becomes a type of Mary as she also bears the Word made flesh. David's dancing is, for Gregory the Great, an example of humility that Christian leaders should emulate (Franke).

▮▮ THE TEXT IN CONTEMPORARY DISCUSSION

This story contains a number of disturbing elements for many contemporary readers. The apparent unfairness of the death of Uzzah is an unsettling reminder of the danger of any dealings with the divine, but the exchange between Michal and David is unsettling in another way. Michal's apparent snobbery is met with a curse on her, depriving her of children. In narrative terms, this is justified as we discussed above, but other readers have led us to consider the complex and difficult position of Michal in the story (Heym). Even without this, the story shows that the same events can have profoundly different interpretations depending on whose view we take. Reading with the eyes of the women in the story uncovers assumptions about the power relations in the story that may need to be questioned.

2 Samuel 7: The Promise of Eternal Kingship

▮ THE TEXT IN ITS ANCIENT CONTEXT

Second Samuel 7 is one of the key chapters in the Hebrew Bible. In it, we see David at the peak of his powers, king of all Israel, at peace in his own city, which is both the political and religious hub of his newly established kingdom. We also see the first inklings of why this hard-fought and longed-for situation, which seems to be the fulfillment of the promise of a land and prosperity for the people of Israel, cannot last. Furthermore, it contains a clue as to how Israel manages to retain its sense of identity and of hope beyond the collapse of the kingdom that has just been established.

It begins with the king established in his palace and at peace with all his enemies, a description that chimes with the book of Deuteronomy (12:10-12) and its prediction that once peace has been established in the land, the Lord will choose a dwelling place. David remarks to the prophet Nathan that he now has a house, but the ark is still in a tent (7:1). Nathan expresses his agreement with whatever David has in mind. That night, however, YHWH speaks to Nathan. In an unprecedentedly long speech, clearly echoing the language and concerns of Deuteronomy, the deity points out that he has never asked for such a house in all his dealings with Israel (7:7). He further points out to David that he has raised him from obscurity and has established a place of safety and security for the people. Rather than David building YHWH a house, YHWH will build a house, in the sense of a dynasty for Israel. One of his offspring will be established forever in his kingdom, and it will be him who will build the house (7:11). YHWH explicitly refers to the cautionary tale of Saul and declares that this time the promise will not be rescinded even if the king commits sins against him. The house and the kingdom will be established forever. Nathan relates all this to David. The change in Nathan's message reminds the reader that his previous acquiescence with David's plan was not God's will; not everything a prophet says is from God.

David responds with an extended prayer (7:18-29), again an unusual feature in the books of Samuel. He does little other than repeat back to God his own promises and describe his deeds to him, acknowledging his own humility and his own dependence on God's favor.

■ THE TEXT IN THE INTERPRETIVE TRADITION

Three crucial points come out of this declaration for later tradition. First, YHWH is in control of David's destiny. Second, YHWH is not tied to any temple, and so the destruction of any temple is itself of no eternal consequence. The third is the promise of an eternal kingdom with the possibility ruled out that God, as he has done in the past to Eli and Saul, will rescind the promise. For readers who have seen the destruction of Jerusalem and the failure of David's line, what can this mean? The reference in 1 Samuel 7 to the offspring of David who builds the temple is most easily attributed to Solomon, but his kingdom was irrevocably split under the reign of his son. The obvious rejoinder that this was due to the sins he and his heirs committed is not open to us, as that explanation is forestalled. If this passage is to mean anything, it can only be that it refers to a throne and a house that have as yet to be established and a kingship that is beyond the political exigencies of this world.

Christian readers have long interpreted this passage as a prophecy of the coming Messiah. Yet the New Testament seems to betray some uneasiness about aligning Jesus to the Davidic tradition. The genealogies have to reckon with the nature of Jesus' relationship to any Davidic line given that he is God's son, not Joseph's. Jesus is also depicted as reacting rather negatively to those who address him as "the son of David" (Mark 12:36-37) and as resisting some of the political and military expectations that seem to have become part of the expectations of a Davidic messiah. All the same, in Acts 13:34-36, Paul explicitly refers to the promises that were made to David being fulfilled in Jesus' resurrection, contrasting Jesus and David who, as a human being, "after he had served the purposes of God in his own generation, died" (Acts 13:36). This is followed up by a long tradition that reads allegorically David as a type of Christ, ruling, defeated, and restored, which idealized the king. Protestant commentators, uncomfortable with this type of hermeneutic, tend to lay more stress on his humanity and fallibility.

THE TEXT IN CONTEMPORARY DISCUSSION

For modern readers, especially those with some critical training, the tension between interpreting this passage as a much-edited failed prophecy of the eternal establishment of Solomon or some other successor's dynasty and responding to the tradition's verdict that it is a reference to a future messianic king is an acute example of the need for a sort of binocular reading of the text. Is it possible to hold such readings in tension without being justly accused of attempting to have one's interpretative cake and eat it? Again, however, is this not symptomatic of the inescapable dilemmas of any sort of revelation of a divine purpose in human affairs? It will always be possible to read the text differently, and the final option for the reader will always be a decision, not an inevitable conclusion. It is a decision that is always also aware of its provisionality. What the biblical text does do, however, is make that provisionality, and the need for decision, exceptionally clear. It also reminds us that such decisions depend on the context within which the text is read, whether the biblical canon or a particular interpretive tradition: Christian, Jewish, text-critical, or skeptical.

2 Samuel 8–10: Building Up Trouble

THE TEXT IN ITS ANCIENT CONTEXT

In the succeeding chapters, we begin to see that the picture at the beginning of 2 Samuel 7 is already shadowed by intimations of trouble ahead for the kingdom. David still has enemies who need to be subdued. He attacks the Philistines and the Moabites and reduces them to servitude (8:2). He attacks and cripples the army of Hadadezer of Zobah and defeats the Arameans, killing twenty-two thousand of them when they come to Hadadezer's aid, putting a garrison in place to subdue them and gain tribute (8:5). He gains such a reputation that Toi, king of Hamath, voluntarily offers him tribute (8:10). All this accumulated wealth is dedicated to YHWH. The Edomites are also defeated, losing eighteen thousand men (8:13-14).

Although these victories are presented as signs of the LORD's favor, we should also be aware that Israel is now in the situation of garrisoning the territory of powerful albeit defeated enemies. David may have won some new allies, but he has also created lasting resentments. He may be able to subdue any potential rebellion against his rule for now, but he is now ruling people who have not consented to his rule and who have no kinship to him. Unifying Israel was difficult enough. Will this new expanded kingship ever know peace?

Potential conflict is embedded in the list of David's administration at the end of 2 Samuel 8. We are assured that he rules justly over Israel (8:15), but does that term necessarily include these subject peoples? Do they now harbor the kind of resentments that Israel felt under Philistine rule? David is now dependent on an inner cabal. In charge of the army is David's nephew Joab (8:16). We already know the threat any general may pose, and in Joab's case, there is an explicit history of differences between him and his uncle (4:39). This circle contains priests who are named before the secretary (8:17), showing the importance of the mutual support of the religious and political establishments in Israel. There is also Benaiah, described as being in charge of the Cherethites and Pelethites

(8:18). These turn out to be elite troops whose loyalty is to the king. The fact that there is a need for such an imperial guard, which is distinct from the people's army, indicates a potential source of tension intrinsic in the kind of kingship David is establishing. A final note says that David's sons were priests. Not only is this at odds with at least the Deuteronomists' accounts of how priests are appointed (Deut. 18:5), it is worryingly reminiscent of the situation with both Eli and Samuel. Hereditary priesthood has proven to be an unreliable institution.

The persistence of potential points of resistance to David's rule in Israel is highlighted in 2 Samuel 9. Jonathan's lame son Mephibosheth reenters the story when David enquires whether any of Saul's descendants are left. The declared reason for this is his desire to show them favor in Jonathan's memory (9:1). This might be plausible but does not necessarily rule out the more practical point that David would do well to nip in the bud any possibility of Saul's heirs becoming a rallying point for disaffection from his rule. David brings Mephibosheth to his palace and feeds him at his table, having restored all Saul's lands to him. We should remember, however, that Saul protested that he came from the least of the families in the least of the tribes. What would his ancestral lands consist of? Not only that, but David's apparently generous gesture of feeding Mephibosheth is, it turns out, less than it seems. He instructs Ziba, an old servant of Saul, and his family to provide the food for Mephibosheth by their labor on Mephibosheth's own lands (9:9-10). David is thus not out of pocket, and Ziba's family now has a cause for resentment against him.

Further trouble ensues when the new king of the Ammonites treats David's ambassadors with disrespect and then hires men from a number of neighboring kingdoms, including the Arameans, to defend himself against reprisals from David (10:6). Joab and his brother manage to defeat the combined armies, but this spurs the Arameans into launching a concerted campaign on their own behalf (10:15). They in turn are defeated, and all the allied kings make peace with David (10:19), but once more, thousands have been killed and any ill-feeling against Israel has material to fuel it. The peace that prevails in the area is one based on fear and is therefore bound to be uneasy and volatile. Being "like other nations" is not a comfortable fate.

▮ The Text in the Interpretive Tradition

In the history of interpretation, the stress in this story has often been on the kindness and charity of David to his potential enemy Mephibosheth in loyalty to his dead friend. The tendency of the tradition to read David's actions favorably and to give him the benefit of the doubt means that it is taken as an example of the love of one's enemy that Jesus enjoins, but this may tend to reduce the disabled Mephibosheth to an opportunity for David's charity, with consequences for the view of disability in Christian tradition (Schipper).

▮ The Text in Contemporary Discussion

For modern readers, 2 Samuel 8–10 has an uneasily familiar ring in an era where successive new countries and new governments seek to establish themselves, proclaiming peace and stability by repressing old injustices and then being led into reprisals against disaffected groups that simply add to a stock of resentment. Is the message that there is no political utopia and that even at its height, the Davidic empire, like all empires, contained the inevitable seed of its own destruction? An African proverb tells us, "You can't have the wood without the termites." The very processes necessary to build the kingdom import the justification and the means for others to tear it down or seek to rebuild it in their interests.

2 Samuel 11–12: Bathsheba: David's Plans and God's Purposes

▌THE TEXT IN ITS ANCIENT CONTEXT

The next chapter shows a kingdom that is not at peace but is now provoking wars on its own account. Second Samuel 11–12 is among the most extraordinary pieces of writing in the Hebrew Bible. Not only do they show a remarkable sophistication in their narrative technique, but they also tell a story that puts Israel's greatest hero in an uncompromisingly unfavorable light. Here is a king who will resort to deception, adultery, and murder involving loyal members of his entourage without any reference to his God but who apparently also believes himself to be the arbiter of justice.

The beginning of the chapter makes the point that David is now separated from his army. They are off fighting the Ammonites, while he is safe in his palace. A domestic drama ensues that is, tellingly, missing from the Chronicler's account of the same military campaign in 1 Chronicles 20. In short, David summons Bathsheba, the wife of Uriah, one of his loyal commanders, and makes her pregnant (11:5). When he learns of her pregnancy, he calls Uriah back and does all he can, including using alcohol, to induce Uriah to sleep with Bathsheba. This is all in contravention of the rule that active soldiers abstain from sex that he himself self-righteously invoked in 1 Samuel 21. When this fails, he notoriously sends a letter to Joab by Uriah's hand containing instructions for Uriah to meet his death (11:14). On hearing the news that he has died, David sends a subtle threat to Joab, who alone knows the whole story (11:25), and marries Bathsheba, ensuring that his child is part of his royal household (11:27).

In all this, David has reckoned without God. Nathan appears and traps him into condemning himself by leading him on so that he pronounces judgment against a fictional character who has stolen and killed a poor man's sheep (12:1-4). David's punishment is that the son born to Bathsheba will die. His response to the child's subsequent illness is flagged by the narrator as incomprehensible to his own courtiers. He mourns until the son dies and then ceases mourning (12:20). Readers are left with contradictory assessments of this behavior. Does it show David's faith in divine justice, or is it blatant cynicism? The upshot is that Bathsheba bears a second child, who turns out to be Solomon (12:24). What kind of a birth story is this for one of Israel's most prominent figures?

All this having occurred, Joab sends his own message to David, warning him that his reputation will be threatened unless he comes down to finish the siege of Rabbah himself (12:27-28). David is now the victim of his own concern with reputation. At the end of 2 Samuel 11, he seemed to have saved his own name and acquired a desirable new wife and child. On the contrary, he learns not only that he has offended God (11:26), whom he did not seem to consider before, but also that he has risked jeopardizing his standing with the army. His once unmatched awareness of and control over the important channels of information has lapsed. He forgot about what God knew, he took no account of the army's perceptions, and Joab now has damning evidence that he could use against him if occasion arises. It is Joab, who now has David and the kingdom's reputation in his hands, who has to recall David to his duty. For the time being, they are both better served by the continuance of David's rule—for the time being.

▌ THE TEXT IN THE INTERPRETIVE TRADITION

In the traditional interpretation of David, this scene sets the seal on the depiction of David as the archetypal penitent. Convicted by Nathan, he repents of his sins in a way that becomes a model for later generations of Christians. This reading is strengthened by the penitential psalms, such as Psalm 51, that are also attributed to him. He thus becomes an endorsement of the sacrament of confession in Catholic and Orthodox tradition, and of the use of the Psalms in self-examination by Protestant readers.

▌ THE TEXT IN CONTEMPORARY DISCUSSION

Contemporary readers may find it difficult to see a marked change in David's behavior after this episode, however. Readers have argued as to whether his apparent reconciliation with his son's death shows a mature spirituality or a cynical relief that the punishment has fallen on the child rather than him. Whatever may be true, his subsequent career is marked by the kind of swings between hostility and sentimentalism about his sons that are reminiscent of Saul. The tensions we have outlined throughout that beset any hereditary monarchy are explored here in a series of stories of great but disturbing power. David is shown to be much less astute in managing his own family than he has been in managing those around him on his way to the kingship. Political leaders worldwide are still beset by these problems, exacerbated by the prevalence of the media. The peccadilloes of a Bill Clinton and the complex relationship between Saddam Hussein and his sons are cases in point.

2 Samuel 13–18: Absalom, the Beloved Enemy

▌ THE TEXT IN ITS ANCIENT CONTEXT

The tension between father and sons, which is exacerbated in the case of a king and his potential heirs, has seldom been so well explored as in the following chapters of 2 Samuel. So far, we have heard nothing of his sons except for lists of their names and their mothers. Now they become the focus of the story in a series of interlinked masterpieces of the laconic narrative style of this book. In particular, they revolve around the glamorous but flawed figure of Absalom.

The first we hear of Absalom is in relation to his sister Tamar, who is the object of their half brother Amnon's passion. Deceived by his pretended illness, she visits his room only for him to rape her and then spurn her (13:14-17). With her life destroyed, as no one else will marry her if Amnon does not, she seeks refuge with her brother. David, we learn, is furious (13:21), but does nothing to Amnon, his favored firstborn. Absalom, enraged by his half brother's attack on his sister, bides his time for two years and then invites all his brothers and his father to a feast. It is here that he has Amnon killed and then flees to the king of Geshur's protection for three years (13:37).

Characteristically, the Hebrew is highly ambiguous about David's attitude to Absalom in a way that most translations cannot capture.

It is Joab, again, who takes the initiative in persuading David to invite Absalom back through an elaborate charade involving a wise woman and a story about a family where one son has murdered another and is now banished (14:5-7). She succeeds, as Nathan did, in trapping David into swearing an oath. The banished son should be allowed to return. David sees through the ruse too late and finds himself obliged to permit Joab to bring back Absalom (14:21).

Again, rather than a touching family reconciliation, there may be realpolitik at work here. Absalom in exile is a constant and uncontrollable potential rival and rallying point for dissent. Joab may be acting in the kingdom's interest in bringing him back where he can be watched, as David did in the case of Mephibosheth. More self-interestedly, Joab may be establishing himself in Absalom's good books against the day when David—who has forced Joab to put up with a great deal—becomes more of a liability than an asset to the kingdom.

David's subsequent refusal to meet Absalom simply fuels his son's resentment. Absalom cunningly begins to eat away at David's power by interrupting the flow of petitioners to the king and presenting himself as the only true hope for justice. After four years, he asks permission to go to Hebron (15:7), the place where finally the rest of Israel besides Judah had accepted David as king and has himself proclaimed as the new ruler of Israel. David's response is to call for the mass evacuation of the city (15:14). Only ten royal concubines are left. On the flight, there is a succession of encounters, the significance of which only becomes apparent on David's return. He meets Ittai the Gittite, another anomalous inhabitant of Gath, Goliath's hometown, who proclaims his loyalty. (15:21). He sends the ark back to Jerusalem (15:25), saying that its fate will show what God's will is. He learns that a trusted councilor, Ahitophel, is now advising Absalom and, in typical fashion, arranges for the elderly Hushai to spy on Absalom's court (15:34)

Old stories come back to haunt him. He meets Ziba, Mephibosheth's servant, who tells him that Saul's grandson is expecting the restoration of his kingdom. David rewards Ziba with the grant of Mephibosheth's property (16:4), reversing his earlier judgment. He meets another Saulide, Shimei, who abuses him roundly (16:7). David prevents his bodyguard from harming him, saying that if his own son has turned on him, he can hardly blame Shimei, who is doing the Lord's own bidding (16:11).

In the meantime, Hushai has persuaded Absalom that he has truly defected from David and proceeds to undermine the wise counsel of Ahitophel, who tells Absalom to sleep with the concubines left behind to signal the total break with his father (16:21). Hushai lets this pass, but then he opposes Ahitophel's advice that a swift targeted assassination of David would lead to the speedy end of the conflict. Instead, Hushai appeals to Absalom's vanity and counsels a pitched battle involving the whole army with Absalom at its head (17:11). Absalom agrees, and Hushai activates the network of informants that David has set up through the guise of the return of the ark. Ahitophel, seeing that he has been ignored and knowing what the outcome will be, hangs himself (17:23).

Sure enough, when battle is joined, David's forces under Joab defeat Absalom's. Absalom himself is caught in a tree by his much-vaunted hair, and Joab dispatches him, despite the public orders of David that Absalom is to be spared (18:14). An extraordinary account of the way in which the message of Absalom's death is brought to David ensues, playing on the reader's memory of the other occasions in which a messenger has brought David news of the death of someone whose actions have posed a threat to his kingship. Here this motif reaches an apotheosis as different messengers vie over how the news that David's son, who had become the embodiment of all that the so-called Laius complex so dreads, is now dead. The beloved son has been thwarted in his attempt to kill and supplant his father. David's reaction, as so often before, is public mourning for the one whom others might expect he would be glad to see removed from the scene. This time, however, there is no poetic outburst, denunciation of the killer, and protestation of royal innocence, only the broken repetition of his son's name and the wish that he had died in Absalom's stead (18:33).

■ The Text in the Interpretive Tradition

The theological appropriation of such stories has to reckon with the fact that God is generally absent throughout these chapters. It is the dynamics of the human family that are the focus of interest, as well as the way in which personal loyalties and feelings conflict with the necessities of statecraft. Absalom becomes a key example of the perils of pride and of personal vanity and extravagance, often at the expense of recalling the depth of his grievance against his father. Through the imagery of Absalom's death scene—a corpse hanging by the neck and entangled in branches—Cassiodorus likened his actions against his father David and subsequent fate to that of Judas Iscariot's betrayal of Jesus Christ (Franke, 383).

■ The Text in Contemporary Discussion

The story of Absalom represents the tensions between father and son and the tension inherent between the human reactions of David as father and the political judgment of David as king. As in the episode with Bathsheba, David has to be recalled by Joab to his kingly duties and his responsibilities to the whole people. This is the nearest the Hebrew Bible comes to a story of patricide, and we may remember that Plato's main reason for banning poets from his Republic was that their stories are full of examples of sons killing fathers, something no government can risk encouraging. In this respect, the Hebrew tradition seems to have gone further in suppressing such stories. David's love for his son risks alienating the rest of his people; this story certainly encourages reflection on the difficulties of drawing the boundary between the personal and the political in any political system. An egregious example from British history is the short and inglorious rule of Richard Cromwell as Lord Protector in succession to his father Oliver, a role for which he had little inclination, aptitude, or training. The propensity for political systems that apparently have no place for the hereditary principle to throw up familial dynasties seems to continue unabated: the Nehru-Gandhi family in India, the Assad regime in Syria, and the Kennedy and Bush dynasties in the United States show that these issues persist in contemporary politics in a range of regimes.

Such close relationships can engender persistent tensions. At the time of this writing, the horrible revenge reportedly exacted by the North Korean leader Kim Jong-un on his uncle for alleged corruption, which extended to the killing of his family and associates, is a reminder that the personal and the political are intertwined in many political systems. Kim Jong-un himself only came to power because his elder brother fell out of favor with their father. Close family ties may mean that perceived betrayals lead to exceptional and drastic reprisals as personal hurt and family honor are brought into the equation and often override political considerations.

2 Samuel 19–20: Coming Home to Roost

■ THE TEXT IN ITS ANCIENT CONTEXT

Second Samuel 19–20 seems to show that the proverbial chickens are coming home to roost for David. First of all, this time the public act of mourning, instead of acting as a potential healing of the rifts in the kingdom and strengthening David's position, backfires. Once again, it is Joab who has to recall David to his duty to set aside his feelings as a father and act as king (19:5-7), bluntly pointing out that his days as king are over unless he reassures his followers that he would not prefer that they had all died so that Absalom could have survived. The rest of Israel is also in turmoil, knowing that they had thrown in their lot with Absalom and now fear David's reprisals.

David rallies by appointing Absalom's general Amasa as head of the army instead of Joab, straining the latter's loyalty yet again (19:13), and using Amasa to bring Judah back to their leader. Shimei reappears, and David appears to pardon him, swearing that he will not put him to death; he does not swear that his successor will be bound by this oath, however. More to the point, Mephibosheth reappears, alleging that the story Ziba had told was a fabrication designed to get hold of Mephibosheth's lands (19:27). The king, now apparently bereft of his former astuteness in dealing with deceptive characters, takes the easy way out by dividing the land between them, only for Mephibosheth to get the last word and renounce the land. A final encounter with the elderly Barzillai catches the ambivalent tone of this return. Barzillai refuses David's offer to become part of the court, but offers his servant Chimcham instead. Returning with David is not a reward he seeks.

This return, far from healing the rifts in the kingdom reopened by Absalom's appeal to the non-Judahites at Hebron, rubs salt in the wound. Judah and the rest of Israel are set at loggerheads as to which can claim David as their own. The problem is compounded by the actions of a Benjamite called Sheba, who persuades the other tribes that they have no stake in David anymore and should follow him instead, which they promptly do (20:2). David is apparently back where he was in 2 Samuel 2, king only of Judah. He calls on his new commander, Amasa, to muster the Judahite army, but Amasa, suspiciously, fails to return by the appointed time. David then turns to Joab's brother, instructing him to hunt down Sheba before he can consolidate his power (20:6). Joab joins his brother and in the process of the hunt meets and kills Amasa, concealing his body so that the troops are not distracted from their purpose. Sheba retreats to his ancestral city, which is then besieged (20:14). Through the intervention of a wise woman, the inhabitants are persuaded to kill Sheba and throw his head over the wall in return for the safety of the city (20:22).

The chapter—and the connected narrative of 2 Samuel—ends with a repeat of the list of David's chief men that is found at the end of 2 Samuel 8. After all that has happened, what has changed? Joab still commands the army, despite David's apparent attempts to discharge him; Jehoshaphat, Benaiah, Zadok, and Abiathar retain their roles. Two things are different, however. David now has an official in charge of forced labor. Significantly, there is no mention of his sons serving as priests (20:23-26). The relationship between ruler and ruled has changed, as has the succession to the kingdom. Both of these changes bode ill for the future stability of a kingdom that has already all but fallen apart and has only just been reconstituted.

It is quite striking how incidents from David's past now come back to haunt him and are read rather differently. It is clear from this material just how flimsy a construct the united kingdom of Israel under David has been. Matters that were thought to be settled turn out to be far from solved, and readers can legitimately wonder how subversive these texts are when it comes to the monarchy. David here is hardly a hero. In one way of looking at it, all he has brought to Israel is to draw people into a series of deadly conflicts, which stem from the tensions in his own family. He has also installed the kingly response of forced labor.

▌ THE TEXT IN THE INTERPRETIVE TRADITION

Both Ambrose and Augustine account for the fact that David mourns for his treacherous son Absalom, but not for the innocent child in 2 Samuel 12, as a result of his knowledge that Absalom, deprived of the possibility of repentance, is lost to him forever in eternal punishment. David's seeming contrition and humility in the encounters that mark his progress to and from the city adds to the picture of him in later tradition as the archetypal penitent, although this masks the reality of the long revenge he later plans. In this context, his presumed authorship of the penitential psalms is also explained.

▌ THE TEXT IN CONTEMPORARY DISCUSSION

David serves here as a warning of the dangers of a charismatic leader whose personal ambitions and relationships spill out into the politics of his community. Contemporary history can supply all too many parallels. Where is the line between the private life and the public duty of a politician? How far should political careers be judged by private misjudgments and misdeeds? On the one hand, in France, the fact that President Mitterand maintained two families remained secret in a way that would be unthinkable in the United States or the United Kingdom and did not lead to his political downfall. On the other hand, in a later generation the marital misadventures of the later president Nicolas Sarkozy were a factor in changing public perceptions of his competence, although his successor François Hollande's own problems in this regard put this in a new perspective.

2 Samuel 21–24: Rereading David

▌ THE TEXT IN ITS ANCIENT CONTEXT

The final four chapters of the books of Samuel are anomalous. Rather than continuing the narrative sequence of the rest of the books, they seem to assemble a number of stories and poems that relate oddly to what has gone before. Second Samuel 21 tells the story of a famine, which YHWH announces is due to a continuing guilt on the house of Saul because he killed the Gibeonites. This seems rather strange in the context of the rest of Samuel, where the accusation laid at Saul's door is his failure to eradicate the Amalekites. Be that as it may, David agrees to hand over seven sons of Saul to be impaled by the Gibeonites as recompense (21:5). He spares the life of Mephibosheth (21:7), because of his loyalty to Jonathan his father, but the story makes no mention of the oath David swore to Saul that he would not cut off his progeny (1 Sam. 25:21-22). Perhaps he takes the typically evasive view that all he is doing is handing them over to the Gibeonites; what happens to them then is not his responsibility.

Once the sons are killed, however, the mother of two of them, Rizpah (the concubine over whom Ishbaal and Abner fell out in 2 Sam. 2:7), sits in vigil to protect their bodies from birds and animals (21:10). David takes that as a sign and retrieves the bodies of Saul and Jonathan from Jabesh-gilead and ensures them proper burial in Saul's father's tomb (21:12). Other names from previous chapters surface in puzzling ways. Both Merab and Barzillai are mentioned, prompting us perhaps to reflect on their motives in a new way.

Further material comes to light, recording a series of fights against giants. On each occasion, it is not David who kills the giant. Indeed, Elhanan is credited with the killing of Goliath (21:19). It is hard not to see a retrospective problematization of the picture of David as the brave young warrior confronting impossible odds on his own. Here David is surrounded by equally competent warriors. The key moment of the encounter between David and Saul is also thrown into question. If David did not kill Goliath, then what is the justification for his rise to prominence in Saul's court?

Second Samuel 22 is a psalm attributed to David on an occasion of his deliverance from his enemies. It is a fine example of the genre, but again contains material that sits uneasily with what we have read in the rest of Samuel. In particular, it represents David as claiming that he has been rewarded for his righteousness (22:21-25) as the singer harps on his blamelessness before God. Is there an irony here? Does the story of David not rather show that he has indeed been dealt with according to his righteousness, but that he has been far from blameless? His actions, intentional and unintentional, have led not to a serene monarchy in perfect accord with God, but to the fractious, unstable, and unjust kingdom depicted in 2 Samuel 20.

Second Samuel 23:1-7 contains what are presented as David's last words. This is surprising, as in the preceding narrative he is not yet dead and his story will continue into 1 Kings. Again, is there irony here? David is represented as having an everlasting covenant with God and as the just ruler in contrast to those who are wicked and who can only be touched by a spear. Yet spears abound in the stories of Samuel, most notably the spear David took from the sleeping Saul, which had been hurled at David and Jonathan. By that token, are David and Jonathan, whom Saul attempted to touch with a spear, to be counted among the wicked? How far is this text pointing to the contrast we have seen elsewhere between the pious David who traditionally lies behind the Psalms and the David we encounter in so much of Samuel who is far from a model of piety?

Chapter 24 recounts the brave deeds of David's champions. The main body of Samuel has kept silent about these for the most part. It commonly represents a military campaign by simply stating that "David went up" against a city and took it. Now we are reminded that he always, of course, went up in the company of mighty warriors whose exploits are not recorded in the books of Samuel but who have driven its story. It is surely not a coincidence either that the final name in the list is the one that haunts David's memory, then and now: Uriah the Hittite, here praised as a member of the band of thirty and thus one of the elite group of Israel's greatest fighters (23:19). Again, the contrast between what he deserved and what he received at the hand of David is reinforced.

The final chapter of this section, and thus of the books of Samuel, represents David as the instrument not of God's favor but of his anger. At YHWH's instigation, David numbers the people of Israel but then realizes that he has committed a grave sin (24:1). Through the prophet Gad, David is offered three choices: three years of famine, three months flight before his foes, or three days of pestilence (24:12-13). David prefers to fall in to God's hands than into human hands, and so the days of pestilence ensue, killing seventy thousand people.

This leads to an extraordinary encounter between David and the angel of destruction on a Jebusite threshing floor in Jerusalem, where David pleads for the punishment to be on him and his house rather than Israel (24:17). Nowhere in the rest of Samuel do we find such an incident, which could put a very different theological interpretation on the fate of the Davidic monarchy and how it relates to the survival of Israel. Is Israel's ultimate destruction explicable as a kind of transferred punishment for the shortcomings of David, just as his nameless son by Bathsheba dies for his sins? Or is the demise of the Davidic dynasty God's price for the survival of Israel?

The same incident also puts an odd twist into the story of the building of the temple as Gad instructs David to buy the threshing floor in order to set up an altar. The site of the altar is the site of David's confrontation with an angel of YHWH who is charged with the destruction of Jerusalem. If this is related to the temple, then it becomes not a home for God or a celebration of his bounty, but a mechanism by which the fatal intentions of God are averted.

▌The Text in the Interpretive Tradition

God's reaction to David's decision to take a census of the people has long consequences in the interpretive tradition. The book of Chronicles makes Satan the instigator of the census (1 Chron. 21:1). This adds a level of complication, in that Satan as a tempter is markedly absent in most of the Hebrew Bible. His role becomes prominent in the New Testament, however, and in subsequent Christian interpretation. The seeming disparity between the accounts in Samuel and Chronicles is thus fertile ground for subsequent reflection on the nature of human sinfulness and the role of demonic temptation in human ill doing.

▌The Text in Contemporary Discussion

Put together, these anomalous final chapters cast a disconcerting retrospective light over the career of David and his significance in the books of Samuel. What other stories have we not heard, and what other motives have been hidden and suppressed? This peculiar "appendix of deconstruction," as Walter Brueggemann has called it (Brueggemann 1988), does not simply serve to throw open to question an otherwise straightforward story, however. Rather, it simply heightens the sense any attentive reader must grasp of how complex and enigmatic the story told in the books of Samuel really is. These final chapters also reinforce our sense of how aware these texts are of the intrinsic limitations and paradoxes of any human institution and any human communication. In doing so, they point for theologically minded readers to the way in which any communication between God and human beings is inevitably bound up in the same limitations. It is part of the power of the Bible's claim to be such a communication that it so subtly and clearly raises these issues, leaving the reader to make his or her decision as to how to respond.

Works Cited

Alter, Robert. 1999. *The David Story: A Translation with Commentary of 1 and 2 Samuel*. New York: W. W. Norton.

Augustine. 2007. *City of God*. Translated by Henry Bettenson. London: Penguin.

Brueggemann, Walter. 1988. "2 Samuel 21-24: An Appendix of Deconstruction?" *Catholic Biblical Quarterly*, vol. 90, 383–97.

Exum, J. Cheryl. 1992. *Tragedy and Biblical Narrative: Arrows of the Almighty*. Cambridge: Cambridge University Press.

Fewell, Danna Nolan, and David M. Gunn. 1993. *Gender, Power and Promise: The Subject of the Bible's First Story*. Nashville: Abingdon.

Franke, John, ed. 2005. *Joshua, Judges, Ruth, 1–2 Samuel*. Ancient Christian Commentary on Scripture, Old Testament 4. Downers Grove, IL: InterVarsity Press.

Frontain, Raymond-Jean, and Jan Wojcik, eds. 1980. *The David Myth in Western Literature*. West Lafayette: Purdue University Press.

Frymer-Kensky, Tikva. 2008. *Reading the Women of the Bible: A New Interpretation of Their Stories*. New York: Schocken.

Gordon, Robert P. 1986. *1 and 2 Samuel: A Commentary*. Exeter, UK: Paternoster.

Harding, James E. 2013. *The Love of David and Jonathan: Ideology, Text, Reception*. Sheffield: Equinox.

Hastings, Adrian. 1997. *The Construction of Nationhood: Ethnicity, Religion and Nationalism*. Cambridge: Cambridge University Press.

Heym, Stefan. 1984. *The King David Report*. London: Abacus.

Jeffrey, David Lyle, ed. 1992. *A Dictionary of Biblical Tradition in English Literature*. Grand Rapids: Eerdmans.

Josipovici, Gabriel. 1988. *The Book of God: A Response to the Bible*. New Haven: Yale University Press.

McCarter, P. Kyle. 1980. *1 Samuel: A New Translation with Introduction, Notes and Commentary*. AB 8. Garden City, NY: Doubleday.

———. *2 Samuel: A New Translation with Introduction, Notes and Commentary*. AB 9. Garden City, NY: Doubleday.

McKenzie, Steven L. 2000. *King David: A Biography*. Oxford: Oxford University Press.

Pyper, Hugh S. *David as Reader: 2 Samuel 12.1-15 and the Poetics of Fatherhood*. Leiden: Brill.

Schipper, Jeremy. 2006. *Disability Studies and the Hebrew Bible: Figuring Mephibosheth in the David Stories*. LHB 441. New York: T&T Clark.

1, 2 KINGS

Gale A. Yee

Introduction

Like the books of Samuel, 1 and 2 Kings was originally one book in the Hebrew canon, continuing the story of the monarchy's decline that was readily apparent from 2 Samuel 9, which recounted the dysfunctional family relations in King David's household, onward. The book of Kings narrates the stories about David's son Solomon, the division into two kingdoms after Solomon's death, the events leading up to the conquest of the northern kingdom of Israel by the Assyrians, and finally to the destruction and exile of Judah by the Babylonians.

Composition

Critical examination of the book of Kings was important for theories about the composition of a major portion of the Old Testament (for a fuller discussion, see Römer). In 1943, the German scholar Martin Noth argued that the final form of the books of Deuteronomy, Joshua, Judges, 1–2 Samuel, and 1–2 Kings was due to a single individual working during the Babylonian exile in the sixth century BCE. Because these books shared similar theological themes and concepts with the book of Deuteronomy, Noth referred to these books collectively as the "Deuteronomistic History" (DH), and called its author/editor the "Deuteronomist" (Dtr). As an editor, Dtr conscientiously incorporated older documents and traditions for his work, such as the stories about the prophets Elijah and Elisha. Dtr even named some of his sources: "the Book of the Acts of Solomon" (1 Kgs. 11:41); "the Book of the Annals of the Kings of Judah" (1 Kgs. 14:29); and "the Book of the Annals of the Kings of Israel" (1 Kgs. 16:27). However, as an author, Dtr shaped these sources and older traditions to compose a particular narrative history of the two kingdoms that articulates his own theological intents and purposes.

American scholar Frank Moore Cross built on Noth's theory by positing a "double-redaction" of the DH. Instead of a single individual working during the exile, Cross noticed an earlier version of the DH that concluded in 2 Kings 22–23, describing the achievements of King Josiah in the seventh century BCE. This first edition of the DH ended with 2 Kgs. 23:25: "Before [Josiah] there was no king like him, who turned to the LORD with all his heart, with all his soul, and with all his might, according to all the law of Moses; nor did any like him arise after him." This Josianic edition underscored two themes. The first was YHWH's promises to David's dynasty in Judah, in spite of the fact that some of the Judean kings kept some of the "high places" of worship. The second was the "sin of Jeroboam," worship at the illegitimate sanctuaries of Dan and Bethel that infected practically every northern monarch and precipitated the ultimate fall of Israel. These two themes converged with the stories about Josiah, who destroyed the altar at Bethel and purged the nation of its idolatrous gods and practices. This seventh-century Josianic edition was then updated in a Deuteronomistic school to form a sixth-century exilic edition of the DH. Other scholars have even posited further editions during the Persian period (late sixth–fifth centuries BCE). The Deuteronomists responsible for these editions were probably high officials of the scribal class in Judah that shared a particular ideology and rhetorical style (Römer, 45–49).

Sense Units

This commentary divides 1 and 2 Kings into the following sense units:

> 1 Kgs. 1:1—2:46: Solomon's Succession to the Throne
> 1 Kgs. 3:1-28: Solomon the "Wise" Man?
> 1 Kgs. 4:1—11:42: Solomon's Bureaucratic Rule
> 1 Kgs. 12:1—16:34: The Divided Kingdom
> 1 Kgs. 17:1—22:53: The Ministries of the Prophets Elijah and Micaiah
> 2 Kgs. 1:1—8:29: The Ministry of the Prophet Elisha
> 2 Kgs. 9:1—12:21: The Rise of the House of Jehu and the Demise of the House of Omri
> 2 Kgs. 13:1—17:41: Events Leading to the Fall of Israel
> 2 Kgs. 18:1—20:21: The Reign of Hezekiah
> 2 Kgs. 21:1—23:30: The Reigns of Manasseh and Josiah
> 2 Kgs. 23:31—25:30: The Final Days of Judah and Its Kings

Theological Framework

Beginning in 1 Kings 15, after the narratives regarding Jeroboam I, Dtr provides a specific theological framework to introduce each of the ruling monarchs that will continue to the end of 2 Kings. The kings of Judah are presented according to the following pattern:

- The date the king took office, correlated with the rule of his rival in Israel (15:1—"In the eighteenth year of King Jeroboam son of Nebat, Abijam began to reign over Judah.")
- His length of reign (15:2a—"He reigned for three years in Jerusalem.")
- The name of the queen mother (15:2b—"His mother's name was Maacah daughter of Abishalom.")

- Dtr's judgment on his rule (15:3-5—"He committed all the sins that his father did before him . . .")
- Other deeds, if any (15:6—"The war begun between Rehoboam and Jeroboam continued all the days of his life.")
- Citation of sources (15:7—"The rest of the acts of Abijam, and all that he did, are they not written in the Book of the Annals of the Kings of Judah?")
- Burial (15:8a—"Abijam slept with his ancestors, and they buried him in the city of David.")
- Name of successor (15:8b—"Then his son Asa succeeded him.")

For the kings of Israel, Dtr follows a similar pattern, but adds the city in Israel where the king had his capital and omits the name of the queen mother: "In the third year of King Asa of Judah, Baasha son of Ahijah began to reign over all Israel at Tirzah; he reigned twenty-four years. He did what was evil in the sight of the Lord . . ." (1 Kgs. 15:33-34).

The most important section in this framework is Dtr's judgment on the king's rule. A certain king may have been a very capable leader, economically and politically. Or the king may have been caught up in the larger imperial politics of the ancient Near East that may have influenced his religious policies. The Dtr, however, is only concerned with how faithful he was to God's covenant. For him, "evil" kings were those who worshiped other gods or allowed their worship in the land; those who allowed shrines and sanctuaries to YHWH, such as the "high places" outside of Jerusalem; those who did not listen to God's prophets; those who participated in religious rituals that Dtr regarded as illicit. According to Dtr, the ultimate destruction of both Israel and Judah was due to their infidelity to YHWH alone by worshiping foreign gods from the moment the people crossed the Jordan and entered the land promised to their ancestors.

1 Kings 1:1—2:46: Solomon's Succession to the Throne

▌ THE TEXT IN ITS ANCIENT CONTEXT

First Kings 1–2 provides a literary bridge from the end of 2 Samuel to 1 Kings. First Kings begins forebodingly, with the detail that old King David could not get warm. Instead of piling on yet another blanket, his servants search the land for a young virgin who will join his harem to be his attendant and share his bed. One of the hallmarks of a king's royal status is the number of his wives, concubines, and sons, and David accumulated many as he gained power (see 2 Sam. 3:2-5; 5:13; 16:20-23). Scholars have remarked on the different ways David's private relationships with his women reflect issues in his public life (Berlin). Because David is unable to "know" Abishag sexually in spite of her beauty, she becomes a signifier of the impotence of his leadership at the end of his rule. The biblical author, as is typical, does not provide access to Abishag's thoughts about being taken from her home to service the king sexually.

Because of his deterioration and the fact that he has not named an heir, David's sons jockey to replace him. Solomon's rival is his half brother Adonijah son of Haggith, who is not only next in line but good looking to boot. Adonijah presumptuously declares, "I will be king," and, like his older brother Absalom, who also had royal ambitions (2 Sam. 15:1-7), gathers a small band of chariots, horsemen, and fifty men to run before him. The declining David does not reproach him for his displays of royal privilege (1:5-6).

Adonijah has powerful people from the military and religious sectors of the kingdom supporting him: Joab, David's mighty general and son of David's sister Zeruiah, and Abiathar the priest. Solomon has his influential supporters as well: Zadok the priest, Nathan the prophet, Benaiah the leader of David's bodyguard, and his mother Bathsheba, the bathing beauty of 2 Samuel 11. Those supporting Adonijah go back to the time when David was king of Judah at Hebron. Those supporting Solomon only come on the scene when David moves his capital to Jerusalem. The parties thus represent the old guard versus the young "turks" in the dynamics of power (Ishida). The members of each party compete with each other for the same position in the realm: Adonijah and Solomon for the kingship; Haggith and Bathsheba as future queen mother; Joab and Benaiah as commander of the army; and Abiathar and Zadok as chief priest (1:7-8).

A sacrificial banquet, hosted by Adonijah, who invites all of David's sons and Judean officials but not Solomon or his supporters, becomes the catalyst for some harem politics to secure the throne for Solomon. Nathan the prophet exploits the jealousy and fears among royal wives to spur Bathsheba into action. He declares that the son of her rival Haggith has "become king" and gives her advice to save her own life and that of her son Solomon. He and Bathsheba cleverly maneuver an impotent, senile old king into proclaiming Solomon as his successor, and, with great fanfare, Solomon is anointed king at the spring of Gihon (1:9-40). When the news of this anointing reaches the banquet, Adonijah's guests abandon him and he himself flees to grasp the horns of the altar, its most sacred part. Solomon spares his life only on the condition that Adonijah "proves to be a worthy man" (1:41-53).

First Kings 2 begins with David on his deathbed giving his final instructions to Solomon. Exhibiting the hallmarks of Deuteronomistic redaction, David exhorts Solomon to adhere to God's covenantal demands as written in the torah/law of Moses in order to prosper in his rule (2:3). God's unconditional promise to David of an eternal dynasty (2 Samuel 7) now becomes conditioned upon the complete fidelity of his successors to God's commands (2:4). We will soon see that the rest of Kings narrates the failures of Israel and Judah to remain faithful to God, resulting ultimately in the destruction of the kingdom and the exile of the people at the end of the book. Solomon himself will initiate this falling-off by worshiping the gods of his many foreign wives (1 Kings 11). After his torah counsel, David instructs Solomon to assassinate Joab, David's right-hand man in military affairs, and Shimei, who had cursed him publicly (2:5-10). David then dies, ending a career riddled with murder by proxy (Halpern 2001).

In the next scene (2:13-46a), Adonijah, in either a shrewd or stupid move, asks Bathsheba to request from Solomon the hand of Abishag, David's last concubine, in marriage. Surprisingly or perhaps cleverly, Bathsheba agrees. The way Solomon behaves toward Bathsheba, rising up and bowing down in her presence and giving her a seat of honor, reveals the high position that Bathsheba achieves as mother of the king. This lends credibility to the notion that she understood very well the effect Adonijah's request would have on her son. Sexual relations with a woman from the former king's harem evoked strong responses in the male politics of gender (cf. 2 Sam. 3:7-8; 16:20-22). Solomon predictably interprets the request as a step to advance Adonijah's thwarted royal ambitions. He has Adonijah assassinated and then deals with Joab and Shimei according to his father's wishes. This unit concludes with the detail, "So the kingdom was established in the hand of Solomon" (2:46b).

■ THE TEXT IN THE INTERPRETIVE TRADITION

Much intriguing speculation exists on the voiceless minor character Abishag (Stahlberg). The Talmud records her saying to David, "Let us marry." When David replies, "Thou art forbidden to me," because he has attained his legal allotment of eighteen wives, she implicitly ridicules his impotence, at which point David shows that he still has what it takes in his old age and has sex with Bathsheba thirteen times (*Sanh.* 22a). Because she is from Shunem, Abishag is linked with the "black but/and beautiful" Shulammite, Solomon's beloved (Song of Sol. 1:5; 6:13). Jerome allegorically personifies Abishag as wisdom herself, "so glowing as to warm the cold, yet so holy as not to arouse passion in him whom she warmed" (*Letter 52 to Nepotian* 2–3). She is the subject of a number of poems that reconstruct her feelings and experiences of being taken from her home to nurse and sleep with a decrepit king (Baumgarten; Curzon). The aging Earl of Hauberk in Aldous Huxley's *After Many a Summer* (1939) records in his diary, "I have tried King David's remedy against old age and found it wanting." In Stefan Heym's novel *The King David Report* (1972), Abishag is given a prominent, if not flattering role, as "stupidest woman in Israel," a sexually ripe concubine whose torrid affair with Adonijah leads to his downfall. In Joseph Heller's novel *God Knows* (1984), David's first love was and still is Bathsheba, who won't have anything to do with David, but still gives Abishag friendly advice about David's personal hygiene and eating habits.

■ THE TEXT IN CONTEMPORARY DISCUSSION

Although royal males in their attempts to obtain the throne are the subject of 1 Kings 1–2, feminist scholars highlight the important roles that harem women play within these political dynamics. Abishag becomes a symbol of David's decline, and Adonijah's request for her hand in marriage leads to his murder. Bathsheba's collusion with Nathan successfully procures the throne for her son, and her sly request that Solomon approve Adonijah's bid for Abishag secures it.

In today's political arena, the wives of male politicians often exert tremendous influence on public policy, albeit informally and behind the scenes. Rosalind Carter and Nancy Reagan were First Ladies who had much influential sway on their presidential husbands. Only more recently have the wives of presidents, such as Hillary Rodham Clinton and Michelle Obama, assumed a more visible role.

1 Kings 3:1-28: Solomon the "Wise" Man?

■ THE TEXT IN ITS ANCIENT CONTEXT

Now that his rivals have been eliminated, Solomon sets about consolidating his state and securing his rule over it. The first and last details describing Solomon's reign—his marriage to Pharaoh's daughter (3:1) and his love for his many foreign wives (11:1-10)—form a bracket around

Solomon's story. Although his wisdom will be underscored throughout, the subtext of Solomon's narrative lays the blame for his decline on his unwise entanglements with foreign women, recurring Deuteronomistic specters thought to seduce Israel away from YHWH (Num. 25:1-3; Deut. 7:3-4; Josh. 23:11-13). His first foreign wife is the daughter of the Egyptian pharaoh, mentioned several times in this story (3:1; 7:8; 9:16, 24; 11:1-2). As a place of enslavement, genocide, and unrelenting oppression, Egypt occupies a significant negative site in the Israelite consciousness. And yet, Solomon seems to appropriate aspects of this empire in establishing his rule as his story unfolds: the large harem (beginning with the pharaoh's daughter), the procuring of "wisdom" (the province of the elite class, 4:30), the stratification of society into the haves and have-nots, the large building projects, the forced labor, the accumulation of wealth, and the brutal taxation. Although Solomon "loved the LORD" (3:3), eventually building YHWH a great temple, he simultaneously "loved many foreign women" (11:1). Even though the adverse consequences of empire building will eventually lead to Solomon's deterioration, what the reader remembers is his love for foreign women and their gods, which seems to displace its real causes.

This tolerance for foreign religions is hinted in the report that Solomon often sacrificed at Gibeon, "the principal high place" (3:4). In Deuteronomistic theology, worship at the high places is usually forbidden, because Jerusalem is the central and normative locus of worship (1 Kgs. 12:31; 15:14; 22:43; 2 Kgs. 14:13, et passim). That Solomon is sacrificing in Gibeon when the ark resides in Jerusalem is rather unsettling. YHWH appears to him in a dream, saying: "Ask what I should give you" (3:5). Because he is only "a little child," faced with the task of governing "a great people," Solomon requests "an understanding mind" and the ability to "discern between good and evil" (3:9). Solomon's dream and the self-deprecating allusion to his youth parallel that of Tuthmoses IV of Egypt (*ANET* 449) and other propagandistic accounts that supply divine legitimation of a king's rule. Because Solomon asks for "understanding to discern what is right" (3:10) and does not ask for riches or honor, God will also give Solomon riches and honor all his life (3:13). Nevertheless, this promise to Solomon of wisdom, riches, and honor is conditional. Solomon must walk in the ways of YHWH, keeping God's statutes and commandments (3:14), a condition that Solomon will not always keep, as we shall see. The narrative ends with Solomon waking up from his dream, returning to Jerusalem to stand before the ark of the covenant. He then offers sacrifices and a feast at the only legitimate place of worship, according to the Deuteronomist (3:15).

Although it originally may have been an independent folktale about the judgment of an unknown ruler, the familiar account of the two prostitutes before Solomon now provides an illustration of Solomon's newly acquired wisdom (3:16-28). Various reasons why the story has two *prostitutes* before the king have been proposed: perhaps the designation explains why these women live together with infants but no husbands; perhaps to highlight that all levels of social strata were able to find justice before the king; perhaps to foreground Solomon's dilemma in deciding between two women, who were considered disreputable and deceptive by nature because of their occupation.

The contours of the case are filtered through the eyes of the plaintiff. According to the plaintiff, the defendant gave birth to a son three days after the birth of her own. During the night when no one else was in the house, the defendant's son dies because "she lay on him" (3:19). While the plaintiff slept, the defendant allegedly took the plaintiff's son and replaced him with her own dead son at the plaintiff's breast. When the plaintiff awoke to nurse, she discovered that her son was dead, but in a closer look knew that the infant was not her son. The defendant refutes her accuser by declaring, "No, the living son is mine and the dead son is yours," arguing back and forth before the king (3: 20-22). The king resolves the conflict by commanding a sword be brought and slicing the infant in two. The true mother is revealed when, moved with compassion, she pleads to the king to not kill her son, but give him to the other woman. The other woman declares: "It shall be neither mine nor yours; divide it" (3:24-26). The Hebrew text is ambiguous regarding the true mother. English versions, for example, the NRSV and NIB, have the king respond, "Give *the first woman* the living boy," even though the Hebrew only says, "Give her the living boy" (3:27), without clearly designating either the plaintiff or the defendant. Biblical scholars have argued for one or the other as the true mother (Garsiel 1993; Wolde).

Although this story ostensibly reveals Solomon's wisdom after God grants him this gift, the process leading toward his judgment would not pass muster in present-day courtrooms. Solomon simply accepts the testimony of the plaintiff without question and does not ask for the defendant's version of the case. He does not probe more deeply how the plaintiff knew that the defendant switched babies in the middle of the night if she was indeed asleep. Why did she not wake up when the dead baby was put at her breast (3:20)? Solomon does not investigate the crime scene for any clues. Instead, he rather recklessly endangers the life of an infant to provoke a reaction from the true mother.

Scholars have pointed out intertextual contrasts between 1 Kings 3 and 2 Kgs. 6:24-31, which also involves two mothers wrangling before the king over one living son. One of these mothers demonstrates compassion for her son; the other, a lack. However, their case is much more gruesome than the one judged by Solomon. During a siege that has been starving the population, the plaintiff had made a pact with the defendant to cook and eat her son that day, and the defendant's son the next day. However, after the plaintiff's son was consumed, the defendant reneged on her side of the bargain and hid her son. The king, seeing no way to resolve this dispute, tears his clothes and irrationally seeks vengeance on the prophet Elisha. Second Kings 6 seems to provide a negative counterpart to the all-wise Solomon, a negativity that is already imbedded in 1 Kings 3 (Lasine; Pyper).

▌ THE TEXT IN THE INTERPRETIVE TRADITION

The story of Solomon's judgment over the prostitutes is perhaps the most well-known, interpreted, and even parodied of his narrative (Ipsen, 134–35). Ephrem the Syrian and Augustine interpreted the story as an allegory in which the two women represent the church and the synagogue, in which the Jews symbolized by the false mother kills her son Christ. Augustine also saw Jewish Christians who tried to enforce the law onto gentiles like the false mother (Conti, 15–21).

Because the text does not explicitly point out which woman is the true mother, the interpretive tradition had different ways to resolve the ambiguity. For example, Rabbi Joseph Kara (1065–1135 CE) thought one could distinguish between a day-old child and one who was three days old on the basis of the birth blood of each. Radbaz (1480–1574 CE) conjectured that Solomon noted the facial similarity between the living child and that of the plaintiff and between the dead infant and that of the defendant (Garsiel, 232–34).

In chapter 14 of Mark Twain's *Huckleberry Finn*, Jim provides a negative reading of this story, based on his experiences as an African American slave, to contradict Huck's understanding of Solomon as the "wisest man." Jim uses a dollar bill to substitute for the child desired by both women. A wise person would go around the neighborhood to find out to which of the two women the money belongs, and then hand it over to the right one. But Solomon would "whack de bill in *two*" and give the pieces to the two parties. Jim declares, "what's de use er dat half a bill?—can't buy noth'n wid it. En what use is a half a chile? I wouldn' give a dern for a million un um." Because Solomon had this large harem, he must have had "'bout five million chillen runnin' roun' de house." He does not value children as a man who only had one or two children. But Solomon, "*He* as soon chop a chile in two as a cat. Dey's plenty mo'. A chile er two, mo' er less, warn't no consekens to Sollermun, dad fatch him!" In the world of slavery, slaves are commodities that are bought and sold. Their intrinsic humanity to the slaveholder is of "no consekens." Jim thus comes off as a wiser man than Solomon in this chapter.

◼ THE TEXT IN CONTEMPORARY DISCUSSION

Of the Solomon traditions, the common lectionaries only contain selections of his dream at Gibeon (3:5-15) and of his prayer at the temple's dedication (8:22-30, 41-43). These readings highlight Solomon's wisdom and piety, while omitting his ruthless elimination of his rivals (1 Kings 2) and his adoption of the oppressive trappings of empire. For the people in the pews, they thus present a one-sided picture of Solomon that supports the idealized traditional reputation as a wise and discerning leader, a reputation that should be counterbalanced with a more critical assessment of his rule.

One of the bitterest aspects of divorce proceedings is over the custody of children. These proceedings often take months, even years, of expensive litigation and emotional turmoil. Although dividing the family property down the middle can be a fair distribution between divorcing partners, "splitting the baby" according to Solomonic justice cannot be an option when it comes to their children. Determining the best interests of the child in our day and age takes much more wisdom than that demonstrated by Solomon in this text.

Feminist scholarship has highlighted the fact that the only narrated example of Solomon's wisdom was on behalf of prostitutes. Within the economics of the texts, one of the most vulnerable members of society, widows who have no male family members to support them may have to resort to prostitution in order to survive. When one focuses on the perspective of the women as prostitutes, one considers the systemic economic circumstances that force women into prostitution, in ancient times and modern, and what kind of justice they can appeal to when their rights are violated (Bird, 197; Ipsen, 134).

1 Kings 4:1—11:42: Solomon's Bureaucratic Rule

◼ THE TEXT IN ITS ANCIENT CONTEXT

The different editorial and ideological layers in these chapters make it is difficult to determine their historical reliability about Solomon and his presumed tenth-century rule. Their narratives have analogues to eighth- and seventh-century-BCE Assyrian inscriptions, persuading scholars to regard them as later retrojections to create a magnificent past for Israel (see also Moore and Kelle, 244–57; Römer, 99). Although Solomon is depicted "in all his glory" (see Matt. 6:29 // Luke 12:27), there is a dark undercurrent revealing Solomon as just another dictatorial and oppressive king like those in other ancient Near Eastern empires. In order to secure his rule, Solomon reorganized his kingdom into twelve administrative districts that cut across tribal lines, staffing them with Judeans who had family or close ties with the Davidic dynasty (4:7-19). Through this redistricting, Solomon was able to constrain and exploit the powerful northern tribes through heavy tax burdens, from which his own tribe of Judah was exempt. First Kings 4:22-28 describes the exorbitant monthly demands from each of these districts, especially for luxury foods, such as meat, that go well beyond subsistence.

Solomon embarked on a number of expensive building projects to trumpet his successes and wealth, but these were realized at a heavy cost (1 Kings 5–7). He had to conscript thousands of his own people and foreigners into corvée labor groups to work on these buildings (4:6; 5:13-18; 9:20-21), taking them away from agricultural production, which was the major source of Israel's economy. The indigenous trees in Israel were not suitable for the great building projects that Solomon desired. In order to purchase and import the celebrated cedars of Lebanon, Solomon had to pay the foreign king Hyram of Tyre an enormous fee in wheat and fine oil (5:11), adding more to the people's tax burden.

The major and most famous building project was the Jerusalem temple (1 Kings 5–8). The three-part floor plan of the temple was similar to Canaanite temples that have been excavated from the same period. This is not surprising since Canaanite craftsmen were involved in the construction (see 7:13). The temple consisted of a vestibule, a nave, and an inner sanctuary, often referred to as the holy of holies (6:2-10). The construction reflected the stratification of the society. The three divisions marked the intensifying degrees of exclusivity, the vestibule having more public access; the nave, more limited; and the holy of holies, forbidden except to the most senior priests and only on special occasions. The rich latticework and carvings, the costly stones, the great bronze pillars and basins, the numerous vessels and accoutrements of gold and silver, and so forth (1 Kings 7) all have a flip side. This great extravagance for the few came at the cost borne by most of the population.

First Kings 6:1 notes that Solomon began this construction "in the four hundred eightieth year after the Israelites came out of the land of Egypt." Long after Israel was freed from Egyptian slavery, Israel ironically had to endure forced servitude and exploitation again under its own king. The building and its furnishings are described in all their opulence, but in the midst of these details of conspicuous consumption is an important condition in both the temple's construction and inauguration accounts: If Solomon obeys all of God's commandments, God will keep the promise made to David and dwell with Israel and not forsake them (6:11-13; cf. 8:56-61). Here the royal ideology of the monarchy that highlights God's promises to the Davidic dynasty stands in tension with the Mosaic covenantal demands that the people, including Israel's king, remain obedient to God's torah (Brueggemann, 88–89). We will soon see that Solomon was not successful in following God's commandments.

The section 1 Kgs. 9:10—11:42 narrates Solomon's downhill slide in his questionable dealings with foreign kings and foreign women, the slave labor of foreign peoples, his staggering greed, and his eventual idolatry. This decline is particularly evident when one compares 10:14—11:8 with Deut. 17:16-17, which stipulates that the king

- must not acquire horses for himself;
- must not return to Egypt in order to acquire more horses;
- must not acquire many wives for himself, or "else his heart will turn away";
- must also not amass silver and gold for himself in great quantity.

Solomon, however, commits all of these infractions in chapters 10–11, depicting a king who shaped his regime into the likeness of Egypt, who had oppressed their ancestors, sending his people back to Egypt to stockpile wealth and horses and adding women to his already substantial harem (Sweeney 2007, 146–47).

Solomon's rule, which began propitiously when Solomon "*loved* the Lord" (3:3), now comes to a shameful close because he "*loved* many foreign women," who turned his heart away from God to worship their own alien deities (11:1-8). Although a hint of disapproval exists, the Deuteronomist presents the negative economic aspects of Solomon's rule—the forced labor, his extreme taxation, his ostentatious materialism—rather neutrally, as opposed to the explicit censure of the king's economic exploitation found in 1 Sam. 8:10-18 and Dtr's advocacy for the most helpless in society (see Deut. 10:18; 24:17-22; 27:19). What comes under his unequivocal condemnation is Solomon's love of many foreign women, who persuade him to sacrifice to their gods. The reader is left with the lasting impression that Solomon's downfall was due to his sexual relationships with women and not to his material self-indulgence and economic oppression (Jobling, 61–64). Because of these marriages, God raises up three major adversaries against Solomon (Hadad, Rezon, and Jeroboam), whose rebellions sow the seeds for the division of the kingdom after Solomon's death (11:14-43). The most significant of these adversaries is Jeroboam, who was in command of Solomon's forced labor in the tribe of Joseph (11:28). After receiving a prophecy from the prophet Ahijah that God will "tear the kingdom from the hand of Solomon" and give to Jeroboam the "ten tribes" (11:31), Jeroboam flees to Egypt, only to return after Solomon's death to become the first king of the northern kingdom (12:20).

The Solomon narrative concludes with the Deuteronomistic citation of its source (the Book of the Acts of Solomon), Solomon's length of rule in Jerusalem, his death, and his succession by his son Rehoboam (11:41-21).

◼ THE TEXT IN THE INTERPRETIVE TRADITION

The parallel account of Solomon in 2 Chronicles 1–9 omits the negative stories of Solomon's idolatry and revolts in 1 Kings 11 and foregrounds the temple in its exposition.

A number of early Christian allegorical interpretations of Solomon's kingdom and temple exist (Conti, 24–64). For example, according to Ephrem the Syrian (c. 306–73 CE), the twelve officials who administered Solomon's kingdom (1 Kgs. 4:7) foreshadowed the twelve apostles of Jesus. The Venerable Bede (c. 672–735 CE) believed that the three floors of the temple (1 Kgs. 6:6) reflected a hierarchical ordering of the lifestyles of the faithful: married people, those who practice continence, and virgins, "levels distinguished according to the loftiness of their profession but all belonging to the house of the Lord" (Conti 2008, 31).

Over the centuries, Jewish and Muslim traditions have presented the story of Solomon and Sheba (1 Kgs. 10:1-13) as a contest of body and mind between an independent and boundary-crossing woman and a man who is eager to keep her subservient. By the Middle Ages, the main focus of the queen's visit had shifted from international to sexual politics, so that in postbiblical and Islamic versions, the queen's sparring match with Solomon was depicted as a threatening attempt to subvert the traditional roles of gender. In the same vein, an Ethiopian legend in the *Kebra Negast* ("Glory of the Kings") records Solomon cleverly seducing the queen after she had made him swear that he not take her by force. They beget Menelik I, the first emperor of Ethiopia (Lassner 1993).

◼ The Text in Contemporary Discussion

The Solomon narratives reveal that the steep income disparity between the haves and the have-nots that we see so blatantly in our own day is not a new phenomenon. Solomon heavily taxed his rural population for both material and human resources in order to support the luxurious lifestyles of his court and build his grandiose monuments. Each month, the court received from one of the provinces not only the choicest grains and flocks but also exotic animals like deer, gazelles, roebucks, and fatted fowl (4:22-24). Similarly, in our day, meat is usually found only on tables in the so-called first world and especially in the United States. Our excessive consumption of meat is having disastrous effects on the environment globally. Moreover, Solomon's forced labor gangs have some analogues to the trade in human trafficking today. Although the former is state-run, while the latter is illicit, both involve coercion and much human suffering.

These narratives are also cautionary tales for us today. They raise serious questions about the abuse of power by a nation's leadership. Solomon's disproportionate wealth and exploitation of the people to obtain it would have enormous consequences. Resistance and protests plagued the last days of his rule. Nowadays, we have food riots over grain and water shortages as a result of the diversion of good farmland to feed cattle, not people. History has already shown us that indifference of the wealthier classes to the poverty and destitution of the people often results in armed conflict. With Solomon, as we will see, this indifference resulted in the division of his kingdom. These texts obligate us to attend to the most vulnerable in our midst so that our global world does not fracture any more than it already has.

1 Kings 12:1—16:34: The Divided Kingdom

◼ The Text in Its Ancient Context

Ahijah's prophecy in 11:31-40, that God will wrench the kingdom from Solomon and give to Jeroboam "the ten tribes," becomes fulfilled in this unit. After his father's death, Rehoboam goes up to be crowned in the important northern city of Shechem, perhaps as a positive gesture toward the northern tribes, or as a presumptuous declaration of his sovereignty over them (Seow, 100).

Having heard that Solomon has died, Jeroboam, his rebellious corvee overseer, returns from Egypt where he had fled from Solomon's wrath (11:40). Along with the tribes, he urges the new king to lighten the hard service and heavy yoke that Solomon had imposed on them. Recall the daily extravagant provisions that the northern tribes had to supply the Jerusalem court (4:22-28) and the corvée labor that built Solomon's building projects (5:13-18). Rehoboam first consults his father's seasoned advisors, who recommend that he "lighten the yoke" appointed by his father. However, rejecting their advice, he turns to a group of courtiers he grew up with, disparagingly described as "boys" to underscore their contrast with the elders. These middle-aged associates—Rehoboam was evidently forty-one years old when he ascended the throne (14:21)—encourage a reply that hints at Rehoboam's or perhaps their own "daddy issues": "My little 'thingie' [Sweeney 2007, 163] is thicker than my father's loins!" (12:10). Given the seemingly huge size of Solomon's own harem (11:3), this would have been an extravagant claim by his arrogant offspring. Rehoboam then declares that rather than lightening the heavy yoke, he will intensify the burdens that his father had laid upon the people (12:14). Predictably, the northern tribes reject Rehoboam as king and return back to their homes. Rehoboam foolishly tries to regain control by dispatching Adoram, his official in charge of corvée labor, to the northern tribes, who promptly stone Adoram to death. Their next victim possibly would have been Rehoboam had he not hastily jumped into his chariot and fled back to Jerusalem (12:16-18).

As the newly crowned king of Israel (12:20), Jeroboam is confronted first with a political problem with religious implications. The Jerusalem temple and its cult continue to be a significant focus of the people's worship, because it houses the ark of the covenant. The northern tribes venerate the ark because it resided in several of their sanctuaries before it was brought to Jerusalem (Judg. 20:26-27; 1 Sam. 3:3; 6:21—7:1). Even though Ahijah prophesied that if Jeroboam follows God's statutes and commandments his dynasty will endure (11:38), Jeroboam still fears that allowing pilgrimages to Jerusalem will turn the people's allegiance back to Rehoboam. To prevent the cross-border excursions, he establishes two shrines at Dan and Bethel, polar ends of his kingdom, installing two calves of gold, of which he declares, "Here are your gods, O Israel, who brought you up out of the land of Egypt" (12:26-33). While the calves themselves are not idols, but simply the beasts of burden that carry the invisible God, for the Josianic Deuteronomist they become reified as "the sin of Jeroboam" throughout his history (see 1 Kgs. 13:34; 14:16; 2 Kgs. 3:3; 10:29; 13:2, et passim). From his southern perspective, the only legitimate place of worship is the temple in Jerusalem. In the dangerous memory of Israel, the calves also conjure up the image of the idolatrous golden calf that Aaron made for the Israelites in the wilderness, underscoring the illegitimacy of Jeroboam's cult (Exodus 32; see Knoppers, 92).

In the next episode, the Deuteronomist continues to portray the competitors of the Jerusalem cult as illicit. While Jeroboam is offering incense at Bethel, a man of God from Judah directs a prophecy at the altar, proclaiming that Josiah, a descendant from the Davidic dynasty several hundred years later, will sacrifice on this altar the priests of the high places established by Jeroboam (13:2-3; cf. 12:31-32). Later in the DH, Josiah will eventually tear down this altar with its gruesome ashes and purge the land of its idolatrous cult (2 Kings 23).

Jeroboam's story ends tragically. When his son Abijah falls ill, Jeroboam tells his unnamed wife to disguise herself, go to Shiloh, and consult with Ahijah, the same prophet who had declared that Jeroboam would rule an enduring house like David's (11:38). However, because Jeroboam made for himself "other gods and cast images," provoking God to anger, Ahijah now proclaims that God will put an end of his dynasty (14:7-11). Ahijah then orders the wife back home, prophesying her son's death, which comes to pass when she crosses the threshold of her house. The seeming passivity of the wife prompts feminists to speculate whether the wife was a victim of domestic violence (Branch, 83–107).

From this point on, the Deuteronomist provides a particular theological frame for the rival kings of Israel and Judah (see the introduction). The most important part of his framework is his religious judgment on the rule, whether he obeyed God's law and banished idols, high places, and so on from the land or let them flourish. A particular king may have been an important political leader and good ruler, but is condemned by the Dtr for religious reasons. For example, given the propensity in Israel for regicide (assassination of kings; see 1 Kgs. 15:27; 16:9-10, 15-16), it is significant that the kings who had the longest reigns in Israel are censured by the Dtr: Jeroboam I (twenty-two years), Basha (twenty-four years), Ahab (twenty-two years), and Jeroboam II (forty-one years).

■ THE TEXT IN THE INTERPRETIVE TRADITION

A version of the LXX contains an alternative account that portrays Jeroboam more negatively (Sweeney 2007, 165–67). Although 12:26 describes his mother Zeruah as a widow (11:26), in this version she is a prostitute named Sarira. The unidentified wife of Jeroboam also receives a name. When Jeroboam flees to Egypt from Solomon's anger, the pharaoh Sausakim (MT Shishak, 12:40) gives him his sister-in-law, Ano, as wife, who bears him a son, Abijah. The version then recounts Jeroboam's gathering the Israelite tribes at Shechem and building fortifications there. At this point, Abijah becomes sick and Jeroboam directs Ano to seek God's counsel. Abijah dies, according to the prophecy Ahijah gives to Ano (see 14:12-13, 17-18). The LXX expansion highlights Rehoboam as an immature teenager and insinuates Jeroboam's role in instigating the revolt by placing him in Israel before the North's rebellion. Jeroboam's marriage into Shishak's royal family reinforces Jeroboam's culpability even more when Shishak later invades Judah after the division (14:25-28).

The Old Testament figure of Ahab was one of the biblical prototypes for Captain Ahab in Herman Melville's *Moby-Dick*. Because Jeroboam is Ahab's predecessor and the prophetic condemnation of the kings of Israel because of his "sin" (see 15:25) will determine the fate of Ahab, his story finds a particular analogue in Melville's tome. The ship *Jeroboam* in *Moby-Dick* becomes the forerunner of Captain Ahab's *Pequod*, and two members of its crew correspond to members of Jeroboam's household: the death of the shipmate Macey parallels Jeroboam's stricken son Abijah, and Gabriel parallels the prophet Ahijah (Bartel, 44–46).

■ THE TEXT IN CONTEMPORARY DISCUSSION

Lord Acton remarked in a letter to Bishop Mandell Creighton in 1887: "Power tends to corrupt, and absolute power corrupts absolutely. Great men are almost always bad men." Rehoboam's folly in not heeding the wisdom of his older advisors presents a cautionary tale about leadership and the abuse of power. In response to the people's request to ease up on the heavy burdens his father had laid on them, Rehoboam arrogantly responds: "Whereas my father laid on you a heavy yoke, I will add to your yoke. My father disciplined you with whips, but I will discipline you with scorpions" (12:11). History throughout reveals that tyrannical rulers and oppressive systems of power will face resistance when the subjugated will not take it anymore: from the slave rebellions against Rome, to the civil rights marches against racism of the last century, to the recent Occupy movement against corporate greed. The text raises questions about what it means to be a leader. Is it true that power corrupts and absolute power corrupts absolutely? How do we prevent or resist the corruption of power without becoming corrupt ourselves?

1 Kings 17:1—22:53: The Ministries of the Prophets Elijah and Micaiah

▌THE TEXT IN ITS ANCIENT CONTEXT

These chapters highlight the ministries of the prophets Elijah (chs. 17–19, 21) and Micaiah (ch. 22) in their clashes with King Ahab of Israel (c. 873–852 BCE) of the powerful royal dynasty of Omri. According to 16:29-34, Ahab not only walked in the sins of Jeroboam but also angered God even more by marrying a foreign woman, Jezebel, daughter of the king of the Sidonians, and worshiping her gods Baal and Asherah. Recall that Solomon's marriages to foreign women and his apostasy led to his own deterioration (1 Kings 11). Also important in understanding these chapters is that both the kings of Israel and Judah continued Solomon's exploitative economic policy of extracting the surpluses from their agrarian subjects to support their building projects, wars, and extravagant lifestyles. This one-sided systemic extraction resulted in the impoverishment of the nation's peasant base.

In 17:1, Elijah appears out of nowhere to proclaim a drought in God's name that will afflict Israel. This declaration is a direct polemic against the worship of the Baal, the Canaanite god responsible for rain and fertility in the land. Although the veneration of Canaanite deities is expressly condemned in the Hebrew Bible, this represents only a part, though an important one, of the rich pluralism in Israelite belief and practice. The worship of Baal and even the goddess Asherah was accepted or at least tolerated in the early stages of Israel's religious development (Dever; M. S. Smith 2002). However, not only does 1 Kgs. 17–22 reflect the developing "Yahweh-alone" theology that belittled these deities (Lang, 13–56; M. Smith 1971, 34–37), but their worship is linked to a royal system of exploitation, in which the majority of the population suffered under the oppression of a small group of ruling elites (Brueggemann 2000, 202–3). Misery from the three-year drought particularly afflicted the marginalized classes of society, as is evident in Elijah's encounter with the starving widow and her malnourished son in Jezebel's own Phoenician hometown of Sidon (17:8-34). Meanwhile, Jezebel murders God's own prophets (18:4, 13), but hosts banquets for the 450 prophets of Baal and the 400 prophets of Asherah, while the rest of the nation starves (18:19). Ahab too seems more concerned about grass for his horses and mules than food for his own people (18:5).

According to the Kurkh Monolith, Ahab possessed enough horses to pull two thousand chariots in a campaign against the Assyrian king Shalmaneser III (Grabbe 2007, 131, 142–43). However, Obadiah's protection of God's prophets from Jezebel's persecution reveals that even some high-level members of the royal court resisted the oppressive policies (18:3, 13).

The confrontation on Mount Carmel between YHWH and Baal is about who can end the drought and bring rain to the land. It is also about the religio-political systems that undergird their worship (18:20-46). This narrative dramatically pits the 450 prophets of Baal against God's lone prophet, Elijah. Two altars for two bulls are prepared. The challenge is which god will answer by fire to consume his sacrificial altar. The Baal prophets go first, calling out to their god from morning till noon with no answer. Elijah taunts their efforts, and they set about gashing themselves, intensifying their raving until past midday with no response. Then, in some spectacularly theatrical moves, Elijah builds an altar with twelve stones symbolizing the twelve tribes of Israel and digs a large trench around it. He dismembers his bull and places the pieces on the wood of the altar. He commands four jars of waters be splashed on the altar three times. He prays one little prayer and immediately God answers with fire, consuming the whole altar and even the water in the trench. Elijah has all the prophets of Baal assassinated, and then tells Ahab to eat and drink, "for there is a sound of rushing rain" (18:41), proving that YHWH, not Baal, makes the life-giving waters flow.

The next clash between Elijah and Ahab, which occurs in 1 Kings 21, foregrounds the ruling elite's abuse of power over land ownership. Ahab wants a vineyard in Jezreel belonging to a man named Naboth, who refuses Ahab's offer of either a better vineyard or a reasonable price, because he regards the land as an inheritance that should not be bought or sold outside of the family to which it belonged (see Num. 27:1-11; Deut. 25:5-10; Jer. 32:6-12). Knowing Mosaic custom, Ahab reacts by pouting and refusing to eat, whereupon Jezebel admonishes him, saying basically, "Aren't you the one who rules Israel?" (21:1-7). Jezebel regards land as a tradable commodity to which the monarch has a privileged claim (Brueggemann 2000, 257–65). She instigates an illegitimate seizure of his land and engineers his death (21:8-16). God then orders Elijah to meet Ahab and prophesy his death sentence because of his wife's deeds: "Thus says the Lord: In the place where dogs licked up the blood of Naboth, dogs will also lick up your blood" (21:19). Jezebel also does not escape censure: "The dogs shall eat Jezebel within the bounds of Jezreel" (21:23).

Elijah seemingly disappears in 1 Kings 20 and 22, but Ahab does not. These chapters deal with Ahab's wars with the Arameans (present-day Syria; for the historical problems dealing with chs. 20 and 22, see Sweeney 2007, 237–58). Although a number of anonymous prophets interact with Ahab in 20:13-15, 22, 28, 35-42, the major prophet confronting Ahab in 1 Kings 22 has a name: Micaiah. Three years have passed since Ahab last fought, but then later made a peace treaty with, the king of Aram (22:1; see 1 Kings 20). Because of this ill-advised treaty, an unnamed prophet condemns Ahab to death (20:42), a sentence that will be fulfilled in 1 Kings 22. Ahab makes an alliance with Jehoshaphat, the king of Judah (c. 870–846 BCE), to recapture Ramoth-Gilead, a strategically important city near the border between Israel and Aram. Jehoshaphat first wants to consult the "word of YHWH" before entering into combat (22:5). Because war involved the participation of YHWH the Divine Warrior, it was a holy affair. Kings thus did not commence battle without consulting the prophets, who informed them about the divine will.

Ahab thus assembles four hundred court prophets and asks if he should go into battle. Though they guarantee his victory, Jehoshaphat still wants another prophetic opinion. Ahab replies that there is another prophet, Micaiah, who can be consulted, "but I hate him, for he never prophesies anything favorable about me, but only disaster" (22:8). Nevertheless, at Jehoshaphat's prompting, Ahab sends for Micaiah, while the court prophets continue to affirm Ahab's victory over the Arameans (22:9-12).

When Ahab asks Micaiah whether the army shall proceed against Ramoth-Gilead, Micaiah prophesies victory. Suspicious of this response in light of past experience, Ahab demands Micaiah to tell "the truth in the name of YHWH" (22:15-16). Micaiah responds with two visions, the first of Israel scattered like sheep without a shepherd, and the second of God in his heavenly court, who asks for a volunteer to be a lying spirit in the mouths of Ahab's prophets. The gist of these visions is that the Lord has decreed disaster for Ahab (22:17-23). Ahab indeed dies ignobly by the end of the chapter (22:29-36). His bloody chariot is washed by the pool of Samaria. Dogs lick up his blood, fulfilling Elijah's prophecy (21:19), and to add insult to injury, prostitutes also wash themselves in it (22:37-38). First Kings concludes with the ascension of his son Ahaziah to the throne, who not only continues the "sin of Jeroboam" but also walks in the way of his father and mother, citing both Ahab and Jezebel in their idolatrous worship of Baal (22:51-53).

▌ THE TEXT IN THE INTERPRETIVE TRADITION

According to the final verses of the book of Malachi, God will send Elijah before "the great and terrible day of the Lord" (4:5). Elijah thus will be seen as the harbinger of the Messiah in Jewish tradition. At Passover celebrations, a cup is usually left out for the arrival of Elijah. Elijah is included in Sirach's "praises of famous men" (Sir. 48:1-12). In the Christian ordering of the books of the Hebrew Bible, the book of Malachi is placed last in the canon, immediately before the Gospels, so that Elijah appears to herald the coming of Jesus. The Gospels describe John the Baptist, the forerunner of Jesus, in the manner of Elijah, a "hairy man, with a leather belt around his waist (2 Kgs. 1:8; cf. Matt. 3:4; 11:14; 17:10-13; Luke 1:16-17). Elijah also appears at Jesus' transfiguration on the mountain along with Moses (Matt. 17:1-13; Mark 9:2-13; Luke 9:28-36). Elijah is one of the prophets referred to in the Quran as a precursor of Muhammad. Martin Luther compared Elijah to the Reformers, and the prophets of Baal to the Roman Catholic Church. In some Jewish legends, the son of the widow of Zarephath, whom Elijah healed (17:17-24), will later become the prophet Jonah.

Ahab's wife, Jezebel, was most likely a very powerful woman in her time, part of the ruling class of an agrarian society, wielding considerable authority in her position as queen. However, she has been demonized even in the early developments of the tradition. The *zebul* of her original name, "Prince, nobility," was distorted into *zebel*, "dung" (Dutcher-Walls 2004; Yee, 848). In the New Testament, the book of Revelation depicts a strong woman "who calls herself a prophet" as a Jezebel, seducing her flock into fornication and idolatry (Rev. 2:19-23). Modern-day dictionaries have also nominalized her name to describe a shameless, scheming woman. This characterization can be found in numerous depictions of Jezebel and women like her in theological treatises, sermons, novels, poetry, and theater (Gaines; Snyder). She is perhaps most memorably embodied in the actress Bette Davis as a spoiled, conniving southern belle in the motion picture *Jezebel* (Warner Bros., 1938). (For a semifictional account of Jezebel by a biblical scholar that tries to rehabilitate her notoriety, see Beach 2005.)

■ THE TEXT IN CONTEMPORARY DISCUSSION

Prophets emerged in ancient Israel during the time of the monarchy to announce God's judgments regarding a particular king's wars, foreign agreements, religious allegiances, and domestic economic and political policies. They condemned a king's abuses of power. They were also described as performing miracles, healing the sick, and making fire come down from the sky.

The question these texts raise for us now is whether such prophets exist in our own time. The stereotype of a prophet is that of a fortune-teller, one who sees and predicts the future. A prophet should be regarded instead as one who sees and analyzes the *present*, one who reads the signs of the times and declares the disastrous future results if things do not change. Such a person must be knowledgeable of contemporary affairs and skilled in some sort of social analysis to critique any injustice or exploitation. Individuals, such as social activists, public policy makers, ecologists, artists, poets, and musicians can all be prophetic in their own way.

Ahab and Jezebel's seizure of Naboth's land has disturbing parallels throughout history in which colonizers from Europe seized lands in Asia, Latin America, and Africa, robbing their indigenous peoples of their rich resources. This colonization continues in our own global economy today, where big corporations exploit the so-called third world of its resources and cheap labor for money and profit. Land and its inhabitants become commodities that can be bought and sold. Where are the prophets today who will hold these corporations accountable?

Popular culture usually lists Jezebel as one of the "bad girls of the Bible." Such stereotyping affects all women who are powerful, competent, independent, and forceful. Qualities that are usually admired in men are depicted as "bossy, pushy, aggressive, and unfeminine" for women, especially those at high levels of authority. Such women may be threatening to men used to more obedient and submissive women. One must remember that the negative depiction of Jezebel arose out of a male-dominated society that served the religious and political interests of the author. Since then, social roles and attitudes regarding the genders have changed dramatically. When one reads or hears such descriptions for women of today, one must step back and consider the source.

2 Kings 1:1—8:29: The Ministry of the Prophet Elisha

■ THE TEXT IN ITS ANCIENT CONTEXT

Chapter 1 of 2 Kings begins with the detail that after Ahab's death, Moab rebels against Israel, a war that will be taken up in 2 Kings 3. This conflict may have some extrabiblical support in the Mesha Stele (Moabite Stone), which describes Omri's oppression of Moab before Mesha throws off his yoke (Grabbe 2007, 131, 144–46). Omri's dynasty is continued in Ahab's son Azariah (c. 852–851

BCE), who seeks the counsel of "Baal-zebub, the god of Ekron" after a bad fall from his house. The qualifier *zebub* is most likely a distortion of an original *zebul*, or "prince," which alters the god's name to "Lord of the flies." For inquiring of Baal-zebub, Elijah prophesies the king's death (1:1-18).

Wedged between the death of Azariah and the rise of his brother, Ahab's son Jehoram, as king of Israel (2 Kings 3) is the story of the transfer of prophetic power and authority from Elijah to Elisha in 2 Kings 2. It begins with the remarkable statement that God was about to take Elijah up to heaven in a whirlwind, but before this occurs, Elijah and Elisha travel to Gilgal, Bethel, Jericho, and finally to the Jordan River. At the Jordan, Elijah uses his mantle to divide the waters, and the two prophets cross over to the other side on dry ground, reminiscent of other stories where waters are miraculously parted (Joshua 3–4; Exodus 14). Elisha requests a "double share" of Elijah's spirit before he is taken away. According to Deut. 21:17, a double share is the inheritance claim given to the firstborn son of a family. A fiery chariot and horses then appear that separate the two prophets, and Elijah ascends upward in a whirlwind. The use of horses and chariots and whirlwinds may be linked to similar portrayals of ancient Near Eastern storm gods, such as Baal, riding through the clouds, to emphasize YHWH's superior control of the weather (see 1 Kings 18). Elisha declares his kinship with Elijah by crying out, "Father, Father" as the chariot and horses disappear. Elisha then takes up the mantle of Elijah, crosses through the parted waters of the Jordan again, and is joined by the company of prophets. Elisha thus begins his active prophetic ministry during the rule of the Israelite kings Jehoram, Jehu, Jehoahaz, and Jehoash.

Besides his introduction in 1 Kgs. 19:19-21, many of the stories of Elisha preserved in 2 Kings 2–13 have been described as legends and miracle stories, making their historicity suspect. Nevertheless, they provide clues to the social history that formed the context of Elisha's prophetic ministry amid the continued exploitation of the people by the Israelite governing classes (Rentería). For example, scholars think that the company of prophets is primarily composed of the peripheral lower classes and that several of Elisha's miracles are for their benefit (Petersen, 47–48; Schulte, 140). Second Kings 4:1-7 records the miracle of the jar of oil for one of the widows of this company, who, bereft of her husband perhaps because of war, famine, or accidental death in the king's building projects, is compelled to sell her children as debt slaves to pay off creditors. First Kings 18 describes the indifference of the royal court to the starvation of the people during famine. Similarly, the background for the miracle of the stew in 2 Kgs. 4:38-41 consists of the desperate attempts of the company of prophets to find food during famine, during which someone may unknowingly contribute a toxic plant to a shared pot of stew, poisoning the community. This episode is followed by one where Elisha feeds one hundred hungry people with only twenty barley loaves, with some left over (4:42-43). Behind the simple story of the recovery of the ax head from the Jordan (6:1-7) is the reality that the ax head was borrowed (v. 5), probably from one of the elite, who would have been able to possess and lend the expensive commodities necessary for farming like axes, plows, and sickles (cf. 1 Sam. 13:19-21). The average peasant or day laborer from this company would have had to become a debt slave to pay for the ax head.

As we saw in 1 Kings 20 and 22, significant features of monarchic rule are the wars and conflicts of kings. Such wars wreak havoc on the nation's fragile agrarian ecosystem, especially when springs of water are stopped up, fruitful trees are cut down, and the land despoiled (2 Kgs. 3:18, 25). All of these man-made disasters bring much physical and economic suffering to the rest of the population. Narratives of Elisha's prophetic ministry with those in the lower rungs of society, who have been tragically affected by these wars, are interwoven with his dealings with the kings and generals conducting the fighting in this global arena (see chart below). Indeed, the stories of the lowly servant (3:11), the female war captive (5:2-4), and the junior officer (6:12) reveal that the politically subordinate or disenfranchised know more than their masters about the prophetic and healing powers of Elisha (Brueggemann 2001, 52–56; Provan, 185).

> *The campaign of the three kings against Moab (3:1-27)*
> The miracle of the widow's oil, the Shunamite's son, the poisoned stew of the company of prophets, the feeding of the people (4:1-44)
>
> *The healing of the Aramean general, Naaman, of leprosy (5:1-27)*
> The recovery of the lost ax head for the company of prophets (6:1-7)
>
> *Elisha's adventures with the Arameans and the siege of Samaria (6:8—7:20)*
> The restoration of the Shunamite's house and land (8:1-6)
>
> *Elisha's "anointing" of the kings of Aram and Israel (8:7—9:13)*
> Adapted from Long and Sneed, 264

■ THE TEXT IN THE INTERPRETIVE TRADITION

Rabbinic tradition is filled with legends of Elijah's appearances on earth after his translation into heaven. He comes to the aid of the innocent victims and especially those who are impoverished. In one story, Elijah sells himself into slavery in order to provide funds for a poor man. He also cures diseases and helps couples with their marital problems. Rabbinic tradition also preserves legends of Elisha. In one of these, the husband of the widow who was compelled to sell her children into debt slavery (2 Kgs. 4:1-7) is the prophet Obadiah, the same official who hid one hundred prophets of YHWH from Jezebel's pogrom (1 Kings 18). Obadiah appears to his widow at his gravesite and directs her to bring a little cruse of oil to Elisha. The miraculous flow of oil not only sustains the widow through her financial difficulties but also the rest of her descendants (Ginzberg 1956, 589–94, 603–4).

Josephus seems to depict Elisha more positively than Elijah in his writings, perhaps because he does not want to be associated with a prophet thought to be the forerunner of the Messiah in his Roman imperial context. He composed a eulogy for the former and not the latter. He omits scenes that portray Elisha negatively, such as the cursing of the boys who called him "baldhead" (2:23-25) and greatly develops others, such as the curing of the waters of Jericho, just prior to the cursing of the boys (2:19-22). He eliminates or rationalizes many of Elisha's miracles, perhaps to counter gentile depictions of Jewish gullibility. Thus, while clearly preserving the popularity of Elijah for his Jewish audience and depicting Elisha as his subordinate, Josephus portrays Elisha's prophetic ministry in a greatly expanded way (Feldman).

Because prophets raised people from the dead (1 Kgs. 17:17-23; 2 Kgs. 4:32-36), cured lepers (2 Kgs. 5:5), multiplied loaves of bread (2 Kgs. 4:42-44; cf. 1 Kgs. 17:8-16), ascended into heaven

(2 Kgs. 2:11-12), and worked miracles for rich and poor alike, many thought Jesus was one of the prophets (Matt. 16:13-14; Mark 8:27-28; cf. Luke 4:24-27).

Aspects of Elijah's and Elisha's healings, horses and chariot, the passing of the prophetic mantle, and other elements form a biblical layer for Franz Kafka's short story "The Country Doctor" (Barzel). The African American spiritual "Swing Low, Sweet Chariot" is based on Elijah's ascension into heaven (2 Kgs. 2:11), and also to the angels that carried Lazarus to the bosom of Abraham (Luke 16:22).

■ THE TEXT IN CONTEMPORARY DISCUSSION

In 1879, General William Sherman declared "War is hell" to give a reality check to those in the graduating class of Michigan Military Academy who looked on war as all glamour and glory. Much of the background for the so-called miracles that Elisha performs is the hell of war: the death of a family's financial support and the danger of selling one's children into debt slavery (4:1-7); war captives (5:2); famine (4:38-39); starvation (6:24-25; 7:3-4); cannibalism (6:26-31); economic chaos (6:25); and ecological destruction (3:25). To counteract and militate against the trauma of war in its myriad guises, Elisha performs miracles at the local level, but does not critique the roots of war at the systemic level. His prophecy to the kings of Israel, Judah, and Edom deals with whether God will grant them victory over Moab (2 Kings 3), not whether they should engage in war in the first place. These texts encourage us to examine the systemic causes of war to eliminate the monstrous effects of war on the people and the land.

2 Kings 9:1—12:21: The Rise of the House of Jehu and the Demise of the House of Omri

■ THE TEXT IN ITS ANCIENT CONTEXT

For Ahab and Jezebel's abuses of power in illegally confiscating Naboth's vineyard in 1 Kings 21, the chickens finally come home to roost in 2 Kings 9–10. The great dynasty inaugurated by Ahab's father Omri is destroyed by Jehu's merciless assassinations of Ahab's son, relatives, and his formidable wife, Jezebel; the Baal cult sanctioned by their regime is purged from the land.

While Ahab's son Joram (c. 851–843 BCE; Jehoram in 3:1) recovers in Jezreel from a battle wound (8:28-29), Elisha sends one of the company of prophets to anoint Jehu (c. 842–814 BCE), a top-ranking military officer, as king over Israel (see 1 Kgs. 19:16). Jehu will "strike down the house of your master Ahab," thus fulfilling Elijah's prophecy against Ahab in 1 Kgs. 21:20-24. Furthermore, Jehu will wreak God's vengeance on Jezebel for the blood of the prophets (see 1 Kgs. 18:4; 19:10), so that "the dogs shall eat Jezebel in the territory of Jezreel, and no one shall bury her" (9:6-10). Jehu's military comrades proclaim him as king, and he embarks on the demolition of Ahab's house (9:13).

Recurring throughout 2 Kings 9 is the ambiguous question *hashalom*, literally, "Is it peace?" but better translated variously depending on the context: "Is everything okay?" "How goes everything?" "Are you well?" "Is all well [at the front]?" "Do you come in peace?" (9:11, 17-19, 22, 31; Olyan).

Accompanied by his nephew, Judah's king Ahaziah (c. 843–842 BCE; see 8:25-29), Joram ironically meets Jehu at the former property of Naboth the Jezreelite that was unlawfully seized by Jezebel. He asks Jehu, "Do you come in peace?" but Jehu replies, "What peace can there be, so long as the many whoredoms and sorceries of your mother Jezebel continue?" (9:22), alluding to her support of the worship of Baal. Joram then flees, warning Ahaziah of Jehu's treachery, but Jehu kills Joram and leaves him exposed without an honorable burial on the plot of land that belonged to Naboth. Ahaziah is also killed, but he at least gets an honorable burial in Jerusalem (9:27-28).

Jehu's next murderous stop in Jezreel is Jezebel's palace. If she is going to die, she will die looking like the royal queen she is, painting her eyes and adorning her hair. She is described as a "woman at the window," a conventional trope in ancient Near Eastern carved ivories. She too addresses Jehu sardonically, "Do you come in peace?" or "Is everything okay?" (9:30), and taunts him as a Zimri, who also killed his king but whose rule only lasted seven days (1 Kgs. 16:9-20). Her harem eunuchs, sensing a power change in the wind, obey Jehu's command to throw her down from the window, where her blood splatters the walls and horses trample her. Jehu, whose appetite seemingly is not affected by her gruesome death ("he went in and ate and drank"), begrudgingly orders a burial for "the cursed woman" since she is a "king's daughter." Unfortunately, all that remains of Jezebel's body is her skull, feet, and hands, fulfilling Elijah's prophecy over her. Jehu even adds a coarser adage to the prophecy by noting that her corpse will be like *dung* on the field in Jezreel (9:30-37), most likely an allusion to the corruption of her name from *zebul* ("prince, nobility") to *zebel* ("dung").

Jehu's brutal rampage continues with his slaughter of Ahab's seventy "sons" in Samaria. Just as the eunuchs desert Jezebel, so do the rulers, the elders, and the guardians of the descendants of Ahab in Jezreel deliver the decapitated heads of Ahab's male kin to Jehu. On the road to Samaria, Jehu encounters forty-two relatives of the assassinated Judean king Azariah, who are also members of Ahab's lineage, and has them massacred. Finally arriving in the royal capital Samaria, Jehu eliminates the remaining offspring of Ahab's line (10:1-17). He then "with cunning" exterminates the prophets, priests, and worshipers of Baal and demolishes his temple. Just as Jezebel's corpse will be like "dung in the field," Baal's temple is reduced to "a latrine to this day" (10:18-27).

The Deuteronomistic evaluation of Jehu's rule is equivocal. On the one hand, Jehu is praised for wiping out Baal worship from Israel. God promises that his dynasty in Israel will continue to the fourth generation, and indeed his is the longest and most prosperous one in the northern kingdom. On the other hand, it also points out that Jehu did not follow God's torah with his heart. He did not turn from "the sins of Jeroboam," the two golden calves installed at Dan and Bethel (10:28-31). His rule concludes with a detail that "the LORD began to trim off parts of Israel," in which Jehu loses the area of the Transjordan to the Arameans. Whether or not this territorial loss results from Jehu's disobedience to the law is left for the reader to decide (10:32-33). However, the ninth-century prophecy of Hosea is more explicit: God will "punish the house of Jehu for the blood of Jezreel" (Hosea 1:4).

The southern kingdom still has links with the newly destroyed house of Omri in the person of Athaliah, mother of the slain king Ahaziah, daughter of either Ahab or Omri, and wife of Judah's king Joram (Jehoram) (2 Kgs. 8:18, 25-26). When she hears about Jehu's massacre, she begins her own assassination of the Judean royal family, threatening God's promise of an eternal dynasty for

David. However, she is thwarted by her daughter-in-law Jehosheba, who hides Ahaziah's son Joash for six years, while Athaliah rules Judah (2 Kgs. 11:1-30). In the seventh year, the priest Jehoiada, Jehosheba's husband according to 2 Chron. 22:11, stages a coup to return the legitimate king of the Davidic line to the throne. Athaliah hears the noise of the coronation and cries "Treason, treason," but she is put to death outside the temple grounds (11:4-16). Jehoiada enacts a covenantal renewal ceremony "between the LORD and the king and the people," whereupon the people demolish the altars and priest of the cult of Baal, which evidently was instituted during the intermarriage of Judah's kings with the house of Omri. The threatened line of David is now restored in the installation of the seven-year-old Joash after this period of illegitimate female rule (11:17-20).

According to the Dtr's regnal formula, Jehoash (Joash) has a prosperous rule in Jerusalem of forty years, although this may include the six years of Athaliah (836–798 BCE). Under the tutelage of the priest Jehoiada, he is faithful to YHWH, even though he does not eliminate the high places (12:1-3). The narrative about Joash's rule deals with his attempts to repair the temple and arrange for the workers to be financially compensated (12:4-16). However, when the Aramean king Hazael threatens Jerusalem, Jehoash has to deplete the temple and royal treasury that had been built up by his royal predecessors in order to prevent Hazael's attack. The formula concludes with Joash's assassination by his servants (12:12:17-21). According to 2 Chron. 24:23-27, Joash is killed for having murdered the son of Jehoiada, his earlier co-regent (see below). His son Amaziah succeeds him. (For a comprehensive study of 2 Kings 11–12, see Dutcher-Walls 1996.)

▌ THE TEXT IN THE INTERPRETIVE TRADITION

According to Ephrem the Syrian, Jezebel paints her eyes and adorns her head (9:30) in order to seduce Jehu and become one of his wives. He links the episode with the story of Adonijah, who requests Abishag the Shunamite as wife, so that he might be elevated to the throne (1 Kgs. 2:17). According to Ephrem, Jehu would want Jezebel as wife to pacify his troubled and agitated new rule. Ephrem also contrasts Jezebel's ignominious death with that of her husband, Ahab. While Jezebel is trampled by horses and eaten by dogs (2 Kgs. 9:33-37), Ahab receives an honorable burial (1 Kgs. 22:37), because he repents from his sins (1 Kgs. 21:27-29) and she does not (Conti, 185–86).

According to Jewish tradition, the prophet Jonah is a disciple of Elisha, who commissions him to anoint Jehu as king. Athaliah's reign of terror is God's punishment of the Davidic dynasty for the extermination of the priests of Nob (1 Samuel 22). Just as Abiathar is the only son of Ahimelech to survive this slaughter, so is Joash the only son of Ahaziah to survive Athaliah's pogrom. After Jehoiada's death, Joash sets up an idol in the temple, but Jehoiada's son and high priest, Zechariah, bars his entry to the temple on the Day of Atonement, which also happens to be the Sabbath. Joash has Zechariah killed, and his death remains unavenged until Nebuzaradan, captain of Nebuchadnezzar's army, destroys Jerusalem. Before his servants kill him, Joash falls into the hands of the Syrians, who "abused him in their barbarous, immoral way" (Ginzberg 1956, 609–10).

The advent of feminist criticism in the late twentieth century focuses critical attention on the queens, Jezebel and Athaliah, whose portrayals as wives and mothers in these texts belie their formidable power and authority in their husbands' kingdoms (Solvang; Bowen; C. Smith 1998).

■ THE TEXT IN CONTEMPORARY DISCUSSION

These texts describe a regime change through violent assassinations. Our own contemporary world is no stranger to such violence, as seen in the political assassinations of Abraham Lincoln, John F. Kennedy, and Martin Luther King. Each period after such murders is marked by much social instability. The killings by Jehu are depicted as particularly motivated by religious zeal: "to wipe out Baal from Israel" (2 Kgs. 10:28). These texts highlight the acute dangers that arise from intense religious passions, namely, the intolerance of other religions, leading to their persecution and extermination in God's name. History already provides many cautionary tales of this religious intolerance: the Crusades and the extermination of indigenous religions by Spanish colonizers in South America and Native American religions by white settlers. We can also include the terrorist attacks by Islamic fundamentalists today. Is violence at the root of the monotheistic faiths? Does religious fervor have to lead to violence? Where are the voices that resist and critique this violence and move beyond mere tolerance, to learn about and respect other religions in their comprehension of the sacred?

2 Kings 13:1—17:41: Events Leading to the Fall of Israel

■ THE TEXT IN ITS ANCIENT CONTEXT

According to 2 Kgs. 10:30, YHWH declares that Jehu's dynasty in Israel will last to the fourth generation. Second Kings 13 focuses on the second and third generation of the house: Jehoahaz (c. 817–800 BCE, 13:1-9) and Jehoash/Joash (c. 800–784 BCE, 13:10-19). Both are condemned for following in "the sins of Jeroboam son of Nebat." Both regimes are plagued by military confrontations with Aram/Syria. The prophet Elisha appears for the last time during Joash's rule. Hearing news of Elisha's imminent death, Joash goes to him, weeping and crying out, just as Elisha did at Elijah's departure: "My father, my father! The chariots of Israel and its horsemen!" (13:15; cf. 2 Kgs. 2:12). Elisha commands Joash to perform a sign act with a bow and arrow to symbolize "the arrow of victory over Aram" at the battle of Aphek (13:17). However, because Joash only strikes the ground with the arrows three times, instead of five (13:18-19), his victory over the Arameans will be incomplete, keeping Syria as an ongoing player in the politics of Israel and Judah (see the Syro-Ephraimite War below). Even in death, Elisha's miraculous powers live on, raising a dead man to life when his corpse touches the bones in Elisha's grave (13:2-21).

The narrative regarding Jehoash/Joash continues in 2 Kings 14, highlighting the rule of the Judean king Amaziah (c. 798–769 BCE). As soon as he gains power, Amaziah executes the two men who assassinated his father Joash (12:20-21), but spares their children according to law of Deut. 24:16 (2 Kgs. 14:5-6). He then engages in a successful campaign against his southeastern neighbor Edom (14:7). However, he foolishly challenges Jehoash of Israel, who responds with a parable of the thorn bush and the cedar, warning Amaziah that any military encounter will be disastrous (on Jehoash's fable, see Solomon 1985). Amaziah engages in battle with Jehoash anyway, but Jehoash not only defeats and captures him but also strips the Jerusalem temple and royal palace of its treasuries (14:8-14). Amaziah is killed after he flees to his stronghold in Lachish (14:17-20) and is succeeded by his son Azariah/Uzziah (14:21-22).

During the fifteenth year of Amaziah's rule in Judah, Jeroboam son of Joash (Jeroboam II, c. 788–747 BCE) rules in Samaria, representing the fourth generation of the Jehu dynasty (14:23-28). Although he follows in the sins of his namesake, Jeroboam son of Nebat (Jeroboam I), his rule is a prosperous one of forty-one years in Israel. Fulfilling the word of the prophet Jonah, Jeroboam expands Israel's borders from Lebo-Hamath (upper Syria) to the Sea of Arabah (the ideal boundaries of Solomon's kingdom, 1 Kgs. 4:21; 8:65). The reign of his Judean counterpart, Azariah/Uzziah, is also a long one of fifty-two years (c. 792–740 BCE, 15:1-7). Dtr only gives him a qualified approval, because he does not remove the high places. Second Chronicles 26, however, greatly expands on Uzziah's rule and provides a reason for God afflicting him with leprosy, which is missing in 2 Kgs. 15:5. The Deuteronomic focus on the religious aspects of their monarchic rule obscures the fact that Israel and Judah under Jeroboam II and Azariah/Uzziah witnessed dramatic political and economic growth (Premnath, 43–98).

Representing the fifth generation of Jehu's dynasty, Jeroboam II's son Zechariah (c. 747 BCE) is not covered under God's prophecy of 2 Kgs. 10:30. His rule therefore only lasts six months and he is assassinated by Shallum (c. 747 BCE, 15:8-12), beginning a series of unstable regimes that will eventually climax in Israel's destruction. After only one month of rule, Shallum is killed by Menahem (c. 747–737 BCE, 15:13-22), a violent king credited with ripping open the pregnant women of a city that refused to surrender to him (15:16; cf. Cogan). During this time, the powerful Assyrian king Tiglath Pileser III (Pul in the Bible, c. 745–727 BCE) begins his westward expansion to gain access to the economic and military possibilities provided by the Mediterranean Sea. Levying a steep tax on the wealthy, Menahem offers "a thousand talents of silver" to forestall King Pul from attacking Israel, tribute that is confirmed in Assyrian accounts (Grabbe 2007, 134). Menahem is able to hold on to power for ten years when his son Pekahiah (c. 737–735 BCE) succeeds him at his death. Pekahiah rules only two years, when he is assassinated by one of his officers, Pekah (15:23-26; regarding the problematic dating of Pekah's rule, see Na'aman, 74–82). During Pekah's rule, Tiglath Pileser captures the Israelite territories of Gilead, Galilee, and all the land of Naphtali, and activates the initial deportations of Israel to Assyria (15:27-29; Younger, 206–8). Pekah himself will eventually be killed by Hoshea (15:30-31), but his narrative will continue in the account of the Syro-Ephraimite War in 2 Kings 16.

During Pekah's rule in Israel, Jotham (c. 759–743 BCE, 15:32-38) begins his administration in Judah when his father Azaraiah/Uzziah is stricken with leprosy (15:5). He is given a generally positive assessment by Dtr, which is expanded in 2 Chronicles 27. Dtr's judgment on his son, Ahaz, however, is quite negative for a Judean king, describing him as walking "in the way of the kings of Israel" in his idolatrous practices (16:1-4). Scholars have dated his rule variously: 727–715 BCE; 735–715 BCE; 743–735 BCE. Attempting to coerce Judah into joining their alliance against Tiglath Pileser III's expansionism, Kings Rezin of Aram/Syria and Pekah of Israel attack Judah in what is known as the Syro-Ephraimite War (16:5). In response, Ahaz petitions Tiglath Pileser himself to "rescue" him from his northern neighbors, becoming his vassal and sending him tribute. Tiglath Pileser responds by destroying Syria's capital city Damascus and exiling its upper classes (15:7-9).

Dtr greatly expands on Ahaz's covenantal infidelity by describing his commissioning and instillation of a new altar in the temple that represented his loyalty to Assyria (Sweeney 2007, 384–86). Ahaz will be succeeded by his son Hezekiah (16:10-20).

Having undergone a complex editorial process (Long, 180–83), 2 Kings 17 is a significant one in the DH, because it provides an extended theological rationale for the fall of Israel. It begins by describing its last days under king Hoshea (c. 732–722 BCE), who had rebelled against Tiglath Pileser's successor, Shalmaneser V of Assyria, and was subsequently imprisoned by him. After a three-year siege, Shalmaneser's successor, Sargon, conquers Samaria in 722/721 BCE and exiles its upper classes (17:1-6).

Dtr's theological commentary highlights the covenantal infidelity of Israel, who forsakes the God who brought them from slavery in Egypt to worship other gods (17:7-12). They refuse to listen to the prophets sent by God (17:13-15), and persist in the sin of Jeroboam son of Nebat (17:21-22). God therefore removes them "out of his sight," and Israel is exiled from their own land to Assyria "to this very day" (17:23). A later redactional addition will testify that Judah will suffer the same fate (17:19-20).

The chapter then narrates the consequences of the Assyrian policy of bringing in foreign populations to replace the exiles in Samaria (Oded). Because the Assyrians do not worship YHWH, God sends lions among them (17:24-25). The king of Assyria tries to deal with this problem by commanding one of the exiled priests be brought back to teach the foreigners "the law of the god of the land" (17:25-27). However, this priest originally hales from Bethel, one of the illegitimate sanctuaries established by Jeroboam I, implying that his teachings replicate the "sin of Jeroboam" among the people (17:28). Dtr then details the religious syncretism of the "people of Samaria," who will later be called Samaritans. They are ultimately judged as worshiping YHWH, but also as serving "their carved images" (17:29-41).

■ THE TEXT IN THE INTERPRETIVE TRADITION

For the rabbis, Ahaz was an extremely wicked man (*Lev. Rab.* 30.3) who, among other things, seized schools and synagogues (11.7), and introduced the worship of Moloch. However, because he was the son (*Gen. Rab.* 63.1) and father (*Eccl. Rab.* 7; 15.1) of devout kings (*Sanh.* 104a), his place was secured in the world to come. In Milton's *Paradise Lost*, Ahaz is a devotee of one of the fallen angels "against the house of God," Rimmon the Syrian deity associated with Damascus (*PL* 1.467–75) (Baker 1992a, 27).

The early church father Ephrem the Syrian had a number of things to say about the final days of Elisha. Regarding his prophecy to Joash, "the Lord's arrow of victory" (13:17) for him "signifies our Lord and Savior hanging from the wood and giving up his spirit." When Elisha dies, the prophet Hosea takes his place as the head of the company of prophets, because the beginning of Hosea's oracles places him during the time of Jeroboam, son of Joash. The resurrection of the man who was tossed into Elisha's grave foretells the future resurrection of all those who have died (Conti, 197–99). Some church fathers used these stories to further their antisemitic views. Origen argues that in light of Jewish purity laws, especially the prohibition of touching dead beings, the miracle of resurrection of the man who touches Elisha's bones reveals "how unsuitable the Jewish interpretation is." John Chrysostom uses the example of Ahaz's sacrificing his son (16:3) and other examples of illegitimate cult to explain the cruelty of the Jews in condemning Christ (Conti, 200, 207).

Josephus's portrayal of the last six kings of Israel expands on their biblical depictions, making them more violent and more reckless in their dealings with Assyria (Begg).

The Text in Contemporary Discussion

In these chapters, Dtr provides us with a sustained rationale for why Israel was destroyed and its people exiled. It culminates in 2 Kings 17, which argues that throughout its history the northern kingdom abandoned YHWH to worship other gods. We must keep two things in mind when interpreting these chapters. First, Dtr is assessing the history of these kings *after the fact* from his exilic/postexilic social location. Israel was already destroyed, and Judah is not far behind. His explanation is filtered through experiences of hindsight. Second, the intent of his history is *theological*. There are many other reasons—military, economic, political, social—why Israel was destroyed, the most obvious being Assyria's brutal, overwhelming resolve to gain entry to the Mediterranean Sea. Nevertheless, for Dtr, Israel's destruction is an act of divine judgment because it failed to keep God's covenant.

Dangers in interpretation arise when one assesses history from the perspective of "the rear-view mirror." It is first and foremost *an* interpretation of events, not *the* interpretation of events. Moreover, *theological* rationales of calamitous events pose serious issues, particularly when the judgment is on a group other than one's own. For example, some German clergy asserted that the extermination of the Jews by the Nazis was God's punishment of the Jews (Sweeney 2008, 1–22). The destruction caused by recent natural events like tsunamis and hurricanes has been explained by religious fundamentalists as God's castigation for abortion, homosexuality, and feminism. Theological explanations are difficult to substantiate and often originate from the harmful gender, racial, or other ideologies regarding marginal groups. As such, they should be avoided.

2 Kings 18:1—20:21: The Reign of Hezekiah

The Text in Its Ancient Context

Along with David and Josiah, Hezekiah (c. 727/715–698/687 BCE) is one of the most highly acclaimed kings of Judah according to Dtr. Historians have tried to reconcile 2 Kings 18–20 with Assyrian sources about Sennacherib's invasion in 701 BCE, many regarding 2 Kgs. 18:13-16 as the only historically reliable part of the narrative: Sennacherib attacked and captured the fortified cities of Judah; Hezekiah submitted to him; Sennacherib demanded a huge tribute of silver and gold; and Hezekiah gave it to him. The rest of 2 Kings 18–20 has undergone a long traditioning process around this relatively historical piece (Grabbe 2007, 195–200; Grabbe 2003).

The Dtr introduction first describes Hezekiah's cultic reform to centralize worship in Jerusalem, anticipating Josiah's later one (18:1-4). Unlike many of the other Judean kings, Hezekiah removes the high places, pillars, and the sacred pole, a symbol of YHWH's wife Asherah (Dever), and a revered Mosaic relic, the bronze Nehustan (Num. 21:1-9). The recurrence of the word "trust/

rely" defines Hezekiah's reliance on God (18:5, 19-22, 24, 30; 19:10), transforming his story into a theological discourse on faith in YHWH (Brueggemann 2000, 493). This faith and confidence will be tested by the Assyrian envoys. Unlike his father, Ahaz, Hezekiah rebels against Assyria (18:7). However, the juxtaposition of Hezekiah's rule in Judah with the downfall of Hoshea and Israel (18:9-12) implies that Judah will not suffer the same fate, because Hezekiah holds fast to God, who was with him when he rebelled (18:6-7).

Nevertheless, the most historically reliable part of the story seems to challenge Dtr's commendation: Sennacherib's invasion in response to this rebellion, and Hezekiah's handover of tribute for Sennacherib's withdrawal (18:13-16). Instead of withdrawing, Sennacherib sends three officials, the Tartan, the Rabsaris, and the Rabshakeh (chief commander, chief eunuch, and chief cupbearer) to negotiate the surrender of Jerusalem. Details of this Assyrian encounter with Judean officials (Eliakim, Shebnah, and Joah) have parallels in Isaiah 36–37. The Rabshakeh skillfully articulates the shortcomings in Hezekiah's sources of trust. Relying on his ally Egypt is foolhardy, because Egypt is a "broken reed of a staff that will pierce the hand of anyone who leans on it" (18:21). Trusting in God's very self has been abrogated by Hezekiah's destruction of God's high places and altars in his centralization of worship (18:22). Even if Assyria gives Judah two thousand horses, Hezekiah has no riders to put on them, especially if he relies on Egyptian assistance (18:23-24). Finally, God's very self sends Assyria to destroy Judah (18:25). Each of these four arguments has a certain ring of credibility (Nelson, 238).

The Judean officials request the Rabshakeh to speak in the diplomatic language of Aramaic, not Hebrew, so that the populace will not hear his demoralizing words. However, the Rabshakeh arrogantly continues in Hebrew to address those doomed "to eat their own dung and drink their own urine" in a prolonged Assyrian siege (18:26-28). He tells them not to be deceived by Hezekiah into relying on God's deliverance. The gods of Hamath, Arpad, Sephaarvaim, Hena, and Ivvah were unable to save their citizens from Assyrian conquest. YHWH will likewise be unable to deliver Jerusalem (18:29-35). Upon hearing the officials' report on the Rabshakeh's words, Hezekiah sends them to consult the prophet Isaiah, who tells Hezekiah, "Do not be afraid," and that God will put a "spirit" in Sennacherib, so that he will hear a "rumor and return to his own land," where he will be killed (19:1-7).

In the next episode, Sennacherib does hear a report that the Egyptian pharaoh Tirhakah of Cush/Ethiopia has set out against him, but instead of returning to his own land, sends his messengers to intimidate Hezekiah again (19:8-13). Hezekiah then appeals to YHWH in the temple (19:14-19), and Isaiah delivers three oracles to him. The first is directed against Sennacherib, highlighting God's own divine power vis-à-vis the king's human arrogance and future humiliation (19:20-28). The second is a "sign" to Hezekiah that the agricultural fields devastated by Sennacherib's armies will recover in three years, and that a remnant will repopulate the land (19:29-31). The third prophesies that Sennacherib will not enter Jerusalem, because God will defend it for God's own and David's sakes (19:32-34). The chapter concludes with the "angel of the Lord" striking down 185,000 in the Assyrian camp and Sennacherib's returning to Assyria, where he is eventually killed by his sons while he is worshiping in the temple of his god Nisroch (19: 35-37). Hezekiah's trust in YHWH is thus vindicated.

The final two episodes about Hezekiah in 2 Kings 20 seem to describe events before Sennacherib's siege of Jerusalem, because Isaiah prophesies that God will add fifteen years to Hezekiah's life and deliver Jerusalem from the king of Assyria (20:6) and the royal treasury is still full (20:13; cf. 18:15-16). The first episode describes Hezekiah's life-threatening boil (20:7), Isaiah's command that he put his life in order before his death, and Hezekiah's fervent prayer to God to remember his faithfulness and devotion (20:1-3). God responds through Isaiah that God will heal Hezekiah, add years to his life, and deliver Jerusalem from the Assyrians. Isaiah then orders Hezekiah to take a lump of figs and apply it to the boil, to heal it (20:4-7).

The second episode involves envoys of King Merodach-baladan, a Babylonian king who heard Hezekiah was ill. Hezekiah welcomes them and shows them all the wealth in his house, armory, and storehouses (20:12-13). Hezekiah may have entered into an anti-Assyrian alliance with the Babylonian king, which would explain why Sennacherib was not able to capture Jerusalem in a lengthy siege. He would not have been able to divide his forces to deal with conflict on the western side of his empire, and with Merodach-baladan on his eastern flank (Sweeney 2007, 413). However, upon hearing of Hezekiah's overt display of his wealth to these foreigners, Isaiah prophesies that in the future Babylon will come and seize everything in his house, and exile some of his sons, who will become eunuchs—those who cannot bear royal sons—in the palace of the king of Babylon (2:14-18). Although Hezekiah verbally acknowledges the prophecy as good, his inward thought, "Why not, if there be peace and security in my days" (20: 19), reveals a negative side to this positively portrayed character: his disregard for disastrous events in Judah and his dynasty after his own peaceful and secure reign.

▌ THE TEXT IN THE INTERPRETIVE TRADITION

Rabbinic legends describe Hezekiah as banishing the ignorance of the law that had occurred under his father Ahaz, to the point of ordering that anyone who does not occupy himself with the torah is subject to the death penalty. Needless to say, eventually one could search from Dan to Beer-sheba and not find a single person ignorant of torah. The illness that afflicted Hezekiah was punishment for "peeling off" the gold from the temple to send to Sennacherib (2 Kgs. 18:16). Therefore, the disease that plagued Hezekiah caused his skin to "peel off." Hezekiah is praised for having the traditions of Isaiah, Ecclesiastes, Song of Songs, and Proverbs put in writing.

Rabbinic legends narratively expand on characters that are not developed in 2 Kings. Sennacherib's vast army is described in great detail. He himself was contemptuous when he first saw Jerusalem, wondering why he bothered to gather armies and conquer other lands to gain it. It was smaller and weaker than the other cities he had subdued. Two of the officials sent to meet the Assyrian negotiators, Shebnah and Joah (cf. 2 Kgs. 18:18), were actually opponents of Hezekiah's rebellion. They shot a dart into the Assyrian camp containing a letter, saying: "We and the whole people of Israel wish to conclude peace with thee, but Hezekiah and Isaiah will not permit it." When Shebnah and his supporters left Jerusalem to join the Assyrians, the angel Gabriel manipulated Sennacherib into thinking that Shebnah was fooling him. Sennacherib then ordered Shebnah tied to a horse and dragged to death (for more on Hezekiah, see Ginzberg 1998, 266–77).

Hezekiah is chiefly remembered in Christian tradition for his piety and for the extraordinary answer to his prayer for a stay of death (e.g., Cyril, *Lectures* 2.15; 12.22). In New England Puritanism, he was sometimes described as a type of Christ (e.g., Thomas Frink, *A King Reigning in Righteousness* [1758]) and as a moral example for temporal magistrates (Baker 1992b, 352). The poem "Destruction of Sennacherib," by Lord Byron, in his *Hebrew Melodies* (1815), depicts the Assyrian king's perspective on the siege.

▌ THE TEXT IN CONTEMPORARY DISCUSSION

We are presented in 2 Kings 18–20 with an idealized king, a paradigm of piety with an abiding trust in YHWH. God was with Hezekiah wherever he went, prospering in his domestic and foreign policies: his centralization of worship and his rebellion against Assyria. He becomes the total opposite of his father, Ahaz, before him and his son Manasseh after him. Nevertheless, we will soon see that the alternation between good king/bad king is a deliberate Dtr construction. Historical and archaeological reconstructions of the period reveal that Hezekiah's cultic centralization and rebellion against Assyria were foolhardy and had disastrous consequences for the economic and social landscape of Judah. Moreover, we will soon see that the supposedly "evil" king Manasseh actually helped Judah recover from his father's disastrous foreign and domestic policies.

Dtr creates a history "after the fact," from the social location of a community that has experienced the trauma of exile and needs an explanation. The explanation Dtr provides is a theological one: the people were unfaithful to God's covenant. We must keep this in mind as we try to relate Hezekiah's story to our own times. Placing one's trust in God in decisions regarding foreign or domestic policies must work in tandem with dedicated analysis of the broader social and political issues surrounding these policies.

2 Kings 21:1—23:30: The Reigns of Manasseh and Josiah

▌ THE TEXT IN ITS ANCIENT CONTEXT

Dtr sets before us two stereotypical models of kingship in these chapters: one utterly "bad" (Manasseh), the other categorically "good" (Josiah). Neither really resembles his historical personage. Dtr describes "evil" Manasseh as reversing all the cult reforms that his father Hezekiah had instigated, comparing him to the absolute worst king of the northern kingdom, Ahab (21:3, 9). His religious abominations even exceeded those of the pagan nations that YHWH drove out of the land (12:9, 11). Because of Manasseh's colossal failures to keep Deuteronomic law (Deut. 12:29-31; 18:9-12; 19:8-10), an unknown prophet declares that YHWH will "wipe Jerusalem as one wipes a dish," casting the remnant off, giving them over to the hands of their enemies (2 Kgs. 21:12-16).

Although blamed for the eventual fall of Judah, Manasseh's lengthy rule (698/687–642 BCE) was historically much more beneficial to the nation than Dtr presents. Following the conventions of ancient Near Eastern historiography, Dtr alternates bad and good kings before and after Manasseh: Ahaz (bad); Hezekiah (good); Manasseh and Amon (bad); Josiah (good) (Evans, 497). Because Josiah is the "golden boy" of the Deuteronomists, Manasseh is set up as his foil. Although he is presented as one of the "good" kings, Hezekiah's rebellion against Assyria was politically and economically disastrous. Sennacherib ravaged the countryside, and Hezekiah lost valuable land in the Shephelah (Finkelstein and Silberman, 251–64). Inheriting a weakened and humiliated nation, Manasseh was left with the task of rebuilding the state after this catastrophe.

Archaeology reveals that Judah experienced a remarkable resurgence under Manasseh's long reign (Grabbe 2007, 201). Collaborating with networks of village clan-based leaders, whose authority was diminished under Hezekiah, Manasseh began to restore those areas of the countryside that were ravaged by Sennacherib. Providing these networks with economic autonomy, his renewal of the rural areas permitted the veneration of the popular agrarian gods, Baal and Asherah, which would later provoke the wrath of the Deuteronomists (Finkelstein and Silberman, 264–67; Halpern 1991, 60–65). Working his position as vassal to his advantage, Manasseh's connections with Assyrian markets enriched his treasuries, trading in luxury goods from Arabia and exporting olives from the Judean highlands for the mass production of oil in the Assyrian-ruled city of Ekron (Finkelstein and Silberman, 267–70; Gitin, 84–87). Despite the biblical condemnation of his regime, Manasseh's rule was a peaceful and prosperous one for Judah. He is succeeded by his son Amon, who is assassinated by court servants, and Amon's son Josiah is placed on the throne by "the people of the land" (21:19-26).

Josiah's birth and rule were already foretold in 1 Kings, when Jeroboam I was offering incense at Bethel, one of his illegitimate sanctuaries. A man of God prophesies against the altar, "A son shall be born to the house of David, Josiah by name; and he shall sacrifice on you the priests of the high places who offer incense on you, and human bones shall be burned on you" (1 Kgs. 13:2). Dtr exalts Josiah among the other Judean kings by describing him as "walking in *all* the way of his father David," and, like Moses and Joshua, "he did not turn aside to the right or to the left" (2 Kgs. 1:2; Deut. 5:32; Josh. 1:7). There was no king before or after him "who turned to the LORD with all his heart, with all his soul, and with all his might, according to the law of Moses" (23:25).

During repairs on the temple, the high priest Hilkiah finds "the book of the law." Hilkiah reports its "discovery" to Josiah, who hears the words of this book as a prophetic judgment from God, "because our ancestors did not obey the words of this book" (22:3-13). Like Moses and Joshua (Exodus 24; Joshua 24), Josiah renews the covenant with the people (23:2-3) and sets about purging the land of idolatrous worship. He begins first with Jerusalem and its environs (23:4-14) and then proceeds to Bethel, the site of the prophecy in 1 Kgs. 13:2, which foretells the destruction of the altar that Jeroboam I erected. Josiah not only tears down the altar but also defiles it by having human bones burned on it, fulfilling the earlier prophecy before moving on to other cultic sites in Samaria (23:15-20). Josiah then centralizes his liturgical reform by instituting the national celebration of Passover held in Jerusalem (22:21-23).

Scholars believed that the "book of the law" was an earlier form of the book of Deuteronomy. However, because of its similarities to early seventh-century Assyrian vassal treaties, they now think that Deuteronomy was composed in the seventh century, just before or during Josiah's reign. Deuteronomy is thus not an ancient scroll that is suddenly "discovered" in the temple but the composition of a Deuteronomistic school (Römer, 45–65). In spite of Josiah's good deeds, he is not able to reverse God's judgment against Judah and Jerusalem because of Manasseh's offenses (23:26-27).

Josiah is killed by Neco, pharaoh of Egypt, at Megiddo, and his son Jehoahaz is anointed king by the people of the land (23:28-30).

▌ THE TEXT IN THE INTERPRETIVE TRADITION

Second Chronicles 33:11-13 has Manasseh captured by the Assyrians, who imprison him in Babylon. He repents of his sins, and God returns him to Jerusalem, where he eliminates the foreign gods and restores the worship of YHWH in the land. The remorse of the one who was considered to be the cause of Jerusalem's destruction provided hope and encouragement to the postexilic returnees to Yehud. The apocryphal work Prayer of Manasseh claims to be the one he utters in 2 Chron. 33:13, although this is unlikely. (See "Prayer of Manasseh" in this commentary.)

Manasseh's contrition is expanded by Josephus (*Ant.* 10.40–46), who concludes that Manasseh "underwent such a change of heart in these respects and lived the rest of his life in such a way as to be counted a blessed and enviable man after the time when he began to show piety toward God" (*Ant.* 10.45). Rabbinic legends describe the king of Babylon casting Manasseh into a heated oven, whereupon Manasseh remembers a prayer his father Hezekiah had taught him about calling on YHWH during times of tribulation. However, angels stop his prayer from reaching God, but God, knowing that he would be shutting the doors to anyone who repents if he did not accept Manasseh's penance, receives Manasseh's prayer through a small opening under the throne of his glory. A wind carries Manasseh back to Jerusalem (Ginzberg 1998, 279–80; Hulbert).

According to rabbinic legends, Josiah sought prophetic confirmation after hearing God's judgment against Jerusalem. He consulted Huldah, not Jeremiah, because he believed that a woman would be more compassionate than a man and deliver a more temperate oracle (*b. Meg.* 14b). Knowing that the temple would be destroyed, he hid the ark of the covenant and all its accessories to protect them from enemy desecration (*Yoma* 52b). Although he instituted a purge of foreign worship, Josiah was deceived by the people, who hid their idolatrous ways from his inspectors (*Lam. Rab.* 1.53). Because of this deception and for disobeying the counsel of Jeremiah to allow the Egyptians passage through his land, Josiah was struck by three hundred darts in the clash between him and the Egyptians (Ginzberg 1998, 282–83). Josephus remarks that Jeremiah composed a lament for Josiah's funeral (*Ant.* 10.78).

▌ THE TEXT IN CONTEMPORARY DISCUSSION

The biblical portrayals of Manasseh and Josiah are ancient examples of demonization and angelization. Demonization is a rhetorical strategy of depicting rival individuals or groups as embodying all that is considered evil or wicked in a particular context. Angelization is its very opposite, representing an individual or group as all good or virtuous. Neither characterization adequately exemplifies the person or groups in question. Demonization is often used to cast targeted individuals or groups as the other. We have seen that Dtr attributes the destruction of Jerusalem to Manasseh by demonizing his rule, even though he historically helped Judah recover from the disastrous foreign policies of his father Hezekiah, who is angelized by Dtr in spite of them.

We often demonize or angelize individuals in our own time. The Bush Administration demonized Saddam Hussein in order to invade Iraq in the 1990s. The Nazis demonized a whole ethnic group, the Jews, in order to justify the Holocaust. Pro-choice advocates are often contemptuously regarded as "baby-killers." The poor are often vilified as "parasites" and "on the dole." Liberals often label conservatives as "rigid," "ignorant," and "intolerant." Many Roman Catholics "angelized" their parish priests, until the sex scandals that have rocked the church revealed an insidious side to their behavior. Evangelicals have angelized many televangelists until revelations of their financial or sexual corruption have surfaced.

Demonization or angelization of persons or groups close off discussion and further inquiry that would reveal a more unbiased, truthful state of affairs. Our examination of Manasseh and Josiah cautions us to recognize demonization or its opposite when they occur in our own time, and to examine such stereotypical characterizations more fully.

2 Kings 23:31—25:30: The Final Days of Judah and Its Kings

■ THE TEXT IN ITS ANCIENT CONTEXT

Although in the larger context of Egyptian and Babylonian imperial politics it was probably inevitable that Judah would be conquered and destroyed by the Babylonians, Dtr still judges its demise theologically. The final kings of Judah—Jehoahaz, Jehoiakim, Jehoiachin, and Zedekiah—all "did what was evil in the sight of the LORD as their ancestors had done" (23:32, 37; 24:9, 19). Therefore, God's very self sends their enemies—Chaldeans, Arameans, Moabites, and Ammonites—to attack Judah to fulfill the words of the prophets, because God refuses to forgive Judah for the "sins of Manasseh" (24:2-4). God's wrath is unequivocal for Dtr: "Jerusalem and Judah so angered the LORD that he expelled them from his presence" (24:20).

Jehoahaz (609 BCE) rules Jerusalem three months before he is imprisoned at Riblah by Pharaoh Neco, the same king who had his father Josiah killed (23:29-33). After levying a large tribute tax on Judah, Neco installs Josiah's son and Jehoahaz's half brother Eliakim as a puppet king in Jerusalem, and changes his name to Jehoiakim (608–597 BCE). In 605 BCE, the Babylonian king Nebuchadnezzar defeats the Egyptians at the battle of Carchemish in Syria and Judah becomes a vassal of Babylonia. Jehoiakim submits to Babylonian rule for three years, but he seizes his chance to rebel, probably after Babylon's costly battle with the Egyptians in 601 BCE. Recovering two years later, Nebuchadnezzar strikes back against Judah with the aid of Judah's neighbors Aram, Moab, and Ammon. Jehoiakim conveniently dies during Nebuchadnezzar's siege of Jerusalem in 597 BCE, and his unfortunate eighteen-year-old son Jehoiachin succeeds him (24:8-9).

Jehoiachin surrenders to Nebuchadnezzar, who carries him off to Babylon along with the queen mother, his harem, the officials, the elite of the land, and anyone in positions to instigate a rebellion (24:10-16). Nebuchadnezzar appoints Jehoiachin's uncle Mattaniah as his puppet king and changes his name to Zedekiah. Nebuchadnezzar's conquest, deportation, and installation of "a king of his liking" in 597 BCE are confirmed in the Babylonian Chronicle (*ANET* 563–64).

Twenty-one-year-old Zedekiah becomes Judah's final king (597–586 BCE). His rule is hampered by several factors, the first being the brain drain of Judah's top officials in the 597 deportation, leaving second-tier advisors. Second, he is appointed by the colonizer, while the "legitimate" king, Jehoiachin, is in exile. Third, his administration is plagued by the pro-Egyptian and pro-Babylonian partisan politics at court. These politics are particularly evident in the book of Jeremiah (see Jeremiah 27–28; 37–38). Unfortunately, Zedekiah sides with the pro-Egyptian party and rebels against Nebuchadnezzar, who besieges Jerusalem in 587 and ultimately conquers it in 586 BCE. Zedekiah is captured when he tries to escape, and is brought to Nebuchadnezzar at Riblah. Zedekiah witnesses the death of his sons before he himself is blinded and taken in chains to Babylon (24:20b—25:7). The temple is burned, and all the treasures that were not seized in 597 are taken away. Furthermore, the remaining elites are exiled in a second deportation (25:9-17) (on the two forced migrations, see Ahn). The only ones allowed to remain are "some of the poorest people of the land," who probably constituted the crucial agrarian economic base of Judah (25:12; cf. 24:14).

To establish some stability in the land, the Babylonians appoint a prominent Judean, Gedeliah, as governor at the new capital, Mizpah. However, Ishmael and his men, most likely anti-Babylonian partisans, assassinate Gedeliah and flee to Egypt to escape Babylon's wrath (25:22-26). Their story is recounted in greater detail in Jeremiah 40–43.

The book of 2 Kings ends ambiguously, with the release of King Jehoiachin from prison by King Evil-merodach of Babylon. He is given a privileged seat at the foreign king's table and a pension for as long as he lives (25:27-30). Although the Davidic dynasty has been disgracefully terminated in Judah, the fact that its exiled king is freed from prison and attains some sort of status, albeit in a foreign court, can be interpreted as a sign of hope for a renewed kingship.

◼ THE TEXT IN THE INTERPRETIVE TRADITION

Leviticus Rabbah 19.6 describes the "abominations" of Jehoiakim in 2 Chron. 36:8 variously. He disobeys the prohibitions of Lev. 19:19 and Deut. 9:11 by wearing garments that mix wool and linen together. He is guilty of disguising his circumcision; tattooing the names of idols on his body; having incestuous relations with his mother, daughter-in-law, and father's wife; and executing men to violate their wives and seize their wealth. When Nebuchadnezzar comes up against Jerusalem, he tells the Sanhedrin, who meets him at Daphne of Antioch, that he only wants the insurgent Jehoiakim. If the Sanhedrin deliver him up, Nebuchadnezzar will withdraw. Like the city of Abel Beth-maacah, which saved itself by surrendering Sheba son of Bichri (2 Sam. 20:14-22), the Sanhedrin seize Jehoiakim and slide him down the city walls of Jerusalem into the hands of the Babylonians. Nebuchadnezzar takes him in chains around the cities of Judah, kills him, and puts his carcass on an ass. Another version states that Jehoiakim is cut into olive-sized pieces and thrown to the dogs.

Jehoiachin fares better than his father in *Leviticus Rabbah* 19.6. When Nebuchadnezzar tells the Babylonians that he has installed Jehoiachin as Jehoiakim's replacement, he is told a proverb: "Do not rear a gentle cub of a vicious dog, much less a vicious cub of a vicious dog." Regretting his decision, he then informs the Sanhedrin at Daphne of Antioch that if they deliver Jehoiachin to him, he will withdraw from attacking the temple. When Jehoiachin hears this, he takes the keys of the temple to the roof and bids God to take them, at which point a hand from heaven seizes them. Another version says that the keys remain suspended in midair. Nebuchadnezzar then puts Jehoiachin into solitary confinement. The Sanhedrin begins to worry that the house of David will cease, if Jehoiachin does not beget a son. They devise a plan involving Nebuchadnezzar's wife, Shemirah, to persuade her husband to let Jehoiachin have sexual relations with his wife. When they are about to have sex, the wife notices the onset of her menstrual period. Because Jehoiachin obeys the law and refrains from sex during her impurity, God pardons all his sins.

■ THE TEXT IN CONTEMPORARY DISCUSSION

The book of Kings thus ends the sordid history of Israel's failure to keep God's torah. It is not history as we understand it today, describing "what really happened." Rather, it is a selective history, told from a biased perspective. The Deuteronomistic History records that from the moment the Israelites crossed the Jordan and settled in the land (Joshua and Judges), they were seduced away from their covenanted partner, YHWH, to worship the gods of the land. They even wanted kings "like the other nations," rejecting YHWH as king (1–2 Samuel). First and Second Kings continue the story with wise king Solomon, blinded by his love for foreign women and their gods, the division of the kingdom into Israel and Judah, the "sin of Jeroboam," which ultimately led to Israel's fall, and then to that of Judah, who refused to learn from Israel's mistakes. For Dtr, the end of this glorious nation is the people's continual infidelity to their God and God's covenant.

The conclusion to the book of Kings prompts us to think about the way we also construct history. All histories are written from a selective partisan perspective, even those that claim to be objective. One commonly hears the saying "History is written by the victors," and this is true. The book of Kings compels us to wonder about the voices that are not recorded in its stories: those of the poor, the marginalized, the soldiers who lost their lives or those who were maimed in the continual wars of the kings, the citizens who starved during the horrible sieges, and the peasants whose crops were crushed or seized by invading armies.

What about histories in our own time? Do American history books adequately tell the stories of the indigenous peoples whose lands were appropriated in the name of Manifest Destiny; or the horrors of slavery and the Civil War, the most shameful period of our history? Does this history focus primarily on European immigrants, ignoring those from Asia, Africa, South America, and the Caribbean? What we learn from the book of Kings is that its history is not disinterested, is not nonpartisan. How can we critically examine the histories of peoples, groups, and nations in our own time?

Works Cited

Ahn, John J. 2011. *Exile as Forced Migrations: A Sociological, Literary, and Theological Approach on the Displacement and Resettlement of the Southern Kingdom of Judah*. BZAW 417. Berlin: de Gruyter.

Baker, David W. 1992a. "Ahaz." In *A Dictionary of Biblical Tradition in English Literature*, edited by David L. Jeffrey, 27. Grand Rapids: Eerdmans.

———. 1992b. "Hezekiah." In *A Dictionary of Biblical Tradition in English Literature*, edited by David L. Jeffrey, 352–53. Grand Rapids: Eerdmans.

Bartel, Roland. 1975. "Melville's use of the Bible in *Billy Budd*." In *Biblical Images in Literature*, edited by Roland Bartel, James S. Ackerman, and Thayer S. Warshaw, 30–64. Nashville: Abingdon.

Barzel, Hillel. 1975. "The Biblical Layer in Franz Kafka's Short Story 'A Country Doctor.'" In *Biblical Images in Literature*, edited by Roland Bartel, James S. Ackerman, and Thayer S. Warshaw, 89–102. Nashville: Abingdon.

Baumgarten, Murray. 1992. "Abishag." In *A Dictionary of Biblical Tradition in English Literature*, edited by David L. Jeffrey, 6–8. Grand Rapids: Eerdmans.

Beach, Eleanor F. 2005. *The Jezebel Letters: Religion and Politics in Ninth-Century Israel*. Minneapolis: Fortress Press.

Begg, Christopher T. 1996. "The Last Six Kings of Israel According to Josephus: Ant 9,228–278." *ETL* 72:371–84.

Berlin, Adele. 1982. "Characterization in Biblical Narrative: David's Wives." *JSOT* 23:69–85.

Bird, Phyllis A. 1997. *The Harlot as Heroine: Narrative Art and Social Presupposition in Three Old Testament Texts*. Minneapolis: Fortress Press.

Bowen, Nancy R. 2001. "The Quest for the Historical Gebirâ." *CBQ* 63:597–618.

Branch, Robin G. 2009. *Jeroboam's Wife: The Enduring Contributions of the Old Testament's Least-Known Women*. Peabody, MA: Hendrickson.

Brueggemann, Walter. 2000. *1 and 2 Kings*. Smyth & Helwys Bible Commentary. Macon, GA: Smyth & Helwys.

———. 2001. *Testimony to Otherwise: The Witness of Elijah and Elisha*. St. Louis: Chalice.

Cogan, Mordechai. 1983. "'Ripping Open Pregnant Women' in Light of an Assyrian Analogue." *JAOS* 103:755–57.

Conti, Marco, ed. 2008. *1–2 Kings, 1–2 Chronicles, Ezra, Nehemiah, Esther*. Ancient Christian Commentary on Scripture, Old Testament 5. Downers Grove, IL: InterVarsity Press.

Curzon, David. 1994. *Modern Poems on the Bible: An Anthology*. Philadelphia: Jewish Publication Society.

Dever, William G. 2005. *Did God Have a Wife? Archaeology and Folk Religion in Ancient Israel*. Grand Rapids: Eerdmans.

Dutcher-Walls, Patricia. 1996. *Narrative Art, Political Rhetoric: The Case of Athaliah and Joash*. Sheffield: Sheffield Academic.

———. 2004. *Jezebel: Portraits of a Queen*. Interfaces. Collegeville, MN: Liturgical Press.

Evans, Carl D. 1992. "Manasseh, King of Judah." *ABD* 4:496–99.

Feldman, Louis H. 1994. "Josephus' Portrait of Elisha." *NovT* 36:1–28.

Finkelstein, Israel, and Neil A. Silberman. 2001. *The Bible Unearthed: Archaeology's New Vision of Ancient Israel and the Origin of Its Sacred Texts*. New York: Free Press.

Gaines, Janet H. 1999. *Music in the Old Bones: Jezebel through the Ages*. Carbondale: Southern Illinois University Press.

Garsiel, Moshe. 1993. "The Story of David and Bathsheba: A Different Approach." *CBQ* 55:244–62.

———. 2002. "Revealing and Concealing as a Narrative Strategy in Solomon's Judgment (1 Kings 3:16-28)." *CBQ* 64:229–47.

Ginzberg, Louis. 1956. *Legends of the Bible*. Philadelphia: Jewish Publication Society of America.

———. 1998. *The Legends of the Jews*. Vol. 4, *From Joshua to Esther*. Baltimore: Johns Hopkins University Press.

Gitin, Seymour. 1997. "The Neo-Assyrian Empire and Its Western Periphery: The Levant, with a Focus on Philistine Ekron." In *Assyria 1995: Proceedings of the 10th Anniversary Symposium of the Neo-Assyrian Text Corpus Project, Helsinki, September 7–11, 1995*, edited by S. Parpola and M. R. Whiting, 77–103. Helsinki: The Neo-Assyrian Text Corpus Project.

Grabbe, Lester L., ed. 2003. *"Like a Bird in a Cage": The Invasion of Sennacherib in 701 BCE*. JSOTSup 363. London: Sheffield Academic.

———. 2007. *Ancient Israel: What Do We Know and How Do We Know It?* New York: T&T Clark.

Halpern, Baruch. 1991. "Jerusalem and the Lineages in the Seventh Century BCE: Kinship and the Rise of Individual Moral Liability." In *Law and Ideology in Monarchic Israel*, edited by Baruch Halpern and Deborah W. Hobson, 11–107. JSOTSup 124. Sheffield: JSOT Press.

———. 2001. *David's Secret Demons: Messiah, Murderer, Traitor, King*. Grand Rapids: Eerdmans.

Hulbert, W. G. 2008. "Good King and Bad King: Traditions about Manasseh in the Bible and Late Second Temple Judaism." *Stone-Campbell Journal* 11:71–81.

Ipsen, Avaren E. 2008. "Solomon and the Two Prostitutes." In *Marxist Feminist Criticism of the Bible*, edited by Roland Boer and Jorunn Okland, 134–50. Sheffield: Sheffield Phoenix.

Ishida, Tomoo. 1999. "Solomon's Succession to the Throne of David." In *History and Historical Writing in Ancient Israel: Studies in Biblical Historiography*, 102–36. Leiden: Brill.

Jobling, David. 1991. "Forced Labor: Solomon's Golden Age and the Question of Literary Representation." *Semeia* 54:57–76.

Knoppers, Gary N. 1995. "Aaron's Calf and Jeroboam's Calves." In *Fortunate the Eyes That See: Essays in Honor of David Noel Freedman in Celebration of His Seventieth Birthday*, edited by Astrid B. Beck, Andrew H. Bartelt, Paul R. Raabe, and Chris A. Franke, 92–104. Grand Rapids: Eerdmans.

Lang, Bernhard. 1983. *Monotheism and the Prophetic Minority: An Essay in Biblical History and Sociology*. Sheffield: Almond.

Lasine, Stuart. 1989. "The Riddle of Solomon's Judgment and the Riddle of Human Nature in the Hebrew Bible." *JSOT* 45:61–86.

Lassner, Jacob. 1993. *Demonizing the Queen of Sheba: Boundaries of Gender and Culture in Postbiblical Judaism and Medieval Islam*. Chicago: University of Chicago Press.

Long, Burke O. 1991. *2 Kings*. FOTL. Grand Rapids: Eerdmans.

Long, Jesse C., Jr., and Mark Sneed. 2004. "'Yahweh Has Given These Three Kings into the Hand of Moab': A Socio-Literary Reading of 2 Kings 3." In *Inspired Speech: Prophecy in the Ancient Near East. Essays in Honour of Herbert B. Huffmon*, edited by John Kaltner and Louis Stulman, 253–75. London: T&T Clark.

Moore, Megan B., and Brad E. Kelle. 2011. *Biblical History and Israel's Past: The Changing Study of the Bible and History*. Grand Rapids: Eerdmans.

Na'aman, Nadav. 1986. "Historical and Chronological Notes on the Kingdoms of Israel and Judah in the 8th Century BC." *VT* 36:71–92.

Nelson, Richard D. 1987. *First and Second Kings*. IBC. Atlanta: John Knox.

Oded, Bustenay. 1979. *Mass Deportations and Deportees in the Neo-Assyrian Empire*. Wiesbaden: Reichert.

Olyan, Saul. 1984. "*Hašalôm*: Some Literary Considerations of 2 Kings 9." *CBQ* 46:652–68.

Petersen, David L. 1981. *The Roles of Israel's Prophets*. Sheffield: JSOT Press.

Premnath, D. N. 2003. *Eighth Century Prophets: A Social Analysis*. St. Louis: Chalice.

Provan, Iain W. 1995. *1 and 2 Kings*. Peabody, MA: Hendrickson.

Pyper, Hugh S. 1993. "Judging the Wisdom of Solomon: The Two-Way Effect of Intertextuality." *JSOT* 59:37–53.

Rentería, Tamis H. 1992. "The Elijah/Elisha Stories: A Socio-Cultural Analysis of Prophets and People in Ninth-Century B.C.E. Israel." In *Elijah and Elisha in Socioliterary Perspective*, edited by Robert B. Coote, 75–126. Atlanta: Scholars Press.

Römer, Thomas C. 2007. *The So-Called Deuteronomistic History: A Sociological, Historical, and Literary Introduction*. New York: T&T Clark.

Schulte, Hannelis. 1994. "The End of the Omride Dynasty: Social-Ethical Observations on the Subject of Power and Violence." *Semeia* 66:133–48.

Seow, Choon-Leong. 1999. "The First and Second Books of Kings: Introduction, Commentary, and Reflections." In *The New Interpreter's Bible*. Vol. 3, *1 and 2 Kings, 1 and 2 Chronicles, Ezra, Nehemiah, Esther, Tobit, Judith*, edited by Leander E. Keck, 1–295. Nashville: Abingdon.

Smith, Carol. 1998. "'Queenship' in Israel? The Cases of Bathsheba, Jezebel and Athalia." In *King and Messiah in Israel and the Ancient Near East: Proceedings of the Oxford Old Testament Seminar*, edited by John Day, 142–62. Sheffield: Sheffield Academic.

Smith, Mark S. 2002. *The Early History of God: Yahweh and the Other Deities in Ancient Israel*. Grand Rapids: Eerdmans.

Smith, Morton. 1971. *Palestinian Parties and Politics That Shaped the Old Testament*. New York: Columbia University Press.

Snyder, Josey B. 2012. "Jezebel and Her Interpreters." In *Women's Bible Commentary*, edited by Carol A. Newsom, Sharon H. Ringe, and Jacqueline E. Lapsley, 180–83. Louisville: Westminster John Knox.

Solomon, Ann M. V. 1985. "Jehoash's Fable of the Thistle and the Cedar." In *Saga, Legend, Tale, Novella, Fable: Narrative Forms in Old Testament Literature*, edited by George W. Coats, 126–32. JSOTSup 35. Sheffield: JSOT Press.

Solvang, Elna. 2003. *A Woman's Place Is in the House*. JSOTSup 349. New York: Continuum.

Stahlberg, Lesleigh C. 2009. "From Biblical Blanket to Post-Biblical Blank Slate: The Lives and Times of Abishag the Shunamite." In *From the Margins 1: Women of the Hebrew Bible and Their Afterlives*, edited by Peter S. Hawkins and Lesleigh C. Stahlberg, 122–40. Sheffield: Sheffield Phoenix.

Sweeney, Marvin A. 2007. *1 and 2 Kings: A Commentary*. OTL. Louisville: Westminster John Knox.

———. 2008. *Reading the Hebrew Bible after the Shoah: Engaging Holocaust Theology*. Minneapolis: Fortress Press.

Wolde, Ellen van. 1995. "Who Guides Whom? Embeddedness and Perspective in Biblical Hebrew and in 1 Kings 3:16-28." *JBL* 114:623–42.

Yee, Gale A. 1992. "Jezebel." *ABD* 3:848–49.

Younger, K. L., Jr. 1998. "The Deportations of the Israelites." *JBL* 117:201–27.

1, 2 CHRONICLES

Alejandro F. Botta

Introduction

In the same way that Deuteronomy offers a second presentation of the law, the books of Chronicles offer a second recounting of the history of Israel. Christian Bibles include 1 and 2 Chronicles among the "historical books" after 1 and 2 Kings. In the Hebrew Bible and in Jewish tradition, both books of Chronicles constitute a unity, with the name of *dibrê hayyāmîm* ("the events of the days") and are found in the Writings (*ketubim*), the third section of the Hebrew Bible. Chronicles had already achieved authoritative status by the second century BCE, but with the exception of Jerome, the church fathers didn't pay much attention to Chronicles. Neither did it enjoy a prominent place in Jewish tradition. The great Jewish scholar Don Isaac Arbarbanel (1437–1509) stated, "my transgressions do I mention today; I have never read this book in my life and never researched its issues—never before today!" (Kalimi 2009a, 236).

The book itself, like most of the literary works composed before the Hellenistic period, does not include a title or the name of its author. The name given to it by the Jewish sages and church fathers reflects their intention to describe or qualify its content.

Authorship and Relationship with Ezra and Nehemiah

The Talmud attributes part of the authorship of Chronicles and Ezra-Nehemiah to Ezra, and part of it to Nehemiah (*b. Bat.* 15a). Medieval Christian scholars were not so certain. Hugh of St. Cher (c. 1200–1263 CE), a French Dominican, affirmed that the author was unknown, although he trusted the veracity of its content (Saltman, 55).

In the nineteenth century, the great majority of biblical scholars considered the book of Chronicles to form a unity with Ezra and Nehemiah. Nowadays, pioneered by the work of Sarah Japhet

(1968; 1993) and Hugh G. M. Williamson (1977), the consensus has moved into considering the book of Chronicles and Ezra-Nehemiah as two different and independent works. The major arguments behind such a shift are differences in language and style peculiarities (Japhet 1968) and the "substantive differences in theology, purpose, and perspective" (Klein 2006, 10) between Chronicles and Ezra-Nehemiah. Immediate divine retribution, a central theological motif in Chronicles, is not that relevant in Ezra-Nehemiah. The almost complete disregard for the exodus tradition and the Mosaic tradition is not as significant in Chronicles as it is in Ezra-Nehemiah. In Chronicles, there is hope of a future reunification with the northern kingdom (2 Chr. 30:1-31), something absent in Ezra-Nehemiah. The "Levitical sermons," a prominent feature of Chronicles, are completely absent in Ezra-Nehemiah. The most recent major commentaries on Chronicles by Gary Knoppers (2003) and Ralph Klein (2006) have both adopted such a position.

Date

There is a certain agreement among scholars that Chronicles is a postexilic composition. But as Klein states, "the evidence for a more specific date within that period is thin and ambiguous" (2006, 13). The suggested dates by scholars range from 520 BCE to 160 BCE. Chronicles doesn't indicate any Hellenistic influence, so there is some consensus to date the book during the Persian period (539–332 BCE) (Kalimi 2005a, 65).

Literary Characteristics

Chronicles begins with a long genealogical section focused on biblical characters who are significant for the author's theological purposes. Genealogies fulfill various functions in the Bible. Some are meant to show the relationship between Israel and the neighboring nations (Gen. 10:1-32; 19:36-38; 22:20-24; 25:1-6); others are used to bridge the temporal gap between events (Gen. 5:1-32; 11:10-27; Ruth 4:18-22); and others to bring together traditions from different origins (Gen. 5:1; 6:9) (Wilson 1977; Johnson 1988, 77–82). One of the characteristics of ancient historiography was the inclusion of discourses or speeches. As the Greek historian Thucydides (fifth century BCE) stated regarding the uses of speeches in his history, "the speeches are given in the language in which, as it seemed to me, the several speakers would express, on the subject under consideration, the sentiments most befitting the occasion" (*History of the Peloponnesian War* 1.22). Chronicles includes several speeches and prayers: Solomon's prayer at the dedication of the temple (2 Chron. 6:14-42); Jehoshaphat when facing the Ammonites and Moabites (2 Chron. 20:6-12); and a number of speeches labeled by Gerhard von Rad as "Levitical sermons" (2 Chron. 15:2-7; 16:7-9; 19:6-7; 20:15-17, 20; 29:5-11) (von Rad 1966, 269–76). These speeches and sermons are a valuable source of information about Chronicles' theological perspectives.

Chronicles as Legitimate Historiography

With the emergence of history as a scientific discipline under the leadership of figures like Leopold von Ranke (1795–1886), the positive valorization of Chronicles by the church fathers and medieval scholars suffered a strong blow. A more positive attitude toward the Chronicler was developed during the second half of the twentieth century under the influence of scholars like Gerhard von Rad (1901–1971) and Martin Noth (1902–1968). Contemporary scholarship tends to accept Chronicles as a valid historiographical work (Graham, Hoglund, and McKenzie; Kalimi 2005a; 2005b). As Japhet (1993, 32) states, "A consideration of the work's relevant features, such as aim, plan, form, and method, must lead to the conclusion that Chronicles is a history, an idiosyncratic expression of biblical historiography." The Chronicler acts as a historian when he gathers material and sources about the past of his community, decides what is significant for his time, and connects diverse events from his sources to produce a coherent narrative about the past. The difference between a mere past event and a historical event is, after all, how significant that event is for the present community. As Isaac Kalimi (2009b, 192) states, Chronicles "represent the principle of 'each generation with his own historiography and historian.' . . . Chronicles is the 'right' composition, 'the true one,' for its time, place, and audience."

Sources

Chronicles abounds in citations of works used by the author to compose his narrative. The book of the kings of Israel and Judah is cited several times, although sometimes with a slightly different name (2 Chron. 16:11; see 20:34; 25:26; 27:7; 28:26; 32:32; 33:18; 35:26; 36:8); there is also a mention of the midrash of the books of Kings (2 Chron. 3:22; 24:27). The Chronicler also refers to prophets or prophetic records like the acts of Samuel the seer, the acts of Nathan the prophet, the acts of Gad (1 Chron. 29:29), the prophecy of Ahijah, and the visions of Iddo (2 Chron. 9:29). The Chronicler is also familiar with the genealogical information provided by the books of Genesis, Exodus, Numbers, Joshua, Samuel, and Ruth. There is a citation of what is written "in the law of the Lord" (1 Chron. 16:40), which possibly refers to the Pentateuch; and a reference to a book of laments, unknown to us, that included a "lament of Josiah" (2 Chron. 35:25). The author seems to know the books of Isaiah (2 Chron. 28:16-21), Jeremiah (2 Chron. 36:21), and Zechariah (2 Chron. 36:9). The Chronicler also used information from lists (1 Chron. 6:1-15), and three canonical psalms (Psalms 96; 105; 106) are cited in 1 Chronicles 16. Without being exhaustive, this list of sources shows evidence of a dedicated historian at work.

1 Chronicles 1:1—9:44: Genealogical Registry of Israel

■ THE TEXT IN ITS ANCIENT CONTEXT

The genealogical register of Israel is further divided into subsections, which will be listed below.

Israel's Ancestors (1:1—2:2)

The first chapter of Chronicles is based on genealogical information from the book of Genesis. The author distinguishes an antediluvian generation (1:1-23) and a postdiluvian generation (1:24—2:2), similar to Assyrian and Babylonian cosmogonic genealogies. The Chronicler begins the genealogy with Adam in order to emphatically place the people of Israel in the context of universal history. "Indeed, one can only appreciate the experience of Israel within its land if one has some understanding of lands and peoples relevant to Israel and how they are related to Israel" (Knoppers 2003, 295).

Judah's Lineage (2:3—4:23)

This section consists of three parts: (a) 2:3-55, the genealogies of the tribe of Judah; (b) 3:1-24, the house of David; and (c) 4:1-23, additional genealogies of the house of Judah. The first part (2:3-55) stresses both the divine election of Judah and God's intolerance toward unfaithfulness as exemplified in the case of Er, who "was wicked in the sight of the Lord, and he put him to death" (v. 3), and of Achar, "the troubler of Israel who transgressed in the matter of the devoted thing" (v. 7). The importance of Ram (2:9-17), who is not the firstborn but occupies the first place on the list, is due to his ancestral relationship to David. In 2:13-15, David is listed as the seventh son of Jesse (according to 1 Sam. 16:6-9; 11-13; 17:13-14, Jesse had only four sons). Later tradition adopted the Chronicler's view, as represented in the Dura-Europos fresco (Kalimi 2009a, 123–32). David's sisters are only mentioned here (2:16-17).

The descendants of Caleb are listed in 2:18-24. The first part of the genealogy (2:18-20) deals with Bezalel, a silversmith (see Exod. 31:2; 35:30), who although belonging to a period prior to David, is associated with David and the tabernacle in view of the future construction of the temple by Solomon. The second part (2:21-24) establishes a connection between Judah and a group of descendants of Gilead. It follows the descendants of Jerahmeel (2:25-41), and an additional list of descendants of Caleb (2:42-55).

David's nineteen sons are enumerated (3:1-9), as are the kings of Israel (3:10-16) and the postexilic generation (3:17-24). The extension of David's genealogy to such a late period reflects the importance of David's descendants even during the restoration period (see Haggai 2). The best known of the genealogies contained in 4:1-23 is the one dedicated to Jabez (4:9-10) and his prayer granted by God. The Hebrew version of this prayer presents some difficulties and perhaps would be best translated, "if you blessed me and enlarged my borders, and if your hand might be with me, and that you would extend lands of pasture." This way, the greatest honor Jabez deserves could be attributed to the extension of his territory due to prayer and not to military force. The two genealogical sections of Judah (2:3-55 and 4:1-23) "form an envelope around the genealogy of David and his descendants, who are the centerpiece of the tribe of Judah in chapter 3" (Klein 2006, 142).

Descendants of Simeon (4:24-43)

The tribe of Simeon comes after that of Judah due to geographical proximity. The cities that are listed in 4:28-33 were considered part of Judah from ancient times (see Josh 19:2-8). In times when the people of Israel are dispersed and the prophets are proclaiming the future restoration of Israel (Jer. 16:14-15; 23:7-8; Zeph. 2:7-9), "the author revives the ideal of a larger tribal federation" (Knoppers 2003, 374).

The Tribes of Transjordan: Reuben, Gad, and Manasseh (5:1-26)

This section enumerates the descendants of Reuben (5:1-10), Gad (5:11-22), and the half-tribe of Manasseh (5:23-26). At the beginning of this section, the Chronicler clarifies the reason why Reuben, Jacob's firstborn, does not come first in his genealogy (see Gen. 29:31-32). The author's interest in demonstrating that God often discards the firstborn (see 1 Chron. 2:3; 26:10) seems to emphasize the fact that before God there are no natural rights, only the benefit of divine election. The section dedicated to Gad (5:11-22) points to the theology of the Chronicler when explaining the reason for military success. They cried to God in the battle (see 2 Chron. 14:11-15; 20:5-30; 32:20-21) and God granted their wish (see 1 Chron. 12:19; 15:26; 2 Chron. 25:8; 32:8) because they trusted in him (see 2 Chron. 32:10); therefore, the Hagrites and all those who were with them "were given into their hands" (5:20). The section dedicated to Manasseh (5:23-26) explains the reason for the exile of the northern tribes (see 2 Kgs. 17:7-23). Israel had transgressed against God (see 2 Chron. 36:14), idolatry being one of the main issues; thus God sends a foreign army to punish his people (see 2 Chron. 36:17), and the consequence is the exile (see 2 Chron. 36:18-20).

Descendants of Levi (6:1-81)

The section is divided into two parts: the genealogy of the Aaronide priests and other Levites (6:1-53), and the settlements of the Levites (6:54-81). The lineages of David and Aaron (see 1 Chron. 2:10-17; 3:1-16) are the only cases in which the generations are enumerated from the patriarchal era until the exile. The importance the Chronicler attributes to the Levites is evident in the number of verses dedicated to the tribe of Levi. Together with Judah and Benjamin, they capture the attention of the Chronicler in the genealogy section.

Tribes of the Central Mountainous Region (7:1-40)

Surprisingly, in the genealogies of both Manasseh and Ephraim, there is no mention of any stay in Egypt. Manasseh appears to be associated with Aramean groups in Canaan, from where he takes his wife (7:14-19), leaving aside the tradition of the stay in Egypt and emphasizing the continuity of the occupation of his territory (the northern part of the territory east of river Jordan). Something similar happens with the genealogy of Ephraim (7:20-29), who according to the Genesis narrative is born and dies in Egypt (Gen. 41:50-52; Exodus 16). However, in Chronicles, Ephraim is in no way associated with Egypt. Rather, Ephraim is presented as originally from and settled in Canaan. The narrative of the murder of his sons as the result of a conflict with Gath's men and the foundation of three cities by his daughter Seerah, "who built both Lower and Upper Beth-horon, and Uzzen-sheerah" located in Canaan, does nothing but reinforce the local Canaanite emphasis, which the author of Chronicles places on Ephraim's sons. In a similar vein, Joshua is presented as already established on the land, in contrast to the conqueror role he is given in the book that bears his name. His leadership in the conquest is omitted in Chronicles.

Additional Descendants of Benjamin (8:1-40; 9:1a)

This new chapter, concerning the tribe of Benjamin, is structured in two sections: a list of Benjamite ancestral houses (8:3-32), and a genealogy of the family of Saul (8:33-40). While the previous section dedicated to Benjamin was centered on the military census (7:6-12), the current chapter is centered on geographical distribution.

The Postexilic Community (9:1b-44)

On concluding the descendants of Jacob (1 Chronicles 1–8), the Chronicler adds a final section listing the inhabitants of Jerusalem, paying special attention to the priestly families (9:10-13), the Levitical families (9:14-16), and the gatekeepers (9:17-33).

◼ THE TEXT IN THE INTERPRETIVE TRADITION

The fact that many of the names found in this section are not found in other books of the Hebrew Bible led the Jewish sages to argue that the people listed in the genealogies are actually people mentioned in other parts of the Bible, but under different names. The medieval Jewish scholar David Kimḥi commented that "even though what is written here cannot be found in any of the prophetic books you should not ask how Ezra [the author of Chronicles according to Kimḥi] knew all these things . . . for they are all traditions" (Berger, 69). Theodoret of Cyrus commented that the purpose of the genealogies was to establish that "all human beings are derived from a single man and how our Savior, the Son of God descended from it." Some chapters deserved especial attention by Theodoret, like the genealogy of Judah, because of its connection with the genealogy of Jesus (Conti, 246).

◼ THE TEXT IN CONTEMPORARY DISCUSSION

The genealogical section has a provisionary summary in the opening of chapter 9: "So all Israel was enrolled by genealogies; and these are written in the Book of the Kings of Israel" (9:1). It is likely that its main purpose is to delimit the essential character of exilic Israel; those who cannot prove their genealogically "pure" connection with the ancestors become suspicious. As with many contemporary communities of faith, the exilic community struggled to set standards that would clearly establish who belonged to the community and who did not. In times of crisis, when what is perceived as the core set of beliefs and practices is threatened, those criteria that determine who is and who is not a member of the community tend to become more specific and enforceable. Could this be the intention of the God who claimed through Isaiah of the exile, "I am about to do a new thing; now it springs forth, do you not perceive it?" (Isa. 43:19). Do statements of faith or genealogies serve or hinder the expected inclusive character of the community of the kingdom, here and now?

1 Chronicles 10:1—12:40: Death of Saul and David's Coronation

◼ THE TEXT IN ITS ANCIENT CONTEXT

The death of Saul (10:1-14) is paralleled in 1 Sam. 31:1-13. For the Chronicler, the reign of Saul is more than a prologue to the history of David. Saul's unfaithfulness will be remembered throughout the Chronicler's work (2 Chron. 26:16, 18; 28:19, 22; 29:5-6, 19; 30:7; 33:19; 36:14). It is summarized in 10:13, where Saul dies for disobeying the LORD by not keeping his commands and for seeking guidance from a medium instead of the LORD.

The account of the death of Saul and his sons begins after 9:35-44. The battle takes place on Mount Gilboa, and the results are disastrous. Saul is terrified of what might happen to him if he falls into enemy hands. His apparent self-inflicted death on the battlefield is the only case of suicide in the Bible (see 2 Sam. 1:10, where Saul dies instead at the hand of an Amalekite). The Chronicler replaces "his armor-bearer and all his men" from 1 Sam. 31:6 with "all his house died together," highlighting the end of the dynasty (10:6).

This is the only place in Chronicles where Yahweh directly intervenes to make a dynastic change. The Chronicler clearly points out that the death of Saul is a punishment for his sins. As Klein states, "What happened in the transition from Saul to David . . . was divine retribution at work, and even more, divine providence" (Klein 2006, 291), two essential elements of Chronicles' understanding of history.

King David's coronation is described in 11:1—12:40. Even though the material for this section comes from 2 Samuel 5, the Chronicler presents it with intent to highlight the divine intervention in favor of David. During Saul's reign, David established his power center in Hebron (1 Sam. 30:31), and according to 2 Sam. 2:4, this is exactly the place where he is anointed king over the house of Judah. In Chronicles, all Israel is "together with" David, while in Samuel the tribes only "came" to David. Then David made a covenant with all the elders who had declared their union with the house of David: "we are your bone and flesh." According to the Chronicler's theological perspective, all this happened in accordance with what God had already announced through Samuel (1 Sam. 15:28; 16:1-3).

The new dynasty needs a capital in neutral territory, and Jerusalem is the chosen place (11:4-9). Once again, it is "all Israel" who marches instead of "the king and his men" (2 Sam. 5:6). From this moment and until today, Jerusalem will be the city of David par excellence. The verse "David became greater and greater, for the LORD of hosts [*sabaoth*] was with him," summarizes the essential elements of David's ascent to the throne (1 Chron. 11:9 // 2 Sam. 5:10); "popular and divine election coalesce in establishing David's rule" (Knoppers 2004, 575).

▌ THE TEXT IN THE INTERPRETIVE TRADITION

Rabbinic commentaries on the death of Saul focus on the question of whether it is legitimate to take one's life when the alternative is facing unbearable pain or torture. The rabbis portrayed the transition from the house of Saul to the house of David as inevitable, irrespective of Saul's behavior, because the "scepter shall not depart from Judah" (Gen. 49:10). Saul's reign was, therefore, provisional and did not have any future. Gregory of Nazianzus compared the transition from Jebus to Jerusalem with the Christian transition from temple to word (Conti, 248). Augustine read the destiny of David as an example of how futile it is to resist the will of God. Commenting on all the men who come to Hebron, Augustine states: "Obviously it was of their own will that these men made David king; the fact is clear and undeniable. Nevertheless, it was God, who effects in human hearts whatsoever he wills, who wrought this will in them" (*Admonitions and Grace* 14.45, in Conti, 248).

▌ THE TEXT IN CONTEMPORARY DISCUSSION

Around the year 1000 BCE, Jerusalem became the capital of the nation of Israel and its religious and political center. Since then, the "City of David," which never ceased to be the religious center of the Jewish people, has witnessed wars; famine; destruction and rebuilding; and foreign occupation by Greeks (Hellenistic), Romans, Byzantine Christians, Muslims, the Ottomans, the British, and Jordanians throughout the centuries. It was not until 1967 that Jerusalem was reunited and reestablished as the capital city of Israel. Today, the ancestral Jewish claim is challenged by Islam, which after its expansion out of the Arabian Peninsula and violent conquest of Jerusalem in 637 CE, occupied the land and built the Al-Aqsa Mosque (completed in 705 CE) on top of the Temple Mount. Alternative narratives are sometimes not equally legitimate and should be examined thoroughly, but is the loss of human life in these successive occupations worth being right?

1 Chronicles 13:1—16:43: Transferring the Ark to Jerusalem

■ THE TEXT IN ITS ANCIENT CONTEXT

First Chronicles 13:1-4 contains an episode not found in the book of 2 Samuel. It introduces the first failed attempt to transfer the ark of the covenant to Jerusalem, which could in no way be the religious center of Israel if the ark was not there. David's procedure indicates his role as popular leader. It is not by royal decree that the decision is made, but rather after consulting with the commanders and leaders. Such a move needed to have the support of all Israelites, and their priests and Levites (13:1-2). The festive occasion, a narrative climax, precedes the tragedy that follows—from general rejoicing to experiencing the fear of divine mystery. Uzzah, who with all good intentions tries to stop the ark from falling, is killed by God and causes quite a stir (13:10). David retracts his original idea as a response to the uncontrollable divine action, and decides not to take the ark "into his care into the city of David" (13:13). Rather, he takes it to the house of Obed-edom the Gittite. Paradoxically, the ark ends up in the house of a Philistine at the service of the royal household. Contrary to David's fears, "the LORD blessed the household of Obed-edom and all that he had" (13:14).

In 2 Samuel, the first attempt to take the ark to Jerusalem is immediately followed by a second try, this time successful (2 Sam. 6:12-19). In 2 Sam. 6:12, the transfer is triggered by the news that David receives of the Lord's blessing of the house of Obed-edom. In Chronicles, David's religious zeal is presented as the initial cause of this new attempt. According to Knoppers, the Chronicler's accounts of David's attempt to retrieve the ark "ultimately ratify the historical primacy, central status, and continuing privileges of the Jerusalem Temple" (2004, 593).

The Chronicler points out the distinction between the Levites and the "descendants of Aaron," the Aaronide priests (15:4), and then sets out the list of Levites according to their families (Kothar, Merari, Gershom, and so forth): "no one but the Levites were to carry the ark of God" (15:2). In 2 Samuel, the ark is transferred by David, while in Chronicles it is a collective endeavor in which the elders of Israel and the military leaders also take part. Chronicles emphasizes that the Levites are the ones who carry the ark, followed by the main strata of the Israelite society, the military, civilian, and religious groups.

The organization of worship that follows (16:4-42) has no parallel in the Deuteronomistic history and can be attributed to the Chronicler's composition. Once again, David is the one to name ministers, to invoke—literally to "remember"—praise, and to thank the Lord. As a corollary to the above description, the Chronicler includes a song of thanksgiving and praise ordered by David, "by Asaph and his kindred" (16:7-38). The reference to Asaph is important, as the texts that mention him in place of Heman or Ethan are considered very ancient. The psalm of the Chronicler includes parts of Psalm 105 (vv. 1-5); 96 (vv. 1-3); and 106 (vv. 47-48). By including these postexilic psalms, "the Chronicler establishes a continuity between the worship life established by David and that of his own day" (Klein 2006, 370).

▌ THE TEXT IN THE INTERPRETIVE TRADITION

The unexpected death of Uzzah while transporting the ark demanded an explanation. David Kimḥi suggested that it was David's mistake to try to carry the ark on a wagon (Num. 7:9 states that sacred objects had to be carried on shoulders) and proposes that David reasoned that God's commandment was only valid for the time of the wilderness (Berger, 126). Salvian the Presbyter stated that Uzzah "was undutiful in his very act because he went beyond his orders," and because "even what seems to be a very little in fault is made great by the injury to God," he deserved his punishment (Franke, 344).

▌ THE TEXT IN CONTEMPORARY DISCUSSION

The ark narrative seems to value the sacredness of objects more than human life. Uzzah's good intentions expressed in his attempt to prevent the ark from falling from the wagon do not mitigate God's anger and subsequent reaction. A contemporary commentator justifies God's behavior by stating that "the fate of Uzzah is a fearful warning against over-familiarity with God. His attitude to the thing should have been as reverent as his attitude to the Person" (Wilcock, 67). I disagree. Uzzah's literary killing (of course, gods do not kill people) justifies the death of another innocent victim, adding to the long list of religion-based (literary and real) murders.

1 Chronicles 17:1—21:30: David's Kingdom Is Consolidated

▌ THE TEXT IN ITS ANCIENT CONTEXT

Nathan's oracle (17:4-14) is of fundamental importance for the development of the concept of covenant between God and Israel. In both Samuel and Chronicles, Nathan's oracle is preceded by an introduction (1 Chron. 17:1-2; 2 Sam. 7:1-3). The Chronicler omits the second part of 2 Sam. 7:1, "the LORD had given him rest from all his enemies around him," and substitutes the rhetorical question in Samuel—"Are you the one to build me a house to live in?" (2 Sam. 7:5)—with a negation: "You shall not build me a house to live in" (1 Chron. 17:4). This clarifies that God is not against the construction of the temple, but rather against the man who was ready to begin the construction. God offers the reasons by means of the prophet, explaining that since leaving Egypt, God has lived in a tent and tabernacle. Both of these are synonymous and contrast with "house," which indicates a construction with walls. The passage then turns from the negative statement (it won't be David who builds the temple) to the positive one: it will be God who builds the house of David to assure his descendants, and it will be from these descendants that the person who will build the temple will come (17:7-15 // 2 Sam. 7:8-16). God's covenant with David will be perpetuated in Solomon, from whom God will never withdraw his steadfast love (17:13)—the opposite of what happened with Saul, David's predecessor.

David responds to Nathan's oracle with a prayer (17:16-27), which consists of two parts: 17:16-22 and 23-27. The first responds to the content of the first part of Nathan's prophecy: God's benevolence toward David (vv. 7-8). David responds, praising God for his promise to establish David's house, and the enumeration of God's promise to Israel (vv. 9-10a). David also refers to the exodus, conquest, and the covenantal relationship between God and Israel (vv. 20-22). The second part of the prayer (vv. 23-27) claims the fulfilling of God's promise on the establishment and continuity of the Davidic dynasty.

Chapters 18–20 present a summary of David's battles against the Philistines, Moabites, Ammonites, and Arameans based on 2 Samuel 8–21. In what follows, David orders a census and acquires the land to build the temple (21:1—22:1 // 2 Sam. 24:1-4, 8-25). The Chronicler follows the narrative of 2 Samuel in this case as well, noting, however, that it was not God who incited David to "go, count the people of Israel and Judah" (as in 2 Sam 24:1) but "Satan," who perhaps shouldn't be understood as the devil but as "an emissary of the deity carrying out God's punishment of Israel" (Stokes, 106).

▉ THE TEXT IN THE INTERPRETIVE TRADITION

Eusebius of Caesarea, commenting on Nathan's prophecy, suggests that Solomon is not the subject of the prophecy, or even the subsequent Davidic kings, who didn't last, but the Messiah ("Christ" in Eusebius's mind), "whose kingdom continues and will continue lasting for endless time" (Conti, 260). After the destruction of the second temple by the Roman army in 70 CE, Jewish interpreters also projected into the messianic era some of the promises to David: "More than God wishes to dwell in a house, He wishes to dwell in Israel's hearts. It is the function of the Messiah to make the hearts of Israel the true House of HaShem" (Eisemann 1987, 248). Regarding the coronation of David (20:2), Kimhi comments on how David could stand a crown that weighed a talent of gold, mentioning previous medieval interpreters that assumed that actually the crown was suspended over his head (the precious stone on top of it was a drawing stone, keeping the crown in the air), but concluding that David wore the crown only for brief periods, therefore being able to withstand its weight.

▉ THE TEXT IN CONTEMPORARY DISCUSSION

The project to build a temple, faced by a prophetic reminder of the continuous presence of the God of Israel with his people and with David, makes it clear that God doesn't need a house, and that God is happy with a mobile structure (tent, tabernacle). Communities of faith spend fortunes to improve their "temples." The transformation from "sacred places" to "sacred hearts" (hearts are also mobile!) as proposed above by Moshe Eisemann is a healthy development within religious traditions. Once fiercely attached to certain sacred real estate and ready to wage savage wars to defend or conquer those places, such a movement focuses on the inner presence of God instead of his territorial presence in a place of worship. Paul writes, "Our body is a temple of the Holy Spirit within you" (1 Cor. 6:19). Would it be more in accordance with the divine will to reallocate all the resources spent on "houses of worship," in "sacred places," toward enriching the lives of those sacred vessels that are human beings? It is noticeable that, as described in Revelation (21:22), there is no temple in the new Jerusalem.

1 Chronicles 22:2—27:34: Preparation for Building the Temple

◼ THE TEXT IN ITS ANCIENT CONTEXT

This section is structured around David's decisions before his death regarding the building of the temple. Chapter 22 consists of three sections: verses 2-5 describe David's initial preparations; verses 6-16, the charge to Solomon; and verses 17-19, his command to the leaders of Israel. Each of these sections has a rhetorical center—David's thoughts (v. 5); David's words to Solomon (vv. 7b-16); and his words to the leaders (vv. 18-19). Each of the following subsections begins with "David said" or "David commanded," emphasizing David's leadership in the whole project. In this way, Nathan's oracle in 1 Chron. 17:11-14 begins to be fulfilled: "I will raise up your offspring after you, one of your own sons, and I will establish his kingdom. He shall build a house for me, and I will establish his throne forever." In this project, it will not be the Israelites who will be subjected to forced labor (as Solomon would do in 1 Kings 5:27), but rather "aliens residing in the land." The term *gerim* is used in Chronicles when referring to the Canaanites who remained in Israel (2 Chron. 2:16); 8:7-10) as free men with limited legal rights. The description of Solomon as "young and inexperienced" is in harmony with the description of him in 1 Kings 3:7, a young child "who does not know how to go out or come in" (see also 1 Chron. 29:1, where David describes him as "young and inexperienced"). Rehoboam is the other king to whom a similar description applies ("young and irresolute," 2 Chron. 13:7), which suggests that these are not mere descriptive terms but rather pejorative reflections of the immaturity that characterizes both kings.

The changes in the obligations of the Levites after the construction of the temple are explained in 23:26-28. Because they will no longer need to transport the tabernacle, they are assigned additional tasks established in the Pentateuch (23:25-26) as assistants to the Aaronide priests, emphasizing the subordination of the Levites to the priests (23:28-32). Music is central to the worship service and here related to the task of worship prophets. It seems evident that Levites also played this role (see 2 Kings 23:2 // 2 Chron. 34:30).

The army is organized in twelve divisions (27:2-15), each of them of consisting of 24,000 men. All the chiefs are part of the list of the heroes of David (2 Sam. 23:8-11; 1 Chron. 11:10–30). Jashobeam of the tribe of Judah is one of the sons of Judah, and is assigned to lead the first division during the first month (Nisan = March–April). He is also named commander in chief of the army during that period. In a similar fashion, all commanders for the rest of the months are listed.

◼ THE TEXT IN THE INTERPRETIVE TRADITION

A midrash reports that God says to David: "'If you were to build it, it would stand eternally, and never be destroyed.' And David said to Him, 'Would this not be all the good?' But God answered him, 'I know that [Israel] will one day sin before Me. I intend to pour My anger upon the [physical] building [rather than on the people themselves, for that reason I do not want a temple which can never be destroyed]" (Yalkut Shimoni to Samuel 145; interpolations by Eisemann 1987, 288).

Some Christian interpreters focused especially on 22:9-10, stating that the reign of Solomon (whose name means "peaceable") was not that long, came to an end, and that the name Solomon was also given to Christ ("he is our peace," Eph. 2:14) (Theodoret of Cyrus, in Conti, 264). Eusebius also argued that Nathan's prophecy (22:10) was really fulfilled by Jesus (*Proof of the Gospel* 6.12, in Conti, 264).

■ THE TEXT IN CONTEMPORARY DISCUSSION

The allocation of such a large amount of materials and human effort to the construction of a place of worship makes us wonder: What is the best way to allocate the resources of religious communities? A symbol of power and prestige for the Jerusalem elite, the temple would hardly serve in any way the well-being of the rest of the population, and it reminds us of the failed intention of Gen. 11:4—"let us make a name for ourselves; otherwise we shall be scattered abroad upon the face of the whole earth." David's existential needs (a memorable building, an everlasting lineage) are the literary reflection of our human "unbearable lightness of being."

1 Chronicles 28:1—29:30: Solomon's Investiture

■ THE TEXT IN ITS ANCIENT CONTEXT

Although chapters 28–29 relate Solomon's enthronement, the central figure is David. David gathers all Israel's officers (28:1), David says (28:2), David provides (29:1), David says (29:10, 20), David calls to bless the Lord (29:20). This version is different from the story in 1 Kings 1–2, where the people play a mere anecdotic role (see 1 Kings 1:39b-40). In these two chapters, their role is fundamental.

David's speech (28:2-10) focuses on three topics: the construction of the temple, Solomon's divine election, and an exhortation to keep the commandments of God. In the same way that Moses could not enter the promised land and it fell to Joshua to lead in the final possession of this promised land, it will be Solomon and not David who will lead the construction of the temple. The promise of a lasting kingdom for Solomon, which in 1 Chron. 17:4 is unconditional, appears conditioned here depending on his effort to keep God's commandments and ordinances. The conditional character of the divine promise extends to the leaders of all Israel (28:8). From the perspective of the postexilic community, it is clear that the motive by which the Davidic dynasty had been displaced and the people taken into exile was the king and his leaders' lack of observance of the divine commandments. In the same way that the plans of the tabernacle were revealed to Moses and then drawn (Exod. 25:9, 40), so too the plans of the temple were revealed to David and then drawn up (28:2, 12, 18-19). The difference between the times of Moses and the Chronicler is that Moses receives the revelation orally, while the revelation to David is in writing (28:19). For the postexilic community, the inspired word has become the inspired text. David becomes not only the architect of the temple but also the one who dictates the order of service and establishes the hierarchical order of the staff who serve the temple. Even if Solomon is the builder, David is the intellectual author of the whole project.

David's prayer (29:10-19) contains three parts: the doxology (vv. 10b-13), the presentation and dedication of the voluntary offering to God (vv. 14-17), and the supplication (18-19). David asks God that Solomon may faithfully uphold "your commandments, your decrees, and your statutes," a clear reference to the Torah, so the temple may be built.

If it were not for the narrative in 1 Kings 1–2 describing the way Solomon reaches the throne, it would be impossible to understand the bloody family conflicts and palace intrigues that facilitated his ascent to the throne in the narration of the Chronicler (29:20-25). The Chronicler adds the offering of sacrifices by "all the assembly" (29:21) to the narrative of 1 Kings, pointing to the unity of the people in support of the new king ("and all Israel obeyed him," 29:23).

The Chronicler then presents a summary of David's reign (29:26-30), highlighting David's reign over "all Israel" (29:26) without mentioning the fact that while he reigned in Hebron, the territory under his command covered only the tribe of Judah (see 1 Kgs. 2:11). In 29:28, he points out that David achieved everything a king could wish and died "in a good old age, full of days, riches, and honor."

▉ THE TEXT IN THE INTERPRETIVE TRADITION

John of Damascus interpreted God's refusal to allow David to build the temple as a clear indication of the need to separate the political from the religious office. He writes, "Emperors have not preached the word to you, but apostles and prophets, shepherds and teachers" (*On Divine Images, Second Apology* 12, in Conti, 270). Augustine used 1 Chron. 28:9 to argue for the choice of free will, but also maintained that God's grace does not depend on it (*On Grace and Free Will II*, in Conti, 271). Bede interpreted the measures of the temple allegorically. Its height, one 120 cubits, was connected with the pouring of the Spirit onto the same number of men (Conti, 271).

▉ THE TEXT IN CONTEMPORARY DISCUSSION

The conditional aspect of the blessings promised to God's servants is perhaps one of the most important components of the evolving theology of the Hebrew Bible that has been left behind by contemporary communities of faith. Was the church of Germany still in a covenantal relationship with God after supporting Hitler's program? Were the communities of the United States that supported slavery and segregation? Are those who discriminate based on race, gender, or sexual orientation? On the other hand, how can contemporary communities of faith living in a world where gods do not intervene in human affairs interpret the consequences of departing from faithfulness?

2 Chronicles 1:1-17: Wisdom and Wealth of Solomon

▉ THE TEXT IN ITS ANCIENT CONTEXT

See parallels to these verses in 1 Kgs. 3:1-15 and 1 Kgs. 10:26-29. First Chronicles 29:28 shows Solomon already sitting on David's throne, and the opening verse of 2 Chronicles states that he "established himself in his kingdom" (see 1 Kgs. 2:12; 2:46b), an expression that denotes the king's overcoming certain obstacles or conflicts (see 1 Chron. 11:10; 2 Chron. 12:13; 13:21; 17:1; 21:4). Solomon's convocation (1:2-6.) resembles David's in 1 Chron. 28:1. The purpose is to demonstrate that "all Israel" is present in this act of worship.

The Chronicler omits God's appearance to Solomon in a dream and moves directly to God's speech (1:7-13) following its parallel in 1 Kgs. 3:5-14: God's question (2 Chron. 1:7b), Solomon's response (2 Chron. 1:8-10), and God's reaction (2 Chron. 1:11-12). Solomon, previously described as "young and inexperienced" (1 Chron. 29:1), will demonstrate maturity and humility when he asks for wisdom to lead his people. God provides him with "riches, possessions, and honor" (1:12) because of this request, which "demonstrated that Solomon indeed had the wherewithal to build the temple" (Klein 2012, 28).

▮ THE TEXT IN THE INTERPRETIVE TRADITION

Solomon's request for wisdom (1:10) has offered biblical interpreters a rich source for homiletic applications. John Chrysostom commented that the believer should "ask nothing worldly, but all things spiritual, and you will surely receive" (Conti, 274). The nineteenth-century rabbi Malbim (Meïr Leibush ben Yehiel Michel Wisser) clarifies that "wisdom" refers to value (ethical) judgment while "knowledge" refers to information or axiomatic truths (Eisemann 1992, 5). Gregory of Nazianzus praised Solomon as "the wisest of all people, whether before him or in his own time," who also knew "the furthest point of wisdom to be the discovery of how very far off it was from him" (Conti, 274).

▮ THE TEXT IN CONTEMPORARY DISCUSSION

Solomon is certainly a controversial figure. The biblical portrait exalts him as a man of prudence and a great builder, but also as a king who burdened the people with excessive taxation and subjected them to forced labor. "Wisdom and knowledge" are essential components of good leadership, but there is a change in attitude from the very beginning of Solomon's reign. Solomon's sense of entitlement eventually moves away from the best interest of his people. It is too common a development of political leaders.

2 Chronicles 2:1—9:31: Construction, Dedication of the Temple, and Solomon's Achievements

▮ THE TEXT IN ITS ANCIENT CONTEXT

David has already charged Solomon with completing the preparations for the building of the temple (1 Chron. 22:14), which prompts Solomon to force seventy thousand men "to bear the burdens" and "eighty thousand to quarry in the hill country" (2 Chron. 2:2). He also requests the help of Huram ("Hiram" in Kings), king of Tyre, who provides skilled craftsmen, cedar, cypress, and algum timber for the project. The Chronicler emphasizes that the laborers forced to work on the temple are not native Israelites but foreigners (2 Chron. 2:17-18; see 1 Chron. 20:3; 22:2; and 1 Kgs. 5:13-18).

Solomon builds the temple on the site God showed to David (1 Chron. 21:28—22:1); the site is also identified as Mt. Moriah, where Abraham was ordered to sacrifice Isaac (Gen. 22:2), also known as God's mountain (Gen. 22:14).

After its construction, the temple is dedicated to the Lord (5:2—7:22 // 1 Kgs. 8:1—9:8). The assembly gathers in Jerusalem during the seventh month (named Tishri after the exile, but Ethanim in the preexilic period, see 1 Kings 8:2) to bring the ark to the temple. The assembly includes the leaders and "all the Israelites" (5:3). The seventh month is the month of the Feast of the Tabernacles (Sukkot, Lev. 23:34; Deut. 16:13-16; 31:10). In 1 Kings, the priests are in charge of moving the ark, but here the task falls to the Levites, according to what David prescribed (1 Chron. 15:2; see Deut. 10:8; 31:25; Num. 3:31). The sacrifices offered by Solomon and "all the congregation of Israel" resemble the sacrifices offered by David and the people when the ark was moved from Kiriath-jearim to Jerusalem (1 Chron. 13:5).

Solomon's speech (6:3-42) follows the pattern of David's speech in 1 Chron. 28:2-10. After his speech, Solomon turns to the bronze altar, extending his hands in prayer (see Exod. 9:29). Solomon praises God for fulfilling his promise to David, and asks that God keep his promise that the Davidic dynasty be perennial, as long as "your children keep to their way, to walk in my law as you have walked before me" (6:16). The general statement of 1 Kings "to walk before me as you have walked before me" becomes more specific in Chronicles: "to walk in my law as you have walked before me." After the exile, to walk before God becomes to walk in God's law (torah). Second Chronicles 6:18-21 reflects tension between a belief in God's transcendence (see 2 Chron. 2:4-5; Isa. 56:7) and his presence in the temple. Solomon's prayer (6:22-23) suggests that oaths previously made in the tent of meeting or other sacred place (see Lev. 6:3-6; Num. 5:13; Judg. 11:11; Amos 8:14) should now be made in the temple.

The final act of the temple's dedication is the offering of sacrifices. The Chronicler adds two miracles to the story narrated in 1 Kings (7:1-10 // 1 Kgs. 8:54-66). First, fire descends from heaven, consuming the burnt offering (7:1), in the same way that fire from heaven consumed David's offering (1 Chron. 21:26). Second, God's glory fills the temple, preventing the priests from entering the precinct (7:1b-2).

God's answer to Solomon's prayer (7:11-22 // 1 Kgs. 9:1-9) offers a good example of the Chronicler's theology of retribution (7:13-15). The people complete four actions, which lead to God's forgiveness: "if my people who are called by my name humble themselves, pray, seek my face, and turn from their wicked ways, then I will hear from heaven, and will forgive their sin and heal their land" (7:14). The notion of humbling oneself appears previously in 1 Chron. 17:10; 18:1; 20:4, and becomes a key element in the Chronicler's theology from this point forward (see 2 Chron. 16:6-7; 30:11; 32:26; 33:12, 19, 23; 34:7; 36:12). Praying has been connected to the rebuilding of the temple (see 1 Chron. 17:25; 2 Chron. 7:1) and to petitions for salvation (2 Chron. 32:20-24; 33:13). To seek God's face (2 Chron. 11:16; 15:4, 15; 20:4) and "to turn from their wicked ways" also appear as theological concepts in 2 Chron. 15:4; 30:6, 9; and 36:13.

In 8:1-18, the Chronicler contradicts the story in 1 Kgs. 9:11-14. In 1 Kings, Solomon gives away the cities to Hiram of Tyre for 120 talents of gold. The Chronicler considers the promised land sacred, and giving it away is not a proper act for a king like Solomon.

The visit of the queen of Sheba (9:1-28 // 1 Kgs. 10:1-28) follows the parallel story in Kings with little variation. As no other king before or after, he is a source of wisdom beyond the borders of Israel. Verses 13-28 again highlight the wealth of Solomon and his passion for luxury items: he orders "two hundred large shields of beaten gold" and three hundred smaller shields also of beaten gold (9:15-16).

■ THE TEXT IN THE INTERPRETIVE TRADITION

The temple built by Solomon received a number of allegorical interpretations. Origen states, "Let us seek to find in the Church the truth of each statement made about the temple. If all Christ's enemies are made the footstool of His feet, and Death, the last enemy, is destroyed, then there will be the most perfect peace. Christ will be Solomon, which means 'Peaceful,' and the prophecy will find its fulfillment in Him" (*On John* 23). Bede commented on the visit of the queen of Sheba, "The sending of the Ethiopian queen of the treasures of the nations to Jerusalem signifies that the Church would bring gifts of the virtue and of faith to the Lord" (*Commentary on the Acts of the Apostles*, in Conti, 68). The Jewish sages, however, interpreted such visits in more somber ways; Nebuchadnezzar, the Babylonian king that would destroy Solomon's temple, was a descendant of the fruit of her visit (*Alphabet Ben Sira* 21b).

■ THE TEXT IN CONTEMPORARY DISCUSSION

Today, The Temple Mount is an issue of contention. Now, the Al Aqsa mosque (the third most sacred place for Sunni Muslims) stands on top of where the temple stood, and Jews are not allowed to pray in any portion of the 1,555,000-square-foot plaza. According to Arab leaders like Yasser Arafat, there was never a Jewish temple in Jerusalem and there is no connection between the city and the Jewish people. This is a widespread belief in Muslim countries. Israeli security forces are on guard (especially during the anniversary of the destruction of the temple) against a handful of Jewish religious radicals who believe that destroying the Al Aqsa mosque would allow the third temple to be built. Perhaps our species will reach a day when our mother Earth will be considered humanity's one and only sacred place, and every human being her priest and caretaker.

2 Chronicles 10:1—12:16: The Schism of the Kingdom and Reign of Rehoboam

■ THE TEXT IN ITS ANCIENT CONTEXT

After the death of Solomon, the nation of Israel experiences a political schism (10:1—11:4). When the assembly of northern tribes challenges the oppressive taxes that enabled Solomon to pursue his building projects, his son Rehoboam chooses to heed the advice of his young friends and punish the people's disrespect with additional oppressive measures instead of following the advice of Solomon's advisers. As a result, the northern tribes reject Rehoboam as their king and secede. The Chronicler shows that he believes Judah is still part of his ideal "all Israel" by replacing "all the house of Judah and Benjamin" (1 Kgs. 12:23) with "all Israel in Judah and Benjamin" (11:3). As Japhet states, "the people remains one even after the monarchy is split into two, and all its elements and tribes continue to be represented in the kingdom of Judah" (1989, 230).

Afterward, Rehoboam engages in some building projects (11:5—12:16). The list of cities fortified by Rehoboam (11:5-12) does not have a parallel story in Kings. In the northern kingdom of Israel, Jeroboam undertakes religious reforms that revoke the Levites' ability to function as priests. As a result, the priests migrate to the southern kingdom of Judah (11:13-17 // 1 Kgs. 12:31-32; 13:33). For the Chronicler, everything Jeroboam does in matters of religion is reprehensible.

In addition to the reference to David's wives and concubines, 11:18-21 is the only place in Chronicles where the author mentions the names of wives, concubines, and children of a king (Rehoboam in this case). Rehoboam favors Maacah, daughter of Absalom, over the rest of his wives and appoints her son, Abijah, as his successor. Following Solomon's example, Rehoboam appoints his sons in strategic positions to assure his control of the country.

Chronicles adds parenthetical comments to the parallel story in Kings about Pharaoh Shishak's attack on Judah (12:1-12 // 1 Kgs. 14:25-28). The first refers to the consolidation of Rehoboam's dominion and his unfaithfulness to God's law (12:1). The narrative sequence makes clear that Shishak's attack results from Rehoboam's and the people's infidelity. Shishak lists 150 cities captured during his campaign in his inscription at Karnak, most of them situated in northern Israel. This passage is composed with Sennacherib's campaign in mind (2 Kings 18–19). In the cases of both Rehoboam versus Shishak, and Hezekiah versus Sennacherib, the stories highlight the consolidation of power and the subsequent arrogance that brings divine punishment. Also in both cases, the humbling of the leaders and kings prevents the destruction of Jerusalem.

Rehoboam does not receive a favorable judgment: "He did evil, for he did not set his heart to seek the LORD" (12:14). "To set one's heart to seek the LORD" will become an essential component of the Chronicler's definition of faithfulness. Not to do so leads one to sin.

▌ THE TEXT IN THE INTERPRETIVE TRADITION

When elaborating on the confrontation between Rehoboam and the people in Shechem, some commentators try to portray it as a misunderstanding; Arbarbanel, for example, states that Rehoboam should have explained to the people how beneficial Solomon's reign had been to them instead of conceding that he oppressed them with a heavy yoke (10:11) (Eisemann 1992, 77). The medieval Jewish scholar David Kimḥi also considered the complaints unjustified considering the peace the land enjoyed during Solomon's reign (Eisemann 1992, 76). Ambrose, however, highlights the fact that justice serves political leaders well while injustice undermines their rule. Augustine condemns Rehoboam for rejecting the counsel of the elders, but emphasizes that this happened to fulfill God's plan (Conti, 78–79).

▌ THE TEXT IN CONTEMPORARY DISCUSSION

The oppressive practices of Solomon are evident in this passage, but as the reception history shows, it was hard for some interpreters to accept that the complaint by the people and their request for lower taxes was fair. Communities of faith find it difficult to criticize biblical heroes like Solomon. The question remains, How one can adjudicate a political confrontation like the one depicted here without any additional evidence? It is clear that Rehoboam's reaction was neither wise nor practical, but was the peace and tranquility under Solomon worth the heavy taxes?

2 Chronicles 13:1—16:14: Abijah, Son of Rehoboam, and Asa, Son of Abijah

▌ THE TEXT IN ITS ANCIENT CONTEXT

Rehoboam' son Abijah follows him to the throne of Judah (13:1—14:1 // 1 Kgs. 15:1-2; 6-8). His sermon in 13:4-12 belongs to a significant literary form in Chronicles called "Levitical sermons." The theological message is clear: The northern kingdom has not only rebelled against the Davidic dynasty but also against God himself. In 13:13-21, Chronicles departs from the narrative in Kings to tell the story of the victory of Judah against Israel. Israel has a larger army, but they are no match for God's chosen dynasty. Judah triumphs "because they relied on the LORD, the God of their ancestors" (13:18). Later, Chronicles makes it clear that God himself struck Jeroboam, causing his death.

Asa, son of Abijah, follows his father (14:2—16:14 // 1 Kgs. 15:1-24), and enjoys ten years of peace (14:2-15). He acts as Davidic kings are supposed to act (14:2). Asa "took away the foreign altars and the high places, broke down the pillars, hewed down the sacred poles" (14:3), and also kept the laws and commandments. The blessings are manifested in a period of peace and in the success of his building program. According to the Chronicler, prosperity is a direct consequence of being faithful. God's peace is challenged by a foreign invasion (14:9-15). An Egyptian army led by a Cushite king (perhaps Osorkon I) attacks Judah, and Asa brings his troops to face an enemy much more numerous and powerful. But Judah is not alone. Asa cries to the Lord and the Lord acts by defeating the enemy.

In 15:1-7, the spirit of God commands his prophet Azariah, Son of Oded, to address the king. The speech is another example of the theology of the Chronicler, and it has also been characterized as a Levitical sermon. In the sermon, the Chronicler promises peace, prosperity, and blessings to those who seek the Lord (15:3-6; see Hosea 3:4). Asa reacts immediately to the prophet's demands (15:8-19). He receives the support of all the people of Judah, Benjamin, and the refugees that had fled the northern kingdom of Israel and who had remained faithful to God. The reforms conclude with a covenant renewal, where the people "with all their heart and with all their soul" commit to the Lord. As a consequence, God gives them rest and peace. King Asa even decides to remove his mother, Maacah, as the queen mother because of her devotion to Asherah, although she is not put to death, as the people's oath in 15:13 would have implied. The Chronicler states that Asa was not completely effective in removing all the high places of worship (in clear contradiction with 14:3), but still describes him as a king with a true heart.

Asa cannot counteract Israel's strategic fortification of Ramah, a city in the territory of Benjamin (4.3 miles north of Jerusalem), and has to resort to an alliance with the King of Aram, Ben-hadad, who resides in Damascus, to prevent its completion (16:1-14). The alliance produces the expected results. After Ben-hadad attacks the northern kingdom, Asa is able to take the fortification materials from Ramah to fortify Geba and Mizpah, two other cities in the territory of Benjamin. The story in Kings does not pass judgment on Asa's actions, but the Chronicler is critical of this foreign alliance. The prophet Hanani comes to Asa (16:7-10) and expresses God's condemnation of Asa for his lack of trust in the God of Israel. The theology of the Chronicler demands that kings should put their trust only in God. Asa's reaction is very different from his reaction to the oracle of the prophet Azariah (15:1-7); instead of obeying, he becomes angry. Instead of returning to God, Asa throws Hanani in jail. A king that leaves God cannot act justly with the people or his prophets. When Asa becomes sick, he fails again to look for God's assistance (see Exod. 15:26). Of course, nothing good can come from this act of disloyalty to the Lord. Asa does not recover, and dies.

■ THE TEXT IN THE INTERPRETIVE TRADITION

The speech of the prophet Azariah was interpreted by some commentators (Kimḥi and the eighteenth-century rabbi Yechiel Hillel Altschuler (Metzudos) as referring to the future, to what will happen if his message is ignored (Eisemann 1992, 106–7). The future without a "true God" symbolizes the years of exile that are coming, where life among idol worshipers equals a life without God. Theodoret of Cyrus reads it as portraying the impiety of the ten tribes who, because of their unfaithfulness, had been deprived of their priests and teachers (Conti, 281).

■ THE TEXT IN CONTEMPORARY DISCUSSION

Azariah's speech reflects an ancient cosmic vision dominant in the history of the Western world until the beginning of modernity. Today, the idea of gods that mingle in human affairs is not compatible with our understanding of the universe and should be left behind. We have learned that there is no assurance whatsoever that peace, prosperity, and blessings will come to those who seek the Lord. Perhaps the tragic deaths of Jesus, Mahatma Gandhi, Martin Luther King, and millions of observant Jews who perished in the Shoah are a painful reminder of that. We can, however, work with the idea that those who seek the Lord will be able to live a *meaningful* life, a life with purpose and fulfillment.

2 Chronicles 17:1—21:1: Jehoshaphat, Son of Asa

■ THE TEXT IN ITS ANCIENT CONTEXT

A faithful king, Jehoshaphat (17:1—21:1 // 1 Kgs. 15:24b; 22:1-36, 41-50a), is one of the Chronicler's favorite kings (along with Josiah and Hezekiah). The ongoing hostilities between the northern and southern kingdoms leads Jehoshaphat to fortify cities and to establish garrisons and outposts to prevent Israel from invading Judah. In this unstable situation, Jehoshaphat shows his faithfulness to God by rejecting Baal (17:3) and trusting God. Jehoshaphat's loyalty to God brings him prosperity and security. The mention of "great riches and honor" is similar to the Chronicler's rendering of the reigns of David and Solomon (see 1 Chron. 29:28; 2 Chron. 1:12). His educational efforts offer a concrete example of Jehoshaphat's faithfulness. He sends officials, Levites, and priests to teach

God's law in the cities of Judah. "2 Chronicles 17 is unique in reporting a royal mandate for disseminating torah" (Knoppers 1994, 63–64). This "mission" is, however, peculiar since teaching God's law was a prerogative of the priests (Lev. 10:11; Jer. 18:18; Ezek. 7:26). The exact nature of the "book of the law" that the group carried with them is uncertain. The existence of such a book is assumed in Deuteronomistic texts (Deut. 28:61; Josh. 1:8; 2 Kgs. 14:5). As a result of Jehoshaphat's faithfulness, God imposes fear on the surrounding countries, which not only refrain from attacking Judah but also bring Jehoshaphat tribute, increasing his wealth.

The passage 18:1—19:3 describes an alliance between Judah and the northern kingdom intended to attack the Aramean enclave of Ramoth-Gilead. The Chronicler explains, "Jehoshaphat had great riches and honor" (18:1), and did not need to enter into an alliance with Ahab, king of the unfaithful northern kingdom. However, Ahab "incited" him to do it (NRSV, "induced"), an expression that always has a negative connotation and outcome in the Bible. In the midst of optimistic oracles of victory and triumph, Jehoshaphat wants to hear what Micaiah son of Imlah (a prophet Ahab disliked because he always prophesied disasters) has to say. Micaiah reluctantly declares the word of God: disaster will indeed be the outcome of the battle (18:16). The parallel text in 1 Kgs. 22:32 reports that during the battle, Jehoshaphat, surrounded by the enemy, cries to his soldiers for help; in Chronicles, he asked God for help and is rescued (18:31). Ahab is wounded and does not outlive the day (18:34). Jehoshaphat returns to Jerusalem only to be admonished by the seer Jehu, son of Hanani (19:2).

After that, Jehoshaphat continues his reforms (19:4-11) by traveling around the country to bring the people back to the Lord and by appointing judges that will "judge not on behalf of human beings but on the Lord's behalf" (19:6). Jehoshaphat sets up a final appeals court in Jerusalem presided over by Amariah, the chief priest for religious matters, and by Zebadiah son of Ishmael, for civil matters (19:11).

In 20:1—21:1, the Chronicler reformulates the story in Kings to focus on God's reward for Jehoshaphat's piety. As is usual in Chronicles, the author highlights the religious elements, leaving aside the political or economic aspects of the conflict. The Chronicler reports that Jehoshaphat's reaction to the invasion was pious: "he set himself to seek the Lord, and proclaimed a fast throughout all Judah" (20:3). The Levite, Jahaziel son of Zechariah, proclaims an oracle of salvation: "Do not fear or be dismayed; tomorrow go out against them, and the Lord will be with you" (20:17; see Exod. 14:13-14; 1 Sam. 17:47). In the final section, the Chronicler reports again about the destiny of any alliance with the unfaithful. Jehoshaphat of Judah accepts a partnership with Ahaziah of Israel to build a fleet, and as expected the ships wreck and are not able to reach their destination (20:35-37).

▌ THE TEXT IN THE INTERPRETIVE TRADITION

Jehoshaphat was praised by Augustine, for he "possessed the justice that David first possessed and did not commit the sins that David later committed" (*Against the Pelagians* 2.21, in Conti, 282). Basil the Great exhorts one to take God's forgiving attitude as an example saying, "If you see your neighbor committing sin, take care not to dwell exclusively on his sin, but think of the many things that he has done and continues to do rightly" (*On Humility*, in Conti, 283). The Jewish sages saw

Jehoshaphat's alliance with Ahab negatively, and stated that Moses himself had to intercede centuries earlier for Jehoshaphat's life (*Sifre to Deuteronomy* 33:7). And according to a midrash it was Jehu's admonition that moved him to reform the judiciary.

▌The Text in Contemporary Discussion

The Hebrew Bible contains a strong message against political alliances with the impious, emphasizing trust in God as the only viable source of legitimation, political stability, peace, and prosperity. The risks of such alliances, as reflected in the alliance between Jehoshaphat and Ahab, are great and the danger of compromising the values of God's people is real. Today, globalization makes it difficult not to engage in alliances and partnership with countries where the freedoms that Western democracies consider basic human rights are limited or nonexistent. How can we work for human rights in countries like China and North Korea, where political persecution is the norm; or Muslim countries, where women are second-class citizens, gays and lesbians, are punished by death, and opting out of Islam also carries the death penalty? How are our values being compromised when we engage in alliances and partnership with such countries?

2 Chronicles 21:2—23:21: From Jehoram, Son of Jehoshaphat, to Athaliah, Mother of Ahaziah

▌The Text in Its Ancient Context

Jehoram, son of Jehoshaphat (21:2—22:1 // 1 Kgs. 22:50b; 2 Kgs. 8:17-24), marries a daughter of Ahab and falls to her idolatrous practices. He systematically kills every other possible candidate to the throne. The questionable behavior of the king naturally brings political calamities, and Jehoram is unable to maintain control over his dominion as the Edomites achieve liberation from the Judahite yoke (21:8-11). The Chronicler includes in this section a letter from the prophet Elijah (21:12-15), which is absent from the parallel story in Kings. The letter clearly reflects the Chronicler's theology of immediate retribution. Jehoram's sins are enumerated, and the prophet foretells the consequences of his behavior (21:13-15). This prophecy is fulfilled, and Jehoram dies a painful death (21:16-20).

Azariah, the youngest son of Jehoram, is then made king by the people (22:2-9 // 2 Kgs. 8:25—10:14). All of his older brothers had perished. Several kings appear in the Bible as being put in office by the people (Joash, Uzziah, Josiah, and Jehoahaz; see 2 Kgs. 11:12-20; 14:21; 21:24; 23:30 // 2 Chron. 23:1-3; 26:1; 33:24; 36:1). The Chronicler adds to the story in 2 Kings, suggesting that it was his mother and bad counselors who led him astray (22:3-4). The Chronicler alters Ahaziah's death story to reflect his pernicious alliance with the northern kingdom. His father's piety, however, prevents him from incurring the ultimate dishonor, and his body is properly buried.

Athaliah, mother of Ahaziah, follows him to the throne (22:10—23:21 // 2 Kgs. 11:1-20). In this section, the Chronicler follows the parallel story in Kings with only minimal variations. Details surrounding the foreign character of the troops brought to the house of the Lord (2 Kgs. 11:4) are omitted because they do not suit the theology of the Chronicler. Joash becomes king and Athaliah is sentenced to death by the priest Jehoiada, who leads a religious reform to return to traditional Yahwism.

■ THE TEXT IN THE INTERPRETIVE TRADITION

Augustine used the Philistines and Arab invasion of Judah (21:16-17) as an example of God's stirring up enemies "to lay waste those countries that he judges to be deserving of such punishment" (*On Grace and Free Will*, 21:42; Conti, 284–85). In a similar vein, Rabbi Yechiel Hillel Altschuler Metzudos explains that "God stimulated Philistia's natural greed" (Eisemann 1992, 156). Athaliah's story, however, is what captured most of the attention of the Western world. In 1691, Jean Racine wrote a play about her, and Mendelssohn and Handel used it as the basis for musical compositions.

■ THE TEXT IN CONTEMPORARY DISCUSSION

Religious-based violence was a common phenomenon in the world of the Bible, but today, with some exceptions, violence in the name of religion or religious orthodoxy is something that most religions reject. Centuries ago, however, millions died as a result of religious wars. The Islamic conquest of the Middle East, North Africa, and half of the Iberian Peninsula (seventh to eighth centuries); the Christian Crusades (eleventh to thirteenth centuries) and the Spanish *Reconquista* (eighth to fifteenth centuries); and the European religious wars among Christian factions of sixteenth and seventeenth centuries are just a few clear examples of how religious irrationality can lead people to abhorrent, violent behavior. Violence in the name of religion makes many wonder if religious convictions are the cause for more harm than good.

2 Chronicles 24:1—28:27: From Joash, Son of Ahaziah, to Ahaz, Son of Jotham

■ THE TEXT IN ITS ANCIENT CONTEXT

Joash's reign (24:1-27 // 2 Kgs. 11:21—12:21) is clearly influenced by the life and death of Jehoiada the priest. While Jehoiada is alive, Joash acts faithfully (24:2). After Jehoiada dies, the king abandons the beliefs of his advisor and faces the disastrous consequences of such defiance. During his faithful period, the king restores the temple, but after the death of Jehoiada, the king and the nobles reject the faithful priest's reforms and even kill Jehoiada's son, the prophet Zechariah. His last wish, "May the LORD see and avenge!" (24:22) will be fulfilled. Verses 23-27 provide additional information to the story about Joash in Kings: the army of Aram attacks Judah and Jerusalem "with few men" (24:24), but they achieve a decisive victory because God has abandoned Joash. He is wounded in battle and killed in his bed by his own servants.

The reign of Amaziah (25:1—26:2 // 2 Kgs. 14:1-17) follows a similar pattern to the reign of Joash. There is a period of faithfulness and prosperity during which the king listens to God's prophet and accepts his advice (25:1-13), followed by unfaithfulness and disaster when the king disregards the message of the prophet (25:14-24). His first action is to take revenge for his father's death, killing those responsible but not their children (see Deut. 24:16; Jer. 31:29-30; Ezek. 18:20). The Chronicler expands the only verse in Kings about the campaign against Edom. There is a census before the campaign (see 1 Chron. 21; 2 Chron. 14:8; 2 Chron. 17:14-19), and the king hires mercenaries from the northern kingdom, but a prophet prevents them from participating in the battle. God is not with Israel. Still, if the people of the northern kingdom return to God with all their hearts, God will return to them (see 2 Chron. 15:2). The victory is not the result of human efforts but the direct consequence of relying on God. Paradoxically, it is the booty that Amaziah brings back with him that causes his future downfall. He takes the Edomite gods and worships them. A prophet rebukes the king, but is threatened. Amaziah's destiny is sealed.

The theology of the Chronicler is evident in the differences from the story in Kings, particularly when narrating Amaziah's war against Joash, king of Israel (25:17-28). The announcement of the prophet of God to Amaziah is fulfilled (25:20), and the king faces a terrible defeat, followed by the plundering of the royal residence and the temple.

Two different periods marked by the king's faithfulness (16:3-15) and unfaithfulness to God (26:16-23) also characterize the reign of Uzziah (26:3-23 // 2 Kgs. 14:21—15:4). In his youth, the king follows the good counsel of Zechariah, "who instructed him in the fear of God; and as long as he sought the LORD, God made him prosper" (26:5). But arrogance leads to transgression, and the king encroaches on the privileges of the priests to make the offerings (26:18). The story in Kings does not explain why Uzziah becomes leprous. For the Chronicler, it is clear; God struck him (26:20). Before falling in disgrace, Uzziah leads successful military campaigns. His building projects improve the defense system of the city of Jerusalem and support agriculture, "for he loved the soil" (26:10). His last days are spent in isolation due to his illness, and his son Jotham exercises authority until Uzziah dies. The sequence of faithfulness, prosperity, arrogance, and disgrace is apparent here once more.

Uzziah's leprosy is a living example for Jotham, his son, of the consequences of violating the sanctuary's holiness (27:1-9 // 2 Kgs. 15:33-38). He continues to reinforce the defensive fortifications in Judah. The Chronicler adds to his canonical source in 27:3b-6. Jotham's triumphs in battle and the tribute he receives are the result of his faithfulness because "he ordered his ways before the LORD" (27:6).

The Chronicler portrays Ahaz, son of Jotham, quite negatively (28:1-27 // 2 Kgs. 16:1-12). While in Kings one finds the expression "the LORD his God" (2 Kgs. 16:2), the Chronicler omits "his God," emphasizing the distance between this king and God. The most important event during his life is the Syro-Ephraimite War (see 2 Kgs. 15:27; 16:5; Isa. 7:1-17; Hosea 5:8-15). The result of this war, which exemplifies Ahaz's unfaithfulness, differs considerably in Chronicles from the text in Kings. Jerusalem does not fall in Kings; it does in Chronicles, and booty and captives are taken away from the sacred city. The captives taken by the northern kingdom will return, however, due to the intervention of the prophet Oded. The prophet points out that despite the constant strife between the northern and southern kingdoms, they are still one people.

God shows his displeasure with both Judah and Israel, but denounces the northern kingdom for repeated unfaithfulness (28:13b). The war leaves Judah vulnerable, whereupon the Edomites and the

Philistines take advantage of the situation. Ahaz should ask the Lord for help, but against Isaiah's advice (Isaiah 7), he asks the king of Assyria for help (28:16), and Ahaz is forced to accept Assyrian hegemony. The temple of God is shut down and the Baals are worshiped. It is possible that Ahaz even used the temple to worship pagan deities (see 2 Kings 16), but the Chronicler omits that possibility in order to preserve the sanctity of the temple. According to the Chronicler, Ahaz's burial outside of the royal burial ground, separated from his ancestors, is his punishment (see 2 Kgs. 16:20).

▌ THE TEXT IN THE INTERPRETIVE TRADITION

Uzziah's punishment for encroaching on the rights and privileges of the priests was used as a model in the early church to assure the exclusive rights of priests and bishops to perform their duties: "so also do you do nothing without the bishop. . . . So every lay person shall not be unpunished who despises God, and is so mad as to affront his priests and unjustly to snatch that honor to himself" (*Constitutions of the Holy Apostles* 2.27, in Conti, 292). Also Pseudo-Dionysius stated, "Surely, there was nothing unseemly in the fact that Uzziah burned incense in honor of God. . . . And yet the Word of God bars anyone who has taken over a task that is not for him" (*Letter* 8, in Conti, 293). The Jewish sages interpreted Uzziah's transgression as sinful pride and concluded that "one of the causes of leprosy is unjustified pride" (Tanchuma Metzora 3, in Eisemann 1992, 205).

▌ THE TEXT IN CONTEMPORARY DISCUSSION

The example of Uzziah is instructive in the sense that he tries to prevent the political powers from encroaching on the religious realm, thereby preventing an unsafe concentration of power. Such radical separation of "church and state" is one of the bases of Western democracies and the natural outcome of the Enlightenment. Within the religious communities themselves, however, the exclusive rights of priests to perform certain functions and rites has developed in a tradition of discrimination against females and sexual minorities, who have been traditionally excluded from clergy positions. Islam and Roman Catholicism are examples of such discriminatory practices.

2 Chronicles 29:1—33:25: Hezekiah, Manasseh, and Amon

▌ THE TEXT IN ITS ANCIENT CONTEXT

The restoration of the temple and the renovation of the covenant are the first steps in Hezekiah's religious reform (29:1-36). Hezekiah's speech offers another good example of the Chronicler's theology. The sin of the ancestors brought God's ire on the people, but Hezekiah becomes an agent of divine reconciliation. The sacrifices for the rededication of the temple follow the instructions of Lev. 17:6 and Num. 18:17, including offerings and burnt offerings (see Leviticus 1), and sacrifices of peace (see Lev. 7:11).

From a private family celebration (Exod. 12:1-2), the Passover became a public festival (30:1-27). It also offered the occasion to call the northern kingdom to return to God (30:6). The Passover is celebrated by all the people at the temple. Letters are sent to all Israel emphasizing the religious unity of the people and inviting them to return to the Lord (30:6, 9). The holy city is cleansed from shrines for Baal, and the Levites offer sacrifices for the people. The arrival of ritually impure refugees from the northern kingdom presents a theological challenge that the Chronicler resolves by inserting Hezekiah's prayer, asking God to pardon those people.

Sennacherib reigned in Assyria from 721 to 681 BCE. His campaign in Canaan aimed, among other things, at punishing disloyal vassals. The story in Chronicles of the Assyrian invasion (32:1-33) contains differences from the story in Kings: it adds a description of the defense system prepared by Hezekiah, omits the alliance with Egypt (an act for which previous kings have been punished), and omits the paying of tribute to Assyria. These omissions are meant to uphold the image of Hezekiah as a just king, who dies honored and respected by all the people (32:33).

Manasseh becomes king when he is only twelve years old, and the Chronicler portrays the first part of his fifty-five-year reign (33:1-20) as a systematic program to overturn the religious reforms of his father, Hezekiah. Immediate retribution follows, and Manasseh is taken captive by the Assyrians. When he prays to God (33:12), God hears his prayer and restores him (an event not mentioned in Kings). The Chronicler demonstrates that God hears the prayers of the humble (see 2 Chronicles 6). After Manasseh turns back to God, he begins a building program to repair the walls of Jerusalem (33:14; see 1 Chron. 11:8; 2 Chron. 26:9; 27:3-4), reorganizes the army in Judean cities (see 2 Chron. 11:5-12; 14:6; 17:12-19), and restores the Yahwistic faith. All of these actions are appropriate for a just king. The summary of Manasseh's reign reflects two aspects of his behavior: his apostasy and his repentance. The brief reign of Amnon (33:21-25) closely follows the description in Kings (2 Kgs. 21:21-22), adding that Amnon never repented (33:23). He is portrayed as an evil king whose death at the hands of his servants seems to be the natural consequence of his impiety.

▌ THE TEXT IN THE INTERPRETIVE TRADITION

John Chrysostom writes, "For so Manasseh had perpetuated innumerable pollutions, having both stretched out his hands against the saints, and brought abominations into the temple, and filled the city with murders and wrought many other things beyond excuse, yet nevertheless after so long and so great wickedness, he washed away from himself all these things. How and in what manner? By repentance and consideration" (*Homilies in the Gospel of Matthew* 22:6, in Conti, 299).

▌ THE TEXT IN CONTEMPORARY DISCUSSION

The Bible postulates that repentance leads to God's forgiveness and restoration. No matter how serious the crimes of the kings of Israel, there is always a chance to return to God and make amends. The rabbis came to terms with the fact that leaders are prone to sin. Sforno commented on the expression "When a leader sins . . ." (Lev. 4:22): "for, after all, it is expected that he will sin." Today we see quite often how political leaders trespass accepted social norms or engage in questionable behavior, and ask for forgiveness from their families and constituents. After a while, they are back running for office. While forgiveness seems to work well within the political realm, there are few attempts to introduce the concept of forgiveness in our legal system, which more often than not fails to reach those in positions of leadership. Should the Chronicler's concept of repentance-forgiveness-restoration have a wider role in the way we deal with social trespasses and crimes?

2 Chronicles 34:1—36:23: Josiah and Last Kings of Judah

▊ THE TEXT IN ITS ANCIENT CONTEXT

Josiah (34:1—36:1 // 2 Kgs. 22:1—23:30 // 1 Esd. 1:1-33), along with David, Solomon, Asa, Jeho-shaphat, and Hezekiah, belongs to a select group of kings favored by the Chronicler. He becomes king at a very young age, which suggests that the group who brought him to power, the "people of the land," dictated most of his policies. The Chronicler reinforces the positive evaluation of Josiah found in 2 Kgs. 22:1-2 by adding information about his early piety (34:3-7).

In Chronicles, the discovery of the book of the law (34:8-33) is the consequence of a program of religious reform already in place instead of, like in Kings, the result of a fortuitous finding. Josiah's reforms seem to be patterned according to the regulations of Deuteronomy 12 (cf. 2 Chron. 34:24 with Deut. 27:9-26; 28:15-68). The book makes Josiah aware of how unfaithful his father has been. The prophet Huldah confirms his sense that God's punishment is on the horizon (34:24), but the imminence of the punishment does not prevent the renewal of the covenant. The book of the law then becomes the book of the covenant (34:30). The narrative closely follows the story in Kings, but prophets become Levites in Chronicles (34:30; cf. 2 Kgs. 23:2) in harmony with the Chronicler's attribution of prophetic ministry to the Levites (see 1 Chron. 25:1; 2 Chron. 20:14; 29:30).

The Passover celebration is the climax of Josiah's reign. It takes place in Jerusalem, following the precedent established by Hezekiah. The Chronicler considers this celebration a return to the faithful days of Samuel. Paradoxically, the faithful king Josiah dies tragically for not heeding the word of God conveyed to him by Pharaoh. Instead of retreating from battle, Josiah rides to his death.

The death of Josiah leaves the "people of the land" in power again. They skip the firstborn Eli-akim and set Jehoahaz on the throne (36:1-4). Pharaoh Neco intervenes, deposing and deporting him to Egypt. Neco declares Eliakim the new king, changing his name to Jehoiakim.

Eliakim/Jehoiakim reigns for eleven years (36:5-8), but the destiny of Judah has already been decided. Their alliance with Egypt makes them an enemy of Babylon, and Egypt is no match for the powerful Babylonians. After they defeated the Egyptian army in 605 BCE, there was no one who could oppose their might. The city of Jerusalem was captured on March of 597 BCE and the elite deported to Babylon. According to Kings, Jehoiakim dies in Jerusalem, but in Chronicles he is taken captive to Babylon.

Jehoiachin, son of Eliakim/Jehoiakim, seems to have been a precocious rebel. The Chronicler reports that at the age of eight he has already begun to do what is bad in the eyes of the Lord (36:9-10). Immediate retribution follows, and within a year he is taken captive to Babylon with the rest of the vessels of the temple.

Jehoiachin's brother Zedekiah was supposed to rule under Babylonian supervision (36:11-13), but the urge to rebel was growing among the elite and the people. After eleven years, Zedekiah rejected Jeremiah's message and rebelled against Nebuchadnezzar. The consequences were tragic; in July 587, after a short-lived rebellion, the Babylonians destroyed the city and the Temple and took thousands as exiles to Babylon.

The last verses in Chronicles (36:14-23 // Ezra 1:1-3) fulfill Jeremiah's words of hope (Jer. 25:11-12; 29:10), as Kalimi states, "showing the fulfillment of God's word in history is one of the Chronicler's literary features" (2005a, 148). The exile comes to an end, and the people return to the land. God has kept his promise.

▌THE TEXT IN THE INTERPRETIVE TRADITION

Kimhi quotes the sages (*b. Yoma* 52b) who clarified that the scroll was found rolled to the passage of the admonitions (Deut. 28:15), "the Lord will drive you" and so on, as one of the consequences of the passage that begins "But if you will not obey the Lord . . . , then all these curses shall come upon you and overtake you" (Berger, 274). Josiah's reform received high praise, which tended to expand its reach. Some commentators note, "With zeal immense, Josiah, himself a prince, acted in such a way as no one before or after him had ever done!—Idols he dethroned, destroyed unhallowed temples. Burned with fire priests on their altars; all the bones of false prophets were dug up; the altars burned. The carcasses to be consumed did serve for fuel" (Pseudo-Tertullian, *ANF* 4:153–54, in Conti, 301). Josiah's tragic death was explained as a result of his not listening to the words of the Lord (Jerome, *Against the Pelagians* 2.22, in Conti, 302).

▌THE TEXT IN CONTEMPORARY DISCUSSION

Religious tolerance is one of the values sorely missing in Scripture. Religion played a different role in ancient societies, where there was no difference between a secular and a religious realm as understood today by most Western societies. On the one hand, it would be extremely difficult for us to grasp what was really at stake behind such religious zeal. On the other hand, it would be a terrible mistake to accept or to justify contemporary expressions of religious intolerance because they are based on ancient texts that religious communities today accept as divinely inspired.

Works Cited

Ben Zvi, Ehud. 2006. *History, Literature and Theology in the Book of Chronicles*. London: Equinox.

Berger, Yitzhak. 2007. *The Commentary of Rabbi David Kimhi to Chronicles: A Translation with Introduction and Supercommentary*. BJS 345. Providence: Brown University.

Conti, Marco, ed. 2008. *1–2 Kings, 1–2 Chronicles, Ezra, Nehemiah, Esther*. Ancient Christian Commentary on Scripture, Old Testament 5. Downers Grove, IL: InterVarsity Press.

Eisemann, Moshe. 1987. *Divrei Hayamim I*. New York: ArtScroll.

———. 1992. *Divrei Hayamim II*. New York: ArtScroll.

Franke, John R. 2005. *Joshua, Judges, Ruth, 1-2 Samuel*. Ancient Christian Commentary on Scripture, Old Testament 4. Downers Grove, IL: InterVarsity Press.

Graham, M. Patrick, Kenneth G. Hoglund, and Steven L. McKenzie, eds. 1997. *The Chronicler as Historian*. Sheffield: Sheffield University Press.

Japhet, Sara. 1968. "The Supposed Common Authorship of Chronicles, Ezra and Nehemiah." *VT* 18:330–71.

———. 1989. *The Ideology of the Book of Chronicles and Its Place in Biblical Thought*. Frankfurt am Main: Peter Lang.

———. 1993. *1 and 2 Chronicles: A Commentary*. OTL. Louisville: Westminster John Knox.

Johnson, Marshall D. 1988. *The Purpose of Biblical Geneaologies with Special Reference to the Setting of the Geneaologies of Jesus,* 2nd ed. Cambridge: Cambridge University Press.

Kalimi, Isaac. 2005a. *An Ancient Israelite Historian: Studies in the Chronicler, His Time, Place and Writing*. Aasen, Norway: Van Gorcum.

———. 2005b. *The Reshaping of Israelite History in Chronicles*. Winona Lake, IN: Eisenbrauns.

———. 2009a. *The Retelling of Chronicles in Jewish Tradition and Literature: A Historical Journey*. Winona Lake, IN: Eisenbrauns.

———. 2009b. "Placing the Chronicler in His Own Historical Context: A Closer Examination." *JNES* 68:179–92.

Klein, Ralph W. 2006. *1 Chronicles: A Commentary*. Hermeneia. Philadelphia: Fortress Press.

———. 2012. *2 Chronicles: A Commentary*. Hermeneia. Philadelphia: Fortress Press.

Knoppers, Gary N. 1994. "Jehoshaphat's Judiciary and the Scroll of YHWH's Torah." *JBL* 113:59–80.

———. 2003. *1 Chronicles 1–9. A New Translation with Introduction and Commentary*. AB 12. New York: Doubleday.

———. 2004. *1 Chronicles 10–29: A New Translation with Introduction and Commentary*. AB 12. New York: Doubleday.

Rad, Gerhard von. 1966. "The Levitical Sermons in I & II Chronicles." In *The Problem of the Hexateuch and Other Essays*. Edinburgh and London: Oliver & Boyd, 267–80.

Saltman, Avrom. 1978. *Stephen Langton Commentary on the Book of Chronicles*. Ramat Gan, Israel: Bar-Ilan University Press.

Stokes, Ryan E. 2009. "The Devil Made David Do It . . . Or *Did* He? The Nature, Identity, and Literary Origins of the *Satan* in 1 Chronicles 21:1." *JBL* 128:91–106.

Wilcock, Michael. 1987. *The Message of Chronicles*. Downers Grove, IL: InterVarsity Press.

Williamson, H. G. M. 1977. *Israel in the Book of Chronicles*. Cambridge: Cambridge University Press.

Wilson, Robert R. 1977. *Genealogy and History in the Biblical World*. New Haven: Yale University Press.

Ezra-Nehemiah

Katherine E. Southwood

Introduction

A key theme in the books of Ezra and Nehemiah is the return from exile and the rebuilding of the temple in Jerusalem. Readers are told within the first few verses of Ezra that the Lord "stirred" the spirit of Cyrus king of Persia to build a temple in Jerusalem and to allow those in exile to return there and build it (cf. Isaiah 44–45). This description of events is often compared to scholarly interpretations of various sources of evidence, each with its own bias, concerning the postexilic context, Persian attitudes to local religions, the movement of populations, and taxation. Cyrus posed a fatal threat to the Neo-Babylonian Empire. He attacked Babylonia in 539 BCE, and after a battle at Orpis the Babylonian ruler Nabonidus was captured. Cyrus entered Babylon, the capital city, in triumph the same year. One of the most prominent sources connecting Cyrus's rise to power and the rebuilding of the Jerusalem temple is the Cyrus Cylinder. Although its propagandistic and stereotypical nature should be noted, the Cyrus Cylinder is a vital piece of evidence that portrays the potential, under Persian imperial leadership, for exiled communities to return to their homelands: "The cities beyond the Tigris, whose dwellings had long lain in ruins. . . . All their people I gathered, and brought them back to their dwelling places." Despite the favorable bias of both presentations of Cyrus, events may have been more connected to the economic organization of the empire into taxable satrapies and provinces, as described by Herodotus, while the portrayal may have been more concerned with gaining the loyalty of subjects and ensuring against rebellions.

Indeed, we have no evidence of any formal Persian policy or recognition of the gods of subject peoples. Nevertheless, there is evidence of the Persians responding to the requests and complaints of the local peoples, including those relating to cultic practice. For example, some of the letters found at Elephantine illustrate Persian authorization for the rebuilding of a Jewish temple that was previously destroyed (TAD A4.9) following a failed request for help from the Jerusalem temple and another, twice drafted, request to the Persians (TAD A4.7; A4.8).

Numerous other inscriptions also illustrate how the Persians reacted to local cultic matters. The Xanthus trilingual inscription, in Aramaic, Greek, and Lycian, which authorizes a cult in Xanthus, shows how the Persian government dealt with the establishment of a local cult. It is striking that nothing within the inscription suggests that the Persians provided any financial support for the cult except to give permission for it to be established. All the expenses, including the donation of land, seem to have been provided by the local community requesting to have the cult established. Likewise, with some similarities to Ezra and Nehemiah, the Udjahorresnet inscription portrays how Udjahorresnet, a high official in contact with the Cambyses, made a petition concerning all the foreigners who dwelled in the temple of Neith in order to have them expelled and to demolish their homes and all their unclean things that were in the temple. Thus, while the Persians continued what was already general policy in the Near Eastern empires—to declare their personal piety in the inscriptions of how they were diligent to obey their god(s) and follow his (their) will, and so on—it is probable that exiled communities such as those described in Ezra would have been expected to support the rebuilding of the temple themselves.

The restoration of the temple provides a physical symbol in the text for the restoration of the postexilic Judean community. As such, striking similarities between the books, and the leaders themselves, occur. Both Ezra and Nehemiah are Jewish officials or leaders (Ezra 7:1-10; Neh. 2:1-2) who become concerned about the state of affairs among the Jews in Jerusalem. Both seek permission from the Persian monarch to carry out their mission (Ezra, implied in 7:6; Neh. 2:1-4); both preside over a number of significant reforms in the Jewish communities in Jerusalem; both write of their experiences in the first person; both are threatened by "foreigners," whether through intermarriage (Ezra 9–10; Neh. 9–10; 13:1-3, 23-31) or harassment (Ezra 4–6; Neh. 4:1-2; 6). Although only a little of the text appears at Qumran, this perceived threat from outsiders may be relevant for discerning the influence of the Ezra material on the sectarian Qumran community, which may have understood itself as the continuation of the postexilic community, as the image of the "holy seed" (Ezra 9:2), developing into a "plant root" in the Damascus Document, a manuscript that forms part of the literature discovered at Qumran dating from about 100 CE, may indicate (CD XVII; Blenkinsopp 2009, 189–227). Likewise, although 1 Maccabees does not refer to Ezra and Nehemiah, the author may nevertheless have been influenced by this construction of Jewish identity (Becking, 143–54).

Opposition to ethnic intermarriage, which emphasizes the perceived threat posed by so-called foreigners, concludes both books. As such, despite the material's age, it is relevant as an illustration of the logic of, and flaws of, ethnic exclusivity nowadays. Rather than interpreting difference as a source of wonder and interest, the narratives represent the failure to tolerate foreign influence. However, what is interesting about this portrayal of ethnic identity is its probable development as a result of return-migration from exile to the homeland (Southwood 2012). As such, the text provides an illustration of the complex impacts migration can have on identity, both for those who migrate and for receiving communities.

The lack of any definite conclusion within both books has activated two responses. Initially, there has been some speculation in later texts regarding the fate of the two leaders. Second Maccabees

1:18-36 depicts Nehemiah as a model legitimating the activities of Judas Maccabeus, but also connecting him to the first temple through the fire on the altar that was never to go out (Lev. 6:12-13). Similarly, despite rabbinic tradition's having Ezra die in Babylon, Josephus eulogizes Ezra, claiming "it was his fate, after being honoured by the people, to die an old man and to be buried with great magnificence in Jerusalem" (*Antiquities* 11.158). The second response to the indefinite, incomplete endings of both books has been the apparent disappearance from written records of the two figures until Ezra's revival in the apocalyptic work *4 Ezra* around the year 100 BCE. Soon afterward, he becomes the second Moses in rabbinic tradition.

Ezra 1–6: The Return from Exile and Rebuilding of the Jerusalem Temple

▋ THE TEXT IN ITS ANCIENT CONTEXT

One controversial area within Ezra concerns the various supposedly "authentic" documents that are used to substantiate the temple's legitimacy both in terms of YHWH's support and of Persian imperial endorsement. These documents consist of Cyrus's decrees, which occur in both Hebrew and Aramaic and frame the first section of the book (Ezra 1:2-4; 6:3-12), and of correspondences between the Persian king Darius and officials in Yehud—Rehum the chancellor and Shimshai the secretary, and colleagues, Tattenai, the governor, and Shethar-bozenai (Ezra 4:6-22; 5:6—6:12)—who accuse the Jews of rebellion but eventually establish, having found Cyrus's decree at Ecbathana, the temple's entitlement to be rebuilt (Ezra 6:1-12). Finally, an edict from King Artaxerxes (Ezra 7:11-27), which bestows Ezra with power in Yehud, establishes, at a narrative level, the complete support of the Persian authorities concerning the Jerusalem temple.

The chronology of these letters is confused. Ezra 6:22 refers to the king of Assyria either as a deliberate anachronism or a mistake. Likewise, if taken as a whole, the narrative concerning the rebuilding of the temple jumps from the reign of Darius (522–486 BCE) to his successor Ahasuerus's reign (486–465 BCE; Ezra 4:6), following which point the narrative jumps to correspondence with Artaxerxes I (465–424 BCE; Ezra 4:7-23), before returning to Darius (Ezra 4:24).

Many scholars doubt the supposed authenticity of the Cyrus decree for some of the following reasons. First, like the Cyrus Cylinder, with which the decree is compared and which mentions only "Sumer and Akkad," the Ezra documents suggest direct Persian interest in Yehud. Second, Cyrus is referred to as "king of Persia," an epithet that only occurs in Jewish documents (Ezra 1:1, 8; 4:3, 5; Dan. 10:1). Third, the Cyrus Cylinder is propagandistic and illustrates Persian toleration of local cults, like the Assyrians and Babylonians tolerated such cults. However, the "decrees" within Ezra actually promote the Jerusalem temple. Fourth, there is no reason why Cyrus would have specifically supported a minority ethnic group at such an early point in his reign. Finally, the decrees themselves are full of Jewish theology, relating to the size of the temple, its vessels, and using the designation "the Lord God of Israel," language that recalls how the Israelites left Egypt (Exod. 12:35-36). However, there is no reason for a Persian king to have embraced such language or concepts (Grabbe, 272–75).

Similarly, objections pertain to the documents concerning the reported rebellious nature of the Jews from the officials in Yehud. Despite the careful writing of such documents in the style of and according to standardized literary conventions for letter writing, and in the Aramaic language, the contents of such documents are nevertheless highly suspect. A similar argument may be made concerning the census of returnees in Ezra 2, which may mimic the beginning of the book of Numbers, as the Israelites resumed their journey toward the promised land. Since linking the return from Babylon and the exodus is prominent in Isaiah 40–55, there is reason to suspect the author of Ezra may be using the same underlying concepts, despite the formal presentation of the material.

▌ THE TEXT IN THE INTERPRETIVE TRADITION

The influence of the return narrative in Ezra is significant. Much of the postbiblical Jewish theology and literature concerns a hope for restoration from foreign domination and the gathering of one people around a new and glorified temple. For example, the rise of Jewish nationalism in the Second Temple period is particularly pronounced (Goodblatt). First and Second Maccabees sharply differentiate between Jew and non-Jew/Judaism and Hellenism. Likewise, *1 Esdras* 3–4 (the tale of the bodyguards) illustrates how the builder of the Second Temple came to accomplish this feat and depicts the wisdom of a Jewish youth in contrast to his gentile colleagues within the Mesopotamian court. Similarly, the book of Tobit envisages the return from exile, the rebuilding of the Jerusalem temple, and then in the end time the rebuilding of a glorious Jerusalem. This rebuilt temple later becomes an eschatological expectation in literature such as *1 Enoch* 91, and in the literature from Qumran where the community stands in opposition to the Jerusalem temple, it constitutes an interim temple, and inspires hopes for the establishment of a future temple. Similarly, the author of the *Apocalypse of Abraham* maintains eschatological hopes for a restored temple and sacrificial system for Israel. Later in the book of Revelation, the image of the eschatological temple becomes somewhat dominant.

▌ THE TEXT IN CONTEMPORARY DISCUSSION

The major themes of the narrative within Ezra 1–6 are the importance of exclusivity in rebuilding the temple and community in Jerusalem and the level of opposition the community encounters from "foreigners," or those who are already on the land. Particularly revealing is the narrative within Ezra 4:1-5, when a group of people, deemed by the author "adversaries of Judah and Benjamin," have their offer to assist in the rebuilding of the temple rejected. Following this, the "people of the land" weaken and trouble the rebuilding work and hire councilors to frustrate it (after which point the Aramaic documents accusing the Jews of rebellion appear in the narrative). Labeling such perceived opponents "people of the land" is interesting, especially in light of the fact that in the rest of the Hebrew Bible, as well as in later rabbinic literature, it usually refers to "Israel." Nevertheless, within Ezra, such "nations of the land" are placed in a dichotomous relationship to the "children of Israel" who are confined to the group that came out of exile and who must be purified from the uncleanness of the people of the land: "And the children of Israel, which were come again out of exile, and all such as had separated themselves unto them from the uncleanness of the nations of the land" (Ezra 6:21). Such binary distinctions between return-migrants and those who have remained in their homelands are not uncommon in light of modern discussions of ethnic identity. For example, ethnic Japanese who were born and raised in Brazil have, on return to Japan, experienced alienation and marginalization and as a result no longer understand Japan as their real homeland. They experience the return as a "re-diasporization" (Southwood 2012).

Ezra 7–8: The Figure of Ezra

■ THE TEXT IN ITS ANCIENT CONTEXT

The character of Ezra only emerges within the narrative at chapter 7, where he is introduced with Aaronic lineage, as a "priest" and "a scribe of the law of the God of heaven" who "had set his heart to study the law of the LORD, and to do it, and to teach the statutes and ordinances in Israel" (Ezra 7:1-5, 10, 12). This illustration of Ezra's legitimacy is further emphasized through a royal edict from Artaxerxes, which establishes Ezra's authority in terms of royal support (Ezra 7:11-26). The blessing at the end of the letter also emphasizes Ezra's divine support and ensures that readers understand that it is YHWH who has stirred the Persian monarch into action: "Blessed be the LORD, the God of our ancestors, who put such a thing as this into the heart of the king . . . and who extended to me steadfast love before the king and his counselors, and before all the king's mighty officers" (Ezra 7:27-28).

Finally, the letter refers to the "good hand of God" upon Ezra, a phrase that, alongside the "eye of God," occurs several times throughout the book to emphasize divine favor (Ezra 8:18 cf. 5:5; 7:6, 9, 28; 8:18, 22, 31).

Several critical issues arise in relation to the letter. Initially, it is specified that Ezra is to "make inquiries" concerning Judah and Jerusalem according to the law he possesses (Ezra 7:14). Precisely what is meant by such a term is unclear, and one cannot straightforwardly assume that it amounts to the same thing as "impose" the law, as the intermarriage episode in Ezra 9–10 may be thought to imply. Nevertheless, one wonders what utility an investigation regarding the law may have had. Elsewhere in Ezra, the verb that is used refers only to searching for records (Ezra 4:15, 19; 5:17; 6:1), and it does not occur in Imperial Aramaic, so there is very little evidence to hand that might help us understand the nature of Ezra's mission. A second problem is how to interpret the term "law." Should we imagine the Aramaic term for law has the same resonances as the Hebrew term *torah*, or might we suggest that what is at stake is the Deuteronomic lawcode? Or should we assume that Persian law is at stake since the letter supposedly arises from Artaxerxes, the Persian monarch? Is the "law" being referred to as some kind of a preliminary version of the Mosaic law, which would later become the Pentateuch? The Aramaic term for "law" that is used here also occurs in Daniel, where it refers to law more generally and includes instructions, edicts, and "the law of the Medes and Persians" (Dan. 2:9, 13; 6:5, 8, 12, 15; 7:25). Again, therefore, the language used is unclear and open to interpretation.

Finally, the letter suggests that all the silver and gold in the satrapy of Babylon is to be given to the temple in Jerusalem, alongside anything freely given and to be used for purchasing animals, grain, and drink. Any other needs are to be paid for from the royal treasury (Ezra 7:19-22). This superabundant generosity sounds more like the "wishful thinking of a Jewish apologist" than reality, and raises the question of why Ezra does not occupy a more official role such as satrap or governor of the territory of Judah, including Jerusalem (Grabbe, 326).

Chapter 8 opens with a list of the heads of the fathers and the genealogy of those who returned from exile in Babylon (8:2-14). The list is organized into families in which a remote ancestor is named and then the immediate head of the family; thus, the list begins with the son and grandson of Aaron (Ithamar and Phinehas). Interestingly, the list contrasts rather sharply with the list provided within Ezra 2 and Nehemiah 7. The list's authenticity is debated; nevertheless, one of its functions appears to be to legitimize the group who returned from exile to Jerusalem through their priestly heritage. There follows a narrative concerning the fast by the Ahava, conducted in order that the group should humble themselves before God and to ask for safe passage, since Ezra claims to have been too ashamed to ask the king for help (Ezra 8:22). This marks a stark contrast to Nehemiah, who travels with letters, army officers, and cavalry from the king (Neh. 2:9).

■ THE TEXT IN THE INTERPRETIVE TRADITION

The figure of Ezra, who is often portrayed as lawgiver, has influenced later Jewish tradition, appearing as a paradigmatic scholar and as the second Moses. The introduction of the Hebrew square script is attributed to him, as well as the bringing together of the collection of the canonical writings of the Hebrew Bible after the exile. Although modern scholars have argued for separate authorship of Chronicles and of Ezra–Nehemiah, the Babylonian Talmud declares Ezra to be the author of the books of Chronicles and large portions of Ezra (*B. Bat.* 15a; *Sanh.* 93b; Williamson 1977; Japhet). Furthermore, the image of Ezra reading the law with a scroll can be found in the synagogue of Dura-Europos (c. 250 CE).

■ THE TEXT IN CONTEMPORARY DISCUSSION

One of the many themes running throughout Ezra, but especially dominant within chapters 7–8, is the search for validity and authority. Such concerns are as real today as they were when Ezra was written. For example, many legal systems that are considered authoritative initially require that laws are valid, sometimes with the result that communities sense a moral obligation to obey the law. However, the perspective of the author or editor of the material in Ezra regarding the dominant source of authority is somewhat complex. Rather than acting autonomously, the Persian kings are portrayed as puppets who carry out YHWH's will for the good of the group who are returning from exile, just as YHWH "hardened" Pharaoh's heart in the struggle to leave Egypt (see Knowles). Likewise, what brings the law legitimacy is the idea of divine support and having the correct lineage. In many ways, the need for such recognition suggests some degree of instability and self-doubt. Rather than assuming divine support, evidence of such must be searched for in records and documents and behind the actions of those in power. Rather than assuming legitimacy, genealogies must be consulted or invented to prove the fact. Matters of power and legitimacy certainly do not disappear in later literature. In many ways, Paul's thinking on the matter is similar to that of the author or editor of Ezra, as he claims "every person is subject to higher powers, for there is no power but of God: the powers that exist are ordained of God" (Rom. 13:1). However, such thinking may be at risk of almost divinizing those in power. Ezra's God is a God who also appointed the Babylonians, and as such, the author sees the exile itself as punishment from God rather than the misuse of power from those in authority (Ezra 9:6-15). A stark contrast to this logic is the example of Micaiah ben Imlah, who speaks truth to power (1 Kings 22).

Ezra 9–10: Ethnic Exclusivity

▌THE TEXT IN ITS ANCIENT CONTEXT

The contentious issue of intermarriage occurs several times throughout Ezra–Nehemiah (Ezra 9–10; Neh. 10:29-32; 13:23-30). Unlike its representation in Nehemiah, which exemplifies the problematic relationship between language and ethnic identity, Ezra 9–10 illustrates the complexity of ethnic intermarriage when placed at the intersection of religious, cultural, and social identities.

The episode is narrated using a variety of different techniques. Initially, a narrative section, which is placed on the lips of the character Ezra, uses reported speech to describe in negative terms the occurrence of intermarriage (Ezra 9:1-5). Within this description is the powerful and loaded self-ascription "the holy seed," who are accused of having "intermingled" with "the people of the lands" (Ezra 9:2). The metaphor emphasizes the community's need to separate from other nations, and to be holy (Deut. 7:3-6), and also underlines the significance of legitimate participation within the community. Only those whose lineage, or "seed," is unsullied may be considered authentic members of Israel (Ezra 2:59-62; Neh. 7:61-64; Ezra 8:1; Neh. 9:2).

There follows an extended penitential prayer on the lips of Ezra that consolidates the ideological connection between "the people of the land" and "abominations" by linking the exile to iniquity and by claiming that intermarriage would be exactly the type of forsaking of commandments that could again risk exile or worse (Ezra 9:14). As such, ethnic intermarriage adds to an already deep-seated source of shame and sinfulness since in response to a "tent peg" of grace—that is, the return from exile to the land—Israel returns to its former behavior. The prayer's portrayal of those who are already living in the land, who had not returned from exile, is particularly derogatory, claiming that the land is unclean as a result of "the filthiness of the people of the lands, with their abominations, which have filled it from one end to another with their uncleanness" (Ezra 9:11). As such, powerful, negative language linked to purity is utilized in order to emphasize the absolute, primordial, ethnic differences between those who returned from exile, who understand themselves as "Israel," and those who remained in the land.

Ezra 10 then reverts to third-person narration, reporting how the community then takes action against those who have intermarried by making a covenant to "cast out" the wives and children of those who have intermarried (Ezra 10:3). It is unclear exactly what is meant by "cast out"; the language is atypical and is unparalleled in the case of formal divorce procedures. Indeed, other pertinent instances of the term may indicate the literal sense in which "cast out" is intended; in cases where a newly married woman's lack of virginity is exposed, she is "cast out" to be stoned to death, as is a woman who has been raped (Deut. 22:21-24). Likewise, when Tamar's irregular sexual exploits are revealed, Judah commands: "cast her out and let her be burned" (Gen. 38:24). Nevertheless, action is taken to ensure that those who have intermarried have two choices; either they must "separate themselves" from the foreign women of the land (Ezra 10:11, 16; cf. Neh. 9:2) or "be separated" from the congregation (Ezra 10:8). Again, loaded terminology, this time relating to ritualized separation for the maintenance of holiness (Ezek. 44:23; cf. Num. 8:14; Deut. 10:8; 29:20), is applied in this instance polemically in order to further polarize and exacerbate ethnic differences between those who returned to the land from exile and the so-called people of the land. Finally, a list is provided naming all those who had intermarried and pledged to cast out their wives (Ezra 10:18-43).

◼ THE TEXT IN THE INTERPRETIVE TRADITION

A variety of explanations exist in response to this challenging narrative. Despite the constantly loaded, ritualized terminology that dichotomizes the people of the land from those who self-ascribe the title "holy seed" and "Israel," some nevertheless maintain that the author's, or editor's, motivations were purely religious. For example, Charles Fensham claims that the "influence of a foreign mother, with her connection to another religion, on her children would ruin the pure religion of the Lord and would create a syncretistic religion" (124). However, a number of scholars now contextualize the issue with reference to the resounding influence throughout the narrative of the exile and the move back from exile. For example, Peter Bedford recognizes that "the text confirms the Babylonian exile to be the defining experience for Judeans . . . one cannot claim to be a Judean apart from it" (152). As such, the main threat to the community is of "going native" lest by assimilating with "the peoples of the lands" the community end up cutting itself off from its roots (Bedford, 154). Similarly, the centrality of ethnicity to the intermarriage episode should be emphasized since such a pronounced ethnic identity emerged as a result of the rediasporization experienced by the exiled community on return to their homeland, which, rather than being the same place that had lived on in the hopes of the exiles, had instead changed dramatically.

The issue of intermarriage arises in numerous contexts after Ezra–Nehemiah. Most prominently, the Qumran material attests strong concerns about intermarriage with gentiles. For example, 4QMMT reports a community who claims to have "separated" themselves "from the multitude of the peoples," and like Ezra, the material uses Deuteronomy 7 to warn against the perils of intermarriage. Similarly, William Loader points out that the *Apocryphon of Jeremiah*, *4QTestament of Qahat*, and *4QVisions of Amran*, texts found at Qumran, also display hostile attitudes toward gentile intermarriage, designating the offspring of such relationships as "half-breeds" (cf. Lev. 19:19; Deut. 22:9; Loader 2009).

◼ THE TEXT IN CONTEMPORARY DISCUSSION

In the modern state of Israel, within ultra-orthodox Jewish movements, some rabbis exercise their religious authority to classify certain marriages as illegitimate on the basis of one partner's supposed lack of Jewishness (Eskenazi and Judd). As such, the effects of immigration continue to give rise to tensions between settlers from different ethnic backgrounds or of divergent religious persuasions such as Ashkenazi and Sephardic Jews, Muslims and Christians, or modern orthodox and reform movements (Eskenazi and Judd, 227).

Modern research arising from social anthropologists concerning ethnicity and intermarriage often explains the phenomena in instrumental terms. Unlike Ezra's representation of Israel and the people of the land as inherently, or primordially, different, modern social scientists would focus more on the economic, social, and political circumstances that give rise to ethnic consciousness. As such, ethnicity itself is to be understood merely as an ideological construct devised by humans to gain power where threats to identity are perceived. Similarly, endogamous, or in-group, marriage may be seen as a measure intended to prevent the diffusion of power to those who are not affiliated to the dominant group. In other words, a tool through which difference is symbolized and accentuated.

To cite a classic example, during the 1950s, urban migrants on the Copperbelt used individualized terms to refer, physically and socially, to more proximate groups, but they resorted to general "tribal" labels when referencing migrants from elsewhere, thereby accentuating differences between distant and familiar groups and emphasizing this difference. As such, a case can easily be made for Ezra 9–10 being as much about power relations as it is about identity.

Nehemiah 1:1—2:8: News of Jerusalem and Permission to Rebuild from Artaxerxes

▌ THE TEXT IN ITS ANCIENT CONTEXT

Nehemiah 1–7 and 10–13, sometimes referred to as the Nehemiah memoirs, recount the missions of the book's namesake, the first beginning around 445 BCE and ending in 433, and the second occurring several years later. Many scholars take the view that chapters 8–9 have been misplaced as a result of some error in transmission, since these chapters include the character of Ezra, who is not mentioned in the rest of the book of Nehemiah, and since this would make for a smoother transition between Ezra 8 and 9 (where the present narrative suddenly jumps from Ezra's preparations to depart for Jerusalem to the intermarriage affair).

Nehemiah 1:11b—2:8 can be described as a court narrative wherein a Jew who has won the respect of a monarch displays wisdom and has a request granted. Numerous examples of narratives of this type, which were a standard element of Hebrew Diaspora legend, can be found, such as the tales of Daniel (Daniel 1–6), Joseph (Genesis 41), Esther (Esther 7–8), Judith (Judith 12), and Ahiqar (see Tob. 1:22). In many of these narratives, as in Nehemiah, the Jew is described as a cupbearer. Nehemiah is cupbearer to Artaxerxes (Neh. 1:11), Joseph to Pharaoh (Gen. 40:1; 41:9), Ahiqar to Esarhaddon and Sennacherib (Tob. 1:22). Many scholars speculate that cupbearer meant one who tasted wine for poison since Xenophon's *Cyropaedia* (1.3.9) suggests that it is a well-known fact that the king's cupbearers, when they proffer the cup, draw off some of it with the ladle, pour it into their left hand, and swallow it down—so that, if they should put poison in, they may not profit by it. There is also speculation about whether cupbearers were eunuchs. The narrative of Ahiqar, found at Elephantine among the Aramaic documents, designates the main protagonist as a eunuch. Likewise, the Septuagint has a variant that makes an interesting misspelling (*oinochoos*, "cupbearer" of Alexandrinus, to *eunouchos*, "eunuch," found in Vaticanus Sinaiticus, and Venetus manuscripts). However, the narrative itself does not appear to be concerned about Nehemiah's role in the Persian court apart from how such a role functions in relation to the condition of Jerusalem. Instead, it is Nehemiah's influence over Artaxerxes, and his request to rebuild Jerusalem, that is at stake.

Why would the Persians have permitted the refortification of Jerusalem? One reason may be the numerous revolts that occurred against Persian domination, especially in Egypt. Although there is no evidence of any imperial strategy concerning Jerusalem, Kenneth Hoglund defends this perspective. Despite some difficulties with this argument, Hoglund's treatment of the Greek sources is commendable. As Jacob Wright comments, "Hoglund has emphasized to biblical research that Ctesias's account of the Megabyzos-rebellion is most probably completely unreliable. Thus, it seems quite plausible that the imperial administration would have desired to tighten its control over the Levant after the intervention of the Delian League and the continued Greek naval operations in the eastern Mediterranean in the decade of the 440's" (81). Unlike the reasons for, or even the questionable historical plausibility of, the Persian monarch's motivations, Nehemiah's motivations are made clear from the outset. The first chapter of Nehemiah is dominated by a penitential prayer (see Boda), detailing Nehemiah's grief-stricken response to the news regarding Jerusalem's present condition. Nehemiah's confession of personal and national sin responds to the echo of Deuteronomistic theology, which views Hebrew misfortunes as punishment for covenantal disobedience (Deut. 28:15-68). Nehemiah also prays that God remember his promises of restoration to the faithful (Deut. 30:1-5). This has many similarities with Ezra's penitential prayer, which also uses Deuteronomistic theology to interpret the cause of the exile as disobedience, and involves mourning and fasting (Ezra 9:5-15).

▌ THE TEXT IN THE INTERPRETIVE TRADITION

The difficulties in transmission are not aided by looking to different versions of the text. In addition to the canonical book, the Greek and Latin texts have different enumeration. The Septuagint version, dated to around the second or first century BCE, contains a compilation of 2 Chronicles 35–36; Ezra 1–10; and Neh. 7:73—8:13. This is known as Esdras α, although in the Latin version it is called 3 Ezra and in some modern translations, such as NRSV, it is known as 1 Esdras. Despite the assumed error in transmission, there are striking similarities between the characters of Ezra and Nehemiah themselves, as well as between the narratives within the books. In both cases, the characters serve Persia in Yehud, initiate their missions with prayer, and deal with an intermarriage crisis. Furthermore, in narratives, they recount opposition from those within Yehud and describe rebuilding work. Both characters are given first-person narration that offers the reader their interpretation of events and that often slides into individual prayer.

Klaas Smelik compares the function of Nehemiah's role as cupbearer at this point to that of seventeenth- and eighteenth-century court Jews who played a significant role in the administration of the various courts in the German Empire. Such court Jews in return for their services attained special privileges, such as personal fortunes as well as political and social influence (see Smelik). Interestingly, 3 Ezra contains a unique account of a competition between three pages at the Persian court, one of whom is identified with the Judean Zerubbabel (3 Ezra 3:1—5:6), an account whose nearest parallel in the history of literature is the Daniel narratives (Daniel 1–6). It is possible, however, that this literary topos penetrated the imagination of Hebrew writers through the Greek fascination with the Persian court, as writers such as Xenophon and Ctesias illustrate. Given this court setting, it is ironic that the narrative designates Artaxerxes as "this man," a phrase that can sometimes be interpreted as disrespectful in tone (Neh. 1:11).

■ The Text in Contemporary Discussion

As Tamara Cohn Eskenazi observes, the cupbearer narrative is dominated by repeated instances of the Hebrew terms *ra* and *tov* ("evil" and "good"), which use the full semantic range of said terms instead of inserting synonyms (Eskenazi 1988). Interestingly, Joseph Fleischman argues that the term *ra* is chosen thoughtfully by Nehemiah in light of Zoroastrian overtones. As such, Nehemiah's dialogue with Artaxerxes shows incredible political, religious, and social astuteness. Given the challenges of interreligious dialogue today, this strategy may be of interest to contemporary readers. Rather than emphasizing the differences between Yahwism and Zoroastrianism, the character Nehemiah draws attention to the similarities in a carefully thought-through manner, thereby creating a common language through which both parties could successfully interact. Although Nehemiah's use of such a tactic may be interpreted as manipulative, the tactic itself is nevertheless effective.

Nehemiah 2:9—7:3: Opposition to Rebuilding

■ The Text in Its Ancient Context

This section of Nehemiah forms part of the so-called Nehemiah memorandum. This possibly independent block that is cast as autobiography orbits around themes such as social, cultic, and economic life in Yehud. Moreover, it contains a repeated refrain-like, stylized vocative, remembrance formula, "Remember [me] . . . Oh my God" (Neh. 5:19; 6:14; 13:14, 22, 29, 31). As such, the sense of the narrative appears as an account of personal actions given before God.

The narrative describes how Nehemiah, having received a commission to serve Persia in Yehud, discovers the city's walls need attention. Following a secretive inspection of the walls by night, Nehemiah's rebuilding project encounters persistent opposition from the start. We are presented throughout the narrative with the move and countermove of Sanballat and Tobiah, and Nehemiah respectively (Neh. 2:11-20; 3:33—4:17; 6:1-19). Each episode depicts total resistance to any interference from outsiders, a theme comparable to that of the rebuilding of the temple in Ezra 4–7; just as foreigners on the land and officials stirred up trouble and made accusations against those who were rebuilding the temple in Ezra, a similar treatment of those who are rebuilding the wall is depicted in Nehemiah.

The opposition facing Nehemiah and his rebuilding project can be divided into two camps. Nehemiah's potential rivals: local individuals with power who apparently worked together to mutual advantage with Sanballat, Tobiah, and Geshem the Arabian, and Nehemiah's fellow Yehudites on the land. However, Lester Grabbe argues that the personality of Nehemiah may also account for some of the opposition, stating that "time and again his actions are confrontational or, at best, insensitive. He evidently had the knack of antagonizing those around him" (Grabbe, 298).

Nehemiah's opponents use a number of other antagonistic tactics to obstruct the restoration of Jerusalem's walls, including anger, ridicule, and sarcasm in Nehemiah 4, when Sanballat mocks the Jews, asking, "What are these feeble Jews doing?" (v. 2). Although there are some problems with the Hebrew at this point, the general force of the derision against Nehemiah is humiliation; even a fox could cause the wall to topple down. The next tactic listed is to "conspire together" and hinder the work (Neh. 4:8). Following this, the fear of attacks against the wall mounts, causing Nehemiah to arm those who work with weapons to the extent that the building goes on with a tool in one hand and a weapon in the other (Neh. 4:13, 17-18). Following this, another tactic employed against Nehemiah is coercion and pressurization. A meeting is called between Sanballat, Geshem, and Nehemiah, which Nehemiah fails to attend. Following this, several invitations to meet are sent to and refused by Nehemiah (Neh. 6:1-4). Finally, the accusation of rebellion is leveled against the building project and against Nehemiah.

Accusations concerning rebellion are a recurring form of opposition. Such opposition is marked in both the Ezra and the Nehemiah narratives at numerous occurrences, in Hebrew and in Aramaic of the term "rebel," *mrd* (Ezra 4:12, 15, 19; Neh. 2:19; 6:6), a serious accusation in light of the political context (see above). This accusation comes to a head in Neh. 6:4-7, where Sanballat writes a letter stating that Nehemiah proposes to "become their king," and accuses Nehemiah of having "appointed prophets to preach about you saying 'There is a king in Judah'" (Neh. 6:7). The accusation is clearly designed, as with some of the Aramaic letters in Ezra, to insinuate sedition on the part of the Jews against the Persian authorities. The completion of the building work is mentioned in Neh. 6:15, but again, this is in the context of opposition to Nehemiah with letters going to and from Tobiah designed, according to Nehemiah, "to make me fearful" (Neh. 6:19). Finally, at the beginning of Nehemiah 7, as soon as the gates are set on their hinges Nehemiah establishes a guard routine.

▌ THE TEXT IN THE INTERPRETIVE TRADITION

Although the realities of Persian taxation lie behind the narrative (see the introduction), the narrative itself appears to be written to preserve the identity and survival of the "Israelite" community (as defined by Nehemiah). This is evidenced in the interpretative tradition, where it is Nehemiah, rather than Ezra, who appears in the praise of the fathers in Jesus ben Sirach (27) as the biblical prototype, and as the initiator of the postexilic refortification of Jerusalem (Neh. 49:13; cf. 2 Macc. 2:13). Why is Nehemiah so prominent in later literature? One reason is that Nehemiah's account of events is very compelling. However, despite this later admiration for the figure Nehemiah, the extent of reliability within the memoirs is questionable. Although the opposition, specifically the political opposition, against Nehemiah is plausible in the context of Achaemenid domination, it is interesting to note that much of the language looks suspiciously like hyperbole. Grabbe argues that "one has the impression that a set of murdering bandits is about to fall upon the poor builders of the wall, that they were opposed by a set of vicious and wily foes who are described in particularly demonic terms" (Grabbe, 299).

Furthermore, the language used draws on the examples of other biblical narratives. "Do not be afraid" is Israel's great battle cry (Deuteronomy 20), the declaration of war through the blowing of the shofar. The phrase "Our God will fight for us" (Neh. 4:20; cf. Judg. 3:27; 6:34; 7:18; 1 Sam. 13:3) presents a picture of Nehemiah as an archetypal leader of Israel. Such stereotypical, resonant language is also evident in Nehemiah's report of the financial crisis (Nehemiah 5). The "great cry" of the people (Neh. 5:1) is mentioned using the same term as the cry against Pharaoh, and the psalmist's cry for God's deliverance from injustice (Exod.14:10; 22:23; Ps. 107:6, 19-20).

THE TEXT IN CONTEMPORARY DISCUSSION

It is interesting to note the underlying ethnic division between the characters. Sanballat is given the appellation "Horonite" (cf. Josh. 16:3, 5; Blenkinsopp 1988, 216). The name Sanballat itself appears to be Babylonian (Williamson 1985, 182). Likewise, although Tobiah is a Hebrew name, the appellation he is given is "the Ammonite." Geshem is called an "Arab" (Neh. 2:19). Although the term *goy* may have different connotations in Nehemiah from its modern usage, it is interesting to note that "enemies" are often mentioned alongside a derogative, exclusionary application of this term (Ezra 6:21; Neh. 5:8, 9, 17; 6:6, 16; 13:26). Such ethnic separation and opposition is a general theme in the books and is seen particularly through attitudes toward intermarriage. Many modern ethnic movements rely on this kind of tactic; ethnic unification is achieved by creating a common enemy (Southwood 2011; 2012). For example, political leaders often utilize ethnic division in order to serve their own agenda of seeking to consolidate an electorate by calling for unification against a real or imagined common enemy. Similarly, colonization during the ongoing conflicts in the Greater Horn of Africa led diverse populations to be united into single parties and movements against the colonial administrators who were perceived as a common enemy.

Nehemiah 7:4—9:37: Ezra's Reading of the Law and the Nation's History

THE TEXT IN ITS ANCIENT CONTEXT

In Nehemiah 7, we find a list, repeated from Ezra 2, of those who returned and repopulated Jerusalem. The repetition may function as a device for continuity within the books, linking the end of the reconstruction effort with its beginning. The second appearance of this Golah list is introduced by the idea that Nehemiah wanted everyone to be registered according to their lineage. According to Kenton Sparks, these lists determine group membership using participation in the experience of exile as a determining factor. Effectively to be perceived as a "true" Israelite, one must "demonstrate an ethnic origin within the people of Israel and only when this pedigree could be established with written documentation" (Sparks, 314–15).

There follows an account of Ezra's reading of the law that disrupts Nehemiah's memoirs. This disruption, coupled with the introduction of Ezra in Neh. 8:1 and absence of Nehemiah, leads many scholars to conclude that this chapter initially belonged between chapters 8 and 9 of Ezra. Furthermore, the date given is the seventh month, before the intermarriage episode in Ezra 9–10, which occurs on the ninth month (Neh. 8:2; Ezra 10:9). Grabbe argues that two separate traditions are combined in Nehemiah 8: a tradition that strongly associates the reading and promulgation of the Torah of Moses with Ezra, and a separate tradition that associates the reading and promulgation of the same law with Nehemiah the Levite, and the people as a whole, without any mention of Ezra (Grabbe, 336). Whatever the original chronological setting of the events, it is interesting to note that they occur on the date later celebrated as the Jewish New Year.

The narrative details how Ezra reads from the book of Moses (Neh. 8:1–3), the Levites explain the law (Neh. 8:7-8), and the people are told to rejoice rather than mourn, because the day is holy (Neh. 8:9–12). Instructions to dwell in booths are found, and booths are prepared, something that had not occurred since the days of Joshua son of Nun (Neh. 8:17), and the celebration of reading the law lasts eight days (Neh. 8:18). A variety of significant details may be observed within the narrative.

Initially, Ezra reads facing the square; thus within a small space a concentration of the population occurs. As such, Ezra's law is conceived of within the narrative as being in the form of a document, not just a set of teachings. Furthermore, the law is portrayed as accessible to all. Ezra symbolically conveys the accessibility of the law to nonpriests by choosing thirteen lay leaders to stand with him while he reads. Furthermore, we are informed that they read "distinctly, and gave the sense, and caused them to understand the reading" (Neh. 8:8). The general implication of the threefold description of the Levites' work is that the law is for the entire Israelite community, rather than being unapproachable, in the ark within the holy of holies.

◼ THE TEXT IN THE INTERPRETIVE TRADITION

The importance of public reading is highlighted by several scholars as an instrument for dissemination of ideologies. For example, David Goodblatt assigns the public reading of Scripture, found in numerous texts, an important role in the rise of ancient Jewish nationalism. Just as Moses and Josiah read the law, so too does Ezra and many after him (Deut. 31:9-13; 2 Kgs. 23:1-3). Goodblatt cites numerous early accounts of such public reading of Scripture. For example, in the fourth century BCE, Hecateus of Abdera writes that the high priest "announces what is ordained, and the Jews . . . fall to the ground and do reverence to the high priest when he expounds the commandments to them. At the end of their laws there is even appended the statements: 'These are the words that Moses heard from God and declares unto the Jews'" (Goodblatt, 36). Similarly, the letter of Aristeas reports that the completion of the finished translation of the Torah into Greek was read out to the assembled Jewish community. Also, 1 Macc. 3:46-60, which describes the assembly of the forces of Judas the Maccabee at Mizpah, may refer to a public reading from the Torah (1 Macc. 3:48). By the time of Philo and Josephus in the first century CE, we have clear statements asserting regular public reading of Scripture on the Sabbath (Goodblatt, 24–48). It is also interesting to note that although the origins of the synagogue service are disputed, the practice of public reading from Scripture may be connected to the emergence of the synagogue institution (see Runesson). The reference to Joshua son of Nun may also lend further nationalist overtones to the celebrations.

■ THE TEXT IN CONTEMPORARY DISCUSSION

The ninth chapter of Nehemiah presents, liturgically, national history from creation and election to exodus and the metaphor of entering the land: a metaphor all too pertinent for those who returned from exile. This presentation of a common history may function as a means of underlining, explaining, and consolidating Israelite ethnic identity (Hutchinson and Smith, 6–7). Interestingly, this commemoration of a shared history is an occasion of mourning and separating from foreigners (Neh. 9:2). The prayer acknowledges both God's long-suffering in continuing to fulfill the Abrahamic covenant despite disobedience, and God's justice in using foreign domination as punishment, namely, by Assyria and Babylonia. The sense of a history of shame that emerges from Nehemiah 9 is similar to the sense of guilt within Ezra's prayer (see Ezra 9:6-7). Unlike many modern ethnic histories, which recount past triumphs, it is interesting that in Ezra and Nehemiah national unity is forged on a history of disappointment and disgrace. Nowadays, shame and guilt are often viewed as entirely negative, but the way such emotions are applied within Ezra–Nehemiah also shows that they have the potential to be used creatively and positively.

Nehemiah 10–13: Obligations for the Renewed Community

■ THE TEXT IN ITS ANCIENT CONTEXT

The tenth chapter of Nehemiah is a list of signatories to agreements concerning religious obligations. These obligations include the agreement not to intermarry with people of the land (cf. Exod. 34:16; Deut. 7:1-4), not to conduct business on the Sabbath (cf. Exod. 23:10-11; Lev. 25:2-7), to give up crops and the exaction of debts in the Sabbatical year, and to provide an annual one-third shekel tax for the temple personnel (cf. Num. 18:8-32). Other obligations listed include the wood offering (see Lev 6:5-6) and the firstfruits (see Exod. 23:19; 34:26; Deut. 26:1-11). The ceremony concludes with a commitment by all "to walk in God's torah which was given by Moses the servant of God and to observe and do all the commandments of the LORD" (Neh. 10:29). Interestingly, like the prohibitions against intermarriage in Exodus and Deuteronomy, throughout Ezra and Nehemiah the movement of females is emphasized (see Deut. 7:3; Ezra 9:2; Neh. 10:30; 13:25).

This has led some scholars to the conclusion that the focus on intermarriage within Ezra and Nehemiah concerns female inheritance. For example, Eskenazi states that "the fear of mixed marriages with their concomitant loss of property to the community makes most sense when women can, in fact, inherit" (Eskenazi 1992, 35). There are numerous problems with this argument (Southwood 2012, 79–83). One problem in particular is the reverse of the argument, that if male members of the community married foreign women they could also receive land and dowry, and so increase the community holdings.

As H. G. M. Williamson points out, the similarities between this chapter and Nehemiah 13 are striking (Williamson 1985, 331).

> Mixed marriages 10:31; 13:23-30
> Sabbath observance 10:32; 13:15-22
> The wood offering 10:35; 13:31
> First fruits 10:36-37; 13:31
> Levitical tithes 10:38-39; 13:10-14
> Neglect of the temple 10:40; 13:11

The list of correspondences may indicate that Nehemiah had taken some steps to deal with such problems, following which the community entered into an agreement to prevent their occurrence; thus, rather than indicating two separate incidents, Nehemiah 10 relies on Nehemiah 13. However, Grabbe doubts that Nehemiah ever had the authority to make any major reforms since "he was only the governor of a small province, and he answered to the satrap (a provincial governor) of all the central government." Therefore, it is a reasonable inference that the governor in turn had to deliver a set amount to the satrapal treasury. As such, a "one-off cancellation of some debts might be possible, but it could be disastrous for the local economy if this happened too widely and too frequently" (Grabbe, 306).

Chapters 11 and 12 of Nehemiah are a utopic presentation of Jerusalem as a city built by clergy, populated by those who are blessed, and dedicated with joy. Indeed, unlike the temple's dedication in Ezra, which was accompanied by both shouting and weeping that could be heard from afar (Ezra 3:13), in Nehemiah only the rejoicing can be heard from afar (Neh. 12:43). Oded Lipschits argues that the section of the text is an ideological creation, or a utopian picture in which Jerusalem is envisaged as ruling over all the old area of Judah as a kingdom and also includes all the places in which Jews lived in the Persian period. A list of those who repopulate Jerusalem, which has military overtones, is provided. This names Judahites (11:1-4), Benjamites (11:7-9), priests (11:10-14), Levites (11:15-18), gatekeepers (11:19), and the "remnant of Israel" (11:20-21). The list has important parallels with 1 Chron. 9:1-17, which is alleged to be a list of those who first returned from exile. By implication, those who were originally exiled are the same remnant community who return. However, the broad geographical distribution of postexilic Judahite settlements that the list suggests in 11:27-36 does not so much reflect the historical realities of the day as recall the ideal territorial possessions in the promised land (see Joshua 15). As such, a similar technique of using evocative language to recall stories about Israel's history in order to narrate the return from exile to Jerusalem is used. Just as the events in Ezra 1 are portrayed as a second exodus, the events in Nehemiah 11 portray the Israelites as entering and inheriting the promised land.

Chapter 12 of Nehemiah describes a processional dedication of the wall, starting with another list that records priestly and Levitical families and high priests (vv. 1-26). Subsequently, 12:27—13:3 reports that the people gather to dedicate the wall and even purify the wall itself to make the city holy. Two groups, each composed of priests and Levites, begin the ceremonial procession at the

Valley Gate. One group ascends to the top of the thick wall in a counterclockwise direction, while the second group proceeds the opposite way. The two groups meet at the temple, where they celebrate with singing, sacrifice, and attention to practical matters that David prescribed for the temple service. The list of Levites highlights the singers who are depicted as carrying out their musical service antiphonally (Neh. 12:8-9).

The thirteenth chapter reports events that occur on Nehemiah's second mission to Jerusalem. The narrative describes how while Nehemiah was away the community had violated some of the stipulations made formerly (Nehemiah 10). For example, Tobiah the Ammonite is housed in the temple, portions have not been assigned to the Levites and temple singers, the Sabbath has been violated, and intermarriage has occurred, including intermarriage between priests and gentiles (cf. Lev. 21:14; Ezek. 44:22). Unlike in Ezra 9–10, the intermarriage crisis in Nehemiah focuses on the issue of language, something that is crucial to ethnic identity (Southwood 2011).

▌The Text in the Interpretive Tradition

The influence and legacy of Nehemiah's and Ezra's intermarriage reforms are strong. Some Second Temple authors considered intermarriage detrimental to Jews because of gentile immorality (Philo, *Spec. Laws* 3.29; Josephus, *Ant.* 4.8.2; 8.5.191–93). Similarly, Tobit insists that his son should "marry a wife of the seed of your fathers" rather than "take a strange wife, who is not of your father's tribe" (Tob. 4:12). Aramaic Levi also assumes that Israelite seed is holy (see *Testament of Levi* 9:9-10). As Hannah Harrington illustrates, the ongoing influence of Ezra and Nehemiah's marriage reforms is evident in several Dead Sea Scrolls. Harrington notes that like Ezra–Nehemiah, "the Qumran authors who discuss intermarriage do not offer a reasonable acculturation process for the non-Israelite partner. Instead, most adopt a priestly stance to holiness which configures it in cultic terms" (259). As such, intermarriage, even among the laity, compromises the holiness of Israel. This is especially clear within 4QMMT, where we find not only a similar ideology to that of Nehemiah's reforms but also the mirroring of certain key terms such as "the holy seed," "impurity," "intermingle," "sacrilege," and "abomination." Similarly, the author of the *Temple Scroll* quotes almost verbatim from Exod. 34:15-16 and interprets the passage in light of Ezra–Nehemiah's perspective on intermarriage. Likewise, the Damascus Document fails to endorse intermarriage through appealing to cultic language: intermarriage is a desecration of Israel's holiness. Again, in the *Genesis Apocryphon*, the insistence on appropriate genealogy and the concern about defilement mirrors what is found in Nehemiah 13. Finally, in 4QFragments, the concern about unions with foreigners continues. As such, while the intermarriage episodes in Ezra and Nehemiah are not explicitly cited, the language and ideas within the texts is nevertheless dependent on Ezra–Nehemiah (Harrington).

▌The Text in Contemporary Discussion

The building of the wall and the reforms mentioned lead Grabbe to conclude that Nehemiah's goal may have been "to make Judah into an isolated puritanical theocratic state" by "creating his own religious and ideological ghetto" (Grabbe, 309–10). Nehemiah is depicted as a powerful and influential, albeit short-tempered, religious leader. Many religious movements today rely on charismatic leaders. However, such charisma must go hand in hand with ethical, righteous, even inclusive principles if the goal is to establish anything more than the formation of isolated, sect-like groups. The problem lies in deciding and interpreting what constitutes righteous behavior.

Works Cited

Becking, B. 2011. *Ezra, Nehemiah, and the Construction of Early Jewish Identity.* FAT 80. Tübingen: Mohr Siebeck.

Bedford, P. R. 2002. "Diaspora: Homeland Relations in Ezra–Nehemiah." *VT* 52, no. 2:147–65.

Blenkinsopp, J. 1988, *Ezra-Nehemiah: A Commentary.* OTL. London: SCM.

———. 2009. *Judaism, the First Phase: The Place of Ezra and Nehemiah in the Origins of Judaism.* Grand Rapids: Eerdmans.

Boda, M. J. 2008. "Redaction in the Book of Nehemiah: A Fresh Proposal." In *(Dis)Unity of Ezra and Nehemiah*, edited by M. J. Boda and P. Redditt, 25–54. Hebrew Bible Monographs 17. Sheffield: Sheffield Phoenix Press.

Eskenazi, T. C. 1988. *In an Age of Prose: A Literary Approach to Ezra-Nehemiah.* SBLMS. 36. Atlanta: Scholars Press.

———. 1992. "Out from the Shadows: Biblical Women in the Postexilic Era," *JSOT* 54:25–43.

Eskenazi, T. C., and E. P. Judd. 1991. "Marriage to a Stranger in Ezra 9–10." In *Second Temple Studies 2: Temple and Community in the Persian Period*, edited by T. C. Eskenazi and K. H. Richards, 266–85. JSOTSup 175. Sheffield: Sheffield Academic Press.

Fensham, F. C. 1982. *The Books of Ezra and Nehemiah.* NICOT. Grand Rapids: Eerdmans.

Fleischman, J. 2012. "Nehemiah's Request on Behalf of Jerusalem." In *New Perspectives on Ezra-Nehemiah: History and Historiography, Text, Literature, and Interpretation*, edited by I. Kalimi, 241–66. Winona Lake, IN: Eisenbrauns.

Goodblatt, D. 2006. *Elements of Ancient Jewish Nationalism.* Cambridge: Cambridge University Press.

Grabbe, L. L. 2004. *A History of the Jews and Judaism in the Second Temple Period.* Library of Second Temple Studies 47. London: T&T Clark.

Harrington, H. 2011. "Intermarriage in Qumran Texts: The Legacy of Ezra-Nehemiah." In *Mixed Marriages: Intermarriage and Group Identity in the Second Temple Period*, edited by C. Frevel, 251–79. LHB/OTS 547. New York: T&T Clark.

Hoglund, K. 1992. *Achaemenid Imperial Administration in Syria-Palestine and the Missions of Ezra and Nehemiah.* SBLDS 125. Atlanta: Society of Biblical Literature.

Hutchinson, J., and A. D. Smith, eds. 1996. *Ethnicity.* Oxford Readers. Oxford: Oxford University Press.

Japhet, S. 1968. "The Supposed Common Authorship of Chronicles and Ezra–Nehemiah Investigated Anew." *VT* 18:330–71.

Knowles, M. D. 2004. "Pilgrimage Imagery in the Returns in Ezra." *JBL* 123, no. 1:57–74

Lipschits, O. 2002. "Literary and Ideological Aspects of Nehemiah 11." *JBL* 121, no. 3:423–40.

Loader, W. 2009. *The Dead Sea Scrolls on Sexuality: Attitudes Towards Sexuality in Sectarian and Related Literature at Qumran.* Journal for the Study of Judaism Supplement Series 40/2. Grand Rapids: Eerdmans.

B. Porten and A. Yardeni (eds.). 1986. *Textbook of Aramaic Documents from Ancient Egypt* (TAD). Winona Lake, IN: Eisenbrauns.

Runesson, A. 2003. "Persian Imperial Politics, the Beginning of Public Torah Readings, and the Origins of the Synagogue." In *The Ancient Synagogue from Its Origins until 200* c.e.: *Papers Presented at an International*

Conference at Lund University, October 14–17, 2001, edited by B. Olsson and M. Zetterholm, 63–89. ConBNT 39. Stockholm: Almqvist and Wiksell.

Smelik, K. A. D. 2012. "Nehemiah as a 'Court Jew.'" in *New Perspectives on Ezra-Nehemiah: History and Historiography, Text, Literature, and Interpretation*, edited by I. Kalimi, 61–72. Winona Lake, IN: Eisenbrauns.

Southwood, K. E. 2011. "'And They Could Not Understand Jewish Speech': Ethnicity, Language, and Nehemiah's Intermarriage Crisis." *JTS* 62, no. 1:1–19.

———. 2012. *Ethnicity and the Mixed Marriage Crisis in Ezra 9–10: An Anthropological Approach*. Oxford Theological Monographs. Oxford: Oxford University Press.

Sparks, K. L. 1998. *Ethnicity and Identity in Ancient Israel: Prolegomena to the Study of Ethnic Sentiments and Their Expression in the Hebrew Bible*. Winona Lake, IN: Eisenbrauns.

Williamson, H. G. M. 1977. *Israel in the Books of Chronicles*. Cambridge: Cambridge University Press.

———. 1985 *Ezra, Nehemiah*. WBC 16. Waco, TX: Word.

Wright, J. L. 2004. *Rebuilding Identity: The Nehemiah-Memoir and Its Earliest Readers*. BZAW 348. Berlin: de Gruyter.

ESTHER

Judy Fentress-Williams

Introduction

The Jewish Diaspora of the fifth or fourth centuries BCE was a community of dual realities, double consciousness, and multiple identities. The theme of multiple identities is present the story of Esther as it employs literary devices of suspense, irony, and plot twists to engage the question of "how" to survive as a Jew in the Persian court. Unlike the court tales in Daniel, where the heroes openly defy the law of the land in their adherence to the Torah, Esther portrays a heroine who works within the system to obtain salvation for her people. Esther manipulates the king like his advisors do, and in so doing saves her people from genocide. The averted genocide gives way to the slaughter of the Jews' enemies and the institution of a new, non-Mosaic, holiday.

Esther is one of the five books of the Hebrew Scriptures that constitute the festival scroll known as the Megilloth. The narrative provides the rationale for the celebration of Purim. Set in Susa, the winter capital of the Persian Empire, the action takes place in the time of the Jewish Diaspora in the Persian Empire, during the fifth or fourth century BCE. The story's heroine is Esther, a Jewish woman who becomes queen of Persia and is thereby able to save her people from genocide.

There are three ancient versions of Esther. There is the canonical, Masoretic (Hebrew) Text that contains no overt reference to the divine. The two Greek translations of a Hebrew text contain additional passages that include prayer and multiple references to God. These additions to Esther afford us a glimpse into the history of translation and development of text (Fox, 269).

The story of Esther opens with a banquet given by the Persian king Ahasuerus (Xerxes) for his officials and ministers that lasted 128 days. This is followed by a seven-day banquet for all the people in the citadel of Susa. The king's banquet is characterized by a lack of restraint, as the king orders the officials to "do as each one desired" (1:8). The queen hosts an additional banquet for the women.

A crisis arises when the drunken king demands the queen's appearance and she refuses. His anger with Queen Vashti is sated when his advisors convince him to depose her. The rash decision leaves the king without a queen. Again, the advisors come to the rescue with a recommendation that will provide a replacement. Young virgins are brought into the palace and undergo a yearlong process of preparation, after which time they "audition" for the role of queen. In the end, Esther, a Jewish girl who is keeping her identity secret, is selected as the new queen.

Almost immediately after becoming queen, Esther is forced into a difficult position because she is a Jew and Haman, the king's top official, has a plan to annihilate her people. Esther is challenged by her cousin Mordecai to champion her people lest she be deceived into thinking her position as queen will protect her. She executes a carefully developed plan of her own as she prepares a banquet for the king and Haman followed by a second banquet where she finally reveals her identity and begs the king's mercy for herself and her people. Esther is successful in gaining the king's favor and exposing Haman. The Jews are allowed to defend themselves against Haman's plot. They kill their enemies, and Haman is impaled on the pole he had built for Mordecai. This victory is followed by the inaugural celebration of the Feast of Purim.

Esther 1:1—2:18: Esther Becomes Queen

▎ THE TEXT IN ITS ANCIENT CONTEXT

Ahasuerus, or Xerxes, would have reigned from 486 to 465 BCE. The narrative's placement in this historical context does not mean that Esther is a historical account. To the contrary, a number of the details in the narrative do not jibe with the information we have about Persia in the fifth century BCE. For example, neither of the queens' names in the book of Esther, Vashti and Esther, appears in the Persian annals. Furthermore, Mordecai presents the reader with some chronological challenges. If he was with those carried away in the Babylonian captivity, he would have to be well over one hundred years old during the third year of the Persian king's reign. These along with other examples suggest that Esther is something other than a strict historical account. One may safely conclude that the historical elements of the Persian Empire during the fifth century are in service to the narrative.

Esther is often categorized as a novella because it is a continuous narrative. It also has the characteristics of a court tale—a story of Jews in the Diaspora whose survival is linked to their identity. Moreover, the presence of reversals and plot twists introduce the elements of a comedy. In fact, the extravagant details (the feasts of the king) and excessive elements (the number of the Jews' enemies killed) have led some scholars to conclude that Esther is a particular type of comedy, namely carnivalesque. The carnivalesque employs humor and chaos to subvert the dominant culture or power. This term helps us understand the function of the comedic in the face of potential genocide. Esther is a narrative court tale with comedic elements.

▎ THE TEXT IN THE INTERPRETIVE TRADITION

The book of Esther follows the structure of a court tale. In these stories, the Jews in the Diaspora must make the decisions that will enable them to survive in the foreign, potentially hostile environment. The court tale depicts the foreign king as powerful, impulsive, and easily influenced by his advisors, who are rivals of the Jewish characters and community. The advisors convince the king to make a decision that goes against Jewish identity, piety, and/or existence. What is perfectly acceptable for the dominant culture could be prohibited in the Jewish community. Even in the Diaspora, the Jews are a people "set apart." They must choose to risk well-being or life itself in order to obey the law and thereby preserve identity. In so doing, they are saved and sometimes the foreign king acknowledges the God of Israel (Dan. 3:28-29, 6:26-27).

As a court tale, the narrative is careful to set up the divide between the power of the ruling nation and the relative helplessness of the Jewish Diaspora. Esther has two names—her Jewish name, Hadassah, which is suppressed in favor of Persian name, Esther. When she is taken along with the other women to become a part of the king's harem, Mordecai instructs her to keep her identity as a Jew a secret. Although the narrative focuses on Esther, the reader should note the king's rash actions of deposing his queen and then finding another result in a number of women who spend the rest of their lives relegated to the harem.

Esther's hidden identity along with her two names highlights the presence of dual consciousness for the Diaspora community. Esther must exist both as a Jew and as a Persian, and as the narrative unfolds, she must make decisions about how and when to claim her respective identities. Her choices have consequences. As was the case in Daniel, the consequences are life and death. Unlike the court tales in Daniel, Esther is not identified as a Jew. The temptation for Esther is to keep her ethnicity hidden and not risk exposure to persecution. She is not asked to take a position of prayer, worship a foreign idol, or violate dietary laws. For all we know, she is not keeping kosher. For Esther, it is not a specific Jewish observance that threatens her people so much as their very identity as Jews.

Both Jewish and Christian audiences are interested in the character of Esther and as a result read this as a narrative of Esther's ascent to the throne instead of the story of Vashti's exile. This reading is encouraged by the fact that there is little character development for any of the characters. No reason is given for Vashti's refusal, and we do not know if Esther is conscripted into the king's service willingly or not. What we know is that these two women along with the other characters are in service to this plot, which leads the reader through a variety of plot twists on the way to the final goal of the triumph of the Jewish community over those who seek to do them harm. In contrast to Vashti's disfavor, Esther has the favor of those she encounters. In the interpretive tradition, Vashti is demonized to justify her rejection. In a narrative with underdeveloped characters that are either clearly good or evil, Esther is the heroine and Vashti becomes the antitype, the defiant wife who threatens the stability of the kingdom.

■ THE TEXT IN CONTEMPORARY DISCUSSION

Esther did not find its way into the canon with ease. The absence of a direct reference to God meant that it was one of the last books to be granted canonical status, aided by its connection to the festival of Purim (Crawford, 77). It is also distinguished as one of the few canonical books that bear the name of a female who is also the protagonist. As a result, the text is of interest to many who want to explore the role of women in the Bible. Esther takes a position of power in a foreign environment. However, her power is still limited by gender. The queen is not an equal with the king, as Queen Vashti discovers. Both queens must navigate a world where their power is limited. In the opening narrative, Vashti's open defiance of the king is grounds for her removal, even though her refusal may have been out of a sense of virtue or propriety, and Esther's compliance with the wishes of her cousin and the eunuch work in her favor. Contemporary audiences are concerned with mixed messages: Esther complies in contrast to Vashti's refusal, but saves her people when she too defies a royal decree and appears unbidden before the king. Esther's compliance and subsequent boldness may reflect the dual consciousness that is a key to survival in the Diaspora.

Esther 2:19—8:3: Mordecai and Haman

▌ THE TEXT IN ITS ANCIENT CONTEXT

The Diaspora community that originally received the Esther story knew that in order to survive, they needed to occupy the world and worldview of the Persian Empire while living in and preserving an alternative worldview—another, equally real set of rules. Their survival is connected to their ability to move from one to another and to know when they need to exchange one lens or set of rules for another. It should come as no surprise that the book of Esther uses verbal dyads and sets up characters in pairs as foils to one another. Esther is a story with two angles of vision—in other words, the structure of the narrative reflects the worldview of the characters in the narrative (Levenson, 10).

In this second sense unit, the narrative action is played out through a contest between the characters Mordecai the Jew and Haman the Agagite. A postexilic audience would hear in these ethnographic modifiers not only a difference in racial/ethnic background but also a history of antagonism. Haman is an Amalekite, but he is referred to as an Agagite. Agag is the name of the Amalekite king whose life was spared by King Saul in 1 Samuel 15. Saul's decision was made in defiance of God's direct command to destroy all of the Amalekites because of their mistreatment of Israel. Although the prophet Samuel killed Agag, the reference to Haman as an Agagite signals the reader to recall Saul's failure to successfully execute the ban on the nation of Amalek.

The narrative turns on the responses the Jews make to the rules and/or situations presented by the dominant society. The first is Mordecai's response to the edict that everyone must bow to Haman. This legislation comes as a result of Haman's elevation in 3:1. The efficiency of the text in detailing Haman's promotion contrasts the elaborate nature of the banquets described earlier. We are not told how or why he is promoted. What matters in this court tale is that Haman is promoted and that the king orders that everyone bow to him. Mordecai, like the heroes in the court tales of Daniel, must take a stand when confronted with a "law of the land" that is in opposition to Jewish practices. At issue here is, first, the command that a Jew cannot bow to a descendant of Agag (Exod. 17:14-16; Deut. 15:17-19; 1 Samuel 15) and, second, adherence to the law requires knowledge of the law. Mordecai's refusal stems from his Jewish identity that is based on the observance of the law. His behavior enrages Haman and is the impetus for his plot to kill Mordecai and his people. Following the lines of a court tale, Haman convinces the unsuspecting king (with the incentive of a bribe) to issue an edict for the extermination of the Jews on the date chosen by the casting of lots, Purim.

When he hears about the edict, Mordecai responds in a way that again betrays his heritage. He enters into the ritual of mourning by tearing his clothes and putting on sackcloth and ashes. Other Jews also enter into mourning, but it is Mordecai's behavior that gets the attention of Queen Esther. Mordecai wants Esther to plead the case of her people before her husband the king. Esther's response reflects not her intentions but the confines of the Persian kingdom. She tells Mordecai that if she approaches the king without being invited, she will be put to death (4:11). Mordecai's exchange with Esther asserts the reality or worldview of the Jewish community over that of the Persian Empire. In this clash of culture, there is only one right answer, and that is to speak out on behalf of her people.

Mordecai's response makes no direct reference to God, but hints at the divine when he says that if she does not help, "help will rise for the Jews from another quarter" (4:14). Esther responds to Mordecai's challenge by choosing to act: she decides she will risk her life for that of her people. Her preparation involves fasting, the antithesis of the feast. Esther does not have to defy an edict that goes against the Torah or her identity as a Jew; in Esther, there is danger simply in being identified as a Jew. In such a world, the book of Esther raises the question of identifying with the oppressed group when one can blend in to the dominant society, what African Americans refer to as "passing for white." If given the opportunity to move in the world of the dominant culture/society/race as one of them, would one willingly choose to identify with their people and take on suffering if one could avoid it? In the Diaspora, where is the line between assimilating to survive and losing one's primary identity? The fact that this dilemma is posited before the queen is of significance. As queen, Esther is in one of the highest positions in the foreign power. If she cannot ignore her Jewish identity, then no one can. Moreover, Mordecai's challenge reminds Esther and the reader that denying one's identity will not save you, even if you are a favored queen.

Once Esther decides to act, the narrative shifts its attention from a contest between Haman and Mordecai to one between Haman and Esther. Both are close to the king and have the opportunity to exercise influence. Haman tricked the king into signing an edict that calls for the extermination of the Jews. Now Esther must find a way to manipulate the king to achieve her desired end. Unlike the court tales in Daniel, the Jews will not witness a supernatural resolution to their situation. They will fast and pray, but in the Diaspora they must also be cunning. Esther successfully gains an audience with the king, and his words convey his willingness to please her: "what is your request? It shall be given you, even to the half of my kingdom" (5:3). She extends an invitation to one banquet, which is the platform for a second invitation. Esther's request is carefully orchestrated to increase the king's desire to give it to her (he is not a patient man) and to elevate the dramatic tension. What could she want that requires two banquets? Once her request is made, the comedic reversal moves to its climax. The king is enraged near the end of the story just as he was in the beginning. His anger in chapter 1 resulted in Vashti's deposition and Esther's appointment. Similarly, the anger of the king means that Haman will be removed and Mordecai will take his position. The lots that were used to set the date of the Jew's annihilation will serve as the name of the Jewish festival that commemorates Haman's defeat and demise. Esther's plan is successful. Thus, although the absence of God is a theological issue, God's absence may be a literary device intended to re-create in the narrative the feeling of the Diaspora community—one that has come to expect God, but doesn't always readily find an obvious divine manifestation.

◼ The Text in the Interpretive Tradition

Haman and Mordecai are positioned by virtue of their ethnicity, as enemies. Such a contrast, informed by dual realities of an oppressed population, leaves little room for subtleties. In all the ways that Mordecai is faithful, loyal, and good, Haman is duplicitous, self-serving, evil, and proud. The contrast between the two is the foundation of Jewish and Christian interpretive traditions. Haman becomes the epitome of the enemy of the Jews; he is linked to Agag and Esau (Carruthers, 134). In Christian traditions, Haman is seen as the model both for elevation of the undeserving and the enemies of the church. Christians who saw the Roman Church as the enemy equated the pope with Haman's rise to power (Carruthers, 135). In Jewish and Christian traditions, much is made of Haman's pride and his anger, both of which limit him. It is his pride that blinds him to Esther's plan, and his anger separates him from reason.

In Jewish tradition, Mordecai's refusal to bow down to Haman is not tied to the prohibition against bowing down to a descendant of Ahab, but to a more obvious prohibition. *Esther Rabbah* asserts that there was an idol adorning Haman's robe, and it was to the idol that Mordecai refused obeisance (Carruthers, 139). Mordecai is the embodiment of the faithful Jew in the Diaspora. He knows how far to assimilate without forgetting his observance of the law. In the end, he is honored and elevated in the foreign kingdom.

◼ The Text in Contemporary Discussion

Esther offers contemporary communities the opportunity to face the reality of evil in a world where God does not appear to be present. Although she is the queen, her life is endangered by virtue of being a Jew. Her adopted homeland became hostile in a very short period of time. The post-Shoah world is well aware of how quickly one's home can turn into a battleground and how the lives of a community can be summarily discounted and disregarded. The challenge of the Shoah is that the genocide was allowed to happen. Why was there no Esther or Mordecai? Was God even more absent than in the book of Esther?

Esther 8:4—10:3: The Revenge of the Jews

◼ The Text in Its Ancient Context

True to the court-narrative form, the king is unable to reverse the edict calling for the extermination of the Jews, but he does allow the Jewish community to defend itself. Not only is Haman killed on the stake he prepared for Mordecai, but those seeking to do harm to the Jews on that day are killed as well. In Shushan, eight hundred enemies of the Jews are killed. In the surrounding verses, the Jews "fought for their lives" (JPS), killing 75,000 of their enemies. In the end of the story, we see the excess of the Jews "standing their ground" mirroring the extravagance of the two feasts at the story's beginning. On the following day, a celebratory feast is held called Purim, named after the lots that Haman cast in his plot to destroy the Jews.

As a comedic novella, we expect the reversals that come at the end. The death Haman plans for Mordecai becomes his own. Mordecai replaces Haman and inherits his holdings. And perhaps most importantly, Esther "daughter of Abihail, along with the Jew Mordecai, gave full written authority, confirming . . . Purim" (9:29). Just as Haman was responsible for the edicts that went out to announce the massacre of the Jews, Esther, the would-be victim of Haman's wickedness, gives a command that is "fixed" and "recorded." Purim will be remembered by generations to come.

▌THE TEXT IN THE INTERPRETIVE TRADITION

The revenge in the story of Esther makes interpreters uncomfortable. In early Christian traditions, Esther is condemned along with her people for vindictiveness and impiety (Fox, 50). In a number of these early traditions, the condemnation of Esther often became the foundation on which anti-Semitic remarks would be made. In later traditions, there has been a tendency on the part of Christian interpreters to downplay or ignore the magnitude of the revenge in the story. Both of these responses reflect a tendency on the part of the interpretive traditions to fix or explain something that is simply an accurate reflection of the human experience. Perhaps our discomfort in the account of the Jewish people exacting revenge results from the way in which it resonates with that part of us that has suffered.

▌THE TEXT IN CONTEMPORARY DISCUSSION

Esther is not the first court tale that involves revenge. The officials of Babylon who orchestrate the scenario that places Shadrach, Meshach, and Abednego in the fiery furnace are themselves tossed into the furnace with their families. Similarly, after Daniel emerges unscathed from the lion's den, his accusers and their families are thrown in. In Esther, Haman, the enemy, and his family are killed. What is of interest in this narrative is that in spite of Haman's punishment, there are still members of the community who want to kill the Jews. The Jews, acting in self-defense, kill tens of thousands of their enemies. The excessive bloodletting at the end of Esther resonates with the Quentin Tarantino films *Inglourious Basterds* or *Django Unchained*. These films offer a retelling of history that allows the victim to exact revenge on those who inflicted suffering. Esther reminds us that those who have witnessed the horrors of genocide are forever marked by that violence and that in the absence of some sense of adjudication, the imagination craves the opportunity to remember the story in such a way that the victims have the right to gain the upper hand over those such as Haman who embody unexplainable evil in our world.

Works Cited

Carruthers, Jo. 2008. *Esther through the Centuries*. Malden, MA: Blackwell.

Crawford, Sidnie White. 2000. "Esther." In *Women in Scripture*, edited by Carol Meyers, 74–77, 289–292. New York: Houghton Mifflin.

Fox, Michael V. 1991. *Character and Ideology in the Book of Esther*. Eugene, OR: Wipf & Stock.

Levenson, Jon D. 1997. *Esther: A Commentary*. OTL. Louisville: Westminster John Knox.

INTRODUCTION TO WISDOM AND WORSHIP: THEMES AND PERSPECTIVES IN THE POETIC WRITINGS

Timothy J. Sandoval

Introduction

This article provides a general introduction to the poetic writings of the Hebrew Bible. It describes features of biblical poetry in general, then discusses the two major "genres" constituting the poetic writings: first, the biblical Wisdom literature (Proverbs, Job, Ecclesiastes) as well as the Song of Songs; and second, those texts related to worship in ancient Israel, especially the Psalms. This article also describes the important role of scribes—and others—in the production and transmission of biblical wisdom and worship texts, and concludes with brief reflections as to the challenges and possibilities that individuals and communities face when appropriating the Bible's poetic books today.

Biblical Poetry

"All which is not prose is verse; and all which is not verse is prose," Moliere once quipped. Biblical scholars, however, seldom settle for such blunt, and in this case tongue-in-cheek, distinctions. Some have written entire books cataloging the array of tropes, literary features, and strategies that when present in a text might be said to distinguish "biblical poetry" from prosaic narrative compositions (Watson 1984; 1995). Others have called into question the very possibility of distinguishing adequately between prose and poetry in the Bible, preferring to understand prose and poetry as standing on different ends of a continuum of biblical literary style (Kugel). As Luis Alonso Schökel has contended, it is impossible to "distinguish strictly between prose vocabulary and poetic vocabulary" or to "distinguish techniques which are exclusively poetic" (19).

Even as scholars debate the distinctions between biblical poetry and prose, several literary features or characteristics are widely recognized as signaling whether a biblical text might be regarded as poetry. The most ubiquitous of these characteristics, and certainly the most commonly acknowledged feature, is the presence of parallelism, or a correspondence of the second half of a line of Scripture with its first half. Although not completely unrecognized prior to the modern period, Anglican bishop Robert Lowth in his *De sacra poesi Hebraeorum* (1753) most famously described this characteristic of biblical poetry. Lowth described three major types of parallelism: synonymous, antithetic, and synthetic. In synonymous parallelism, the second half of a line essentially repeats the thought of the first half using a similar or related terminology ("An evildoer listens to wicked lips; / and a liar gives heed to a mischievous tongue," Prov. 17:4). With antithetic parallelism, the second half of the line presents the same or related message as the first half by using contrasting terms ("A wise child makes a glad father, / but a foolish child is a mother's grief," Prov. 10:1). Synthetic parallelism is the most elastic of Lowth's categories. With this sort of parallelism, the second half of the verse in some sense expands or builds on the first half to complete it ("Haughty eyes and a proud heart— / the lamp of the wicked—are sin," Prov. 21:4).

Lowth's description of biblical parallelism has proven to be "extraordinarily tenacious" and is still widely cited even as scholars have made important refinements to his analysis and categorization of different types of parallelism (Kugel, 15). Most importantly, the parallelism between two parts of a poetic line of Scripture is not a simple correspondence in meaning, as Lowth's term "synonymous" might suggest; nor need there be a direct correspondence between terms in each line as the designations "antithetic" or "synthetic" could imply. As Adele Berlin writes, parallelism "involves many types of linguistic repetition or equivalences—grammatical structures, semantic terms, words, and sounds" (309). For Kugel, it is the sequencing within a poetic line that is most important. The second part of the line expands on the first part, "carrying it further, echoing it, defining it, restating it, contrasting with it," and "it is this, more than any aesthetic of symmetry or paralleling, which is at the heart of biblical parallelism" (51).

Although the significance of parallelism as one indicator of biblical poetry cannot be denied, scholars have also sought to correct a one-sided view of its preeminence as the primary sign that a biblical text is poetry. Most scholars, like Wilfred G. E. Watson, who offers a taxonomy of features and tropes in biblical poetry, rightly view parallelism as only one characteristic of a poetic text. It is not "*the* characteristic of Hebrew poetry" (Watson 1995, 118, emphasis mine). In fact, parallelism is also sometimes a technique of biblical prose, and some poetic lines do not employ parallelism (Kugel, 70; Berlin, 304).

Hence, scholars have cataloged other important characteristics of biblical poetry besides parallelism. In the poetic tradition of some languages, rhyming and meter—a fixed and regular rhythmic pattern (e.g., iambic pentameter)—are important features of poetry. Although rhyming words can be found in biblical poetry, some scholars suggest it is not a prominent device of biblical poetry (Berlin, 310). By contrast, many students of the Bible have long contended that meter is in fact a feature of biblical poetry and have attempted to count syllables, thought units, and analyze accent patterns to demonstrate this. The nature, and even the existence, of meter in biblical poetry, however, has been increasingly contested. Although certainly biblical poetry at different points makes use of specific, identifiable, and recurring patterns of sound, which is rightly called rhythm (Berlin, 308), most scholars would concede that meter—a regular and relatively inflexible pattern of sounds—is not present in the same way that it is, for instance, in certain traditions of English or classical Greek poetry. As Michael Patrick O'Connor writes, "no consensus has ever been reached in the matter of Hebrew meter because there is none" (O'Connor, 138, cited by Peterson and Richards 1992, 42).

Besides identifying parallelism and the rhythmic patterns of syllables or accents, scholars also point to other aspects of biblical texts that suggest their poetic quality. As Berlin has noted, biblical poetry deploys a host of rhetorical strategies: hyperbole, merismus, personification, rhetorical questions, and so forth. Alliteration, plays on words, and paronomasia, as well as repetitions and refrains, also can be discovered in the poetic books of the Bible. A high density of literary tropes or metaphorical and symbolic language, which for some theorists is the most important indicator that a text is poetic, is also present in biblical poetry (Berlin, 311–13). However, like parallelism, such rhetorical or literary features are not unique to biblical poetry.

Biblical Wisdom Literature

If deciding what constitutes biblical poetry is a somewhat complicated task, discerning which of these biblical poetic texts should be described as "Wisdom literature" is likewise not self-evident. Scholars generally do agree that Proverbs, Job, and Ecclesiastes constitute the three Wisdom books of the Hebrew Scriptures. Likewise, a good number of psalms, such as Psalms 1; 36; 37; 49; 73; 119; 127; 128; 133 have been called "wisdom psalms." The wisdom psalm designation, however, is not precise, and scholars debate which psalms are best said to be related to the wisdom tradition. Some also reckon the Song of Songs as a wisdom composition, but it shares few significant characteristics with indisputable wisdom compositions. Outside of the Hebrew canon, the deuterocanonical (or apocryphal) books of Ben Sira (Sirach) and Wisdom of Solomon are also regularly reckoned as Wisdom books, while examples of wisdom works can also be found among the Dead Sea Scrolls (for example, 4QInstruction) and throughout the literature of the ancient Near East, especially ancient Egypt.

So just what *does* constitute Wisdom literature? How is it, for instance, that three texts as remarkably distinct as (1) Proverbs, with its poetic instructions (1–9) and lists of short sayings (10–29); and (2) Job, with its exploration of the possibility of disinterested piety (1:9), its extended "dialogue" between Job and his "friends" (3–27), and its divine speeches "from the whirlwind" (38–41); and (3) Ecclesiastes, with its skeptical (or joyful?) evaluation of limited human possibilities in the face of inevitable death, all come to be understood as part of the same literary, intellectual, and moral tradition that is called wisdom? How is that certain other texts, including some psalms, likewise are said to share in this tradition? And why is it that most psalms and the Song of Songs are often *not* regarded as wisdom texts? The answer to these questions, of course, is that despite important differences, Proverbs, Job, Ecclesiastes, and a number of other texts not only share much in common but also share *more* with each other than they do with other sorts of biblical literature, including most psalms and Song of Songs. Indeed, Proverbs, Job, Ecclesiastes, and the other wisdom texts noted above share what might be called a set of "family resemblances," as Michael V. Fox and others have similarly put it (Fox, 17).

Vocabulary

One family resemblance that Proverbs, Job, and Ecclesiastes share is a common vocabulary or terminology. Terms derived from the Hebrew words for wisdom, knowledge, understanding, folly, and so forth are prominent in these texts.

> Folly is a joy to one who has no sense,
>> but a person of understanding walks straight ahead. (Prov. 15:21)

> So I turned to consider wisdom and madness and folly . . ." (Eccles. 2:12)

> Who is this that darkens counsel by words without knowledge? (Job 38:2)

> This wisdom characteristic can also be found in some wisdom psalms (e.g., Ps. 49). However, it is not prominent in most Psalms, or in the Song of Songs.
> A cluster of moral terms related to the Hebrew words for justice, righteousness, wickedness, and so forth are also widely represented in Proverbs, Job, and Ecclesiastes:

> the same fate comes to all, to the righteous and the wicked, to the good and to the evil. (Eccles. 9:2)
> The house of the wicked is destroyed,
>> but the tent of the upright flourishes. (Prov. 14:11)
> See, God will not reject a blameless person,
>> nor take the hand of evildoers. (Job 8:20)

Certain wisdom psalms also make use of this moral vocabulary ("The wicked borrow, and do not pay back, / but the righteous are generous and keep giving," Ps. 37:21), although such rhetoric is of course common to other psalms as well. Song of Songs, however, again does not share this wisdom family trait and makes little use of the moral language common to wisdom books.

Teaching

A further easily discernible characteristic that most biblical works that belong to the wisdom family share is a rhetorical emphasis on teaching. This is particularly evident in Proverbs, especially in chapters 1–9, which explicitly sought to teach its ancient readers or hearers what it meant to be wise and just, as its scribal authors and redactors understood wisdom and justice:

> Hear, my child, your father's instruction,
>> and do not reject your mother's teaching. (Prov. 1:8; cf., e.g., Prov.1: 2-6; 2:1; and see
>> sections "Wisdom's Morality" and "Israel's Worship" below)

Although the mode of teaching present in Job and Ecclesiastes is not as obvious as in Proverbs, an instructional emphasis can be discerned in the pages of these books as well. Early on in Job, for example, the satan figure prominently announces one of the questions this book self-consciously explores—the possibility of disinterested piety: "Does Job serve God for nothing?" (1:9). Later, the dialogues between Job and his friends attempt to reckon with the related questions of why Job suffers and why the wicked prosper (see Job 21). In exploring these and other concerns, the text is not merely engaging in an intellectual exercise of moral philosophy but also instructing the reader or hearer in what the scribes who produced Job regarded as key questions emerging from the moral rhetoric of Wisdom literature. These questions seem related to the retributive, or cause-and-effect, rhetoric of traditional, didactic wisdom texts like Proverbs (see section "Israel's Worship" below).

In Ecclesiastes, the voice of Qohelet (or "the Teacher," perhaps the historical author or a literary invention of the scribal authors) asks, "What do people gain from their toil?" (1:3) and explores the fundamental moral question of what is "good for mortals to do" (2:3). Qohelet's famous refrain—which is also a conclusion of his investigations—that there is nothing better than to eat and drink and enjoy what one can (e.g., 2:24; 3:13) is also a form of instruction. As Eccles. 12:9 explicitly puts it, "Besides being wise, the Teacher also *taught* the people knowledge, weighing and studying and arranging many proverbs." Yet for humans who inevitably face death and who witness or experience injustice (e.g., 2:12-19; 9:1-10), Qohelet's instruction is also a vehicle for a deeper sort of critical reflection on the value of traditional wisdom teaching like that encountered in Proverbs.

The teaching emphasis of other biblical books sometimes designated as wisdom works is also not as direct as in Proverbs. Most of the psalms, for instance, are not directly concerned with instruction, but with other matters (offering praise [Psalm 150], structuring lament [Psalm 3]; celebrating torah [Psalm 119]). Even those psalms that are regularly designated as wisdom psalms are sometimes only indirectly instructional. For instance, rather than offering the hearer much specific moral teaching via a rhetoric of wisdom, knowledge, and folly, Psalm 37 appears most concerned to motivate the reader or hearer to remain steadfast in righteousness in the face of persecution and the prospering of the wicked. Similarly, unless the Song of Songs is understood in allegorical terms as revealing the love of the divine for Israel (or of Christ for the church), the erotic poetry of that book can likewise be viewed as instructional only in very broad rhetorical terms.

Solomon

King Solomon is the great patron of wisdom in ancient Israel and in ancient Judaism. Much as Moses was identified with the giving of torah and David with the composition of the Psalms, Solomon is the Israelite ancestor associated with Wisdom literature. A connection with King Solomon is thus a further family trait that can suggest a text belongs to the biblical wisdom tradition.

Solomon's legendary wisdom is recounted in the early chapters of 1 Kings. In 1 Kings 3, rather than petition the divine for "long life, or riches, or for the life of your enemies" (v. 11), Solomon requests the ability to govern well and "to discern between good and evil" (v. 9). He subsequently receives from the divine "a wise and discerning mind" unrivaled among humans before or after him

(v. 12). First Kings 4:29-34 reiterates the fact that Solomon possessed "very great wisdom" and notes his composition of 3,000 proverbs and 3,005 songs, while in 1 Kgs. 10:1-10 the queen of Sheba marvels at Solomon's legendary wisdom and verses 23-25 recall in summary fashion both his great wisdom and wealth.

Several of the collections that make up the book of Proverbs are directly or indirectly related to Solomon (1:1; 10:1; 25:1). Ecclesiastes does not explicitly name Solomon but does allude to Qohelet (or "the Teacher") as "the son of David, king in Jerusalem" (1:1; cf. 1:12). The presentation of the royal figure in 1:12—2:26 likewise seems at least in part designed to evoke memories of King Solomon. Job is not attributed or related to Solomon, but its status as Wisdom literature is never questioned, being secured by the other wisdom family traits the book demonstrates. By contrast, Psalm 72 is directly related to Solomon but is usually classed as a "royal psalm" and not Wisdom literature. The erotic poetry of the Song of Songs, of course, likewise alludes directly to Solomon (1:1, 5; 3:7-11; 8:11-12), but this connection with the legendary king is essentially the book's only wisdom characteristic.

International Influence, Universal Perspective

Although King Solomon is the great patron of wisdom in ancient Israel, the biblical wisdom texts also belong to a broader ancient Near Eastern literary tradition and share many family traits, including a kind of universal moral perspective, with a range of texts from Egypt and Mesopotamia. Because of its affinity with this international tradition, the Israelite wisdom books have sometimes been said to represent a foreign or non-Israelite element in biblical literature. In the past, for instance, some scholars argued that verses in Proverbs that invoke Israel's deity, YHWH, are late or secondary reworkings of a literature that is basically non-Israelite.

Sections of Proverbs are, of course, attributed to non-Israelites. A certain Agur speaks at 30:1, and the mother of Lemuel is the author of the instruction at 31:1-9. What's more, Prov. 22:17—23:11 (or 24:22) is also almost certainly influenced by the Egyptian Instruction of Amenemope. The character of Job, though not necessarily the book's author, is also a non-Israelite. But claims about biblical wisdom's foreignness are overstated. The Bible's Wisdom literature certainly shows affinities to other ancient Near Eastern works, but so do other parts of the Bible (cf. biblical and ancient Near Eastern creation stories, flood stories, covenant texts, and so forth). The Wisdom literature, like the rest of the Bible, belongs to a broader ancient Near Eastern cultural milieu and is largely the product of scribes, at least some of whom would have been multilingual and engaged in managing international relations for the Israelite and Judahite (and later Judean) political and economic elite. It is thus to be expected that the work of these comparatively cosmopolitan Israelite and Judahite (and later Judean) scribes would reflect their intimate knowledge of the scribal wisdom works of neighboring peoples.

However, it is true that Israelite wisdom books appear, on the one hand, less concerned with certain themes prominent in other parts of the Bible that scholars have sometimes regarded as central to Israelite identity and, on the other hand, more concerned with broader, universal questions of ethics or morality. Proverbs, Job, and Ecclesiastes do not, for instance, much mention torah, the cult, the Sinai covenant, or the exodus. Rather, the book of Proverbs emphasizes a general and broad moral instruction and the formation of character through the attainment of virtues and values that the ancient sages believed were necessary to produce good and flourishing human lives (see "Wisdom's Virtues" below). More critical or self-consciously reflective wisdom books like Job and Ecclesiastes likewise explore issues that other ancient Near Eastern texts also address. Job's wrestling with the suffering of the righteous, for instance, finds parallels in a text such as the Babylonian Theodicy. Likewise, the famous call in Ecclesiastes to eat, drink, and enjoy life in the face of inevitable death is a perspective echoed in works such as the Mesopotamian Epic of Gilgamesh and the Egyptian Harpers' Songs.

Genre and Forms

Texts that belong to the Wisdom literature family also often participate in the same genres and share certain literary forms. Michael V. Fox suggests there are two main wisdom genres from the ancient Near East: "didactic Wisdom and critical (or speculative) Wisdom" (17). Didactic wisdom regularly takes the form of a wisdom "instruction," the teaching of traditional values and virtues passed down usually from a father to a son. In biblical Wisdom literature, the instruction form is primarily evident in the poems of Proverbs 1–9, where the parental voice—identified as both male and female at the outset in 1:8 (see also 4:3; 6:20; 10:1; 15:20; 23: 22; 28: 7; 29:3, 15, 17; 30:17), but as male in 4:3—is closely identified with the words spoken by personified Woman Wisdom, who also instructs the book's addressee. The instruction form is also evident at 22:17—23:11 (24:22), a passage that is likely dependent on the Egyptian Instruction of Amenemope, and at 31:1-9, where the voice of another female teacher, the mother of Lemuel, instructs her son. Didactic wisdom books, however, can also incorporate forms besides the instruction (see below).

According to Fox, critical wisdom books "reflect and comment *on* doctrines and values" that didactic Wisdom literature seeks to directly inculcate in its hearers (17, italics original). This genre is represented by texts such as Job and Psalms 49, 73, and 88. Fox does not regard Qohelet as a species of critical wisdom—though others surely would. For him, although "Qohelet contains much critical or reflective material . . . it presents itself as a teaching about how to live one's life and is to be classed as didactic" (17–18). Most psalms and the Song of Songs, however, belong to neither the genre of didactic wisdom or critical wisdom. The genres of the psalms are diverse (see "Worship and the Psalms" below), and Song of Songs is best described as ancient erotic poetry, though there is a long tradition in both Judaism and Christianity of interpreting the book as an allegory of God's love for Israel or Christ's love for the church.

Besides the "instruction," the literary form perhaps most commonly associated with biblical Wisdom literature is the *mashal*, regularly translated as "proverb" in English. The short, usually two-line proverb, or *mashal*, is prevalent in Proverbs 10–29 and is common to wisdom books obviously dependent on Proverbs (such as Sirach). Ecclesiastes also includes relatively long sections of short proverbs (see 7:1-13 and aspects of 5:1-12 and 9:17—11:6), even if these proverbs seem sometimes to be more intentionally arranged and deliberately ironic and provocative than most of the sayings in Proverbs—for example:

> A good name is better than precious ointment,
>   and the day of death, than the day of birth. (7:1)

> Sorrow is better than laughter,
>   for by sadness of countenance the heart is made glad. (7:3)

The *mashal* is a form not regularly associated with non-wisdom psalms or Song of Songs, although like Job, the poetry in these books is often presented in couplets that regularly deploy parallelism, as do most *meshalim*.

Some biblical scholars have sought to understand biblical proverbs in light of the study of the short, pithy, usually one-line folk saying easily identifiable in a host of cultures (e.g., "A stitch in time saves nine"; "One who chases two rats will kill nothing," a Yoruba proverb cited by Pachocinski, 292). For these commentators, the short sayings that make up much of the book of Proverbs (especially chs. 10–29) likely find their origin in the oral, folk wisdom of the Israelite peasant population. Others, however, have emphasized the literary as opposed to oral quality of the two-line *mashal* in the Bible and have identified the royal court, the temple, or some sort of formal educational institution as the most likely social setting for the development of the *meshalim* of Proverbs and for the origins of Wisdom literature more generally.

However, the term *mashal* does not denote only the kind of short saying (or proverb) that is common in Proverbs 10–29. The prophetic allegories in Ezekiel 17 and 24, for instance, are each represented as a *mashal*. What's more, in Prov. 1:6, the term is paralleled to "figure" and "riddles," which suggests that the word can also refer to some sort of deflected discourse in need of interpretation. As Fox concludes, the *mashal* can be broadly understood as a "trope" or some sort of symbolic language, or more narrowly as a short saying or a proverb (54–55).

Both didactic wisdom and critical wisdom literature, of course, deploy other identifiable forms besides the instruction or the *mashal*. Another ancient form adapted by Ecclesiastes, for example, is the royal testament (1:12—2:11) whereby a king recounts his own greatness and exploits. Job too contains a multitude of forms. The book, for instance, opens and closes with a prose tale that frames an extended wisdom dialogue between Job and his friends (Job 3–27), while the words attributed to Elihu later in the book (Job 32–37) are related to Israel's hymn tradition. Other easily identifiable forms taken up by wisdom texts include an acrostic poem (Prov. 31:10-31), the macarism or beatitude (e.g., Ps. 1:1; Prov. 3:13; Eccles. 10:17), and numerical sayings (e.g., Prov. 6:16-19; 30:18-31).

Wisdom Morality: Virtues and Their Value

If "teaching" in the tradition of Solomon is a characteristic of Wisdom literature and the "instruction" and the *mashal* are among the prominent literary forms used to present wisdom lessons, what exactly does Wisdom literature teach or instruct one in? What are the universal moral perspectives and questions that the texts address with their vocabulary of wisdom and righteousness, wickedness, and folly?

Wisdom's Virtues

Several scholars (such as Brown) have pointed to the prologue of Proverbs (1:2-7) as key to understanding that book's moral goals, which are themselves foundational to the moral vision of the wisdom tradition in ancient Israel. After the superscription of 1:1, which gives the book its name—*Mishle* (Hebrew), or Proverbs—the prologue highlights the book's moral purposes largely, though not simply, through a series of infinitive constructions. The text seeks to instill three types of virtues: intellectual virtues ("wisdom," "insight," v. 2), social virtues ("justice, righteousness, and equity"; v. 3), and practical virtues ("shrewdness," "prudence," i.e., "cunning," v. 4). The design of the poem, not usually evident in English translations, literarily suggests that the book's authors especially prized the social virtues of verse 3, which stands at the pinnacle of the prologue's structure (see Brown, 23–30).

Both simple youth and advanced sages (see 1:4-5) can be instructed in the virtues that constitute the way or path of wisdom, a metaphorical complex important to Wisdom literature's moral discourse, especially in Proverbs 1–9. In wisdom thinking, there are only two moral options: the way of wisdom and righteousness, which leads to life, and the path of folly and wickedness, which leads to death. All who proceed in wisdom's way will increase in wisdom, or as Prov. 1:5-6 puts it, "gain in learning" and "acquire skill" to understand wisdom's moral teaching. The one who follows wisdom's way will learn to comprehend a "proverb" (or trope), a "figure," and "riddles." These words might designate specific genres that Proverbs deploys, although genuine riddles do not seem to be present in the book. By contrast, all of the terms individually, and when paired, connote some sort of figurative discourse or a discourse in need of interpretation. Thus, rather than naming specific forms of speech that might be found in Proverbs, they more probably together describe the character of the book's moral discourse and the project of acquiring and advancing in wisdom more generally. Following wisdom's way will produce intellectual, social, and practical virtue, as Prov. 1:2-4 claims. But wholly following the "way" of this teaching is not a simple activity. To travel wisdom's path fully will demand some hard interpretive work, like the unraveling of a riddle or the exploration of a trope.

The final verse of Proverbs' prologue introduces a further important concept for biblical Wisdom literature: the fear of the Lord (e.g., 1:7; 8:13; 9:10; Job 1:1; 28:28; Eccles. 12:13). The fear of the Lord is a much-discussed concept. As Fox recognizes, it can refer to a certain awe and respect of the holy Other. However, the notion of the fear of the Lord also retains traces of literal fear of a powerful deity, a fear that can motivate adherence to wisdom's way, as do the promises of rewards and punishment in Proverbs and elsewhere in Wisdom literature (Fox, 69–71). The emphasis on fear of the Lord as the beginning of wisdom (or knowledge) at the end of the Proverbs prologue places the intellectual, social, and practical virtues of wisdom's way (see 1:2-4) in intimate connection with a fundamental religious virtue, although ancient writers and readers would not have distinguished moral and religious virtues, or presuppose a religious-secular split in the way many contemporary people do. All the virtues belong to wisdom, which itself is intimately related to YHWH and YHWH's creation (see Prov. 8:22-31).

The prologue of Proverbs thus points toward key aspects of wisdom discourse, especially in didactic wisdom literature, which sages in different books build on, reflect on, and sometimes, as with the critical impulses of Job and Ecclesiastes, interrogate. Much of the content of the virtues and values that didactic wisdom offers are introduced early in Proverbs (chs. 1–9). The antisocial behavior of violent, greedy people is clearly denounced (1:10-19), and one should not withhold good from, or plan harm to, a neighbor (3:27-29). Chapter 6 warns against standing surety (vv. 1-5), laziness (vv. 6-11), deceptive behavior (vv. 12-15), arrogance, false testimony, and sewing "discord" (vv. 16-19), the last being a topic also taken up in 3:30-35. All of these practices or vices can contribute to social conflict and so highlight the premium the sages placed on social virtue noted above (1:3). Wisdom's concern with social stability, albeit in a clearly patriarchal vein, is also evident in the energy Proverbs invests in warning a male addressee of the "strange" or "foreign" woman, who on the literal level of the text is another man's wife with whom he might commit adultery (see Prov. 2:16-19; 5:3-20; 6:24-35; 7:1-27; 22:14; cf. Fox, 134–41, and below). Wise persons will know how to employ practical virtues—shrewdness and cunning—to promote and maintain social virtue and avoid vice, although the wisdom tradition knows such practical "wisdom" can often be used for ill rather than good. Wisdom literature's prizing of intellectual virtue is evidenced in Proverbs 8, which informs the hearer of Woman Wisdom's divine origins and her intimate relationship to the structure of the cosmos (see 3:19-20).

The virtues of wisdom's way introduced in Proverbs 1–9 are reiterated and expanded in the proverb collections of 10–29 (31). The short sayings in these chapters promote the virtues of diligence and hard work (10:4; 21:5), honesty in speech (16:13) and business dealings (11:1; 16:11), avoidance of adultery or the strange woman (22:14), kindness and generosity to the poor (14:31; 19:17) and social justice (21:3), as well as humility and fear of the Lord (11:2; 22:4). The sayings also acknowledge the efficacy of intellectual and practical virtues, but subordinate these to the divine will (16:1, 9; cf. 2:7).

Most of wisdom's virtues as presented in Proverbs are highlighted in one way or another in Job as well. In his self-defense, for example, Job claims to be one who embodied wisdom's virtues, especially social virtue: "I put on righteousness, and it clothed me; my justice was like a robe and a turban" (29:14). Job claims to have "delivered the poor" and the "orphan who had no helper" and to have made the "widow's heart sing"; he was "a father to the needy" and championed the cause of the "stranger" (29:12-16; cf. 30:24-25; 31:13-21). He likewise was sexually virtuous (31:1, 9), feared god (31:23; cf. 1:1), understood the limited value of wealth as opposed to wisdom (31:24-25; see also "Wisdom's Desirability" below), and was honest in speech and his dealings (31:30, 38-40). The poem treating wisdom's great value and inaccessibility (ch. 28), and the divine speeches (chs. 38–41), which highlight the mystery of creation, likewise point to this wisdom book's interest in esoteric intellectual matters.

Despite Ecclesiastes' more ambiguous instructional intentions, its author—whether Qohelet or a circle of scribes—likewise knows of wisdom's central social virtues, even if the text recognizes they are too often absent in society (3:16-17; 4:1-6). The book's intellectual curiosity is evident in its fundamental question about the "good" in human life and the Teacher's investigations into human strivings (e.g., 1:3-11; 2:1, 12). At Eccles. 7:16-17, wisdom's emphasis on practical virtue is also recognizable in Qohelet's famous exhortation: "Do not be too righteous, and do not act too wise; why should you destroy yourself? Do not be too wicked and do not be a fool; why should you die before your time?"

Wisdom's Desirability

Besides introducing virtues and values important to wisdom's way, Proverbs 1–9 also functions fundamentally to underscore for its addressee the *value* of wise instruction and the *worth* of following wisdom's way and acquiring wisdom's virtues. Most important to this rhetorical work of valuing wisdom's way are economic and erotic discourses, but they are not the only sorts of images the text deploys to describe wisdom's worth or desirability. Woman Wisdom, for example, does not merely cry out (1:20-33) like a prophet (cf. Jeremiah 7) to be heard and followed but also insists that wisdom, insight, and understanding should be passionately pursued as one might search for precious silver and treasure (2:4). Those who find wisdom are said to be "happy," and wisdom is described as more valuable than "silver," "gold," and "jewels" since "nothing you desire can compare with her." Wisdom's ways are "pleasantness" and "peace" (3:13-18), and wisdom affords security amid uncertainty in life (3:21-26).

The personification of wisdom as a woman is one of the most significant aspects of Israelite Wisdom literature (see esp. Prov. 1:20-33; 8:22-36; Sirach 24; Wis. 6:12-20; 7:22-28; cf. Job 28). Historical-critical scholarship has sought the origin of this figure in a number of ways. Some have understood her as simply a literary personification. Others suggest she is a hypostatization of YHWH's wisdom, while others underscore the influence of ancient goddess figures in her depictions, for example, Egyptian Ma'at, or more likely, Isis. Yet, whatever her provenance, the figure of Wisdom is also part of the effort of the ancient patriarchal authors to describe for a male audience the desirability or worth of their moral perspectives, their way of wisdom. Wisdom is not only valuable like material wealth. She is also presented in terms of a desirable, marriageable woman. In Prov. 4:5-8, the addressee is encouraged to "acquire" (cf. Boaz's marriage, or "acquisition," of Ruth in Ruth 4:10) and to "love" Wisdom, to "not forsake" her, and to "embrace her." If the addressee does these things, if he attains to wisdom's virtues, Woman Wisdom will not only "keep" and "guard" him but also bring him "honor," as might the ideal wife of the ancient patriarchal imagination. As Prov. 4:9 promises the addressee, Wisdom will "place on your head a fair garland" and "bestow on you a beautiful crown," images that many scholars (though not all) associate with ancient marriage customs (cf. Song 3:6-11).

In binary fashion not uncommon to patriarchal discourse, in Proverbs 1–9 Woman Wisdom— a symbol of the right way of wisdom and righteousness—is regularly contrasted with the strange or foreign woman (see 2:16-19; 5:3-20; 6:24-35; 7:1-27; cf. Woman Folly in 9:13-18). Literally understood, the patriarchal text presents the strange woman as an illegitimate and dangerous sexual partner for its imagined young male addressee; she is another man's wife and the opposite of the addressee's (potentially) real wife (see 5:15-20). The addressee of Proverbs is urged to be content with his own real wife but also to seek Woman Wisdom, whose desirability is constructed in erotic terms associated with legitimate patriarchal marriage. The addressee's real wife, but especially Wisdom, whom he might acquire like a wife, can save him from the dangers of illicit sex with the strange, adulterous woman (2:16-19; 6:24) and more generally from the illicit "way" of folly and wickedness, for which the strange woman is also a trope.

The image of desirable, valuable wisdom is also present in Job, where "the price of wisdom is above pearls" (Job 28:18; cf. 28:15-19). Qohelet likewise knows that "wisdom excels folly as light excels darkness" (2:13), even if such a statement in Ecclesiastes is designed to relativize wisdom's worth. Images of desirable, personified Wisdom in the Hebrew Bible not surprisingly also influenced later Jewish reflection on wisdom, for example, in Philo and the New Testament (John 1; 1 Cor. 1:18-21; Col. 2:3). Woman Wisdom (or in Greek, *sophia*) has likewise proven an important, generative biblical-theological image for critical feminist theologians.

Wisdom's Moral Rhetoric

One of the oft-noted features of the moral discourse of especially didactic wisdom texts such as Proverbs, or the words of Job's friends in Job 3–27, is a cause-and-effect rhetoric.

> A slack hand causes poverty,
>> but the hand of the diligent makes rich. (Prov. 10:4)

> I have not seen the righteous forsaken,
>> or their children begging bread. (Ps. 37:25)

This act-consequence rhetoric of biblical Wisdom literature has been much discussed. Klaus Koch, for instance, famously argued that such rhetoric is evidence that some biblical texts (such as Proverbs) present an inherent relationship between deeds and their results so that any punishment or reward for wrongdoing or virtuous activity was essentially an automatic byproduct of the act itself; it did not necessarily require the divine to act as the agent of retribution to mete out punishments and rewards.

Koch's view regarding acts and consequences in the Bible has been criticized and refined by other scholars. Nonetheless, a strong retributive rhetoric is undeniably present in much Wisdom literature and the moral import of such rhetoric is important to grasp. Some readers understand the cause-and-effect rhetoric in books like Proverbs in strong, literal fashion as promising and threatening real material and social rewards and punishments: if one keeps wisdom, one will prosper, but if one strays to the way of folly, misfortune awaits. This simplistic ideology, then, is sometimes thought to stand in stark contrast to Job and Ecclesiastes, which are characterized as offering critical, more nuanced responses to traditional wisdom's act-consequence schema. These critical wisdom works understand that a simple retributive moral view of the cosmos does not accurately reflect reality, since sometimes the wicked prosper, the righteous suffer, and wisdom does not always secure a flourishing life for those who follow its way (see Crenshaw).

The retributive rhetoric of much Wisdom literature, however, should not be understood in overly literal terms or caricatured as fundamentally naive about the vagaries of human experience. Wisdom writers never understood their retributive rhetoric to represent the way the world actually and always operates. Even scholars who believe that traditional wisdom's cause-and-effect rhetoric implies a strong retributive principle to be at work in the real world have long noted that the sages recognized "exceptions" to their retributive rule. Others suggest that such retributive rhetoric may have formed part of a pedagogical strategy that would have proved effective for instructing young students (see Prov. 1:4; Crenshaw, 267).

Yet if the retributive rhetoric of wisdom texts like Proverbs is part of a pedagogical strategy and not merely a series of literal promises of reward and punishment, it is also more than this. Didactic wisdom literature in particular functions fundamentally as moral instruction that seeks to form the character of its hearers or addressees by promoting a range of values and virtues it regards as essential (though perhaps not sufficient) for attaining a good and flourishing life. Wisdom literature's retributive rhetoric is thus a piece of this tradition's larger discursive moral work. The certainty of its rhetorical structure—if this, then this—supports the ancient sages' broader certainty that wisdom is integrally related to the divine act of creation. Wisdom's virtues belong to the very structure of the cosmos that YHWH created (Prov. 8:22-31). A child or unreflective youth might initially follow wisdom's way out of a hope for the real rewards or fear of the real punishments articulated by wisdom's retributive rhetoric. But this is not the end of wisdom's way. More mature students who learn to understand wisdom's tropes and figures—its broader symbolic moral discourse—would come to do so not through any external motivation of rewards and punishment, but because the acquisition of wisdom's virtues—the aligning of oneself with the genuine moral structure of YHWH's created cosmos—has become its own reward.

Israel's Worship: A Brief Overview

Understanding the Bible's poetic (and other) texts that relate to worship in ancient Israel is just as challenging a task as reckoning with biblical poetry's wisdom texts. It can be instructive to first gain an overview of the particulars of worship in that milieu—the *where*, *what*, *when*, and *who* of worship in ancient Israel. Yet even this seemingly straightforward undertaking can be vexing, for the study of ancient Israel's worship must reckon with several core issues or questions, each of which are complicated topics in and of themselves, taking different shapes depending on how the biblical sources and the data from the material remains of the ancient Levant are construed and prioritized, as well as how they are correlated to different epochs in ancient Israelite history. Hence, only a few of the most significant aspects of Israel's worship as attested in the Bible and in the material remains can be offered here before considering the way Scripture's poetic books, especially the Psalms, reflect Israel's worship practices and theology.

The Hebrew Scriptures testify to the fact that Israel's worship—its practices and ideological and theological expressions of devotion to their deity or deities—originated and developed in the often tumultuous and conflicted spiritual, socioeconomic, and political struggles of Israelite and Judean individuals and communities. Israel's worship reflected the effort of these individuals and communities to understand their existence and construct meaning for themselves in light of the divine reality that they understood themselves to have encountered. Put otherwise, worship in ancient Israel, as attested in the Bible and by the material remains of the ancient Levant, cannot be construed as monolithic. To the contrary, it developed over the centuries, taking different forms at different times and places, and was often contested by social actors.

Sites of Worship

One of the central questions for understanding the Bible's world of worship has to do with *where* worship happened in ancient Israel. Much of biblical literature, especially the Deuteronomist school and texts allied to the Deuteronomistic perspective, identify the temple in Jerusalem on Mount Zion as the most important site of worship. This centralization of worship is often associated with the religious reforms instituted by King Josiah of Judah in the late seventh century BCE (2 Kings 23). Yet the biblical texts also reveal that worship at different moments in the history of ancient Israel and Judah was quite diverse and not confined to the Jerusalem temple. For example, in a text that purports to recount events early in Israel's history, a certain Elkanah worshiped and sacrificed at Shiloh, where Eli was priest (1 Samuel 1). The Bible also speaks of important shrines at Bethel and Dan that were sanctioned by the monarchs of the northern kingdom of Israel, where official communal worship practices would have been carried out (1 Kgs. 12:25-33). So too the texts allude to "high places" where devotees would have also worshiped the divine outside of central sites like Bethel, Dan, or Jerusalem (1 Kgs. 12:31).

Yet worship in ancient Israel was likely not limited to these more or less official sites. Patrick D. Miller (62–76), for instance, notes that together the Bible and archaeological data suggest that extended families or clans could be associated with particular shrines, while some domestic households were also sites of religious practices. Judges 6:11; 19-24; and 8:22-27, for example, appear to allude to the shrine associated with Gideon's clan, while Jer. 19:13 and 32:29 attest to (non-Yahwistic) domestic rooftop worship.

Content of Worship

Besides the "where" of worship at temples, high places, and in family settings, an important issue for understanding ancient Israel's worship is a consideration of *what* took place at temples, shrines, and other cultic sites. Central here are, of course, the prayers and songs of individuals or the gathered community to which the Psalms testify (see "Worship and the Psalms" section below). Yet just as important are Israel's system(s) of offerings and sacrifices, which themselves are related to particular sites of worship and conceptions of holiness and purity. The Bible mentions an array of offerings and sacrifices that formed part of ancient Israel's worship. Several of these can be mentioned here briefly.

Tithes and offerings of firstfruits were offered primarily in thanksgiving to the deity. In large part, they served to support priestly service (Num. 18:12-32; Deut. 14:27-29; 18:3-5; 26:12; Neh. 10:37-38; 13:10-12), but also could be consumed by worshipers (Deut. 14:22-26; Miller, 118–20). The "burnt offering" (*'olah*), however, was fully consumed on the sacrificial altar (Lev. 1:9). The *'olah* sacrifice may have served to elicit divine favor or to call the deity's attention to a worshiper's plight. It also at points seems to have served an expiatory function (Leviticus 1) and could be associated with occasions of celebration as well (Lev. 22:17-22; Num. 15:1-11; Miller, 107–9). In contrast to the *'olah*, only a small part of the *minhah*, or "grain offering," was consumed on the sacrificial altar, with the remainder going to the priests as their portion (Lev. 2:9-10).

In contrast to both the *'olah*, which was fully consumed by sacrificial fire, and the grain offering, which was primarily the priestly portion, the meat of a well-being sacrifice (*zevah shelamim*)—whether offered as thanksgiving, in payment of a vow, or as a general freewill offering—was to be primarily consumed by the worshiper (Leviticus 3; Miller, 113).

According to Leviticus, a further sacrifice, the *hatta't*, or "purification offering" (in the past, often called the "sin offering"), functioned to purify the holy sanctuary from uncleanness that may have attached to it either through ritual impurity or impurity caused by unintentional sin (Leviticus 4–5; see especially Milgrom, 253–93). The *hatta't* is also the central offering in the Yom Kippur, or Day of Atonement, sacrificial ritual (Leviticus 16). A further sacrifice, the *'asham* (Leviticus 5), or "reparation offering" (sometimes rendered as "guilt offering"), like the *hatta't*, was "expiatory in some sense," or was "intended to deal with particular kinds of sins and their effects or with violations of the sacred." It served "primarily to make reparation for an offense of which one is guilty" (Miller, 117).

Occasions of Worship

Closely related to the where and what, or the site and content, of Israel's worship, is the *when* of Israel's worship. Worship in ancient Israel was both prompted by the intermittent needs of individuals and the community and structured into a regular cycle of religious celebration.

The different genres of the Psalms are testimony to particular moments of individual or communal crisis (such as illness [6], military threat [46]), or celebration and thanksgiving (such as healing [30], military victory [18], or a royal marriage [45]), that might provoke worship and be structured in and through worship practices (see "Worship and the Psalms" section below). Alongside such occasional moments of worship, the Bible also attests to Israel's worship of the divine at regular, recurring moments. Leviticus 23 and Numbers 28–29, for instance, record versions of the Bible's cultic or worship calendar. The Tamid, or "daily offering," was a sacrifice offered in the morning and evening (Num. 28:1-8), while other offerings were associated with the Sabbath day (Num. 28:9-10) and the new moon (28:11-15). The superscription of Psalm 92 identifies this text as a song for the Sabbath-day worship.

The complex traditions of cultic celebrations in the Bible also record a number of communal festivals. Three of the communal pilgrimage festivals were particularly important: (1) The spring Festival of Passover (Pesach), which celebrated the Hebrews' escape from Egypt (and at some point in ancient Israel's history incorporated a distinct agricultural festival of unleavened bread); (2) The Festival of Weeks or Pentecost (Shavu'ot), which marked the end of the grain harvest seven weeks after Passover; and (3) Booths (Sukkot), the fall harvest festival. The Psalms of Ascent (120–34) are often thought to be associated with pilgrims' ascent to Jerusalem for the celebration of the communal feasts.

Functionaries of Worship

Most Israelite women, men, and children would have participated in ancient Israel's worship life in important ways, such as by taking part in sacrificial meals and pilgrimage festivals, by offering prayers, making vows, uttering blessings, and likely in household worship rituals (see Miller, 203). Yet in the ancient patriarchal context, official worship leadership in Yahwistic religion would have predominantly fallen to adult male members of the community.

The central institution of the priesthood was likely reserved exclusively for males, and the Bible suggests that priestly responsibilities lay in three main areas (so Miller, 165–71): (1) Divination, or the discerning of the divine will, by, for instance, the casting of the Urim and Thummim (Deut. 33:8); (2) teaching torah, especially as this pertains to rituals associated with sacrifice and questions of uncleanness and holiness (Leviticus 13); (3) offering sacrifices and manipulating the blood of sacrifices (Leviticus 1–7).

Despite clear roles for priests, the priesthood itself was a contested institution that evolved throughout biblical history in relation to the roles of various priestly families and in terms of the status of various religious shrines or sites of worship. For example, the Levites likely originally held full priestly rank (as in Deuteronomy), but were according to certain texts demoted to the status of cultic assistants in a later epoch (Num. 3:5-10; 1 Chron. 23:2-6; Ezek. 44:10-16; see Miller, 162–65, 171–74). Other biblical texts similarly attest to "priestly politics" in ancient Israel and to the rise of the Zadokite or Aaronide priesthood (see 1 Kgs. 1–2).

Yet besides priests and Levites and their roles in worship, the Bible also attests to the role of other nonpriestly functionaries in ancient Israel's worship life, both women and men. Male and female musicians, singers, and dancers, for example, appear to have played important roles in worship contexts. As Ps. 68:25-26 (English vv. 24-25) states:

> Your solemn processions are seen, O God,
>> the processions of my God, my King, into the sanctuary—
> the singers in front, the musicians last,
>> between them girls playing tambourines.

A number of sometimes-obscure references in the Psalms likewise appear to suggest a role for singers, instruments, and musicians in biblical worship, while the antiphonal structure of certain Psalms (Psalms 122; 133; 136) is often thought to suggest participation in worship by a gathered assembly and not merely cultic functionaries. Although there are no clear data, in the family context, elders—women and men—likely would have held leadership roles in worship.

Objects of Worship

In the Bible, worship is primarily directed toward YHWH, the principal deity of the Israelites and Judahites (and later Judeans). Yet the fact that the ancient Israelites and Judahites worshiped deities besides YHWH is also well attested in the Bible. This worship, however, is regularly censured as illegitimate especially by the Deuteronomistic redactors of the Bible, and other allied voices, which sought to present the exclusive worship of YHWH as normative. Although certain texts in the Hebrew Bible may reveal a monotheistic impulse (such as the later chapters of Isaiah), exclusive worship of YHWH in the Hebrew Bible cannot usually in the strict sense be called monotheism, the belief in the existence of only one deity. Rather, it is monolatry, the exclusive devotion to one god, without denying the existence of other deities.

Jeremiah 44 is only one rather full example of a passage that alludes to the worship of a deity outside the realm of official Yahwism, although again with a negative evaluation that reflects the influence of Deuteronomistic theology. The text indicates that some ancient Judahites, apparently with significant leadership of women, worshiped a female deity. In Jer. 44:17-19 (cf. 7:16-18), first Judahite men and women and then only women—all refugees in Egypt from the destruction of Jerusalem by the Babylonians in 586 BCE—proclaim:

> we will do everything that we have vowed, make offerings to the queen of heaven and pour out libations to her, just as we and our ancestors, our kings and our officials, used to do in the towns of Judah and in the streets of Jerusalem. . . . And the women said, "indeed we will go on making offerings to the queen of heaven and pouring out libations to her; do you think that we made cakes for her, marked with her image, and poured out libations to her without our husbands' being involved?"

Besides the Queen of Heaven (likely the Mesopotamian deity Ishtar), the Bible probably speaks of another female deity worshiped by some ancient Israelites and Judahites. Allusions to the "asherah" in the biblical texts usually seems to refer to what was likely a tree or wooden cult object. At other points, however, it is possible that the text understands Asherah to be a female deity (2 Kgs. 23:4), who was worshiped alongside YHWH and who was well-known in the ancient Levant. Two now-famous inscriptions from Israelite sites at Kuntillet 'Ajrud and Khirbet el Qom, dating from the eighth century BCE, which mention YHWH and his Asherah, are likely allusions to this Israelite goddess. Some scholars also note that the depiction of Woman Wisdom, who is intimately related to YHWH in texts like Prov. 8:22-31, is reminiscent of ancient Near Eastern goddess figures and may in fact preserve a memory of the veneration of a female deity in Israel as well.

Worship and the Psalms

Although historians of ancient Israel have long described how the Bible testifies to the origins and development of Israelite religion, the biblical texts themselves imagine the major institutions, practices, and theologies of Israelite worship in light of a larger story of the divine's interaction with the descendants of Sarah and Abraham as recounted in the Pentateuch. In this larger story, the people's rescue from Egypt by their deity YHWH is the most important event. In the biblical narrative, the Torah, including instructions regarding Israel's sacrificial system, the roles of priests and other functionaries, the pilgrimage festivals, and even the Deuteronomic insistence on a single (Jerusalem) temple as a site of exclusive worship of YHWH, are all directions given to the Israelites in light of their escape from Egyptian slavery.

Outside the Pentateuch, Israel's other great worship text—the Psalms—also acknowledges this broader story of salvation, and recognizes identification with this narrative as a meaningful framework for Israel's worship life (Pss. 22:4-5; 66:5-7; 80:8; 83:9-11; 135:8-9). Indeed, the Psalter itself has been shaped into "five books" that parallel the structure of the five books of Moses, which transmit the people's foundational story. Certain "historical psalms," such as Psalm 136, also liturgically recall the people's history with their God—"who struck Egypt through their firstborn . . . , and brought Israel out from among them . . . who divided the Red Sea in two . . . and made Israel pass through the midst of it . . . , but overthrew Pharaoh and his army in the Red Sea" (136:10-15).

Yet Israel did not understand the encounter of the divine as belonging only to the great salvific moments of history. Adherence to the instruction of torah formed a kind of present response to the deity's past salvific work on behalf of the people. Likewise the Psalms reflect the ongoing encounter of individuals and communities with the deity in the midst of the rhythms of daily life. Indeed, upon hearing the moments of the great salvation story recited publicly in Psalm 136 (above), gathered worshipers likely would have proclaimed in antiphonal fashion an ongoing present relationship with the divine rescuer with the words, "for his steadfast love endures forever." Indeed, Israel's response to the deity in worship can in part be traced via the genres or forms of speech deployed throughout the Psalter.

Scholars long ago reached a broad consensus regarding the genres of most of the psalms in the book of Psalms. These forms or genres suggest how individual psalms may have functioned in Israel's worship. Psalms of individual or communal lament, for example, reveal human voices yearning for relief from the realities of suffering and injustice (individual lament psalms might include 3; 5–7; 13; 17; 22; 25–28; 31; 38–40; 42; 43; 51; 54; 57; 69–71; 120; 139; 142; communal laments might include 9; 12; 44; 58; 60; 74; 79; 80; 94; 137). Songs of thanksgiving express human gratitude for divine responses to petitions—for rescue, provision, and justice (18; 30; 32; 34; 40; 65–67; 75; 92; 103; 107; 116; 118; 138). Hymns of praise orient humans in relation to an exalted deity. They recall not only the divine majesty that worshipers might experience but also reveal and call forth joyful aspects of worship (Psalms 8; 19; 66; 100; 104; 111; 114; 148; 145–150; see Pleins).

The forms or genres of other psalms likewise point to their place in Israelite worship. As was already noted, the Songs of Ascent (Psalms 120–134) may have been associated with the practice of pilgrims "going up" to Jerusalem for one or another of the great festivals. A number of other psalms focus on Zion (Psalms 46; 48; 76; 87; 125), or the king, who likely played an important role in the official cult and in maintaining the institutions of worship (Psalms 2; 24; 29; 45; 47; 72; 93; 95–99; 101; 110). Certain psalms also seem clearly composed with liturgical contexts in mind (Psalms 15; 24), while the antiphonal structure of others suggests a concrete usage in acts of worship (Psalms 123; 133; 136). Still other psalms, as already mentioned, celebrate torah (Psalms 1; 119) or deploy wisdom vocabulary and forms to, for instance, help worshipers reckon with the anomalous realities of evil befalling righteous persons and the prosperity of the wicked (Psalms 36; 37; 49; 73; 127; 128; 133).

Conclusion: The Wisdom and Worship of Scribes, Others, and Us

An important question remains: Exactly *whose* ideas of wisdom and *whose* vision and models of worship does a reader encounter in the Bible's poetic books? To describe the wisdom and worship of these texts as "biblical" or even as "Israelite," "Judahite," or "Judean" is not only tautology but also perhaps obscures as much as it reveals when asking about the figures behind the Bible's wisdom and worship texts. As with most other biblical literature, it is likely that the poetic books as we have them in their *final* form in the Hebrew Bible are the product of intellectually or educationally elite scribes or sages. These scribes would have been overwhelmingly male and socially well-placed individuals.

Ideological critics of the Bible have often, and rightly, demonstrated the hidden biases of biblical writers, especially in terms of gender and class identification. Critical readers of the Bible must not ignore how socially well-placed, most often male, writers shaped biblical perspectives. Given the high status the Bible has among people of faith, especially Christians, this work of ideological critique must continue so that the particular perspectives of these elite men of ancient Israel are not unduly universalized as adequate and obligatory for all peoples, everywhere, and in every historical moment. Only the most conservative understanding of the Bible as inspired Word of God permits such an identification between certain meanings of the words of the biblical texts (as presented by contemporary authoritative interpreters) and theological and ethical demands the texts place on contemporary people of faith.

Although the poetic books are in the end products of intellectually elite scribes, the interests and values of the sages who produced this literature should not be uncritically collapsed into the interests of the 1–2 percent of the population of ancient Israel that constituted the economic and political elite of that society. Just as surely, scribal interests should not be viewed as identical to the 80–90 percent of the population that made up the peasant agricultural population. Though the scribal "class" would have been socially distinct, marked by education and elevated literacy, it was likely also quite diverse. Certainly the Bible at points suggests some scribes held high positions in the political institutions of ancient Israel, and these individuals likely identified closely with the economic and political elite (2 Sam. 8:17; 20:25; 1 Kgs. 4:3). Yet some scribes also would have been occupied with mundane tasks—for example, the penning of economic records and marriage contracts—making such strong identification with rulers and aristocrats less likely. Still others would have been more ambiguously placed at different levels in the administration of religious, economic, and political institutions of the court and temple. In any case, these scribes and sages likely understood their work and social station as qualitatively distinct from other social actors, whether peasant agriculturalists, artisans, or social elites (Sir. 38:24—39:11). As Ben Sira puts it, if scribes were not occupied with agriculture or handcrafts, they were "concerned with prophecies" and preserving "the sayings of the famous" and "seeking out meanings of proverbs" and parables (Sir. 39:1-3; cf. Prov. 1:2-6).

Indeed, besides managing religious, political, and economic institutions, largely on behalf of the political and economic elite, some master scribes or sages in Israel and Judah (and later Judea) also produced, read, and taught literarily, ethically, and theologically sophisticated texts like Psalms, Job, Proverbs, Ecclesiastes, and Song of Songs. They were, in other words, the guardians (and in part the creators and authors) of ancient Israel's literary, ethical-theological, and historical traditions. This is important since, as David Carr has explained, ancient scribes were not trained to serve as mere bureaucrats and copyists. A scribe's education was not merely about learning to read and write, or how to document financial transactions. Rather, scribal education in ancient Israel likely was largely concerned with moral instruction and centered on the study of culturally significant texts—like the Bible's poetic books. Scribes learned these texts, however, not by simply or primarily copying them, but in large part by hearing them dictated and by memorizing them. By becoming intimately familiar with culturally significant texts, scribes came to internalize the virtues, values, and perspectives of the texts they learned. The traditions a scribe learned and wrote on skin or shard also came to be written "on the tablet of the [scribe's] heart" (Prov. 3:3; 7:3; Carr).

One important moral impulse that the scribal voices in the Bible's poetic writings articulate is a cry for social justice—a purview often more closely associated with the prophets. Psalm 72, for instance, recounts the role of the ideal king who was to "judge your people with righteousness and your poor with justice" (v. 2). Proverbs likewise seeks to instill social virtue—"justice, righteousness, and equity"—in its hearers (1:3) and praises the rule of monarchs who ensure justice is done in their realms (e.g., Prov. 16:10, 13; 20:26, 28; 29:4, 14). The text also insists on fair economic practices (Prov. 11:1; 16:11; 20:10, 23) and demands justice in the legal sphere for the poor and marginalized (Prov. 22:22-23). The wisdom patriarch Job too claims to have protected the poor, widow, orphan, and traveler (Job 29:12-17), while the royal, Solomon-like figure in Ecclesiastes laments the absence of justice in his context (Eccles. 3:16—4:3).

Of course, the Bible's social justice—the justice and righteousness that the sages and scribes who produced the Bible envisioned—is not necessarily what many people today imagine when reflecting on social justice. Biblical social justice, for the most part, lacks the egalitarian impulse of most contemporary versions of justice emerging from liberal, Enlightenment thought. It likewise is not essentially concerned to eliminate poverty, as are many contemporary expressions of yearning for social-economic justice. Rather, the Bible's social justice is in general paternalistic and patriarchal.

As was the case elsewhere in the ancient Near East, in the Bible the king and other social-political elites—rulers and patriarchs of the community—were to act as a "father" to the community and to care for those in their charge. Those at the pinnacle of the patriarchal order were ultimately responsible to ensure that those lower in the chain of social-economic being—the poor and the needy—were cared for. Special concern was also to be directed toward those with liminal social status due to their not being clearly or firmly associated with a patriarchal household—widows, the fatherless, and foreigners. Even the eighth-century prophets, it seems, do not offer a vision of an economic revolution. Intolerable to them was not the *existence* of the needy (and certainly not a system of patriarchal privilege), but the gross *oppression* of the poor by those who were to be responsible to care for them. The economically and socially vulnerable were supposed to be assisted and protected. Their status, however, was not necessarily to be fundamentally transformed.

Though rhetorically distinct and emerging from an educational and literary context that likely was not as morally urgent as prophetic demands for social justice, the Bible's poetic voice of justice was nonetheless, like prophetic preaching, also a form of rhetorical and ideological "social control" over the political and economic elite. The powerful social positions inhabited by the political and economic elite made them vulnerable to ethical failures precisely in the social and economic realms; it made them liable to oppress the poor and to take advantage of the marginalized. Sagacious scribes addressed this reality not through prophetic oracles or visions but by transmitting and promoting a social-justice ideology that acknowledged the legitimacy of political and economic elites only insofar as they were agents of social justice.

In a real sense, then, it is a patriarchal, paternalistic, scribal vision of wisdom and worship that we encounter in the poetic books of the Bible. The literary and ideological "fingerprints" of male sages are most visible on the literature. However, this fact should not be overstated. With just a bit of (sometimes knotty) detective work, one can also discover traces of the fingerprints of others.

Scholars have for some time debated the methodological challenges involved in recovering female and nonelite voices in the Bible. These challenges revolve around questions like a text's relationships to its author, the weight that should be given to comparable literature where other voices are in fact named, or the nature of speech acts and the manner in which language carries traces of the voices of social actors who have "already" addressed a topic of discourse. Despite such debates, it is certain that the intellectually elite, male scribes ultimately responsible for the Bible's poetic books did not live in an ideological vacuum. Nor did the literary tradition over which they were guardians develop in a social vacuum. Hence we can expect that the voices of women and nonelite others in the discourses that the scribes developed were not completely erased.

For example, although the patriarchal tradition has erased her name, Proverbs itself records the instruction of a queen mother to her son Lemuel (31:1-9). Comparative studies of instructional texts, however, has revealed that her voice belongs to a chorus of other socially and economically well-placed women throughout the ancient Near East who attained scribal training and mastered a sage's learning (Fontaine). It is also likely that the sages or scribes who produced Proverbs drew on the wisdom of the broader Israelite and Judean agricultural, folk population when crafting their collections of wise sayings, especially in Proverbs 10–29. Certainly Prov. 25:1, with its note that King Hezekiah's men "transmitted" the subsequent proverbs, reminds the reader of the elite scribal context of wisdom. Nonetheless, especially the first half of many of the lines in the sayings collected in Proverbs 25–29 might well be derived from folk sayings, to which women and other nonelites surely contributed. Likewise, the Song of Songs, a text that many believe includes a strong female voice, may be related to popular love songs, which in folkloric traditions are in fact sometimes composed by women (Fontaine). What's more, it is probable that many of the laments, praises, hymns of thanksgiving, and pilgrimage songs of the Psalms were formed out of the responses to the real-life situations of the entire worshiping community of ancient Israel and Judah, not merely that of the male scribal intelligentsia.

The Bible's vision of wisdom and worship is thus not merely that of elite male figures. It rather includes, even if in submerged and dialogical fashion, the voices of the entire community of YHWH. Yet the ability to hear nondominant voices in the Bible is not merely a question of finding the right method to excavate those voices. It is also related to hermeneutics and the role of interpreters in understanding biblical texts. Simply put, the social contexts and experiences—or subjectivity—of some contemporary readers provide them with a different lens through which to read biblical texts, or differently attuned ears with which to hear submerged voices. Some women readers may thus more aptly than many male interpreters ask about, identify, and describe female voices in biblical books and more deftly uncover the patriarchal assumptions of those texts. Likewise, readers from non-Western cultures, where folk proverbs remain much more common than in Western societies, may be better situated to hear the oral wisdom of the agricultural peasant population of ancient Israel in the midst of the written scribal texts that make up Wisdom literature. So too poor and marginalized readers in the contemporary world bring a knowledge of the brutal realities of different sorts of social and economic oppression that can "thicken"—and sometimes problematize—understandings of the Bible's persistent concern with the needy. Put otherwise, if the voices of the whole people of YHWH in the ancient biblical texts are going to be heard, what is needed is something like what Cheryl B. Anderson has called "inclusive biblical interpretation." Such an approach to biblical interpretation promotes diverse readings of the Bible by the whole diverse people of God today and not merely the analyses of ecclesial and academic experts.

Hearing a full range of voices in the biblical texts by "reading against the grain" of the biblical texts with interpreters whose concerns and perspectives are different from our own may initially prove difficult for some readers; it may even at times prove scandalous. To have one's charitable giving and deeds challenged through an analysis of how the Bible's paternalistic views of justice may not be sufficient to liberate the poor from poverty can be difficult. To acknowledge the Bible's celebration of sexuality and the erotic in the Song of Songs in the midst of communities where anxiety around such subjects—especially with young people and sexual minorities—runs high likewise can prove exceptionally challenging. To ascribe positive agency to the strange, adulterous woman of Proverbs 7, whose sexuality is depicted as dangerous for young men, may prove downright offensive—at least initially so. However, to read against the grain this way *with* the strange women and *with* some feminist interpreters would not be to glorify adultery or to sanction through the Bible the throwing off of all sexual norms, as some might fear. It would rather be to imagine this strange woman as an active subject who claims control over her own sexuality in the midst of a patriarchal culture that dictated her choice of sexual partners and valued her primarily in terms of her ability to mother sons (see Fontaine). It would be to ask how the Bible's wisdom and worship traditions can speak today in contexts where patriarchy and sexism are as entrenched as ever. This sort of reading, like other readings associated with the Song of Songs' celebration of the erotic, or Wisdom literature's paternalistic economic justice, can create space in which a faithful and prayerful community of Bible readers might discern together a divine word of good news for all of God's people today. Indeed, throughout history, Jews and Christians have attempted to discern the Bible's vision of wisdom and worship in order to achieve for themselves and their communities, in their own times and places, better wisdom for life and more faithful worship of their God. Contemporary readers of these books are invited to continue in this tradition.

Works Cited

Anderson, Cheryl B. 2009. *Ancient Laws and Contemporary Controversies: The Need for Inclusive Biblical Interpretation.* Oxford: Oxford University Press.

Berlin, Adele. 1996. "Introduction to Hebrew Poetry." In *The New Interpreter's Bible.* Vol. 4, *1 and 2 Maccabees, Introduction to Hebrew Poetry, Job, Psalms,* edited by Leander E. Keck, 301–14. Nashville: Abingdon.

Brown, William P. 1996. *Character in Crisis: A Fresh Approach to the Wisdom Literature of the Old Testament.* Grand Rapids: Eerdmans.

Carr, David M. 2005. *Writing on the Tablet of the Heart.* Oxford: Oxford University Press.

Crenshaw, James L. 1998. *Education in Ancient Israel: Across the Deadening Silence.* New York: Doubleday.

Fontaine, Carol R. 2002. *Smooth Words: Women, Proverbs and Performance in Biblical Wisdom.* London: Sheffield Academic.

Fox, Michael V. 2000. *Proverbs 1–9: A New Translation with Introduction and Commentary.* AB. New York: Doubleday.

Koch, Klaus. 1983 (1955). "Is There a Doctrine of Retribution in the Old Testament?" In *Theodicy in the Old Testament*, edited by J. L. Crenshaw, 57–87. Philadelphia: Fortress Press.

Kugel, James L. 1981. *The Idea of Biblical Poetry: Parallelism and Its History.* New Haven: Yale University Press.

Lowth, Robert. 1753. *De sacra poesi Hebraeorum.*

Milgrom, Jacob. 1991. *Leviticus 1–16: A New Translation with Introduction and Commentary.* AB. New York: Doubleday.

Miller, Patrick D. 2000. *The Religion of Ancient Israel.* Louisville: Westminster John Knox.

O'Connor, Michael Patrick. 1980. *Hebrew Verse Structure.* Winona Lake, IN: Eisenbrauns.

Pachocinski, Ryszard. 1996. *Proverbs of Africa: Human Nature in the Nigerian Oral Tradition.* St. Paul, MN: Professors World Peace Academy.

Peterson, David L., and Kent Harold Richards. 1992. *Interpreting Biblical Poetry.* Minneapolis: Fortress Press.

Pleins, J. David. 1993. *The Psalms: Songs of Tragedy, Hope, and Justice.* Maryknoll, NY: Orbis.

Sandoval, Timothy J. Forthcoming. "Education: Hebrew Bible." In *Oxford Encyclopedia of Bible and Gender Studies.* New York: Oxford University Press.

Schökel, Luis Alonso. 1988. *A Manual of Hebrew Poetics.* Rome: Editrice Pontificio Istituto Biblico.

Watson, Wilfred G. E. 1995. *Classical Hebrew Poetry: A Guide to Its Techniques.* 2nd ed. Sheffield: Sheffield Academic Press. [originally published by JSOT Press, 1984]

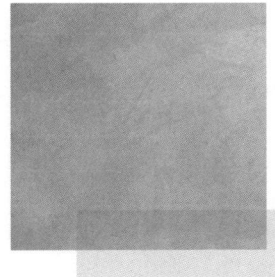

JOB

Alissa Jones Nelson

Introduction

Job is not a text that lends itself to simple resolution. The format of the book itself seems to kick against any barriers imposed by unified hermeneutical perspectives. It holds in tension multiple genres, characters, voices, time periods, perspectives, and perhaps authors. It is a complex and difficult book, but this very complexity is what has made the book of Job such a ubiquitous text across religious, philosophical, literary, and artistic traditions, from Barth to Gutiérrez, Kafka to Camus, Milton to MacLeish, Blake to the Coen brothers.

The complexity of Job begins with its language and structure. The Hebrew is notoriously difficult to translate, due to obscure or unintelligible words and phrases. The book is also difficult to date with any certainty. Scholars generally agree on a date somewhere between the seventh and second centuries BCE, which is admittedly far from precise. The setting for the narrative is clearly the patriarchal era, but there are notable parallels with the book of Jeremiah and the Suffering Servant in Second Isaiah (both of which are more reliably dated to the sixth century BCE), and the questions Job raises surrounding issues of retribution, YHWH's power and justice, and the expectation of future liberation also resonate with the Babylonian exile, although there are no direct allusions to this context in the text itself.

The earliest reference to Job as a figure is Ezek. 14:14, 20, but this may be a reference to an earlier prose narrative or to an oral tradition, not to the book as we have it. We cannot date the book based on its relationship to other biblical passages, because many of these related passages also have uncertain dates. While the text as we have it certainly resonates with exilic themes, it lacks references to important issues in later Second Temple wisdom literature, which seems to indicate a final date of composition between the Babylonian captivity and the Second Temple period (Perdue, 78–84). Similarities between Job and Babylonian wisdom texts and traditions (The Babylonian

Theodicy, The Just Sufferer, I Will Praise the Lord of Wisdom, The Dialogue between a Man and His God) also point to some connection with a Babylonian context. The structure of the text seems to indicate different stages of composition, which may also represent a range of time periods. Perhaps we can safely argue that the final form of the text dates to the exilic or postexilic period, while admitting that we are unsure when it began or precisely how it reached its present state.

The authorship of the book is another open question. Most scholars agree that the author was an Israelite. Some argue that a single author composed the entire book (Wilson; Hartley), perhaps pulling material from earlier written or oral traditions (e.g., the prose prologue and epilogue, the interlude on wisdom in Job 28); others identify internal "inconsistencies," which they argue may indicate multiple authors and redactions of the book (Clines 1989; Perdue). Scholars have speculated that the author may have been a member of the upper class of Judahite society who was exiled to Babylon, perhaps wealthy, perhaps an intellectual, perhaps a court official. The author was not only skilled in terms of eloquence and argumentation but also appears to have been well-educated and somewhat unorthodox.

Even the genre categorization of Job is open to debate. While the book has traditionally been identified as Wisdom literature, some scholars argue that other genres might be more appropriate designations. Gerhard von Rad (1966; 1972) is perhaps the most well-known proponent of the book as Wisdom literature. Timothy J. Johnson builds on von Rad's thesis that "apocalyptic literature is the child of wisdom" and identifies the book of Job as an apocalypse (von Rad 1972, 179). Alternative genre identifications include dramatic lament, Greek tragedy, drama, comedy, and parody.

David Clines succinctly summarizes efforts to resolve these interpretive dilemmas as "intelligent speculation" (1989, lvii). Some scholars suggest that portions of the book they have identified as additions or interpolations should be removed in order to aid interpretation. The issue, however, is that one's interpretive bias, the themes one identifies as the "main" themes of the text, and the potentially anachronistic criteria by which one determines what counts as "coherence," inevitably impinge on one's choice of what portions of the book to amend or excise. As Kenneth Ngwa notes (360), one's analytical beginning determines to a large extent where one ends in interpreting Job. I would argue that the nature of the text requires the reader to embrace and explore contradictions and complexities rather than attempting to uncover or create a more or less synthetic reconciliation. It is much more interesting to wrestle with what may seem to be strange twists and turns in the text, and the ways in which more or less distinct components function in the text as we currently have it. This is what the remainder of this chapter will attempt to do.

Job 1–2: Prologue—Calamity Befalls a Righteous Man

▌ THE TEXT IN ITS ANCIENT CONTEXT

The book opens with the assertion that Job is a man from the land of Uz. There have been many debates over where exactly Uz is. Edom has been suggested, as per Gen. 36:28; Lam. 4:21; and 1 Chron. 1:42. Hauran, a location in northern Palestine, is also a candidate. The key point is that it is not in Israel; Job is not an Israelite. This attempt to give the story a universal, transnational appeal is consistent with Wisdom literature as a genre. The concept of a chosen people or a special covenant between God and Israel is not mentioned, although the name of God (YHWH) is used repeatedly. The relationship is intimate but not explicitly national. It is clear that this is the Israelite God, but God's special connection to Israel is not part of the narrative.

From the beginning, Job's wholeness (Heb. *tam*, which also has the connotation of "integrity") and uprightness (*yashar*) are particularly important. These personal qualities also extend to his wealth and his family; three daughters and seven sons, both numbers representative of wholeness or completeness in ancient Near Eastern (ANE) contexts, further emphasize Job's *tam*; seven thousand sheep and three thousand camels also emphasize not only his wealth but also his *tam*. Ten is another important number representing perfection, which is included here by association (ten children, one thousand oxen). These numbers are also a way to emphasize the staggering extent of Job's wealth, his completeness in a material sense.

Tam means whole or complete rather than without sin, but one must maintain right relationships with God and others in order to maintain this wholeness; Job's actions on behalf of his children illustrate this concern. *Yashar* in Hebrew, translated "upright," also has the sense of straightness, directness; with Job, what you see is what you get. The dialogues bear this out. These qualities are the core of Job's integrity, and the words themselves recur throughout the text to emphasize their centrality to the conflict between Job and his interlocutors. Job's blamelessness is integrity, not sinlessness. Job also feared God, which is identified as the source of wisdom (Job 28). Job trusts and relies on God, which is one more reason why his suffering is so devastating to him.

Job's accuser ("the satan") is an interesting conundrum. He appears among the children of God and seems not to be out of place there; he is God's functionary. God controls his actions, which is why the satan needs permission to afflict Job, and also why God is ultimately responsible for all of the calamities that befall Job.

The ash heap (2:7-8) represents mourning, social isolation, and poverty. Job's suffering is physical, emotional, social, and psychic; he has been afflicted in every possible sense. Gustavo Gutiérrez declares that Job is "a sick as well as a poor man" at this juncture (6).

The use of *barak* to mean both "bless" and "curse" is intriguing and problematic. We can infer from the surrounding text that Job's statement in 1:21 is indeed "blessed be the name of the Lord," since the very next verse assures us that Job did not sin by charging God with wrongdoing. Then again, perhaps this qualification indicates that Job may have sinned by cursing God in spite of acknowledging God's right to do what God has done, and the next verse is meant to reassure us that Job is still *tam* in spite of this slip. In either case, the ambiguity is interesting, both here and in his wife's statement in 2:9. In Job 1:5, where Job is concerned about his children's sin, and in 1:11 and 2:5, where the satan incites God against Job, *barak* certainly seems to carry a negative connotation, but again the potential ambiguity is intriguing.

When Job's friends finally arrive (Job 2:11-13), they engage in traditional mourning rituals, tearing their clothes, sprinkling dust on their heads, and sitting with Job on the ground. They are silent for seven days, which may refer both to the traditional period of mourning and to the seven days of creation, as creation becomes a theme in the dialogues that follow. The primary mourner must be the first to speak, and Job breaks the silence in a spectacular fashion in Job 3.

▋ THE TEXT IN THE INTERPRETIVE TRADITION

Other biblical texts (Ezek. 14:14, 20; James 5:11) emphasize the endurance of Job in his trials; many later interpretive traditions also emphasize aspects of the "patient" Job based on Job's responses to suffering in the prologue. These themes fit nicely with questions and issues that would have been current at the time of the Maccabean revolt (165 BCE) and the destruction of the temple (70 CE) as well as the persecution of early Christian communities. In both the Septuagint and the apocryphal *Testament of Job*, the iconoclastic Job of the dialogues is intentionally softened in favor of an example of patient endurance and the development of a theology of resurrection. This tradition of Job the Patient is then carried forward by Eusebius, Augustine, Jerome, and Gregory the Great into medieval Christian interpretation, and beyond that into the Renaissance by influential figures such as Francis Bacon and John Donne. The Qur'an and Islamic traditions around Job (Ayyub, in Arabic) also develop this saintly view of Job as a long-suffering prophet of God, an example of patience, fortitude, and wisdom. In early Christian literature as well as art and architecture, Job is most often depicted as the patient sufferer, or alternatively as an athlete or warrior battling the satan, who is equated in early Christianity with the figure of the devil. The first interpretation makes endurance primarily a passive task, while the latter emphasizes the active nature of Job's struggle, the idea of victory and a prize to be won (Ambrose). As we will see, these interpretations become problematic when compared to Job's lengthy dialogue with his friends and, ultimately, with God.

Job's wife and her enigmatic outburst in 2:9 are also a key focus in interpretive tradition. Rabbinic commentary, the Septuagint, the Targum, and the *Testament of Job* all seek to give a better explanation for her behavior than what we have in the Masoretic Text. In the biblical text, Job's wife is never given a name, a history, or a place of origin and is consequently a secondary character. She is not mentioned as an agent in her children's births or in mourning their deaths. Her outburst to Job in 2:9 is thus without explicit context, although the reception of her character in subsequent interpretive texts testifies to some common points of understanding. It is interesting that the only woman who speaks in Job is also the only person who speaks without a lengthy explanation. Her presence is implied in the epilogue, perhaps; many interpreters assume that she takes part in Job's "having" ten more children, although birth is not explicitly mentioned. Rabbinic midrash assigns Job a new wife in the epilogue, namely Dinah, Jacob's daughter. Job's (first) wife is only mentioned twice more, as a literary device to illustrate Job's suffering (19:17) or to support his oath of innocence (31:10). As we encounter her in Job 2:9, we are left to speculate about the cause of her enigmatic statement.

Her cryptic comments have invited exposition in the Qur'an and Islamic tradition as well as among interpreters from Augustine, Jerome, Gregory the Great, and Martin Luther to Ellen van Wolde, Sarojini Nadar, and F. Rachel Magdalene. It is interesting that both the Septuagint and the *Testament of Job* present a nuanced and mostly sympathetic picture of this woman and her involvement in Job's suffering while the patristic tradition and medieval and Reformation Christian communities largely portray her as a foolish woman at best and as an agent of the satan at worst. In many Islamic and Christian interpretive traditions, she is portrayed as gullible rather than evil; this is often identified as a problem for women generally (Thomas Aquinas; Luther). Modern and post-modern interpretations have again picked up the ambiguity of her character and have demonstrated a keen interest in fleshing out Job's wife, as we will see below.

The identity and function of the satan have also been issues in interpretive tradition. Second Temple Jewish tradition, and later Christian tradition, identified Satan as a proper name and an independent personality; in the text of Job, the satan seems to be an office, a function, a sort of prosecuting attorney (Hartley, 71–72) rather than a discrete character (Perdue, 84–85). Nevertheless, subsequent interpretations have often read the character of the satan in Job as synonymous with this later concept of Satan.

▌▌The Text in Contemporary Discussion

A particularly interesting cluster of contemporary interpretations focuses on the character of Job's wife. In line with the expansions introduced by the Septuagint and the *Testament of Job*, as mentioned above, there seems to be a common desire across temporal and cultural contexts to flesh out this interaction and to allow her to explain herself, her relationship to her husband, and the suffering that leads to her outburst (Clines 1989; Gravett 2012; Hartley; Klein; Magdalene; Nadar; Ngwa; van Wolde 1995). This speaks to a wide variety of contemporary social and political issues, including the recovery of female characters in the biblical texts; an analysis of their portrayal and their agency (or lack thereof), which might be relevant for women in religious communities today; questions about the role of women in marriage relationships and religious leadership; and political issues related to gender (in)equality and to the disproportionate suffering of women in contexts of conflict (e.g., Afghanistan and Darfur) and disease (e.g., the HIV/AIDS pandemic), where they are marginalized as actors and yet often suffer more than their male counterparts. Job's wife in the Hebrew text stands as a reminder of the many women who are marginalized, denied agency, and even made scapegoats in their suffering. Efforts to give Job's wife a voice, to resolve the ambiguity of her involvement in Job's drama, and to assign her a role that underlines both her agency and her narrative marginalization testify to the ancient and contemporary recognition that this simplistic portrayal of an otherwise central female character is insufficient and unsatisfactory. In this sense, the reception of Job becomes a critique of patriarchy even, or perhaps especially, in patriarchal contexts.

Job 3: Job's First Monologue—Curse and Lament

▌The Text in Its Ancient Context

The genre of this section involves both curse (Job 3:1-10) and lament (3:11-26); the first section focuses on Job's wish that his suffering would never have begun, and the second focuses on his questions about why he continues to suffer, as well as his implicit wish for death.

Sheol is a reference to the netherworld, and Job here expounds on the idea that it is a place of quiet and rest compared to the suffering of his present condition. It is the great leveler; thus the wicked and the righteous, kings and slaves are all alike there. Conceptions of Sheol in the ANE are many and varied, but what is important here is how Job constructs this place, as a final refuge from his suffering. This will be a theme he picks up again and again in the dialogues.

Whereas the satan had accused God of hedging Job in for his own protection (Job 1:10), Job sees this same hedging in (3:23) as obscuring his vision, preventing him from walking in the way of wisdom as he had previously done. It is yet another source of suffering.

■ THE TEXT IN THE INTERPRETIVE TRADITION

Interpreters have variously understood this chapter as a structured and coded lament according to fixed criteria (Hartley; von Rad 1972) and as a passionate outburst intended to convey something that is fundamentally incommunicable (Gutiérrez; Tamez 1986, 2004). In either case, it is certainly a stunning expression of emotion, and we are afforded the opportunity to understand the depth of Job's suffering and consequent despair before being launched into the theological debates that follow.

The theme of creation recurs throughout this chapter. It has been interpreted as a new strand of wisdom theology in the exilic context, one that counters traditional structures and opposes another new strand, which emphasizes the formation of and obedience to torah. The creation theme is evident in Job's opposition of light and darkness, which calls to mind the original creation of the world. Job's longing for chaos may represent a longing to annihilate the entire order of creation (Clines 1989; Perdue) or simply to undo the day of his own birth (Wilson). If we accept the former interpretation, we could argue that this monologue is the primary thing God rejects in God's speeches. Job's assertion that the order of creation is not "good," as God declared it in Genesis, requires God to respond defensively and to explain its goodness in terms other than those Job attempts to impose.

■ THE TEXT IN CONTEMPORARY DISCUSSION

The above-noted shift in terms and perspective is an important point for contemporary debates about theodicy; the book of Job asks readers to acknowledge that human understandings of what constitutes "justice" and what role God plays in the process of maintaining a just order in God's creation are fundamentally subjective and perhaps flawed. It is important in contexts such as these to be responsive to efforts to reframe the terms in which this debate takes place.

The purpose of Job's curse and lament is to set the stage for the increasingly acrimonious dialogues in the following chapters. Here we are reminded that the story of Job is fundamentally a drama; Job 3 forces us to confront the violence of Job's emotions, the depth of his suffering, and the human aspect of his suffering; as readers, we are reminded that we should not forgo compassion in favor of intellectual debate. For those interpreters who see the suffering of the innocent as a primary theme in the book of Job, this chapter is an essential part of the issue. The question of how a person of faith responds to suffering (Clines 2003; Gutiérrez) is not merely an intellectual or philosophical question. The first step, as in Job 3, is to sit in silence with the sufferer and listen to the outpouring of grief. What comes next, as we will see below, is more complex.

The issues raised here and carried forward as themes throughout the book resonate with contemporary questions of social justice. What is the purpose of suffering, if any? Why do the innocent suffer? Alternatively, if one subscribes to the doctrine of original sin, is there such a thing as innocent suffering? How do one's opinions on these matters influence one's approach to injustice and suffering in the world? Is the book of Job relevant to these questions? These are issues to be explored in the following sections.

Job 4–27: Dialogues—On Righteousness, Suffering, and Justice

■ THE TEXT IN ITS ANCIENT CONTEXT

The dialogue between Job and his friends is not unique among comparable Wisdom literature in the ANE, but it is the only Israelite literature to develop this form. Scholars have speculated that the content of the dialogues, particularly the issues of retribution, righteous suffering, and God's justice, either reflect a contest or debate between two types of sages in exile or outline common questions the Israelites were posing in light of their experience of exile. In either case, the text reflects a debate in which tragic events were the impetus for some parties to defend traditional concepts of retribution and find comfort in authority based on received wisdom, while others questioned everything. These various responses to loss also raised questions about which groups and which theologies would shape the future of the Israelites in their radically new context (Perdue, 91).

Both Job and his opponents appeal to esoteric knowledge, to revelations and visions that cannot be substantiated, only asserted. Theological arguments on all sides of the issues are based on this kind of "mantic wisdom," which seems to become more mainstream in the context of exile. This could be the result of an encounter with another kind of wisdom practiced in the ANE, that of skilled ritual practitioners such as the priests of Babylon. This is also a basis for the growth of apocalyptic literature (Johnson). The traditional divisions between "seers" and "sages," between prophets and religious leaders or temple functionaries, seem to be blurring in the absence of a centralized religious practice based around the temple (Perdue, 91–92). Thus Job's challenges to his friends are also challenges to priestly theology and the primacy of the temple in mediating and effectuating God's relationship with the Israelites. Israelite Wisdom literature exhibits a tension between knowledge of God derived from torah and knowledge derived from creation; as a non-Israelite, Job develops the latter theme, which allows him more autonomy and gives more weight to individual experience as an arbiter of wisdom. This is not a new issue, but Job develops it more fully and drives it in new directions (Perdue).

Job also subverts traditional images of God as Israel's protector. He turns these metaphors around to cast God as a destroyer and himself as a person mistakenly identified as an enemy of God. God the Divine Warrior in Job 6 and 16 looses his arrows against Job. God the Creator, who sets limits on chaos to preserve his creation, in Job 7, 26, and 27 treats Job like one of the chaos monsters who must be subdued. A particularly poignant passage in the context of exile is 10:1-17, where Job laments that no one can rescue him from God's hand. In the creation narratives, God's hand fashions humankind, and Job evokes this metaphor as a personal interaction in 10:8-12. In the

Deuteronomistic history and in the Psalms, God's hand signifies a power that repeatedly saved the Israelites. In Job's case, being in God's hand is the problem rather than the solution. God's creative and sustaining power has turned destructive. This is particularly evocative and emotive in an exilic context; where God's hand was once seen as a source of deliverance, it is now seen at best as having failed to prevent disaster and at worst as having directly imposed it. In another moving passage, Job 27:2-3, Job insists that God has denied him justice at the same time as he acknowledges that he lives only by the spirit or breath of God. This again calls to mind the creation narrative, wherein God breathes his own breath into human beings to give them life. Job will not give up his complaint as long as he lives, but he knows that his life continues only because God wills it. The poignancy of Job's cognitive dissonance here reflects a larger context in which the Israelites are trying to decide how to proceed into a collective future.

Job first mentions the idea of an umpire, someone to intervene between him and God, in 9:33. In 13:6, he begins to use explicitly legal language (argument, plea), and in 13:13-23 he sets the terms God should abide by in court. In 16:18-22, Job laments the impossibility of any mediator intervening between him and God, but in 19:23-27 he reiterates his intense desire that such a thing were possible. In chapter 23, he begins to consider the details of a legal case against God. Job 23:6 is an explicit reference to the covenant; the Hebrew *yarib* is a legal accusation of a breach of an agreement or covenant. The problem is that Job does not know where to find God to subpoena him, but God clearly knows where to find Job, since he has afflicted Job so severely. Job laments his disadvantage here and wishes that he could hide from God just as God hides from Job. The difficulty in locating God might also be a reflection of an exilic context, as the temple, the place where YHWH has traditionally been found, is no longer an option. Job is confident in his ability to win his case but not in his ability to compel God to participate.

▊ The Text in the Interpretive Tradition

It is interesting that in rabbinic interpretation, where the Hebrew text would have been the primary source, the interpretive tradition is much more varied than traditions of the saintly Job found in Christian and Islamic interpretation, as we saw above. Rabbinic tradition is far more likely to emphasize the iconoclastic Job and to debate issues such as when he lived, whether he was a Jew or a gentile, what the reason was for his suffering, and whether he worshiped God out of love or fear. One explanation for the greater diversity of rabbinic interpretations is that rabbinic tradition lacked the rigid theological structures that dominated early Christian and Islamic communities (Vicchio 2006a). It is also interesting to note, however, that the grief-stricken, angry Job of the dialogues survived in medieval Christian liturgy, particularly in the Office for the Dead, where Job's laments were quoted extensively for their pathos and the emotional catharsis they lent to the bereaved. The tradition of Job as an avenue for the expression of grief in the face of suffering, death, and persecution thus has an older, if less ubiquitous, history. The use of Job in laments over HIV/AIDS in South Africa is an example of the contemporary continuation of this tradition (West with Zengele; West).

Even in these darker interpretations, both ancient and contemporary, Job 19:23-27 is often included as a beacon of hope, a belief in the resurrection of the dead and a panacea for suffering.

At several points in the text, Job seems to explicitly deny the possibility of resurrection (14:7-12; 16:18-22). This has not prevented generations of interpreters from seeing in 19:23-27 a theology of resurrection or even a prefiguration of Christ. For example, whereas the Hebrew text presents 14:14 as a seemingly rhetorical question ("If a man dies, will he live again?"), the Septuagint renders the same verse as a positive assertion ("For though a man die, he will live again"). The iconoclastic Job of the Hebrew text is intentionally softened in the Greek text and subsequent interpretations in Greek-speaking communities, providing an example of patient hope in the face of persecution by promising justice in the afterlife. Interpreters who carry forward this theme and find in Job a doctrine of resurrection, both the concept of bodily resurrection and the idea of a soul/body dualism and concomitant ideas of the afterlife of the soul, include Clement, Origen, Jerome, Gregory, Aquinas, and Luther as well as contemporary interpreters such as Janzen.

There are solid arguments against this interpretation, including the idea that the Redeemer (Wilson suggests that a less theologically loaded translation of the Hebrew *go'el* would be "Vindicator"; Clines [1989] suggests "Kinsman" or "Champion") is a personification of Job's plea, his affidavit in the legal case he wants to bring against God (Clines 1989); the idea that the Champion is God because God can be both judge and vindicator (Gordis; Hartley; see Isaiah 39); and the idea that the Champion is some other heavenly being, a personal god or an angel, a counterpart to the satan, who will vindicate Job in the heavenly council where the satan had condemned him (Terrien; Pope; Habel). A key question related to the identity of the Vindicator is *when* Job hopes this vindication will take place. The question hinges on how one interprets *'akharon* ("later," "finally," "at the last"). Does this refer to the end of Job's suffering? The end of Job's life? Or does it have eschatological significance? Job's statement in 19:26 offers little help, as the phrase "after my flesh has been thus destroyed" could refer to the current destruction of boils and skin disease or to the final destruction of death. Gerald Wilson argues convincingly that Job is expressing an impossible desire (conveyed repeatedly in the rhetorical Hebrew phrase *mi yitten*, or "who will give?"). The key point here is not *who* or *when*, but *whether*, and ultimately the answer is no (Wilson, 209). This is consistent with Job 16:19-20, in which Job laments the impossibility of any mediator between himself and God, and which provides a key by which we may also read 19:23-27 (Clines 1989, 465–66).

Furthermore, Job has been hoping for public vindication; the publicness of the affirmation of his righteousness is particularly important to him. He does not want to be thought of as a sinful man who deserved what he got, and the communal and social aspects of his suffering are particularly galling to him (as we will see in Job 29–31). Thus it seems more likely that Job is here referring to restoration and vindication in this life. This is partly an argument from context, because a theology of resurrection in Israel had not been developed by the time of the exile, and partly an argument from the text itself, because a belief in eventual restoration after death would undermine the fear of death, which Job expresses throughout the remainder of the book. If the solution to Job's suffering is simply that he will be restored in the afterlife, then the discussion should end here, and Job should have no more cause for complaint (Saadiah 1988). The argument that Job is here referring to an individual resurrection or afterlife ignores the context of these verses in the overall trajectory of Job's argument and the book as a whole. Thus Job desires intensely that God will vindicate him before his death, but he believes that in fact God is his enemy and will soon kill him. The focus is Job's repeated demand for a face-to-face encounter with God in a legal dispute (Clines 1989, 455–56).

Later Christian interpretive traditions read the themes of the New Testament as presented in a coded form in the Old Testament; hence Job is often viewed as a prefiguration of Christ by the early church fathers, including Ambrose, Augustine, Jerome, and Gregory the Great. Job's patience and humility in the face of the satan's affliction is likened both to a retelling of the story of Adam and Eve, wherein this time the protagonist manages to resist the woman's and the satan's temptations (John Chrysostom), and to Jesus' resistance of temptation in the desert (Gregory the Great). In all these cases, Job's integrity and patient acceptance of undeserved suffering at the hand of God paves the way for a concept of innocent suffering that undergirds both the incarnation and the salvific function of Christ's atonement (Hartley; Wilson).

Early Christian interpretation also emphasizes the issue of original sin as both an explanation for Job's suffering and as a way of absolving God of responsibility. According to this theology, no human being is innocent; thus questions of innocent suffering become irrelevant. Clement of Rome saw in Job proof of this theology. Early church fathers, including Jerome and Augustine, as well as later Reformers, such as John Calvin, supported and developed this interpretation, based primarily on 9:1-2 and 14:4-5.

As we saw above, early traditions tend to polarize Job as either the saint or the iconoclast. In medieval Jewish interpretation, Saadiah is one of the first to merge these traditions. He takes the tension between these two portrayals seriously, as do Maimonides and Gershonides (see also Vicchio 2006b, 97–98). Saadiah also takes up the theme of innocent suffering, offering three possible resolutions for this dilemma: suffering builds character; suffering is purification; suffering is a test. Saadiah underlines God's responsibility for Job's suffering and refuses to ascribe to the idea of life after death as a solution. In Job's case, death is final; Job himself does not believe in life after death. In Saadiah's view, this proves Job's uprightness. If Job had believed in an afterlife, his endurance of suffering could not have been disinterested; the very fact that he thinks death is the end proves his righteousness and disinterested service of God.

Scholars have been frustrated by the fact that the neat tripartite structure (three dialogue cycles, in the first two of which the friends speak in an established order and each receives an individual response from Job) breaks down in the third cycle, wherein Bildad's speech is quite short, and Zophar does not speak at all. Many have tried to rearrange the text so that this structure is preserved. Verses in Job 24 are redistributed to Zophar (Clines 2006); verses in Job 27 are ascribed to Bildad (Hartley). Again, it seems to me that it is more interesting to address the themes of the text than to attempt to re-create a structure for the speeches based on a potentially anachronistic concept of "coherence," which may have been significantly less important to the author(s) of Job than it appears to be to the book's interpreters.

Job's friends have sometimes been interpreted as corporate personalities representing distinct priestly and theological traditions whose theology in the exilic context is under serious strain (Hartley). Job has also been interpreted as a corporate personality, perhaps an alternative option to the traditional Israelite identification with the corporate personality of Jacob (van Wolde 2002) or the representative of a more abstract group, the poor and marginalized (Dussel). It seems clear that this text is not simply the story of extraordinary events in the life of a unique individual, although it is certainly that as well. Efforts to universalize the story by placing Job and his friends outside the nation of Israel, setting the story in the patriarchal period, and incorporating wisdom traditions from other ANE societies make it clear that this is not simply the history of one extraordinary individual and his encounter with God. Nevertheless, the themes of the text and the use of Israel's personal name for God also create a close resonance with a particularly Israelite context.

The encounter with Job's pain inspires fear rather than compassion in his friends; they have to malign his integrity in order to retreat into a comforting theological world where such visions do not trouble them (Wilson). This is an understandable reaction to the horrors of conquest and exile. Job is challenging the basis of an established theological understanding of the world; he does so because to him it seems horrible, but the friends find his viewpoint even more disconcerting (Gutiérrez). These differing perspectives are both understandable reactions to suffering. Integrity and experience are most important to Job; stability, security, authority, and intellectual understanding are primary for his friends. Both Job and his friends are willing to sacrifice Job himself to prove their respective points. Job's repeated appeals to his friends for compassion, and his insistence that those who do not suffer cannot understand his plight except by falling back on retributive principles, is consistent with liberation theologies and their various interpretations of these dialogues as Job's progress toward a more empathic and nuanced understanding of the poor and marginalized through his own experience of suffering (Job 24; see Tamez [1986, 2004]; Dussel; Gutiérrez).

▌THE TEXT IN CONTEMPORARY DISCUSSION

Each of Job's comforters affirms retributive principles in a distinct way, yet their arguments have the same ultimate results in terms of their views of God, their views of humanity in general, and their views of Job in particular. Job's challenge to the retributive principle is not only a challenge to his friends but also to a long tradition of Wisdom literature and the organizing principles of the Israelite covenant relationship with YHWH. Clines (2003) is arguably right when he asserts that the book has nothing to say about the meaning of suffering generally; but it certainly addresses one of the core principles of the Israelite conception of the organization of YHWH's creation, and as such it has wider implications.

Job raises key questions about the authority of tradition. Job's friends defend traditional wisdom principles and by implication traditional religious hierarchies. Job's challenge to authority begins with the friends and extends beyond them to the principles they espouse and ultimately to God as the governor of the created order. In this sense, Job not only undermines the traditional content of wisdom teaching but also explodes the context, the pedagogical method, of being instructed. He refuses to bow to authority in the sense that traditional wisdom teaching demands; his own experience is his authority. This has interesting implications for contemporary discussions about theological and interpretive authority. Job becomes a blueprint for a theological world in which the vernacular voice, the interpretive insight based on personal experience over intellectual investigations (if indeed the two things can be separated), has the same authoritative force as the academic voice. Tradition is no longer the arbiter of acceptable theology.

In this context, we see evidence of the emergence of a theological concern with the individual. The extraordinary experience of a unique individual is the basis for both the questions and the answers Job provides. Job makes experience his theological starting point, while the friends make theological ideas their starting point (Rayan; Pyeon; Nam; Wilson). Tradition is inadequate to address Job's unique situation. This is consistent with a historical context in which the community is concerned with shaping a new and challenging future. Thus experience has become a corrective to the conceptual. The impossibility of dissociating idea from experience, truth from life, is a key theme throughout the book. It is also a key theme in contemporary debates about the meaning of suffering. Such a debate can never be purely philosophical; to disregard the concrete experience of those who suffer is to contribute to their suffering.

Job believes that God perverts justice, a position his friends find abhorrent. In many contemporary contexts, God's responsibility for suffering is an explicit reason for loss or lack of faith; in Job's case, it is a catalyst for reorientation of faith. Job's early wish that he would simply be allowed to die is replaced first by a vain hope that he might encounter God in a court setting on equal footing and then by a serious legal challenge to the conditions of his suffering and to God as the party responsible for it. Where some interpretive traditions have found the answers to Job's questions in the idea of the afterlife, as we saw above, contemporary discussions question whether this is an adequate explanation. One of the central tenets of liberation theologies and religious social justice movements is the idea that suffering cannot be addressed simply by asserting that the injustices of this life will be set right in the next. In these contexts, the argument is that the impetus for action rests with human communities; it is the responsibility of people of faith to act on behalf of those who suffer, and arguments insisting that sufferers must deserve their suffering and that the appropriate response is patience and fortitude in the hope of a reward in the hereafter perpetuate and legitimize structural injustices and are therefore part of the problem rather than the solution.

Job's suffering leads him to recognize the link between poverty, despair, and hopelessness that goes hand in hand with the lack of any prospect for change (Wilson, 59–60; Gutiérrez). The purpose of human life according to the book of Job may indeed be to acquire wisdom, but wisdom is not simply the reiteration of traditional authority structures or the maintenance of consistent principles in the face of a chaotic reality. The purpose of human life is to come to terms with experience, as Job tries to do. If wisdom is indeed know-how, gaining "mastery in life that will lead to blessing, satisfaction, and even prosperity" (Wilson, 3), then Job makes a powerful argument that retributive theology will not help a person achieve this goal. Thus Job provides a counternarrative to the dominant Deuteronomic themes of the Old Testament and the retributive understanding of traditional Wisdom literature, undermining retributive perspectives and reflecting a new understanding of how to live in a strange new context.

The question of wisdom at stake in the book of Job is the question of how to react appropriately to suffering, whether one's own or that of others (Clines 2003; Gutiérrez). As we saw above, the first step Job advocates in chapter 3 is to empathize with grief and anger. The second step, as outlined in the dialogues, is to confront both the structural issues that contribute to suffering and the authority figures who legitimize them. Contemporary debates over social justice in religious contexts are also attempts to achieve this, and they, like Job, often face similar resistance from traditional theologies and hierarchical structures, whether religious, political, or social. Antonio Negri's neo-Marxist reading sees Job as an allegory for humanity as a whole, subject to immense suffering as traditional estimations of meaning and value are destroyed one after the other, but finally restored by recognizing themselves as possessors of divine power and wisdom, able to govern their own world justly according to new principles of freedom, equality, and a common fight against oppression. This reading also resonates with themes in a variety of liberation theologies, which see in Job various possibilities for a structural understanding of poverty and an empathy leading to advocacy for the oppressed and marginalized (Gutiérrez; Tamez 1986; 2004; Dussel; West).

Job 28: Interlude—On Wisdom

◼ The Text in Its Ancient Context

This chapter depicts a wide-ranging and eloquent search for wisdom. In Job 28:23, the Hebrew emphasizes "God himself," God alone. God alone knows the way to wisdom, because God not only sees everything but also created everything; in this process, he "saw," "declared," "established," and "searched out" wisdom (28:27). And wisdom, perhaps ironically considering the repeated trope that no one knows the way to it (28:1-22), turns out to be precisely what tradition said it was: to fear the Lord and turn away from evil (28:28). This is also precisely the behavior Job is praised for in 1:1, 8; and 2:3. To be sure, wisdom is not a matter of intellect; it could be argued that this is the fundamental mistake the friends are making, pressing the case for wisdom as an understanding and acceptance of principles such as retribution. Nevertheless, the idea that the fear of the Lord is the beginning of wisdom is not new or unique to Job (see Prov. 1:7; Eccles. 12:13).

◼ The Text in the Interpretive Tradition

Most commentators argue that this is an interpolation with little connection to its context (Hartley; Terrien; Newsom; Habel). Clines (2006, 908–9) argues that unless it can be attributed to one of the speakers, it is an "aberration." He thinks Elihu is the most likely of all the characters to attempt to answer the question, "Where shall wisdom be found?" Thus he asserts that this chapter is properly placed as the final speech of Elihu, because its theme (wisdom is the fear of the Lord) is consistent with the last lines of Elihu's final speech in the text as we have it (888). Clines advocates reordering the text so chapter 27 is Zophar's final speech, the Elihu speeches (Job 32–37) come next, and Job 28 is properly identified as Elihu's final speech (Clines 2006, 908). This is an interesting proposal and seems to solve quite a few issues with the text, but it is not the only theory.

Wilson argues that the fact that Job 27 and 29 both begin with identical phrases, indicating that Job is still speaking ("And Job again took up his discourse and said . . ."), demonstrates that Job 28 is also Job's speech, because it is sandwiched between these introductions. However, one could just as easily argue that the absence of such a clause at the beginning of Job 28 indicates that it alone is not Job's speech. Whereas Clines sees Elihu as the most likely speaker, Wilson (299) argues that the theme is closest to Job's words. According to the theology of the friends, "the world works according to discoverable principles, and Job needs to submit to those principles in order to achieve and maintain a life of wisdom and blessing. . . . In Job's mouth, the words of Job 28 stand firmly against the common assumptions of the sages" (Wilson, 305; see also Jones).

Sophia Magallanes agrees that the poem in Job 28 is appropriately placed in Job's mouth as a precursor to his vow of innocence, and it aligns with God's eventual response to Job in arguing that one understands divine justice through mundane, earthly matters rather than through abstract theological principles. In contrast to Wilson, Magallanes argues that this chapter provides convincing evidence that the text of Job expounds rather than rejects the traditional wisdom of Proverbs; justice only "appears to be absent in the world when the way of the God-fearer is hidden" (Magallanes, 202). Thus it is both poetic allegory and essential context for Job's final speech.

Scott Jones argues that the poem is intended not as a hymn to wisdom but as a critique of the way people like Job's friends have traditionally sought wisdom. In Job 28, Job rejects the earthly realm as providing adequate assistance in his struggle; he is thus encouraged to continue his battle with his attention focused beyond his friends in particular and beyond the created order in general.

It is clear from the above discussion that Job 28 still represents an enigma in the interpretive tradition of the book of Job. There are many attempts to explain its inclusion and to identify its speaker, but none that achieves wide scholarly consensus.

▮ THE TEXT IN CONTEMPORARY DISCUSSION

Regardless of how one chooses to explain Job 28, the key question is why an unattributed speech is included and what wisdom has to do with the other themes we have identified in the text. The simplest answer to the first question seems to be Wilson's, that Job is the speaker and that Job 28 is simply part of the structure of Job's discourse, as identified in chapters 27 and 29. While acknowledging that the simplest answer is not necessarily the best one, I would also argue that attempts to relocate and redistribute this speech, while interesting, are not ultimately more convincing than Wilson's argument. Attempts to use thematic issues to determine which speaker is most likely to have uttered this poem depends to a great extent on the interpreter's subjective opinion. It is perhaps more enlightening to analyze the ways in which an interpreter's assignment of Job 28 affects her or his overall interpretation of the important themes in the book as a whole. If Job 28 is ascribed to Elihu, then whether wisdom does in fact constitute fear of the Lord, as the Israelite wisdom tradition advocates, is an open question. If the same speech is put in the mouth of Job, then we have a reiteration of this primary principle of Wisdom literature, because God eventually affirms Job as having spoken rightly. In the latter case, the fear of the Lord has a new face, as Job's harsh language throughout the dialogues is here assessed as being consistent with fearing God and living wisely.

These options are instructive for debates about appropriate ways to bring ancient faith traditions into contemporary life. Some religious communities advocate adhering to the ancient traditions as closely as possible; others advocate translations and interpretations of these traditions that are more or less radical in their reassignments; still others reject ancient traditions and attempt to embrace the principles and motivations behind them. Job potentially provides support for each of these approaches, but the book also seems to fall more heavily on the side of those who embrace ambiguity and tension and are open to reinterpreting tradition based on new experiences and perspectives. Hence we have interpretations of Job's suffering in Hindu communities (Sitaramayya), appropriation of Job's laments in contexts of HIV/AIDS in South Africa (West with Zengele), and challenges presented by liberation theologies (Tamez; Dussel; Gutiérrez), all of which use Job to challenge existing religious structures and indeed standard uses of the book of Job itself, particularly those advocating patience and endurance in the face of suffering.

Job 29–31: Job's Final Monologue—Statement of Righteousness

■ THE TEXT IN ITS ANCIENT CONTEXT

In Job's final speech, he looks backward and forward in a more integrated manner than he has done thus far. He seems to have reached the end of his tether but still manages to confidently assert his rights (Clines 2006, 1036). He also seems to turn his back on his friends and turn his full attention to God (Wilson). Job's speech in chapter 27 was a short oath. Job 29–31 is much more expansive. These chapters reflect a neat tripartite structure, with Job's nostalgic reflection on his past (29), lament over his present circumstances (30), and his final oath of innocence (31).

Job's reflection on his past, "when the Almighty was still with me" (29:5a), may indicate that the ruptured relationship with God is one of Job's primary concerns (Wilson, 313). Nevertheless, the loss of wealth and status also seem quite important to Job, and "when the Almighty was still with me" could equally refer to the blessings associated with this state as to any Christianized sense of direct relationship with God, especially given the fact that this lament is followed by 29:5b-10, which clearly indicate the association of the Almighty's presence with earthly blessing and respect. Job craves approval, but it is also true that he helped the poor, orphans, widows, the blind, the needy, and strangers (29:13-16); and it is clear that Job expected to be rewarded with ease in return for his righteousness (29:18-20). His longing for his formerly privileged place in society is the theme of 29:21-25. Again, this is consistent with the context of exile, wherein the issue is not only physical and psychological pain but also a loss of status, being shamed and reviled.

Job's suffering is particularly galling because it is both intense and public; it seems the two things are interrelated in key ways. Job 30:1-15 laments Job's humiliation and describes his tormentors in particularly harsh terms, as less than human (30:1, 6-7). Job laments the passing of his honor and prosperity (30:15b, c) before he describes the extreme physical and psychological pain that torments him (30:16-31). This is further complicated by the pain Job experiences because God does not answer when Job cries out to God; God is afflicting Job in a way that Job would not afflict a human being in need (30:25-26). The spirit of God that paradoxically keeps Job alive in previous sections is now being poured out (30:16). It is clear that Job believes the problem is not that God is unaware; God is paying close and careful attention (30:20), and in the context of defeat, exile, and Diaspora, this itself is the problem.

Job next makes a series of "disavowals" (Clines 2006, 1013). Job's oaths in this chapter are serious; in his context, one who makes an oath and fails to fulfill it is inviting unmitigated disaster. Of course, Job does not think he can be proven wrong, and it is hard to imagine what further disaster could possibly befall him. Job's affidavit considers themes that resonate with standard tropes in Old Testament literature: dishonesty, adultery, injustice and the proper treatment of slaves, unfair or unsympathetic treatment of the disenfranchised (the poor, widows, and orphans), greed, placing trust in wealth or idols (a key prohibition in the Old Testament and an ostensible reason for the exile), revenge or rejoicing in the downfall of enemies, a failure of hospitality (another key Old Testament theme, particularly in stories about the patriarchs), covering up sin, and mistreatment of the land and the tenant farmers who till it (also a common Old Testament theme, where the land has a corporate personality, is able to cry out and weep, and is a key component in the covenant). Job disavows all of these errors; in an Israelite context, he disavows any violation of torah.

Finally, in Job 31, Job gives a forceful account of his belief in his own innocence. He is so confident of being able to answer all claims against him that we would wear any accusation as a crown for all to see, thus making a public affirmation of his innocence, which, together with the cessation of his suffering, is the primary thing he has wished for throughout his dialogue. Here his words end, with the Hebrew verb *tammu*, the same root used to describe Job as blameless and upright, integrating Job's affidavit with the idea that his words, like himself, are blameless and whole. God will eventually confirm this.

▌▐ The Text in the Interpretive Tradition

This section skillfully moves the reader away from Job as an object of pity and toward a view of the Job of previous days, a man of power, wealth, and a sense of entitlement. Some interpreters have found in these passages more cause to chastise Job than to praise him, although he himself clearly thinks the actions he describes are evidence of his worthiness and integrity. It is up to the reader whether to hold Job to the standards of his own time, in which case he is rather remarkable for his insistence on "the importance of motivation in ethics," or to judge him by the standards of contemporary ideals and to find him wanting, for example in his owning of slaves, his treatment of his wife as property, his brooking no dissent or disagreement, and his failure to challenge a system that privileged him and disadvantaged others (Clines 2006, 1038; Tamez, 1986, 2004; Gutiérrez).

▌▐ The Text in Contemporary Discussion

Job's failure to address the systematic injustices of his society, from which he certainly profited, provides the impetus for much contemporary discussion around the book, including assertions that Job didn't go far enough in addressing the question of suffering because he is primarily (Tamez 1986, 2004) or solely (Clines 2003, 2006) concerned with his own unique case. This can be read as evidence that the wealthy can never fully understand the plight of the poor (Clines 2003); it can also be a testament to the power of experience to overcome prejudice (Tamez 1986). I would argue that this aspect of the book should not be read anachronistically through a contemporary lens, which demands that Job must see things our way if he is to be a hero for the marginalized. However, I would also argue that in the context of the exile, many aspects of social structure were being questioned; the challenge for interpreters is to allow the book to address the questions that it meant to address and not import new questions, which the book perhaps could not have envisioned.

Arguably, the issue is not the social structure of ancient Israelite society; the issue is how one should respond to suffering, and what role God plays in the governance of the world. Of course, the question of how one should respond to suffering could equally be explored in the context of changes to the systematic ways in which social structures perpetuate it, but in this case the text seems to be focused on undeserved suffering, particularly in the context of covenant and exile. In relation to contemporary debates, however, the book as a whole provides ample interpretive fodder for arguments against passivity, quiescence, and apathy in the face of injustice, whether its perceived source is one's friends, one's God, or one's society at large.

Job 32–37: Elihu's Monologue—Theology of Retribution

▌ The Text in Its Ancient Context

At the end of Job 24, Job challenges his friends to prove him wrong. Their dwindling speeches in Job 25 seem to indicate that they are unable to do so. Elihu's stated purpose in intervening is to prevent Job's words from being taken as wisdom merely because his three friends could no longer muster an argument against him. This is the textual basis on which this new voice is introduced, although many interpreters would argue that this is a later addition. Elihu's compulsion to speak (32:17-22) is part of the prophetic tradition and evidence of the spirit of God compelling him to speak, as in the case of Jeremiah. Job also depicts himself as compelled to speak by his suffering (7:11; 10:1). This is perhaps further evidence that the distinction between "seer" and "sage," discussed above, was blurring in the context of the exilic search for new religious authority.

Elihu represents a more nuanced but still ultimately traditional view of the principle of retribution. One particularly interesting passage in this context is Job 33:23-28: here Elihu develops the earlier theme of a mediator, envisioning an angel with the authority to declare a person *yashar* ("upright"). There is some tension between the angel's defense of the person's *yashar* and the person's own confession of sin and "perverting the right." It seems that Elihu is advocating a sort of middle ground between Job's position and that of the friends, arguing that Job should not abandon hope of a mediator, but that he should also be prepared to confess to having "perverted the right." This is perhaps a more palatable version of the principle of retribution, but in the larger context of the book as well as the larger context of the exile, it still falls short of a satisfactory explanation for the apparent chaos of events.

▌ The Text in the Interpretive Tradition

Many commentators loathe Elihu (Terrien; Gordis; Newsom; Habel), while a few defend his appeal as a passionate young man who argues from emotion as well as intellect (McKay). Most interpreters agree that this section is a later addition to the text, although some argue that it adds nothing new and should be lifted out entirely. Some think that Elihu merely sets the stage for God's arrival (Timmer); others think his function is more nuanced, an artistic development appropriate to the larger structure of the text (Saadiah; Wilson). They argue that this section heightens the drama of God's appearance in the whirlwind, anticipates "the rather bombastic character of the divine appearance," and prepares the reader for Job's ultimate restoration by indicating that things are not hopeless (Wilson, 359). We might also see in Elihu a response to Job's request in 31:35 that someone would hear him. Saadiah thinks Elihu's advice is sound; the fact that Job does not respond to him indicates that Elihu has won his argument with Job. Alternatively, Thomas Aquinas sees the divine speeches as a rebuttal of Elihu who, like Job, suffers from a lack of wisdom. In any case, these chapters illuminate one more response to Job's suffering, which can certainly be characterized as innovative but which does not fundamentally change either Job's complaint or God's response to it.

Several commentators use Elihu's speeches as a means to resolve the tension in Job. Rashi argues that Job is indeed pious but not perfect; Job's primary problem is hubris, and consequently his failure is an intellectual rather than a moral one. Elihu provides Job a way out of this dilemma by reminding him of the need for humility. Rashi argues that God's speeches confirm Elihu's advice to Job, and Job's response in 42:6 indicates his adoption of perfect humility. Job's suffering is caused by a lack of wisdom and is the price he must pay to acquire wisdom (Maimonides, Gershonides). Aquinas agrees that the major lesson of Job is the importance of acquiring wisdom and the concomitant importance of humility regarding one's own opinions and status. He also sees Job's lack of reverence as an issue that Elihu correctly identifies as problematic. Luther and Calvin pick up this theme. Luther argues that Job's suffering causes him to complain too much and to fail to demonstrate appropriate reverence for God. Job's friends accuse him of sinning before he suffered; Luther thinks Job sinned as a result of his suffering. Calvin takes this further. He is offended by Job's impudence far more than by the content of his speeches. Calvin supports Elihu's argument that suffering is instructive, but argues that Elihu's response is not enough for the impudent Job, which is the reason God must eventually speak to Job directly. Calvin ultimately returns to the theology of the three friends; human beings must simply submit to God's power.

According to Clines, Elihu goes beyond the theology of the other friends and has a more nuanced concept of the suffering of the righteous. God uses suffering to instruct the righteous, and they may choose to listen and experience restoration or they may resist and face death. Elihu challenges the polarization of the righteous and the wicked; one can fall into sin and still be righteous. Elihu also believes that God communicates through the workings of nature, an idea borne out in God's speeches. Ultimately, Clines argues, Elihu doesn't go far enough. He still views suffering as punishment for wrongdoing, even if the ultimate aim is different. Elihu is sympathetic to Job, and his view of the natural world is partly accurate but still implies that human beings are the center of everything. As we will see below, this anthropocentric view of creation proves to be particularly problematic.

With regard to the key passage in 33:23-28, Wilson suggests that Elihu considers himself the messenger; Habel sees this angel as a heavenly mediator, a counterpart to the satan in the prologue. According to Clines, we must assume that the angel is carrying out God's bidding rather than acting in opposition to God, because Elihu argues that God uses suffering for communicative and redemptive purposes. This theme is also present in Job 5:1 and 16:20; Clines sees the mediator here as a prophetic voice whose duty is to convey God's will to human beings, a task that is consistent with other angelic interventions in the Old Testament. Thus the mediator is not someone who intercedes for Job, but someone who proves to Job that God is in the right (Clines 2006). However, in 33:24, the angel does appear to ask God to spare the person from death; we cannot be sure what the ransom is, but the implication is that the word of the angel seems to provide some form of compensation for divine justice. The surprising thing is that deliverance appears to come before repentance; it is a divine act of pity. This is consistent with certain prophetic texts, wherein repentance is often depicted as an act of gratitude for forgiveness rather than a precondition for it. The notion that repentance precedes forgiveness is arguably a Christian anachronism. If we accept this premise, perhaps the ransom is not concrete at all but merely a poetic device (Clines 2006). Job 33:26 seems to imply a thanksgiving offering rather than an atoning sacrifice, which may also be an anticipation of Job's own restoration prior to the sacrifice in Job 42.

■ THE TEXT IN CONTEMPORARY DISCUSSION

Elihu is not only young; the word for *young* he uses in Job 32:6 also indicates a lack of social standing. He affirms an initial respect for age and the tradition of wisdom, but the words that follow do not reflect this in practice. One of Elihu's innovations is to propose that the divine spirit gives life to human beings but also provides them with wisdom. In contrast to the idea that observation and experience are the source of wisdom, and therefore that greater age means more opportunities for observation and experience and hence more wisdom, Elihu says that the spirit of God can inspire anyone, including someone as young as he is. Thus Elihu underscores the challenge to authority, another recognized theme in the book.

In Job 33, Elihu seems to find Job's protestations of innocence less problematic than his demands that God answer his complaints. Elihu argues that God does not need to answer Job, and moreover that God speaks to human beings in visions and through suffering, which is meant to correct their behavior. In other words, Job's suffering *is* God's communication, and Job should expect nothing further. However, God is merciful and does sometimes redeem sinners and extend their lives. Retribution need not be final; it is a teaching tool, designed to initiate turning or returning to God. Elihu believes that suffering comes to all people as a means of identifying sin, encouraging repentance, and ultimately restoring the person; suffering is instructive. This is a consistent theme in Job's interpretive tradition, from patristic to medieval to Reformation Christian communities. It is also a theme in contemporary discussions about the reasons for suffering, from the parenting trope that "suffering builds character" to the Christian tradition that encourages the sufferer to identify the ways in which God uses suffering to instill spiritual principles or to test faith. The theology of divine providence becomes especially problematic in this aspect, that suffering must be explained as somehow beneficial to the sufferer. This concept certainly has precedence in the wisdom tradition, but is developed in Job with particular reference to exilic concerns.

Thus, in spite of a certain amount of innovation, Elihu is still basing his theology (if not his speech) on received wisdom rather than on experience. God is sovereign and cannot be swayed by human behavior; human initiative is limited to observation and response, and learning how best to do this constitutes the search for wisdom. The innovation of Job, and one of the great sources of Job's continued relevance in contemporary religious and nonreligious contexts alike, is to undermine this foundation and to base his theology (or lack thereof) on lived experience.

Job 38:1—42:6: Theophany—God Responds and Job Relents

▌ THE TEXT IN ITS ANCIENT CONTEXT

This section begins as God answers Job out of the storm, which is a common setting for a theophany (2 Kgs. 2:1, 11; Pss. 18:7-15; 50:3; Ezek. 1:4; Nah. 1:3; Zech. 9:14) and also calls to mind God's appearance to the Israelites on Mount Sinai at the time of the exodus (Exod. 19:16-20). This detail is particularly important at this juncture, as this is also the first time since the prologue (with the exception of Job 12:9) that the personal name YHWH rather than the generic term for God has been used. In the storm imagery and in the use of the name God revealed to Moses, readers are reminded that this is the God of the covenant, who initiated a special relationship with the Israelites. This lends another dimension of meaning to what follows, as God's redefinition of justice resonates with a wider redefinition of the terms of the covenant as gratuitous rather than retributive.

The speeches of YHWH make use of the ANE genre of onomasticon—lists of items presented to illustrate and embody a particular category. In this case, the purpose seems to be to indicate by extension that there is no part of the created world outside of God's authority; the lists cover wild and domesticated animals, wild and cultivated land, as well as the heights of the heavens, the depths of the sea, and even symbolic places such as Sheol and the "innermost parts" of human beings. The form of these chapters also develops the genre of disputation, demonstrating the knowledge of a wise master against that of a student.

The symbol of the waters, as well as the great beasts Behemoth and Leviathan, represent YHWH's control over chaos. In other ANE texts (such as the Epic of Gilgamesh, the *Enuma Elish*, and the Atrahasis Epic), the waters threatened to overwhelm the gods who originally unleashed them; in the case of YHWH, readers are meant to infer that his strength and control are incontestable.

Some commentators hypothesize that Behemoth may be a hippopotamus, and Leviathan either a whale or a crocodile. Behemoth and Leviathan may simply be ciphers for the strongest land and sea creatures imaginable, thus reinforcing YHWH's dominion over the entire earth. Alternatively, it has been suggested that both beasts represent mythical chaos monsters. Various ancient texts (Herodotus, *Hist.* 2.68–71) and Egyptian hieroglyphs (ceiling of the Ramesseum) depict hippopotami and crocodiles in conjunction or succession; hence their association here is not without precedent. In ancient Egypt, only the pharaohs or the gods could hunt the hippopotamus, and such a hunt was considered a battle against evil. Defeat of the great beast also confirmed the hunter's right to rule. The description of Leviathan is similar to that of Lotan in Ugaritic literature, a mythic sea creature that Baal defeats in order to prove his supremacy. In any case, the primary purpose here is to establish YHWH's control over the forces of chaos and disorder and thus his authority over the created world.

In the wider context of Wisdom literature, the mysteries of the world illustrated in YHWH's speeches are also the means by which human beings confront the mysteries of God. Whereas Job confronts YHWH directly in the whirlwind, Wisdom literature teaches that readers can also confront God in the world around them. Wisdom literature is itself a search for explanation(s) in the context of certain historical periods and events; in this case, it is a search for meaning after the wrenching events of exile. In Wisdom literature, knowledge is a function of relationship and trust; hence Job's relationship with YHWH takes primacy over his ability to answer the questions YHWH poses in these speeches. Experiential reality, not rational speculation, is the foundation of wisdom in this context.

YHWH's speeches shift the tenor of the book from dialogue to examination. YHWH questions Job and challenges Job to instruct him. The initial emphasis is on Job's lack of wisdom. However, emphasis gradually shifts from Job's ignorance to YHWH's power; this is particularly evident in the shift from "who" questions to YHWH's direct references to himself as "I," and then the emphasis on "can you" questions directed at Job beginning in 38:31. Additionally, the focus gradually shifts from Job personally to humanity generally. These shifts in the series of apparently unanswerable questions that YHWH poses to Job seem to be an effort to reorient Job's perspective to take in the wider purview of creation, to see his suffering as a small issue in the grand scheme of things.

The question remains: Are these speeches an effective response to Job's complaint? The key point is that Job appears to accept them as such. While the reasons behind the lack of retributive organizing principles in YHWH's created world are not clearly stated, the affirmation that they are in fact lacking is enough for Job to achieve one of his key goals, his own vindication in the eyes of his friends. It is an interesting compromise. Job still fears God for naught, since his righteousness has not yet been directly affirmed, thus confirming YHWH's victory in the original wager with the satan; nevertheless, the possibility of Job's righteousness exists, and Job appears to accept this as his answer. Job may in fact repent, or not; the ambiguity of Job's response (which we will address in the next section) seems to indicate that YHWH's confirmation of the bankruptcy of retributive theology, rather than Job's response to this confirmation, is the central issue here.

▌ THE TEXT IN THE INTERPRETIVE TRADITION

Job's ultimate response to God in 42:6 has been the subject of much exegetical debate, with many interpreters concluding that the philological ambiguity of the verse is deliberate and so subverts the possibility of closure at the end of the dialogues because these issues cannot be simply resolved. William Morrow identifies three major interpretive possibilities in the meaning of Job's final statement: "Wherefore I retract [or "I submit"] and I repent on [or "on account of"] dust and ashes"; "Wherefore I reject *it* [implied object in 42:5], and I am consoled for dust and ashes"; "Wherefore I reject and forswear dust and ashes" (Morrow, 211–12). Another possibility is presented by Leo Perdue (125–26), among others: "I protest, but feel sorry for dust and ashes." Morrow identifies the major themes of Job's response in accordance with each translation as repentance, consolation, and rejection, respectively. Perdue's translation could be termed the "ironic" or "defiant" response. These basic themes accurately categorize the majority of interpretations of this verse.

Like many other issues in the book of Job, the choice of translation of this verse among interpreters rests primarily on thematic rather than philological grounds. The overall theme(s) identified by an interpreter of Job will affect her or his translation of this ambiguous verse, and her or his translation of this verse will deeply affect the identification of overarching themes in the book.

Perhaps, as in the case of the use of *barak*, this ambiguity is a deliberate literary device designed to subvert simplistic resolution.

Some interpretations argue that the message of YHWH's speeches and Job's responses is that YHWH's justice is greater than human justice (Gutiérrez; von Rad 1972); others argue that the beauty of creation is itself consolation for suffering (Gordis); still others argue that the problem is not innocent suffering but proper conduct in the face of suffering (Clines 2006). While commentators disagree on the overall purpose behind the speeches as well as whether they are an effective response to Job, most agree that the speeches contain both confirmation of YHWH's control over creation and disavowal of retribution as the organizing principle behind YHWH's created world.

None of these interpreters is able to definitively overcome the challenges posed by the opposite perspective, but the very existence of these counterchallenges is what makes the book itself, and particularly the concluding sections, so endlessly compelling. If, as Clines argues, the book of Job was intended to subvert closure, then we are in agreement with von Rad that "truth can be opposed to truth" and that this dissonant opposition can be a positive rather than a negative factor in biblical interpretation (Clines 1990; von Rad 1972, 312).

▌ THE TEXT IN CONTEMPORARY DISCUSSION

YHWH challenges Job to establish the retributive order he and his friends seem to desire, to reward the righteous and punish the wicked. YHWH's speeches emphasize the point that Job has neither the knowledge nor the power to accomplish this. YHWH has the power and yet does not use it solely to this end. Many interpreters (von Rad 1975; Gutiérrez; Tsevat) have made a leap here to say that the issue is one of grace; human beings are expected to trust God without any guarantee of reward, as Gutiérrez says, "gratuitously." Others (Clines 2003, 2011; Perdue) argue that the text does not clearly indicate this interpretation; its concern seems to be to establish that one cannot assume that those who suffer are wicked. This is an important message, both in the context of Israel's exile and in contemporary contexts of suffering.

YHWH's first speech uses vivid imagery and mythic symbols to establish his control over the world he created. If YHWH does not govern the world according to retribution, it is not because he cannot, but because he will not. YHWH binds the wicked as he binds the sea; the sea is still destructive and indicative of chaos, but within the limits of YHWH's control. The same principle applies to the wicked. Again, in the case of this long list of wild animals, YHWH's power over them and their simultaneous threat to humanity and civilization indicates YHWH's control over forces dangerous to humankind without the elimination of these dangers. YHWH sustains the wild ox and ass in spite of the fact that they are of no use to humankind, as their domesticated relatives are. Images of warhorses and carrion birds also call to mind human death, which is part of the scheme of things and not something to be avoided.

YHWH's second speech focuses more directly on the core of Job's challenge, the issue of justice and just governance of the world. Both speeches emphasize the fact that YHWH's concern is for creation as a whole, not humanity specifically. In contemporary environmental debates, this passage has been used to encourage the development of theologies of the environment as well as more generally to counteract a theology that sees human beings as the focus and pinnacle of creation. YHWH's speeches here support a more symbiotic view of creation, where human beings are part of a natural order rather than tasked with directing or controlling it. By implication, such interpretations also challenge economic principles of unlimited growth as well as the idea that the righteous have the right to material prosperity and protection from chaos (Stokes Musser).

Job 42:7-17: Epilogue—A Righteous Man Restored

■ THE TEXT IN ITS ANCIENT CONTEXT

The burnt offering God demands in Job 42:7-9 indicates that it is Job's friends who have sinned; burnt offerings are characterized as sin offerings. The friends are accused of folly, of rejecting God or refusing to follow the way of the righteous that leads to true wisdom. The implication is that Job has followed the way of true wisdom, in spite of the fact that he complained in Job 3 that this way was hidden from him.

The remainder of the chapter is devoted to a description of Job's restoration. The doubling of all of his possessions, with the exception of his children, is particularly interesting (Job 42:10-12). This is not merely an indication that Job was restored to his former status and then some. It is also evocative of the Israelite law that a thief should restore double what he has taken. In some sense, this seems to be an admission of guilt on God's part, an indication that God was wrong to inflict suffering on Job and therefore owes some form of restitution.

The restoration of Job's family structure is also a key issue in the epilogue (Job 42:13-15). Much is sometimes made of Job's decision to grant his daughters an inheritance along with his sons. However, as Clines points out, daughters were permitted to inherit in the case that a father had no sons, and this condition may simply be a reflection of Job's enormous wealth. Equally, the basis for the daughters' inheritance seems to be their beauty rather than any sense of equity or protofeminist impulse on Job's part (Clines 2011). Van Wolde (1997) thinks this aspect is proof that Job has accepted his lack of control over his own fate and that of his children, typified by his scrupulous offerings on their behalf in the prologue. Job has learned to let go and enjoy things, and this new-found hedonism is the source of his behavior toward his daughters. In any case, the primary point of the text seems to be that Job was ultimately restored, that he even lived double the length of years ascribed to the average mortal (42:16), and by implication that the Israelites could expect a similar restoration.

■ THE TEXT IN THE INTERPRETIVE TRADITION

Interpretive tradition raises two primary issues in the epilogue: What is it that Job has spoken which God identifies as "right," and does Job's material restoration undermine the idea that it is possible to serve God gratuitously?

On the first question, Daniel Timmer (302–3) argues that Job and the friends are praised and chastised respectively for speaking *to* God, not *of* God. The subject of God's approval is Job's repentance or turning, and the subject of his disapproval is the friends' apparent failure to respond in this way to God's appearance; this is illustrated by Job's sin offering on their behalf, as Job facilitates their repentance. He sees the book as an example of wisdom pedagogy, both in form and content. Speaking to God not only involves pious submission but also allows for willful rebellion as a means to achieving the ultimate end of reverence for and "attachment to" God, which both undergirds and surpasses the wisdom enterprise (Timmer, 305).

Other interpreters argue that these verses provide the context in which we learn what was really at stake in Job's struggle: not the understanding or accomplishment of justice, but the understanding and accomplishment of undeserved generosity, as manifested in Job's prayer for his friends, as well as the acknowledgment of undeserved suffering, in that God does not accuse Job of sin. In this sense, Job has spoken of God what is right (Merkur). Still others see in this affirmation a legitimation of anger and lament as responses to suffering that do not undermine integrity or continued relationship with God (West).

Nam translates Job 42:7 as an argument that Job has spoken of God "constructively." The issue for him is one of efficacy rather than one of truth. Job's speeches have afforded God the opportunity to speak in return, and it is this situation rather than the content of Job's speeches that God affirms.

On the second question, some interpreters evade the issue by arguing that the epilogue was originally a separate story, together with the prologue, and so is not meant to address the issues raised in the dialogues and God's subsequent speeches. This assumes, unfairly I think, that the author or editor who put the two stories together was not capable of integrating them properly. Other interpreters have proposed more interesting theories. Gutiérrez interprets Job's restoration as the author(s)'s desire "to give human and material expression of the deep spiritual joy that Job has experienced in his final encounter with God" (12). Clines (2011) argues that it may be the case that Job's restoration is contingent on his willingness to make the required offering on behalf of his friends. This selfless act is confirmation of Job's reorientation, and it is that which is the prerequisite of Job's restoration. Van Wolde (1997, 2002) thinks that Job's restoration is an argument for a type of righteous hedonism, learning to enjoy the blessings of God rather than being bound by legal structures that attempt to delimit and earn such blessings.

Dan Mathewson argues that the epilogue is evidence of Job's struggle with "desymbolization" and "resymbolization." Thus the epilogue is not as simple as it seems; we cannot interpret it in the same symbolic world Job previously inhabited, because the poetic dialogues have intervened between the two. A goal of the survivor of trauma is "symbolic wholeness" or, in Job's case, "resymbolization," yet the divine speeches indicate that there can be no stasis in a world where chaos is limited but not eliminated. Perhaps the book of Job indicates that symbolic wholeness itself is impossible; it is not simply the previous symbolic wholeness of Job's world that is rejected, but any symbolic wholeness at all. Like suffering itself, the book of Job can never be fully synthesized.

It is also significant that this restoration of Job's wealth and family would have been understood among his friends and detractors as evidence of God's favor. This public vindication is something that Job has been longing for since the third chapter, and perhaps this is less a material reward for Job than a confirmation of the "rightness" of his behavior, and consequently of the possibility that a sufferer can be righteous and that a mortal can contend with God.

◼ THE TEXT IN CONTEMPORARY DISCUSSION

At the end of the book, we are left with as many questions as we had at the beginning. Job accepts his restoration as compensation for his suffering, or at least we must assume he does, since we hear no more from him directly. Job's friends are castigated but ultimately forgiven, and the process of their expiation is itself evidence of Job's reorientation away from retribution and toward gratuitousness as an organizing principle of life in the world YHWH has created. In one sense, Job has certainly been right: he complained that YHWH does not govern the world according to the principle of retribution, and YHWH's speeches confirmed that this is so. Job's acceptance, whether we categorize it as repentance, consolation, rejection, or silent defiance, nevertheless confirms that retributive justice is not something human beings can expect from YHWH. Van Wolde (1997) argues that the possibility of disinterested belief comes after God's speeches reorient Job's perspective, not before. It is this transition, rather than Job's initial patience, that proves the outcome of the divine wager. Job is fundamentally a story of progress toward the possibility of gratuitousness. Thus the epilogue does not simply reinscribe the principle of retribution. It leaves open the possibility that restoration, blessing, and vindication are things Job, and perhaps the exiled Israelites and contemporary readers as well, may hope for, although not something that can be earned. Just as Job's faith is or has become disinterested, God's blessings are also disinterested, and a person should enjoy to the fullest those blessings God chooses to bestow.

All interpreters see something of themselves in Job. This is no less true for Augustine or Maimonides than it is for Gutiérrez or Clines. This is a primary reason why Job is considered one of the great works of ancient literature and has been influential well beyond the religious traditions for which it is considered Scripture; it shows each reader something of her- or himself, and in so doing, it also points to the truth that all interpretation is a subjective endeavor.

Works Cited

Calvin, John. 1952. *Sermons from Job*. Edited by L. Nixon. Grand Rapids: Eerdmans.

Clines, David J. A. 1989. *Job 1–20*. WBC 17. Dallas: Word.

———. 1990. "Deconstructing the Book of Job." In *The Bible as Rhetoric: Studies in Biblical Persuasion and Credibility*, ed. M. Warner. 65–80. London: Routledge.

———. 2003. "Does the Book of Job Suggest that Suffering Is Not a Problem?" In *Weisheit in Israel: Beiträge des Symposiums, "Das Alte Testament und die Kultur der Moderne,"* anlässlich des 100. Geburtstags Gerhard von Rads (1901-1971), Heidelberg, 18.-21. Oktober 2001, edited by David J. A. Clines, Hermann Lichtenberger, and Hans-Peter Müller, 93–110. Münster: LIT Verlag.

———. 2006. *Job 21–37*. WBC 18a. Nashville: Thomas Nelson.

———. 2011. *Job 38–42*. WBC 18b. Nashville: Thomas Nelson.

Dussel, Enrique. 1983. "The People of El Salvador: The Communal Sufferings of Job." *Concilium* 169:61–68.

Gershonides. 1946. *Commentary on Job*. Translated by Abraham Lassen. New York: Bloch.

Goodman, L. E. 1988. *The Book of Theodicy: Translation and Commentary on the Book of Job by Saadiah Ben Joseph Al-Fayyumi*. New Haven/London: Yale University Press.

Gordis, Robert. 1978. *The Book of God and Man: A Study of Job*. Chicago: University of Chicago Press.

Gravett, Emily O. 2012. "Biblical Responses: Past and Present Retellings of the Enigmatic Mrs. Job." *Biblical Interpretation* 20: 97–125.

Gregory the Great. 1850. *Morals on the Book of Job*. 4 Vols. Trans. Charles Marriott. Oxford: Parker.

Gutiérrez, Gustavo. 1987. *On Job: God-Talk and the Suffering of the Innocent*. Translated by Matthew J. O'Connell. Maryknoll, NY: Orbis.

Habel, Norman C. 2004. "The Verdict on/of God at the End of Job." *Concilium* 4:2–38.

Hartley, John E. 1988. *The Book of Job*. NICOT. Grand Rapids: Eerdmans.

Janzen, J. Gerald. 2009. *At the Scent of Water: The Ground of Hope in the Book of Job*. Grand Rapids: Eerdmans.

Johnson, Timothy Jay. 2009. *Now My Eye Sees You: Unveiling an Apocalyptic Job*. Sheffield: Sheffield Phoenix.

Jones, Scott C. 2009. *Rumors of Wisdom: Job 28 and Poetry*. Berlin: de Gruyter.

Klein, Lillian R. 1995. "Job and the Womb: Text about Men, Subtext about Women." In *A Feminist Companion to Wisdom Literature*, edited by Athalya Brenner, 186–200. Sheffield: Sheffield Academic.

Luther, Martin. 1960. *Preface to the Old Testament*. Vol. 35, *Luther's Works*, edited by Theodore Bachmann. Philadelphia: Muhlenberg.

Magallanes, Sophia. 2011. "Bringing Wisdom Back Down to Earth: A Wisdom Reading of Job 28." PhD diss., Azusa Pacific University.

Magdalene, F. Rachel. 2006. "Job's Wife as Hero: A Feminist-Forensic Reading of the Book of Job." *BibInt* 14, no. 3:209–58.

Maimonides, Moses. 1956. *Guide for the Perplexed*. Translated by M. Friedlander. New York: Dover.

Mathewson, Dan. 2006. *Death and Survival in the Book of Job: Desymbolization and Traumatic Experience*. New York: T&T Clark.

McKay, J. W. 1979. "Elihu—A Proto-Charismatic?" *ExpTim* 70:167–71.

Merkur, Dan. 2004. "Psychotherapeutic Change in the Book of Job." In *From Genesis to Apocalyptic Vision*. Vol. 2, *Psychology and the Bible: A New Way to Read the Scriptures*, edited by J. Harold Ellens and Wayne G. Rollins, 119–39. Westport, CT: Praeger.

Morrow, William S. 1986. "Consolation, Rejection, and Repentance in Job 42:6." *JBL* 105, no. 2:211–25.

Nadar, Sarojini. 2003. "Re-Reading Job in the Midst of Suffering in the HIV/AIDS Era: How Not to Talk of God." *OTE* n.s. 16, no. 2:343–57.

Nam, Duck-Woo. 2003. *Talking about God: Job 42:7-9 and the Nature of God in the Book of Job*. New York: Peter Lang.

Negri, Antonio. 2009. *The Labor of Job: The Biblical Text as a Parable of Human Labor*. Translated by Matteo Mandarini. Edited by Roland Boer. Durham, NC: Duke University Press.

Newsom, Carol A. 2003. *The Book of Job: A Contest of Moral Imaginations*. Oxford: Oxford University Press.

Ngwa, Kenneth. 2009. "Did Job Suffer for Nothing? The Ethics of Piety, Presumption and the Reception of Disaster in the Prologue of Job." *JSOT* 33, no. 3:359–80.

Perdue, Leo G. 2007. *Wisdom Literature: A Theological History*. Louisville: Westminster John Knox.

Pope, Marvin H. 1965. *Job*. AYB. New Haven: Yale University Press.

Pyeon, Yohan. 2003. *You Have Not Spoken What Is Right about Me: Intertextuality in the Book of Job*. New York: Peter Lang.

Rayan, Samuel. 2006. "Wrestling in the Night." In *Voices from the Margin: Interpreting the Bible in the Third World*, edited by R. S. Sugirtharajah, 407–28. 3rd ed. Maryknoll, NY: Orbis.

Sitaramayya, K. B. 2001. *The Marvel and Mystery of Pain: A New Interpretation of the Book of Job*. Bangalore: MCC.

Stokes Musser, Sarah. 2012. "Comfort in the Whirlwind? Job, Creation, and Environmental Degradation." *WW* 32, no. 3:286–93

Tam, Edman P. C. 2002. "Silence of God and God of Silence." *AJT* 16, no. 1:152–63.

Tamez, Elsa. 1986. "A Letter to Job." In *New Eyes for Reading: Biblical and Theological Reflections by Women from the Third World*, edited by John S. Pobee and Barbara Von Wartenburg-Potter, 50–52. Geneva: WCC.

———. 2004. "From Father of the Needy to Brother of Jackals and Companion of Ostriches: A Meditation on Job." *Concilium* 4:103–11.

Terrien, Samuel. 1957. *Job: Poet of Existence*. New York: Bobbs-Merrill.

Thomas Aquinas. 1989. *The Literal Exposition on Job: A Scriptural Commentary Concerning Providence*. Translated by Anthony Damico. Edited by Martin D. Yaffe. Atlanta: Scholars Press.

Timmer, Daniel. 2009. "God's Speeches, Job's Responses, and the Problem of Coherence in the Book of Job: Sapiential Pedagogy Revisited." *CBQ* 71:286–305.

Tsevat, Matitiahu. 1981. *The Meaning of the Book of Job and Other Biblical Studies*. New York: Ktav.

van Wolde, Ellen. 1995. "The Development of Job: Mrs. Job as Catalyst." In *A Feminist Companion to Wisdom Literature*, edited by Athalya Brenner, 201–21. Sheffield: Sheffield Academic.

———. 1997. *Mr. and Mrs. Job*. Translated by John Bowden. London: SCM.

———. 2002. "Different Perspectives on Faith and Justice: The God of Jacob and the God of Job." *Concilium* 1:17–23.

Vicchio, Stephen J. 2006a. *The Image of the Biblical Job: A History*. Vol. 1, *Job in the Ancient World*. Eugene, OR: Wipf & Stock.

———. 2006b. *The Image of the Biblical Job: A History*. Vol. 2, *Job in the Medieval World*. Eugene, OR: Wipf & Stock.

———. 2006c. *The Image of the Biblical Job: A History*. Vol. 3, *Job in the Modern World*. Eugene, OR: Wipf & Stock.

von Rad, Gerhard. 1966. "Job XXXVIII and Ancient Egyptian Wisdom." In *The Problem of the Hexateuch and Other Essays*, 281–91. Translated by E. W. Trueman Dicken. Edinburgh: Oliver & Boyd.

———. 1972. *Wisdom in Israel*. London: SCM.

———. 1975. *Old Testament Theology*. Vol. 1, *The Theology of Israel's Historical Traditions*. Translated by D. M. G. Stalker. London: SCM.

West, Gerald O. 2008. "The Poetry of Job as a Resource for the Articulation of Embodied Lament in the Context of HIV and AIDS in South Africa." In *Lamentations in Ancient and Contemporary Contexts*, edited by N. C. Lee and C. Mandolfo, 195–214. Atlanta: Society of Biblical Literature.

West, Gerald O., with Bongi Zengele. 2004. "Reading Job 'Positively' in the Context of HIV/AIDS in South Africa." *Concilium* 4:112–24.

Wilson, Gerald H. 2007. *Job*. New International Bible Commentary. Grand Rapids: Baker Books.

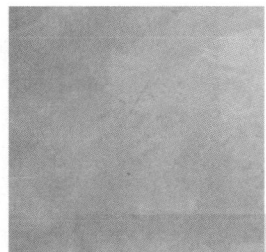

PSALMS

W. Derek Suderman

Introduction

The Psalms have long been a treasured part of Jewish and Christian Scripture, functioning as a songbook, devotional and liturgical resource, source of comfort, and basis for messianic hope, as well as a window into ancient worship and liturgy. With its range of emotions and evocative language, the Psalms continue to "speak" to and for people in a fresh and compelling way in the contemporary world. In the words of Dietrich Bonhoeffer: "Whenever the Psalter is abandoned, an incomparable treasure is lost to the Christian church. With its recovery will come unexpected power" (Bonhoeffer, 162).

The term *psalm*, from the Greek *psalmos*, is *mizmor* in the Hebrew, referring to song or instrumental music. The Hebrew title, *sepher tehillim*, or "book of praises," underscores its concluding emphasis. Within the threefold Jewish Scripture (*Tanakh*), the book of Psalms is the first book in the "Writings"; it also plays a vital role within Christian Scripture, given that New Testament writers cite the Psalms—and Isaiah—more than any other scrolls.

Far from homogenous, however, the book of Psalms represents an anthology with a long compositional history, including material emerging from early in the preexilic period to well after the postexilic return to the land. Just as a contemporary hymnal gathers material from previous ones, remnants of prior collections can also be found (see 72:20). A recurring blessing and "amen" formula divides the Psalms, in their current shape, into five "books"—see Pss. 41:13; 72:18-19; 89:52; 106:48—similar to the five books of Moses, Genesis–Deuteronomy (Mays, 42).

While lament dominates the first three books of the Psalms (1–89), the tone shifts to praise and thanksgiving in the final two (90–150). The Dead Sea Scrolls, dating from 250 BCE to 70 CE, suggest that books 1–3 were already stable by this point, while more variation in order and content appears in books 4–5 (Wilson, 120–21).

The Language and Genres of the Psalms

The Psalms employ poetic language, whose perhaps most striking feature is the consistent appearance of parallel lines. The psalmists employ "antithetical" parallelism, on the one hand, to make a stark contrast.

> for the LORD watches over the way of the righteous,
> but the way of the wicked will perish. (1:6)

"Synonymous" parallelism, on the other hand, seems to say the same thing twice.

> For I know my transgressions,
> and my sin is ever before me. (51:3)

Even here, however, there is a slight difference between the two lines, and even an "intensification" from one line to the next. Reading the space between the two lines as "how much more so" allows the reader to explore the more subtle difference between transgressions and sin on one hand and "knowing" and having my sin constantly before me on the other (Alter, 11).

The Psalms also use metaphor and imagery to great effect; the enemies are lions and bears, God is a rock or a mother hen protecting her brood, and so on. In addition, the Psalms employ similar vocabulary and return to certain motifs again and again. Indeed, repeating the same or related words can be used to signal emphasis, organize a particular psalm, or make intertextual connections. For this reason, this commentary will draw attention to key terms and refer the reader to places with linguistic and thematic connections to the passage under consideration.

Finally, Hermann Gunkel's work in the early twentieth century was a watershed in studying psalms, since he initiated the systematic investigation of their patterned language and so identified various genres or types (see Gunkel 1967; 1998). Although the sequence and specific elements within psalms vary, characteristics can be identified for lament, thanksgiving, hymns, royal, wisdom, and torah psalms (see Gerstenberger 1988, 9–21).

Lament or prayer (*tefillah*) psalms speak persuasively to convince God and others to respond favorably to the psalmist. They generally include an invocation to YHWH, a description of distress, and an appeal for help (see Psalm 6). These psalms often contain imprecations that call on God to punish the enemy and usually conclude with a statement of confidence or affirmation that YHWH has heard. Approximately one-third of the Psalter consists of laments, far and away the most numerous genre in the book.

Thanksgiving (*todah*) psalms publicly acknowledge answered prayer before a social audience. They typically describe a past situation of distress, how the psalmist called out to God, and the deliverance experienced (see Psalm 116). Thanksgiving psalms often conclude with an invitation to the social audience to join the psalmist in recognizing God's deliverance.

Hymns or psalms of praise (*tehillim*) typically recount God's attributes, deeds, and steadfast love, whether for Zion, Israel, humanity generally, or the broader creation. At its most basic, the psalmist cries *halelu yah* ("Praise YHWH").

Royal psalms relate to the king but do not constitute a unique genre; rather, they build on others, including lament (Psalm 21), thanksgiving (Psalm 18), or hymns (Psalm 2). Though some royal psalms have been recognized as messianic within both the Jewish and Christian traditions (Psalm 2), others understood as messianic are not self-evidently "royal" (22).

Wisdom psalms contain distinctive vocabulary, forms, and even organizational features; Psalm 119 is structured as an elaborate acrostic. Some scholars have attributed these elements to individual study and see wisdom material as reflecting primarily written rather than oral language, while others attribute such elements to liturgical changes in a postexilic setting.

Like royal psalms, torah psalms can be identified by content but reflect a mixture of distinct genre types (wisdom in Psalms 1; 119; a hymn in Psalm 19). Despite their relatively small numbers, the strategic location of royal, wisdom, and torah psalms within the organization of the Psalter highlight their significance.

Determining the ancient settings for various genres has proven more difficult than describing their genre characteristics, in part because psalm material was modified and reused in different contexts over time. The setting of individual laments has proven particularly vexing, with proposals ranging from individuals in distress anywhere (Gunkel 1967, 19–20), spoken by the king in a national assembly (Mowinckel, 1:225–28), used in judicial proceedings in the temple (Schmidt), and spoken by individuals in small, liturgical gatherings (Gerstenberger 1988, 13–14). While the first and last of these options hold the most promise, certainty eludes us.

In any case, the implied rhetorical setting that permits the psalmist to address both God and a broader social audience proves most significant for the ancient and contemporary function of these psalms, whatever the precise ancient setting(s) from which they emerged.

"Voice(s)" in the Psalms

While psalms are often described as prayers and therefore considered direct communication between humans and God, they consistently reflect a social element. While at times psalmists call on different groups to respond (Ps. 118:1-4), even individual laments include the three components of God, the psalmist, and others (Westermann, 169).

While the psalmist's own voice is primary, he often quotes the hostile speech of adversaries or articulates the words of support he wants others to articulate. Even the voice of God appears periodically, which, in their ancient setting, would have been articulated by a cultic functionary on behalf of the divine. Within the psalms, we hear the voice of each of the parties Westermann identifies.

Thus it is helpful to think of psalms as *oral* speech, as Gunkel suggested, which is said out loud and so able to address both a divine and social audience. The psalms also represent *potential* speech not limited to ancient contexts but reembodied in the contemporary world. As will be seen repeatedly, both potential and danger lie in how these words are used; contemporary religious communities who claim the Psalms as part of their Scriptures play the essential role of discerning among competing and even contradictory claims (Suderman 2012, 214).

In contemporary use, people tend to monopolize the "voice" of the Psalms by consistently casting themselves individually or collectively as the speaking subject(s). While often appropriate, this can become particularly discordant when psalms call on God's vengeance to destroy the enemy, leading some readers to wonder why such material is in the Bible at all (see Psalms 69; 109; 137). Christian lectionaries commonly skip over offending verses or omit entire psalms (Holladay, 304–15), in part because it is not clear how these can legitimately represent *our* words.

A potential antidote to this tendency lies in recognizing the various social roles reflected in the Psalms beyond that of the speaking subject and then identifying with those who *hear* rather than speak these words. For instance, rather than functionally eliminating calls for God to destroy the enemy, we may fruitfully consider whose contemporary voice such words may represent, and even when they may be appropriately spoken about us. More than merely a window into ancient culture and liturgy, the Psalms also function as a mirror for looking at ourselves more deeply.

A second and related temptation lies in monopolizing the "voice" of legitimate interpretation. While the strength of Western scholarship has been its insistence on placing psalms in their ancient contexts, this focus has also insisted on a historical and cultural gap between the ancient world and our own. While helpful, this emphasis can also prompt less attention to the contemporary function of this material within religious communities and even a pejorative view of "precritical" or non-Western perspectives.

Instead, we do well to recognize insights from devotional and liturgical readings, the broader history of interpretation, as well as global and lay perspectives. Indeed, the way in which many continue to read the Psalms reflects a closer affinity to the broader history of interpretation than Western biblical scholarship. As we attend to the gains of Western scholarship, we should also consider its limitations and drawbacks.

David and the Psalms

The Psalms have traditionally been associated with David, the "sweet singer of Israel," based on his association with music and prominence in the headings of the Psalter. While several headings relate specific psalms to contexts within his life (see Psalms 3; 51), the psalms themselves provide few clues as to their historical settings. Several other figures appear within the Psalm headings, including the "sons of Korah," Asaph, Solomon (72; 127), and even Moses (90).

With the emergence of Western biblical criticism, scholars began to question and then largely reject the headings as accurate depictions of authorship, and so sought other authors and historical contexts. Gunkel and his followers shifted the focus of Psalms scholarship away from authorship to determining the genre and social settings of particular psalms. The discovery of ancient texts at Ugarit, written in a Canaanite dialect very similar to biblical Hebrew, provided direct parallels to vocabulary and grammatical structures in the Psalms.

In recent decades, "canonical criticism" has prompted interest in the shape and organization of the Psalms and has reinvigorated discussion of the role and significance of David vis-à-vis the Psalms. Where Brevard Childs described the Psalm headings as representing early "midrashic exegesis" (Childs 1971), Gerald Wilson noted that "orphan" psalms were increasingly linked to a biblical figure or setting, with the number of "David" psalms increasing from the Hebrew to the Septuagint, Qumran, and Syriac Psalters (Wilson, 155–56); in effect, the Psalms became *more* linked to David over time rather than less so. Indeed, the Hebrew phrase *ledavid*, usually rendered "of David," was understood as the dative "concerning" or "about David" in the Greek Septuagint.

Thus, rather than claims of authorship, these headings function in a later stage of composition to place the psalms within the broader context of other scriptural scrolls, where they function as ancient "cross-references" to orient the reader (Mays, 11–13). To claim this element as reflecting historical authorship on one hand or to dismiss it as "unoriginal" on the other fails to recognize the ancient function and contemporary potential of this element.

The "Ancient Context(s)" of the Psalms

The long and complex compositional history of the Psalms complicates what we refer to as their "ancient context(s)." For instance, "ancient context" could mean either the earliest level of material within the psalm, where and when it was written, or the social setting in which it was initially used. It could also refer to a specific psalm's broader cultural context, including its radical transformation from sun or Baal worship to celebrating torah or praising YHWH (Psalms 19; 29). Alternatively, "ancient context" could also refer to the enhanced function a psalm could take beyond its original intent by its location within the larger scroll, as when a preexilic royal enthronement psalm prompts messianic expectation after exile (Psalm 2).

Thus, for our purposes, "ancient context" has at least a dual meaning: the setting in which the psalm arose or was originally used (its ancient social setting and function) and the role of a particular psalm within the book of Psalms itself. As a cathedral can be constructed, modified, and continue to function over time, it may be best to recognize that psalms have the potential to pass through and function differently within multiple contexts.

Psalms 1–2: Introduction

■ THE TEXT IN ITS ANCIENT CONTEXT

Psalms 1–2 function as a joint introduction that orients the book to wisdom, torah, and messianic categories (Mays, 42–44).

The first psalm begins: "Happy is the one who does *not* walk . . . , stand . . . , or sit," before introducing its positive counterpoint as those who "delight in the law of YHWH [*torath yhwh*]." While the psalm primarily employs wisdom terminology (happy, advice, way), it thus also introduces the key phrase that introduces each of the Psalter's torah psalms (Pss. 1:2; 19:7; 119:1). The idyllic scene then builds on wordplay, where both trees and humans "prosper/flourish" (1:3), and the psalm ends with characteristic wisdom vocabulary, contrasting the "ways" and fates of the righteous and wicked. The psalmist's concluding confidence introduces a basic tension, since later laments reflect settings where the righteous do *not* prosper and the wicked appear to triumph (see Psalms 9–10; 73).

Psalm 2 is a royal psalm that portrays the opposition of rival kings to God and divine support for "his anointed" (*al meshiho*); while the righteous "meditate" on the law (1:2), the peoples "meditate" on emptiness (2:1). Divine first-person speech underscores God's connection with Zion and emphatically describes the king as "my son," language central to the Davidic covenant and common in the ancient Near East, but it is unique here in the Psalms (2:2; cf. 2 Sam. 7:14; Mays, 47). Scholars have proposed the initial setting for this material as an enthronement festival that celebrates the monarchy, similar to those found in other ancient Near Eastern sources. In any case, Psalm 2 depicts the king as a militaristic leader, which prompts a warning directly aimed at would-be rivals. The concluding "Happy is the one . . ." introduces the only wisdom element in this otherwise royal psalm, which both links back to the start of Psalm 1 (1:1) and introduces "refuge," a repeated motif in the book. Though initially a royal enthronement song, the fall of the monarchy combined with the Davidic covenant promising a descendant on the throne "forever" transformed it into a messianic one (Psalm 89; 2 Sam. 7:11-17).

■ The Text in the Interpretive Tradition

While Christian interpreters identify the "anointed" as Christ, they differ in how this is understood. Both Origen and Jerome saw Jesus speaking in Ps. 2:3, with the latter reading "chains" as "the heavy burden of the law." Luther, however, saw this Psalm as David speaking of Christ, with the "rod of iron" representing "the holy Gospel, which is Christ's royal scepter in his Church." Rather than reading it as directly about Christ, Calvin read Psalm 2 as David depicting his own rule, which then becomes a "type" for Christ (Holladay, 169–72, 193, 197).

While the church fathers' interpretations of the Psalms articulate a consistent polemic against the Jews that implies awareness of a Jewish audience, there is little corresponding material from [redundant?] rabbinic sources; though it contains some material reaching back to the third century, the *Midrash on the Psalms* (*Midrash Tehillim*) emerged in the thirteenth century (Gillingham, 45).

While Rashi articulates his own interpretation of Psalm 2, he also notes that rabbinic tradition read it in light of the Messiah (Holladay, 151). Thus the debate between the emerging Jewish and Christian traditions lay not in whether Psalm 2 was messianic, but rather in whether Jesus fulfilled this role. While Psalm 2 is a significant "messianic" psalm within the Christian tradition, it does not appear in Jewish liturgy (cf. Psalms 72; 110; Holladay, 144).

■ The Text in Contemporary Discussion

Messianic readings of the Bible have had long-standing effects. The biblical claim of YHWH's strong support for the king and expectation of dominion has been used to support the "divine right" of kings and the imperialistic aspirations of Christendom. Contemporary claims to national "exceptionalism" reflect a similar tendency to read one's own country as the rightful heir to the status of ancient Israel and thus claim divine sanction for military and socioeconomic domination (see Psalm 18).

The tendency to read into the first-century context later assumptions regarding the parting of the ways between Jews and (gentile) Christians can cloud the mutual understanding of contemporary members of both groups. For instance, on one hand it is problematic to treat first-century documents claiming Jesus to be the Messiah as "Christian," since Jesus' disciples and most (if not all) New Testament writers were Jews; on the other, it is also problematic to treat Jesus' fulfillment of messianic expectation as self-evident (see Psalm 22; Luke 24:13–35). Greater recognition of the diversity of Judaism(s) in the first century as well as the interpretive methods and assumptions of various groups hold promise for improving our understanding of both Jewish and Christian traditions.

Psalms 3–8: Refuge in the Midst of Enemies

■ THE TEXT IN ITS ANCIENT CONTEXT

Psalms 3–8 are each identified as "of David," which both distinguishes them from the introduction and inaugurates the Davidic collection extending through books 1–2 of the Psalms (3–41; 42–72). In so doing, this section begins the lament that dominates the first three books of the Psalms (3–89) and also reflects the three subjects intrinsic to lament: God, the psalmist, and others (Westermann, 169).

Psalm 3 begins with the invocation "Oh YHWH" characteristic of lament psalms that, in a polytheistic context reflected in Babylonian parallels, immediately identifies the specific deity being addressed. In characteristic fashion, this invocation leads to a description of distress, in this case being surrounded by enemies, and a call for God to act or intervene (3:1-2, 7). This psalm also reflects the dynamic of shifting to address various audiences that appears repeatedly in the Psalms, speaking first *to* YHWH, then *about* God, and finally *to* the divine once again. The final verse reflects a shift in tone characteristic of lament, deriving confidence from articulating pain and being heard. Heard in light of the heading's setting of David's fleeing Absalom, David's grief at his son's death may highlight the relative restraint of the psalm (2 Sam. 18:33); "break the teeth" proves defensive and less strident than appeals to destroy the enemy elsewhere (cf. Psalms 109; 137). Psalm 4, which also complains of enemies, again reflects a shift in audience where the psalmist calls on his social audience to speak against his ostracized status (4:2-6). By exhorting listeners to "trust in YHWH," this section also introduces a significant motif in the Psalms.

Psalm 5 addresses God persistently, identifying slander and wicked speech as its key concern (5:9; cf. 3:2; 4:6). The psalmist calls on God to allow the rebellious enemies' schemes to fall on themselves, in contrast to those "who take refuge in you" (5:10-11; cf. 2:11). References to God as "king" and to the "holy temple" become significant motifs elsewhere (93, 99).

Psalm 6 again speaks of enemies, although the major concern here appears to be sickness (6:2); Psalm 30 gives thanks for deliverance from such a context. Where the previous addressed God saying "you hate all *evildoers*" (*po'ale 'aven*, 5:5), here the psalmist explicitly challenges his social adversaries: "Depart from me, all you *evildoers*" (6:8; cf. 4:2); the NRSV's rendering of the latter as "workers of evil" obscures this connection. The confidence that God has heard "my *prayer* [*tefillah*]" prompts the change in tone and concluding conviction that the enemies will be stopped (6:8-10).

Psalm 7 again claims refuge in YHWH amid enemies. In addition to characteristic calls for God to "rise up" and "awake," the psalmist's claim of innocence and integrity provides the basis for God's attention (7:3-5, 8; cf. Job 1:1; 9:20-22). The appeal to God as judge functions alongside the conviction that the wicked's own designs will entrap them (7:9). With no indication that the situation has changed, Psalms 3–7 each conclude with a shift in mood and a statement of confidence or affirmation. In their ancient setting, this change may have responded to a cultic official's "oracle of salvation" affirming the initial petition.

Psalm 8 reiterates divine sovereignty, linked to creation rather than the king (cf. Psalm 2). In language reminiscent of Genesis, the psalmist marvels that the creator of the universe "remembers" them. The transfer of royal attributes to humanity (glory, honor, crown, dominion) reflects God's care for human creatures despite hardship, challenging ancient conceptions of the human role as slaves at the whim of the gods, as reflected in the Babylonian creation account.

■ THE TEXT IN THE INTERPRETIVE TRADITION

Psalm 8 has been employed repeatedly within both the Jewish and Christian traditions, but in divergent ways; what has served as a "hymn of creation" for Jews has been a messianic psalm for Christians. Translation emerged as a point of dispute from the beginning, particularly over *ben 'adam* ("son of man") in 8:4. This psalm has long prompted messianic interpretation within the Christian tradition, beginning already in the New Testament (see Ps. 8:2; Matt. 11:25; 21:16; Luke 10:21). Perhaps the most striking example appears in Ephesians 1, which claims "that the one who sits at the right hand of God (Ps. 110:1) is the one who has put all things in subjection under his feet (Ps. 8:6)" (Gillingham, 3–4, 22; Eph. 1:20-23).

Psalm 6 has also had particular significance as one of seven "penitential psalms" within the Christian tradition (cf. Psalm 51).

■ THE TEXT IN CONTEMPORARY DISCUSSION

While psalms are often described as prayers to God (Brueggemann, 34), Psalms 3–7 prove characteristic of laments in that they consistently address a social as well as divine audience and so reflect multiple social roles that enhance their function as potential speech (Suderman 2010, 165–69).

Thus, while "evildoers" have been associated with magic workers in the ancient world (Mowinckel, 2:4–8), they can also be read as those who benefit from the social, economic, political, and military configuration of our globalized world. Beyond providing words to speak, laments also provide lessons in empathy for the voices of others and the opportunity to recognize where we may even have functioned as an "enemy" or been part of a system perpetrating such misdeeds (see Psalm 141). Thus the contemporary function of lament requires communities of discernment that do not identify exclusively with the speaker but are committed to attend to and evaluate the laments they hear (Suderman 2012, 212–17).

Finally, while the elevated status of humans in Psalm 8 represents good news for victims of abuse and those on the socioeconomic margins, overemphasis on human "dominion" can also provide ideological cover for minimizing the human impact on the environment. Biblical depictions of creation where humanity does *not* lie at the center may be particularly important in light of contemporary ecological concerns (see Psalm 104; Job 38–41).

Psalms 9–16: Confronting Hostile Speech

■ THE TEXT IN ITS ANCIENT CONTEXT

Psalms 9–10, joined as one psalm in the Septuagint, reflect an acrostic poem (see Psalm 119) that has been disrupted by a middle section, calling into question the confidence of the outside frame (9:17—10:10; Gerstenberger 1988, 72–73). Psalm 9 begins with thanksgiving for past deliverance that underscores God's continuing role as king and, therefore, judge (9:4-16; cf. 89; 93–99). While Psalm 9 continues the confident tone of Psalm 8, God blots out the "memory" (*zikram*) of the wicked and "remembers" (*zakar*) them for judgment (9:5-6, 12; cf. 8:4).

The middle portion, however, articulates lament and abandonment. Here the way of the wicked endures (10:5), offering three quotations of the enemy reflecting "dismissals of God and assertions of self-sufficiency and autonomy" (Brueggemann, 225; see 10:6, 11, 13). The initial confidence that God will not "forget" (*shakach*; Ps. 9:12, 18) contrasts with the nations who "*forget* God" and the wicked who believe that "God has *forgotten*" (9:17; 10:11). While the psalmist reasserts God's commitment to the "cry of the afflicted," the success of the wicked prompts the call for YHWH to "rise up" and "not *forget*" (Ps. 10:12) and so exercise divine kingship by executing justice (10:15-18).

Psalm 11 builds on God's role as a judging king (11:1, 4-7), but addresses a plural, social "you" and never God directly. Psalm 12 returns to appeal directly to God for help from hurtful speech, again quoting the adversary (12:4). The voice of YHWH responds directly to the beginning of this psalm and the earlier call: "I will now *rise up*" (v. 5; cf. 9:19; 10:12). While salvation oracles generally lie outside of the psalms themselves (Gerstenberger 1988, 81), the divine "I" here counteracts the adversarial speech of the enemies.

Psalm 13, the shortest lament in the Psalter, provides a characteristic example of this genre and repeats its basic question four times: "How long . . . ?" This emphatic repetition underscores the sense that God has "forgotten" and "hidden your face" (Ps. 13:1-2; cf. 10:11). Psalm 14, virtually identical to Psalm 53 in the "Elohistic Psalter" (Psalms 42–83; see below), both quotes the apathy of the fool and directly challenges those seeking to "confound the plans of the poor" (14:1, 6; cf. 6:8), providing a scathing indictment of contemporaries (14:3-4). The last verse of Psalm 14 also employs language familiar from the prophets to directly address the despair of exile (Jer. 30:3; Amos 9:14; Gerstenberger 1988, 220).

Psalm 15 reflects an entrance liturgy centered on requirements to access the temple (cf. Psalm 24). Hope for "deliverance . . . from Zion" (Ps. 14:7) leads into questions by worshipers seeking to enter sacred space and the response of cultic functionaries (15:1-5). While emphasis on ethical requirements rather than ritual elements may reflect a later reinterpretation of an earlier liturgy (Gerstenberger 1988, 88), they also contrast directly with the wicked in previous psalms; those allowed access are right-doers (*po'el tsedeq*; cf. 5:5; 6:8; 14:4); speak truth (*'emeth*) "in his heart" (cf. Psalm 9); does not slander (cf. 12:4); and so on (15:2-5).

Finally, Psalm 16 reiterates confidence that again contrasts the psalmist with the wicked. Whereas others say "there is no God" (14:1), the psalmist "takes refuge," saying, "you are my Lord" (16:1-2). The psalmist, responding in part to the earlier frustration over the prosperity of the wicked (10:4), repeats that he has chosen YHWH, a choice that has prompted gladness, security, and recognition of "the path of life" (16:9-11).

■ THE TEXT IN THE INTERPRETIVE TRADITION

Where Origen generally sees enemies allegorically as "vices" and other "enemies of the moral and spiritual life," an increasingly gentile church also used this vocabulary against the Jews. Nonetheless, "while the church fathers were not slow to identify their enemies, they were usually reluctant to curse them or to establish precedents for other Christians to do so" (Thompson, 54–56).

In light of ongoing research into the early differentiation between emergent Judaism and early Christianity as well as the long-standing negative effects of such exegesis, we do well to heed Thompson's caution: "*The history of Christian anti-Jewish exegesis . . . ought to stand as an object lesson of what* not *to do with the Psalms*" (Thompson, 70).

◼ THE TEXT IN CONTEMPORARY DISCUSSION

With social media and instant communication, contemporary culture knows the potential for both life-giving and damaging "speech." These psalms draw particular attention to malicious speech by repeatedly quoting hostile voices, witnessing to social isolation and estrangement. Such quotations also allow the psalmists to go beyond conventional limits and articulate "'unspeakable' complaints against God" (Jacobson, 49, 55).

The wicked's claim that "there is no God" (Ps. 10:4; 14:1) also proves striking given the rise of "new atheism." In contrast to contemporary debates, however, here this claim reflects a lack of accountability beyond oneself more than deductive reasoning or an abstract philosophical stance (Mays, 81–82); most significantly, suffering leads the psalmist *to* rather than *away from* God.

Psalms 17–22: Zion Theology and the Davidic King

◼ THE TEXT IN ITS ANCIENT CONTEXT

Psalm 17, twice identified as a "prayer" (*tefillah*; heading, v. 1), calls for rescue from the wicked enemy. The psalmist contrasts his rightful speech with the arrogant speech of the wicked and again calls for YHWH to "Rise up!" (v. 13), a phrase initially linked to lifting the ark of the covenant to symbolize God's presence in battle (see Num. 10:34). While the psalmist's claims of innocence and righteousness frame the psalm (17:3-4, 15), God's sword and other military imagery link it to the following.

In Psalm 18, the king gives thanks for answered prayer through military success, with a parallel version appearing within the narrative of David (see 2 Sam. 22:1-51). The psalm describes divine support that provides the king with training and strength for battle (18:34, 39). The Hebrew root for "salvation/victory" (*yasha'*) appears five times in various forms, culminating with:

> . . . exalted be the God of my *salvation*,
>> the God who gave me vengeance
>>> and subdued peoples under me. (Ps. 18:46b-47)

While victory is related to the psalmist's righteousness and blamelessness (18:20-25), the psalm's Zion theology directly links God to the Davidic king or "his anointed" (*meshiho*, v. 50), who destroys the enemy with divine aid (cf. Psalm 89a).

Psalm 19, one of three torah psalms (cf. Psalms 1; 119), appears in the midst of this description of royal power. While initially describing the "glory of God" in the heavens in a manner similar to

Canaanite sun worship (19:1-6), the second section glowingly describes the "law" (*torah*) in six parallel lines, with the final verse again linking law to "meditation" (*hegyon*; cf. Ps. 1:2; Josh. 1:8). While the dramatic shift in vocabulary and theme has led many to treat it as combining two unrelated poems, Psalm 19 also holds together as it stands and even provides a "polemic" against sun worship (Sarna, 74). Its placement amid royal psalms both builds on references to legal vocabulary (Ps. 18:22, 30) and embodies the central role the law was to hold in the life of the Israelite king (Deut. 17:18-19). It also illustrates how the meaning of material can be transformed (cf. Psalm 29). Psalm 19 reflects the positive view of law (*torah*) assumed within the Old Testament (Exod. 20:1-3; Deut. 30:11-19), so that "Torah study is an act of worship" (Sarna, 95).

Psalm 20 reiterates divine protection for the king, initially addressing the monarch with a series of well-wishes ("May YHWH answer you . . .", 20:1-5 [author's translation]), moving to speak about the king and YHWH to a broader social audience (20:6-8), and concluding with a summary appeal to God: "Give *victory* to the king, O Lord." While the psalm assumes a seamless link between the temple/Zion, the anointed, and victory/salvation, it also rejects pride in military might "in the name of the Lord our God" (20:7). While Psalm 21 initially addresses God, it is not clear whether the second section speaks to God or the king (Gerstenberger 1988, 106). In either case, this psalm adds the benefits of long life and economic prosperity to military victory and dominion, while underscoring the key elements of the king's trust and God's steadfast love (*hesed*; v. 7).

Psalm 22 expresses both a sense of abandonment and trust. The initial "My God, my God, why have you forsaken me?" contrasts with the ancestors' experience of deliverance (22:4-5) and the assurance of the preceding psalms. The psalmist repeatedly speaks of being surrounded by hostile forces, which leads to calls for God to not be distant; the offer to praise God and tell of his deliverance constitutes the "vow" the psalmist commits to fulfill (22:22-24). The end of the psalm uses king language to describe YHWH rather than the anointed, reiterated in reference to God's justice (cf. Psalm 96).

◼ The Text in the Interpretive Tradition

Psalm 22 figures prominently within the New Testament portrayal of Jesus' passion. Before the addition of chapters and verses, "My God, my God, why have you forsaken me?" (22:1) functioned not only as Jesus' cry of anguish embodying the righteous sufferer but also as the incipit or effective "title" of the psalm itself (Matt. 27:46; Mays, 105).

While Augustine consistently reads the Psalms through Christ, he can speak either from an exalted position or from within the human condition; in effect, "Christ can speak *to* or *as* his body, the church" (Thompson, 56–57). Thus, for Augustine, Psalm 22 could be seen as either Christ himself or "Christ the body" speaking (Gillingham, 39).

Where Luther's "prophetic and Christocentric approach" saw Psalms 22 and 23 speaking directly of Christ, Calvin argued that—since Jesus *did* die—Psalm 22 was best understood in light of David and only secondarily of Christ or the individual Christian. Similarly, Calvin believed that Psalms 18 and 23 represented "types" that foreshadowed rather than predicted Christ (Gillingham, 144–45).

◼ THE TEXT IN CONTEMPORARY DISCUSSION

Whereas some have contrasted Christianity as a religion of peace with other traditions as inherently violent and some such as the "new atheists" have linked religion itself to violence, the potential for both peace and violence lies within the biblical tradition itself (see Psalm 149). While the Psalms generally insist on a divine monopoly on violence, the king's role as God's earthly representative provides the most notable exception (Firth, 3). In this sense, Psalm 18 provides a precedent that links divine support to military victory, a logic historically used by Christian leaders to legitimate political, national, and military interests.

To accept a mandate for human violence, however, assumes a direct correlation between a specific contemporary power and ancient Israel, sidestepping repeated biblical injunctions that victory does *not* depend on "chariots and horses" but trust in the divine (Ps. 20:7; cf. Exod. 14:13-14; Ps. 33:16-17). For Christians, such a mandate is also tempered by the New Testament's repeated transformation of a conquering messiah (Psalms 2; 18; 89a) into one who embodies suffering (Psalm 22).

In *The Prophetic Imagination*, Walter Brueggemann describes an ongoing struggle between "royal" and "prophetic" trajectories in the Bible. With this reasoning, Zion psalms seem to reflect the imperialist aspirations that the prophets (and we should) critique. Ben Ollenburger, however, has shown that Zion theology is based on God's kingship and thus places all creation and all nations, including their military might, under divine authority and God's "exclusive prerogative." Thus "the monarchical language of Zion symbolism does not legitimate 'imperial monarchy,' it prohibits it" (Ollenburger, 158–62).

Psalms 23–33: Trust in God's Steadfast Love

◼ THE TEXT IN ITS ANCIENT CONTEXT

The pastoral imagery of Psalm 23 may be the most familiar of the Psalms, speaking *about* rather than *to* God throughout. Beyond the link to David's childhood, "shepherd" was a term used for royalty in the ancient Near East, so that "the LORD is my shepherd" resonates with describing God as king (Pss. 10:16; 47:7-8; 93:1). "Setting a table" reflects hospitality and casts God as a gracious host committed to the guests' welfare (Anderson and Bishop, 183); where elsewhere enemies pursue the psalmist, here it is "goodness and mercy [*hesed*]" that do so.

Psalm 24, which begins with a cosmic description of YHWH as creator (24:1-2; cf. Psalms 74, 104), contains an entrance liturgy with a call and response among different voices (cf. Psalm 15). The psalm moves from liturgical and ethical motifs to military ones, with the concluding reference to "YHWH of hosts/armies [*yhwh tsebaʾoth*]" highlighting a divine-warrior motif (cf. Psalm 84). Psalm 24 also illustrates the difficulty of determining a psalm's "ancient context," with proposed settings including the ark of the covenant entering the temple during the preexilic period (Gunkel 1998, 316–17), pilgrims coming to Jerusalem for a religious festival (Sarna, 103), and worshipers approaching the Second Temple or a synagogue after exile (Gerstenberger 1988, 119).

Psalm 25 is an acrostic poem that incorporates aspects of lament alongside statements of confidence (cf. Psalms 34; 119). It declares the psalmist's *trust* in God, appeals to divine *steadfast love*, asks for God's guidance, and seeks forgiveness. In Psalm 26, the psalmist claims innocence grounded in his integrity (26:1, 11; 37:37; cf. Job 1:1, 8; 9:20-22). Oriented by God's steadfast love and truth (v. 2), the psalmist does not associate with the wicked but loves the temple (26:4-5, 8; cf. 1:1; 141).

Psalm 27 again reflects confidence and links a fulfilled life to the temple (27:4; 26:8), while also appealing for divine intervention and teaching (27:7-12). The concluding dual call to a social audience to "wait for the LORD" reaffirms the psalmist's confidence, even though the situation has not changed.

Psalm 28 begins with a lament to God that turns into thanksgiving for answered prayer addressed to a social audience. A concluding assertion of God's support for "his anointed" (*meshiho*) leading to a final appeal on behalf of the people may reflect a later broadening of material beyond an individual supplicant (cf. 3:8; Gerstenberger 1988, 129).

Psalm 29 begins by addressing the "sons of gods" (*bene 'elim*), a divine council common within ancient literature and assumed elsewhere in Scripture (82:1; Gen. 1:26; Job 1; Jer. 23:18). The sevenfold repetition of the "voice/sound of YHWH [*qol yhwh*]" punctuates the psalm and underscores the cosmic power of this deity, while the concluding description of *YHWH* as king directly counters Canaanite mythology, which used the same description for Baal. In effect, Psalm 29 redeploys language and imagery used to describe the rival storm god Baal within Canaanite mythology to affirm YHWH's sovereignty instead.

Psalm 30 again gives thanks for answered prayer, describing the psalmist's prior state, his own cry, and YHWH's response. Reference to God's anger and the psalmist's impending death suggests the psalm arises from a setting of illness (cf. Psalm 6), while the exhortation for a social audience to join the psalmist in praise reflects the public setting key to thanksgiving (cf. Psalm 116).

Psalm 31 intermingles lament and calls for respite from enemies with confident praise for answered prayer, concluding with "blessed be the LORD" and a call for broad social recognition (31:21-23). Once again, this response reflects the psalmist's "taking refuge" and *trusting* in God. The social appeal to "Love the LORD, all you his saints [*hasidayw*]" reflects the mutuality of covenant commitment (31:23; cf. 30:4), since both God and the saints/faithful ones demonstrate "steadfast love" (*hesed*). The final exhortation to "be strong" and "take courage" broadens the call familiar from Joshua to the community (see Josh. 1:6-9).

Psalm 32 begins with a description of distress, confession, and forgiveness that broadens to a social exhortation for each of the faithful to pray (v. 6). The divine voice describes God's commitment to teach and guide (32:8; cf. 25:4) before contrasting the wicked with the righteous who trust in YHWH and whom steadfast love surrounds. In effect, this psalm gives thanks for having experienced the forgiveness requested earlier (32:5; cf. Psalm 25).

Psalm 33 concludes this section with a communal hymn celebrating God's steadfast love shown in creation and to Israel, reiterating the major emphases of the preceding psalms and calling for joyful response. YHWH's role as cosmic king makes human military preparation useless (33:14-17), while the community affirms its trust and hope in God's *hesed* (33:20-22).

■ THE TEXT IN THE INTERPRETIVE TRADITION

Both Jewish and Christian medieval interpreters contrast the "praise of God's loud voice" in Psalm 29 with the "still, small voice" found in 1 Kgs. 19:12. However, where Rashi connects "wilderness of Kadesh" to Sinai and so sees God's voice giving torah (29:8), the *Glossa Ordinaria*, a medieval collation of biblical notations from the church fathers, identifies the same phrase with "the Jews, who do not have the sanctity of the law, that is spiritual understanding" (S. Davis, 73). Jewish interpreters Rashbam and David Kimchi link the divine voice to creation and the Messiah respectively, while Bruno de Segni ties it to inspired teaching that leads to baptism (S. Davis, 69–73).

While very different from Western or academic readings, David Adamo argues against portraying indigenous African interpretation as "fetish, magical, unchristian and uncritical." Rather, he describes how contemporary African Independent Churches recognize the "power in names" and so interpret Psalm 29 as a psalm of "protection . . . defense, liberation, healing, and success" (Adamo, 141, 135).

Jesus' final words on the cross in Luke's Gospel are: "into your hand I commit my spirit" (Ps. 31:5; Luke 23:46). While this statement contrasts with Mark and Matthew's "My God . . . why have you forsaken me?" (Ps. 22:1; Matt. 27:46; Mark 15:34), in both cases Jesus embodies the suffering of lament rather than a militaristic messiah (Psalms 2, 18, 72, 89a).

Psalm 23 has long been a liturgical resource, functioning as a "funeral psalm" alongside Psalm 22 and 116 as early as the fourth century (Gillingham, 55).

■ THE TEXT IN CONTEMPORARY DISCUSSION

Psalms 29 and 19 draw on broader Canaanite mythology and so raise the issue of how previous traditions and understandings can be appropriately incorporated into the tradition. Missionary movements have often insisted that new adherents break from all aspects of prior culture. For instance, church-run residential schools sought to "assimilate" Native American peoples into (European) Canadian culture by systematically eliminating their indigenous language, traditions, and religious perspectives, with grave ongoing consequences. Postcolonial critics have also drawn attention to "marks of colonial hermeneutics" amid links between Christian evangelization and Western imperialism (Sugirtharajah, 61–73).

Psalms 29 and 19 reflect the ongoing dynamic of religious contextualization or syncretism whereby ancient traditions are adapted and transformed, in these cases shifting their significance to emphatically underscore that it is *YHWH's* "voice" (*not* that of Baal) that thunders (29) and *YHWH* (*not* the sun) who orients their lives through *torah* (19). This has been a long-standing issue, as attested in the "Christianization" of the winter equinox as a celebration of Jesus' birth (Christmas) and the transformation of spring fertility celebrations into a commemoration of the resurrection (Easter).

Psalms 34–41: Sickness, Enemies, and Land

■ THE TEXT IN ITS ANCIENT CONTEXT

Psalms 34–41 reflect motifs of forgiveness, social solidarity, and wisdom. The final psalms conclude book 1 with a confident tone, ending in a doxology (41:13). This feature, the first of several in the

Psalms (72:18-19; 89:52; 106:48), was either introduced late in the composition process or provided the "pattern" for later conclusions that divide the current Psalter into five books (Mays, 13).

Psalm 34 incorporates various wisdom elements into thanksgiving for deliverance. Like Psalm 25, it has both an instructional purpose and an acrostic structure (cf. Psalm 119). The psalm employs characteristic wisdom vocabulary and motifs, including a contrast between the righteous and wicked, a "happy . . ." saying (v. 8; cf. 2:11), "turn from evil" (v. 14; Ps. 37:27; Prov. 16:6; Job 1:1), and "fear of the LORD" (v. 11; Prov. 1:7). The latter instructional motif addressed to "sons" extends beyond biological offspring to address students or apprentices as well (cf. Prov. 4:1). References to "taking refuge" in God and "servants" reflect broader motifs in the Psalms (cf. 2:11; 90:16; 102:14, 28).

Psalm 35 is an individual lament calling for divine deliverance that merges military and court language, including "fight" (v. 1); "violent witnesses" (v. 11); and pleading with God to contend (*ribah*) with his persecutors, support his cause (*rib*), and "judge" according to God's justice (*tsidqeka*) (35:1, 11, 23, 24). Since others' support has been denied to him (35:11-16), the psalmist wishes for God to dole out the same treatment that he has received (35:4-8; cf. Psalm 109). The concluding verses divide his social audience into those who "rejoice" in his plight and those who "desire my vindication [*tsidqi*]" (35:26-28; cf. 40:14-17). Psalm 36 again reflects social division and the potential for social solidarity, speaking from a setting where the wicked slander and plot (36:3, 4). The psalmist praises God's steadfast love and calls for it to continue (36:5-10), which reinforces the link between God's *hesed* and righteousness (*tsedeq*) and echoes the previous psalm's call for divine judgment (Ps. 36:10; 35:24).

Psalm 37, another acrostic wisdom poem (cf. Psalm 34), addresses the prosperity of the wicked, insisting that this is temporary and soon to be rectified; the claim that "I have not seen the righteous forsaken" seems hard to fathom (37:25). The court language found both here and in Psalm 35 resonates with the "prophetic lawsuit" tradition as well (Isa. 3:13; Hosea 2:2); *meditating* on wisdom and having "the law of their God in their hearts" also sound familiar (vv. 30-31; cf. Ps. 1:2; 19:14). The psalm's focus on land (*'erets*), which appears six times (37:3, 9, 11, 22, 29, 34), can be read in deeply contrasting ways, either as a means of legitimating the status quo or as a "utopian" vision of a future that challenges and overturns the present (Brueggemann, 243–53).

Psalm 38 assumes a link between sin and sickness, seeing YHWH as both the court of appeal and the enemy to be defended against (38:1-8; cf. 39:9-10). The psalmist also complains of social isolation and enemies (38:18-20; 41:5-9), including those who "meditate" on treachery (38:11-12; cf. 1:2; 2:1). Psalm 39 reflects on the passing nature of human mortality as a breath (*hevel*), employing the key term in Ecclesiastes often translated as "vanity" (39:5, 6, 11; Eccl. 1:2). Psalm 40 moves from public thanksgiving to reflect on God's steadfast love and truth and a call to demonstrate this once again through the psalmist's rescue; the closing distinction between opponents and supporters reflects the psalmist's self-identification with God (40:14-16; cf. 35:26-28).

Psalm 41 again links sin and sickness, with the psalmist's confession undergirding the conviction that he will be sustained through his illness. The psalmist calls out for mercy and expresses confidence rooted in his integrity (41:12; cf. 26:1, 11), while his plight is compounded by an intimate friend who has forsaken him (v. 9; cf. Psalm 55).

Psalm 41 concludes with a doxology that closes book 1: "Blessed be the LORD . . . Amen and Amen." With slight variations, similar doxologies divide the Psalter into five books (see Ps. 72:18-19; 89:52; 106:48).

▐ THE TEXT IN THE INTERPRETIVE TRADITION

Like Psalm 45, Psalm 34 does not appear prominently within the New Testament but soon becomes a key christological psalm. Of particular interest, Clement sees Christ addressing believers with the appeal "Come, O children, listen to me," effectively portraying Jesus as divine wisdom (34:11; cf. Prov. 8:32). Later, the psalm also begins to be used within the Eucharist, building on the phrase "taste and see that the Lord is good" (34:8; Gillingham, 24–26, 52).

▐ THE TEXT IN CONTEMPORARY DISCUSSION

The psalmists' experiences of rejection, social isolation, and stigmatization prove all too common in the contemporary world. The view of sickness as divine punishment for sin has affected responses to a wide range of contemporary issues, including HIV/AIDS, people struggling with addictions, mental health issues (see Psalm 88), and so on; Job provides a striking example of the type of social isolation such debates can prompt. An opposing tendency, perhaps particularly prominent in the West, has been to remove sickness from the spiritual arena altogether, which undercuts prayer regarding such matters.

While Psalm 37 assumes that the righteous will enjoy the land and the wicked will be cut off from it (Ps. 37:2, 22; cf. Deuteronomy 28), Brueggemann illustrates how Jesus' words in the Sermon on the Mount push this claim to a future "utopia" and so reflects a judgment of the present that does not live up to this expectation. While he points to the dispossession of small farmers at the hands of agribusiness as an example of its contemporary relevance (Brueggemann, 249–53, 257), farmers in developing nations have also repeatedly called for Western countries to halt agricultural subsidies to allow them to compete in the global market. Indigenous peoples in the Americas continue to call for the recognition of land rights, treaties, and redress for their sustained marginalization and displacement. In short, land remains a contentious issue.

The conclusions of Psalms 35 and 40 underscore the crucial social challenge such issues represent. While complex, discerning amid multiple voices remains a crucial and ongoing task of contemporary faith communities (Suderman 2012, 216).

Psalms 42–49: The Voice of the Community

▐ THE TEXT IN ITS ANCIENT CONTEXT

Psalm 42 begins book 2 (Psalms 42–72) with this series of psalms attributed to the "sons of Korah" (42–49) as well as the "Elohistic Psalter" (42–83), which prefers to use "God" (*'elohim*) rather than YHWH, which dominates the rest of the Psalter (Anderson and Bishop, 13). This section changes from a primarily individual to an increasingly communal voice that reflects Zion theology liturgically centered on the kingship of God (cf. Psalms 93–99).

Psalms 42–43, linked by the threefold refrain "Why are you cast down, O my soul" (42:5, 11; 43:5), continue to complain against enemies epitomized in the taunt: "Where is your God?" (42:3, 10). They also introduce the tone of this section by referring to both past and future liturgical experiences related to the temple (42:4; 43:4), linking the psalmist's thirst for God with religious pilgrimage (cf. Psalm 120).

Psalm 44 provides the Psalter's first corporate cry for help (Mays, 176), not in a penitential mode but with a communal claim of innocence (44:17-22). While the first part recalls past success where God's support rather than military prowess or weaponry was the decisive element (44:4-7), the second articulates a communal lament after defeat; just as victory was linked to God's support, here defeat is seen as a sign of God's rejection (44:9-16; cf. Psalm 18). The imagery of sheep without a shepherd and being scattered among the nations builds on ancient Near Eastern royal imagery (Psalm 23) and reflects affinity with prophetic material, leading some to suggest an exilic or postexilic setting (44:11; see Isa. 53:6; Jer. 23:1-3; Mays, 178–79). "Rouse," "awake," "rise up," "my king and my God," and the concluding appeal for God's steadfast love reflect the shared vocabulary of individual and communal laments.

Identified as a "love song" in the heading, Psalm 45 reflects a royal wedding procession, with the vocabulary, imagery, and even direct address to a "daughter" proving similar to the Song of Solomon (45:10-12; see Song of Sol. 3:5-11). While the explicit voice of a "scribe" at the outset is unique (Mays, 181), links between the military, wealth, justice, and the king prove common in the Psalms (Psalms 2; 72; 89). The phrase "your throne, O God" introduces a tension into the psalm given the distinction between God and the anointed monarch in the next verse; at the same time, this phrase also resonates with the surrounding psalms' royal depiction of God (45:6-7; cf. Ps. 82). The appeal to "forget your people and your father's house" suggests the bride is a foreigner (v. 10; cf. Ruth 1:16), recalling long-standing antipathy to such unions (Deut. 7:3-4; 1 Kgs. 11:1-8; Ezra 9:12-14).

Psalms 46–48 are hymns that celebrate YHWH as cosmic king and God's intimate association with the temple and city of Jerusalem. Psalm 46 identifies God as "our refuge and strength," whose bond to the "city of God" assures its defense (46:4-5; 48:3, 10). "YHWH of hosts/armies [*yhwh tseba'oth*]" here underlines the divine role as cosmic peacemaker, who destroys military weaponry and says, "Be still and know that I am God" (46:7-11; 48:8). Psalm 47 calls on all peoples to sing to YHWH and extends God's dominion over the peoples to "us," as God's heritage (47:1-4). God reigns over nations and creation from his "holy throne" (Ps. 47:7-8; 93), with a strong military connotation both in resolving conflict and subduing others on Israel's behalf (46:9; 47:3). Psalm 48 again links God to Zion, where the city's inviolability is matched by the awe of foreign kings (48:1-8). The description of the city and temple prompts address to God and reflection on divine *hesed* as well as an invitation for pilgrims to walk around the city in awe (48:9-14); military armament and strong defenses pale in significance to the conviction that "all human affairs are under the direction and governance of God" (Sarna, 166). Strikingly, however, in these psalms, the human king has disappeared, reinforcing the basic conviction that victory is based on God's action rather than military prowess.

Psalm 49 provides a wisdom reflection, identified as a proverb and riddle addressed to a broad audience (v. 4). The frequent claim to *"trust* in God" elsewhere contrasts with "those who *trust* in their wealth" here, an object lesson for the shared fate of both the "wise" and "fool" who cannot take riches with them (49:6, 10–11; cf. Eccles. 2:14). A repeated refrain underscores the mortality of humans and animals (49:12, 20).

■ THE TEXT IN THE INTERPRETIVE TRADITION

Though not prominent in the New Testament, Psalm 45 became significant at an early stage within the Christian tradition. Like the Song of Solomon, it was interpreted as depicting the relationship between God and people and Christ and the church (Mays, 181–82). This psalm was employed in early church controversies to both argue for the divinity of Christ, reading Ps. 45:7 as addressing *Christ* as God, and to link him to the Old Testament and so counter Marcion and his followers (Gillingham, 24–26, 30).

Based on Psalm 46, Luther's anthem "A Mighty Fortress Is Our God" reflects his contentious time period, linguistic prowess, and dedication to make the Psalms accessible to a wider public (Gillingham, 140–41).

■ THE TEXT IN CONTEMPORARY DISCUSSION

Biblical reference to the hiddenness and even absence of God has become particularly poignant in the wake of the Holocaust (44:24; cf. 13:1; 88:14; 89:46; Job 13:24). David Blumenthal identifies Psalm 44 as a "psalm of rage" expressed "at our enemies" but also "at those who betrayed us, by action and inaction. And we rage at God" (Blumenthal, 94); his multilayered reading, which draws on Elie Wiesel's *Night*, is stunning (Blumenthal, 94–110). Marvin Sweeney calls for people to recognize and reject the tendency to blame victims for their own victimization, and advocate for increased human responsibility in light of God's absence (Sweeney, 228–41; cf. Blumenthal, 108–9).

Treating the Nazi regime as an aberration too easily insulates the Christian tradition from recognizing the devastating potential of anti-Jewish interpretation and rhetoric present within it for millennia. The Holocaust forces Christians to recognize how we can and have become the very "enemies" the psalmist condemns.

Psalms 50–64: Lament and Confession

■ THE TEXT IN ITS ANCIENT CONTEXT

The section of Psalms 50–61 begins with the first psalm attributed to Asaph (50; cf. 73–83). This section also includes the first psalms "of David" in book 2 (42–72), where contextual headings become the norm rather than the exception (cf. Psalms 3, 142).

Psalm 50 portrays a court scene where God functions as both prosecutor and judge (Mays, 194), addressing Israel as "my faithful ones [*hasidai*]" and "my people" (50:5, 7). The initial critique of liturgy does not reject sacrifice itself, but insists on God's overarching ownership of any offering (50:10–11; Mays, 196). God's concluding address articulates several charges, while thanksgiving and cries for help recognizing God's sovereignty reflect a proper liturgical stance.

Psalm 51, whose heading sets it after Nathan confronts David for his indiscretion with Bath-sheba, represents perhaps the most well-known prayer of confession in the Psalter. Following a characteristic lament structure—address, complaint, petition, and vow of praise (Anderson, 82–83)—its opening imperatives to God set the tone ("Have mercy," "blot out," "wash," and "purify" in 51:1-2), while three distinct terms for sin underscore its main theme. In the "precritical" period, the claim "Against you, you alone have I sinned" prompted significant reflection in light of the heading (v. 4); in contrast, biblical critics have frequently cited this statement as evidence that David could *not* have articulated this prayer. While hyssop reflects an ancient purification ritual (51:7; cf. Exod. 12:22; Lev. 14:51), the psalmist's appeal for a "clean heart [*leb*]" suggests improved judgment, since the heart is the site of the will in the Old Testament (see Exod. 9:7, 35; 1 Kgs. 3:9). The divine spirit/breath (*ruach*) allows the psalmist to be taught and in turn to teach other sinners to return/repent (51:10-13). The tension between God's having "no delight in sacrifice" but then the psalmist's affirming that "you *will* delight" in them (51:16, 19) has led many scholars to see the last two verses as an addition rehabilitating temple ritual, perhaps in the postexilic period (Gerstenberger 1988, 214).

Psalm 52 immediately addresses a mighty one (*gibbor*) who "boasts," "plots," and "loves evil more than good" (52:1-4). The psalmist contrasts the mighty one who trusts in wealth (49:6) with his trust in God's steadfast love (*hesed*, 52:6-9). Psalm 53 represents a minor variation of Psalm 14, with the change from YHWH to God characteristic of the Elohistic Psalter. While it does not contain a contextual heading, the initial reference to a "fool" (*nabal*) resonates with the account of David's confrontation with Nabal (1 Samuel 25). Psalm 54 calls out for divine aid, with the appeal to God's might (*gibbur*) linked to the confidence that enemies will receive their due from the divine (54:1, 5; 52:5; 53:5). This thanksgiving exemplifies the previous instruction to offer thanks and call on God (54:6; 52:9; cf. 50:14-15).

Psalm 55, which simply reads "of David," is an individual lament that addresses multiple audiences. While initially speaking to God, the turning point appears when the psalmist levels a direct accusation to someone in his social circle: "But it is *you*, my equal . . ." (v. 13; cf. Ps. 41:9). This direct accusation, similar to Nathan's strident critique of David (2 Sam. 12:7), precedes address to yet another audience *about* both the "friend" and God rather than *to* either of them. The psalm complains of both a covenant violation and seemingly innocent but in reality violent words (55:20-21); it is unclear whether v. 22 reflects what should be said or whether these are the "smooth words" of the adversary. Encouraging God's vigorous response, the psalmist ends with a claim to "trust in you."

Psalms 56–57, which the headings again place in contexts in which David was under duress, call for God and express confidence in the divine. The first centers on declarations of trust in God (56:3-4, 10-11). Where the previous psalm lamented the friend's words (*debarayw*, 55:21), here persecution aimed at the psalmist's *word/cause* elicits trust in God's *word* (56:4-5, 10); the psalmist's praise of the divine word rather than God himself proves unique and is underscored by repetition (56:10; Gerstenberger 1988, 227). Psalm 57 claims refuge in God, under the "shadow of your wings" (57:1; cf. Ps. 91:4). What begins as a lament shifts to thanksgiving for how the enemies, who are described as ravaging wild animals, have fallen into their own trap (v. 6). Here again God's steadfast love and truth ground the psalmist's confidence (57:3, 10), while a repeated refrain exalting God frames the last section (57:5, 11).

Psalm 58 depicts an inversion of justice (cf. Psalm 82), where rulers promote violence and reflect the tendencies of the "wicked." The psalmist calls for God to stop their aggression, again employing the metaphor of hostile animals (58:6-8; cf. Ps. 3:7). The conclusion underscores the basic concern of the psalm; the righteous rejoice because they "envision vengeance" as a certainty (cf. Psalm 94); vengeance is not itself the point but confirms that "there are gods judging on the earth [*yesh-'elohim shophetim ba'arets*]" (58:10-11; see Psalm 82; 94).

Psalm 59 repeats the call for deliverance from enemies, whose destruction once again provides the means for recognizing God's supremacy (59:13). Praise for God's steadfast love intermingles with the protective description of the divine as fortress, refuge, and strength (59:16-17).

Psalm 60 moves from the call of an individual beset by enemies to a communal lament by those who have suffered a military defeat. God's rejection prompts a call for victory and a reversal of God's absence from "our armies" (60:1-5, 10-12; cf. Ps. 89:39); the divine promise to which the psalmist appeals appears elsewhere as well (60:5-12; cf. Ps. 108:6-13; Gerstenberger 1988, 240). While the psalm depicts military defeat as reflecting divine anger, the solution lies not in armament but in God's victory on behalf of Israel; the claim that "he will tread down our foes" reflects the Zion theology described elsewhere (see Psalm 18).

Psalm 61, a first-person counterpart to Psalm 60, also calls for divine protection from the enemy and mentions God's dwelling (61:4; cf. 60:6). While the motif of finding refuge "under the shadow of God's wings" reappears (v. 4; cf. 57:1; 91:4), in the second part God has already "heard" the psalmist's vows. The psalm shifts to appeal for the longevity of the king, employing the language of the Davidic covenant linked to God's steadfast love and faithfulness (*'emeth*, 61:6-7; cf. Ps. 89a; 2 Sam. 7:12-16). Whether the speaker is an individual, a representative of the community, or the king himself, the appeal for the king here again reflects characteristics of Zion theology (Mays, 215).

Psalms 62–63 express trust and confidence in God. Psalm 62 twice repeats the refrain "For God alone my soul waits" that identifies God as "my rock and my salvation, my fortress" (62:1-2, 5-6). Most of the psalm speaks to a social audience, briefly addressing plural adversaries directly before speaking *about* them and finally exhorting his listeners to "trust in God" (62:3-8; cf. Ps. 55:13). The psalm underscores the motif of refuge, concluding with a brief address affirming God's divine steadfast love and expressing confidence that God will "repay all according to their work" (62:7-8, 12). Psalm 63, the last in this sequence linked to a setting in the life of David, again describes how the psalmist's soul thirsts for God and links an experience of awe in the sanctuary to his recognition of divine *hesed* (63:1-5; cf. 42:4). Here too the "shadow of your wings" appears as an image of refuge, while the final verses contrast the fate of his adversaries with that of the king (63:7, 10-11; cf. 61:4).

Psalm 64 is another lament psalm concerned primarily with the speech of the enemy. In places where the wicked's schemes and speech appear as swords and arrows aimed toward the psalmist, he expresses confidence in God's in-kind response (64:2-8). The psalm concludes with an exhortation for the righteous and upright to also "take refuge in him" (64:10).

▌THE TEXT IN THE INTERPRETIVE TRADITION

Within the Christian tradition, Psalm 51 has been the most prominent of seven traditional "penitential psalms" (6; 32; 38; 51; 102; 130; 143), used heavily from the early church fathers to the present. It has been prominent within liturgy, monastic traditions, and private devotion. For Luther, the penitential psalms were particularly significant, since they provided the means for individual Christians to approach God directly through Christ and so bypass the system of indulgences he opposed (Gillingham, 52–53, 138).

◼ THE TEXT IN CONTEMPORARY DISCUSSION

Psalms 50–64 illustrate the complex issue of "voice" so central to the Psalms. How should the community of faith respond when an abused party, such as David surrounded by his enemies, becomes an abuser, epitomized in his covetous action with Bathsheba and murderous cover-up of Uriah? Comparable issues arise at both individual and group levels, where a past victim of abuse goes on to abuse others, or where an oppressed or marginalized group gains the upper hand and employs its newfound power to subordinate, persecute, and oppress others.

In contemporary parlance, Psalm 51 reflects the voice of a (purportedly) penitent "offender," while lament psalms represent the cries of (purported) "victims." While reading the Psalms in an age of "terror," intergroup conflict, and xenophobia can reinforce the assumption that "enemies" are necessarily foreign and external, Psalm 55 reminds us that they may also be "intimate enemies" such as a close associate or even family member (Sheppard, 70); elsewhere Ulrike Bail has demonstrated the potential of reading Psalm 55 in light of domestic violence and abuse (Bail, 1998). Furthermore, reading the preposition in the heading "of David [*ledavid*]" as the also plausible "*to* David" allows the reader to hear Psalm 55 as the voice of Bathsheba—or even Uriah—confronting David, and thus complicates our understanding of the commonly employed confession in Psalm 51.

In so doing these psalms also illustrate the complexity of discerning the appropriate contemporary function of psalms material, since they simultaneously confront the social audience with both "offender" and "victim" voices. The rhetorical presence of a social audience in these psalms again underscores the role of contemporary communities to hear, evaluate, and respond to the voices they hear (Suderman 212, 216–17).

Finally, although most critical scholarship has moved away from reading psalms in light of David, such a stance isolates scholars from many lay and non-Western readings, and also from the broader history of interpretation. Just as too strong an emphasis on confession can eclipse the possibility of lament or claims of innocence, so critical scholarship can monopolize the "voice" of legitimate interpretation and so overlook the ongoing significance of "precritical" interpreters and global voices.

Psalms 65–72: Communal Praise and Thanksgiving

◼ THE TEXT IN ITS ANCIENT CONTEXT

This section concludes both book 2 of the Psalter (42–72) and a David collection (see Ps. 72:20). Psalms 65–68 are identified as both a psalm (*mizmor*) and a song; though not unprecedented for psalm headings (see Psalms 30; 45; 46; 48), the latter element appears most often in book 5 to introduce the "Songs of Ascent" (Psalms 120–134).

Psalm 65 articulates communal praise and thanksgiving directly to God, describing divine response to prayer, control over the mountains and seas, and provision. God's control over creation and mention of both Zion and temple resonate with Zion theology (65:1, 4; cf. Psalm 18), while the link to fertility recalls the critique and transformation of Baal worship elsewhere (cf. Psalm 29).

Psalm 66 extends worship beyond the temple, addressing different audiences. The psalm initially addresses "all the earth," calling for a communal thanksgiving for God's action exemplified in the exodus and entering the land (66:1-8). Turning to God, the psalmist describes times of hardship as a process of testing and purification and then vows to sacrifice in the temple to express his individual thanksgiving (66:10-15). The final section, directed to "all you who fear God," recalls God's response to prayer and concludes by affirming God's steadfast love (*hesed*, 66:16-20).

Psalm 67 articulates a communal blessing that effectively transfers Aaron's blessing from the mouth of a priest to the corporate "us" of the community (67:1; cf. Num. 6:24-26; Gerstenberger 2001, 32). While it follows a similar pattern as the previous psalm by speaking *of* God, then *to* God, and finally *of* God again, here the community desires that God bless the people (67:1, 7) rather than calling on the peoples to bless God (66:8, 20). Repetition underscores the psalmist's hope that God will be recognized by those peoples beyond Israel who experience divine judgment and guidance (67:2-5).

Psalm 68 links mythological elements to the particular history of Israel to underscore the sovereignty and power of God. The initial appeal for God to "rise up" against his enemies calls upon God to enact the contrasting fate of the "righteous" and "wicked" (68:1-3; cf. 1:5-6). The psalm draws on several motifs associated with Baal, including the depiction of God as "rider on the clouds/heavens," his link to rains and fertility, and reference to the divine voice (cf. Psalm 29). The psalm also reflects competition between Mount Zion (perhaps Mount Sinai) and the mountain of Bashan as rival cultic centers (68:15-16), and corresponds directly to the ancient "Song of Deborah" (68:7-8; cf. Judg. 5:4-5; Gerstenberger 2001, 38). Reference to God as "father of orphans" places the divine in the role of a kinsman-redeemer (68:5; cf. Exod. 22:22-24), before portraying God as king entering the temple and receiving tribute from the nations (68:24-31). The repetition of divine might or power underscores God's sovereignty (68:28, 33-35).

Psalm 69 is an individual lament that cries to God for help, gives voice to extended curses or imprecations against enemies, and concludes with praise and exhortation to a social audience. The psalmist draws on water as a symbol of chaos to describe his persecution by enemies as drowning. While he grounds his appeal on God's steadfast love, truth, and mercy, drastic imprecations against enemies underscore his anguish (69:22-28; cf. Psalm 109) and precede a social exhortation to the lowly (69:32-33). The final call for God to rebuild Judah reflects a postexilic context for the present psalm, which incorporated elements of an older lament (Gerstenberger 2001, 52).

Psalm 70 calls for God's intervention, repeating almost verbatim from Ps. 40:13-17, with minor changes such as the name of God. This psalm reflects the basic social division often implicit in lament, contrasting those who "seek my life" and speak against the psalmist with those who seek God and speak accordingly.

Psalm 71, one of only six before Psalm 72 without a heading, alternates between descriptions of trouble and the psalmist's trust and hope in God (Mays, 234). References to both "my youth" and old age reflect a long-standing relationship with God, while the metaphorical depiction of God as the psalmist's midwife underscores the intimacy of this relationship (v. 6; cf. Ps. 139:13-15; Jer. 1:5). The final commitment to meditate on God's justice resonates with the depiction of the faithful elsewhere (71:24; 1:2; 19:14).

Psalm 72, whose heading is best rendered "to" or "for Solomon," describes the attributes of a righteous king who demonstrates judicial wisdom, support for the vulnerable, exercises "dominion" over a broad swath of territory, and receives service and tribute from other monarchs. Here the well-being (*shalom*) of both people and land are intimately linked to and even derive from the king (72:3, 7), while the blessing of the nations through him resonates with Abram's call (72:17; Gen. 12:3). The grammatical ambiguity of the repeated Hebrew verb form can be read as either a series of desires ("May he judge . . ." NRSV) or future action ("He shall judge . . ." KJV). Regardless, this psalm presents a portrait of an ideal king and probably emerges from a coronation liturgy (cf. Psalm 2). The initial link to Solomon illustrates the biblical ambiguity of such a depiction; renowned for wisdom, exceptional wealth, and expanding the kingdom of Israel, Solomon also embodies what a king should *not* be (1 Kgs. 3–11; Deut. 17:14-18).

Psalm 72 concludes book 2, with the marker noting the "end of the prayers of David" standing in tension with several psalms "of David" appearing later in the book (86; 101; 138). This editorial marker reflects the end of a Davidic collection that precedes the current form of the Psalter, and so witnesses to the complex compositional history of the book (see Jer. 51:64; Prov. 25:1).

▮ THE TEXT IN THE INTERPRETIVE TRADITION

Seeing Psalm 72 as fulfilled in the visit of the magi reflects an ancient interpretive tradition already present in Tertullian's *Against the Jews* in the second century and illustrated in the illuminated *St. Albans Psalter* in the twelfth (cf. 72:10-15; Matt. 2:11; Gillingham, 26, 100–101). In contrast to its prominence as a traditional "messianic" passage often employed during Advent within the Christian tradition, Psalm 72 does not appear within Jewish liturgy (cf. Psalms 2, 110; Holladay, 144).

Rashi's discussion of Psalm headings provides an intriguing counterpoint to contemporary debates. Rabbinic tradition interpreted Ps. 72:20 as "All these are the prayers of David" and so saw David as the writer of the entire Psalter, but Rashi reads this phrase as "they were concluded." However, whereas modern critical scholars point to this verse as evidence of an earlier collection, Rashi appeals to the order in which psalms were found to explain its current position. Thus, though Psalm 72 concluded David's writing, it was discovered before others attributed to David that appear later in the book (Hailperin 1963, 232–33).

New Testament writers drew on Psalm 69 to depict the life and significance of Jesus (see 69:4, 9; John 2:17; 15:25), with the passion narratives in all four Gospels describing Jesus being given a drink of sour wine on the cross (69:21). While the psalm seems striking in its vindictiveness, Romans employs Psalm 69 in its call to "build up the neighbor" (Ps. 69:9 // Rom. 15:3), after explicitly prohibiting the execution of vengeance by leaving it "for the wrath of God" (Rom. 12:18-21; cf. Psalms 109, 149).

◼️ THE TEXT IN CONTEMPORARY DISCUSSION

Debate over the appropriate extent and role of government continues in the contemporary world, and political advertising and propaganda abound. Psalm 72 paints a picture of an ideal king as an instrument of peace (*shalom*), a righteous judge, and a strong ruler who appears at the very center of the people's well-being; even rain and produce appear implicated in the nature of the king.

David Jobling has explored this psalm's role as royal propaganda, pointing out internal inconsistency in the psalm's transition from a "mythic" to a more "political" description of the king. He suggests that the psalm promotes a "tributary" model of production where the centralized king consumes goods and produces ideological self-justification, while those on the periphery produce goods and consume ideology (Jobling, 95, 123).

On the other hand, Walter Houston sees Psalm 72 linking the monarch to a central concern for justice. Where Psalm 82 critiques those who are supposed to judge justly but do not, this psalm provides an appeal for the king to live up to lofty ideals and so, by subordinating the monarchy to justice, "effectively demolishes the doctrine of the divine right of kings" (Houston, 360; cf. Psalm 82; Deut. 17:14-20).

Psalms 73–83: Cries from a Context of Destruction

◼️ THE TEXT IN ITS ANCIENT CONTEXT

Psalms 73–83 begin book 3 with a collection of Asaph psalms, shifting from an individual under duress to a community reeling from the destruction of the temple and Jerusalem. The despair of exile and destruction underlies the repeated call for God to act on Israel's behalf.

Psalm 73 is a wisdom reflection that contemplates the dissonance between the claim that God blesses the righteous and observing the prosperity of the wicked (73:3-12; cf. Ps. 1:6). While the psalmist "almost stumbled" in light of this quandary, visiting the sanctuary convinces him that this success is temporary. In effect, this psalm reframes the issue by contrasting those far from the divine with the psalmist's conviction to remain near God (73:27-28), seeing intimacy with God rather than material gain as the reward for faithfulness.

Psalm 74 is a communal lament that reflects an exilic setting in which the sanctuary has been destroyed and desecrated (74:3, 7). While the opening query asking why God has cast off his people effectively frames book 3 (Ps. 74:1; 89:38; cf. 44:10, 24), the cry "how long?" prompts a recital of God's role as saving king. Seven emphatic appearances of the pronoun "you" in five verses underscore that God gained victory over the forces of chaos and ancient Canaanite deities (sea, Leviathan, streams, the sun, 74:13-17). The psalmist calls on God to *remember* the people that God has redeemed and his dwelling in Zion, as well as the insolence of the enemy (74:2, 18, 22). The concluding appeal for God to "rise up" and "plead your case" arises from the imperative call to attend to covenant; God's role as king implies both bringing order to the cosmos and acting on behalf of this covenant people (cf. Psalm 68; 93).

Psalms 75–76 affirm and praise God's justice. A brief corporate expression of thanks to the divine introduces God's direct speech and his commitment to judge, albeit on a divine—rather than human—timetable (75:1-5). The psalm then shifts to describe God's role in judging (75:6-8). The final verses reiterate each party's commitments, with the individual vowing to praise and the divine reaffirming that the wicked will be cut off and the righteous exalted, thereby addressing the concern of Psalms 74–75 (75:10; cf. Ps. 1:5-6). While "boastful" can be read as the hubris of Babylon (see Assyria in Isa. 10:12), it also reflects a more immediate social adversary elsewhere (75:4; cf. 5:5; 52:1; 73:3); both provide cogent possibilities (Mays, 249). Psalm 76 is a hymn that again praises divine judgment and commitment to save. God's sovereignty over military forces reflects the divine-warrior motif present elsewhere (76:3, 6; cf. Exod. 15:1-3; Isa. 59:16-20).

Rather than cry to God, Psalm 77 moves from an initial description of the psalmist's distress to reflect on God's wondrous deeds. A series of rhetorical questions, beginning with "Will YHWH cast [us] off forever?" (77:7, author trans.; cf. 74:1; 89:38), question central divine attributes (steadfast love, graciousness, compassion) (77:7-9; cf. Exod. 34:6-7). Psalm 77:10 marks a shift in focus from the "I" of the early section to the divine "you" in the latter (Brueggemann, 261–67); the psalmist remembers "your way" (77:13, 19), again intermingling God's action in delivering Israel from Egypt with divine sovereignty over the chaotic waters (cf. 74; Exod. 15:1-10). Remembering God as Israel's redeemer moves beyond being God's people to God's family or next of kin (77:15; cf. Ps. 74:2; 78:35; Isa. 43:1, 14). While its economic role is more often recognized, here God also plays the role of *avenger*, who defends and metes out punishment for those who violate family members (Deut. 19:4-12).

Psalm 78 provides instruction punctuated by characteristic wisdom terminology: teaching, words, proverb, and riddles (78:1-2; cf. Prov. 1:6-8). It seeks to derive lessons from the past by contrasting God's faithful deeds with the people's repeated rebellion from the time of the exodus until that of David. While divine anger and judgment figure prominently (78:21, 31, 58-59), the psalmist also insists on God's restraint and deliverance (78:38; cf. Exod. 34:5-6; Nehemiah 9), culminating with the establishment of the temple and the Davidic line (78:67-72).

Psalms 79–80 cry out for God's response to the destruction of Jerusalem through the restoration of Israel. The graphic portrayal of the desecration of both temple and bodies prompts both the cry "how long?" and the call to shift God's anger away from Jerusalem and onto the nations (79:1-6). The appeal for God *not* to remember former sins and to show compassion reiterates elements from the previous psalm (79:8; 78:38-39), while the concluding call for vengeance leads to a vow of praise (79:10-13). Psalm 80 continues the communal appeal for God to turn from anger, calling on the divine warrior (YHWH) God of hosts/armies, to "restore us . . . that we may be saved" (80:3-4, 7, 19). While the vine also appears as a metaphor for Israel in the prophets (80:8, 14; cf. Jer. 2:21; Ezek. 19:10), this psalm calls for God's response in the aftermath of the catastrophe more than explaining why God has "broken down its walls" (80:12; cf. Isaiah 5).

In Psalm 81, God answers the previous psalms. After introductory verses, God recounts his response to the people's cry (81:6-7; cf. Exod. 2:23-25). The divine admonition centers on the beginning of the Ten Commandments, both in terms of God's identity as the one who "brought you up out of Egypt" and in terms of the commandment to not follow other gods (81:9-10; cf. 78:58; Exod. 20:1-2). The call for Israel to listen/obey provides the central motif (81:8, 11, 13; cf. Deut. 6:4); as in Deuteronomy, God's "turning" to judge the nations is here directly linked to Israel's obedience (81:14; cf. 80:14; Deut. 28:1, 15).

Psalm 82, identified by J. Clinton McCann Jr. as "the single most important text in the entire Bible" (2011), takes place within the "divine assembly" and underscores God's fundamental commitment to justice. While it appears only here in the Old Testament, this phrase has direct parallels in Ugaritic documents, where it builds on the status of El as the chief deity in the Canaanite pantheon (similar to Zeus in Greek mythology) and resonates with several Old Testament passages that also refer to a divine council (Sarna, 169; cf. Gen. 1:26; Job 1–2; Jer. 23:18). Since those charged with maintaining justice are not executing this task properly, *God* laments "How long?" (82:1-5). The psalm concludes with the psalmist's voice calling on God to judge and so fulfill the royal role others have abdicated. While the psalm depicts the failure of judges, the gods (*'elohim*) here can be understood as either humans with exalted status or "divine beings" (Sarna, 173–75). In either case, Psalm 82 emphasizes that the God of Israel is fundamentally committed to justice and willing to intervene when it is not practiced.

Psalm 83, the last linked to Asaph (cf. 50), calls on God to come to Israel's defense. A counterpart to the divine voice previously speaking of "my people" (81), here Israel's status as "your people" undergirds the psalmist's claim that its adversaries are also those of God (83:1-5). In doing so, the psalm lists traditional enemies and draws on God's past action as added motivation (83:6-12; cf. Amos 1–2). The conclusion seeks both the destruction of the enemy and their recognition of YHWH's unique status (83:16-18; cf. Exod. 14:4, 18, 25; Isa. 45:3, 6).

▌ THE TEXT IN THE INTERPRETIVE TRADITION

The use of Psalm 82 within different contentious settings proves intriguing. In John's Gospel, Jesus himself quotes from verse 6, "You are all gods," to refute a charge of blasphemy (John 10:34). Later, arguing against Marcion's proposal that the God of Jesus is different than the creator God, Tertullian insists that Ps. 82:1 reflects "other beings being judged as non-Gods" (Gillingham, 26). While Psalm 82 appeared commonly in the early church fathers, it did not receive as much attention as others in later liturgical use (Gillingham, 53).

The rabbinic *Midrash on the Psalms* (*midrash tehillim*) discusses these same verses, but with a different focus. The rabbis explain Ps. 82:1 as a "Judge among judges," referring to the apparent use of gods (*'elohim*) for human beings elsewhere (Exod. 22:8). The reference to "ye are godlike beings" and mention of *'adam* ("mortals") in the next verse led the rabbis to link the passage with Adam being driven from the Garden of Eden. The concluding verse affirms the basic conviction stated elsewhere: "Remove these mortal judges, and Thou alone be King and Judge" (Braude, 2:59–60; cf. Psalms 93–99).

▌ THE TEXT IN CONTEMPORARY DISCUSSION

The contemporary globalized world also faces significant disorientation, with protracted financial and ecological crises, as well as ongoing violence and insecurity that transcend national, ethnic, or religious boundaries. Like the psalmist, we too live in a world where we perceive the "righteous" and the "wicked," and are tempted to claim national or religious exceptionalism whereby *we* are the "righteous" by definition. While societies, governments, and religious traditions all too often claim the prerogative to function in ways they prohibit for others, these psalms insist that God is king, not just of one fiefdom but of the cosmos (see Psalms 93; 97).

In this context, several things stand out. First, the psalmist calls on the wrath of God to punish the nations, with the recognition that Israel itself has also been subject to divine judgment. Being God's people does not provide an exception to suffering, but heightens the responsibility to follow the divine will (Psalms 78; 81). Second, the call for divine judgment is grounded in God's justice, exemplified in addressing the plight of the weak, orphan, and lowly (Psalm 82); the psalms undercut the tendency to play personal piety over against social concerns. Another temptation lies in too quickly assuming the "enemies" to be other nations or entities, without recognizing the extent to which the psalmists implicate social systems (94) or even close friends (Psalm 55); more than merely about "them," it is crucial to consider when this may critique "us" or even *me*.

Finally, the psalmist's appeal for God to "save" does not represent an escapist spiritual cry uninterested in physical and social reality, but a demand for social liberation and rehabilitation in the here and now. Where contemporary thinking is often dualistic, pitting body against spirit or worldly existence with life eternal, the psalms repeatedly challenge such a dichotomy.

The destruction of Jerusalem, pillaging of the temple, and Babylonian exile represent the most traumatic but also one of the most transformative moments in the history of ancient Israel. As these psalms attest, this experience challenged the wisdom tradition's conviction that God rewards the righteous and punishes the wicked (73), contested the liturgical tradition's view of the status of the temple and Jerusalem (79), and raised profound questions about the justice, character, and presence of God (76; 82). This crisis prompted both introspection and reflection on past experience (75; 77; 78) and passionate appeals for God's intervention (80; 83).

Psalms 84–89: From Joy in the Temple to Personal and Corporate Despair

▌THE TEXT IN ITS ANCIENT CONTEXT

While references to the sons of Korah frame books 2 and 3 (Psalms 84–88; cf. 42; 44–49), Psalms 84–89 also include psalms linked to David (86) and Ethan (89), shifting from rejoicing in the temple to the agony of exile (Ps. 84; 89b). Psalm 84 also reflects a shift back to using YHWH as the dominant name for the divine, after the conclusion of the "Elohistic Psalter" (see Psalm 42).

Psalm 84 contains both a hymn and a pilgrimage song praising the temple (Gerstenberger 2001, 123–24), with its exuberance reinforced by three "Happy are . . ." sayings (84:4, 5, 12). This focus and the fourfold use of "YHWH (God) of hosts/armies," a designation consistently linked to Zion and the temple in the Psalms (24:10; 46:7, 11; 48:9; 69:6), both forms a thematic link with the preceding section and signals the shift away from God (*elohim*) as the default term for the divine (84:1, 3,

8, 12; cf. 80:4, 7, 14, 19). The psalm refers to both "your anointed/messiah [*meshihekah*]" and God as a shield (84:9, 11), introducing the royal motif that dominates Psalm 89 and frames this section.

Psalm 85 recalls when YHWH forgave in the past and calls for God to do the same in the present, articulating its existential anguish with the query "Will you be angry with us forever?" (85:1-7; cf. 79:5). The fourfold use of the Hebrew term *shub* connects how YHWH had previously *restored* Jacob and *turned* from anger to the contemporary call to *restore* and *revive* again (85:1-6). Wrath and anger reflect language typically linked to exile and imply an exilic setting (85:3, 5; cf. 2 Kgs. 17:18; 23:26; Isa. 12:1; Jer. 4:8, 26; Ezek. 7:12-14). The final section expresses confidence in God's response and describes a hopeful future. Where the psalmist calls for divine steadfast love, God will speak peace (*shalom*) to his faithful (85:8); "steadfast love and faithfulness/truth will meet; justice and *peace* will kiss" (85:10).

Psalm 86, the only one attributed to David in book 3, draws on characteristic phrases and motifs from lament and thanksgiving psalms in an "anthological style." The relationship between a servant and "my Lord," terms appearing three and seven times respectively, reflects the dominant motif that both provides a paradigm for prayer and links to the royal depiction of David in Psalm 89a (Mays, 278–79). To do so, the psalmist again draws directly on the depiction of YHWH as "merciful and gracious . . ." found in Exodus 34 (Pss. 86:15; 103:8; Exod. 34:6-7; Joel 2:13; Jon. 4:2).

Psalm 87 extols Zion and even addresses it directly as the "city of God," a hymnic feature with ancient Near Eastern parallels (87:3, Gerstenberger 2001, 139). Rather than focusing on the temple and its connection to Israel, however, this psalm links foreign nations to God, even describing traditional enemies as being born in Zion, an oddity reiterated by YHWH (87:4-6). Where Psalm 83 called for the destruction of traditional enemies, here foreign nations are incorporated into the liturgical center of Israel. While unusual, a radical opening to the nations appears elsewhere as well (see Isa. 19:24-25, 66:20-21; Amos 9:7).

Psalm 88, identified with both the "sons of Korah" and "Heman the Ezrahite," provides an unusual yet powerful individual lament. The psalm emphatically addresses God throughout, who functions as both the court of appeal and the enemy; God has put him in the depths (88:6), divine wrath confronts him (88:7, 16), God has prompted the psalmist's utter social isolation (88:8, 18), and has "cast me off" (88:14; cf. 74:1; 77:7; 89:38). The description of repeatedly calling on God leads to rhetorical questions about God's steadfast love, faithfulness, and righteousness, precisely those elements praised elsewhere (88:9-12; cf. 85:9-11; 86:13, 15; 89:1-2). Where individual laments typically conclude with a statement of confidence or vow of praise, this psalm contains no hopeful emotional turn or shift in tone; what begins with a cry to the "God of my salvation" ends in despair.

Psalm 89, consisting of two strongly contrasting sections (89:1-37, 38-52), centers on the reliability of God. Psalm 89a immediately introduces the key terms *steadfast love* and *faithfulness*, which appear repeatedly and often in parallel (89:1, 2, 24, 33, 49). The psalmist first speaks to God and then quotes the divine, a pattern that repeats itself throughout the first section of the psalm; the divine voice reiterates God's covenant with David and so introduces its dominant motif (89:3; 2 Sam. 7:16). The psalmist then praises YHWH's control over the mythological forces of chaos (89:6-12; cf. Psalms 74; 104) and then quotes a vision (cf. Isa. 1:1; Dan. 8:1). Here God speaks again to underscore God's intimate relationship with the king and weave him into the very fabric of the cosmos, such that he controls not only his enemies but even the sea and rivers (89:19-25). God again reaffirms the covenant with David, reiterating the king's status as God's son and the eternal inviolability of the covenant (89:26-37; cf. 2 Sam. 7:12-16; Ps. 2:7). Thus the psalmist links God's *faithfulness* reflected in control over creation to divine *steadfast love* embodied in a divine commitment to the Davidic king.

"But *you*" marks a dramatic shift to the second section of the psalm. Where in Psalm 89a this emphatic pronoun had been used six times to underscore God's control over creation (89:9-12, 17), in 89b the psalmist directly accuses God of betraying the covenant with David—the very subject of previous praise (89:38; cf. 89:34). He bemoans the realities of exile: the crown lies in the dust, the scepter has been removed, and the throne is discarded. Finally, the psalm moves from accusatory description to a call for action and a shift in focus from the singular "servant" to "servants" (89:3, 20, 39, 50). A dual "how long?" coupled with two calls for God to "remember!" urge God to act, and surround the climactic question that reflects the existential crisis of the psalm: "Lord, where is your *steadfast love* of old, which by your *faithfulness* you swore to David?" (89:46-51). Thus Psalm 89 reflects the basis for the expectation of an ideal, future "messiah"; the Babylonian exile coupled with the Davidic covenant provides the context for a *future* king who would restore the monarchy.

While the final verse of Psalm 89 forms an editorial closing for book 3, its muted praise in comparison to other parallel elements reflects the tone at the end of this section (cf. 41:13; 72:18-19; 106:48); Psalm 89 ends in despair over the plight of the king that parallels the depressed tone at the end of Psalm 88. A chasm has opened between the divine promise and Israel's experience, where the overthrow of the Davidic king reflects nothing less than God's violation of covenant (89:39).

◼ The Text in the Interpretive Tradition

Psalms 88–89 illustrate the debates over psalm superscriptions and their implications. Jerome reads *mahalath le'annoth*] in the heading of Psalm 88 as "the *mysterium* of the Church gathered together" to praise God and proceeds to read the psalm as Christ speaking. Abandoned by his disciples, Jerome links "you have made me a thing of horror to them" to the Jews shouting "Crucify him!" (88:8). Rashi, in contrast, reads *mahalat* as "sickness" and relates the entire poem to the collective Israel that "is now suffering the hardships of exile." For him, the psalm represents the voice of "the entire Jewish people . . . 'whom the nations once respected but now despise'" (Shereshevsky 1982, 125).

Rashi also considers the attribution of these psalms, agreeing with the superscription that Psalm 89 was composed by Ethan against a rabbinic tradition linking it to Abraham. He explains the dual superscription of Psalm 88 by suggesting that Heman is the musician and performer of a psalm that was written by the sons of Korah (Hailperin, 234; cf. Psalm 72).

◼ The Text in Contemporary Discussion

Where lament psalms "have been largely purged from the life and liturgy of the church," this represents a "costly loss" since limiting appropriate religious speech to praise and thanksgiving does not adequately reckon with the struggles of lived experience (Brueggemann, 44, 98–110). The deep despair of Psalm 88 reflects the experience of many who deal with depression and forms of mental illness, overwhelmed and perceiving no way out of a negative situation. This psalm has the potential to be a powerful resource that both provides a "voice" for those who are struggling and a call for empathetic response from others. The struggle with profound social isolation reflected in Psalm 88 challenges contemporary faith communities to support and hold onto hope for those who cannot do so themselves.

Psalm 89 also proves significant. On the one hand, it cautions against simply claiming God's promises and treating the divine as a mechanistic force to be controlled. On the other hand, it also reflects the profound disorientation of having a bedrock understanding (i.e., God's commitment to the Davidic monarchy) fundamentally challenged by experience. However, this tension does not prompt a turn *away* from but rather a turn *to* God; where contemporary "new atheism" has found a receptive audience, Psalms 88–89 and biblical lament more generally reject such a move. Though its strident tone may be unnerving, Psalm 89 reflects the audacity to call for YHWH to live up to covenant responsibilities, and thus the intimacy of the underlying relationship.

Psalms 90–100: YHWH Reigns

▐ THE TEXT IN ITS ANCIENT CONTEXT

The move from book 3 to book 4 marks a significant shift from despair to hope. While the placement of royal psalms at the "seams" of books 1–3 (2; 72; 89) underscores the failure of the monarchy, book 4 (90–106) responds to the call for God to reestablish the Davidic king by reiterating God's steadfast love and faithfulness but shifts the focus to YHWH-as-king rather than a mortal monarch (Psalms 93; 95–99; Wilson 209–14, 217).

Psalm 90, identified as a prayer (*tefillah*), provides a communal plea for God to turn from anger and wrath. The only one attributed to Moses, this psalm fulfills his role of interceding on behalf of the people in a moment of crisis (see Exod. 17:1-7; 32:7-14). Where humans are called to repent, the psalmist acknowledges sin (90:3, 8) and then calls on YHWH to turn and demonstrate divine compassion and steadfast love (90:13-14; cf. 86:15; Exod. 34:6-7; Joel 2:13; Jon. 4:2). While Psalm 90 picks up several motifs (anger, the short time span of life, "how long?") and continues the shift from servant to servants noted in the previous psalm, it does not mention the "anointed," David, or the Davidic covenant. Even as it reiterates a call for God's steadfast love, the final appeal for God to uphold the work of *our* hands provides a striking contrast to the previous focus on the king (90:14; cf. 89:49-51).

Psalm 91 depicts divine protection for those who trust in God, culminating in a series of promises spoken in the first-person voice of God. Shelter, shade, and the metaphor of a bird with her brood under her wings provide images of divine protection (90:1-4; cf. Ruth 2:12; 3:9); claiming God as "my refuge" appears most frequently in the Psalms, with prayer seeming to be the epitome of seeking refuge in YHWH (e.g., Ps. 2:12; 7:1; 11:1). Military imagery, ranging from large, corporate elements to individual ones enhances the depiction of divine protection from a litany of dangers. Both military and natural imagery prove defensive, so that even though the "wicked" will receive their recompense, the recipient of the promise looks on as a bystander rather than enacting it himself

(91:8; Exod. 14:13-14; cf. Psalms 18; 149). Final promises appear in the voice of God: "I will deliver ... protect ... answer ... be with them ... rescue ... satisfy ... and show them my salvation" (91:14-16). Reference to those "who love me," a term used elsewhere both for God's love for Israel and in contexts of marriage, underscores the intimacy of this relationship (Gen. 34:8; Deut. 7:7; 21:11).

Psalm 92, which the heading associates with the Sabbath, provides a liturgical hymn that declares God's steadfast love and faithfulness, and so responds to the query at the end of book 3 (89:49). The psalm shifts to praise YHWH directly, reiterating the temporary nature of the current prosperity of the wicked (92:7-9; cf. Psalm 73). The concluding depiction of the righteous as a flourishing palm tree recalls Psalm 1, here linked to the temple rather than the torah (92:12-15; cf. 1:2-4).

Psalm 93 introduces the "YHWH reigns" motif, which dominates book 4 (96:10; 97:1; 98:6; 99:1). While it shares vocabulary and characteristics with royal psalms (Psalms 2; 72; 89), here these attributes are directly tied to God rather than an earthly king: YHWH reigns, wears royal robes, is established and enthroned. The sound/voice (*qol*) of the rivers and "mighty waters" provide the backdrop for heightening YHWH's majesty (93:3-4; cf. Psalms 29; 104). Some scholars have linked Psalms 93 and 95–99 to an "enthronement festival" celebrating YHWH's kingship in preexilic Israel (Mowinckel, 1:106–13). In its current setting following the description of the fall of the monarchy in Psalm 89, however, Psalm 93 addresses the crisis of exile through *divine* rule rather than reestablishing the Davidic line, meeting concerns voiced earlier in an unexpected way (see Ps. 89:49).

Psalm 94 begins with the strident call,

> O Lord, you God of vengeance,
>   you God of vengeance, shine forth!

While at first glance out of place amid assurance, praise, and "YHWH reigns" psalms, this cry reflects the logical implications of the former: as king, God's royal responsibility is to ensure the proper functioning of justice (cf. Psalms 72; 82). The cry for vengeance reflects the lament "How long?" arising from the litany of abuses of society's most vulnerable (94:1-6). Justice is the fundamental issue at play; where the wicked assume God to be inert (94:7), vengeance here "is not an arbitrary or vindictive act, but a judicial intervention against the guilty" (Sarna, 192). The lack of immediate comeuppance for the wicked underlies the angst of the psalm (cf. Psalm 73). Nonetheless, the repeated final conviction that God "will wipe them out" expresses confidence that the current situation will be rectified, and corresponds to the double calls for vengeance and the cries "How long?" at the outset (94:23; see vv. 1, 3).

Psalm 95 opens with a hymn of praise and thanksgiving to YHWH, whose identification as a "great king above all gods" highlights the polytheistic context this section assumes (95:1-3). Depicting the people as God's flock (cf. Ps. 80:1) and exhorting them to hear *his* voice provides an implicit caution against following the voices of others (the floods, Ps. 93:3-4; the enemy, 55:3; charmers, 58:5). God's voice concludes the psalm, sounding a note of caution by recalling past disobedience in the wilderness.

Psalms 96–99 continue the motif of YHWH as king. Psalm 96, linked elsewhere to Asaph and celebrating David bringing the ark of the covenant into Jerusalem (1 Chron. 16:23-33), calls for public praise and recognition of YHWH and depicts all rivals as idols (96:4-5; cf. 97:9). While it briefly mentions the sanctuary, the listeners are to declare "among the nations 'YHWH reigns'" (96:10, author trans.). This royal status, underscored by a litany of adjectives concerning God's majesty, is exemplified in divine mastery over creation and establishing justice. This in turn forms the basis for the variations to come.

> He will judge the world with righteousness [*tsedeq*],
> and the peoples with his truth [or faithfulness, *'emunatho*]. (96:13)

Psalm 97 again asserts that "YHWH reigns" (97:1; cf. Ps. 93:1; 99:1), with the divine throne based on righteousness and justice. Third-person description shifts momentarily to directly address YHWH, where "your judgments" provide the reason for rejoicing and the implicit basis for being exalted above other gods; here again YHWH's commitment to justice differentiates this God from other would-be deities (97:8-9; cf. 82). The concluding verses directly exhort those who "love YHWH" to hate evil and give thanks, confirming God's commitment to the faithful and righteous (97:10-12); God's people are also to embody the divine characteristics described at the outset.

Psalm 98 praises God's marvelous deeds and celebrates God's *yeshu'ah*, a key term variously rendered as "victory," "salvation," "liberation," and "deliverance" (98:1-3). This effusive praise again responds to the despairing question at the end of Psalm 89, reiterating that God "has remembered his steadfast love and faithfulness" (98:3; cf. 89:49), but linking this commitment to the "house of Israel" rather than the "house of David." The psalmist calls for the earth, including the sea and floods, to praise YHWH; the last verse reiterates God's role as judge.

Psalm 99, again beginning with "YHWH reigns" (99:1, cf. 93:1; 97:1) and praising God's justice, links this claim to divine holiness and the status of the temple and Zion. Being "enthroned upon the cherubim," which generally refers to the ark of the covenant (99:1; Exod. 37:7-9; 2 Sam. 6:2), proves unusual in the Psalms. While the other contexts where the term *cherubim* appears depict God as a divine warrior who fights on behalf of the people (Ps. 18:10; 80:1), this psalm does not mention enemies but immediately links the term to Zion, later referred to as God's "holy mountain" (99:2, 9). Similarly, the communal designation "YHWH our God," which appears sparingly in the Psalter but four times in this psalm, resonates with Deuteronomic language and corresponds to the key role of Moses, Aaron, and Samuel as intermediaries (99:6).

Psalm 100 is an exuberant communal entrance liturgy, presumably to a service in the temple (100:4), that calls on all of the earth to praise YHWH. The imperative to worship (*'ibdu*, 100:2; cf. 2:11) could also be translated as "serve," with the corresponding noun "servant" (*'ebed*; cf. 89:50; 90:13, 16) providing an implicit contrast with those who *serve* other gods or idols (cf. 97:7). Both the depiction of God as shepherd (v. 3, cf. Psalm 23) and the confirmation of YHWH's steadfast love and faithfulness are familiar, and again respond to the despairing question discussed earlier (100:5; 98:3; cf. 89:49).

▌ THE TEXT IN THE INTERPRETIVE TRADITION

The *Midrash on Psalms* resolves the dilemma of "orphan psalms" here by extending the attribution of Moses in Psalm 90 to this whole section (90–100), matching these eleven Psalms with Moses' blessing of the eleven tribes (Deut. 33:6-26; Braude, 2:87–88). Psalms 90–93 are also recited in both Sabbath and festival services (Holladay, 142).

From early on in the Christian tradition, these psalms were interpreted christologically. For instance, Justin Martyr sees Psalm 96 as a prediction of Christ's rule after resurrection (Holladay, 163–64). Psalms 96 and 98 continue to be used in the Advent season, with the former showing that "Christ has come, and will come again" and the latter providing the inspiration for Isaac Watts's hymn "Joy to the World" (Mays, 309–10, 312).

The basic conviction that "YHWH reigns" undergirds central prayers in both Jewish and Christian traditions: "Blessed are you, YHWH our God, *eternal king/king of the universe*" and "*Thy kingdom* come, thy will be done on earth as it is in heaven."

THE TEXT IN CONTEMPORARY DISCUSSION

The intimate connection between "YHWH reigns" and justice cannot be overemphasized. As Nahum Sarna notes, in Psalm 94, God's "people" are those being oppressed, while the "wicked" are the "corrupt, privileged upper classes" who "control the levers of power," including the legal system itself (Sarna, 195, 202). Where "lady justice" is often portrayed blindfolded with balance scales in one hand and a sword in the other, projecting an image of unbiased objectivity and the right to punish, in this psalm justice is neither blind nor disinterested, but rather *for* the widow, stranger, and orphan. As the divine king, God accepts the responsibility to function as the defender of the outcast who will also return to "judge the earth" in the future, which acts as both hope and warning for life in the present.

This recognition undercuts the tendency to think in dualistic categories, separating spiritual "salvation" from physical or social "liberation"; the term *yeshu'ah* (and the derivative name Jesus) hold these together. Similarly, though "justice" is often treated as a social phenomenon and "righteousness" related to personal piety, both commonly translate the term *tsedeq*. Claiming YHWH as king cuts through such artificial divisions and pushes adherents to recognize physical and spiritual, social and individual realms as inseparably under the rule of God.

Finally, while Psalm 91 is commonly used as a "call to worship" in Christian liturgy, the devil also quotes it to tempt Jesus to claim special messianic protection: "If you are the Son of God . . ." (Matt. 4:5-6; Luke 4:9-11; cf. Ps. 91:11-12). While people may gravitate toward psalms of comfort and assurance rather than the strident language of lament, Jesus' temptation demonstrates that the former are not immune from misuse either but reflects the hermeneutical wrestling with Scripture central to both Jewish and Christian traditions.

Psalms 101–106: Praise to God and Social Warning

THE TEXT IN ITS ANCIENT CONTEXT

Psalm 101, the first of two attributed to David in book 4 (see also 103), reflects a royal inauguration or celebration (Mays, 321). Beginning by singing of steadfast love and justice, the psalm centers on the king's commitment to blamelessness and integrity (101:2-3; cf. 18:23-25). The psalmist's commitment to turn away from and root out slander, deceit, wickedness, and evil parallels his dedication to the "faithful" and the blameless, while the dual promise to destroy reflects the royal role of responding to evil (101:5-8; cf. 94:23; 18:40). While the close association between God and king implies that enemies of one are also adversaries of the other (cf. 139:21-22), in the Psalms such violence is generally reserved exclusively for YHWH or the king as God's representative (Firth, 3).

Psalm 102, immediately identified as a prayer, moves from a typical invocation to a description of distress reflecting physical torment and derision from "enemies." The extended introduction leads to God's "indignation and anger" as the main culprit, so that God is both the court of appeal and the source of affliction (102:10; cf. Ps. 38:1-3; 88; 106:32). "But you" marks a shift from the transitory nature of human life to the eternal nature of God, and from a focus on the individual to plural "servants" (102:12-14). God's response to the prayer of the downtrodden emerges from divine kingship and the restoration of Zion (Mays, 325). Recording the prayer also provides an opportunity for future generations to move from lament to praise (102:1, 17, 21). The psalm concludes by contrasting the ephemeral nature of the psalmist with God's role as creator and confidence about the future of "your servants' children."

Psalm 103, again "of David" (cf. 101), "blesses" YHWH as divine king. The opening call to "not forget" initiates a string of participles that describe God's attributes and actions on behalf of "my soul" (forgiver, healer, redeemer), culminating in the description of YHWH quoted from Exodus that effectively links God's commitment to justice with the characteristics of steadfast love and compassion (103:8; cf. Exod. 34:6-7). Like the previous, this psalm contrasts the transitional nature of humanity with the eternal steadfast love of the divine, creator king (103:15-19) with the conclusion calling on the entire heavenly court to join the psalmist to "bless YHWH."

Psalm 104, another hymn beginning with "bless YHWH" (104:1; cf. 103:1), focuses on the cosmic scale even as it is framed by personal references to "my God" (104:1, 33). While alternating between third-person description of God and momentary direct address to YHWH has led some to argue for a composite nature or different voices present in the psalm (Gerstenberger 2001, 222), the overriding motif is clear: YHWH is the creator, sustainer, and provider of the cosmos. Although the created elements and God's role in setting limits prove similar to the creation account in Genesis 1 (104:8-9), here humanity does not represent its climax (104:23; cf. Psalm 8). The next section praises YHWH directly, both grounding creation in wisdom (cf. Prov. 8:22) and reiterating divine control over the cosmos, including the mythological elements of the sea and Leviathan (104:24-26; cf. 74:12-17). The psalmist's final call for the destruction of sinners and the wicked underscores that the God of creation also remains committed to justice on the social plane.

Psalm 105 calls for people to give thanks and remember (*zikru*) YHWH's "wonderful works" (105:5), centered on the Abrahamic covenant of land (Mays, 337). It illustrates how God has remembered his covenant with Abraham and ties it to torah obedience (105:8, 42-45). The psalm identifies Abraham, Moses, and the people as God's servant(s), rather than the Davidic king (cf. 89:3, 20, 39); even the term "anointed/messiah" refers to the patriarchs rather than the monarch here (105:15; cf. 89:38, 51).

Psalm 106 provides a counterpoint to the previous, again rehearsing Israel's story from the exodus until living in the land, only this time concentrating on the rebellion of the people (cf. Psalm

78). The initial call to give thanks to YHWH "for his steadfast love endures forever" reflects a liturgical refrain (106:1; cf. Psalm 136), while those who embody God's concern with justice and righteousness are described as "happy" (106:3; cf. 99:4; 103:6). While the psalmist's appeal for YHWH to remember him links this psalm to the previous (106:4-5; cf. 105:42-44), a communal declaration of sin introduces its main subject. Where God acted to save and redeem, the people forgot, disobeyed, and prostituted themselves, leading to divine discipline and anger. Even so, the final verses reiterate the thrust of the psalm: while the people sin and rebel, God repeatedly delivers by hearing their cry, remembering covenant, and showing steadfast love (106:43-46; cf. Exod. 2:23-25). The communal call to "save us" shifts to address God once again and corresponds to the psalmist's initial request to experience salvation (106:4, 47), while the call to "gather us from the nations" reflects an exilic context (106:47; cf. Deut. 30:1-4; Isa. 56:3-8; 66:18).

The final verse provides an editorial conclusion to book 4, similar to the previous (v. 48; cf. Ps. 41:7; 72:18-19; 89:52).

▮ THE TEXT IN THE INTERPRETIVE TRADITION

As one of seven traditional "penitential psalms" (cf. Psalm 51), Psalm 102 has functioned liturgically in various settings. Along with the Songs of Ascent (120–34), the penitential psalms have been used to pray for the souls of deceased individuals in the "Office for the Dead," which became an official rite in the fifteenth century. As early as the fourteenth century, the penitential psalms, along with many other psalms, were also included in booklets called "Prymers," or "first prayers," that functioned both as devotional resources and reading instruction (Gillingham, 55, 103).

▮ THE TEXT IN CONTEMPORARY DISCUSSION

Environmental and ecological issues continue to prompt significant debate. As a hymn praising God's work and role in creation, Psalm 104 is striking in part because here humanity appears as part of creation but not as its culmination or climax (104:23; cf. Genesis 1–2; Psalms 8; 72). Also, rather than concentrate on the act of creation, here God continues to be at work, limiting, sustaining, and providing.

While in the West, the type of mythological perspective underlying Psalm 74 or 104 may seem like a relic of the distant past, the conviction that this particular God controls elements that others worship can still be readily witnessed in animistic traditions today. Nonetheless, if one considers idolatry as treating something created as the Creator or mistaking the finite for the infinite, it is worth pondering what populates our own pantheon in the West. For instance, might our modern "gods" include giving free rein to the market and its "forces" as the arbiter of worth; pursuing military campaigns in support of ambiguous "national interests," acting as a contemporary version of sacrificing our sons and daughters (Ps. 106:37-38); pushing for productivity such that it becomes a contemporary fertility "god" or our own version of Baal, which refuses to recognize limits? At what point does humanity's modification of climate systems, destruction of species, and attempts to modify and even control ecological systems take "dominion" too far (cf. Gen. 1:26; Ps. 8:6)?

Ellen Davis notes that Psalm 104 proves unusual in that it does not reflect "a primordial struggle with chaos monsters" prevalent in ancient Near Eastern literature; even the sea and Leviathan, elements that elsewhere embody chaos and seem to work against the divine, are here dependent on God for their ongoing nourishment (104:25-26; cf. 74:12-17). Indeed, only the last verse and its mention of humanity suggest the possibility of opposition to God's creative and sustaining action (E. Davis, 63). In effect, perhaps humans can also represent rebellious forces of chaos that need to be limited for the good of creation (104:6-9). A critical rereading of the Bible that recognizes "the present fact of Creation" and places humanity within creation rather than outside or above it has become a crucial task (Berry, 94–95). What may at first glance appear as an ancient, superstitious relic holds contemporary significance after all.

Psalms 107–112: Imprecation and Assurance

◼ The Text in Its Ancient Context

Psalm 107 begins book 5 with the same liturgical thanksgiving refrain as the previous psalm: "for his steadfast love endures forever" (107:1; 106:1; cf. 136). Where the previous called on God to "gather" Israel from the nations, here the psalmist calls on the "redeemed of YHWH" who *have been* gathered to give thanks (Ps. 106:47; 107:3). The psalm then provides four examples reflecting the same pattern: an initial portrayal of distress, a refrain describing how each "cried to YHWH," God's liberating response, and a refrain calling on them to give thanks in recognition of God's steadfast love. The final section links God's sustenance of creation to divine concern for those in distress (107:33-43), while the final appeal to the "wise" reinforces the instructional purpose of the psalm and reiterates YHWH's steadfast love as its core teaching. In contrast to Psalms 105–106, the focus here lies on God's response to the cry of those in distress without reference to Israelite history.

Psalm 108, attributed to David and drawn directly from parts of two previous psalms, links individual praise with a communal call for divine support of military victory (Pss. 57:7-11; 60:5-12; cf. 18). In its present form and setting, this psalm addresses God to reiterate frustration for having been cast off (108:11; cf. 89:38). While reference to "us" can be read as the broader community, in light of the heading and royal expectations elsewhere this could also be heard as the voice of Davidic descendants, would-be claimants to the throne (Psalms 2; 18; 89). In either case, the psalm reflects a postexilic setting and yearning for divine aid.

Psalm 109, attributed to David, is the first lament in book 5. Calling out from a setting of persecution and hateful speech, debate continues on whether the unusually extensive middle curse section reflects the words of these adversaries, as suggested by the NRSV's addition of "they say" (109:6), or those of the psalmist himself (109:6-19; Gerstenberger 2001, 258–59). In either case, the psalmist affirms these words against his accusers (v. 20), and so we cannot avoid these drastic imprecations as expressing the desires of the psalmist. The adversaries here are identified as *satan*, a Hebrew term that most frequently depicts people rather than supernatural beings in the Old Testament (109:6, 20; cf. 1 Kgs. 11:14, 23, 25). Here it appears as "accuser" or perhaps prosecuting attorney in a courtlike setting, which roughly corresponds to the role of "the *satan*" in the heavenly court in Job 1–2. The crisis in the psalm arises from a lack of *hesed* understood as "social solidarity," which leads to a direct appeal for God's *hesed* to fill this void (109:12, 16, 21, 26; Brueggemann, 275–80). The shift from curses to direct address to YHWH, emphatically marked by "but *you*" (109:21), introduces the appeal for God to rectify the situation that leads to praise and the confident assertion of God's alignment with the "poor and needy."

Psalm 110 provides reassurance based on two statements in divine first-person speech. The introductory phrase "YHWH says [*ne'um yhwh*]," which appears only here in the Psalter, typically introduces oracles in prophetic books (110:1; cf. Isa. 43:10, 12; Jer. 1:8, 15, 19; Amos 4:6, 8-11). The invitation to "my Lord" to "sit at my right hand" probably derives from an enthronement ceremony, whereby the king was recognized as divinely empowered and appointed to act as God's representative (Mays, 351–52); as elsewhere, kingship is here linked with Zion and ruling over enemies (cf. Psalm 2). A divine oath formula (*nishba' yhwh*) introduces another divine statement that adds a priestly role to the king (110:4); in its only other occurrence in the Psalms, this phrase reiterates God's commitment to the Davidic king (Ps. 132:11). The concluding verses portray "my YHWH" as a conquering king and universal judge on his day of wrath (cf. Ps. 2:8-9; 18:34-40).

Psalms 111–112 function together to describe YHWH and the benefits for those who fear him. Both begin with *halelu yah* (111:1; 112:1; cf. 146–150) and then follow a twenty-two-line acrostic pattern, where each begins with the subsequent letter of the Hebrew alphabet (cf. 119). The final verse of Psalm 111 and the first of 112 hinge the psalms together, with wisdom reflection on the "fear of the LORD [YHWH]" (111:10; cf. Prov. 1:7; 9:10) leading to "Happy is the one who fears YHWH"; similarly, "all those who do *them*" (111:10) anticipates delighting in "his commandments" (112:1; cf. 1:2), linking "fear of YHWH" to torah observance (cf. 19:9; 119). These psalms portray those who "fear YHWH" as mirroring divine attributes, including righteousness (111:3; 112:3, 9), graciousness and mercy (111:4; 112:4), justice (111:7; 112:5); uprightness (111:8; 112:2, 4), and enduring forever (111:3, 10; 112:3, 9). Finally, those who fear YHWH trust in God (112:7) and reflect divine concern for the poor (112:9; cf. 82:4; Mays, 359–60). These psalms end with the prominent wisdom motif contrasting the righteous and wicked, though here the "desire of the wicked" perishes rather than the wicked themselves (112:10; cf. 1:6).

◼ THE TEXT IN THE INTERPRETIVE TRADITION

Psalm 110 is the most cited psalm in the New Testament; the Gospels depict Jesus using it to problematize the idea of the anointed (*christos* in Greek, *messiah* in Hebrew): "The LORD says to my lord, 'Sit at my right hand until I make your enemies your footstool'" (Ps. 110:1). Jesus argues that, since David refers to "my Lord," "how can he be his [David's] son?" (Matt. 22:45; Luke 20:44).

Psalm 110 remained significant within the Christian tradition, in part because it explained the interim period between Jesus' death and resurrection and his return in the eschatological future (Acts 2:32-36; Heb. 1:3-4, 13; 1 Pet. 3:22; cf. Psalm 8). This psalm also reflects the repeated divine forbearance in the Psalms, where the success of the wicked and suffering of the righteous represent a temporary hiatus awaiting divine intervention to set things right (cf. Psalms 73; 94; 102).

In contrast to its significance in the Christian tradition, Psalm 110 does not appear within Jewish liturgy (cf. Psalms 2; 72; Holladay, 144).

Psalm 109, with its drastic imprecations against enemies, was cited in Jesus' passion accounts and provided the opportunity for anti-Jewish rhetoric from the early church on. For instance, Luther paints this with a broad brush as a "psalm David composed about Christ, who pronounces 'terrible curses' upon Judas and 'everyone of Judas's ilk,' including 'Judaism as a whole' as well as 'all schismatics and persecutors of the Word of Christ.'" Building on his "two kingdoms" theology, Luther suggests "it is permissible to curse on account of the Word of God; but it is wrong to curse on your own account for personal vengeance or some other personal end" (Thompson, 55, 59–60, 63).

■ THE TEXT IN CONTEMPORARY DISCUSSION

Cursing or imprecatory psalms such as Psalm 109 continue to generate much debate. While lament psalms have largely fallen out of use in liturgical contexts, Brueggemann (102–7) has argued for their ongoing significance for giving voice to the voiceless and challenging the status quo. Some have argued for the cathartic effect of imprecation, where voicing the desire for vengeance constitutes handing over responsibility for executing it, and thus "surrendering retribution" to God (Firth). In contrast, Amy Cottrill believes that Psalm 109 represents a "revenge fantasy" that contemporary readers must resist on the grounds not only that it may prompt violence but also that the language in itself is violent (Cottrill, 147–56).

While Cottrill helpfully warns of the potential for using imprecations to justify violence, the "satanic" reading of Psalm 91 in the Gospel accounts of Jesus' temptation reminds us that the abuse of psalms to obscure God's will rather than discover it is not unique to lament, but can be found in psalms of comfort and praise as well. Lament psalms—including those with strident curses against the enemy—hold the potential to promote empathetic understandings and responses, perhaps especially when we step away from the role as "speaker" and into that of their social audience in order to attend to the voice(s) of others in distress. This possibility underscores the vital role of contemporary communities committed to hear and discern such speech (Suderman 2012, 212–16; see Psalm 137). In so doing, we may even move from being the "hero" of the psalm to identifying with the "enemy" who needs to repent and turn from wrongdoing (see Psalm 141).

In relation to New Testament material and the broader Christian tradition, Psalm 110 raises a related issue. David Firth has argued that the perpetration of violence in "I" psalms is restricted to God, with the only exception being that of the king as God's representative (Firth, 3). While Psalm 110 illustrates this exception (110:5-6; cf. Ps. 2:9), its use in the New Testament corresponds to the general trend that does not reject the possibility of vengeance but restricts its implementation. Jesus' call for his followers to forego retribution and pursue love of enemies (Matt. 5:38-48) does not make the New Testament immune from calls for vengeance; indeed, the lament "how long?" and accompanying cry for vengeance from martyrs under the divine throne challenges common notions of "heaven" (Rev. 6:10; cf. 79:10). Once again, however, God's response reflects divine forbearance; while the "cry" is recognized as legitimate and the outcome assured, God does not act immediately. Similarly, also faced with a context of persecution, Paul instructs his listeners to "pursue (*diokontes*) the love of strangers, and bless those who persecute (*diokontas*) you" and to "never avenge yourselves, but leave room for the wrath of God" (Rom. 12:13-14, 18-19). The last verse, with its quotation from Deuteronomy, underscores the point: "For it is written: 'Vengeance is mine, *I* will repay,' says the LORD" (Rom. 12:19; cf. Deut. 32:35; Ps. 94:1). While the desire for vengeance does not disappear in the New Testament, it is clear that meting this out reflects a divine and not human prerogative.

Christian history has seen the repeated religious justification of human violence, a tendency that remains a persistent temptation. Mays points to the persistent prophetic critique of the monarchy and the eschatological way in which Psalm 110 points to God's coming kingdom as two important qualifications that guard against its use as contemporary political propaganda (Mays, 353; cf. Psalm 72).

Psalms 113–119: Praise of the Cosmic God, Giver of Torah

▌ THE TEXT IN ITS ANCIENT CONTEXT

Beginning with *halelu yah*, Psalm 113 calls on the "servants of YHWH" to praise God. It portrays God in cosmic terms as "on high" and "above the heavens," but without mention of temple or Zion (113:4). God's commitment to reverse the fortunes of the poor and needy and the "barren woman" illustrate YHWH's concern for those on the margins.

Psalm 114 is a hymn of praise, unusual in that it neither addresses the divine nor recounts YHWH's deeds directly (Mays, 364). Rhetorical questions addressed to the sea, Jordan, mountains, and hills introduce YHWH's presence as the key element of the psalm. Economical in its use of words, this psalm again links God's action in Israel's particular experience with divine control over mythological forces (cf. Psalm 74).

Psalm 115 is a communal hymn centered on the issue of "trust." Briefly addressing God to affirm divine steadfast love and truth, the remainder of the psalm responds to the taunt of the nations: "where is your God?" (cf. Ps. 79:10; Isa. 36:18-20). It also critiques those who worship idols they have made, which reflects a temptation in the postexilic period (cf. 106:36, 38; Isa. 44:9-20). Whereas others *trust* in idols, the psalmist exhorts Israel, the priesthood, and those "who fear YHWH" to *trust* in God; in return, YHWH will be "their help and shield" and will bless them (115:9-13). The ending reciprocates divine blessing, with the people committing to bless YHWH forever; *halelu yah*!

Psalm 116, which is divided into two in Greek and Latin Bibles, gives thanks for deliverance from distress. The opening "I love YHWH" proves unique in the Psalms (Mays, 370) and links to the main motif of the previous, since "love" moves beyond emotional attachment to connote strong loyalty (Gen. 25:28; Exod. 20:6). The psalm follows a clear thanksgiving pattern with an opening, a description of distress and divine response, and a commitment to praise and fulfill a vow. The death of the faithful is "costly" or "grievous" to YHWH, since death eliminates their praise (116:15, Mays, 370; Ps. 115:17). The final reference to the congregation and temple underscores that thanksgiving reflects a public testimony meant to inspire and exhort the broader community, while *halelu yah* provides an opportunity for others to join the psalmist's thanksgiving (116:17-19).

Psalm 117 exemplifies the basic elements of a hymn: a call, this time for all peoples, to "praise YHWH" and an affirmation of the steadfast love and truth/faithfulness of YHWH.

Psalm 118 combines hymnic elements with others derived from individual thanksgiving. The initial verses again underscore divine steadfast love with an antiphonal call consisting of a familiar liturgical element of thanksgiving to the same groups identified in Psalm 115 (118:1-4; cf. 106:1; 107:1; 136). The psalm then shifts to a tightly structured song in which an individual voice gives thanks for deliverance from enemies, leading to the rhetorical query: "what can mortals do to me?" (v. 6; cf. 56:11). The psalmist illustrates the motif of divine help by contrasting "taking refuge" in God and trusting in mortals, "cutting off" (literally "circumcising") the surrounding threat (118:7-13). The psalmist's emphatic repetition of "the right hand of YHWH" and verbatim repetition of the praise from the "Song of the Sea" in Exodus 15 underscores a connection to the exodus (118:14; Exod. 15:2; cf. Isa. 12:2). The remainder of the psalm reflects a liturgical setting with several speakers, including an entrance appeal and response (cf. Ps. 24:7-10), individual thanksgiving and communal response, a communal blessing linked to a procession, and a declaration of thankful intimacy (118:19-29). The return to the same thanksgiving refrain frames the psalm with God's steadfast love (cf. vv. 1-4; Mays, 374).

Psalm 119, the longest chapter in the Bible, is an extended hymn that praises God and declares loyalty to law (*torah*). This third torah psalm (cf. Psalms 1; 19) is an elaborate acrostic poem structured in eight-verse blocks, with each section corresponding to consecutive letters of the Hebrew alphabet; 22 letters and 8 verses per letter result in 176 verses of poetic text. The psalm repeatedly employs seven terms related to torah: "decrees," "statutes," "commandments," "ordinances," "word," "precepts," and "promise/saying"; with few exceptions, at least one of these terms appears in each verse of the poem. Just as it employs motifs and vocabulary from each genre of the Psalms, Psalm 119 also draws on material from other scriptural books. After initial "happy are . . ." sayings (119:1-3), the remainder of the psalm addresses God, continually emphasizing commitment to *your* law, *your* decrees, *your* statutes; a momentary shift to directly address evildoers underscores this basic pattern (119:115; cf. 6:6). The psalmist's stance as God's "servant," a term that appears fifteen times, is not restricted to a Davidic king (89:3, 20, 39) or exceptional figure such as Abraham (105:6, 42) or Moses (105:26), but anyone committed to following God's torah. Though individual in form, Psalm 119 serves a didactic function to instruct its listeners (Gerstenberger 2001, 316).

▮ THE TEXT IN THE INTERPRETIVE TRADITION

Psalms 113–118, referred to as *hallel* or "praise," became a significant liturgical unit used during the Passover in early Judaism (Gerstenberger 2001, 280) that continued to be recited during the home Passover seder meal as well as in the daily liturgy for all three major pilgrim festivals: Passover, Feast of Weeks (Pentecost), and Feast of Booths (Holladay, 143).

The New Testament already draws on Psalm 118 to portray Jesus and his passion, referring to the builder's rejection of the cornerstone and the crowd using the phrase "blessed is he who comes in the name of the LORD" as Jesus enters Jerusalem (118:22, 26). Psalm 118 was later one of Luther's favorites. Reading Israel as "the elect children of God," Luther emphasizes the central motif of trust, while also tying the psalmist's setting of being surrounded to his own conflict with "the pope and his vermin"; interestingly, Luther also reinterprets "cutting them off," saying that "we Christians crush the heathen through our prayers" (118:10-14). Luther read "I shall not die" as referring to "eternal life," the "gates" as the parish, Jesus Christ as the king of Palm Sunday and the rejected "cornerstone . . . , and the builders who reject him are the Jewish and papal leadership who fail to recognize God's marvelously free grace" (Hals 1983, 278–82).

◼ THE TEXT IN CONTEMPORARY DISCUSSION

As addressed repeatedly, the psalmists cry out from social—as well as physical—distress. Therefore, Psalms 116 and 118 prove significant in that they reflect structured moments of public and social rehabilitation and reentry (Jacobson, 133). While this is sometimes practiced in our day when overcoming sickness, within the criminal justice system the opposite is often the case. Whereas North American society thrives on social shame and stigmatization in criminal justice proceedings, it lacks an equivalent to transform an individual's status or symbolically reintegrate former offenders into their communities, a complex issue that relates to earlier discussions on confession and abuse (cf. Psalms 51; 55).

Finally, the postexilic setting of this section and its role in identity formation proves striking. As Psalm 119 reflects, the gift of torah is to be celebrated and cherished, and comes with the expectation of obedience; far from an unbearable burden or impossibility, Psalm 119 revels in the law as God's blueprint for abundant life (cf. Deut. 30:11-20). Counterintuitively, it was the temple's destruction and the Babylonian exile (587 BCE) that gave rise to the birth of the synagogue, a transformation that helped Judaism to survive the second temple's destruction. To this day "the Talmud" refers to the *Babylonian* rather than the Jerusalem Talmud as the more authoritative collection in the Oral Torah, which witnesses to Babylon's vital significance as a center of Jewish learning well into the Common Era.

Psalms 120–134: Pilgrimage "Songs of Ascent"

◼ THE TEXT IN ITS ANCIENT CONTEXT

Psalms 120–134 are a series of short psalms identified in their headings as "Song(s) of Ascent." The latter Hebrew term appears in reference to "going up" to Jerusalem (122:4) and relates to an offering associated with temple liturgy. While different genres of psalms appear in this section, their liturgical language and frequent references to Jerusalem and Zion reflect a connection to pilgrimage (Mays, 385–86).

Psalm 120 is an individual lament calling for YHWH to rescue the psalmist from malicious speech. The final verses express frustration about living with one who "hates peace," reflecting the social aspect of this term as well-being or good relationships and suggesting physical conflict: "I [am] *peace*, but when(ever) I speak, they [are] for war" (120:6-7). Here the psalmist claims a direct link to or even embodiment of *shalom* that the NRSV's "I am *for* peace" does not capture.

Psalm 121 is a poem of assurance directed to a social audience that moves from an initial rhetorical question to a declaration of confidence that unites cosmic and intimate aspects of the divine, seeing YHWH both as creator and "my help" (121:1-2; cf. 40:17; 70:5). The response, presumably spoken to the initial speaker by a liturgical leader or functionary (Gerstenberger, 2001, 324), focuses on YHWH's role as "your *keeper*"; indeed, the Hebrew root "keep" (*shamar*) appears six times (121:3-8). Both in theme and vocabulary, this psalm proves reminiscent of other psalms of assurance (cf. Psalm 91).

Psalm 122, the first of three ascent songs attributed to David (see also Psalms 124; 131), exemplifies a pilgrimage song. Reference to being "within your gates" and rejoicing in the opportunity to "*go up*" to Jerusalem and enter the temple suggest it functioned as a "song of arrival" for pilgrims (122:1-4). Reference to the thrones "of justice" and "of the house of David" may refer to dispute mechanisms initiated by David and carried into the postexilic context (122:5, cf. 2 Sam. 8:15; 15:1-6; Mays, 392–93). Wishes for the peace of Jerusalem for the temple's sake illustrate its liturgical significance within pilgrimage traditions (cf. 120:6-7).

Psalm 123 calls for mercy and shifts from the previous speech about God to address YHWH directly. The metaphors of a male and female servant underscore both the expectancy and subordinate position of the psalmist. The double call for mercy or favor corresponds to the negative doublets in the final verses; they "have had more than enough of contempt" (123:3-4). The move from the voice of an individual to a communal "we" suggests the individual functions as a representative or spokesperson for a larger group.

Psalm 124, a second ascent song "of David" (cf. 122), articulates communal thanksgiving that builds on the motif of YHWH, maker of heaven and earth, as "help" (124:8; cf. 121:1-2). Initial repetition underscores that this has been experienced as YHWH's being "on our side" (literally "for" or "of" us; cf. Josh. 5:13-15). Though water imagery is used, the primary concern here concerns when "men (*'adam*) rose over us" (124:2, author trans.). The threefold repetition of "our souls" (124:4, 5, 7) emphasizes that their whole being was threatened; whereas "soul" implies a distinction from the body, the Hebrew *nefesh* reflects one's whole being or self. The liturgical "blessed be YHWH" introduces the metaphor of an escaping bird, which describes the fulfillment of a wish elsewhere (124:6-7; cf. 11:1; 55:6; 102:7).

Psalm 125 employs the physical attributes of Zion to depict the eternal stability of "those who trust in the LORD." Where elsewhere the psalmist complains of being surrounded by enemies or the wicked, here the hills around Jerusalem illustrate how YHWH "surrounds his people" (125:2; cf. 34:7). The "the staff of wickedness," which appears only here in the Old Testament, may refer to the external threat of foreign domination or to the internal one of injustice (Mays, 398). The concluding verse reiterates the psalm's focus on the people: "Peace be upon Israel" (cf. 128:6); by extending the *shalom* of Jerusalem and the temple to those who trust in YHWH (125:1; cf. Ps. 122:6-7), the psalm provides a poignant affirmation for pilgrims from beyond the city walls.

Psalm 126 speaks of the restoration of Zion and looks forward to an even more complete restoration of the people. The phrase "the LORD turned the captivity of Zion" applies characteristic language from the prophets to Zion itself (cf. Deut. 30:3; Jer. 29:14; Amos 9:14). The restoration most probably refers to the restoration of the temple in the postexilic period, though the New

Jewish Publication Society translation renders the entire psalm as a hope for the future. The symmetry of the psalm emerges from several repetitions ("restore," 126:1, 3; "then," twice in 126:2) that moves from a broader recognition of what YHWH has done "for them" to a corporate recognition of God's action "for us," and then an appeal for a future, more complete restoration (126:2-4). The metaphor of a wadi or seasonal stream underscores the need for restoration, while the images of sowing and reaping build on ancient Near Eastern motifs that reflect current difficulty and anticipated joy (Mays, 400).

Psalm 127, one of two psalms linked to Solomon (see also Psalm 72), employs "house" in two different ways to highlight YHWH's central significance. The initial depiction of building, guarding, and work without God as empty (127:1-2) plays on Solomon's reputation as a house-builder and this motif within wisdom literature (cf. 1 Kgs. 6:1; 7:1; Prov. 9:1; 14:1). The second section uses "house" as family or offspring (cf. 2 Sam. 7:5, 11) and "inheritance" to refer to children (literally "sons") rather than possessions or land (cf. Deut. 4:21; 26:1). The parent is "happy" in part because offspring will be able to speak "in the gate," the traditional place of adjudication and decision (cf. Ruth 4:1-6; Job 5:4; Prov. 31:23, 31).

Psalm 128 declares "happy" those who "fear YHWH," which the parallel phrase "walk in his ways" links to torah obedience (128:1, 4; cf. 112:1), because they will enjoy blessings of produce, wife, and children. While the last "blessing" of witnessing the well-being of Jerusalem and long life has a singular verb form and so addresses everyone who "fears YHWH," the final "peace be upon Israel" extends this blessing to the larger people (cf. 125:5). The psalm also emphasizes Zion's special status as the site from which divine blessing comes.

Psalm 129 extends the form of individual thanksgiving to the community (129:1-2; cf. 124:1-2). Withstanding extended abuse from enemies leads to a confident affirmation of YHWH's righteousness and initiates a series of imprecations against "all who hate Zion," which again reflects the close identification of the psalmist and the holy hill (129:5-8).

Psalm 130, the sixth "penitential prayer" in the Psalter (see Psalm 51), employs the form of an individual lament to exhort Israel to hope in YHWH. An initial invocation, cry, and reflection on sin and the possibility of forgiveness address God directly. The remainder describes how "my entire being (*naphshi*)" hopes and waits for YHWH, which is then reiterated in the exhortation to Israel. The psalm affirms God's steadfast love as the key element for addressing sin and, like the previous, concludes by moving from the individual to focus on the community, Israel.

Psalm 131, another "psalm of David" (cf. 124), continues the motif of hope by emphasizing the psalmist's patient rather than haughty stance. The metaphor of a weaned child provides the emotional draw of the psalm, while the call for Israel to "hope in YHWH" repeats the conclusion of the former (131:3; 130:7).

Psalm 132 reiterates God's commitment to the Davidic covenant and reasserts the intimate connection between Zion and the messiah. It alternates between the voice of the psalmist and direct quotations of the vows of, first, David (132:1-5; cf. 2 Samuel 6–7; Gerstenberger 2001, 363) and then YHWH (132:11-12; cf. 2 Sam. 7:12-16; 1 Kgs. 2:4; 11:38-39). The final section provides God's affirmative response and commitment to act on behalf of the priests, the faithful, and David "my anointed/messiah" (132:14-18). The psalm reasserts the link between the dominant Davidic king as servant and anointed (132:10, 17; cf. Ps. 89:4) and the divine warrior, represented by the ark and might of YHWH. Where book 4 downplayed the Davidic messiah in favor of YHWH as king, here this figure reappears in familiar style (cf. Psalms 2; 89a).

Psalms 133–134 together close the Songs of Ascent. Psalm 133 describes in glowing terms the harmony when "kindred [literally "brothers"] live together in unity" (133:1), affirming the pilgrims' communal experience. The dual images of oil running down Aaron's head and beard and dew on Mount Hermon witness to divine anointing and abundance. Psalm 134 concludes the Songs of Ascent with a blessing, addressed to "all you servants/worshipers of YHWH" (134:1). Lifting arms in the night paints a picture of ancient worship, perhaps the liturgical conclusion of a pilgrimage festival. In any case, "the psalm now stands in a literary rather than a liturgical location" (Mays, 415). It concludes in symmetry that embodies the intimacy between God and people: just as God's servants *bless* YHWH, the psalm concludes with "May YHWH . . . bless you." The divine depiction as "maker of heaven and earth," a phrase unique to book 5 of the Psalter (134:3; cf. Ps. 115:15; 121:2; 124:8; 146:5), reiterates the one being worshiped as the source of blessing.

▍ THE TEXT IN THE INTERPRETIVE TRADITION

The Songs of Ascent (120–134) have continued to function liturgically, having been used to pray for the souls of deceased individuals in the "Office for the Dead," during Easter, and in medieval "Prymers" or "first prayers" (Gillingham, 55, 103; see Psalm 102).

Psalm 126 illustrates the flexibility of such material, having been used as a reading for thanksgiving, advent, and lent. In the first case references to sowing and reaping function in a straightforward sense, while the latter builds more figuratively on its rich language. The description of kindred/ brothers "living together in unity" has prompted the use of Psalm 133 as a reading for the Lord's Supper, and already Augustine pointed to this psalm as significant for founding monastic communities (Mays, 400, 414).

▍ THE TEXT IN CONTEMPORARY DISCUSSION

The Songs of Ascent witness to the significance of pilgrimage and place, with consistent reference to Jerusalem and Zion underscoring their special status. The connection between adoration and place, however, has been a mixed blessing. Within the Christian tradition it was the special status of the "Holy Land" that prompted Christian crusaders to "go up" to Jerusalem, also as a form of pilgrimage.

The link between pilgrimage and communal identity is further underscored in the contemporary setting, where some Jews refer to moving to Israel as "making *aliyah*" or "going up," adopting pilgrimage language to speak of permanent relocation. At the same time, within contemporary Israel and Palestine, there are interweaving narratives of historic injustice and tragedy, victimhood and victimization, strength and weakness, hope and despair, identity and land. With this context in mind, the opening "Psalm of Ascent" proves particularly striking.

> Too long have I had my dwelling among those who hate *peace* (*shalom*).
> I am *peace*, but when I speak they are for war. (120:6-7)

The psalm speaks of deep-rooted animosity and suspicion, with a sense of victimization that is raw and urgent. While the issue here seems intractable, Psalm 120 also functions as an invitation to begin to "go up."

A contemporary challenge lies in attending to the many contemporary and discordant voices within Israel and Palestine, and empathetically discerning what we hear (Psalms 44; 55; 137). The call to "pray for the peace of Jerusalem" and the possibility of pervasive well-being remains both suggestive and elusive (122:6). We pray for the day when Jewish, Muslim, and Christian inhabitants of these lands may say together: "How very good and pleasant it is when kindred live together in unity!" (Ps. 133:1).

Psalms 135–145: From Distress to Praise

▮ THE TEXT IN ITS ANCIENT CONTEXT

In addition to reflecting a wide range of emotions, settings, and genres, Psalms 135–145 include the final Davidic collection of the Psalter, which frames book 5 (138–145; cf. 108–110).

Psalm 135 is a hymn celebrating the sovereignty of YHWH, whose opening and conclusion reflect a liturgical call and response that invites different groups to "praise" and then "bless" YHWH (135:1-4, 19-21). The psalm shifts to first person to describe YHWH's status "above all gods," reflected in God's control over creation and mythological forces as well as the nations (cf. Ps. 74:12-17; 104:24-26; Psalm 105); the God of the cosmos is also the one who has acted on behalf of Israel in the exodus and provided the gift of land. Momentary address to YHWH introduces confidence in God's judgment and compassion (v. 13), a telling contrast to the inaction of idols (cf. Ps. 115:4-8; Isa. 44:18). The servants of Pharaoh and those who make and trust in idols provide the negative foil for the servants of YHWH and so reinforce the close identification of YHWH with "his people" Israel.

Psalm 136 represents another antiphonal hymn, where a leading voice speaks the initial lines and the gathered assembly responds with the chorus: "for his steadfast love endures forever." In doing so, the psalm recounts and celebrates God's role in creation, the exodus, and providing the land (cf. Psalm 105).

Psalm 137, a communal lament for Jerusalem, stands in stark contrast to the previous psalms. Set in Babylon, Zion exists as a memory rather than a lived reality. The prior conviction of Zion's inviolability adds salt to the wound when captors ask for a "song of Zion" (137:3-4; cf. 48:8-14; 132:13-18), while reference to a "foreign (*nekar*) land" implicitly links Babylon to the idolatry condemned elsewhere (Ps. 135:15-18; cf. Deut. 31:16; Josh. 24:20-23; Prov. 7:5). While direct address to "daughter Babylon" mirrors the earlier speech to Jerusalem, here the psalmist articulates drastic, vengeful wishes that shock contemporary readers: "Happy is the one who seizes and dashes your children against the rock" (137:9). While a few passages in the Old Testament refer to such harsh treatment in military contexts (e.g., 2 Kgs. 8:12; Hosea 10:14; Nah. 3:10), this passage reflects a desire for Babylon to be paid back in kind rather than personal vengeance. Memory is a key element here: the captives remember Zion and curse themselves if they "do not remember" Jerusalem (137:1,

5-6), which then grounds the imperative plea for YHWH to also remember. This psalm implicitly questions whether God will remember the covenant with Zion and David voiced in earlier psalms (89a, 132), or whether divine steadfast love will not prove trustworthy. The vengeful wishes here should not lead the reader to disregard the existential crisis it reflects (see section below).

Psalm 138 begins the final "of David" collection (138–145) with thanksgiving, shifting back and forth between direct address to and speech about YHWH. The initial vow to "give you thanks . . . before the gods (*'elohim*)," rendered "angels" in the Septuagint, suggests a polytheistic context (cf. Psalm 82); "your holy temple" contrasts with the Babylonian context, during which the temple lay in ruins. This psalm returns to praise God's steadfast love and truth/faithfulness (cf. Ps. 25:10; 86:15) for responding to the psalmist's distress, and sees his own praise as anticipating that of the "kings of the earth" (138:2-4). The "height" of YHWH draws attention to divine attention to the lowly, while the psalmist enjoys divine protection from enemies. The final praise for God's steadfast love reflects a liturgical formula used elsewhere and prompts an appeal for it to be sustained (138:8; Ps. 136).

Psalm 139, a second psalm "of David" that addresses God throughout, portrays YHWH's intimate knowledge and care for the psalmist. An initial description leads to a series of rhetorical questions confirming the pervasive divine presence; Jonah provides a case in point for one attempting to flee from God's presence (139:7; Jon. 1:3). "You knit me together in my mother's womb" introduces the next part of the psalm, leading to what at first glance seems a dramatic shift in tone from meditating on God's thoughts to calling for the destruction of the wicked (139:17-22). However, the strident imprecations here reflect the logic of the psalm, extending the shared intimacy between God and the psalmist to claim that God's enemies are those of the psalmist as well (cf. Ps. 26:5; 31:6). The concluding call for God to "search me" reflects a commitment to introspection and self-critique that proves significant after such strident self-identification with God.

Psalm 140, another "psalm of David," is an individual lament that calls on YHWH for deliverance from violent men. The psalmist intermingles statements of confidence with pleas for help, before calling for the destruction of the enemy by allowing the adversaries' designs to fall on themselves (140:6-10; 69:22). The psalm concludes with a confident assertion addressed to a social audience regarding divine justice for the poor and needy, and anticipates thanksgiving from the righteous.

Psalm 141, yet another "psalm of David," inverts the usual language of individual lament to ask God to preserve the psalmist himself from evil. An initial invocation calling on YHWH to come quickly moves to an appeal for the psalmist's prayer and liturgical gestures to be counted as sacrifices. The psalmist then appeals to God to guard him from joining forces or even becoming one of the "evildoers" (131:3-4; cf. 6:8). While "guard my mouth" addresses the persistent issue of malicious speech, the psalmist also asks God to keep him from evil, wickedness, and evildoers. Although the translation of 141:5-7 proves elusive, the motif continues since the psalmist's commitment to "delightful" words contrasts with his wicked potential, further underscored by the resonance between "my mouth" and the "mouth of Sheol" (141:3, 7). The psalmist looks to YHWH for orientation and to seek refuge (141:8), reiterating a key theme from early in the Psalter (Ps. 2:12; 7:1; 11:1; cf. 144:2). The final appeal to "guard me" transforms the trap described elsewhere as the vindictive attack of the enemies to the seductive allure of joining forces with "evildoers" (141:9; cf. 140:5).

Psalm 142, set as David "in the cave" by a contextual heading (cf. 1 Sam. 22:1; 24:3-4; Psalms 3; 51), is an unusual individual lament that begins by describing an appeal to YHWH in the third person rather than an invocation directed to God. Three consecutive imperatives to "attend," "rescue," and "bring me out" exemplify the psalmist's stance of taking refuge in God (142:5-7). The concluding vow to praise describes recognition and social rehabilitation among the righteous (cf. Psalm 88).

Psalm 143, the third consecutive prayer/lament (*tefillah*) of David (v. 1; cf. 141:2; 142:1), employs characteristic vocabulary to call directly on God for help from enemies. Following an invocation appealing to "your faithfulness" and "your righteousness," the beleaguered psalmist's loss of spirit prompts him to "remember" and "meditate" on God's past action, so that his entire being (*nephesh*) thirsts for God (143:1-6). Appeals for YHWH to "answer," "not hide your face," "rescue," and "teach me" are grounded in divine steadfast love and the psalmist's trust (143:7-10). This in turn leads to the final appeal for God's righteousness and steadfast love to manifest themselves by preserving the psalmist on one hand and dealing harshly with the enemies on the other.

While literary dependence is difficult to demonstrate, Psalm 144 combines vocabulary and motifs from previous psalms to address a new setting (Gerstenberger 2001, 427). The initial description of God, including that he "trains my hands for war," and the high depiction of humans resonate elsewhere (Ps. 144:1-7; cf. Ps. 8:4; 18:1-2, 9, 34). The psalm calls on the cosmic YHWH to respond to the psalmist's plight, brought on him by foreigners and their emptiness (144:7-8, 11; cf. 137:4; 139:20). The commitment to "sing a new song," linked to God's rescuing "his servant David" from enemies, resonates with royal psalms (144:9-11; cf. Ps. 18:1; 89:4, 21; 132:10). The concluding wishes for the well-being of the community (144:12-14; cf. 128:1-3) and happiness for "the people whose God is the Lord" (144:15; cf. 33:12) suggest that here again the well-being of the people is intimately tied with that of the Davidic king (cf. Psalm 72).

Psalm 145 is an acrostic hymn that provides the "climax" for book 5 and introduces the praise that closes the Psalter as a whole (Wilson, 225). The only psalm whose heading reads a "*praise* (*tehillah*) of David," it alternates back and forth between praises to God and descriptions about the divine. Heard as the voice of David, the opening proves particularly striking since it highlights *God* as king, and so reiterates the major motif from book 4 (145:1; 93:1; 97:1; 99:1). The initial praise culminates in the quotation of the description of YHWH from Exodus, acclaiming God's compassion and steadfast love (145:8; cf. Exod. 34:6; Ps. 86:15; 103:8), which in turn leads to the emphatic insistence that "the Lord is good to *all*, and his *compassion* is over *all* that he has made." From this point on, the word "every/all" (*kol*) appears fourteen more times (seventeen in total in this psalm), which gives the psalm a breathless "comprehensiveness" as it underscores the divine-king motif and insists on God's concern for the lowly and those who cry out (145:11-19; Mays, 437–38). The psalmist reiterates the basic conviction from the outset of the Psalter that YHWH "watches over *all* who love him (the 'righteous'), but *all* the wicked he will destroy" (145:20; 1:6). This double "all" asserts comprehensive surety, despite the counterevidence in the intervening psalms themselves. The final intention to praise YHWH and claim that "*all* flesh will bless his holy name" serves a double purpose, forming an inclusio with the first verse of this psalm and introducing the central motif of the final section (146–150; Wilson, 225–26).

∎ THE TEXT IN THE INTERPRETIVE TRADITION

Within Jewish liturgy, Psalm 137 is significant in that it is used daily in the "blessing after meals" on weekdays, and so links the home meal to remembering the "altar of the sacrifice in the temple" and the "loss of the temple in Jerusalem" (Holladay, 145).

While Babylon and Jerusalem already begin to function symbolically within the New Testament, the early church fathers tend to interpret this psalm allegorically. In a particularly striking example, Augustine provides an allegorical interpretation that builds on Origen and Jerome to interpret the children of Babylon as "newly-born evil desires" that his listeners should eliminate by dashing them against the "rock," which is Christ, before they become deep-rooted habits. For Augustine, this psalm also represents an ecclesial lament that recalls the church's persecution by its adversaries that predicts rather than advocates for divine judgment, with the goal of repentance (Thompson, 57–58).

∎ THE TEXT IN CONTEMPORARY DISCUSSION

The drastic imprecations of Psalm 137 illustrate the vital significance of attending to "voice" for interpreting psalms. While this psalm can be interpreted as vindictive and hopelessly violent, its utter disorientation and despair also provides an opportunity for empathy with the millions of contemporary people who have been ravaged and displaced by war. Where dealing with imprecations in the psalms can be treated as an abstract philosophical problem—or even a reason to dismiss or even functionally eliminate offending biblical material—an empathetic hearing of Psalm 137 as an expression of posttraumatic stress moves beyond a justification of violence or call for militant action by those seeking to inflict it on others; the same words can have a very different function and significance when spoken by a traumatized refugee rather than a president or (para)military commander. The issue becomes particularly complex when these people may be one and the same (cf. Psalm 55). Unfortunately, in many contemporary settings, people do not suffer from *post*traumatic stress, since their distress is ongoing. Psalm 137 does not call on God to give the psalmist or his community the strength or skill to enact vengeance, even as it dramatically evokes the anger and despair of displacement (cf. Ps. 18:34, 47; 149:6-9; see Psalm 109).

Psalm 141 proves particularly significant in this regard. Where the psalmists repeatedly cry out to YHWH to free them from the vicious speech and wicked actions of the enemy, this psalm reflects how tempting it can be to collude with these "doers of evil." Psalm 141 should give us pause, since it reflects the possibility of becoming one of the wicked and so challenges the tendency to always see ourselves on the side of right, justice, and equity (see Psalm 44). Within the Christian tradition, the request here resonates with the familiar phrase from the Lord's Prayer: "Lead us not into temptation"; the concluding introspection following the imprecation of Psalm 139 points in a similar direction.

Psalms 146–150: Praise YHWH—Hallelujah!

▌THE TEXT IN ITS ANCIENT CONTEXT

Psalms 146–150 enact the concluding call of the previous psalm for all flesh to bless YHWH (Ps. 145:21). Each psalm begins and ends with *halelu yah* ("praise YHWH!"), calling for praise in ever-broadening circles: from an individual voice (David, 146), to Israel and Jerusalem (147), the angels and creation (148), and finally "all flesh" (150; Wilson, 193–94). Rather than an isolated section or summary of book 5, these psalms function as a doxological conclusion to the Psalter as a whole.

Psalm 146 fulfills the individual praise promised earlier (145:21). The psalmist begins with direct address to "my soul" and a vow to lifelong praise before addressing a social audience, exhorting his listeners to not trust in princes, whose spirit is temporary (147:1-4); again, this motif proves particularly striking if heard as the voice of David (cf. 145:21; Wilson, 226). The wisdom saying "happy are those . . ." emphasizes hope in God as "maker of heavens and earth," "doer of justice," and "giver of food" (146:5-7), which lead to a series of emphatic statements: "*YHWH* sets . . . *YHWH* opens." The fivefold repetition of the divine name and use of participles emphasizes that *this* God is active, with a strong focus on liberation and the plight of the socially marginal. The final verse extends the previous claim into the future, so that "YHWH reigns" (93:1; 97:1; 99:1) here becomes "YHWH will [continue to] reign *forever*" (v. 10). *Halelu yah*!

Psalm 147 elicits communal praise for YHWH, reiterating God's care for the downtrodden and stance against the wicked. Again the psalmist describes YHWH with a string of participles focused on divine social commitments and God's role as creator. God does not delight in military might (the "strength of the horse") but in those who "fear him" and hope in divine steadfast love (147:10-11), just as those whose delight lies in YHWH's torah are "happy" (Psalm 1:2). The LXX takes the subsequent *halelu yah*, a call to Jerusalem and Zion themselves to "praise YHWH," as the beginning of a new psalm, and divides it here (147:12; Gerstenberger 2001, 444). In any case, the peace of the city derives from YHWH and no one else (147:14). Where the prince's spirit is fleeting, God's spirit and word act together (146:3-4; 147:18); Israel is distinct not by its own merits but because it alone has received this word. While the term *torah* does not appear, word, statutes, and ordinances all relate to this term elsewhere (cf. Deut. 4:5-8; Psalm 119). The gift of torah is yet another reason for praise: *Halelu yah*!

Psalm 148 expands the praise still further, with six consecutive imperative calls to heavens, angels, hosts, and the cosmos to "praise him!" (148:1-4). The sequence and all-encompassing call to creation, including the mythological elements of sea monsters and the deeps, recalls the Genesis creation account and underscores God's sovereignty and control (148:7; Gen. 1:21 cf. Psalms 74; 104). The final call to all of humanity underscores the special status of "his people," "his faithful ones," and "the children of Israel." *Halelu yah*!

Psalm 149 builds on the previous psalm, but concentrates on the faithful (149:2, 5, 9; 148:14). The initial call to praise invites listeners into the company of the faithful, linking the children of Zion with YHWH as king, who "takes pleasure in his people" (149:4; cf. Ps. 93:1; 147:11). Where elsewhere vengeance is reserved for God or the Davidic king (18:47; 79:10; 94:1; 99:8), this psalm calls on the people themselves as agents for vengeance and judgment in a highly unusual fashion. Given the ambiguity of the Hebrew verb forms here, it is unclear whether this section should be read as a wish ("Let . . .") or future ("The high praises of God will be . . ."), and so scholars debate whether this passage is best seen in light of a historical link to "theologically sanctioned violence" or as referring to an eschatological future (149:5-9; Gerstenberger 2001, 454–55; cf. Psalm 72). In either case, the focus here lies in the judgment of ruling and socioeconomic elites and salvation for the humble (149:4; Brueggemann, 125); the tables are turned so those formerly bound are liberated, while those who acted with impunity are bound (146:7; 149:8; cf. 2:3). *Halelu yah*!

Psalm 150 concludes the Psalter with a resounding call to "praise," repeating the imperative *halelu* twelve times in its six verses. The psalm moves from describing YHWH to a picture of liturgical worship (150:1-5); the blowing of the shofar (ram's horn) was used as a summons in liturgical and military contexts (150:3; see Lev. 25:9; Josh. 6:8-9; Judg. 6:34). The concluding call to praise for "anything that breathes" summarizes not only the concluding "Hallelu" psalms (146–150) but also the entire Psalter, rearticulating the previous call (150:6; see Ps. 145:21; Wilson, 194). *Halelu yah*!

▌▌ THE TEXT IN THE INTERPRETIVE TRADITION

While the *Midrash on the Psalms* describes the reason for vengeance in Psalm 149 as the nations' treatment of Israel, it also limits this to foreign kings rather than the "common people" (149:8; cf. 2:2). Further, it draws on other passages to transform this psalm's unusual call for the "faithful . . . to execute vengeance on the nations" into God's vengeance, an interpretive move similar to Paul in Romans 12 (see Ps. 109; also "Contemporary Discussion" below, p. 597; cf. Deut. 32:43; Nah. 1:2; Braude 2:384).

Similarly, the exceedingly rare phrase in the Greek Bible of "two-edged" (literally "two-mouthed") sword links this passage to the "son of man" in Revelation (cf. Ps. 149:6 LXX; cf. Sir. 21:3; Rev. 1:16; 2:12), where it is both limited to Christ and transformed into his speech (cf. Heb. 4:12). In a similar vein, within Revelation the conquering "lion of Judah" is revealed as the slaughtered lamb, while the people tread a path of martyrdom rather than vengeance (Rev. 5:5-6; 6:10-11).

Where Christians may assume that the psalmist's call for God's vengeance represents an Old Testament problem (Ps. 75; 83; 94), the setting of oppression and persecution prompts similar language in the New Testament as well (cf. Ps. 79:10; Rev. 6:10). The key shift in the New Testament lies not in the absence of God's judgment, but in the conviction that it is *God's* role to execute vengeance and not that of the believing community (cf. Psalm 18; Matt. 5:38-45; 25:31-46; Rom. 12:17-21; Rev. 6:11).

▌▌ THE TEXT IN CONTEMPORARY DISCUSSION

The Psalms' concluding call to praise YHWH is based on who God is; humans join in as one part of the larger creation, a cosmic chorus praising its maker. This hymnic language does not eclipse the deeply personal and emotional language of much of the Psalter, but rather provides its grounding and orientation.

We may wonder why Psalm 149 ruins such a wonderful litany of praise. Rather than sidestep this psalm, perhaps it too can be a significant hermeneutical irritant for our time. In an "age of terror," it is important for Jews and Christians alike to recognize calls for religiously based violence within our own traditions rather than merely critiquing those beyond them. For communities of faith dedicated to following Jesus Christ as Lord—and not Caesar(s), ancient or contemporary—such calls to become instruments of divine vengeance represent a temptation rather than fulfillment of the divine will. Once again, the dilemma represented by this passage lies not so much in the presence of such words in Scripture as in the orientation and basic commitments of the community dedicated to interpret it (see discussion of Psalm 109). Indeed, while there are many historical examples where biblical violence has been employed to legitimate or sanction their own, to treat such a passage in this way in the Christian tradition fails to recognize the transformation of vengeance reflected in the New Testament.

At the same time, Psalm 149 underscores that the anticipated praise of YHWH by all nations, peoples, and rulers has yet to become a reality. We live with the ongoing tension of a promise and conviction yet to be fulfilled. Against persistent appearances to the contrary, the Psalms challenge contemporary listeners to declare that God does watch over his people, and that injustice and oppression will not have the last word. As we join in the resounding praise, we also do so aware that we may be part of the systems and powers that God opposes and will bring to judgment (Psalm 141). Rather than triumphant imperialism or smug self-satisfaction, the cacophony of praise at the end of the Psalms prompts ongoing introspection (cf. Psalm 139), whereby we evaluate whether we are indeed abandoning ourselves in the radical trust of God (Brueggemann, 126–29).

Works Cited

Adamo, David Tuesday. 2009. "Psalm 29 in Africa Indigenous Churches in Nigeria." In *Psalm 29 Through Time and Tradition*, edited by Lowell K. Handy, 126–43. Princeton Theological Monograph Series 110. Eugene, OR: Pickwick.

Alter, Robert. 1985. *The Art of Biblical Poetry*. New York: Basic.

Anderson, Bernhard W., and Steven Bishop. 2000. *Out of the Depths: The Psalms Speak for Us Today*. 3rd ed. Louisville: Westminster John Knox.

Bail, Ulrike. 1998. "'O God, Hear My Prayer': Psalm 55 and Violence Against Women." In *Wisdom and Psalms: A Feminist Companion to the Bible*, edited by Athalya Brenner and Carole R. Fontaine, 242–63. Sheffield: Sheffield Academic Press.

Berry, Wendell. 1993. "Christianity and the Survival of Creation." In *Sex, Economy, Freedom and Community: Eight Essays*, 93–116. New York: Pantheon.

Blumenthal, David R. 1993. *Facing the Abusing God: A Theology of Protest*. Louisville: Westminster John Knox.

Bonhoeffer, Dietrich. 2005. *Prayerbook of the Bible: An Introduction to the Psalms*. In *Life Together and Prayerbook of the Bible*, edited by Geffrey B. Kelly, 141–81. Translated by Daniel W. Bloesch and James H. Burtness. Dietrich Bonhoeffer Works 5. Minneapolis: Fortress Press.

Braude, William G., trans. 1959. *The Midrash on Psalms*, 2 vols. Yale Judaica Series 13. New Haven: Yale University Press.

Brueggemann, Walter. 1995. *The Psalms and the Life of Faith*. Edited by Patrick D. Miller. Minneapolis: Fortress Press.

Childs, Brevard S. 1971. "Psalm Titles and Midrashic Exegesis." *JSS* 16, no. 2:137–50.

Cottrill, Amy C. 2008. *Language, Power, and Identity in the Lament Psalms of the Individual*. LHB/OTS 493. New York: T&T Clark.

Davis, Ellen F. 2008. *Scripture, Culture, and Agriculture: An Agrarian Reading of the Bible*. Cambridge: Cambridge University Press.

Davis, Stacy. 2009. "Not Elijah's God: Medieval Jewish and Christian Interpretation of Psalm 29." In *Psalm 29 Through Time and Tradition*, edited by Lowell K. Handy, 69–78. Princeton Theological Monograph Series 110. Eugene, OR: Pickwick.

Firth, David G. 2005. *Surrendering Retribution in the Psalms: Responses to Violence in Individual Complaints*. Waynesboro, GA: Paternoster.

Gerstenberger, Erhard S. 1988. *Psalms, Part 1: With an Introduction to Cultic Poetry*. FOTL 14. Grand Rapids: Eerdmans.

———. 2001. *Psalms, Part 2, and Lamentations*. FOTL 15. Grand Rapids: Eerdmans.

Gillingham, S. E. 2012. *Psalms Through the Centuries*. Vol. 1. Oxford: Wiley-Blackwell.

Gunkel, Hermann; Joachim Begrich. 1998. *Introduction to Psalms: The Genres of the Religious Lyric of Israel*, Translated by James D. Nogalski. Mercer Library of Biblical Studies. Macon, GA: Mercer University Press.

Gunkel, Hermann. 1967. *The Psalms: A Form-Critical Introduction*. Second Edition. Trans. Thomas M. Horner. Biblical Series 19. Philadelphia: Fortress Press. Translated from vol. 1 of the second edition of *Die Religion in Geschichte und Gegenwart* (Tubingen: J.C.B. Mohr [Paul Siebeck], 1930).

Hailperin, Herman. 1963. *Rashi and the Christian Scholars*. Pittsburgh: University of Pittsburgh Press.

Hals, Ronald M. 1983. "Psalm 118." *Int* 37, no. 3:277–83.

Holladay, William Lee. 1993. *The Psalms through Three Thousand Years: Prayerbook of a Cloud of Witnesses*. Minneapolis: Fortress Press.

Houston, Walter J. 1999. "The King's Preferential Option for the Poor: Rhetoric, Ideology and Ethics in Psalm 72." *BibInt* 7, no. 4:341–67.

Jacobson, Rolf A. 2004. *"Many Are Saying": The Function of Direct Discourse in the Hebrew Psalter*. LHB/OTS 397. New York: T&T Clark.

Jobling, David. 1992. "Deconstruction and the Political Analysis of Biblical Texts: A Jamesonian Reading of Psalm 72." *Semeia* 59:95–127.

Mays, James Luther. 1994. *Psalms*. IBC. Louisville: John Knox Press.

McCann, J. Clinton, Jr. 2011. "The Single Most Important Text in the Entire Bible: Toward a Theology of the Psalms." In *Soundings in the Theology of Psalms: Perspectives and Methods in Contemporary Scholarship*, edited by Rolf A. Jacobson, 63–75. Minneapolis: Fortress Press.

Mowinckel, Sigmund. *The Psalms in Israel's Worship*, vol. 1 and 2. The Biblical Resource Series. Translated by D.R. Ap-Thomas. Grand Rapids: Eerdmans, 2004.

Ollenburger, Ben C. 1987. *Zion, the City of the Great King: A Theological Symbol of the Jerusalem Cult*. JSOTSup 41. Sheffield: JSOT Press.

Sarna, Nahum M. 1995. *On the Book of Psalms: Exploring the Prayers of Ancient Israel*. New York: Schocken.

Sheppard, Gerald T. 1991. "'Enemies' and the Politics of Prayer in the Book of Psalms." In *The Bible and the Politics of Exegesis: Essays in Honor of Norman K. Gottwald on His Sixty-Fifth Birthday*, edited by David Jobling, Peggy Lynne Day, and Gerald T. Sheppard, 61–82. Cleveland: Pilgrim.

Shereshevsky, Esra. 1982. *Rashi, the Man and His World*. New York: Sepher-Hermon Press.

Suderman, W. Derek. 2010. "Are Individual Complaint Psalms Really Prayers? Recognizing Social Address as Characteristic of Individual Complaints." In *The Bible as a Human Witness to Divine Revelation: Hearing the Word of God through Historically Dissimilar Traditions*, edited by Randall Heskett and Brian Irwin, 153–70. LHB/OTS 469. New York: T&T Clark.

———. 2012. "The Cost of Losing Lament for the Community of Faith: On Brueggemann, Ecclesiology, and the Social Audience of Prayer." *JTI* 6, no. 2:201–18.

Sugirtharajah, R. S. 2001. *The Bible and the Third World: Precolonial, Colonial, and Postcolonial Encounters*. Cambridge: Cambridge University Press.

Sweeney, Marvin A. 2008. *Reading the Hebrew Bible after the Shoah: Engaging Holocaust Theology*. Minneapolis: Fortress Press.

Thompson, John Lee. 2007. *Reading the Bible with the Dead: What You Can Learn from the History of Exegesis That You Can't Learn from Exegesis Alone*. Grand Rapids: Eerdmans.

Westermann, Claus. 1981. *Praise and Lament in the Psalms*. Translated by Keith R. Crim and Richard N. Soulen. Atlanta: John Knox.

Wilson, Gerald H. 1985. *The Editing of the Hebrew Psalter*. SBLDS 76. Chico, CA: Scholars Press.

Zenger, Erich. 1996. *A God of Vengeance? Understanding the Psalms of Divine Wrath*. Louisville: Westminster John Knox.

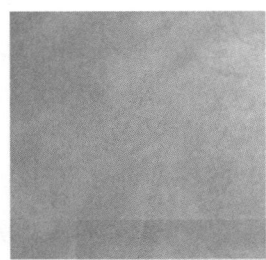

PROVERBS

Carole R. Fontaine

Introduction

Proverbs is a composite text, like so many others in the Bible, woven of discrete blocks of material drawn from different times and places. Some individual proverbs probably began as oral compositions in the towns and villages of Israel and Judah as early as the Iron I period of settlement (c. 1200–1000 BCE). Like all Wisdom literature, the book reflects an international awareness because of its scribal origin as a product of the bureaucracies of teachers, counselors, administrators, and scribes of indigenous monarchies (1 Sam. 8:15-18; 20:23-26; 1 Kgs. 4:1-6). Later, the sages in the Second Temple period maintained administrative contacts with the empires that colonized them (Perdue, 105–7). The final editing of Proverbs probably can be placed within the late Persian or early Ptolemaic periods, with a final point for dating the collection before the persecution of the Jews by the Seleucid monarch Antiochus IV Epiphanes in 175 BCE.

Individual proverbs are composed in parallelism, the primary feature of Hebrew poetry, where the second line of a verse restates the first in some way (synonymous = basic identity; antithetic = contrast; or synthetic/formal = second part advances the first). Most proverbs are composed as two-line verses, but longer compositions (especially in 1–9 and 30:1—31:31) pile up parallelisms, creating much longer compositions. In general, the sages favor antithetic parallelism because they present options between what is good and approved and what is not. By adopting this rhetorical form, they invite hearers to make correct decisions. The poetry of Proverbs also uses syntactical variations: uncommon word order, omission of verbs, or distributive use of adjectives so that they refer to elements in both lines of the verse, and so forth. These features require the hearer—often fancied to be a student of the sage—to puzzle over meanings, thereby enhancing his or her growth as an astute user of purposeful language.

Given the diversity of content and social circumstances, it is no coincidence that early Christian missionaries often began their work by translating Proverbs into local dialects, since in traditional societies such forms represent hallowed knowledge. The use of proverbs—biblical or otherwise—globally in modern development work and as measures of psychological and cognitive competence connects these ancient oral forms to modern endeavors.

The book will be divided into "sense units" as follows:

Proverbs 1:1-33: Wisdom Introduced
Proverbs 2:1—6:35: Instructions by the Sage Parent
Proverbs 7:1—9:18: A Triad of Females: Wisdom, Folly, and Strange Woman
Proverbs 10–15: Antithetic Teachings Collection
Proverbs 16:1—22:16: The Royal Collection
Proverbs 22:17—24:22: The Egyptian Teachings
Proverbs 24:23-34: More Sayings of the Wise
Proverbs 25:1—29:27: More Sayings of Solomon
Proverbs 30:1—30:33: Teachings and Numerical Sayings
Proverbs 31:1-9: A Mother's Instruction
Proverbs 31:10-31: Acrostic on the Strong Woman

Proverbs 1:1-33: Wisdom Introduced

■ THE TEXT IN ITS ANCIENT CONTEXT

Proverbs 1:1-7: A Course in Wisdom

Proverbs begins with a theological syllabus from the Second Temple period, introducing Solomonic authorship (1 Kgs. 4:29-34; cf. ascriptions in Prov. 1:1; 10:1; Eccles. 1:1; Song of Sol. 1:1; Psalms 72; 127). Solomon's legendary knowledge made him the envy of surrounding peoples (1 Kings 10). Solomon could not have been the author of the whole books of Proverbs, Qoheleth, or Song of Songs, since some sections are in late Biblical Hebrew. The Solomonic ascription protects these often secular, not particularly religious or "Israelite," wisdom books from being disqualified from the canon. In that sense, Solomon has indeed "authored" the appearance of wisdom within the biblical tradition.

Jews—especially the elite, learned class of the postexilic period—found themselves living in a more cosmopolitan world as provinces of Persian or Hellenistic empires. Traditions of Greek philosophy were known, which called for a new articulation of the source of Jewish knowledge, the Torah. In highlighting Solomon's legendary wisdom, sages and students found a secure, Jewish base for their work and daily ethics.

The opening treatise offers an organic approach to study: Wisdom teaches moral and ethical values (not simply facts), and the "course" will use a literary method, teaching the skillful use of language as well as mastery of social skills (wise dealing, etc.). Whether a son leaving the family to take up a scribal post at the court, or an already learned sage, all can "hear and gain in learning."

Willingness to accept correction, regardless of age or status, is a key feature of wisdom. Understanding hidden meanings of riddles and metaphorical turns of phrase helps develop cognitive skills, and "cultural competence" is learned through interpreting complex, multilayered speech as proverbs and "enigmas" (NRSV "figure," 1:6).

The passage ends with the "motto" (Fox 2000, 67–71) in 1:7: "'fear of the Lord' is the beginning of wisdom." This fear is a key term for the religion of ancient Israel *and* a way of being that roots all thought and action in a creaturely relationship before God. This is *the* prerequisite for learning and having "wisdom." Fools who reject wisdom and reproof are not simply untutored or stupid; they make an existential *choice* that distances them from God and wisdom.

Proverbs 1:8-19: The Father's Instruction

A section of "instructions of the father" (sage) to the youth (student) begins—a form familiar from Egyptian literature (the *sebayit*; see below, Prov. 22:17—24:22). Instructions incorporate proverbs and miscellaneous forms to make longer poetic units. The sage inhabits the role of the patriarchal father, the final authority for the socioeconomic unit (*bet 'ab*) of the extended family. Probably composed after the proverb collections, this section of the book probably reflects a more educational or professional context of scribal training as the real "life setting" (Perdue, 86–89).

Egyptian parallels appear: a "garland" reflects the headdress symbolizing status and excellence; "pendants" are signature seals indicating scribal office and personal name (1:9; cf. 3:3; 4:9; 7:3; allusions in Deut. 6:6-9; Sir. 6:29-31; Prov. 6:21; 3:22). In 1:11-14, the deceptive speech of temptation is used by the "father" to depict the wicked path of sinners of Ps. 1:1. Such behavior ends in death in the form of Sheol/the Pit (1:12). Evil acts inevitably bring about their own punishment, at least in Proverbs—a theory known by modern interpreters as the act-consequence relationship, and a concept dear to the hearts of educators of every time and place ("What goes around comes around").

The "Torah of the Mother," equal to the father's, appears as a source of knowledge to which the child/scribe must attend with all seriousness (1:8; 4:3; 6:20; cf. 31:1-9, 26). Women were important household managers and first teachers to children, but this may also refer to their social roles under later empires (Fontaine 2002). This instruction ends with irony: the wicked intend a bloody fate for innocents, but finally, the blood shed is *their own*, and their fate is in Sheol! A nature proverb in 1:17 highlights act and outcome: even birds will avoid a net when they see it, but the sinners of 1:10-19 don't.

Proverbs 1:20-33: Wisdom Calls

Woman Wisdom's poem ends this unit. She is a personified Scold, knowing mother, cosmic goddess figure, or good Israelite prophet. The prophets echo in her speech: she makes known thoughts and words (1:23-24; cf. Isa. 65:2, 12; 66:4; Jer. 7:13, 24-27) leading to life or death. This composite figure is the male sage's counterpart. She speaks frequently in chapters 1–9. In fact, she is the most talkative female in the entire Bible. She is the subject of admonitions (imperative proverbs) to young men; poems of praise for her by the sage are intermixed with her self-praise ("aretalogies") in Proverbs 1–9. These are often juxtaposed with warnings against her "evil twin," the negative female

(2:16-19; 5:1-23; 6:20-35; 7:1-27). In fact, both are hybrid characters—part goddess figures, part real women—and serve as inverted "mirror" images of each other (Yoder 2001, 73–74).

■ The Text in the Interpretive Tradition

Proverbs 1:1-7: Solomon, a Wise Sinner

Solomon is almost a folklore character by the time we reach New Testament times, appearing in sayings of Jesus in the Gospels (Matt. 1:6-7; 6:28-29; Luke 12:27), and in the apocryphal Wisdom of Solomon as Wisdom's royal lover (Murphy 1988; Wis. 6:12; 7:10; 8:9). Qumran also reworks this material (4Q525). Church fathers revere Solomon as a scriptural king in Jesus' lineage, thus promoting an explanation of why Christians may learn rhetoric or science from foreign philosophers (Jerome, *Letter to Magnus*; Clement of Alexandria, *Strom.* 1, 3, 5). Language skills count, since the "true" gospel meaning of Hebrew texts might be a hidden riddle that Christians must solve. Magical Solomon appears in the Pseudepigrapha (*The Testament of Solomon*), the Qur'an ("The Ant" sura), Christian Ethiopia (*Kebra Nagast*), Jewish (*Tg. Esther Sheni*), and Islamic folklore (Fontaine 2002).

Proverbs 1:8-19: The Father's Instruction

All later authorities agree that it is the duty of fathers to teach their sons the ways of righteousness, and to take the father's instructions at face value. Ideas here inform Heb. 12:5-6, and subsequently the idea of harsh discipline of children as "love" becomes standard for both Christians and Jews, but for different reasons: Jews because they must teach the hard truths of surviving persecutions (*b. Sanh.* 101a; *Gen. Rab.* 42:1), Christians because they must be ready to emulate Christ's suffering (Clement of Alexandria, *Strom.* 3.18).

Proverbs 1:20-33

By the time of Paul's writings, Jesus Christ is the "Sophia" of God, in a way that both nods to the Hebrew tradition, but also normalizes the tricky issue of such an exalted, preexistent female figure (1 Cor. 1:24; see discussion of Prov. 8:1-36) by providing a link to Jesus as wisdom/*logos* in John's prologue (1:1-18). Jews and Christians begin to part ways: Wisdom's female voice can be read as identical to the Torah's, God's, Christ's, or the Gospel's. The Torah is referenced in Wis. 9:18, Sir. 15:1, and *Pirqe Aboth* 6. For Christians, Christ is the true referent in speech by or about Wisdom (Gregory of Nyssa, *Against Eunomius* 3.2). Wisdom's cry and human lack of response applies to any situation the writers find worthy of their concern or scorn. Martin Luther explains, using 1:28: God does not hear the prayers of "Jews, heretics, and schismatics," because proud minds preclude knowledge of God (Luther, *Lectures on Romans* 10).

■ The Text in Contemporary Discussion

Proverbs 1:1-7

In the developing world, the use of proverbs still flourishes for purposes of teaching or deciding legal matters (Fontaine 1982; Oha, 21). Child-rearing proverbs are frequent: "Treat a son like a *raja* for the first five years, like a slave for the next ten, and like a friend thereafter" (from North India, White, 16); "Children are not dogs; their parents are not gods" (Haiti); and "A child is a certain worry, but an uncertain joy" (Old English). A brief survey of "proverbs" in professional databases shows that, worldwide, proverbs are taken as an index of cultural values (Healey and Sybertz, 34–35), and the ability to interpret these figurative speech acts is often used to assess both cognitive and psychological states (Katz and Ferretti).

Proverbs 1:8-19

Adopting the voice of an eternal Wisdom linked to fear of the Lord, Solomon's authority, or the father's authority is a strategy for control. What the text *actually* conveys is cultural content such as customs, values, and other very much time-bound views. Similarly, content is also heavily conditioned by gender, ethnicity, and social status, along with the political and historical circumstances of its authors' worlds. By speaking as the authority, the text takes on a power it might not have otherwise, dripping with grave implications of cosmic punishments. But who is *really* speaking in the instructions and poems of Proverbs 1–9, and why should we listen? Audiences are taking it "on faith" that what the author tells us is true—though subject peoples like women, the poor, and colonized peoples might well beg to disagree. Yet, even in the ethico-moral realm, the sages present us with truths that hold in their own time, place, and status: we dispute elements of their program, but we cannot doubt their sincerity.

Proverbs 1:20-33

The mother may be the best clue to understanding Prov. 31:10-32, but Woman Wisdom (Hebrew *hokmah*; Greek *sophia*) is a goddess-like figure (see note on Proverbs 8), familiar from surrounding cultures as well. Ordinary mothers rarely appear shouting from the tops of the town or the marketplace (1:20-21), telling their erring children "what's what"! Wisdom's words, harsh and scolding, show her as a direct distributor of "the fear of the Lord," using language as her method, by way of her counsel, knowledge, and reproof (1:23-25, 29-33). She intends to mock and scoff when disaster strikes fools.

Ignoring advice and refusing correction are foolish choices, both then *and* now. The authoritative voice of Gaia, in the form of global warming, melting glaciers, and ice caps, flammable drinking water, mass extinctions, and polluted atmosphere, is today speaking loudly to her human children, without much response. Ecological interpretations of the figure of Woman Wisdom abound, making this passage especially relevant in ecotheology. Is Wisdom the personified "self-revelation of creation," always paired with divine self-revelation teaching mortals the ways of God and earth (Rad, 149–62)? Ecotheologians claim she is the voice of Earth—the evangelist of the interdependent web of creation who teaches us deep ecology (Habel and the Earth Bible team, 23–34; Wurst, 48–64). Both her anger here and industry as the wife in Proverbs 31 point to a wisdom of attentiveness to what is actually before us. Wisdom suggests a biblical way to authorize a repentant, deeply "local" attention to the economic and environmental practices that have global impact. Immediate action is required, though like the thieves of 1:8-19, the powerful tell us there will be no consequences, so like the stubborn children of 1:20-30, we refuse Mother Earth's reproof. We must wait to see if humanity is capable of hearing what Earth Wisdom cries out to us from her vantage point on the heights of our cities and from the corruptions of our market-driven world: perhaps it is not too late if we do not scorn her insights and repent.

Proverbs 2:1—6:35: Instructions of the Sage Parent

■ THE TEXT IN ITS ANCIENT CONTEXT

A number of instructions by the father/sage appear together in these chapters (2:3-22; 3:1-12; 3:27-33; 4:1-27; 5:1-23; 6:1-35). Long passages about Wisdom (2:1-15; 3:13-18, 19-26; 4:1-19) and her protection against undesirable women (2:16-19; 5:1-23; 6:20-35) form an alternating antithesis in the instructions. We also see embedded proverbs (3:32-33, 35; 5:21), 'ashrey ("happy" or "blessed") sayings (3:13), nature wisdom (6:6-11), admonitions (positive or negative commands, 3:5, 9, 11, 27-31), and numerical sayings (6:16-19; see entry below on 30:1-33, 30:14-31; Amos 1:3-2:8), common in Ugaritic literature, following the pattern of x and x + 1.

Ostensibly, the father addresses the youth using the formula "my child" (lit. "my son") in 2:1; 3:1, 11, 21; 4:1 (plural), 10, 20, forming a marker for the boundaries of different instructions (5:1-6, 7-23; 6:1-5, 20-35). Favorite topics occur: wisdom as intellectual pursuit (2:1-11; 3:5-7), personification (3:13-20; 4:5-13), with the latter now flanked by negative females (Hebrew "strange woman" ['ishah zarah]; NRSV "loose woman," 2:16a; 5:3-23), "foreign woman" (nokriyah; NRSV "adulteress," 2:16b-19), "adulteress" ('eshet ra', "evil woman," 6:24-35), and prostitute (zonah, 6:26). All of these variations of sexually dangerous women stand in antithetic contrast to the fine figure of Woman Wisdom and her earthly variation, one's own wife (5:18-20). At the same time, they flesh out the portrait of female wickedness to complement the descriptions of male wickedness, forming a nice synonymous topic.

Proverbs 5 begins an ongoing discourse on the "wrong woman." Egyptian instructions often counsel the young would-be scribe or diplomat not to approach women in their professional work. In Israel, professional ethics says the same, but adds much more personal descriptions of the harm, based on biblical law and the difficult inheritance problems for Second Temple communities after return from exile. This may be why the "strange woman" (that is, "not known") and the "foreign woman" are more dangerous than prostitutes. Mythology of goddesses who descend to the underworld or kill their partners also contributes to the warnings (2:16-19; 6:26; 7:22-27; 9:18).

The wicked of both sexes display similar traits: "perverse or scornful, deceptive speech" (2:12, 16; 3:34), a negative "way" (2:12, 15; 4:14-15, 19), pleasure in their wicked acts (2:14; 4:16-17), and final punishments (2:22; 3:25, 32-33). Wicked/fool and righteous/wise (2:20-21; 3:27-35; 4:18) form a key topical antithetic pair. The same is true of the contrast between Woman Wisdom and negative females (cf. 2:16-19 to 3:13-18; 4:6, 8-9, 13). The "path" or "way" of each side of either pair is illustrated by their deeds and traits (2:8, 12-15, 18-19, 20; 3:8, 17, 23, 31; 4:11-12, 14-15, 18-19, 26-27).

Other key themes are: wisdom's cosmic origin (2:6-9, 3:19-20), and the image of a Tree of Life (3:18). Egyptian goddesses influence imagery: Ma'at, patroness of scribes, is usually shown with the ankh (life) and a symbol of wealth in either hand; Isis and Hathor appear as sacred trees, as does Canaan's own mother goddess, Asherah, who was worshiped in the Jerusalem temple (Murphy 1998). "Fear of the Lord" gets its standard treatment (2:5; 3:7). In 6:20-35, the mother's torah (v.

20b) once again urges memory, respect, and reproof, acting just like light illuminating darkness (13:9; cf. Ps. 119:105).

▮ THE TEXT IN THE INTERPRETIVE TRADITION

Positive statements about wisdom inform the later traditions: torah, Tree of Life, cosmic genealogy, rich benefits, and wisdom's role in history all appear in later Jewish writings (4Q525 2 ii + 3; Wis. 3:10-11; 7:8-13; 10:15-21; Sir. 1:26-27; *1 En.* 32:6). A favorite observation in 3:11-12, "the Lord reproves the one he loves," citing a father's discipline of the child, is well used (Clement of Alexandria, *Strom.* 1.5; to Luther, *Letter to Elector John of Saxony*), but it is *not* to be considered an evil end dealt out to sinners. The "strange" woman is expanded at Qumran in the so-called Wiles of the Wicked Woman (4Q184; cf. 4Q525, frg. 15). The strange woman could be an allusion to wicked Hellenistic culture (Clement of Alexandria, *Strom.* 1.5).

▮ THE TEXT IN CONTEMPORARY DISCUSSION

Sages share a strongly biased, patriarchal view of the world. The adolescent males they teach must submit to self-control and often violent authority in order to one day join in the social control of inferiors. After all, if God "himself" punishes *his* loved sons as a father does, then oppressive control is divinely authorized by the plain sense of the text. Negative females represent the ultimate expression of male fear of loss of control projected onto the mythological plane of the dark underworld. Warnings against her suppress many levels of male causality; her oily words are usually effective. Patriarchal bad faith is at work here: Is there a recognition that women in ancient society, owned and denied rights or choices, might actually *not* be all that accepting of the situation?

Studies of proverbs in Africa show a similar trend (see Schipper). Obododimma Oha, writing of female devaluation in Igbo proverbs, demonstrates that these units of folklore are far from neutral. A continual attempt is made rhetorically by male speech and literary forms to portray women as intellectually and morally inferior, all presented as a cultural truth that none can contest. The Igbo say that "proverbs are the palm-oil with which words are eaten." Students of masculinized rhetoric make clear that the oil, in the case of proverbs, is rancid indeed (Oha, 87–102). But perhaps our sages are correct: women released from men's control will indeed be the death of them, as the patriarchal ceilings of male heavens fall, as this proverb from Africa notes: "When sleeping women wake, mountains move" (www.worldofproverbs.com).

Proverbs 7:1—9:18: A Triad of Females—Wisdom, Folly, and Strange Woman

▮ THE TEXT IN ITS ANCIENT CONTEXT

Proverbs 7:1-27: Warning against Woman Stranger

Another teaching on the strange woman begins with a description of commandments as law (Deut. 6:6-9) held close to the body (cf. Prov. 3:1-3). Wisdom is here called "sister" and "friend" in lover-like language familiar from Egypt and the Song of Songs (Prov. 7:4; Song of Sol. 4:9-12). Only she can force out the delicious temptations of the strange woman's words.

A view from the sage's window showing the strange woman stalking her youthful victim is constructed like an eyewitness account. Archaeological tableaux from the ancient Near East repeatedly show women—prostitute, goddess, or queen—looking out of a window (Brenner and van Dijk-Hemmes, 120), so perhaps the sage's mother could be the speaker here. Certainly, mothers are concerned with their son's choice of mate (Gen. 27:46) and involved in the making of marriages (Judg. 14:2-4).

Twilight is a dangerous time of mistaken identities, when the Sumerian demoness Ardat-Lili (Lilith in later traditions) lurked at crossroads looking for male victims, just as the strange woman, now "decked like a prostitute" (7:10), does. Body language is telling: she is loud-voiced, direct, brazen, and bold in presentation of her desire. Seduction is primarily verbal: rich, absent husband, a lush bed invoking fertility and luxury. Lusty males descend to the level of trapped animal or slaughtered beast (7:22-23). She is the embodiment of the crooked path (7:25-27) leading to a mythological death.

Proverbs 8:1-36: The Cosmic Genealogy of Wisdom

Woman Wisdom speaks in self-praise, similar to the *Aretalogies of Isis* in Egypt (8:17). The setting in 8:1-5 directly recalls 1:18-22 but is less scornful. Open and affirming, this exalted figure addresses the untutored with her splendid offers: learning, life, and success (8:5-6, 14-19, 21, 35-36). Fear of the Lord and the emphasis on language recur in 8:13, 6-9. Excellence in counsel (8:14-16) makes her the *real* reason leaders succeed. The origin of her exceptional nature in 8:22-31 is cosmic: she is the firstborn of the Lord's creation, saw it all, and perhaps even assisted as a "master craftswoman" (8:30a), or perhaps a beloved royal child, constantly in God's company, frolicking in joy at YHWH's work (8:30b; the meaning of 'amon in 30a is disputed).

The Hebrew text bristles with ambiguities. "Created" in 8:22 could be translated as "acquired," with the latter including an aspect of sexual creation (Gen. 4:1b). "God acquired me first" *before* starting creation suggests a preexistent entity that YHWH engages for his creation project. If God created Wisdom in a sexual way as the very first thing done in creation (Egyptian mythology of Ma'at may be of influence here, Fontaine 2002), this is hardly a better reading for patriarchal theology's relentless rejection of all things female. In 8:24, the phrase "I was brought forth" refers to the female's labor in giving birth (literally "I was given birth to"), not a male god "begetting." This strengthens the image of a darling daughter found later in 8:30. Who is the mother here? YHWH is the only possible referent for the act. Once born, baby girl Wisdom delights in the diversity of the entire created world, including humanity (8:30-31), a laughing link between heaven and earth (Wurst, 48–64). The way of Wisdom is linked to the power of primal knowledge, God's power to create and order—she has seen it all, and participated. Who wouldn't make her their choice, and thrive?

Proverbs 9:1-18: Invitations to Wise and Foolish Banquets

The conclusion to Proverbs 1–9 ends with significant metaphorical ambiguity, as audiences discover once again just how similar are the words of personified Folly and Wisdom, if one does not take into account the differing outcomes of their offers. The two banquets (9:1-5, 13-18) could not be more different, although the invitations sound exactly the same. Verses 1–6 present Wisdom inviting the untutored (9:4, cf. 8:5) inside her house, offering bread and spiced wine. The seven pillars in 9:1 may refer to the folk idea that seven mountain pillars held up the firmament over the earth, or other sets of seven (cf. 1 Kgs. 7:17; Prov. 26:16; Clifford, 105). Whatever the case, spacious luxury is indicated, for "seven" carries the meaning of completion. Wisdom's feast might echo a dedicatory celebration of a finished temple or palace (1 Kgs. 8:1-5), a scene from Ugaritic epics about Baal's new palace (*KTU* 1.4.6; *ANET* 134).

Mixed wine has a place in ancient practice, whether watered (John 2:10) or spiced (Song of Sol. 8:2). "Bread," meaning any staple food, refers to Wisdom's spiritual teachings (cf. Isa. 55:1; Sir. 15:3). Openly searching, she calls in 9:3 from places in town where she cannot be ignored (8:2; 9:14; cf. 1:20-22, busy roads and city gates where business happens), but we note that she has a female staff in 9:3 (cf. Prov. 31:15). Her offerings (the sages' teachings) sate the deepest hunger and thirst. Wisdom, the hostess with the mostest, offers life to her guests, something other goddesses seldom do (Ugaritic Anat kills those who rebuff her; *ANET* 151).

Proverbs 9:7-12 inserts a number of wisdom sayings, thus interrupting the immediate juxtaposition of wise and foolish banquets. Many scholars move these verses to the end of Proverbs 9. Scoffers and evildoers have a ready and cynical answer—or even violent action—to every reproof. The helpful sage may be the one who suffers (Prov. 22:10). The entire teaching of Proverbs 1–9 is summarized in verse 10: the fear of the Lord is the beginning of wisdom, leading to a long and successful life (9:11-12).

We conclude with Woman Folly's banquet (9:13-18). Like the would-be adulteress of Prov. 7:11a, Woman Folly (but "foolish woman," Fox 2000, 253–62) is painted in negative images. Since *'eshet-kesilut*—"woman/wife of foolishnesses" (pl.)—occurs only here in the Hebrew Bible, perhaps we should contrast her also with the wife of substance (*'eshet-hayil*) in Prov. 31:10, and understand her as a "wife of fools" (see note 31:10). Traits from the adulteress are reassigned (cf. 2:16-19; 5; 6:20-35; 7), depicting a disruptive, active female persona. Inhabiting high places (where wealthy homes and palaces are located), she calls to the gullible outside like a sideshow barker at her door. Her invitation has deep meaning—it *does* encapsulate truth, but should one embrace the ethical gray zone it highlights? (The sages would answer no.) Instead of Wisdom's transparency, Folly suggests stolen water (intercourse? cf. 5:15-20) is sweeter than one's own; illicit bread spices consumption with secret pleasure. Like the fertility goddesses who invited kings or champions to marital banquets only to slay them and take their power, or punish their rebuffs (Clifford, 107), Folly's menfolk are the walking dead in the sages' eyes.

▌ The Text in the Interpretive Tradition

Proverbs 7:1-27

Here the strange woman is clearly designated as someone's wife, so all strictures concerning adultery apply (Deut. 22:22-25; *b. Sotah*), though if she is married to a foreigner, other laws than Israelite ones would be in force. Here, the Qumran expansions of the mythological filth and death are extreme in their misogyny (4Q184; cf. 4Q525, frg. 15). The Talmud comments on the connection to demons and twilight in 7:9 (*b. Ber. 3b*). Warnings about the strange woman are taken to refer to attractive Christian heresy and governments in *t. Hul.* 2:22-24. Adultery is particularly heinous for women, reflecting inappropriate agency in one meant to be fully subject, even in body, to her husband (Eph. 5:22-24). Paul (1 Corinthians 7) and the Christian fathers may not be enthusiastic about marriage compared to virginity, but a Christian wife is *far* less dangerous than the liaison presented here (Jerome, *Pammachius* 47).

Proverbs 8:1-36

Assorted themes are carried forward in Sir. 1:4, *Ahiqar*, the *Odes Sol.* 33:5; 41:9; *2 En.* 24; 25:4, 26; 28:4; 30:8; and the *T. Sim.* 5:2. The most important tradition developed concerning Wisdom's genealogy is in the prologue to the Gospel of John, where the Second Temple Jewish *Sophia* of our sages is transmuted into Greco-Roman *logos* of Stoic philosophers and Christian theologians. Proverbs 8 sparks Paul's thinking (1 Cor. 1:24; Col. 1:15-17; Heb. 1:2-3, 6a, 8-10), and the Christian fathers follow. By the time of the fourth century CE, Proverbs 8 becomes critical for the debate over whether Christ was created by or coexistent with the Father (Arians versus Nicenes). Gregory of Nyssa (*Against Eunomius* 3.2) extensively harmonizes female Wisdom with the Christ-Wisdom of the Gospels and Letters—warning the prudent in his audience *not* to take the texts' meaning literally, "absolutely and without examination" at first reading—something seldom said of masculine metaphors! Luther follows the trend (*Commentary on Romans* 1:2): it is the glorious Gospel that has been set up for humanity before creation. Wisdom becomes a cover symbol for the Word, extending the Logos theology of the New Testament.

Proverbs 9:1-18

The image of Wisdom, the life-giving hostess, appears in the New Testament and late wisdom (Sir. 15:3; 24:21; John 6:35-40). The seven-pillared house finds expansive interpretation in Jewish and Christian interpretation: seven firmaments (*Midrash Proverbs*), days of creation (*b. San.* 18a), seven sacraments, gifts of the Holy Spirit, and so on (Fox 2000, 297–98). Byzantine liturgies read this passage for Holy Thursday; the West used 9:1-5 for feasts of the Virgin Mary. Hippolytus of Rome glosses Wisdom's house as the Virgin's pregnancy, producing the bodily incarnation itself (*On Proverbs*, frg. 2).

◼ THE TEXT IN CONTEMPORARY DISCUSSION

Proverbs 7:1-27

Biblical scholars have struggled much to separate the composite wicked woman into her various aspects: an in-group or out-group woman married to another (adulteress); a prostitute, often of foreign descent (Rahab, Delilah); a strange woman—someone not from the speaker's own ethnicity; a woman worshiping in a cult that is forbidden in Israel (7:14-20); and/or a reference to foreign goddesses like Inanna, Ishtar, or others who are noted for either descending to the underworld or killing their human partners (Inarash, Aphrodite, etc.). Translations that blur these distinctions are not especially helpful for discussions of biblical sexuality. Whichever aspect of the "bad girl" paradigm we might find emphasized in different texts, it is clear that only Wisdom or the woman of substance could counteract her dreaded influence.

Male fears of adultery in the past (and some modern traditional cultures) stem from the reality of arranged patriarchal marriages: young women often found themselves given for life—without choice or consent—as glorified property to a much older man, to be used functionally for his bed, hearth, and comfort. Prostitutes were equally at risk under patriarchy: supposedly, only dire family economics could account for it, and daughters sold as debt slaves were at the sexual mercy of their owners (Exod. 21:7-8; Lev. 19:29; Neh. 5:5). Foreign women as wives represented a major threat to the transfer of property, and might promote participation in or tolerance of foreign cults.

Today, adultery can still carry broad economic and violent consequences, but is not so likely to be mythologized, though the trope of the "divorced wife" and "cuckolded husband" are used as a figure of fun or torment in male culture. Where an ideology of romantic love exists, "cheating" can create a radical rupture for the innocent partner, creating a sense of loss, betrayal, and descent to the depths. Divorces caused by adultery can be rancorous and costly, economically and psychologically. Considered a moral and ethical rift in a committed relationship, adultery today is different from times in the past because wives currently have more recourse and choices in how they might deal with male infidelity.

The exact nature of Lady Folly is complex too: she could be a degraded foreign goddess, an adulteress, a foreigner, idolater, or any combination thereof. She and Wisdom speak in similar language in Prov. 9:1-18; Wisdom/Folly function as a gendered pair expressing a *single* male ideology of the female other. Texts dependent on Proverbs 7–9, such as the Wiles of the Wicked Woman at Qumran (4Q525 15; 5Q16; 4Q184 1), easily portray the negative archetypes from 7:1—9:18 in ways that suggest fear of the goddess, the witch, the faithless or murderous midwife of neighboring mythologies. On the positive pole of the female other archetype, Wisdom of Solomon (8:9; 7:28; 8:16) depicts a goddess-bride Wisdom who ennobles her king, as though she were the Greco-Roman Isis rising from the wave, loving those who love her (Apuleius, *The Golden Ass*).

Proverbs 8:1-31.

Happy are those who find Wisdom! For biblical theologians and feminists, the figure of Lady Wisdom/wife of substance and her negative variations—multifaceted Lady Folly and the unfortunate wives appearing in Proverbs—are a source of fascination and speculation. First mother who is made manifest by her child Jesus, or cosmic sender of whom he is *the* prophet par excellence, Wisdom has been located in the earliest Jesus movement (see Schüssler Fiorenza). Other scholars posit a gnostic "myth" of Sophia, come down from heaven to guide men, as a basic trope for the equation of Jesus/Christ with Sophia. In the Nag Hammadi gnostic texts, some see Wisdom as the precursor of the paradoxical speaker in the disturbing "The Thunder, Perfect Mind" (McGuire 1994, 39–54), where a list of extreme juxtapositions (Madonna-whore, life-death, etc.) proclaimed by a single female character lend credence to Wisdom/Folly as a *single* entity, bifurcated into positive or negative forces. By highlighting Wisdom's genealogy and activities, modern scholarship has accounted for reasons why she morphed into certain aspects of the Messiah or Holy Spirit for Christians or Torah, the Shekinah, or Kabbalistic Tree of Life for Jews.

For believing women, so often excluded from the "salvation history" of call, covenant, election, and redemption, Wisdom suggests new ways to relate to the biblical traditions. Her connection with Jesus Christ in subsequent texts gives welcome relief from the imagery and theologies of male-only religion, as in the "Re-Imagining" movement in Christology of the late twentieth century (see Cole, Ronan, and Taussig). Indeed, happy are women and men who find themselves able to return to the tradition, enhanced and enlarged by Wisdom, who supports their varied aspirations.

Proverbs 9:1-18

Banquets, good and bad, continue to function as powerful images of social interaction, exchanges of power, and ultimately redemption from the trials of poverty and disgrace. Perhaps representing philosophical symposia of Hellenistic philosophy as their key referent (Fox 2000, 303–6), or as scenes rooted in the everyday life of families, villages, and cities, feasts were important. Some took place at seasonal, religious, or socially critical times of change (births, marriages, death; Matt. 22:1-14; 25:10; Mark 6:21; 12:39). Other banquets in New Testament Gospels (Luke 5:29-32; 12:35-38; 14:7-24; 20:46) harmonize with Wisdom's in Proverbs 9. Other banquets could become scenes for disgrace (see the banquets in Esther), with unanticipated, and deadly, outcomes.

Folly's invitation to a banquet of wickedness can be related to the world of globalized economies and corporate control of resources. In the face of world poverty and despair, lavish gluttony of "the good life" is enshrined everywhere ("competitive eating" competitions, corporate retreats, political fundraising, etc.). "Stolen water is sweet, and bread eaten in secret is pleasant," remarks Folly truth-fully out of *her* wisdom, and the same is true today. How sweet are the corporate profits from buying up potable water in the developing world and then selling it back at a profit. The secret profits of global banking industries or wholly arbitrary, outrageous health-care fees levied on ordinary people by big corporations for profit are sweet to those who benefit. Global manipulation of currencies in developing companies creates debt that allows outsiders to capitalize on the subsequent disasters ("disaster capitalism"). These are common examples of the secret doings that keep the rich getting richer in games rigged to their advantage. African proverbs used at the United Nations with NGOs in Western countries, in Somalia, and in other African contexts express the dynamics of rich/poor: "When elephants fight, the grass gets hurt" (Healey and Sybertz, 36–37).

Proverbs 10–15: Antithetic Teachings Collection

▊ THE TEXT IN ITS ANCIENT CONTEXT

Ascription to Solomon (*mishlay*, "proverbs-of"; cf. commentary on 1:1-7) may reflect the presence of significantly older material in the collections of Proverbs 10–30. Since the meanings of proverbs are "decoded" by their application in social settings, whether oral or literary (Fontaine 1982), it has been said that "a proverb in a collection is dead." While scholars are limited with respect to social use, sound observations may still be made. The antithetic collection uses antithetic proverbs to the virtual exclusion of all other forms. Antithetic word pairs build up these divergent observations, pressing for the affirmation of one and renunciation of the other as a matter of "common sense." The "way of wisdom," introduced in Proverbs 1–9, is given flesh and sinew by the piling up of so many keenly examined examples, but "faith statements" play their part as well, contradicting what even casual observers of life know to be true: the righteous *do* fail occasionally; the wicked often live long and prosper.

The cast of characters from Proverbs 1–9 reappears in this collection, as they pursue their "way" to found their "house," neatly tying up Wisdom's teachings and object lessons from her cosmic vantage point with everyday examples in the human realm. Fathers (10:1; 13:1; 15:5) and mothers (10:1; 15:20) appear together. Sons (translation mine)—lazy or diligent, attentive to education or not, corporally punished for their own good, secure into the following generations—are found in 10:1, 5; 13:1, 22, 24; 14:26; 15:11 ("son of *'adam*" = mortal), 20, but daughters appear not at all. This is a serious lacuna in the sages' ideology of worthy females: Are there no intelligent, pious daughters who could benefit from the sages' teachings? Is it useful to urge a morality on young men if young women are not also indoctrinated to uphold it? Good wives were critical to any successful household (11:16, 22; 12:4; 14:1). Where are the proverbs that teach young women about their duties? The mother was thought to instruct her daughters in all they needed to know, but the sages' blindness to this educational task underscores the gendered nature of their teachings. The "house" motif, the domestic sphere in which women hold paramount power, occurs in 11:29; 12:7; 14:1, 11; 15:6, 25, 27, where men who leave daily decisions to the industrious wife or servant are contrasted with fools who constantly interfere without cause. Perhaps this reflects a mother sage's point of view in keys to selecting a good mate: at home, fools make tiresome partners.

The wise/righteous person is shown with a good understanding of the role of speech, a favorite wisdom theme (10:6, 11, 13a, 14, 18-21, 31-32; 11:9, 12, 13; 12:6, 13, 14, 17-19, 22; 13:1-3, 5; 14:3, 5, 7, 25; 15:1-2, 4, 7, 14), compared to the fool or wicked, who delights in lies, strife, slander, scoffing, and other deceptive or ignorant linguistic behaviors. The poor are a topic as well: although some poverty results from laziness (10:4), the sages call out the unfair advantage of the rich in their dealings with others, suggesting that poverty may be a consequence of a stacked deck or a well-placed bribe (10:15; 13:7-8, 23; 14:20-21, 31; 15:15). Compassion to the poor neighbor renders one "happy" (blessed) in 14:21; God prefers such behavior (14:31). All the days of the poor are hard, but better that than living with hate or without knowledge of God (15:15-17).

Faith statements that contradict common observations usually invoke God or following sage advice as the guarantor of a final good outcome in 10:3, 22, 27, 29; 12:2-3; 14:27; 15:3, 25, 29.

▌ THE TEXT IN THE INTERPRETIVE TRADITION

The sayings of Solomon are received by the tradition as true and worthy of transmission and obedience—whether taken literally or metaphorically—by both Christian and Jewish authors. Ben Sira repeats many of the antithetic sayings with some slight variation or elaboration (cf. Sir. 7:17 with Prov. 10:27; Sir. 3:17-24 with Prov. 11:2; 15:33). In Sir. 20:5-8, the saying in Prov. 15:23 is further amplified: the wise wait to use a "word in season" (Prov. 15:23, "How good!"), whereas fools never manage it, because they are talkative but have nothing truthful to say (Sir. 20:5-8a). The pseude-pigraphical work of *Ahiqar*, among others, also reuses sayings from this section (see, e.g., v. 156 = Prov. 10:32; v. 168 = 11:11; 14:11). Proverbs 11:24 undergirds 2 Cor. 9:6; Acts 13:10 references the straight path of Prov. 10:9. Proverbs 10:12 becomes the kernel of a beloved passage on love in 1 Cor. 13:1-8a, and finds its way into 1 Pet. 4:8. Rabbinic stories like those of Rabbi Akiba's long-suffering wife show Prov. 12:10 in narrative use vindicating the woman's view over her neighbor's (*b. Ketub.* 62b). The church fathers also appeal to the wisdom of these proverbs (e.g., Clement, *Strom.* 1.6, 10; 2.7, 11, 13, 18; Jerome, *Against Rufinus* 3.43; *Pelagians* 1.33; 2.1), assuming their truth content to be self-evident and useful.

◾ THE TEXT IN CONTEMPORARY DISCUSSION

Modern observers of action and its relationship to the character of the actor often reject the stark contrasts of the antithetical sayings: black-and-white characterizations like those of the sages have yielded to a modern world of many shades of gray. This rejection of hard-and-fast rules is hardly modern, however: in Job and Qoheleth, we find serious questions about the reliability of retribution. Modern sayings suggest instead: "No good deed goes unpunished"; "Nice guys finish last"; "The cockroach knows well how to dance in the sun, but the fat chicken prevents him" (Africa); or "Keep your head down and your mouth shut." As always, context determines how much "truth" is ascribed to the proverb/saying, and whether it should be understood literally (see Katz and Ferretti).

Proverbs 16:1—22:16: The Royal Collection

◾ THE TEXT IN ITS ANCIENT CONTEXT

Dating is more certain here: the monarchy of Judah ended in the Babylonian exile of 587/586 BCE. Many scholars date "royal sayings" about kings and counselors ("the wise") before that time. Regional wisdom texts from times of the biblical monarchies show similarities to the themes in this collection: warnings against taking part in or even witnessing angry disputes are common. Calm, deliberative speech and careful listening are the hallmarks of the sage and the wisdom ideal, fostering the goal of patient, generous responses in a heated moment. A diplomat must know better than to befriend hot-headed, ill-tempered, loud-mouthed fools who often stir up strife by slander and gossip just because they can.

Earlier wisdom themes appear, but in many, features used to describe sages or the righteous *now* describe the (ideal) king (16:10, 12, 13, 15; 20:8; 21:1), whom sages manage with persuasive speech at times of quick anger, or petulant use of power (19:12; 20:2). Differences between wise and malicious speech dominate this collection (16:1, 10, 13, 21, 23-24, 27-28; 17:4, 5, 7, 14, 20, 27-28; 18:2, 4, 6-8, 13, 17, 20-21, 23; 19:5, 9, 22, 28; 20:19-20; 21:6, 28; 22:10-12, 14). This is the case because the profession of court counselor relies on influential speech to achieve goals (16:13; 18:20-21). Other elements of life at court come in for comment: bribes appear in 17:8, 23; 18:16; 19:6; 21:14 but show a range of evaluations that characterize the more nuanced proverbs of the Royal Collection. When neutrally appraised, they are effective "gifts" that work almost magically to open doors

(17:8; 18:16; 19:6). In Prov. 21:14, the gift becomes an outright "bribe," which averts retribution, and in 17:23, bribes lead to perversion of justice by the wicked who accept them. Wives are a "good thing," a sign of God's favor (18:22); wise wives are "from the Lord" (19:14). "Better-than" sayings heighten contrasts (17:12; 19:1), or suggest, counterintuitively, that sometimes "less is more" (21:9). The sages recommend poverty and integrity over wealth and pride (16:8, 19). Bread and water with quiet calm trump a fractious feast (17:1). A mere corner of an exposed rooftop is preferable to a house with a fretful wife (21:9, cf. 19:13); better a deserted island than a miserable wife (21:19).

Court experience puts a worldly twist on the more simplistic faith affirmations of Proverbs 10–15. Things do *not* always work out as people expect, even thoughtful plans (16:1, 7, 9; 19:21), one's "way" (16:2, 9; 20:24), outcomes (16:3, 33), speech (16:1b), or observed events (16:25; 21:31). Actually, human circumstances are determined finally by God who alone knows inner reality and final outcome. Even wisdom cannot prevail against the Lord (21:30). How can a mortal ever understand God's ways (20:24) under such circumstances? Still, following wisdom's general program of behavior is the best strategy available (22:4).

■ The Text in the Interpretive Tradition

Fourth Ezra 3:34, *Pss. Sol.* 5:16, *2 Bar.* 38:1, *2 En.* 50:5, Clement of Alexandria (*Paed.* 2.10; *Strom.* 2.18), Jerome, and many others use content, form and vocabulary of the Royal Collection as they evaluate local rulers. Jerome considers "contentious wives" (Prov. 21:9, 19) enough to cancel out all wifely virtues, even their origin from God (Prov. 18:22; 19:14; *Against Jovinianus* 1.28), recommending virginity as the only safe path. *Pirqe Aboth* 1 and 2 discuss the ideal of silence and wise words, but find wives deleterious to their achievement. In *b. Ber.* 19b, Prov. 21:30 provides a "rule" (God may confound wisdom or rabbinic logic) that helps resolve contradictions in texts, interpretations, or common practice.

■ The Text in Contemporary Discussion

The sages in this collection show a keen attention to "what works": in their role as counselors to the great, they suggest appeasement of the powerful (16:13); refusal to rescue a violent person, since it is pointless (19:19); refusal to guarantee a neighbor's loan (17:18); hiding from danger (22:3), and refusing friendship to gossips (20:19). While these worldly tips betray the weary cynicism of "don't get involved," they are also balanced with a recognition of how persuasive language can positively affect a situation (e.g., 16:13, 21, 23-24; 17:10), just as malicious, lying speech destroys harmony (e.g., 16:27-28; 17:4; 18:6-8; 19:28).

The power of language seen in 18:21, "Death and life are in the power of the tongue," is nicely demonstrated by the Teacher from Galilee. In Luke 10:30-37 and Matt. 22:15-22, Jesus manages to follow *all* of wisdom's rules, but twists them to critique power relations without incriminating himself. Lawyers, Pharisaic disciples, and Herodian spies all try to draw Jesus into a quarrel, but he answers softly, crafting wisdom speech (the parable or saying) to raise subversive interpretations. In Luke 10, he presents a Samaritan who violates wisdom's goal of noninvolvement in dicey situations and surpasses the Jewish elites' righteousness, thereby enlarging the vision of the "neighbor" across boundary lines. In Matt. 22:15-22 (cf. Mark 12:13-17; Luke 20:20-26), Jesus sidesteps an explosive question with a question and response of his own: pay feudal taxes to the one who owns everything; but for the devout Jew, Caesar owns nothing, creates nothing but misery, so pay *him* nothing! "God is the All-Provider, not Caesar" becomes the message for the poor in the crowd around this sage. Jesus refuses the quarrel but reframes the encounter, and gives it a double-sided "takeaway" lesson: "Render unto Caesar what is Caesar's."

Proverbs 22:17—24:22: The Egyptian Teachings

■ THE TEXT IN ITS ANCIENT CONTEXT

Here monarchic and colonial sages make use of a twelfth-century-BCE instruction from Egypt, that of the sage Amenemope. Returning to the format of instructions in Proverbs 1–9, the title "The Words of the Wise" (22:17a) is followed by admonitions, "Incline . . . hear . . ." with a motivation: what follows is "pleasant," lip-ready, and generates trust in YHWH (22:19-21). Aramaisms throughout this section reflect the international character of diplomatic and bureaucratic training. Features found in the Egyptian forerunner of Prov. 22:17—24:22 have provided explanations for some textual difficulties in the biblical text, allowing for better translations (Fox 2009, 709–12).

Standard themes are featured in 22:17—24:22: good and bad speech (22:24-25; 23:9; 24:7-9, 28-29), treatment of the poor (22:22-23, 23:10-11), work ethic and riches (22:29; 23:4-5; 23:19-21; 29-34; 24:10), court manners and good sense (22:26-27, 23:1-3; 23:6-8), the blessings of wisdom (23:12-16, 22-25; 24:3-6; 24:13-14), prostitutes and adulteresses (23:26-28). Students are to refrain from envy, avoid the bad and emulate the good, making their parents very happy indeed (23:15-16, 22-25).

■ THE TEXT IN THE INTERPRETIVE TRADITION

The New Testament endorses the general tone and teachings of this section of Proverbs: the admonition against too much wine and strong drink (23:19-21, 29-35) underlies Eph. 5:18. The repayment for all one's deeds in 24:12 undergirds statements about Christ's judgment in Matt. 16:27; Rom. 2:6; 2 Tim. 4:14-15; and 1 Pet. 1:17. God and emperor/king (24:21-22) viewed as objects of reverence and obedience ("fear") are found in 1 Pet. 2:17. Many of this collection's themes are also echoed in the *Syr. Men.*, Clement, Ambrose, John Cassian, and Athanasius.

■ THE TEXT IN CONTEMPORARY DISCUSSION

It is remarkable to observe how easily an Egyptian text from the world of the polytheistic occasional enemy Egypt fits in with the biblical messages from Proverbs. Often, interpreters stress a radical discontinuity between Israel and the world of the "other," as though Israel had a totally unique vision of ethics, right behaviors, or the role of the divine in securing justice or punishing wickedness. The earlier Egyptian text corresponds closely to that of Prov. 22:17—24:22, with respect to attitude toward life, duty, and the role of the divine in assuring justice. This suggests that the "us/them" antithesis—at least between wisdom teachings from various cultures—has been overdrawn by later writers.

Second, there is a compelling statement here of an ancient cross-cultural ethic of duty to the innocent, poor, and disenfranchised. Amenemope rehearses this theme, with emphasis on land tenure, in the form of honoring boundary markers of inherited fields (Amenemope 6:13—9:9), and this is repeated in Prov. 22:28; 23:10-11. Both texts give the same reason: the divine Creator is the advocate of the poor, the widow, the disabled, and the stranger, and punishes those who abuse them (Prov. 22:23; Amenemope 21:5-6; 24:11-14; 25:9-6). Such universally held sentiments by the sages of the region provide evidence that can serve to inspire a global interfaith ethic: *everyone* now is our neighbor, and we have duties of rescue (intervention) toward them. Ignorance is *no excuse* in Prov. 24:12. The judgment scene in Matt. 25:31-46 endorses this very ethic for the followers of Jesus.

Proverbs 24:23-34: More Sayings of the Wise

■ THE TEXT IN ITS ANCIENT CONTEXT

A title (24:23a) begins this small collection of lengthy admonitions, ended by an extended vignette ("example story") on laziness (24:30-34). Proper judgments, industriousness, false witness, revenge, and poverty are all covered here. The strong emphasis on working the land (24:27, 30-34) continues a hallowed biblical fixation: without land, there is no life (Ezra 5). Family inheritance must be worked properly and not become the property of outsiders (Ruth 4:1-10), for it represents the well-being of future generations.

Proverbs 24:29, simply put, "*Don't* do unto others as they have done to you," is a precept critical to Jewish and Christian teachings as a "Golden Rule," and is based on the basic community ethics of Jewish law. Revenge is forbidden, reserved *only* for God (Deut. 32:39-42), for punishment is certain, even if delayed. Leviticus 19, the "heart" of the Holiness Code, entwines duty to land, the poor, and fair judgment with laws forbidding vengeance, false witness, slander, taunting the handicapped, bearing a grudge, and hatred of the neighbor (Lev. 19:9-18), for "you shall love your neighbor as yourself" (Lev.19:18b). Ultimately, even the land/field/vineyard has "standing" before God, and can charge humans with misuse (Job 31:38-40).

■ THE TEXT IN THE INTERPRETIVE TRADITION

Second Enoch 50:4 counsels avoiding vengeance. Sirach 10:30 counsels work as an antidote to want. Jesus' teachings focus on lessons learned in working fields, fishing, and observing nature (Matt. 6:28-30; 12:33; 13:3-9, 18-33, 36-40, 47-49; John 4:34-38). In James 5:4, the cries of defrauded harvest workers are heard by God. The scholars' work—studying the Torah—is the fields and vineyards that must be worked diligently in the Babylonian Talmud (*Mas. Eruvin* 21b:28-31).

■ THE TEXT IN CONTEMPORARY DISCUSSION

Interpreters debate whether the ethics of the sages tilt toward the elite, but proverb collections show considerable nuance: one must be impartial, but the scale tilts on the side of advocacy for the poor. The sages of Proverbs are well aware of the tendencies by the avaricious "haves," which put economic justice at risk for the "have-nots." From their administrative vantage point, kings and administrators have the job of carefully monitoring the behavior of the wealthy for such unfair practices.

Proverbs 25:1—29:27: More Sayings of Solomon

■ THE TEXT IN ITS ANCIENT CONTEXT

Two collections of "other proverbs of Solomon" for the court professionals in training, 25:1—26:28 and 27:1—29:27, are bound together here under one title (25:1), ascribed to the "officials of King Hezekiah" (715–687 BCE), who collected them together. Kings, counselors, messengers, and military leaders figure in stories of Hezekiah's clashes with invading Assyrians, showing each side using proverbial speech (2 Kgs. 18:21: Egypt is a "broken reed"; 2 Kgs. 19:3b, a mother unable to give birth easily). Proverbial sayings in this unit share similar sharply crafted images to convey meaning, perhaps deliberately arranged to instruct court officials (Van Leeuwen).

Proverbs 25:1—26:28

Typical wisdom themes unite the sections, but there are also differences: Proverbs 25–26 does not show the strong antithetic character of Proverbs 10–15, but makes use of sharply crafted similes. Parallels to the Egyptian instructions are evident as well. Professional duties are the most important topics in Proverbs 25: Well-timed, reasoned persuasion is likened to rich or desirable items: gold apples in silver setting (25:11), gold jewelry (25:12), and soft words convince—and break bones (25:15)! Cold weather or water, so precious and welcome in a hot climate, are compared to faithful messengers (25:13) and good news from afar (25:25). Less desirable similes (comparisons to rainless clouds [25:14], implements of war [25:18], rotting teeth and lame feet [25:19], vinegar in a cut, along with moths and worms [25:20], muddied water sources [25:26]) lend color to sayings about negative items. Proverbs 26 has less striking language, but uses stark juxtapositions to raise issues of ambiguity: Does every context not call for its own application of wisdom theories or language (26:4-5), just as different sorts of people require different responses (26:1, 3, 23-26)? Honor for a fool is like bad weather during agricultural seasons or setting a stone in a slingshot (26:1, 8); those who use fools for messengers might as well cut themselves or drink poison (26:6), for fools whom one hires are like archers who shoot friend and foe alike (26:10). Worst, perhaps, is the fool's use of language: proverbs told at the wrong time hang useless like crippled legs (26:7) or a thorn in the hand of a drunk (26:9), making it difficult to judge whether to indulge their folly with wise answers (26:4-5). The retribution for a "sin" may be inherent and congruent in verse 27: a pit might swallow its digger; a stone might fall back on its mover (cf. Ps. 7:16; Eccles. 10:8-9).

Proverbs 27–29

Antithetic sayings return as the colorful language of Proverbs 25–26 takes a back seat. Proverbs 29 uses an acrostic (alphabetic) form to signal its unity: 29:1 begins with 'aleph, the first letter of the alphabet, and 29:27 begins with a tav, the final. Standard wisdom themes are reviewed but show less coherence, and YHWH sayings are less frequent here than elsewhere.

In Proverbs 27, fools and their havoc appear in 27:3, 22, along with unseemly praise, boasting (27:1-2), contentious wives (27:15-16), jealous, envious enemies, and inappropriate friends or kin throughout the chapter. The chapter ends with nature wisdom advising good practices on the land (27:23-27). The world can be uncertain (27:1, 20), filled with paradox: a friend may wound by truth-telling; an enemy is all kisses (27:6); a close neighbor might be better than faraway kin (27:10b).

Proverbs 28 and 29 concern public governance, based on whether righteous, wise leaders are in power or hasty (28:20, 22), wicked (28:3, 15), cheating fools who are a danger to everyone. The two types form antitheses in 28:2, 4, 5, 7, 8, 10, 12, 28, and throughout: people flourish under the former, but hide or cry out under the latter. "Torah" appears in 28:4, where it may refer to the teachings of this collection that uphold Mosaic laws, which institutionalize care for the poor, the widow, orphan, and stranger (see Leviticus 18–20). It is clear that a "preferential option" and God's blessing are aimed at the welfare of the poor: rulers who understand the rights of the poor and take action to guard them win God's favor (28:4-5, 8, 25, 27; 29:2, 7, 13-14, 26), whereas wicked rulers who raise taxes and gouge the poor are fools who will bring about rebellion eventually (28:2-4, 12, 15-16, 29:2, 4, 7, 16, 27). The sages criticize those who put profit first (28:8; 29:4), using the proverbial image of a growling lion, familiar in antiquity in reference to kings, heightening the portrait of predatory behavior by wicked elites (28:15; cf. Ezek. 32:2, Prov. 19:12; 20:2; 30:29-31). Ultimately, it is the Lord who made both the rich and the poor; elites do not deserve more than their fair share. The marked differences between the righteous and the wicked, the unjust and the upright, make them into each other's worst nightmare, "abominations," in 29:27.

■ THE TEXT IN THE INTERPRETIVE TRADITION

The book of Tobit puts Prov. 25:2 into the mouth of the angel Gabriel, but with a twist: in Prov. 25:2, God's glory is to conceal; the king's glory is to search out hidden things (injustice, plots, etc.). In Tobit 12:7, 11b, it is "good" to conceal a king's doings, but it is good to reveal the "works of God," acknowledging God's honor and glory. The rabbis of *b. Shab.* 30b worry about 26:4-5: Is a sage to answer a fool, or not? They resolve the dilemma by specifying that 26:5 refers to improper readings of the Torah: *that* foolishness *must* be corrected! Proverbs 29:24 seems to be based on Leviticus 5: witnesses must come forward, or they are accessories to the crime. The most important legacy is in 25:21-22: students are advised to "love their enemies" in very concrete ways by providing sustenance. This may provoke a change of heart (?), but even should it not, it pleases God. Romans 12:17-21 is based on these verses. Proverbs 26:11, the fool who commits his idiocies repeatedly, like a dog who returns to its vomit, is found in 2 Pet. 2:22, where it is used of those who fall away from the true faith, and linked to a nonbiblical proverb about swine.

■ THE TEXT IN CONTEMPORARY DISCUSSION

The sages join the rural Hebrew prophets (Amos, Micah) and the Teacher from Galilee in offering scathing analyses of elite profit-taking and rigging the system in the favor of the "haves." Astute observations of what the way of the wicked looks like "on the ground" is thoroughly explored here; obedience is not simply a matter of "right" (monotheistic) theology and pure cultic worship. The denunciation goes much deeper in Proverbs, to the heart of the worldview that secures the sages' ethical practice: one must *choose* to be good. Bearing witness to economic cheating, corrupt court processes, trumped-up quarrels used to distract, and the power of wicked propaganda against the innocent is obligatory. The humility of the sages is their protection: they may hold themselves in high esteem, but they have learned not to trust in themselves and their own wisdom (26:12, perhaps a comment on 26:4b and 5b; cf. Prov. 3:5, 7). YHWH has made *all* citizens of the planet (even the flocks and fields), and cares about them all, not just successful elites.

Romans 12:17-21 is nested in a longer discussion, but vengeance is forbidden, not just for legal reasons but also because it fractures a community and makes reconciliation among kin unlikely. Our proverb as applied in Romans goes a step further: no hope of future gain should motivate those who follow Christ. They must opt for love over all else, even the natural human desire to settle scores with enemies in their own coin—an eye for an eye! Evil must be fought with good, not passivity where the righteous give way to the wicked (Prov. 25:26). The enemies may not turn to friends, but God's pleasure is assured—and the enemies *may* succumb to God's peace after all (16:7). "In the end, love wins."

This deep insight into the way that Christians, and before them, Jews, must think and act their way out of the trap of retributive violence is the basis of nonviolent resistance to worldly wickedness. Taking a cue from the life of Jesus (among others), great visionaries like Mahatma Gandhi, Martin Luther King Jr., and Bishop Desmond Tutu, along with Tibetan Dalai Lamas, have demonstrated that this text is not dead, but deeply influential—for some, even extending down into daily diet in a refusal to take part in the suffering of animals, also creatures of worth. Those who would be good and wise may never just "pass by on the other side" or keep silent when justice is at stake, even if attempting to correct a wicked fool may seem doomed to failure.

Proverbs 30:1-33: Teachings and Numerical Sayings

◼ THE TEXT IN ITS ANCIENT CONTEXT

Another discrete section opens here consisting of extended passages (30:1b-4, 5-6, 7-9, 11-14, 15-16, 18-19, 21-23, 24-28, 29-31, 32-33) incorporating admonitions (30:6, 10, 32b), individual sayings (30:5, 15, 17, 20, 33), and numerical sayings incorporating nature wisdom (30:15-16, 18-19, 21-23, 24-28, 29-31). The title "The Words of Agur" (30:1) may refer to authorship, collection, or patronage, and some scholars read the NRSV's "an oracle" as a place name, meaning "from/of Massa" in northern Arabia. If the latter is correct, then Agur was not an Israelite, lending another piece of evidence to the international nature of wisdom teachings.

The world-weariness of verses 30:1b-4 is not without antecedents: the Egyptian Dialogue of a Man with His Soul and other cynical or "contest" dialogues often express ennui and despair at humanity's inability to know the "whole story," as does Qoheleth (e.g., Eccles. 1:2-11). The rhetorical questions in 30:4 have many echoes in Job's dialogues and recall YHWH as Creator in Job 38–42, questioning his upstart worshiper on cosmic subjects. The extended units here often sound like a riddling contest, inviting the audience to puzzle over what unites the items listed. Items in 30:15-16 are all ones thought to be insatiable, and unite to identify "greed" as the topic; "inexplicable movement" is the referent that binds 30:18-19; "crushing weight" is the topic of 30:21-23; in 30:24-28, "size doesn't matter" is illustrated by the unclean critters that still have a valuable lesson to teach; "swaggering movement" is the answer in 30:29-31.

■ THE TEXT IN THE INTERPRETIVE TRADITION

The speaker in 30:4 raises weary questions, based in cosmic, natural, or intimate sources of knowledge: Who can go between heaven and earth, wrap up water, or discern identities? While some traditions claim Enoch went up and down between heaven and earth (*1 En.* 72–82), the questions here, and their echo in Job 38:4-30, 34-38 and 39:4, make clear only the Lord has or could do these things. Humans, even sages, are deeply limited creatures! Nature wisdom featured in 30:15-16, 24-28, and 29-31 reminds us that the world of field, flock, and wilderness are also players in God's drama of creation, and the choice of animals considered unclean underscores that *all* of nature has something to teach. These creatures can illustrate interpreters' own personal views. Jerome (*Against Jovinianus* 1.28) uses the sucking leech in verses 15-16 (the "daughters" are the two prongs at either end that suck blood) as a condemnation of all *women* by reading "women's love" for "barren womb," and linking it further to the unloved woman and uppity maid of 30:23. Reading this with all of Proverbs' previous negative sayings about wives, Jerome concludes that *any* wife is a dreadful choice, since woman's love is "the grave . . . the parched earth, and . . . fire" (Schaff 1995).

■ THE TEXT IN CONTEMPORARY DISCUSSION

The collection of things that look different on the surface but share a hidden connection (at least as the sage views them) suggests both the encyclopedic knowledge essential for those in the "education and counsel" business, but also a form of intelligence that is holistic and contextual. Categories are at work here that the sages' forms unlock for the student: What similar features do "small" things (30:24-28) share? Can these function as a lesson for students about aspects of wisdom (providing food for winter, 30:25; managing one's environment, 30:26; ability to work together without oversight, 30:27; ability to change venues, 30:28)? Yes, of course, they can, in the hands of masterful teachers: understanding the hidden connections in nature (30:15-16, 18-19, 21-23, 24-28, 29-31) serves to illuminate *human* categories of behavior (women under patriarchy searching for personhood via motherhood, 30:16, 23; male-female relations, 30:19; changes in status, 30:22-23; and the self-aggrandizement of leaders, 30:31b). The sage of Proverbs 30 reminds us that the "little" folk of lower status or size in these numerical sayings *also* have worthy or surprising things to teach. The author's own pleasures in knowledge when its grasps "things too wonderful [that is, unexpected and difficult to understand] for me" (30:18) is palpable.

Proverbs 31:1-9: A Mother's Instruction

■ THE TEXT IN ITS ANCIENT CONTEXT

This "royal" instruction reminiscent of Egyptian instructions aimed at monarchs (Fox 2009, 883; 2000, 82–83) gives us finally an instruction purportedly composed by an unnamed mother for her son, Lemuel, thus providing examples of the mother's torah featured elsewhere (1:8; 6:20; 31:26). As the father's voice in instruction, coupled with cosmic Lady Wisdom's speech, opened the whole book, here at the end, Proverbs 31 balances the ending with a mother's instruction (31:1-9), followed by a look at Lady Wisdom at home in 31:10-31 as the woman of substance. This forms a deliberate inclusion of parental teaching paired with an appearance of female Wisdom. Clearly, this is a sign of editorial decisions at work.

While no "Lemuel" (= Solomon?) is known in the Bible, we find a second mention of Massa (see note on "oracle" in 30:1ab), a region in northern Arabia. The queen mother regards her son as exceedingly dear (31: 2), a "son of my womb," and so her prohibitions take on an especially urgent tone. She warns against too much engagement with women (harem politics, perhaps), which can undercut effective leadership (cf. the courtly riddle contest in 1 Esd. 4:13-32). Wine is also called out as a potential danger, but the queen is attentive to wisdom's theme of the "right season/time": kings *shouldn't* drink, but condemned criminals and the destitute *should* be given wine to numb the pain of their condition (31:6-7). Kings must *never* forget their duties (31:4-5), but those at the far end of the status continuum ought to be allowed to forget (31:6-7. cf. 1 Esd. 3:18-24 for wine's strength). The ultimate duty of a king, then, is not to abuse the pleasures or resources of his status, but to raise his voice for the voiceless (31:8-9) in judgment and in governance.

Proverbs 20:1 already commented on the effects of intoxicants that "lead astray," and it is followed directly by the "dread anger" of a king in 20:2. Proverbs 20:8 speaks of a king's unimpaired judgment as he "winnows" evil (sifts the evidence). Similarly, in Prov. 28:15-16 and 29:14 we have associations seen in the queen mother's teaching: angry kings who oppress the poor are swept away. The secret to a long, successful rule is knowledge of the rights of the poor and enforcing them. Lemuel's mother is speaking authoritatively here, blind neither to the tendencies of kings nor the faults of members of her sex.

∎ THE TEXT IN THE INTERPRETIVE TRADITION

The Talmud (*b. Sanh.* 43a:18-19) offers intriguing comments on 31:5-7 in the context of executions of proven criminals: judges and witnesses should *not* drink, for it impairs judgment, but the condemned *should* be given drink to "benumb" their minds. The rabbis report that the women of Jerusalem provided the condemned with wine into which frankincense had been mixed as they were taken to the place of execution, giving compassionate care for the moment of death. They even went so far as to provide the money for the wine and drug out of their own pockets, suggesting that they took the sentiments of Lemuel's mother to heart. These practices illuminate the ministries women provided to Jesus during the passion event: Mark 14:3 (= Matt. 26:6-7) speaks of a woman giving "final care" to Jesus (Matt. 26:10-12; Zaentz). She anoints him with an expensive natural analgesic (unspecified in Matthew 26, but probably "myrrh" [Mark 15:23], used in treatment of leprosy, as was frankincense), perhaps already available in the host's, Simon the Leper's, household. The wines given to Jesus during his agonizing execution may also be part of the Jerusalem women's service to the condemned: women ("daughters of Jerusalem" in Luke 23:27-28) were among the crowd looking on (Matt. 27:55-56), and the wines offered to Jesus are "mixed" with palliative drugs ("gall" in Matt. 27:34, 48; Mark 15:36; Luke 23:36; John 19:29 specifies hyssop, also a fumigant and analgesic). It is easy to imagine one of them commissioning a bribe that facilitated the provision of their medicaments to Jesus.

◼ THE TEXT IN CONTEMPORARY DISCUSSION

The advice offered by Lemuel's royal mother is precious, not only for its example of motherly concern about the right use of life's pleasures and their impact on essential duties, but also because of the balance her instruction provides to the father's voice and all the negative proverbs found throughout the book. In Prov. 31:1-9, we finally hear a female voice, one endowed with worldly experience, knowledge of legal proceedings, and compassion for the destitute and condemned. The words of this woman offer sound advice, insightful conclusions, and a finely tuned sense of how situational ambiguity moderates individual precepts. Her advice ranges from her most intimate relationship ("son of my womb") to the greatest possible extent—the huge mass of the poor and needy who require the voice of another to give words to their distress. One of the voices that performs this noble task is that of the mother.

Proverbs 31:10-31: Acrostic on the Strong Woman

◼ THE TEXT IN ITS ANCIENT CONTEXT

The crowning achievement of an unknown editor's defense of woman occurs in Prov. 31:10-31, an acrostic poem in praise of the strong woman or woman of substance. Designed with each successive letter of the Hebrew alphabet beginning a new line, its use as an exercise for students is highly likely, and its content fits with that goal. There have been many warnings about the attractions of the "wrong" (= exogamous) woman, but now they are balanced out by a portrait of the woman the sages *do* recommend. The Hebrew term that describes this affluent, industrious, and wise woman, *ḥayil*, when used of men, describes full adult strength and capacities (power and courage), but may also refer to wealth (e.g., Gen. 34:29; Num. 31:9; 1 Sam. 14:48; Job 20:18). The portrait of her wealth and industry in a variety of household, financial, and market venues suggests that this woman is not merely a "good wife": instead, she is a "strong woman," or better, given the sociological setting of the Persian and Hellenistic periods, "woman of substance" (Yoder 2001, 77).

This wife and mother is one with many resources: her bride price and her dowry speak of wealth (31:11-12), and her access to female staff, fields, profits from her textile work, provisions of exotic imports for her family, her real estate and its usufruct all betoken great luxury, suggesting a daughter of a wealthy elite who brings economic advantages into her marriage. Like Woman Wisdom, she is the making of her man (31:16, 18, 20-24), offering many of Woman Wisdom's gifts. Wealth and honor (3:15; 8:11; 31:10), a luxurious house and staff (9:1, 3; 31:15, 21, 27), and a secure future are hers to bestow. Both figures appear at gates (1:21; 8:3; 31:31); both are hard to acquire (1:28; 8:17; 31:10); both reward their men with good things (3:16; 4:8; 8:18, 21; 31:11-12) and fine reputations (3:4, 16; 31:23). Both are able to "laugh" at the future (1:26; 8:30; 31:25), since both exemplify the teachings of wisdom and their benefits. Equally as important as their wealth, they both teach compassionate care for others (1:24; 4:6; 31:20, 27). In verse 26, we learn that when this wise woman speaks, it is with the "torah of kindness" (*torath-hesed*) on her tongue, invoking the "covenant love" (*hesed*) that God supplies in abundance to those who are part of the covenant community. She is indeed, as her husband and children attest, "a woman who fears the Lord" (31:30).

▌THE TEXT IN THE INTERPRETIVE TRADITION

Proverbs 12:4 taught that an *'eshet-hayil*, the "woman of substance" like the one we see in 31:10-31, is a "crown for her husband," and Proverbs 31 amplifies this with examples. Later interpreters had qualms about the merits of marriage, often castigating woman as bringer of sin and death (1 Tim. 2:11-15; cf. Sir. 25:24; 42:13-14). Sirach 26:1-4 makes clear that if one *must* have dealings with women, the "good wife" of Proverbs 31 is the best and most desirable of the lot. Even Clement of Alexandria (*Paed.* 3.11), while excoriating harmless adornments of women (based on 1 Tim. 2:9; 1 Pet. 3:1-4), finds that the industry and piety of the wife of 31:10-31 make her a "store of excellence" worthy of his blessing.

▌THE TEXT IN CONTEMPORARY DISCUSSION

The "woman of substance" is no mirage, but a composite of the economic activities of elite women in the complex, vibrant colonial economies supervised by elites during the Persian and Hellenistic Empires, though her activities have precursors in the monarchic period that gave us Abigail, Jezebel, and other powerful wives. As Christine Elizabeth Yoder points out, this is "women's work" raised to a level of theological validation as an outcome of "fear of the Lord" (Yoder 2001, 108–9). While that is better than venomous proverbs, this wife is still objectified and viewed from a male perspective as both an acquisition of and means to men's material gratification—just as Woman Wisdom is to the sages who praise and seek her, as YHWH did before them in 8:22-31. The woman of substance presents a largely unattainable model for real women (not unlike a "virgin mother"), because she reflects the activity of *many advantaged* women, not just one. While she is naturally viewed from a male author's point of view—all authors speak out of their own subject position at some level—her description also reveals the biases of the elite class of sages.

"Wisdom is good with an inheritance!" (Eccles. 7:11a, RSV). What a difference status makes! This is no average woman, as details and contrasts reveal. Boasting of the future is usually forbidden (27:1), but not for her (31:21, 25). Yes, she works hard—but not on tedious cleaning or childcare; she has staff to take care of that. Moving around the city, vocally bartering with merchants, wearing fine clothes or jewelry—all these activities are discouraged by the sages when lesser women are involved, but in this woman, they are exemplary. Strong woman has no need to nag a lazy, drunken, quarrelsome, violent fool of a husband: *she* has her *own* resources, which *she* manages to the welfare of those for whom *she* cares. After all, how much trouble can her fortunate man cause the household, while sitting in the city gates, basking in the glow of her wealth?

Poor women, then and now, are not so lucky.

Works Cited

Brenner, Athalya, and F. van Dijk-Hemmes. 1996. *On Gendering Texts: Female and Male Voices in the Hebrew Bible.* Leiden: Brill.

Clifford, Richard. 1999. *Proverbs: A Commentary.* OTL. Louisville: Westminster John Knox.

Cole Susan, Marian Ronan, and Hal Taussig. 1997. *Wisdom's Feast: Sophia in Study and Celebration.* Kansas City: Sheed & Ward.

Fontaine, Carole R. 1982. *Traditional Sayings in the Old Testament: A Contextual Study.* The Bible and Literature 5. Sheffield: Almond.

———. 2002. *Smooth Words: Women, Proverbs and Performance in Biblical Wisdom.* Sheffield: Sheffield Academic.

Fox, Michael V. 2000. *Proverbs 1–9: A New Translation with Introduction and Commentary.* AB. New York: Doubleday.

———. 2009. *Proverbs 10–31: A New Translation with Introduction and Commentary.* AYB. New Haven: Yale University Press.

Habel, Norman C. 2000. *Readings from the Perspective of Earth.* Earth Bible 1. Cleveland: Pilgrim.

———. 2003. "The Implications of God Discovering Wisdom in Earth." In *Job 28: Cognition in Context*, edited by Ellen van Wolde, 281–97. Leiden: Brill.

Habel, Norman C., and the Earth Bible Team. 2001. "Where Is the Voice of Earth in Wisdom Literature?" In *The Earth Story in Wisdom Traditions*, edited by Norman C. Habel and Shirley Wurst. Earth Bible 3. Sheffield: Sheffield Academic.

Healey, Joseph, and Donald Sybertz. 1996. *Towards an African Narrative Theology.* Maryknoll, NY: Orbis.

Katz, Albert N., and Todd R. Ferretti. 2003. "Reading Proverbs in Context: The Role of Explicit Markers." *Discourse Processes* 36, no. 1:19–46.

McGuire, Anne. 1994. "The Thunder, Perfect Mind." In Searching the Scriptures, Vol. II: A Feminist Commentary, edited by Elisabeth Schüssler Fiorenza, 39–54. New York: Crossroad.

Murphy, Roland E. 1988. "Wisdom and Eros in Proverbs 1–9." *CBQ* 50:600–603.

———. 1998. *Proverbs.* WBC. Nashville: Thomas Nelson.

Newsom, Carol A. 1989. "Woman and the Discourse of Patriarchal Wisdom: A Study of Proverbs 1–9." In *Gender and Difference in Ancient Israel*, edited by Peggy L. Day, 142–60. Minneapolis: Fortress Press.

Oha, Obododimma. 1998. "The Semantics of Female Devaluation in Igbo Proverbs." *African Study Monographs* 19, no. 2:87–102.

Perdue, Leo G. 2008. *The Sword and the Stylus: An Introduction to Wisdom in the Age of Empires.* Grand Rapids: Eerdmans.

Perkins, John. 2005. *Confessions of an Economic Hit Man.* New York: Plume.

———. 2008. *The Secret History of the American Empire: The Truth About Economic Hit Men, Jackals, and How to Change the World.* New York: Plume.

Rad, Gerhard von. 1972. *Wisdom in Israel.* Translated by J. D. Martin. London: SCM.

Schaff, Philip, trans. 1995. The Nicene and Post-Nicene Fathers, Second Series, Vol. 6: Jerome: Letters and Select Works. Hendrickson Publishing (www.ccel.org/schaff/npnf206.vi.vi.I.html, accessed 3/15/2004).

Schipper, Mineke. 1991. *Source of All Evil: African Proverbs and Sayings on Women.* Ivan R. Dee.

Schüssler Fiorenza, Elisabeth. 1994. *Jesus: Miriam's Child, Sophia's Prophet.* London: Continuum.

Van Leeuwen, Raymond. 1988. *Context and Meaning in Proverbs 25–27*. SBLDS 96. Atlanta: Society of Biblical Literature.

White, Sarah C. 2009. "Men, Masculinities, and the Politics of Development." *Gender and Development* 5, no. 2:14–22.

Weber, Elke U., Christopher K. Hsee, and Joanna Sokolowska. 1998. "What Folklore Tells Us about Risk and Risk Taking: Cross-Cultural Comparisons of American, German, and Chinese Proverbs." *Organizational Behavior and Human Decision Processes* 75, no. 2:170–86.

Wurst, Shirley. 2001. "Woman Wisdom's Way: Ecokinship." In *The Earth Story in Wisdom Traditions*, edited by Norman C. Habel and Shirley Wurst, 48–64. Earth Bible 3. Sheffield: Sheffield Academic.

Yoder, Christine Elizabeth. 2001. *Wisdom as a Woman of Substance: A Socioeconomic Reading of Proverbs 1–9 and 31:10-31*. Berlin: de Gruyter.

———. 2009. *Proverbs*. Nashville: Abingdon.

Zaentz, Paula Rendino. 2008. "Matthew 26 and Mark 14: Spikenard and Women's Healing Ministries to Jesus." Unpublished paper.

Ecclesiastes

Micah D. Kiel

Introduction

The author of Ecclesiastes weaves a web of dicta, reflections, and wisdom aphorisms shaped by tradition, experience, and context. The book squirms beneath difficult questions about the relationship between God, experience, and justice: Do people get what they deserve? Does God act in predictable ways? What is the nature of life, and how are we to live? The questions are timeless; the answers, however, assert an epistemological skepticism that have long left Ecclesiastes marginal to some.

Ecclesiastes is attributed to "the son of David" (meaning Solomon), although the name Solomon is never used. Solomon is associated with much of the Wisdom literature, so such an ascription here is not surprising. Solomon did not write Ecclesiastes, however. Linguistic analysis proves that it was written during the Persian period, probably sometime between 450 and 325 BCE. The author also is referred to as Qoheleth, which in Hebrew most literally means "gatherer." This word is commonly used as a proper name for the author of the work.

The book makes no discernible references to historical places, figures, or events. Details suggest that a Palestinian origin is most likely. Historical research about the Persian period—especially its economics—illuminates Qoheleth's words. Taxation was widespread and highly organized. Coins were minted in unprecedented numbers and became the basis of economic activity. Inscriptions of this period portray concern about economic issues. Ecclesiastes reveals a similar preoccupation. Qoheleth's opening reflection on meaninglessness is immediately made concrete in the economic realm: accumulated wealth and all of its accoutrements (houses, vineyards, herds, and silver) are nothing but a chasing after the wind (2:1-8).

The economic system under the Persians was marked by mobility. There was opportunity to move up or down the economic ladder, often rapidly. At the same time, excessive debt was rampant. Many borrowed money to feed their families. People were forced to work in prisons to pay off debt.

There is even evidence that rich individuals owned their own prisons in which they could hold those unable to pay back their debts (Seow, 31).

Ecclesiastes also appropriates language similar to that used in the dissemination of land grants (Seow, 24). These grants were distributed rather arbitrarily, often at the whim of rulers or other elites. The land also was not inherited by offspring. The prospects of wealth accumulation or, the opposite, rapid descent into destitution, provide a crisp backdrop against which Qoheleth's message can be understood. At times, Qoheleth despairs at the capricious economic context, observes indeterminacy, and recommends nothing other than mirth (8:15; 9:7). At the same time, many of the book's idioms, and even its very depiction of God, are analogies that come from this economic context. Thus God is depicted as capricious, a deity whose future actions are unknowable (3:16-22). Qoheleth evinces an epistemological uncertainty that parallels the relationship between Persian leadership and rapid economic change.

One must also have a sense of Qoheleth's canonical and theological contexts in order to understand the edge to his words. Qoheleth interacts with a specific theological ideology that claims there is a close connection between actions and consequences. This formulation is given expression in Deuteronomy: "If you will only obey the LORD your God . . . all these blessings shall come upon you" (28:1-2). The opposite is also true: "But if you will not obey the LORD your God . . . then all these curses shall come upon you" (28:15). This ideology, sometimes called "Deuteronomistic" because of its source in Deuteronomy, is a perspective that has influenced large portions of the Old Testament.

This close connection between act and consequence finds a particular formulation in Israel's Wisdom literature: "Those who listen to me will be secure and will live at ease" (Prov. 1:33). Later Wisdom literature reaffirms this rigid connection between act and consequence: "You who fear the Lord, trust in him, and your reward will not be lost" (Sir. 2:8). If the Wisdom literature gives us any access to life among ruling elites and their education system, then such a tidy formula—that God repays according to action—might serve their ruling interests well: by offering a clear definition of God; by claiming to know how and why God acts; and, most importantly of all, by ordering obedience.

In such a context, Ecclesiastes stands out. Contrary to a doctrine of close connection between actions and consequences, Qoheleth recommends a pursuit of pleasure, because life's events contradict such a tidy theological formulation: "There are righteous people who perish in their righteousness, and there are wicked people who prolong their life in their evildoing" (7:15). Experience contradicts the theological party line: "the same fate comes to all, to the righteous and the wicked, to the good and the evil, to the clean and the unclean" (9:2). Qoheleth, like the author of Job, offers life's experiences as a rebuttal to the widely held theological dictum that God treats people according to their actions. Ecclesiastes, then, is situated not only in a specific historical context of rapidly shifting economic opportunities. It also interacts with conventional theological formulations, often refusing to accept them wholesale.

Ecclesiastes 1:1-11: Philosophical Musings of a Teacher

▌The Text in Its Ancient Context

The book opens with the repetition of the Hebrew word *hevel*, which evokes a puff of smoke or a vapor. *Hevel*'s connotations—something brief, fleeting, and indeterminate—are hard to convey in English. Most translations, following the Septuagint and Vulgate, use "vanity" or "meaningless." Starting with *hevel* sets an immediate agenda: when scrutinized, life appears to be little more than an abridged vapor.

In Eccles. 1:4-11, Qoheleth attempts to prove that all is *hevel* by contemplating the created order. Such contemplation is common in Wisdom literature. The regularity of creation is often used to support the idea that God is in control of the universe (Sir. 16:26-30). It can also be used to judge deviations from its regularity (*1 En.* 80–81). In Job, God brags about creation's workings in order to make Job's complaints seem minuscule in comparison. Qoheleth's response to creation is quizzical. The sun rockets around the earth. Streams flow, do not fill, yet do not run dry. The wind blows and returns. Scrutiny of such things is deemed "wearisome; more than one can express" (1:8). The experience of creation is too magnificent to be summarized, yet too vexing to comprehend.

The poetry is skillfully constructed so as to support this conclusion. Pronouns are avoided. Instead, the nouns themselves (generation, sun, sea, wind) are repeated. The poetry thus embodies the very idea that life is repetitive, that there indeed is "nothing new under the sun" (1:9).

The ultimate metaphor in which all of these reflections are grounded, however, is economic. The Hebrew word *yitron*, meaning "advantage" or "profit," is used ten times in Ecclesiastes, and it reinforces the idea that economics (both real and metaphorical) are central in the thought of the author. The word conveys a sense of surplus, an amount beyond what is necessary. Given what we know about the economics of the day—it was a "lively economic environment" (Seow, 22)—such an operative analogy throughout the text should not be surprising. Qoheleth assumes that his audience is shrewd enough to understand the concept of *yitron*: if an activity does not produce a surplus, he deems it a waste of time.

▌The Text in the Interpretive Tradition

In Rom. 8:20, Paul uses the Greek word *mataiotēs* ("futility"), which is the Septuagint's translation of *hevel* in Eccles. 1:2. The confluence of this word with Paul's broader reflection in chapter 8 about creation suggests that Paul may intentionally be interacting with Ecclesiastes. For Qoheleth, the vapor-like quality of life came from monotony, regularity, and a sense that nothing has changed. Paul also connects creation with futility. Because of his apocalyptic worldview, he concludes that the futility is not God's doing, nor the fault of creation itself, but is instead something that has been imposed on it. Because life is *hevel*, Qoheleth will eventually advocate the pursuit of happiness because nothing is assured and everything is meaningless. Paul, however, looks forward to a day when the futility of creation will be fixed though liberation, it will be "set free from its bondage"

(Rom. 8:21). Thus Qoheleth and Paul both sense a futility in the created order, but their respective points of view lead to drastically different responses to that basic observation.

In a completely different context, Ephrem the Syrian (d. 373 CE) finds the image of the unfillable sea (Eccles. 1:7) as a type of Christ. In an acrostic hymn, Jesus, as the sea, is the one into whom the endless Jewish symbols, similes, and typologies flow: "Since it [i.e., Jesus/sea] is a wondrous gulf, all creatures cannot fill it. . . . Therefore, the sea is Christ Who is able to receive the sources and springs and rivers and streams that flow forth from within scripture" (McVey, 302–3). While the supersessionism of such a perspective is unpalatable, Ephrem's reading here is remarkable in its subtle appropriation of the image from Ecclesiastes.

■ THE TEXT IN CONTEMPORARY DISCUSSION

While much of the discussion of creation in the Bible demonstrates differences between the ancients and ourselves, here in Ecclesiastes, one might find Qoheleth's contemplation of the created order relevant. Science and all of its learning has not removed the basic experience of being flummoxed by nature. The most learned of our astrophysicists, observing colliding particles and getting brief glimpses of the origins of the universe at the quantum level, are continually surprised by what they find. We best not have God enter at the point where science, for the moment, cannot explain something. Qoheleth here offers a different way: a quizzical reaction to the mysteries of the world's working. We want to know more; the eye is not satisfied with seeing, nor the ear with hearing (1:8). This speculation, for Qoheleth, leads ultimately to pessimism. The regularity of the created order suggests that things have never changed, that there is nothing new anywhere.

Ecclesiastes 1:12—2:26: Uselessness of Seeking Wisdom

■ THE TEXT IN ITS ANCIENT CONTEXT

We might think of the next section in Qoheleth as the reflections of a workaholic. No matter how hard one works, what is crooked will stay crooked. Qoheleth, using the ancient literary form of a fictional royal biography, lists accomplishments and things acquired: great deeds, houses, vineyards, flocks, and so on. Qoheleth's employment of this biography, however, is ironic. None of this allows one to corral the vapor that is life.

Even pursuit of wisdom is nothing more than a chasing of the wind, for "in much wisdom is much vexation" (1:18). All is still *hevel* ("vanity" or "meaningless") because a life of wisdom provides no discernible advantage—the wise one dies just like the fool; one fate befalls everyone. Qoheleth goes one step further: pursuing wisdom may actually make it worse! Increased wisdom only brings increased pain and vexation (1:18). Ignorance is bliss.

■ THE TEXT IN THE INTERPRETIVE TRADITION

Martin Luther has an extended treatise, "Notes on Ecclesiastes," in which he attempts to tackle the problems that Qoheleth presents. He does so obliquely, however, by changing God's role, thereby blunting the force of Qoheleth's skeptical theological suppositions. For example, in 1:15 Qoheleth proclaims that what is crooked cannot be made straight. From this observation, Luther argues that what Qoheleth says is true for human beings. Luther says that anyone who claims his or her life "has gone at all times just as he had proposed" should be accused of lying. The solution, Luther says, is "to commit everything to God" (Luther, 26–27). This does not face the critique head-on because Qoheleth suggests that even God cannot be observed to fix such problems.

▌THE TEXT IN CONTEMPORARY DISCUSSION

Qoheleth here offers a deeply skeptical view of the human condition. To those in a Christian context, one might jump to the afterlife to avoid his skepticism: Why despair over a terrestrial end when something better awaits? Qoheleth had no such luxury. For most of the Hebrew Bible, the afterlife as a place of ongoing reward or punishment was not a part of the belief system. The conspicuous lack of an afterlife, however, does not make Qoheleth's thoughts irrelevant. Such reflections should force the reader to linger on the questions of existential angst one finds here. Who has not, after a long and frustrating day, asked "What's it all for?" Who has not laid awake at night, anxious about the future? Even at night, our hearts are not at rest (see 2:23). At the very least, Qoheleth gives honest expression to what it is often like to be a human.

Ecclesiastes 3:1-15: A Time for Everything, Yet Undesignated

▌THE TEXT IN ITS ANCIENT CONTEXT

The poem in the third chapter of Ecclesiastes proceeds with paired opposites: birth/death, plant/pluck, weep/laugh. The paired phrases are not given grammatical subjects; they tumble forward in infinitival constructions governed only by prepositions and the noun for "time," *'eth*. The poetry obfuscates who acts. This suggests that God is the actor, making the poem "an invitation to embrace God's grace and to have faith that situations will change" (Tamez, 58).

The prose section that follows the poem is built on the same theological foundation. He *knows* that it is good to be happy (3:12) and that God's work endures forever (3:14). This is Qoheleth at his most optimistic and faithful. God is in control of history, God appoints times and seasons for everything, and that which God does should induce awe (3:14). Problems arise, however, because humans can discern little about the actual big picture. Verse 11 summarizes the vexing situation in which humans find themselves: God has made a time suitable for everything and given humans a sense of time—a past and a future—yet what God has actually done in the past and what God will do in the future are beyond human ken. In his own words: "that which is, already has been; that which is to be, already is" (3:15). It is as if Qoheleth has a pile of puzzle pieces in front of him, but no idea what the picture looks like, and thus no idea where to start putting it all together.

▌THE TEXT IN THE INTERPRETIVE TRADITION

The specific pairing in the poem of a time to be born and a time to die is used frequently in early Christian authors with reference to baptism. The language and imagery is similar to that of Paul in Rom. 6:3-4. Cyril of Jerusalem, for example, in his second lecture on the mysteries addressed to those preparing for baptism, says: "What Solomon said in another context is applicable to you: 'A time for giving birth, a time for dying,' although for you, contrariwise, it is a case of 'a time for dying and a time for being born'" (Cyril of Jerusalem, 165).

◼ THE TEXT IN CONTEMPORARY DISCUSSION

One cannot read Ecclesiastes 3 without hearing jangly 1960s pop music in the background. The song "Turn! Turn! Turn! (To Everything There Is a Season)," written by Pete Seeger and made popular by The Byrds, has made this text one of the most recognized in the Bible.

Peace advocates often use Eccles. 3:8 ("a time for peace") to claim that *now* (in whatever context they may be situated) is the time for peace. This problematically ignores the fact that verses 9-15 suggest we will not know when any of these times are. God is the one who decided when a time is suitable (3:11). Humans are blessed with a sense of past, present, and future, but yet are cursed with an inability to discern completely God's actions: "yet they cannot find out what God has done from the beginning to the end" (3:11).

Ecclesiastes 3:16—4:8: Epistemological Nihilism

◼ THE TEXT IN ITS ANCIENT CONTEXT

In 3:16-22, Qoheleth reinforces the epistemological skepticism from the previous section. He begins with a simple observation: wickedness and righteousness often do not have their rightful places. Then Qoheleth lets the reader in on his own inner dialogue ("I said in my heart . . ."), which attempts to resolve the tension in the distortion of justice on the earth. The first option is that God will judge the righteous and the wicked (3:17), for there is a time appointed for everything. This idea, which echoes 3:1-15, is not developed.

Qoheleth whispers another option to himself (3:18): what is perceived as lack of justice is little more than God testing humans. The concept of testing finds a natural home in the wisdom tradition. In a pedagogical setting, trouble and problems in life are seen as God testing the individual, who, if successful, will emerge better and stronger on the other side (e.g., Sir. 2:1; 4:17), like gold that has been tested in fire. The trial burns off impurities, leaving behind a stronger, purer original (Prov. 27:21). This is not where Qoheleth takes the idea of testing, however. The test instead is meant to show humans that they are but animals. Animals and humans share the same fate: death and decomposition. The reflection culminates with the phrase: "Who knows?" (3:21), a stark contrast to 3:12 and 14, when Qoheleth happily claimed, "I know." Upon further reflection, things have changed.

Modern Bibles start Ecclesiastes 4 in the middle of what is really a continuation of the flow of thought until 4:8. In 4:1-3, Qoheleth's gaze turns to the oppressed. He does not specify the nature of the oppression, but it is broad and systematic. The oppressors oppress the oppressed (the word is used in a similarly repetitive way in Hebrew), and there is no one to comfort them. Conspicuously absent is the sentiment of texts such as Ps. 69:33 and Sir. 4:16 that God will hear the cry of the poor or oppressed. Because of this, the dead are better off than the living, because they no longer have to see such injustice. Better yet, however, are those who have never been born because they have never seen the oppression at all. Again, for Qoheleth, ignorance is bliss (cf. 1:18).

▮ THE TEXT IN THE INTERPRETIVE TRADITION

Much of the history of the interpretation of this portion of Ecclesiastes has been spent trying to make it say something other than what it actually says. Ambrose of Milan (d. 397), in his treatise *Death as a Good*, struggles to explain Qoheleth's statement that death is preferable to life (4:2). Death is not bad for one who is pious, of course, because of the Christian belief in the afterlife, but the death of one who is impious will lead to hell. Ambrose proceeds to say that death is preferable for the impious as well, because at least he or she will cease to sin. Such a reading, of course, is done through the lens of later Christian eschatology, and does not accurately explicate Qoheleth's intentions.

▮ THE TEXT IN CONTEMPORARY DISCUSSION

One might not immediately associate Ecclesiastes with the pervasive biblical concern for social justice, but this text suggests that the concern may be close to Qoheleth's heart. Noticing and calling out oppression and oppressors puts Qoheleth in a long line of biblical texts that do the same with similar vocabulary, such as Exodus and Amos. Amos, for instance, insists that God rushes to alleviate the plight of the oppressed. In Exodus, God hears the cry of the Israelites in slavery and decides to fight on their behalf (2:23-25). Wisdom literature tends to focus on the oppressed with a more pedagogical goal, that proper care of the oppressed is a way of honoring God (e.g., Prov. 14:31). In Ecclesiastes 4, however, God is conspicuously absent. One comes away rather frustrated. God is not isolated as the champion of the oppressed, nor are humans given a directive to change their treatment of the same. Despite his clear exposition of the problem of oppression, it is ultimately not clear what Qoheleth would want us to do.

Ecclesiastes 4:9—5:20: Contemplating the Oppressed

▮ THE TEXT IN ITS ANCIENT CONTEXT

In 5:8-9, Qoheleth returns to oppression, a topic already mentioned in 3:16-17 and 4:1-3. Here, however, the oppressed are defined as the poor, framing the issue in a specifically socioeconomic way. The oppression of the poor stems from economic structures, layers of bureaucracy, and unchecked power. Most scholars see here a reference to the system of satraps in the Persian world (Seow), or the political world of Ptolemaic Egypt (Tamez). In either scenario, one finds a series of powerful individuals who looked out for the power of each other to the detriment of the poor.

Striking, again, is Qoheleth's response to the poor and oppressed. God is absent. There is not even a strong condemnation of those who are aggressively oppressing. In 5:13, it seems clear that even riches are fleeting, but this is far from a vision of social justice. The action he does prescribe is enjoyment. Qoheleth notes that everything is temporal, picking up the theme from the opening chapter. Individuals should hope that God gives something good, and when it arrives, enjoy it. Such a directive makes sense in the unstable economic conditions of the Persian context.

▮ The Text in the Interpretive Tradition

Whether Qoheleth's original intentions or not, Eccles. 4:9-16 has, across the centuries, been read to emphasize the importance of community. Qoheleth's example of a "threefold cord" (4:12) is an evocative metaphor for finding strength in numbers in a spiritual group. Gregory of Nyssa uses Ecclesiastes to support the idea that an individual committing to a life of celibacy should not do so alone, but should have a spiritual guide, because two are better than one (Wright, 237; Gregory of Nyssa, 70).

▮ The Text in Contemporary Discussion

Qoheleth here offers a powerful condemnation of an economy based on greed and backroom collaboration. Evil is not just personal but also structural. The challenge lies in the fact that the solutions to such problems are not personal, individual ones. Structural evil will not be solved by simply changing ourselves. Solutions require collective action, engaged communities, and most importantly, a comprehensive revaluation of what is good. Qoheleth seems to give voice to this very idea in 5:10-20—that those who love money and riches will never be satisfied and that they provide no real benefit to life.

Ecclesiastes 6:1—7:14: Who Knows What Is Good?

▮ The Text in Its Ancient Context

In 5:18-20, Qoheleth says to enjoy while you can, but at the beginning of Ecclesiastes 6, Qoheleth claims that God will prevent an individual from enjoying possessions because the things God gives a family are suddenly enjoyed by a stranger. It's almost as if, in juxtaposing these two suppositions, Qoheleth wants to represent the paradox that is life. Given the capricious economic context in the Persian period, it would make sense that there could be some anxiety over a family actually retaining their possessions (Seow, 210).

In Eccles. 6:12, Qoheleth asks, "who knows what is good?" This is a typical question for the author (e.g., "who knows?" in 3:21). The "better than" sayings in chapter 7 purport to answer the question of 6:12. What Qoheleth deems to be "better" comes as a shock. Mourning, sorrow, rebuke, and sadness are "better" than laughter, feasting, and songs. Although in the form of proverbial wisdom, Qoheleth subverts expectations. The episode ends with Qoheleth saying that God makes both good and bad so that humans have no idea what will happen (7:14).

▮ The Text in the Interpretive Tradition

Midrash Qoheleth offers an extensive reflection on 7:1, trying to explain the text's claim that the day of death is better than the day of birth. The midrash suggests that at birth, one's station in life is not yet known, while at death, it is. Thus one can rejoice at death if good deeds have led to a good life, while rejoicing at birth would be premature. The midrash uses the analogy of two ships, one leaving the harbor and the other arriving. Although everyone rejoices as one leaves, a wise person holds the opposite view: "there is not cause to rejoice over the ship which is leaving the harbor because nobody knows what will be its plight . . . but when [a ship] enters the harbor all have occasion to rejoice since it has come in safely" (as cited in Christianson, 190). This metaphor does not stray far from Qoheleth's main intention, that for epistemological reasons (i.e., that humans do not know what will happen to them) or for anthropological ones (i.e., humans have no ability to influence the outcome of their lives), humans need to rethink the causes and occasions for both joy and sorrow.

▌ THE TEXT IN CONTEMPORARY DISCUSSION

I was shocked recently to find out that the crib my wife and I had purchased five years earlier had been deemed "illegal" because it no longer cohered to the most recent safety standards. Our society spends a lot of time, money, and energy in order to prolong life. I do not suggest we abdicate the civic responsibility of safety standards. When it comes to life, however, we often value quantity over quality. Much of the focus of our health-care system is designed to prolong life (a noble pursuit, to be sure); but does this ignore the importance of quality of life? Qoheleth's words challenge our society. Even if someone lives to be two thousand years old, he says, it would be better to be a stillborn child if there is no enjoyment during those years (6:4-9).

Vexing, however, are Qoheleth's collateral statements suggesting that enjoyment itself is difficult, if not impossible. The things given in life for enjoyment may be taken and given to another (6:2). The appetite is never satisfied (6:7). Humans are not even given the ability to dispute their lot in life, because "the more words, the more vanity" (6:11). Everything, as Qoheleth has already said, is but a chasing of the wind.

Ecclesiastes 7:15-29: An Accounting of Everyday Life

▌ THE TEXT IN ITS ANCIENT CONTEXT

In 7:15, Qoheleth enters fully into a critique of the conceptual underpinnings of much of Israel's Wisdom literature. Texts such as Deuteronomy (e.g., 4:40; 28:1-2, 15) and Proverbs (e.g., 3:1-2, 24-26) avow a connection between act and consequence. With one experiential observation, Qoheleth undermines such simplistic theological formulations: he has seen "everything"—one righteous sufferer or prosperous sinner fractures the formula.

Qoheleth's responses to a lack of justice vary; here he recommends moderation. This raises certain questions, however. How can he recommend that one not be too righteous (7:16)? Likewise, saying the opposite: "Do not be too wicked" suggests that a moderate amount of wickedness is appropriate. Some have suggested that Qoheleth here is being sarcastic, or that he speaks against an overly confident wisdom. This may be a point where scholars overthink the problem: in a book that often uses hyperbole (e.g., the preferred status of a stillborn baby in 6:4-6), his point here is simple. The observation in 7:15 obliterates the traditional "Deuteronomistic" formula. In 7:16-18, we find absurdity, a parody of attempts to express a tidy formula that can efficiently encapsulate the totality of humanity's interactions with God. If his formula seems ridiculous, that is exactly the point: any tidy formula will wilt in the face of the human condition; life and experience are too complex.

◼ THE TEXT IN THE INTERPRETIVE TRADITION

In 7:26, Qoheleth refers to a woman who is a trap and more bitter than death. Similar sentiment about women is extant in other Wisdom literature (e.g., Prov. 25:24; Sir. 9:1-9; 25:16-26), and so we should not be surprised to find it here. Many early Christian commentators laud "Solomon" for such words and often use them as a resource to explain the benefits of celibacy or virginity. For example, Pseudo-Clement of Rome (third century CE) warns consecrated men from consorting with women with "much silliness, without fear of God" (Wright, 256).

Although scholars argue about whether Qoheleth was misogynistic, there is an unfortunate legacy stemming from 7:26. Qoheleth's description of the "bitter woman" finds its way into what has been described as "one of the most malignant and destructive texts of Western culture," the *Malleus Maleficarum*, a treatise written to help identify witches in the fifteenth century (Christianson, 39). It explains that a woman is more bitter than death because death only kills the body, but "the sin which arose from woman destroys the soul" (as cited in Christianson, 40).

◼ THE TEXT IN CONTEMPORARY DISCUSSION

Feminist critics of Scripture have rightly balked at Qoheleth's words in 7:26-29. Such words force modern interpreters to confront the social, cultural, and religious differences between the time of the text and our own. The exegetical details are always important, however. Qoheleth may not have intended to repudiate all women everywhere (as some across the centuries have interpreted the text). In its literary context, he may simply be trying to contrast the personified woman, Wisdom, with another personified woman, Folly (see Seow, 270–73). Nevertheless, there are legitimate reasons to be skeptical of a text from a patriarchal culture that evinces misogynistic language. Texts have the power to promulgate a hierarchical relationship between genders, and modern interpreters should have their ears attuned to such readings of texts.

Ecclesiastes 8:1—9:18: Eat, Drink, and Be Merry

◼ THE TEXT IN ITS ANCIENT CONTEXT

These two chapters build on and offer some similar observations to the central themes at play throughout the book. Qoheleth's reflections on life lead to one conclusion: enjoy yourself while you can; as the poet Robert Herrick says, "Gather ye rosebuds while you may." Qoheleth's observations go beyond just the inevitability of death, but that while alive there is no way to predict people's fates. The basic observation in 8:14 could summarize much of Ecclesiastes: the righteous are treated like the wicked, and the wicked are treated like the righteous. This leads to the conclusion that all is vanity. Qoheleth expands on this observation in 9:1-8, making it more explicit by pairing opposite groups of people (righteous/wicked, good/evil, clean/unclean, good/sinners) to whom the "same fate" comes (9:3).

◼ THE TEXT IN THE INTERPRETIVE TRADITION

Gregory the Great (d. 604 CE) coordinates Eccles. 8:14 with the theology of Job. The fact that justice is not apparent in the world, he says, has no doubt been ordained by God. Gregory comes to this conclusion because of two contextual factors. First is his belief in an afterlife, which was not necessarily operative in Qoheleth's own theological tool kit. From Gregory's afterlife-influenced point of view, those doing the evil are "hastening onward to those torments that are without end" (as cited by Wright, 261). Second, Gregory conflates the situation in Job, in which the prologue describes God's role in the genesis of Job's ordeal, with the situation in Ecclesiastes, where the point seems to be the opposite: God's conspicuous absence.

◼ THE TEXT IN CONTEMPORARY DISCUSSION

Qoheleth, one might say, is preoccupied with death. In this way, he shows some similarities to modern philosophy. The existentialist philosopher Martin Heidegger speaks of "being-towards-death." He says that the experience of life always leaves one with a sense that there is "constantly something still to be settled," that we all die (Heidegger, 279). For Heidegger, there is a "not yet" that belongs to individuals, as long as they exist, which is a "coming-to-its-end" (286). The connection between being and death is part of the experience of existence itself: "death is a way to be" (289), which an individual assumes as soon as he or she comes into existence. He quotes German poet von Tepl: "As soon as man comes to life, he is at once old enough to die" (*Der Ackermann aus Böhmen*). Authentic living, for Heidegger, must exist toward the inevitability of death "without fleeing it or covering it up" (305).

Qoheleth agrees with these sentiments. He similarly suggests that death needs to be part of our very self-understanding (e.g., 9:2-3, 5). The inevitability of death must be part of our lived experience: "no one can anticipate the time of disaster" (9:12). Death is the great equalizer and reveals nothing about how a person has lived her or his life (contrary to Sir. 11:28). For Qoheleth, the experience of "being-towards-death" should influence not only our theological formulations but also how we live our lives: "Go, eat your bread with enjoyment, and drink your wine with a merry heart" (9:7).

The critique that might be leveled against Heidegger and Qoheleth is their individuality. Qoheleth's observations about the lack of justice in the world are, for the most part, personal reflections, not indictments of structural injustice. Likewise, Heidegger insists that an individual's "ownmost possibility," by which he means death, is "non-relational" (308). This is part of his existentialism, just as the individual-based reflections of Qoheleth are in keeping with the approach of the wisdom tradition. One might ask them: "Where is 'the other'?" Qoheleth's sober realization of death's inevitability could be directed outward, recommending solidarity with those around the world who live a truly contingent existence, where, because of war or extreme poverty, death is a daily reality.

Ecclesiastes 10:1—11:6: A World Gone Awry

▊ The Text in Its Ancient Context

Chapters 10–11 depict a world on the brink of chaos. One cannot trust in governmental officials (10:5-6; 16-17). Rulers and slaves have traded places (10:7). One can again see the historical context—marked by economic turmoil—as the impetus behind such reflections. Evidence suggests regular turnover among the rulers and elusive economic security (Seow, 23–26, 325) because of such rapid changes and the policies correlated with them. Qoheleth presses this point by moving from words about kings and rulers to quotidian, agrarian situations. Camouflaged pits with nets suddenly trap those who dug them (10:8). Woodworkers will be threatened by their craft (10:9). The world has gone askew.

The call to "send out your bread upon the waters" (11:1) and to "divide your means" (11:32) are often thought to advocate foreign and diversified investments in order to avoid any vicissitudes that might threaten economic viability. On the other hand, there is nothing here specifically about profit, as one might expect from economic advice. All Qoheleth says is that "you will get it back" (11:1). Seow coordinates the saying in 11:1 with the Egyptian Instruction of Anksheshonq, which says: "Do a good deed and throw it in the water; when it dries you will find it" (Seow, 342). Perhaps Qoheleth advocates doing a good deed without expecting anything in return. This fits Qoheleth's overall observations, that human actions in no way guarantee any kind of commensurate response; the "consequences of human actions are often contrary to expectations" (Seow, 343).

▊ The Text in the Interpretive Tradition

Interpreters have long recognized 11:1-2 as Qoheleth's clearest call for charity and concern for others. *Midrash Qoheleth*, later Christina interpreters, and modern authors such as Louise Erdrich all recognize "the passage's implicit and poetic urging of generosity" (Christianson, 219–20).

Authors as early as Alcuin (d. 803) allegorize this text and conflate it with New Testament imagery of the sowing of seeds. This turns it into a call for evangelization. This interpretation remains prevalent today in Christian evangelical contexts. The Internet is replete with sermons connecting Eccles. 11:1 with evangelization, often asserting that if one casts bread (i.e., sows), then one will reap a harvest of believing souls.

▊ The Text in Contemporary Discussion

Richard Wilbur's 2010 poem offers what one interpreter called a "midrash" on Ecclesiastes 11:1.

> We must *cast our bread*
> *Upon the waters*, as the
> Ancient preacher said,
>
> Trusting that it may
> Amply be restored to us
> *After many a day.*

That old metaphor,
Drawn from rice farming on the
River's flooded shore,

Helps us to believe
That it's no great sin to give,
Hoping to receive.

Therefore I shall throw
Broken bread, this sullen day
Out across the snow,

Betting crust and crumb
That birds will gather, and that
One more spring will come. (see Works Cited, p. 641)

This poem is constructed of Haiku in which the first and last lines of each stanza rhyme. It recapitulates the image of Qoheleth into a different context, but seems to retain the central idea of hope for a future, although one more selfish and less focused on charity.

Ecclesiastes 11:7—12:14: The End of All Things

■ THE TEXT IN ITS ANCIENT CONTEXT

The consensus suggests that 11:7—12:8 is a reflection on youth and old age. Many scholars argue that the text was originally intended to be an allegory. Some elements work well allegorically: dimly lit windows represent poor eyesight (12:3); women who cease to grind represent a lack of teeth (12:3). Other elements, such as terrors in the road or being afraid of heights (12:5), do not. Choon-Leong Seow (376–82) suggests that Qoheleth combines the imagery of old age with eschatological language so as to depict the end of humanity itself. Qoheleth's talk of death, to this point in the book, has remained abstract. Here at the end, a "cosmic doom" that depicts "the end of human existence" (379) forcefully imposes on the reader "the finality of death" (380).

A short epilogue concludes the book in the third person, not Qoheleth's customary first person. Based on such observations, most scholars consider the epilogue extraneous to the core of the book because it came from the hand of a different author. The final two verses show the widest variance: "Fear God, and keep his commandments; for that is the whole duty of everyone. For God will bring every deed into judgment." Most conspicuous here is the mention of the commandments, an emphasis lacking in Qoheleth's reflections throughout the book. Qoheleth sporadically refers to judgment, but does not generally refer to God. We have, at the very end, the intrusion of a later redactor into the text of Ecclesiastes.

■ THE TEXT IN THE INTERPRETIVE TRADITION

Medieval French Talmudist Samuel ben Meir (d. 1158) was the first to attribute the end of Ecclesiastes to an editor (Christianson, 249). Those who avoid this observation, however, have tended to find in the text's final two verses a powerful way of framing the skepticism of most of Qoheleth's message. Thus St. Bonaventure says that it cannot be properly understood without reading all of it (Christianson, 253). While some suggest that a "faithful" ending may have helped such a skeptical book become canonized in both the Jewish and Christian traditions, no direct evidence supports such a conclusion.

■ THE TEXT IN CONTEMPORARY DISCUSSION

Endings matter, especially in Ecclesiastes. Some say that the "conservative" ending is an intrusion into Qoheleth's intentions and unfairly frames his original intent. It is worth noting, however, that recommending the commandments (Eccles. 12:13) does not necessarily contradict any of Qoheleth's teachings or observations. The final words could be read as an appropriate response to Qoheleth's skepticism that one must eventually arrive at a more faithful belief. On the other hand, such a view might give too much weight to the ending and simultaneously must ignore the possibility of redactional activity.

Should we be so flummoxed, however, to find diverse traditions within a biblical text? All of Scripture is the product of tradition; it does not fall into our laps straight from the lips of God. Sometimes traditions are woven together to constitute whole biblical texts. At other times, changes and emendations are made after the time of the "original author" (to the extent that such a thing can even be discussed). Scripture is diverse. To find diversity within a specific book only demonstrates the diversity of the canon. No book embodies that diversity better than Qoheleth, whose observations, brash honesty, and bold recommendations push faith communities to rethink and reexamine the most sacredly held truths and ideals. In a way, whether original or not, the final two verses show Qoheleth considering that which we thought he had rejected, which is the very posture his readers must adopt in order to read his words with open hearts and minds.

Works Cited

Basil of Caesarea. 1950. *Ascetical Works*. Translated by Monica Wagner, CSC. FC 9. Washington, DC: Catholic University of America Press.

Christianson, Eric S. 2007. *Ecclesiastes through the Centuries*. Oxford: Blackwell.

Cyril of Jerusalem. 1969. *The Works of Saint Cyril of Jerusalem*. Vol. 2. Translated by Leo P. McCauley, SJ. FC 64. Washington, DC: Catholic University of America Press.

Davis, Ellen F. 2000. *Proverbs, Ecclesiastes, and the Song of Songs*. Louisville: Westminster John Knox.

Gregory of Nyssa. 1967. *Ascetical Works*. Translated by Virginia Woods Callahan. FC 58. Washington, DC: Catholic University of America Press.

Heidegger, Martin. 1962. *Being and Time*. Translated by John Macquarrie and Edward Robinson. San Francisco: Harper & Row.

Limburg, James. 2006. *Encountering Ecclesiastes: A Book for Our Time*. Grand Rapids: Eerdmans.

Luther, Martin. 1972. *Ecclesiastes, Song of Solomon, 2 Samuel 23:1-7*. Translated by Jaroslav Pelikan. Luther's Works 15. St. Louis: Concordia.

McVey, Kathleen E., trans. 1989. *Ephrem the Syrian: Hymns*. Mahwah, NJ: Paulist Press.

Seow, Choon-Leong. 1997. *Ecclesiastes: A New Translation with Introduction and Commentary.* AB 18C. New York: Doubleday.

Tamez, Elsa. 2000. *When the Horizons Close: Rereading Ecclesiastes.* Translated by Margaret Wilde. Eugene, OR: Wipf & Stock.

Wilbur, Richard. 2010. "Ecclesiastes 11:1" from *Anterooms: New Poems and Translations.* Copyright © 2010 by Richard Wilbur. Reprinted by permission of Houghton Mifflin Harcourt. All rights reserved. Reprinted by permission of The Waywiser Press (http://waywiser-press.com). UK and Commonwealth rights reserved.

Wright, J. Robert, ed. 2005. *Proverbs, Ecclesiastes, Song of Solomon.* Ancient Christian Commentary on Scripture: Old Testament 9. Downers Grove, IL: InterVarsity Press.

SONG OF SONGS

Hugh R. Page Jr.

The Song of Songs is a song (Heb. *šîr*) purportedly composed by or making specific reference to Solomon (1:1). It is, in reality, a pseudonymous work. The interpretive literature on the book is vast, and accessible summaries can be found in the more recent commentaries of Tremper Longman III (2001) and J. Cheryl Exum (2005). Scholarly agreement is far from uniform, even among more contemporary commentators, about its content and structure. Some, like Longman, treat it as a poetic "anthology" (Longman, 48). Others are convinced that it is a unified composition with a coherent organizing theme. Exum attempted early on in her engagement of the book to employ a hybrid strategy, synthesizing both of the aforementioned approaches, but eventually abandoned this in favor of reading it as a literary "whole" (Exum, 37). Marvin Pope in his now classic magisterial treatment in the Anchor Bible Commentary series argues that "characterization of the Song as an Anthology is not especially helpful" (Pope, 37). Evidence can be marshaled in favor of either position, so this is an issue about which there is likely to be healthy disagreement among interpreters well into the future.

Insofar as it treats love—in its concrete and ethereal dimensions—as a topic for serious intellectual and spiritual musing, a solid case can be made for its inclusion in the Bible's corpus of Wisdom literature. While not a new suggestion, it is worthy of consideration because within the Song, the taxonomy and lexical inventory used to talk about love (e.g., Heb. *dôd*, *'āhēb*, *ra'yāt*, and *'ahăbâ*) are crucial didactic elements—as crucial as the words used with reference to prudent behavior and its religious underpinnings in Proverbs, Ecclesiastes, and other exemplars of the wisdom genre. In pedagogical contexts, I have found it useful to follow those who see the Song of Songs as a libretto or script for a ritual performance. From my vantage point, one finds in it at least four main voices: (1) a male voice, (2) a female voice, (3) a narrator (or chorus), and (4) Love (Heb. *'ahăbâ*).

The latter of these voices, Love, invites readers to ponder its mysterious calling and to yield themselves to its urgings. In some respects the Song of Songs is reminiscent of the Sumerian cycle of poetry focused on the gods Inanna and Dumuzi (Wolkstein and Kramer) as well as the *hieros gamos* ("sacred marriage") tradition preserved in the Ugaritic tale (CAT 1.23) describing the conception and birth of Dawn and Dusk (Coogan and Smith, 155–66). Resonances to love poetry in ancient Egypt, Canaan, and Mesopotamia have also been noted (Longman, 49–54). It is possible that the liturgical function of what we have in the Song of Songs is to explain the divine etiology of love. Its internal rhetoric emphasizes that the locus of human meaning is found in the unquenchable desire for, and the process of seeking union with, one's beloved, and in recognizing the transcendent moments that are part of the quest that such a quest generates.

From a form-critical standpoint, the *Sitz im Leben* ("life setting") and date of the book are virtually impossible to discern from internal data. Certain linguistic features suggest that the book is either relatively late in composition or hails from an Israelite provenance in which lexical archaisms were prevalent. For example, one particular grammatical element recurring in the text—the use of the prefixed Hebrew particle *šin* as a relative pronoun—could be indicative of either an early or late date. It also contains a number of words that appear only once in the entirety of the Hebrew Bible (see Pope, 33–34). Such a specialized lexicon suggests that the book had a didactic thrust not unlike other works within the biblical wisdom corpus. It views the cosmos as an *esoteric* landscape in which the beloved is at once an archetypal concept and a palpable presence in the human realm. It asserts that the concrete and infinite are part of a single cosmic reality. The physical textures of life are honored through fulsome descriptions of the natural world, the spectrum of human emotions, and the template of the human body. Love occupies a central place in the book, but also poses the ultimate paradox. Giving oneself and one's possessions to pursue and seek communion with it will make one an object of contempt (Heb. *bûz*). Thus 8:6-7 can be said to provide the *axis* around which it and indeed life itself revolves. The quest for and union with one's beloved are those essential features of a terrestrial pilgrimage leading to the *šalhebetyâ* (8:6)—the ineffable flame—in whose presence light, peace, and wholeness are found.

1:1—3:11: Voices of Love and Nocturnal Visions

▌ THE TEXT IN ITS ANCIENT CONTEXT

The first three chapters of the Song of Songs model a structural pattern discernible throughout the book: juxtaposition of poetic monologues by what appear to be representative male, female, and unidentified voices. A woman speaks in 1:1-3, inviting an unnamed suitor, perhaps a monarch, to shower her with kisses and to spirit her away (1:4a). A scene shift immediately follows to a royal abode. In the remainder of verse 4, we have an invitation given to a host of young women present (1:3)—or perhaps to a chorus—to celebrate and remember.

> Let us rejoice because of you.
> Let us keep your love always in mind.
> Those who are just love you far more than wine. (1:4)

Soliloquies celebrating the attractiveness of the two lovers follow in the remainder of chapter 1 and in chapter 2. Pastoral imagery abounds (1:7-8, 17) as the comely features of the lovers and the natural surroundings in which their attachment to one another deepens are described in evocative detail. Throughout, one senses that the similarity of nature's rhythms to those of human love is a secret this section is intended to reveal. The agony of unfulfilled longing (3:1-3) and the joy of union with one's beloved (3:4) are revealed in a night vision, the timelessness of which is expressed antiphonally here and later on in the book: "Don't rouse or push Love until the time is right" (2:7; 3:5; 8:4).

◼ THE TEXT IN THE INTERPRETIVE TRADITION

Jewish and Christian expositors have made innumerable interpretive forays into the Song of Songs. Pope offers a selective summary of this rich tradition and notes the presence of Jewish allegorists who see the Song as expressive of YHWH's relationship with Israel, Christian allegorists for whom it is emblematic of the bond between "Christ and the church," and later Jewish mystical traditions that see reflected in the Song "the union of active and passive aspects of the intellect" (Pope, 89). One can readily imagine the rich interpretive possibilities that emerge from applying such paradigms to Song of Songs 1–3.

◼ THE TEXT IN CONTEMPORARY DISCUSSION

Love maintains much of its allure as modern trope and mystery in twenty-first-century life. However, there is reticence to discuss, particularly in faith communities, love and relationships using evocative imagery like that found in the Song. In the West, there remain, at times, strong unspoken taboos that prevent frank discussion about longing and the consummation of desire, even within the parameters of committed long-term partnerships. The Song certainly urges modern readers to "push the envelope" and be more daring in claiming ownership of our emotions and our bodies. We also have to be cognizant of the patriarchal milieu from which the Song comes, the relatively narrow understanding it has of the human gender binary (male/female), and the heteronormative paradigm it reifies. Interpretive readings that reach beyond these cultural signifiers toward the book's core message about love will be better able to deploy it in support of theologies that nurture inclusive communities of conscience.

4:1—8:4: Awakening and Being Intoxicated by Love

◼ THE TEXT IN ITS ANCIENT CONTEXT

How does one comprehend—at a deeper level—the rationale for and implications of the baroque language in this section's evocative monologues? Moreover, what are we to make of the following recommendation in 5:1?

> Friends, Lovers:
> Eat, drink, become inebriated!

Exum's intriguing suggestion about "conjuring" in the Song offers important insight: "The Song casts a spell with words: through seductively beautiful poetry the lovers materialize and dematerialize in a continual play of seeking and finding" (Exum, 6). This raises the possibility of seeing the

Song, in its entirety, as a literary talisman—a *conjurational* implement of power—capable of making the Love that can "stand toe to toe" with Death a reality (8:6). Therefore, the final command in 5:1 (Heb. *wĕšikrû*) could be translated, in context, "be spellbound." It is a directive that should perhaps shape one's approach to this second section in its entirety. As Exum suggests, the Song "invites us to become lovers too" (7).

■ THE TEXT IN THE INTERPRETIVE TRADITION

Strikingly, Ambrose of Milan sees in Song. 5:1 allusions to Christ communing with the faithful and encouraging them toward greater perfection. A host of other early Christian commentators have noted elements in this section of the Song with important dimensions of the church and the life of faith. Some of the more interesting are Gregory of Nyssa's identification of the frankincense in Song. 4:13-15 with Christ's divinity and his comment on the absence of the beloved in 5:6 as emblematic of the transcendence of Christ; Theodoret of Cyr's reading of Song of Songs 6:5 as a reference to the God's ineffable light; and Ambrose of Milan's suggestion that the nursing-breast imagery in 8:1 alludes to Christian baptism (for the aforementioned references, see Wright, 339–62).

■ THE TEXT IN CONTEMPORARY DISCUSSION

The strength of interpretive paradigms developed after the Enlightenment is that they stress the value of empirical evidence. When applied to biblical studies, evidence-based approaches treat the Bible purely as an ancient artifact from which information can be mined using scientific methodologies. It becomes an object subject to scholarly and ecclesial gaze—an ossified recipient of our querying. To subject a book like the Song to such treatment deprives it of the vitality it was intended to have. Jewish and Christian allegorists allowed the Song to fire their imaginations. We too should take Exum's lead and allow the evocative poetry in 4:1—8:4 to conjure the lovers in the text as well as the courage we need to love in our generation and live with the consequences—not always salutary—of a life guided by its dictates.

8:6–14: Love Gives Voice to Life's Greatest Paradox

■ THE TEXT IN ITS ANCIENT CONTEXT

It is in this final section that the Song of Songs most displays the traits of a classical treatise in the genre of speculative wisdom, albeit with a haunting resonance to Canaanite mythology. Love (Heb. *'ahăbâ*) speaks of its vitality and boasts of its power. Both make it a worthy opponent for two forces most emblematic of the life cycle in the ancient Syro-Palestinian imagination: waters and death. To place it as a "seal" on one's thoughts ("heart") and actions ("arm") is to become its devotee and to be warmed by its powerful "divine fire"—the meaning of Hebrew *šalhebetyâ* (8:6). This unquenchable inferno is the iconic hypostasis of the celestial force made manifest in the human longing, the drive to seek the ineffable, and the physical consummation of desire between lovers. One detects unmistakable reminiscences of Ugaritic myth—that is, of the cosmic battle between Ba'lu, the Canaanite storm god, and Yammu, the deification of the sea, whose sobriquets are "Prince Sea" and "Judge

River." One also detects resonances of the story of the continuous battle between Baʻlu and Môtu, the personification of death.

> They fight each other like heroes
> Môtu is strong, as is Baʻlu
> Like raging bulls, they go head to head
> Môtu is strong, as is Baʻlu
> They bite one another like serpents
> Môtu is strong, as is Baʻlu
> Like animals, they beat each other to a pulp
> Môtu falls, Baʻlu collapses. (CAT 1.6.6.16–22)

The protagonists fight to a virtual draw, both falling exhausted from a contest in which neither can claim absolute supremacy. The implication here, and in the Song of Songs, is that Love and Death are engaged in a timeless battle, which is ongoing in the celestial and terrestrial realms. While neither can claim victory, Love's ability to hold its own against its fearsome foe is reason for hope in the divine and human realms.

Nonetheless, the author—or perhaps an editor—of the Song of Songs wonders aloud why it is that in spite of the undeniable truth of Love's remarkable power, those who yield themselves to its inspiration are fated to be misunderstood and shunned by others (8:7). The scene then shifts, perhaps intentionally, to present a parallax view of how the all-encompassing essence of love is made known in the preparation of an earthly lover for the arrival of her beloved (8:8-9) and the feeling of all-encompassing wholeness (Heb. *šālôm*) that her visage engenders (8:10).

▌The Text in the Interpretive Tradition

Both the Pauline Letters (e.g., Rom. 12:10; 1 Corinthians 13) and the Johannine corpus (e.g., John 13:34; 1 John 14:18) in the New Testament celebrate the centrality, transformational power, and mystery of love (1 John 4:8, 16, 18). In the Fourth Gospel, it is the focus of Jesus' "new commandment" to love one another as Jesus has loved them (John 13:34; 15:12, 17). It is tempting to imagine here and elsewhere that early Christian tradition is in conversation with the tradition of love in Song. 8:6-7. Although editors of the most recent edition of the Greek New Testament (Aland et al., 887–901) identify no quotations or allusions to the Song of Songs in the Gospels, Acts, epistolary texts, or the Apocalypse, it is hard to imagine that a passage like 1 Cor. 13:8, "Love [*agapē*] does not fall," is neither in conversation with nor alluding to Song. 8:6. Among early Christian expositors on this text are Ambrose of Milan, for whom the "seal" in 8:6 is Christ; Augustine of Hippo, who opines on the soteriological impact of love; and Cyril of Jerusalem, who uses Song. 8:7 as a proof text for the actions of the women who came to anoint the body of Jesus after his death (for the aforementioned and additional citations from other early Christian exegetes see Wright, 364–66).

▌The Text in Contemporary Discussion

The mystery of love and its transformational power have long been celebrated in music, literature, and art. Moreover, certain musical genres such as blues, rhythm and blues, and soul explore its physical, emotional, social, political, and spiritual dimensions. It is perhaps the late twentieth century's failure to realize the teleological goals expressed in this musical tradition that gave rise to hip-hop culture, whose countercultural thrust offers a strong critique of an older generation that failed either to create Martin Luther King Jr.'s "Beloved Community," or to board the "Love Train" of which the 1970s soul ensemble The Spinners so movingly sings. Nonetheless, today's Bible readers and interpreters have a remarkable opportunity to retrieve the Song of Songs from its place in the archive of potentially scandalous and incredibly difficult biblical texts to which it is often relegated.

The impetus for this reclamation can and should be Song. 8:6-7, which has the ability to function as a window onto a long series of conversations in the ancient world about love. This same text can also be the starting point for a radical reorientation of traditional approaches to Scripture reading. Rather than beginning with the Gospels or taking a yearlong blended (combination of readings from the Old Testament, New Testament, and Psalter) book-by-book approach such as that advocated by the Center for Biblical Studies' "Bible Challenge" (see http://thecenterforbiblicalstudies.org and related links), one could imagine using Song. 8:6-7 as an eschatological antiphon with which to begin and end *lectio divina* or to supplement other strategies of engagement. At a time when the comparative study of Scriptures is not just an activity localized in the academy, but an essential activity in the promotion of interfaith relations as well, texts like Song. 8:6-7 allow clergy and laity to focus on larger—at times intractable—life issues and ponder ways that an appropriate array of texts, biblical and other, can be brought into an illuminating and empowering dialogue with one another. Such a process would certainly eliminate some long-standing barriers standing in the way of our being advocates for a vision of love and loving as all-encompassing and fully embodied acts of solidarity linking the hearts and minds of those willing to risk the "disdain" (Song. 8:7) of others and sit before the *šalhebetyâ* (8:6).

Works Cited

Aland, Barbara, Kurt Aland, Johannes Karavidopoulos, Carlo M. Martini, and Bruce M. Metzger, eds. 2005. *The Greek New Testament.* 4th ed. Stuttgart: Deutsche Bibelgesellschaft/United Bible Societies.

Coogan, Michael D., and Mark S. Smith. 2012. *Stories from Ancient Canaan.* 2nd ed. Louisville: Westminster John Knox.

Exum, J. Cheryl. (2005). *Song of Songs: A Commentary.* OTL. Louisville: Westminster John Knox.

Longman, Tremper I., III. 2001. *Song of Songs.* Grand Rapids: Eerdmans.

Pope, Marvin H. 1977. *Song of Songs: A New Translation with Introduction and Commentary.* AB. Garden City, NY: Doubleday.

Wolkstein, Diane, and Samuel Noah Kramer. 1983. *Inanna: Queen of Heaven and Earth.* New York: Harper & Row.

Wright, J. Robert, ed. 2005. *Proverbs, Ecclesiastes, Song of Solomon.* Ancient Christian Commentary on Scripture, Old Testament, 9. Downers Grove, IL: InterVarsity Press.

Themes and Perspectives in the Prophets: Truth, Tragedy, Trauma

Carol J. Dempsey

Introduction

Perhaps no other collection of texts is as rich as Israelite prophetic literature, whose authors knew how to imaginatively and effectively communicate messages of woe and visions of hope. As beautiful as the prose and poetry of these texts may be, they are not without bias and oftentimes reflect the culture and thought of the day, all of which has sparked lively debates and discussions among scholars and general audiences alike. Though time-bound, Israel's prophetic literature has a timeless quality that calls listeners in new contexts to hear the message of the prophets anew. The prophets of old continue to call people of all generations to right relationship so that all life may flourish and so that the vision of the new heavens and the new earth can become realized. The following article explores the richness of Israel's prophetic literature and invites readers to consider what it means to become poets and prophets of a new day characterized by justice, righteousness, loving-kindness, and humble walks with God.

Prophetic Writings in Their Ancient and Historical Contexts

Definitions and Canon

Lush in content and form, stunning in imagery and rhetoric, Israel's prophetic literature grew out of the lived experience of its prophets. It reflects the activities of the nation's prophets as they passed judgments, provided vision, acted symbolically, and offered comfort to the people of their respective communities. Written in prose and poetry, prophetic literature describes so-called prophets who live suspended between heaven and earth. As messengers of the divine, the prophets gazed into heaven's windows and offer a picture of Israel's God seated on the throne, tending to the business of the heavenly court. As ordinary yet highly gifted human beings, the prophets presented an earthly view of reality that seems sordid and grim on the one hand but magnificent and hope-filled on the other. They had the uncanny ability to see both what was and what could be, all of which is described quite vividly in Israel's prophetic literature.

The Hebrew canon of the Bible is divided into three divisions: the Torah, the Prophets (*nebiim*), and the Writings (*ketubim*). The Prophets are further subdivided into two categories: the "Former," or Nonwriting Prophets, and the "Latter," or Writing Prophets. The literature of the former prophets includes Joshua, Judges, 1–2 Samuel, and 1–2 Kings. The latter prophets include the Major Prophets—Isaiah, Jeremiah, Ezekiel—and the Book of the Twelve: Hosea, Joel, Amos, Obadiah, Jonah, Micah, Nahum, Habakkuk, Zephaniah, Haggai, Zechariah, and Malachi.

The classification of the Former Prophets as prophetic is somewhat unusual because of the historical nature of these texts, and yet these books attest to the times in which the prophets are said to have lived and to have been active. The Deuteronomistic history attests to God's speaking to Israel through the prophets. The books of Chronicles, and most notably 1 Chron. 29:29, present the prophets as Israel's first historians.

Unlike the Hebrew canon, the Christian canon follows the divisions of the Septuagint (LXX) and has a fivefold division: the books of Law, History (containing the Former Prophets), Poetry, the Major Prophets, and the Minor Prophets. The ordering of the first six books of the Minor Prophets is also different in the Christian canon, which has Hosea, Amos, Micah, Joel, Obadiah, and Jonah coming before the other texts.

Three other books associated with the prophetic corpus but that are not part of the block of material known as the Major or Minor Prophets are the books of Baruch, Lamentations, and Daniel. The backdrop to the book of Baruch is the fall of Jerusalem and the exile in 587 BCE. This book is not part of the Hebrew or Palestinian canon of sacred texts but is found in the Greek Septuagint. Roman Catholic and Greek Orthodox regard Baruch as one of the seven deuterocanonical books. For Protestants, Baruch appears in the apocryphal texts of the Bible.

The background of the book of Lamentations is also the fall of Jerusalem in 587 BCE. The inspiration and canonicity of Lamentations has been acknowledged, but its location in the canon varies: the Hebrew tradition places the book among the Writings; the Greek and Latin traditions place Lamentations among the Prophets.

A similar situation exists for the book of Daniel. This book portrays the Judahites in exile. The two prayers in Daniel 3 and the stories of Susanna and Bel and the Dragon, chapters 10 and 14 respectively, are found in the Greek and Latin version of the text but not in the Hebrew canon. Roman Catholic tradition accepts these passages as canonical, but Protestant tradition rejects them as apocryphal. The Hebrew text places Daniel among the Writings, but the Greek, Catholic, and Protestant canons place Daniel among the Prophets.

Origins

When considering the origins of prophetic literature, no one definitive person or group can be named as author of the texts. Some texts may have been written by the prophet, others by tradents, and still others by anonymous authors and editors who preserved and added to an emerging body of texts. The words, actions, and symbolic gestures of the prophets remained alive throughout Israel's history, and generated new words and accounts that resulted in books such as Isaiah, Micah, and Obadiah.

Ancient Near Eastern Context

The earliest records of prophetic activity come from the city of Mari, located in upper Mesopotamia on the Euphrates River. In this region and specifically in the royal archives of Mari, about fifty letters have been found from the reign of Zimri-lim (around 1775–1761 BCE). Zimri-lim was the last Mari ruler before he was defeated by the Babylonian king Hammurabi. These letters were written by officials and administrators and contained communications from intermediaries delivering divine messages intended for the king. A few letters were also written to Yasmah-Addu, Zimri-lim's predecessor. In essence, a message was given from a god to an intermediary or prophet, who in turn told the message to a letter writer, who wrote it down and then gave it to the king. The intermediaries were both professional and nonprofessional men and women who received the messages in dreams and visions, often at the temple and sometimes during sacrificial rites. Interestingly, none of the Mari texts show that prophecy was associated with any one individual in particular. Most of the messages sent to the king concerned military, political, and religious matters; some even warned the king about various undertakings yet to occur. Many of the messages served to support the king in his leadership role. The Mari texts provide evidence showing that prophecy was not restricted to the Bible and is part of a much larger religious tradition. Additionally, the Mari texts show that divine communication happened through intuitive divination that took the form of a verbal message.

One other set of texts that reflect prophetic activity has been found. These less-well-known tablets, which date to the Neo-Assyrian period, roughly the eighth to seventh centuries BCE, preserve the proclamations of nine women and four men known as prophets who were contemporaneous with Isaiah and Micah.

Additionally, three Aramaic inscriptions indicate prophetic activity in the ancient Near East. First, the Deir ʿAlla inscription (750–650 BCE) shows that predictive texts were known in the Transjordan, not far from Israel, in the eighth century BCE. Second, the Zakkur inscription (805–775 BCE) contains the standard "fear not" formula for salvation proclamations from both Neo-Assyrian and biblical texts. Third, the Amman Citadel inscription (late ninth century BCE) seems to show some evidence of prophetic content, but no scholarly consensus exists on this point.

For most of the twentieth century CE, scholars did not think that the socioreligious phenomenon of "prophecy" existed in Egypt. Recently, however, attempts have been made to find evidence of prophetic activity in various Egyptian texts. The only Egyptian text that may exhibit the phenomenon of prophecy, however, is *Wenamun*, a story about an Egyptian official on an adventurous journey to Byblos. His task is to acquire timber for the Amun-Re temple at Karnak. During his journey, the official encounters many obstacles and is eventually arrested. His fate changes when someone appears to him in a trance and announces that he should be set free. The official, however, is not an Egyptian; he is a Phoenician, and thus the story is better suited as a Levantine prophecy and not an Egyptian one.

Attempts have also been made to locate prophetic activity at Ugarit, Ebla, Emar, and among the Hittites. All of these attempts, however, have not yielded conclusive evidence.

Finally, research into prophetic activity in the ancient Near East has proven to be helpful to the study of prophecy in ancient Israel. The literature makes clear that prophecy was common in the ancient Near East and must not be confined to Israel. Moreover, expressions such as "thus says . . ." found in ancient Near Eastern texts and also in Israel's prophetic corpora show some similarities of prophetic activity between the ancient Near East and Israel. Unlike Israelite prophetic literature, however, ancient Near Eastern literature does not show significant cases where prophecy questioned the monarchy. Ancient Near Eastern prophecy tended to support and encourage the monarchy, which is strikingly different from Israel's prophetic literature.

Israel's Prophets: Their Diverse Roles as Seekers of Truth

Although prophecy in Israel seems to share some similarities with ancient Near Eastern prophecy, the Israelite prophetic tradition had its own distinctive character. For instance, ancient Near Eastern prophecy often made no distinction between prophet and priest, which was not the case for Israel. Some of those who were later recognized as prophets may have been priests, as in the cases of Jeremiah and Ezekiel, but others, such as Hosea and Micah, were not priests.

In Israel, various types of prophets existed: the shamanistic prophets, known for their ecstatic activity, were often itinerant and usually prophesied in groups; the cultic or temple prophets, like Jeremiah, were associated with the priesthood and were sometimes found proclaiming in the temple; the court prophets, such as Daniel, who was both a prophetic and wisdom figure, advised the king. Others were free prophets, who began their work around the mid-eighth century BCE. These prophets included Amos, Hosea, Micah, and Isaiah. For them, their primary authority was God. They often stood on the periphery of Israelite society and worked to provoke social and religious change.

Israel's prophetic literature uses three terms to characterize Israel's prophets. Appearing about four hundred times in this literature, the most important and common term is *nābî*, which is frequently used in 1–2 Samuel, 1–2 Kings, Jeremiah, and Ezekiel. The term *ḥōzeh*, usually translated as "seer," is associated with those prophets who have a vision. Three striking examples appear in Num. 24:4, 16; and Ezek. 13:16, 23. The third term is *rō'eh*, used more than a dozen times in the Hebrew Bible and usually translated as "diviner." This person could discover things that were hidden, as in the case of 1 Sam. 9:9. Saul's servant suggests that Samuel be consulted to help find missing donkeys. Related terms include "man of God," as in the cases of Samuel (1 Sam. 9:6-10) and Elisha (2 Kgs. 5:8, 14-15). In Amos 3:7, God reveals to Amos that no punishment will befall the people without their knowing the divine intentions that will be made known to the people through God's "servants the prophets." Some of Israel's prophets have also been compared to a "sentinel" (Jer. 6:17), a "watchman" (Ezek. 3:16-21; 33:1-9), a "lookout" (Isa. 21:6), and a "refiner" (Jer. 6:27-30), each implying a specific task for which the prophet was responsible.

Scholars today debate whether all of Israel's prophets were actual historical persons. Despite such historical questions, the Bible's prophetic books do offer a comprehensive picture of the "prophetic persona" and the prophets' diverse roles as seekers of truth. The Bible portrays Israel's prophets as everyday people, for the most part, but scholarly arguments based on the form and style of the prophetic texts suggest that the prophets were well educated. The prophets were the keepers of the covenant and the guardians of justice, righteousness, and loving-kindness. The prophets were unrelenting on issues concerning justice (Amos 5:21-24; 8:4-6), and they frequently challenged institutions, systems, structures, attitudes, and mind-sets that were often considered "sacred" (Isa. 1:10-20; 58:1-14; Jer. 7:1-15).

Prophecy was a charism that called Israel's prophets to remain faithful to their God, their vocation, the task to be done, and the mission to be accomplished. As divinely inspired persons, Israel's prophets were called to comfort (Isa. 40:1-2), confront (Hosea 4:1-3), offer hope (Jer. 30:31-34; Joel 2:21-29), proclaim (Mic. 1:1-16), envision (Jer. 31:31-34), energize (Isaiah 25), shed light (Amos 6:1-8), exhort (Hosea 6:1-3), intercede (Hab. 3: 1-16), announce judgment (Hosea 4:1-3), proclaim salvation (Isaiah 62), and keep alive the gift of imagination (Ezekiel 1). Hence, their mission was multifaceted.

The prophets had an ethical mission: to help liberate creation from pain and suffering, inclusive of both victims and perpetrators of injustice (see, e.g., Isa. 42:1-4; 52:13—53:12; Joel 2:21-22). They also had a theological mission: to make known that Israel's God was a God of justice and compassion (Mic. 7:18-20). Their mission was also political: they had to advise political, social, and religious leaders of the day (Jer. 38:14-28). Finally, Israel's prophets were to be forever in dialogue with God, who would reveal what needed to be said and done (Mic. 6:6-8). As keepers of the covenant, Israel's prophets were heralds of good news, calling people back to right relationship (Isa. 1:16-17).

The biblical texts suggest that the experience of the prophets was an intuitive one, as exemplified by the opening words of Jeremiah's call narrative: "The word of the Lord came to me thus . . ." (Jer. 1:4). When first called to serve as a prophet, some of the prophets were initially reluctant (see Jer. 1:4-10 and Isa. 6:1-9), but God divinely and freely bestowed the gifts needed for this vocation (Jer. 1:6-10), enabling the prophets to say, "Here am I; send me!" (Isa. 6:8).

As passionate people who felt deeply about the pressing issues of their day, the prophets experienced all sorts of emotions related to their vocation (Habakkuk 1). They felt joy, delight, fear, frustration, pain, and most notably righteous anger over the people's apostasy, idolatry, and other transgressions (Micah 3). Perhaps the best example of a passion-filled prophet can be found in the book of Jeremiah, where the prophet complains to his God (Jer. 15:10-18), expresses utter frustration, though not without a sense of confidence and hope (Jer. 20:7-18), and then prays to his God for understanding (Jer. 32:16-25). Through the person of Hosea, Israel came to know the struggle within God's heart, which vacillated between love, remembrance, frustration, fidelity, and compassion (Hosea 11:1-9). Because of an inner compulsion that often welled up inside of them, the prophets had to speak; the spirited and Spirit-filled word of God had to go forth even when the prophet would rather not proclaim it (Jer. 20:9). The prophets were in touch with God's Spirit and filled with this Spirit, the source of their proclamation and the inspiration behind their mission (e.g., Mic. 3:8).

The prophets often began their proclamations with the phrase "Thus says the LORD," a typical prophetic messenger formula and later addition lending both authority and credence to the prophets' words. Many times, the prophets delivered God's word with graphic detail (Ezekiel 21). Their message was always related to their divine mission of establishing justice in the land. For example, Micah upbraided the political, social, and religious leaders of his day because they had acted unjustly. He also addressed the priests and prophets who had corrupted their religious offices (Mic. 3:1-7, 9-12). The prophets often spoke out against idolatry (Ezek. 14:6-8; Hab. 2:18-20), a stance that not only supported torah but also firmly established the sovereignty of Israel's God over all other gods.

Although the word of the prophets was often harsh, foreboding, and reflective of the influences and mores of their times, this word was always the graced word, inviting people to change their ways (Ezek. 18:30-32) and to be transformed into the holy and godly human beings they were meant to be (Gen. 1:27; Lev. 20:26).

The prophet's word was sometimes delivered through symbolic action. The prophets would perform some sort of symbolic gesture, the meaning of which only came to light much later on in the life of the community. Micah lamented, wailed, and went barefoot and naked to draw attention to the community's sinfulness (Mic. 1:8). Jeremiah sported the yoke of oxen to symbolize to his people that they were about to go into Babylonian captivity (Jeremiah 27).

With respect to the prophet's vision, the prophetic books make clear that Israel's prophets read the signs of the time. Because they studied both their community and world events, they knew what was about to befall Israel and Judah, and they warned their communities and the surrounding nations of their fate if they did not chart a new course. They were also graced to see God's vision of unity and peace for all creation, beautifully expressed in Isa. 2:1-4; Mic. 4:1-5; and Isa. 65:17-25. The prophets heralded a vision of a new kind of leadership that would help to usher in the reign of God and a new world order (Isa. 9:1-7; 11:1-9; 32:1). One can say that they were double-visioned: they saw what was and what could be, giving both sight and insight to their listeners.

Ninth Century BCE: Elijah and Elisha

In the ninth century BCE several prophets were active: Balaam (Numbers 22–23), Samuel (1–2 Samuel), Nathan (2 Sam. 7:1-17; 12:1-15; 1 Kgs. 1:1-45), and Ahijah (1 Kgs. 11:29-39; 12:12-15; 14:1-18), among others (see also 1 Kings 12–14).

Immediately following the division of the kingdom of Israel, two strong prophetic figures emerged in the ninth century: Elijah and Elisha. The Elijah cycle of stories is found in 1 Kings 17–19, 21; 2 Kgs. 1:1—2:18. Elijah was a Yahwist prophet in the tradition of Moses, active during the reign of King Ahab. He was noted for his struggle against Baalism, which is highlighted in Elijah's confrontation with the prophets of Baal on Mount Carmel (1 Kings 18). Elijah wins the contest and establishes God's power and Baal's impotence. He also has a marvelous encounter with God at Horeb (1 Kgs. 19:9-19) and later curses King Ahab and his house for his abuses of power (1 Kgs. 21:1-29). According to the biblical text, Elijah is taken up to heaven by a whirlwind as chariots of fire appear between him and his successor Elisha (2 Kgs. 2:1-18).

Elisha's cycle of stories recount his many miracles, visionary proclamations, and his alleged legitimation of King Jehu's rule (2 Kgs. 2:1—10:35). The stories particularly reveal his concern for his marginalized followers.

Preexilic Predictions of Tragedy: From Amos to Jeremiah

During Israel's and Judah's preexilic period (922–587 BCE), some people enjoyed prosperity and peace, while others at the bottom of the economic pile suffered many hardships. The prophets tried to mitigate the unjust oppression that some suffered at the hands of others. In both kingdoms, religious apostasy and idolatry were rampant; injustices and transgressions were many. Political, social, and religious institutions were sunk in the mire of sin and corruption. Civil war raged intermittingly; nations and kingdoms made poor alliances and ineffective coalitions. On the world scene during this time, Assyria rose to its zenith of power only to be defeated by Babylon, which later succumbed to Persia.

Many of the preexilic prophets warned against alliances and coalitions, upbraided kings, large landowners, and other political and social leaders because they had become corrupt and had blatantly disregarded torah. These prophets also addressed the religious leaders of their day, many of whom had become hypocrites (see, e.g., Micah 1–3). The prophets also passed judgment on the ordinary folk who were not faithful to covenant and the law, and they addressed those nations that took advantage of Israel and other peoples (Amos 1–2; Isaiah 13–23). Despite their harsh words, these prophets saw the reign of God dawning on the horizon when all nations, all peoples, would come together in peace on God's holy mountain (Isa. 2:1-4; Mic. 4:1-5). That day, however, would not arrive until all corruption and wickedness had been rooted out. Hence, turmoil, chaos, and devastation paved the way to restoration, renewal, and transformation.

The preexilic period ended in 587 BCE, when the southern kingdom of Judah collapsed, the capital city of Jerusalem was burned, the temple was destroyed by the Babylonians, and the inhabitants of Judah were exiled to either Babylon or Egypt. These events ushered in the exilic period of prophetic activity (587–539 BCE). The books of Amos, Hosea, First Isaiah, Micah, Zephaniah, Nahum, Habakkuk, and Jeremiah describe all these events.

Exilic Promises of Comfort and Hope: From Ezekiel to Second Isaiah

The exilic years found the Israelites without land, a king and monarchy, and a temple. They wondered if their God had abandoned them completely. Life in Babylon, however, was not a terrible experience for the Israelites. In fact, when they were freed from exile, many chose to stay in Babylon rather than start the hard work of rebuilding and reestablishing themselves as a people and a community in Yehud. These exilic times, though, did bring a certain degree of sadness, despair, and lamentation to the Israelites. They had lost so much! The prophetic texts of this period include Obadiah, Ezekiel, and Second Isaiah. These prophets often delivered a message of comfort (see, e.g., Isa. 40:1-2; 43:1—44:28). God would redeem the people; the temple would be rebuilt; the people would be reestablished on their land; and the land and community would flourish.

When Cyrus of Persia defeated the Babylonians, he issued an edict that essentially ended the Israelites' exile. The people were now free to return to their land. Some did; some did not. This edict began the postexilic period in Israel's history (539–333 BCE).

Postexilic Return, Restoration, and New Challenges: From Haggai to Jonah

The postexilic period is also known as the restoration or Persian period. The prophetic texts of Third Isaiah, Joel, Jonah, Haggai, Zechariah, and Malachi focus on shoring up life in the community and on rebuilding the temple. The community faced many economic problems, struggled with divided opinions among themselves as to how life should be lived, and faced hostility from neighboring Samaria as to who had the right to claim the old territory of Judah. Zerubbabel's rejection of the Samaritans' offer to help rebuild the temple set in motion the enmity between the Jews and the Samaritans that continued into the next century. The people also faced the problem of religious ritualism whereby maintaining rituals took preference over one's relationship with YHWH and the living out of social justice. Thus this time was a mixture of hope and disillusionment for the people, with restoration becoming part of Israel's future and not its present lived reality.

Literary Dimensions and Perspectives of the Prophetic Writings

Israel's prophetic texts use many different forms. They include symbolic action reports (Isa. 20:1-6), commissioning reports (Jer. 1:4-10), vision reports (Amos 7:1), biographies (Jeremiah 37–44), woe proclamations (Mic. 2:1-5), dirges (Ezek. 32:17-19), laments (Amos 5:1-3), judgment speeches (Mic. 1:2-7), *rib*, or courtroom, scenes (Mic. 6:1-5; Hosea 4:1-3), parables (Isa. 5:1-7; Jer. 18:1-11), disputation speeches (Mic. 2:6-11), complaints (Hab. 1:2-17), prayers (Hab. 3:1-16), prophetic historiography (Isaiah 36–39; Jeremiah 52, which is basically the same as 2 Kgs. 18:13—19:37), taunt songs (Isa. 14:3-22), and legends (2 Kgs. 4:1-7), among other forms.

Written predominately in poetry, the prophetic literature uses a variety of rhetorical elements such as numerical word pairs (Amos 1–2), merisms (Jer. 46:12), imagery (Ezek. 17:1-10), rhetorical questions (Amos 3:3-8), extended metaphors (Mic. 3:1-3), similes (Hosea 9:10), anthropomorphism, which ascribes human qualities to God (Zeph. 1:4), and personification (Ezekiel 16), among other literary techniques.

Major Themes in the Prophetic Writings

Covenant

At the heart of prophetic preaching was the Sinai covenant, which established a relationship between God and the Israelites. A myriad of images such as shepherd and flock (Isa. 56:11; Ezek. 34:8-10; Zech. 11:16-17), vine and vinedresser (Isa. 5:1-7), potter and clay (Jer. 18:1-11), and father and son (Jer. 31:9) gave expression to this relationship. Oftentimes, marital imagery captured the covenant relationship between God and the people of Israel. God was the husband; Israel was the wife (Hosea 1–2). The Deuteronomic perspective on covenant throughout the prophets emphasizes the demands of the covenant and puts those demands in the context of God's great love for the people (Deut. 4:37; 7:8; 10:15). Repeatedly, the people are called to respond with love (Deut. 6:5; 10:12).

The prophets exposed the people's violations against covenant and warned of the divine consequences that would follow these transgressions. Some of the transgressions included apostasy (Jer. 2:19), idolatry (Isa. 2:8, 20), swearing, lying, murder, stealing, adultery (Hosea 4:1-3), and profaning the Sabbath (Ezek. 20:12-13a). At times, the people even pleaded with God not to break covenant with them even though they had transgressed (Jer. 14:13-22).

Finally, the prophets proclaimed that even though Israel had broken the covenant and had suffered divine consequences, God's covenant plan remained constant (Isa. 59:21). Four prophets in particular heralded the vision of a new covenant: Second Isaiah (Isa. 42:1-9; 49:1-13; 54:9-10; 55:3-5), Jeremiah (Jer. 31:31-34), Ezekiel (Ezek. 34:23-31; 37:24-28), and Hosea (Hosea 2:16-23). Along with a new covenant, the people would be given a new heart and a new spirit that would enable them to follow God's ordinances and statutes, which would in turn allow them to live in peace and prosperity in the land.

Justice

The prophets called Israel to do good and correct oppression, to seek and execute justice (Isa. 1:7), and to wait for God continually (Hosea 12:6). Because life in Israel was essentially hierarchical, the erosion of justice on the part of some of Israel's political and religious leaders took its toll on the common good. Injustice prevailed in the land, because the Israelites themselves had forgotten God and God's ways. Various prophetic texts suggest that some of the more economically and socially powerful Israelites preyed on their own kin. These situations often went unchecked by Israel's political and religious leaders, but not by prophets (Isa. 5:8-30; Jer. 5:20-29; 9:4-11; Mic. 2:1-5, 8-9; Hab. 1:2-4; 2:6-20). Amos railed against Israel's injustices and warned the people that justice would prevail "on that day" (Amos 2:6, 16; 3:14; 5:18, 20; 6:3; 8:3, 9, 11, 13).

For the prophets, injustice would never be the people's enduring experience. The experience of darkness and utter futility characterized by the absence of justice would one day be transformed into light with the coming of God, who would clothe the people in garments of justice and salvation (Isa. 60:1-3; 61:10; 62:1). Israel's God is a God of justice (Isa. 30:18) who loves justice (Isa. 61:8) and who makes justice part of the new covenant (Hosea 2:19)

Apostasy and Idolatry

Two of Israel's main transgressions were apostasy and idolatry. Apostasy often resulted in idolatry. Apostasy consisted of acts of rebellion against God and God's laws and an abandonment of faith in God and God's covenant (Isa. 1:2-9; Jer. 5:1-17). Jeremiah denounced Judah's apostasy and infidelity and warned the people about the tragic events that would befall them because of their transgression (Jer. 5:6).

Idolatry was the worship of and trust in gods other than YHWH (Isa. 2:6-9, 12-22; Jer. 2:9-19; Ezek. 16:23-29; 23:7, 30). Idolatry was often described as sexual promiscuity, adultery, and unbridled lust. The prophets repeatedly warned the Israelite community against worshiping idols (Isa. 44:9-20; 45:16), which took the form of "the work of human hands" (Isa. 2:8; 37:19; Jer. 1:16; Mic. 5:12), molten images (Isa. 40:19; Jer. 10:14), abhorrent objects (Isa. 66:3; Jer. 4:1; Ezek. 5:11), and abominations (Isa. 44:19).

Idolatry included a wide variety of moral failures, such as oppression of the vulnerable, murder, and adultery (Jer. 7:6, 9; Ezek. 22:2-12). The most abominable form of idolatry was the kind connected with child sacrifice (Isa. 57:5; Jer. 7:31; 19:5; 32:35; Ezek. 16:20-21; 20:31; 23:39). Ezekiel, Hosea, and Micah addressed both apostasy and idolatry and made known to the people the consequences of their actions (Ezek. 6:1-7; Hosea 8:1-14; Mic. 1:2-7). Forgetfulness of God led to forgetfulness of God's ways, which resulted in political, social, economic, and religious corruption and chaos that ended in the destruction of both Israel and Judah.

The prophets proclaimed that God would reestablish Israel in right relationship marked by faithfulness and the end to idolatry (Isa. 2:17-18; 30:22; 31:7; Ezek. 11:18-20; 36:25; 37:23; Hosea 2:14-23). When idolatry would come to an end, the name of YHWH would be the only divine name on the earth (Zech. 14:9; Mal. 1:11).

Worship

Israelite prophetic literature lists a whole range of expressions of personal and communal worship: prayer (Isa. 1:15; 37:4; 56:7; Hab. 3:1-19); singing (Isa. 12:5; 26:1; 30:29; 42:10; Jer. 20:13; Amos 5:23; 8:10); lamentation and fasting (Isa. 58:3-5; Jer. 9:20; 14:12; 36:6, 9; Ezek. 32:16; Amos 8:10; Joel 1:14; 2:12, 15; Jon. 3:5; Zech. 7:5; 8:19); sacrifices and offerings (Isa. 1:11; 19:21); vows (Isa. 19:21; Jon. 1:16; Mal. 1:14); festivals (Isa. 33:20; Ezek. 36:38; Hosea 2:11; Zech. 8:19); and pilgrimages (Isa. 30:29; Ezek. 45:17; 46:11; Hosea 2:11; 9:5; Amos 5:21; Nah. 1:15; Zech. 14:16-19).

For the prophets, justice was the precondition of worship. Praxis and worship were inseparable. Israel's sacrifices and expressions of worship were useless and unacceptable to God unless the community first practiced justice (Isa. 1:10-20; 29:13-14; 58:6-14; Jer. 6:16-21; 7:21-28; Amos 4:4-5; 5:14-15, 21-28; Hosea 6:4-6; Mic. 6:6-8). Right relationship with God, with one another, and with all creation was integral to the renewal, restoration, and transformation of the community. Worship was to give expression to this right relationship.

True, False, and Corrupt Prophets

Not all who made proclamations in God's name were considered true prophets. In ancient Israel, false prophets coexisted with true prophets. The deciding factor determining a true or false prophet depended on whether the prophecy was fulfilled. For this reason, many people within the Israelite community recognized those gifted "seers" as poets, and only later on were they acknowledged as prophets. Like the true prophets, the false prophets engaged in ecstatic activities (1 Kgs. 18:19-40; 22:5-23), experienced dreams, and delivered their contents to the people, but these dreams were later condemned (Deut. 13:1-3; Jer. 23:25-38; Ezek. 13:9). Unlike the true prophets, the false prophets led the people astray, especially when they spoke in the name of Baal (1 Kgs. 18:19-40). They oftentimes gave the people a false sense of confidence (Jer. 4:10; 6:14; Ezek. 13:10) that served to undermine the message of the true prophets, thereby creating conflict. Only true prophets stood in the council of God, and only true prophets were called and sent by God (Isa. 6:1-13; Jer. 1:4-10). Jeremiah 28 describes an exchange between Jeremiah and Hananiah and provides an example of conflict and opposition that also existed among the prophets. The prophets also railed against those who were true prophets but who corrupted their prophetic office for self-serving purposes (Mic. 3:5-7).

Judgment and Suffering

Many prophetic proclamations were words of judgment. Amos inaugurated the concept of the Day of the Lord, which was a time of judgment and condemnation (5:18-20) for a people guilty of many social injustices (2:4-5, 6-8; 4:1-3; 5:7-12). Isaiah condemned worship that represented external gestures empty of any true reform of daily behavior (Isa. 1:10-17; 29:13). Israel was indicted for sins against covenant Decalogue (Hosea 4:1-2), idolatry (Hosea 2:7, 10; 4:12-13; 8:4-6), corrupt legislation (Isa. 10:1-4), oppression of the poor (Isa. 3:14-15; 10:2; Ezek. 22:29), and other social iniquities (Mic. 2:1-11; 3:1-11). Not only was Israel judged but also its enemies (Jer. 25:31). Oftentimes, the prophets depicted a courtroom scene that featured God making a case against the people (Isa. 3:13-15; Mic. 6:1-5). Divine judgment was seen as the reason why Israel and Judah were destroyed.

Not only did the people suffer under divine judgment but also the land and the natural world (Isa. 24:1-24; 33:7-9; Jer. 4:23-28; 7:16-20; 12:4; 14:1-9; 23:9-12; Hosea 4:1-3; Amos 4:6-10; 8:4-8; Zeph. 1:2-6). Because the people rejected God, God suffered (Isa. 1:2-3; 54:6; Jer. 2:1-37; 15:5-9; 18:13-15; Hosea 11:1-9; 13:4-6). The prophets also depicted God suffering with those who were suffering (Isa. 15:5; 16:9-11; Jer. 9:10, 17-18; 31:20; 48:30-36). The prophets themselves suffered because of their mission (Jer. 11:18—12:6; 15:10-21; 17:14-18; 18:18-23; 20:7-12, 14-18).

Law

Central to the preaching of the prophets was a focus on the law. Going forth from out of Zion (Isa. 2:3; Mic. 4:2), God's law was set before the people (Jer. 44:10; Ezek. 20:11), and they were called to walk in its statutes and ordinances (Ezek. 20:19). For the prophets, the torah was a way of life that safeguarded right relationship with God, self, and others. Many people, however, rejected torah (Isa. 5:24; Jer. 6:19; Ezek. 5:6; Amos 2:4), forsook it (Jer. 9:13; 16:11), forgot it (Hosea 4:6), or transgressed it (Isa. 24:5; Hosea 8:1).

The prophets taught that if people followed torah they could be transformed into a new humanity and pursue a godly life instead of a life of oppression and violence (Isa. 2:2-5). Repeatedly, the prophets put the people on notice when they broke torah (Isa. 24:5). Jeremiah proclaimed that rejection of God's commands led to expulsion from the land (Jer. 16:13; 44:23). Habakkuk preached that torah is ineffective when people commit violent acts and corrupt justice (Hab. 1:4). Zephaniah announced the judgment of God against the Israelites because of a long list of sins that included priests who did violence to torah because they had profaned what was holy (Zeph. 3:4). For Israel's prophets, torah was at the heart of ethical living; torah safeguarded covenant relationship.

Repentance

Torah created the backdrop for repentance, and the prophets continually called the people to "repent," to "return" to God (Jer. 24:7; Joel 2:12-13; Zech. 1:3; 10:9; Mal. 3:7). The prophets portrayed God as desiring a mutual relationship based on both parties' returning to each other. Even though the people had committed egregious transgressions, they were encouraged to return to God (Jer. 15:19; Zech. 1:3; Mal. 3:7). The prophets made clear, however, that repentance included amending one's ways (Jer. 26:13).

Isaiah and Zechariah called for repentance in the face of exile (Isa. 44:22; 55:7; Zech. 1:6). Jeremiah issued one of the most poignant pleas for repentance in all of prophetic literature (Jer. 3:6—4:2). He declared Judah's sinfulness, expressed God's anger, emphasized the need for the people to acknowledge their guilt, highlighted God's compassionate intercession on Judah's behalf, and proclaimed Judah's future restoration to God and the land.

If the people repented and turned back to God, then God would repent of the calamities set in motion against the people and the land. Disaster and punishment would not occur, and hope for salvation would become a reality (Isa. 45:22; 58:9-14; Joel 2:13-14).

Divine Sovereignty, Creation, Hope

The prophets depict God as Lord of heaven and earth, lord of everything (Isa. 14:26; 66:1). This God is the true God, the living God, the everlasting King (Jer. 10:10). Israel's God is above all other gods (1 Kings 18), reigns over all nations (Jer. 10:7), is the only God (Isa. 45:5-6, 14, 18, 21-22; 46:9; Joel 2:27), and is incomparable (Isa. 40:18). This God is the "Lord of hosts" (Amos 4:13) and the commander in chief who musters up armies for battle (Isa. 13:4).

To make known God's sovereignty, the prophets often used images from the natural world in their messages. In a divine indictment of the people, Isaiah and Micah featured God appealing to the earth and the heavens as witnesses (Isa. 1:2; Mic. 6:1-2). Catastrophic events in the heavens and on earth announced the coming of God (Joel 2:10; Nah. 1:5). Creation imagery and related metaphorical language became part of the prophets' poetic expression in an attempt to shake the people out of their state of lethargy, indifference, or despair. The prophets even went so far as to depict God as a wild animal—a lion (Isa. 31:4; Jer. 49:19; Hosea 11:10; Amos 3:8) and a bear (Hosea 13:8).

As the sovereign Lord over all, Israel's God had an important relationship with creation. God sustained and nurtured creation, maintained the fixed orders of the world such as day and night (Jer. 31:35-36), disrupted them (Isa. 13:10; Ezek. 32:7-8; Joel 3:15), and governed the weather patterns, giving rain for seedtime and promising a harvest in the fall (Isa. 30:23; Jer. 5:24). When God summoned creation, creation responded (Amos 1:2; 9:5-6).

The prophets described the inextricable link between human behavior and the moral order of creation. When humankind transgressed, the human community and the natural world suffered the consequences of divine chastisement. Jeremiah even linked the people's faithlessness to the well-being of creation (Jer. 4:22-26; 9:12-13) and condemned Judah's leaders for the unmaking of creation (Jer. 12:10-11).

The prophets also tied the renewal of the people's relationship with God to the restoration of creation. As humankind turned from their sinfulness and returned to their God, so they were restored to the land and the land itself was restored to its splendor. The prophets' vision of hope included the wilderness blossoming in glory, beauty, and splendor (Isa. 35:1-2; 41:18-20) and the flourishing of the mountains (Joel 3:18; Amos 9:13b). Ezekiel proclaimed that the covenant of peace included the giving of rain and the restoration of fertility (Ezek. 34:25). Hosea proclaimed a covenant that included the beast of the field (Hosea 2:18). This covenant would result in security for God's people (Hosea 2:19-22; Ezek. 34:25) as well as a full flourishing of the earth (Hosea 2:21-22). Harmony restored among the human community had a strong impact on the rest of creation (Isa. 11:6-9). The promise of salvation became reason for all creation to rejoice and celebrate (Isa. 42:10-12; 44:23). For the prophets, the natural world had a significant place in God's plan of salvation (Isa. 44:23; 45:8; 49:13).

Salvation

The concept and imagery of salvation are multifaceted and rich, particularly in the book of Isaiah, where salvation is a key term. Isaiah's vision of salvation was a universal one, extended to all (Isa. 45:22; 52:10). Salvation was eternal (Isa. 45:17; 51:6, 8) but only if the people returned to fidelity to their God (Isa. 45:22).

In the prophets, God, the source and foundation of salvation (Isa. 12:2; Jer. 3:23; Hab. 3:18), donned a helmet of salvation (Isa. 59:16-17). God's salvation was cause for joy and gladness (Isa. 25:9) because it was everlasting (Isa. 45:17). Even when the people had all gone astray, God's salvation was always a promised gift (Isa. 56:1) even when it seemed distant (Isa. 56:11). Oftentimes, salvation was for God's sake, the sake of God's holy name (Ezek. 36:22-32; cf. Isa. 42:25; Jer. 14:7-9; Dan. 9:15-19). The prophet was clothed with garments of salvation (Isa. 61:10). As righteousness rained down, so also salvation sprang up like plants (Isa. 45:8). Waters drawn from the wells of salvation would quench all thirst (Isa. 12:3). City walls were bulwarks of salvation (Isa. 26:1; Jer.1:18-19; 15:20). Many of the prophetic texts depict the prophets announcing proclamations of salvation even in the midst of their messages of judgment and doom (Mic. 2:12-13).

The key figure ushering in a time of salvation was the servant (Isa. 49:6), God's instrument and righteous branch in whose days Judah would be saved (Jer. 23:5-6). This ruler would be from Bethlehem (Mic. 5:2) and would deliver the people from the Assyrians (Mic. 5:6). This servant would establish justice, free captives from prison, and release those from the dungeon who sit in darkness (Isa. 42:7).

God

Oftentimes, Israel's prophets portrayed God as a violent God, inflicting punitive chastisements on a wayward people. This violence was reflective of the prophets' culture and times and a belief in a theology of retribution (see, e.g., Deuteronomy 28). In attempting to proclaim Israel's God as the sovereign one who was more powerful than all other gods and earthly rulers and forces at work in the culture, the prophets had to depict Israel's God in human ways as a God of unsurpassable power and might, who is larger than life and capable of leveling peoples, nations, and lands (see, e.g., Mic. 1:2-7; see also the proclamations to the nations in Isaiah 13–23; cf. Jeremiah 46–51; Amos 1:2—2:16).

The prophets depicted God as a warrior judge (Isa. 13:4-5; 42:13; Jer. 21:5; Ezek. 21:5; Amos 1:3—2:16; Joel 2:11; Zeph. 3:17; Zech. 13:7-8) who brandishes a lethal sword (Ezek. 21:1-32). God is a roaring lion in Isa. 5:8-30, an agonizing parent (Isa. 1:2-9), a teacher (Isa. 48:17-19), an artist and creator (Isa. 44:24-28), a designer and crafter of symbols (Jer. 11:11-19), a weaver of visions and maker of dreams (Amos 7:1-3), one who raises up prophets (Jer. 1:4-10), replaces stony hearts (Ezek. 36:22-36), acts as a shepherd (Ezek. 34:11-16), who is sovereign over all nations (Isa. 25:1-10), who sustains, redeems, heals, renews, restores, and transforms life (Isa. 43:1-13, 25; Hosea 14:4-9), and who desires to be one with humankind (Jer. 31:31-34; Hosea 6:4-6).

Much of the God-language in Israel's prophetic literature is predominantly male and reflects many of the roles assumed by males in their respective cultures and societies. For example, just as men are fathers, so God is described as "Father," or as an "Everlasting Father" (Isa. 9:6; 63:16; cf. Jer. 3:4, 19; Mal. 1:6). Just as men are kings, so God is named "King" (Isa. 41:21; Jer. 10:10; 51:57; Ezek. 20:33; Zeph. 3:15). Just as men are bridegrooms, so God is a bridegroom (Isa. 62:5). Just as men are husbands, so God is a husband (Isa. 54:5; Jer. 31:32). Furthermore, God the Lord is the God of hosts, the commander in chief of the heavenly and earthly powers (Isa. 1:9; 44:6; Hosea 11:5; Amos 3:13; Nah. 2:13; Zeph. 2:9; Zech. 1:3; Mal 1:4). Israel's God is the "Holy One of Israel" (Isa. 10:20; 41:16; Jer. 50:29), the "God of Israel" (Isa. 29:23; Jer. 9:15; Ezek. 8:4; Zeph. 2:9), the "Creator of Israel" (Isa. 43:15), the "Holy One of Jacob" (Isa. 29:23), the "Mighty One of Jacob" (Isa. 49:26; 60:16), the "God of Jacob" (Isa. 2:3; Mic. 4:2), the "God of David" (Isa. 38:5) and the "Lord, who redeemed Abraham" (Isa. 29:22). Julia M. O'Brien's recent study offers a rigorous critique of the God metaphors used in prophetic literature.

One point is certain: the prophets were trying to send a strong warning that one more powerful than those in power was going to establish justice by toppling over abusive, domineering, controlling, unjust leadership who had a monopoly on power. Interestingly, the biblical text and evolving history have shown that such violent and aggressive use of power has not succeeded in hastening the reign of God or ushering in peace. Violent uses of power often led to more violence, and that situation still exists today. In this way, the prophetic texts remain prophetic, beckoning people to turn their swords into plowshares and their spears into pruning hooks for the sake of a new world order. For the prophets, God was, ultimately, a God of compassion, which is the deepest expression of justice (Mic. 7:7-18). This point, however, does not preclude constructive consequences for wrongdoing.

Reception History and the Prophets

The interpretive tradition helps offer a number of interesting perspectives about the message of the prophets. These perspectives also are colored by the historical contexts in which they arose.

Perspectives from the Church Fathers

Israelite prophetic literature provided a foundation for Christian interpretation and preaching among the church fathers. Living and preaching in a time that is now considered precritical, many of the fathers read the prophets as foretelling the person of Jesus. Irenaeus identified the four faces of the living creatures in Ezekiel 1—the lion, the man, the ox, and the eagle—as representing the fourfold picture of Christ in the Gospels. For Tertullian, Ezekiel's vision of the dry bones was proof of the resurrection. Cyril of Alexandria posited that Jonah's journey in the fish was to be understood as a foreshadowing of Christ's death and resurrection. Although he saw the rebuilding of the "tent of David" as the restoration of the Jews by Cyrus, he argued that the deeper meaning of the text was to be found in Christ: the fallen tent was the fallen race suffering from death, and the restitution of the tent occurred when Jesus was resurrected and with him those who believed in him.

The church fathers believed that the "new covenant" in Jeremiah was a prophetically prefigured the Christian faith. For them, Jeremiah was a prophet under the old covenant and, as such, was heralding the gospel when he spoke of "the new covenant." The fathers viewed Isaiah as a prophet who was proclaiming the good news of Jesus to the world. For example, John Chrysostom viewed Isa. 7:14 as a prophecy that showed how Jesus was to be conceived, born, and nurtured. For Augustine, Isa. 7:14 pertained to Christ's being born as a visible man of a human virgin mother. This Christ was also a hidden God since God was Jesus' Father. For Bede, the name Immanuel signified both natures of Jesus' person. Jerome believed that Isaiah contained all the sacred mysteries of Jesus and that many of the passages from Isaiah prefigured the events of Jesus' life. For Jerome, Isaiah was an evangelist and an apostle in his proclamation of Jesus. Isaiah is the prophet quoted most in the church fathers' writings.

A few church fathers rejected the standard allegorical approach to the prophets and tried to understand the prophetic message from the historical situation as intended for the audience at the time of a particular prophet. In his commentary, Theodore of Mopsuestia (c. 350–428 CE) tried to identify the historical background of each prophet. He gave much attention to the tension that existed between how Nineveh is portrayed in Jonah and how the city is portrayed in Nahum.

Finally, Martin Luther and John Calvin took a view of the prophets similar to many of the early church fathers. Luther published interpretations of Jonah (1526), Habakkuk (1526), and Zechariah (1527). He set the prophets within their historical setting, established their historical sequence on the basis of the books' superscriptions, commented on the prophetic office, and at times offered christological readings of some texts. In his work on Ezekiel 38–48, Luther took a strong christological approach to the interpretation of the prophecy. Calvin often applied the prophets' message to Christ and his church (McKinion; Duguid, 231–32).

Perspectives from the Rabbis

Talmudic tradition does not arrange the prophetic books in chronological order. The rabbis chose a thematic or theological basis for the texts' ordering and concluded that Jeremiah should appear first among the prophets because, like the book of Kings that precedes it in the Hebrew canon, Jeremiah was concerned with destruction. Ezekiel came next because it began with destruction but concluded with consolation. Isaiah followed Ezekiel because Isaiah was concerned with consolation, one of the text's main themes. The Book of the Twelve followed Isaiah (Dempster, 75–76). This rabbinic concern with destruction and consolation represented an underlying preoccupation with several interrelated issues in the prophets: the destruction of the temple and Jerusalem, the exile of the people from the land of Israel, the restoration of the Jerusalem temple, and the return of the exiled people to the land. Talmudic tradition maintains that Jeremiah wrote the book. Rabbinic tradition questioned the canonical status of Ezekiel, since the text often conflicts with halakic statements found in the Torah.

For the rabbis, the most important prophet was Isaiah, who announced a vision of world peace for all nations (Isa. 2:2-4; Mic. 4:1-5). They viewed Isaiah as a book of comfort because it looked forward to the time when the Jews would bring torah to all peoples, and exiled Jews would return home. Isaiah was also popular because of the book's fervent loyalty to the Davidic monarchy in the first part, the prophecies of salvation and descriptions of a suffering yet vindicated figure in the second part, and the recognition of one God throughout the book as a whole.

The rabbis used midrash as their main method for interpreting the prophets. Two components determined the nature of midrashic interpretation: the text and the interpreter. Midrashic interpretation was verse-centered and philologically focused, beginning with biblical words and phrases. The rabbis saw the interrelatedness of biblical verses, and oftentimes a prophetic verse would shed light on another prophetic verse or even texts in the Torah or the Writings. For example, midrash associates Hab. 3:5 with Ps. 91:6 to describe the pestilence that overwhelms those who perpetuate deeds of darkness. Finally, the talmudic rabbis realized that the Bible's prophetic literature was only a small part of what was actually uttered. For the rabbis, the last of the biblical prophets marked the final departure of God's spirit from Israel. Thus prophecy belonged to the past. Therefore, the word of God was to be sought in the Torah and in the prophecies already delivered.

Interpreting the Prophets Anew: Contemporary Perspectives

The interpretation of the prophetic message continues today. Various perspectives address the meaning of the text and shed new light on how the prophet can be "read" with greater depth.

Feminist and Liberationist Perspectives

Two of the more controversial approaches to the biblical text have been feminist and liberationist perspectives, challenging the way people hear and read the biblical text and how they live their lives. These two approaches address patriarchy and hierarchy, two social aspects at the heart of Israel's culture and prophetic literature.

Broadly understood, patriarchy involves systems of legal, social, economic, and political relations that not only validate but also enforce the notion of male superiority and the sovereignty of males as heads of families over other dependent persons in any given household. Patriarchy violates women because it denies women the right to be autonomous. Within a patriarchal and hierarchical societal structure and household, women are denied the right to construct culture, to control property, to maintain bodily integrity, to formulate their own decisions, and to express their own views and opinions. Patriarchy restricts and prohibits women's participation in Israelite culture.

Alice L. Laffey (152) has argued that "a patriarchal culture is, by its nature, hierarchical." With respect to prophetic literature, Laffey points out that this particular kind of culture sets parameters around worship. Only the priests have charge of the temple and the altar (Ezek. 40:45-46), and the only animals fit for sacrifice to God are males without blemish (Ezek. 43:22, 23, 25; 45:18, 23; Mal. 1:14). The only appropriate wives for priests are virgins of the stock of the house of Israel (Ezek. 44:22). Other men could marry widows and divorcées, but these types of women were inappropriate for priests (Ezek. 44:22). Additionally, while all males were circumcised, women were not, and any woman who belonged to an Israelite man was subsumed under the male's circumcision.

Another topic that feminists and liberationists have addressed in prophetic literature is the marriage metaphor. Israel's lived experience of marriage influenced the biblical portrait of marriage, gender, and sexuality. Just as women are presented as sexually subordinate to men, who control their sexual reproduction, Israel is subordinate to God's control. The prophetic image of Samaria and Jerusalem as God's wife highlights this subordination.

Nancy Bowen explores the metaphorical violence of a jealous husband against his wife in prophetic literature by examining Hosea 1–3; Jeremiah 2–3; and Ezekiel 16 and 23. She points out that when relationships are hierarchically structured, the one deemed "superior" by society (the husband) often asserts control over the "subordinate" one (the wife). This assertion of control sometimes takes the form of physical violence, as in the case of Ezekiel 16. This structural situation that gives way to physical violence has also been deemed psychologically violent, as several other scholars have noted in their exploration of the book of Hosea (Pressler; Perdue et al.; Baumann).

Furthermore, because Jerusalem and Samaria are unfaithful, they deserve to be punished by God, the faithful spouse. The punishment includes a host of violent acts, such as being stripped naked (Ezek. 16:39; 23:26; Hosea 2:3), public exposure, defamation and mockery (Ezek. 16:37, 57; 23:10, 29; Hosea 2:3, 10), mutilation (Ezek. 23:25, 34), gang rape (Ezek. 16:40), stoning (Ezek. 16:40; 23:47), and death (Ezek. 16:40; 23:10, 47). Feminist interpreters often understand such imagery to be pornography, because it involves objectification, dominance, pain, and degradation.

The work of T. Drorah Setel is foundational to the discussion on prophetic pornography. Setel argues that significant congruencies exist between biblical, and especially prophetic, texts on the one hand and modern pornographic depictions of female sexuality on the other hand. She notes that in both cases objectified female sexuality is used as "a symbol of evil" (Setel, 86). Athalya Brenner points out further that even though feminist definitions of pornography vary, two claims remain constant: pornography restricts female choice to an actual act of slavery, and it serves to accentuate the nature and meaning of male power. With respect to Jeremiah 3 and Ezekiel 16, Brenner argues that "pornography preserves and asserts male social dominion through the control of female sexuality" (186).

Israel's infidelity to God is described metaphorically as harlotry. Feminist and liberationist studies have focused on this theme in Isa. 1:21; Jeremiah 2–3; Ezekiel 16; 23; Hosea 1–3; and Mic. 1:6-7. Prophetic literature presented harlotry and spiritual whoredom as violations of covenant with God. Israel sought other gods and trusted in foreign powers and often solicited protection from foreign powers instead of trusting only in God. Thus Israel was guilty of apostasy (Bellis; Setel; Weems 1989; Ortlund). According to Gale Yee, Hosea feminizes the Israelite male leadership as an adulterous woman who has broken her marital vow.

Feminist and liberationist studies have also focused on the female gender used to speak of a city, country, and people. Examples of cities include Rabbah (Amos 1:14) and her daughters (Jer. 49:3), Samaria (Ezek. 16:46; Hosea 13:16; Amos 3:9) and her daughters (Ezek. 16:53, 55), Zion (Isa. 1:27) and her daughters (Isa. 1:8; Zech. 2:10), Jerusalem (Isa. 51:17; Ezekiel 16) and her daughters (Mic. 4:8; Zeph. 3:14; Zech. 9:9), Sidon (Isa. 23:4) and her daughters (Isa. 23:12), Tyre (Isa. 23:15) and her daughters (Ezek. 26:6, 8), Sodom (Ezek. 16:46, 48-49) and her daughters (Ezek. 16:53, 55-56), daughter of Gallim (Isa. 10:30), daughter of Tarshish (Isa. 23:10), Bethlehem Ephrathah (Mic. 5:2), Gaza (Amos 1:7), Rahab (Isa. 51:9), Gebal (Ezek. 27:9), and Tehaphnehes (Ezek. 30:18).

Examples of countries that are personified as women include Moab (Isa. 16:2), Egypt (Isa. 19:14; Jer. 46:11, 24; Ezek. 23:21), Edom (Ezek. 16:57; 32:29), Elam (Ezek. 32:24), Judah (Jer. 3:7-8, 10), the land of the Philistines (Ezek. 16:27, 57), Israel (Amos 5:2; Jer. 18:13), and Babylonia (Isa. 47:1; Jer. 50:42; Ezek. 23:17; Zech. 2:7). Laffey comments, "A woman may be understood to have much in common with a city or a country: she may be more or less valuable, more or less beautiful, large or small, a greater or lesser source of nurture, faithful or unfaithful. It is a compliment to a city or a country to personify it; it is an insult to women that cities and countries are so personified!" (162).

Two striking instances where female imagery is used to cast aspersions on infidelity and wickedness of cities occur in Jeremiah and Ezekiel. Unfaithful Zion is compared to a woman dressed in crimson, decked with ornaments of gold, and eyes enlarged with paint, beautified for her lovers (Jer. 4:30). In Ezekiel, the poet uses two promiscuous sisters, Oholah and Oholibah, to describe the sordid state and wicked deeds of Jerusalem and Samaria (Ezekiel 23).

The prophets condemned Israel's enemies by means of female imagery that connotes vulnerability, powerlessness, and inferiority. For example, the Egyptians will be like women (Isa. 19:16); the Babylonians will become women (Jer. 50:37; cf. Jer. 51:30); the hearts of the warriors of Moab and Edom will be like the heart of a woman in labor (Jer. 48:41; 49:22); and the Assyrian troops have become like women (Nah. 3:13).

Last, the gendered city Daughter Zion has drawn much attention from feminist interpreters. Carleen Mandolfo builds on her earlier dialogical approach to the Psalms and brings the voice of Daughter Zion into conversation with the voices addressing or depicting Zion throughout the prophetic corpus. Mandolfo presents Daughter Zion as someone who has found her own voice. A collected volume of essays responds to Mandolfo's thought and work and offers additional insights on the Daughter Zion metaphor (Boda, Dempsey, and Snow Flesher). Christl Maier has studied the use of this metaphor and its personification in relation to feminist perspectives on the body. I have looked at the metaphor of Jerusalem/Zion in its transformative state in Isaiah 60–62 (Dempsey 2009).

Ecological Perspectives

One of the most fruitful dialogues taking place is that between Israel's prophetic writings and ecology. Norman Habel and colleagues have created a series of ecojustice principles, reading the Bible through this ecological lens. Texts and topics discussed include Isa. 24:6 and the notion of a curse destroying the earth; the vision of land in Jeremiah 32; desolation in the book of Ezekiel; prophecies against the mountains in Ezekiel 6, 35, and 36; the earth community in Hosea 2; the relation to ecojustice and anthropological justice in Isa. 65:17; and the wolf, the lamb, and the little child as transformative agents for the earth community in Isaiah 11. Guiding these studies is the notion that earth and all its communities of life are intrinsically good and can no longer be viewed from an anthropocentric, objectified perspective. The writings advocate for the voices of indigenous peoples who know how the Earth suffers from the oppression that came with colonization. They argue that these voices must be heard and listened to in light of the current ecological crisis (Habel and Wurst 2001).

A second study collection of essays of this nature edited by Norman C. Habel and Peter Trudinger introduces readers to an ecological methodology of hermeneutics. Prophetic texts studied include Lamentations 1–2; Hosea 4:1-3 and the grievance of earth; Joel and the presence of the earth community in this text; the book of Amos and the voice of the earth within this text; and the book of Jonah and the role that nonhuman characters play in this book. Each of these articles adopts a geocentric perspective for interpreting the text instead of the usual anthropocentric perspective. Texts are reread with a member of the earth community as subject. For example, in Lamentations 1–2, Jerusalem is the focus of analysis. This city, a nonhuman subject, suffers on account of humankind's behavior, is cursed because of human sin, and has its voice co-opted for human purposes. Hosea 4:1-3 is read from the perspective of the land to demonstrate that creation actively mourns the subversion of the created order, which results in the languishing and perishing of animals, birds, and fish who live in the land. This article and the others in the collected volume argue for readers to appreciate the role that earth, understood as the entire ecosystem, plays in the relationship between God and creation. They call for a radical change of posture, one that acknowledges earth as a subject in the biblical text, and specifically in the prophets. Unique to this work is the retrieval of earth's voice expressed through creative stories and poetry that conclude some of the volume's chapters. Thus a voice previously unnoticed or suppressed within the biblical text and its interpretation comes to life in ways that are prophetic and profound.

Ellen Davis works from the premise that Israel's earliest prophetic writers were distinctly agrarian and thus their voices remain prophetic for today regarding local and global issues involving food production. One section of her work focuses specifically on Amos and Hosea, two "agrarian" prophets who, as Davis argues, understood completely that the health of human lives and culture was bound up inextricably with the care of the land and the just distribution of its harvest. Davis uses the prophets' writings to expose the destructive practices and assumptions that currently dominate the global food economy. Related to Davis's work, Matthew J. M. Coomber's study looks at land and land ownership in relation to globalization and the impact that it has on the poor of the planet.

Most recently, in "Jeremiah 14:1-9: From Drought to Starvation: A National Experience, A Global Reality," I link the great drought in Jeremiah to present-day depletion of water sources, the availability of water, and global climate change. I have also written on other prophetic texts from an ecological perspective, focusing on the natural world's suffering caused by human violence, greed, abuse, and the lack of reverence for life in general. Reflecting on various texts from both the Major and Minor Prophets, I make the claim that a systemic connection exists between human sinfulness and ecological destruction. I also point out that within prophetic literature, an inherent link exists between the redemption of humankind and the restoration of the natural world. The prophets offer an eschatological vision that can provide people with a basis of hope and a paradigm for faithful, holistic living today (Dempsey 1999; 2000).

Perspectives from Trauma and Disaster Studies: Encountering Jeremiah

Trauma and disaster studies, a new interdisciplinary conversation, arose in the twentieth century. These studies involve insights from cognitive psychology, counseling, sociology, literary criticism, and anthropology. Using the insights gleaned from this field of inquiry, Kathleen M. O'Connor investigates the book of Jeremiah. She shows how every passage anticipates disaster, speaks about it, and offers ways of coping with its life-changing consequences. She points out that the text addresses the victims of the Babylonian assaults in Judah in the sixth century BCE, which involved invasions, displacements, and deportations.

Looking at the metaphorical broken family in the Jeremiah text, and then moving on to Jeremiah's war poems, weeping poems, biographical stories, confessions, sermons, and the text's final chapters, O'Connor illuminates the suffering of Jeremiah and his community, the impact violence has had on them, and the wounds they have endured. She concludes that despite its elements of disaster and trauma, the book of Jeremiah is a work of hope and resilience, one that shows readers how dwelling in the midst of devastation can be a way forward to the rediscovery of life and God (O'Connor 2011).

Prophetic Literature and Communications Studies

Besides trauma and disaster studies, other interdisciplinary approaches to the Bible have developed. Another way to view the biblical text is through the lens of communication studies, which explains how people use communication to exert influence and to construct knowledge, identities, relationships, and societies. One topic that generates much discussion in prophetic literature, in communications studies, and in the lived experience of life today is conflict. Using the text of Jeremiah 37–39, Elayne Shapiro and I explore the nature of conflict from the biblical studies and communications studies lenses. We first deal with the text's biblical content that features Jeremiah's tense interaction with King Zedekiah in the final days before Judah falls to the Babylonians. Then we examine the biblical narrative from the perspective of conflict theory, which involves a struggle between at least two interdependent parties who perceive incompatible goals, scarce resources, and interference from others in achieving their goals. They focus on the dialogue between Jeremiah and Zedekiah to show how the text illustrates that Jeremiah was so concerned with the content of his message, that he ignored the impact on the receiver. As a consequence of Jeremiah's obliviousness to communication skills, his receiver becomes defensive. Defensiveness blocks Zedekiah from benefiting from the content of Jeremiah's conversation with him. Both sender and receiver contribute to the debacle. The study serves as a model of how to identify and deal effectively with conflict in daily life (Dempsey and Shapiro).

Conclusion

Truth, tragedy, and trauma are but three characteristics of Israelite prophetic literature whose poets saw things as they were and dreamed of things as they could be. The prophetic texts provide a glimpse into the world of an ancient people whose struggles, hardships, depravity, hopes, and aspirations reflect the human condition in all its beauty and shame. The world of the ancestors is not so different from contemporary times as nations jockey for position in the global arena and the prophets of today sound the alarms about climate change, globalization, life-threatening violence, hunger, growing poverty, the loss of habitat, and social, political, economic, and religious injustices. The prophets of old, however, continue to remind the listeners and readers of prophetic literature today that, despite the world's condition, all of life lives under divine promise, and the final word to be received and taken to heart is not a word of judgment or doom; rather, the final word is always a word of hope (Isa. 65:17-25; Mic. 7:18-20; Hosea 14:1-9; Joel 2:21-22).

Works Cited

Baumann, Gerlinde. 2001. "Prophetic Objections to YHWH as the Violent Husband of Israel: Reinterpretations of the Prophetic Marriage Metaphor in Second Isaiah (Isaiah 40–55)." In *Prophets and Daniel: A Companion to the Bible (Second Series)*, edited by Athalya Brenner, 88–120. Sheffield: Sheffield Academic.

Bellis, Alice Ogden. 1994. *Helpmates, Harlots, Heroes: Women's Stories in the Hebrew Bible*. Louisville: Westminster John Knox.

Boda, Mark, Carol J. Dempsey, and LeAnn Snow Flesher, eds. 2012. *Daughter Zion: Her Portrait, Her Response*. SBLAIL. Atlanta: Society of Biblical Literature.

Bowen, Nancy R. 2006. "Women, Violence, and the Bible." In *Engaging the Bible in a Gendered World*, edited by Linda Day and Carolyn Pressler, 186–99. Louisville: Westminster John Knox.

Brenner, Athalya. 1993. "On 'Jeremiah' and the Poetics of (Prophetic?) Pornography." In *On Gendering Texts: Female and Male Voices in the Hebrew Bible*, edited by A. Brenner and F. van Dijk-Hemmes, 177–93. New York: Brill.

———. 1995. "On Prophetic Propaganda and the Politics of 'Love': The Case of Jeremiah." In *A Feminist Companion to the Latter Prophets*, edited by Athalya Brenner, 256–74. Sheffield: Sheffield Academic.

Coggins, Richard, and Jin H. Han. 2011. *Six Minor Prophets through the Centuries*. Oxford: Wiley-Blackwell.

Coomber, Matthew J. M. 2010. *Re-Reading the Prophets through Corporate Globalization: A Cultural-Evolutionary Approach to Economic Justice in the Hebrew Bible*. Piscataway, NJ: Gorgias.

Davis, Ellen F. 2009. *Scripture, Culture, and Agriculture: An Agrarian Reading of the Bible*. New York: Cambridge University Press.

Day, John. 2010. "Hosea and the Baal Cult." In *Prophecy and the Prophets in Ancient Israel*, edited by John Day, 202–24. LHB/OTS 531. New York: T&T Clark.

Dempsey, Carol J. 1999. "Hope amidst Crisis: A Prophetic Vision of Cosmic Redemption." In *All Creation Is Groaning: An Interdisciplinary Vision for Life in a Sacred Universe*, edited by Carol J. Dempsey and Russell A. Butkus, 269–84. Collegeville, MN: Liturgical Press.

———. 2000. *Hope amid the Ruins: The Ethics of Israel's Prophets*. St. Louis: Chalice.

———. 2009. "From Desolation to Delight: The Transformative Vision of Isaiah 60–62." In *The Desert Will Bloom: Poetic Visions of Isaiah*, edited by Joseph Everson and Hyun Chul Paul Kim, 217–32. SBLAIL 4. Atlanta: Society of Biblical Literature.

———. 2014. "Jeremiah 14:1-9: From Drought to Starvation: A National Experience, A Global Reality." In *By Bread Alone: Approaching the Bible through a Hermeneutic of Hunger*, edited by Sheila E. McGinn, Lai Ling Ngan, and Ahida Pilarski. Minneapolis: Fortress Press.

Dempsey, Carol J., and Elayne J. Shapiro. 2011. "Jeremiah: Defensiveness and Conflict (Jeremiah 37–39)." In *Reading the Bible, Transforming Conflict*, edited by Russell A. Butkus, Anne Clifford, and Carol J. Dempsey. Theology in Dialogue. Maryknoll, NY: Orbis.

Dempster, Stephen G. 2012. "Canon, Canonization." In *Dictionary of the Old Testament Prophets*, edited by Mark J. Boda and J. Gordon McConville, 71–77. Downers Grove, IL: InterVarsity Press.

Duguid, Iain. M. 2012. "Ezekiel: History of Interpretation." In *Dictionary of the Old Testament Prophets*, edited by Mark J. Boda and J. Gordon McConville, 229–35. Downers Grove, IL: InterVarsity Press.

Dobbs-Allsopp, F. W. 2009. "Daughter Zion." In *Thus Says the Lord: Essays on the Former and Latter Prophets in Honor of Robert R. Wilson*, edited by John J. Ahn and Stephen L. Cook, 125–34. New York: T&T Clark.

Ellens, J. Harold, and Wayne. G. Rollins, eds. 2004. *Psychology and the Bible: A New Way of Reading the Scriptures*. Santa Barbara: Praeger.

Ferreiro, Alberto, ed. 2003. *The Twelve Prophets*. Ancient Christian Commentary on Scripture, Old Testament 16. Downers Grove, IL: InterVarsity Press.

Habel, Norman, and Peter Trudinger, eds. 2008. *Exploring Ecological Hermeneutics*. Atlanta: Society of Biblical Literature.

Habel, Norman C., and Shirley Wurst, eds. 2001. *The Earth Story in Psalms and Prophets*. Sheffield: Sheffield Academic.

Junior, Nyasha. 2006. "Womanist Biblical Interpretation." In *Engaging the Bible in a Gendered World*, edited by Linda Day and Carolyn Pressler, 37–46. Louisville: Westminster John Knox.

Keefe, Alice A. 2001. *Woman's Body and the Social Body of Hosea*. JSOTSup 338. Sheffield: Sheffield Academic.

Laffey, Alice L. 1988. *An Introduction to the Old Testament: A Feminist Perspective*. Philadelphia: Fortress Press.

Maier, Christl M. 2008. *Daughter Zion, Mother Zion*. Minneapolis: Fortress Press.

Mandolfo, Carleen R. 2007. *Daughter Zion Talks Back to the Prophets: A Dialogic Theology of the Book of Lamentations*. Atlanta: Society of Biblical Literature.

McKinion, Steven A., ed. 2004. *Isaiah 1–39*. Ancient Christian Commentary on Scripture, Old Testament 10. Downers Grove, IL: InterVarsity Press.

O'Brien, Julia M. 2008. *Challenging Prophetic Metaphor: Theology and Ideology in the Prophets*. Louisville: Westminster John Knox.

O'Connor, Kathleen M. 2006. "The Feminist Movement Meets the Old Testament: One Woman's Perspective." In *Engaging the Bible in a Gendered World*, edited by Linda Day and Carolyn Pressler, 3–24. Louisville: Westminster John Knox.

———. 2011. *Jeremiah: Pain and Promise*. Minneapolis: Fortress Press.

Ortlund, Raymond C., Jr. 1996. *Whoredom: God's Unfaithful Wife in Biblical Theology*. Grand Rapids: Eerdmans.

Perdue, Leo G., Joseph Blenkinsopp, John J. Collins, and Carol Meyers, eds. 1997. *Families in Ancient Israel*. The Family, Religion, and Culture. Louisville: Westminster John Knox.

Pressler, Carolyn. 2006. "The 'Biblical View' of Marriage." In *Engaging the Bible in a Gendered World*, edited by Linda Day and Carolyn Pressler, 200–211. Louisville: Westminster John Knox.

Schüssler Fiorenza, Elisabeth. 2001. *Wisdom Ways: Introducing Feminist Biblical Interpretation*. Maryknoll, NY: Orbis.

Setel, T. Drorah. 1985. "Prophets and Pornography: Female Sexual Imagery in Hosea." In *Feminist Interpretations of the Bible*, edited by Letty M. Russell, 86–95. Philadelphia: Westminster Press.

Sherwood, Yvonne. 1996. *The Prostitute and the Prophet: Reading Hosea in the Late Twentieth Century*. New York: T&T Clark.

Stienstra, Nelly. 1993. "YHWH Is the Husband of His People: The Marriage Metaphor in the Book of Hosea." In *YHWH Is the Husband of His People*, 96–126. Kampen, the Netherlands: Kok Pharos.

Streete, Gail Corrington. 1997. *The Strange Woman: Power and Sex in the Bible*. Louisville: Westminster John Knox.

Weems, Renita. 1989. "Gomer: Victim of Violence or Victim of Metaphor?" In *Interpretation for Liberation*, edited by Katie Geneva Cannon and Elisabeth Schüssler Fiorenza. *Semeia* 47 (1989): 87–104.

———. 1995. *Battered Love: Marriage, Sex, and Violence in the Hebrew Prophets*. Minneapolis: Fortress Press.

Wilken, Robert Louis, with Angela Russell Christman and Michael J. Hollerich, eds. 2007. *Isaiah Interpreted by Early Christian and Medieval Commentators*. The Church's Bible. Grand Rapids: Eerdmans.

Yee, Gale A. 2003. *Poor Banished Children of Eve: Women as Evil in the Hebrew Bible*. Minneapolis: Fortress Press.

ISAIAH 1–39

Marvin A. Sweeney

Introduction

Isaiah 1–39 is part of the larger sixty-six-chapter book of Isaiah, which is attributed to the prophet Isaiah ben Amoz, in Isa. 1:1. Isaiah was a Jerusalemite prophet who spoke during the reigns of the Judean kings Uzziah (783–742 BCE), Jotham (742–735), Ahaz (735–715), and Hezekiah (715–687/686).

The late eighth century BCE saw a number of events that had a major impact on the kingdoms of Israel and Judah. First was the Syro-Ephraimitic War in 735–732, in which Israel and Aram invaded Judah in an effort to force Judah to join their anti-Assyrian alliance. When King Ahaz of Judah appealed to Assyria for assistance, the Assyrian king Tiglath Pileser III destroyed Damascus, reduced Israel, and subjugated Judah. Second was the destruction of the northern kingdom of Israel by the Assyrians in 724–721, following its revolt against the Assyrian Empire. Third was Hezekiah's revolt against Assyria in 705–701, which saw the Assyrian king Sennacherib's invasion of Judah and siege of Jerusalem. Although the book of Isaiah claims a great victory for YHWH and Hezekiah, Assyrian records and archaeology confirm that Judah was devastated, although Jerusalem remained intact and Hezekiah remained on the throne.

Throughout this period, Isaiah advised against military confrontation with Assyria. Isaiah's theological worldview was heavily informed by the Davidic/Zion stream of ancient Judean thought, which posited an eternal covenant between YHWH, the royal house of David, and the city of Jerusalem. According to the Davidic/Zion tradition, YHWH would defend the house of David and the city of Jerusalem forever (see 2 Samuel 7). Isaiah therefore viewed political and military alliances between Judah and other nations as unnecessary and potentially dangerous. He consistently argued for reliance on YHWH as the best course for Judah's security.

Although the superscription attributes the book to the prophet Isaiah, interpreters since antiquity have recognized that major portions of the book were composed by other writers. Isaiah 40–66 appears to presuppose the conclusion of the Babylonian exile and the rise of King Cyrus of Persia in 539 BCE (see Isa. 44:28; 45:1), as well as later periods.

The Babylonian Talmud (c. 600 CE) attributes the book of Isaiah to King Hezekiah of Judah and his colleagues (*b. B. Bat.* 14b). The medieval commentator Rabbi Abraham Ibn Ezra (1089–1167 CE) hints at the possibility of a different author beginning in Isaiah 40. By the late eighteenth century, modern critical scholars recognized Isaiah 1–39 as a work based on the prophecies of Isaiah ben Amoz and Isaiah 40–66 as the work of later prophets from the exilic period and beyond. Bernhard Duhm's 1892 commentary first argued that the book of Isaiah presented the work of Isaiah ben Amoz in Isaiah 1–39, an anonymous prophet known as Deutero-Isaiah in Isaiah 40–55, and a third prophet known as Trito-Isaiah in Isaiah 56–66. Subsequent interpretation recognizes Trito-Isaiah as the work of multiple writers.

More recent scholarship focuses on reading the various components of the book of Isaiah as a literary whole. When Isaiah 1–39, 40–55, and 56–66 are read as a single work, they present the vision of Isaiah ben Amoz that spans some four to five hundred years of Judah's and Jerusalem's history and YHWH's activity in the world from the time of the Assyrian invasions in the late eighth century BCE through the anticipated recognition of YHWH as the sovereign ruler of all creation from the Jerusalem temple, the holy center for creation.

The process of the formation of the book over this period of time points to efforts in ancient Judaism to read Isaiah as a book that addresses later times as well. Second Isaiah and Trito-Isaiah both contain extensive intertextual citations of texts from Isaiah 1–39 that indicate reflection on the meaning of Isaiah's prophecies in relation to the end of the Babylonian exile and the early Persian or Second Temple period when the temple was rebuilt. Indeed, the final form of the book of Isaiah appears designed to persuade later generations of Jews that YHWH is indeed the true G-d of creation and that they should return to Jerusalem to acknowledge YHWH as the true sovereign of a restored Israel and Judah and the world at large.

The final form of the book of Isaiah is therefore designed to demonstrate YHWH's role as the true sovereign of creation and G-d of Israel/Judah. The first half of the book, in Isaiah 1–33, presents YHWH's plans to reveal worldwide sovereignty at Zion. These chapters argue that failure to recognize YHWH results in disaster, such as that realized by King Ahaz of Judah during the Assyrian invasions of Israel and Judah, whereas adherence to YHWH will result in security and restoration. The second half of the book, in Isaiah 34–66, argues that the time of restoration is at hand. Based on the model of King Hezekiah during the Assyrian siege of Jerusalem, the people need to turn to YHWH, who will return them to Jerusalem at the center of a restored creation.

The book of Isaiah is preserved in two major manuscripts from Qumran. The iconic 1QIsa[a], which dates to the late second century BCE, presupposes a proto-Masoretic text, although it includes many exegetical variations, including a clear division between Isaiah 33 and Isaiah 34 to mark the two halves of the book. 1QIsa[b], which dates to the first century BCE, preserves a proto-Masoretic text. Isaiah appears in some twenty-one other manuscripts from Qumran as well.

Jewish tradition reads the book of Isaiah as a book of comfort (*b. B. Bat.* 14b–15a) that antici-pates the restoration of Jerusalem in the aftermath of disaster and exile. Selections from Isaiah are read throughout the year in the Jewish worship service as Haftarah readings, that is, readings from the Prophets that accompany the reading of the Torah portion at the center of the Jewish worship service. Many of the Haftarah readings from the ninth of Av, the Jewish day of mourning for the loss of the temple and other disasters, in the late summer through Rosh Hashanah, the Jewish Near Year, in the early fall, are drawn from Isaiah to anticipate divine restoration and blessing at the beginning of the New Year. According to Jewish tradition, Isaiah was put to death by Hezekiah's evil son Manasseh, who sawed Isaiah in half after accusing him of being a false prophet (*b. Yev.* 49b; see also the pseudepigraphical work *The Martyrdom of Isaiah*).

Christianity also views the book of Isaiah as a key text in articulating Christian theology. Isaiah is quoted extensively throughout the New Testament, especially as a book that anticipates the coming of Christ. Indeed, Isaiah holds out a vision of an ideal world that Christianity understands to be realized through Jesus Christ. The reference to the birth of Immanuel in Isa. 7:14; the portrayal of the ideal king as the "Prince of Peace" in Isa. 9:1-6; and the Suffering Servant in Isa. 52:13—53:12 all play key roles in Isaiah's anticipation of Christ in the New Testament and Christian thought. The first part of Handel's *Messiah* (Dublin 1742) is based largely on texts from Isaiah.

Both Judaism and Christianity employ elements from Isaiah's commissioning vision in Isaiah 6, particularly the song of the Seraphim, "Holy, holy, holy, is the L-rd of Hosts, the whole earth is filled with [G-d's] glory" (6:3), as part of their respective worship services.

In the aftermath of the Shoah (Holocaust), both Jewish and Christian interpreters have begun to rethink the meaning of Isaiah. Isaiah's commission in Isaiah 6 to render the people blind, deaf, and dumb without the possibility of repentance, for instance, implies that G-d deliberately punishes innocent humans to reveal divine glory. Some maintain that Isaiah's commission calls not for accept-ance of evil even when it comes from the highest authority, but instead for human beings to exercise moral responsibility in their own right to bring about the ideal world that Isaiah holds forth.

Isaiah 1: Prologue to the Book of Isaiah: YHWH's Intention to Purify Zion

▌ THE TEXT IN ITS ANCIENT CONTEXT

Isaiah 1 begins with the superscription for the book in 1:1. The superscription identifies the book as "the vision of Isaiah son of Amoz," and states that his focus is on Judah and Jerusalem. It places the prophet in the reigns of the Judean kings Uzziah (783–742 BCE), Jotham (742–735), Ahaz (735–715), and Hezekiah (715–687/668). Major events during this period include the Syro-Ephraimitic War (735–732), the fall of northern Israel to the Assyrian empire (722/1), and the Assyrian inva-sion of Judah and siege of Jerusalem (701).

Isaiah 1:2-20 constitutes the speech of the accuser in which the prophet lays out YHWH's charges that the people of Jerusalem, Judah, and Israel act like the people of Sodom and Gomorrah by not following divine guidance. Isaiah 1:21-31 constitutes the speech of the judge in which the prophet likens Jerusalem to unrefined ore that must be smelted to purge the city of its alleged sins. Once the process of punishment is complete, the prophet looks forward to Zion's restoration.

▌ THE TEXT IN THE INTERPRETIVE TRADITION

Most modern scholars maintain that Isaiah 1 consists primarily of oracles by Isaiah son of Amoz, but it has been edited to serve as the prologue both to the book of Isaiah as a whole and to the first portion of the book in either Isaiah 1–39 or Isaiah 1–33 (Fohrer; Tomasino). It can function in this role because it presents an overview of the major concerns of the book, namely, YHWH's judgment against Jerusalem and Israel and the ultimate restoration of Jerusalem and Israel. Interpreters have noted its parallels with Isaiah 34, which opens the second half of the book of Isaiah, and Isaiah 66, which closes the book of Isaiah as a whole (Evans).

Christian tradition reads Isaiah 1 as a summary of the sins of Israel that calls for the coming of Jesus. Paul quotes Isa. 1:9 in Rom. 9:29 as part of his larger argument for justification by faith. Protestant Christian interpretation generally reads Isa. 1:10-17 as an indictment of temple ritual practice, although Jewish interpreters generally note that it condemns ritual practice that is not accompanied by proper moral and spiritual outlook (see Leviticus 19).

Jewish tradition reads Isa. 1:1-27 as the Haphtarah, or Prophetic Reading, for Shabbat Ḥazon, "the Shabbat of Vision," the first Shabbat after Tisha b'Av, "the ninth of Av," in late July or early August that commemorates the destruction of the First and Second Temples. The passage rehearses the theme of judgment that explains the destruction, but it points to restoration at the end.

▌ THE TEXT IN CONTEMPORARY DISCUSSION

Isaiah 1 is an indictment of human wrongdoing and rejection of G-d, but it looks forward to restoration once the people have been purged by divine punishment. In the aftermath of the Shoah or Holocaust, contemporary theologians recognize such statements as a form of theodicy, that is, they defend G-d against charges of divine wickedness, absence, and impotence by asserting that human beings—and not G-d—must be responsible for evil in the world.

Isaiah 2–4: YHWH's Plan for Worldwide Sovereignty at Zion

▌ THE TEXT IN ITS ANCIENT CONTEXT

Isaiah 2–4 begins with its own superscription in Isa. 2:1, which identifies the following material as "the word which Isaiah ben Amoz envisioned concerning Judah and Jerusalem" (author trans.). The unit presents the prophet's announcement concerning the preparation of Zion/Jerusalem for its role as the center for YHWH's worldwide sovereignty.

The Jerusalem temple was considered the holy center of creation. The portrayal of Jerusalem here as the site of the holy temple of YHWH, to which the nations would flock to learn divine instruction and bring an end to war, appears to presuppose the role that major temples played in Mesopotamian culture. During the Babylonian Akitu or New Year's festival, representatives of the nations subject to Babylonian rule would carry idols of their national gods in procession through the streets of Babylon to honor the Babylonian king. When the procession reached the temple of Marduk, the king would climb the steps to the top of the temple. There he would be granted the tablets of destiny, which gave him the right to rule the Babylonian Empire—and thus all creation—for another year on Marduk's behalf.

Following Isa. 2:2-4, the prophet presents three addresses that outline how the ideals expressed in this passage will be achieved. The first, in Isa. 2:5-9, begins with an invitation to the house of Jacob to join the nations' pilgrimage to Zion. But the passage quickly turns to accusations that the people have abandoned YHWH to follow foreign gods. As an adherent of the Davidic-Zion tradition, which maintains that YHWH alone protects the royal house of David and the city of Jerusalem, Isaiah opposed foreign alliances.

The second address, in Isa. 2:10-21, presents the prophet's announcement of the coming day of YHWH, when YHWH will punish foreign nations that threaten Israel (e.g., Isa. 13:6, 9; Joel 1:15; 2:11, 31; 3:14; Obad. 15) or those within Israel who allegedly oppose YHWH (e.g., Amos 5:18-20; Zeph. 1:7, 14; Mal. 4:5). The oracle focuses on the downfall of all who are high, mighty, and arrogant, and holds that YHWH alone will be aggrandized on the coming day of punishment.

The third address, in Isa. 2:22—4:6, focuses on the purging of Jerusalem and Judah. Following the plea in Isa. 2:22 to abandon human self-reliance, the passage turns to the punishment of the male leaders of Jerusalem and Judah in Isa. 3:1-11. The address then focuses on the leading women of Jerusalem and Judah in Isa. 3:12-4:1 who will be judged, stripped of their fine clothing, and left bereft of their husbands once the men have been killed or exiled. The passage concludes with an idyllic portrayal of a restored Jerusalem following the purge of the city.

▌ THE TEXT IN THE INTERPRETIVE TRADITION

Many modern interpreters maintain that Isa. 2:2-4 (cf. Mic. 4:1-5) dates to the Babylonian exile in the sixth century BCE, because of the analogy with the Akitu festival and the passage's many affinities with Second Isaiah. Like Second Isaiah, the passage envisions peace among the nations who will recognize YHWH as the sovereign deity of all creation and the nations of the world. Isaiah 2–4 summarizes the message of the book of Isaiah as a whole, which envisions a process in which YHWH will bring punishment upon Jerusalem as a means to purge and restore the city, thereby to reveal YHWH's role as sovereign of all creation and the nations at large.

When read as part of the prophecies of Isaiah ben Amoz, the portrayal of judgment in Isaiah 2:5—4:6 functions as Isaiah's means to explain how the Assyrian Empire will be able to overrun Israel and Judah; namely, because the king and people do not place their faith in YHWH's promises of protection, YHWH brings the Assyrians to punish them for infidelity.

In both Jewish and Christian tradition, the passage is read as an eschatological portrayal of the future restoration of Jerusalem. The New Testament presupposes Isa. 2:2-4 in defining the imagery of the city on the hill in the salt and light parable of the Sermon on the Mount in Matt. 5:13-16. The city of light is a beacon to the good works of Jesus' followers and the glory of G-d in heaven.

The reference to the city on a hill informs John Winthrop's 1630 sermon extolling the Massachusetts Bay Colonists to make their city (Boston) a shining example for the world.

Rabbinic commentators such as Abraham Ibn Ezra and David Kimḥi read the passage as a portrayal of the days to come when the temple would be rebuilt and the Messiah would come. The restoration of Zion is a key theme in both biblical and modern Zionist thought. Indeed, the BILU Zionist pioneers took their name from the first letters of the Hebrew words in Isa. 2:5, "O House of Jacob, come and let us go" (*bet ya'aqov, lekhu venelkhah*).

■ The Text in Contemporary Discussion

The idyllic imagery of Isa. 2:2-4, with its portrayal of the nations beating swords into plowshares and spears into pruning hooks, expresses one of the most important ideals of human life. Indeed, Isa. 2:4 serves as an unofficial motto for the United Nations. The English translation of the passage is inscribed on the Isaiah Stone, located in Ralph J. Bunche Park just across the street from the United Nations headquarters in New York City.

But Isaiah 2–4 also employs images of divine judgment against all who are high, mighty, and arrogant. Although many read such accusations as justified indictments against sinful human beings, readers must remember that Isaiah was attempting to explain the realities—whether anticipated or realized—of foreign invasion in his own time. In the aftermath of the Shoah, or Holocaust, such attempts to explain evil by accusing the victims are coming increasingly under criticism. In the end, readers must remember that the prophets faced the same problems that contemporary thinkers face, namely, how to explain evil while simultaneously positing an omnipotent and moral G-d. Our own responsibility to establish an exemplary city on a hill becomes paramount.

Isaiah 5–12

Isaiah 5–12 is a lengthy unit that focuses on the Assyrian invasions of Israel and Judah and the restoration of Jerusalem and the Davidic monarchy once YHWH defeats the Assyrians. It includes two basic subunits, the prophet's announcement of judgment against Israel and Judah in Isaiah 5 and the prophet's explanation of the significance of divine judgment in Isaiah 6–12. Isaiah 6–12 includes three basic subunits, Isaiah's vision of YHWH in Isaiah 6; the account of YHWH's judgment against Judah during the Syro-Ephraimitic War in Isaiah 7:1—8:15; and the announcement concerning the fall of Assyria and the restoration of the Davidic kingdom in Isaiah 8:16—12:6.

Isaiah 5: Announcement of Judgment against Israel and Judah

■ The Text in Its Ancient Context

Isaiah 5 begins with the so-called vineyard allegory in Isa. 5:1-7, in which the prophet sings about his "friend's" unsuccessful efforts to grow good grapes in his vineyard. As the allegory progresses, it becomes evident that Isaiah's "friend" is indeed YHWH and that the vineyard with its sour grapes represents the people of Israel and Judah. A series of "woe" oracles then follows in Isa. 5:8-24, in which Isaiah, speaking on YHWH's behalf, charges the people with a series of crimes that illustrate their refusal to follow divine torah, "instruction" (5:24). The prophet's charges include illegal acquisition of land and houses (5:8-10), drunkenness and failure to heed the needs of the poor (5:9-17), impious demands for divine action (5:18-19), the confusion of good and evil (5:20-21), and the subversion of justice (5:22-23). YHWH's announcement of judgment, which portrays the approach of the Assyrian army, then concludes the subunit in Isa. 5:25-30.

■ THE TEXT IN THE INTERPRETIVE TRADITION

Modern interpreters maintain that Isaiah 5 is the product of Isaiah, but they note its intertextual relationships with the new song of the vineyard in Isa. 27:2-13, a sixth-century text, which looks forward to the restoration of Israel and Judah once the punishment is completed. The use of the "woe" oracle is particularly important because it warns of impending danger if the nation loses sight of its obligations for justice and righteousness in the world.

■ THE TEXT IN CONTEMPORARY DISCUSSION

The approach of an enemy army is a terrifying prospect in both the ancient and the modern world. We in the United States have been blessed in that we have not suffered a foreign invasion since the War of 1812. Nevertheless, Isaiah's warning applies to us as well, insofar as he envisions leadership that is more interested in serving its own interests rather than those of the nation at large. Gridlock in the US Congress is a case in point, as our nation suffers from the inability of our Congressional representatives to arrive at compromises that will serve the larger good.

Isaiah 6: Isaiah's Commission Vision

■ THE TEXT IN ITS ANCIENT CONTEXT

Isaiah 6 presents the prophet's autobiographical account of his vision of YHWH in the Jerusalem temple. Interpreters are divided as to whether this is a commissioning account or a later reflection concerning the prophet's failure to convince the people to repent. The issues include the placement of the chapter after Isaiah 1–5 rather than at the beginning of the book and YHWH's commission to render the people blind, deaf, and dumb so that they are unable to repent, which seems to contradict the prophet's efforts throughout the rest of Isaiah 1–39.

The account is an example of a throne vision in which YHWH appears to a human enthroned in the earthly or heavenly temple (1 Kings 22; Ezekiel 1; Daniel 7). The vision takes place in the year of King Uzziah's death (742 BCE), before the Syro-Ephraimitic War and the Assyrian invasions of the late eighth century. It is based on the imagery of the interior of the Jerusalem temple during worship. The prophet stands by the column at the entrance to the temple, where the king stands (2 Kgs. 11:14; 23:3) so that he can see into the interior of the temple (1 Kings 7). YHWH is enthroned over the ark of the covenant, which resides in the holy of holies of the temple. The portrayal of YHWH's train or robes billowing out of the temple is based on the imagery of smoke from the thick incense generated by the ten incense burners in the great hall of the temple. The portrayal of the seraphim (fiery angelic figures) is based on the imagery of the ten menorahs or candlestands, each with seven lamps, burning within the thick incense smoke. Their hymn, "Holy, holy, holy, is YHWH of Hosts, the whole earth is full of [G-d's] glory" (author trans.), represents the song of the Levitical choir during the temple liturgy. The rumbling noise is from the heavy doors that are opened at sunrise to inaugurate the daily morning worship service. The placement of a hot coal on Isaiah's lips emulates the mouth-purification ceremonies practiced by Mesopotamian *baru* priests to prepare themselves to speak divine words. YHWH instructs Isaiah to render the people blind, deaf, and dumb so that they cannot repent and thereby save themselves. Isaiah does not object to YHWH's plans. Instead, he simply asks, "how long?" and YHWH responds with a vision of destruction (based on the Hebrew verb *sh'h*, which underlies the term Shoah) that will result in a surviving remnant of only 10 percent of the people. That remnant then constitutes "the holy seed" that will restore Jerusalem and Israel.

▌ THE TEXT IN THE INTERPRETIVE TRADITION

Modern scholars have raised questions as to whether Isaiah 6 is the work of the prophet or not. Although some maintain that it is a later composition (e.g., Kaiser, 115–21) its portrayal of coming judgment in which the people are rendered blind, deaf, and dumb is a signal that it might represent the prophet's reflection on his inability to motivate the kings and people to change. Ezra 9:2 cites "the holy seed" from Isa. 6:13 as part of Ezra's portrayal of the restoration of Jerusalem in keeping with Isaiah's prophecies.

The New Testament cites Isa. 6:9-10 frequently. In Matt. 13:14; Mark 4:12; and Luke 8:10, the quote appears to validate the disciples of Jesus who understand his words. In John 12:39 and Acts 28:25, it appears as part of larger discussion concerning the failure of Jews to recognize Jesus as the Messiah. Although such comments were generated by early Christianity's attempt to argue for its own perspective, the condemnation of Jews would have repercussions throughout the Middle Ages and the modern period, culminating in the Shoah (Holocaust). The song of the Seraphim, "Holy, Holy, Holy . . ." constitutes part of the Trisagion (thrice holy) in Christian liturgy.

Judaism reads Isa. 6:1-13, together with Isa. 7:1-6 and 9:5-6, as part of the Haftarah for Exod. 18:1—20:26, which recounts the revelation of Torah at Sinai. The Haftarah aids in helping Jews to understand G-d as the sovereign monarch who stands behind the Sinai revelation. The song of the Seraphim, "Holy, Holy, Holy . . ." constitutes part of the Kedushah (sanctification) of the morning and Musaf (additional) worship service in Judaism.

▌ THE TEXT IN CONTEMPORARY DISCUSSION

Mordecai Kaplan, the founder of Reconstructionist Judaism, finds a particularly disturbing issue is the moral character of YHWH's charge to the prophet to render the people blind, deaf, and dumb so that divine purpose might be realized (Kaplan). Such a position is an expression of teleological ethics, that is, the end result justifies the means. But the sacrifice of generations until that purpose is achieved hardly constitutes an example of ontological ethics, that is, the question of whether an act is good or evil in and of itself. Interpreters have noted that Isaiah does not challenge YHWH like

Abraham (Genesis 18), Moses (Exodus 32; Numbers 14), Job, and others do when confronted with the possibility of divine evil. Ironically, Isaiah's ideal vision of world harmony among the nations (Isa. 2:2-4) is not realized and the book ends with the portrayal of the corpses of those who would resist YHWH (Isa. 66:24). Elie Wiesel (111) states that we can say anything to G-d from within Jewish tradition. The same applies to Christianity. Perhaps we should learn from this that Isaiah should have objected, just as we must object when confronted with evil even from the highest of authorities.

Isaiah 7:1—8:15: YHWH's Judgment against Judah

■ THE TEXT IN ITS ANCIENT CONTEXT

Isaiah 7:1—8:15 presents an account of Isaiah's encounter with King Ahaz of Judah during the Syro-Ephraimitic War. Since the reign of King Jehu of Israel (842–815 BCE), the northern kingdom of Israel had been allied with the Assyrian Empire, which ensured that Israel would no longer be threatened by Aram as it was during the reigns of the Omride kings, that is, Omri (876–869 BCE), Ahab (869–850), Ahaziah (849), and Jehoram (849–842). But when King Pekah (737–732) came to the throne, he sought an alliance with Aram so that he might oppose the Assyrian Empire and bring an end to the crushing tribute that Israel had to pay. The Syro-Ephraimitic alliance therefore attempted to include all the small kingdoms of western Asia so they could present a united front against Assyria. King Jotham of Judah and his son Ahab refused to join the alliance. As Assyrian allies themselves, they knew that the Assyrians would devastate any kingdom that broke a treaty, and they likely distrusted an alliance based on two powers that had been at war with each other a century earlier. Consequently, northern Israel and Aram attacked Jerusalem in 734 BCE in an effort to force it into the Syro-Ephraimitic coalition.

The narrative portrays the fear of the house of David at the news of the Syro-Ephraimitic invasion of Judah. King Jotham apparently had passed away for reasons unknown to us, and his twenty-year-old son Ahaz was the new king. Ahaz was inspecting the water system of Jerusalem, located at the Upper Pool by the Fuller's Field ("fuller" means "one who does laundry"), which would have been located in the Kidron Valley east of Jerusalem outside the city's walls. The people of the city had access to the water through an underground tunnel, which represented a weak point in the city's defenses. Insofar as David had conquered Jerusalem by means of this tunnel (2 Sam. 5:8), Ahaz was considering how to defend the site. Isaiah's approach with his son, symbolically name Shear Jashub (Hebrew for "a remnant will return"), signaled the prophet's message that Ahaz should rely only on YHWH to defend the city, in keeping with YHWH's promise that the sons of David would sit on the throne of Israel in Jerusalem forever (2 Samuel 7). Of course, that would mean that many Judeans would die in keeping with the name of Isaiah's son, "(only) a remnant will return/survive." Ahaz preferred more practical means, however, and summoned the Assyrians to assist him as recounted in 2 Kings 16. Upon recognizing Ahaz's failure to trust in YHWH, Isaiah then proclaims that Judah will suffer as the Assyrians will invade and devastate the country, leaving

Judah to suffer under increased tribute. Although many believe Isaiah's advice to be impractical, it was based on the premise that the Assyrians would have invaded Aram and Israel anyway once their armies moved south to attack Jerusalem. The Assyrians destroyed Damascus and subjugated Israel, stripping it of its outlying territories. Pekah was assassinated. Ahaz's impetuousness did not result in an Assyrian reward; rather, it put him in Assyria's debt and resulted in heavier obligations to Assyria.

▮ THE TEXT IN THE INTERPRETIVE TRADITION

Modern critics, particularly Peter Ackroyd, have noted that the Ahaz narrative in Isaiah 7:1—8:15 is formulated as a counterpoint to the presentation of Hezekiah in Isaiah 36–39. Ahaz appears to be unwilling to trust in YHWH or Isaiah, and Judah suffers invasion and subjugation to Assyria as a result. Hezekiah places his trust in YHWH and Isaiah in Isaiah 36–37, and the city of Jerusalem is delivered as a result. The two narratives thereby characterize their respective segments of the book. Isaiah 1–33 speaks especially of judgment like that experienced by Ahaz, whereas Isaiah 34–66 anticipates deliverance and restoration like that experienced by Hezekiah.

Matthew 1:23 cites the birth of Immanuel (Hebrew, "G-d is with us") in Isa. 7:14 as a prophecy that predicts the birth of Jesus. The Gospel, however, cites the Greek text of the Septuagint, which states that the boy will be born to a *parthenos*, "virgin," in keeping with Hellenistic tradition that celebrates children born to gods—for example, Zeus—and human virgins. The Hebrew text reads, *'almah*, "young woman," irrespective of her status as a virgin. Jewish interpreters understand Immanuel to be a son of Isaiah.

▮ THE TEXT IN CONTEMPORARY DISCUSSION

Just as Israel was invaded by Aram (Syria) and other nations, such as Egypt, Assyria, and Babylonia, in antiquity, so modern Israel has been invaded or attacked repeatedly by Syria, Egypt, Hezbollah, Hamas, and other Arab nations in modern times, for example, in 1948, 1967, 1973, 2006, and 2012. Israel stands at a geographical crossroads in the ancient and modern Middle East, and it is therefore a tempting target. Many see the Palestinian issue as the key issue of the Middle East, but the refusal by many Arab and Muslim countries to view Israel as a legitimate state for Jews is just as crucial.

Isaiah 8:16—12:6: Announcing the Fall of Assyria and Restoration of the House of David

▮ THE TEXT IN ITS ANCIENT CONTEXT

Isaiah 8:16—12:6 presents Isaiah's announcements concerning the fall of Assyria and the restoration of the Davidic kingdom. It includes two major components, namely, (1) prophetic instruction concerning YHWH's signs to Israel and the House of David in Isa. 8:16—9:6 (9:7 in NRSV) and (2) the prophet's announcement concerning the fulfillment of YHWH's signs in Isa. 9:7—12:6 (9:8—12:6 in NRSV).

Isaiah 8:16—9:6 begins with an expression of the prophet's frustration that Ahaz will not listen to him. He therefore announces his intention to "bind up the testimony and seal my instruction [torah] among my teachings" while he waits for YHWH, who is hiding the divine face from the house of Israel. He envisions the people walking in great darkness until such time as a new and righteous Davidic monarch will emerge who will be recognized as "the prince of peace."

Isaiah 9:7—12:6 announces the fulfillment of YHWH's signs. The passage begins with a lengthy sequence of oracles, all based on the formula "YHWH's hand is stretched out still," which condemn the northern kingdom of Israel in Isa. 9:7—10:4 for a variety of misdeeds. This oracular sequence constitutes the prophet's comment on the fall of the northern kingdom of Israel to the Assyrian empire in 722/721 BCE. With Israel destroyed, Isaiah then turns in Isa. 10:5—12:6 to a condemnation of the Assyrian Empire, particularly its king (presumably Sargon II), for his arrogance in threatening Jerusalem and claiming to be the true power in the world. In Isa. 10:5-34, Isaiah likens the Assyrian king to the Egyptian Pharaoh of the exodus, when he announces that the Assyrian king will fall just like a tree that has been trimmed. YHWH will grow a new, righteous Davidic monarch from the stump of Jesse. The prophet holds in Isa. 11:1-16 that the new monarch will be wise and righteous, that he will reunite Israel and Judah, and that he will swoop down on the enemies of Israel and Judah, resulting ultimately in the return of exiles from Assyria and Egypt. The concluding hymn in Isa. 12:6 draws its language from the Song of the Sea in Exodus 15, especially in verses 1-3, and various Psalms, such as 105:1 and 118:14, 21, to praise YHWH for restoring Israel and Judah.

◼ THE TEXT IN THE INTERPRETIVE TRADITION

Modern interpreters debate compositional issues in Isaiah 8:16—12:6. Although many view the royal oracle in Isa. 9:1-6 as Isaiah's anticipation of the birth of Hezekiah, they see the royal oracle of Isa. 11:1-16 as a postexilic composition. Isaiah 11 was more likely written in the time of King Josiah of Judah (640–609 BCE), who was known for his program of religious reform and national restoration. The reign of Josiah saw many editions of the narrative and prophetic books, such as Joshua–Kings, Isaiah, Amos, Hosea, and portions of Jeremiah that were edited to support the Josian reform. Isaiah 11, with its vision of a child king who would reunite Israel and Judah to bring home the exiles from Assyria and Egypt, is an example of such work. The hymn in Isa. 12:1-6 points to a liturgical setting for the performance of Isaiah, perhaps in the monarchic period as well as in the second temple of the Persian period and beyond.

Isaiah's royal oracles have been a source of constant attention in Christianity insofar as they are read as predictions of the coming of Jesus. The reference in Isaiah 8:23—9:1 (9:1-2 in NRSV) to the people who have seen a great light appears in Matt 4:15-16 as part of the evangelist's introduction to Jesus' career in the Galilee. Likewise, the phrase "a child is born" in Isa. 9:6 stands in the background of the birth of Jesus in Matt. 1:23. Isaiah 9:1-6 plays a key role in Handel's oratorio *The Messiah* (Dublin 1742), which is performed especially at Christmastime to celebrate Jesus' birth and life. Paul cites Isa. 11:1, 10, in Rom. 15:12 as part of a larger argument that the new Davidic king is a sign to the nations.

Talmudic tradition views Isa. 9:1-6 as a reference to the birth of Hezekiah. The talmudic Rabbi Bar Kappara thought that Hezekiah was supposed to be the Messiah, but the attribute of justice (*middat ha-din*) argued against this claiming that David was not made the Messiah and that Hezekiah was less worthy (*b. Sanh.* 94a). Isaiah 10:32—12:6 functions as the Haftarah reading for the eighth day of Passover because of its exodus references, its portrayal of the downfall of an oppressive king, and its vision of exiles restored to Israel and Judah from Egypt and Assyria.

■ THE TEXT IN CONTEMPORARY DISCUSSION

The celebration of the downfall of an oppressor expresses an important ideal in both Christianity and Judaism. In Christianity, such ideals are expressed through the coming of Christ, who brings down the oppressive powers of the world. In Judaism, such ideals are expressed especially in the celebration of Passover and the release of the people of Israel from Egyptian bondage. We may also remember the joyous celebrations at the end of World War II, when both Nazi Germany and imperial Japan surrendered. The famed picture of the sailor kissing the nurse in Times Square is a lasting reminder of the joy experienced as a result of the end of the war. At the same time, we must remember the limits of military power. The killing of Osama bin Laden, however satisfying given his crimes, did not bring the war on terrorism to an end.

Isaiah 13–27

Isaiah 13–27, concerned with the preparation of the nations for YHWH's worldwide sovereignty, constitutes a distinctive section within the book of Isaiah as a whole. It contains two basic components. The first is the announcement concerning the nations in Isaiah 13–23, including Babylon (Isaiah 13–14), Moab (Isaiah 15–16), Damascus (Isaiah 17–18), Egypt (Isaiah 19–20), the Wilderness of the Sea (Isa. 21:1-10), Dumah (Isa. 21:11-12), Arabia (Isa. 21:13-17), the Valley of Vision (Isaiah 22), and Tyre (Isaiah 23). The second concerns the restoration of Zion/Israel at the center of the nations. All of the nations mentioned were part of the Persian Empire, which indicates that the book of Isaiah associates YHWH with Persian rule.

Isaiah 13–14: The Pronouncement Concerning Babylon

■ THE TEXT IN ITS ANCIENT CONTEXT

Like all of the oracles against the nations in Isaiah 13–23, Isaiah 13–14 begins with a superscription that labels the following text as the *massa'*, or "pronouncement," concerning Babylon. The prophetic pronouncement functions as a means to depict YHWH's actions in the world.

Isaiah 13–14 is a lengthy oracle that anticipates the downfall of Babylon on the day of YHWH. The day of YHWH tradition is well known in the Prophets as a day when YHWH will act against enemies, including those who threaten Jerusalem, Judah, and Israel (e.g., Joel 1–2; Obadiah; Zeph. 1:2-18), and even against Jerusalem or Israel itself when viewed as acting contrary to YHWH's expectations (e.g., Isa. 2:6-21; Amos 5:18-20). King Hezekiah of Judah allied with the Babylonian prince Merodach Baladan in his attempt to revolt against the Assyrians in 705–701 BCE. The aim of the revolt was to strike Assyria from both west (Judah and its allies) and east (Babylon and its allies) and thereby divide Assyrian efforts to put down the revolt. Isaiah's opposition to this alliance is evident in Isaiah 39, where Isaiah condemns Hezekiah for receiving the Babylonian embassy in preparation for the revolt.

A short oracle against the Philistines is appended in Isa. 14:28-32 to account for one of the nations subdued by Hezekiah as he prepared for revolt.

▌ THE TEXT IN THE INTERPRETIVE TRADITION

Most scholars recognize that Isaiah 13–14 is the product of later editing, particularly in the sixth century BCE, when the Persians conquered the Babylonian Empire and allowed exiled Jews to return to Jerusalem to rebuild the temple. Isaiah 13 in particular appears to have been composed to anticipate the work of Second Isaiah in Isaiah 40–55, which announced the end of the exile and called on Jews to return to Jerusalem. The passage appears to have reworked an older anti-Assyrian oracle in Isaiah 14 that celebrated the battlefield death of the Assyrian monarch Sargon II in 705 BCE. His defeat was so complete that his body laid unrecovered and unburied on the battlefield (see Isa. 14:19-20). Sargon's death was an important catalyst for Hezekiah's revolt in 705 BCE. The brief anti-Assyrian oracle in Isa. 14:24-27 points to the original Assyrian referent of the oracle and demonstrates how earlier Isaian prophecies could be reread in reference to later events following the lifetime of the prophet.

Interpreters have long noted the portrayal in Isa. 14:12 of the fall of Helel son of Shachar, "the Shining One, son of the Dawn," from heaven down to Sheol (the netherworld where all of the dead go; see esp. Erlandsson). Although this was originally meant as a reference to Sargon II, later interpreters viewed it as a description of a fallen angel from heaven who would then become the Satan figure. Thus the Vulgate translates the phrase into Latin as Lucifer, "light bearing" (in reference to the morning star, Venus), which became a name for Satan in the Christian tradition. Although the downfall of Lucifer comes to play a role in Christian eschatology, early Protestant interpreters such as Luther and Calvin denied that this text referred to Satan, preferring instead to see it as a historical reference to Babylon. Jewish interpreters tended to read the name in relation to the Babylonians. Rashi saw it as a reference to Venus, the morning star, which symbolized the Babylonian goddess Ishtar, and Kimhi understood it as a reference to Nebuchadnezzar.

▌ THE TEXT IN CONTEMPORARY DISCUSSION

Many interpreters read Isaiah 13–14 as an oracle proclaiming the downfall of Iraq during the 1991 Gulf War, especially when Saddam Hussein parked Iraqi fighter jets by the ruins of Ur, located in the territory of ancient Babylonia, in an attempt to protect them from allied forces. Saddam Hussein attacked Israel with Scud missiles in an attempt to draw Israel into the war and thereby prompt Arab allies of the United States such as Egypt and Syria to reconsider their participation in the US-led alliance. Iraq's Scud missiles lacked precision guidance systems, and they generally struck civilian rather than military targets. Israel was not an active member of the alliance—indeed, the United States, in an effort to attract Arab nations into the alliance, had advised Israel to stay out of the war altogether. Nevertheless, Saddam Hussein hoped to draw on the anti-Jewish sentiments of America's Arab allies by deliberately attacking Israel despite the fact that it was not directly involved.

Others see environmental concerns addressed in this text, particularly in Isa. 14:7-8 in which the trees celebrate the downfall of the King Babylon because he would no longer come to cut them down (Tucker, 161). Mesopotamian rulers were known for their expeditions to Phoenicia (modern Lebanon) to cut down cedars and other trees to decorate their imperial palaces.

Isaiah 15–16: The Pronouncement concerning Moab

∎ THE TEXT IN ITS ANCIENT CONTEXT

Isaiah 15–16 is Isaiah's oracle concerning Moab, located east of the Jordan River and Dead Sea in modern-day Jordan. The oracle describes Moab's distress at a foreign invasion, likely the Assyrian king Tiglath Pileser III, during the Syro-Ephraimitic War (734–732 BCE). The city names indicate a flight from the region north of the Wadi Arnon, which would have been Israelite territory settled by Reuben and Gad prior to the ninth-century-BCE war between Aram and Israel. Seeing Israel's defeat by Aram, King Mesha of Moab seized Israelite territory north of the Arnon, as recorded in his famed Moabite Stone. In Isa. 16:6, the prophet recalls Moab's arrogance.

∎ THE TEXT IN THE INTERPRETIVE TRADITION

Although this text was likely written by Isaiah, it was reused in later contexts. It likely provided support for Josiah's interests in reestablishing Davidic rule over Moab in the late seventh century BCE. Portions of the oracle were reused in Jeremiah's oracle concerning Moab in Jer. 48:29-38.

∎ THE TEXT IN CONTEMPORARY DISCUSSION

Isaiah 16:3-5 is frequently cited in support of causes for social justice. Gene M. Tucker, for example, understands this section to be a reference to refugees from war. He states, "The visionary poet sees the answer to the problems of refugees from war to be in a ruler descended from David, on the throne in Jerusalem. The passage is messianic in this hope for an anointed one in the future. Its vision of a time of peace under a just ruler reiterates the themes of 11:1-5" (Tucker, 169).

Isaiah 17–18: The Pronouncement concerning Damascus

∎ THE TEXT IN ITS ANCIENT CONTEXT

Isaiah 17–18 constitutes the prophet's pronouncement against Damascus, the capital of Aram (Syria), but the reference to Ephraim and Israel in Isa. 17:3 indicates that it addresses the Syro-Ephraimitic coalition that threatened Jerusalem and Judah in 734–732 BCE. The woe oracle against

Cush (Ethiopia) in Isaiah 18 presupposes King Hosea of Israel's embassy to Cush in 724 BCE, in preparation for its ultimately fatal revolt against Assyria. Isaiah is opposed to such alliances, as they indicate a failure to put trust in YHWH.

■ THE TEXT IN THE INTERPRETIVE TRADITION

The Aramaic *Targum Jonathan* reads the reference to Cush in Isa. 18:1 as India, which prompted medieval Jewish interpreters such as Rashi and Kimhi to read Isaiah 18 as a depiction of the eschatological war against Gog of Magog (Ezekiel 38–39).

■ THE TEXT IN CONTEMPORARY DISCUSSION

The prophet's condemnation of Damascus raises the issue of judgment against the Assad regime of modern Syria, which is also creating for itself a heap of ruins. Hafez al-Assad was a member of the minority Alawite sect of Shia Islam who served as air force commander under the leadership of the Baathist party. He came to power by instigating two internal military coups in 1969 and 1970 to oust the leadership of his own Baathist party. Under his rule as president of Syria, Hafez al-Assad (1971–2000) was known for its belligerency against Israel, particularly the Yom Kippur War of 1973, and its suppression of dissent, particularly the killing of some twenty thousand Muslim Brotherhood supporters in Hama in 1982. Although many saw his son, Bashar al-Assad (2000–present) as a potential reformer, the outbreak of the Syrian civil war, which has now seen over one hundred thousand killed, has dashed any such hopes. Many are concerned about the future of Syria, insofar as the Syrian rebels are heavily influenced by al-Qaeda and other Islamic extremists. Assad himself is supported by Hezbollah soldiers, who are allies of Iran.

In both Isaiah 17–18 and in this modern example, we find some of the fatal consequences that come with the lust for, and desire to cling to, power. Assad's desperation to hold on to power has led to the use of chemical weapons against his own people. In one attack on August 21, 2013, over 1,400 Syrian civilians, including women and children, were killed in a gas attack apparently launched by the Syrian army. The Assad regime has responded by claiming that the attack was carried out by the Syrian rebels, but the rebels lack access to such weapons and the means to deliver them. This desperate move has now led Assad's allies to join with a United Nations resolution to strip him of his chemical arsenal, and may ultimately lead to his undoing.

Isaiah 19–20: The Pronouncement against Egypt

■ THE TEXT IN ITS ANCIENT CONTEXT

Isaiah's pronouncements against Egypt in Isaiah 19–20 presuppose the role that Egypt played in the late eighth century in instigating revolt against the Assyrian Empire. Isaiah was opposed to military alliances between Judah and foreign powers. He points to internal struggle within Egypt during the late eighth century that eventually brought the Egyptian twenty-fifth (Ethiopian) dynasty to power as a sign of Egyptian instability. Isaiah 19:16-25 may presuppose the Assyrian conquest of Egypt in 671 and the subsequent rise of the twenty-sixth (Saite) dynasty as an Assyrian ally. Isaiah's walking about Jerusalem naked and barefoot in Isaiah 20 following the conquest of Ashdod by Sargon II in 715 BCE is a prophetic symbolic action meant to demonstrate the fate of those who would support an Egyptian and Ethiopian-inspired revolt against Assyria.

■ THE TEXT IN THE INTERPRETIVE TRADITION

Egypt ultimately became a major center for Jewish life in antiquity, prompted initially by the movement of refugees from the eighth-century Assyrian invasions and subsequent political and trade relations in the Persian, Hellenistic, and Roman periods. Although Egypt was the birthplace of the Greek Septuagint in the Hellenistic period, the emergence of antisemitism in the Roman period placed the Egyptian Jewish community at risk (see Schäfer).

■ THE TEXT IN CONTEMPORARY DISCUSSION

Although Egypt was the site of an important Jewish community from antiquity through the medieval and early modern periods, the Egyptian government expelled the bulk of its Jewish community and seized its property in the aftermath of the creation of modern Israel in 1948. President Anwar Sadat of Egypt signed a treaty with Israel in 1979 that saw the return of the Sinai to Egyptian control, but Sadat was assassinated in 1981 for his initiative and the treaty has remained rather cold to this day. The ongoing political and religious struggles between factions raise great concerns for the future of the treaty and for the Christian community in Egypt.

Isaiah 21: Pronouncements concerning the Wilderness of the Sea, Dumah, and Arabia

■ THE TEXT IN ITS ANCIENT CONTEXT

Isaiah 21 is not a single text, but it is a sequence of prophetic pronouncements concerning the Wilderness of the Sea in Isa. 21:1-10; Dumah in Isa. 21:11-12; and Arabia in Isa. 21:13-17. The reference to Babylon's fall in 21:9 indicates that the Wilderness of the Sea refers to Babylon. The term refers to the marshy area where the Tigris and Euphrates join and flow out into the Persian Gulf, that is, the modern Shatt al-Arab Waterway. Hezekiah's Babylonian ally in his revolt against Assyria (see Isaiah 39), Prince Merodach Baladan, used the area as a base to hide from the Assyrians and to conduct guerrilla operations against them. Dumah is the name of an Arabian Desert oasis conquered by the Assyrian king Sennacherib in 689. It is associated with Seir, another name for Edom. The Assyrians conducted campaigns against the Arabian tribes in the late eighth and seventh centuries. The present oracle presupposes Sennacherib's defeat at Kedar in the northern Arabian Desert in 689.

■ THE TEXT IN THE INTERPRETIVE TRADITION

A. A. MacIntosh points to the reference to Elam and Media in Isa. 21:2 as an indication that Isaiah 21 is a palimpsest, that is, a text that has been rewritten in relation to later circumstances. Babylon fell to a combination of Elamites and Medes in 539 BCE under the leadership of Cyrus. It appears that the concern with the anticipated downfall of Merodach Baladan has been updated to account for Babylon's fall to Cyrus.

Isaiah 21:9 is cited in Rev. 18:2 as part of the scenario concerning the fall of Babylon (Rome).

■ THE TEXT IN CONTEMPORARY DISCUSSION

The reference to the watchtower in Isa. 21:8-9 inspired the title of *Watch Tower*, the publication of the Jehovah's Witnesses. The Jehovah's Witnesses believe that the destruction of the present world order through Armageddon is imminent and that the kingdom of G-d is at hand. The image of the watchtower in Isa. 21:8-9 therefore symbolizes their watchfulness in preparing for the advent of G-d's kingdom. The downfall of Babylon was symbolic of the eschatological age in Christianity when Christ would be revealed to all (Revelation 18–19).

Isaiah 22: The Pronouncement concerning the Valley of Vision

■ THE TEXT IN ITS ANCIENT CONTEXT

Isaiah 22 is called the pronouncement concerning the Valley of Vision, but the contents of the oracle make it clear that it refers to Jerusalem after the lifting of Sennacherib's siege in 701 BCE. Although Isaiah 36–37 claims a great victory over Sennacherib, his records indicate that Hezekiah saved the city and his throne by capitulating to the Assyrians. Isaiah points out the cost of the siege, namely, Jerusalem was spared but the land of Judah was devastated.

Isaiah refers to Hezekiah's water tunnel, built in preparation for the revolt. He condemns Shebna, a major government official under Hezekiah, for building his own tomb at a time of national threat. An ancient inscription marking the tomb of Shebna has been discovered in the Kidron Valley east of biblical Jerusalem in the Arab Silwan village.

■ THE TEXT IN THE INTERPRETIVE TRADITION

Isaiah 22:13, "let us eat and drink, for tomorrow we will die," appears in 1 Cor. 15:32 to characterize Paul's opponents who do not believe in Jesus' resurrection. The reference to the key of the house of David in Isa. 22:22 appears in Rev. 3:7 to indicate to the church in Philadelphia that the door (to Christ) is open to them.

Talmudic tradition holds that Shebna was the high priest who shot an arrow to the Assyrians with the message that all Jerusalem—except Hezekiah and Isaiah—were ready to surrender (*b. Sanh.* 26ab; see also Rashi).

■ THE TEXT IN CONTEMPORARY DISCUSSION

Premature celebrations of victory often mask reality. Japan celebrated a premature victory over the United States at Pearl Harbor in 1941 without realizing that they had planted the seeds of their own national destruction. Likewise, although the United States was able to claim victory in Iraq, it now has little influence in Iraq. From politicians who claim victory too early to office workers who Twitter about promotions before they have been secured, this text serves as a valuable warning against the sorts of hubris that lead people to snatch defeat out of the jaws of victory.

Isaiah 23: The Pronouncement against Tyre

▌THE TEXT IN ITS ANCIENT CONTEXT

Isaiah's pronouncement concerning Tyre targets one of Hezekiah's principal allies in his revolt against the Assyrians. Tyre was the dominant Phoenician city, and it was the major sea power of the day, with a powerful navy and extensive trade relations. But when Sennacherib unexpectedly subdued the island city in 701 BCE, Hezekiah's western allies quickly abandoned him, leaving him to face the Assyrians alone.

▌THE TEXT IN THE INTERPRETIVE TRADITION

The oracle has been updated in Isa. 23:13-18 to account for Tyre's fall to the Babylonians in 588–572 BCE. Like Jerusalem, the oracle anticipates that Tyre will rise again in seventy years (cf. Jer. 25:29 on Jerusalem).

▌THE TEXT IN CONTEMPORARY DISCUSSION

The issue of being abandoned by one's allies that is raised in Isaiah 23 is still applicable in a plethora of modern contexts, whether it be betrayal on an international scale or within the family relationships. Modern Lebanon fell victim to its internal divisions between its Maronite Christian, Druze, and Muslim populations. The Palestine Liberation Organization (PLO) moved into Lebanon following its failed attempt to take over Jordan in 1971, and thereby played an important role in destabilizing the country. The Lebanese civil war of 1975–1990 saw the disintegration of Lebanon as a coherent modern state. Israel invaded Lebanon in 1982 to counteract the PLO, and later withdrew in 2000 following its failure to establish Maronite Christian control of the country. Lebanon is now dominated by Hezbollah (Party of G-d), a heavily armed Shiite Muslim militant military organization and political party backed by Iran. Lebanon never signed a peace treaty with Israel following the 1948 war of independence. Hezbollah attacked Israel from southern Lebanon in 2006, raining missiles on Haifa and other parts of the country, and Israel counterattacked with air, naval, and ground units. In the aftermath of the conflict, both the Lebanese government and the United Nations abandoned their commitments to disarm Hezbollah, leaving Israel to feel abandoned by a major governing body to which it belongs.

Isaiah 24–27: YHWH's New World Order: Salvation for Zion/Israel

▌THE TEXT IN ITS ANCIENT CONTEXT

Isaiah 24–27 concludes the oracles concerning the nations in Isaiah 13–27 with an extensive prophetic announcement concerning YHWH's new world order based in Zion. This section envisions a future withering of creation and judgment against the earth in Isa. 24:1-23 followed by a prophetic announcement of YHWH's blessing in Isaiah 25:1—27:13. This latter section includes YHWH's blessing of the earth at Zion in Isa. 25:1-12 and its results in Isa. 26:1—27:13, including an account of Judah's petition to YHWH for deliverance in Isa. 26:1-21; YHWH's defeat of Leviathan in Isa. 27:1; and an exhortation to Israel to accept YHWH's offer of reconciliation.

Isaiah 24:1-23 presents the prophet's announcement of YHWH's punishment of the earth. The portrayal of a devastated and withered land is a typical element of blessings and curses speeches, for example, Leviticus 26 and Deuteronomy 28–30, that posit natural catastrophe as a consequence of human failure to abide by the divine will. The prophets employ them constantly for the same purpose (e.g., Isa. 34:11-17; Jer. 5:6; 19:7-9; Hosea 4; 13:7-8). The imagery presupposes the period of the late summer prior to the onset of the fall rains and the New Year that inaugurates the restoration of divine rule over the world of creation. In the present instance, the withered earth presages the fall of the "city of chaos" (Isa. 24:10), that is, Babylon, and the recognition of YHWH's reign.

Isaiah 25:1-12 inaugurates the announcement of blessing with a portrayal YHWH's blessings for Zion. The imagery includes a banquet for the nations at Mt. Zion in which death will be banished forever. Such a banquet is based on the celebration of the fall festival of Sukkot, "Booths," which celebrates the completion of the summer harvest and anticipates the onset of the fall rains. In Mesopotamian cultures, the fall rains were celebrated as the time when fertility gods, such as Tammuz, were returned to life from the netherworld.

Isaiah 26:1-21 presents Judah's petition to YHWH for deliverance. The liturgical dimensions of the passage emerge here insofar as it employs an initial hymn of praise in 26:1b-6 to celebrate YHWH's deliverance of the land from the wicked city of chaos. The imagery of childbirth in 26:17-18 complements the imagery of resurrection of the dead in 26:14 and 19 to give expression to YHWH's life-giving deliverance of the people.

Isaiah 27:1 presents a brief reference to YHWH's defeat of Leviathan, the seven-headed chaos monster of the deep known also in Ugaritic/Canaanite mythology (see also Ps. 74:13-14; Isa. 11:15-16). Leviathan's defeat symbolizes YHWH's deliverance of the people from Babylonian exile.

Finally, Isa. 27:2-13 presents the new vineyard allegory in which YHWH finally gets the vineyard to produce fruit (cf. Isa. 5:1-7). The vineyard metaphor portrays Israel's taking root in the aftermath of exile to grow once again. With its restoration, the exiles of Israel will return from Assyria and Egypt.

▌THE TEXT IN THE INTERPRETIVE TRADITION

Many interpreters view these chapters as the so-called Isaiah Apocalypse, insofar as Isaiah 24–27 employs motifs of cosmic chaos and restoration, the resurrection of the dead (see Isa. 26:14, 19), and a view of the future that suggests the end of time. But these motifs are not necessarily apocalyptic. Like many prophetic writings, Isaiah 24–27 employs mythological motifs to portray divine action in the world (see, e.g., Amos 7–9; Isaiah 49–54; Habakkuk 3; Ezekiel 8–11), and the references to "in that day" in the passage are simple references to the future. Overall, the passage simply points to the downfall of an unnamed, exalted city of chaos (Isa. 24:10, 12; 25:2-3; 26:5), likely Babylon, which will precede the recognition of YHWH's sovereignty throughout the world.

The overthrow of Babylon, the restoration of good relations between Israel and the nations in these chapters (cf. Isa. 2:2-4), and the intertextual resignification of earlier prophetic texts in these chapters point to the late sixth century as the setting for composition, although Isa. 27:2-13 might be earlier. Isaiah 24–27 would then play an important role in binding together the prophecies of Isaiah ben Amoz in Isaiah 1–39 and those of the exilic prophet Deutero-Isaiah in Isaiah 40–55 to form a sixth-century edition of the book at the onset of Persian rule. This period saw the restoration of the Jerusalem temple with Persian support, thereby opening a new era for Jerusalem's relationship with foreign nations.

Paul cites Isa. 25:8 in his discussion of resurrection in 1 Cor. 15:54 and Isa. 27:9 in his discussion of forgiveness of sins in Rom. 11:27.

Rabbinic tradition views the city of chaos as Jerusalem and understands the entire block to be concerned with Jerusalem's restoration.

◼ THE TEXT IN CONTEMPORARY DISCUSSION

The twentieth century saw two major attempts by world powers to establish an international body to which nations could turn to settle conflicts. The creation of the League of Nations was the first attempt in the aftermath of World War I, and the creation of the United Nations in the aftermath of World War II was the second. Although hardly perfect, the United Nations played important roles in the creation of the modern state of Israel in 1948 and the containment of the Cold War to regional conventional conflicts rather than all-out nuclear war. Although the United Nations is frequently politicized and rendered ineffective and irrelevant by many of its member states, it still remains an important institution for achieving peace and justice in the world.

Isaiah 28–33: YHWH's Plan for Jerusalem: Announcement of a New King

◼ THE TEXT IN ITS ANCIENT CONTEXT

The first portion of the book of Isaiah concludes with a block of material in Isaiah 28–33 that focuses on the prophet's instruction concerning YHWH's plans for the deliverance of Jerusalem and the emergence of a new king. The oracles in this block each begin with an introductory "Woe" (Isa. 28:1; 29:1; 29:15; 30:1; 31:1; cf. 33:1), with the exception of the culminating unit in Isa. 32:1, which begins with "Behold!" This block includes five subunits, namely, Isa. 28:1-29; 29:1-24; 30:1-33; 31:1-9; and 32:1—33:24.

Isaiah 28:1-29 begins the sequence with the prophet's instruction concerning YHWH's purpose in bringing Assyrian rule. The oracle condemns the leadership of both the northern kingdom of Israel and the southern kingdom of Judah for self-indulgence, gluttony, and drunkenness, all metaphors for royal incompetence. The imagery of the covenant with death presupposes the Canaanite "marzeah" ritual, which celebrates descent into the underworld, perhaps at the outset of the dry summer season.

Isaiah is well familiar with agricultural metaphor and frequently employs it to makes his points. In order to produce dill, cumin, wheat, and so on, the produce must first be crushed.

Isaiah 29:1-24 presents the prophet's instruction concerning YHWH's purpose in assaulting Jerusalem. The term Ariel, "lion of G-d," recalls the lion as symbol of the tribe of Judah (Gen. 49:8-11) and serves as a pun on the Hebrew term, *har'el*, which designates the temple altar hearth (see Ezek. 43:15-16). The first "woe" oracle in 29:1-14 portrays YHWH's "conquest" of Jerusalem with a foreign army just as David conquered it with his own soldiers (2 Sam. 5:6-9). Isaiah 29:11-12 calls on readers to view the book of Isaiah as a sealed vision. The second "woe" oracle, in 29:15-24, focuses on the realization of YHWH's purpose for Zion so that the blind and the deaf (see Isaiah 6) will sanctify YHWH.

Isaiah 30:1-33 presents the prophet's instruction concerning YHWH's delay in delivering the people from Assyria. This oracle expresses Isaiah's dissatisfaction with Hezekiah's embassy to Egypt to enlist support for his revolt against Assyria. As in Isaiah 7, the prophet opposes military alliances as a denial of the power and sovereignty of YHWH. Consequently, YHWH will delay deliverance until the people show greater trust. In the end, a teacher will arise to guide the people to throw out their idols so that YHWH will strike down Assyria. Within the context of the final form of the book of Isaiah, this would refer to Second Isaiah and his or her successors in Isaiah 40–66.

Isaiah 31:1-9 presents the prophet's warning concerning reliance on Egyptian aid in Hezekiah's revolt against Assyria. Only YHWH will protect Jerusalem much like a lion or hovering birds protect their prey.

Isaiah 32:1—33:24 concludes the sequence with a presentation of prophetic instruction concerning the future, righteous king. The first portion of this subunit, in Isa. 32:1-20, presents the prophet's vision of the righteous king whom the blind, deaf, and dumb will see when their eyes, ears, and minds are opened to YHWH's purpose (see Isaiah 6). In keeping with Isaiah's view of YHWH as the true Creator, such recognition will result in the blooming of the wilderness and the people will be secure (see Isa. 40:1-11). The second portion of this subunit, in Isa. 33:1-24, begins with a woe oracle that introduces a liturgical presentation of the new king in conjunction with the downfall of Israel's oppressor. In the end, the people who were rendered blind, deaf, and dumb in Isaiah 6 will see the king in his beauty in 33:17 and a secure Jerusalem in 33:20, in which YHWH serves as the ultimate king.

■ THE TEXT IN THE INTERPRETIVE TRADITION

Scholars have argued that most of the material in Isaiah 28–33 was written by Isaiah ben Amoz, but some elements represent later composition. The liturgical composition in Isaiah 33 appears to be the product of the final fifth-century edition of the book, in the time of Ezra and Nehemiah. Isaiah 33 closes the first portion of the book of Isaiah with a vision of the new king and the restored Jerusalem. Its liturgical character indicates that the book could have been presented as part of a temple liturgy. Isaiah 30:19-33; 32:1-8, 15-20, which points to Josiah's restoration as the projected outcome of the prophecies of Isaiah, appears to have been composed for the Josianic edition of Isaiah in the late seventh century.

The authors of the Dead Sea Scrolls apparently saw the references to the future teachers of Israel in Isa. 30:19-33 as a reference to their own Righteous Teacher who formed the group in the early second century BCE and led them to the site of Qumran, where they awaited G-d's final apocalyptic war against the wicked of the world. Although they anticipated a restoration of Jerusalem, events did not turn out as expected and both Qumran and the Jerusalem temple were destroyed in the Zealot revolt of 66–74 CE. The Great Isaiah Scroll from Qumran (1QIsaᵃ) has a gap between Isaiah 33 and Isaiah 34, indicating that this is the main structural division of the book.

Many of these texts appear in the New Testament. The reference to speaking in tongues in Isa. 28:11 appears in 1 Cor. 14:21 as part of Paul's efforts to prompt the people to trust in prophets and not in those who speak in tongues. Nevertheless, Isa. 28:11-13 was influential in promoting such practice among Pentecostal and charismatic Christians (see Mark 16:17; Acts 19:6; 28:1-6; 1 Corinthians 12–14). The precious cornerstone of Isa. 28:16 appears in Paul's characterization of Torah in Rom. 9:33, and its reference to trust appears in his discussion of justification by faith in Rom. 10:11. It also appears in Peter's characterization of Scripture in 1 Pet. 2:6. The deep sleep of Isa. 29:10 appears as part of Paul's polemic against Israel in Rom. 11:8. The motif of vain worship in Isa. 29:13 appears in the polemics against Pharisees (rabbinic Jews) in Matt. 15:7 and Mark 7:6. The destruction of the wisdom of the wise in Isa. 29:14 factors into Paul's discussion of the demise of those who do not believe in Christ in 1 Cor. 1:19. The reference to the potter and the clay plays a key role in Paul's argument in Rom. 9:19-21 that humans cannot resist G-d.

Rashi read Isa. 30:19-33 as a reference to the days of the Messiah, but other medieval interpreters, such as Kimhi, read it as a reference to Hezekiah. Rashi, Kimhi, Ibn Ezra, and others read the righteous monarch of Isa. 32:1 as a reference to Hezekiah. The vision of the king in his beauty in Isa. 33:17 is a reference to a vision of the Shekinah, or presence of G-d, according to Rashi, although Kimhi sees it as a reference to Hezekiah once again (for comments by Rashi, Kimhi, Ibn Ezra, and others, see Rosenberg, ad loc.).

Isaiah 27:6-28:13; 29:22-23 functions as the Haftarah reading for Exod. 1:1—6:1. The Haftarah's themes of judgment leading to restoration thereby accompany the narrative of Israel's enslavement in Egypt with its initial promises of deliverance from Egyptian bondage.

▌THE TEXT IN CONTEMPORARY DISCUSSION

YHWH's delay in bringing about the restoration of Jerusalem following the Assyrian punishment is a major factor in the conceptualization of divine action in the book of Isaiah. It becomes a means to defend the integrity of G-d in the aftermath of the Assyrian invasions; that is, the claim that Judah and Israel deserve punishment protects YHWH from charges that the deity failed to live up to the terms of the eternal covenant with the house of David and the city of Jerusalem. Indeed, the postponement of restoration until after the Babylonian exile, again after the building of the Second Temple, and even again until after the reforms of Ezra and Nehemiah, testify to the faithful vision of G-d's power, fidelity, and integrity in the book of Isaiah over against the experience of invasion, reversal, and subjugation. Such an issue is particularly important in the aftermath of the Shoah, in which we continue to ask questions about G-d's presence, morality, and power in the face of unspeakable evil. Such questions point to continued faithfulness in G-d together with a corresponding faithfulness to truth that is inseparable from our relationship with G-d. We do not yet have all the answers, but we continue to strive to achieve them.

Isaiah 34–35: Prophetic Instruction concerning YHWH's Return of Exiles to Zion

■ THE TEXT IN ITS ANCIENT CONTEXT

Isaiah 34–35 introduce the second half of the book of Isaiah, in chapters 34–66, with an emphasis on the judgment of the nations, here represented by Edom, and the return of the exiles to Zion, a major concern in Isaiah 40–66. Edom is condemned in biblical literature for its role in the Babylonian destruction of Jerusalem (Ps. 137:7; Jer. 49:7-22; Lam. 4:21-22; Ezek. 25:12-17; Obadiah). Isaiah 34 presents a number of parallels with Isaiah 1: the call to attention (Isa. 1:2; 34:1); YHWH's vengeance (Isa. 1:24; 34:8); unquenchable burning (Isa. 1:24; 34:10); YHWH's mouth has spoken (Isa. 1:20; 34:16); the sword of punishment (Isa. 1:20; 34:5-6); sacrificial blood and fat (Isa. 1:11-15; 34:6-7); Sodom and Gomorrah (Isa. 1:7-10; 34:9-10); and wilting leaves (Isa. 1:30; 34:4). Isaiah 35 portrays the return of the exiles to Jerusalem as a second exodus, much like Second Isaiah.

■ THE TEXT IN THE INTERPRETIVE TRADITION

The Great Isaiah Scroll from Qumran (1QIsaiahᵃ) has a gap of several lines between Isaiah 33 and Isaiah 34, indicating the fundamental structural division of the book. Various scholars have confirmed the literary division of the book at this point.

■ THE TEXT IN CONTEMPORARY DISCUSSION

The recollection of the exodus in Isaiah 35 points to one of the most important holidays in Judaism, the Passover, which celebrates the exodus from Egypt. The exodus is recounted each year at the Passover seder, a home dinner service that celebrates Jewish freedom from oppression and return to the land of Israel. The appearance of this motif in Isaiah 35—and indeed throughout the entire book of Isaiah—points to the importance of the Passover observance in antiquity as well as in modern times.

Isaiah 36–39: Narratives concerning YHWH's Deliverance of Jerusalem and Hezekiah

■ THE TEXT IN ITS ANCIENT CONTEXT

The Hezekiah narratives found in Isaiah 36–39 also appear in 2 Kings 18–20, albeit it in somewhat different form. Because these chapters contain the last references to the prophet Isaiah ben Amoz in the book of Isaiah, many interpreters presume that they form an appendix to an early form of the book that focuses only on the eighth-century prophet. More recent discussion has recognized the transitional function of these chapters as the concluding reference to the Babylonian exile in Isaiah 39, which points forward to the so-called Second Isaiah, beginning in Isaiah 40. Overall, these chapters point to YHWH's deliverance of Jerusalem as a result of Hezekiah's turning to YHWH, which anticipates the calls for recognition of YHWH's deliverance at the end of the Babylonian exile in the second part of the book.

Isaiah 36–37 presents the account of YHWH's deliverance of Jerusalem during the 701-BCE siege of the city by the Assyrian monarch Sennacherib. Following the unexpected death in battle of Sargon II in 705, King Hezekiah of Judah and Prince Merodach Baladan of Babylon planned a two-pronged revolt against Assyria. Sennacherib proved able to meet the challenge, and conquered Tyre in his initial counterattack in 701. With the fall of Tyre, Hezekiah's western allies abandoned him, leaving Judah open to Assyrian attack. The Assyrian army overran Judah, destroying the city of Lachish and all other cities in Judah while laying siege to Jerusalem. When the Assyrian Rab Shakeh, chief cupbearer (a high administrative title), demanded Jerusalem's unconditional surrender, Hezekiah spread the document before YHWH in the temple and appealed for help. Isaiah answered on YHWH's behalf, indicating that YHWH would deliver Jerusalem due to Hezekiah's faithfulness. According to the account, YHWH's angel killed 185,000 Assyrian troops, and Sennacherib himself was assassinated by his own sons in the temple of his god, Nisroch. Sennacherib's records, however, claim that he forced the capitulation of Hezekiah, and returned to Assyria with many captives and much booty. He was assassinated by his sons some twenty years later, in 681 BCE. Scholars argue that Sennacherib was compelled to negotiate a settlement with Hezekiah that left Jerusalem intact and Hezekiah alive so that he could move against Merodach Baladan in Babylonia. As a result, both Hezekiah and Sennacherib claimed victory.

Isaiah 38 presents the account of Hezekiah's recovery from illness prior to the revolt. Again, the narrative stresses YHWH's response when the king turns to YHWH. The Isaian account includes Hezekiah's prayer, which is absent in the Kings narrative, to accentuate Hezekiah's faith in YHWH.

Isaiah 39 recounts the embassy of Merodach Baladan to Hezekiah in preparation for the revolt. Isaiah opposed Hezekiah's revolt and condemned Hezekiah's willingness to ally with the Babylonians, arguing that someday his sons would be carried off as captives to Babylon.

◼ THE TEXT IN THE INTERPRETIVE TRADITION

As noted above, many scholars recognize that Isaiah 36–39 serves as a transitional narrative within the book of Isaiah as a whole. The concluding reference to Babylonian exile in Isaiah 39 anticipates the return from Babylonian exile beginning in Isaiah 40. Hezekiah's faithfulness therefore serves as a model for the response of the exiles to YHWH in the second part of the book. But the Hezekiah narratives also function as a means to contrast Hezekiah with the presentation of Ahaz in Isaiah 7.

Ahaz rejects Isaiah's calls for him to trust in YHWH and sees Jerusalem subjugated to the Assyrians as a result, but Hezekiah turns to YHWH during the revolt and sees the deliverance of the city from the Assyrian siege. Interpreters note the location of Isaiah's encounter with Ahaz at the conduit of the Upper Pool by the Fuller's Field in Isaiah 7, and that the Assyrian Rab Shakeh stands at the same location when demanding the surrender of Jerusalem in Isaiah 36–37. When compared with the Hezekiah narratives in 2 Kings 18–20, differences in the text (e.g., the inclusion of the prayer of Hezekiah in Isaiah 38) indicate that Hezekiah appears far more pious and faithful in the Isaian version than in Kings, where Hezekiah immediately submits to Sennacherib at the outset of 2 Kings 18. Overall, the Isaian text presents Hezekiah as a repentant monarch who turns to YHWH in time of crisis.

◼ THE TEXT IN CONTEMPORARY DISCUSSION

The Hezekiah narratives demonstrate the importance of accounting for literary and theological perspective in the interpretation of biblical literature. Although Isaiah 36–39 claims a great victory for Hezekiah, Sennacherib's records also claim a great victory for the Assyrians. Indeed, both were correct; Sennacherib forced Hezekiah's submission, and both Hezekiah and Jerusalem survived the Assyrian onslaught. Such a lesson should be borne in mind when reading biblical literature in general. When the prophets claim that Israel was punished with exile because the people sinned, does this mean that Israel actually committed sins that justified national catastrophe? Or is this a means to explain disaster as an act of G-d and thereby to defend the power, presence, and righteousness of G-d in the world when disaster strikes? In the aftermath of the Shoah (Holocaust), modern theologians continue to struggle with the notion that human suffering must be explained by human sin.

Works Cited

Blenkinsopp, Joseph. 2000. *Isaiah 1–39*. AB 19. New York: Doubleday.

Childs, Brevard S. 2001. *Isaiah: A Commentary*. OTL. Louisville: Westminster John Knox.

Erlandsson, Seth. 1970. *The Burden of Babylon: A Study of Isaiah 13:2—14:23*. ConBOT 4. Lund: Gleerup.

Evans, Craig A. 1988. "On the Unity and Parallel Structure of the Book of Isaiah," *VT* 38:129–47.

Fohrer, Georg. 1962. "Jesaja 1 als Zusammenfassung der Verkündigung Jesajas." *ZAW* 74:251–68.

Kaiser, Otto. 1983. *Isaiah 1–12: A Commentary*. OTL. Philadelphia: Westminster.

Kaplan, Mordecai. 1926. "Isaiah 6:1-11." *JBL* 45:251–59.

Rosenberg, A. J. 1982–1983. *The Book of Isaiah*. Judaica Books of the Bible. New York: Judaica.

Schäfer, Peter. 1998. *Judeophobia: Attitudes towards the Jews in the Ancient World*. Cambridge, MA: Harvard University Press.

Sweeney, Marvin A. 1996. *Isaiah 1–39, with an Introduction to Prophetic Literature*. FOTL 16. Grand Rapids: Eerdmans.

———. 2008. *Reading the Hebrew Bible after the Shoah: Engaging Holocaust Theology*. Minneapolis: Fortress Press.

Tomasino, A. J. 1993. "Isaiah 1.1—2.4 and 63-66 and the Composition of the Isaianic Corpus." *JSOT* 57:81–98.

Tucker, Gene M. 2001. "Isaiah." In *The New Interpreter's Bible*, edited by Leander E. Keck, 6:25–305. Nashville: Abingdon.

Tull, Patricia K. 2010. *Isaiah 1–39*. Smyth and Helwys Bible Commentary. Macon, GA: Smyth & Helwys.

Wiesel, Elie. 1982. *Souls on Fire: Portraits and Legends of Hasidic Masters*. New York: Vintage.

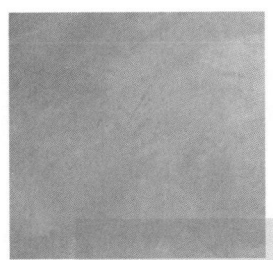

ISAIAH 40–66

Chris A. Franke

Introduction

The book of Isaiah deals with people, places, and events spanning several centuries, from 733 BCE to some time around 515 BCE. Chapters 1–39, referred to as First or Proto-Isaiah, focus on the time when Israel and Judah were under Assyrian rule. An ominous message to King Hezekiah announces the rise of the Babylonian Empire in Isaiah 39. The result is that nothing will be left of his kingdom, Judah, and his Davidic lineage will come to an end. The backdrop of the following chapters, 40–66, includes the Babylonian destruction of Judah and the exile of many of its citizens in 587 BCE; the rise of the Persian Empire under Cyrus the Great in 539 BCE; and the restoration of life in Jerusalem after Cyrus allowed all exiles to return home. While the name Isaiah never appears in 40–66, Isaiah 1–39 and 40–66 share common features, including emphasis on Jerusalem/Zion, reference to the Davidic monarchy, and common images and names of God.

Chapters 40–66 treat two different eras. Chapters 40–55 are addressed to exiles living in Babylon during the rule of Cyrus (538–515 BCE). Their liberation from Babylonian oppression is soon to come. Chapters 56–66 recount the situation in the newly formed Judah, now called Yehud, after the exiles return home and are united with those who had remained in the land after the fall of the kingdom.

Chapters 40–55 are usually identified as Second or Deutero-Isaiah and 56–66 as Third or Trito-Isaiah. Scholars disagree about the authorship of these two sections of the book of Isaiah. Some hold that they represent two different authors or prophets. The mostly hopeful messages of Deutero-Isaiah (abbreviated as DI) and its Babylonian setting are very different from the more somber and sometimes threatening tone and setting in Yehud of Trito-Isaiah (abbreviated as TI). Others see continuity between the two. The strongest defense of single authorship is the consistent literary style throughout. A geographical change does not in itself warrant asserting a new author. In this article, the book of Isaiah is abbreviated as BOI. DI indicates chapters 40–55 and TI chapters 56–66. The view here asserts a single authorial voice.

Other suggestions describing the authorship of DI include the following. Ulrich Berges proposes that cultic representatives are the authorial group responsible for the composition of 40–55 (Berges, 587–88). The people who were sent into exile after the destruction of Jerusalem surely included the priests familiar with temple worship and other cultic activities. They could also be responsible for composition of prayers and/or psalms used in worship.

Lena-Sofia Tiemeyer (26–30) proposes the possibility of female authorship of 40–55. In support of this view, she cites the many metaphors that compare God to a woman, the references to female socio-sexual roles, descriptions of tasks related to motherhood, and the absence of negative images of women.

Isaiah 40:1-31: Israel's God Is Incomparable

▌ THE TEXT IN ITS ANCIENT CONTEXT

Chapter 40 is the beginning of another major section of the BOI. It represents momentous changes of time, place, and mood from chapters 1–39, which are set in mid- to late eighth-century Jerusalem. The time and place of Isaiah 40–55 is 539 BCE, when Babylonia succumbed to Cyrus the Great of Persia. DI's message is addressed to the community of exiles living in Babylon. The chapter begins with words of comfort and reassurance and promises change for those living under Babylonian rule (40:1-2).

What is known about the exiles who lived in Babylonian territory? Some scholars describe their living conditions as relatively benign. Life continued in exile with little if any disadvantage to the exiles. However, data from sociological and psychological sciences reveal a very different view of people forcibly removed from a secure existence in their homeland. Living as minorities in a foreign country offered little if any security or civil rights. "The Judean experience of deportation . . . was a severe and traumatic personal, social, and psychological event" (Moore and Kelle, 364). Convincing people who suffered under such conditions for half a century that God was on their side would have been a difficult task. They would need constant and reliable reassurance that God is aware of their existence. DI not only acknowledges their long term of suffering but in a stunning admission also acknowledges that they "received from YHWH's hand" twice as much punishment as they deserved for their sins. Their fortunes are soon to be reversed. A way will be prepared in the wilderness, and God will lead them back home.

Isaiah 40–66 is filled with a variety of images demonstrating YHWH's power and will to save. The long poem in 40:12-31 is the first of many such demonstrations. The prominent image of God in these verses is of a powerful, all-knowing, everlasting Creator. The literary device of the rhetorical question is used here and elsewhere in DI. It often appears in connection with repetition, another technique by which DI gets the attention of the audience: "To whom then will you liken God?" (40:18) and "To whom then will you compare me?" (40:25). The intent is not to demand answers of the audience but to assert the obvious. No one can be compared to YHWH. YHWH is incomparable. The author takes an argumentative or polemical tone. The defensive aspect of the polemic is because the other side of the issue is all too obvious to the audience. They have good reason to doubt.

■ THE TEXT IN THE INTERPRETIVE TRADITION

Anyone who has ever listened to Handel's *Messiah* will be familiar with the BOI. The libretto contains seventeen citations from the BOI (Davies, 464–84). The Messiah to whom Handel points is Jesus as described in the Synoptic Gospels. Mark's Gospel begins with an allusion to the BOI, showing John the Baptist preparing way of the Lord (Mark 1:2-3). Since the New Testament cites the BOI more times than any other Old Testament text, it is not surprising that Handel's librettist, Charles Jennens, used numerous texts from Isaiah. The librettist repeats Isa. 40:1-5 almost word for word in the first three pieces. The only phrase omitted is the troubling "double payment from the LORD for all her sins." Other citations from Isaiah 40 in the *Messiah* include 40:9, which describes the messenger who brings the good news, and 40:11, describing God the shepherd gently leading the lambs.

■ THE TEXT IN CONTEMPORARY DISCUSSION

The frequent use of motifs and ideas from the BOI in the New Testament and later Christian interpretations has led many Christians to believe that the only way to understand Isaiah is through a christological lens. Knowledge of events in Israel's history as well as an awareness of how these texts were used well before New Testament times is crucial to a wider view of the importance of the BOI. From early on in Jewish tradition, selections from Isaiah 40–60 that recall the destruction of the temple and the exile from Judah were read in synagogues before the high holy days (Paul, 71). The message of comfort in 40:1 is the first of these readings, which mark the period of personal and national mourning for Jews. Sabbath readings in current Jewish liturgy are filled with selections from the book of Isaiah. Both Jewish and Christian traditions have appropriated texts from Second Isaiah for liturgical use.

Isaiah 41:1—44:8: The Nations and Their Gods Are Put on Trial/ God Reassures Israel

■ THE TEXT IN ITS ANCIENT CONTEXT

DI has been called the "spider poet" because of the tangled web of connections found throughout 40–55 (Kim, 178). Chapters 41:1—44:8 illustrate this phenomenon. Motifs include the nations, the making of idols, Israel/Jacob as God's chosen, the servant, and transformation of the wilderness. Many of these motifs appear throughout the rest of 40–66. God is portrayed as warrior, attorney or judge, a woman giving birth, king, comforter. Literary genres adapted from ancient Near Eastern documents include terminology reflecting a courtroom trial, hymns used in liturgies, and rhetorical questions, all of which would be familiar to DI's audience in Babylon.

Isaiah 41 begins with a courtroom setting. God puts the nations on trial, demanding proof that they and their deities are powerful. Are they able to control events, predict the future? Do they have power enough to terrify or harm others? As evidence that it is YHWH who is able to control events, predict the future, and terrify nations, God has called up Cyrus the Persian king to defeat the Babylonian Empire in 539 BCE. The gods are unable to prove that they can control and predict the future. They remain silent and ineffectual in contrast to God's powerful acts on behalf of Jacob/ Israel. A distinctive feature in this section is God speaking in the first person, emphatically asserting that "I have held my peace, I have kept still," "I will cry out," "I will lay waste mountains," "I will turn the rivers into islands," "I will lead the blind," "I will turn the darkness before them into light," "these are the things I will do," "I will not forsake them" (Isa. 42:14-16). An English translation of 41:1—44:8 reveals over 130 occurrences of first-person pronouns.

The courtroom scene in 43:9-13 brings a new and far more serious challenge to the nations. They have no witnesses who can prove that their gods exist. The nations were initially asked to show that they and their gods were powerful. YHWH now asserts that

> before me no god was formed,
>   nor will there be any after me. (43:10)

thus denying the nature or existence of the gods.

While the nations tremble with fright, YHWH comforts Jacob/Israel: "Do not fear, for I am with you" (43:5). The "fear not" formula appears throughout DI, beginning with God's opening message to the exiles (40:9). It underlies the prophet's message in 41:1—44:8. The phrase "fear not" is adapted from an ancient Near Eastern literary-theological motif used to indicate that the gods support their kings and people. Shalom Paul cites an example of the goddess Ishtar reassuring Assyrian kings that she will deliver their enemies for destruction (Paul, 166). Also familiar in these documents is the phrase "grasping the right hand," which demonstrates that a king or god supports his people. DI uses this formula in 41:10 and 13 to indicate divine support.

The hymn of praise in 42:10-12 is a familiar genre frequently used in their worship services. All are commanded to lift up their voices and sing to give glory to YHWH and declare God's praise! The hymn genre most likely originated in a cultic setting. When a group of people gathers to worship, part of their worship includes praying and singing. Motifs for these prayers include complaint, lament, and thanksgiving, which are used in Isaiah 40–66. All of these genres reflect significant events with which the audience was familiar. These features will immediately direct the audience's attention to the significance or tone of the message.

◼ THE TEXT IN THE INTERPRETIVE TRADITION

Scholars reading Isaiah 40–66 over the years have proposed a wide variety of strategies to understand its complicated features. One of the most significant contributions to understanding the literary dimensions of DI was made by James Muilenburg in his commentary in *The Interpreter's Bible*. Using the results of form-critical studies of Isaiah 40–66, he showed that the prophet used typical forms of the time but tweaked them, adding to or altering the formulas to give new depth and nuance to the message.

The cult of the Babylonian gods is described in some detail beginning in Isa. 41:6-7. DI emphasizes idolatry and especially the construction of images of Babylonian deities in chapters 40–47. The disparaging polemics against the construction and worship of statues is evidence that the exiles in Babylon were familiar with and perhaps attracted to these practices. Accentuated here is YHWH's power over nations, kings, and their deities; the idea that YHWH is "the first and the last"; and the idea that "there is no god besides me" and "no savior besides me."

Some have referred to DI as the exponent of monotheism in Israel. While one might speak of incipient monotheism in DI, it is not so much a question of how many gods there are but rather what kind of a god YHWH is. Israel's repeated attention to a single deity over the course of their history is the background of the later development of a full-fledged monotheism. See Mark Smith's discussions of this fascinating and complicated aspect of Israelite history and religion (Smith 1990; 2001).

■ THE TEXT IN CONTEMPORARY DISCUSSION

The BOI often uses the metaphor of regeneration of land, plant life, and waters and compares these to the condition of human existence. The repeated references to life-giving water in DI and TI reflect the devastated conditions of the land reduced to a wasteland by the ravages of war. Recent interest in ecological issues has encouraged Bible scholars to address this issue.

Patricia K. Tull brings these issues to her study of Isaiah, demonstrating that Isaiah uses "plant imagery to tie human spiritual and societal health to environmental well-being" (Tull, 27). She indicates that it is sometimes impossible to tell when the text is to be understood literally or metaphorically. Referring to a group of farmers who studied Genesis 3, she cites their observation that "when humans are disconnected from God, the soil will be the first to suffer."

Isaiah 44:9-20: The Folly of Making and Worshiping Images of Deities

■ THE TEXT IN ITS ANCIENT CONTEXT

Scattered through Isaiah 40–48 are references to features of Babylonian religion, especially the making and use of images of gods in the Babylonian pantheon. DI's perspective on images, artisans who make them, and those who worship them is consistently negative and critical. Isaiah 44:9-20 features a detailed description of the construction of *images* or *idols* (for DI the terms are synonymous), from the planting of the trees used for carvings to the iron workshop in which images are forged. The tone of this anti-idol passage is scathing sarcasm and ridicule. DI derides those who burn wood to cook their meals and warm their hands and then bow down to a statue made of the same kind of wood. Such a person is a "shepherd of ashes with a deluded mind" (44:20, author's trans.).

A recent commentary by Shalom Paul is a rich source of background information for Babylonian history, literature, religion, and culture during the time of the formation of Isaiah 40–66. Paul describes an event during the reign of Babylonian king Nabonidus, who made dramatic changes in the Babylonian cult. One of the most significant was to change the order of the gods in the pantheon. The chief god Marduk was deposed and replaced with another god. Nabonidus also canceled celebration of a religious holiday, which enraged the populace. Marduk's priests, understandably upset, published a document attacking Nabonidus's behavior, claiming that he "looks at representations [of the gods] and utters blasphemies" (Paul, 13).

DI's familiarity with the Babylonian scene is clear from the details included in the anti-idol passages. He takes for granted that his audience living under Babylonian rule for decades is familiar with these practices. Understood in light of the political situation in Babylon, it is not difficult to understand DI's polemical tone. In the words of DI, Marduk's "devotees shall be put to shame" (44:11) when their emperor deposed their chief god. Critique of the gods is critique of Babylonian politics. DI's exilic audience would relish the disarray of Babylonian's inept and divided leadership.

▌ THE TEXT IN THE INTERPRETIVE TRADITION

DI uses satire in several poems that describe Babylonian practices and politics; for example, Isaiah 46–47. *Satire* is used to ridicule, diminish, or attack an individual, an institution, or a culture. It evokes in the audience feelings of scorn or contempt for the subject. Putting the drudgery of the artisans in elegant, poetic language heightens the level of ridicule and mockery. Some consider this literary feature to be beneath the soaring language of DI. However, reading it in light of oppressive conditions in Babylonia makes DI's satirical critique a fit way to disempower an oppressive empire.

▌ THE TEXT IN CONTEMPORARY DISCUSSION

What significance might this satire on images of deities have for diverse religious groups? Orthodoxy has a tradition of the veneration of icons. The veneration of the Bible itself is a traditional practice for some Christians. Hindu practices include processions of images of deities as part of its tradition. Another way to reflect on this question is to ask: How is the divine made present in the world?

"Laughing at Idols" is the title of an article by George M. Soares-Prabhu (1995, 110), who critiques DI's ridiculing the Babylonian practice of making statues of their gods. He interprets Isa. 44:9-20 from his perspective of religion and politics in India, where many world religions exist "in tolerable harmony," and contrasts this with DI's "inadequate view of God." Soares-Prabhu highlights the value of pluralist Indian interpretations as a corrective to intolerance often seen in Western religions, which emphasize monotheism. Familiarity with interpretations of the Bible from the perspective of the social location of the reader opens up the richness of the biblical text for all cultures.

Isaiah 44:21—45:24: A Reminder to Israel—You Will Be Created and Freed by God

▌ THE TEXT IN ITS ANCIENT CONTEXT

The message of hope in 44:1-6 is resumed in verse 21 after the polemic against the image makers. DI again asserts that, while they cannot predict the future, predictions made by God's messengers will be fulfilled. The ruins of Jerusalem and other cities of Judah will be rebuilt and repopulated (44:26), and the foundation of the new temple will be laid (44:28). As proof that this will happen, DI introduces Cyrus, king of Persia, who has defeated the hapless Nabonidus, ruler of Babylonia. God's purpose will be carried out by Cyrus, who YHWH calls "my shepherd" (44:28).

It must be kept in mind that the audience for these messages is the exiles living in Babylonia under Babylonian rule. They are familiar with the Babylonian scene. They know about the coming of Cyrus, the fall of Nabonidus, and would also be familiar with the form and style of official messages about Babylonian kings. The motif of rebuilding cities and their temples is often attributed to kings in Mesopotamian documents (Paul, 247). To get the attention of this audience, DI uses a variety of examples with which the exiles would be familiar.

One of the most deeply disturbing ideas for the exiles was the loss of the Davidic monarchy and the temple. God's promise of the permanence of these institutions had been broken. DI explains that God's covenant promise of an eternal Davidic line continues through Cyrus, who now takes on David's title as "the anointed one" (45:1). As a caution to those who are critical of a foreigner as the anointed one, DI makes several striking comparisons. God is a potter, and the critics are the clay pots. The potter asks if the clay can criticize its maker. In two other images, God is a father and a mother. The critics are again asked if anyone questions their parents about who they are making. No answer is needed: the critics' position is ridiculous. To dispel further objections, God announces that Cyrus "will build my city and set my exiles free" (45:13).

◼ THE TEXT IN THE INTERPRETIVE TRADITION

The ramifications of the assertion that God is sole creator of all things are far reaching. God can make Cyrus king and can strip other kings of their robes, signs of their power. For DI, the belief that God is one can result in only one conclusion: all nations will "follow you," "bow down to you," "come over in chains," and must admit that "God is with you alone" (45:14). This is described as a "fantasy nourished by resentment at subjection to the great powers" (Blenkinsopp, 262). Such a sentiment can be understood by any people at any time who live under the oppression of a powerful empire.

◼ THE TEXT IN CONTEMPORARY DISCUSSION

Bible scholar Ada María Isasi-Díaz speaks of her experience living in exile from Cuba and her yearning to return home lest she forget her own country (Isasi-Díaz, 149–63). She found solace and understanding in Psalm 137, a lament of exiles yearning for their homeland. This psalm asks God to remember the fall of Jerusalem. It includes the desire for vengeance against the enemy, much like that against Babylon in Isa. 45:13-14, and expresses the wish that the babies of the enemies will be dashed against the rock. Isasi-Díaz asks: What is the theology behind this psalm?

Her personal experiences influence how she reads such texts. Seeing injustice against the poor and experiencing the effects of sexism in her church and ethnic prejudice as a Cuban living in America shaped her hermeneutical strategy. Rather than trying to read a text "objectively," that is, trying to come to the original meaning of the text, she realized the importance of clarifying her own perspective and her purpose for reading that text. She emphasizes the three-way relationship between "the reader, the writer, and the text." A reader's questions influence what the text could have meant in the past and what it means today. She describes her approach to the text as "oppression-liberation."

The language of Psalm 137 and Isa. 45:13-14 can express both personal and community grief for suffering terrible losses, including the loss of order in their world. Isasi-Díaz, while uncomfortable with the strong and vengeful sentiments, prays this psalm because it has a cathartic effect. It allows her to express a troubling feeling. She also notes that there is a great difference between words of vengeance and acts of vengeance.

Isaiah 46:1-13: Babylonian Street Scene—A Procession of Idols Carried on Beasts of Burden

▌ THE TEXT IN ITS ANCIENT CONTEXT

Chapter 46 is the polar opposite of the triumphant march of the exiles returning home in Isaiah 40. Bel and Nebo, chief gods of Babylonia, are carried in an ignominious procession out of their homeland into captivity. One of the motifs in previous chapters has been the folly of making images and worshiping them. This begins in 40:18–20 and is repeated in every succeeding chapter.

This scene in 46:1–7 would have been familiar to the exiles in Babylon. On the occasion of the New Year festival, the images of Bel and Nebo were carried in a procession through the streets. Bel is a title for the god Marduk, Babylon's protector. Nebo was his son, who during the New Year celebration was to write down the fate of the cities for the coming year. A very different occasion in Mesopotamian culture was transporting images of gods out of a threatened or destroyed city. Yet another example was seizure of the statues by the conquering enemy. This was done for economic reasons, to confiscate the precious metals and stones set in the statues. It also mocked the impotency of gods of the defeated nation.

Chapter 46 describes the gods as heavy loads on weary animals. They all stoop and stumble and bow down. The phrase "bow down" can refer to obeisance to a high authority, such as a king, or an act of worship of a god. But here it highlights their utter ineffectuality and proves that they are unable to "save" or "deliver" anyone. God addresses Jacob/Israel, emphasizing that, unlike these statues, which can save no one, "*I* carried you from the beginning." "*I* made," "*I* will bear," "*I* will carry," "*I* will save" (46:3-4). Furthermore, God accuses them of being "rebels." Here, as elsewhere in these anti-idolatry passages, the offenders are rebellious Israel. God reminds them,

> I am God, and there is no other;
>   I am God, and there is no one like me. (46:9)

This recalls the infamous first idol-making event at the foot of Mount Sinai, when people worshiped the golden calf as their god (Exod. 32:1-14). YHWH initially threatened extermination of the community but relented from this plan.

Chapter 46 contrasts the downward spiral of Bel and Nebo and their supporters with the elevation of YHWH, who insists that "I will fulfill my intention" to a "stubborn" and perhaps unconvinced group of exiles. YHWH's word has been spoken; deliverance is at hand.

■ THE TEXT IN THE INTERPRETIVE TRADITION

Previous scholarship approached DI (as well as other prophetic texts) with the idea that it was made up of conventional genres, short units that originated in the spoken word. In the process of writing, these shorter units were thought to have been brought together to connect similar themes or motifs. However, the poetry of DI transcends more traditional techniques and adds nuance to conventional formulas (Franke 1994, 263). An example of the literary genius of this prophet/poet is the image of procession to contrast the fate of Jacob/Israel and that of their captors. Procession for the enemies in 46:1-2 means going into captivity. In Isaiah 47, deposed Babylon falls from her throne to earth, down to the underworld. Processions for the exiles will lead them out of captivity back to their homeland in 40:3-5; 48:20-21; and 51:9—52:2. This extended image is an essential aspect of the prophet's message to the exiles; it is far more than a mere assemblage of loosely related themes.

■ THE TEXT IN CONTEMPORARY DISCUSSION

While DI's message is often characterized as a message of comfort and consolation to those living under Babylonian rule, a crucial element in chapter 46 is the accusation against Jacob/Israel of idolatry, and warnings of the consequences. Just as Isaiah 40 begins with comfort to the disconsolate, it also includes a brief polemic against idolatry, accusing the audience of comparing God to an idol made by human hands. In many of the anti-idolatry sections in DI, the issue is not denying the existence of God. The offense is comparing God to idols or considering them equals to Israel's God. The prophet's audience is not Babylonians. It is the exiles living in Babylon who have taken on the religious practices of their captors.

Isaiah 47:1-15: The Fall of Virgin Daughter Babylon

■ THE TEXT IN ITS ANCIENT CONTEXT

Chapter 47 is a pivot on which the main ideas and message of DI turn (Franke 1991). In the previous chapters, the disconsolate exiles lived in fear of their conquerors, doubted that God could or would come to their rescue, needed constant encouragement that they had not been forgotten, and wondered if they were still being punished for their infidelities. DI describes numerous examples of differences between the god of Jacob and the gods of the Babylonian Empire in 40–46. The critique of the Babylonian images and especially the artisans who made them pervades this section. While YHWH was powerful and carried the people, the Babylonian deities could not even move but had to be carried by those who worshiped them.

Here God speaks directly to "virgin daughter Babylon." In the ancient world, cities were often described figuratively as women needing protection of kings. In satirical language, God ridicules all of Babylon's claims. She thought: she'd be queen forever; she was secure; she'd never be widowed; and she would never lose her children. She thought she could hide her evil deeds. She thought her astrologers could predict her future or use magic to control events.

From the beginning words in 47:1, it is clear that Babylon's future will be grim. Instead of being seated on a throne, she will sit in the dust, on the ground. Even more, she will go into "darkness," intimating her passage to the underworld.

To Babylon's humiliation, she will be stripped of her garments: veil and robe will be removed, legs uncovered. In summary, her "nakedness" and "shame" will be seen by all. The latter terms indicate exposure of her genitalia. For her crimes—showing no mercy to the exiles and especially abusing the elderly—there will be no one to save her. Just as the Babylonian deities in chapter 46 bowed down and went into captivity, so Virgin Daughter Babylon will exchange her royal status for that of slavery.

This poem has features similar to satirical laments for the dead elsewhere in Isaiah (14:3-21), as well as in lamenting the death of gods in ancient Near Eastern literature (Anderson, 60–82). These laments include the hubris of the gods or nations in their belief that they will rule forever. They also fall from their thrones, sit on the ground, and descend into the underworld.

▮ THE TEXT IN THE INTERPRETIVE TRADITION

The fall of Babylon has been interpreted from the perspective of anthropology as a rite of passage (Kruger). The various details of Babylon's passage—loss of status, the shame of removing her garments and exposure, doing menial work—portray her as a queen turned slave. This description is an example of a sociocultural antitype of Babylon's status as queen. It can also be read as an antitype of the status of Jerusalem/Zion. Later chapters describe the elevation of Zion's status from widow to bride, rejected and captive to redeemed, and barren to mother of many. DI uses the fall of Babylon as a contrast to the rise of Jerusalem.

▮ THE TEXT IN CONTEMPORARY DISCUSSION

In chapter 47, Babylon is portrayed as the object of God's punishment. She is subjected to physical abuse and punishment, which strips her of her power. She loses her husband and children and remains alone with no one to save her. How are readers today to understand this in a meaningful way? What theological problems does such a view create?

One of the most significant challenges in reading the Bible in the modern world is how to deal with the ancient Near Eastern view of women that pervades biblical texts. In the ancient world, women were viewed as the property of men. It was commonly accepted that the ideal male was powerful, able to provide his city/family with food, shelter, and protection. Sexual fidelity is not included in the list for men. The ideal female was submissive, in need of protection, faithful to her spouse. Women were the property of their male protector, husband or father or brother. They were second-class citizens at best.

In recent years, scholars have discussed this question by providing important background information to the origins of this point of view. The *Women's Bible Commentary*, now in its third edition (Newsom, Ringe, and Lapsley), provides data to support the need of a more informed view of this matter in biblical texts, both Old and New Testament.

It is no longer justifiable for interpreters to take the biblical view of women and men as acceptable views for the world today. Citing biblical views about women out of context is not sufficient evidence to draw conclusions and make rules for society today. It is not only insufficient but also damaging to both women and men. In this matter as well as many others, a contextual view of society and culture is essential to understand values and practices in the Bible.

Isaiah 48:1-22: God Warns Israel and Announces a New Exodus

▐ THE TEXT IN ITS ANCIENT CONTEXT

In this chapter, several literary techniques are used by the author/editor to make connections to earlier sections, and also to segue to following material. Chapter 48 links chapters 40–47 and 49–55 by motifs or themes. These include God as Creator, Holy One of Israel, Redeemer. Cyrus, identified as "the one whom YHWH loves," is the ruler who will defeat Babylon. God declares past and future events to Jacob/Israel to demonstrate the power and reliability of the divine word over against the lifeless idols and images. However, exiles persist in their stubbornness and obstinacy.

A striking feature amid these accusations against intransigent Jacob/Israel is the depth of God's passionate reaction to their treachery. God's response is mixed. On the one hand, the people's infidelity enrages God almost to the point of exterminating them. God's reputation is at stake, only deferring from punishing them "for my name's sake," "for my own sake." God is incredulous at their behavior: "Why should my name be profaned?" (48:9-11). On the other hand, God speaks as a teacher or parent "who teaches you for your own good," observing wistfully that things would have been different if only "you had paid attention to my commandments" (48:17-19).

In the final verses (48:20-21), DI urges the audience to "go out from Babylon, flee from Chaldea" and reminds them of the exodus from Egypt. This recalls 40:1, the good news of a "highway for our God" on which they would be led through the wilderness. Øystein Lund (227–29) shows that 48:17-22 returns to several key themes in 40:12-40: YHWH's knowledge of the future and power over military and/or political events. The repetition of words or motifs at the beginning and end of a section is called an inclusio. It is a structuring device to indicate the beginning and end of a section within a text. It functions much like chapter divisions do in books today. Chapter 48 is a turning point in the direction of Isaiah 40–55. The terse statement in 48:22—"no peace for the wicked"—also points to the very end of the BOI, since it anticipates similar threatening sentiments in 57:21 and 66:24.

▐ THE TEXT IN THE INTERPRETIVE TRADITION

Scholars refer to Isaiah 48 as the "problem child" of biblical criticism because of its range of motifs, grammatical peculiarities, contradictions in God's past and present actions, and excessive repetition. Some of God's actions are harsh and seemingly contradictory to the message of consolation with which DI begins. Scholars vary wildly in their assessment of this chapter. A form-critical approach fails to solve the problems. One proposal asserts that certain material was added by another writer or editor. Another eliminates repetitious features.

In a commentary that stands outside the prevailing thought of most Isaiah scholarship in the first half of the twentieth century, Charles Cutler Torrey (372–80) views Isaiah 48 as an integrated whole. It begins and ends on a note of rebuke and acknowledges that Israel, though unworthy, is the chosen people. Torrey also notes a close connection in time between the composition of Isaiah 46 and 47, as well as to motifs throughout Isaiah 40–66.

■ THE TEXT IN CONTEMPORARY DISCUSSION

Chapter 48, more than any other chapter in the BOI, deals with Israel's relationship with God in all its permutations. It highlights the tension between Israel's dependence on God and its obduracy to God's word. Walter Brueggemann sees this originating in "the tension deep within the character of Yahweh" (Brueggemann, 100), speaking of the motifs of displacement and restoration that underlie Isaiah 48. He applies this to our own Western culture with the disappearance of certitude and the difficulties of maintaining a social infrastructure.

From one perspective, the problem is God's credibility and dependability. From another, it is the people of God. Rémi Lack describes the problem well: the only obstacle to salvation is the apathy of the people and their refusal to accept that a foreigner, Cyrus, is the instrument of that salvation (Lack, 106).

Works such as Brueggemann's and Lack's, which read the BOI as an integrated whole, are examples of canonical readings. This method of exegesis is a more recent development in biblical scholarship, which offers yet another way to read and understand complicated biblical texts.

Isaiah 49:1—52:12: Daughter Zion, the Servant, and the Role of the Nations in Judah's Future

Chapter 49 begins a new section of DI. Previous characters and places important in Isaiah 40–48— Cyrus as God's anointed, the artisans and their ineffectual statues, and Babylon—are no longer mentioned. The word pair Jacob/Israel occurs for the last time in 49:5-6 and is replaced by Jerusalem/Zion. Key figures—Zion/Jerusalem, the nations, and the servant—are intertwined in 49:1—52:12. These three figures are treated in three separate sections.

Zion/Jerusalem

■ THE TEXT IN ITS ANCIENT CONTEXT

A major emphasis in Isaiah 49–55 is on Zion/Jerusalem. From the beginning of DI, the biggest challenge was to convince the exiles that God is not only willing to save them but also has the power to do so. The message of comfort and consolation with which DI begins (40:1) is repeated in 49:13; 51:3, 12. However, Zion remains unconvinced by these claims. YHWH has abandoned and forgotten her (49:14). The term "abandoned" is often used of a husband leaving his wife. Zion challenges God in 51:9 to "Awake, awake, put on strength!" Isaiah scholar Luis

Schökel describes 51:9—52:6 as a "bold and affectionate dialogue" between Zion and her husband (Schökel, 179).

The first words God uses to answer Zion's accusation relate to Zion as a wife and mother. The most convincing argument is the image of a mother's relationship to her child. God asks a rhetorical question, "Can a mother forget her nursing child or show no compassion for the child of her womb?" (49:15). The motifs of mother and child and wife continue through to 49:26. God promises that soon Zion will have so many children that she will need a bigger tent in which to live. God reminds Zion that "you are my people" (51:16). God responds to Zion by mirroring her previous command to "wake up" and orders her to "rouse yourself," "wake up," and "depart!" Captive Jerusalem must rise from the dust, remove the bonds from her neck, and garb herself in festive apparel. Her redemption is at hand.

■ THE TEXT IN THE INTERPRETIVE TRADITION

It has long been clear that the Bible is filled with many images of God as male: king, warrior, husband, father. However, the increase of women scholars in biblical studies has given rise to a wider context for interpreting texts. Much of the terminology in chapters 49–54 emphasizes feminine roles to describe God's relationship to Zion. The interpretive history of DI has been expanded with the awareness of significant images and metaphors for women. Previously overlooked ideas are now highlighted and brought to the fore. Interest in feminist and gender issues, especially in the BOI, has grown within recent years. Hanne Løland in her book on gendered God language in the Bible reads three texts in DI that compare God to a woman and emphasize the bodily connections between mother and child. In 42:14, God is portrayed as a pregnant women giving birth to her child. In 46:3-4, God has carried Israel from pregnancy through birth through to old age. Last, the comparison intensifies in 49:15. God asks (rhetorically) whether a mother can forget her nursing child or have no compassion for the child of her womb. Here YHWH is compared to a mother who loves her child. Some scholars are uneasy with the idea that God would be portrayed in feminine imagery and protest that God's love is contrasted to or greater than that of a mother. However, the same protest could be raised in comparing God with a warrior, or father, or some other masculine figure.

■ THE TEXT IN CONTEMPORARY DISCUSSION

One of the most important features of DI's emphasis on Jerusalem/Zion in recent scholarship is the recognition of the importance of feminine figures. The difficulty and beauty of moving into postmodernity is that there is not just one correct interpretation of a given text. The nature and identity of communities that read texts influences how and why interpretations vary. One rabbi explains it this way, asking, "How do donkeys read the Bible?" The answer is: they look for stories about donkeys. When reading a text, everyone brings personal experiences to their interpretation of that text. When women began studying the Bible in seminaries and universities, they brought new questions, ideas, and insights to the fore. Studies of Zion/Jerusalem in Isaiah 40–66 have increased in recent years as scholars, both women and men, incorporate the identity and role of Zion into their reading of the BOI.

Nations

▌ THE TEXT IN ITS ANCIENT CONTEXT

The term "nations" (Heb., *goyim*) appears throughout Isaiah 40–55; it is a synonym for "coastlands" and "peoples." These chapters contain several descriptions of who or what the nations are and why they are significant in DI. Richard Clifford calls chapter 49 "a press release to all the nations" (Clifford, 150). The coastlands are addressed by the servant who functions as a "light to the nations" (49:1-6). Zion/Israel, once called the slave of rulers, changes places with the nations. The message to the nations is that their rulers will work as ignominious servants, prostrating themselves and licking the dust of the feet of Zion and her children (49:22-23). The oppressors become the oppressed. A technique frequently used in DI called *inner-biblical allusion* is the citation of another biblical text to enhance meaning. The image of Zion's oppressive rulers losing their power is a foil to a text in Jer. 13:18, which portrays the opposite situation: Israel's king and queen mother lose their crowns and must take a lowly seat when Babylon destroys Judah (Willey, 203). In Isaiah 49, the tables are turned. A somewhat different view of the role of the nations is also alluded to in this section. For example, the "coastlands" wait for God and hope in God's powerful arm (51:5). In 52:10b, all nations and "the ends of the earth shall see / the salvation of our God."

▌ THE TEXT IN THE INTERPRETIVE TRADITION

An important aspect of biblical studies is textual criticism. Since there are many ancient manuscripts of the Bible in various languages, text critics study these texts to arrive at an authoritative reading of a given word or words when more than one possible reading exists. For Isaiah scholars, the discovery of the Isaiah manuscript among the Dead Sea Scrolls has given much insight into the BOI. With respect to Isa. 52:5, one of the scribes of the Dead Sea Scrolls made a change in the translation of verse 5, as did the Greek translator in the Septuagint. This may reflect ancient concerns about the meaning and/or significance of this verse. Joseph Blenkinsopp observes that attempts at "a coherent reading of 52:1-12 have not been successful" (Blenkinsopp, 340).

▌ THE TEXT IN CONTEMPORARY DISCUSSION

Past and present interpretations of the role of the nations in DI have vigorously debated the question of whether DI's prophecies were nationalistic or had a universalistic, inclusive view of the nations, including them among the redeemed. When referring to the nations, some Isaiah commentaries have used highly charged theologized perspectives that go far beyond evidence in the text. The term *goyim* has been translated as "heathens," "pagans," or "gentiles." The messenger "who brings good news" in 52:7 is called an "evangelical herald of the Gospel" in a recent Christian commentary (Lessing, 9). Yet other Christian interpreters see these texts as encouraging missionary work to convert pagans. However, the contemporary concept of conversion is not a feature of Old or New Testament religion (see "Conversion," in Anchor Bible Dictionary, Vol. 1, pp. 1131–33).

The Servant

▌THE TEXT IN ITS ANCIENT CONTEXT

The identity and role of the servant in DI is one of the most controversial issues in the BOI.

Reading the servant passages in the context of the Babylonian exile and its aftermath is essential to understanding the servant's role.

Questions asked about the servant abound: Who is the servant? Is the servant an individual, or are there many? Can the servant be identified with any individual important in Israelite history? Is it a collective term applied to all Israel? What is the role or work of the servant? Is the servant a prophet, teacher, priest, or the author of Isaiah 40–55? What is the reason for the servant's suffering?

In 49:1—53:12, the servant appears three times. In 49:1-7, he is called from birth by God to restore the survivors of Israel but laments that his work has been in vain. In 50:4-10, his role is to teach and sustain the weary community. However, he is not well received and endures persecution at their hands. The longest section devoted to the servant is Isa. 52:13—53:12. Though 52:13 begins with an announcement that the servant will prosper and be lifted up, this positive view does not continue. The servant's life is a pattern of rejection, misery, and continual violence from birth until his ignominious death. In the end, the righteous servant who intercedes on behalf of the community will see his descendants prosper, and he will be numbered among the great ones.

The role and possible identity of the servant can be more clearly understood within the sociopolitical setting of the exiles' life under Babylonian rule (Gottwald, 499–501). The prophet's ringing praises of Cyrus the Persian as liberator of the exiles (44:28—45:4) could be seen as threats to the Babylonian Empire. Some among the exiles supported the prophet's view; others feared that his words would bring retaliation against the exiles for their antigovernment stance. Alternately, a pro-Babylon position among the exiles is not hard to imagine. After living there for years, many adapted to this new life, perhaps supporting the status quo of Babylonian rule and their own social and political security. The execution of a traitor can be seen as an understandable response by the Babylonian government (Ceresko, 1–14).

▌THE TEXT IN THE INTERPRETIVE TRADITION

The identity and role of the servant is one of the most discussed issues in DI scholarship. In the late 1800s, Bernhard Duhm proposed that four sections in DI—42:1-4 or 7; 49:1-4; 50:4-9; and 52:13—53:12—were so different in composition, style, and content that they must have come from another author and were inserted into the BOI at a later time. A distinction was made between Israel/Jacob as servant and the innocent servant in these four passages, which came to be called the Suffering Servant Songs. Most scholars today consider the so-called Servant Songs consistent with the literary style and content of the rest of DI. Other occurrences of the term "servant" elsewhere in DI refer to Israel and allude to the suffering of the exiles. The sociopolitical explanations of Norman Gottwald and Anthony Ceresko relating to the servant in Isaiah 52–53 are understandable within the Babylonian context before the return to Judah. They may also shed light on the continuing challenges for community life after the return as described in Isaiah 56–66.

■ THE TEXT IN CONTEMPORARY DISCUSSION

Many Christian interpreters identify the "Suffering Servant" exclusively with Jesus and identify those who attacked the servant with Jews. Two problems arise with these views. To speak of Jesus, who lived in the first century CE, would be meaningless to exiles living in Babylonia in the sixth century BCE. In addition, this view fans the fires of antisemitism for those who hold such a misinterpretation today.

Contemporary interpretations of the Suffering Servant have been meaningful to indigenous people in countries around the world. Jorge Pixley (95–96) relates accounts of Latinas in San Salvador and Nicaragua who worked in communities to change their impoverished conditions. Offering educational opportunities and organizing groups of women resulted in the slaying of those who encouraged social action. Pixley compares the deaths of such leaders to that of the servant in Isaiah, calling them martyrs. Attempts at social transformation can and do result in persecution if the government feels threatened.

Another comparison is made between the Suffering Servant and the *minjung* of Korea. This term refers to people who are politically oppressed, economically exploited, socially alienated, religiously discriminated against, and denied education (Moon, 113). In Kwangju, capital of the poorest region in the country, protesters in 1980 demonstrated against the government, which had ignored their plight for years. Peaceful rallies were put down by military paratroopers, and in the end more than three thousand people were killed or injured. Moon compares the Suffering Servant to the *minjung* who gave their lives to liberate others.

Isaiah 54:1-17: Zion Transformed from Barren Woman and Destroyed City to Mother of Many and Rebuilt City

■ THE TEXT IN ITS ANCIENT CONTEXT

The addressee and subject of God's messages in previous chapters is Zion (Isa. 49:14—50:2, 51:2-3; 51:11—52:9). She is described as a barren woman; bride; mother; widow; divorced woman; an afraid and abandoned woman grieving the loss of her children; one who suffered devastation and destruction, famine and sword and captivity; and a destroyed and soon to be rebuilt city. In six verses (54:1-6), the prophet lists all the previously used epithets of the defeated people and then overturns them.

A tent that will be enlarged for all of Zion's children is a metaphor for the expansion of her descendants throughout the world. The dispossessed will now advance to possess and populate the nations (54:3). The shame of abandonment, widowhood, or divorce will be forgotten because God "your Maker is your husband . . . your Redeemer" (54:5).

One of the most striking declarations in this section is God's admission that

> for a brief moment I abandoned you . . .
> in overflowing wrath for a moment
>   I hid my face from you. (54:7-8)

Her husband acknowledges her terrible suffering and unjust punishments and promises to amend his ways. In terms of the marriage metaphor, it is understandable that one or both parties might admit their shortcomings. While it is not typical to hear God acknowledge fault in this or any relationship in the Bible, this sentiment was earlier expressed in Isa. 40:2 with God's admission that Jerusalem's penalty was excessive.

Another view of Zion in 54:11-17 is as a city about to be rebuilt. A new Jerusalem is described in fantastical terminology. The image of a bejeweled city recalls descriptions of Mesopotamian palaces (Paul, 427). Jerusalem's children will be taught by God and will live in great prosperity. The city will never be taken over by oppressors; no weapons will be strong enough to overtake it. No one will be able to speak against her.

▌ THE TEXT IN THE INTERPRETIVE TRADITION

Does God apologize to Zion for having abandoned her, or is God's wrath against the people justified? Two commentators on Isaiah 40–66 explain God's treatment of Zion in verses 6-7. Instead of "a brief moment," Paul translates "in a fit of rage," reading the Hebrew term *rega'* as an "antonym of love," not a measure of time. He further explains that the "Lord's rapprochement with Israel is based not on their regret but on His love" (Paul, 423). Blenkinsopp reads God's statement as a standard accusation used in Assyrian treaties as the result of breaking a treaty (Blenkinsopp, 363). It seems jarring or out of place amid the effusive language of joy to introduce such explanations or defenses of God in these passionate reassurances to Zion.

▌ THE TEXT IN CONTEMPORARY DISCUSSION

One of the most basic discussions in the Bible, both Old and New Testament, relates to the questions of God's anger and why throughout history innocent people have suffered. The way scholars have interpreted Isa. 54:7-8 serves as an example of the wide range of explanations. Some consider that God's wrath is justified; people deserve punishment for their sinful acts. Others emphasize that a relationship between God and people is based not on strict rules or punitive treatment, but on a familial model that emphasizes love, acceptance, understanding, and forgiveness.

Isaiah 55:1–13: God's Word Is Reliable

▌ THE TEXT IN ITS ANCIENT CONTEXT

This short chapter is a dense and complicated review of past motifs and allusions to future themes woven together by the underpinnings of the reliability of God's word. As such, it functions to link Isaiah 40–54 to 56–66. The entire BOI is connected by the assertion in 1:20, repeated in 40:5 and 58:14, that "The mouth of YHWH has spoken."

The word that goes forth from God's mouth will accomplish God's purpose for the exiles. Several images are used throughout 55:1-13 to illustrate their future. They will be given the basic sustenance of water and bread and also lavished with wine, milk, and rich food. Offers of such fare to people living in disadvantaged conditions would catch the audience's attention. God's word is compared to rain and snow falling from the heavens; just as these water the earth providing seeds for the sower and bread for the eater, God's word will provide life for the people. Similar images of renewed fertility continue in 55:12-13. A once thorny, weed-filled wilderness will be replaced by the growth of fragrant trees. Those who suffered as they were led into captivity through a hostile desert environment will return to fruitful land and an everlasting memorial that will never be "cut off." The transformation of the wilderness announced numerous times in DI will become a reality.

Another image of transformation, in 55:3-4, recalls God's covenant with David. In a radical change to the original terms of this agreement—that there would always be a Davidic descendant on the throne in Jerusalem—God alters the promise and makes an eternal covenant with the exiles, who will return to Jerusalem. The Davidic monarchy is not mentioned elsewhere in DI; it perhaps is inserted here to allude to the importance of the Davidic kingship in First Isaiah.

■ THE TEXT IN THE INTERPRETIVE TRADITION

A problem with God's promise of a permanent Davidic dynasty is that neither the dynasty nor Jerusalem survived. Here is another reason for exiles to doubt God's power and/or will to restore them. How was DI's audience to understand the arcane reference to the new "everlasting covenant" in 55:3? Many commentaries and articles have taken on these cryptic verses. Some reconceptualize the promise, referring to the "democratization" of the Davidic monarchy in which leadership resides in the entire community. Another explanation is that roles filled by individuals in the past will be taken over by a wider circle of people in the future (Clifford, 192).

■ THE TEXT IN CONTEMPORARY DISCUSSION

Chapter 55 sums up motifs from previous chapters. It also functions as a connection with the following chapters. In Isaiah 56–66, the issue of leadership in Jerusalem in the postexilic period continues to be problematic. Reference to the "memorial" and "everlasting sign" of the regeneration of the land is considered by some to be a garden or park that memorializes the return home. Others view it as a metaphor for the renewal of creation. Jewish tradition has interpreted the "memorial, / for an everlasting sign" that will never be cut off (55:13) as a reference to the Sabbath. This refers to the importance of keeping the Sabbath in 56:4-7, as well as the promise to the foreigner and eunuch that they will not be cut off from the community in Jerusalem. It does not, however, resolve the underlying issue—the continuing problem of fulfillment of God's promises to the exiles.

Isaiah 56:1—59:21: Problems after the Return—Relationship between the Returnees and Those Who Remained in Judah

■ THE TEXT IN ITS ANCIENT CONTEXT

Chapters 56–66 (TI) are set in Yehud (a term for Judah as a Persian province) after the exiles return to begin life in what remained of their ravaged homeland. The returnees, the Diaspora, include those who left Babylonia as well others who were exiled elsewhere after the destruction of Jerusalem. They joined people who remained in the land after 587 and eked out an existence with no infrastructure: no economic security, no food, and no governing bodies.

Chapters 56–66 continue in a literary style similar to that of 40–55. The same themes and motifs appear with variations. Two major sections in TI (Isa. 56:1—59:21 and 63:1—66:24.) reflect the current troubled realities of life in Yehud. Chapters 60–62, however, focus on hopes for the future in a restored Jerusalem and temple.

In this mixed community, disagreements reach a high pitch. Factions argue about who is in charge, what is considered evidence of faith, what rules govern worship, and who is allowed to participate in this new community. One group emphasizes an inclusive viewpoint, accepting participation by all regardless of ethnicity or background. Another is more exclusive in perspective, especially with respect to foreigners and the indigenous populace.

Chapters 56–59 describe bitter conflicts in the newly constituted Yehud. Issues in Isaiah 56 include proper observation of the Sabbath, rules about sacrificial offerings, and the role of foreigners and eunuchs in worship. The latter are assured that if they keep the Sabbath and the covenant they will not be separated from the community. God will gather outcasts because "my house shall be called a house of prayer / for all peoples" (56:7).

Another issue is misuse of authority by leaders. The shepherds and sentinels who are supposed to protect their community are compared to wild animals and dogs with voracious appetites for food and drink (56:9-12). Leaders are referred to as offspring of a sorceress and are accused of slaughtering their children (57:3-5). Their adulterous mother, the sorceress, is the focus of the attack in 57:6-13. Her sexual behavior is explicitly described in what can be called the most violent, lurid polemic in the Bible. Imagery relating to adultery committed by a woman is found in other prophetic literature. In the book of Hosea, the prophet's wife Gomer is accused of being unfaithful. However, it is not found elsewhere in Isaiah 40–66.

Chapters 58–59 return to the theme of the divided community and inadequate ritual behaviors. The issue in 58:1-9 is the efficacy of fasting. People protest that, while they fast and humble themselves, God does not acknowledge their acts. However, their behaviors belie the significance of fasting: they oppress their workers, quarrel with one another, and engage in acts of violence. An air of sarcasm and impatience underlies God's accusations that they fast only for show. God redefines fasting as acts of social justice: freeing the oppressed; sharing food with the hungry, homes with the homeless, clothes with the naked; and satisfying needs of the afflicted (58:6-7, 10). The grievous nature of the people's offenses intensifies in 59:1-4. Their hands are filled with blood, and they speak lying words; they have corrupted the court system. God's defense is that their own sins prevent them from seeing God's face and hearing God's word.

Chapters 58–59 have a homiletic tone. People claiming to seek God's presence indulge in unacceptable behaviors. If they change these behaviors, they will dwell in the light of God's presence. Conditions that guarantee God's guidance and sustenance are laid out in 58:10-14. People respond with a lament in which they admit their sins and take responsibility for the divisions within the community (59:9-15). In fact, their offenses have contributed to the continuing chaotic conditions.

God grows increasingly indignant at their vile behavior and asks: "Shall I be appeased for these things?" (57:6); "Have I not kept silent and closed my eyes and so you did not fear me?" (57:11); and

"Do you call this a fast, a day acceptable to the LORD?" (58:5). Specific references to God's wrath continue in 57:16-17. A finale to all this bloodshed and violence is a spectacular theophany of God as an angry warrior (59:15a-19). God, appalled at the lack of justice, puts on garments of vengeance and a mantle of fury. God's wrath will punish all adversaries and enemies; they will be repaid according to their deeds.

▌ THE TEXT IN THE INTERPRETIVE TRADITION

The eunuch laments that he has no children to carry on his name (56:5). But God promises that, if he observes the covenant, he will not be forgotten, and will be given an everlasting "monument and a name" (Heb., *yād vāshēm*). Yad Vashem is the name of a holocaust memorial complex in Jerusalem that preserves the memory of the six million people killed during World War II. Names, photos, films, and other artifacts of those killed ensure that they will have an "everlasting name that will not be cut off."

▌ THE TEXT IN CONTEMPORARY DISCUSSION

The BOI begins with a blistering critique of people who bring sacrifices and burnt offerings while oppressing the poor in their community (Isa. 1:10-20). God refuses to acknowledge their prayers and warns that they will be devoured by the sword unless they defend the *widow and the orphan*. This phrase is used throughout the Bible; it refers to the neediest in society, who have no means of supporting themselves. Isaiah 58:13 repeats the accusation from Isa. 1:12 that people are "trampling the Sabbath," and redefines the meaning of fasting and Sabbath observance as restoring justice, freeing the oppressed, feeding the hungry, sheltering the homeless, and clothing the naked.

Of all the passages in the Bible cited as a command to the faithful, the one most often repeated is the command to care for the widow and the orphan. Unfortunately, all too many well-intentioned believers direct their attention to other offenses. As a result, the oppressed and needy continue to be ignored, not seen or heard. Society often overlooks the existence of the poor. Data from the National Coalition for the Homeless shows 3.5 million people (1.35 million of them children) experience homelessness in a given year (DeYoung et al., 875).

Isaiah 60:1—62:12: Restoration of Jerusalem and Its Inhabitants

▌ THE TEXT IN ITS ANCIENT CONTEXT

An issue continuing throughout Isaiah 40–66 is the deferment of God's promise of comfort and deliverance. From the very beginning (Isaiah 40), the disconsolate exiles protested that their

> way is hidden from the LORD,
>> and [their] right is disregarded by [their] God. (40:17)

When the exiles returned to their homeland, hopes of a new and improved life failed to materialize. Life in a fractured and fractious community as described in Isaiah 56–59 brought different problems.

Chapters 60–62 form a stark contrast to the surrounding sections, 56–59 and 63:1—65:16, which portray difficulties, intrigues, and rancorous disagreements among groups in Yehud. From beginning to end, chapters 60–62 emphasize the glorious future of the once devastated Jerusalem. It will be restored to include Zion's children, and also kings and peoples of other nations. Numerous images describe the return of fertility to land and people, the radiance of rebuilt Jerusalem, and the shining beauty of the city and its inhabitants, all of which demonstrate the reversal of Zion's fortune.

One of the most notable features of 60–62 is the reappearance of feminine images of Zion. These include the feminine forms of address, as well as references to Zion as a wife, bride, and mother, as in 49, 52, and 54. Chapter 60 swarms with feminine grammatical forms. Recalling 49:15-21, Zion is again directly addressed by God in 60:1-22 (Wells, 198–202). A key image of the city's restoration in chapter 60 is that of light. Zion will be radiant as nations are drawn to her. God's everlasting glory will replace the light of sun and moon. Also repeated from DI is God's apology (60:10). Because people received a double portion of shame, they will now possess a double portion of everlasting joy (61:7).

Much of Isaiah 60–62 uses motifs and language from 40–55, often showing how the situation of Zion/Jerusalem is renewed and transformed. The people begin a new life in Yehud with a mixed group that includes returnees, those who had stayed in the remains of a destroyed Jerusalem, as well as foreigners with no national or ethnic connections to the original Jacob/Israel community.

▮ The Text in the Interpretive Tradition

The relationship of the nations/foreigners to the returnees is introduced in two ways. Striking images describe the reversal of status among foreigners, kings, nations, and the renewed Zion. Foreigners will build the city walls; kings will bow down to Zion and bring their wealth to her (60:10-12). They will also do the work of shepherding and farming while the once oppressed will serve as priests and ministers of God (61:5-6). Are foreigners accepted or rejected in this new community? One view is that 60:2-7 portrays a tolerance, even acceptance, of gentiles whose offerings God regards as "acceptable on my altar" (Smith-Christopher, 126–27). Reading the same verses, another view is that in Isaiah 60–63, foreigners are viewed in a negative light because of their ancestry, ethnicity, and/or national identity. One explanation for these differing views is that in a later period a *redactor* (editor) of TI acknowledged that foreigners were eventually incorporated into the community.

▮ The Text in Contemporary Discussion

It could be said that cognitive dissonance is a consistent feature of the audiences' mind-set throughout Isaiah 40–66. They hold in tension a belief in God's promise of comfort and extravagant prosperity alongside an experience of continuously deferred hope. Some interpreters have characterized views of the future in TI as *eschatological* or *apocalyptic*. The term *eschatology* refers to an end time or climax of history. The term *apocalyptic* is applied to types of literature that arose in the Hellenistic and Roman period around 333 BCE, several centuries after the destruction of Babylon. Works such as the books of *Enoch* and Daniel anticipated catastrophic and imminent upheavals: earthquakes, massacres, world war against unholy nations, and the like. Referring to DI or TI as eschatological or apocalyptic is misleading and vague. When people in any age imagine a better future in positive and exaggerated terms, it does not necessarily indicate that they are thinking of the end time, or the last days. It can be a sign of hope for what is to come.

Isaiah 63:1—66:24: The People Lament God's Unfulfilled Promises and Community Divisions Continue

■ THE TEXT IN ITS ANCIENT CONTEXT

Chapters 60–62 describe the restoration of Jerusalem and its inhabitants. Jerusalem's radiant light replaces sun and moon. Daughter Zion's fortunes are reversed. Violence ceases. Absent from this idyllic picture is any note of the bitter divisions among the community that marked chapters 56–59. The last chapters of the BOI (63–66) return to the somber view of the state of affairs in Yehud with an additional feature. A contrast is drawn between the fates of two groups within the community. Those engaging in illegitimate ritual practices are "destined to the sword," while God's servants will rejoice in Jerusalem.

Chapter 63 begins with the appearance of a mysterious figure whose garments are splattered with the blood of Edom. God is portrayed here as a warrior who has taken vengeance against Edom, a longtime enemy of Israel. A number of commentators, offended by the violent image, deny that the wrathful warrior could be God. However, the motif of God's wrath throughout Isaiah 57–59, and the warrior image elsewhere in TI (in 59:15b-19 and 66:14b-16), are consistent with God as an angry warrior. A major difference between these passages is that in chapter 59 God's anger is directed against injustices within the Jerusalem community; in chapter 63, it is aimed at Israel's enemies.

The remaining chapters consist of a lament in which people bemoan the loss of God's help (63:7—64:12), and God's response to their desperate pleas (65:1-15). Jerusalem's destiny is portrayed in chapter 66 in surprising and graphic images of reward for the faithful and punishment for the intransigent reprobates.

In the lament, people again remind God of unfulfilled promises. The tone of their complaints reaches a desperate pitch. They ask: Where is the one who led Moses through the sea? Where is your zeal and your might, your compassion? They blame God for hardening their hearts and causing them to sin. Still suffering from the loss of their nation and their temple, they ask, "Will you keep silent, and punish us so severely?" (64:12). God speaks in self-defense, asserting that though "I held out my hands all day long" (65:2), rebellious people angered God with idolatrous rituals. God warns them that they will receive full payment for their actions and promises to destine them to slaughter (65:1-15).

Not all will be destroyed in the fiery blast of God's anger. A group within the community, the servants who did not forsake God, will inherit blessings. The contrasting destinies of these two groups are listed in 65:13-15. The chosen, God's servants who have followed God's commands, will live and rejoice in a glorious new Jerusalem. God is about to create a new heaven and earth where all ills will be forgotten. Descriptive language for this new state of life in chapter 65 is taken from earlier Isaiah texts, including the peaceable community, where predatory animals and their prey will eat together (11:6-9), and from the blossoming wilderness of Isaiah 35.

The last chapter alludes to previous motifs from chapters 60–62. One of the most striking is the recurrence of Jerusalem as a mother and wife. In 66:7-13, Zion/Jerusalem is portrayed as a woman giving birth after a speedy labor, nursing the child from her glorious bosom, carrying the baby in her arms, and dandling the baby on her knees. God is also compared to a mother and to a midwife who assists in the delivery of the child. These images emphasize physical features of a mother giving birth and caring for her child. Her birth pains last for only a moment. Her womb is opened: 66:9 literally translated is "breaking" (the membrane). She nurses the child from her "consoling breast" and "glorious nipple" (Franke 2009).

These images are complicated. Zion/Jerusalem and God are portrayed as mother. In previous chapters, these same images appear in similar combinations. God is a woman gasping in labor pains (42:13-14); God is compared to both a father and to a mother in labor (45:10), and to a nursing mother who has compassion for the child of her womb (49:5). Some scholars disagree that God is portrayed here or anywhere as a woman and read these passages as a contrast, saying that God's love is greater than that of a mother. It is difficult to defend such a position in view of the passages cited above. Images of Zion as a bride, a once barren woman, a mother who has lost her children, a woman once captive now dressed in beautiful garments, a widow, a divorced woman, a wife rejected and then taken back by God are recapitulated in glowing portrayals of God and Jerusalem/Zion in Isaiah 60–62 and 65–66.

The BOI contains a pastiche of ideas and forms. Ritual offenses are contrasted with emphasis on appropriate offerings and Sabbath observance. Many nations will be called to Jerusalem to bring offerings to God on Mount Zion. The last verse, 66:24, describes a ghastly scene: the bodies of all who have rebelled against God burn in unquenchable fire. However, in Jewish tradition, books of the Bible should end with a positive perspective. Therefore, verse 24 is sometimes followed by the repetition of verse 23:

> From new moon to new moon,
>   And from Sabbath to Sabbath,
> All flesh shall come to worship before me
> All flesh will come to worship before God.

▌ The Text in the Interpretive Tradition

While the violence of the Divine Warrior image is shocking, it has been used from New Testament times to the present. The bloodied warrior appears in Revelation 14, describing the fall of Babylon. The son of man and others wield sharp sickles, harvesting the earth of evil. The "wine press of God's wrath" yields vast quantities of blood. It has also been used to illustrate and justify war in US history in the name of truth and justice. The Divine Warrior inspired Julia Ward Howe to compose a Civil War song still sung today in many contexts. Recall the first verse of this song.

> Mine eyes have seen the glory of the coming of the Lord,
> He is trampling out the vintage where the grapes of wrath are stored,
> He hath loosed the fateful lightning of his terrible swift sword;
> His truth is marching on. Glory, Glory, Halleluiah.

Another use of Isaiah 66 is found in Brahms's *Eine Deutsches Requiem*. Grieving mourners long for the one who has died, but they are reassured: "I will again behold you, and your heart will be joyful. . . . Look at me. . . . I have found comfort at last. I will give you comfort, as one whom his own mother comforts."

Selections from the BOI have caused difficulties for some Roman Catholic authorities that have recently made changes in the liturgy. The document *Liturgiam Authenticum* aims at using transcendent language and warns against Isaiah texts because they often portray God as too human. However, use of images taken from human life and experience in the BOI is what makes it such an important text in Judeo-Christian tradition. The Bible is *the primary* source of "sacred vocabulary." Problematic texts should be used, explored, read, and discussed. Texts that make a divine-human connection and cause problems for readers are precisely those texts that advance the development of theological and religious thinking.

■ THE TEXT IN CONTEMPORARY DISCUSSION

After the destruction of the Twin Towers on 9/11, the world was forever changed. Scholars responded to this event, realizing the need to address directly questions of vengeance and violence in the Bible, both Old and New Testaments. At the annual meeting of the Society of Biblical Literature that followed 9/11, many research and study groups changed their direction and began to focus on these issues in the Bible, in religion, in churches, and in other religious bodies. This topic now forms a major body of study in areas of scholarship (Franke and O'Brien). Religious groups— Jews, Christians, and Muslims—also make this issue part of interfaith discussions.

Works Cited

Anderson, Gary A. 1991. *A Time to Mourn, a Time to Dance: The Expression of Grief and Joy in Israelite Religion*. University Park: Pennsylvania State University Press.

Berges, Ulrich. 2010. "Farewell to Deutero-Isaiah or Prophecy without a Prophet." In *Congress Volume Ljubljana 2007*, edited by André Lemaire, 575–95. VTSup 133. Leiden: Brill.

Blenkinsopp, Joseph. 2002. *Isaiah 40–55*. AB. New York: Doubleday.

Brueggemann, Walter. 1998. *Isaiah 40–66*. Westminster Bible Commentary. Louisville: Westminster John Knox.

Ceresko, Anthony R. 2002. *Prophets and Proverbs: More Studies in Old Testament Poetry and Biblical Religion*. Quezon City, Philippines: Claretian.

Clifford, Richard J. 1984. *Fair Spoken and Persuading: An Interpretation of Second Isaiah*. New York: Paulist.

Davies, Andrew. 2007. "Oratorio as Exegesis: The Use of the Book of Isaiah in Handel's *Messiah*." *BibInt* 15:464–84.

DeYoung, Curtiss Paul, Wilda C. Gafney, Leticia Guardiola-Saenz, George E. Tinker, and Frank M. Yamada, eds. 2009. *The Peoples' Bible*. Minneapolis: Fortress Press.

Franke, Chris A. 1991. "The Function of the Satiric Lament over Babylon in Second Isaiah (xlvii)." *VT* 41:408–18.

———. 1994. *Isaiah 46, 47, and 48: A New Literary-Critical Reading*. Biblical and Judaic Studies 3. Winona Lake, IN.: Eisenbrauns.

———. 2009. "'Like a Mother I Have Comforted You:' The Function of Figurative Language in Isaiah 1:7-26 and 66:7-14." In *The Desert Will Bloom: Poetic Visions in Isaiah, Ancient Israel and Its Literature*, edited by A. Joseph Everson and Hyun Chul Paul Kim, 35–55. Atlanta: Society of Biblical Literature.

Franke, Chris, and Julia M. O'Brien, eds. 2010. *Aesthetics of Violence in the Prophets*. New York: T&T Clark.

Gottwald, Norman K. 1985. *The Hebrew Bible: A Socio-Literary Introduction*. Philadelphia: Fortress Press.

Isasi-Díaz, Ada María. 1995. "By the Rivers of Babylon: Exile as a Way of Life." In *Reading from This Place*. Vol. 1, *Social Location and Biblical Interpretation in the United States*, edited by Fernando F. Segovia and Mary Ann Tolbert, 149–63. Minneapolis: Fortress Press.

Kim, Hyun Chul Paul. 2009. "The Spider Poet: Signs and Symbols in Isaiah 41." In *The Desert Will Bloom: Poetic Visions in Isaiah*, edited by A. Joseph Everson and Hyun Chul Paul Kim, 159–80. SBLAIL. Atlanta: Society of Biblical Literature.

Kruger, Paul A. 1997. "The Slave Status of the Virgin Daughter Babylon in Isaiah 47:2: A Perspective from Anthropology." *JNSL* 23:143–51.

Lack, Rémi. 1973. *La symbolique de livre d'Isaïe: Essaie sur l'image littéraire comme élément de structuration*. AnBib. Rome: Pontifical Biblical Institute.

Lessing, R. Reed. 2011. *Isaiah 40–55: A Theological Exposition of Sacred Scripture*. St Louis: Concordia.

Løland, Hanne. 2008. *Silent or Salient Gender? The Interpretation of Gendered God-Language in the Hebrew Bible, Exemplified in Isaiah 42, 46 and 49*. Tübingen: Mohr Siebeck.

Lund, Øystein. 2007. *Way Metaphors and Way Topics in Isaiah 40–55*. FAT. Tübingen: Mohr Siebeck.

Moon, Cyris Heesuk. 1999. "Isaiah 52:13—53:12: An Asian Perspective." In *Return to Babel: Global Perspectives on the Bible*, edited by John R. Levison and Priscilla Pope-Levison, 107–13. Louisville: Westminster John Knox.

Moore, Megan Bishop, and Brad E. Kelle. 2011. *Biblical History and Israel's Past: The Changing Study of the Bible and History*. Grand Rapids: Eerdmans.

Muilenburg, James. 1956. "The Book of Isaiah: Chapters 40–66." In *Interpreter's Bible*. Vol. 5, *Ecclesiastes, the Song of Songs, Isaiah, Jeremiah*, edited by George A. Buttrick, 381–773. New York: Abingdon.

Newsom, Carol A., Sharon H. Ringe, and Jacqueline E. Lapsley, eds. 2012. *Women's Bible Commentary*. 3rd ed. Louisville: Westminster John Knox.

Paul, Shalom M. 2012. *Isaiah 40–66: Translation and Commentary*. Eerdmans Critical Commentary. Grand Rapids: Eerdmans.

Pixley, Jorge. 1999. "Isaiah 52:13–53:12: A Latin American Perspective." In *Return to Babel: Global perspectives on the Bible*, edited by John R. Levison and Priscilla Pope-Levison, 95–100. Louisville: Westminster John Knox.

Schökel, Luis Alonso. 1987. "Isaiah." In *The Literary Guide to the Bible*, edited by Robert Alter and Frank Kermode, 165–84. Cambridge, MA: Belknap Press of Harvard University Press.

Smith, Mark. 1990. *The Early History of God: Yahweh and the Other Deities in Ancient Israel*. San Francisco: Harper & Row.

———. 2001. *The Origins of Biblical Monotheism: Israel's Polytheistic Background and the Ugaritic Texts*. Oxford: Oxford University Press.

Smith-Christopher, Daniel L. 2002. *A Biblical Theology of Exile*. Minneapolis: Fortress Press.

Soares-Prabhu, George M. 1995. "Laughing at Idols: The Dark Side of Biblical Monotheism (an Indian Reading of Isaiah 44:9-20)." In *Reading from This Place*. Vol. 1, *Social Location and Biblical Interpretation in the United States*, edited by Fernando F. Segovia and Mary Ann Tolbert, 149–63. Minneapolis: Fortress Press.

Tiemeyer, Lena-Soria. 2011. *For the Comfort of Zion: The Geographical and Theological Location of Isaiah 40-55*. Leiden: Brill.

Torrey, Charles Cutler. 1928. *The Second Isaiah: A New Interpretation*. Edinburgh: T&T Clark.

Tull, Patricia K. 2009. "Persistent Vegetative States: People and Plants and Plants as People in Isaiah." In *The Desert Will Bloom: Poetic Visions in Isaiah*, edited by A. Joseph Everson and Hyun Chul Paul Kim, 17–35. SBLAIL. Atlanta: Society of Biblical Literature.

Wells, Roy D. 2009. "'They All Gather, They Come to You': History, Utopia, and the Reading of Isaiah 49:18-16 and 60:4-16." In *The Desert Will Bloom: Poetic Visions in Isaiah*, edited by A. Joseph Everson and Hyun Chul Paul Kim, 187–216. SBLAIL. Atlanta: Society of Biblical Literature.

Willey, Patricia Tull. 1997. *Remember the Former Things: The Recollection of Previous Texts in Second Isaiah*. SBLDS. Atlanta: Scholars Press.

JEREMIAH

Kelly J. Murphy

Introduction

The name Jeremiah likely derives from the Hebrew "YHWH exalts," but the prophet is better known as the "weeping prophet" because of the grief-filled words that constitute the book of Jeremiah. In fact, the English word *jeremiad* stems from Jeremiah's name, designating a genre of literature in which an author laments the current state of affairs in his or her society, customarily predicting looming disaster (see Carroll 2008, 229). Accordingly, the biblical book of Lamentations is traditionally ascribed to the prophet because of its mournful tone. Jeremiah has long been a favorite of artists and theologians: Michelangelo painted the prophet on the ceiling of the Sistine Chapel, where Jeremiah holds his chin in his hands and appears deeply troubled, and a Romanesque sculpture often identified as a reflective Jeremiah is located at the Church of St. Pierre, Moissac in southern France. Martin Luther King Jr. once wrote, "[Jeremiah's] life and character are full of surprises that stimulate thought on great moral and religious problems" (King 1992, 181), and Dietrich Bonhoeffer drew on Jeremiah while imprisoned by the Nazis. Yet for contemporary readers, entering the textual world of the book of Jeremiah can be disorienting and disturbing. Somewhat famously, John Bright once called the book a "hopeless hodgepodge" (Bright 1986, lvi). There is no clear chronological order to the events described in the book, the pages brim with violent, disquieting imagery, and the world of ancient Israel can seem far too different from our own.

The book itself is initially set in the period of Josiah, an era marked by a series of both religious and political reforms in ancient Israel that might have held a promise of hope for the tiny nation of Judah, surrounded by the dominant empires of Assyria, Egypt, and Babylon, as they struggled to survive amidst the political turmoil that rocked the ancient Near East during and following Josiah's reign. Yet from the outset of the book, readers know Judah's fate: Jerusalem will fall to the Babylonians in 587 BCE, and the people will be exiled from the land. In short, the book is placed in one of the most troubling, and theologically and politically important, periods for the composition of the Hebrew Bible: the events leading up to the Babylonian exile, the beginning of the exile itself, and its aftermath.

Composition, Structure, Literary Elements

As Bright's "hopeless hodgepodge" comment suggests, the book of Jeremiah displays no clear order and is combined of a mix of poetry and prose. In the past, many biblical scholars assumed that the poetic oracles derived from the "historical" Jeremiah, while his scribe Baruch was responsible for the biographical material, and a later writer/editor (perhaps influenced by the so-called Deuteronomists, with their Deuteronomy-inspired theology) wrote the additional prose sermons. According to the superscription in Jeremiah 1:1-3, the prophet is the son of Hilkiah, a member of a priestly family and from the city of Anathoth (see 11:18-21). More recent scholarship proposes that not all of the poetic oracles can be attributed to the historical Jeremiah, about whom not much can be known with any certainty, and that the book overall is the result of a long history of composition and the work of many authors/editors. In its final form, the book is likely the result of an exilic or postexilic community. The complex redactional history of the book is perhaps most clearly evident when the Masoretic text (Hebrew) and the Septuagint (Greek) versions are compared; the Septuagint is considerably shorter and appears to preserve an earlier form of the book.

Various genres are embedded in the pages of Jeremiah, which, combined with the lack of a chronological narrative, makes it is difficult to delineate the structure of the book clearly. Generally, scholars divide the book into two major parts: Jeremiah 1–25 (before the fall of Jerusalem) and Jeremiah 26–52 (the fall of Jerusalem and its aftermath). Despite—or because of—its complicated redactional history, the book demonstrates substantial familiarity with other biblical texts, alluding to stories from Genesis, Exodus, the books of Joshua–2 Kings, the book of Hosea, the book of Job, and the Psalms.

Key Themes

Several key themes and words span the book. First, the book emphasizes that YHWH is sovereign, powerful, and the creator of all (e.g., 10:10-13). Israel/Judah belongs to him (e.g., 2:3; 10:16; 51:19), but consistent throughout is the idea that an enemy from the north is descending on the land. Although at times Jeremiah blames the oncoming disaster on the people's moral and ethical failures, the major concern of the book is that the people "go after [hālak]" other gods and have not remained faithful to YHWH. Thus any disaster that comes is the fault of the people. Yet the book also repeatedly calls on the people to šûb, or "to return/repent." In this way, while destruction is assured, there also remain occasional moments of hope. Nevertheless, the realities of war, loss, and trauma overflow from the pages and resonate in the voices of its characters.

Like many biblical prophetic books, the book of Jeremiah is largely centered on men: the two major characters are YHWH, principally depicted as a vengeful, warrior god ("YHWH of hosts"), and Jeremiah, the reluctant and sometimes bitter prophet. Though there are occasional positive images of women, females primarily function as stock characters intended to shame Israel/Judah as a whole or the men of Israel/Judah in particular. When women appear, they are usually the familiar figures of the adulterous wife or the unfaithful daughter.

As is often noted, a plethora of voices appear in the book: YHWH, the people, the kings, Jeremiah, the other prophets, the land itself, and occasionally even the women speak. At times, the polyvocal nature of the text makes it difficult to determine the speaker; such ambiguity literarily represents the chaos of the period the book depicts. Yet in spite of the many divine speeches, YHWH's silence also marks the book: in the final laments voiced by the prophet, the deity fails to respond and God is strikingly absent from many of the events surrounding life in Judah after the fall.

Jeremiah 1:1-19: Introduction and Call Narrative

■ THE TEXT IN ITS ANCIENT CONTEXT

The opening of the book of Jeremiah consists of two parts: a superscription, which places the prophet in a specific historical context (1:1-3), and a call narrative, which includes two visions (1:4-19). Together 1:1-3 and 1:4-19 serve as a prelude, launching the reader into the devastating period of ancient Israelite history that followed the fall of the Assyrian Empire and the rise of the Babylonian Empire, ultimately resulting in the destruction of Judah and the ensuing exile.

The book begins Jeremiah's prophetic activity in the thirteenth year of the reign of King Josiah (627 BCE), and claims that it ends with the captivity of Jerusalem in 587 BCE (1:1-3). However, other Jeremianic texts suggest that the prophet continued to be active after the destruction of Jerusalem (see 40:1; 42:7; 43:8; 44:1, 24-25). According to this timeline, Jeremiah lived through the reign of five Judahite kings: Josiah, Jehoahaz, Jehoiakim, Jehoiachin, and Zedekiah. Yet the book does not proceed chronologically through their reigns, but rather jumps between events in different periods with no clear timeline; O'Connor notes that the "messy date-line conveys the interruption of time that accompanies trauma and disaster" (O'Connor 2012a, 132). Overall, the text claims that Jeremiah had a prophetic career of forty years, recalling the forty years Moses wandered in the wilderness. For later readers who are aware of how the events that take place during the reign of these kings will progress, the superscription casts a portentous tone over the book. Though the book begins with the phrase "the words of Jeremiah," 1:2 quickly identifies the source of these words: YHWH. Divine speech plays a central role in the book, which includes over one hundred uses of the formulaic phrase "Thus says YHWH" (parallel language is found throughout the ancient Near East, including at Mari, where the phrase "Thus spoke Annunitum" [a deity] appears in a prophetic text; see Petersen 2002, 16), as well as numerous instances of "the word of YHWH came to me." Thus the superscription establishes from the outset the close relationship between the deity and the prophet, while also underscoring that Jeremiah speaks for YHWH, granting divine authority to both the prophet's words and the book overall.

Jeremiah 1:4-19 opens by emphasizing the divine word: "Now the word of YHWH came to me" (1:4). Form critically, 1:4-10 is a call narrative, and as such it aligns with the call narratives of other key figures in the Hebrew Bible (e.g., Moses [Exod. 3:11; 4:10-11] and Gideon [Judg. 6:11-24]).

Such call narratives typically follow a prescribed order: the deity addresses the appointed person and gives a task (1:4-5), the appointed individual objects by citing inadequacy for such an undertaking (1:6), the deity offers assurances that he will be with the person (1:7-8), and then the deity provides a sign as proof (1:9-10). In particular, 1:10 will serve as an important verse as the book unfolds, for after putting "his words" in Jeremiah's mouth, YHWH proclaims,

> See, today I appoint you over nations and over kingdoms,
> to pluck up [*nātaš*] and to pull down [*nātas*],
> to destroy [*'ābad*] and to overthrow [*hāras*],
> to build [*bānâ*] and to plant [*nāṭaʿ*].

Like the superscription, the call narrative also contains parallels with the figure of Moses. Both Jeremiah and Moses claim problems with speech (Jer. 1:6; cf. Exod. 4:10-12), and the deity promises to give them both the means to speak (Jer. 1:9; cf. Exod. 4:10-12). The final editors of the book portray Jeremiah as the "prophet like Moses" foreshadowed in Deut. 18:15-22. Despite the similarities, there are also noteworthy differences. The text recounts Jeremiah's call from the first person, and Jeremiah, alone out of all of the prophetic figures in the Hebrew Bible, is appointed as a prophet before his birth (1:5). Like Jer. 1:1-3, 1:4-10 functions as a prelude, introducing themes that will run like threads throughout the following pages: Jeremiah is a "prophet to the nations" (1:5, 10), the disaster will come from the north (1:13), and while destruction looms, there is also language of rebuilding and hope (1:10).

Jeremiah 1:11-19 consists of two visions. In the first, Jeremiah sees "a branch of an almond [*šāqēd*] tree" (1:11). YHWH then interprets the vision: "You have seen well, for I am watching [*šōqēd*] over my word to perform it" (1:12). The wordplay in Hebrew serves as a reminder to the reader: YHWH is with Jeremiah and will do what he promises. The second vision is of a "boiling pot, tilted away from the north" (1:13). Again, YHWH interprets the vision: disaster from the north approaches Jerusalem and Judah, a direct result of the misdeeds of the people, who have been worshiping other gods (1:14-16). Jeremiah 1:15 emphasizes the idea that all nations are under YHWH's control. Although later readers often immediately associate the "disaster from the north" with Babylon, it is not until 20:4-6 that the text names Babylon as the enemy chosen by God to punish Judah for its offenses. Though many scholars have attempted to identify a precise location for this "boiling pot from the north" (see Holladay 1986, 42–43), it seems more likely that this is metaphorical language that draws on mythological and cosmic images (see O'Connor 2001, 490; Clements 1988, 21).

The visions end with YHWH's directive that Jeremiah "gird up his loins" and proclaim to the people of Judah everything the deity commands him (1:17). While the preceding visions focused on the ominous threat approaching Judah, 1:17-19 focuses on the prophet himself. The attention on Jeremiah introduces several more themes that will follow in the book. First, Jeremiah will have enemies among the established leaders of Judah, including the kings and priests, as well as the people of the land (1:18). Additionally, the passage reiterates that YHWH will be with Jeremiah to deliver him from his enemies, and that the deity has outfitted him appropriately: he is "a fortified city, an iron pillar, and a bronze wall" (1:19), invoking warfare imagery. While Jeremiah will be protected as a "fortified city," Jerusalem itself—YHWH's own city—is doomed. As the first sense unit of the book ends, the reader is left with an uneasy feeling: Jeremiah, in true prophetic fashion, will stand with only God on his side, and an (as yet unidentified) enemy is set to destroy the people of Judah, sent by their own God.

■ THE TEXT IN THE INTERPRETIVE TRADITION

That Jeremiah is informed of his prophetic mission "in the womb" sets him apart from other prophets. Accordingly, in rabbinic tradition, Jeremiah is described as one of four men whom YHWH created directly (along with Adam, Jacob, and Isaiah); the rabbis use Jer. 1:5, which reads "before I formed [i.e., "created"] you in the womb, I knew you" to draw this conclusion (*Pesiq. Rab.* 26:1). Additionally, rabbinic commentary focused on the introductory material that sets the stage for Jeremiah as a prophet like Moses. For the rabbis, the line "one of the priests of Anatoth" (1:1), which connected Jeremiah to a priestly line associated with wrongdoing (cf. 1 Kgs. 2:26-27), leads to the interpretation that Jeremiah lamented, "Among the priests my name is deprived of the respect due it" (*Pesiq. Rab Kah.* 13:13). What follows is a comparison between the fates of Moses and Jeremiah, where Jeremiah laments all the good that happened to Moses and contrasts it with all the bad that befell him: for example, Moses is blessed (Num. 6:24), while Jeremiah is cursed (Jer. 29:22). In other rabbinic texts, however, the comparison between Moses and Jeremiah concentrates on their similarities: both were prophets for forty years, both prophesied concerning Judah and Israel, the people revolted against them, one was cast into water and the other into a pit, both were saved by a slave, and both spoke words of reprimand (*Pesiq. Rab Kah.* 13:6). Another midrash reports that Moses had the voice of a boy from birth (*Exod. Rab.* 1:24), a parallel with Jer. 1:6.

In Christian tradition, Tertullian and Irenaeus both based arguments for human life in the womb based on Jer. 1:5, while Maximus of Turin and Jerome compare the stories of Jeremiah and John the Baptist in the womb to illustrate that even before birth God consecrated these men (Wenthe, 3-4). Additionally, Jer. 1:5 was used by Ambrose to argue for the twofold nature of Christ: the divine aspects of the Christian savior came from the deity, while the human characteristics came from his human mother without negatively affecting his divinity (Wenthe, 4). Finally, both Athanasius and Ambrose invoked the passage in arguments against the Arians, claiming that while some, like Jeremiah, are created, Christ was begotten but not created and, per Athanasius, "he is the Father's image and eternal word, never having not existed" (Wenthe, 4).

■ THE TEXT IN CONTEMPORARY DISCUSSION

The opening chapter of the book continues to speak today, transcending the boundaries of both temporal and cultural differences. The first words of Jeremiah are marked by both despair and hope and are set in a period of historical trauma and disaster; accordingly many scholars and theologians argue that the book is especially pertinent in addressing the fears and concerns of contemporary trauma and disaster survivors (see O'Connor 2012a, 2012b; Weems 2004). Jeremiah's words have been used to grapple with events ranging from the Nazi Holocaust, terrorism, war, colonization, to wanton violence and natural disasters. One contemporary message of the book—even if the following pages may be far from universally uplifting—is that it is possible for disaster survivors to move from having been "pluck[ed] up" to "rebuild[ing]" (1:10); in other words, from disaster to recovery.

Although the introduction to the book problematically blames the victims for the looming disaster, O'Connor notes that such a direct cause-and-effect correlation, while nevertheless insufficient, does "make space for recovery to begin" (2012a, 72). Similarly, Stulman and Kim suggest that 1:10 provides "hope in crisis" (2010, 100) and may help victims toward a "reestablishment of agency" (104). Accordingly, the book of Jeremiah can be a useful, if also challenging, resource for trauma survivors.

Additionally, Jer. 1:5 has played a significant role in the ongoing debate about abortion. On the one hand, opponents of abortion frequently cite the passage as proof that the fetus is a human being from conception. On the other hand, since 1:5 is poetry, others suggest that it is "difficult . . . to know if this passage is meant literally or metaphorically" (Friedman and Dolansky 2011, 48). Drawing any certain conclusions about what the ancient poetry means is challenging at best.

2:1—4:4: Divine Pleas and Indictments

■ THE TEXT IN ITS ANCIENT CONTEXT

Jeremiah 2:1—4:4 begins with the "word of YHWH" coming to Jeremiah (2:1). O'Connor calls this section a "drama of the broken family" rather than the more commonly used "broken marriage metaphor" (O'Connor 2012a, 35; also see 145n1). It is not simply the married couple that is affected by the charge YHWH levels against Judah and Israel; rather, YHWH indicts the couple's offspring as well (2:9). Israel and God are a "broken family" (O'Connor 2012a, 35).

In Jer. 2:1—3:5, the deity relates his intention to divorce Judah for its apostasy, particularly citing Judah's devotion to Baal, a Canaanite god, rather than to YHWH. Intriguingly, the reference to Jerusalem in 2:1 is missing from the Septuagint; the remainder of the passage is directed to Israel (the northern kingdom) and thus may reflect an original composition intended to entice the northern kingdom to reunite with Judah as a part of Josiah's reforms (see 1 Kings 1–11; Holladay 1986, 62–63). Later redactors appear to have added Jerusalem and Judah to the oracle. As is often noted, the following passages draw heavily from the imagery found in Hosea: Jer. 2:1-3 romanticizes the postexodus wilderness period (see Hosea 2:14-20), and YHWH describes Israel as his wife, recalling the "devotion of [her] youth" (2:2; see Hosea 2:15). But according to this oracle, things quickly went amiss once the Israelites entered the promised land. In particular, "the prophets prophesied by Baal, and went after [*hālak*] things that do not profit [*lōʾ-yôʿilū*]" (2:8). The verb for "to profit" in Hebrew comes from the root *yaʿal*, which can also mean "to help or "to be of use." The Hebrew wordplay between the name of Baal and the verb underscores the futility of worshiping Baal, who cannot help or be of use. The indictment is to the point: YHWH's designated officials and people have failed to perform their roles and have worshiped worthless deities (see Hosea 2:8-17).

Ambiguity runs rife throughout the passage: at times, it seems that Israel (the northern kingdom) is male, while Judah (the southern kingdom) is depicted as the unfaithful wife—O'Connor suggests that they are blended together in 3:20 (see O'Connor 2012a, 36–37). Moreover, at times Israel seems to refer only to the northern kingdom, while in other passages it seems to refer to the two kingdoms together. Yet the predominant theme is the unfaithfulness of *both* Israel and Judah, which is expressed through the use of the marriage metaphor commonly found throughout the prophetic books of the Hebrew Bible (e.g., Hosea 1–3; Isaiah 40–55; Ezekiel 16): YHWH, the loyal husband, has been abandoned by Israel/Judah, the faithless wife. Here and throughout Jeremiah, the text draws on the widespread ancient Near Eastern depiction of cities as female, and this gendered imagery is (largely) employed negatively. The text describes Israel/Judah-the-woman as shameful and degraded (e.g., 2:22-24; 2:29—3:5). Any Israelite male is thus also shamed and degraded, forced to understand himself as female according to the textual metaphor (see O'Connor 2001, 492; Claassens 2013, 126; Weems 2005, 216).

Form critically, 2:9-14 is often called a "prophetic lawsuit," where YHWH formally accuses Israel of wrongdoing and makes it explicit that the fault sits with the people, who "changed its gods . . . for something that does not profit [ya'al]," again invoking Baal (2:11). The result is that the "land is a waste" (2:15), foreshadowing the oncoming exile. The mention of Egypt and Assyria implicates the people for making treaties with these foreign powers and thus not relying on YHWH alone (2:18; 2:36). Jeremiah 2:29—3:5 reiterates the image of Israel as adulterous wife, and sets the stage for the question posed in 3:1. The text of Deut. 24:1-4 lurks behind the passage: a man cannot remarry a woman who has married another man. Left unanswered is the question: If a human man cannot take back a wife who has gone astray, can YHWH? Jeremiah 3:6 continues the marriage metaphor and purports to relate an exchange between YHWH and the prophet during the reign of Josiah. In contrast with the preceding verses, there is a clear contrast between the northern kingdom, who abandoned YHWH first, "and yet her false sister Judah did not fear" (3:8). Though YHWH thought Judah would not go astray after seeing how Israel was "cast off" (3:8), nevertheless Judah strayed, only insincerely repenting. For this reason, 3:11 states that Israel is less guilty than Judah, and 3:12 calls for Israel to *šûb*, to return/repent.

The metaphor then switches from that of an adulterous wife to a parent-child relationship between God and Israel/Judah: "Return [*šûb*], O faithless children" (3:14). The following verses paint a picture of a compassionate God allowing his errant children to return to their homeland, a time when "all nations" shall assemble in Jerusalem (3:17) and both Israel and Judah will "come from the land of the north to the land that I gave your ancestors for a heritage" (3:18). In 3:22b, the speaker shifts from YHWH to the children, who admit their wrongdoing and seek to return (3:22-25). YHWH speaks again in 4:1-4. In 4:1, the Hebrew *'im*, "if," is repeated three times: *if* the Israelites return (*šûb*), *if* they remove (*šûb*) the abominations from before YHWH, and *if* they swear to worship YHWH in "truth, justice, and righteousness," then the other nations of the world shall be blessed and praised through them (4:2). The text echoes with the promise to Abraham in Gen. 12:2-3 (through Israel all nations will be blessed). The passage ends by calling for the people to both break up fallow ground and to stop sowing among thorns, as well as to circumcise themselves to YHWH and remove the foreskins of their hearts (4:4; see Deut. 10:6): the repetition of "removing" throughout the verse implies the need to begin again and suggests that the foreign gods are the problem (Allen 2008, 62). However, the passage ends with an ominous warning,

> or else my wrath will go forth like fire,
>   and burn with no one to quench it,
> because of the evil of your doings. (4:4)

■ THE TEXT IN THE INTERPRETIVE TRADITION

Despite the divine indictments, some early Jewish interpretations focused on the theme of hope for repentance. For example, one rabbinic interpretation explains the Hebrew letters in Jeremiah's name (*yrmyh*) as composed of the Hebrew words *yôd* ("ten"), *rm* ("to journey up"), and *yh* ("the Presence [of the deity]") (*Pesiq. Rab Kah.* 13:11). Accordingly to the story, "in ten stages the Presence journeyed up and away" from the temple, descending and remaining on Mount of Olives for three and half years, where three times a day he repeated the words of Jer. 3:22 in the hopes of getting his people to repent (*Pesiq. Rab Kah.* 13:11).

In the New Testament, the author of the Gospel of John invokes the depiction of God as the "fountain of living waters" from Jer. 2:13 and applies it to Jesus (John 4:10-11). Early Christian interpretation also focused on the "fountain of living water" as well as the "broken cistern": Theodoret of Cyrus claims that the mystery of the Trinity is revealed in the phrase "fountain of living water," while Augustine asserts that Christ was the fountain of living waters, and those who do not believe in Christ rely on the broken cisterns (Wenthe, 17). Drawing on the harvest imagery of the choice vine gone wild in Jer. 2:21, Origen describes how the church has replaced Israel (Wenthe, 24–25). Finally, based on 4:4, many early Christian interpreters noted that spiritual circumcision replaced physical circumcision (Wenthe, 41–43).

Carl Rakosi's poem "Israel" draws from the KJV's rendering of Jer. 3:6: "Hast thou seen that which backsliding Israel hath done?"

■ THE TEXT IN CONTEMPORARY DISCUSSION

From the beginning, there are two troubling aspects of the book for contemporary readers: the negative depiction of women and how the book blames the victims of the expanding Babylonian Empire for what befalls them.

The negative depiction of women throughout Jeremiah—and especially how violently they are treated throughout the book—can isolate even readers who are able to place the book within its historically patriarchal confines. Yet as Renita Weems notes, if "women readers can hold their disgust at bay long enough to stay with the poetry and press certain questions" (218), then female (and male) readers can decide to "face the language of sexuality in Jeremiah" and "to speak up about the ways in which religious texts distort reality, re-inscribe sexual abuse, force connections where there are none, and hide behind language about authority to maintain the status quo" (219; see also O'Connor 2012a, 2012b). As readers, we can ignore the realities of gendered language in Jeremiah—or we can fight against and challenge them.

While for the author(s) of Jeremiah, placing the blame on the victims is clearly a theological explanation for the sociopolitical events that surrounded the fall of both Israel and Judah, for contemporary victims of violence, natural disasters, illness, and the like, it can be difficult to find much to redeem in 2:1—4:4. However, placing the blame on the people, while problematic, also hands victims some power over their situations; in other words, they can do something in the future to change what happens to them and thus "gain a sense of control" (O'Connor 2012a, 44). Even if such blame-the-victim language is ultimately unsatisfying, it is nevertheless an "effort to make meaning" in an uncertain, traumatized world (2012, 44). Thus, for modern readers, this is a text that provides "vital, explosive speech that both reveals and heals wounds" (O'Connor 2012a, 45). In short, the book helps illustrate to victims how to speak again in the face of tragedy.

Jeremiah 4:5—6:30; 8:4—10:25: The Foe from the North

▐ THE TEXT IN ITS ANCIENT CONTEXT

The largely poetic material found in 4:5—6:30 and 8:4—10:25 is united by a common theme: the approach of an unnamed enemy from the north and the predicted devastating results, which YHWH confirms through the repeated prophetic messenger formula, "Thus says YHWH" (Jer. 4:27; 5:14; 6:6, 9, 16, 21-22; 7:3, 20-21; 8:4; 9:7, 15, 17, 22-23; 10:2, 18). Despite the focus on the enemy, it is never identified specifically; rather, enemy is often described as a wild animal as in Jer. 4:7 and 5:6 (cf. Ezek. 5:17) and overall depicts the disaster as cosmic in scope (see Jer. 4:23-28). Although it is difficult to date the oracles with any precision and many of the prose narratives may have been edited or added later, there are indications that the warnings are addressed to both the northern and southern kingdoms, and some material may stem from before the invasion of 587 BCE (see Holladay 1986, 132–38).

From a literary perspective, the text is marked by polyvocality. A number of voices speak in this unit, including those of "YHWH, Jeremiah, a narrator, the people, the northern kingdom, daughter Zion, and the foe" (O'Connor 2001, 493). As is often noted, the clamor of voices makes it difficult to determine the speaker. Yet the reality of the war and destruction is pervasive amid the din: 4:7-8 underscores the futility of the situation, as a lion—often depicted in the Hebrew Bible, along with other wild animals, as Israel's enemy and a sign of danger and terror—is coming. There is nothing the people can do to stop it, and so they are implored to put on sackcloth and lament,

> The fierce anger of YHWH
> has not turned [*šûb*] away from us. (4:8)

While the book often uses the verb *šûb* to call the people to repent, here the verb casts a dark shadow over whether YHWH's anger will turn from the people.

The narrator blames various leaders in Jer. 4:9—the kings, officials, priests, and prophets. Jeremiah 4:10 returns to the prophet: "Ah, YHWH God, how utterly you have deceived this people and Jerusalem, saying, 'It shall be well with you,' even while the sword is at the throat!" Although the NRSV reads, "I said," presumably intending the first-person speaker to be understood as Jeremiah, other texts preserve, "they said," perhaps indicating the prophets from 4:9 (Carroll 1986, 161). As Carroll notes, this places the blame not on the prophets but on YHWH, who misled them by giving them prophecies of peace rather than destruction ("it shall be well with you"; 4:10; 14:13-16, 23:17; see also Mic. 3:5). The support of prophets other than Jeremiah differs from the largely critical attitude toward the prophetic office that weaves throughout the book (Carroll 1986, 161; see 14:13-16; 23:9-40; 27–28; 29:21-23). The protest is strikingly bold: YHWH allowed the prophets to make false prophecies of peace. There is no divine response to this claim; rather, 4:11-18 reiterates that the impending disaster is Jerusalem's own fault, though here the metaphor shifts from that of a lion to an oncoming wind that will punish rather than "winnow" or "cleanse" (4:11). In Jer. 4:19, an unknown speaker, sometimes identified as Jeremiah and sometimes identified as the land personified, speaks again, momentarily letting the reader witness the torment felt by those facing the destruction of the people and city.

> My anguish, my anguish! I writhe in pain!
>> Oh, the walls of my heart!
> My heart is beating wildly;
>> I cannot keep silent;
> for I hear the sound of the trumpet,
>> the alarm of war.

From a feministic perspective, Bauer translates 4:19 as "My belly! My Belly! I-writhe-in-labor," reading "labor" with the Septuagint and Vulgate instead of "wail" with the Hebrew MT (Bauer 1999, 63–66). In this interpretation, the prophet himself takes on the female metaphor applied to the city, and so "Female Israel (earlier identified as 'Daughter My People') and the prophet Jeremiah have merged to cry out in light of the impending devastation" (Bauer, 64). Next, the phrase "I looked" is repeated four times in 4:23-26. What the speaker sees is destruction: quaking mountains and hills, an absence of people, a sky without birds, the land turned to desert, and the cities destroyed. A moment of hope is found in 4:27, "yet I will not make a full end," but 4:28 reiterates that YHWH will not "turn back [šûb]" from the oncoming devastation. Daughter Zion is addressed in 4:29-31 as both a whore and a mother giving birth amid the destruction and chaos, and the chapter ends with the haunting image of the woman "gasping for breath" and "fainting before killers" (4:31).

Jeremiah 5:1-13 restates the divine hesitation at bringing about the disaster, while also providing a kind of "theodicy" to justify YHWH's actions (Carroll 1986, 174). The first six verses of the chapter recall the story of Abraham and Sodom in Gen. 18:23-32. If Jeremiah can find just one person who "acts justly and seeks truth," then YHWH will forgive and the disaster can be averted. First, Jeremiah searches among the poor, but they refuse to turn (šûb) from their ways; next, Jeremiah seeks a just person among the rich, but there too he fails to find even one (5:3-5). The result is death by wild animals: lion, wolf, and leopard (5:6). Jeremiah 5:7-11 reiterates the adulterous ways of YHWH's people. Since the people failed to heed the prophets, YHWH puts fire into the mouth of Jeremiah and vows to bring a nation from "far away" (5:15). This nation will "eat up" the harvest, the children, the flocks, and the fig trees, and will destroy the fortified cities in which the people naively put their trust (5:16-17). Though 5:18 looks forward to "those days," the days of the exile, promising an incomplete end, the following verses enumerate the reasons the people deserve their fate, and the passage ends by again indicting the failure of the leaders, both the priests and, especially, the prophets, pointedly stating that YHWH's people "love to have it so" (5:30-31).

Daughter Zion appears again in 6:1-30, and a number of voices merge, including the voice of YHWH, the enemy, Jeremiah, and the people. Perhaps most powerfully, though YHWH calls on the people to repent, any repentance is pointless (6:26). Jeremiah is working with "rejected silver"

(6:30) that cannot be used; the people have failed. There is no escaping the army that comes rushing like the "roaring sea" (6:23).

When the poetic oracles resume in 8:4, the text returns to the theme of Israel's disobedience and the approaching disaster. The passage opens with a fivefold repetition of *šûb*: to return (8:4 [2×], 5 [2×], 6). Why, asks YHWH, do the people refuse to "turn back"? Drawing on the notion from Proverbs that wisdom is discovered by observing the natural world (e.g., "Look to the ant!" in Prov. 6:6), YHWH compares the people with storks, turtledoves, swifts, and cranes, which know their place (8:7), while his own people claim to be "wise" but do not know theirs.

In the first-person lament in 8:18—9:3, it is difficult to discern the speaker: is it Jeremiah who wishes "O that my head were a spring of water, and my eyes a fountain of tears, so that I might weep day and night for the slain of my poor people!" (9:1)? Or is it YHWH? Scholarly opinion is divided (for different explanations, see Allen, 111; Carroll 1986, 235–36). O'Connor attributes the words to YHWH, and suggests that in this way the text holds a "promise of healing," for "it puts aside punishment, eschews questions of causality, and understands God in radically different terms from much of the rest of the book" (O'Connor 2001, 497). Jeremiah 8:21-22 reads—from either Jeremiah, the city, or YHWH's perspective—

> For the hurt of my poor people I am hurt,
>> I mourn, and dismay has taken hold of me.
> Is there no balm in Gilead?
>> Is there no physician there?
> Why then has the health of my poor people
>> not been restored?

Gilead, located in Deut. 3:16 east of the Jordan River, is associated here with balm and healing, yet the section that stretches from 8:4—10:40 offers little hope.

Jeremiah 9 articulates the divine wish to leave Israel in the desert "for they are all adulterers" (9:2; see Exodus 32–34; Numbers 14), ending with yet another divine promise to "turn Jerusalem into rubble" (9:10) because Israel abandoned the torah and followed other gods (9:12). Funeral imagery dominates 9:17-21: death has entered Jerusalem because of the people's unwillingness to devote themselves to YHWH, and while God delights in "kindness, justice, and equity," Israel remains "uncircumcised in heart," unwilling to realize that ritual actions alone (like physical circumcision) will not save them.

In Jeremiah 10, the MT is arranged differently than the Septuagint, lacking 10:6-8, 10. Additionally, verse 11 is in Aramaic and not Hebrew. The Septuagint is likely older than the MT, and the Aramaic is likely a later addition to the MT; in short, 10:6-8, 10, praises YHWH as a God like no other and ascribes a kind of monotheism to the text that is not otherwise seen in the Septuagint, while the Aramaic of 10:11 claims that any gods who did not "make the heavens and the earth" shall perish (see Petersen, 100–102). As Brueggemann notes, the gods described in 10:1-6 are "characterized by a series of negatives": they cannot move, speak, walk, do evil, do good, nor make (Brueggemann 1998, 103). In contrast, in 10:10-16, YHWH makes, establishes, stretches out, utters, makes rise, brings out, and forms (Brueggemann, 103). Many scholars wish to place these verses in an exilic context, since "idolatry was a particular temptation for the assimilating community in Babylon" (O'Connor 2001, 498). However, since YHWH is the one who "formed all things" and Israel is his (10:16), there remains some hope: surely the creator God can return his people to their land.

Jeremiah 10:17-25 changes the overall thrust of the chapter. YHWH speaks, "I am going to sling out the inhabitants of the land" (10:18). The concluding words portray Mother Zion without her children, standing amid ravaged tents (10:20). Again, the speaker remains ambiguous in this passage: Is it Jeremiah or the personified city? Nevertheless, 10:23-25 ends by acknowledging YHWH's power while also imploring the deity for both mercy (10:24) and justice (10:25). The final plea for divine wrath to punish the "nations" quotes Ps. 79:6-7, and overall, 10:17-25 may be a passage written in an exilic context (see Carroll 1986, 263–65).

■ THE TEXT IN THE INTERPRETIVE TRADITION

In rabbinic tradition, Jeremiah's anguished cries "My anguish! My anguish! I writhe in pain!" (4:19) are connected to his birth; following these words, he opened his mouth and accused his mother of being faithless. When his mother asks, "What makes this infant speak thus? Surely on no account of mine!," the text reports that Jeremiah spoke not of his birth mother, but from the womb knew Jerusalem would be destroyed because of her unfaithfulness (*Pesiq. Rab.* 26.1/2).

In Christian tradition, Jerome identifies "the lion who seeks to destroy" (4:7) as Nebuchadnezzar in the historical sense, but also as the devil (Wenthe, 44). Both Origen and Theodoret of Cyrus invoke Jer. 9:25-26 to illustrate that spiritual circumcision is more important than physical circumcision (Wenthe, 87).

In more contemporary reuses, the "Battle Hymn of the Republic" draws on Jer. 6:9-15: "My eyes have seen the coming of the glory of the Lord; He is trampling out the vintage where the grapes of wrath are stored." Holocaust survivor Elie Wiesel would remember Jer. 10:25 ("and all the birds of the air had fled") when he returned to Auschwitz, writing, "Then and only then did I remember that, during the tempest of fire and silence, there were no birds to be seen on the horizon; they had fled the skies above all the death-camps. I stood in Birkenau and remembered Jeremiah" (Wiesel, 126; cited in Carroll 1986, 170).

■ THE TEXT IN CONTEMPORARY DISCUSSION

The violence, despair, and war-filled oracles that focus on the cosmic battle coming from the north are often troubling for contemporary readers. In a modern world that is still ravaged by war—and both the physical and sexual violence that often accompany it—these verses can be overwhelming, especially because they clearly illustrate that the oncoming disaster comes directly from the deity. For that reason, the question posed in Jer. 5:19 is especially timeless, "Why has YHWH our God done these things to us?" The question of theodicy, while unanswerable, remains vital to contemporary theological discussions among people of all faiths.

Despite this, positive images can also be found in the otherwise terror-filled depictions contained in these oracles. While the largely male-centered text of Jeremiah often uses the image of a woman in labor negatively, birth also has a "powerful, life-giving nature" (Claassens, 122). If readers see the anguished cries of 8:18—9:3 as Jeremiah's, then such a reading might help them to contest "traditional gender roles," and "to grasp something of the notion of gender as performative" (Claassens, 127). Such an interpretation enables us to understand that dichotomies like "masculine" and "feminine" are largely constructed by societies and opens a window into healthy dialogue about other possible understandings of gender. Similarly, if it is God who speaks in anguish in 8:18—9:3, the text provides an opportunity for thinking constructively about images of the divine in the Hebrew Bible that are not exclusively male and violent (O'Connor 2012b, 277). Finally, Jer. 4:23-28 reminds readers that human actions have an effect on the natural world, while giving the earth itself a voice to mourn (O'Connor 2012b, 277).

7:1-15; 7:16—8:3; 26:1-24: The Temple Sermon and Related Material

■ THE TEXT IN ITS ANCIENT CONTEXT

The material in Jer. 7:1-15, often called the "Temple Sermon," interrupts the poetic material found in 4:5—6:30 and 8:4—10:25, and is followed by another prose passage in 7:16—8:3 that, although closely related to the Temple Sermon material, many scholars suggest is a secondary addition. Jeremiah 26:1-23 also retells the Temple Sermon, though with some differences. According to 26:1, Jeremiah preached the sermon in the year 609 BCE, when King Jehoiakim ascended to the throne following Josiah's death in the battle against Neco II at Megiddo. Prior to Jehoiakim's ascension, Josiah's son Jehoahaz ruled for a brief three months before Neco II deported him to Egypt, replacing him with Jehoiakim. Despite the claim that the sermon took place in 609 BCE, it is likely that these texts are either exilic or postexilic compositions, although they may contain kernels of the "historical" Jeremiah's own views about the corruption of the temple and its personnel.

Jeremiah 7:1 begins, not surprisingly, with "the word that came to Jeremiah from YHWH." The prophet is commanded to stand at the gates of the temple and to implore the people to listen to YHWH's warning: "Amend your ways and your doings, and let me dwell with you in this place" (7:3). However, the Hebrew can be read in two ways: either YHWH is to dwell *with* Judah in the temple, or, alternatively, the text reads "I will *let you* dwell in this place" (see Holladay 1986, 236–37). In the second case, the meaning is clear: if the people repent and reform, they will be spared the punishment of exile. The Judahites are then warned that they should not fool themselves into thinking that YHWH will not let his temple be destroyed: "Do not trust in these deceptive words: 'This is the temple of YHWH, the temple of YHWH, the temple of YHWH'" (7:4). Literarily, the threefold repetition emphasizes how naive the authors of the sermon believed the Judahites to be; despite Jeremiah's warnings, no one understood that God would let the temple be destroyed (see 4:10; 14:13-16; 23:17 on the prophets who falsely prophesied peace). What YHWH wants from his people is not empty words in a building that they believe to be important, but rather ethical and moral behavior based on the covenant (7:5-15). If the Judahites wish to avoid exile, they must repent. The language evokes the book of Deuteronomy: act justly, protect the marginalized, refrain from murder, and remain faithful to YHWH alone (7:5-7). In exchange for these actions, YHWH promises to dwell in the temple.

Despite the possibility of a reprieve offered in Jer. 7:5-7, 7:8-11 casts a dark shadow over YHWH's previous words: the people stand in the temple and claim, "We are safe!" Jeremiah 7:9 implicates the Judahites as transgressing five of the Ten Commandments (see Exod. 20:1-17; Deut. 5:6-21): stealing, murdering, committing adultery, swearing falsely, and going after (*hālak*) other gods. The temple has become nothing more than a "den of robbers" (Jer. 7:11). Next, the text shifts the reader's attention both geographically and temporally as YHWH reminds the Judahites of his former dwelling place in Shiloh, a shrine to YHWH in the northern kingdom where he no longer dwells (see Josh. 21:1-2; 1 Sam. 1:3, 9). Like the "offspring of Ephraim," symbolizing the northern Israelites, who according to the theology of the books of Joshua through 2 Kings disobeyed YHWH and subsequently fell to the Assyrians in 721 BCE, YHWH will also cast the Judahites out of his sight (15:15).

In Jer. 7:16-20, YHWH forbids Jeremiah to intercede on behalf of the people, while 7:21-28 suggests that sacrifices are not necessary, again moving away from an emphasis on ritual action: "For in the day that I brought your ancestors out of the land of Egypt, I did not speak to them or command them concerning burnt offerings and sacrifices" (7:22). Jeremiah 7:29—8:3 details Judah's ultimate destiny and the fate of the dead—including a lack of burial. Perhaps most interestingly, this exilic or postexilic passage recalls the writer(s)' memories of Judah's religious practices, which are quite distinct from the "YHWH-alone" religion that later develops as the norm. In particular, the text records how the people felt compelled to stay faithful to the "Queen of Heaven," as well as the practice of sacrificing the firstborn child. Scholarly identification of the "Queen of Heaven" varies, from Ishtar, a Mesopotamian goddess identified with the planet Venus, to Astarte, a Canaanite goddess of fertility and war and beyond (see below on Jeremiah 44; Cohn 2004; Ellis 2009). Likewise, the extent of child sacrifice in ancient Israel remains a matter of scholarly dispute.

Jeremiah 26 begins what scholars generally recognize as the second half of the book, largely repeating the Temple Sermon from 7:15-22. Like in 7:15-22, Jeremiah is commanded to warn the errant Judahites that their ways could lead to the same end that befell Shiloh. The difference is what follows in 26:7-24, which records Jeremiah's run-in with the priests and the prophets and the trial for his life. Accusing Jeremiah of treason, the authorities call for Jeremiah to be put to death. However, a new character is introduced: Ahikam the son of Shaphan, who is later identified as the father of Gedeliah, saves Jeremiah (see 2 Kgs. 22:12, 14).

▌ THE TEXT IN THE INTERPRETIVE TRADITION

The Aramaic Targum of Jeremiah radically changes 7:4, reading, "Do not trust in the words *of the prophets of* falsehood *who say, 'In front of* the Lord's temple *you are worshiping; in front of* the Lord's temple *you are sacrificing; in front of* the Lord's temple *you are paying homage: three times in the year you appear before him'" (Tg. Jer.* 7:4). In accordance with the rabbinic idea that repetition in scriptural texts holds an unlocked meaning, the Targum thus connects the threefold repetition of "YHWH's temple" to the three annual pilgrimages in ancient Israel (see Exod. 23:14; 34:23; Deut. 16:16; see

Hayward 1987, 26). In the Talmud, Jer. 7:4 is understood as a prediction of the destruction of both the First and Second temples (*b. Naz.* 32b). In a discussion that ends with a citation of Jer. 7:24, a midrash notes that Jeremiah was one of three prophets of his time: the other two included Huldah, who prophesied to the women, Zephaniah, who prophesized in the temple, and Jeremiah, who was sent to the city squares (*Pesiq. Rab.* 26:2).

In the New Testament, the phrase "den of robbers" appears in Jesus' words at the temple in Matt. 21:13. Additionally, like the Temple Sermon text, the interpretive tradition warns against placing too much emphasis on structures and buildings rather than on ethics and actions. For example, Jerome notes of the church "we are not to put our faith in the splendor of its buildings" (Wenthe, 65).

■ THE TEXT IN CONTEMPORARY DISCUSSION

For contemporary readers, the Temple Sermon might seem no longer applicable: it represents the problems and wrongdoings of the ancient Israelites, not our own. Yet for the author(s) of these passages, it seems clear that being faithful to God is not enough; people must act justly, shun violence toward their neighbors, and care for the destitute. Buildings and material goods are not important, but behaviors and actions are. Such a message speaks especially to the privileged members of the Western world, where material goods such as large houses or fancy cars are often seen as indicators of prosperity and divine blessing, whereas being poor or underprivileged is often attributed to some "bad" action of the affected individual or group. Thus the Temple Sermon can speak to modern people that focus primarily on their own well-being (spiritually or materially) while ignoring responsibility toward the greater community.

Jeremiah 11:1-17: The Broken Covenant

■ THE TEXT IN ITS ANCIENT CONTEXT

Jeremiah 11:1-17 begins a prose narrative that focuses on how Israel and Judah broke the covenant with YHWH. Jeremiah 11:6-8 invokes the memory of Israel's ancestors in Egypt and God's deliverance, while also proclaiming that they "walked in the stubbornness of an evil will" (11:8). Jeremiah 11:9 returns to the present and calls for the people to turn back (*šûb*) from their ways. The following section specifically lists the "house of Israel," the northern kingdom, as also implicated in the deity's accusations (11:10). The accusation is that both Israel and, in particular, Judah are no longer serving YHWH, but rather are serving many gods (11:13).

In 11:14-17, the focus shifts from YHWH's accusing the Judahites through Jeremiah to YHWH's directly addressing the prophet himself, again commanding that Jeremiah not pray for the people (see 7:16; 14:11; also Exod. 32:30-35). Jeremiah 11:15 personifies Judah as YHWH's beloved, who has done "vile deeds" that cannot be erased with vows or sacrifices (see 6:20; 7:21-22). The speaker appears to change in 11:16, stating "YHWH once called you," referencing a green olive tree (see Hosea 14:7; Ps. 52:10). Jeremiah 11:17 reminds readers that YHWH of hosts "planted" Israel, recalling the language of "to plant" and "to pluck up" in 1:10. The phrase translated into

English as "YHWH of hosts" literally means "YHWH of armies," and conjures the image of God as masculine warrior (11:17). The decision appears final: destruction is coming.

■ THE TEXT IN THE INTERPRETIVE TRADITION

Jeremiah 11:6, which places Jeremiah's prophecies in the towns of Judah and streets of Jerusalem, reflect the midrashic idea that he was assigned to the city squares while Huldah preached to the women and Zephaniah preached at the temple (*Pesiq. Rab.* 26:2).

In his *Homilies on Jeremiah*, Origen argues that "the word that came to Jeremiah" in 11:1 means Christ was with and spoke through Jeremiah, noting the use of the "Word" in John 1:1, and stating, "And I could say that Christ was with Moses, with Jeremiah, with Isaiah, with each of the righteous" (Wenthe, 94).

■ THE TEXT IN CONTEMPORARY DISCUSSION

A clear set of rules governs the world depicted in 11:1-16: good things will come to those who follow the rules of the covenant, while those who disobey the stipulations set forth will be punished. Yet as both ancient and contemporary audiences know all too well, life is rarely so neatly ordered. Good people suffer, innocent people die, and the wicked all too often go unpunished. As such, the Temple Sermon can be less satisfying than other theodicy-oriented protests, such as those found in the book of Job or in the following laments of the prophet and the people in the book of Jeremiah.

Jeremiah 11:18—20:18: Laments and Symbolic Actions

■ THE TEXT IN ITS ANCIENT CONTEXT

The material found in 11:18—20:18 is both bracketed and punctuated throughout by Jeremiah's personal laments (11:18-23; 12:1-6; 15:10-21; 17:14-18; 18:18-23; 20:7-13; 20:14-18), while also containing laments by the people (14:1-10, 19-22) and the deity (12:7-13; 14:17-18; 15:5-9). The language is reminiscent of both the lament Psalms (e.g., Psalm 3; 4; 7; 28; 31) and the book of Lamentations. Dispersed throughout these chapters is also a series of what scholars name "symbolic action reports"; these narratives report "prophetic behavior that is designed to convey a message" (Petersen, 20) and are found throughout the book of Jeremiah (13:1-11; 16:1-4; 19:1-2, 10-11; 25:15-29; 27:1-3, 12; 28:10-11; 32:1-15; 43:8-13; 51:59-64). Although some scholars have attempted to attribute the laments and symbolic actions to the historical Jeremiah, overall the sense unit located in 11:18—20:18 appears to be the result of later reworking, providing both a way to understand the events of 587 BCE and following, and giving later exilic readers a means to mourn their current situation (see Allen, 144–45; Carroll 1986, 277–78).

Even if only as a literary character, within these verses Jeremiah as an individual begins to emerge: he is a lonely, suffering, tormented prophet who faithfully carries out the actions prescribed to him by the deity but also laments his own situation and role in the unfolding events. For example, in 11:18-20 Jeremiah bewails how, as a prophet announcing to his fellow Judahites their wrongdoings, he has been like a "gentle lamb led to the slaughter" and the people "devised schemes" against him; thus, he asks that YHWH punish them. Though the ending of Jeremiah 7 was ambiguous about the fate of the prophet, the short prose narrative in 11:21-23 indicate that the people of Jeremiah's own hometown of Anathoth sought the death penalty against him (see 1:1; 7:12). The oracle is grim: YHWH will punish Anathoth, and the young men will die by the sword and the sons and daughters by famine. The promise of death by sword and famine reveals the realities of warfare: children die and people starve. In both the face and aftermath of the Babylonian invasion, such realities would have been familiar to any survivors (19:9; see 2 Kgs. 6:24-29). Jeremiah 12:1 returns to a second lament by the prophet, in which he "lay[s] charges" against YHWH (from the Hebrew verb *rîb*, meaning "to dispute" or "to conduct a lawsuit"). The idea of bringing charges against the deity invokes biblical courtroom language found elsewhere (see, e.g., Job 21) and emphasizes the question of divine justice. The questions of "Why?" and "How long?" from 12:1, 4, illustrate how Jeremiah's laments continue to escalate: "God becomes the object of Jeremiah's complaint" (Petersen, 111). Overall, Jer. 12:1-4 raises the question of theodicy (see Hab. 1:13; Job 21:7). In this lament, the book departs from the traditional language of the books of Joshua through 2 Kings or the book of Proverbs, with their rigid notion of cause and effect for human suffering, to a demand for a more satisfying answer.

In Jer. 12:5-13, YHWH answers, and like Jeremiah's words, the deity's words are filled with sorrow. However, as commentators often point out, the deity fails to respond to Jeremiah's question of theodicy (Brueggemann, 120). Poignantly, the deity states that he has

> . . . given the beloved of my heart
> into the hands of her enemies. (12:7)

The shepherds, who symbolize Israel and Judah's kings, have destroyed God's vineyard (12:10-11; see Isa. 5:1-7). Personified in 12:11, the land mourns for the deity. In 12:9, it was the wild beasts that "devoured," yet by 12:12 it is "the sword of YHWH" that devours. The passage ends in a short prose section that is likely the addition of a later editor (12:14-17). While the preceding material was mournful in tone, these verses offer a word of hope. Though YHWH "plucks up" Judah (see 1:10), he will later have compassion on the people and restore them to the land. Jeremiah 12:17 threatens that any nation that does not listen will be "uprooted and destroyed," recalling the prelude (1:10). Nevertheless, "there is hope, if [the other nations] learn to swear by YHWH's name" (O'Connor 2001, 500). Here Jeremiah truly is a "prophet to the nations" as foretold in the opening chapters of the book (see Carroll 1986, 292).

Jeremiah 13:1-11 introduces the first symbolic action performed by the prophet: YHWH commands him to buy a linen loincloth, wear it, and then hide it near a rock by the Euphrates (13:1-5). "After many days," YHWH tells Jeremiah to find the loincloth, which is now *šāḥat*—ruined (13:6-7). YHWH then explains the strange action: just as the loincloth is ruined, so too will the deity ruin Judah and Jerusalem, which like the loincloth will be "good for nothing" (13:8-9). As Brueggemann explains, "The proper use of a loincloth is to be worn by a man. It is to be worn, not hidden and buried. Thus Israel's proper use is to cleave to Yahweh, not to be autonomous, stubborn, or committed to other gods" (Brueggemann, 128). The loincloth, which "clings" to the person wearing it (13:11), is now ruined, as is the close relationship between YHWH and Israel.

In Jer. 13:12-14, YHWH dictates that Jeremiah tell the people that "every wine-jar should be filled with wine" (13:12); when the people question this action, Jeremiah is to tell them that YHWH is about to make all the inhabitants of Jerusalem drunk, and will "dash them one against another, parents and children together. . . . I will not pity or spare or have compassion when I destroy them" (13:13-14). The verb translated as "destroy" (*šāḥat*) derives from the same Hebrew root as "ruin" in the loincloth story (13:9). The remainder of Jeremiah 13 is composed of a series of oracles that implore the Judeans to listen and turn away from arrogance (see 13:15, 17), ending with a decree from YHWH that he himself will shame Israel for its iniquities (13:22-27). Jeremiah 13:22 contains some of the most disturbing gendered imagery in the book: Judah's "skirts will be lifted"—an act intended to cause shame and associated with sexual assault—and she will be violated. As O'Connor bluntly states, "God rapes her; Judah is destroyed" (O'Connor 2012a, 54).

Jeremiah 14:1—15:21 contains oracles concerned with drought and war, marked by lament language voiced by the people as they ask YHWH to help them despite knowing that they have acted in the wrong (14:7-9). Their cry for aid is sternly refused in 14:10. YHWH again tells the prophet that he is not to intercede on their behalf (see 7:16; 11:14; 14:11). The repetition of "sword, famine, and pestilence" (see 14:12, 13, 15, 16) describes what awaits the people and their lying prophets, who are promising peace to the people (14:13). The following verses, spoken by YHWH, reiterate the coming sword and famine (14:17-19). Another lament voiced by the people ensues, as they confess their sin and profess their faith in YHWH (14:20-22).

Despite the prominence of hope in the people's laments, Jeremiah 15 indicates the hopelessness of the situation: even if Moses or Samuel, famous for their appeals to YHWH on behalf of the people, stood before him, YHWH would not save those addressed here (15:1). These people are destined for four things: pestilence, sword, famine, and captivity (15:2), which the text connects with four kinds of destroyers, including "swords to kill, dogs to drag away, and the birds of the air and the wild animals of the earth to devour and destroy [*šāḥat*]" (15:3). Jeremiah 15:4 places the responsibility for the forthcoming destruction on Manasseh, who ruled from 698 to 642 BCE and is blamed throughout the book of Kings for Judah's demise (see 2 Kgs. 23:26-27). Yet in the book of Jeremiah, where the people are regularly regarded as bringing about their own fate by their failure to return, the mention of Manasseh seems to clearly indicate a later addition. Jeremiah 15:5-9 includes a lament by the deity himself, followed by another of Jeremiah's laments in 15:10-21. Famously, Jeremiah complains that he was ever born: "Woe is me, my mother, that you ever bore me, a man of strife and contention to the whole land!" (15:10; cf. Job 3:2-12). By stating that he has neither "lent" nor "borrowed," Jeremiah establishes his innocence—and yet the people curse him (see Carroll 1986, 327). Though many English translations of the passage continue in 15:11 with "YHWH said," the Septuagint reads, "So be it YHWH," placing the words in Jeremiah's mouth (see Carroll 1986, 325). Jeremiah 15:15-18 also continues in the lament of an individual to the deity, with Jeremiah stressing his innocence and challenging the deity even more than he did previously (Petersen, 113). Each lament grows in agitation and anguish. YHWH's response is located in 15:19-21, where the repetition of *šûb* ("return") is featured, and once again the response, while assuring, fails to address the specific complaints voiced throughout 15:15-18, yet again drawing another parallel with the response Job receives from the deity in Job 38–41 (see Carroll 1986, 333). Jeremiah is reminded of his prophetic duty (15:20); this is the last time the deity will respond to a lament.

In Jer. 16:1-4, YHWH instructs Jeremiah not to take a wife or to have children—any children born shall "die of deadly diseases," and there will be no one to mourn them or bury them (16:4). Likely, this passage is a symbolic action that works as a literary device rather than a biographical account of the historical Jeremiah's marital status. The passage continues by forbidding a variety of mourning practices (16:5-9), for YHWH promises "to banish from this place, in your days and before your eyes, the voice of mirth and the voices of gladness, the voice of the bridegroom and the voice of the bride" (see 7:34; 25:10; 33:11). Again, the text reiterates that the forthcoming disaster is because of the sins of both Judah's ancestors and the current generation (16:10-13), and though YHWH claims he will not show mercy (16:13), the following verses offer yet another occasion for hope: the saying "As YHWH lives who brought the people of Israel up out of the land of Egypt" shall become "As YHWH lives who brought the people of Israel out of the land of the north and out of all the lands where he had driven them," returning them to their own land (16:15). Jeremiah 16:16-18 turns again to the language of divine judgment and wrath: "carcasses of their detestable idols" have polluted the land, and so Judah will pay double for their iniquity (16:18; see Lev. 11:10-12). The chapter ends with a hymn of praise (16:19-20) and a divine promise that all the nations will know YHWH (16:21; see Jer. 10:5, 8, 14-15; Isa. 2:2; 60:3; Mic. 4:2).

Jeremiah 17 begins with further polemic against those who rely on idols rather than YHWH. Drawing again on drought language, 17:5-8 illustrates that those who trust in idols made by human hands shall "live in parched places in the wilderness" (17:6), while those who rely on YHWH will be like a "tree planted by the water" (17:8). Jeremiah 17:12-13 returns to the idea of YHWH as hope (see 14:8), reminding the reader that YHWH is the "fountain of living waters" (see 2:13). Jeremiah 17:14-18 contains another of Jeremiah's personal laments, beginning, "Heal me, O YHWH, and I shall be healed" (17:14); the passage continues with Jeremiah imploring the deity to shame his persecutors, but to protect Jeremiah himself, even as Jeremiah urges YHWH to "bring on the day of disaster" (17:18). There is no divine response to the lament.

The chapter ends with YHWH instructing Jeremiah to stand in the "People's Gate," and to remind those who pass through to honor the Sabbath; if they do not, YHWH will "kindle a fire" in the gates of Jerusalem, a fire that "cannot be quenched" (17:27). Fire that destroys the city—tied here to a failure to observe the Sabbath—connects the verses found in 15:14 and 17:4 (see Carroll 1986, 367). The text is clear: failure to stay faithful to YHWH brings disaster on the city.

In yet another symbolic action, which draws on the language of "plucking up" and "breaking down" from 1:10, YHWH commands Jeremiah to visit a potter's house, where he witnesses a potter reshaping a new pot out of clay from a previously spoiled attempt (18:1-4). In 18:6, YHWH then compares the potter's action with his own abilities; surely he too can rework the flawed pot that is Israel ("Can I not do with you, O house of Israel, just as this potter has done?"). Should a nation turn from its evil, YHWH can turn from his plan to "pluck up and break down and destroy it" (18:7-8). Similarly, if YHWH is "build[ing] and plant[ing]" a nation but it turns toward evil, he can likewise change his mind (18:9-10). Jeremiah 18:11-12 reports that YHWH implores the people to turn from their ways since he is a "potter shaping evil against you," but the people refuse. In 18:13-17, YHWH laments their ways, ending with his decision to

> . . . show them my back, not my face,
>   in the day of their calamity.

Jeremiah's lament in 18:18-23 finds the prophet bitterly complaining about his enemies and asking YHWH to "deal with them while you are angry" (18:23). YHWH does not respond.

Jeremiah 19 continues the theme of potter, pots, and divine judgment with another symbolic action. YHWH commands Jeremiah to buy a potter's jug and to take the elders of the people and the senior priests to the Potsherd Gate, located in the "valley of the son of Hinnom," also called Topheth, a place associated with the sacrifice of children to Baal and Molech in biblical tradition (see Deut. 18:10; 2 Kgs. 16:3; 21:6; Isa. 20:33; Jer. 7:31). Repeating the warning of a forthcoming disaster (19:1-9), Jeremiah is to break the jug before the people and say, "Thus says YHWH of hosts: So will I break this people and this city, as one breaks a potter's vessel, so that it can never be mended" (19:10-11). The story of the shattered pot is embedded in a longer sermon against the practices associated with Topheth, and as such "it incorporate[s] the kings, people, and houses of Jerusalem" into the condemnation of those religious observances (Carroll 1986, 386). The passage ends with Jeremiah returning to the temple's court and again announcing that the disaster is coming because the people have refused to listen (19:14-15).

Jeremiah 20 includes a short pericope that describes how Pashhur, the "chief officer" at the temple, arrests the prophet and places him in the stocks (20:1-2). Upon his release, Jeremiah says to him, "YHWH has named you not Pashhur but 'Terror-all-around'" (20:3). Pashhur's act will result in all of his family and friends dying in Babylon (20:6). Jeremiah 20:7-18 contains the last of Jeremiah's personal laments, in which he claims to have been tricked by the deity (20:7), noting that no one will listen to him and he is weary of his prophetic role (20:9). Again, he curses the day of his birth (20:14-18). The sense unit ends on a personal note of misery, anguish, and despair. The deity does not respond; Petersen notes that while traditionally lament language is hopeful because it anticipates a response, Jeremiah's laments "make clear that a response—at least the hoped-for response—was not, finally, forthcoming" (Petersen 116).

▌ THE TEXT IN THE INTERPRETIVE TRADITION

Both the Jewish and Christian traditions customarily credit Jeremiah with writing Lamentations because of the prevalence of lament language in the book of Jeremiah. Early Jewish interpreters often depicted the reasons for Jeremiah's laments, including that he was born knowing of Jerusalem's eventual destruction (*Pesiq. Rab.* 26:1/2).

Rembrandt's *Jeremiah Lamenting the Destruction of Jerusalem* captures the anguish of the prophet, while Igor Stravinsky, Ernst Krenek, and Leonard Bernstein (among others) have written modern compositions of the laments, often borrowing from the book of Lamentations. Gerard Manley Hopkins's "Thou Are Indeed Just, Lord" is inspired by the question of theodicy posed in Jeremiah's laments (cf. Jer. 12:1).

◼ The Text in Contemporary Discussion

More than any other texts from the book of Jeremiah, it is Jeremiah's laments and weeping that stand out in contemporary discussion; these are the sections of the text that make the prophet appear both human and relatable. For modern readers who face traumatic situations, Jeremiah's weeping can be a window into recovery once they have moved past the stage of numbness that follows (see O'Connor 2012a, 2012b). Moreover, Jeremiah's laments in particular are a clarion call that reminds readers that it is difficult to be a prophet and to speak truth. Any number of modern-day "prophets" attest to this, from Malcolm X to Martin Luther King Jr., from Simone Weil and Dietrich Bonhoeffer to Oscar Romero. Perhaps most importantly, Jeremiah's laments provide a means by which contemporary people can invoke age-old questions of theodicy, can call God to court and ask for answers, and can voice their experiences of present-day sufferings. Yet the text is also increasingly marked by YHWH's silence and his failure to respond to the prophet's cries. Such divine silence is disturbing, but philosophers and theologians such as Simone Weil and Gustavo Gutiérrez, in their different ways, find in such silence and mystery a means by which the experiences of human suffering and violence can be wrestled with rather than ignored (see Nava 2001).

Jeremiah 21:1—23:40: The Fall of Jerusalem and the Question of Hope

◼ The Text in Its Ancient Context

Jeremiah 21 begins with a prose narrative that professes to take place during the reign of Zedekiah (597–587/586 BCE), one of Josiah's sons and a descendant of David, who was placed on the throne by the Babylonian king Nebuchadrezzar following the initial Babylonian conquest of Jerusalem in 597 BCE. According to the text, Jeremiah repeatedly warned Zedekiah to accept Babylonian rule and not to rebel. In Jeremiah 21, the familiar "word of YHWH" comes to Jeremiah and he is instructed to tell Zedekiah that YHWH has given them into the hands of the Babylonians (21:4-7). Jeremiah 21:8 includes a speech addressed to the people of the land rather than to the monarch, and it follows a covenant formula from the book of Deuteronomy: "I am setting before you the way of life and the way of death" (see similar language in Deut. 15:19, 30). In Jeremiah, ironically, the people are advised to surrender to the Chaldeans (i.e., the Babylonians) rather than fight against them in order to follow "the way of life." Those who do not will "die by the sword, famine, and pestilence" (21:9). To faithfully follow YHWH is to let the Babylonians—YHWH's chosen instrument of punishment—attack and take the city.

The prose narrative ends and once again the book returns to both poetic oracles and smaller prose units throughout Jeremiah 21:11—23:40. This section of text is largely concerned with the fate of the Davidic monarchy. Zedekiah's pleas for divine help are chillingly refused; YHWH himself will fight against the city (21:5). Jeremiah 22:6 recalls 8:22, citing Gilead.

> You are like Gilead to me
> like the summit of Lebanon;

though it ends direly,

> but I swear that I will make you a desert,
> an uninhabited city.

The brief section in 23:1-8 looks forward to the restoration of the monarchy following the Babylonian exile, but overall the poetry and prose in 21:11—23:40 are marked by a critique and distrust of the institutions of Jeremiah's day—the kings (21:11—22:30) and the priests and the prophets (23:9-40).

At the end, the passage turns from a critique of the monarchy to a critique of prophecy. The fulcrum of this section is that Jeremiah is a true prophet; according to Jeremiah, the people tragically listened only to the false prophets. If a new branch of David is to sit on the throne in Jerusalem, then the audience of the book of Jeremiah must accept that Jeremiah's words carry authoritative, divine weight.

▌ THE TEXT IN THE INTERPRETIVE TRADITION

In rabbinic tradition, the association between Gilead and Lebanon in Jer. 22:6 leads the rabbis to claim that YHWH showed Moses the temple (*Mekilta de-Rabbi Ishmael, Amalek* 2:87). Among the early Christian interpreters, Ambrose uses 22:13 to caution against extravagant homes, writing, "The person who builds with justice builds not on earth but in heaven" (Wenthe, 165). Theodoret argued that the "righteous branch" of 23:5 foreshadowed Christ (Wenthe, 166), while Ephrem the Syrian and Origen used Jeremiah's words about false prophets to caution against listening to them (Wenthe, 180).

References to Gilead abound in popular culture; sometimes these are positive and align with the idea of comfort and healing found in Gen. 27:25 and Jer. 8:22, as exemplified by the African American hymn "There Is a Balm in Gilead." At other times, references cast aspersions on Gilead and seem to conform to the more negative images of Gilead and its ruin such as in Jer. 22:6 (see also 46:11). For instance, Margaret Atwood's *The Handmaid's Tale* takes place in a totalitarian nation called the "Republic of Gilead," where the character Moira calls the hymn "There Is a Bomb in Gilead" (Atwood 1998, 218).

▌ THE TEXT IN CONTEMPORARY DISCUSSION

Jeremiah 21–23 focuses on the fall of Jerusalem and the failure of the kings, priests, and prophets during a time of national crisis. Such a text reminds readers that ancient peoples also looked to their leaders during moments of uncertainty; like other prophetic books, this passage places responsibility in the hands of the people themselves (Jer. 21:8). If the people want to save themselves, they must abandon the divine city and accept their fate; if they wish to remain and fight the Babylonians, they will die abandoned by YHWH. The passage is a stark warning that what seems like the right or the easiest course of action is not always the correct course. In the contemporary world, when we often want to blame political leaders for their actions, we also frequently fail to take into account our own inactions. We too are responsible for "choosing life," for taking care of the ecological well-being of the earth, the health and welfare of others, and political crises both near and far.

Jeremiah 24:1—25:38; 27:1—29:32: Prophets, Prophecies, Power, and Politics

◼ THE TEXT IN ITS ANCIENT CONTEXT

Jeremiah 24:1-10; 25:1-38; 27:1-22; 28:1-17; 29:1-32 largely focus on the relationship between prophets, prophecies, politics, and power, particularly the overarching theme that all power ultimately comes from YHWH. These chapters are united in their depiction of Babylon as YHWH's tool for punishing the errant Judahites, of Jeremiah as a true prophet, and a prophet to the nations. While Jeremiah 24 introduces the metaphor of those who remain in Jerusalem as "bad figs," Jeremiah 27 concludes with a reference to what will happen to those "bad figs" that did not go to Babylon as commanded.

Prophets in ancient Israel (and in the context of the larger ancient Near East) are often described as communicating with their god(s) in a variety of ways: through symbolic actions, judgment oracles, woe oracles, lawsuits, laments, and hymns (see Petersen, 28–30). Often, prophets report visions, such as in Isaiah 6 or Ezekiel 1–3. While visions play a prominent role in many prophetic books, the book of Jeremiah contains only a few. In 24:1-10, Jeremiah receives a vision of two baskets of figs: one is full of ripe, good figs, and the other is full of bad figs that could not be eaten. The surprising divine revelation is that the good figs represent the exiles: those who go to Babylon (Jer. 24:4-5; see Ezek. 11:14-15). In biblical writings, figs are associated with security and economic prosperity (see 1 Kgs. 4:25; 2 Kgs. 18:31; Isa. 36:16). Recalling the words of Jer. 1:10, those who go to Babylon will build (*bānâ*) and plant (*nātaʿ*); those who stay in the land will be overthrown (*hāras*) and uprooted (*nātaš*). The text also invokes the covenant formula, "they shall be my people and I will be their God," found in 7:23; 11:4; 30:22; 31:1, 33; 32:38. Additionally, YHWH promises that he will give these exiles a "heart to know me" (24:7; see 31:33-34), while 24:8 explicates that King Zedekiah, his officials, the remnant of Jerusalemites who remain in the land, and the exiles who fled to Egypt are the "bad figs," whom YHWH will "make a horror, an evil thing" to "all the kingdoms of the earth." Such a description starkly contrasts the promise to Abraham in Genesis 12, which is alluded to in Jer. 4:2; rather than becoming a blessing, Israel/Judah will become a "horror." The "bad figs" are destined for "sword, famine, and pestilence," and will be "utterly destroyed" (24:10).

Literarily, the passage is set during the rule of Zedekiah, following the deportation of Jehoiachin to Babylon in 597 BCE (see 2 Kgs. 24:8—25:30; 2 Chron. 36:9-21). The book of Jeremiah portrays Zedekiah and his supporters negatively, if at times ambiguously (see 22:27; 29:17; 2 Kgs. 24:10-17; see Applegate 1998). The passage reflects the three major geographical areas of interest during this tumultuous period: Babylon, where many were exiled beginning in 597; Judea, where a remnant remain; and Egypt, where others had already and would continue to go into exile (see Jeremiah 43). Although some scholars see this as an example of an actual vision Jeremiah had while at the temple (see Bright, 194; Allen, 275–76), others posit that the chapter is a later addition to the book (see Carroll 1986, 482–88). Carroll sees this later addition as a "propaganda" piece for those who returned to Jerusalem after the exile but traced their lineage to the first exiles who left with Jehoiachin in 597 BCE; the image thus supports through a divine revelation the returnees' claim to leadership positions in Jerusalem following their absence from the land (Carroll 1986, 482–88; see Brueggemann, 212). In short, the text clearly identifies with the exiles; those who remained or who fled to Egypt are left without hope.

Jeremiah 25 then goes back in time to the reign of Jehoiakim and the first year of Nebuchadrezzar's reign (25:1). Jeremiah complains to the people of Judah and Jerusalem that he has been speaking to them for twenty-three years, but they fail to listen, and he notes that he is part of a long line of prophets, whom "YHWH persistently sent you," and, like those who came before him, the people did not listen to those prophets either (25:4-7). Accordingly, enemies from the north—including King Nebuchadrezzar of Babylon—will attack, and YHWH will make the people "an object of horror and of hissing, and an everlasting disgrace" (25:8-9). Despite the use of "everlasting," 25:11 specifies the period of the exile as seventy years (25:11). In 25:12, YHWH promises, "after seventy years . . . I will punish the king of Babylon and that nation" (see Jeremiah 50–51). The addition of seventy might be the result of "the actual end of the exile and the return of deportees to the homeland" (Brueggemann, 222).

In another symbolic action report, YHWH commands Jeremiah to take a cup filled with "the wine of wrath," and sends Jeremiah to a list of nations who must drink from it (25:15). The result is madness and the coming sword (25:16). The list of nations is long (25:19-26) and concludes with "the king of Sheshach shall drink." Sheshach is a code word for Babylon, "a cryptographic device whereby letters of the alphabet in reverse order are substituted for letters in the proper order" (Carroll 1986, 500). In English, the letters *a–b–c* would become *z–y–x*; in Hebrew, the root *b–b–l* becomes *s–s–q*. The chapter ends with war imagery: YHWH of hosts is "summoning a sword" (25:29), he will "roar from on high" (25:30), "clamor will resound to the ends of the earth" (25:31), and the dead "shall not be lamented, or gathered, or buried; they shall become dung on the surface of the ground" (25:33). The deity, like a lion, will destroy the land "because of his fierce anger" (25:38).

Jeremiah 27:1 returns to the reign of Zedekiah. The passage is marked by a symbolic action: Jeremiah is to make a yoke of straps and bars and put them on his neck (27:2), and then he is to send word to the kings of a number of nations who have sent envoys to Jerusalem in the hopes of making a treaty against Babylon with Zedekiah (27:3). The yoke, used agriculturally with oxen, represents "political subjection" (Allen, 306). The message is this: YHWH has given Nebuchadrezzar his "servant" all of their lands. Any nation that refuses to "put its neck under the yoke of the king of Babylon" will experience the deity's divine wrath: famine, pestilence, and destruction (27:1-8). Such symbolic actions reiterate that prophets were speaking to their immediate contexts rather than predicting far-off events; even more so, Jeremiah's symbolic wearing of the yoke illustrates the strange behaviors associated with biblical prophets. Jeremiah's message clearly outlines that any earthly political power comes not through the hand of the king but rather through the will and strength of the Israelite deity.

Next, YHWH announces that the people "must not listen to your prophets, your diviners, your dreamers, your soothsayers, or your sorcerers" when they speak against serving Babylon (27:9). The only way to be saved and to keep their own lands is to obey YHWH (27:10-11), and Zedekiah should ignore the Judahite prophets who encourage him to rebel against Babylon; these prophets are "prophesying a lie" and were not sent by YHWH (27:14-15). Jeremiah implores the priests and the people not to listen to the prophets who claim that the stolen vessels from the temple will soon be returned to Judah (27:16). Rather, "serve the king of Babylon and live" (27:17), for a time is approaching when the remaining vessels will also be carried off to Babylon (27:21-22). Yet 27:22 ends on a note of hope: one day YHWH will return these stolen items to the temple.

Jeremiah 28 illustrates the interplay of power, politics, and prophecy in a scene that places Jeremiah into direct contest with another prophet: Hananiah, who challenges Jeremiah in the temple before priests and "all the people" (28:1), claiming that YHWH has told him that he broke the yoke of the king of Babylon, and that within two years the exiled king, people, and stolen property will be returned (28:2-4). The prophetic showdown continues as Jeremiah responds, at first by saying, "May YHWH do so!" (28:6). But he follows this with a reminder of the prophets who preceded them: it is only when the word of a prophet comes true that it can be known that YHWH sent that prophet (28:8-9; see Deut. 18:20). In response, Hananiah takes the yoke from Jeremiah's neck and breaks it (28:10). YHWH responds through Jeremiah by explaining that Hananiah has only succeeded in certifying the oncoming disaster; as a punishment, Hananiah will be dead within a year (28:16). Jeremiah's prophecy is then shown to be true: "In that same year, in the seventh month, the prophet Hananiah died" (28:17).

Next, Jeremiah sends a letter to the priests, prophets, and people in exile in Babylon. Within the letter is the prophetic messenger formula, "Thus says YHWH of hosts" (29:3). The command is surprising: live and prosper in the land of Babylon. The people are commanded to build houses, plant gardens, take wives, have children, and to marry their daughters so they too might "multiply there" (29:5-6). Moreover, they are to pray to YHWH on *behalf* of Babylon, for "in its welfare you will find your welfare" (29:7). The chapter continues to focus on the prophets and their power plays: the prophets among the exiles should not be allowed to deceive them because YHWH did not send them (29:8-9). Jeremiah 29:16-20 is absent from the Septuagint. Those who remained in Judah will suffer YHWH's wrath, and he will make them "like rotten figs that are so bad they cannot be eaten" (29:17). The letter concludes by addressing three specific prophets in Babylon: Ahab son of Kolaiah, Zedekiah son of Maaseiah, and Shemaiah of Nehelam, who will die as a result of their lies (29:21; 29:31-32).

▌ THE TEXT IN THE INTERPRETIVE TRADITION

In a rabbinic tradition, Jer. 24:6 is used in conjunction with Amos 9:15 to claim that once the Israelites are again "planted" in the land, they will not again be plucked up again (*Mek. R. Ish, Shirata* 10:10). A story in the Talmud relates that the prophets Ahab and Zedekiah from Jeremiah 29 were put to death because they asserted that YHWH commanded them to sleep with Nebuchadrezzar's daughter—connected to the captivity of Hananiah, Mishael, and Azariah from the book of Daniel, these two prophets were proven false when they were also thrown into the furnace but did not survive (*b. Sanh.* 93a).

In early Christian interpretation, the "bad figs" became a symbol for the synagogue, while the "good figs" symbolized the church (Wenthe, 181). Jerome emphasized that it is right to "seek the peace of the city or the land" where a person lives based on 29:7; similarly, Augustine urges people to pray for their kings, saying that Jeremiah gave the exiles "the divine command to go obediently . . . counseled them also to pray for Babylonia" (Wenthe, 198–99).

▪ THE TEXT IN CONTEMPORARY DISCUSSION

For contemporary readers, questions of power and politics remain especially pertinent. The vision of the good and bad figs is one of God's merciless judgment, and one in which the deity is depicted as ultimately unforgiving. Such a black-and-white view of human morality can be comforting if we want those who do wrong to be punished, but such a categorical vision of the world is difficult to maintain. Surely not everyone who remained behind in Jerusalem and Judah were "bad figs." After all, as the text claims, many of those who stayed behind did not have the privilege of leaving because they were not among the elite of Jerusalem. Accordingly, this passage challenges contemporary readers to think behind the final form of the text and to examine the motives and contexts of the writers (see Weems, 119). Today the text dares readers to think about how we might address those who are left in frightening situations, in war zones and in occupied territories, or in the aftermath of natural disasters. Do we blame them for "bringing it on themselves," such as certain conservative Christian leaders blamed Hurricane Katrina on American "sinfulness"? If read with the victims and with those left behind, such a dichotomous text encourages readers to recoil from too easily accepting that there is always a "good guy" and a "bad guy" in any given situation, but rather to acknowledge that real life is often far more complicated than such easy oppositions. Moreover, it is a powerful reminder that such simple dichotomies often come at the expense of those who, materially, have the least.

Additionally, these passages with their emphasis on power and politics call on those in power to act conscientiously (see Masenya 2010, 148–49). These passages also call on people—both privileged and marginalized—to attempt to discern "true" prophets from "false" ones; as Weems notes, "Despite appearances, when it comes to prophets and their preaching, it is never easy to tell true ones from false ones—not back then and not now" (Weems, 23). Only history—per Deuteronomy—can tell the difference between a true and a false prophet.

Jeremiah 30–33: The Book of Consolation

▪ THE TEXT IN ITS ANCIENT CONTEXT

Jeremiah 30–31 is frequently called "the Book of Consolation" or "the Little Book of Comfort," though an overarching hopeful theme unifies all of Jeremiah 30–33. Set amid so much lamentation, war imagery, and violence, "readers are simply not prepared for the explosive beauty of the 'little book of consolation'" (O'Connor 2012a, 103). Some scholars argue that this material may have originally been written for the northern kingdom, while others suggest an exilic writer later redacted the chapters (Stulman 2005, 258–59). R. E. Clements calls these chapters "the pivotal center for the entire book" (Clements, 8).

The Book of Consolation opens with YHWH instructing the prophet to "write in a book all the words that I have spoken to you" (Jer. 30:1). Since the unit opens with the divine instructions for Jeremiah to write "in a book/scroll" the words dictated to him, it is possible that parts of Jeremiah 30–31 were once part of an individual "book" (see Holladay 1989, 155–67). In Jeremiah 30–31, the phrase "the days are coming" frames the chapters, reiterating that these passages look to the future rather than the present (30:3; 31:27, 31, 38). The repeated use of the prophetic messenger formula, "Thus says YHWH," delineates the separate oracles (Jer. 30:2, 5, 12, 18; 31:2, 7, 15-16, 23, 35, 37; 32:3, 14-15, 28, 36, 42).

The oracle in Jer. 30:5-11 sets the stage for many of the important themes and metaphors that run throughout the Book of Consolation. The current situation is one of "terror without relief" (30:5); this is a topsy-turvy world where life is so calamitous that men are suffering pain "like a woman in labor" (30:6). Unusual for the book of Jeremiah is a somewhat positive depiction of a woman in labor, for here labor equals new life (Claassens, 122). Invoking both the exodus tradition and the promise of an eternal Davidic king (30:8), the passage ends on a note of hope: though YHWH will punish Israel/Judah (also reiterated in the oracle in 30:12-17), he will not make an end of them (see 30:11). The oracle in 30:18—31:1 focuses on rebuilding Jerusalem, while 30:22 invokes the covenant formula, "And you shall be my people, and I will be your God," indicating a future time when the relationship between YHWH and the people will be repaired. Yet 30:24 is a reminder that this restoration is in the future: "in the *latter days* you will understand this." Jeremiah 31:2-6 and 7-14 likewise invoke the exodus and wilderness traditions; in particular, 31:4 recalls Miriam with her tambourine (see Exod. 15:20-21; Stulman, 269). Jeremiah 30:5-6 may contain clues that this oracle once spoke to the northern kingdom. For example, the divine promise to "bring them [i.e., the survivors or remnant] from the land of the north" (31:8) elicits Jeremiah's initial predictions of an oncoming enemy from the north in Jeremiah 2–6, but may also be left over from Jeremiah's attempts at Josiah's behest to bring to Jerusalem some of the people who survived the Assyrian destruction of the northern kingdom in 721 BCE. In any case, "the text offers hope" to anyone living in exile or uncertainty; thus the audience might have originally been the "Judean exiles residing in Babylon during the sixth century" (Stulman, 258).

The short oracle in Jer. 31:15-22 is perhaps one of the most famous of the book of Jeremiah: Rachel weeps for her exiled children, and the text promises that her children shall be restored. Jeremiah 31:22 ends with gender reversal: a woman who courts a man (see 30:6), stressing the curious idea of YHWH forgiving his faithless wife and restoring her to the land—but also perhaps imagining a "changed order of relationships" in the gendered world of ancient Israel (O'Connor 2012b, 276). Jeremiah 31:23-34 emphasizes that with the return shall also come a new/renewed covenant: "And just as I have watched over them to pluck up and break down, to overthrow, destroy, and bring evil, so I will watch over them to build and to plant, says YHWH" (31:28; see 1:10). The focus, however, is still on the future: YHWH *will* watch over them to build and to plant. In this future period, children will be responsible for their own sins (cf. Ezek. 18:1-32, from which Jeremiah appears to draw, but which places such individual responsibility in Ezekiel's own period). Jeremiah's world remains ambiguous, trauma-filled, and uncertain. Nevertheless, in the future, the covenant will be rewritten into their hearts, from the "least of them to the greatest" (31:34).

Chronology falls apart in Jeremiah 32, which is set just prior to the siege of Jerusalem, when Zedekiah reigns and Jeremiah is imprisoned. Zedekiah approaches Jeremiah and implores him for help, but the prophet remains silent and Zedekiah merely repeats Jeremiah's prophecies about the city's fall to him (32: 3-5). When Jeremiah finally speaks, it is about an entirely different matter and seems to have happened before his imprisonment; the word of YHWH came to him and predicted that his cousin would arrive and ask Jeremiah to purchase a plot of family land (32:7-8). Jeremiah does so and then has Baruch take the deed of purchase and bury it in a jar (32:14). The symbolic action that Jeremiah recounts is one of hope: "houses and fields and vineyards shall again be bought in this land" (32:15). The land Jeremiah purchases becomes symbolic for all of the land of Israel.

Scholars regularly divide Jeremiah 33 into two sections: 33:1-13 and 33:14-26. The first section depicts the coming devastation with utter brutality, but closes by imaging Jerusalem once again filled with "the voice of mirth and the voice of gladness, the voice of the bridegroom and the voice of the bride, the voices of those who sing, as they bring thank offerings to the house of YHWH" (33:11), an about-face of 7:34; 16:9; and 25:10, which promised to bring an end to these things. Jeremiah 33:14-26 is missing from the Septuagint and is likely a late addition to the MT, which focuses on the restoration of the house of David: there remains a future for Israel (a message that would certainly have been good news to the exiles in Babylon). In short, the Greek and Hebrew texts of Jeremiah illustrate how later interpretive communities used (and sometimes added to) the textual tradition to address their own concerns and needs—and the presence of 33:14-26, often dated to as late as the Persian period, attests to the ongoing legacy of Jeremiah and his words.

▌ THE TEXT IN THE INTERPRETIVE TRADITION

The image of Rachel weeping over her children in Jeremiah 31:15 draws on the story from Genesis 35, which records the death of Rachel. There the text reports how she named her last son Ben-oni, "son of my sorrow" (Gen. 35:18). Though Genesis is silent on the precise location of Rachel's burial, the book of Samuel locates her grave in Ramah (see 1 Sam. 10:2). The Jeremiah text appears to combine known traditions and is an excellent example of intertextuality in the Hebrew Bible.

Targum Jeremiah also illustrates interpretive differences. Instead of a "voice heard in Ramah," the *Tg. Jer.* reads "the height of the world": the Hebrew root *rmh* ("height") evokes "the highest heaven where God's throne is" (Hayward, 133 n. 13). Similarly, Rachel is no longer the one weeping; rather, "the house of Israel" weeps. The Targum draws on the idea that Jeremiah was at Ramah with the exiles before they left for Babylon (Jeremiah 40); Israel weeps because Jeremiah did not choose to go with them (Hayward, 131 n. 13).

The New Testament employs the image of a "new covenant" from the Book of Consolation (see Matt. 26:27-28; Mark 23–24; Luke 22:20; 1 Cor. 11:25; 2 Cor. 3:6), while Matt. 2:17-18 cites Jer. 31:15 in one of the fulfillment prophecies; namely, Herod's slaughtering of the children is understood as a fulfillment of the Jeremianic prophecy "foretold" by Rachel's weeping over her own children. Similarly, many early Christian interpreters drew on the image of Rachel weeping. For example, Ephrem the Syrian wrote that the passage was fulfilled in a "historical sense" when the sons of Judah and Benjamin where first sent to Ramah and then exiled to Babylon (see Jer. 40:1) and fulfilled in a "spiritual" sense when Herod slaughtered the innocent children (Wenthe, 208). Jeremiah 31:29-30, along with the "new covenant" in 31:31-32, would also be important for early Christian interpreters, since it claims individual responsibility for wrongdoing rather than inherited guilt from the wrongdoings of an individual's parent. Augustine wrote, "In this new covenant through the blood of the Mediator, the paternal decree having been cancelled, humankind by rebirth begins to be no longer subject to the paternal debts that bind them at birth" (Wenthe, 211). Numerous interpreters also used 31:31 as proof that the New Testament replaced the Old Testament, including Augustine, Irenaeus, John Chrysostom, and Theodoret of Cyrus (Wenthe, 212–13).

Beyond early Jewish and Christian interpretations, the Book of Consolation continues to be used in contemporary interpretations of the book of Jeremiah. For instance, Verdi's *Nabucco* (i.e., Nebuchadrezzar) is an Italian opera that in act 2 draws on Jeremiah 30 (the other three acts use Jeremiah 21; 50). In poetry, William Cowper's "Ephraim Repenting" draws on Jer. 31:18-21. Additionally, the image of Rachel weeping for her children often appears in art, including in a sculpture by Linda Gissen that was commissioned by a Roman Catholic bishop in the diocese of Richmond, Virginia, to teach about and honor those who died in the Nazi Holocaust.

▮ THE TEXT IN CONTEMPORARY DISCUSSION

The image of Rachel weeping for her children continues to speak across the ages, "for all the lost ones are the same to this mother, regardless of their generation" (Brueggemann, 287). The text has been invoked in discussions of the Nazi Holocaust, when examining the prevalence of gun violence in the United States and the frequent related death of young children, to other instances of violence against children, such as the kidnapping of young Nigerian girls in 2014. Rachel refuses to be consoled, and, similarly, contemporary readers can refuse consolation as they fuel both their outrage and social action in the face of senseless violence. The promise of return also offers hope to those who grieve.

In a book that otherwise often presents troubling images of women for contemporary readers, Jeremiah 30–33 provides positive descriptions of women who are "symbols" for the rebuilt life imagined by the text (O'Connor 2012b, 275). Here childbirth equals life (31:8), the voice of the bride will be heard (33:11), and the text depicts a different kind of relationship between men and women (31:22). Similarly, Jeremiah 30–33 delivers an opportunity to imagine God as healer, mother, and justice-seeker, images often associated with women (O'Connor 2012b, 277; see Jer. 30:17; 31:20, 33-34; 33:6). Broadly speaking, Jeremiah 30–33 functions as an integral part of "survival" literature for people clinging to hope in what might seem to be otherwise hopeless situations (see Weems, 123). Set in the middle of the book, it can speak to those people who are *still* suffering and *still* attempting to survive in the face of what may seem like hopeless situations.

34:1—36:32: Two Groups, Two Scrolls

▮ THE TEXT IN ITS ANCIENT CONTEXT

Jeremiah 34 again returns the book to the past; namely, Nebuchadrezzar's siege against Jerusalem and Judah. While Jeremiah predicts Zedekiah's own exile, he also promises that the king will "die in peace," and his death will be accompanied by all of the appropriate funeral rites known to ancient Israel, including spices and laments (34:3-5; see 52:8-11). Jeremiah 34:8-10 reports that Zedekiah made a covenant with the people in Jerusalem and allowed all Hebrew slaves to go free. Historically, this may have been done to help prepare the city for the Babylonian attack, especially in order to provide more people to fight. Many scholars suggest that this may reflect the period when Babylon temporarily stopped their march toward Jerusalem to deal with Egypt (see 37:3-15). However, 34:11 records an abrupt reversal of Zedekiah's proclamation of freedom.

The remainder of the passage outlines the ongoing problem of Israel's unfaithfulness. First, YHWH invokes the exodus tradition and the injunction to set free Hebrew slaves every seventh year (34:12-14). Citing the Judahites "turn[ing] [*šûb*] around" and taking back the slaves after their manumission, YHWH says, "You have not obeyed me by granting a release to your neighbors and friends; I am going to grant a release to you, says YHWH—a release to the sword, to pestilence, and to famine. I will make you a horror to all the kingdoms of the earth" (34:17). The covenant with Abraham is now void; the corpses of the Judahites will become food for animals (34:20). Gone are the promises of the appropriate funeral rites. Instead, YHWH promises to bring the Babylonians back to the city, where they take it and "burn it with fire" (34:22). Words of comfort are absent; the towns of Judah will become "a desolation without inhabitant" (34:22).

While Jeremiah 34 reiterates that Zedekiah and his officials stand in a long line of those disloyal to YHWH, Jeremiah 35 focuses instead on a group that is capable of maintaining righteousness. Again, the time period is set before the exile, although now the text returns to the days of Jehoiakim, sending the reader even further back into the history of Judah; such a temporal shift exemplifies that Judah's wrongdoing long precedes the reign of Zedekiah. Jeremiah is commanded to visit a group called the Rechabites (see Exod. 3:1; 18:1; 2 Kgs. 10:15-28; 1 Chron. 2:55; Neh. 3:14). The Rechabites lived according to a series of strict regulations: drinking no wine, building no houses, neither planting nor owning fields or vineyards, and living in tents (35:6-7). In short, the Jeremiah text depicts the Rechabites as nomadic tent-dwellers. Their unusual presence in Jerusalem is the result of the oncoming Babylonian army (35:11). When Jeremiah takes the Rechabites to the temple and offers them wine, they steadfastly refuse, citing the above-mentioned precepts (35:8-10). As is often noted, the Rechabites become the perfect counterexample to the people of Judah and, especially, to Zedekiah's actions in the preceding chapter. In contrast with Jeremiah 34, Jeremiah 35 ends with a promise of hope rather than devastation: for their faithfulness, the Rechabite descendants will continue to thrive for "all time" (34:19).

Jeremiah 36 returns to the fourth year of King Jehoiakim. Jeremiah is instructed to write YHWH's words on a scroll, summarizing all the words the deity spoke to Jeremiah since the days of Josiah "until today" (36:2), in the hopes that when Judah hears of the forthcoming disasters, they may "turn" (*šûb*) from their evil ways (36:3). Jeremiah dictates these words to Baruch, his scribe, and orders him to go and read the words on a fast day before all the people in the hopes that they might "turn" (*šûb*) (36:5-7). Next, the narrative moves forward into the fifth year of Jehoiakim during a fast, when Baruch reads the scroll in the hearing of Gemariah the secretary; Jeremiah's message is subsequently reported to the officials (36:9-13), who summon Baruch to bring the scroll and read it to them. Upon hearing it, the officials decide to tell the king (36:14-16), but they first instruct Baruch to go into hiding with Jeremiah (36:17-19). Following this, the scroll is read before the king (36:20-21), who, piece by piece, burns the scroll in a fire. The arrogant act appears to symbolize an attempt to nullify Jeremiah's words (for an alternative explanation, see Carroll 1996, 31–42). The king ignores the officials' warnings to heed the words of the scroll and instead orders that Baruch and Jeremiah be arrested; however, YHWH hides them (36:23-26). The final scene returns to another divine message from YHWH, in which the prophet is instructed to write the words again on a second scroll (36:27-28). Jehoiakim's fate is spelled out: his descendants will not sit on the throne, his body will not receive proper burial, and his children, servants, and all the people of Jerusalem and Judah will suffer "all the disasters with which I have threatened them" (36:31-32). The passage blames the king for the oncoming disaster, while the second scroll reiterates the divine origin of the prophecy, which cannot be ignored.

Although some scholars have attempted to find an original, historical book of Jeremiah behind this scene (see Holladay 1989, 253), Carroll suggests that the chapter is a fictional story based on 2 Kgs. 22:8-13 (Carroll 1986, 662–68). While the chapter may not reflect historical reality, it nevertheless contains important symbolic value: the chapter establishes Baruch as an authority, sent by Jeremiah and divinely commissioned to continue Jeremiah's prophetic mission. For Carroll, "Chapter 36 belongs more to Baruch's story than it belongs to Jeremiah's" (1996, 33). Additionally, Jeremiah 36 is an important chapter in the book, because it is one example of how "the book starts reflecting on itself" (Carroll 1996, 33). Scroll after scroll is recorded in the upside-down chronological world of Jeremiah, but the book continues to live long past the disaster the prophet predicted.

▌ THE TEXT IN THE INTERPRETIVE TRADITION

The Mishnah records the existence of the Rechabites during the Second Temple, when a particular day was provided for them to make offerings (*m. Ta'an.* 4:5), while a midrash explains that the covenant made with Jonadab was greater than that made with David; Jonadab's covenant, based on Jer. 35:19, was unconditional, while the covenant made with David was conditional, citing Ps. 132:12 and 89:33 (*Mek. R. Ish., Amalek* 4:131). Often, the Rechabites are held in high regard in rabbinic literature (e.g., *Mek. R. Ish., Amalek* 4:120).

Similarly, early Christian readers also elevated the Rechabites as worthy of emulation, including Jerome: based on a comparison of the Rechabites, who lived outside in tents, to Moses who wandered in the desert, and to the followers of Christ who were first simply fishermen, Jerome claimed that "solitude [is] paradise," while Theodoret of Cyrus praised the Rechabites but also imagined "what sort of people . . . they would have been if they had heard the law of the gospel" (Wenthe, 230–31).

An apocryphal work titled *The Story of Zosimus* or *The History of the Rechabites* includes an expanded version of Jeremiah 35 (see Charlesworth 1985, 443–62).

▌ THE TEXT IN CONTEMPORARY DISCUSSION

Unlike other places in the book of Jeremiah where all of the people are guilty, the story of the Rechabites provides readers with an alternate case. While the Rechabites are not Israelites, and so are in some way the "Other," they are nevertheless lifted up as an example of a faithful group blessed by the deity. The book of Jeremiah overall pays little attention to this group; nevertheless, they can be an example of resistance to cultural norms and imperial policies even as the text depicts them as "Other" and exotic (see Davidson, 189–207).

Additionally, the act of the king burning the scroll because it contains words that he is uncomfortable with is not an unfamiliar action in the modern world. Carroll writes, "In the twentieth-century book burning has become an art form" (1996, 39). From the burning of Jewish books by the Nazis, the banning of certain books in school libraries, to burnings of the Qur'an in the United States, the "art" of book burning continues to be a way that people express their discomfort over what might seem "other," strange, or dangerous to them. Yet what makes us uncomfortable can also teach us, challenge us, and offer us an opportunity for healing.

Jeremiah 37:1—45:5: The Baruch Account

■ THE TEXT IN ITS ANCIENT CONTEXT

In 45:1, the text names Baruch as the narrator of the preceding material, reiterating that Baruch was the scribe who wrote down the messages Jeremiah received from YHWH (36:32); Jer. 37:1—45:5 is often called the "Baruch account" and consists largely of third-person narratives about Jeremiah. O'Connor compares the Book of Consolation with the Baruch account, writing, "Whereas the little book of consolation promise that future life will be radiantly idyllic, the Baruch document focuses on immediate problems of brute survival" (O'Connor 2001, 518). Gone is the time for predictions and dire warnings; the siege and its aftermath unfold.

Jeremiah 37–38 focuses on Jeremiah's imprisonment during the reign of Zedekiah, once again radically shifting the chronological timeline. Again the book returns to the brief lull in the Babylonian invasion of Jerusalem as they dealt with the approaching Egyptian army (32:1, 3). Zedekiah implores Jeremiah to pray for him and the people (37:3). However, the deity's response is dire; Jeremiah is to tell the king that the Babylonians will return—and even their wounded men alone could destroy the city (37:10). Jeremiah 37:11-16 describes Jeremiah's arrest—charged with attempting to desert to the Babylonians—and imprisonment in the house of the secretary Jonathan, where he is placed in a cistern, likely a former repository for water storage. In 37:17-21, Jeremiah is brought before Zedekiah, who asks if there has been any reply from YHWH; Jeremiah answers in the affirmative, "You shall be handed over to the king of Babylon" (37:17). Zedekiah moves Jeremiah to the "court of the guard," which would have been located in Zedekiah's own house (37:21). In a haunting reminder of the realities of war, the text reports "a loaf of bread was given him daily from the bakers' street, until all the bread of the city was gone" (37:21).

Jeremiah 38 gives a slightly different version of this same story. As in the previous chapter, Jeremiah preaches that the city will fall at the hands of the Babylonians (38:2-3). Here the officials complain to the king that Jeremiah is "discouraging" both the soldiers and the people left in the city (38:4; see 21:8-10; 32:3-5; 34:2-5). Zedekiah allows Jeremiah to be imprisoned, but in this version of the story he is thrown into a cistern in "the court of the guard" (38:6). Lowered into the cistern by ropes, Jeremiah sinks into the mud (38:6), which may indicate a period close to 587/586 BCE and the ultimate destruction of Jerusalem when the cistern waters were beginning to dry up. Jeremiah

38:7-13 tells the story of Jeremiah's rescue from the cistern by a man named Ebed-melech, meaning "servant of the king," who is identified as a Cushite (often translated as Ethiopian) and a eunuch in the king's house. Notably, it is not Jeremiah's native supporters who rescue him, but rather a stranger and an Egyptian. In 38:14-28, the king again asks the prophet for divine support for his revolt, but Jeremiah declines to give him any reassurance, only repeating that surrender is the only way to ensure survival (see 20:1-16; 21:4-10; 27:1-11). Zedekiah fears for his life if he surrenders to the Babylonians, but Jeremiah assures him that he and his house will survive (38:20). However, if he continues to rebel, Jerusalem will burn, and Jeremiah reports a vision in which the women remaining in Zedekiah's house taunt him as they are led out, recalling Jeremiah's own previous imprisonment in the muddy cistern,

> Your trusted friends have seduced you
>   and have overcome you;
> Now that your feet are stuck in the mud,
>   they desert you. (38:22)

Zedekiah swears Jeremiah to secrecy about their conversation and moves Jeremiah from the cistern to house arrest (37:28).

Jeremiah 39 reiterates that Jeremiah's prophecies have been true all along. Zedekiah flees, but is captured by the Babylonians in the plains of Jericho, and brought before Nebuchadrezzar (39:3-6; see Jeremiah 52; 2 Kgs. 25). The results are gruesome: Zedekiah's sons are slaughtered "before his eyes," along with the nobles of Judah, and Nebuchadrezzar then "put out the eyes of Zedekiah" (a common practice in ancient Near Eastern warfare; see Judg. 16:21; 2 Kgs. 24:18—25:7), binding him in chains and taking him to Babylon (39:6-7). The king's house, the houses of the city, and the walls of Jerusalem are destroyed, and the "rest of the people" of the city are exiled to Babylon (39:8-9), although "some of the poor people who owned nothing" are left behind and given vineyards and fields to work (39:10). The Babylonian king then commands that Jeremiah be looked after but not harmed, and he is given to Gedaliah, one of Jeremiah's allies (39:11-14; see 26:24). The chapter closes with "the word of YHWH" that comes to Jeremiah: Ebed-melech will not be harmed because he trusted in YHWH, though Jerusalem is doomed (38:15-18).

The next two chapters describe life in Judah following the Babylonian invasion, when Gedaliah, a descendant of the Shaphan family who seems to have supported the Babylonians and warned against rebelling, functions as a Babylonian appointed governor (40:7). Jeremiah 40:1 places the prophet in Ramah, where he is offered release by the captain of the guard and the chance to accompany the captives being exiled to Babylon. However, Jeremiah is also given the opportunity to return to Gedaliah and to stay with the people, or to "go wherever you think it right to go" (40:5). Surprisingly, Jeremiah returns to Gedaliah rather than accompanying the exiles to Babylon (40:6). Mizpah, which means "watchtower" or "lookout" in Hebrew, is established as the capital following the destruction of Jerusalem (2 Kgs. 25:24-25). When the surviving remnants of Judah come to Gedaliah at Mizpah, he instructs them to serve the Babylonian king and to gather food (40:7-12).

The following material reports the assassination of Gedaliah at the hands of Ishmael son of Nethaniah (40:14-15; 41:1-3). The day following Gedaliah's assassination, a group of eighty men from Shechem, Shiloh, and Samaria arrive in traditional mourning attire to make offerings: their beards shaved, clothes torn, and bodies gashed (41:5). Ishmael meets them as they enter Mizpah and slaughters all but ten, throwing them into a cistern (41:6-7, 9) and taking the remaining people before setting out to the Ammonites (41:10; on the strange story of Ishmael, see Carroll 1986, 710–12). Upon hearing of this, Johanan son of Kareah, who had initially warned Gedaliah of the assassination plan, follows after Ishmael and his captives, meeting them at the pool of Gibeon (40:12). The captives with Ishmael join Johanan's forces (41:13-14), while Ishmael escapes to the Ammonites (41:15). The chapter ends by reporting that Johanan, the leaders of the forces, and the remaining people, including soldiers, women, children, and eunuchs, set out with the intention of fleeing to Egypt, fearing the Babylonians on account of Gedaliah's assassination (41:16-18).

Jeremiah 42:1 begins with Johanan and all of the remaining people approaching Jeremiah to ask for divine instruction (42:1-3). Jeremiah agrees to intercede with the deity on their behalf, and they agree to do as YHWH commands them (42:4-6). Ten days later, YHWH answers: remain in the land and YHWH will "plant you, and not pluck you up; for I am sorry for the disaster that I have brought upon you" (42:10; see 1:10). However, if the people are determined to go to Egypt, then "there you shall die" (42:16). There will be no remnant or survivors (42:17). Jeremiah 42 reports that the various leaders, including Johanan, accuse Jeremiah of lying and Baruch of inciting Jeremiah against them (43:2-3). As a result, the people go to Egypt, settling at Tahpanhes (43:4-7). Jeremiah and Baruch go with them to Egypt (43:6), where the word of YHWH again comes to the prophet, instructing him to perform yet another symbolic action (42:8-13). Jeremiah is to take large stones, bury them in the clay pavement before the Pharaoh's house in Tahpanhes and in the presence of the Judeans, and say to them, "Thus says YHWH of hosts, the God of Israel: I am going to send and take my servant King Nebuchadrezzar of Babylon, and he will set his throne above these stones that I have buried, and he will spread his royal canopy over them" (43:10). What will follow is, predictably, disaster: Nebuchadrezzar will ravage Egypt and destroy their gods; and pestilence, captivity, and the sword will come to all who are destined for them (42:11-13).

YHWH next reminds the exiles that they have seen the "disaster that I have brought on Jerusalem and the towns of Judah," especially because they made offerings to other deities (44:2-3). Moreover, the deity repeats that he continually sent prophets to warn them but that the people "did not listen or incline their ear" (44:5). Then YHWH accuses the people of continuing to make offerings to other gods while in Egypt (44:8), blaming their ancestors and their wives, their own crimes, but especially the offenses "of your wives, which they committed in the land of Judah and in the streets of Jerusalem" (44:9). The people reply in 44:15-19, stating that they will continue to make "offerings to the Queen of Heaven," claiming that when they did so in the past they prospered, but when they stopped, their lives took a turn for the worse (44:18). Jeremiah 44:20-30 reiterates the fate of these people: they shall all perish by sword and by famine, and Egypt will fall to its enemies just as Judah fell to Babylon.

The final section explains that when the words of YHWH came to Jeremiah, Baruch wrote the words in a scroll (45:1). The passage returns the story to the fourth year of Jehoiakim's reign, addressing YHWH's words to Baruch, and recalling Jer. 1:10 once again: "breaking down" what was built and "plucking up" of what was planted will happen (45:4). While Baruch's future is bleak, he will survive: a "prize of war" in the oncoming disaster (45:5).

▌ THE TEXT IN THE INTERPRETIVE TRADITION

While Baruch is mentioned only a few times in the book of Jeremiah, he lives on in both the Jewish and Christian interpretive traditions. A talmudic passage notes that both Jeremiah and Baruch were descendants of Rahab, a prostitute (*b. Meg.* 14b; see *Pesiq. Rab Kah.* 13:5). Another rabbinic discussion revolves around whether Baruch is also a prophet; one story recounts how Baruch complained that he was not, but was reminded by YHWH that after the exile there was no longer a need for prophecy because "there is no flock, what need is there of a shepherd?" (*Mek. R. Ish, Pisha* 1:148–66). Baruch is counted among the prophets in the Talmud (see *b. Meg.* 14b–15a).

In Christian tradition, Baruch is attributed with writing the deuterocanonical work Baruch, as well as the Syriac *Apocalypse of Baruch*, the Greek *Apocalypse of Baruch*, and a work referred to as *The Rest of the Words of Baruch* (*4 Baruch*). In the Eastern Orthodox Church, Baruch is considered a saint, and both Peter Paul Rubens and Henry Miller Block depicted the image of Jeremiah dictating to Baruch in paintings. Dietrich Bonhoeffer, when imprisoned by the Nazis after speaking out against the injustices he witnessed, wrote to a friend and fellow prisoner, "we shall have to repeat Jer. 45.5 to ourselves every day" (Bonhoeffer 1997, 279).

One notable component of Jeremiah 44 is the vilification of the Israelite's worship of the "Queen of Heaven." Despite the book's negative imagery, the text here (and in Jer. 7:18) may give contemporary readers a glimpse into what might have been the realities of ancient Israelite religion before it became more masculinized in the writings of later editors and redactors; in other words, it is possible that ancient Israelite women (and men) worshiped a female deity called the Queen of Heaven (see Jeremiah 44). As O'Connor notes, the women who worshiped the Queen of Heaven are "resourceful, independent women" who "become religious agents, taking worship into their own hands, as are many women today" (O'Connor 2012b, 273). In the contemporary world, such texts can encourage women to take up leadership roles within their own religious and nonreligious communities and can offer a counter-reading to the otherwise problematic gendered language of Jeremiah. Kathleen Norris's poem "Cakes for the Queen of Heaven" invokes Jeremiah 44 and reflects on gender relations in the book of Jeremiah and beyond.

▌ THE TEXT IN CONTEMPORARY DISCUSSION

On the one hand, the narrative in the Baruch account attests to the possibility of human choice; though Zedekiah repeatedly asks for Jeremiah's advice, he also repeatedly misses opportunities to "turn" from his ways and reform. Similarly, those who end up in exile in Egypt also miss their opportunity to listen to the divine command and do as they have been told. Yet the narrative also includes the story of Ebed-melech, which exemplifies both how one individual can save another's life and illustrates that it is possible to take an alternate position from the status quo. In more contemporary examples, it is possible to lift up the figures of Dietrich Bonhoeffer or Martin Luther King Jr. as those who were willing to call for reform and to exemplify such reform in their own lives.

On the other hand, it is important for contemporary readers to remember that exile is not always a matter of choice—and the results of resistance can be brutal.

The murder of Gedaliah offers a different problem for modern readers, where the question of theodicy resurfaces, and again God is entirely silent. Though Gedaliah remained in the land, a "good fig," he did not live; rather, he was brutally murdered. The deity is absent from these events, and the divine silence is troubling. Yet this silence is also "essential"; it allows the voices of the victims "to be heard" (Stulman, 328) rather than subsumed under divine explanation. In the face of unspeakable tragedy, perhaps divine silence is more appropriate and more akin to human experience.

Jeremiah 46:1—51:64: Oracles against the Nations

▌ THE TEXT IN ITS ANCIENT CONTEXT

Jeremiah 46–51 consists of a series of "oracles against the nations" (OAN), a scholarly designation for a genre of literature commonly found in the prophetic material. Literarily, the oracles often begin by denouncing the enemy nations and then move on to a condemnation of Israel itself (see the book of Amos). Remarkably, despite the fact that Jeremiah was designated as a "prophet to the nations" in 1:10, there are only six chapters devoted to the OAN, while much longer sections consisting of prophecies concerning foreign nations are found in Isaiah 13–23 and Ezekiel 25–32 (see Petersen, 110). Outside of the Major Prophets, Obadiah and Nahum consist almost entirely of OAN.

The placement and order of the OAN in Jeremiah are different in the Septuagint and the Hebrew MT, the latter of which is found in contemporary English-language Bibles. In the Septuagint, the OAN begin in Jer. 25:14 (49:34 in the MT) and continue through Jeremiah 32. In the Septuagint ordering, the OAN follow the divine claim that the exile will last for seventy years, after which the deity will punish the nation from the north that he has first sent on Judah (Jer. 25:11-13). The Septuagint begins with Elam and concludes with Moab. The Hebrew MT, however, begins with Egypt and ends with Babylon.

Jeremiah 50–51 of the MT, written in both poetry and prose, is largely devoted to the fate of Babylon. For most of Jeremiah, the Babylonian invasion is depicted as appropriate; it is the will of YHWH and a just sentence for the people's inability to stay faithful to their God. However, in these passages, Babylon is depicted negatively: "Babylon must fall for the slain of Israel" (51:49). While some of the material may stem from the prophet himself, scholars suggests that because of the mix of poetry and prose, the blend of military (Jeremiah 50) and hymnic (Jeremiah 51) material, and the abrupt about-face concerning the role and fate of Babylon, the final two chapters are likely a collection of oracles from exilic and/or postexilic writers who are hoping for a return to the land (see Petersen, 127–28; also Isaiah 5–12; 13–14; 36–37; Jer. 15:17-18).

The OAN are united by a number of literary themes and metaphors. Perhaps most predominately, these oracles feature significant warfare imagery: Egypt's defeat is linked to the "Day of YHWH," when the deity would intervene in history to ultimately destroy Israel's enemies (e.g., Joel 2; Amos 5). Moreover, these texts frequently invoke "YHWH of hosts"—or, more literally,

"YHWH of armies" (Jer. 46:10, 18, 25; 48:1, 15; 49:5, 7, 26, 35; 50:18, 25, 31, 33, 34; 51:5, 14, 19, 33, 57, 58). The Hebrew *ḥereb* ("sword") appears repeatedly, accompanied by terrifying imagery and usually wielded by the deity. For example,

> A sword against the Chaldeans, says YHWH,
>   and against the inhabitants of Babylon,
>   and against her officials and her sages!
> A sword against the diviners,
>   so that they may become fools!
> A sword against her warriors,
>   so that they may be destroyed!
> A sword against her horses and against her chariots,
>   and against all the foreign troops in her midst,
>   so that they may become women!
> A sword against all her treasures,
>   that they may be plundered! (Jer. 50:35-37; see also 46:10; 49:37)

Frequently, the text depicts the warriors of the foreign nations mockingly—as beaten and fleeing (46:5), as compared to women (48:41; 49:22; 51:30), and as captured (51:56). The deities of the other nations are also discredited: YHWH defeats the Egyptian bull god Apis (46:15); Chemosh, the god of Moab, will be exiled and his people ashamed of him (48:7, 13); the Babylonian gods Bel and Marduk are "shamed" and "dismayed" (50:2), while 51:44 recounts how YHWH will

> . . . punish Bel in Babylon,
>   and make him disgorge what he has swallowed.
> The nations shall no longer stream to him;
>   the wall of Babylon has fallen,

reversing the image of 55:34 (Carroll 1986, 848).

The section concludes with a final symbolic action report in Jer. 51:59-64. According to this short narrative, Baruch's brother Seraiah (Jer. 32:12) accompanied Zedekiah to Babylon, and Jeremiah sent a scroll with him that included "all the disasters that would come on Babylon" (51:60). Jeremiah commanded Seraiah to read the scroll in Babylon, and then to tie a stone to it and throw it into the Euphrates River, saying, "Thus shall Babylon sink, to rise no more, because of the disasters that I am bringing on her" (51:64). The sense unit ends with the words "Thus far are the words of Jeremiah," a conclusion that leads many to suggest that Jeremiah 52 is a later addition.

Despite the terrifying war imagery and violence depicted in the OAN, there remains an element of hope that runs throughout the OAN—not just for Israel but also for the very nations that the oracles are prophesying against (see 46:26; 48:47; 49:6; 49:11; 49:39). With the exception of Babylon, each nation is promised a restoration (see 46:26; 48:47; 49:6; 49:11; 48:39). Babylon, however, will fall: ironically, it will fall to an "enemy from the north," recalling especially Jeremiah 1–4, where the "enemy from the north" approached, threatening Israel (also see 50:3, 9, 41; 51:48). The fact that Babylon will fall at the hand of an "enemy from the north" reinforces the cosmic and mythological nature of the threat throughout the book; it was always bigger and more terrifying than even the mighty Babylonian Empire. The people are urged to flee Babylon and to return home (51:46, 50). In the future when Israel is restored to the land, the "iniquity of Israel shall be sought, and there shall be none; and the sins of Judah, and none shall be found; for I will pardon the remnant that I have spared" (Jer. 50:20).

▌ THE TEXT IN THE INTERPRETIVE TRADITION

In contemporary Judaism, Jer. 46:13-28 is the *haftorah* (the reading from the Prophets) for the *parashah* (the reading from the Torah) of Exod. 10:1—13:16, and "counterposes the theme of Israelite servitude in Egypt in the *parashah* with a promise of Egypt's eventual destruction (Jer. 46:14-24)" (Fishbane 2002, 97).

In the Christian tradition, Jerome calls on believers to listen to Jeremiah's command to flee from Babylon in 51:6, connecting this passage with Rev. 18:2, to illustrate the seductive allure of "Babylon" while reminding his readers that nevertheless, "heathenism has been trodden down, the name of Christ daily exalted higher and higher" (Wenthe, 269).

In contemporary poetry, verses from Jeremiah 51 inspired both Edna St. Vincent Millay's "Make Bright the Arrows," and Thomas Hardy's "In Time of 'The Breaking of Nations.'" Jeremiah 51:7 is depicted in Simeon Solomon's 1859 drawing *Babylon Hath Been Given a Golden Cup*.

▌ THE TEXT IN CONTEMPORARY DISCUSSION

The vivid descriptions of violence, disturbing images of divine retribution, and bloody images of God as divine warrior in the OAN are difficult texts and not usually what one associates with "sacred" Scripture. YHWH is both vengeful and a god who flippantly uses and discards nations for his own purpose. At first, Babylon is YHWH's instrument in punishing Israel, but later God decides to take retributive actions against Babylon for performing the very actions that the text of Jeremiah claims God impelled Babylon to do. On the one hand, it is easy to dismiss these chapters as examples of the "unsophisticated" thought of ancient Israel, a time and a place far removed from our own. On the other hand—difficult though it may be—the OAN also provide an opportunity for contemporary readers to wonder about our own internal depictions of the deity: Do we imagine that God hates those whom we ourselves hate, those who seem "other" and foreign? Do we picture our God as loving and kind to us, but as a warrior to those who stand in our way? Moreover, in what ways do the realities of war depicted in the OAN continue to the present—including and especially against women and the marginalized (see Jeremiah 46)?

If contemporary readers of the OAN can move beyond the disturbing language, there are elements that may continue to be useful rather than simply disturbing. For example, with Stulman, if these texts emerged out of the "*world of worship and not warfare*, their weapons are rhetoric and imagination"—and therefore can be of use for people "who find themselves on the margins of society without power, temple, land, or hope," where "the only power they wield is the power of theater, which reimagines and reframes social reality" (Stulman, 384–85). Again, the book of Jeremiah gives voice to those who have suffered and may find themselves afraid to speak. Additionally, the occasional moments of hope and restoration for the enemy nations throughout the book of Jeremiah indicate that God can forgive. Examples such as Jer. 49:11 serve as stark textual prompts amid difficult language that God cares for the orphans and widows, even of his enemies.

Such a divine example can impel modern readers to move toward forgiveness—or at least, some form of reconciliation—for their own enemies after the appropriate healing has occurred. Perhaps this is the point of the vengeful, violence-filled OAN (or the imprecatory psalms, such as Psalm 137): there are "psychological benefits" to venting, honestly expressing feelings of rage and hurt (see Strawn 2013, 412). Such violence—especially when it is written and not acted out physically—becomes the space for recovery from trauma and disaster, returns agency and voice to survivors, the colonized, and the marginalized (see Strawn; O'Connor 2012a, 2012b; Weems).

Jeremiah 52:1-34: Historical Appendix

■ The Text in Its Ancient Context

As noted throughout, the book of Jeremiah renders both its characters and its timeline ambiguous at various points. The present form of the book now contains what scholars often deem a "historical appendix" (Jeremiah 52). In short, this chapter reiterates the story of Zedekiah's reign, the fall of Jerusalem, the series of deportations, and the release of Jehoiachin (Jer. 52:31-34; see 2 Kgs. 25:27-30). As is often observed, the chapter is a nearly word-for-word repetition of 2 Kgs. 24:18—25:21, 27-30, while 52:4-16 occurs in Jer. 39:1-2, 4-10. Overall, the addition of Jeremiah 52 appears to serve as proof that Jeremiah's prophecies were fulfilled (similarly, see Isaiah 36–39).

Jeremiah 52:4-6 indicates that the Babylonian siege lasted two years, ending only in the eleventh year of King Nebuchadrezzar (587/586 BCE). The enduring siege resulted in famine (52:6), and the text repeats the story of Zedekiah's flight and capture. Jeremiah 52:13 reports the devastating reality of the loss of the temple. In 52:15, the text records that some of the poorest people, along with others left in the city, are deported to Babylon; this is in contrast with the earlier deportation in 597 BCE, which largely included only the elite of the city. However, 52:16 also notes that some of the poorest people remained, "to be vinedressers and tillers of the soil." The remaining people will be a source of conflict in the Persian period of return (see Ezra-Nehemiah). The chapter continues with a lengthy list of all that was removed from the temple (52:17-23), a regular practice of conquering armies in the ancient world. Jeremiah 52:24 includes that "the chief priest Seraiah" was also deported (see 1 Chron. 5:40; Ezra 7:1).

The book concludes with the release of Jehoiachin from his Babylonian imprisonment, though he must remain in Babylon. The addition may have been a later editorial attempt to end Jeremiah in an encouraging way: a descendant of the Davidic line still lives and may yet return. Yet, as is fitting for Jeremiah, it is also ambiguous and open-ended: the former king is not returned to his land.

■ The Text in the Interpretive Tradition

One of the issues resulting from Jeremiah 52 in Jewish tradition is that the dates do not correspond with those provided in the book of Kings. One talmudic passage explains the two different biblical dates listed for when Nebzaradan entered the temple (the 7th of Av in 2 Kgs. 25:8-9, but the 10th of Av in Jer. 52:12), by noting that the enemy entered the temple on the 7th of Av, vandalized it on that day and the 8th, kindled a fire in it on the 9th, but the major damage was done on the 10th of Av; nevertheless, the priority goes to when the catastrophes begin (*b. Ta'an.* 29a).

In Christian tradition, Chrysostom used Jer. 52:14-16 and the fact that only a small number of people remained in Jerusalem and Judah to argue, in a homily on Romans, that God saves people through "much kindness" and "faith"—but not because of their "own resources" (Wenthe, 271).

◼ THE TEXT IN CONTEMPORARY DISCUSSION

Jeremiah ends with the fall of Jerusalem and Judah in 587 BCE, returning to the tragedy about which the prophet so drastically forewarned his contemporaries. For the readers of the final form of the book, this ending is not a surprise—the destruction of Jerusalem had already been foretold, told, and retold throughout the book. Furthermore, the original audience may have been those who survived the disaster itself. While the ending might be read as one that offers hope—a Judahite king is still alive, being treated with some kindness in Babylonian captivity, and thus hope for return and a new Davidic king is not entirely lost—the reappearance of the central tragedy of the book reminds readers of how the book of Jeremiah might function, as many scholars have suggested, as "survival" or "trauma" literature. The polyvocal text—with its jumble of poetry and prose, its displaced chronology, its violence and its hope, the speech *and* the silence of its characters—is ultimately a work that gives voice to readers' human experiences, both comforting and catastrophic. The book allows readers to imagine themselves in different places: as invaders and as exiles, as Babylon and as Jerusalem, as the powerful and the marginalized, as male and female, as divine and as human, and, perhaps most importantly, as a prophet who can give voice to the sometimes harsh reality of human experience and the catharsis of lament, as well as to the knowledge of divine presence *and* divine silence.

Works Cited

Allen, Leslie C. 2008. *Jeremiah: A Commentary*. OTL. Louisville: Westminster John Knox.

Applegate, John. 1998. "The Fate of Zedekiah: Redactional Debate in the Book of Jeremiah." *VT* 48, no. 3:301–8.

Atwood, Margaret. 1998. *The Handmaid's Tale*. New York: Anchor Books.

Bauer-Levesque, Angela. 1999. *Gender in the Book of Jeremiah: A Feminist-Literary Reading*. New York: Lang.

Bonhoeffer, Dietrich. 1997. *Letters and Papers from Prison*. Edited by Eberhard Bethge. Rev. ed. New York: Simon & Schuster.

Braude, William G. 1978. *Pešikta dĕ-RaḇKahaňa: R. Kahana's Compilation of Discourses for Sabbaths and Festal Days*. Philadelphia: Jewish Publ. Society of America.

———. 1968. *Pesikta Rabbati: Discourses for Feasts, Fasts, and Special Sabbaths*. New Haven: Yale University Press.

Bright, John. 1986. *Jeremiah: A New Translation with Introduction and Commentary*. AB. New York: Doubleday.

Brueggemann, Walter. 1998. *A Commentary on Jeremiah: Exile and Homecoming*. Grand Rapids: Eerdmans.

Carroll, Robert P. 1986. *Jeremiah: A Commentary*. OTL. Philadelphia: Westminster Press.

———. 1996. "Manuscripts Don't Burn: Inscribing the Prophetic Tradition; Reflections on Jeremiah 36." In *Dort ziehen Schiffe dahin*, edited by M. Augustin et al., 31–42. Frankfurt am Main: Peter Lang.

———. 2008. "Century's End: Jeremiah Studies at the Beginning of the Third Millennium." In *Recent Research on the Major Prophets*, edited by A. Hauser et al., 217–31. Sheffield: Sheffield Phoenix.

Charlesworth, James H. 1985. *Expansions of the "Old Testament" and Legends, Wisdom and Philosophical Literature, Prayers, Psalms, and Odes, Fragments of Lost Judeo-Hellenistic Works.* New York: Doubleday.

Claassens, L. Julianna. 2013. "'Like a Woman in Labor': Gender, Postcolonial, Queer and Trauma Perspectives on the Book of Jeremiah." In *Prophecy and Power: Jeremiah in Feminist and Postcolonial Perspective*, edited by C. Maier and Carolyn J. Sharp, 117–32. London: Bloomsbury.

Clements, R. E. 1988. *Jeremiah*. IBC. Atlanta: John Knox Press.

Cohn, Herbert. 2004. "Is the 'Queen of Heaven' in Jeremiah the Goddess Anat?" *JBQ* 32, no. 1:55–57.

Davidson, Steel. 2013. "'Exoticizing the Otter': The Curious Case of the Rechabites in Jeremiah 35." In *Prophecy and Power: Jeremiah in Feminist and Postcolonial Perspective*, edited by C. Maier and Carolyn J. Sharp, 117–32. London: Bloomsbury.

Ellis, Teresa Ann. 2009. "Jeremiah 44: What If 'The Queen of Heaven' Is YHWH?" *JSOT* 33, no. 4:465–88.

Epstein, Isidore. 1961. The Babylonian Talmud. London: Soncino Press.

Fishbane, Michael A. 2002. *Haftarot: The Traditional Hebrew Text with the New JPS Translation*. Philadelphia: Jewish Publication Society.

Freedman, H., and Maurice Simon. 1983. *Midrash Rabbah*. London: Soncino Press.

Friedman, Richard Elliott, and Shawna Dolansky. 2011. *The Bible Now*. New York: Oxford University Press.

Hayward, Robert. 1987. *The Targum of Jeremiah: Translated, with a Critical Introduction, Apparatus, and Notes.* Wilmington, DE: Michael Glazier.

King, Martin Luther, Clayborne Carson, Ralph E. Luker, and Penny A. Russel. 1992. *The Papers of Martin Luther King, Jr. January 1929–June 1951 Volume 1.* Berkeley: University of California Press.

Holladay, William Lee. 1986. *Jeremiah 1: A Commentary on the Book of the Prophet Jeremiah, Chapters 1–25.* Hermeneia. Philadelphia: Fortress Press.

———. 1989. *Jeremiah 2: A Commentary on the Book of the Prophet Jeremiah, Chapters 26–52.* Hermeneia. Minneapolis: Fortress Press.

Lauterbach, Jacob Zallel. 1976. *Mekhilta de-Rabbi Ishmael.* Philadelphia: Jewish Publication Society of America.

Masenya, Madipoane. 2010. "Jeremiah." In *Africa Bible Commentary*, edited by Tokunboh Adeyemo et al., 147–56. 2nd ed. Nairobi, Kenya: WorldAlive; Grand Rapids: Zondervan.

Nava, Alexander. 2001. *The Mystical and Prophetic Thought of Simone Weil and Gustavo Gutiérrez: Reflections on the Mystery and Hiddenness of God.* Albany: State University of New York Press.

Norris, Kathleen. 1989. "Cakes for the Queen of Heaven: A Poem in Praise of Darkness." *Journal of Feminist Studies in Religion* 5, no. 2:79–82.

O'Connor, Kathleen M. 2001. "Jeremiah." In *The Oxford Bible Commentary*, edited by John Barton and John Muddiman, 487–527. Oxford: Oxford University Press.

———. 2012a. *Jeremiah: Pain and Promise.* Minneapolis: Fortress Press.

———. 2012b. "Jeremiah." In *Women's Bible Commentary*, edited by Carol A. Newsom, Sharon H. Ringe, and Jacqueline E. Lapsley, 267–77. 3rd ed. Louisville: Westminster John Knox.

Petersen, David L. 2002. *The Prophetic Literature: An Introduction.* Louisville: Westminster John Knox.

Strawn, Brent A. 2013. "Sanctified and Commercially Successful Curses: On Gangsta Rap and the Canonization of the Imprecatory Psalms." *Theology Today* 69, no. 4:403–17.

Stulman, Louis. 2005. *Jeremiah.* Nashville: Abingdon.

Stulman, Louis, and Hyun Chul Paul Kim. 2010. *You Are My People: An Introduction to Prophetic Literature.* Nashville: Abingdon.

Weems, Renita J. 2004. "Jeremiah." In *Global Bible Commentary*, edited by Daniel Patte, 212–25. Nashville: Abingdon.

Wenthe, Dean O., ed. 2009. *Jeremiah, Lamentations.* Ancient Christian Commentary on Scripture, Old Testament 12. Downers Grove, IL: InterVarsity Press.

Wiesel, Elie. 1981. *Five Biblical Portraits.* Notre Dame: University of Notre Dame Press.

LAMENTATIONS

Wilma Ann Bailey

Introduction

The book of Lamentations consists of a collection of five poems generally believed to have been composed subsequent to the conquest of Jerusalem by a Neo-Babylonian military force in 587/586 BCE. Most of the poems appear to be a response to that conquest or a similar event. They are focused on the plight of those who survived the carnage of war and remain in Jerusalem, a destroyed and depopulated city, whether by choice or happenstance after the elite and ruling families were carried away into exile. The authors of the poems are unknown, though tradition ascribes them to the prophet Jeremiah, which is why the book appears after Jeremiah in Christian Bibles. In Jewish Bibles, it appears in the collection known as the "Writings," following the book of Qohelet (Ecclesiastes). The Hebrew title for the collection is taken from the first word, 'êkâ, which is usually translated into English as a cry of distress, "How?" or "Alas!"

Laments are poems that express sorrow or grief and secondarily other emotions that are outcomes of pain and loss such as anger and bewilderment. The Hebrew word qînâ (plural qînôt) is sometimes translated "lament" and sometimes "dirge" in English Bibles. The two genres are similar. But unlike dirges, which are usually described as funeral songs, laments tend to have a hopeful element expressed, for example, in the form of an appeal to God for relief. Oddly, the word qinah itself is not used in the book of Lamentations, though it is used in other books such as Jeremiah, Ezekiel, Samuel, 2 Chronicles, and Amos. It may be that the ancient Israelites classified these poems differently. That is, they may not have thought of them as qînôt. Sigmund Mowinckel, a Norwegian scholar working in the first half of the twentieth century and using form-critical categories, identified two types of Laments in the Bible: national and personal. "Communal" rather than "national" may better describe the laments in the book of Lamentations because there is no nation, certainly not in the modern sense, in the aftermath of the fall of Jerusalem.

This article, which relies heavily on the author's research and writing for a commentary on Lamentations in the Believers Church Bible Commentary series (in process, Herald Press), will use Mowinckel's classifications because his work—in Western scholarly circles—is considered central in illuminating the genre. He points out that the "I" language found in many laments, though appearing to be an individual's voice, may in fact be a communal voice. According to Mowinckel, characteristics of the national lament include an invocation, a statement of complaint, a request for help, motivations for the request, a promise of sacrifice, expressions of thanksgiving, and a statement of assurance that the prayer has been heard (Mowinckel, 229–30). Few biblical laments actually exhibit all of these characteristics, though most have several. The sine qua non identifying mark is the statement of loss or complaint. Something has gone terribly wrong, and the lamenter is giving voice to it. Laments are a common biblical genre, and they appear outside of the book of Lamentations. According to Toni Craven, 40 percent of the psalms are laments (Craven, 26). It is believed that biblical laments were originally set to music and therefore sung. The sounds, tones, and rhythms are as significant as the meaning of the words. Nevertheless, they can stand by themselves because the pathos comes through.

Lamentations 1:1—5:22: We Have Known Grief

◼ THE TEXT IN ITS ANCIENT CONTEXT

Four of the five poems in the book of Lamentations are structured as alphabetic acrostics, each line of poetry starting with a subsequent letter of the Hebrew alphabet in order. The Hebrew alphabet has twenty-two letters, yielding twenty-two verses in each chapter. The third poem is a triple acrostic. Each letter is repeated three times at the beginning of three lines in a row. The last poem, chapter 5, is the only one not structured as an acrostic, which may be a testimony to its independent origin. The acrostic structure may have been chosen as a mnemonic device or for aesthetic reasons. It has also been suggested that meaning is attached to the structure, in that it reflects the idea that grief must be fully expressed and then brought to an end. Life must go on.

The conquest of Jerusalem destroyed not just human lives, walls, and buildings but also political, social, and economic structures of southern Israelite life. It also caused a theological crisis. Zion and Davidic theologies, to which many in the southern tribe of Judah adhered, believed in the inviolability of Jerusalem and that there would always be a Davidic descendant on the throne of Israel. Now there was no throne, no independent Israelite state. Surviving Davidic descendants were imprisoned in Babylon. Something was needed to replace the weakened Davidic theology, but it had not yet emerged. Furthermore, one school of Israelite thought blamed disaster, whether personal or communal, on sin. Sin, it argued, caused God to either withdraw divine protection or directly use an enemy to punish. The poems in Lamentations express this conventional theology (a theology that is still dominant in the twenty-first century CE), but they also challenge it. The voices in the poems, for example, confess that they have sinned, but they seem to be at a loss as to what those sins were. They seem to not know what they could have done to merit such punishment. There is no listing of sins in the book or confessions of specific sins. One finds only vague allusions to rebellion or transgression. Moreover, the close juxtaposition of phrases describing the suffering of children to the confessions is a statement of protest, implying that the children, at least, had not done anything to merit the suffering they are experiencing. Therefore, it cannot possibly be just. A theology that always connects suffering to sin must confront the question of the justice of God. A just God would not cause the suffering of innocent children. The remnant is clearly struggling with how to understand God's role in the disaster. Through the lament form, the writers describe their situation in using both descriptive and metaphorical language. They express their feelings about it and their hopes for change or revenge. This essentially is the function of biblical lament.

▌THE TEXT IN THE INTERPRETIVE TRADITION

The primary way in which the book of Lamentations is used in the synagogue and church is as a lectionary reading in the liturgy. In the Jewish tradition, it is chanted in its entirety on the ninth of Ab, a summer (in Israel) fast day that mourns the Babylonian destruction of Jerusalem in 587/586 BCE, by the Romans in 70 CE, and other tragedies that have befallen the Jewish people. In Christian liturgical traditions, it is read in part or whole during Holy Week, most often on Good Friday, thereby associating it with the passion of Christ.

Outside of its function in the liturgy, the best-known part of the book is the middle section of chapter 3, which contains words of comfort, hope, and reassurance. The New Revised Standard Version (NRSV) translates them this way:

> The steadfast love of the Lord never ceases,
> > his mercies never come to an end;
> they are new every morning;
> > great is your faithfulness. (3:22-23)

Readers have tended to give primacy to this part of the book because it is consistent with common theological understandings about the nature of God. God is good and compassionate. It is also used as an interpretive pivot for the rest of the book. Chapter 3 begins with a complaint uttered by a person who is described as a *geber*, a word usually translated as "strong man." In the interpretive tradition, as articulated by Delbert Hillers, it has been assumed that this person is to be understood in one of three ways: as "everyman," an actual historical individual, or Israel, collectively (Hillers, 109, 122). However, *geber* is not used to describe an ordinary person elsewhere in the Bible. It describes an outstanding man, a militarily competent man, or prominent person. In Lamentations, it is a *geber* who feels that he is under attack by God. The point is, If such a man can be defeated, what hope is there for the ordinary person, whether male or female? Conventional statements about God's mercy and compassion in the middle of the chapter are interpreted to counteract the statements of despair uttered by the *geber*. But that is not enough to make the central section of chapter 3 the prevailing theology of the book. The additional content and complaints in the chapter and chapters 4 and 5, suggest that the *geber* and the lofty statements of chapter 3 must play an important but perhaps more limited role in the interpretation of Lamentations in the thought of the ancient redactors.

Traditionally, Lamentations has been read as a reflection on sin and deserved punishment. That assessment has been changing because of a greater willingness to confront the theological difficulties that emerge when the question of innocent suffering is raised. The Zion figure prominent in chapters 1 and 2 has drawn the attention of scholars and other readers of the text and lead them to a different way of interpreting it. Tod Linafelt, who has studied Lamentations alongside other contemporary examples of "literature of survival," sees the Zion figure rather than the *geber* as the interpretive key (Linafelt, 20–25). Survival literature is a witness that the catastrophe did not exterminate a people. There are survivors, and life will continue. He points out that God is thought to be the cause of the suffering in Lamentations but also the one to whom one appeals for relief, revenge, or an explanation as to why the suffering has occurred. This creates a theological and ethical problem, particularly because Zion, like most places in the Hebrew Bible, is feminine in grammatical gender and personified in female imagery. Zion, Linafelt writes, is like an abused woman. She must accept the abuse and confess that she deserves it. Texts in the Bible (though probably not Lamentations because it is more a read than studied text) have been used inappropriately to counsel abused women, insisting that they must have done something wrong to incur the wrath of the abuser.

However, the Zion figure along with other female imagery in Lamentations may be interpreted in another way, as being there to engender sympathy and protest against interpretations that blame Zion and therefore the Jewish people for its own destruction. In chapters 1 and 2, Zion is imaged in multiple female roles: a princess, a widow, a lover, an abandoned woman, a refugee, a woman forced into servitude, a mother who has lost her children, a wanton woman, and a virgin daughter of Judah. Many of these images envision Zion as a victim who deserves sympathy. Her former lovers have deserted her. Her friends have betrayed her. She has suffered. She has lost her home, her place, her status. In some of the images, but clearly not all, Zion is given agency and therefore held culpable for the things that have befallen her.

Carleen Mandolfo constructs a theory about Lamentations which places it in dialogue with prophetic books that also use the Zion imagery. In the prophetic books, Zion is silent in the face of critique, but in Lamentations, she points out, Zion speaks. Zion's speaking in Mandolfo's interpretation is not just to the context of the book of Lamentations but to the prophets as well (Mandolfo, 59). She points out that the power dynamics in the dialogue between God and Zion must be taken into consideration. God has more power, but that does not mean Zion does not have a credible theological voice (Mandolfo, 85).

God in Lamentations is a literary character who reflects one theological point of view, and Zion is a literary character (or set of characters) that reflect other theological points of view, and then there is the distinct voice of the narrator who also has a theological point of view. When the narrator blames Zion for having sinned, Zion does not respond to the narrator's charge; rather, she appeals to God to notice her suffering. She blames her lovers (generally understood to be political allies) for having deceived her. The pattern of the shifting of blame is similar to that of the man and woman in the garden in Genesis 3. Zion's appeals suggest a theological position that even when one bears some responsibility in a wrong, God's compassion can mitigate the punishment.

In Lamentations, God is spoken about, but God speaks only once, in a recollection of the composer of the third poem. There, in 3:35, the poet confesses that God did respond when called on. The message that God brought was "Do not be afraid" (author's translation). This standard formulaic phrase is found in many places in the Bible. Usually, the context is a theophany. Typically, either God or a divine messenger appears and says, "Do not be afraid," before providing further instructions. In Lamentations, the phrase is followed not by further words from God but by the poet affirming that God has redeemed him, has seen his affliction, and will bring about justice. In Lamentations, the narrator describes what he (or she) understands to be God's role in the suffering, as does Zion and the *geber*. God never agrees or disagrees with the role assigned by the narrator, Zion, or the *geber*, but God does speak a word of comfort and hope. In four of the five poems, however, God is silent.

Chapter 4 contains a poignant description of the aftermath of war. Starvation and a collapse of the social structures are highlighted. The poet draws attention to the persons who in the poet's estimation have suffered the most: the children who are starving and abandoned, and the elite who have been debased. This poem focuses on the religious elite, the prophets and priests. They are blamed for having brought on the crisis by "pouring out the blood of the righteous" (Lam. 4:13 author's translation). This idea is consistent with Jeremiah 35, where it is the elite, the shepherds, who are to be blamed for the disaster, not the ordinary folk. The chapter ends with a call for vengeance against Edom. Edom did not attack Jerusalem, but it took advantage of it after the Babylonian army completed their work, leaving the city open and vulnerable according to the book of Obadiah.

The fifth chapter of Lamentations is different from the others, not just in that it lacks the acrostic structure, but in its character. More so even than chapter 4, it highlights socioeconomic differences in ancient Israelite society and the differences between the way in which the conquest affected the wealthy and the poor. The chapter, like the others, is primarily complaint, but it is the complaint not of all Israelite society but only the elite. The elite now live as the poor do every day. The complaint is that this is not right. The social order has been turned upside down. The elite in the normal order are those who rule. But in the aftermath of the war, "servants [or slaves]" are ruling over them. The rich complain that they have been reduced to grinding and gathering wood and other chores that the lower class normally performs for them every day. The elite used to own the resources, but now they have to pay for them, like the poor do. They are outraged by the injustice of it all. But they seem incapable of realizing that what they are now experiencing is the everyday lot of their former servants, the poor, and the ordinary people in ancient Israelite society.

▌ THE TEXT IN CONTEMPORARY DISCUSSION

Lamentations raises a number of issues that merit discussion in contemporary times. One is the question of sin and its relationship to suffering. In both Jewish and Christian traditions, sin is thought to be a cause of suffering. This leads to the next step, where the sufferer is said to be the cause of his or her own suffering or alternatively that God is punishing the sufferer because of sins that he or she committed. In Lamentations, Zion assumes that she must have committed some grievous sin to merit the suffering that she is experiencing, but she is at a loss to know what the sin is. To be sure, sometimes individuals do suffer as a result of their bad behavior, but too often this line of thinking leads to blaming victims both as individuals and as religio-ethnic groups such as the Jews or a socioeconomic group such as the poor for their own oppression. Blaming the victim diverts attention from structures, powers, and policies that sin against individuals and communities causing suffering and scapegoating. When God is thought to be punishing persons or groups for sins, oppressors or those who stand by can justify their actions or inactions as being complicit with God's justice. This theology also suggests that if the individual or group stops sinning, the suffering that is a result of punishment meted out by God may be mitigated. God is merciful and will forgive if confession is made or repentance ensues.

The notion that sin and suffering are related can have a positive impact in that suffering created by humans can be corrected by humans. If the sin is one's own, one can stop sinning and the suffering will come to an end. If someone else or some institution is causing the suffering, the institution can be forced to change its ways. Justice can be brought to unjust situations. These things are not outside the control of the human community because they are not just a matter of fate or happenstance. This theology of sin has justified evil but also spawned great works of justice and charity. Both Jewish and Christian traditions also recognize that some suffering is not attached to sin. This is more difficult to understand and more difficult to correct. The book of Job deals with that issue, as do portions of Lamentations (e.g., 2:11-12; 4:2-4). They do not provide answers to this difficult question, but they do recognize it is there and pose a challenge to conventional theologies that posit God as all good, all just, and all-powerful. Harold Kushner struggles with this issue in his well-known book, *When Bad Things Happen to Good People* (see the 2004 reprint of this classic).

Another issue raised by Lamentations is the hiddenness of the real culprits in disaster. Is it the tornado or flood, or is it a weakening climatic system caused by human intervention, or is it caused by unseen divine forces? The book raises the issue of the role of God in disaster and how the role of God is to be interpreted in Scripture. God speaks only once, and then a word of comfort, yet several of the voices in the book including Zion, the *geber*, and the narrator blame God for the disaster. Jerusalem was destroyed by an armed Babylonian force, not God, but God is blamed. The theological notion in play is that God is the cause of all that happens, both good and bad. The Babylonian fighting force was simply a tool for God. The images that we create of God in circular fashion shape our images of God as they get passed from generation to generation. We might ask ourselves, What are our images God, Where did they come from, and, Why do they continue? Why do we blame God when humans have clearly created a disaster? Is God the scapegoat for humans, or are humans the scapegoat for the actions of God?

Calls for vengeance, which are not rare in biblical poems of lament, are discomforting for modern readers. Contemporary theologies teach that vengeance is never an appropriate response to experienced evil. Most modern readers dismiss the calls for vengeance as a reflection of a more primitive mind-set. This, too, is a way to claim superiority over other people without attempting to understand the function of these calls for vengeance in the ritual of ancient Israel. The question is, Is a call for vengeance to be equated with taking vengeance, or is it a way to express how one feels? If one is granted permission to emote, does that mitigate the need to act on one's feelings? What is the function of the calls for vengeance, and what did it mean in its ancient literary context? Is there a place in the liturgy or spiritual practice for calls of vengeance today?

Lamentations is essentially a tool to help people and groups move through the grieving process. It is not meant to be used alone. It is one part of the liturgy, one part of acts of mourning such as tearing one's clothing and putting ashes on one's head. It accompanies the visits by families and friends and the wailing of the professional mourning women. The book in effect gives permission to mourn and grieve losses in a way that is emotive and at times disturbing. One is freed to say exactly what one thinks at the moment. Some Western communities have moved away from rituals of mourning altogether. Even after a death, rituals celebrating a person's life have taken their place. Is this a move in a healthier direction, or is this a way to distance one's self from the pain of the loss?

The structure of Lamentations suggests that mourning should be expressed fully and emotively, and then mourning should be brought to an end. It is inappropriate to be like Jacob, who upon being led to believe that his son Joseph had been torn apart by a wild animal said that he will "go down to Sheol to my son, mourning" (Gen. 37:35). A time for mourning must give way to a time for dancing according to Eccles. 3:4. That is the way of the world. The community cannot afford to lose the input and productivity of one of its own to perpetual mourning. One must get on with life not only for one's own sake, but also for the sake of the living community.

Works Cited

Craven, Toni. 1992. *The Book of Psalms*. Collegeville, MN: Liturgical Press.

Hillers, Delbert. 1992. *Lamentations*, revised edition. Anchor Bible. New York: Doubleday.

Kushner, Harold S. 2004. *When Bad Things Happen to Good People*. New York: Knopf Doubleday.

Linafelt, Tod. 2000. *Surviving Lamentations: Catastrophe, Lament, and Protest in the Afterlife of a Biblical Book*. Chicago: University of Chicago Press.

Mandolfo, Carleen R. 2007. *Daughter Zion Talks Back to the Prophets*. Atlanta: Society of Biblical Literature.

Mowinckel, Sigmund. 1979. *The Psalms in Israel's Worship*. 2 vols. Translated by D. R. AP-Thomas. Nashville: Abingdon.

EZEKIEL

Corrine L. Carvalho

Introduction

The book of Ezekiel is set against the backdrop of the fall of Jerusalem. The book contains several dates that cover a twenty-year span, from July 593 BCE to March 573. For the original audience, these dates were ominous. As the book opens, Judah is a colony of Babylon. The king Jehoiachin and his staff have been exiled to Babylon in 597, and a puppet king, Zedekiah, rules in his stead. But after a rebellion by Zedekiah, the Babylonians besiege Jerusalem, destroying the city in 587, and exiling a significant number of its elite citizens. Judah ceases to exist as an independent state, and the religious identity of its citizens is seriously compromised. Even by 573, there is no indication that the nation would be restored.

The prologue of the book (1:1-3) introduces its main character, Ezekiel, a priest who was exiled in the first deportation of 597 BCE. This opening marks Ezekiel as part of the elite class, whose work supported the royal ideology of the time. The oracles in the book express the experience of destruction and exile from this specific social location. Ezekiel represents the male elite of the preexilic period who lost status, prestige, and honor in the fall of their city.

The book is clearly written from the perspective of male urban elites. For them, Judah's identity is threatened by their loss of land ownership, the destruction of the temple, and the treatment of the Davidic monarchy. The book views the ideal society as one based on male patriarchal privilege, and both disaster and restoration are defined in terms of male landowners.

The elite perspective is also found in more subtle elements of the book, such as the literary quality of the book. The oracles display a profound familiarity with various literary and intellectual traditions not just in Judah but also in the wider context of the ancient Near East. The author deliberately uses earlier traditions to create new and startling images. The oracles are detailed and intricate, while the book is more organized than most prophetic texts, including Jeremiah and Isaiah.

The preservation of Ezekiel's oracles in written form is a deliberate part of this text. The prophet is depicted as made mute by God in chapter 3 and told to eat a scroll, indicating that the written version of the oracles is more important than their oral form.

A priestly perspective permeates the book as well. Ezekiel is not an elite male who happened to be a priest. Rather, the depictions of sin and restoration both are told in priestly terms. Sin leads to urban defilement. Defilement prompts God to abandon the temple, and that divine abandonment results in the fall of a city bereft of its divine warrior. The image of God on a throne borne by cherubim, an image tied to God's presence in the temple, provides structure to the book. Ezekiel has a vision of this enthroned God within the temple in chapter 1. God leaves the city in chapters 8–11 and returns as a mark of restoration in chapter 43. The book ends with a nine-chapter vision of a restored Israel, at whose center stands an ideal temple inhabited by God on this throne.

The book is told from a male perspective. Women are hardly mentioned, and when they are, they serve male concerns. Two chapters (16 and 23) personify the city as a woman in a way that indicates the presumption that female behavior is only important for the way it affects male honor. Human women appear most prominently in the condemnation of female prophets in 13:17-23 and the death of the prophet's wife in 24:15-18, but these also reflect male concerns. Unlike the book of Lamentations, for example, there are no poems that describe the fall of the city from the experience of wives and mothers.

In this patriarchal culture, male honor becomes the uppermost social value. Shame only exists insofar as honor is possible. Much of the book's rhetoric flows from the shame the male elite experienced in the fall of their city and their new status as forced laborers in exile. But in a surprising twist, the book does this by encouraging the male elite to embrace their experience of shame. It accomplishes this by the way it depicts God. The book aims to preserve the honor of YHWH by casting God as the ultimate male head of household. This rhetorical strategy makes the human male elites inferior to this divine head of household; the book uses the notion of shame to recast them as underlings of this sovereign Lord. The purpose of the shameful defeat of the male elite was to reveal to them their true status as low-class persons with no rights in comparison to their patriarchal divine head.

The book insists that God's actions, whether in Israel's glorious past, in their present state of shame, or in their future restoration, are all predicated on the preservation of divine honor. Two repeated phrases drive this idea home. First, the text repeatedly states that God acts for the sake of the divine name or reputation. Second, God constantly asserts that "I am YHWH." Both statements are assertions of divine honor and prerogative. God does not act out of love; "he" acts only to assert his divine right.

These social assumptions make it difficult for contemporary audiences to appreciate the book. In fact, some contemporary scholars have wondered whether its author suffered from mental illness. The book presents vivid images of a God actively destroying the city, shaming its citizens, constantly reminding them that they deserve nothing. Readers expecting a loving, nurturing God will not find it here. The rhetoric of the book is meant to shock and aggravate its audience, so that they question their own assumptions about human election and divine power.

Contemporary readers often want to reject the view of God the book projects. Interestingly, the book hints that the ancient audience had a similar reaction. Ezekiel 33:32-33 states that the people came to hear Ezekiel, not because they believed he was a prophet, but because they considered him an entertainer. They too wanted to distance themselves from the theology he presented.

The book of Ezekiel insists, however, that its audience needs to face what tragedy and loss reveal about the nature of God and humanity. Its setting urges its readers to hear the voices of people like Ezekiel, those marked by tragedy and unspeakable loss. It reminds its audience that even today war refugees suffer not just economic hardship but also shame, especially when they undergo a significant loss of status. The book calls on today's elite to recognize that an elite status is just an illusion, one that draws faith communities away from God. Those who truly understand God's power are those for whom "exile" becomes part of their innate identity.

Ezekiel 1–3: The Opening Vision

■ The Text in Its Ancient Context

The first three chapters, sometimes referred to as the call of Ezekiel, describe Ezekiel's first prophetic experience and set out the book's view of the prophetic office. They also introduce the three main characters in the book: the measly mortal Ezekiel, the kingly God, and the rebellious people. The first three verses introduce Ezekiel as an elite priest who now lives in Babylon as an exile.

Ezekiel's call begins with a vision of God in the temple of Jerusalem before the fall of the city. Most prophetic visions were short; Amos sees a basket of fruit (8:2), and Micaiah is shown a battlefield (1 Kgs. 22:17). Ezekiel's vision of a portable throne is striking for the level of detail that it utilizes. Similar to Isaiah's vision of God enthroned above the seraphim in Isaiah 6, Ezekiel 1 describes heavenly beings that support the throne (identified as cherubim in 9:3), the appearance of the throne, the sounds of the wings, and the clothing of God. The vision progresses from bottom to top, and as it gets closer to describing God, the language begins to fail.

God does not speak until the second chapter, where the prophet is given an overview of what he is being called to do. The speech characterizes the people of Israel as rebellious. This term, often used in the Pentateuch to describe the people when they sinned, is applied in a variety of ways in Ezekiel. Sometimes their rebellion takes the form of violating God's laws (Ezekiel 20). Other times, it refers to political rebellion (17:12-15). Ezekiel 2:7-9 describes them as hard as a stone, meaning that they are unrepentant and stubborn in their rebellion.

God defines Ezekiel's role as prophet. Chapter 3 describes the prophet as a sentinel on a city's walls whose job it was to warn the inhabitants of an advancing enemy. This book views the prophet as someone who warns Israel of its fate unless they take immediate steps to prevent it. But the book has already noted that they will not be warned, foreshadowing their refusal to recognize him as a prophet. They are stubborn, unwilling to change, so that Ezekiel's message contains words of "lamentation and mourning and woe" (2:10).

These chapters make clear that Ezekiel has no agency in what will follow. He is dragged to Jerusalem in a vision in chapter 1 and returned to Babylon, stunned, in 3:15. God addresses him throughout the book, not as a "man of God" (the title for prophets in the historical books), but as a "mere mortal" (literally "son of man"). Ezekiel is simply God's mouthpiece. This point is driven home at the end of the call narrative, when God makes the prophet mute except when pronouncing an oracle (3:24-27). Since Ezekiel cannot speak on his own, the things he says in the rest of book are to be viewed as God's own words.

▌ THE TEXT IN THE INTERPRETIVE TRADITION

The opening vision of the book of Ezekiel, which is repeated in chapters 8–11 and 40–48, became a prominent image in both the Jewish and Christian traditions. Ezekiel's text became the springboard for descriptions of other heavenly journeys found in later Jewish apocalyptic texts. In postbiblical Judaism, it became the basis for a stream of Jewish mysticism called "Merkabah mysticism" (*merkabah* is the Hebrew word for "chariot"), which viewed the chariot as an allegory for heaven itself (see Sweeney).

A different allegorical tendency is seen in Christian exegesis, which viewed the four faces of the cherubim as allegories for Christian Scripture. On the one hand, they represented the four parts of the Christian Old Testament (Law, History, Wisdom, Prophets) mirrored by the four parts of the New Testament (Gospels, Acts, Epistles, Revelation). On the other hand, they foreshadowed the four evangelists, where each of the four evangelists is represented by one of the four animals in the vision. The wheel within the wheel became a standard metaphor for the relationship of the Old and New Testaments: the New was hidden within the Old (Stevenson and Glerup, 11). These interpretations are prominent up through the Reformation period, when they began to wane. Reformers identified the enthroned figure in this vision as Christ (Beckwith, xlvi and 16–20).

▌ THE TEXT IN CONTEMPORARY DISCUSSION

One of the biggest challenges for contemporary readers of the book is to recognize the social location of the original audience of the book. The book's rhetoric is aimed at justifying the fall of Jerusalem as an act of God. In order to do this, it portrays its citizens as fully deserving of such violence. Contemporary readers often want to identify with the character of God, and thus rush to judge these ancient people as sinful and rebellious.

Contemporary discussions of the book, however, assume a different starting point. The book reached its final form after the destruction of the city. Death, violence, degradation, and displacement were everyday realities for the book's original audience. That reality undercut every pillar on which Israelite identity depended: gone were its political, religious, and social institutions. No longer were they Israelites whose nation was founded on a covenant with YHWH. They were forced laborers in Mesopotamia, displaced refugees in Egypt, and colonized farmers in a land occupied by a foreign army.

Daniel Smith-Christopher applies the insights of refugee studies to the exilic literature of ancient Israel. He notes that one of the most prominent results of such a tragedy is an overwhelming feeling of loss of control. If the event(s) is viewed as capricious or unprovoked, then a community has more difficulty overcoming feelings of dread and foreboding. Individuals and communities who fare best after trauma are those who take some responsibility for their fate, which restores a sense of control. Kathleen O'Connor's (2002; 2012) analysis of Jeremiah and Lamentations couples this perspective with the insight that the other prominent result of trauma is loss of language, especially when the trauma overwhelms the person or community. Literature of trauma attempts to provide language for overwhelmingly tragic experiences.

What distinguishes an exilic text like Lamentations from that of Ezekiel is that, while Lamentations describes the fall of the city from the perspective of its human inhabitants, the book of Ezekiel puts the description of the disaster into the mouth of God. These descriptions then become folded into a rhetoric of castigation. As a result, the same events that the book of Ezekiel describes seem to be exalted rather than mourned. It hides the fact that both texts affirm the breadth of the disaster that the people of Judah experienced. Neither book backs away from how horrible those events were; they do not minimize them, ignore them, or belittle them. The honesty with which Ezekiel speaks of the city's horrors alone gave their suffering purpose or meaning.

Ezekiel embodies how war feels to former elites rendered helpless. Since he is portrayed as a righteous sufferer, the prophet's portrayal tempers the book's overt rhetoric that the punishment was deserved. His fate shows that not all sufferers had been evil sinners, and that tragedy strikes all alike.

Ezekiel 4–7: Oracles before God Leaves

■ THE TEXT IN ITS ANCIENT CONTEXT

Ezekiel's prophetic activity begins in earnest in chapter 4. The first oracles take the form of symbolic acts, a form the book inherits from the Israelite prophetic tradition. For example, Isaiah walks around naked for three years as a sign that Israel will be left with nothing once God's punishment comes (20:2-4). Ezekiel does three complicated symbolic acts. First, he acts out the sieges of Samaria and Jerusalem (4:1-17), then he shows the various ways people will die when the city falls (5:1-12), and last, he prophesies against mountains (6:1-7). Each of these is followed by an explanation of the symbolic public performance.

Behind these texts is the reality of siege warfare that shaped so much of the cultural memory of the ancient world. Throughout the ancient Near East, literature can be found that describes cultural fears of sieges. Many of them contain similar descriptions of death through violence, disease, and even cannibalism. Ezekiel 4:9-17 focuses on the realities of gradual communal starvation. Chapter 5 reflects the varieties of ways people die in times of ancient war; even those who survive the war itself (represented by the hair in the prophet's hem in v. 3) are still vulnerable to violent deaths in exile.

While similar events are described in the book of Lamentations, the insistence that this fate is deserved makes Ezekiel's versions more difficult to appreciate. Chapter 6, in particular, blames ritual sins as the cause for the destruction. In keeping with the book as a whole, the chapter characterizes sin as defilement. God promises to destroy the religious institutions of Judah, symbolized by the destruction of altars, because their worship has become idolatrous. While this may be a reference to worship of other gods, the same language is also used for any ritual irregularity even in the worship of YHWH.

This section introduces other major themes that will permeate the book. First, the detail of God's command that Ezekiel cook his food on human dung (4:12) reinforces the uneven power structure that is at the heart of Ezekiel's relationship to God. Second, the reader will experience the siege, fall, and destruction of the city through the character of Ezekiel. Since the book depicts the prophet as fully controlled by God, even when that experience horrifies him, it represents the reality that the Judeans' fate was also forced on them.

Ezekiel 6:7 contains the first of many repetitions of the phrase, "then you shall know that I am the Lord." This phrase, which punctuates the book, sums up the reason for the horrible events it describes: to reveal God to the world. What is shocking about Ezekiel's version of divine self-disclosure is that God is revealed not through acts of mercy and kindness but rather through violence and destruction. Even chapter 7, which contains the first oracles in the book in a poetic form, seems to relish the violence that it describes. Here the audience encounters multiple vibrant pictures of the realities of siege warfare, which unrelentingly blame the victim for its violent fate.

▌ The Text in the Interpretive Tradition

Pre-Enlightenment texts rarely commented on how the prophet is depicted in the first six chapters of the book. That focus has shifted in the modern period. With the rise of psychoanalysis in the nineteenth century, many scholars began to ask whether the prophet suffered from some sort of psychosis. The most recent example is David Halperin's conclusion that Ezekiel had been molested as a child and blamed his mother. While these interpretations flow out of the odd language of the book, they fail to deal directly with the book's own testimony that Ezekiel's "trauma" was the fall of the city. By assigning the "real" meaning of these disturbing oracles to the author's personal psychosis, interpreters distance themselves from the horrors that the text describes.

Another way scholars have distanced themselves from the text's overt meaning has been the recent trend to view exilic texts like Ezekiel that describe the horrors of the war and its aftermath as propaganda by the former ruling elite to project themselves as the true Israel. Hans Barstad states that texts that describe the land as empty or the whole country as devastated were myths designed to assert the exiles as the "true" Israel. He concludes that the fall of the nation did not disrupt most people's lives, only the lives of the elite.

Such approaches to exilic literature distance contemporary readers from the texts' explicit content. The images of devastation in the book of Ezekiel must have resonated enough with the post-fall community for it to be preserved even though the texts are so shocking. This history of interpretation demonstrates common approaches to disturbing biblical texts: they are either ignored, trivialized, or resisted.

▌ The Text in Contemporary Discussion

Contemporary witnesses to war remind us that the tragedies of war are experienced at every level of society. The book aptly describes the multiple ramifications of a war-torn society. Although the most obvious deaths come from enemy fire (swords in the ancient world), death takes many forms as a nation-state crumbles. In fact, it is telling that the book pays less attention to death in armed combat and more to the tragedy of a lingering death through disease and famine. During a siege, when a city is cut off from its food and water supplies, food rations become insufficient to keep the population healthy. Those weakened through starvation are more vulnerable to illness, and, as food supplies rot or water becomes contaminated, those sickened by food-borne illnesses are more likely to die.

Contemporary readers who use a variety of stances to distance themselves from the shocking language of the book can fail to recognize that what it describes is the reality of many people even in today's world. War destroys communities, not just with bombs or guns, but through the destruction of reliable sources of clean water and food. Even today, those who have escaped war-torn countries find themselves in refugee camps, where they are still vulnerable to violence and lacking adequate food and clean water.

This section of Ezekiel begins and ends with the twin companions to death by the sword: death through starvation and disease. It represents the reality of those who have lived through war only to find that their safety is still precarious. To hear Ezekiel is to hear the fate of too many in our world today.

Ezekiel 8–11: God Leaves the City

■ THE TEXT IN ITS ANCIENT CONTEXT

The opening oracles of Ezekiel are followed by another vision report, which describes the prophet's second visionary journey to Jerusalem about three years before its siege. Here the prophet sees the chariot throne described in chapter 1 leave the temple and its city because of the defiling sins of the urban elite.

Chapter 8 has a clear ritual focus. The sins that it describes are ritual sins, and their effect is ritual defilement. In the ancient world, the rituals associated with temples were designed to keep this divine residence protected from contact with the profane world. Courtyards that surrounded temples formed circles of protection from anything ritually unclean. Priests were charged with ensuring this security.

Although the exact nature of the rituals that the prophet describes in chapter 8 is unclear, they are obviously not producing the effects the worshipers hoped for. Instead of guaranteeing their security, they cause the city's only divine resident, YHWH, to leave. In the ancient world, cities were under the protection of a patron deity; once that deity left, the unprotected city was vulnerable to enemy attacks. These chapters follow this motif of divine abandonment. They linger over descriptions of God's chariot throne and detail God's slow progression outside of the city. YHWH is first transported to the door of the sanctuary building (9:3, repeated in 10:18). From there it flies up to the east gate of the inner courtyard (10:19), and finally leaves the city in 11:23. At this point, the reader knows that the city is doomed.

The passage also describes a variety of heavenly beings that carry out God's decrees. The creatures that bear God's throne are explicitly identified as cherubim (9:3), multiformed creatures that served as divine guardians throughout the ancient Near East. It also introduces six heavenly executioners who slay sinners (9:1-2). Finally, there is a recorder who marks those whom the executioners should spare (9:3-4). We are never told how many, if any, the recorder marks for survival. Instead, the passage focuses on the widespread death wrought by the executioners (9:5-6).

In the midst of chapter 11 is a brief oracle of hope. Verses 17-20 look for the return of the exiles and the restoration of Israel, even though the city has not yet been destroyed. As with all of the oracles of restoration in the book, this one will not be motivated by the people's behavior: they do not repent and are no better than when God sent them away. The remedy to this problem is a heart transplant (replacing a dead heart [stone] with one that is alive) and the infusion of a new spirit. The result will be a community that will keep God's commandments, thus not defiling the land again.

▋ The Text in the Interpretive Tradition

The Christian tradition was fascinated by the marking of the righteous. Christians noted that this angel marked the people with the Hebrew letter *tau*, which was shaped like a cross. Therefore, Origen states that the mark prefigures the rite of baptism, which includes marking the baptized with the sign of the cross on their forehead (Stevenson and Glerup, 34–35). This interpretation persists even into the Reformation period, where the divine figure is identified as Christ.

One of the difficulties of this passage is that, although the angel seems to mark some people as righteous, the chapter describes the destruction of the whole city. Steven Shawn Tuell (185–202) compares how this passage is treated in both rabbinic writing and in Calvin. While the rabbis state that the righteous are punished for not preventing their neighbors from sinning, Calvin distinguishes between the physical death felt by everyone in the city and the spiritual salvation of the righteous through the gift of eternal life.

▋ The Text in Contemporary Discussion

While on the surface these chapters seem to address only ancient assumptions about divine activity, beneath them is a more troubling question that has plagued many communities of faith. Where is God when disaster strikes? If God is powerful, how can tragedy happen? Images of divine abandonment were one way ancient peoples negotiated the tension created by their assertions of divine beings who are powerful and can control the world over against their experience of communal tragedy. The motif of divine abandonment protects the belief in a powerful God. Israelite texts that use the images of abandonment also strive to maintain God's justice. This is not a capricious and untrustworthy god, but rather one who acts according to principles of justice. It is fascinating to see how much blame this community was willing to accept in order to maintain that their God is both powerful and just, despite the fall of the city.

This is not just an ancient problem, though. Even today, people who have experienced great tragedy often describe their suffering as God's will. Some fundamentalists like Pat Robertson have claimed that natural disasters, such as Hurricane Katrina, are punishments from God for the legalization of abortion. To many other American Christians, such claims are not only untrue but also offensive. Using human tragedy as an opportunity to make a political statement seems like the basest abuse of religious authority. As a result, many American Christians are reluctant to say that national calamity is God's judgment for sinful behavior. Yet even with this reluctance, many of them still find comfort in the belief that God has a purpose in their suffering even if that purpose is not clear in the midst of the tragedy.

Ezekiel 12–13: True and False Prophets

▌ THE TEXT IN ITS ANCIENT CONTEXT

These two chapters focus on the role played by prophets in the years leading up to the fall of the city. These oracles are dated to three years before the siege of Jerusalem, while Zedekiah, the king appointed by the Babylonians, was on the throne. Although the city had been enjoying peace for seven years, these chapters depict this time as Judah's last chance to listen to its prophets.

Although there are many accounts of prophets preserved in the Bible, the fact is that there were many more prophets who existed at any given time in Israel. The biblical texts preserve glimpses of the controversies that arose when prophets disagreed. In these two chapters, it is clear that inhabitants of Jerusalem either don't believe prophets like Ezekiel who warn that the city will fall or they believe that these warnings pertain to some distant future. Ezekiel calls their complacency "rebellion" (12:2).

The two chapters condemn both the prophets who give false hope and the people who do not believe the prophets who warn of disaster. Chapter 13:17-23 includes an indictment of female prophets. Although this passage is our only evidence of a professional class of female prophets in Judah, the details of their activities accords well with what we know of female prophets in Mesopotamia. Female prophets tended to work in groups, have less prestige than male counterparts, and use divination as an accepted vehicle for prophetic statements. It is important to notice that Ezekiel's criticism of them is not based on gender; all prophets who prophesy "out of their own imagination" (13:1 and 17), whether they are male or female, are condemned.

In contrast to these false prophets, chapter 12 characterizes Ezekiel as a true prophet. In this symbolic act, performed in Babylon, Ezekiel's metaphoric flight closely mirrors the final fate of Zedekiah, as related in 2 Kgs. 25:4-7. Although the passage may have been revised or added after the fall of the city, the rhetorical effect of this detailed account marks Ezekiel as an unusually accurate prophet.

That characterization is reinforced in 12:6 and 11, two of the three times in the book when Ezekiel himself serves as a prophetic sign (the other is in 24:24). Ezekiel embodies the prophetic message. In both passages where he serves as a sign, the text states that what happens to him will happen to the whole community. Ezekiel is not only a priest of the temple but also the embodiment of the perfect prophet and its message.

▌ THE TEXT IN THE INTERPRETIVE TRADITION

These chapters in Ezekiel also do not garner as much attention as the visionary material in the book. Like many Old Testament passages that deal with false prophets, the description of false prophets in chapter 13 becomes an occasion for Christian exegetes to talk about heretics in their own day, as is found in Jerome's commentary on Ezekiel (Stevenson and Glerup, 45–50).

The Text in Contemporary Discussion

While this passage focuses on the failure of the prophets in a time of crisis, Ezek. 7:26 castigates other religious leaders as well. The ancient Israelites, like people today, turned to their religious leaders for guidance in times of crisis. Notice, however, that this passage does not place all of the blame on the religious leadership's failure to discern the situation properly. It also condemns the people who hear only what they want to hear. Although it may be easy to understand why they would have ignored a prophet who was not even in the city, the text makes clear that the real problem is the people's unwillingness to confront their own responsibility for their nation's fate. The book of Ezekiel reminds its readers that not only are political and religious leaders responsible for communal ethics but responsibility also rests equally with those who hear the message but choose not to listen.

Today's world is not that different. Perhaps a stark example is found in the media treatment of the sermons of President Obama's pastor, Rev. Jeremiah Wright. During Obama's first run for the presidency, Wright's review of America's history of colonial expansion and racist policies, including how these attitudes should temper responses to the events of 9/11, were often used to present him as a false and even dangerous prophetic voice. Yet, when his sermons are heard within the context of African American liberation theology, he demonstrated the connections between white treatment of indigenous peoples, race-based slavery, and contemporary politics. It remains a message many people do not want to hear.

Ezekiel 14 and 18: Moral Responsibility

The Text in Its Ancient Context

In any disaster, people immediately begin to wonder who is to blame. These two chapters demonstrate that the ancient world was little different from our own. Both of these chapters, however, virulently deny that the blame for the fall of the city could be displaced either onto an earlier generation or onto some small segment of the population. Ezekiel does not let anyone in his own generation off the hook.

Chapter 14 seems to be responding to the assertion that the prophets had not adequately warned the people, and are to blame for the city's fall. The chapter assumes the three major activities of ancient prophets: people could ask them to get an oracle from God on their behalf; they could deliver oracles that had been revealed to them for the whole community; and they could intercede to God on behalf of the people. Ezekiel 14 asserts that these prophetic functions have all been in place, so the true prophets are not to blame.

Chapter 14 keeps the blame on the people in three ways. It denies oracles of salvation to those who are sinners (vv. 7-8), and it promises punishment for false prophets (vv. 9-11). More prominently, however, it deals with the question of intercession. In 14:12-20, the longest section of the chapter, the oracle asserts that Israel's sins are so great, God will respond to no one's intercessions on their behalf, not even three legendary righteous heroes from Israel's past: Noah, Daniel, and Job. All three of these figures were blameless individuals who suffered in spite of their righteousness. Because this chapter is about the responsibility of the prophetic voice in the national crisis, the chapter is really about Ezekiel's inability to avert the disaster that befell Jerusalem. By using the characters of Noah, Daniel, and Job, the chapter projects Ezekiel as another innocent sufferer whose pleas for the people God rejects.

Chapter 18 deals with a different issue: the question of intergenerational punishment. There are many biblical texts which assert that God punishes later generations for the sins of an earlier generation. The Ten Commandments, for example, state that God will punish "children for the iniquity of parents, to the third and the fourth generation" (Exod. 20:5). Ezekiel's lengthy chapter goes through various scenarios of parents and children committing sins, each time stating that the sinner alone deserves punishment. This was clearly a hotly debated topic at that time. The proverb that is quoted in 18:2 is also quoted and denied in Jer. 31:29-30. The denials of this view in both Ezekiel and Jeremiah make sure the generation that experienced the fall of the city would recognize that they alone were responsible for its fall.

Last, it must be recognized that chapter 18 is not about individual responsibility; it is about intergenerational punishment (Joyce). The book of Ezekiel is more ambiguous about individual responsibility. While it asserts that God holds individuals responsible for their sins, it also knows that many innocent people suffered in the various deportations by the Babylonians and in the destruction of the city. Chapter 14's portrayal of innocent sufferers suggests that Ezekiel was one of those whose suffering was not the result of his sinful behavior. In addition, ancient texts tend to focus on the suffering of landowners and their individual responsibility without questioning that the result of their punishment is often meted out on their whole households (wives, children, servants, and slaves), regardless of their personal behavior.

■ THE TEXT IN THE INTERPRETIVE TRADITION

With both of these chapters, patristic writers focused on the efficacy of repentance for the forgiveness of sins. John Chrysostom uses 14:12-23 to argue that the righteousness of a person's ancestors will not save a person; they only serve as a model of righteous behavior (Stevenson and Glerup, 54). Augustine and Ambrose, among others, apply a similar message to chapter 18. Repentance brings life, which, for these Christian exegetes, means eternal life (Stevenson and Glerup, 76–85).

In the Reformation, these chapters became the basis for discussions about repentance and grace. The discussion of repentance in chapter 14 led William Greenhill, for example, to note that repentance is the work of the Spirit, while Calvin tempers Ezekiel's statement that Noah, Job, and Daniel were saved by their righteousness (Beckwith, 72–80). Similarly, the discussion of salvation in chapter 18 led Reformers to discuss the efficacy of adherence to the law, the question of double predestination, and whether one who has been saved can turn back to sin (Beckwith, 98–108).

Another passage that draws comment is the statement in 18:23 and 32, repeated in 33:11, that God takes "no pleasure in the death of the wicked." John Sawyer notes that, although Luther does not pay much attention to the book of Ezekiel throughout his writings, he quotes this verse some sixteen times in a variety of settings (2011, 4).

◼ THE TEXT IN CONTEMPORARY DISCUSSION

American culture valorizes rugged individualism to such a degree that it often masks communal interdependency. Yet, even with the rhetoric of the individual, there are ways that questions of intergenerational and intercommunal responsibility leak out. Statistics show that a higher percentage of those incarcerated suffered from child abuse than is found in the general population. Those abused as children experience increased rates of substance abuse, mental illness, and symptoms of post-traumatic stress disorder. On a communal level, it is also clear that one generation's misuse of natural and financial resources is felt more by later generations than by those who wrought the damage. Later generations do, in fact, suffer for the acts of earlier generations.

Communities suffer the effects of the sins of individuals, especially when those individuals have a leadership role. Workers often pay an undue price for fiscal mismanagement of a company's resources. Families can be torn apart when a parent abuses alcohol or becomes violent. Here is where it is important to remember the book's social location. Ezekiel 14 and 18 do not deny that much suffering is undeserved, but these chapters attempt to make those in leadership positions recognize that their own elite status does not release them from liability. They have sinned, and God holds them accountable.

Ezekiel 15, 17, and 19: Parables, Allegories, and Laments

◼ THE TEXT IN ITS ANCIENT CONTEXT

These three chapters use literary genres found more often in nonprophetic texts. Chapters 15 and 17 are extended allegories, a category associated with proverbial literature. Chapter 19 is a dirge, or funeral song. The use of vines, plants, and lions to represent the nation and its leaders is found in both the literary record and Judean iconography. Prophetic texts such as Isa. 5:3; Hosea 10:1; and Jer. 2:21 liken Israel to a vine. The king is a plant in Isa. 11:1, while the nation is an olive tree in Jer. 11:16-17. Royal seals from Judah show that the symbol for the Davidic monarchy was a lion. While chapter 15 uses the vine to represent the fate of the city as a whole, chapters 17 and 19 focus on the role the final kings of Judah played in these turbulent times. The details of the allegories are complicated, and scholars disagree about what each element of the symbols means, but even with this ambiguity, certain things are clear.

First, the poems maintain the focus of blame on the inhabitants of Jerusalem. Nowhere is Babylon condemned for its attacks on Judah. In chapter 19, the nation is consumed in an act of self-immolation (19:12-14). Second, Ezekiel objects to Zedekiah's rebellion against Nebuchadnezzar (17:11-21; see also 2 Kgs. 24:20—25:1). When royals made treaties, they swore by their patron gods to uphold the treaties. Ezekiel uses this to cast Zedekiah's rebellion against Babylon as a rebellion against God.

Last, these poems are the work of a literary master. The author creatively uses poetic forms that fit different situations to deliver damning indictments against the nation and its leadership. Chapter

19's use of the dirge is especially delicious: it is a funeral song delivered while the king is still alive, a bit like running the obituary for a sitting president. The artistry is found in the creative ways the author uses traditional forms and motifs to deliver detailed oracles about the international politics of his day.

∎ THE TEXT IN THE INTERPRETIVE TRADITION

In the Christian tradition, chapter 17 receives far more attention than either chapter 15 or 19. In part, this is because Jesus' speech in John 15 that he is the vine and believers are the branches shares more vocabulary with Ezekiel 17 than with similar images in either Isaiah or Jeremiah (Manning, 36–40). While Jerome picks up on this idea and identifies the vine as Christ, Origen focuses more on the branches, interpreting the image as the church (Stevenson and Glerup, 75–76).

∎ THE TEXT IN CONTEMPORARY DISCUSSION

Sometimes a political cartoon can capture outrage better than words; these chapters are verbal cartoons. They remind readers that, although much of the rhetoric in the book seems to address individuals, the book is really a critique of the international policies that led to the nation's fall. In today's world, criticism of American policies during periods of disaster is often labeled unpatriotic. These poems challenge contemporary communities of faith not to confuse patriotism with naiveté or, worse, self-righteousness.

In post-9/11 America, criticism of American policies, especially in the Middle East, is often deemed anti-American. Yet Ezekiel's assertions that Judah's quest for aid from Egypt was a root cause for the fall of the city, especially in a time when Egypt was Judah's only ally, is a far more radical statement than contemporary critiques of America's policies throughout the Middle East. What Ezekiel proposes means either total capitulation to Babylon or full destruction of the city, yet he bases these claims on a sense of Judah's true identity as completely under God's control. Patriotism is not blind acquiescence to political powers, but stems rather from a broader sense of a nation's ethical identity. Sometimes the most patriotic thing a person or group can do is protest.

In the 1960s, feminists often noted that the personal is political. These poems put a different spin on this adage: the spiritual is political. The focus on international politics as the arena for faith-based decisions adds a different lens for our current debates about religion and politics. While the media often casts disagreements over personal decisions such as abortion and marriage equality as religious issues, faith-based critiques of war or foreign policies are often ignored. The biblical text insists that faith-based groups should ponder the relationship between international relations and religiously informed ethical principles.

Ezekiel 16 and 23: City Leaders as God's Wives

∎ THE TEXT IN ITS ANCIENT CONTEXT

These two chapters, so troubling to contemporary readers, take another common metaphor found in Israelite prophetic literature, that the city is like God's wife. Ezekiel's version develops it in creative and disturbing ways. That creativity is designed to provoke outrage in the readers, a task it still accomplishes today.

The personification of capital cities as women is found in Jeremiah and Hosea in particular. The metaphor works because of the ancient understanding of marriage. In Israel, husbands and wives were not equals; men had legal control over their wives. As was true for any subservient person within the household, the male head of household was allowed to beat his wife (and slaves and children) as punishment for their wrongdoings. Wives who were caught in adultery could be stoned to death, while those suspected of adultery had to undergo a ritual ordeal to prove their innocence. Male honor was preserved through the behaviors of his dependents. Women's actions were evaluated by whether they brought honor or shame to their male partners.

Jerusalem and Samaria were like wives, because they were dependent on God for all they had. They owed complete allegiance to God, who could punish them for any challenge to his male-defined authority. Worshiping other gods was tantamount to adultery, punishable by death. One of the goals in both chapters is to get the male audience to accept their shameful, dependent status in relationship to God.

In these two chapters, Ezekiel's use of the metaphor is far more graphic than what is found in other prophetic books. In fact, many modern translations of the texts tone down the sexually explicit language of the Hebrew text. Both chapters review Israel's history, describing the founding of the nation and its subsequent history. In both historical reviews, the wives are completely undeserving of God's notice of them. Neither text states that the marriage was based on love. The details in the chapters distinguish the two versions of the metaphor. Chapter 16 deals with the history of Israel's religious practices, practices cast as idolatrous and therefore deserving of capital punishment. Chapter 23, on the other hand, again deals with international relations. The lovers are allies of Judah, and the courting of those allies is depicted as "whoring" after illicit lovers.

The graphic rhetoric makes it all too easy to forget that these female figures are metaphors and are not descriptions of real Judean women at the time. In fact, the wicked women actually personify the male elite of these cities. These chapters require the male audience to identify with the sexually uncontrolled female figure, although they might rather identify with the male husband. Rhetorically, these passages feminize their male audience.

Feminization was one way to shame a man. It casts the man as someone who was controlled and subservient. In ancient Near Eastern literature, the defeat of soldiers is likened to rape and the labor pains of a woman who dies in childbirth. Prisoners of war were stripped, mutilated, and sometimes castrated in order to shame them. These chapters pick up on the rhetoric of shaming but make the one doing the shaming not the Babylonians but rather God. In Ezekiel, God's masculinized honor is maintained through the shaming of his dependents, turning them into women.

▌THE TEXT IN THE INTERPRETIVE TRADITION

Within the commentary tradition, these chapters were rarely used to substantiate the subjugation of women. In the patristic period, two trajectories of interpretation can be found. First, God's washing of the infant in 16:9 becomes a foreshadowing of Christian baptism (Stevenson and Glerup,

57–59). Second, the passage was also used to condemn contemporaneous opponents; for Jerome, these were heretics, while for Calvin, they were papists. Andrew Mein (159–83) notes that these later authors accept Ezekiel's gender hierarchy, and thus use female metaphors as insults.

Since the rise of second-wave feminism, the gendered assumptions that undergird these texts have been challenged. Drorah Setel was the first to compare texts like these to pornography because they turn the audience into voyeurs of female sexual activity and sexual assault. Feminist scholars have noted that the texts have too easily been used to substantiate domestic violence, sexual assault as "punishment," and the natural sinfulness of women (Weems).

Feminists have employed a counter-reading to the texts, one that deconstructs the rhetoric of legitimate male control. They note the ways the texts actually encapsulate male fear of women. Others have noted that Ezekiel itself is supposed to be a counter-reading of the prevailing male rhetoric (Patton).

■ THE TEXT IN CONTEMPORARY DISCUSSION

Although this text is not about real women, it inadvertently hints at the fate of women and children during wartime. In the ancient world, since male honor was demonstrated by the fate of their households, women and children were pawns used to demonstrate defeat. In ancient iconography, this was accomplished by showing the conquering king as the one who protects women and children (Chapman), but the literature attests to a much different fate. Women were raped or forced to become slaves in the households of the conquerors. As slaves, they were sexually available to the men of the household. Men and children were put on the front lines of the conqueror's army without armor, so that they would be killed while exhausting the weaponry of the opponent.

The fate of women and children in war is not much different in the modern world. Still today, more women and children die in armed conflict than do combatants (see Indra). Rape is still used as a military tactic; in the former Yugoslavia, women were systematically raped and impregnated as an element of ethnic cleansing. In the Republic of Congo, the rape of women and children reinforced the army's destruction of male opponents (see Kristof and WuDunn).

Given that Ezekiel's audience would have been one that had seen such acts of war, it invites today's readers to think about what these metaphors sound like to contemporary audiences who have undergone similar fates. Are they heard as substantiating such activity, or do they in fact undercut the claim by any human in power to have the right to perform such actions? Do these texts substantiate sexual assault, or do they undercut the power claims that are constituent of such crimes?

Ezekiel 20: A History of Sin

■ THE TEXT IN ITS ANCIENT CONTEXT

Chapter 20 is the longest review of Israel's history in the book. It focuses on the wilderness period, when God revealed the law to the Israelites. The passage focuses on the people's response, throughout characterizing them as sinful and disobedient. Earlier prophets also focused on the wilderness period as the time that was constitutive of the Israelite community. Hosea, for instance, depicts it as a honeymoon period, when God had first taken Israel as a bride, and she was still faithful to him (2:15). As in chapters 16 and 23, Ezekiel depicts the Israelites as never deserving God's favor, opening with the charge that they committed idolatry while still slaves in Egypt (20:7). Because Israel is so weak, undeserving, and unexceptional, all of God's actions on behalf of Israel have been and will be done for one reason alone: to enhance YHWH's international reputation.

The chapter uses irony in its radical theology. In this review, God reveals laws three times to the people (18:11-12, 19-20, 25-26). The first two times, the laws, which are characterized by observation of the Sabbath, are life-giving, meaning that if the Israelites had obeyed them, they would have prospered, but the people reject these laws. The third time, God decides to punish them for their disobedience by giving them laws that, when they follow them, actually cause them to sin (vv. 25-26). The irony is that these are the only laws the Israelites follow. Once defiled, Israel's punishment by God is justified.

The passage ends with an oracle of restoration in 20:40-44. This restoration, however, is not a reversal of the earlier assessment of Israel's worthiness. It only occurs to reinforce to the world that YHWH is powerful. The key to the success of the restoration will be Israel's acceptance of its unworthiness. Once they "loathe" themselves (v. 43), restoration can proceed.

▌▌ THE TEXT IN THE INTERPRETIVE TRADITION

In 20:25, the laws revealed to the Israelites are called "statutes that were not good." This reference to divinely revealed evil laws has led to a long history of interpretation. In the patristic period, Christians identified the "bad laws" as Jewish torah. Early Christians like Augustine and Chrysostom, following Paul's view of the law, viewed these laws as ultimately unable to save a sinner (Stevenson and Glerup, 86–87). In the Middle Ages, Christians used this tradition in their polemical writings against Jews. To counter this trend, Jewish interpreters like Rashi and Kara viewed the sinfulness of that particular generation to have been so great that it undercut any good that came from observing torah (Harris, 79–83). Reformers like Calvin, on the other hand, used the passage to discuss the relationship between faith and observing the sacraments, as well as keeping the Sabbath (Beckwith, 113–15).

▌▌ THE TEXT IN CONTEMPORARY DISCUSSION

Although Ezekiel 20 is a review of Israel's history, it is clearly told with an ideological focus in mind. The history is meant to characterize the people as unworthy and depict God as all powerful. This chapter offers particular challenges to people of faith. First, the events it recalls are those usually used either to illustrate the goodness of God or to exalt heroes like Moses. Ezekiel's twist on the tradition is as surprising to contemporary audiences as it was to the ancient one.

The chapter also offers the tantalizing possibility that laws touted as religiously binding might in fact lead people to sin. Prior to the nineteenth century, the biblical slave laws were used as justification for Christian slavery, yet today Christians view these as "not good" laws, ones that do not affirm life, but rather led people to sin. Today, many Christians use biblical laws about sexuality to limit access to marriage for members of contemporary society. Ezekiel 20 invites readers to question whether these also might be laws that do not affirm life, but rather lead to sin and injustice. It undercuts the equation that a law that is divinely revealed must be good, by stating that God can reveal laws that are meant to be disobeyed.

Ezekiel 21-22 and 24: The End Is Near

■ THE TEXT IN ITS ANCIENT CONTEXT

Chapters 21–24 are the final oracles before the report of the fall of Jerusalem reaches the prophet. Chapters 24 and 33, which bookend the oracles against foreign nations, deal explicitly with the final destruction of Jerusalem. In the chapters under consideration here, the condemnation of the city intensifies the motifs found in earlier chapters of the book, as they paint an inevitable portrait of Jerusalem's doom.

Chapter 21 contains various oracles that center on the image of the sword. City walls were breached so that soldiers could enter the city and slay its inhabitants. Neo-Assyrian reliefs that depict siege warfare in this period show that swords were used not just to kill people but also to dismember and behead them. The clipped nature of the language in these poems conveys the sense of panic as the walls were breached.

Chapters 22 and 24 focus on the filth of the slaughter through its images of blood and defilement. These disturbing images would have been all too familiar to survivors of the devastation. There must have been pools of blood and human waste where the slaughtering occurred. The sights and smells would have assaulted any human sensibility. The depiction of the walled city as an iron pot in which body parts float in 24:6-13 re-creates the horror of the city's fall. These poems masterfully capture the reality of warfare through flashes of images that encapsulate that destruction. They are also disturbing in their attribution of that destruction to God. Although usually it is the victors who write history, here we have the historical witness of the defeated Judeans. In a kind of photographic negative of the Assyrian reliefs, it is as if those dismembered bodies rose up to tell their story.

The final verses of chapter 24 mark a turning point in the book. For the book of Ezekiel, the destruction of the temple in Jerusalem is Judah's final punishment. The passage once again uses the character of Ezekiel to personalize the experience of national collapse. The death of his wife, who was his "delight," symbolizes the destruction of the temple, the delightful possession of the Judeans. But the sign that the chapter focuses on is not the loss of wife and temple, but rather on God's command that these losses cannot be mourned. Mourning was an important ritual in the ancient world. It was a public act that both provided communal support for the mourner and paid honor to the dead. The inability to mourn the dead is the final horror endured by the survivors, leaving them alone and shamed.

■ THE TEXT IN THE INTERPRETIVE TRADITION

The Ancient Christian Commentary on Scripture lists no patristic commentary on these chapters, and contemporary research into the history of interpretation of the book of Ezekiel has done little to fill this gap. The silence, however, is deafening. It demonstrates a common interpretive move made when biblical texts contain disturbing images: dismissing them through silence. It also helps explain why the heart of Ezekiel's message has failed to inform the Christian tradition in a significant way. While contemporary Christians may be familiar with Ezekiel's visions or his image of the dry bones (Ezekiel 37, see below), they are often completely unfamiliar with the violent images that permeate the book.

Recent biblical scholarship has sought to redress this lapse by wrestling with the interpretation of violent texts. A volume devoted to violent images in the prophets, for example, looks at the aesthetic function of violent images (Franke and O'Brien). These studies challenge contemporary readers to consider the role that violent images in film, art, and music play today, and how that function relates to contemporary theologies.

▌THE TEXT IN CONTEMPORARY DISCUSSION

The close of this section in Ezekiel reminds readers that death is not the worst of war's horrors. Those who survive often face a perennially interrupted life. The modern world is not so different. Ezekiel's use of mourning rituals to signify major social disruption resonates with the experiences of refugees today. Ezekiel 24 uses mourning to signify the disruption to basic social practices within refugee populations. Jeremiah 16 similarly talks about the interruption to both mourning and marriage rituals. Gregory Lee Cuéllar, who reads Isaiah 40–55 through the lens of Mexican immigrant experience, notes similar themes of disruption. Simple family-based rituals become political statements when a community has minority status. Ezekiel 24 depicts mourning as a basic human right whose denial is an ultimate horror for those who could not mourn Judah's dead or bury the mutilated bodies of loved ones, let alone weep at family gravesites.

Although these texts address the experience of the defeated, they also invite readers to ponder what such violence does to its perpetrators. Here, God personifies the stance of the perpetrator, and it is not a very pleasant portrayal. Readers are struck by the text's attempt to justify violence, the smug self-assurance that might makes right. The victims in the passages are not individuals but a faceless mass, eventually reduced to dangling body parts. Yet the reader's sympathy remains with the victims and not the perpetrator. YHWH seems more monster than hero.

Is this chapter really about God? Or is it about how perpetrators of violence turn themselves into God in order to commit acts that horrify normal human sensibilities? Trauma literature gives voice to those whose experiences have left them without words; like the book of Lamentations (O'Connor 2002), these chapters in Ezekiel provide language for those traumatized by national defeat.

Ezekiel 25–32 and 35: Oracles against Foreign Nations

▌THE TEXT IN ITS ANCIENT CONTEXT

Many prophetic collections contain a section of oracles condemning nations other than Israel and Judah. Chapters 25–32 in Ezekiel show signs of conscious editing, which indicate that they play an important rhetorical function in the book. For example, seven nations are condemned, and the last nation, Egypt, is denounced seven times. The oracles are placed just after the notice of the fall of Jerusalem and mark the book's turn toward oracles of restoration.

Although this section, along with a recapitulation in chapter 35, contains oracles against some of the minor nations that surrounded Israel, the bulk of the material focuses on Tyre to the north and Egypt to the south, both economic titans at the time. Surprisingly, there are no oracles against Judah's military enemy Babylon. Instead, the focus is on the two neighbors of Israel that Babylon was unable to defeat. The poems that make up these oracles use metaphoric and mythic language to create vivid pictures of these two nations. These poems reflect a Judean perspective on the unique culture of each nation.

The oracles against Tyre (26:1—28:19), the capital of the Phoenicians, focus on its relative security from enemy attacks (chapter 26, which describes the city's location) and its economic prosperity (chapter 27, which depicts Tyre as a merchant ship). Phoenicia was one of the few nations in the Levant with natural ports, which afforded it a bustling trade on the Mediterranean. As a result, its wealth was not solely dependent on the unreliable rains on which the agricultural economy of the rest of the Levant depended. The geography of its main city, Tyre, also accorded it protection against siege. Built on an island that was connected to the mainland only at low tide, the siege works of the Babylonian army were ineffective against it. In Ezek. 29:18-20, Ezekiel sounds almost sorry for the unsuccessful effort of the Babylonians, stating that God will reward Babylon's thirteen-year effort by giving them Egypt instead.

The oracles against Egypt (29:1—32:32) use language that engages Egyptian religious iconography in order to subvert its claims to power. Although it may seem odd to find such vitriol against an ally of Judah who did in fact come to Judah's aid (albeit unsuccessfully), Ezekiel blames Egypt for presenting itself as a nation on which Judah could have relied. These oracles are framed by two condemnations of the Pharaoh, who is depicted as a reptilian creature whom God fishes out of the Nile, which Pharaoh claims to have created. At the end of the oracles, Egypt and its warriors have their proper reign, enthroned in the depths of the land of the dead surrounded by the dead armies of Judah's other enemies (32:17-32; see also 31:15-18).

Both sets of oracles castigate the foreign kings for their hubris, and both do so in part by engaging Israel's traditions about Eden. Although most contemporary readers of the Bible are familiar with Eden from the story of the creation of Adam, for the Israelites Eden was simply God's garden, a lavish place filled with every good tree, marvelous gems, and springs that watered the earth. In 28:2-19, Tyre's king is mocked for claiming to be a god, responsible for his own wealth, rather than a creature of God banned from Eden. In 31:2-18, both Assyria and Egypt are ridiculed for likening themselves to the loftiest tree in Eden; as punishment, God chops them down, felling all of their allies in the process.

The strong language in the oracles against Tyre and Egypt reveal that for this author, the real threat to Judah was not military defeat but rather cultural colonization. Both of these nations were attractive to Judeans, because their economic dominance seemed to protect them against invasion. In addition, Egypt housed Judean refugees after the fall of the city. This section of Ezekiel reveals the author's fear of the loss of Judah's cultural identity that would result from both appeasing these neighbors and settling in their lands.

The Text in the Interpretive Tradition

Although much of this material receives little comment in the Christian tradition, the interpretation of the prince of Tyre in chapter 28 has a long history within both Judaism and Christianity. The passage describes a person created with every kind of wisdom and glory who then falls from his exalted position because of his own pride. Although very early Jewish texts identified this figure as Adam before being driven out of Eden, later sources say that he is Hiram, who supplied the Israelites with material for the temple (Patmore, 59–69).

Christian tradition, on the other hand, linked this story to the creation and fall of Satan. Although the Bible contains no clear story of the fall of Satan, it was a popular legend, dating back to at least the Hellenistic period. Christians looked for evidence of this tradition in the Bible, offering various texts as evidence for the tradition. The language of exalted creation and fall due to sin suit this purpose handily (Stevenson and Glerup, 90–97).

The Text in Contemporary Discussion

A major threat to the identity of a colonized nation is cultural hegemony. In our postcolonial world, the effects of European colonization around the globe are felt today not just in terms of economics but also through its effects on culture. The triad of Babylon, Tyre, and Egypt in Ezekiel represents three different types of colonization that were at play both in the ancient world and today: military, economic, and political. For Ezekiel, it is the allure of those nations, which are economically and politically attractive, that makes them so dangerous.

In our postcolonial world, the same holds true. While there is far less military occupation of the Southern Hemisphere by the North, cultural hegemony continues through a global economy that depends on maintaining economic disparity, and through the promise of military "aid" that uses the rhetoric of alliance to mask the reality of dependence. Egypt's horses are today's US fighter planes.

This section of the book also hints at the kind of cultural annihilation that refugee populations experience. While Egypt did provide a safe haven for Judean refugees, this section of the book invites contemporary US readers to recognize the struggle that refugees from Somalia, Liberia, and Southeast Asia face in their attempts to maintain vestiges of their cultural identity. These texts ask if this lifeline is really a noose that will destroy the very identity of those seeking aid. These chapters warn Judah of the allure of dominant cultures, even when the other choice may be military collapse.

Ezekiel 33: The Fall of Jerusalem

The Text in Its Ancient Context

Chapter 33 closes off the oracles condemning Judah; placed after oracles against Judah's neighbors, it recapitulates themes found in chapters 1–24. It does this in a way that relieves Ezekiel of any responsibility for the nation's destruction. First, it reiterates the image of the prophet as a sentinel, found in 3:16-21. Second, it reviews the discussion of individual sin and salvation found in chapter 18. Most importantly, though, the second half of the chapter focuses explicitly on Ezekiel. His mouth is opened to speak freely (cf. 3:25-27) just as news of the fall of the city comes to the exiles. This loosening of his mouth marks the end of his function as sentinel; the prophesied events have now come to pass.

The passage ends with a summary characterization of the people. In the beginning of the book, they are characterized as rebellious and unwilling to listen. Even after the notice of the fall of the city, they still fail to believe Ezekiel. They assert that, although God has destroyed those living in Judah, the exiles must be blessed since God seems to be giving the land to them (33:24). Even after Ezekiel announces that they are mistaken, they dismiss him as a mere entertainer (33:30-33). Ezekiel, and subsequently God, have done all that they could do.

▮ THE TEXT IN THE INTERPRETIVE TRADITION

Christian exegetes use the two passages about the prophet as sentinel to talk about the office of the bishop. In Greek, the word for "bishop" (*episkopos*) means "overseer" or "watchman." In the patristic period, both this chapter, along with 3:16-21, are used as a paradigm for the role of the bishop. While everyone must speak when they see wrong happening, this is especially true for bishops (Stevenson and Glerup, 25–29, 98–103).

▮ THE TEXT IN CONTEMPORARY DISCUSSION

The depiction of a people only willing to hear what they want to hear is eerily familiar. Even today, for example, many people dismiss warnings about how our choices direly affect the environment. Although this chapter seems to be about Ezekiel, it is really about the justice of God. In fact, by making every speech by Ezekiel a direct oracle from God, the book asserts that God sent warning after warning to the people as disaster loomed. In one of the most striking verses in the book, YHWH states, "I have no pleasure in the death of [even] the wicked" (33:11, "even" added for emphasis). Disaster is not God's will; change is.

Since natural disasters happen all of the time, it is easy to dismiss them as meaningless, not reflecting anything about the nature of God or the effects of human sin. But abdicating all responsibility for the extent of natural disasters is even more morally blind. Why is it that the poor and marginalized suffer the effects more than the rich? How do we define safe and adequate housing? What do we count as a disaster? Who benefits from practices that continue the polluting of the atmosphere, and why is there so little will to enact programmatic change? This passage in Ezekiel states that disasters are not God's will; facing communal responsibility for natural disasters and their aftermath is. But, like the ancient Israelites, sometimes it is easier to blame God than it is to change a group's way of life.

Ezekiel 34 and 36: Hope for the Future

▮ THE TEXT IN ITS ANCIENT CONTEXT

Chapters 34 and 36 contain the first lengthy oracles of restoration in the book. Chapter 34 focuses on political restoration, while chapter 36 discusses the restoration of the land. Both chapters start with a summary of what had gone wrong in the past; kings had failed the people, and the land had been laid waste. Both chapters symbolize restoration as the flourishing of nature. In an agriculture-based economy, this is tantamount to a booming stock market.

The oracles in chapter 34 play with shepherding images. In the ancient world, it was common to depict the king as a shepherd of the people, who are the flock. In the ancient world, shepherds did not own the flock; they worked for the flock's owner. In 34:31, God is the owner of the flock, and the kings, who work for God, keep that flock safe. The restoration of the Davidic monarchy is mentioned only twice in the book, here and in chapter 37. What is important to notice in this chapter, however, is that it deals less with human agents of restoration and instead focuses on God. It is God who seeks out the flock, YHWH who restores them. This results in a "covenant of peace" (v. 25), that is, a restoration of all nature.

The oracles of restoration in chapter 36 can be divided into two parts. Verses 1-12 depict the restoration of the land itself, which had been devastated as the Babylonian army advanced southward. Verses 13-21 contain the surprising conclusion that the worst result of the fall of Jerusalem is how it damaged YHWH's reputation among other nations. God defends this reputation first by asserting that the punishment of Judah was deserved, and, second, that the restoration of Israel will occur to prove God's "sanctity" or power.

Verses 22-36 provide a brief outline of Ezekiel's program of restoration. First, God will gather the people from every place they have been scattered. God will first purify them and then give them a new heart along with a new divine spirit. Only then will the people be returned to the land. Once there, nature will respond with bounty. Finally, everyone will recognize that YHWH is the agent of this restoration: Israel will feel shame both for their earlier sins and in recognition of the greatness of God, and the other nations will finally recognize the holiness and power of Israel's God.

The oracles throughout the chapter are couched in ritual imagery. The land that is restored will be the "mountains," a veiled reference to the restoration of the temple on its holy mountain. The sins of the people are compared to the defilement of a menstruating woman (vv. 17-19), and the restoration of the people includes a divine purification ritual (v. 25). God's reputation is equated with sanctity and holiness, while the inhabited cities will teem with people, like the temple teems with flocks on festival days (vv. 37-38).

▐ THE TEXT IN THE INTERPRETIVE TRADITION

Early Jewish literature used the image of the good shepherd as a messianic designation. *First Enoch* 85–90 seems to identify this figure as Judas Maccabaeus, while *Psalms of Solomon* 17 applies it to the restoration of the Davidic monarchy. The Gospel traditions engaged this same imagery, applying it to God and Jesus. The passage with the most explicit connection to Ezekiel 37 is John 10 (Manning, 27–36). Because of these New Testament references, far more attention has been paid to 34:11-31 than to any other part of the book of Ezekiel. The good shepherd was also applied to Christian leaders, especially bishops and abbots, who were charged with caring for their "flock" (Stevenson and Glerup, 104–15).

▌THE TEXT IN CONTEMPORARY DISCUSSION

Tragedy challenges belief in God. It is difficult to believe in a powerful, just, and loving God in the face of innocent suffering. God either seems cruel or ineffective. Ancient peoples faced similar challenges. Ezekiel abandons the notion of a loving God; the word is never used in the book. But the author holds on to two essential divine elements: divine justice and power. Jerusalem's fall was deserved, but its restoration, though undeserved, will demonstrate God's power.

This is not the solution favored by the elite in today's world: people want God to love them and do not want to admit how little control they have over the world writ large. Often people would rather have a loving God who is willing to forgo justified punishments or who is no match for the evil humans do, than one who directly causes disasters in the world.

Twelve-step programs, like Alcoholics Anonymous, view the admission of one's lack of control over addictions and the acceptance of a higher power as an important step in recovery. One of its slogans, "Let go and let God," embodies this surrender to divine power. Although addiction is not the same tragedy as wartime devastation, it does provide a model for equating the acceptance of personal responsibility with the recognition of where human power ends and divine power begins.

Acceptance of divine control is also an important element in Protestant views of divine grace. Luther states that what freed him from worrying about his salvation was his recognition that he would never deserve it. Calvin's view of human depravity especially after the fall shares with Ezekiel the ideas that humans are damaged, unable to do good on their own, but infinitely salvageable because of God's choice to save them. The image is one of profound hope, because its surety stems from God and does not depend on fallible human effort. And reliability is what humans most desire when they feel profoundly their own inability to control the world.

Ezekiel 37: The Valley of the Dry Bones

▌THE TEXT IN ITS ANCIENT CONTEXT

Both chapters 36 and 37 depict restoration as a return from death. In 36:26-27, the heart of stone represents death. While the heart transplant means the body lives, it is the infusion of divine breath or spirit that really represents human life, as is seen in Gen. 2:7. In 37:1-14, the prophet has a vision of a battlefield strewn with dead bodies. Assyrian reliefs indicate that bodies were often left to rot unburied where carrion birds and the ravages of weather would strip them of all flesh. Ezekiel's vision of a valley filled with bones is an image of these desiccated carcasses.

God calls on the prophet to revivify these skeletal remains. The prophet's answer that only God knows if they can be revived (v. 3) shows the hopelessness of dreams of restoration. Yet through the prophetic proclamations, what God promises comes true. The bodies that rise up from field and grave are a metaphor for the restoration of the living, breathing nation (vv. 11-13).

The parallel vision of restoration in verses 15-23 reinforces this metaphoric meaning. In this section, two dry sticks are grafted together representing not just the restoration of Judah but also the future restoration of all twelve tribes of Israel. The northern kingdom, composed of ten tribes, had been exiled by the Assyrians more than a century before the fall of Jerusalem. Those exiles had been scattered throughout Mesopotamia. Yet, within Israel's prophetic tradition, there always remained a hope that all twelve tribes would one day be restored and reunited.

This chapter reiterates the pattern of restoration seen in earlier oracles. First, restoration includes divine purification of the restored community (v. 23; see 36:25). Second, the passage repeats the hope for the restoration of a Davidic king (v. 24; see 34:23-24). Last, it refers to this restoration as a "covenant of peace" (v. 26; see 34:25-29). It also anticipates the final vision of the restoration of the temple in chapters 40–48, first by the insistence on the restoration of all twelve tribes (see esp. 47:21—48:7), and finally by the notice that God will once again restore the temple (37:27-28).

▌ The Text in the Interpretive Tradition

Ezekiel 37:1-14 has often been seen as an image of bodily resurrection. In fact, patristic writers asserted that these verses accurately describe the way bodies would be resurrected after the second coming of Christ (Stevenson and Glerup, 12–24). This became the text's standard interpretation, seen in places as wide ranging as wall paintings in the ancient Jewish synagogue of Dura Europos (Manning, 40–43), to nineteenth-century African American spirituals (Callender).

The Reformers expanded the interpretation of the passage in two ways. First, they focused on the fact that the bones are brought together by prophetic speech. For William Greenhill, this passage is about the efficacy of God's Word; even if it falls on something dead, it can bring it to life. Second, they paid more attention to the image of the two sticks, but for them these did not represent the two nations of Judah and Israel, but rather the division of Jews and gentiles. The question remained whether the oracle was fulfilled with the rise of Christianity that brought together Jews and gentiles, or whether it referred to an unfulfilled oracle about the ultimate conversion of all of the Jews (Beckwith, 179–87).

In modern commentaries, attention has turned to the placement of this chapter within the book as a whole. Recently discovered ancient Greek manuscripts, which agree with Old Latin versions, place this chapter right before chapter 40, which starts the vision of the restored temple (see Lust). The placement of this chapter affects the interpretation of the Gog material that follows. Is it a vision of God's defeat of another human enemy (indicated by its placement in the ancient Greek texts), or is it a vision of God's future cosmic battle (implied by its current placement)?

▌ The Text in Contemporary Discussion

The images in chapter 37 face squarely the feelings of despair felt by those displaced by war. Although the image of a field of dead bodies may seem rather gruesome, it effectively depicts the experience of war refugees who have had to leave the gravesites of loved ones who have died. The art installation *One Million Bones* (onemillionbones.org) in Washington, DC, has a similar task: to provide a visual reminder of the extent of genocide in the modern world and to raise awareness of the survivors. Similarly, Ezekiel 37 should remind us that refugees in our communities, even those grateful for a sense of safety, still yearn for what may seem impossible: a return not to what life was but to the best of what life could be in their land of origin.

Ezekiel 37 does not deny the sense of hopelessness. It does not offer a false sense that the refugee community can change their situation or that the restoration will come easily. What it does do is encourage the community to dream big. But those dreams are not based on human effort, which is not up for the task; they are based on God, for whom all things are possible.

This trust in God is not a way to pacify a disgruntled community. It is not a denial of their communal tragedy. In fact, it is the opposite. It validates the community's sense that their own visions of a better world are not silly, insignificant pipe dreams. Ezekiel 37 states they are what God had wanted all along. This chapter calls on communities of faith to support refugee communities and to experience their visions of a better world as a prophetic voice.

Ezekiel 38–39: God's Role in Israel's Future

▌ THE TEXT IN ITS ANCIENT CONTEXT

Right before the final vision of the book, Ezekiel 38–39 contains a vision of a future attack on the restored nation by a mythic enemy. The enemy in this passage is an unidentified king, Gog, who hails from a mythic land, Magog. He gathers an army from every corner of the globe and marches against people living in unwalled villages. The text states that he does this simply to gather more plunder.

Gog is defeated handily by God; in fact, the battle is not even described, insinuating that it was literally "no contest." Instead, the passage focuses on three postbattle scenes: the gathering of the spoils of war by the Israelites, the burial of the corpses, and the postbattle sacrifice of the enemy. In the first two of these scenes, the details stress the enormous size of this army. It takes seven years to burn all of the spoils, while the pile of bodies becomes a monument. In the third postbattle scene, God feeds the corpses to carrion birds and other beasts in what the text terms a "sacrifice," thus inverting the usual offering made to God at the end of a battle.

The passage ends with the longest recognition formula of the book. It not only states that this will happen so that "they will know that I am YHWH," but also goes on to note that with this battle everyone will recognize that the Babylonian exile occurred because Israel had sinned. In other words, God's defeat of the greatest human enemy anyone could imagine proves that Babylon's defeat of Judah was not the result of God's weakness but rather the result of God's choice to let Babylon win.

▌ THE TEXT IN THE INTERPRETIVE TRADITION

The vision of Gog and Magog has had a significant interpretive history. From as early as Zechariah, the text has served as fodder for later apocalyptic images. Sverre Bøe traces the way that Revelation, especially chapters 19–20, reuses imagery from these chapters in creative ways.

Because Gog cannot be identified with any historic enemy of Judah, this literary figure became a trope for any evil enemy of God's chosen people. Gog represents all that is evil, and Israel becomes the innocent victim whom God vindicates. Jerome views Gog as the antichrist, a view found into the Middle Ages. Reformers, who also identified Gog as Satan, looked to the Jewish community in their own day as the subject of these chapters. Disturbingly, they believed that these chapters dealt with how God would bring about the conversion of all Jews, who currently suffered because they lacked faith in Christ (Beckwith, 190–93).

Today, Christian millennialist groups continue to use the term "Gog" for any archenemy of Christianity. During the Cold War era, for example, some American Christian churches viewed Russia as the new Gog. Today, some Messianic Christians, who view the re-creation of the nation of Israel as a harbinger for the second coming of Christ, identify Arab Islam as the new "Gog."

■ THE TEXT IN CONTEMPORARY DISCUSSION

The celebration of violence in the Gog pericope has often been problematic for Christians living in colonizing countries, such as England, Germany, and the United States, but when the chapters are read from the perspective of the colonized, a vision in which God annihilates evil incarnate makes poetic sense. The chapters tell the story of a people who view themselves as utterly defenseless, whose only hope of survival lies in an otherworldly power.

The victim in this passage is never the aggressor. The attack by Gog is unprovoked and gratuitous, just as the colonization of economically depressed areas of the globe by nations of relative wealth and privilege is also gratuitous, unprovoked, and motivated by the basest of human instincts: greed. The passage unravels the ideology of the colonizer. Not only are the boasts of Gog vain, but they are laughable in light of the source of true power—God. The details of the text serve to highlight this uneven power distribution: as numerous and as well-equipped as the army is, God dispatches them in a moment.

The passage also uses details from nature to undercut the ideology of the colonizer. The passage notes that all of nature recognizes God's power, trembling at the warrior's entrance onto the battle scene. The text mentions "creeping things," for example, worms, bugs, lizards, and locusts, that recognize God's power. Even trees benefit from God's duties as warriors; they avoid being cut down as firewood for seven years, while the Israelites use the spoils of war as fuel for cooking, heating, and light. Gog and his armies are rendered less than geckos and ginkgoes, a beautiful fantasy indeed.

Ezekiel 40:1—44:4: Visions of the Temple

■ THE TEXT IN ITS ANCIENT CONTEXT

The book of Ezekiel ends with a nine-chapter vision of the restoration of the nation of Israel. That restoration begins and ends at the restored temple of Jerusalem. The rest of the vision radiates out from this liturgical center. The vision is told through the eyes of Ezekiel, who is led on a visionary tour by an unidentified heavenly tour guide. These chapters contain no prophetic speeches, except the command to observe the vision and write it down (40:4; 43:10-11).

The opening section of the vision contains the prophet's tour of the temple complex, starting in its outer courtyard (40:5-27), proceeding to the inner courtyard (40:28-47), then into the outer parts of the sanctuary building (40:48—41:26). The tour then proceeds back outside to the inner court, the arena for priestly rituals (42:1-20).

In chapter 43, Ezekiel once again sees God on the portable throne, this time flying back into the temple complex, a vision that ties the restoration to the oracles of condemnation in the first part of the book. The image marks the restoration as the reversal of the problems that led to national defeat. Twice the passage states that God will dwell in this temple "forever" (43:7, 9). This idea is reinforced when the gate through which God traveled is permanently shut (44:2).

God's move back into the temple is followed by a number of items found in other biblical texts that describe the founding of a temple. First, God's presence in the temple requires the restoration of daily sacrifices, seen in the restoration of the altar and the priesthood in 43:13-27. Second, God's indwelling requires the reestablishment of ritual laws (43:11-12) spelled out in the next section. Last, the reality of God's presence in the temple is symbolized by the divine "glory" that emanates from the temple (44:4).

◼ The Text in the Interpretive Tradition

Although Christians today often pay little attention to these final chapters of the book, it was fertile ground for patristic and medieval interpretation. The details were often interpreted allegorically: the temple was the church, and each detail represented some aspect of Christian belief. This trend lasted into the Reformation period, where it was coupled with a focus on Christ as the center of the vision (Tooman, 215–20; Beckwith, xlvi, 205–13).

Ezekiel's temple came to prefigure Mary in the Christian tradition (Sawyer, 7–9), a view that persisted in Catholicism, but not among Reformers. First, just as a temple housed the real presence of God, Mary's pregnant body "housed" the divine Christ. If Mary were to be a dwelling place for God, then like the temple, this "house" had to be pure, free from any defilement. The typology that Mary's body was a temple for Christ led to the tradition that Mary herself had to be pure, and for Christians this meant free from original sin. The doctrine of Mary's "immaculate conception" expresses this belief that she had to have been conceived without the stain of original sin in order for her to function as a pure vessel for Christ.

The doctrine is really about the nature of Jesus, as true God even before Mary's impregnation whose "house" had to be prepared prior to his incarnation within her body. Catholic tradition also looks to the image of the locked gate as an allegory for Mary's permanent virginity. Her purified body is protected from any subsequent defilement or impregnation. If her body is God's temple, then it cannot house anything else.

◼ The Text in Contemporary Discussion

These chapters in Ezekiel are not often read in the church; their focus on detailed measurements of walls and spaces does not seem to be the stuff of spiritual nourishment. But the chapters do invite contemporary Christian communities to consider what it really means to proclaim that Christ is among them. Ezekiel suggests that such a statement should result in concrete changes in how societies are organized, worship is ordered, and people relate to God and each other. The details themselves are not as important as the fact that faith results in concrete changes that are communally visible.

While the Christian tradition often looks down on the practice of sacrifices as something "pagans" do, the fact is, the active sacrificial liturgies in other religions, such as Islam, the shamanistic sacrifices in Hmong communities, and the sacrifices of Hindu religion provide a living witness to the fact that all liturgy is really an acting out of metaphors about the divine reality. If God is among the people, then rituals of feeding provide a way for that community to express that the divine presence should be nurtured, honored, and cared for through ritual hosting and festive feeding. Recognizing how important those rituals are in the biblical tradition helps foster interreligious dialogue with those who still practice forms of sacrifice.

Ezekiel 44:5—48:35: The Blossoming of a World Made Right

■ THE TEXT IN ITS ANCIENT CONTEXT

The final five chapters in the book finish the vision of the restored nation begun in chapter 40. They extend the effects of God's presence in the temple to the nation as a whole. Ezekiel 44:5—46:24 contains the book's ideal laws for this visionary restored community. While the laws in the Pentateuch reflect life in a settled economy, these laws focus on cultic matters, an indication of the book's priestly perspective. Although these laws may seem more practical than visionary, their utopian quality should not be ignored.

The final chapters of the book bring the utopian nature of the vision back to the fore. In the ancient Near East, temples were often touted as a ritual paradise, the site from which all creation bursts forth. In arid lands, this was most often symbolized by an abundance of fresh water; this idea is the basis of the four rivers in Gen. 2:10-14. Ezekiel 47 paints a picture of a fructifying river flowing out from beneath the temple itself and watering the land. The image of the Dead Sea teeming with freshwater fish encapsulates this paradise.

Another idyllic detail is the distribution of land among the twelve tribes of Israel. Each strip of land is equitable, especially since the vision imagines a land of universal fertility. Although some tribes are closer to the nation's center, which might suggest a privileged position, the nation's new geography makes clear that nothing profane can reach God in the temple. Here, the temple is not located inside the capital city, but rather is surrounded by land given to the priests. It is literally set in a ring of holiness. The capital city, with its restored monarchy, is adjacent to this holy area.

In addition to the changes in geography, this utopian vision also changes city and society. The leading monarch is not called a "king" but rather a "prince." The vision makes clear that the monarchy serves primarily a ritual function as leader of lay worship. Second, the king is never identified as Davidic, nor is the capital city ever called Jerusalem. This is new space. The book ends with the renaming of the city. Naming the city "YHWH is there" reinforces the main message of these chapters, that restoration is equated with God taking up residence again in Israel's national temple.

■ THE TEXT IN THE INTERPRETIVE TRADITION

While Jewish tradition focused on the laws in Ezekiel that did not match similar precepts in the Pentateuch (Sweeney, 13–16), Christian exegetes looked at the figure of the king, who, as first among the worshipers, came alternatively to symbolize Christ as well as the priests. In addition, the life-giving waters of Ezekiel 47 became fertile ground for interpretation. Jerome, who saw the temple tour as an allegory for the mystical ascent to heaven (Stevenson and Glerup, 125–47), likened the river to the teachings of the church, while the *Epistle of Barnabas* says that it represents baptism (Stevenson and Glerup, 125–47). The Reformers viewed the river as the proclamation of the gospel (Beckwith, 225–29).

■ THE TEXT IN CONTEMPORARY DISCUSSION

What does paradise look like? In a world where drought destroyed whole communities, where water supplies were scarce and often vulnerable to contamination, paradise could be symbolized by flowing fresh water. But this world does not exist only in the past. Today drought threatens thousands of people daily. In the 1960s, drought in what was then called Biafra resulted in images of starving children. These droughts are exacerbated today by climate change, so that even places that do get rain have been left barren because the timing of those rains can no longer be predicted. For other people, like those in Haiti and Egypt, the need for fresh water has left many people displaced when dams are built to harness that water.

Reading Ezekiel 47 through the lens of these experiences shows that in an ideal world, there would be no need to fight for water or for the crops that result from that water. Utopia is marked by equal and easy access to natural resources. If people all had what they needed, this vision suggests, then wars over land possession would also cease. Society could set up equitable portions of land. It suggests that there would be no need of big government, and communities could look for leaders who primarily led them in praising God. It is not the utopia of big business or corporate greed, but it is a vision of a world set right.

Works Cited

Barstad, Hans M. 1996. *The Myth of the Empty Land: A Study in the History and Archaeology of Judah during the "Exilic" Period*. SO 28. Oslo: Scandinavian University Press.

Beckwith, Carl L., ed. 2012. *Ezekiel, Daniel*. Reformation Commentary on Scripture, Old Testament 12. Downers Grove, IL: IVP Academic.

Bog, Sverre. 2001. *Gog and Magog: Ezekiel 38–39 as Pre-Text for Revelation 19, 17-21 and 20, 7-10*. WUNT 2/135. Tübingen: Mohr Siebeck.

Callender, Dexter E., Jr. 2010. "Ezekiel." In *The Africana Bible: Reading Israel's Scriptures from Africa and the African Diaspora*, edited by Hugh R. Page Jr., 157–63. Minneapolis: Fortress Press.

Chapman, Cynthia R. 2004. *The Gendered Language of Warfare in the Israelite-Assyrian Encounter*. HSM 62. Winona Lake, IN: Eisenbrauns.

Cuéllar, Gregory Lee. 2008. *Voices of Marginality: Exile and Return in Second Isaiah 40–55 and the Mexican Immigrant Experience*. American University Studies 7. Theology and Religion 271. New York: Lang.

Franke, Chris, and Julia M. O'Brien, eds. 2010. *Aesthetics of Violence in the Prophets*. LHB/OTS 517. New York: T&T Clark.

Halperin, David J. 1993. *Seeking Ezekiel: Text and Psychology*. University Park: Pennsylvania State University Press.

Harris, Robert A. 2011. "The Reception of Ezekiel among Twelfth-Century Northern French Rabbinic Exegetes." In *After Ezekiel: Essays on the Reception of a Difficult Prophet*, edited by Andrew Mein and Paul M. Joyce, 71–88. LHB/OTS 535. New York: T&T Clark.

Indra, Doreen, ed. 1999. *Engendering Forced Migration: Theory and Practice*. New York: Berghahn.

Joyce, Paul M. 1989. *Divine Initiative and Human Response in Ezekiel*. JSOTSup 51. Sheffield: JSOT Press.

Kristof, Nicholas D., and Sheryl WuDunn. *Half the Sky: Turning Oppression into Opportunity for Women Worldwide*. New York: Vintage, 2010.

Lust, Johann. 1981. "Ezekiel 36–40 in the Oldest Greek Manuscript." *CBQ* 43:517–33.

Manning, Gary T., Jr. 2011. "Shepherd, Vine and Bones: The Use of Ezekiel in the Gospel of John." In *After Ezekiel: Essays on the Reception of a Difficult Prophet*, edited by Andrew Mein and Paul M. Joyce, 25–44. LHB/OTS 535. New York: T&T Clark.

Mein, Andrew. 2011. "Ezekiel's Women in Christian Interpretation: The Case of Ezekiel 16." In *After Ezekiel: Essays on the Reception of a Difficult Prophet*, edited by Andrew Mein and Paul M. Joyce, 159–83. LHB/OTS 535. New York: T&T Clark.

O'Connor, Kathleen M. 2002. *Lamentations and the Tears of the World*. Maryknoll, NY: Orbis.

———. 2012. *Jeremiah: Pain and Promise*. Philadelphia: Fortress Press.

Patmore, Hector M. "Adam or Satan? The Identity of the King of Tyre in Late Antiquity." In *After Ezekiel: Essays on the Reception of a Difficult Prophet*, edited by Andrew Mein and Paul M. Joyce, 59–69. LHB/OTS 535. New York: T&T Clark.

Patton, Corrine L. 2000. "'Should Our Sister Be Treated Like a Whore?' A Response to Feminist Critiques of Ezekiel 23." In *The Book of Ezekiel: Theological and Anthropological Perspectives*, edited by Margaret S. Odell and John T. Strong, 221–38. SBLSymS 9. Atlanta: Society of Biblical Literature.

Sawyer, John F. A. 2011. "Ezekiel in the History of Christianity." In *After Ezekiel: Essays on the Reception of a Difficult Prophet*, edited by Andrew Mein and Paul M. Joyce, 1–9. LHB/OTS 535. New York: T&T Clark.

Setel, Drorah T. 1985. "Prophets and Pornography: Female Sexual Imagery in Hosea." In *Feminist Interpretation of the Bible*, edited by Letty Russell, 86–95. Philadelphia: Westminster.

Smith-Christopher, Daniel. 2002. *A Biblical Theology of Exile*. OBT. Minneapolis: Fortress Press.

Stevenson, Kenneth, and Michael Glerup, eds. 2008. *Ezekiel, Daniel*. Ancient Christian Commentary on Scripture, Old Testament 13. Downers Grove, IL: InterVarsity.

Sweeney, Marvin A. 2011. "The Problem of Ezekiel in Talmudic Literature." In *After Ezekiel: Essays on the Reception of a Difficult Prophet*, edited by Andrew Mein and Paul M. Joyce, 11–23. LHB/OTS 535. New York: T&T Clark.

Tooman, William A. 2011. "Of Puritans and Prophets: Cotton Mather's Interpretation of Ezekiel in the *Biblia Americana*." In *After Ezekiel: Essays on the Reception of a Difficult Prophet*, edited by Andrew Mein and Paul M. Joyce, 203–27. LHB/OTS 535. New York: T&T Clark.

Tuell, Steven Shawn. 2011. "The Meaning of the Mark: New Light on Ezekiel 9 from the History of Interpretation." In *After Ezekiel: Essays on the Reception of a Difficult Prophet*, edited by Andrew Mein and Paul M. Joyce, 185–202. LHB/OTS 535. New York: T&T Clark.

Weems, Renita. 1995. *Battered Love: Marriage, Sex, and Violence in the Hebrew Prophets*. OBT. Minneapolis: Fortress Press.

DANIEL

Anathea Portier-Young

Introduction

Daniel combines story, prayer, vision, and interpretation in a creative and hope-filled response to domination, state terror, and persecution. One of the earliest exemplars of the literary genre of apocalypse, it makes visible the hidden workings of empire and God. More specifically, Daniel is a *historical* apocalypse. It interprets events and circumstances of the past, present, and future and helps God's people claim their history and identity in a time of unspeakable trauma.

The text of Daniel that is the foundation for this commentary consists of twelve chapters that alternate between Hebrew and Aramaic, with 1:1—2:4a in Hebrew, 2:4b—7:28 in Aramaic, and 8:1–12:13 in Hebrew. This bilingual structure is part of the book's artistry: just as sacred language frames imperial language, so religious identity, belief, and praxis is the ground for all interactions with foreign empires.

The first six chapters contain the stories of four Judean children—their Hebrew names are Daniel, Hananiah, Azariah, and Mishael—who are led captive from their homeland during Babylonia's conquest of Jerusalem. They soon rise to power in the courts of four kings: Nebuchadnezzar, king of Babylon (1:1), his son Belshazzar (5:1), Darius the Mede (5:31), and Cyrus the Persian (6:28). Some of these stories may have originated in a Diaspora setting, perhaps among Jews in Babylonia during the Persian period (between 539–333 BCE), a time when political domination also made space for negotiation and collaboration. The stories appear to have been crafted into a written collection of court tales that provided the basis and beginning for the longer book of Daniel that took shape in Judea in the second century BCE.

The stories coalesce around the figure of Daniel, wise and prayerful youth, interpreter of dreams, bold in speech. They are hero stories: Daniel and his friends provide readers with models of courage, faithfulness, and success against odds. Though prisoners, they have opportunities for education

805

and personal advancement within the foreign government. At the same time, they confront jealousy, conspiracy, and execution. Their stories highlight challenges of negotiating Jewish identity and maintaining faithful praxis in the context of foreign domination.

The court tales in Daniel 1–6 also incorporate diverse literary forms, including prayer, dream report, dream interpretation, divine decree, and royal letter. These forms play a key role in the book's treatment of sovereignty, power, and knowledge. Daniel receives wisdom and insight to interpret dreams as well as divine writing. His interpretations clarify the relationship between human kingdoms and divine kingship. Even while God's people are in exile, God reigns over time and history, appointing kings, humbling them, and bringing kingdoms to an end.

These stories provided a group of visionary scribes with a model for their own nonviolent witness in the face of imperial exploitation and violence. In the year 167 BCE, Judea was a province within the Seleucid Empire. Seleucid king Antiochus IV Epiphanes aimed at the re-creation of his empire through reconquest of Judea, undertaking a campaign of state terror that culminated in religious persecution of Jews as well as plunder and captivity. The apocalyptic visions and discourse in Daniel 7–12 were crafted by scribes who resisted persecution and terror through their teaching, writing, prayer, and martyrdom. They composed the Hebrew and Aramaic book of Daniel as a gift of understanding and hope for the many.

The dream of the statue in chapter 2 provided a model for Daniel 7's vision of a succession of four kingdoms, now imaged as monstrous and predatory beasts, followed by an eternal kingdom granted to one like a human. At the vision's heart is an Ancient of Days seated on a fiery throne. The vision thus shifts attention away from the glamour of earthly imperial armies to focus on divine sovereignty and justice. A second vision in chapter 8 portrays Antiochus's assault on God's sanctuary and provides a timeline for the cessation of sacrifice. Despite the touch and assurances of the man Gabriel, Daniel remains devastated and confused by what he has seen. In Daniel 9, Daniel turns to the scroll of Jeremiah for understanding. He also fasts and prays. He has a vision of a man clothed in linen, then is touched once more by Gabriel, who unfolds for him a future history from the time of the kings of Persia through the wars of the Hellenistic kings, to the time of persecution in Judea and finally the intervention of Michael, protector of Daniel's people (Daniel 10–12). This final discourse culminates with the promise of resurrection and the command to Daniel to go his way and rest.

The biblical book of Daniel may more properly be called books of Daniel: ancient versions witness to a vibrant set of scriptural traditions in Hebrew and Aramaic, on one hand, and Greek, on the other. The ancient Greek texts of Daniel also exhibit multiplicity, so that we have not one ancient Greek version but two. The Hebrew and Aramaic text of Daniel examined here holds the status of sacred Scripture for Jews and Protestant Christians. For Catholics and Orthodox Christians, one or both Greek texts also hold the status of sacred Scripture. These Greek versions are longer, containing the stories of Susanna, Bel and the Dragon as well as additional narrative and two hymns within the story of the three young men in the furnace. Collectively, these stories foreground religious experience, including worship of the one God; they also mark a literary shift from apocalypse to short novel and saint's life.

Daniel 1:1-21: Wisdom in Captivity

■ THE TEXT IN ITS ANCIENT CONTEXT

The setting in Babylon highlights themes of exile, captivity, and alienation. For readers in second-century-BCE Judea, this story setting invited a novel interpretation of their own experience as colonial subjects. Foreign rule created a set of competing demands and loyalties. Would it be possible to remain faithful to God while serving the empire? Would God equip the faithful with the wisdom and strength to speak to ruled and ruler alike the words of truth that would lead to righteousness and life?

Daniel and his friends are given new names in a language that is not their own and that invoke the names of gods they do not worship (Dan. 1:7). They are trained in the literature and lore of a foreign culture that prides itself on reading the future in stars, entrails, and even dreams (1:4-5). Yet Daniel and his friends draw a line at eating the king's food, recognizing in this royal nourishment an act of patronage that demands allegiance and claims the power to sustain and shape human life (1:8). Confident that *God* will sustain and shape them, they ask instead to be given water to drink and parts of plants to eat (1:12). Subsequently, God grants them far more extensive knowledge and wisdom than that of their Chaldean captors. To Daniel, moreover, God grants understanding of visions and dreams (1:17). For the ancient audience of Daniel, this story establishes the source of the book's visionary authority and roots the book's wisdom and promises for the future in the traditions of Judah's past.

■ THE TEXT IN THE INTERPRETIVE TRADITION

Early Jewish and Christian interpretations of Daniel survive in Josephus's *Jewish Antiquities*, various rabbinic midrashim, and commentaries by Jerome and Theodoret of Cyrus, among others. Their treatments of Daniel 1 combine legend, intrabiblical interpretation, allegory, and theological reflection.

Theodoret of Cyrus's reading of Daniel 1 emphasizes the relationship between human free will and divine care. Daniel's choice to abstain from the king's food was simultaneously a choice to follow God's commands. This choice enabled him to enjoy divine mercy, protection, and providential care. This interpretation resonates with modern Christian spiritual disciplines based on Daniel 1, commonly known as "Daniel fasts," entailing a diet of water and plant-derived foods. Those who practice such fasting aim at sanctification and nearness to God while simultaneously expecting greater prosperity in matters of health and even finances (Gregory).

■ THE TEXT IN CONTEMPORARY DISCUSSION

Recent scholarly treatments of Daniel 1 have focused on identity, bodily boundaries, and colonialism. Mary Mills links imagery of food and table and the spaces that contain them with social identity. In the border crossing from homeland to exile, bodily boundaries map the limits of competing sovereignties. In Daniel 1, the king's table contrasts with God's; the latter is invoked by the transfer of Jerusalem's sacred vessels to Babylon; Daniel is also a vessel. By abstaining from the king's food, he maintains his bodily purity, rooting his identity in divinely granted nourishment and wisdom rather than in royal provision and courtly education.

Philip Chia argues that by refusing to eat from the king's table, Daniel and his friends resist colonization. By contrast, Danna Nolan Fewell challenges readings of Daniel 1 as resistance narrative, arguing that the text portrays accommodation and emphasizes the vulnerability of Daniel and his friends as children in exile.

Daniel 1 thus offers a rich resource for youths in particular, who must negotiate identity in complex social spaces, imperial and otherwise. In what ways will they be countercultural? In what ways will they conform to the culture they inhabit? Food, language, education, and naming are central elements in this negotiation.

Daniel 2:1-49: Dreaming and Speaking Empire's End

▌ THE TEXT IN ITS ANCIENT CONTEXT

Daniel 2 is most widely known for Nebuchadnezzar's dream of a giant statue made of metals and clay (2:31-35). The centrality of the dream and its interpretation in this chapter mirrors its Babylonian setting, in which "visions of the night" were believed to convey messages from the gods. Babylonian dreamers and diviners wanted to know first of all whether a dream was favorable or unfavorable (Rochberg 2004). Over time, a more detailed system of interpretation developed. Dream interpreters in Sumer, Babylon, Susa, and elsewhere in ancient Mesopotamia kept records of dreams and the fortunes that followed, handing these on through generations. Interpreters drew on this divinatory tradition to understand symbols within a dream. The audience of Daniel would have connected Daniel's interpretation of Nebuchadnezzar's dreams in Daniel 2 and 4, as well as his confusion concerning his own visions in later chapters, with this Babylonian art of dream interpretation.

The idea of a revealed sequence of kingdoms is found in the diviner's manual *Enuma Anu Enlil*. The surviving tablets of this compendium date to around 650 BCE. Ancient readers might have imagined that this compilation, like the *Ziqīqu* tablets, formed part of the training Daniel and his friends received in the language and literature of the Chaldeans. Here is part of an oracle from this collection (Tablet 20, §11, line 7, Recension A; Rochberg 1988, 211).

> The prediction is given for Babylon: The destruction of Babylon is near. The scattering of the scattered land is near (?). . . . The king to whom they said, "yes." . . . His reign will end. In the m[outh of the god]s (?) his destruction is near. Ur will take away the rule of Babylon. Ur will take supremacy over Babylon.

The book of Daniel is informed by and interacts with biblical as well as Mesopotamian and Hellenistic traditions. In this chapter, we see the seeds of apocalyptic literature taking root within a rich and diverse cultural matrix (see J. J. Collins 1998, 26–37).

■ THE TEXT IN THE INTERPRETIVE TRADITION

The earliest Jewish readers of Daniel 2 understood themselves to be in the time of the fourth kingdom of iron and clay (2:33). They expected God to establish the stone (2:34), that is, the enduring kingdom (2:40-43), in the near future, and they understood that kingdom to be their own. Throughout the later history of interpretation, readers have similarly located themselves at this turning point between kingdoms.

By the first century CE, the fourth kingdom was understood to be Rome. For Christian interpreters in the medieval and Reformation periods, the fourth kingdom was still "Rome," but not the Rome of antiquity. It might be the Holy Roman Empire, the Roman Catholic Church, or another major power. In the seventeenth century, Portuguese Jesuit António Vieira interpreted Daniel 2 in conjunction with Revelation as a prediction of Portuguese independence and imperial expansion in America (Valdez).

■ THE TEXT IN CONTEMPORARY DISCUSSION

Daniel is a bilingual book, switching from Hebrew to Aramaic in 2:4b, continuing in Aramaic through the end of chapter 7, then switching back to Hebrew for the remainder of the book. For Jews, Hebrew was the language of sacred Scripture and of liturgy. It invoked the demands and promises of their covenant with God. Aramaic was a Mesopotamian language that became the lingua franca of the Persian Empire.

In the time of Daniel's composition, Aramaic was the language spoken by the people of Judea; it also remained a language of international commerce and imperial administration. The linguistic structure of the book provides a normative frame around Jewish life and their interaction with the empires that ruled them. Their allegiance was owed finally not to Nebuchadnezzar nor, later, to the Seleucid king Antiochus IV Epiphanes, but to God. The bilingual character of this biblical book alerts us to the languages and registers in which we speak. What do they convey about power, identity, rights, and obligations? What claims do our political rhetoric and our language about God make on us?

Daniel 3:1-30: Into the Furnace

■ THE TEXT IN ITS ANCIENT CONTEXT

The portrait in Daniel 3 of royal folly satirizes the pretensions and preoccupations of empire. In the face of such imperial arrogance, the actions and words of Shadrach, Meshach, and Abednego model courage and fidelity. The narrative of miraculous deliverance confirms the power of God and relative powerlessness of the Babylonian king.

Within the narrative, repetition creates a liturgical rhythm that mimics the king's attempt to command universal worship. At the narrative's beginning, the statue commands attention (3:1-5). Repeated references to the statue are then interwoven with references to the furnace (3:6-18), until the furnace takes the place of the statue as the heart of the narrative (3:19-26). This shift highlights the king's failure: the three young men willingly enter the fire rather than worship the statue (3:18).

The statue is characterized by its material—gold—and its dimensions of sixty cubits high and six cubits wide. Paired with repeated lists of administrative officials, this extravagant display of wealth evokes imperial patterns of economic exploitation such as taxation, tribute, and plunder (see 2 Kgs. 16:8; 18:14; 23:33-35; 24:13). Gold is brilliant, but not strong. The dimensions, while visually impressive, suggest instability. The rapacity of empire produces an unsustainable economic and social system.

By contrast with the Genesis creation story (1:26-27), here the king, not God, creates an image to represent to the world his own power and dominion. The king mimics God but can create only an inert object. Shadrach, Meshach, and Abednego reject the confusion between king and God that the statue represents, and in so doing refuse complicity in the economic and ideological structures of empire.

▌ THE TEXT IN THE INTERPRETIVE TRADITION

The Greek Old Testament, or Septuagint, preserves a longer form of Daniel 3 that is canonical for Catholics and many Orthodox Christians. It includes two hymns, the Prayer of Azariah and the Song of the Three Young Men, as well as narrative sections that introduce the songs and create a bridge between them (3:24-90 LXX; see the entry for "Azariah and the Song of the Three Jews," below)). The Greek text answers Nebuchadnezzar's farcical liturgy with a truly universal counter-liturgy of confession and praise. Through worship, the flames are transformed into a locus of divine presence, anticipating the fiery throne of the Ancient of Days (Dan. 7:9-10).

▌ THE TEXT IN CONTEMPORARY DISCUSSION

Elements of satire in Daniel 3 remind readers that humor has its place in the most serious of moments and in our most sacred texts (Avalos; Valeta; Chan, 16). Satire can be a powerful tool for critique, challenge, and change. Like Daniel's friends, we are immersed in media that market to us habits and systems of exploitation and consumption that are unstable and unsustainable. Advertisements and "reality" shows summon us to worship soulless images that are at best a parody of the image of God. Satire can reveal their absurdity and prompt us to reclaim our faculties of judgment and dedicate our bodies and whole selves to witness for the welfare of humankind and all creation.

Daniel 4:1-37: Royal Madness

▌ THE TEXT IN ITS ANCIENT CONTEXT

Ancient sources suggest that Daniel 4 draws on oral traditions about Babylon's last king, Nabonidus, who ruled from 556 to 539 (Henze, 69). Criticism of Nabonidus's behavior and beliefs had blossomed into a portrait of royal derangement. The account of Nebuchadnezzar's humiliation in Daniel 4 adapted oral traditions about Nabonidus, substituting Judah's conqueror for his successor as the story's main character.

Nebuchadnezzar II was an avid builder. In one inscription, he proclaimed, "the defenses of Esagila and Babylon I strengthened and secured for my reign an enduring name" (Sack, 66). Yet Daniel 4 cautions against mistaking royal work of empire- and city-building for divine power to order and create.

To drive home this point, Daniel makes creative use of the Mesopotamian mythological trope of the "wild man." Its best-known exemplar is the figure of Enkidu in the Gilgamesh Epic. The wild man Enkidu accepts the rule of the king and is thereby transformed into a "civilized" human being, symbolizing transformation of disorder into order and uncharted territory into city and kingdom. Daniel utilizes this trope in its animalization of the king, who has failed to understand the governing order that has established his own kingship and built up his kingdom (Henze, 93–99). He can become human again only when he recognizes the divine sovereign power that orders all things.

▋ The Text in the Interpretive Tradition

In the late eighteenth century, Daniel 4 inspired English poet and artist William Blake's portrait of a debased king in his illuminated *Marriage of Heaven and Hell*. Blake's king is naked, on all fours, mouth gaping, and beard hanging to the earth. Uncomprehending eyes sink beneath a furrowed brow that betrays anxiety even as the swollen orbits suggest age and exhaustion. The king wears a four-pointed crown atop his head of long, thick hair; his drooping face and helpless expression contradict a body thick with muscle. The image satirizes monarchy. At the same time, its caption, "One Law for the Lion and Ox Is Oppression," critiques a liberal democracy, market economy, and industrial revolution that render humans interchangeable with one another (Makdisi).

▋ The Text in Contemporary Discussion

Daniel 4 and the artistic traditions it inspired trade heavily on the trope of madness. They raise questions about what it means to be human in an age of empires, industrialization, technology, and global capitalism. Empire markets exploitation, destruction, and degradation of human beings and natural resources alike as normal, reasonable, and inevitable. For example, in the modern industrial world, transnational corporations advertise to young consumers that fashion and electronics are keys to identity, self-expression, and social success. Low retail prices and ever-changing selections persuade consumers that these goods are disposable. While corporations profit, their laborers and the earth pay the greatest cost. This madness is often hidden from view. How might readers of Daniel today use the arts to help others see the destructive logic and practices of the systems that dehumanize us and degrade creation for what they are? What does Nebuchadnezzar's story teach about human vocation?

Daniel 5:1-30: Writing on the Wall

▋ The Text in Its Ancient Context

Daniel 5 opens with a new king in Babylon, Nebuchadnezzar's son Belshazzar. Historically, Belshazzar was the son not of Nebuchadnezzar, but of Nabonidus. Belshazzar acted as regent in Babylon during his father's ten-year absence from the capital. This detail reminds us that the Daniel stories do not aim at simple historical reportage. Rather, the composers of the stories play with history, deploying familiar motifs and traditions to evoke their associations in popular imagination while at the same time articulating truths about God and empire that cut through time and space.

One such truth is the relationship between empire and idolatry. As Belshazzar and his company drink from the vessels plundered from the Jerusalem temple, they praise gods that are not gods, but are rather the inert materials: "gold and silver, bronze, iron, wood, and stone" (5:4). In the Hebrew Scriptures, the pair "wood and stone" commonly refers to gods made by human hands (Deut. 4:28; 2 Kgs. 19:18; Isa. 37:19). Deuteronomy 29:17 adds to the pair "silver and gold," while Hab. 2:19 parodies the idols of wood and stone that are ornamented with these precious metals. The longer list in Daniel 5 adds two metals, bronze and iron, not found in the other lists (5:4, 23). Together with gold and silver, they are the four metals from which the statue of Daniel 2 was composed (2:32-33). Joined with stone and wood, they suggest that Belshazzar has conscripted his princes, wives, and concubines in idolatrous worship of empire itself.

▌THE TEXT IN THE INTERPRETIVE TRADITION

The writing on the wall in Daniel 5 and the divine will it encoded provided Galileo Galilei (d. 1642) with a metaphor that would prove enormously influential in the philosophy of science. Just as the writing on the wall was inscrutable to all but Daniel, so too nature requires a specialist to decode its language of geometry and proportion (Reeves).

Although Galileo is often conscripted into a modern narrative of warfare between science and religion, he did not conceive of his own work in this way. Galileo found in Scripture a metaphor for his scientific study of nature. They were not opposed to one another, but complementary, as he wrote in 1613: "Holy Scripture and nature proceed alike from the divine Word—Scripture as dictated by the Holy Spirit, and nature as the faithful executor of God's commands" (Galilei, 56).

▌THE TEXT IN CONTEMPORARY DISCUSSION

While Belshazzar stages his feast "for his lords" (5:1), in attendance are also "his wives, and his concubines" (5:2). The repeated possessive pronoun identifies them as belonging to him and subject to his command. After fulfilling his command, the wives and concubines disappear from the story.

A second supporting role is played by the queen (5:10-12). She offers personal counsel and reassurance, recounts history, and names key relationships. She places special value on insight, interpretation, and revelation from the heavenly realm. Belshazzar obeys her command; her prediction proves true. Yet the queen disappears from the story as well. In some respects, she provides a model for breaking out of scripted roles of subservience. In other respects, she reinforces the narrative's gendered hierarchy. How are women's roles scripted in the movies, television shows, and commercials we watch or in the books, magazines, and newspapers we read? How are women's roles defined and performed in our churches, families, and places of work? In what ways do women in authority reinforce, challenge, or displace patriarchal norms? The Geena Davis Institute on Gender in Media (www.seejane.org) provides resources for discussions about women and gender in media. Paired with study of Daniel 5 and other biblical texts, these tools provide a point of entry for discussions of women's roles in church and society.

Daniel 6:1-28: The Lion's Den

■ THE TEXT IN ITS ANCIENT CONTEXT

In earlier chapters, Daniel has repeatedly outperformed his fellow courtiers; by the end of Daniel 5, he has been promoted to high administrative rank. Now in Daniel 6, his success inspires jealousy and conspiracy. Jealousy and conspiracy among courtiers are well-known tropes in ancient Mesopotamian and early Jewish literature, including the Akkadian wisdom poem *Ludlul bēl Nēmeqi*, the Aramaic tale of Ahiqar, and the book of Esther. Karel van der Toorn has argued that the Daniel stories adapted earlier Mesopotamian narrative models to portray Daniel's success at court as well as the opposition he faced.

In addition to adapting a familiar plot, Daniel 6 also borrows the image of the lion's den from Mesopotamian scribes as a metaphor for the scribe's fall from royal favor: the one who previously received a lion's share of honor and material reward (including food) was now to be the lion's meal (see Toorn). By literalizing the metaphor, the storyteller opens wide the doors of imagination and gives new life and meaning to familiar tropes. In the process, literal settings take on new symbolic meanings (Goatly).

■ THE TEXT IN THE INTERPRETIVE TRADITION

Hippolytus of Rome's *Commentary on Daniel* (c. 202–211 CE) is considered the earliest extant Christian commentary on a biblical book. In his allegorical reading, Babylon is the world and the den of lions is Hades. By imitating Daniel's courage and steadfastness, his reader will be brought living out of the den and "found as a sharer of the resurrection" (Hippolytus, 3.31.2–3). The association between Daniel's deliverance from the lions' den and resurrection made this scene popular in early Christian and late antique funerary art (Jensen; Sörries).

■ THE TEXT IN CONTEMPORARY DISCUSSION

Michelle Alexander documents the effects of racial profiling and the War on Drugs in the United States, including mass incarceration and disenfranchisement of a stunning percentage of African American men. Analysis of who benefits and who is harmed reveals a disconnect between stated and actual motives driving these policies and practices. Daniel 6 and other biblical texts that portray incarceration and the manipulation of justice systems can help readers perceive systemic abuse and reclaim the power to reform and transform legislative, judicial, and carceral systems.

The imagery of Daniel 6 also conveys the dynamics and consequences of bullying. Psychologists studying the effects of adult bullying have noted that its victims "feel like slaves and animals, prisoners, children, and heartbroken lovers"; these similes highlight feelings of confinement, objectification, debasement, isolation, vulnerability, betrayal, and loss (Tracy, Lutgen-Sandvik, and Alberts).

Daniel's imagery acknowledges victims' pain, offers models of courage and a source of hope, and underscores the need for strong leadership to prevent bullying.

Daniel 7:1-28: Beastly and Humane Rule

▮ THE TEXT IN ITS ANCIENT CONTEXT

In Daniel 2 and 4, Nebuchadnezzar dreams and Daniel interprets. Now, in chapter 7, Daniel dreams and angels interpret. In the biblical canon, an angelic interpreter first appears in the book of Zechariah (e.g., Zech. 1:9, 13-14, 19-21). Over time, revealing angels became a characteristic feature of Jewish apocalyptic literature. As residents of heaven with special access to the divine court, the angels were also believed to possess divine knowledge. They could travel freely between heaven and earth and mediated between humans and God in roles analogous to priest, prophet, and ruler. Daniel 7 accents each of these roles.

Another key feature of apocalyptic literature is its novel combination of familiar and fantastic imagery, which directs the imagination to see reality in a new light. The symbolism of Daniel's dream in chapter 7 has roots in the biblical books of Genesis, Hosea, and Ezekiel, as well as Canaanite and Mesopotamian mythology and Hellenistic royal iconography (Eggler). Each myth and symbol is refracted through a distinctively Jewish theological lens and given new meaning.

The contrast between the four beasts and the one like a human develops further a dichotomy explored already in Daniel 4. The beasts are monstrous, defying created categories of order. Daniel first sees a beast like a lion with eagle's wings, which appears to represent the Babylonian Empire. Echoing Nebuchadnezzar's debasement and restoration of reason in Daniel 4, its wings are removed and it receives a human heart (7:4). The second beast, like a bear, may represent the Median kingdom; it is portrayed with ribs between its teeth and receives the command to feast on flesh (7:5). The third beast, representing the Persian Empire, is like a leopard with four wings and four heads; its mobility and gaze thus extend toward the four corners of the earth (7:6). The fourth beast, representing the Hellenistic Empires, is mutated more than all the beasts before it; with iron teeth, it eats and crushes; its feet smash what remains (7:7). Its ten horns embody the might and treachery of its kings; it has a mouth for boasting and eyes like a human's (7:8). In each case, form mirrors ontology: predatory and mixed forms convey the violence of imperial rule, while quasi-human faculties of reason, sight, and speech call attention to empire's distorting logic. After the body of the fourth beast is destroyed, sovereignty is given to one like a human. This human form gives bodily expression to the humane rule of the kingdom of the people of the holy ones of the Most High and links that rule with the angels, who, throughout the latter half of Daniel, are also described as sharing visible likeness to humankind.

▮ THE TEXT IN THE INTERPRETIVE TRADITION

In the Gospel of Mark, Jesus alludes to Daniel 7 in his discourse from the Mount of Olives (Mark 13:26). Later, Jesus' self-identification with the figure who comes with the clouds is linked to his divine Sonship and future glorious advent (Mark 14:62). The Gospels of Matthew and Luke add further emphases on the kingdom of the son of man and his future role as judge and advocate (A. Y. Collins, 98–100).

THE TEXT IN CONTEMPORARY DISCUSSION

The book of Revelation adapts Daniel's descriptions of the beastly kingdoms in its portrayal of Rome (13:1-2, 11-14). For the writers of Daniel, the Seleucid Empire seduced, devoured, and exploited its subjects. For the seer of Revelation, it was Rome. In looking for the modern-day analogue to these ancient empires, American scholars have often pointed to the United States (Horsley). Yet political philosophers Michael Hardt and Antonio Negri contend that the role of empire no longer belongs to colonizing or occupying nation-states. In today's global economy, transnational corporations and the economic systems that support their practices of exploitation and segmentation are the new empire.

Readers of Daniel 7 in the twenty-first century must analyze not only ancient text but also modern context. What is the nature of the political and economic systems in which we participate? Do they destroy and devour, seduce, and exploit, or do they enact justice for humankind and for the earth?

Daniel 8:1-27: A Limit to Desolation

THE TEXT IN ITS ANCIENT CONTEXT

At the conclusion of the vision in Daniel 8, Daniel hears a holy one ask how long the assaults on the heavenly sanctuary and host will last (8:13). The response is measured by the number of evening and morning sacrifices: 2,300 evenings and mornings (8:14). This great number of mornings and evenings are not the only measure in Daniel for the cessation of the temple offerings. Later, the angel Gabriel describes the same period as "a half-week" (9:27), that is, three and a half years. The man clothed in linen will similarly declare its duration "a time, two times, and half a time" (12:7; cf. 7:25). These numbers are partly symbolic: they are one-half of seven years. Seven was the number of days of creation, and so symbolized divine order and providence as well as totality, completion, perfection, and sanctity. Half seven symbolized Antiochus's assault on holiness, his failure to undo God's order, and his inability to create and sustain on his own. The 2,300 mornings and evenings are also a source of hope: God has set a limit to the time of desolation.

THE TEXT IN THE INTERPRETIVE TRADITION

The interpretation of Dan. 8:14 was a cornerstone in the premillennial historicist calculations of American Protestant William Miller (d. 1849). Miller interpreted the 2,300 evenings and mornings as years. The desolated sanctuary was the entire earth, and the years of desolation were the pope's rule. At their conclusion, in 1843 (later revised to 1844), Christ would return (Newport). By 1844, Christ's return was not evident. Followers of Miller dealt with this "Great Disappointment" in different ways. Hiram Edson concluded that Christ *had* come—to "the second apartment" of the *heavenly* sanctuary (Newport).

The Text in Contemporary Discussion

The book of Daniel continues to figure prominently in modern-day calculations of the "end times." The data in Daniel suggest that this effort is misguided. At the same time, the impulse to reinterpret biblical prophecy for the present day is very much in keeping with methods practiced in the book itself, as we see further in Daniel 9.

Daniel provided perspective on current events by placing them within a broader narrative and historical framework and interpreting them in relation to God's work in history and plan for the future. The activity of the horn and the period of desolation in Daniel 8 described events and circumstances in the audience's present. The vision and its interpretation helped them to understand their plight in terms not just political but also theological. It also helped them to perceive an end, not to history, but to foreign domination.

Daniel 9:1-27: Study, Fasting, and Prayer

The Text in Its Ancient Context

Daniel's study of Jeremiah's scroll offers insight into the interpretation of Scripture in early Judaism. Daniel approaches interpretation as a sacred and even mystical endeavor. He fasts and humbles his body with sackcloth and ashes, enacting heightened awareness of human mortality and dependence on God. In response to what he has read and seen, he also prays, confessing his people's sins and shame and begging God to hear, see, and forgive, to pay attention and act for the sake of God's city and people. In response to Daniel's pleading, Gabriel comes to him and interprets Jeremiah's scroll. The time of exile has not ended: seventy years are seventy weeks of years (Dan. 9:2, 24-27).

Similar prophetic periodization of history is found in the Apocalypse of Weeks (*1 En.* 93:1-10; 91:11-17), a Jewish historical apocalypse contemporary with the book of Daniel. In this apocalypse, history is divided into ten weeks. Reading Daniel 9 in the context of other early Jewish apocalypses reveals a shared view of time and history. As in the Apocalypse of Weeks, so in Daniel 9 the division of history into weeks of years invokes time's created, sabbatical structure and calls to mind the Jubilee of Lev. 25:8-22. Jubilee was a time of liberation, restoration, and justice and was closely linked with the Day of Atonement. Accordingly, Gabriel declares that the seventy weeks have been appointed to atone for guilt and bring justice (Dan. 9:24).

The Text in the Interpretive Tradition

An exegetical text from Qumran known as 11QMelchizedek (11Q13; mid-first century BCE) may preserve one of the oldest extant references to Dan. 9:25-26 (Campbell). Melchizedek is the central figure in this eschatological text. His role is similar to that of Michael in Daniel: the people are his inheritance, he is a leader among the "sons of God," or angels, and he will be an instrument of God's judgment and will liberate his people in "the last days." Like Daniel and the Apocalypse of Weeks, this text envisions history measured in heptads. Its quotations of Lev. 25:9 and 13 and Deut. 15:2 explicitly link Daniel's discourse with jubilary traditions of justice and restoration.

■ THE TEXT IN CONTEMPORARY DISCUSSION

The apocalyptic timetables in Daniel 9 and the Apocalypse of Weeks are often characterized as expressing a deterministic view of history. Yet this understanding of providence does not negate the emphasis on teaching and justice in both works. Moreover, the prayer in Daniel 9 shifts the focus from the crimes of empire to the community's relationship with God. It offers an avenue from failure to renewal through responsibility and forgiveness. Gabriel's discourse places this understanding of sin and reconciliation within an apocalyptic framework. Even in the midst of appointed times, God remains responsive to petition and confession. Here and throughout the book, Daniel's actions and prayer provide a model for his audience to follow. In the same way, Gabriel's words to Daniel provide the book's readers with wisdom, understanding, and the assurance, "you are greatly loved" (9:23).

Daniel 10:1-21: Vision, Understanding, and Strength

■ THE TEXT IN ITS ANCIENT CONTEXT

Daniel spends three weeks in mourning. During this time, he abstains from meat, wine, and delicacies and refrains from anointing his body. Gavin Flood argues that ascetic practices are a means of transforming subjectivity. They root the self in tradition but also provide a way to transcend the limits of body, culture, cosmology, and individual desire. They create a "new" body able simultaneously to push back against these boundaries and to open itself to the will of God (Flood).

Daniel's abstention precipitates a vision as he stands by the bank of the Tigris River (Dan. 10:3-5), one of the four rivers that flow from the Garden of Eden (Gen. 2:14). The banks of flowing waterways mark a boundary between heaven and earth (Genesis 1), eras (Genesis 6–9), life and death (Exodus 14–15; Carlsson), promise and fulfillment (Josh. 1:2-3). For Daniel, like Ezekiel before him (Ezek. 1:1.3), the riverbank is a space of revelation. At the water's edge, he will learn of his people's future in their own land, the end of empire, and the passage from death to life. In Daniel 12, the detail is added that the man in linen stands above the waters of the stream, while two others stand on each side (12:5-6). The angels who appear to Daniel occupy heaven and earth; they stand in past and future; they are witnesses to death and to the promise of life eternal. The man in linen bridges these divisions to bring understanding and strength to Daniel.

■ THE TEXT IN THE INTERPRETIVE TRADITION

The Jewish apocalypse *4 Ezra* (c. 100 CE) draws on Daniel's portrayal of visionary praxis, including mourning, fasting, and dietary abstinence (*4 Ezra* 6:35; Dan. 9:3; 10:2-3). *Fourth Ezra* also adds a new element. Toward the book's conclusion, the Most High provides Ezra with a cup to drink. Its fiery liquid imparts understanding and wisdom, allowing him to dictate his revelations to the five men who are with him (14:39-48). The Most High declares that seventy of the books they have written contain "the river of knowledge" (14:47). Abstinence has prepared the seer to receive a different kind of substance and sustenance. Moreover, the act of writing places the river within the text, making it possible for others to receive revelation by consulting the books.

▌THE TEXT IN CONTEMPORARY DISCUSSION

Scholars have debated whether visionary texts such as Daniel or *4 Ezra* reflect genuine religious experience or literary convention (Stone). Apocalypses are richly allusive, drawing heavily on earlier prophetic and apocalyptic tropes, images, and symbols. They attribute visionary experience to a figure from the past, creating a fictional narrative to frame their reports of revelation. Does this mean that they do not reflect actual visionary experiences on the part of their authors and their faith communities?

Increasingly, we are learning that ancient visionary praxis relied heavily on reading and interpreting sacred Scriptures (Rowland with Gibbons and Dobroruka). An earlier text like Ezekiel or Daniel could provide a later visionary with an example of mystical asceticism as well as imagery and language to describe her or his vision of God's throne, angels, and divine glory. The sacred text itself was also a gateway to mystical transformation and divine encounter (DeConick).

Daniel 11:1-45: War, Betrayal, and Persecution

▌THE TEXT IN ITS ANCIENT CONTEXT

The angel's discourse in Daniel 11 reveals to Daniel events that will unfold from his time through the death of Antiochus IV Epiphanes. Yet the discourse does not simply foretell events to come; it interprets them. While names and dates can help modern readers establish context for interpreting the chapter, the style of the angel's discourse suggests that more important than the names and dates of particular individuals, battles, negotiations, and betrayals are their character. Kings of the North (Seleucids) and South (Ptolemies) seem almost interchangeable; at times, even these designations are abandoned for pronouns that leave the reader unable to distinguish one actor from another (e.g., 11:11-12). The kings are alike in war making, pride, deception, and weakness. And they do not last.

The discourse highlights themes of sovereignty, wealth, and warfare. A notice at the chapter's beginning suggests that empire's greed will be its undoing: the final Persian king "will heap up greater wealth than all who have gone before, relying on his wealth as his strength" (author's own translation); in so doing, he will wake the kingdom of Greece and so bring about his own downfall (11:2). In later verses, violence, exploitation, and idolatry characterize the rule of Antiochus IV (11:24, 28, 36). The discourse employs critique as a mode of resistance to the military, economic, and religious ideology and practices of empire.

In the year 167 BCE, Antiochus IV undertook a persecution of Jews in Judea. Daniel 11 describes a group of "wise teachers" among the Judeans who will help many of their people to understand the events that are happening, what God asks of them, and what God will do (11:33). Their nonviolent witness and martyrdom (11:33) provide a further example of resistance for the audience to follow.

▌THE TEXT IN THE INTERPRETIVE TRADITION

For the writers of Daniel, the description of the king of the North who "shall exalt himself and consider himself greater than any god, and shall speak horrendous things against the God of gods"

(Dan. 11:36) referred to Antiochus IV Epiphanes. In the first century CE, this verse inspired the portrait of the "lawless one" (literally "human of lawlessness") in 2 Thess. 2:1-8. Among early Christian interpreters, this "lawless one" became further identified with *antichristos*, a term used in 1 and 2 John (1 John 2:22, 4:3; 2 John 7). The label "antichrist" was used to help members of the writers' community discern between teachings and spirits that were of God and those that were not of God and to identify as untrustworthy teachers of false doctrine (Fuller). Over time, *antichristos* evolved from adjective to title, coalescing into a composite portrait of the Antichrist assembled from key passages in Daniel, 2 Thessalonians, 1 and 2 John, and Revelation (e.g., Rev. 13:1-4; Fuller).

▍THE TEXT IN CONTEMPORARY DISCUSSION

In her essay "Queering the Beast: The Antichrists' Gay Wedding," biblical scholar and cultural critic Erin Runions calls attention to interpretations of Dan. 11:37 among culturally conservative Christians in the United States that identify the Antichrist as a gay male. In this stream of interpretation, Runions detects an "apocalyptic logic" driving much political opposition to gay marriage (Runions, 80).

In her 1928 novel *The Well of Loneliness*, lesbian writer Radclyffe Hall reads Daniel differently (Madden). Hearing the words of a spiritual—"Didn't my Lord deliver Daniel, then why not every man?"—leads Stephen, the novel's protagonist, to pose another question that draws on Dan. 8:13 and 12:6: "Yes, but how long, O Lord, how long?" (Hall, 330). Later in the novel, Stephen asks more pointedly: "How long was this persecution to continue? How long would God sit still and endure this insult offered to . . . creation? How long tolerate the preposterous statement that inversion was not a part of nature? For since it existed what else could it be? All things that existed were part of nature!" (Hall, 368).

Same-sex love, "gender-inversion," and "congenital sexual inversion" had been medically pathologized and socially stigmatized. Nor were same-sex unions blessed by the church, though Stephen and others long for this blessing (Hall, 369). Ed Madden has argued that Hall's appropriation of Daniel and other biblical texts simultaneously writes a "reverse discourse" of legitimation and voices a hope of future acceptance.

Daniel 12:1-13: The End of Days

▍THE TEXT IN ITS ANCIENT CONTEXT

The angel's discourse culminates in a prediction of salvation, freedom, life, and knowledge for Daniel's people. The angel also foretells resurrection followed by judgment and reward or punishment for some of those who have died (12:2-3). Daniel draws on earlier traditions even as it articulates a new vision for life after death (Nickelsburg).

The prophet Hosea voiced the hope of some among his people that after two days God would restore their health and after three days raise them up to live in God's presence (Hosea 6:2). Hosea appears to have had in view the continuation of life through healing from sickness, not resurrection from death, yet later interpreters would associate the two (Macintosh, 222).

In Ezekiel's vision of dry bones, God instructs the prophet to declare to the bones that they will live (Ezek. 37:4). God explains that the bones are all Israel (37:11) and God will open their graves and bring them up from their graves (37:12-13) and they will live in their land (37:14). Like Daniel 12, Ezekiel 37 simultaneously envisions bodies raised from the earth and a nation's new beginning and restoration.

Isaiah 24–27 contain a vision of cosmic upheaval, destruction, judgment, and renewal. These chapters foretell the end of death: God will destroy the shroud and swallow death for all time (25:7-8). Daniel 12:2 shares with Isaiah 26:19 imagery of waking from the dust from death to life.

▌THE TEXT IN THE INTERPRETIVE TRADITION

The portrait of Michael as angelic warrior in Daniel 10 and deliverer who would liberate God's people in Daniel 12 influenced later imperial ideology. In the Carolingian Empire, beginning in the eighth century CE, liturgical acclamations called *laudes regiae* were sung at coronations and on festival days. The centerpiece of the *laudes* invoked for the king the protections of Mary and the archangels, with Michael listed as the first of these (Kantorowicz). In a similar vein, Charlemagne's military standards depicted Michael with the legend "Patron and Prince of the Empire of the Gauls" (Johnson). Michael, a figure associated in Daniel with the end of empire, is thus transformed in the Byzantine era into a symbol of empire's divine aid and military might.

▌THE TEXT IN CONTEMPORARY DISCUSSION

For Barbara Leung Lai, the differing portraits of Daniel in Daniel 1–6 and 7–12 represent Daniel's public and private selves. In public, Daniel displays confidence and God-given understanding. In private, Daniel is terrified and confused by his experience. His body manifests his distress. Yet the angel has lifted him to his feet and given him strength and partial understanding. Daniel's story can help pastoral-care providers acknowledge and cope with the dissonance between their public and private experiences and with the psychic and physiological effects of fear and confusion. The predictions and promise to Daniel at the book's end offer hope and assurance not just to Daniel but also to pastors.

The final commands to Daniel also offer practical instruction. Some interpret the commands "go your way, and rest" (12:13), with reference to Daniel's death (e.g., Pace 2008, 343). Yet the word "rest" (*nûaḥ*) does not typically refer to death. Here it may more closely correspond to Sabbath (cf. Exod. 20:11; 23:12). In the face of suffering, despair, weakness, and confusion and in response to God's own work of creation, salvation, and liberation, the reader, like Daniel, is reminded that rest provides a path to renewal and life (cf. Exod. 31:16-17; Deut. 5:15).

Works Cited

Alexander, Michelle. 2010. *The New Jim Crow: Mass Incarceration in the Age of Colorblindness*. New York: New Press.

Avalos, Hector. 1991. "The Comedic Function of the Enumerations of Officials and Instruments in Daniel 3." *CBQ* 53, no. 4:580–88.

Bull, Malcolm, and Keith Lockhart. 2007. *Seeking a Sanctuary: Seventh-day Adventism and the American Dream*. 2nd ed. Bloomington: Indiana University Press.

Campbell, Jonathan G. 2007. *The Exegetical Texts*. Companion to the Qumran Scrolls. London: T&T Clark.

Carlsson, Leif. 2004. *Round Trips to Heaven: Otherworldly Travelers in Early Judaism and Christianity*. Lund: Lund University.

Chan, Michael. 2013. "Ira Regis: Comedic Inflections of Royal Rage in Jewish Court Tales." *JQR* 103, no. 1:1–25.

Charlesworth, James H. 2007. "Can We Discern the Composition Date of the Parables of Enoch?" In *Enoch and the Messiah Son of Man: Revisiting the Book of Parables*, edited by Gabriele Boccaccini, 450–68. Grand Rapids: Eerdmans.

Chia, Philip. 2006. "On Naming the Subject: Postcolonial Reading of Daniel 1." In *The Postcolonial Biblical Reader*, edited by Rasiah S. Sugirtharajah, 171–84. Oxford: Blackwell.

Collins, Adela Yarbro. 1993. "The Influence of Daniel on the New Testament." In John J. Collins. *Daniel: A Commentary on the Book of Daniel*. Hermeneia. Minneapolis: Fortress Press.

Collins, John. J. 1993. *Daniel: A Commentary on the Book of Daniel*. Hermeneia. Minneapolis: Fortress Press.

———. 1998. *The Apocalyptic Imagination: An Introduction to Jewish Apocalyptic Literature*. 2nd ed. Grand Rapids: Eerdmans.

DeConick, April D. 2006. "What Is Early Jewish and Christian Mysticism?" In *Paradise Now: Essays on Early Jewish and Christian Mysticism*, edited by April D. DeConick, 1–24. Atlanta: Society of Biblical Literature.

Eggler, Jürg. 2000. *Influences and Traditions Underlying the Vision of Daniel 7:2-14: The Research History from the End of the 19th Century to the Present*. Göttingen: Vandenhoeck & Ruprecht.

Erdman, David V. 1977. *Blake: Prophet against Empire: A Poet's Interpretation of the History of His Own Times*. 3rd ed. Princeton: Princeton University Press.

Fewell, Danna Nolan. 2003. *The Children of Israel: Reading the Bible for the Sake of Our Children*. Nashville: Abingdon.

Flood, Gavin. 2004. *The Ascetic Self: Subjectivity, Memory and Tradition*. Cambridge: Cambridge University Press.

Fuller, R. C. 1995. *Naming the Antichrist: The History of an American Obsession*. Oxford: Oxford University Press.

Galilei, Galileo. 2012. *Selected Writings*. Translated by William R. Shea and Mark Davie. Oxford: Oxford University Press.

Goatly, Andrew. 1997. *The Language of Metaphors*. New York: Routledge.

Gregory, Susan. 2010. *The Daniel Fast: Feed Your Soul, Strengthen Your Spirit, and Renew Your Body*. Tyndale Momentum.

Hall, Radclyffe. 2005. *The Well of Loneliness*. Hertfordshire: Wordsworth.

Hardt, Michael, and Antonio Negri. 2000. *Empire*. Cambridge, MA: Harvard University Press.

Henze, Matthias. 1999. *The Madness of King Nebuchadnezzar: The Ancient Near Eastern Origins and Early History of Interpretation of Daniel 4*. Leiden: Brill.

Hippolytus of Rome. 2010. *Commentary on Daniel*. Translated and edited by Tom C. Schmidt. CreateSpace. www.chronicon.net. Accessed August 4, 2013.

Horsley, Richard A., ed. 2008. *In the Shadow of Empire: Reclaiming the Bible as a History of Faithful Resistance*. Louisville: Westminster John Knox.

Jensen, Robin Margaret. 2000. *Understanding Early Christian Art*. New York: Routledge.

Johnson, Richard F. 2005. *Saint Michael the Archangel in Medieval English Legend*. Woodbridge: Boydell Press.

Kantorowicz, Ernst H. 1958. *Laudes Regiae: A Study of Liturgical Acclamations and Mediaeval Ruler Worship*. Berkeley: University of California Press.

Landon, Richard. 1990. "The Stillman Drake Galileo Collection." In *Nature, Experiment, and the Sciences: Essays on Galileo and the History of Science*, edited by Trevor H. Levere and William R. Shea, 321–37. Dordrecht, the Netherlands: Kluwer Academic.

Leung Lai, Barbara M. 2008. "Ancient Sage or Dysfunctional Seer? Cognitive Dissonance and Pastoral Vulnerability in the Profile of Daniel." *Pastoral Psychology* 57:199–210.

Macintosh, Andrew. 1997. *Hosea*. ICC. Edinburgh: T&T Clark.

Madden, Ed. 2000. "Gospels of Inversion: Literature, Scripture, Sexology." In *Divine Aporia: Postmodern Conversations about the Other*, edited by John C. Hawley, 123–52. London: Associated University Presses.

Makdisi, Saree. 2003. *William Blake and the Impossible History of the 1790s*. Chicago: University of Chicago Press.

Mills, Mary. 2006. "Household and Table: Diasporic Boundaries in Daniel and Esther." *CBQ* 68, no. 3:408–20.

Newport, Kenneth G. C. 2000. *Apocalypse and Millennium: Studies in Biblical Eisegesis*. Cambridge: Cambridge University Press.

Nickelsburg, George W. E. 2006. *Resurrection, Immortality, and Eternal Life in Intertestamental Judaism and Early Christianity*. Cambridge, MA: Harvard University Press.

Nickelsburg, George W. E., and James C. VanderKam. 2004. *1 Enoch: A New Translation*. Minneapolis: Fortress Press.

Pace, Sharon. 2008. *Daniel*. Smyth and Helwys Bible Commentary. Macon, GA: Smyth and Helwys.

Portier-Young, Anathea. 2010. "Languages of Identity and Obligation: Daniel as Bilingual Book," *VT* 60:1–18.

———. 2011. *Apocalypse against Empire: Theologies of Resistance in Early Judaism*. Grand Rapids: Eerdmans.

Reeves, Eileen. 1991. "Daniel 5 and the *Assayer*: Galileo Reads the Handwriting on the Wall." *Journal of Medieval and Renaissance Studies* 21, no. 1:1–27.

Rochberg, Francesca. 1988. *Aspects of Babylonian Celestial Divination: The Lunar Eclipse Tablets of Enūma Anu Enlil*. Horn, Austria: Ferdinand Berger & Söhne.

———. 2004. *The Heavenly Writing: Divination, Horoscopy, and Astronomy in Mesopotamian Culture*. Cambridge: Cambridge University Press.

Rowland, Christopher, with Patricia Gibbons and Vicente Dobroruka. 2006. "Visionary Experience in Ancient Judaism and Christianity." In *Paradise Now: Essays on Early Jewish and Christian Mysticism*, edited by April D. DeConick, 41–56. Atlanta: Society of Biblical Literature.

Runions, Erin. 2008. "Queering the Beast: The Antichrists' Gay Wedding." In *Queering the Non/Human*, edited by Noreen Giffney and Myra J. Hird, 79–110 Aldershot: Ashgate.

Sack, Ronald. 2004. *Images of Nebuchadnezzar: The Emergence of a Legend*. Selinsgrove, PA: Susquehanna University Press.

Sörries, Reiner. 2006. *Daniel in der Löwengrube. Zur Gesetzmäßigkeit frühchristlicher Ikonographie*. Wiesbaden: Reichert.

Stone, Michael. 2003. "A Reconsideration of Apocalyptic Visions." *HTR* 96, no. 2:167–80.

Theodoret of Cyrus. 2006. *Commentary on Daniel*. Translated and edited by Robert C. Hill. Atlanta: Society of Biblical Literature.

Toorn, Karel van der. 1998. "In the Lions' Den: The Babylonian Background of a Biblical Motif." *CBQ* 64:626–40.

Tracy, S. J., P. Lutgen-Sandvik, and J. K. Alberts. 2006. "Nightmares, Demons, and Slaves: Exploring the Painful Metaphors of Workplace Bullying." *Management Communication Quarterly* 20, no. 2:148–85.

Valdez, Maria Ana Travassos. 2011. *Historical Interpretations of the "Fifth Empire": The Dynamics of Periodization from Daniel to António Vieira, S.J.* Leiden: Brill.

Valeta, David. 2008. *Lions, Ovens, and Visions: A Satirical Reading of Daniel 1–6*. Sheffield: Sheffield Phoenix.

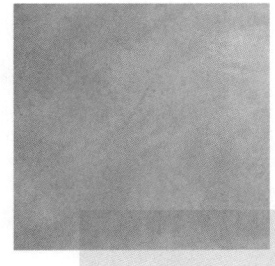

HOSEA

Alice A. Keefe

Introduction

The book of Hosea is the first of the twelve books of the Minor Prophets scroll, composed of collected oracles attributed to the eighth-century-BCE prophet Hosea. The collection originated in the northern kingdom of Israel and was transmitted to Judah after the Assyrian conquest, where it helped to shape—and was shaped by—the emerging Deuteronomistic school. The collection most likely underwent further redaction during the Babylonian exile—a time when Hosea's prophecies resonated with the experiences of a new generation.

Hosea son of Beeri was most likely a native of Ephraim, the name he favored for the northern kingdom of Israel. His oracles evidence extensive knowledge of the kingdom's history, its current domestic and foreign politics, and the duplicitous conduct of its priestly and political leaders. The prophet Hosea situates himself within a lineage of prophets going back to Moses (Hosea 6:5; 9:8; 12:13), and grounds his message in recollection of the sacred traditions of the exodus from Egypt, the forging of the covenant at Sinai, and YHWH's providential care for Israel in the wilderness. As part of his prophetic mission, he marries a woman named Gomer, characterized as a "woman of promiscuity," and gives bizarre and ominous names to their children. This symbolic action points to Hosea's core concern: the failure of the nation to live up to the terms of the Sinai covenant.

According to the book's superscription, Hosea's prophetic activity began sometime in the middle of the eighth century BCE, during the last years of King Jeroboam II of Israel, and continued through the troubled years leading up to the Assyrian conquest in 722 BCE. This was a politically turbulent era in the northern kingdom, marked by palace coups and multiple regicides, war with Judah, and a vacillating foreign policy, all of which opened the way for Assyria's invasion. Meanwhile, the cult of sacrifice at the national shrines functioned as an arm of the royal administration, lending divine sanction to the monarchy and its policies. As a prophetic witness to the era, Hosea denounced the duplicity, faithlessness, and foolishness of Israel's elite establishment. In his eyes, the nation had violated the nation's covenant with YHWH, and divine punishment in the form of historical disaster would soon ensue. While the book includes several oracles offering hope of reconciliation and redemption, the overall tone is dark with warnings of impending national catastrophe.

Hosea 1–3: YHWH's Wife of Promiscuity

▌ THE TEXT IN ITS ANCIENT CONTEXT

The book of Hosea is best known for the marriage metaphor of Hosea 1–3. This trope was a rhetorical innovation that deployed an image of something familiar to Hosea's ancient audience—the structure of Israelite marriage—to evoke a renewed understanding of something less familiar or perhaps forgotten, that is, the requirements of the covenant relationship between YHWH and the nation. Hosea 1:2 reports that the inspiration for this metaphor came in a divine revelation, whereby the prophet was instructed to take "a wife of promiscuity" and have "children of promiscuity." In following this command, Hosea acted out on the stage of his own life a message concerning Israel's covenant with YHWH (portrayed as marriage) and "her" neglect/violation of that covenant (portrayed as wifely infidelity).

Hosea's original audience would have received and understood his marriage metaphor in relation to the meanings that marriage and sexual transgression carried in the ancient world. In modern culture, we tend to think of marriage as being primarily a romantic or personal relationship, and value mutual and equal relations between husband and wife. In Hosea's world, the primary aim of marriage was reproduction and the continuation of the patrilineage, and the relationship between husband and wife was hierarchical and asymmetrical. A wife in ancient Israel was under the authority of her husband, was dependent on him for her subsistence, and owed him exclusive sexual rights so that the paternity of his children could be assured. A wife who strayed sexually was subject to divorce and even death (Num. 5:11-31; Deut. 22:22-24). Her obligation of fidelity, however, was not reciprocal; a husband could enjoy sexual relations with other women, such as prostitutes or concubines, so long as no other man's "rights" over "his" women were violated. Codes of honor and shame provided indispensable support for this social system. A man's honor depended on his ability to maintain sexual control over his wife/wives and daughters. A woman who had illicit sexual relations—even if it was forced on her through rape—brought shame on the men in her family (Gen. 34:31; Lev. 21:9). Hosea's metaphor draws on these social codes, comparing the nation to an adulterous wife giving birth to children of uncertain paternity (powerful symbols of transgression and shame in his world) in order to awaken his audience to the gravity of their own transgression of their covenant obligations to YHWH.

Hosea's marriage metaphor is deployed in different configurations in each of the book's first three chapters. In the third-person narrative of Hosea 1:2-3, the prophet is instructed to marry a woman named Gomer, who is characterized as a woman or wife of *zĕnûnîm*. *Zĕnûnîm* carries the meaning of repeated or habitual sexual transgression, and is best translated as "whoredom(s)" or "promiscuity" (Bird 1989, 80). (Although some older translations render "whore" or "harlot," the term for a professional prostitute, *zônâ*, is not used.) When Gomer gives birth, the children are likewise characterized as children of *zĕnûnîm*, and Hosea gives them ominous names that signal God's displeasure. The name of the firstborn, Jezreel (Hosea 1:4-5), evokes memories of the blood spilled at the town of Jezreel by the usurper Jehu in his bloody coup against the house of Ahab (2 Kings 9–10) and invites comparison between that era and the violent politics of Hosea's own time. The names of the second and third children—"Not Pitied" and "Not My People" (Hosea 1:6-8)—effect ironic reversals of the Mosaic traditions of election and covenant, in which YHWH had pity on the enslaved Israelites and announced they would be his people (Exod. 3:7-9; 19:5). Hosea 1 concludes with the hope for future restoration, figured poetically through a lifting of the curses implied in these names (1:10-11).

In Hosea 2, YHWH accuses his wife, the nation Israel, of chasing after other lovers, believing that it is they, and not her "first husband," who provide her with the gifts of the land's bounty (Hosea 2:5). Outraged, the husband, YHWH, threatens to exercise his legal rights to violently punish and/or divorce her; he promises that he will strip her naked "in the sight of her lovers" (2:10), put an end to "all her appointed festivals" (2:11), and "lay waste" her vineyards and orchards (2:12). Abruptly, these divine threats shift to a promise of reconciliation in the wilderness, a kind of second honeymoon that revives the original intimacy that existed between YHWH and Israel in the years of wandering in the wilderness (Hosea 2:14-15). The chapter ends with YHWH's promise of a new covenant/betrothal that includes the whole of creation and is founded on the virtues of righteousness, justice, *ḥesed* ("steadfast love" or "covenant fidelity"), and mercy (Hosea 2:16-23).

Hosea 3 offers a first-person account of YHWH's command to the prophet to love an adulterous woman. Hosea tells the woman that she must refrain from sexual pleasures for a time, even with her husband; the point being that Israel itself must dwell for a time in a state of separation (or exile), without political leaders or its sacrificial cult. The brief chapter ends with the prospect of the reunification of Israel under a Davidic king. A similar promise of Israel and Judah being "gathered together" under "one head" also is found at the conclusion of Hosea 1 (1:10-11).

While the metaphor of female sexual transgression dominates and unites these chapters, the referent of the metaphor—the actual sins being condemned—is not clear. The motif of the wife chasing after "her lovers" in conjunction with reference to the "feast days of the *ba'alim*" suggests that Israel's sin is pursuit of other gods. Many have understood these "lovers" or *ba'alim* as the fertility gods of ancient Canaan. In this view, Hosea objects to popular participation in a syncretistic fertility cult in which the people sought assurance of agricultural fertility through rituals of worship and sacrifice to the rain god Baal and other deities connected with the powers of nature.

■ THE TEXT IN THE INTERPRETIVE TRADITION

Hosea's marriage metaphor made a lasting impact on the religious language of subsequent generations. In Christianity, marital imagery shaped both ecclesiology, where the church is envisioned as the bride of Christ, and mystical theology, in which the soul unites with the divine. And within both Christianity and Judaism, female sexual transgression, or "whoring," has had a long history as a primary trope for sin.

Perhaps because of the marriage metaphor's influence in Western religious thought, it has attracted considerable attention over the centuries. Much of this commentary has been focused on efforts to reconstruct the biographical facts concerning the relationship between Hosea and Gomer (Sherwood, 40–54). Many premodern commentators were so offended by the thought of Hosea, God's righteous prophet, being sullied by marriage to an "impure" woman that they interpreted Hosea's marriage as occurring only in a dream, as the Jewish exegete Abraham Ibn Ezra suggested (Lipschitz, 20), or as a visionary experience, as the Protestant Reformer John Calvin maintained (43–44). Twentieth-century biblical scholars have generally assumed the literal intent of the marriage, but have filled in the gaps to create a romanticized narrative of Hosea's unrequited love for Gomer, his personal pain at her betrayal, and his heroic forgiveness of her. This preoccupation with the details of Hosea's personal life has been motivated by the premise that the prophet's own emotional turmoil served as his inspiration for understanding YHWH's experience with Israel, suffering from their rejection, but forgiving them and loving them in the end (e.g., Rowley, 97).

The details of Gomer's sexual life have also been the topic of much speculation. Many twentieth-century commentators, building on the thesis that rituals of sacred prostitution were part of the fertility cult Hosea condemns, have argued that Gomer's infidelity involved the performance of ritual sex acts within the fertility cult. She might have been a sacred prostitute who had sex with men at the shrines (e.g., Mays, 25–26), or alternatively, a virgin who had been ritually "deflowered" in bridal rites at the shrines (e.g., Wolff, 14–15).

The view that Hosea opposed a popular fertility cult, in which the worship of nature deities was accompanied by sexual rituals, has served to articulate and reinforce a theological opposition between pagan nature worship and ethical monotheism. Evidence supporting the scenario of a sexualized fertility cult in ancient Israel is slim. In response, some have sought an alternative approach to reconstructing Hosea's religious contexts by attending to the interrelationships between religion, politics, and economics in ancient Israel (Keefe; Yee 2001; Kelle). These interpreters highlight the political and cultural connotations of Baal and the Baalim in Hosea's world, and suggest that Israel's "lovers" are not fertility gods but foreign gods, that is, the state deities of other nations—Israel's allies, trading partners, and/or overlords. From this perspective, the nation's "promiscuity" is a symbol for its deepening investments in international "liaisons" and cosmopolitan orientations (see also Hosea 8:9), and those whom Hosea accuses as "whoring" are not the people in general, but Israel's elite power brokers.

In the twentieth century, many biblical scholars argued that rituals of sacred prostitution were included in Baalim fertility cult under the theory that human sex acts performed in imitation of the sacred marriage of the gods helped to secure the fertility of the land. In recent years, however, this reconstruction of the religious contexts behind Hosea's rhetoric has been challenged. Scholars who have revisited the "sacred prostitution" hypothesis have found no compelling evidence for ritual sex in ancient Israel or neighboring cultures in this era (Toorn; Oden). The existence of a popular fertility cult or widespread Baal worship in Hosea's Israel, as are presupposed by most interpreters, also is uncertain (Kelle, 137–52). Further, the cult practices that Hosea explicitly attacks—rites of sacrifice at the high places and the presence of the bull icon at Bethel—were not foreign accretions, but accepted features of Yahwism in his day (Yee 2001, 351).

■ THE TEXT IN CONTEMPORARY DISCUSSION

Contemporary theological reflection on Hosea 1–3 demands attention to issues of gender and the problematic legacy of patriarchal symbols within Western religious traditions. Feminist readers contend that Hosea's marriage metaphor reinforces patriarchal social structures, silences woman's voice, legitimates violence against her, and identifies women with sin and evil. The metaphor presupposes and legitimates a patriarchal social system in which husbands have a unilateral right to control their wives' sexuality and the legal authority to inflict physical punishment on her if she violates that right. Furthermore, YHWH's threats of violence against the metaphorical woman—threatening to strip her naked in the sight of her lovers, presumably so they can rape her (2:10)—is a highly disturbing motif, and one that some find to be almost pornographic in its conjunction of voyeurism and violence (e.g., Setel). How does a woman who has been battered relate to the image of God as a wife batterer (Weems, 8)? Can this text function as sacred Scripture for her, or for anyone who seeks liberation from the violence that sustains patriarchy?

Another problem with this metaphor is its gender assignments, which link maleness with the divine and femaleness with sinful humanity. Although metaphors posit an "as-if" relation between vehicle and tenor, readers tend to devolve into literalism. Thus the metaphorical comparison of God with a man (a husband) has supported the belief that males have a closer resemblance to the divine than do females. Such is the case, for example, among those Catholic theologians who justify the exclusion of women from the priesthood in part with reference to the Bible's "nuptial mystery" in which God is the husband of Israel (as in Hosea), or Christ is the bridegroom of the church, as in the New Testament. Because God is metaphorically a bridegroom, those who represent him in the church—the priests—must also be male (Sacred Congregation, section 5; Yee 1996, 227–28). Ironically, a metaphor that in its ancient context was intended to critique men of power becomes a tool for the maintenance of male power over women.

Hosea 4:1—5:7: The Land Mourns

■ THE TEXT IN ITS ANCIENT CONTEXT

Hosea 4 opens with an announcement of YHWH's "indictments against the inhabitants of the land" and specifies its cause. Absent are faithfulness, loving-kindness (*ḥesed*), and knowledge of God (Hosea 4:1); these are among the virtues that should bind Israel and YHWH together (Hosea 2:19-20). Instead, there is cursing, lying, killing, stealing, adultery, and bloody murder (Hosea 4:2): sins that closely correspond to the ethical prohibitions of the Decalogue (Exodus 20). As a result of this proliferation of sin, the land will "mourn" and all the animal life that dwells in it will die (Hosea 4:3).

Hosea then turns his attention to Israel's religious leadership and the rituals over which they preside. A certain priest is singled out (Hosea 4:4); he might have been an important official within the royal cult, or perhaps he represents the institution of the priesthood as a whole. This priest is charged with forgetting YHWH's *tôrah* ("law/teaching") and rejecting knowledge (Hosea 4:6). The priests were responsible not only for presiding over sacrifices but also for teaching knowledge of the covenant and its obligations to the people (Deut. 33:10). But the religious leaders have failed in this mission, and as a result, the people "are destroyed for lack of knowledge" (Hosea 4:6). The venerable shrines where the priests officiate are also condemned. Hosea admonishes the people not to "go up" to Gilgal or Beth-aven (literally "house of iniquity"), the latter being Hosea's pejorative term for the national shrine at Bethel (Hosea 4:15).

Throughout this section, Hosea communicates his judgments through further metaphors of sexual transgression. The nation has been led astray by a "spirit of whoredom" (Hosea 4:12; 5:3-4), and consequently the people "play the whore" and "devote themselves to whoredom" (Hosea 4:10, 15). Also, the high places are depicted as places of orgiastic promiscuity where male worshipers consort with prostitutes and dependent females brazenly commit adultery (Hosea 4:13-14).

THE TEXT IN THE INTERPRETIVE TRADITION

Those commentators who believe that rituals of sacred prostitution were part of Canaanite religion find support for this theory in Hosea 4:13-14, reading these verses as literal descriptions of ritual sex taking place at or near the high places (e.g., Mays, 73–75; Wolff, 86–87). Reference to men consorting with whores and qĕdēshôt, a term usually translated as "sacred prostitute," along with depictions of fornicating daughters and daughters-in-law, have led commentators to envision a scenario of orgiastic revelry at the shrines. However, in a society in which female sexual transgression was a grievous crime (see Deut. 22:13-27), it is unlikely that any women other than prostitutes would engage in illicit sex in public locations (Christl, 266; Keefe, 100–101); if read figuratively, these references to public sex appear to be rhetoric designed to provoke shock and shame in its male audience. Worse than the worst imaginable crime—subordinate women in sexual rebellion—is the behavior of Israel's men. Though their crimes are not clearly specified, their participation in the cult is likened to having sex with prostitutes and qĕdēshôt (Hosea 4:14b), terms that pejoratively refer perhaps to the male priests themselves (Keefe, 101–2) or to female cult personnel serving at the shrines (Bird, 87; Wacker, 233–34).

Another approach has been to envision the high places as sites of goddess worship, a view supported by Hosea's sarcastic remarks about the sacred trees standing in the vicinity of Israel's open-air altars (Hosea 4:13b). The tree of life was a well-known symbol for the goddess Asherah, a point that leads to the suggestion that Hosea objects to the worship of Asherah at the high places (Christl; Wacker). Also, some have found hints of goddess worship in Hosea 4:19, emending the text to read "a wind has wrapped her up in her skirts," that is, the skirts of a goddess (Emmerson; Wacker, 221–23).

THE TEXT IN CONTEMPORARY DISCUSSION

This section opens with a disturbing prediction of the withering of the land and all that lives in it. The beasts of the field, the birds of the air, and the fish of the sea that God created at the beginning (Gen. 1:20-31) will be taken away, and as a result, the land will "mourn" (Hosea 4:1-3). Noting the connection with the creation story, DeRoche argues that the text portends a "reversal of creation" in which all life is undone. The root cause of this ecological collapse, says Hosea, is human greed, violence, and perfidy, which poison the land. His prophecy of a world stripped of its animal life is particularly relevant today as disruptions in our global ecosystems threaten the extinction of many species. Heeding Hosea, we might attend to the interconnections between human beings and nature, and consider the role of human sin in the deterioration of the environment, on which we and future generations depend.

Also relevant today is Hosea's scathing criticism of the failures of Israel's religious leadership, who pursue "a spirit of harlotry" rather than teaching knowledge of God and modeling right action. In Hosea's eyes, the self-serving, short-sighted behavior of Israel's priesthood was a significant contributing factor leading toward national catastrophe. Reflecting on these points in relation to our own perilous situation in the modern world, the text invites reflection on the crucial responsibilities of religious leaders today and the far-reaching consequences of failure to uphold those responsibilities.

Hosea 5:8—10:15: They Shall Return to Egypt

■ THE TEXT IN ITS ANCIENT CONTEXT

The oracles in this section address a range of issues relating to warfare, Assyrian tribute demands, and the politics of regicide, along with further attacks on the high places and shrines. Although no certain correlations can be made between particular passages and specific historical events, the oracles reflect the chaotic politics and ill-advised foreign policies of the years leading up to Assyrian conquest.

The historical context for Hosea 5:8-14 is probably the Syro-Ephraimitic War (734–733 BCE). The looming threat of invasion is evoked twice by Hosea's prophetic commands to "blow the horn" in warning of danger (Hosea 5:8; 8:1). The prophet mocks Israel and Judah's feeble attempts to find safety in alliances or the paying of tribute to Assyria or seeking alliance with Egypt (Hosea 5:13; 7:11; 8:9). Ephraim "mixes himself with the peoples," says the prophet, and therefore "foreigners devour his strength" (Hosea 7:8-9).

Hosea 7 comments on the endemic violence swirling around the royal house as one regicide followed another (Hosea 7:2-7; cf. 2 Kgs. 15:8—17:23). In Hosea's eyes, Israel's present monarchy—established by bloodshed and not by divine authorization—has become illegitimate and shall fall (Hosea 8:4; 10:7). The fate of the monarchy is interdependent with that of its premier symbol, the "calf of Samaria" (that is, the calf image at Bethel that authorized the power of the state based in Samaria); it will be carried off as tribute to Assyria (Hosea 8:5; 10:6). Both the monarchy and the calf image are illegitimate human creations (Hosea 8:4) that provide no protection from foreign incursions or divine wrath.

Hosea 9 opens with an oracle of judgment delivered to participants in a harvest festival, most likely the seven-day festival of Sukkot. The celebrants are accused of having loved a "prostitute's pay" on their threshing floors (Hosea 9:1), suggesting, as in Hosea 2, that their sin is a failure to acknowledge YHWH as the source of the land's fertility. Dire prophecies follow concerning the failure of human fertility. The prophet prays for YHWH to give them "a miscarrying womb and dry breasts," and predicts that Ephraim, the fruitful one, shall "bear no fruit," thus negating all hope for the future (Hosea 9:14, 16).

Hosea speaks of the sins of the present through allusions to the primordial sins of Israel's past. Twice he speaks of the nation's guilt with reference to "the days of Gibeah" (Hosea 9:9; 10:9), alluding perhaps to the horrific rape and murder of a woman at Gibeah and the bloody, pointless civil war that ensued (Judges 19–21). Hosea also recalls the sin of Baal Peor (Hosea 9:10), Israel's first "intercourse" with the nations where shared worship and interethnic marriage compromised Israel's identity as God's chosen one (Numbers 25). The shrine of Gilgal is also evoked as the place where YHWH "first began to hate them" (Hosea 9:15), perhaps referencing the "original sin" of the establishment of the monarchy under Saul at Gilgal, an event that Samuel saw as a rejection of YHWH (1 Sam. 8:7-8).

Bitter tropes of reversal unify this section. Those who celebrate the harvest with wine and rejoicing will go hungry and will eat "unclean" bread in Assyria (Hosea 9:1-4). YHWH's promise that Abraham's descendants will be "exceedingly fruitful" (Gen. 17:6) becomes a prophetic "prayer" for sterility and a nation bereft of children (Hosea 9:11-14, 15-17). And for the people who were brought forth out of slavery in Egypt, the trope of a return to Egypt vividly figures the destruction and exile to come (Hosea 7:16; 8:13; 9:6; 11:5).

◼ THE TEXT IN THE INTERPRETIVE TRADITION

Although the bulk of the oracles in this section concerns political issues, theologically oriented commentary has focused on particular passages that contain hope for the future or guidance as to what YHWH requires. It is instructive to note how Jewish and Christian commentators have interpreted the same passages in different ways.

Hosea 6:1-3 places a liturgical prayer for collective restoration in the mouth of the people, expressing hopes of salvation through the metaphor of healing and the image of being raised up by YHWH "on the third day" (Hosea 6:2). The apostle Paul probably had this verse in mind when he wrote that Jesus was raised on the "third day" in accordance with the Scriptures (1 Cor. 15:4), but Tertullian was the first to refer explicitly to this verse as a prophecy of Jesus' resurrection (*Adversus Marcionem* 4.43; *Adversus Judaeos* 13.23). Rabbinic tradition, on the other hand, cites this passage as a proof text for the teaching concerning the resurrection of the dead at the end of time (McArthur).

Hosea 6:6 has been an important text over the centuries for discussions about the role of sacrifice and ritual observance in biblical religions. Here, Hosea announces that YHWH desires "steadfast love" (*ḥesed*), not sacrifice, and knowledge of God, not burnt offerings. Similar views are found in 1 Sam. 15:22 and the oracles of other eighth-century prophets (Isa. 1:10-17; Amos 4:4-5; 5:21-27; Mic. 6:6-8). In Christian contexts, Hosea 6:6 is sometimes taken in support of the view that Jesus' sacrifice replaced the ritual requirements of the Torah. Jesus quotes Hosea 6:6 twice in the book of Matthew in answer to objections from the Pharisees concerning the lax ritual observance of his disciples (Matt. 12:6) and to explain his practice of eating with "unclean" sinners (Matt. 9:9-13). Subsequently, many Christian theologians have read Hosea 6:6 as proving that after Jesus, the ritual requirements of the Torah are nullified.

Rabbinic tradition, however, interpreted Hosea 6:6 as indicating YHWH's progressive revelation to the Jewish people, as the center of Judaism shifted from temple to Torah. Rabbi Yohanan ben Zakkai cited this passage to console a disciple who was grieving over the loss of the Jerusalem temple, fearing that without the cult of sacrifice there was no way to atone for sin. Rabbi Yohanan explained that YHWH had removed the temple to make way for another, and perhaps higher, form of atonement: moral action and covenant fidelity (*Avot D'Rabbi Natan* 9). The rabbinic tradition is clear, however, that the ritual requirements of the Torah, other than those that require a temple, still stand.

■ THE TEXT IN CONTEMPORARY DISCUSSION

This section directs our attention to sins relating to the political realm, inviting us to observe the militarism, duplicitous politics, and realpolitik diplomacy of our own time in a more critical light. Hosea condemns Israel's princes and collaborators who "burn with intrigue and "devour their rulers" (Hosea 7:6-7, RSV), using their power to fight and kill for more power. He mocks their efforts to find security through building strongholds and fortified cities (Hosea 8:14) or by making alliances with the region's strong man, Assyria (Hosea 8:9). Trust in militarism, announces Hosea, leads not to security but to devastation (Hosea 8:14, 10:13-15). And against those who glorify the male "sport" of waging war, Hosea depicts war as bitter carnage in which mothers are gratuitously slaughtered along with their children and pregnant women are ripped open for fun (Hosea 10:14; see also 13:16).

Today nations still go to war proudly proclaiming that God is on "our side." But what if the Almighty is not with "our" nation, but against it? Hosea asks us to imagine that unthinkable scenario through intense metaphors of divine wrath. YHWH will be like dry rot or the maggots that feed on dead bodies (Hosea 5:12), like a lion ripping his prey to shreds (Hosea 5:14), or like a fowler who catches hapless birds in his snares (Hosea 7:12). There is no domestication of the deity here, but multiple revelations of YHWH's absolute power over life and death (Yee 1996, 250). These disquieting depictions of YHWH are a powerful counterpoint to any religious nationalism that complacently assumes God will always be on our side.

Perhaps most disturbing of all are Hosea's images of female sterility and the death of children. The parallel between Hosea's dark prayer that YHWH give them dry breasts and miscarrying wombs and the ancient prayer beseeching the "blessings of the breasts and of the womb" (Gen. 49:25) suggests that Hosea has reversed the ancient blessing formula and transformed it into a curse (Krause, 197). Like his warning prophecy of ecological collapse in which all animal life perishes (Hosea 4:3), Hosea's evocation of universal sterility and a world without children is an intentionally disturbing sign for the approaching annihilation. Today these images appear as more than just prophetic hyperbole. Given the threats to human flourishing and even human survival posed by our modern weapons of mass destruction and our destabilization of the ecosystem, Hosea's prophecies of a lifeless world can remind us of what is at stake in the decisions we, as individuals and as nations, make today.

Hosea 11–14: Divine Pathos and Human Repentance

▊ The Text in Its Ancient Context

In these final chapters, the major themes of Hosea's book are reiterated: Israel's election and redemption out of Egypt, Israel's rebellion and sin, the pending punishment, the call for repentance, and the hope for covenant renewal.

Hosea 11 reviews the story of Israel through the metaphor of Israel as YHWH's adopted child. Called forth from Egypt, and held tenderly within the "bonds of love," they nevertheless soon turned to idolatry and now deserve punishment. As with Hosea's marriage metaphor, this metaphor presupposes the family structures of ancient Israel, in which power relations were asymmetrical and the disobedience of the subordinate family member (wife or child) could be a capital offense (Deut. 21:18-21). But at the same time, family relations may be characterized by love and intimacy, and the pain that comes from discord can be mutual. The parental metaphor makes way for depiction of YHWH as a god of compassion as well as justice; in the midst of announcements of punishment to come, the compassion of YHWH for his child wells up, and the deity recoils from his wrathful intention, proclaiming, "I am God and not man" (Hosea 11:9). In contrast to Samuel, who says that YHWH "is not a man" and therefore will not reverse his judgment on Saul (1 Sam. 15:29), Hosea asserts that YHWH's divinity means he is not bound by his anger, and can choose forgiveness.

In Hosea 12, the story of the grasping and duplicitous Jacob serves as the paradigm for Israel's present sinful condition (Hosea 12:2-4, 12). Israel is also pejoratively termed "a Canaanite" or "a trader" who brags over his ill-gotten wealth (Hosea 12:7). The term "Canaanite" had become a synonym for "trader" in Hosea's time, due to the association of Canaanites with mercantile activities, but the suggestion of Israel becoming like foreign "others" (the Canaanites) is also present.

Hosea 13 opens with a pointed invective against the idolatry practiced within the national cult. Hosea again echoes Samuel's objection to the establishment of the monarchy (13:10) and suggests that trust in the power of their kings is part and parcel of Israel's sin. The coming wrath of YHWH is compared to a wild beast—a leopard, a lion, or a bear—that will rip them to shreds (Hosea 13:7-8), or to the east wind, the sirocco, which will dry up all sources of life-giving water (Hosea 13:15).

As in Hosea 1–3, where threats of punishment and divorce give way to the promise of reconciliation, Hosea 14 closes the book on a note of hope and promise that is set through images of abundant fertility. Hosea 14 begins with a call for Israel to return to YHWH, and gives instructions for true repentance (14:2-4). This is followed by a promise of redemption, figured in images of abundant fertility. YHWH pictures himself as the moisture providing dew, or as a tree under whose shade the people shall flourish like a garden (14:5-8).

▊ The Text in the Interpretive Tradition

Many interpreters have taken Hosea 11 to be the climax or turning point of the book of Hosea. Through the metaphor of YHWH's prodigal son, the story of Israel's election and rebellion is retold, and the audience is prepared to hear yet another oracle of divine rejection and punishment. Instead, the love YHWH bears for his adopted child causes his heart to turn from its wrathful intentions.

Numerous Christian commentators read Hosea's depiction of YHWH's anguished love for Israel, despite its sins, as anticipating the Christian concept of God as love. The doctrine of retributive justice is here "transcended by Hosea's conception of God's holiness as redemptive love" (Ward, 204). For Abraham Heschel, a Jewish theologian, the "divine pathos" so powerfully communicated in Hosea 11 teaches that not only is YHWH a God who demands justice, but "He is also a God Who is in love with His people" (44).

Hosea's references to the Jacob traditions in Hosea 12 are opaque and difficult to interpret. The motif of Jacob weeping and seeking "his" favor may refer to Jacob weeping and pleading with the angel after a night of struggle in Genesis 32 (although this motif is not preserved in the canonical version of the story), or to Jacob's weeping for forgiveness when he encounters Esau the next day (Gen. 33:4). In either case, Jacob's journey, from being a deceiver to a weeping penitent, models the transformation from sin to repentance that the nation must make (Yee 1996, 284).

In Hosea 14:1-3, the prophet instructs the people on the correct attitude of repentance, which will restore divine favor. For this reason, this passage serves as the prophetic reading that follows the Torah reading on the Sabbath between Rosh Hashanah and Yom Kippur, the holy days focusing on repentance for sin.

The use of tree imagery to depict YHWH's providential care (14:5-8) has intrigued many commentators, given that the tree of life was a common iconographic image of the goddess Asherah. This connection has prompted suggestions that Hosea has here appropriated goddess symbolism and applied it to YHWH. Julius Wellhausen's proposed emendation of Hosea 14:8b to read "I am your Anat and your Asherah" (134) has continued to fuel discussion about whether Hosea here is displacing goddess worship by attributing the powers of fertility to YHWH alone (e.g., Wacker).

◼ THE TEXT IN CONTEMPORARY DISCUSSION

In this section, Hosea offers a rich array of divine imagery that can expand our repertoire of metaphors for God. Of special note is the image of YHWH as Israel's parent in Hosea 11:1-4. While most commentators have taken this as a metaphor of YHWH as a father, the depiction of YHWH's parental care for the infant Israel may better describe the activity of a mother. Schüngel-Straumann argues for this point by translating the very difficult text of Hosea 11:4b as a description of YHWH breastfeeding "her" son: "I was for them like those who take a nursling to the breast . . . in order to give him suck" (4–5). Feminine divine imagery is also suggested by the depiction of YHWH as a fruitful tree in Hosea 14:7-8. For Gale Yee, this image of YHWH's providential care resonates with the figure of Woman Wisdom from Proverbs, who is also described as a life-giving tree (Prov. 3:18; Yee 1996, 297). The presence of these female metaphors for the divine in Hosea is somewhat surprising, given that in the history of the biblical traditions, Hosea's influential image of YHWH as a divine husband helped to foreclose on the possibility of imagining "him" as female. Hosea's theological imagination, however, was not so constricted, and his use of feminine and fertility imagery for YHWH contribute to today's quest for a more holistic and inclusive vision of the divine reality.

The incorporation of Greek philosophical ideas (in which the divine is defined as unchangeable perfection) into Christian thought in late antiquity has also made it difficult to imagine God as passionate and capable of changing his mind. But Hosea's YHWH expresses great passion as he wavers between implacable anger and inconsolable love for his people. Such representations of the divine pathos of YHWH underscore his freedom to change his mind and to choose to redeem rather than to destroy. This divine openness to change reminds us of our own human capacity for remorse and repentance; if YHWH can change his mind, so perhaps we humans can change our ways before we, like Ephraim, must "reap the whirlwind" (Hosea 8:7) and suffer the consequences of our present follies.

Works Cited

Bird, Phyllis. 1989. "'To Play the Harlot': An Inquiry into an Old Testament Metaphor." In *Gender and Difference in Ancient Israel*, edited by Peggy L. Day, 75–94. Minneapolis: Fortress Press.

Calvin, John. 1984. *Commentaries on the Twelve Minor Prophets*. Translated by John Owen. Reprint, Grand Rapids: Baker.

Christl, Maier. 2009. "Myth and Truth in Socio-Historical Reconstruction of Ancient Societies, Hosea 4:11-14 as a Test Case." In *Thus Says the Lord*, edited by John J. Ahn and Steven L. Cook, 256–72. New York: T&T Clark.

DeRoche, D. 1981. "The Reversal of Creation in Hosea." *VT* 31:400–409.

Emmerson, Grace. 1974. "A Fertility Goddess in Hos IV 17-19?" *VT* 24:492–97.

Heschel, Abraham J. 1962. *The Prophets*. New York: Jewish Publication Society.

Keefe, Alice A. 2001. *Woman's Body as the Social Body in Hosea*. Sheffield: Sheffield Academic Press.

Kelle, Brad E. 2005. *Hosea 2: Metaphor and Rhetoric in Historical Perspective*. Leiden: Brill.

Krause, Deborah. 1992. "A Blessing Cursed: The Prophet's Prayer for Barren Womb and Dry Breasts in Hosea 9." In *Reading Between Texts: Intertextuality and the Hebrew Bible*, edited by Danna Nolan Fewell, 191–202. Louisville: Westminster John Knox.

Lipschitz, Abe, ed. and trans. 1988. *The Commentary of Rabbi Abraham Ibn Ezra on Hosea*. New York: Sepher-Hermon Press.

McArthur, Harvey K. 1971. "On the Third Day." *NTS* 18:81–86.

Mays, James L. 1969. *Hosea: A Commentary*. Philadelphia: Westminster.

Oden, Robert A., Jr. 1987. "Religious Identity and the Sacred Prostitution Accusation." In *The Bible Without Theology: The Theological Tradition and Alternatives to It*, 131–53. San Francisco: Harper & Row.

Rowley, H. H. 1963. "The Marriage of Hosea." In *Men and God: Studies in Old Testament History of Prophecy*. London: Nelson.

Sacred Congregation for the Doctrine of the Faith. 15 October 1976. "Declaration *Inter Insigniores* on the Question of the Admission of Women to the Ministerial Priesthood." http://www.vatican.va/roman_curia/congregations/cfaith/documents/rc_con_cfaith_doc_19761015_inter-insigniores_en.html (accessed April 3, 2014).

Schüngel-Straumann, Helen. 1987. "God as Mother in Hosea 11." *TD* 34, no. 1:3–8.

Setel, T. Drorah. 1985. "Prophets and Pornography: Female Sexual Imagery in Hosea." In *Feminist Interpretation of the Bible*, edited by Letty Russell, 86–95. Philadelphia: Westminster.

Sherwood, Yvonne. 1996. *The Prostitute and the Prophet: Hosea's Marriage in Literary-Theoretical Perspective*. Sheffield: Sheffield Academic Press.

Toorn, Karel van der. 1992. "Prostitution, Cultic." In *ABD* 5:510–13.

Wacker, Marie-Theres. 1995. "Traces of the Goddess in the Book of Hosea." In *A Feminist Companion to the Latter Prophets*, edited by Athalya Brenner, 219–41. Sheffield: Sheffield Academic Press.

Ward, James M. 1966. *Hosea: A Theological Commentary*. New York: Harper & Row.

Weems, Renita. 1995. *Battered Love: Marriage, Sex, and Violence in the Hebrew Prophets*. Minneapolis: Fortress Press.

Wellhausen, Julius. 1963. *Die Kleine Propheten*. Skizzen und Vorarbeiten 5. 4th ed. Berlin: Reimer.

Wolff, Hans Walter. 1974. *Hosea: A Commentary on the Book of the Prophet Hosea*. Philadelphia: Fortress Press.

Yee, Gale A. 1996. "The Book of Hosea." In *The New Interpreter's Bible*. Vol. 7, *Introduction to Apocalyptic Literature, Daniel, The Twelve Prophets*, edited by Leander E. Keck, 197–297. Nashville: Abingdon.

———. 2001. "'She Is Not My Wife and I Am Not Her Husband': A Materialist Reading of Hosea 1–2." *BibInt* 9, no. 4:345–83.

JOEL

Ronald A. Simkins

Introduction

Nothing is known about the prophet Joel or his father Pethuel, and little is known about the historical context of the book that bears his name. On this all scholars agree; on other interpretive issues regarding the book of Joel, there is little unanimity. The date of the book has been assigned to a range from as early as the ninth century BCE to as late as the Maccabean period for its final compilation. A fifth-century-BCE date, putting it in the mid-Persian period, has attracted many scholars due to the vocabulary and expressions that Joel shares with other late books, such as its emphasis on the role of the temple and cult, and the scribal activity evident from Joel's citation of other biblical texts and references to biblical ideas.

The composition and structure of the book of Joel are also unsettled, though the dividing lines are much clearer. Following Bernhard Duhm, most scholars before the middle of the twentieth century argued that the book was composed in two distinct parts or with multiple layers: 1:1—2:27 represent the oracles of the prophet Joel in response to a past and present catastrophe, and 2:28—3:21 are later apocalyptic oracles addressing a future eschatological hope. The day of the LORD passages in the first part of the book were also interpreted by some as later editorial additions to connect the two parts of the book. Most recent commentators, however, have argued for the unity of the book, noting the symmetry between the two parts (e.g., Wolff), or emphasizing repetition and development of themes, such as the day of the LORD, between the two parts (e.g., Simkins). John Barton continues to support Duhm's division of the book. Regardless of how the composition of the book is understood, the two parts of the book demonstrate a shift in tense and tone. Joel 1:1—2:17 is written in the past and present tenses and is descriptive and prophetic in tone. Beginning in 2:18, the book shifts to the future tense, and by 2:28 the tone becomes eschatological.

The book has an anthological character, with the prophet drawing on numerous prophetic themes. Moreover, the prophet cites many other prophetic texts or traditions, suggesting that Joel was perhaps a learned scribe and an interpreter of the prophetic tradition (see Crenshaw, 26–28, 35–39).

The book of Joel appears to have been occasioned by an unprecedented catastrophe, which is described in 1:1—2:11, and the meaning of the book is shaped by the interpretation of the nature of the catastrophe, the role of the cult in response to the catastrophe, and the relationship of the catastrophe to the proclamation of the day of the LORD.

Joel 1:1-20: Locust Plague and Lamentation

■ THE TEXT IN ITS ANCIENT CONTEXT

The book of Joel begins with the proclamation of an unprecedented catastrophe: locusts have devoured everything in the land (1:2-4). How this locust plague differs from previous plagues is not stated; the text only emphasizes the locusts' voracious appetite. The four terms for locusts in verse 4 have often been interpreted as denoting developmental stages of the common desert locust (*Schistocerca gregaria*)—though only three distinct stages of the locust's metamorphosis are apparent to the casual observer—but the terms elsewhere are used interchangeably. Here the terms are used rhetorically to emphasize the complete destruction caused by the locusts.

Scholars debate the nature of the catastrophe. The references to locusts and their destruction may describe a literal plague, or they may be interpreted metaphorically, referring to an invading enemy army. A few passages (1:12, 19-20) elicit images of drought, which is generally incompatible with locust infestations. Although multiple interpretations are possible, it is unlikely that the locusts are metaphors for an invading army when they are *compared to* an invading nation (1:6) or an army (2:6-9). The drought imagery may refer to the normal dry conditions of summer, whose effects are intensified by the locusts' devastation, or it may be stock poetic imagery used to emphasize the totality of the natural catastrophe.

The remainder of chapter 1 can be divided into a call to lamentation (vv. 5-14) delivered by the prophet to the people, and the lament (vv. 15-20) that the people should cry to God. The call to lamentation can be divided into four strophes (vv. 5-7, 8-10, 11-12, and 13-14), each beginning with an imperative call (v. 5: "wake up," "wail"), followed by a vocative designating those addressed (v. 5: "drunkards," "wine-drinkers"), and then a substantiation clause giving the reason for lamentation (v. 5: "for [the sweet wine] is cut off from your mouth"). The first three strophes then continue with additional lines describing the devastation, but the final strophe concludes with a series of imperatives directed to the temple priests.

The first strophe (vv. 5-7), which begins by calling for drunkards to awake, perhaps suggests for many that Joel's audience has been complacent or foolish in not giving attention to the significance of the locust plague. Other scholars simply note that drunkards, coupled with wine-drinkers, are those who have experienced the consequences of the locusts' devastation firsthand. Similarly, in the third strophe (vv. 11-12), the farmers and vinedressers are called to lament. Both the first and the third strophes emphasize the agricultural devastation caused by the locusts. The second strophe

(vv. 8-10) lacks an explicit addressee in the vocative, but the feminine singular imperative and the reference to the temple in verse 9 perhaps implies a personified Jerusalem. The call to lamentation reaches its climax in the fourth strophe (vv. 13-14), where the priests, the ministers of the altar, are addressed. In both the second and fourth strophes, emphasis is placed on the consequences of the agricultural devastation for the temple liturgy: namely, that the grain and drinking offerings to God at the temple have come to an end.

Joel's call to lamentation demands a liturgical response to the catastrophe. The priests should summon all the people to fast and to assemble at the temple to cry out to God. Verses 15-20 are perhaps the words of the lament that the people should cry. They should bewail that "the day of the LORD is near," or better, that it is "now at hand." The lament identifies the devastation of the locust plague with the day of the LORD, which since the time of Amos has been associated with YHWH's judgment, both on Israel and on the nations. Although in 2:31 and 3:14 Joel perhaps refers to *the final* day of the LORD, in which YHWH will bring an end to human history, inaugurating the eschatological era, in 1:15 (and also 2:1, 11), Joel is only referring to *a* day of the LORD—a present but limited day of God's judgment. As a day of the LORD, the locust plague has not only destroyed the agriculture but also threatens the community of living creatures. Thus the people should cry out to God as even the cattle and wild animals do (vv. 18, 20).

■ THE TEXT IN THE INTERPRETIVE TRADITION

Although the four terms used for locusts in Joel 1:4 refer to a literal locust plague, the interpretive tradition has generally understood the terms metaphorically. One Greek translation, for example, renders them as Egyptians, Babylonians, Assyrians, and Greeks. The Targum interprets the terms to be peoples, tongues, governments, and kingdoms. Ephrem the Syrian (d. 373) and Isho'dad of Merv (c. 850) take the locust terms as metaphors for Tiglath Pileser III, Shalmaneser V, Sennacherib, and Nebuchadnezzar.

■ THE TEXT IN CONTEMPORARY DISCUSSION

By identifying the locust plague with the day of the LORD, the book of Joel raises questions of theodicy and the role of God in natural disasters, even today. Can God's activity or will be discerned in such catastrophes? Many today seem to be willing to identify natural disasters as God's judgment on one corporate sin or another, but such diagnoses demonstrate little more than the prejudices of the interpreters. Joel too thought a natural catastrophe signaled God's activity, the day of the LORD, but his reasoning and response are instructive to us. Joel's diagnosis is not simply based on the destruction caused by the locust plague, but on its effect on the temple: the grain and drink offerings, the daily sacrifices, were brought to an end. In a world in which such events were not explained scientifically (or through natural causality), such a calamitous event was surely an act of God. Joel does not, however, respond with a moral diagnosis to explain God's actions; he does not blame the catastrophe on the people's sins. He calls instead for a fast and the self-abasement of lamentation. As Joel will articulate in the next chapter, God is merciful and gracious (2:13) and will hear the humble cry of his people.

Joel 2:1-11: Invasion by the Army of YHWH

▌ THE TEXT IN ITS ANCIENT CONTEXT

Although the first chapter presents the catastrophic locust plague as a past event, a present and ongoing catastrophe is heralded in chapter 2. Through multiple metaphors, Joel 2 describes the invasion of YHWH's army on a city, presumably Jerusalem and its environs. Scholars disagree on the nature of this second catastrophe and on its relationship with the locust plague lamented in chapter 1. This catastrophe has been understood in three different ways: (1) the invasion of a historical enemy of Judah, such as the Babylonians; (2) the invasion of an apocalyptic army; and (3) a locust plague that is compared to an invading army. Joel's use of metaphor makes option 1 the least likely interpretation; the catastrophe is *compared to* an invading army rather than being a historical army. According to the second option, the locust plague of chapter 1 becomes a metaphor for an eschatological enemy from the north on the day of the LORD. The enemy army would thus be compared to locust-like apocalyptic creatures (compare the apocalyptic army in Rev. 9:1-11). The difficulty with this interpretation is that the description of the invasion in verses 3-9 has a this-worldly orientation and reflects the activity of *real* locusts; apocalyptic language is not otherwise evident in the first part of the book. (Whether it is characteristic of the second part of Joel is debated.) Thus most scholars interpret Joel 2:1-11 as referring to a locust plague that was presently "assaulting" the environs of Jerusalem.

The relationship between this locust plague and the plague whose destruction was lamented in chapter 1 is uncertain. The use of perfect verbs in chapter 1 and primarily imperfect verbs in chapter 2 indicates only the temporal orientation of the oracle in relation to the speaker, not the temporal relationship between the oracles. The locust plague in chapter 2 may thus refer to the same event that is lamented in chapter 1. Nevertheless, because locust plagues in the Middle East often occurred over several years (such as the 1915 plague documented by John Whiting) and because Joel 2:25 refers to the "the years that the swarming locust has eaten" (NRSV), the locust invasion described in chapter 2 may also be interpreted as a continuation of the previous year's infestation.

Verses 3-9 describe the onslaught of a locust plague consisting of innumerable hoppers marching in array. Their destruction is compared to that of fire; their appearance, to that of horses. Their assault on the people is likened to an army attacking a city whose defenses are ineffectual. Although these metaphors present a realistic portrait of a locust plague, verses 1-2 and 10-11 signal the uniqueness of this plague because of its supranaturalistic qualities. The locust infestation is YHWH's own army, whose march heralds the day of the LORD. Using traditional theophanic language, the prophet describes the cosmic convulsions that accompany the locust plague as YHWH the divine warrior marches to battle.

▌ THE TEXT IN THE INTERPRETIVE TRADITION

The Christian tradition has generally interpreted 2:1-11 to be referring to the future, to the second coming of Jesus, when he will come on the day of the LORD to judge the world. This understanding is already apparent in the book of Revelation, where Joel 2 appears to be the inspiration, based on numerous similarities, for the apocalyptic locust army unleashed by the fifth angel (9:1-11). The differences are striking, however. Whereas Joel's locusts act like typical locusts, the locusts of Revelation do not consume the vegetation, as would be expected, but rather torture humans with their scorpion-like tails.

∎ THE TEXT IN CONTEMPORARY DISCUSSION

Joel sees in the locust plague a theophany of YHWH—a visible intensification of God's presence. Biblical theologians have often noted that the Bible portrays God to be actively involved in human affairs, and the prophets discern God's activity in relation to human conduct (most often in terms of the covenant). But this is not the whole story. As Joel makes clear, God's activity and presence are discernible also in the natural world. Indeed, most biblical descriptions of God's theophany emphasize the natural forms of God's appearance. Although God is transcendent, God does not remain outside of the natural world, and it is through creation that God is known. For Joel, the locust plague was as revelatory of God as a divinely spoken oracle.

Joel 2:12-27: Appeal to and Response from YHWH

∎ THE TEXT IN ITS ANCIENT CONTEXT

This unit consists of two parts: an appeal to YHWH, which consists of a call for the people to return to YHWH (vv. 12-14) followed by a call to lamentation (vv. 15-17) and YHWH's response to the people's appeal (vv. 18-27). The transition between the two parts in verses 18-19a, using converted imperfect verbs, presumes that some time has elapsed since Joel's appeal and that the people heeded his call to return to YHWH and to lament.

The prophetic call to return in verse 12 is presented as an oracle of YHWH, and so YHWH addresses the people in the first person ("return to me"), but by verse 13 Joel is again the speaker and YHWH is addressed in the third person. "Return to YHWH" is often interpreted as a call to repent from sin, but Joel enumerates no such sins. Joel's emphasis is not to blame the people (and perhaps no blame could be assessed), but to simply to call the people to turn to "the national God in the hope that YHWH would save the people" (Barton, 77). Joel's confidence that "even now" YHWH can save his people is expressed through Joel's use of a well-known creedal confession in verse 13. Found elsewhere, in Exod. 34:6-7; Num. 14:18; Neh. 9:17; Pss. 103:8; 145:8; Nah. 1:3; and Jonah 4:2, Joel cites a version, also found in Jonah, that underscores YHWH's mercy and eliminates the reference to God's justice or judgment (see Crenshaw, 136–37).

The call to lamentation (vv. 15-17) explains how the people should return to YHWH—through a national assembly of mourning. All should attend, from children to the elderly, even those who would otherwise be celebrating. The people should rend their hearts, and not only their garments (v. 13)—the ritual lamentation should also have an inward motivation. And the priests should bring the people's case to YHWH: YHWH should deliver his people for the sake of his own reputation (v. 17).

YHWH's response to the people's lamentation is a salvation oracle that is characterized by both YHWH's jealousy and compassion. YHWH's jealousy on behalf of the people is an expression of YHWH's passionate commitment to them. No longer will God allow the people to become a mockery to the nations; no longer will the people be put to shame. Compassion is YHWH's response to the people's suffering as a result of the locust plague. Thus YHWH will destroy the locust plague—called the "northerner" in reference to the "enemy from the north" tradition—and YHWH will restore the land from all the devastation caused by the locusts. Similarly, in response to the drought lamented in 1:19-20, YHWH promises to bring the rains in their seasons.

▌THE TEXT IN THE INTERPRETIVE TRADITION

In part because Joel does not enumerate the sins of the people or otherwise denounce their behavior, Joel 2:11-17 plays a prominent role in the Christian liturgies of Ash Wednesday at the beginning of Lent. The general nature of Joel's call to return to YHWH enables the text to be used as a generalized invitation to enter into the period of contrition that prepares Christians for celebrating Christ's redemption.

▌THE TEXT IN CONTEMPORARY DISCUSSION

It is significant that in the face of the devastating locust plague, Joel does not enumerate the sins of the people. He does not blame the people for the catastrophe nor, in Deuteronomic fashion, link the catastrophe to the people's infidelity to the covenant. Joel is also not interested in the question of theodicy; he seeks neither to explain nor justify God in the presence of the destructive plague. Instead, Joel simply asks the people to turn to God in supplication. Openness to lamentation with God is the proper response to such catastrophes. In the shame of their suffering, the people had turned away from YHWH. Joel's call to return is not to indict the people for their sins but to renew their faith in God through visible acts of devotion.

Joel 2:28—3:21: The Coming Day of the LORD

▌THE TEXT IN ITS ANCIENT CONTEXT

The final unit of the book consists of five oracles (2:28-32; 3:1-3, 4-8, 9-17, and 18-21), which take on a future-oriented, eschatological tone that has occasioned many early twentieth-century interpreters to conclude that these final oracles are later additions to the book. Following in this tradition, Barton characterizes this unit as a collection of miscellaneous oracles whose predictions do not amount to a coherent set of expectations (2001, 92). Most recent scholars, however, continue to attribute these oracles to Joel, even though the focus of their utterance no longer seems to be the locust plague. The literary style and scribal character of these oracles is similar throughout the book. What unite these oracles thematically to the first part of the book are references to the day of the LORD. Indeed, in the first part of the book, Joel sees in the unprecedented locust plague the advent of the day of the LORD. In these final oracles, Joel explains in scribal fashion how the day of the LORD will unfold.

"Then afterward" (NRSV), which begins the first oracle in 2:28-32, connects the final oracles temporally to what precedes them. "These things" may refer to YHWH's restoration of the locust devastation described in 2:18-27, or to Joel's call for the people to assemble and lament in 2:12-17. If the latter is the case, then the events predicted in the oracles of this unit are amplification on the events of YHWH's salvation oracle in 2:18-27.

The first oracle, Joel 2:28-32, envisions the outpouring of YHWH's spirit and the cosmic convulsions that will take place on the day of the LORD. In this context, the spirit is associated with prophecy and divine communication (see Num. 11:29), and hence the emphasis on dreams and visions, rather than on empowerment (cf. Judg. 6:34). YHWH will pour out his spirit on "all flesh," which generally refers to everyone, irrespective of gender or ethnicity, but the context limits it to the people of Judah and Jerusalem. In the prophetic tradition, the democratization of YHWH's spirit is characteristic of the coming period of salvation, when God's people will be free from oppression, the righteous will live in peace, and justice will reign on the earth. It is also accompanied by the regeneration of the natural world (see Isa. 32:9-14; 44:1-5; Ezek. 39:25-29), and so corresponds with the agricultural bounty promised in 2:18-27. Although the day of the LORD will bring cosmic upheavals (vv. 30-31) and destruction of the nations (3:1-17), Joel echoes the royal or Zion theology when he declares that YHWH's people—those who call on his name (v. 32)—will remain safe in Jerusalem (see Psalms 46; 48).

As Joel 2:18-27 promised the restoration of the land destroyed by the locusts, 2:28-32 promises salvation for the people who "return to YHWH." Similarly, just as YHWH will destroy the locust army (2:20), so also will YHWH punish the nations who have oppressed his people (3:1-17). In chapter 3, Joel develops the consequences of the day of the LORD for the nations, connecting them to the salvation of God's people in the preceding oracles with the adverbial phrase, "in those days and at that time." The oracles in chapter 3 may be interpreted in reference to the divine warrior hymns, which are attested in early Israelite and royal hymns (Exod. 15:1-18; Judges 5; Psalms 2; 24; 29; 68; 89; 97) but are revived in a number of late eschatological prophecies (Isa. 59:15b-20; 66:14b-16, 22-23; Ezekiel 38–39; Habakkuk 3; Zechariah 14). Based on a mythic pattern of divine conflict, such as found in the *Enuma Elish*, the divine warrior hymns celebrate YHWH's battle and victory over Israel's enemies (see Hiebert, 875–76). In Joel 3, the first two oracles (vv. 1-3, 4-8) describe how the nations have challenged YHWH's sovereignty by oppressing his people. In the third oracle (vv. 9-17), YHWH declares war on the nations, and the natural world convulses as YHWH marches out to battle. No actual battle is described; YHWH's victory is assured. Then YHWH is enthroned in Zion, which becomes an eternal sanctuary for his people. The fourth oracle (vv. 18-21) concludes the hymn with a description of the rejuvenation of the natural world and a reaffirmation that YHWH will indeed render justice on behalf of his people (see further, Simkins, 219–41).

Although the oracles in Joel 3 in their final form correspond to the structure and themes of the divine warrior hymns, this is probably a consequence of Joel's scribal activity. Joel drew on common prophetic traditions to interpret the coming day of the LORD. Scholars have usually noted that verses 4-8 are different in style from what precedes and follows it, they disrupt the flow from verse 3 to verse 9, and thus should be viewed as a later addition. However, if chapter 3 is viewed as a scribal composition, nothing precludes verses 4-8 from being added by Joel as an amplification of the crimes spelled out in verse 3.

■ The Text in the Interpretive Tradition

Because this unit relies so heavily on existing prophetic traditions for defining the day of the LORD, it is not surprising that later writers drew on Joel for interpreting eschatological events. As Joel interpreted the events of his day in light of known traditions, so also later prophets and writers interpreted their current events in light of Joel's prophecies. Thus, on Pentecost, Peter quotes Joel 2:28-32 to explain the outpouring of the Spirit on the followers of Jesus (Acts 2:17-21). According to Peter's speech in Acts, this happened in the "last days," and rather than YHWH, it is Jesus of Nazareth who pours out the spirit. Although Joel seems to limit the outpouring of the spirit to those in Judah, and indeed Peter addresses the men of Judea, perhaps following the text of Joel, the context of Peter's speech extends the outpouring of the Spirit to the Diaspora, all of whom hear the followers of Jesus speaking in their own languages. The tendency to universalize Joel's "all flesh" is complete in Paul, who quotes Joel 3:5, "Everyone who calls on the name of the Lord will be saved," to emphasize that there is no distinction between Jew and gentile (Rom. 10:12-13).

■ The Text in Contemporary Discussion

This unit presents two conflicting voices. On the one hand, Joel 2:28-32 speaks with an inclusive voice, as Paul recognized in Romans. Even though the context of Joel might limit the scope of "all flesh" (v. 28) and "everyone" (v. 32), the reappropriation of the text in new contexts cannot ignore its inclusive tendencies. The mercy of God is available to the one who calls on the name of the LORD. On the other hand, Joel 3:1-21 speaks with an exclusive voice. The inhabitants of Judah and Jerusalem stand in opposition to all the nations, whom YHWH will judge through war. The justice of God is not itself the difficult issue, for YHWH applies the *lex talionis* as the justification for the nations' punishment: The nations will be treated in the same way that they have treated God's people. What is missing, however, at least from our perspective, is the role of the individual. Both Judah (God's people) and the nations are treated as singular collectives; there is no exception for individual choices. The conflicting inclusive and exclusive voices of the text can only be resolved when both voices are heard in tension, giving due weight to both God's mercy and justice, individual and collective.

Works Cited

Barton, John. 2001. *Joel and Obadiah*. OTL. Louisville: Westminster John Knox.

Crenshaw, James L. 1995. *Joel: A New Translation with Introduction and Commentary*. AB 24C. New York: Doubleday.

Duhm, Bernhard. 1911. "Anmerkungen zu den Zwölf Propheten." *ZAW* 31:184–88.

Hiebert, Theodore. 1992. "Joel, Book of." In *ABD* 3:873–80.

Simkins, Ronald A. 1991. *Yahweh's Activity in History and Nature in the Book of Joel*. Lewiston, NY: Edwin Mellen.

Whiting, John D. 1915. "Jerusalem's Locust Plague." *National Geographic* 28:511–50.

Wolff, Hans Walter. 1977. *Joel and Amos*. Hermeneia. Philadelphia: Fortress Press.

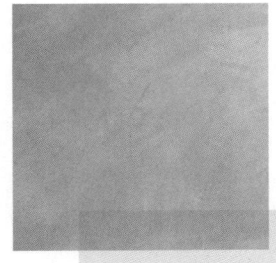

AMOS

M. Daniel Carroll R.

Introduction

The superscription (Amos 1:1; cf. 7:9-11) sets the historical context of the prophet's ministry in the early to mid-eighth century BCE, during the reigns of Jeroboam II of Israel and Uzziah/Azariah of Judah. Amos is said to come from Tekoa in Judah, modern Khirbet Tequʻa, about ten kilometers southeast of Jerusalem. The opening verse mentions an earthquake (see also 6:9-11; 8:8; 9:1, 5; cf. Zech. 14:5), which seismic studies locate between 760 and 750 BCE.

International circumstances had allowed Israel to attain prominence (2 Kgs. 14:25). Aram/Syria, Israel's northern neighbor and principal foe in the second half of the ninth century, was in decline. Assyria was weakened after the death of Adad Nirari III in 783 and would not influence the region again until Tiglath Pileser III assumed the throne in 745. The oracles in Amos 1 and in 4:10; 6:3, 13, if they reflect this setting, suggest that Israel was not as strong as the national ideology pretended. In addition to recent defeats by bordering countries, in the future an unnamed enemy would invade the land (3:11; 6:14). These words would be fulfilled by Assyria.

The book accuses the powerful of oppression, even as they enjoyed a comfortable lifestyle (Amos 3:15; 4:1; 5:10-11; 6:1, 4-6). The judicial system was compromised (5:12, 15), and many had fallen into debt slavery (2:6-8; 8:4-6). Sociological approaches try to reconstruct these mechanisms of exploitation (see surveys in Houston; Coomber). Some argue that the text attacks a form of rent capitalism, others an inequitable tributary mode of production under the monarchy's control. Another possibility is that the mutual obligations of the patron-client relationship had been violated. A cultural-evolutionary perspective suggests that environmental factors, changes in traditional sociocultural roles, asymmetric economic relationships, and the actions of religious elites all played a part. Each option alerts readers to the concreteness of the prophetic message.

Composition, Structure, Literary Elements

From the late nineteenth and into the twentieth century, scholarship attempted to distinguish the *ipsissima verba* ("actual words") of the prophet from later additions. Subsequently, form and tradition critics claimed to identify editorial stages connected to specific historical settings (e.g., Wolff). Several hypotheses about the redactional history have been put forward in the last two decades (see the surveys in Carroll R.; Barton). Some recent scholars contend that the book is a postexilic creation of a scribal class in the Persian province of Yehud in the fifth to fourth centuries BCE. There have also been efforts to correlate the production of Amos with the process of compiling the Book of the Twelve. Similar wording might imply mutual influence between books. For example, Joel 3:16a is repeated in Amos 1:2a, and the mention of Edom at 9:12 anticipates Obadiah.

A second group of scholars defends the authenticity of all or most of the book. Some connect the diverse emphases in the book to different times in Amos's ministry (e.g., Andersen and Freedman). Others look to comparative ancient Near Eastern linguistic and archaeological data as the basis for an eighth-century date (e.g., Paul). New archaeological discoveries, such as the excavations at Tell es-Safi (referred to as Gath in Amos 6:2) and the discovery of extensive copper smelting in the Arabah of Edom (1:11-12), suggest a stronger historical basis than many have considered viable. Evidence from Mesopotamia reveals that prophecies could have been recorded soon after the delivery of oracles. This contradicts the common view that prophetic oracles circulated orally for a long time before being written down.

Literary studies are yet another kind of approach. They presuppose the unity of the book. Its artistry of form and language and intricate theological argument suggest a consistent authorial or editorial hand. Critical scholars increasingly recognize the book's literary features and incorporate them into their redaction studies (e.g., Jeremias). Those who conceive of Amos as part of the Scripture of the church also champion the canonical form. This is the text that Christians read and use for worship and the practice of their faith. The new field of the theological interpretation of the Bible seeks to nurture skills for such readings and values precritical interpretations.

Literary features of Amos include many metaphors and similes, wordplays, rhetorical questions, chiasms, and merism. Recognizable form-critical categories are the messenger formula ("thus says the LORD"), judgment speeches, the proclamation formula ("Hear this"), and the woe-cry. The oracles against the nations (Amos 1:3—2:16) use the $n/n + 1$ graded numerical saying ("For three transgressions of . . . , and for four"). The book has a penchant for series of five and seven items, which will be pointed out in the commentary. Finally, some believe that the entire book exhibits a chiasm with 5:7-8 at its center. A chiasm is a concentric structure, which repeats similar ideas or terminology in a reverse matching sequence. Its climax is in the middle, not at the end of the pattern.

Key Themes

The most important theme is the person of YHWH. This is the battleground of the prophet's ministry. The people celebrate a deity of blessing and victory (Amos 5:18-20), although the recent past had been characterized by disaster (1:3-15; 4:6-11). The book predicts more catastrophes. The deity of the national ideology did not question the exploitation of the poor. Appropriately, the prophetic message denounces Israel's religiosity and announces the destruction of the sanctuaries (3:14; 4:4-5; 5:4-6; 7:9; 8:3; 9:1).

Instead of this YHWH, the book presents a God who is sovereign over all nations (1:3—2:3; 9:7) and manifests power in the natural order (1:2; 4:7-13; 5:7-9; 7:1-6; 8:8-9; 9:5-6). This YHWH of Hosts mandates social justice and will punish Israel for the exploitation of the vulnerable. Other themes include the exodus (2:10; 3:1-2; 9:7), the remnant (3:12; 5:3; 6:9-10; 9:8), and the hope of a restored creation under a Davidic king (9:11-15). The presence of a formal idea of covenant is debated (for the covenant idea, see Stuart).

Amos 1:1—2:16: Preface (1:1-2) and Oracles against the Nations (1:3—2:16)

■ THE TEXT IN ITS ANCIENT CONTEXT

Amos 1:1 combines "words" with "he saw," thereby connecting the prophet's spoken message with the visions (chapters 7–9). Verse 2 is a fitting foreword to the themes of the book: YHWH's roar (3:8; see also 3:4, 12), distressed fields (4:7-9), mourning (NRSV "wither"; 5:16; 8:8, 10; 9:5), Zion (6:1; 9:11), and Carmel (9:3). The force of the message is communicated through the metaphor of a devouring lion. YHWH appears as a lion in several prophets (Isa. 31:4; Jer. 25:38; Lam. 3:10-11; Hosea 5:14; 13:8; Mic. 5:8). The lion conveys power and fear. Importantly, the voice of YHWH comes from Jerusalem and Zion, not Samaria and Bethel. From the beginning, the book discredits the northern kingdom's government and religious system. The future beyond the judgment lay with the southern monarchy (9:11). The Judean Amos probably was a man of means, not a simple shepherd. He is called a *noqed* in 1:1, a term used elsewhere only of a king with huge flocks (2 Kgs. 3:4). According to 7:14-15, Amos was a herdsman, which could suggest that he also owned cattle. Sycamore trees do not grow in the region of Tekoa, so he may have owned other properties. Amos is knowledgeable of international affairs, and, if these messages do come from him, he was quite the poet. No poor shepherd here!

The oracles against the nations in 1:3—2:16 constitute the first of three major sections in Amos. These oracles set the tone of judgment for the rest of the book. These two chapters begin by condemning the transgressions of surrounding peoples before turning their gaze to Judah and Israel. Oracles against the nations is a common genre in the prophetic literature (see Isaiah 13–23; Jeremiah 46–51; Zephaniah 2). These oracles use what is called the *n/n* + 1 formula, where *n* is the number three, but do not list the four transgressions. The purpose may be to convey the habit of wrongdoing or to single out the worst behavior. Some believe that the numbers three and four should be added together, with seven symbolizing the fullness of sin. The repetitive language, with slight variations, interconnects the series (Paul, 7–15).

It is difficult to identify the events that lie behind these indictments, as no specifics are given. Some of these nations were long-standing enemies, so various settings are possible. Perhaps these oracles refer to ongoing skirmishes along national boundaries (see Amos 4:10). The constant thread throughout is cruelty in warfare. "Threshing sledges of iron" in Amos 1:3 might refer to physical torture or could be a figurative expression for ruthlessness (cf. 2 Kgs. 13:7; Isa. 41:15), while 1:11 reveals uncontrolled bloodlust in battle. Philistia and Tyre are denounced for human trafficking, probably of captives taken in war (1:6-10). Ripping open pregnant women bespeaks unbelievable barbarity (1:13; cf. 2 Kgs. 8:12; 15:16), and the desecration of a tomb violated ancient respect for the dead (2:1; cf. 2 Kgs. 23:16).

Amos 1:3—2:3 announces judgment on these other nations for their atrocities; fires will consume the fortresses of their capital cities, symbols of military strength. Several oracles target the leadership, decreeing either death or exile (1:5, 8, 15; 2:3). These persons were most responsible for instigating armed conflicts and the suffering of the casualties. All but the last oracle may allude to Israel's defeats. If so, they put the lie to the boasting of 6:13 and the nation's patriotic theology about the day of the Lord (5:18-20).

The formulaic introduction and endings to the Judah and Israel oracles (Amos 2:4-6, 6-16) echo those of 1:3—2:3. That is, they are transgressors like the other nations and will suffer a similar fate. Their sin, though, is directed inward: violation of the law's demands (Judah) and the socioeconomic exploitation of the poor (Israel). It is difficult to specify with confidence the nature of the abuse. For instance, does 2:6 refer to bribery of judges or to unpaid debts, however small, that lead to debt slavery (see 8:6)? Is the young woman of 2:8 a relative with whom father and son commit sexual impropriety or a debt slave abused by the men of the house? Whatever their exact meanings, all options are unacceptable. Israel also ignored the gracious acts of God in their past and compromised his representatives (2:9-12). Note that the seven transgressions of 2:6-8 are matched by seven kinds of soldiers in 2:14-16. Perfect sin merits complete defeat.

∎ THE TEXT IN THE INTERPRETIVE TRADITION

War was a constant reality in Old Testament times. The prophetic literature does not shy away from describing its horrors or denouncing religious ideologies that legitimated war. These oracles declare that cruelty in war will not go unpunished, as human life is precious in the sight of God. History is not purposeless; it has a moral framework and direction. This section teaches that God judges by turning warlike peoples over to the violence they perpetrate. In the Old Testament, this judgment takes the form of *lex talionis*: punishment corresponds to the crime. Here, to instigate war will mean experiencing the same at the hand of another people (cf. Isa. 10:5-19; Hab. 2:4-17).

Interpreting the oracles of 1:3—2:3 as attacks on Israel, rabbinic commentators emphasized the cruelty of the Gentiles and their punishment as an indication of God's favor (Neusner, 16–17, 63; Sweeney et al., 1036–37). Some church fathers allegorized certain lines. Gregory the Great held that 1:13 referred to the enemies of the gospel. To enhance their reputation (borders), they twist the truth about God in those whose full understanding of the gospel has not yet matured. Tertullian believed that 2:6 predicted the selling of Jesus by Judas (Ferreiro, 86, 88). The Reformers Martin Luther and John Calvin connected the censure of 2:8 with the greed of the priests and monks of their day (Luther, 141; Calvin, 187). For Calvin, the stubborn distortion of the Word of God by the Jews (cf. Acts 7:51) and the lies of the Catholic Church are manifest in 2:4; appeal to tradition (their "fathers") is no excuse (Calvin, 178).

■ THE TEXT IN CONTEMPORARY DISCUSSION

This last century and a half has been the bloodiest in history. The realism of this section of Amos stands as a warning to our society, with its multibillion-dollar military budget and involvements in wars around the world, the ownership of millions of firearms in homes, the violence in our neighborhoods, and our fascination with violence in media. What future might these political policies and lifestyle choices portend?

The assertion that the LORD judges through war does not mean that every war comes from God's hand. To say as much would be to blame God for the evils wrought by human arrogance and greed. What is certain is that God will eventually call human violence to account. History is not a senseless trajectory across the centuries; the prospect of judgment should give us pause about our complicity—personally, socially, and politically—in violence of any kind.

For those who champion social justice, such as liberation theologians, Amos 2:6-8 and its condemnation of oppression is a foundational passage. The anonymity of the exploiters and their victims and the vagueness of the accusations allow for wide appropriation of these verses. Modern oppressors and workers of injustice embody these descriptions in today's societies, and these wrongs demand denunciation by new prophetic voices. These realities, however, cannot be oversimplified. Lai Lung Elizabeth Ngan warns Asian Americans, who can enjoy a privileged status vis-à-vis other minorities, about imitating the actions Amos condemns. Exploitation crosses all classes and ethnicities. Some feminist scholars wonder if the prophet is aware of the disproportionate burdens that poor women bear (such as low salaries, poor nutrition, the care of children), but are appreciative of his recognition of the terrible abuse of women in war (1:13). If the maiden of 2:8 is a debt slave, there may be greater attentiveness to destitute women than some believe.

Amos 3:1—6:14: The Words of God and the Prophet

■ THE TEXT IN ITS ANCIENT CONTEXT

These four chapters provide details that substantiate the condemnation of Israel's social and religious transgressions and the announcement of divine judgment. Chapters 5 and 6 also weave in laments for the losses that this punishment will bring.

"Hear this," declares the prophet in Amos 3:1-2. These lines communicate that to be the chosen people of God carries special responsibility. Israel could not claim ignorance of the ways of YHWH. A series of seven rhetorical questions follows (3:3-6), progressing from an undefined meeting in 3:3 through to encounters that all lead to death and culminating in the disaster God brings to the city—in context, Samaria the capital. YHWH the lion (cf. 1:2; 3:12) has roared this decree through his prophet (3:7-8). The rest of the chapter reveals its sense: an enemy will destroy Samaria's defenses, Bethel's altars, and the extravagant homes of the well-to-do. Oppression reigns, and its fruits sustain the sociopolitical system—practices that would shock even Israel's enemies (3:9-10). Amos 4:1-3 announces the fate of the self-indulgent wives of the powerful, whom he mocks as "cows of Bashan" (a fertile area famous for its cattle; Jer. 50:19; Mic. 7:14). In a change of metaphor, the text says that they will be taken far away to exile, like hooked fish, through breaches in the walls of the defeated city.

A new subsection begins at Amos 4:4. Surprising irony gives bite to the prophetic word. Israel is beckoned to worship at the historic shrines of Bethel and Gilgal, but the people's worship is sin. The sacrifices mentioned in 4:4-5 do not deal with transgression; this is a religion of celebration and gratitude to the national deity. These activities satiate their religious impulses (4:5), but they are disconnected from the recent tragedies of hunger, drought, crop failure, and war (4:6-11). The refrain "yet you did not return to me" is repeated five times, emphasizing their estrangement from God. All their religious fervor was for naught and misplaced. Now they must prepare for a terrifying meeting with YHWH, not at those sanctuaries but face-to-face. Amos 4:13 is the first of three hymns that highlight the power of the sovereign God to judge (cf. 5:8-9; 9:5-6). He is YHWH God of Hosts, a name that includes a foreboding military epithet.

Like Amos 3:1 and 4:1, 5:1 begins with "Hear this word." Amos 5:1-3, following as it does the announcement of 4:12-13, reveals that the encounter with God will mean decimation of the towns in war, surely the conflict foretold in 3:6—4:3. Israel is compared to a young woman dying before reaching her potential in maturity. This oracle opens a chiasm that extends through 5:17. The deaths of 5:1-3 are matched by the ubiquitous laments in 5:16-17. The call to seek God and not the sanctuaries is echoed in 5:14-15 by the exhortation to seek and love the good, which is justice under YHWH God of Hosts. The distortion of justice and righteousness in 5:7 is fleshed out in 5:10-13 as the exploitation of the poor through taxes, bribery in the courts, and the silencing of those who would stand up to defend them. At the heart of this chiasm is the book's second hymn, in 5:8-9. The powerful creator God, who made the stars and controls the daily rhythms of nature, tears down the strong and their fortresses. In this hymn is found the climax of the chiasm and perhaps of the entire book: "YHWH is his name." Once again, as in 4:4-13, the person of God is at stake for the prophet. The YHWH perpetrated and praised at Bethel and Gilgal does not question injustice and in the end cannot save them. The true God indeed would be with them (5:14), but not in the way they had imagined. The prophet's YHWH will punish Israel's perverse theology and the society that it legitimated.

Amos 5:18-27 continues the themes of unacceptable civil religion and defeat. It begins with "woe!" connecting these verses back to the wailing of 5:16-17. This passage can be appreciated as a conceptual chiasm that again announces defeat. The negation of the mistaken common belief in future victory (5:18-20) will be confirmed by a future exile, when Israel will carry with them the foreign gods who were supposed to protect them (5:26-27). The many unacceptable practices of Israel's worship (5:21-23) stand in contrast to an earlier, purer faith (5:25). At the center of this structure is the demand to have justice and righteousness flow—not as intermittent water in the wadis of that dry land, but as a never-ending stream. Once more, religion and ethics are portrayed as inseparable. How different this mandate for justice and righteousness is from the nation's values (cf. 5:7)!

Several literary features highlight the message of divine rejection. Amos 5:20 emphatically repeats the notion of darkness in 5:18, while 5:19 conveys the inescapability of painful judgment. In other words, the triumphal day of the Lord (its earliest mention in the prophetic literature) anticipated by the national ideology will be turned on its head. Defeat not victory is in the offing, and that by God's hand. The emotive verbs with which 5:21 begins demonstrate how visceral is the rejection of Israel's religious practices. Note that 5:21-23 lists seven religious practices, expanding on those mentioned in 4:4-5. Amos 5:26 is a disputed verse in terms of the tense of the verb (past or future) and the apparent reference to astral deities (for a survey of opinions, see Paul, 194–98).

Amos 6 opens with another woe (6:1-7). The first target of the prophetic invective is the powerful, who feel confident in comparing the nation to surrounding peoples. They selfishly enjoy in abundance the finest meat, wine, and oils, while the rest of the population suffers want (cf. 4:6-10). The scene described in these verses could be a *marzeah* feast, apparently a banquet celebrated by the wealthy that might have been connected to funerary rights (cf. Jer. 16:5). This fete is known from different parts of the ancient world, so there may have been influence from other cultures that made the activity even more unacceptable. The fate of this uncaring elite repeats that of the women of 4:1-3.

The second half of Amos 6 broadens the judgment to include all Israel (6:8-14). Here the transgression is national arrogance. Its military is ridiculed in 6:13. The people rejoice in having taken *lo' davar*, literally "no-thing." A great victory indeed! Their fortresses and armies, supposedly the proof of Israel's power, will not be able to shield it from the death and border-to-border destruction of the coming invasion. The foolish confidence of Israel—from the wealthy to the masses—is as incomprehensible as plowing the sea, as imprudent as the manipulation of justice (cf. 5:7).

▌ THE TEXT IN THE INTERPRETIVE TRADITION

Not many lines of Amos are cited in the literature of Qumran and the New Testament. The Damascus Document, however, reinterprets Amos 5:25-26 as a word of encouragement for the Essene community, who successfully took the true Word of God into exile—that is, away from the evil city of Jerusalem. Stephen quotes the Septuagint translation of 5:25-27 in his speech before the Sanhedrin to demonstrate Israel's historic rebellion and idolatry (Acts 7:42-43). This is the first of only two occasions where the words of Amos appear explicitly in the New Testament. The other passage is 9:11, to which James appeals at the Council of Jerusalem in Acts 15 (for other possible allusions, see Sweeney et al., 1038–39).

Rabbi Simla in the third century suggested that Amos 5:4 ("Seek me and live") was a précis of the 613 commandments (*b. Mak.* 23b–24a). Though appreciative of Amos's moral focus, rabbinic commentators were reluctant to accept the comprehensive destruction of the people of God predicted in the book. Some limited the judgment of 5:18-19, for example, to the gentiles and believed that the light of the day of the LORD referred to the redemption of Messiah. Others explained the wounding by various animals in 5:19 as that done to the Jews by the sequence of empires, beginning with Babylon (Neusner, 67–68).

Alberto Ferreiro (95–96) reports that based on the Septuagint's mistranslation, Tertullian, Cyril of Jerusalem, Ambrose, and Augustine saw in Amos 4:13 a prediction of the coming of Jesus ("he makes known to humanity his Messiah"). Further, Athanasius and Ambrose argued against those who said that the creation of the wind in this verse referred to the creation of the Spirit (the word for both is the same in Hebrew). Other passages the church fathers employed in contending with others include Tertullian's interpretation of 5:10 as a general negative description of the Jewish people; John Chrysostom's belief that 5:21-24 substantiated the worthlessness of Jewish rituals;

and Jerome's connection of the boast of 6:13 with the arrogance of heretics. In his comments on 6:1, Tertullian pointed to the conversation with the Samaritan woman at the well (John 4) and the healing of the Samaritan leper (Luke 17:17) as Jesus reversing the condemnation of 6:1 for those responding to him. Chrysostom and Basil the Great warned Christians not to fall into the fleeting and self-destructive excesses of 6:4-6 (Ferreiro, 100, 102, 104–6).

The Reformers also applied the prophetic oracles of Amos 4–6 to their context. Luther, for instance, preached that the victories of the Turks were God's chastisement of Europe to help bring them to faith, just like what had been preached to Israel in 4:6-10 (Luther, 153). He related 5:10 to Germany's political and religious leaders; and Calvin perceived the evils of 5:10-13 as present in his day too (Calvin, 265). Both read their doctrinal frameworks back into Amos's words. In 5:4-6, Luther (158–59) finds the distinction between true faith accepted in grace and the empty religious works of the Catholic Church. Calvin (252–55) uses these verses to teach that the wider preaching of repentance does not contradict the salvation of only the predestined elect; public proclamation renders all beyond excuse and confirms them in their sin.

An outstanding case of the appropriation of Amos's message is the Dominican friar Girolamo Savonarola (1452–1498). In a series of sermons on Amos and Zechariah preached in Florence during Lent of 1496, Savonarola railed against the civil and ecclesiastical authorities of the city for their corruption and for the emptiness of the rituals of the Catholic Church. For this boldness, he was jailed and executed (Barton, 172–74).

▌ THE TEXT IN CONTEMPORARY DISCUSSION

Liberation theologians find prophetic support in Amos 5:7, 10-13, to condemn structural evil. Amos 3–6 also provides material for denouncing religious stances that support oppressive and nationalistic ideologies of the status quo. Some Latin American liberationists developed new liturgies and structures of Christian life (base ecclesial communities) as alternatives to the historic ecclesiastical institutions, which did not condemn oppression and had provided religious backing for unjust ideologies. These theologians utilized a measure of the Marxist critiques of religion against the blessings of dictatorships by many Catholic and Protestant churches (or at least their passive acceptance) and their promotion of a fatalistic, otherworldly religion that did not respond to the needs of the people. The goal of these liberationists was the creation of fresh expressions of the faith that would partner in social transformation (Carroll R. 1992, 91–122, 289–306).

The most well-known verse in the book is Amos 5:24: "But let justice roll down like waters, and righteousness like an ever-flowing stream." Martin Luther King Jr. quoted it in his famous speech on the Washington mall in August 1963. From an African American perspective, this line is also a rebuke of Southern evangelicalism's past support of slavery and segregation. The resiliency of African American Christian faith is evident in its songs, so the hymns of Amos resonate too (see Robertson). Some feminists dislike 4:1, believing it to be a distasteful characterization of women, though it may be more of a mockery of the excesses of a small wealthy elite than of women in general. They do point out, however, that Amos does not use the harlot metaphor prominent in other prophetic books.

The issue of the historical judgments of God was touched on earlier, but a particular dimension of the means of judgment surfaces conspicuously in these chapters: the role of the created order. The power of God in nature appears in the hymns of Amos 4:13 and 5:8-9 (cf. 9:5-6); 4:6-10 cites ecological disasters as divine judgments (cf. 1:2; 8:8-9); and the rhetorical questions of 3:4-5 and 6:12 appeal to the animal world. These passages suggest nature's cooperation with YHWH in judgment, even as human transgressions have ecological impact (cf. Hosea 4:1-3). The future flourishing of the community is also defined by natural bounty (9:11-15). These observations do not mean that the book is concerned directly with ecological matters, nor does it mean that all natural disasters should be identified as divine judgments. At the very least, however, the prophetic message should stimulate reflection on the interconnectedness of human communities and their ethical behavior with the nonhuman world, for good or for ill (Marlow, 120–57 and passim).

Amos 7:1—9:15: Visions of Israel's Future

▮ THE TEXT IN ITS ANCIENT CONTEXT

The last three chapters of Amos contain five visions, three of which are followed by material that illustrates and expands their themes (Amos 7:10-17; 8:4-14; 9:5-10). The book closes with a brief description of a glorious restoration after the judgment of God.

The first two visions describe devastating judgments (Amos 7:1-6). The first is a locust plague (cf. Exod. 10:12-15; Deut. 28:42; Joel 1), which occurs after the second crop (vegetables and legumes) was sprouting and while the grain would be maturing in the fields. The timing could not be worse, as this represented complete agricultural loss. The second vision is more mythological in its mention of the cosmic deep (Gen. 7:11; Isa. 51:10), but the message is similar: complete destruction. The prophet intercedes, pleading for YHWH to forgive and stop. Note the contrast between the nation's delusional hubris and Amos's clear appreciation of Israel's standing before God and in the world ("How can Jacob stand? / He is so small")!

With the third vision, intercession ends. Any hope for reprieve is dashed (Amos 7:7-9). The usual translation of 'anak (this word appears only in this passage in the entire Old Testament) is "plumb line." This has led to the interpretation that the people, represented by the wall, have not lived in conformity to YHWH's standards. This Akkadian loanword, however, means "tin" (Andersen and Freedman, 757–59; Paul, 233–35). This translation fits well in context and reinforces the declaration about the weakness of Israel. In this vision, the mighty fortresses of Israel are made of tin. While at a distance, the impression might be that they are of iron, in truth they are feeble. Once again, the nation is deceived, its boasting empty (cf. 6:13). God rips out a piece of this pathetic wall and throws it in their midst. It follows, then, that the defenses of Israel can protect its illegitimate worship places or the monarchy (7:9).

The narrative of Amos 7:10-17 carries on the thread of the destruction of the religious and political institutions. Bethel was Israel's most important sanctuary, where the civil religion of Israel was celebrated and promoted (7:13). Amaziah, the chief priest, recognizes the threat of Amos's words to that social construction of reality and demands that he return to his own country and earn his keep as a prophet there. Amos's response is to declare that he is not a prophet by trade or descent, but rather by the calling of God. As explained earlier, 7:14 and 1:1 suggest that he was a man of some status. Amos's standing probably gave weight to his words, enough so that his audience would pay attention and the king and his priest worry about his impact. The fate of the priest, along with his family's, encapsulates the coming national experience of judgment (7:17).

The meaning of the fourth vision (Amos 8:1-3) is based on a wordplay: *qayits* ("summer fruit") and *qēts* ("end"). The basket of ripe fruit symbolizes that Israel's end has come. With that will come wailing in the temple (or palace; the Hebrew term is the same for both). Either place was appropriate, as each was central to how the nation had devolved. There would be mourning, not celebratory songs (cf. 8:10; 5:16-17). The text returns to the economic exploitation of the poor and exposes from another angle the elite's perverse view of religion (8:4-6). Once again, the text emphasizes the power of the Creator in judgment (8:7-9). Soon the prophetic word would end, and lack of food (4:6) would be superseded by the absence of a word from God (8:11-13). Amos 8:14 may refer to foreign gods or different appellations of YHWH at various cultic sites (Paul, 268–72). Either option merited censure, as both exhibited syncretistic tendencies.

The final vision pictures the destruction of the temple at Bethel (Amos 9:1-4). Previous passages foretold the breaking of its altars (3:14) and its burning (5:6), but here its demolition is definitive. This was where the false YHWH of the national ideology was constructed and worshiped; this was where everything that was wrong with the nation—socially, economically, politically, militarily—received religious sanction. Here the judgment must begin. The punishment's comprehensiveness here is communicated by merisms—that is, the mention of two extremes with the idea that everything in between is meant.

Like previously, the incomparable sovereignty of the God who will judge Israel is celebrated in a hymn (cf. Amos 4:13; 5:8-9). The nation, although chosen of YHWH, is not exempt from judgment (9:7; cf. 3:1-2). YHWH was involved in the history of its neighbors too (cf. 1:3—2:3). Amos 9:8-10 clarifies that comprehensive punishment did not mean the eradication of Israel. A remnant would be left, even if in exile. This glimpse of hope is expanded in 9:11-15. After the devastation of judgment would come a new government, not of the misdirected northern regime but of the Davidic line (cf. 1:2). From the rubble would rise a people restored to the land, secure and prosperous, no longer attacked by other nations but sharing with them a relationship with YHWH. This time would be the reversal of the want and war of their present condition. This stark contrast has long led many scholars to argue that 9:11-15 is an exilic or postexilic addition, inserted to give hope after the fulfillment of the predicted judgments.

◼ THE TEXT IN THE INTERPRETIVE TRADITION

Some church fathers believed that Amos came from humble beginnings. Thus Gregory the Great pointed out how the Spirit can raise the humble to do great things for God (Ferreiro, 109–10). Irenaeus, Tertullian, Lactantius, and Cyprian believed that Amos 8:9-10 predicted the signs accompanying the crucifixion of Jesus (Ferreiro, 112). The warning of the famine of the word of God in 8:11-13 was taken by both the rabbis and the Reformers as an alert to heed the teaching of the Torah and correct doctrine, respectively (Sweeney et al., 1036; Luther, 182–84; Calvin, 376–80).

Among the Qumran materials, Amos 9:11 is listed in the collection of texts of the Florilegium (4QFlor 1:1-13). Apart from 5:5-26, this is the only passage cited and expounded in that community's literature. Rabbinic commentators understood 9:11-15 eschatologically as descriptions of the messianic era (Neusner, 103; Sweeney et al., 1037). In the New Testament, James quotes Amos 9:11-12 at the Council in Jerusalem (Acts 15:12-21). He grounds his argument for the inclusion of the gentiles on the Septuagint of 9:12 ("so that the rest of humankind may seek the Lord").

In the Christian tradition, Amos 9:11 has been interpreted christologically. Augustine and Chrysostom believed that the raising of the fallen tabernacle of David was a reference to the resurrection of Jesus (Ferreiro, 116). Luther says that the tabernacle of David is his descendants, out of whom Christ would arise, who would build the church (Luther, 189). Likewise, Calvin sees here a reference to the first advent (Calvin, 404–7). Both equate 9:12-15 to the spiritual blessings that accompany Christ's kingdom (Luther, 189–90; Calvin, 407–13).

■ THE TEXT IN CONTEMPORARY DISCUSSION

What has been said earlier about the modern appropriation of Amos holds true in this final section. Here, too, are found the critique of the false consciousness of civil religion, the denunciation of socioeconomic oppression, and the connection between nature and the acts of God. Here also is a model of performing the prophetic office despite official opposition. The narrative of Amos 7:10-17 has empowered advocates of the marginalized in their struggle to proclaim and work for social transformation in YHWH's name. That courageous stance for justice, come what may, is one of this book's enduring legacies. Martin Luther King Jr. said that Christians should be as "maladjusted" as Amos to their context and speak out against injustice (Carroll R. 2002, 57–58).

Finally, Amos 9:11-15 teaches that the oppressions of today and the judgments of those wrongs are not the final word of God (Carroll R. 2002, 70–72). Beyond the losses inherent in those two realities and as a reversal of what we now endure will come the rebuilding, the raising, and the repairing of the ruins, abundance instead of want, and secure roots instead of displacement. We may live now in the place and hour of oppression as we await divine validation, or perhaps in that in-between time after what we believe is God's judgment and as we await God's new tomorrow. This prophetic hope can sustain the weary and encourage perseverance in the march toward justice.

Works Cited

Andersen, Francis I., and David Noel Freedman. 1989. *Amos: A New Translation with Notes and Commentary.* AB 24A. New York: Doubleday.

Barton, John. 2012. *The Theology of the Book of Amos.* Old Testament Theology. Cambridge: Cambridge University Press.

Calvin, John. 1986. *Joel, Amos and Obadiah. A Commentary on the Minor Prophets.* Vol. 2. Edinburgh: Banner of Truth Trust.

Carroll R., M. Daniel. 1992. *Contexts for Amos: Prophetic Poetics in Latin American Perspective.* JSOTSup 132. Sheffield: Sheffield Academic Press.

————. 2002. *Amos—The Prophet and His Oracles: Research on the Book of Amos*. Louisville: Westminster John Knox.

Coomber, Matthew J. M. 2010. *Re-Reading the Prophets through Corporate Globalization*. Biblical Intersections. Piscataway, NJ: Gorgias.

Ferreiro, Alberto, ed. 2003. *The Twelve Prophets*. Ancient Christian Commentary on Scripture, Old Testament 14. Downers Grove, IL: InterVarsity Press.

Houston, Walter J. 2009. *Contending for Justice: Ideologies and Theologies of Social Justice in the Old Testament*. Rev. ed. London: T&T Clark.

Jeremias, Jörg. 1995. *The Book of Amos: A Commentary*. Translated by D. W. Stott. OTL. Louisville: Westminster John Knox.

Lessing, R. Reed. 2009. *Amos*. Concordia Commentary. St. Louis: Concordia.

Luther, Martin. 1975. *Luther's Works*. Vol. 18, *Minor Prophets I: Hosea–Malachi*. Translated by R. J. Dinda. Saint Louis: Concordia.

Marlow, Hilary. 2009. *Biblical Prophets and Contemporary Environmental Ethics*. Oxford: Oxford University Press.

Neusner, Jacob. 2006. *Amos in Talmud and Midrash: A Source Book*. Studies in Judaism. Lanham, MD: University Press of America.

Ngan, Lai Lung Elizabeth. 2004. "Amos." In *Global Bible Commentary*, edited by Daniel Patte, 277–85. Nashville: Abingdon.

Paul, Shalom M. 1991. *Amos: A Commentary on the Book of Amos*. Hermeneia. Minneapolis: Fortress Press.

Robertson, Cleotha. 2010. "Amos." In *The Africana Bible: Reading Israel's Scriptures from African and the African Diaspora*, edited by Hugh R. Page Jr., 172–79. Minneapolis: Fortress Press.

Stuart, Douglas. 1987. *Hosea-Jonah*. WBC 31. Waco, TX: Word.

Sweeney, Marvin A., et al. 2009. "Amos (Book and Person)." In *Encyclopedia of the Bible and Its Reception*, edited by Hans-Josef Klauck et al., 1028–44. Berlin: de Gruyter.

Wacker, Marie-Theres. 2012. "Amos." In *Feminist Biblical Interpretation: A Compendium of Critical Commentary on the Books of the Bible and Related Literature*, edited by Luise Schottroff and Marie-Theres Wacker, 397–405. Grand Rapids: Eerdmans.

Wolff, Hans Walter. 1979. *Joel and Amos: A Commentary on the Books of the Prophets Joel and Amos*. Hermeneia. Translated by Waldemar Janzen, S. Dean McBride Jr., and C. A. Muenchow. Philadelphia: Fortress.

OBADIAH

Joseph F. Scrivner

Introduction

This prophecy of twenty-one verses is the shortest book in the Old Testament. The prophet's name means "servant of YHWH." Outside the book, this name is given for eleven individuals (1 Kgs. 18:3-16; 1 Chron. 3:21; 7:3; 8:38 [9:44]; 9:16; 12:9; 27:19; 2 Chron. 17:7-9; 34:12; Ezra 8:9; Neh. 10:5 [Neh. 10:6]; Neh. 12:25). Yet, none of these fits Obadiah's prophecy. This prophecy is a judgment oracle against the nation of Edom, because it exploited Judah while it was under attack by another, more powerful nation. In fact, Obadiah's language fits the time of Babylon's destruction of Judah in 586 BCE. Yet the prediction of restoration for the dispersed in the book's conclusion likely indicates a final form composed during the exile (586–539 BCE). Produced in this provenance, Obadiah's proclamations provoke reflection on the appropriate response to violent violation.

Obadiah 1:1-21: Speaking Judgment and Restoration

▌ THE TEXT IN ITS ANCIENT CONTEXT

Obadiah can be divided into two uneven sections, with the first focused on God's judgment on Edom (vv. 1-16), prosecuting its case with varying metaphors in the course of three subsections (vv. 1-4, 5-7, 8-16). The second section predicts Judah's restoration, when its exiles will possess its enemies' land (vv. 17-21). These two sections are united by their emphasis on a time of righteous reckoning: judgment on Edom but restoration for Judah.

The first section begins with the use of first-person plural verbs, which convey a decree by YHWH and the divine council. The council has dispatched a messenger with a charge of attack (v. 1). Yet Edom is self-deceived, believing it is protected by its location in the hills (v. 3). Regardless, God promises to bring Edom low (vv. 2, 4).

Obadiah continues by employing "the prophetic perfect" to predict divine judgment on Edom's excessive exploitation (Pagán). Even thieves, plunderers, and grape-gatherers know when enough is enough, but not so for Edom (v. 5). They did not exercise any restraint with Judah. In return, God will repay their voracious violence. Indeed, as Edom turned on Judah, so God will use Edom's allies against it (vv. 6-7).

Obadiah's message of divine retribution progresses in verses 8-16, as this subsection is framed by the motifs of the Day of the Lord and *lex talionis* (vv. 8, 15). God has set an appointed time when divine judgment will be relentless (vv. 8-9). Moreover, since Edom and Judah are "brothers" (vv. 10, 12), Edom should have shown Judah mercy, not enabled and extended its destruction. Indeed, verses 10-14 repeat the phrase "you should not have . . ." in its list of grievances detailing how Edom took advantage of Judah at every turn. Now, the prophet reports,

> As you have done, it shall be done to you;
>   your deeds shall return on your own head. (v. 15)

God will employ the nations as vehicles of vengeance to accomplish this judgment (v. 16).

In the book's final section (vv. 17-21), Obadiah foretells restoration for Judah. In contrast to Edom drinking on God's holy mountain (v. 16), days are coming when Mount Zion will once again be a place of holy refuge and God will give Judah's enemies into its hands (v. 17). These enemies include Edom, who will burn as stubble in Judah's fire (v. 18). Yet God's restoration will not be limited to Edom's destruction. Rather, the formerly dispossessed in Judah will possess the surrounding nations: the Philistines to the west, Ephraim to the north, and the towns of the Negev to the south (vv. 19-20). In addition, the rescued will return to Mount Zion and rule over Edom. Then the kingdom will belong to YHWH (v. 21).

▌ THE TEXT IN THE INTERPRETIVE TRADITION

Two themes from Obadiah's oracle can be highlighted in light of their significant role in the larger biblical tradition. First, an important literary motif is Obadiah's use of hierarchical imagery to denounce Edom's haughtiness. This is a recurrent device in prophetic judgment speeches. The prophets repeatedly condemn the surrounding nations for arrogantly exalting themselves in their abuse of other nations. Accordingly, God will respond in due time, showing them that only YHWH is worthy of exaltation (Isa. 2:11; 3:16; 5:15; 10:12; 37:23; Jer. 13:15; 48:29; Ezek. 16:50; Mic. 2:3; Zeph. 3:11). This applies even in cases when God has used the nation as an instrument of judgment (Isa. 47:1-15).

Another important topic is Israel and Judah's generational conflict with Edom. Of course, this relationship is portrayed as a sibling rivalry in the eponymous narratives about Jacob and Esau (Gen. 25:19-34; 27:1-28:22; 32:3-33:17). Conflict is described again when Edom does not allow Moses and Israel to pass through its land (Num. 20:14-21; see also Deut. 2:2-13). In addition, Edom was sacked by King David and served as Judah's vassal until it successfully revolted (2 Sam. 8:13-14; 1 Kgs. 22:47; 2 Kgs. 8:20-22). This historical relationship should inform one's interpretation of Obadiah and other biblical condemnations of Edom (Ps. 137:7; Isa. 34:5; Jer. 49:7-22; Lam. 4:21-22; Ezek. 25:12-14; Joel 3:19; Amos 1:6; Mal. 1:4-5). Obviously, Edom likely viewed its plunder of Judah in the sixth century as overdue justice. In Judah, however, the perception of Edom's role during the Babylonian campaign only worsened, so much so that one writer in the second century accused Edom of participating in Babylon's destruction of the temple (1 Esd. 4:45).

■ THE TEXT IN CONTEMPORARY DISCUSSION

The issues involved in the specific conflict between Judah and Edom can be extended to tensions within groups as well as between groups. In the early church, for instance, Luke portrays a relatively minor clash between Jewish Palestinians, on the one hand, and Hellenistic Jews, on the other (Acts 6:1-6). A more significant division is that between Jews and gentiles in the early church. The seeds of this struggle are planted in the arguments about Jewish identity for early believers as witnessed in our early writings from Paul in Galatians and Romans. Later, Luke in Acts 15 also portrays this fight, so too with the polemical depictions of Jews in the Gospels of Matthew and John.

Accordingly, an important question for modern readers of Obadiah in particular and the Bible in general is how one can facilitate mutual respect and reconciliation between warring parties. How does one examine deeply rooted distrust with empathy and compassion? Can one find constructive alternatives to cynical accusations and recriminations? Two scholars reflecting recently on Obadiah lament their ability to cite contemporary analogies, one from Korea (Ahn) and another from Africa (Farisani).

In the United States, numerous analogies can also be cited, such as continued obfuscation about slavery and the Civil War (Levine), and disingenuous forgetfulness regarding the role of persistent racial bias in the creation and reproduction of urban decay, poverty, and violence (Sugrue). In each case, few participants and parties want to engage in the necessary spadework found in various attempts at "Truth and Reconciliation" (Hayner). Yet this is likely the only way one can address past wounds and pursue authentic, healing communities. Such should be the charge of those who claim to hear and obey the biblical call for reconciliation.

Works Cited

Ahn, John J. 2009. "Obadiah." In *The Peoples' Bible*, edited by Curtiss Paul Deyoung, Wilda C. Gafney, Leticia Guardiola-Saenz, George E. Tinker, and Frank M. Yamada, 1063–64. Minneapolis: Fortress Press.

Farisani, Elelwani B. 2010. "Obadiah." In *The Africana Bible: Reading Israel's Scriptures from Africa and the African Diaspora*, edited by Hugh R. Page Jr., Randall C. Bailey, Valerie Bridgeman, Stacy Davis, Cheryl Kirk-Duggan, Madipoane Masenya, Nathaniel Samuel Murrell, and Rodney S. Sadler Jr., 181. Minneapolis: Fortress Press.

Hayner, Priscilla B. 2011. *Unspeakable Truths: Transitional Justice and the Challenge of Truth Commissions*. New York: Routledge.

Levine, Bruce. 2007. *Confederate Emancipation: Southern Plans to Free and Arm Slaves during the Civil War*. New York: Oxford University Press.

Pagán, Samuel. 1996. "Obadiah." In *The New Interpreter's Bible*. Vol. 7, *Introduction to Apocalyptic Literature, Daniel, the Twelve Prophets*, edited by Leander E. Keck, 447–49. Nashville: Abingdon.

Sugrue, T. 1996. *The Origins of the Urban Crisis: Race and Inequality in Postwar Detroit*. Princeton Studies in American Politics. Princeton: Princeton University Press.

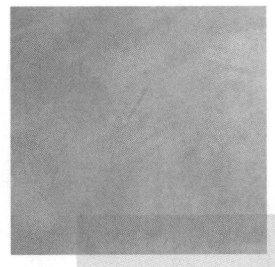

JONAH

Matthew J. M. Coomber

Introduction

The book of Jonah, the fifth book of the Minor Prophets, is one of the most popular stories of the Hebrew Bible/Old Testament. In addition to being read as the prophetic portion of the afternoon service on Yom Kippur, Jonah's story has been popularized in art, theater, and children's stories.

In the Hebrew Bible, the book of Jonah stands in stark contrast to other prophetic writings, in that it only contains five Hebrew words of actual prophecy. Instead, the book follows the absurdist and wayward journey of a prophet who is called to preach to a sinful enemy city so as to save its inhabitants from YHWH's wrath. Rather than piously following this divine command, the prophet flees from YHWH's will, only to be forced to carry out his mission and to struggle with God's compassion for Jonah's oppressors. While the meaning behind Jonah's reluctance to help his oppressors is clear, the authors' intent in transmitting the story has been interpreted in a number of ways. Many interpreters have received the story as a tale of God's acceptance for the outsider, conveying an idea of God's universal love. More recent interpretations, especially those from a postcolonial perspective, view the story as sharing in the frustrations that are experienced by those who suffer foreign oppression.

The book's protagonist, an eighth-century prophet named Jonah ben Amittai, is said to have been active during the time of King Jeroboam II (786–746 BCE). He foretells Jeroboam II's expansion of Israel's borders "from Lebo-hamath as far as the sea of the Arabah" in 2 Kgs. 14:25. In 1 Esdr. 9:23 (Greek), Jonah is listed among the Levites who divorced their foreign wives during Ezra's religious reforms. The Hebrew account, found in Ezra 10:23, lists Eliezer instead of Jonah. Jonah is the only one of the twelve Minor Prophets mentioned by name in the Qur'an (10:98). While the book of Jonah is set in the eighth century, the story's emphasis on God's sovereignty over all nations and themes of forgiveness for the penitent suggests a postexilic composition, with the earlier prophet's name borrowed for storytelling purposes.

The historicity of the book, and its fantastical narrative involving a man who is swallowed by a great fish ("sea monster" or "large sea creature" in the Septuagint) as a means of rescue, has long been a source of controversy among Christian readers. The controversy stems not so much from post-Reformation literalism, but Jesus' references to the story in both Matt. 12:39-41 and Luke 11:29-32, leading some to assert its historical accuracy. This, however, disregards Jesus' frequent use of parables, suggesting that his teachings were not bound to historical accuracy. Modern scholarship widely receives the book of Jonah as a parable or a work of religious fiction to teach a lesson or transmit wisdom.

Jonah 1:1-17: Rebellion against a Divine Command

◼ The Text in Its Ancient Context

The book opens with a common prophetic call, "the word of the Lord came to Jonah," but is followed by a command that not only takes Jonah by surprise but would have also seemed surprising to the ancient audience. YHWH commands his servant to go straight to the Assyrian capital of Nineveh, "that great city," as described in Gen. 10:11-12, because "their wickedness has come up before me" (Jon. 1:2). But whereas YHWH's taking notice of a people's "wickedness" tends to be a harbinger of doom (Gen. 6:5; Deut. 9:5; Jer. 23:11; Hosea 9:15), and the words "come up before me" reflect YHWH's words prior to Sodom's destruction (Gen. 18:11)—a sentence that Jonah would have been happy to deliver—in this story, YHWH's command leads to a chance for repentance. Rather than heed this most offensive command, Jonah chooses to flee.

In the context of the prophetic genre, Jonah's decision to abandon God and his prophetic call so resolutely is shocking; his reaction stands in contrast to the eagerness of most prophets to heed YHWH's call. This prophet's decision to flee YHWH was intended to startle, and the fact that the "wickedness" of Nineveh is not specified leads the reader to focus on Jonah's struggle with his deity's will. From a sociohistorical standpoint, however, Jonah's reaction is most understandable. The Assyrians whom Jonah was called to warn were notorious for their use of physical and psychological terror tactics to subdue weaker states, including Israel. During their eighth-century campaigns into the Levant, the Assyrians inflicted punishments of disfigurement and/or death on regional leaders and resisters, while leaving many areas in economic ruin (Coomber, 103–5). The thought of bringing YHWH's mercy to Nineveh would have been repugnant, and is in juxtaposition to the xenophobic sentiment of Jonah's contemporary books, Ezra and Nehemiah. But despite Jonah's best efforts, his plan to escape YHWH's call ends in spectacular failure.

Jonah's flight emphasizes his desire to challenge YHWH's command in most every way. Whereas YHWH commands Jonah to "arise" (*qôm*) and go eastward to Nineveh, the prophet goes "down" (*yārad*) to the port city of Joppa, "down" into a ship that was headed to Tarshish in southern Spain, which was considered to be the western edge of the world. Jonah then continues his descent by going "down" into the ship's hold, where he lies "down" and falls into a deep sleep.

In response to Jonah's flight, YHWH sends a violent wind that puts the ship and its sailors in mortal danger. The sailors' inability to save the ship by jettisoning cargo and praying to their gods leads the ship's captain to demand that Jonah pray to his god (Jon. 1:5-6), rebuking the prophet who will not rebuke the Ninevites. After successfully prophesying that Jonah's presence caused the storm (1:7), the prophet who refuses to prophesy demands to be thrown into the sea, rather than simply turning the ship back toward Nineveh. After a failed attempt for shore and praying to Jonah's god for forgiveness for killing his prophet, the sailors throw Jonah overboard (1:15). While Jonah's preference for death over heeding YHWH's call further emphasizes the prophet's resolve to avoid his mission in Nineveh, the prophet will not be released so easily. Before Jonah can drown, YHWH sends a "great fish" to swallow him, and he dwells in its belly for three days and three nights (1:17 [16:1 MT]).

This scene in which pagan sailors pray to YHWH, while Jonah refuses to talk to his God, highlights both the prophet's anger and the deity's universal nature. Not only is mercy shown to the sailors by calming the sea, but they also go on to make a sacrifice and vows to YHWH (1:16), perhaps suggesting that further sacrifices would be offered onshore. In a polytheistic world, the sailors' willingness to offer sacrifices to YHWH makes sense, and a total religious conversion should not be assumed. What is emphasized is their acknowledgment of YHWH's place as a major deity among the nations, as found in 1 Kgs. 17:24 and 2 Kgs. 5:15-18.

■ THE TEXT IN THE INTERPRETIVE TRADITION

The dramatic imagery and supernatural events of Jonah 1 have inspired a variety of receptions over the millennia. Jonah's anger at YHWH has been used to address the problems of nationalism, xenophobia, and also particularism and exceptionalism: the latter two being ideas of superiority for one particular group, setting them apart and above all others. Uriel Simon notes that the introduction of the protagonist reveals that his loyalties rest not in obedience to the "Lord of the universe," but with his people, the nation of Israel (Simon, viii). This interpretation of Jonah reflects a midrash composed by first-century teacher Rabbi Ishmael that admonishes a particularism that understood the welfare of Israel to be the supreme value and considers Jonah's disobedience in contrast to the prophets Elijah and Jeremiah. Jeremiah is represented as asserting the dignity of the father (God) and the son (Israel), and thus his prophecy is repeated. Elijah asserted the dignity of the father but not the son, and thus was replaced with Elisha. Jonah, however, asserted the dignity of the son but not the father, and thus God's voice leaves him after two chances (Simon, viii).

Whereas Rabbi Ishmael's midrash—adopted by Rashi, Joseph Kara, David Kimḥi, and Abraham Ibn Ezra—was intended to discourage an exceptionalism that places the state above the divine, Jonah 1 has also been used to promote exceptionalism and empire. English cartographer John Speed's use of Jonah and the fish in his late sixteenth-century map titled *Canaan* (raremaps.com) reflects an English imperialist interpretation of the prophet Jonah as the *sinful* subversive peoples whom the English controlled. The British Empire, however, is seen through the lens of the great city and repentant city of Nineveh, which represented both power and, as unfolds in Jon. 3:5-9, perfect piety (Staffell, 489–92).

From earliest Christianity, as seen in Matthew 12 and Luke 11, theologians have placed importance on the messages of the book of Jonah. Early interpretations often focused on the allegorical, sometimes using Jonah's rebellion as a vehicle for anti-Jewish sentiment. Rather than finding messages of God's universal love, St. Jerome connected Jonah's name—Hebrew for "dove" and a reference to Israel—to read Jonah's rebellion as allegorical to Israel's rejection of the salvation of the gentiles (Pyper, 352). John Chrysostom interpreted Jonah's rejection of God as allegorical to the Jewish people's rejection of Jesus, writing, "It is because you killed Christ . . . that there is no restoration, no mercy anymore and no defense . . . you have eclipsed everything in the past and through your madness against Christ, you have committed the ultimate transgression" (Holmgren, 128). These anti-Jewish interpretations, in contrast with those of Rabbi Ishmael, highlight the cultural subjectivity of biblical interpretation.

During the Reformation, many turned from allegorical interpretations to focus on the story as the human drama of Jonah's disobedience. Contemporary readings commonly view Jonah's rebellion as a satirical work against the intolerance of the postexilic era to promote a more universal view of God, while postcolonial interpretations have been effective in wrestling with the questions that arise when a God of the oppressed takes the side of the oppressors, as addressed in the third section of Jonah, 3:1—4:11, below.

■ THE TEXT IN CONTEMPORARY DISCUSSION

Rabbi Ishmael's use of Jonah's flight as an admonishment of first-century-CE particularism is relevant to the modern world, in which an us-versus-them mentality is used to attack the other, whether due to religious affiliation, political beliefs, or sexual preference. The questions raised by Jonah 1 lead the reader to acknowledge, through the person of Jonah, that our own ideologies should not be assumed to be those of God. The problem of projecting one's ideology onto respected figures is also common in the secular realm, as often happens with the invocation of influential thinkers from "the Founding Fathers" to Karl Marx. The narrative behind the so-called War on Terror, for example, is commonly framed as a clash of civilizations, with Christianity and Islam on opposing sides. Those who engage in Islamophobia—such as Pastor Terry Jones, who engaged in burning the Qur'an, new atheist author Sam Harris, who has claimed that Muslims are intellectually inferior (Crossley, 82–84), or Ann Coulter, who has asserted that the United States "should invade their [referring to Muslim] countries, kill their leaders, and convert them to Christianity" (Crossley, 69)—dehumanize people in ways that make it easier to engage in and accept such atrocities as the Haditha massacre, in which US soldiers killed twenty-four unarmed Iraqi civilians; after six years of court proceedings, no jail time was sentenced.

Chen Nan Jou finds modern value in YHWH's compassion toward the Ninevites. Addressing Christians who see all other religions as incapable of good and who disparage attempts to discern the theological relevance of non-Christian cultures, Chen notes that it is not God's prophet Jonah who is depicted as devout and religious in Jonah 1, but the pagan sailors on the boat. Considering this, and Jesus' willingness to break social boundaries and commune with the others of his time, Chen promotes Jonah as a vehicle for overcoming Christian attitudes of exceptionalism that have impeded interreligious dialogue (Chen, 292–94).

Jonah 2:1-10: Submission in the Face of Divine Will

◼ THE TEXT IN ITS ANCIENT CONTEXT

The second chapter of Jonah, thought by some to be a later addition (e.g., Benckhuysen, 6–9), contains a psalm of thanksgiving. Jonah's psalm can be divided into five parts. The first section, 2:2-3 (2:3-4 MT), recalls the prophet's call for help, suggesting that Jonah's preference for drowning was changed when faced with death. Interestingly, in 2:3 (2:4 MT), Jonah asserts that it was YHWH who cast him into the waters, rather than the sailors, at Jonah's behest (1:12-15). The second section, 2:4-6a (2:5-7a MT), likens Jonah's descent into the sea and the fish's belly as being cut off from God. The psalm's third section, 2:6b-7 (2:7b-8 MT), recalls how YHWH, in his temple, heard Jonah's prayer from the sea's depths and concludes with a thanksgiving prayer and sacrifices. But unlike other psalms of thanksgiving, which offer a means of meditation on the goodness of God, Jonah's psalm continues Jonah 1's absurdist narrative.

The first oddity of Jonah's prayer is that it is composed from the belly of a fish, which is an unlikely location from which to give thanks for salvation; most who venture through a fish's mouth consider themselves anything but saved. Second, Jonah only opens his mouth to give his psalm—his first utterance in the book—after sitting mute for three days in the fish's belly. Third, while thanking God for saving him from death, the prophet appears to assume that he will be exiting the fish from the same direction he entered. Jonah does not repent for the disobedience that led him into his present predicament. Thus the reader is presented with the absurd situation in which an unrepentant prophet reluctantly agrees to seek repentance from a foreign people who tormented Israel.

◼ THE TEXT IN THE INTERPRETIVE TRADITION

The image of Jonah being swallowed by a great fish has ignited the imaginations of artists and theologians alike, leading to interpretations through various mediums. Jewish midrashim have used Jonah's seventy-two hours of silence inside of the fish to offer additional meanings and interpretations to the story. Casting the fish as an ancient beast—supported by the adjective for the fish in the Septuagint, *megalos*, which can mean "ancient"—Rabbi Eliezer writes how entering into the fish was like walking into a synagogue. Jonah and the fish then confront and chase away the sea monster Leviathan (Isa. 27:1; Pss. 74:14; 104:26; Job 3:8; 40:25) before miraculously arriving under the foundations of the temple of Jerusalem, where God listens to Jonah's prayer (Green, 128).

Among early Christians, Augustine of Hippo reflected on Ps. 130:1, celebrating Jonah's time in the fish as a reassurance that no matter how deeply a person might fall into sin, God can always hear their repentance and deliver them (Green, 16–18). In addition to themes of repentance and forgiveness, Jonah's journey in and out of the fish has been interpreted as a promise of resurrection.

In entering into the sea and then being swallowed by a great fish, Jonah became dead to the world, or at least to the sailors who threw him out of their boat. But the certainty of Jonah's demise was wrong. Despite all evidence to the contrary, Jonah was not truly dead, and early Christians used this illusion of death to promote hope in the afterlife. Jesus used Jon. 1:17—2:10 to explain that despite the apparent finality of his demise he would only remain in the tomb for three days

(Matt. 12:40). In the same way, Christians turned to Jonah 2 to convey their hope in life after death, despite the apparent finality seen in a corpse. This message of resurrection is reflected in the carvings on several early-Christian sarcophagi, which reassured loved ones that their deceased's life only appeared to be over (see Lawrence; Britishmuseum.org; livius.org; rome101.com).

THE TEXT IN CONTEMPORARY DISCUSSION

Themes of repentance and deliverance in Jonah 2, highlighted by Augustine, can be beneficial to both those within and outside of Abrahamic faith communities. For those who derive religious significance from Jonah, the idea of a God who listens and gives aid, regardless of how far one has fallen, can be a great source of comfort. In both religious or secular contexts—for example, dealing with a breakdown in international relations or coping with a personal addiction—the idea that people cannot fall so low that they cannot stand back up is powerful.

Jonah 3:1—4:11: Struggling with the Consequences of Divine Mercy

THE TEXT IN ITS ANCIENT CONTEXT

After Jonah's flight from YHWH's command and vow to fulfill the deity's will, the story reopens with the "word of the LORD" once again commanding Jonah to go up to Nineveh to proclaim God's message. This time the prophet heeds (Jon. 3:1-3a). Juxtaposed, the parallelism used in Jon. 1:1-3 and 3:1-3a becomes apparent. While YHWH's call to action is essentially the same, Jonah's response is the opposite. Rather than attempting to flee from God and his mission, Jonah's voiceless response is to do exactly what is asked of him. However, YHWH does not repeat the rationale that is given in 1:2, "for their wickedness has come up before me," but simply relies on Jonah's sense of duty to obey, which Simon reads as a hint that the prophet's external compliance was accompanied by internal opposition (Simon, 25–26).

Upon his arrival at the enemy city of Nineveh, described as a three-days' walk across (Jonah 3:3b), Jonah walks for a day before proclaiming the only words of prophecy in the book: "Forty days more and Nineveh shall be overthrown" (3:4)! To Jonah's great dismay, his few words of prophecy are received with astounding effect. Highlighting the power of an utterance from YHWH and this foreigner's God's identity, the people of Nineveh are instantly moved to repent from their undefined sin (3:5). In hopes that YHWH's anger can be appeased, their king orders not only his people to submit to total repentance but also the city's animals, who are commanded to fast, put on sackcloth, and cry "mightily to God" (3:7-8). The ironic contrast between the Ninevites' and Jonah's reaction to impending doom should not be overlooked: while YHWH's prophet refuses to repent for rebelling against God while in the fish, the nonbelieving inhabitants of Nineveh fully repent for whatever wrong they have committed. And just as the Ninevites are swift to atone for their evil (*ra'*), YHWH is also swift to repent from the evil (*ra'*) that he had planned for them.

Considering that YHWH destroyed Sodom despite Abraham's intercessions in Gen. 18:16-33, a peaceful outcome for Nineveh may not have been a foregone conclusion. But now that Jonah's work has proved successful and the people have repented, Jonah ironically appears to have lost all optimism. Jonah 4 opens with what is commonly considered to be Jonah's second rebellion: the prophet's anger toward God. Whereas the people and the animals of Nineveh have everything to celebrate, a distraught Jonah confesses that his unsuccessful run to Tarshish was an attempt to subvert what he now fears will happen: YHWH will hear to the Ninevites' repentance and give them his mercy (4:1-2). Joseph Blenkinsopp argues that YHWH's merciful nature not only offended the prophet by aiding his enemies but also discredited Jonah's powers of prophecy, as there was apparently a tradition of Jonah predicting Nineveh's demise, as found in Tob. 14:4 and 14:8 (Blenkinsopp, 242).

In Jonah 4:2, the reader is presented with yet another ironic twist. Jonah quotes Exod. 34:6-7, which extols YHWH's attributes of mercy and forgiveness, not as a form of praise, for which they are so often used, but as a protest. That God is indeed merciful and slow to anger has become loathsome to him under his current circumstances. Having played a role in the fruition of God's mercy toward the Ninevites gives him such great despair that Jonah again seeks out death in 4:3, claiming that "it is better for me to die than to live." But rather than granting his servant's request, YHWH questions Jonah's right to be angry in 4:4; in the Septuagint, YHWH asks if Jonah is really that angry. Without a word of response, Jonah leaves to the east of Nineveh and makes a booth for himself, where he sits and waits to see what will become of the city.

Despite Jonah's anger and his desire to die, God does not abandon Jonah, but follows and engages him through three supernatural events. God causes a plant to shoot up and provide Jonah with shelter from the hot desert sun (4:6), sends a worm to attack the plant and cause it to wither (4:7), and finally sends a scorching wind from the east, which combined with the heat of the sun rekindles the prophet's death wish. Yet again, rather than heeding Jonah's desire to be put out of his misery by death, God admonishes the prophet for exercising compassion on behalf of the shade-giving bush, but withholding it for the hundreds of thousands of Ninevites who "do not know their right hand from their left."

▌ THE TEXT IN THE INTERPRETIVE TRADITION

Whereas the contents of Jonah 3:1—4:11 do not contain the vivid and miraculous imagery of the book's first two chapters, the story's conclusion demands much reflection on the part of the reader. Blenkinsopp interprets both YHWH's decision to retract the evil he planned for Nineveh and Jonah's despair at his God's mercy as a wisdom critique of Hebrew prophecy that attempted to wrestle with the sorts of theological problems that accompany prophecy, such as nationalism (Blenkinsopp, 242). By pitting a nationalist prophet against his own god's willingness to extend mercy to an enemy nation, the authors worked to promote a YHWH who was free from the sociopolitical constraints of the prophetic word. Such an interpretation can be taken in a couple of ways. One interpretation is to take the book of Jonah as a rejection of the exceptionalism that is promoted in much of Hebrew prophecy, encouraging readers to abandon their nationalist views.

While traditional interpretations of Jonah's fourth chapter have read YHWH's rebuttal of Jonah as a statement against Hebrew particularism, pitting Jonah's sense of exceptionalism against the more universal outlook of the divine, as discussed above of Jon. 1:1-17, another way of reading

Jonah is found in recent postcolonial interpretations of the prophet's reaction to the forgiveness of his nation's imperial tormenters, shedding new light on the text.

▮ THE TEXT IN CONTEMPORARY DISCUSSION

Jonah's disapproval of God's mercy toward the Ninevites has traditionally been treated as an indefensible position. However, when viewed from the colonized perspective of the protagonist and the book's original audience, new levels of meaning are uncovered. From the perspective of a people who have suffered brutal colonization, the Koreans, Chesung Justin Ryu finds it difficult to condemn Jonah's anger: "As long as the oppression or colonization and its painful memories are ongoing, how can the oppressed hide their anger in learning that their oppressors and colonizers are saved by their God—the God of the oppressed?" (2009, 198). Considering the colonized perspective of Jonah's postexilic authors and audience, Chesung does not believe that the story was intended to mock an angry prophet's particularism, but to share in the silence of an oppressed people (Chesung, 202, 218). In this light, Jonah's anger is not narrow-minded and stubborn, but a legitimate grievance to which the prophet responds with silent resistance.

In her Africana reading of Jonah, Valerie Bridgeman takes issue with YHWH's questioning of Jonah's anger (Jon. 4:4, 9-11), claiming that this storyline can have the negative outcome by demanding silence from those who face oppression and stifling revolution (Bridgeman 2010, 186). To simply assume that the pious answer to YHWH's question concerning Jonah's right to be angry is "no" disregards the context surrounding the text, in which Jonah is asked to aid and abet an enemy in the destruction of his own culture and people; despite any repentance against evil in Nineveh, the Assyrians went on to destroy the northern kingdom of Israel in 722 BCE, some forty years after the story of Jonah's journey is to have taken place. Rather, Bridgeman sees YHWH's question as an invitation for the reader to consider how anger can factor into "justice making, evangelization, and reconciliation" (Bridgeman 2010, 186). In confronting this problem, Bridgeman notes that some black preachers have read Jonah as a message about the dangers of going against God's will, or as a springboard for conversations on releasing hatred for a greater good, even when the hatred may be deserved (Bridgeman 2013).

Chen's postcolonial reception of Jonah finds a message of God's universal love that calls on Christian readers to consider the "undesirables" to whom Jesus preached, and to foster openness and camaraderie with peoples of other faiths so as to bring an end to religious bigotry in our time (Chen, 293–94).

Works Cited

Benckhuysen, Amanda W. 2012. "Revisiting the Psalm of Jonah." *Calvin Theological Journal* 47, no. 1:5–31.

Blenkinsopp, Joseph. 1996. *A History of Prophecy in Israel: Revised and Enlarged.* Louisville: Westminster John Knox, 1996.

Bridgeman, Valerie. 2010. "Jonah." In *The Africana Bible: Reading Israel's Scriptures from Africa and the African Diaspora*, edited by Hugh R. Page Jr., R. C. Bailey, V. Bridgeman, and Stacy Davis, 183–88. Minneapolis: Fortress Press.

Britishmuseum.org.www.britishmuseum.org/explore/highlights/highlight_objects/pe_mla/m/marble_sar-cophagus_carved_with.aspx

Chen Nan Jou. 2004. "Jonah." In *Global Bible Commentary*, edited by Daniel Patte, J. S. Croatto, N. W. Duran, T. Okure, and A. Chi Chung Lee, 291–94. Nashville: Abingdon.

Chesung Justin Ryu. 2009. "Silence as Resistance: A Postcolonial Reading of the Silence of Jonah in Jonah 4.1-11. *JSOT* 34, no. 2:195–218.

Coomber, Matthew J. M. 2010. *Re-Reading the Prophets through Corporate Globalization: A Cultural-Evolutionary Approach to Economic Injustice in the Hebrew Bible*. Piscataway, NJ: Gorgias.

Crossley, James G. 2008. *Jesus in an Age of Terror: Scholarly Projects for the New American Century*. London: Equinox.

Gaines, Janet Howe. 2003. *Forgiveness in a Wounded World: Jonah's Dilemma*. Studies in Biblical Literature 5. Atlanta: Society of Biblical Literature, 2003.

Green, Barbara. 2005. *Jonah's Journeys*. Collegeville, MN: Liturgical Press.

Holmgren, Fredrick C. 1994. "Israel, the Prophets, and the Book of Jonah." *CurTM* 21:127–32.

Lawrence, Marion. 1962. "Ships, Monsters and Jonah." *AJA* 66, no. 3:289–96.

Livius.org. www.livius.org/jo-jz/jonah/jonah-sarcophagus.html

Pyper, Hugh S. 2000. "Jonah." In *The Oxford Companion to Christian Thought*, edited by Adrian Hastings, Alistair Mason, and Hugh Pyper, 352–53. New York: Oxford University Press.

Raremaps.com. www.raremaps.com/gallery/archivedetail/15530/Canaan/Speed.html

Rome101. www.rome101.com/Topics/Christian/Magician/pages/Vat31496_0609_0680WS.htm

Simon, Uriel. 1999. *Jonah*. JPS Bible Commentary. Philadelphia: Jewish Publication Society.

Staffell, Simon. 2008. "The Mappe and the Bible: Nation, Empire and the Collective Memory of Jonah." *BibInt* 16:476–500.

MICAH

Matthew J. M. Coomber

Introduction

The book of Micah is attributed to the work of Micah of Moresheth, an eighth-century-BCE Judean prophet whose prophecies were directed toward both Samaria and Jerusalem in the latter half of the eighth century. The book represents the sixth scroll of the twelve Minor Prophets in the Masoretic Text and is placed between Jonah and Nahum. In the Septuagint, it is the third scroll of the Minor Prophets and is placed between Amos and Joel. According to Mic. 1:1, the prophet Micah's work extended from the reigns of King Jotham (742–735) to King Hezekiah (715–687), making him a contemporary of Isaiah. In the book of Jeremiah, Micah of Moresheth is celebrated as a bold prophet who was not afraid to speak to power during Hezekiah's reign (26:18). He is also listed among the great leaders in 2 Esd. 1:38.

While the book of Micah may be short in length, it is long on scathing attacks against those who use political, religious, or economic power to exploit their neighbors for personal gain. But despite its numerous threats of YHWH's wrath and prophecies of doom, Micah also expresses God's eagerness to maintain relations with God's people.

Considering the book of Micah's ability to address a variety of religious and societal issues, its use within popular religion has probably been less frequent than it deserves. Unlike the book of Exodus, which enjoys an easy-to-follow narrative, Micah's poor preservation, its large number of authors and redactors, and an irregular timeline pose a number of hermeneutical challenges. Additionally, there are disagreements as to Judah's sociopolitical situation at the turn of the seventh century BCE. While Micah's hermeneutical issues will be explored in the following sense units, issues surrounding Judah's historicity should first be addressed.

Traditional views on Judah's history find a thriving, centuries-old kingdom by the late eighth century, the time to which the book of Micah is attributed. However, recent archaeological discoveries indicate that Judah was a largely undeveloped region until Israel's destruction in 721, during Assyria's expansion into the Levant. While the debate over Judah's historicity has been limited almost entirely to academic circles, a later dating of Judah's rise to prominence has very real implications for those who wish to use the Bible in struggles against modern political, religious, and economic injustice, as will be explored below. Regardless of Judah's historicity, and while much of Micah was likely written during the postexilic period, the fact that the book is set in a time of economic development and imperial incursion, rather than within an already well-established state, opens the book to new interpretations.

Another challenge to interpreting Micah has been the book's contextual ambiguity. The transgressions condemned by the prophet are often presented without any information as to who was abusing whom or how these abuses occurred. While the lack of clarity regarding the book's historic context have frustrated attempts to understand the book in its original settings, this ambiguity can also allow the text to step outside of its origins and speak more fluently across culture and time, as discussed in the following sense units.

For the purposes of this commentary, the book of Micah's lack of overarching narrative makes it difficult to divide into clearly defined units. Many ideas and themes within the book are repeated and revisited, leading to a certain amount of repetition from one sense unit to the next.

Micah 1:1—3:12: Attacks against Political and Religious Abuses of Power

▐ THE TEXT IN ITS ANCIENT CONTEXT

The authors of Micah waste little time in laying out the sense of doom and destruction that they want to convey. After a brief biography of the prophet in Mic. 1:1, the text launches into a series of oracles that convey YHWH's rage against both Israel and Judah, foretelling severe punishments for their transgressions. The contextual ambiguity, addressed above, is prevalent here; negligible information is offered as to the nature of Israel and Judah's sins or the identities of their perpetrators and of their victims. But while the details may be understated, a sense of looming doom is not.

Following Micah's biography in 1:1, the book immediately proceeds to a prophecy that foretells the impending arrival of YHWH, who will judge Israel—for the acts of idolatry and corruption that it used to procure its wealth—and Judah for unspecified crimes (1:5-7). In return for their sins, both kingdoms will be laid to ruin at the hands of invading forces (1:15). The impact of YHWH's justice is to be swift and, despite Micah's proclamation, unexpected; in an ironic twist of fate, the inhabitants of the Judean town of Maroth will suffer YHWH's wrath while eagerly awaiting the fruits of its favor (1:12).

Chapter 2 offers more specifics about the nature of the transgressions for which God's people are to be punished. Micah lashes out at those who use their power to steal land from others (Mic. 2:1-2, 9). There are many Hebrew words for oppress, but 'ashaq, which is used in 2:2, refers to violence, robbery, and poverty, and conveys well the serious consequences of land seizures in agrarian societies.

The sociological field of cultural-evolutionary theory reveals that as agrarian societies are absorbed into world systems of trade, a series of societal patterns tends to unfold, regardless of culture or time. As administrative elites are enticed by the earning potential of newly available trade routes, they coerce subsistence farmers into abandoning traditional risk-reducing strategies for the high-risk, specialized cultivation of exportable crops. As heightened risk translates into crop failure, producers are forced to take out survival loans at exorbitant rates, which ultimately leads to default and foreclosure. Administrators then consolidate these lands into huge estates that can be effectively managed for the large-scale cultivation of export goods. In the end, these rulers hoard the benefits of trade as previously self-sufficient subsistence farmers are either forced into wage labor or become displaced (Coomber 2011, 217–19). To combat such suffering, agrarian societies often establish prohibitions against the permanent sale of farmland, as found in biblical texts (Lev. 25:10, 23-28; Num. 27:1-11; Ruth 4:3-6; and 1 Kgs. 21:1-4), Sumerian and Babylonians laws, and in former colonies of the Ottoman Empire (Coomber 2010, 109, 197). In response to their crimes, the Judean landgrabbers would have to watch as foreign armies divided the very estates they had stolen from their neighbors (2:4).

The only hopeful message in Micah 1–3 is found in 2:12-13, which provides assurance that the survivors of YHWH's wrath will be gathered back together like a flock in pasture. The origins and meaning of this passage are much disputed. Whereas Francis Andersen and David Friedman interpret 2:12-13 as a later, postexilic addition (Andersen and Friedman, 32–34), others read these words of hope as mocking the lies of Judah's false prophets who cry peace when there is war (Ben Zvi, 67). Whether taken as original text, postexilic redaction, or example of false prophetic assurances, the "comfort" tone found in 2:12-13 does not last.

Chapter 3 continues with oracles of doom, targeting corrupt politicos and religious leaders who, like the landgrabbers of Micah 2, will be punished by foreign invasion. Without listing their crimes, the authors of 3:1-3 launch a salvo against Judah and Israel's political elites, likening them to cannibals who devour the flesh from people's bones. This imagery, which is graphic to the extreme, would have resonated with the prophets' intended audience. While the Hebrew word *pashat*, commonly translated as "flay," refers to a specific method of butchering that was used in cultic sacrifice (Lev. 1:6), the authors' audience would have also recognized *pashat* as a common Assyrian terror tactic that was widely advertised to discourage rebellion in occupied areas (Andersen and Friedman, 353). At the time of the resulting invasion, YHWH would answer the ruling elites' cries with the same silence with which they had responded to their subjects' cries for justice (3:4).

In Mic. 3:5-8, YHWH's anger focuses on the prophets, who are condemned for neglecting the people by crying "peace" for those who fill their mouths and declaring "war" against those who do not or cannot offer food (3:5). YHWH's anger at the religious establishment, however, appears to pit divine expectations against the religious norms of the time. Most prophets, such as Ezekiel, Jeremiah, and Isaiah, were professionals who expected to be compensated for their craft; this is found in Saul's concern over not being able to offer Samuel food in return for a prophetic request (1 Sam. 9:6-8). Whether or not the prophets of Mic. 3:5-8 were aware that their expectations of payment had offended their God, 3:5-7 proclaims that YHWH will cut them off by removing their ability to practice their craft. It appears that the transgression of the priests and prophets in 3:11 is rooted in willingness to perform their rites for money, but not as YHWH's earthly representatives.

As with the use of *pashat* in Mic. 3:3, the threats leveled against Israel's and Judah's religious and political leaders in this passage were rooted in the geopolitical events of the late eighth century. The threat of Assyrian aggression was realized in Israel's destruction in 721 and during Judah's invasion and near annihilation in 701, and the punishments would have been read in light of these foreign invasions.

▎The Text in the Interpretive Tradition

While the greater geopolitical context of the late eighth century is largely known, the book of Micah offers very little information regarding the nature of the particular transgressions that it condemns; it is possible that those who contributed to the book at later dates were also unaware of the exact nature of these misdeeds. Other than general accusations of corruption and idolatry, Micah's first chapter gives little information as to the crimes that were to bring Israel and Judah's destruction, which led the Presbyterian English commentator Matthew Henry (d. 1714) to focus on more general meanings of the text in his commentary. He warns of "spiritual diseases" to which those who are given great power are exposed, setting a negative example for their subjects (Henry, on Mic. 1:1-7).

The ambiguity of Mic. 2:1-4, which informs the reader only that one anonymous group took land from another anonymous group through unspecified means, lends itself to varied interpretations, mostly involving the sin of coveting another's land. John Calvin, for example, interpreted this passage as a reminder of God's disdain for frauds and plunderers, encouraging the reader to channel his or her desires toward what is right and just (Calvin, 175).

Reading Mic. 2:1-4 through the lens of international capitalism, twentieth-century interpretations have largely read the text as an admonishment of greedy merchants or businessmen who seized land from poor farmers. Such commentators as James Mays and Ralph Smith have framed the contents of Mic. 2:1-2 as a struggle between the interests of Judah's wealthy and poor. Both Mays and Smith view the passage as condemning a small group of merchants who used corrupt government officials to steal arable land from poor farmers (Mays, 64; Smith, 24). Neither merchants nor poor farmers are mentioned in the text, but since the perpetrators and victims are not identified, such speculations are understandable, if not useful. Juan Alfaro takes even greater interpretive license, suggesting that the *mishpakhah* ("family") mentioned in 2:4 refers to a "mafia family" of organized criminals that profited through stealing poor farmers' lands (Alfaro, 25).

The condemnation of corruption among religious elites caught the attention of early Christian commentators who were dealing with corruption in their own times. Jerome drew on the corruption of priests and prophets in Mic. 3:11 to limit the pay of clergy in order to prevent them from chasing the purse rather than the Spirit (Arelatensis, 76:456). Cyril of Alexandria (253–54) referenced Mic. 3:9 to address the problem of those who would "pervert what is right" by corrupting holy texts to suit their own needs. Despite the aforementioned troubles in transmitting the book of Micah, the contents of 1:1—3:12 have resonated with interpreters through the centuries and remain highly relevant in the early twenty-first century.

▌THE TEXT IN CONTEMPORARY DISCUSSION

Despite the fact that the first three chapters of Micah focus on issues that are prevalent in almost any society—problems of political and religious corruption—they are rarely used to confront modern injustices. Perhaps this is due to a lack of an overarching narrative or the cumbersome nature of the book. However, recent archaeological and sociological research has uncovered previously unrecognized levels of relevance that these texts have in addressing modern-day imperialism and economic exploitation.

Considering the vast societal transformations that Judah experienced in the late eighth century as the region was absorbed into Assyria's trade nexus, it is plausible that the land seizures of Mic. 2:1-2 did not represent a few venal individuals who subverted an otherwise just system, as Mays, Smith, and Alfaro suggest, but were the result of a pan-Judean shift in economic policy. Marvin Chaney argues that as Judah was presented with new opportunities to trade wine, olive oil, and cereals with Assyria and its trade partners, Judah's rulers coerced previously autonomous farm families into abandoning their traditional risk-reducing subsistence practices for the specialized, trade-focused cultivation of these crops. As increased risk led to crop failure, survival loans resulted in the foreclosure of family-held lands, allowing ruling elites to consolidate and control the productive efforts of the region. Such forms of exploitation are found in our modern economic context.

Building on Chaney's work, Coomber has used examples of these patterns in agrarian societies that have been absorbed by global capitalism to shed light on Mic. 2:1-4's hidden contexts and consider the relevance of such prophetic complaints in the modern world (Coomber 2010, 2011, 2013). Uncovering connections between trade exploitation in the ancient and modern world not only offers a voice for agrarian workers displaced by market forces, whether Tunisian peasants or Iowan farmers who must to compete against heavy subsidies for corporations (Levins and Galbraith), but can also provide a powerful critique of those who benefit from such injustices today.

Micah 4:1—5:15: Hope for a Restored Relationship with YHWH

▌THE TEXT IN ITS ANCIENT CONTEXT

Commonly considered a postexilic addition, Micah 4 makes for an abrupt transition from the foreboding mood of Micah 1–3. The prophecy of chapter 4 moves the reader forward in time, envisioning a day when YHWH's house not only will be reestablished but also will become the center of worship for the peoples of many nations. While God's role as judge is foretold to be both active and present, YHWH will serve as a vehicle for peace by arbitrating between powerful nations, which will beat their swords into plowshares and spears into pruning hooks as war is rendered a thing of the past (Mic. 4:3-4).

It should be noted that Mic. 4:1-3 is nearly identical to Isa. 2:2-4, raising questions as to which passage was the original. While it has traditionally been thought to have originated with Micah, recent scholarship suggests that the oracle was borrowed from the Isaianic tradition and given greater power through extending God's reign over nations that were far away (Mic. 4:3; cf. Isa. 2:4). This more powerful rendering places Jerusalem not only at the center of Israel but also at the center of YHWH's reign in history.

Immediately following Mic. 3:12, which proclaims Jerusalem would be reduced to "a heap of ruins," Mic. 4:1-8 reverses the city's destruction to make it more powerful than it had ever been. Ben Zvi suggests that this reversal was created to assure postexilic audiences that YHWH's power had not been diminished by Jerusalem's fall, but would be expanded to ensure that the city remained at the center of God's power (Ben Zvi, 104–5, 111–13). By connecting the past of King David's reign to a Jerusalem that would serve as a harbinger of peace to the nations of the world, 5:1-5a would have offered its ancient audience encouragement and pride as they awaited Israel's coming glory.

Connections between Israel's past and future continue into Micah 5, where a ruler from Bethlehem is prophesied to bring peace and security to the land (5:2-6). The placement of this great monarch's origins in Bethlehem, the city of King David's birth, gave ancient audiences a sense of continuity after the interruption in rule of Israel's and Judah's defeats and exile. The power of this coming king, and his mandate by YHWH, is revealed through the grand shift in power that is prophesied in 5:5-6; if the once-great Assyrian Empire decides to invade the once-weaker state of Israel, the Assyrians will be routed and conquered under the promised Bethlehemite ruler. Such words would have bolstered the wounded pride of postexilic audiences.

The greatness of this new era is further emphasized in Mic. 5:10-15, which promotes Israel's dominance into the future and YHWH's ongoing role in human history. The passage depicts YHWH as playing an active role in Israel's affairs, cleansing Israel of military and cultic objects and destroying disobedient nations who stand in the way of God's plans.

▌ THE TEXT IN THE INTERPRETIVE TRADITION

While both Judaism and Christianity have received Micah 4–5 as a portrayal of Zion's coming restoration, there has been significant divergence between Jewish and Christian interpretation. Many of these differences rest in the fact that the fourth and fifth chapters feed into the Christian narrative of Jesus' birth in Bethlehem and also the evangelical image of all nations coming together under God's reign, as described in the New Testament.

The promise of peace found in the imagery of turning weapons of war into tools of farm production, as found in Mic. 4:3 (and also in Isa. 2:4 and Joel 3:10), has captured the hopes and imaginations of its audiences. Rather than an event pertaining to the second coming of Jesus of Nazareth, Maimonides, a twelfth-century-CE rabbinic scholar, interpreted the prophecy of Micah 4 as pertaining to a bright future on earth during the time of the Messiah. In addition to reading 4:1 as a glorious period in which rule would return to Israel and subjugation to wicked kingdoms would become a thing of the past (Maimonides 1975, 171), he interpreted the words of Mic. 4:3, "nation shall not lift up sword against nation," as heralding a virtuous time in which people would "attain much perfection and be elevated to the life of the world-to-come" (Maimonides, 166–67). This passage invited audiences not only to hear the warnings against corruption in the book of Micah, but it also offered the promise of a brighter future.

Many Christian interpretations have taken Micah 4 out of its ancient Hebrew context to address their own religious systems. In *The City of God*, Augustine (18.30) claimed that Micah used the mountain imagery in 4:2 to describe a gathering of nations under Christ. Justin Martyr read Mic. 4:1-3 as a foretelling of Christ's coming and that the beating of swords into plowshares happened when the twelve disciples came together with Christ to "teach to all the Word of God" (Justin Martyr, Mic. 4:1-3). Later, Matthew Henry interpreted Mic. 4:1-8 as a promise to the Christian church of a time in which "the reign of Christ shall continue till succeeded by the everlasting kingdom of heaven" (Henry, on Micah 4). Each of these interpreters reshaped the passage's message to relate to their own religious beliefs and spiritual needs.

The imagery of Mic. 4:3 has also appeared in recent popular culture. The imagery of turning weapons into farm tools has also been used in such popular songs as "Down by the Riverside" and Don Henley's hit single "The End of the Innocence."

■ THE TEXT IN CONTEMPORARY DISCUSSION

Beyond hopes for peace in a distant future, the fourth chapter's powerful and hope-filled imagery of turning weapons of war into tools for peacetime productivity can be an effective tool for promoting nonviolence today. There are many recent examples of Mic. 4:3 being used to address war, from its domestic economic impact to the threat of nuclear annihilation. American president and former general Dwight Eisenhower used a reversal of the peaceful imagery in 4:3 to warn of the rise of a military industrial complex, which he feared would bring about a time in which plowshares would be turned into swords.

The imagery of Mic. 4:3 has also been adopted by a number of antiwar organizations that have taken it upon themselves to help fulfill Micah's prophecy. Operation Plowshares, a Christian antinuclear-weapons group, became famous in 1980 when eight of its members broke into a Pennsylvania nuclear-missile site and successfully damaged warhead nose cones and engaged in other acts of civil disobedience. Another group called Silo Pruning Hooks entered a Missouri Air Force base in 1984, where they used a jackhammer to damage the lid of a nuclear silo. Eight members of the Catholic Worker Movement, who called themselves Pitstop Ploughshares, broke into Shannon Airport in Ireland in 2003, where they caused £80,000 of damage to United States bombers that had been awaiting sorties during the second Gulf War. Many of the aforementioned activists served prison sentences for their faith-based acts of nonviolent resistance to war.

In addition to the above examples of how Mic. 4:3 has been used to address violence in the modern world, the imagery of this verse can also speak to how nations use their money. For example, the fact that the United States allocates vast amounts of national wealth toward its military says a great deal about its fiscal priorities. In the 2013 budget, the US defense department was allocated $525 billion in discretionary spending, as compared to $23 billion for agriculture and $70 billion for education (United States Government, 2013). Whether or not these priorities are in order, the vision found in Mic. 4:3 has the potential to play a powerful role in the conversation.

Micah 6:1-8: The Trial of the Accused

■ The Text in Its Ancient Context

From the early twentieth century, scholars have dated this section of Micah to the postexilic period. But regardless of its time of origin, Mic. 6:1-8 presents audiences with a court setting in which Judah's injustices are placed on trial. The passage opens with a demand that the accused people plead their case before the judgment of YHWH and the whole earth (6:1-2), and concludes with a correctional instruction in 6:8 that was considered by Northrop Frye (206) to be one of history's greatest moral breakthroughs. This trial scene, however, breaks from some of the standard conventions of its time.

Whereas court cases traditionally start with a leveling of charges against the accused, here the deity opens the proceedings in the defendant's box, raising concerns about YHWH's own possible shortcomings and giving the accused a chance to voice any complaints that they may have (6:3-5). Through YHWH's line of questioning, which suggests a sense of confusion and betrayal as YHWH works to understand how it might have offended the people and caused them to go astray, YHWH highlights all that has been done for the people (6:3-5). The accused does not appear to take the opportunity to lodge any complaints, but responds in 6:6-7 with a series of questions as to how the accused might appease YHWH's anger, offering a crescendo of cultic sacrifices from burnt calves to the climax of child sacrifice. Thomas Römer (21) argues that the accused were not referring to some ancient practice that had been replaced by animal sacrifice, but an institution of child sacrifice that coexisted alongside animal sacrifice. The reference to child sacrifice in 6:7, and its rejection in 6:8, is commonly thought to have marked a break from the practice.

Whereas Mic. 6:6-7 is often received as an earnest attempt to make amends with God, Ben Zvi (147) argues that the dialogue's conclusion in instruction, rather than an announcement of salvation, may indicate that 6:6-7 represents a defense against YHWH's charges. Using an intertextual approach, Mignon Jacobs reads 6:6-7 as a complaint against the deity, in which Israel refutes its God for wearying its people by offering a sarcastic list of outlandish sacrificial demands (Jacobs, 177–78).

In the pinnacle of the unit (Mic. 6:8), the voice of the prophet summarizes the Torah, laying out what it means to live well under YHWH: "to do justice, and to love kindness, / and to walk humbly with your God." Whereas the accused party's response to YHWH's anger is cultic sacrifice (6:6-7), 6:8 moves their religious practice beyond temple ritual and into the way they conduct their daily lives. This message is congruent with Isa. 1:11-17, where cultic offerings are also rejected in favor of a lifestyle that promotes the peace and justice of God. In so doing, Mic. 6:8 works to replace the notion that justice is YHWH's job, and places its responsibility on the shoulders of the people.

◼ THE TEXT IN THE INTERPRETIVE TRADITION

The futility of the people's offerings in Mic. 6:6-7 has been received as a push for right living. Ambrose (306–7) looked to cultic offerings of 6:6-7 as a call to turn away from ritual appeasement and concentrate on living "a good life."

One of the most shocking aspects of Mic. 6:1-8 is the suggestion of child sacrifice in 6:7. Clement of Alexandria asserted that the suggestion of child sacrifice spoke out against "those human impulses that are unhelpful in gaining knowledge of God" (Ferreiro, 171).

Calvin read 6:6-7 as the prophet's voice, mocking his audiences' futile remedies for atonement. He relates this to those of his own time who devise means to alleviate their guilt before God. Using the Catholic Church's leadership as an example, Calvin relates the extreme remedy of child sacrifice (6:7) to the mentality of papacy, which will "toil in ceremonies, and if they pour forth some portion of their money, if they sometimes deprive nature of its support, if with fastings and by other things, they afflict themselves, they think that by these means they have fully performed their duties" (328).

◼ THE TEXT IN CONTEMPORARY DISCUSSION

The powerful messages and thought-provoking problems that the authors of Mic. 6:1-8 posed to their audiences can provide modern readers with ample material for discussion. From a faith perspective, the passage raises questions about what it means to live a life of faith under a God who seeks justice, kindness, and humility.

The people's response to the court proceedings of Mic. 6:1-5 is to shield themselves with ritual piety and prescribed laws. The prophet's rejection of these means of atonement can speak to modern "holier-than-thou" attitudes toward spiritual purity, suggesting that piety comes not simply through ritual observance but in how the faithful conduct themselves toward their neighbor and also God. This passage can serve to encourage faith practitioners and communities to move beyond traditional ritual practice and into engaged spiritual practice that centers itself on kindness, justice, and humility, as had been displayed in Pope Francis I's calls to view service to the poor as service to God. He exemplified this sentiment by taking the unprecedented step of washing the feet of prisoners during his first Maundy Thursday service as pontiff. Included in the foot-washing were people of other faiths and women, the latter of whom may have broken liturgical law.

What it means to live in justice, kindness, and humility is left open to interpretation, enabling the text to flow into the varied cultural contexts into which it is received. This ambiguity not only lends the passage an ongoing relevancy but also demands reflection on the part of the reader and encourages conversation with others. The powerful messages of 6:8 can also serve as a rallying cry, tempered with humility, for such justice struggles as the Catholic Worker Movement, School of the Americas Watch, Christian Peacemaker Teams, and the work of liberation theologians from Latin America to India.

The humility aspect of Mic. 6:8 also speaks to the tendency to resolve tensions by blaming an other (see Gen. 3:12-13), which can cause harm to innocent parties and also deny oneself the benefits of self-reflection. An extreme example of blaming the other is found in the followers of

Pastor Fred Phelps, who view the September 11, 2001, attacks as a direct outcome of God's anger against homosexuality, leading them to celebrate at the funerals of fallen service members and the victims of LGBT violence. Pastors Pat Robertson and the late Jerry Falwell also asserted that the 9/11 attacks were a product of God's wrath against "homosexual culture," while adding feminists, supporters of legalized abortion, and the American Civil Liberties Union to their list of scapegoats. While several passages within the Old Testament do promote corporate punishment for perceived sins—recently addressed by Hugh Pyper and Philip Davies—Mic. 6:6-8 presents an opportunity to focus on one's own conduct rather than on the conduct of the "other." Within the context of theologies that perceive God as punishing sin through historic events, Phelps, Falwell, and Robertson laid blame at the feet of those with whom they disagreed, but did not consider how their own failings may have brought about such wrath. The instruction of 6:8 can encourage a spirituality that searches for kindness, justice, and humility within oneself rather than finding fault in others.

Micah 6:9—7:7: Accusations and Verdicts against Corruption, Revisited

■ THE TEXT IN ITS ANCIENT CONTEXT

Following the instruction of Mic. 6:8, the text returns to the problems of corruption that were addressed in Micah 1–3. Addressing "the city," its assembly, and the tribe, YHWH's anger is directed against their "treasures of wickedness" and the wickedness of the temple that houses them. In 6:10-12, the city—commonly thought to be Jerusalem though it could also be Samaria—is presented with a list of crimes, including financial inequity, general violence, and deceit, which will lead to its destruction by foreign invaders, as laid out in 6:13-16.

The accusations of Mic. 6:9-12 reflect those found in Micah 1–3, but offer a wider focus by denouncing the people alongside of their leaders. In 6:11, YHWH condemns an economic practice that was used by merchants and is also supported by the archaeological record: using different weights for the selling and purchases of goods in the temple market (Yeivin, 64–68). What is often lost in English translations, and may give insight into the urgency with which the authors addressed economic injustice in a religious context, is a suggestion that these corrupt activities affected YHWH's well-being. The NRSV translation of 6:11 reads, "Can I tolerate wicked scales / and a bag of dishonest weights?" However, "tolerate" comes from the Hebrew word *zakah*, which means "to be clean" or "pure." In its first-person singular interrogative form in 6:11, the meaning conveyed is "Can I be made pure/clean/innocent by these wicked scales and a bag of dishonest weights?" Arnold Ehrlich (287) and William McKane (195) argue that this is an error in the Masoretic Text, based on the Septuagint's third-person presentation of the verb *dikaiōthēsetai*, which means "shall they be justified?" However, there is precedent to consider that the authors were concerned that YHWH could be tainted by human injustice. If this is the case, 6:11 offers a greater sense of urgency in rooting out injustices pertaining to religious economic practice.

The passage's focus on the violence and deceit of the wealthy and city dwellers in Mic. 6:12 reflects common connotations of monarchic Jerusalem in the postexilic era (Ben Zvi, 164). Whether the text's origins are in the eighth century or after the Babylonian exile, the authors and audience were able to draw on the accusations and curses of 6:13-15, and again in 7:2-3 to help explain the destruction of the unnamed city.

■ THE TEXT IN THE INTERPRETIVE TRADITION

John Calvin and Matthew Henry both interpreted Mic. 6:9-16 as a warning against trapping one-self through fraudulent acts. Calvin saw the individuals in the city as more wicked than the other inhabitants because they not only robbed their neighbors but also set up a system in which the victims were forced to become perpetrators; the general inhabitants were not engaged in sin with the intent of doing harm, but forced to cheat in order to avoid poverty (Calvin, 336). Matthew Henry's commentary adds that for the whole of the city, "what is got by fraud and oppression, cannot be kept or enjoyed with satisfaction" (Henry, on Micah 6).

Early Christian theologians used the agrarian analogy of the harvest in 7:1 as an opportunity to reflect on the works of those who align themselves with the church, writing that not only pagan nations but also those of the church must consider what they are cultivating within themselves. Origen proclaimed, "Let each of us scrutinize himself. Is he an ear of corn? Will the Son of God discover something in him to pick or harvest?" This call for introspection dovetails with the call for humility in 6:8.

■ THE TEXT IN CONTEMPORARY DISCUSSION

In the wake of the financial collapse of 2008, caused largely by the world's most powerful financial institutions' dishonest investments and lending schemes, Mic. 6:9-16 remains pertinent in our time. The passage promotes the idea that God pays attention to financial conduct, suggesting that marketplace dealings are not to be viewed as separate from religious practice. The phrase "that's business," often used to justify questionable financial dealings, did not appear to absolve YHWH's targets in Micah.

The imagery of people using wicked scales and dishonest weights in 6:11, the violence and deceit of 6:12, and the imagery of hunting each other in nets in 7:2 dovetail with the Ponzi schemes of Bernard Madoff and Alan Stanford, as well as recent cases of mutual-fund fraud, misleading mortgage practices, and illegal foreclosures that have left so many in ruin. These biblical images can also speak to prosperity theologians who promise congregants God-given monetary wealth if they donate their money into these pastors' vast coffers.

Whether from a faith or secular perspective, Calvin's aforementioned interpretation of Mic. 6:9—7:7, which considers the inhabitants of the city as unwilling perpetrators of injustice, raises questions about the inherent injustice in our global economy. Many poorer and middle-class citizens in the world's wealthiest nations cannot afford to purchase goods that are not produced by sweatshop labor. In our current economic system, it is difficult for people to prepare for retirement or their children's college education without investing in corporations that are involved in unethical practices. Micah 6:9—7:7 raises a lot of uncomfortable questions that serve as a starting place for conversations on how economics might move beyond bottom-line motivations to consider more equitable approaches to prosperity and growth.

Micah 7:8-20: Hope in a Restoration, Yet to Come

■ THE TEXT IN ITS ANCIENT CONTEXT

The closing verses of Micah return to the themes of hope that are found in Micah 4–5. The passage opens with the city's voice expressing a steadfast faith in YHWH and the idea that even when the prophet falls (7:8) YHWH will execute judgment on the city's behalf. While Mic. 7:9 promotes the idea that Jerusalem's fall was the work of God—an indignity that the city endured for its sins—it will be the enemies of Judah who will suffer the final downfall (7:10).

With a promise of restoration, found in Micah 4–5, the prophet foresees a time when the city's walls will be rebuilt (7:11) and the people of the great empires will come to its gates (7:12). Only this time, the Assyrians and Egyptians will not approach as conquerors seeking the spoils of war, but in shame and with fear as they stand in dread of YHWH's power (7:16-17). The passage offered its ancient readers hope in the face of overwhelming adversity, whether a looming Assyrian invasion or the humiliation of exile. Other renderings of 7:12 view those approaching the city from Assyria and Egypt not as foreigners but as the returning Hebrews who are coming home after the exile, highlighting their penitence and willingness to adhere to YHWH's will.

In the form of a praise offering, the book of Micah concludes with an idyllic picture of a God of justice and mercy. With great hope, the prophet asks what other gods can be compared to YHWH, a God who forgives sins, lets anger abate, and will cast out the people's sins to offer compassion (7:18-20). This closing praise promoted the idea that despite the iniquities of the people, YHWH's covenant had not been broken, but would continue, stronger than ever.

■ THE TEXT IN THE INTERPRETIVE TRADITION

The messages of hope and divine forgiveness in Mic. 7:8-20 have been a focus of interpreters throughout the centuries, and are reflected in the Jewish practice of *tashlik*, which comes from the verb *shlk*, or "to throw," in 7:19. Performed on Rosh Hashanah (the Jewish New Year), the practice consists of participants casting rocks that represent their sins into a body of water. It has been thought to be a good omen to see a fish during this ritual, which can serve to take away the participants' guilt. The sixteenth-century Jewish mystic Moshe Cordovero also drew on Mic. 7:18-20; he viewed this passage as an embodiment of the Jewish ethic of forgiveness (Schimmel, 85–88).

Origen referenced God's forgiveness in Mic. 7:19 as an example of mortal charity. Referencing Micah, he wrote, "The prophet in Scripture says, 'We should cast our sins into the depths of the sea.' John continues, 'He who has food should do likewise.' Whoever has food should give some to one who has none" (94.99). Basil the Great offered another interpretation of this verse, likening the waters in 7:19 to the Christian baptismal waters that wash away the baptized person's sins (Ferreiro, 177). Calvin interpreted this passage as a testament to the power of God's promises, remaining loyal to the covenant made with Abraham, despite Israel's sins (389–90).

■ THE TEXT IN CONTEMPORARY DISCUSSION

The themes drawn from Mic. 7:8-20 in Jewish and Christian interpretive tradition continue to find relevance in the modern world. Calls to trust in God and the levels of compassion the passage promotes are applicable in a number of ways. As addressed in Cordovero's interpretation, this passage could serve as a force for reconciliation. Various religious debates generate anger and hurt within their communities, leading to both violence and schism. A reminder of God's willingness to pardon wrongdoing, slowness to anger, and delight in pity (7:18) can serve as a starting place for healing.

Furthermore, whether in one's spiritual or secular life, the message of hope in the face of overwhelming adversity, as found in 7:8-17, can address such seemingly hopeless cases as healing fractured relations, bringing about peace where there is little cooperation or willingness to work through the aftermath of a tragedy.

Works Cited

Alfaro, Juan I. 1989. *Justice and Loyalty: A Commentary on the Book of Micah*. Grand Rapids: Eerdmans.

Ambrose of Milan. 1972. *Seven Exegetical Works*. Translated by Michael P. McHugh. FC 65. Washington, DC: Catholic University of America Press.

Andersen, Francis I., and David Noel Freedman. 2000. *Micah*. Edited by William Foxwell Albright and David Noel Freedman. AB 24E. New York: Doubleday.

Arelatensis, Caesarivs, ed. 1953. *Corpus Christianorum Series Latina*. Turnhout, Belgium: Brepols.

Augustine. 1954. *The City of God: Books XVII–XXII*. Translated by Gerald Walsh and Daniel Honan. FC 24. New York: Fathers of the Church.

Ben Zvi, Ehud. 2000. *Micah*. Edited by Gene M. Tucker, Rolf P. Knierim, and Marvin A. Sweeney. FOTL 21B. Grand Rapids: Eerdmans.

Calvin, John. 2010. *Commentary on Jonah, Micah, Nahum*. Christian Classics Ethereal Library. http://www.ccel.org/ccel/calvin/calcom28.html.

Chaney, Marvin, L. 1989. "Bitter Bounty: The Dynamics of Political Economy Critiqued by the Eighth-Century Prophets." In *Reformed Faith and Economics*, edited by Robert L. Stivers, 15–30. Lanham, MD: University Press of America.

Coomber, Matthew J. M. 2010. *Re-Reading the Prophets through Corporate Globalization: A Cultural-Evolutionary Approach to Understanding Economic Injustice in the Hebrew Bible*. Biblical Intersections 4. Piscataway, NJ: Gorgias.

———. 2011. "Prophets to Profits: Ancient Judah and Corporate Globalization." In *Bible and Justice: Ancient Texts, Modern Challenges*, edited by Matthew J. M. Coomber, 212–37. BibleWorld. London: Equinox.

———. 2013. "Debt as Weapon: Manufacturing Poverty from Judah to Today." *Diaconia: Journal for the Study of Christian Social Practice* 4, no. 2:143–58.

Cyril of Alexandria. 2008. *Commentary on the Twelve Prophets*. Vol. 2. Translated by Robert C. Hill. FC 116. Washington, DC: Catholic University of America Press.

Davies, Philip. 2011. "Rough Justice?" In *Bible and Justice: Ancient Texts, Modern Challenges*, edited by Matthew J. M. Coomber, 43–55. BibleWorld. London: Equinox.

Ehrlich, Arnold B. 1968. *Randglossen zur Hebräischen Bible: Textkritisches, Prachliches und Sachliches*. Vol. 5, *Ezechiel und die Kleinen Propheten*. Hildesheim: Georg Olms.

Ferreiro, Alberto, ed. 2003. *The Twelve Prophets*. Ancient Christian Commentary on Scripture, Old Testament 14. Downers Grove, IL: InterVarsity Press.

Frye, Northrop. 2006. *The Collected Works of Northrop Frye*. Vol. 19, *The Great Code: The Bible and Literature*. Edited by Alvan Lee. Toronto: University of Toronto Press.

Henry, Matthew. 1935. *Matthew Henry's Commentary on the Whole Bible in Six Volumes.* Vol. 4, *Jeremiah to Malachi.* New York: Fleming H. Revell.

Jacobs, Mignon R. 2001. *Conceptual Coherence of the Book of Micah.* Sheffield: Sheffield Academic Press.

Levins, Richard A., and John K. Galbraith. 2003. *Willard Cochrane and the American Family Farm.* Lincoln: University of Nebraska Press.

Maimonides, Mosheh. 1975. *Ethical Writings of Maimonides.* Ed. Raymond L. Weiss and Charles E. Butterworth. New York: Dover Publications.

Martyr, Justin. 1948. *Saint Justin Martyr: The First Apology, The Second Apology, Dialogue with Trypho, Exhortation to the Greeks, Discourse to the Greeks, The Monarchy; or the Rule of God.* Trans. Thomas B. Falls. The Fathers of the Church 6. New York: Christian Heritage.

Mays, James L. 1976. *Micah: A Commentary.* London: SCM.

McKane, William. 2000. *The Book of Micah: Introduction and Commentary.* New York: T&T Clark.

Pyper, Hugh S. 2010. "Rough Justice: Lars von Trier's *Dogville* and *Manderlay* and the Book of Amos." *Political Theology* 11, no. 3:321–34.

Römer, Thomas. 2010. "Le Sacrifice Humain en Juda et Israël au premier millenaire avant notre ére." In *Archiv für Religionsgeschichte* 1:17–26.

Schimmel, Solomon. 2002. *Wounds Not Healed by Time: The Power of Repentance and Forgiveness.* New York: Oxford University Press.

Smith, Ralph L. 1984. *Micah–Malachi.* Edited by David A. Hubbard, Glenn W. Barker, John D. W. Watts, and Ralph P. Martin. WBC 32. Waco, TX: Word.

United States Government. 2013. *Fiscal Year 2013 Budget of the U.S. Government.* Washington, DC: US Government Printing Office, 2013.

Yeivin, Shmuel. 1969. "Weights and Measures of Varying Standards in the Bible." *PEQ* 101:63–68.

NAHUM

Wilhelm J. Wessels

Introduction

Nahum is a short prophetic book specified in verse 1 as an oracle (*maśśā'*) from YHWH. This short book is a display of YHWH's power over the Assyrians, the enemy of Judah. With impressive rhetoric, a dismayed Judah is challenged to imagine YHWH's victory over their powerful oppressor (Wessels, 55–73). Very little is known about the author and his origin. Although Elkosh is designated as his town of origin, this place is unknown. Some regard Nahum as a cultic prophet or even a scribe, while still others focus on his poetic abilities. The prophet acted in the seventh century, but that is not necessarily the date of the completion of Nahum as a literary work. Very little detail is available from the book itself to determine a date. In Nahum 3:8-9, Thebes is mentioned, a city that was ransacked by Assyrian forces in 667 BCE. The other historical reference is the fall of Nineveh in 612 BCE. The book should most probably be dated after the fall of Nineveh in 612 BCE. The composition and unity of Nahum is also a contentious issue and has implications for the dating of the final text of the book (see Mason, 63, 74–75). Those who believe the book evolved over a long period of time would opt for a postexilic date for the final version of the document (see Roberts, 38–39; Schulz; O'Brien 2002, 14–15).

There are several views on the genre of Nahum. It has been treated, for example, as a prophetic liturgy (Coggins, 9–10), a prophetic refutation speech, a prophetic historical exemplum (Floyd, 18), a propagandistic anti-Assyrian tract, nonviolent resistance literature, a collection of songs of soldiers, and a type of city lament (see Huddlestun). A key characteristic that should be considered when analyzing Nahum is the poetic nature of the book with its use of rhetorical devices and imaginative language and images. The following literary units have been proposed for the discussion of the Nahum's content: 1:1-15 [Heb. 1:9-2:1]; 2:1-13 [2:2-14]; 3:1-17; 18-19.

Nahum 1:1-15: YHWH and the Fate of Judah and Their Enemies

■ THE TEXT IN ITS ANCIENT CONTEXT

The oracles in Nahum concern Nineveh, symbol of power to the Assyrians. The dominance of Assyria forms the background of the discussion. Nineveh was situated on the eastern bank of the Tigris River near Mosul. Sennacherib (705–681 BCE) made Nineveh his capital, and it remained the capital under his successors Esarhaddon (680–669) and Ashurbanipal (668–627) (see Baker, 560–61). Nineveh was finally destroyed in 621 BCE by the Medes. As the enemy of Judah and Israel, Nineveh was also the enemy of YHWH.

Nahum 1:2-8 is a hymn about YHWH in the form of an incomplete acrostic. David Petersen (198) regards Nahum 1 as "a theological prolegomenon" to the book as a whole. The pericope concerns the nature and power of YHWH as the sovereign power. Three aspects of YHWH are highlighted in this short poem: First, his nature is described as jealous, avenging, slow to anger, and great in power (vv. 2–3a); second, his actions are emphasized (vv. 3b–6). His theophanic appearance affects nature and depicts his power. It is stated that his mighty presence will affect the wind, clouds, sea, rivers, and mountains. His enemies should take note of his sovereign power over nature and people. In the third instance, YHWH is presented as both protector of his people and destroyer of his enemies (vv. 7-8). On the one hand, he is described as good: a stronghold in times of trouble who knows the people who seek shelter in him. On the other hand, verse 8 states that he will annihilate his enemies and pursue them into darkness.

This poem serves the purpose of fostering trust in YHWH on the part of the people of Judah. The very nature of YHWH testifies to Judah that YHWH will counter the force of their powerful enemy Assyria. Nahum 1:9-15 reveals an alternating pattern of doom for Nineveh (1:9-11, 14; 2:1) and deliverance for Judah (1:12-13, 15 [Heb. 2:1]; 2:2). In verses 9-11, the people of Judah are assured that the unknown enemy's plans will not succeed. Like fire devours thickets and stubble, so will the enemy be devoured. Nahum 1:12-13 confirms that YHWH's acts will favor his people. The strong enemy will be destroyed. Images of a yoke being broken and a band snapped are used to depict the destruction of the enemy. The doom proclamation directed against the enemy in 1:14 entails a threat of total extinction: their name will be wiped out, images of their gods destroyed, and their death a sure reality. Verse 15 [Heb. 2:1] is an appeal to Judah to celebrate YHWH's victory over the enemy and to show their loyalty to YHWH by keeping their vows.

■ THE TEXT IN THE INTERPRETIVE TRADITION

The book of Nahum was interpreted and applied through the centuries by biblical authors and by proponents from the Jewish and Christian traditions. Scholars have referred to the relationship between the books of Jonah and Nahum. Both concern Nineveh and it inhabitants, but Klaas Spronk (16–17) is convinced that Jonah is a reaction to the uncompromising condemnation of the Assyrians in Nahum, leaving room for the possibility that the nations can also enjoy YHWH's grace. There is also a correspondence between Nah. 1:15 and Isa. 52:7, both referring to the messenger motif, but there is no consensus among scholars on this literary correspondence.

It should be noted that the book of Nahum played an important role in the Qumran community. Fragments as well as interpretations of passages from Nahum testify to this (see 4QpNah [4Q169]). Some of the words from Nahum were regarded as relevant and therefore applied to the context within which this community lived (Coggins, 14). One example mentioned by Jin H. Han (20) is Nah. 1:4, which refers to YHWH's power over the waters of the sea. According to the Qumran commentator, YHWH will release the same power against his enemies (4QpNah, fragments 1 and 2 cited in Berrin, 77). Furthermore, it seems that Nahum 1 had influence on some psalms of thanksgiving (Spronk, 16–17).

When it comes to the use of the book of Nahum in the Christian tradition, several of the church fathers applied aspects of it to their context and experiences. It is clear that Nineveh had become a symbol of all that is evil. Most of these fathers also interpreted the text of Nahum christologically. Huddlestun (106–7) refers to several such persons including Julian of Toledo, Haimo of Auxerre (Nahum 2—judgment of the devil and associates), Athanasius of Alexandria, and Tertullian (Nah. 1:4—referring to the calming of the sea by Jesus). Cyril of Alexandria (c. 375–444) should also be mentioned in this regard. He wrote a commentary on several of the prophets in which he tried to do justice to the historical setting of the text. In his commentary, he easily engages the society of Jesus' time and speaks of Satan, the unholy scribes and Pharisees, and how Christ will crush rulers and authorities as is mentioned in Nahum 1 (Cyril of Alexandria, 292). There are several more such examples from Cyril's commentary on Nahum, where he applies the text in similar fashion. An interesting example of the interpretive tradition of Nahum 1 is Origen's interpretation of the phrase in Nah. 1:9, "no adversary will rise up twice." According to Han (23), "Origen declares that the death penalty resolves guilt. For God does not exact justice from offenders twice" (*Homilies on Leviticus* 11.5). Nahum 2:15 has in particular attracted the attention of Christian interpreters because of the association of the "good news" with the gospel of Jesus Christ in the New Testament (see Rom. 10:15). For a detailed discussion of the interpretive tradition of Nahum, Han (6–30) has much more to offer than space allows here.

■ THE TEXT IN CONTEMPORARY DISCUSSION

The book of Nahum concerns the destruction of the enemy Assyria, emphasizing the sovereignty of YHWH as supreme power. Despite the criticism leveled against the book (see Mason, 57–58), most scholars have high regard for its literary quality and poetic brilliance. It employs metaphors, similes, rhetorical questions, repetitions, and numerous other stylistic devices to highlight the themes it wishes to convey. However, one can also appreciate the problems people experience when reading the book of Nahum. The content of the book raises serious theological issues, not the least of which are the following: How can such brutal and disturbing deeds, portrayed in the book of Nahum with regard to the fate of Nineveh, be ascribed to YHWH? Can YHWH be associated with such atrocious deeds? Nahum should be read as coming from a prophet/poet who has related his experience of oppression at the hands of the Assyrians to his understanding of YHWH. The poet/prophet is clear on this: YHWH alone possesses sovereign power and in exercising this power will counter and surpass the brutal force of the Assyrians. Contemporary interpreters should be careful to avoid a narrow "God is for us alone" theology and therefore should not lose sight of a more inclusive message of "God is for people."

Nahum 2:1-13: The Downfall of Nineveh

▌ THE TEXT IN ITS ANCIENT CONTEXT

In Nahum 2:1-13 (Heb. 2:2-14), the focus is on the downfall of Nineveh. Although the city is not named in the early verses, it later becomes clear that the proclamation is aimed at the city. Verse 1 alerts Judah's enemy of a scatterer that will pose a threat to them. This is followed in 2:1 by a word of encouragement that YHWH will restore his people. In the following verses, a scene is painted of a battlefield of which Judah is the spectator observing the downfall of the powerful Assyrian enemy. This is done in poetic style with skillful application of imagery and rhetoric. In 2:3-5, the siege of Nineveh is described, followed in 2:6-8 with scenes portraying the emotional impact of the carnage on the citizens in the city. The image of a flooded city is presented in verse 6. Verse 7 is difficult, but it seems that the Hebrew word *huzzab* should be understood as "it is decreed" that the inhabitants of the city will be carried away, slave girls lamenting the state of affairs of an empty city (Coggins, 41–42; Roberts, 65–66). According to verse 8, Nineveh is like a dam leaking water, a metaphor for power dwindling. In staccato style, the prophet describes the plundering of the wealth of the city (v. 9) and also the tragic consequences of defeat.

> Devastation, desolation, and destruction!
> Hearts faint and knees tremble,
> all loins quake,
> all faces grow pale! (Nah. 2:10)

Nahum 2:11-12 makes use of a lion metaphor to taunt the king of Assyria and the nobles because of their diminishing power. The chapter ends with a declaration that YHWH will totally destroy Nineveh and its leaders in war and leave Assyria powerless.

▌ THE TEXT IN THE INTERPRETIVE TRADITION

As already noted, the book of Nahum played an important role in the Qumran community (see 4QpNah). A Dead Sea fragment of Nah. 2:11-13 testifies to this. This passage refers to lions, interpreted by the Qumran commentary, according to some, as referring to Antiochus IV Epiphanes (175–163) and probably Demetrius III (died in 88 BCE; Coggins, 15). Others seem to see in the reference to the lion an allusion to Alexander Janneus, who reigned from 103 to 27 BCE (Huddlestun, 106). The Nahum pesher is an invaluable source of information on the Maccabean period. The midrash associates the lion with Nebuchadnezzar, the monarch responsible for the exile (*Exod. Rab.* 29.9; Han, 29).

An interesting example of how some readers interpreted Nahum involves the issue of the "scatterer" mentioned in 2:1. The Septuagint offers the reading "one who breathes on your face." In light of this translation, the church father Cyril of Jerusalem (c. 315–387) relates this to John 20:22-23, where Jesus breathes on the apostles to receive the Holy Spirit. This action according to Cyril represents the restoration of creation after the fall of Adam, when the first breathing of the Holy Spirit took place (see Han, 27). Later in history, there are examples others who made the Nahum text relevant to their time. Luther, for example, says that the "Assyrians perished because they were unable to use their prosperity moderately" (Spronk, 17), and arrives at the conclusion that the pope will similarly be destroyed (see Huddlestun, 107, for more on Luther's interpretation of aspects of the Nahum text). Many interpreters regard Nineveh as synonymous with evil, and its defeat as the demise of evil itself.

THE TEXT IN CONTEMPORARY DISCUSSION

As mentioned above, the issue of violence rears its head particularly in chapter 2. The people of Judah are invited to observe how YHWH destroys their enemy. One possible way to approach the theological dilemma of YHWH's involvement in violence is to regard Nahum as similar to "resistance poetry." In this way, Nahum can be approached with a focus on societal issues and as a reflection of anti-Assyrian sentiments. The issue here is the poetic "overstatement" of expression. Not only is the sovereignty of YHWH stated in awesome overtones and theophanic imagery, creating an atmosphere of awe and reverence, but it also concerns Nineveh. The city and king's destiny is described in language and pictures that are disturbing and even repulsive in nature. By means of these excessive overtones, an atmosphere of emotional tension is created for a functional purpose. This resistance poetry, born out of rage and frustration, depicts the defeat of the enemy in the strongest possible language as an outlet of suppressed or heightened emotions. At the same time, faith is expressed in the supremacy of YHWH, who represents real power. However, it is one thing for the contemporary interpreter to read the book of Nahum with an understanding of its historical context, but it is quite another matter to use it to condone violence in the name of YHWH. Perhaps the book of Nahum should be read for the repulsive effect it can have on the reader or audience when confronted with such brutal and violent scenes and to encourage contemporary readers to search for other nonviolent ways of addressing oppression.

Nahum 3:1-19: Demise and Downfall of Nineveh

THE TEXT IN ITS ANCIENT CONTEXT

Nahum 3 is subdivided between verses 1-17 and 18-19. Verses 1-17 can be further subdivided into two units: 1-7 and 8-17. This chapter describes the demise and downfall of Nineveh. Nahum 3:1-7 is a threat against Nineveh described as an evil city. Again, a scene of war and carnage is depicted showing the literary skill of the poet. What is striking is that YHWH is the antagonist of the adulterous city, announcing that Nineveh will be humiliated as a female. In verses 8-17, the defenselessness of Nineveh is the subject. The city Thebes was found not to be invincible; on what grounds, then, can Nineveh claim to be better than Thebes? Verse 12 employs the simile of a ripe fig to refer to Nineveh, shaken from a tree and falling into the mouth of an eater, meaning her enemy. The powerlessness of Nineveh's army is again depicted by comparing its troops to women.

In the next verses, three media are mentioned that will cause Nineveh's destruction: fire will devour the city, a sword will cut her off, and an enemy will invade the city as young locusts consume a field. The inhabitants of Nineveh can multiply like locusts, but this will still not prevent YHWH from destroying them. The last two verses of chapter 3 are addressed to the king of Assyria, informing him that he cannot rely on his officials to save the day. His situation is to be compared to an incurable wound; he can expect hardship in the future. This news will bring joy to people he had oppressed and who suffered as a result of his unceasingly evil actions.

▌THE TEXT IN THE INTERPRETIVE TRADITION

It is worth mentioning that there is possible influence of Nah. 3:8 on Rev. 17:2, which describes the whore of Babylon (Coggins, 14). There are also other instances of influence of Nahum 3 one can see in Rev. 18:3, 22, with its mention of sorcery (see Nah. 3:4); and in Rev. 17:6, with its allusion to Babylon as "drunken with blood" (see Nah. 3:1, 11). Both Nah. 3:1, 7, and Rev. 18:9-19 lament the burning of the city (Spronk, 113). The commentary on Nahum from Qumran regards the "city of blood" in Nah. 3:1 as "the city of Ephraim," meaning "Jerusalem filled with treachery and lies by the Pharisees" and "Amon is Manasseh, that is, the Sadducees" (Spronk, 114). Jerome regards No-of-Amon (Nah. 3:8) as Alexandria, and Cyril interprets the "eater" of 3:13 as Satan. Even more extreme is Luther's interpretation of Nah. 3:5 ("I will lift up your skirts over your face") as the gospel revealing the prostitution of the pope (see Spronk, 114).

▌THE TEXT IN CONTEMPORARY DISCUSSION

A major issue that confronts readers is the stereotyping and humiliation of females. It was argued above that metaphors are keys for interpreting the book of Nahum. However, the metaphors used in Nahum 3 need careful attention since they are offensive to women. Julia O'Brien (2004, 29–30) has rightly argued that the issues addressed here should be understood in terms of the larger underlying gender concern, that of male honor. An understanding of this underlying issue should sensitize contemporary readers of the text to discern and address such issues in their own societies. The text of Nahum should in no way be used to justify unsavory prejudices and ideologies (see also Han, 31–32).

The book of Nahum poses many interpretive challenges. One thing, however, is clear: this short book demands that its readers confront their own beliefs and prejudices.

Works Cited

Baker, David W. 2012. "Book of Nahum." In *Dictionary of the Old Testament Prophets*, edited by Mark J. Boda and J. Gordon McConville, 560–63. Downers Grove, IL: InterVarsity Press.

Berrin, Shani L. 2004. *The Pesher Nahum Scroll from Qumran: An Exegetical Study of 4Q169*. Studies on the Texts of the Desert of Judah 53. Leiden and Boston: Brill.

Coggins, Richard J. 1985. *Nahum, Obadiah, Esther: Israel among the Nations*. Grand Rapids: Eerdmans.

Cyril of Alexandria. 2008. *Commentary on The Twelve Prophets*. Vol. 2. Translated by Robert C. Hill. FC. Washington, DC: Catholic University of America Press.

Floyd, Michael H. 2000. *Minor Prophets*. Part 2. Grand Rapids: Eerdmans.

Han, Jin H. 2011. "Nahum." In *Six Minor Prophets through the Centuries: Nahum, Habakkuk, Zephaniah, Haggai, Zechariah, and Malachi*, by Richard Coggins and Jin H. Han, 7–35. West Sussex: Wiley-Blackwell.

Huddlestun, John R. 2011. "Nahum." In *The Oxford Encyclopedia of the Books of the Bible*, edited by Michael D. Coogan, 100–119. Oxford: Oxford University Press.

Mason, Rex 1991. *Micah, Nahum, Obadiah*. Sheffield: Sheffield Academic.

O'Brien, Julia M. 2002. *Nahum*. Sheffield: Sheffield Academic.

———. 2004. *Nahum, Habakkuk, Zephaniah, Haggai, Zechariah, Malachi*. Nashville: Abingdon.

Petersen, David L. 2002. *The Prophetic Literature: An Introduction*. Louisville: Westminster John Knox.

Roberts, J. J. M. 1991. *Nahum, Habakkuk and Zephaniah*. Louisville: Westminster John Knox.

Schulz, H. 1973. *Das Buch Nahum. Eine redaktionskritische Untersuchung*. Berlin: de Gruyter.

Spronk, Klaas. 1997. *Nahum*. Kampen, the Netherlands: Kok Pharos.

Wessels, Wilhelm J. 2005. "Yahweh, the Awesome God: Perspectives from Nahum 1." *JSem* 14, no. 1:55–73.

HABAKKUK

Hugh R. Page Jr.

Introduction

A work incorporating first-person narrative, oracles, prudential wisdom, liturgical doxologies (2:14, 20), and an ancient (or perhaps archaizing) Hebrew poem, Habakkuk is best understood as a prophetic pastiche presenting the prophetic insights of an impatient sentinel who bravely takes Israel's deity to task for inaction in the face of injustice. Structurally, this seer's complaint is followed by a vision ensuring recompense—one that he is commanded to record (2:2); a doxology (2:20); and a prayer filled with reminiscences of God's power and exploits as Divine Warrior. It concludes with a reaffirmation of trust in YHWH from this emotionally shaken, though confident, visionary. Habakkuk offers an evocative model for context-specific theological reflection and social activism in the twenty-first century, that is, one that in no way limits the agency of those who identify and seek redress for injustice. The book takes seriously the role of the sacred in reform initiatives and allows for the deployment and rearticulation of ancestral traditions as points of reference in fashioning spiritualities of resistance that eschew facile hopes for immediate earthly intervention by a divine patron. It presents readers with, in the words of Cheryl Kirk-Duggan, "a matrix of injustice, theodicy, and triumph" (197).

The date and life setting for the book of Habakkuk are difficult to establish with any degree of certainty. The prophet's name, derived from a Hebrew root meaning "to embrace" or "clasp," suggests that perhaps the one delivering the prophecy has either seized or been emotionally taken by the message relayed in the book. It has been proposed that the oracles in Habakkuk were delivered between 609 and 597 BCE (Roberts, 82–83). Reference to the "raising up" of "the Chaldeans" (1:6), along with the eschatological thrust of its oracles, suggest a sixth-century-BCE origin for this prophetic anthology. The presence of ancient mythological motifs akin to those in Ugaritic and Sumero-Akkadian lore have suggested to some scholars a much earlier date for Hab. 3:1-15 (e.g.,

Hiebert; and Roberts, 84, 151–57). Insofar as the reappropriation of traditions focusing on creation and cosmic warfare is common to biblical literature produced in the exilic period, especially in Isaiah 40–66, this poem may serve as the interpretive fulcrum for the entirety of the book.

Habakkuk 1:1—2:1: An Impatient Seer Calls God to Task

▮ THE TEXT IN ITS ANCIENT CONTEXT

In the popular imagination, prophets, seers, and visionaries are viewed as enjoying a particular closeness to God. For some, that unique connection suggests an implicit harmony, an ongoing meeting of the minds, between the source and recipient of a revelatory experience. However, the Hebrew Bible reveals a far more complex reality. We see evidence of prophets struggling with and seeking to make sense of their vocation and instructions (e.g., Isa. 6:1-13; Jer. 11:18-23; Ezek. 4:9-14; 11:13; 37:3). In Jonah, perhaps the theological linchpin of the Book of the Twelve Minor Prophets, we even have a parody focusing on the fraught relationship between God, seer, and mission. At times, the adversarial relationship between prophet and God is central to the rhetoric and structure of Habakkuk.

The book, which is identified as an oracular record of a vision (i.e., "The oracle that the prophet Habakkuk saw"), opens with the prophet registering a complaint to YHWH, the essence of which can be summed up in a single question: Why in the face of pervasive and enduring "wrongdoing" (1:3) and injustice (1:4) has the LORD failed to act? Operating from the presupposition that the righteous should always triumph over the wicked, a concept echoed in both Deuteronomic (e.g., Deut. 7:12-15) and sapiential traditions (e.g., Prov. 11:8; 12:7), Habakkuk calls Israel's God to task for failing to function as either loving patriarch or omnipotent suzerain.

▮ THE TEXT IN THE INTERPRETIVE TRADITION

Habakkuk has a fascinating interpretive history. Jewish and Christian readers have pondered its more opaque passages and sought to mine its oracles for gems of wisdom to sustain people of faith in times of crisis. The book is a point of reference for several New Testament writers (see the indexes in Aland et al., 888, 900). The Old Greek/Septuagint version of Hab. 1:5 is quoted directly in Acts 13:41 at the conclusion of Paul's homily on salvation history in the synagogue of Antioch. Hebrews 10:37-38 quotes and offers an eschatological interpretation of Hab. 2:3-4. In the Pauline corpus, we find two additional quotations of Hab. 2:4 in Rom. 1:17 and 3:11 respectively. Passages alluding to Habakkuk are found in 2 Pet. 3:9 (Hab. 2:3); 1 Cor. 12:2 (Hab. 2:18-19); and Luke 13:6 (Hab. 3:17).

Biblical manuscripts and a detailed commentary (Hebrew—pesher) exploring the eschatological implications of Habakkuk are extant in the Dead Sea Scrolls corpus. Such indicate the esteem in which the book was held among those for whom the sectarian community founded at Qumran was a spiritual sanctuary. In the Habakkuk pesher (1QpHab), "the wicked," "righteous," and "Chaldeans," referenced in Hab. 1:4, 6, are understood to be the opponents of the community, those aligning themselves with the mysterious "upright teacher," and—perhaps—the armies of the Roman

Empire respectively (Graham, 475; Reventlow, 31–32). Engagement of the book by a vast array of Jewish and Christian interpreters from late antiquity to the modern era illustrates its broad applicability in a variety of life settings (see Graham).

■ THE TEXT IN CONTEMPORARY DISCUSSION

Habakkuk reminds those in all generations to stand at their "watchpost"; speak truth to power, whether spiritual, temporal, or—in some cases—ultimate; and await appropriate responses to any "complaint" made on behalf of those without agency (Hab. 2:1). In our own world, application of the laws maintaining our social fabric all too often appear "slack" (1:4), and justice, it seems, at least for those radically "othered" or at the bottom of our social or economic hierarchies, "never prevails" (1:4). The deaths of Trayvon Martin (Sanford, FL, 2012), Jonathan Ferrell (Charlotte, NC, 2013), and Renisha McBride (Dearborn, MI, 2013); the disproportionate impact that stop-and-frisk practices by the New York City Police Department have on people of color living in the city's boroughs (on which see http://www.nyclu.org/issues/racial-justice/stop-and-frisk-practices, accessed January 27, 2014); and the insensitive representations of Asian peoples and cultures in cinema (e.g., the 2012 movie *Cloud Atlas*) and television (e.g., season 9, episode 14 of the CBS serial *How I Met Your Mother*) raise major concerns about the ways in which negative racial stereotypes influence public perceptions of African Americans and Latino/a cultures in the United States. The marginalization and mistreatment of the LGBTQ community by several mainstream Christian denominations raises comparable concerns. The same can be said regarding policies governing colonization and ideologies (e.g., that of Manifest Destiny) promoting territorial expansion that resulted in the genocide of native peoples here and in others parts of the world. Habakkuk issues a clarion call to those who would assume the prophetic mantle to speak evocatively about what needs to be done to address injustice and set things right.

Habakkuk 2:2-20: The Divine Sovereign Responds— Words to Ponder

■ THE TEXT IN ITS ANCIENT CONTEXT

The LORD provides an intriguing answer to Habakkuk's query, instructing him to record clearly what he is told. Patience is counseled (2:2-3) and a reminder given that the upright should rely on faithfulness to sustain them (2:4). Warnings are given against pride (2:4), wealth, and arrogance (2:5), those who exploit and despoil (2:6-8), those profiting from ill-gotten gain (2:9-11), the bloodthirsty (2:12-13), the wrathful (2:15-17), and idol makers (2:18-19). Two remarkable doxologies are strategically placed in this extensive collection of "Woe" admonitions. The first affirms the pervasive influence of YHWH's presence (2:14). The second demands silence in light of the LORD's presence in the sacred precinct (2.20). The rhetoric of the speech seems intended to elicit awe and reverence rather than directly to address Habakkuk's primary concerns. Sapiential musings that reduce the complexities of human behavior to moral binaries (2:4) offer little solace when injustice is rampant and political upheaval is about to consume one's homeland (1:6).

◼ THE TEXT IN THE INTERPRETIVE TRADITION

Habakkuk 2 has given rise to considerable theological, musical, and esoteric musings. In the Qumran community, Hab. 2:4 is seen as a reference to the upright adherents of Torah teaching (Reventlow, 31). Pauline thought owes undeniable indebtedness to Hab. 2:4. Along with Gen. 15:6, it is certainly one of the texts that inspired the itinerant apostle from Tarsus. M. Patrick Graham has noted fascination with this chapter among Christian apologists ranging from antiquity to the Protestant Reformation, among whom he numbers Cyril of Alexandria, Martin Luther, and John Calvin. He notes that both Luther and Calvin affirmed the christological import of Hab. 2:4 (see Graham, 475–76). Arthur Ainger's nineteenth-century hymn "God Is Working His Purpose Out" is an extended reflection on Hab. 2:14. George Root's hymn "The Lord Is in His Holy Temple" builds a theme expressed in Hab. 2:20 (Carpenter and Williams, 627). In recent years, Hab. 2:2 has been popularized as a mantra for focused pursuit of one's vision by musical artist and preacher the Rev. Joseph Simmons, also known as "DJ Run" of the pioneering rap group Run-D.M.C. (see http://www.youtube.com/watch?v=SC2oh6s6d7o). These passages are likely to continue firing the imaginations of future interpreters.

◼ THE TEXT IN CONTEMPORARY DISCUSSION

In the worldview of the Bible, the God of Israel sheds light on elements of the divine plan to selected women and men from time to time. On some occasions, those celestial communiqués are straightforward responses to queries (Exod. 3:13-15). On others, they are either voluntary disclosures accompanying theophanies (Gen. 12:1-3), or tantalizing clues that have to be either wrestled from mysterious envoys (Gen. 32:22-32), or secured through deft negotiation (Gen. 18:16-33). In a few very special cases, such as Job 38–41 or Hab. 2:2-20, a revelatory experience with the ineffable confronts a seeker with oblique advice shrouded in unfathomable mystery. Many members of today's Jewish and Christian communities would no doubt speak of their relationship with God in similar terms. A stern rebuke like that in Job 38:2—"Who is this that darkens counsel by words without knowledge?"—might cower an anguished soul into accepting its place in the cosmos. A firm admonition like that of Hab. 2:20—"The Lord is in his holy temple; let all the earth keep silence before him!"—might well have the same impact. However, the literary texture of Habakkuk allows for a more nuanced encounter with God and lived experience. Habakkuk, after all, ignores the divine "gag order." He speaks, as should all people of conscience.

Habakkuk 3:1-19: The Prophet Prays with Steely Resolve

◼ THE TEXT IN ITS ANCIENT CONTEXT

In what appears to be an inversion of the pattern encountered in Job 38–41, it is Habakkuk—not YHWH—who has the final word in this high-stakes verbal game of challenge and riposte. It is the prophet who recounts the cosmogonic march from Teman (Hab. 3:3) to rescue the faithful (3:13), acknowledges the devastating realization that disaster in his own world is imminent (3:16), refuses to embrace despair (3:18), and affirms his fidelity to the one who is his "salvation" and "strength" (3:18-19). Inclusion of this ancient poem and the prophet's admonitions to his God makes Habakkuk an instructional manual for those who would make themselves open to the incursions of the spirit without succumbing to the strictures of Deuteronomic thought, the narrow binaries of the sages, the eschatological musings of apocalyptic separatists, or the fatalistic strains expressed in Qohelet (Eccles. 1:1-11).

■ THE TEXT IN THE INTERPRETIVE TRADITION

Habakkuk is an enigmatic figure who—like Enoch, Elijah, Joseph of Arimathea, and Mary Magdalene—spawned fanciful speculation in antiquity, some of which is retained in apocryphal and pseudepigraphic sources (see Bel 33–39; and the *Martyrdom of Isaiah* 2:9). Habakkuk 3, one of the most intriguing chapters of this prophetic anthology, has also received considerable attention. The Septuagint deploys Egyptian solar imagery to make sense of 3:5 (Reventlow, 23). Augustine views the entire poem as discourse between Habakkuk and Jesus (Graham, 475). William Hayes Ward long ago posited that the poem was likely part of liturgical worship in the Jerusalem temple (Ward, 6). Among more recent commentators, Roberts (84) and Anderson (260) argue convincingly that this poem has an ancient pedigree. Many of its interpretive cruxes are intractable and unlikely to be resolved in the near future. Whatever its age or original provenance, it is integral to the canonical form of the book and confronts all readers with the question: Why did Habakkuk lift up this *tefilla* ("prayer"); and why should every subsequent generation of readers follow his example?

■ THE TEXT IN CONTEMPORARY DISCUSSION

In the presence of inexplicable tragedy, few options are left to those who trust that the universe is governed by a compassionate and all-knowing divine sovereign, and yet feel exposed, unprotected, and abandoned. One option is the modification or rejection of one's core beliefs. Another option is to seek communion with—and answers from—that celestial monarch through prayer. Yet a third choice is to reaffirm one's allegiance to and faith in that deity: even in that God's apparent absence. In Habakkuk, we have a model, indeed a *prophetic paradigm*, for seeking connection with, challenging, and asserting continuing fidelity to YHWH. Its main features are steely resolve and a commitment to healing and personal empowerment through "talking back" to—*signifying on* (in *Africana* parlance) as it were—God.

The book of Habakkuk affirms that the one thing of which we are never deprived is our voice, our ability to affirm the painful particularities of our circumstances, and to demand that God hear and respond. As S. D. Snyman has noted, prophets such as Jeremiah and Habakkuk acknowledge that "struggle" is part of the spirituality articulated in Scripture; that there are occasions when God's responses to us "remain incomprehensible"; and that there are those instances when, in confronting ambiguity or apparent divine absence, "conversation with God is in itself enough" (see the summary of Snyman's position in Lombaard, 43). For Kent Keith, author of ten maxims for leadership known as the "Paradoxical Commandments," Habakkuk offers an eleventh adage by which to live: "The world is full of violence, injustice, starvation, disease, and environmental destruction, *Have faith anyway*" (Keith, xiv–xv). The reader can take these proposals an additional step further and suggest that in Habakkuk we are reminded that when confronting despair, the one thing we should *never* do is to remain silent.

Works Cited

Aland, Barbara, Kurt Aland, Johannes Karavidopoulos, Carlo M. Martini, and Bruce M. Metzger, eds. 2005. *The Greek New Testament*. 4th rev. ed. (9th printing). Stuttgart: Deutsche Bibelgesellschaft / United Bible Societies.

Anderson, Francis I. 2001. *Habakkuk*. AB. New York: Doubleday.

Carpenter, Delores, and Nolan Williams, eds. 2001. *African American Heritage Hymnal*. Chicago: GIA.

Graham, M. Patrick. 1999. "Habakkuk, Book of." In *Dictionary of Biblical Interpretation*, edited by John H. Hayes, 475–78. Nashville: Abingdon.

Hiebert, Theodore. 1986. *God of My Victory: The Ancient Hymn in Habakkuk 3*. HSM 38. Atlanta: Scholars Press.

Keith, Kent M. 2008. *Have Faith Anyway: The Vision of Habakkuk for Our Times*. San Francisco: Jossey-Bass.

Kirk-Duggan, Cheryl. 2010. "Habakkuk." In *The Africana Bible: Reading Israel's Scriptures from Africa and the African Diaspora*, edited by Hugh R. Page Jr., 197–201. Minneapolis: Fortress Press.

Lombaard, Christo. 2012. *The Old Testament and Christian Spirituality*. International Voices in Biblical Studies. Atlanta: Society of Biblical Literature.

Reventlow, Henning Graf. 2009. *History of Biblical Interpretation*. Vol. 1, *From the Old Testament to Origen*. Translated by Leo G. Perdue. Resources for Biblical Study. Atlanta: Society of Biblical Literature.

Roberts, J. J. M. 1991. *Nahum, Habakkuk, and Zephaniah*. OTL. Louisville: Westminster John Knox.

Ward, William Hayes. 1911. "A Critical and Exegetical Commentary on Habakkuk." In John Merlin Powis Smith, William Hayes Ward, and Julius August Bewer, *A Critical and Exegetical Commentary on Micah, Zephaniah, Nahum, Habakkuk, Obadiah, and Joel*. New York: Charles Scribner's Sons.

ZEPHANIAH

Jin Hee Han

Introduction

The book of Zephaniah introduces the prophet as the son of Cushi, suggesting an African connection (Bennett 1996, 659), whose lineage includes King Hezekiah of Judah (Zeph. 1:1). The historical background is set in the late seventh century, probably before Josiah's Deuteronomic reform, which removed the kind of religious practices that Zephaniah berated. One of the twelve Minor Prophets, Zephaniah follows Nahum and Habakkuk. The rationale behind the order of the Twelve is not transparent, but Nahum's condemnation of Nineveh and Habakkuk's search for God's justice and grace form a suggestive backdrop to the prophecy of Zephaniah, who announces divine judgment for all nations and salvation for the faithful remnant of Israel. The book is made of the following sections: oracles of doom and destruction (1:2-13); the great day of YHWH (1:14-18); repentance and redemption (2:1-3); oracles against the nations (2:4-15); the remnant of Israel (3:1-13); and the celebration of YHWH rejoicing over the divine work of salvation (3:14-20).

Zephaniah 1:2-13: Doom and Destruction

▮ THE TEXT IN ITS ANCIENT CONTEXT

The prophet sounds an alarm setting forth God's announcement of the total devastation of the world in Zeph. 1:2. The catastrophe will clear away both humans and animals, for corruption has become so extensive as to leave no living thing untouched (1:3). It is going to be even more sweeping than Noah's flood, which did not include the fish of the sea (see Gen. 6:7). The prophet identifies the primary basis of judgment as Judah's worship of other gods. The NRSV translates Zeph. 1:3 as God causing the wicked to stumble, but the original Hebrew actually envisions divine judgment removing "the stumbling blocks along with the wicked" (author's own translation). The prophetic catalog of venerated objects that incurred God's wrath in Judah and Jerusalem includes the Canaanite god Baal, idols, the host of the heaven (referring to the stars), and the Ammonite god Milcom (1:4-5). Zephaniah 1:5b adds another offense: the duplicity of conflating the worship of God with that of Milcom, which may be another name of the deity Molech, who is associated with child sacrifice (see Lev. 18:21; 20:2-5). The honoring of Milcom, whose Hebrew (*malkām* in Zeph. 1:5) can be translated "their king," may also suggest idolatrous worship of human kings (1:5). These wrongful worshipers have committed the offense of abandoning God (1:6).

In Zeph. 1:7, the prophet proclaims the sobering day of YHWH (1:7), anticipating the forthcoming poem "The Great Day of YHWH" (1:14-18). To deal with the rampant corruption that has contaminated the universe, God institutes a sacrificial meal for consecrated guests (1:7). The meaningful worship is set in contrast with the ruinous cult of Judah and Jerusalem. The latter half of 1:7 contains a humorous play on words, making it ambiguous as to whether the guests are to partake of the feast or to be slaughtered as ritual sacrifice. The faithful remnant of Zeph. 3:12-13 would constitute the former kind of guests, while the powerful officials and princes of 1:8 would be the latter.

On the anticipated day of YHWH, God is expected to punish the noble and the royal (1:8b); those dressed in foreign attire (1:8c); those who leap over the thresholds, an imitation of a practice of Canaanite priests (1:9a; see also 1 Sam. 5:4-5); and those who participate in treacherous economic exploitation in the name of loyalty to their master, whether they are serving their king or another god (Zeph. 1:9b). Wailing will be heard throughout Jerusalem in the Fish Gate and the Second Quarter and in the Mortar, which all have been associated with the bustling of profit-seeking commerce (1:10-11a). On the day of God's judgment, both traders and trading will be finished (1:11b). The prophet imagines God searching through Jerusalem with lamps to seek out those who are complacent while denying God's relevance in human affairs (1:12). The prophet predicts the catastrophic collapse of the rich who trust in their wealth more than God (1:13), recalling the curses compiled in Deuteronomy 27–28.

■ THE TEXT IN THE INTERPRETIVE TRADITION

The prophetic oracle of doom in Zeph. 1:2-13 is marked by the vision of God's exhaustive judgment. Judah and Jerusalem are clearly the offenders, but animals are also included in the cosmic carnage. The midrash compares God's action to destroy the whole creation to that of a king who punishes his prince and the teacher who led him astray (*Gen. Rab.* 28.6; cf. *b. Sanh.* 108a). Citing Hosea 4:1-4a and Isa. 59:1-4, Cyprian (546) argues that the thoroughgoing destruction is necessary to purify the polluted creation.

The comprehensive list of offenses that focus on idolatrous worship combines cultic aberrations with economic exploitation and complacency (Zeph. 1:4-8). The internal social ills are linked with the issue of foreign clothing, whose offensive nature may have to do with foreign influence that promotes corruption (Theodore of Mopsuestia, 291). Martin Luther (327) ridicules the donning of foreign clothes in 1:8 as an act of abandoning one's own religion and culture. The rich who profit from godless pursuits will be exposed by God's search through Jerusalem with lamps, which the Jerusalem Talmud imagines as a picture of the Lord, who examines the heart of the people (*y. Pesah.* 27a).

■ THE TEXT IN CONTEMPORARY DISCUSSION

Zephaniah's depiction of cosmic upheaval fuels the modern discussion on faith and ecology. Due to their sins of idolatry and predatory exploitation of nature, human beings risk losing the privileged status described in Gen. 1:28 when they fail to live up to the creator's charge (Kay, 226). The prophetic word threatens to cancel even the covenant of Noah in Genesis 9, which is supposed to be eternal (Berlin, 82). The prophet's critique of a corrupt cult that causes the cosmic catastrophe is in consonance with the idea of faithful worship that enables the worshiper to endure evil and experience order, as Jon D. Levenson charts in *Creation and the Persistence of Evil*.

Zephaniah 1:14-18: The Day of YHWH

■ THE TEXT IN ITS ANCIENT CONTEXT

In Zeph. 1:14-18, the prophet offers a full description of the consequences of the day of YHWH that he mentioned in 1:7 (see also Isa. 13:6, 9, 13; Jer. 30:7; 46:10; Ezek. 30:2-3; Joel 1:15; 2:1-2, 11; Amos 5:18-20; 8:9-14; Mal. 4:5). Following Amos, Zephaniah treats it as a day of disaster for Judah, who may have thought that it was set aside for her enemy nations. The scope of destruction on the day includes the whole earth (echoing Zeph. 1:2), providing a dramatic backdrop to God's salvation of the remnant of Israel in 3:8-20. However, the oracle maintains its focus on those who "have sinned against YHWH" (1:17; see Sweeney 2003, 97).

The day is approaching fast and accompanies ominous cries (1:14). Zephaniah delineates the day as a time of divine wrath and assembles no less than eight words to depict a hopeless situation (1:15). This day of despair reveals enemy forces attacking Judah and Jerusalem (1:16), and the prophet explains the havoc as YHWH's punishment against the sinners (1:17). No treasure will shield them from the attackers when YHWH unleashes sweeping destruction that the prophet hyperbolically presents as the end of "the whole earth" (1:18).

■ THE TEXT IN THE INTERPRETIVE TRADITION

Zephaniah 1:14-18 has been interpreted in a number of ways. Origen (107–13) cites the passage as the source of inspiration for Paul's language in Rom. 2:5-6, which announces the day of God's final judgment and whose darkness is contrasted with God, the light of the spiritual world. Theodore of Mopsuestia (292) interprets the day of YHWH as a specific time in history when God's decrees are fulfilled. Gregory the Great expects the day of YHWH to open up minds that are closed to truth; and for the church, it will be like the day of a wedding marked by "the happiness of the elect, those who will be found worthy to rejoice" (1990, 72). Luther (334–35) calls the day of YHWH a day of Babylonian captivity rather than the final day of history. According to Calvin (226), the oracle of the day of YHWH confirms that there is no salvation apart from God.

THE TEXT IN CONTEMPORARY DISCUSSION

Zephaniah's eschatological expectation of a day when God would restore justice is far from a defeatist's delayed wish fulfillment. It challenges worshipers to seek the redress of contemporary social ills in light of God's concern for the oppressed and sovereignty over history. The prophet's call for justice reverberates in Jürgen Moltmann's theology of hope, which inspires mission in service of justice. The prophet's perspective on the day of YHWH anticipates Wolfhart Pannenberg's eschatology, in which the future facilitates the construction of peace in this world in light of the eschatological kingdom of God.

Zephaniah 2:1-3: Repentance and Protection

THE TEXT IN ITS ANCIENT CONTEXT

In Zeph. 2:1, the prophet calls on the people of Judah, the "shameless nation," to gather together. This imperative of assembly serves as a pun. On the one hand, it summons them to communal repentance; on the other hand, it threatens to dispose of the people like stubbles of grain gathered to be thrown away. The prophet emphasizes that time is running out; each of the three lines of 2:2 begins with the sentence-starter "before." As the doom brewing for the whole world (1:14-18) is about to unleash its destructive forces against the nations (2:4-15), the prophetic word offers the last chance for the humble who have kept the law of the Lord to find the path of salvation, which is to be accomplished through seeking out YHWH and doing God's demands for justice and humility (2:3a). To the urgent exhortation the prophet adds the cautious qualifier "perhaps" (2:3b; see also Amos 5:15), underscoring that deliverance is purely YHWH's doing. It is not the prophet's to guarantee it, much less the outcome of the works of righteousness by the pious. God has set aside the humble among God's people (see also Zeph. 3:12-13), who will be instrumental in Judah's possible salvation (2:3). By contrast, the nations that lack humility and willingness to seek YHWH will meet destruction (2:4-15).

THE TEXT IN THE INTERPRETIVE TRADITION

The midrash finds in Zeph. 2:1 a mandate of self-correction before correcting others, for Judah cannot criticize the sins of other nations or exhort them to follow her example until she first heeds God's call to repentance and is found worthy for God's salvation (*Lam. Rab.* 3:50). Zephaniah's words cause the monastic church father Pachomius (36) to grieve over the imminent end of the age with no adequate instruction in faith available; he attributes the egregious situation to the lack of mortification as a pious practice.

THE TEXT IN CONTEMPORARY DISCUSSION

In his book *Option for the Poor*, Norbert Lohfink observes that Zephaniah displays a distinctive interest in the poor, while most prophets direct their oracles against the kings and the nobles. Lohfink's insight exerts important influence on liberation theology, which observes the link between poverty and spirituality. While the world faces extinction, the poor and the humble on the margin have the possibility of salvation by God (see Sobrino). Through "the orthopraxis of the marginalized," God's peace and justice come true (Bail, 456).

Zephaniah 2:4-15: Against the Nations

▌THE TEXT IN ITS ANCIENT CONTEXT

Oracles against the nations (Philistines, Moabites, Ammonites, Ethiopians, and Assyrians) underscore God's sovereignty over the world. These declarations contain puns in Hebrew whose sound effects are left out in English versions. For example, one could paraphrase the translation as follows: "Gaza shall be zapped; Ashkelon, shattered; Ashdod, pushed away; and Ekron, eradicated" (Zeph. 2:4). The seacoast of Canaan, where Philistines and Cherethites dwell, will be devastated and repopulated by the remnants of Judah (2:5-7). Moab and Ammon will become like Sodom and Gomorrah (Gen. 19:24-38) as a punishment of the offense of humiliating the people who belong to the Lord of Hosts (Zeph. 2:8-10). God's wrath will destroy other gods, and the world will worship God alone (2:11). The Ethiopians, who represent the farthest corner of the world, will also be under God's judgment (2:12). The oracles against the nations conclude with Assyria, for whom these other nations have been vassals. God will annihilate Assyria, the enemy from the north, and its capital city Nineveh for their arrogance (2:13), and their lair will be inhabited by wild animals (2:14-15). The hubris of Nineveh and her dilapidation serve as a lesson of history that promises no eternal glory—no matter how powerful and proud she may be. The tale serves as a comfort for those who have been hurt by her aggression (2:15).

▌THE TEXT IN THE INTERPRETIVE TRADITION

Early church fathers find the spread of the gospel alluded to in the prophet's vision of God whom each will worship in his or her own place. John Chrysostom (2:69–70) regards Zeph. 2:11 and 3:9 as comments on the actualization of Isaiah's peaceable kingdom (Isa. 11:1-9), which will come true when all nations serve God under one yoke in their own place. Based on Zephaniah's vision, Augustine reflects on God who gathers the predestined believers into one body of Christ (2004, 248). In his homily on Psalm 97, Jerome (192) imagines churches secure with Christ as their foundation, although they are like islands beaten by the waves of the ocean. Whereas Luther (340–42) maintains that Judah would also be destroyed, leaving only the faithful remnant to be saved, Calvin (240) acquires a message of hope for Judah, in that divine retribution is moved to other nations.

▌THE TEXT IN CONTEMPORARY DISCUSSION

The prophet underscores God's central role in the course of the history of the nations and their international affairs. Their offenses include worshiping other gods, menacing God's people, and boasting that their power will be eternally secured as exemplified in the pride of Assyria. The prophet's critical assessment of proud nations lends a theological corrective to political powers that seek their glory and preservation by imperial militarism that threatens the livelihood of other nations, and also by exploitative colonialism that leaves other peoples impoverished. This theme provides biblical support for postcolonial interpreters and those who combat ills of imperialism in the contemporary world.

Zephaniah 3:1-13: The Remnant of Israel

▌THE TEXT IN ITS ANCIENT CONTEXT

Commentators debate over whether one should read Zeph. 3:1-13 as condemning Judah or other nations. The identity of the city denounced in 3:1 is ambiguous. Does "the oppressing city" refer to Nineveh or Jerusalem? The immediately preceding passage may invite one to posit that the verse is a continuation of the oracle against Assyria in 2:13-15; however, the ensuing verses reveal that Judah is being depicted in 3:1 as the place of the impurity and oppression.

The first offense of the city is the rejection of instructive correction and trust in God (3:2). Its evil outcome manifests itself in the societal ills marked by rampages of rapacious political leaders and irresponsible religious leaders (3:3-4). The main offenders are leaders: officials, judges, prophets, and priests, all of whom the prophet casts with beastly images. The inclusion of judges among the culprits may represent the collapse of the system of justice. By contrast, YHWH's rule is marked by justice (3:5). God expects the judgment against the nations to be a good lesson for the oppressing city that needs cleansing, but the city compounds her guilt by rejecting correction and exacerbating corruption (3:6-7).

Recalling the day of YHWH in Zephaniah 1, the prophet announces that God will initiate legal proceedings against the oppressing city, render a verdict, and execute her punishment, which will affect the whole world (3:8). The time of judgment will be followed by a new era, when the pure community emerges, transformed to worship God in unity (3:9-10). The day will reveal that, whereas the proud who have rebelled against God will be removed (3:11), the humble remnant will find security in God's presence, empowering them to do right (3:12-13).

▌THE TEXT IN THE INTERPRETIVE TRADITION

The Hebrew homonym *yônâ* in 3:1 could mean either "oppressing" or "dove." The Septuagint construes it as "dove," and the midrash adds another pun by scathing the city for acting like a dove and ignoring the lesson from Nineveh the city of Jonah (*yônâ*; *Lam. Rab.*, proem 31). Theodore of Mopsuestia (299) regards the dove as signifying Israel, which is charming but refuses to trust in YHWH. Luther (349) suspects that by the "dove" the prophet secretively refers to the Holy Spirit present in Jerusalem.

Cyprian (555) construes the prophet's call for patience (3:8) as a charge to wait for the day when God avenges the wrongs that the faithful go through during the time of persecution. The prophet's vision of "pure speech" (3:9) leads the medieval Jewish philosopher Ibn Ezra to argue that it means the universal use of Hebrew (*Commentary on Ecclesiastes* 5.1). The image of the pure speech and one accord (3:9) provides Gregory the Great (1844–1850, 2:541–42) with the vision of the universal worship of God. Augustine (1998, 868–69) concludes that the prophet speaks of the day when the world will worship God.

THE TEXT IN CONTEMPORARY DISCUSSION

The prophet's criticism of leadership portrays how the people suffer when leaders fail to do what they are called to do and, more seriously, when they do the opposite, as Sweeney observes with the prophets and priests (2000, 520). Civil rights activist Howard Thurman (1028–29) charges modern religious workers to pay attention to Zephaniah's criticism of prophets and priests so that they may not fall into the pit of professional banality and the loss of moral sensitivity. Christian Marxist writer José Miranda (120) finds God waging a war of liberation against the powerful oppressors in Zeph. 3:1-13. God places the oppressors under judgment, and Israel's humble remnant will see God's salvation.

Zephaniah 3:14-20: The Jubilation of YHWH

THE TEXT IN ITS ANCIENT CONTEXT

The book ends with an uplifting message of hope that dwells on the glorious prospect of the salvation of Israel. Jerusalem, the "daughter Zion" that represents Israel, is exhorted to sing a song of jubilation (3:14), for Judah has been saved by YHWH, the king of Israel, who now fills Jerusalem with courage (3:15-16). The book reaches its climax in the portrayal of the divine warrior (see also Exod. 15:3), who fights on behalf of God's people and takes delight in the people who have been saved (Zeph. 3:17). The NRSV's rendering of God, who "will renew you in his love" (3:17), is based on the Greek and the Syriac. The Hebrew says, "He will be silent in his love" (author's own translation), which ironically juxtaposes the scene of God engaged in loud jubilation in the same verse. The Hebrew could be translated alternatively as "[God] will bring you to silence," creating a picture of God soothing the people (Roberts, 220, 222). God is restoring the joy of feast, taking away guilt and disaster (3:18). In the reversal of fortunes, God who expels Jerusalem's internal oppressors and external aggressors will heal the poor who have suffered at their hands (3:19). God will bring those who were dispersed in humiliation, and their restoration will be a theme of praise for the whole world (3:20).

THE TEXT IN THE INTERPRETIVE TRADITION

The Targum finds in the "Song of Zephaniah" (3:14-20) a depiction of the Lord dwelling among the people through Shekinah (the manifestation of God's presence among the people). The Talmud depicts the messianic end time as "when the highhanded disappear from Israel" (*b. Sanh.* 98a). The coming of the Messiah and the restoration of Israel based on Zeph. 3:20 is reflected in the traditional Jewish liturgy.

Cyril of Jerusalem (117–18) derives the blessing for candidates of baptism from the exhortation to sing and rejoice over God's deliverance. Zephaniah's vision of God's joy inspires Theodoret of

Cyrus (218) to dwell on the love of God in Christ, who gives his life. Theodore of Mopsuestia (304) constructs a scene in which God the king removes troubles and restores Zion out of divine love. The reversal of fortunes reminds Luther (364) of the early martyrs who were despised like refuse, but are now signs of blessings. Now God's song causes the redeemed to give thanks to the Lord, for in this unusual passage God sets aside divine majesty to show love for the redeemed (Calvin, 304). The Baptist preacher Charles Haddon Spurgeon (271) lifts up the unique nature of this scene of divine jubilation, recalling that God did not sing at the creation and simply rated it as "very good" (Gen. 1:31), but redemption gives joy to the Trinity.

■ The Text in Contemporary Discussion

Zephaniah portrays God as the divine warrior, a depiction deeply rooted in the ancient conceptual world of Old Testament times (see Miller). The militaristic overtone of this portrayal of God is troublesome for contemporary sensitivities that value peace, and some interpreters warn against the danger of using divine violence to legitimate individual and nationalistic pursuits as God's will (Heffelfinger, 341). Most significantly, the divine warrior in Zeph. 3:14-20, and elsewhere in the Bible, exerts divine power on behalf of the people who have no one else to whom they can turn. The book that began with the prospect of the world's annihilation caused by the people and their leaders—along with their national self-aggrandizement—then concludes with God's exuberance over the divine work of salvation. The prophet calls on the redeemed to join with the song of joy and thanksgiving for God, who alone can save.

Works Cited

Augustine of Hippo. 1998. *The City of God against the Pagans*. Cambridge Texts in the History of Political Thought. Cambridge: Cambridge University Press.

———. 2004. *Letters 156–210*. WSA II/3. Hyde Park, NY: New City Press.

Bail, Ulrike. 2012. "Zephaniah; or The Threefold Jerusalem." In *Feminist Biblical Interpretation: A Compendium of Critical Commentary on the Books of the Bible and Related Literature*, edited by Luise Schottroff and Marie-Theres Wacker, 450–59. Grand Rapids: Eerdmans.

Bennett, R. A. 1996. "Zephaniah." In *The New Interpreter's Bible*. Vol. 7, *Introduction to Apocalyptic Literature, Daniel, and the Minor Prophets*, edited by Leander E. Keck, 657–704. Nashville: Abingdon.

Berlin, Adele. 1994. *Zephaniah: A New Translation with Introduction and Commentary*. AB 25A. New York: Doubleday.

Calvin, John. 1984. *A Commentary on the Twelve Minor Prophets*. Vol. 4. Translated by John Owen. Geneva Series Commentary. Edinburgh: Banner of Truth Trust.

Chrysostom, John. 1998. *Commentary on the Psalms*. 2 vols. Translated by Robert C. Hill. Brookline, MA: Holy Cross Orthodox Press.

Coggins, Richard, and Jin H. Han. 2011. *Six Minor Prophets through the Centuries*. Blackwell Bible Commentaries. Chichester, UK: Wiley-Blackwell.

Cyprian. 1978. "The Treatises." In *ANF* 5:421–564.

Cyril of Jerusalem. 1969. *The Works of Saint Cyril of Jerusalem*. Vol. 1. Translated by Leo P. McCauley, SJ, and Anthony A. Stephenson. FC 61. Washington, DC: Catholic University of America Press.

Ferreiro, Alberto, ed. 2003. *The Twelve Prophets*. Ancient Christian Commentary on Scripture, Old Testament 14. Downers Grove, IL: InterVarsity Press.

Gregory the Great. 1844–1850. *Morals on the Book of Job*. Vol. 2. Library of Fathers of the Holy Catholic Church 21. Oxford: Parker.

———. 1990. *Forty Gospel Homilies*. Translated by David Hurst. CS 123. Kalamazoo, MI: Cistercian.

Heffelfinger, Katie M. 2012. "Zephaniah." In *Women's Bible Commentary*, edited by Carol A. Newsom, Sharon H. Ringe, and Jacqueline E. Lapsley, 339–42. 3rd ed. Louisville: Westminster John Knox.

Jerome. 1964. *The Homilies of Saint Jerome*. Vol. 1. Translated by Sister Marie Liguori Ewald, IHM. FC. 48. Washington, DC: Catholic University of America Press.

Kay, Jeanne. 1989. "Human Dominion over Nature in the Hebrew Bible." *Annals of the Association of American Geographers* 79:214–32.

Levenson, Jon D. 1988. *Creation and the Persistence of Evil: The Jewish Drama of Divine Omnipotence*. San Francisco: Harper & Row.

Lohfink, Norbert F. 1987. *Option for the Poor: The Basic Principle of Liberation Theology in the Light of the Bible*. Translated by Linda Maloney. Berkeley, CA: Bibal.

Luther, Martin. 1975. *Luther's Works*. Vol. 18, *Lectures on the Minor Prophets I*. Edited by Hilton C. Oswald. St. Louis: Concordia.

Miller, Patrick D. 1973. *The Divine Warrior in Early Israel*. HSM 5. Cambridge, MA: Harvard University Press.

Miranda, José Porfirio. 1974. *Marx and the Bible: A Critique of the Philosophy of Oppression*. Maryknoll, NY: Orbis.

Moltmann, Jürgen. 1967. *Theology of Hope: On the Ground and the Implications of a Christian Eschatology*. New York: Harper & Row.

Origen of Alexandria. 2001. *Commentaries on the Epistle to the Romans: Books 1–5*. Translated by Thomas P. Scheck. FC 103. Washington, DC: Catholic University of America Press.

Pachomian Koinonia: Instructions, Letters, and Other Writings of Saint Pachomius and His Disciples. 1982. Vol. 3. CS 47. Kalamazoo, MI: Cistercian.

Pannenberg, Wolfhart. 1984. "Constructive and Critical Functions of Christian Eschatology." *HTR* 77:119–39.

Roberts, J. J. M. 1991. *Nahum, Habakkuk, and Zephaniah: A Commentary*. OTL. Louisville: Westminster John Knox.

Sobrino, Jon. 1984. *The True Church and the Poor*. Maryknoll, NY: Orbis.

Spurgeon, C. H. 1992. *Faith's Checkbook: A Devotional*. New Kensington, PA: Whitaker House.

Sweeney, Marvin A. 2000. *The Twelve Prophets*. Vol. 2. Berit Olam. Collegeville, MN: Liturgical Press.

———. 2003. *Zephaniah: A Commentary*. Hermeneia. Minneapolis: Fortress Press.

Theodore of Mopsuestia. 2004. *Commentary on the Twelve Prophets*. Translated by Robert C. Hill. FC 108. Washington, DC: Catholic University of America Press.

Theodoret of Cyrus. 2006. *Commentary on the Prophets*. Vol. 3. Translated by Robert C. Hill. Brookline, MA: Holy Cross Orthodox Press.

Thurman, Howard. 1956. "The Book of Zephaniah: Exposition." In *The Interpreter's Bible*. Vol. 6, *Lamentations; Ezekiel; Daniel; Hosea; Joel; Amos; Obadiah; Jonah; Micah; Nahum; Habakkuk; Zephaniah; Haggai; Zechariah; Malachi*, edited by George A. Buttrick, 1007–36. New York: Abingdon-Cokesbury.

HAGGAI

J. Blake Couey

Introduction

The book of Haggai contains one of the Bible's clearest pictures of early postexilic Jerusalem. Its four units mix prophetic speeches with brief narrative segments. Each unit has a specific date, together covering a period of four months in 520 BCE. It describes the work of the prophet Haggai, whose name is fittingly related to the Hebrew word for "festival." Haggai encourages his community to rebuild and rededicate the temple of YHWH in Jerusalem, which had been destroyed by the Babylonians in 587 BCE (Hag. 1:1—2:19). He also makes bold but cryptic promises concerning Zerubbabel, the governor of Judah and a descendant of King David (2:20-23). Haggai's vision of postexilic Jerusalem is thus thoroughly traditionalist, seeking some degree of restoration for the two most important institutions of the preexilic period—the temple, and the monarchy.

In its final form, the book celebrates Haggai's success as a prophet—an unusual phenomenon in the Hebrew Bible, as other prophets typically face great opposition (e.g., Jer. 26:7-11; Amos 7:10-13)—and reaffirms the centrality of the second temple in postexilic Judaism (Petersen, 36). The prophecies in Zechariah 1–8 concern similar issues and are dated around the same time; consequently, some commentators have proposed that the two books are an editorial unity (e.g., Meyers and Meyers, xliv-xlviii), but others disagree. Haggai and Zechariah were remembered for their roles in the reconstruction of the temple in Ezra 5:1; 6:14.

Haggai has received minimal attention from later interpreters. Selected texts appear in discussions of ritual purity or the character of God in rabbinic Jewish sources, and a few verses have attracted notice in Christianity for their perceived christological significance. The book may likewise seem to hold little significance for contemporary readers; however, it is a helpful model for encouraging a hurting, disillusioned community, and it offers profound reflections on the connections between past, present, and future during times of rapid change. Its ambivalent attitude toward the Persian Empire also deserves attention in a global, postcolonial age.

Haggai 1:1-15: Rebuilding the Temple

▎ THE TEXT IN ITS ANCIENT CONTEXT

This unit opens with a prophetic speech criticizing the postexilic community for their hesitancy to rebuild the temple (Hag. 1:1-11). Although it concerns the larger community, it is addressed to "Zerubbabel . . . governor of Judah" and "Joshua . . . the high priest" (1:1), who are also remembered for their leadership in Ezra and Zechariah. The term "governor" refers to a position of political authority in the Persian administrative system, although it is unclear precisely how much power the governor of Judah would have held at this time. The position of high priest gained increased power in the postexilic period in the absence of the monarchy.

Ezra 3 suggests that the foundations of the new temple had been laid when the first Judean exiles returned from Babylon in 538 BCE. Haggai 1 is set eighteen years later (1:1), and the temple remained unfinished. For Haggai, this is an affront to YHWH's honor (1:8). In ancient Near Eastern religion, temples were understood as the locus of divine presence on earth. The concern for building a "house" for Baal in Ugaritic myths suggests that the lack of a temple diminished a deity's status. According to Ezra 4:4-5, the delay in rebuilding the temple resulted from conflict between the returning exiles and local populations, but Haggai blames it solely on the indolence of the people, who are more concerned with the state of their own homes (Hag. 1:4, 9). Scholars disagree over the translation of the Hebrew *sapun* (NRSV "paneled") in verse 4. In other biblical texts, it refers to fine cedar paneling (e.g., 1 Kgs. 7:3; Jer. 22:14). Some commentators suggest that, by itself, the word simply means "covered" or "roofed," and that the postexilic Jewish community would not have been able to afford such luxurious homes (e.g., O'Brien, 142–43). Haggai's description, however, may be rhetorically exaggerated to heighten the contrast between the people's houses and YHWH's house (Petersen, 48–49). The community's attitude contrasts sharply with David's anxiety in 2 Sam. 7:2 that he lives in a palace while the deity lacks a temple. The prophet does acknowledge the difficulties faced by the postexilic community in Hag. 1:5-11, but he explains their lack of prosperity as the result of YHWH's anger. The language of these verses echoes biblical and ancient Near Eastern futility curses associated with broken treaties or covenants (Kessler, 130–33; cf., e.g., Lev. 26:26; Deut. 28:38, 48). Other prophets similarly understand drought and other natural disasters as divine punishments (e.g., Hosea 2:9, 12; Amos 4:7-10).

Haggai 1:12-15 is a narrative recounting the community's response to Haggai's speech (1:12-15). Resumption of work on the temple is attributed simultaneously to multiple causes: the leadership of Zerubbabel and Joshua, the initiative of the community, the prophetic encouragement of Haggai, and the empowerment of YHWH's spirit. Even before the work has resumed, God already promises to be "with" the people in Hag. 1:13, echoing similar promises from other prophetic books (e.g., Isa. 7:14; 43:2). It is this promise that motivates them to rebuild the temple. Some commentators treat these verses as a separate unit from the rest of the chapter, due to the parallel date formulas in verses 1 and 15 (e.g., Petersen, 55–60). Rather than marking a separate pericope, however, the second formula underscores Haggai's success as a prophet by quantifying the speediness with which the people responded to his message.

Haggai supported Persia's imperial agenda, although perhaps unintentionally, through his passionate advocacy for rebuilding the temple. Local temples were an integral part of the Persian administrative system, which explains their financial support for temple construction (see Ezra 6:8-9). The references to Darius and the use of Persian regnal years in dating formulas further reinforce the validity of their rule. Although the construction of the second temple served Persian interests, it also played an indispensable role in the survival of the postexilic community. The temple would become the chief symbol of their identity and the center of their religious activity, as seen in later texts, such as 1–2 Chronicles and Malachi.

∎ The Text in the Interpretive Tradition

The single-minded focus on the temple in this unit has been a problem for many Christian readers; Augustine, John Calvin, and the editors of the Geneva Bible, among others, understood the text to refer to the "spiritual" temple composed of believers, with reference to 1 Cor. 3:16-17 (Ferreiro, 22; Coggins, 137). Nonetheless, interpreters have been able to connect individual verses to particular Christian beliefs or practices; for instance, Calvin saw in Hag. 1:13 a proof text for election through divine grace. A lack of sympathy for Haggai's project persists among some modern commentators, who dismiss the prophet's concerns as excessively nationalistic. The potentially anti-Judaic overtones of such readings have been noted by more recent interpreters (Kessler, 2–4; O'Brien, 137–38).

∎ The Text in Contemporary Discussion

In today's world, many disenfranchised persons find themselves in situations like that described in Haggai 1, such as residents of distressed neighborhoods or refugee and migrant communities. This unit demonstrates the difficult balance that must be maintained when challenging such groups to action. Haggai's explanation of the people's hardships may come across as victim blaming, yet his words helped counteract their feeling of powerlessness. How does one honor the agency of persons in distress without reductively attributing their complex situations to their own choices? The prophet's demand that the people rebuild the temple before repairing their own homes also raises questions. While it may be appropriate to expect individuals to make economic sacrifices for the good of their communities, at what point does it become unjust to ask persons who are already economically distressed to ignore their own well-being?

It is difficult for contemporary readers to appreciate fully the tremendous importance of the temple for the postexilic Jewish community. Nonetheless, Christian readers should avoid using this unit to caricature Second Temple Judaism as materialistic or nationalistic, as some interpreters have done. The temple functioned as a tangible symbol of God's presence with the community and their continued status as God's people. To understand the concerns of the text more sympathetically, one might think of the trauma experienced by congregations whose places of worship have been vandalized or destroyed.

Haggai 2:1-9: Disappointment and Hope

▌ THE TEXT IN ITS ANCIENT CONTEXT

Nearly one month after the previous episode (Hag. 2:1), some members of the postexilic Jewish community were disappointed by the edifice that they had begun rebuilding. Over sixty-five years after the first temple was destroyed, it is doubtful that many in Haggai's audience could actually remember it (but see Ezra 3:12), yet it looms in their collective memory as a sign of a better past. Other prophetic texts portray preexilic Judah as a nation plagued by inequality (e.g., Isa. 1:10-17), however, suggesting that the temple's "former glory" resulted in part from oppressive policies toward the poor and vulnerable. Haggai agrees that the second temple cannot compare to its predecessor, but he minimizes that difference by referring to the two structures as if they were the same building (Kessler, 165–67).

In Hag. 2:4-5, the prophet encourages the people using language that occurs throughout the Hebrew Bible. These references to familiar traditions subtly but powerfully reestablish the community's connection to their history (Kessler, 170–71). The admonition "take courage" (Heb. *hazaq*, literally "be strong") is especially associated with Joshua, the successor to Moses (Deut. 31:7; Josh. 1:6), and it may be used here to connect the postexilic high priest with his earlier namesake. The command "do not fear" is a staple of salvation oracles in Isaiah (e.g., Isa. 35:4; 41:10). Verse 5 evokes the exodus traditions, situating the current community in their ongoing covenantal relationship with YHWH.

The focus shifts to the future in Hag. 2:6-9, which announces imminent divine activity. Again, the prophet relies on traditional themes. The verb "shake" (Hebrew *ra'ash*) in verses 6-7 occurs frequently in descriptions of cosmic upheaval accompanying YHWH's appearance (e.g., Judg. 5:4; Ps. 18:7). Verse 7 evokes another familiar motif, the pilgrimage of foreign nations to Jerusalem (e.g., Isa. 2:2). As in other exilic and postexilic texts, these nations financially support the community in Jerusalem (Isa. 45:14; 61:6). Here, their support does not appear to be offered willingly, and it is only their wealth—not the nations themselves—that comes to Jerusalem. The suggestion that the temple's construction would be funded by foreign wealth obliquely acknowledges its funding by the Persians. By reframing this support as the result of divine activity rather than an imperial handout, however, Haggai undercuts claims of Persian supremacy. In verse 9, YHWH promises to bless the temple with *shalom*; in this instance, "prosperity" is an appropriate translation of the Hebrew term, but its range of meanings also includes "peace" and "wholeness."

▌ THE TEXT IN THE INTERPRETIVE TRADITION

Haggai 2:6-9 has received more interpretive attention than other parts of the book. The phrase "treasure of all nations" in verse 7, which could also be translated "desire of all nations" (e.g., Vulgate; KJV), has traditionally been taken as a reference to Christ. Allusions appear in music for Advent and Christmas, such as Handel's *Messiah* or the hymn "O Come, O Come, Emmanuel." Other interpreters, including Augustine, associated it with Christ's second coming (Ferreiro, 226). Similarly, verse 6 is quoted in Heb. 12:26-27—the only unmistakable quotation from Haggai in the

New Testament—with eschatological overtones. For many Christian readers, the promised "splendor" in Hag. 2:9 is also fulfilled by Christ. In rabbinic Jewish texts, it is taken as a prediction of the greater size of the second temple (Coggins, 147; Neusner, 67–68), which Calvin accepts as a valid but partial fulfillment of the prophecy.

◼ THE TEXT IN CONTEMPORARY DISCUSSION

During times of rapid change, it can be tempting to look back wistfully on a selectively remembered past. While space should be allowed for appropriate grief, this sense unit cautions us that excessive indulgence in nostalgia may hinder a community from living wholeheartedly into its future. Moreover, the text encourages us to be sensitive to persons with very different experiences of the past. Some white Americans, for example, have positive memories of the 1950s, while many African Americans remember the same period as a time of institutionalized segregation and racial injustice. The "good old days" were not equally good for everyone.

The denigration of foreign nations in verses 7-8 might make contemporary readers uncomfortable, especially in contexts in which hypernationalism poses problems. One should remember that these words were written for a community adjusting to imperial subjugation. It may be unrealistic and even unfair to expect victims of recent injustice to forswear resentment against their oppressors—especially when one's instinctive sympathies lie with the oppressors. Most contemporary American readers of Haggai, after all, have far more in common with citizens of the Persian Empire than the postexilic Jewish community.

Haggai 2:10-19: Ritual Questions

◼ THE TEXT IN ITS ANCIENT CONTEXT

In Hag. 2:11-13, the prophet asks the priests for a "ruling" on two scenarios concerning "holy" and "unclean" objects. As understood in the ancient world, uncleanness is a state of ritual impurity that impedes contact with the deity. It is not the same thing as sinfulness, although there is overlap between the categories. The transmission of uncleanness via dead bodies, which is the premise for Haggai's second scenario, is discussed in Num. 19:11-22.

The priests' rulings indicate that uncleanness can be easily transmitted, but ritual holiness cannot. Based on these rulings, Haggai declares the people's "work" unclean in verse 14. It is not clear to whom he refers. Some commentators have argued that he means the Samaritans, whom the returned exiles would have regarded suspiciously. Although Ezra 4 describes tension between the two groups at the time of the temple's reconstruction, the book of Haggai shows no awareness of such conflict. Recent scholarship generally assumes that the verse refers to the entire postexilic community. Apparently, they had begun to make offerings again, but the temple structure had not been sufficiently consecrated. As a result, their offerings became unclean through contact with the impure altar, and that uncleanness was transmitted to all of their agricultural produce ("work of their hands," Hag. 2:14).

Nonetheless, the tone of verses 15-19 is largely positive. The prophet promises that their fortunes will change dramatically once some task related to the temple's reconstruction is completed (2:15, 18). Verse 18 implies that this task would be completed on the same day as the proclamation of the oracle. It cannot simply be the rebuilding of the temple, which the previous units indicate had been going on for two months. The reference to the "foundation" in verse 17 probably indicates the formal dedication of the temple, involving a ceremonial foundation stone (see Ezra 3:10-11; Zech. 4:9); ancient evidence confirms the existence of a similar ritual in Babylon (Petersen, 88–90). As a result of this ceremony, the community would be able to offer acceptable sacrifices again, restoring their contact with the deity and making future blessings possible (2:19).

◼ THE TEXT IN THE INTERPRETIVE TRADITION

Not surprisingly, given its concerns with purity issues, this unit has been more significant in Jewish interpretation than in Christian interpretation. The Jerusalem Talmud, for instance, depicts a spirited rabbinic debate over whether the priests answered Haggai's questions correctly and suggests that Haggai cursed the people by declaring their offerings unclean (Coggins, 148; Neusner, 49–51).

◼ THE TEXT IN CONTEMPORARY DISCUSSION

For the same reasons that traditional Christian interpretation has largely ignored this unit, some contemporary readers may have difficulty sympathizing with its concerns—particularly readers from Protestant traditions that place little value on ritual. Nonetheless, these verses encourage reflection upon the character of God and the nature of worship.

For Haggai, ritual is only effective when specific expectations are met. Other prophetic texts famously condemn thoughtless or hypocritical worship, such as Amos 5:21-24, yet Haggai cautions that good intentions do not always make worship acceptable to God. Ritual actions belong to complex symbolic systems informed by rich traditions, apart from which their meaning may be compromised. At the same time, the people are not without recourse. God communicates to them through priests and prophets, making it clear how divine demands can be satisfied so that God may bless the people.

Haggai 2:20-23: A Promise to Zerubbabel

◼ THE TEXT IN ITS ANCIENT CONTEXT

The speech in Hag. 2:20-23 has the same date as the previous unit. Directed to Zerubbabel, it is the only speech in the book addressed to a single individual. Verse 21 repeats language from Hag. 2:6 to announce future divine activity, although without the same sense of imminence. In verse 23, the phrase "that day" resonates with "this day" in Hag. 2:18, placing the temple dedication on the same trajectory as these future events. The climax of these events is the divine election of Zerubbabel, a descendant of King David (1 Chron. 3:19). Appropriately, Hag. 2:23 uses language associated with David, including the term "servant" (2 Sam. 7:5; Ps. 132:10) and the verbs "take" (2 Sam. 7:8) and "choose" (Ps. 78:70). The promise to "make [Zerubbabel] like a signet ring" alludes to Jer.

21:24-25, in which the exiled King Jehoiachin/Jeconiah—Zerubbabel's grandfather—is compared to a signet ring removed from YHWH's finger. The reversal of that image may imply the restoration of the Davidic monarchy, especially if Persia is imagined as one of the "kingdoms" overthrown in Hag. 2:22. Such hopes are only given restrained expression, though, and even that is deferred to the future. While the oracle stops short of advocating rebellion against Persia, it is surely no accident that the first verse in the book acknowledges Darius's kingship, but the final verse announces Zerubbabel's election.

This oracle might seem out of place following units that focused on the temple. Temple building and repair, however, were chiefly royal prerogatives in the ancient world. The Davidic monarchy and the Jerusalem temple were closely connected institutions in preexilic Judah (2 Samuel 7; 1 Kings 8). It would only have been natural, then, for Zerubbabel's role in the reconstruction of the temple to have forced the question of his royal status, and this connection is even clearer in Zech. 6:11-13.

◼ THE TEXT IN THE INTERPRETIVE TRADITION

The messianic implications of these verses were not lost on early Christian interpreters, who regarded Zerubbabel as a prototype of Christ. For example, Ambrose connected the signet ring language in Hag. 2:23 with that in Song 8:6, which was also interpreted christologically (Ferreiro, 229). Rabbinic Jewish interpreters noted the connection between Jer. 21:24 and Hag. 2:23, which they harmonized by supposing that Jehoiachin must have repented, causing God to rescind the oath that Jehoiachin's line would cease (Neusner, 55–56).

◼ THE TEXT IN CONTEMPORARY DISCUSSION

Despite its cautious depiction of the future, this text almost certainly raised expectations that were disappointed. We do not know what happened to Zerubbabel. Persian rule persisted for another two centuries, only to be replaced by Greek and then Roman rule, and the Davidic family seems to have faded in prominence. We should recognize that this text contains a failed promise, a problem that is only partially mitigated by its association with Christ in the Christian tradition. How does one navigate the theological questions raised by this claim? At the very least, we should remember that speaking about God's future activity remains incredibly risky, even when undertaken with great care. Persons of faith might even find it reassuring that God is not limited by our hopes for the future but remains free to act in new and surprising ways.

Works Cited

Calvin, John. 1950. *Commentaries on the Twelve Minor Prophets*. Translated by John Owen. Grand Rapids: Eerdmans.

Coggins, Richard, and Jin H. Han. 2011. *Six Minor Prophets through the Centuries*. Blackwell Bible Commentaries. Malden, MA: Wiley-Blackwell. [Cited as Coggins]

Ferreiro, Alberto, ed. 2003. *The Twelve Prophets*. Ancient Christian Commentary on Scripture, Old Testament 14. Downers Grove, IL: InterVarsity Press.

Kessler, John. 2002. *The Book of Haggai: Prophecy and Society in Early Persian Yehud*. VTSup 91. Leiden: Brill.

Meyers, Carol L., and Eric M. Meyers. 1987. *Haggai, Zechariah 1–8*. AB 25B. New York: Doubleday.

Neusner, Jacob. 2007. *Zephaniah, Haggai, Zechariah, and Malachi in Talmud and Midrash: A Source Book*. Lanham, MD: University Press of America.

O'Brien, Julia M. 2004. *Nahum, Habakkuk, Zephaniah, Haggai, Zechariah, Malachi*. AbOTC. Nashville: Abingdon.

Petersen, David L. 1984. *Haggai and Zechariah 1–8*. OTL. Philadelphia: Westminster.

ZECHARIAH

Amy Erickson

Introduction

The superscriptions in Zechariah 1–8 (Zech. 1:1, 7; 7:1) locate Zechariah's prophetic activity in the early reign of the Persian king Darius (520–518 BCE), prior to the completion of the Second Temple (dedicated in 515 BCE). Haggai's prophetic activity dates roughly to the same period (see Ezra 5:1; 6:14), and for both prophets, the rebuilding of the temple is an essential precursor to the realization of the postexilic community's future prosperity and well-being. Zechariah 1–8 consists of a series of vision reports framed by hortatory speeches. The apocalyptic prophecies in Zechariah 9–14, while difficult to situate historically with any precision, reflect a later time period, perhaps the mid-fifth century BCE. At that time, Greece's program of military expansion led the Persians to fortify the empire's western borders, resulting in an increased military presence in the province of Yehud (Petersen 1995; Cook 2011). Given these differences, the majority of scholars divide Zechariah into two (Zechariah 1–8; 9–14) or even three (Zechariah 1–8; 9–11; 12–14) discrete collections.

While readers will appreciate the different themes and literary styles in the two parts of the book, there is continuity across the material as well. The book as a whole expresses a priestly theology, similar to that reflected in Ezekiel and the Holiness strands of the Pentateuch (Leviticus 17–26). Also evident in both parts of the book is an apocalyptic worldview. While the apocalyptic literary features in Zechariah 1–8 appear in a more nascent form ("proto-apocalyptic"), they are evident in the prophet's radical eschatology and in the sharp distinctions Zechariah makes between the present time and the coming age, heaven and earth, and the faithful and the wicked (Cook 1995, 125–33). Although Zechariah 9–14 is not a full-blown apocalypse, many of the hallmarks of apocalyptic thought take clearer form in the second part of the book (Collins). This material details not only God's disruptive entrance into the earthly plane at the start of the coming new age and a final battle waged in Jerusalem, but also the tribulation and suffering that a portion of humanity must endure prior to the divine implementation of a new age.

Both parts of the book arise from experience of life in Yehud (formerly Judah), a colony in the Persian Empire. The population of Yehud consists of returnees from exile in Babylon, the nondeported population of the land, inhabitants of Samaria, and officials from the Persian Empire (who may also be returnees). That there were tensions among these groups is evident in the books of Ezra and Nehemiah. For its part, the book of Zechariah refers to these groups, but the distinctions between them figure minimally in his visions of restoration.

The nature of prophetic books produced during the Persian period reflects changes in practices of reading, writing, preaching, and teaching. In contrast to prophets from earlier periods who were depicted as preaching God's word channeled through them to a "live audience" (e.g., Jeremiah 7), after the exile, the locus of revelation begins to shift from the mouth of the prophet to the word on the scroll (Sommer). While the prophet's oral performance of his message provides the book with its starting point, the scroll of Zechariah was shaped by producers who were interacting more and more with religiously significant written texts (Mason). Consistently engaging earlier prophetic literature, Zechariah advocates for Israel to view its present and future both in light of its past failures, captured in the prophets' words of judgment, and its testimonies to YHWH's desire to bless Israel and the world.

Zechariah 1:1-6: "Do Not Be Like Your Ancestors"

∎ THE TEXT IN ITS ANCIENT CONTEXT

Zechariah begins with a sermonic address that implores the audience to depart from the ways of their ancestors. Memories of exile and Jerusalem's destruction are marshaled to encourage the people to embrace a new way of being. Zechariah's rhetoric seeks to form a community whose memory of the past runs deep but does not predetermine its future. Restored to Jerusalem and awaiting the return of YHWH, Zechariah conditions the final restoration and reconciliation with YHWH on the people's return to YHWH (1:3). The report in Zech. 1:6 indicates that the people do indeed repent, which sets the stage for the visions that follow to imagine YHWH's return to the temple in Jerusalem.

∎ THE TEXT IN THE INTERPRETIVE TRADITION

The early church fathers highlighted the tension between divine grace and human free will in this passage. Augustine's interpretation of this passage is strongly shaped by his debate with Pelagius, who taught that humans could achieve moral perfection on their own and thus earn God's grace. Augustine argued that while Zechariah "simultaneously commends" divine grace and human free will, ultimately it is God who extends grace to the people and enables them to repent and return (Ferreiro).

∎ THE TEXT IN CONTEMPORARY DISCUSSION

Zechariah 1:1-6 raises fundamental questions about identity. To what extent are peoples' lives shaped by the behavior of our ancestors? How might communities negotiate the intersections between their memories of the past and their vision of the future? In the opening verses of Zechariah, the prophet does not palliate or deny the community's history of pain, rebellion, and alienation from God. Nor does he encourage Israel to reinvent its identity apart from its past. Indeed, through allusion and image, the book of Zechariah weaves together language from Israel's prophetic traditions and stories of its past to address the community's present concerns and anxieties. And yet, the book's warnings and exhortations, formulated out of prophetic messages of judgment, lead the people to make a choice for a fundamentally different future. Zechariah's way of interacting with authoritative texts may offer a model for contemporary communities to engage Scripture, balancing the voices of the tradition with the context and needs of later readers in complex and creative ways.

Zechariah 1:7—2:13: Visions of God's Return to Jerusalem

▌ THE TEXT IN ITS ANCIENT CONTEXT

Zechariah 1:7—2:13 contains the first three of Zechariah's eight visions. In form, these visions have much in common with prophetic symbolic visions (Jer. 1:11-12, 13-14; 24; Amos 7:7-9; 8:1-3; see Niditch). However, different from most of the visions in Amos and Jeremiah, Zechariah's visions aim to express hope rather than judgment and introduce of a new figure: the interpreting angel. The angel, who translates the meaning of the obscure visions to the prophet, becomes a hallmark of apocalyptic literature (Daniel 7–12). Scholars often characterize Zechariah's visions as proto-apocalyptic; as such, the material evinces an apocalyptic perspective but lacks the formal features of later apocalyptic texts. This perspective is evident in the idea that a divine plan is unfolding in the heavens that will have radical repercussions for earth in the near future, but the divine program is hidden from most of God's people. Even the prophet, with his privileged view of events unfolding on a transcendent plane, needs an angel to explain the significance of his visions.

The movement of Zechariah's eight visions can be seen to reflect a move from the periphery of the world to its center, the temple (the fifth vision), and back out to the periphery (Stead). These first three visions communicate God's intention to return to Jerusalem, which is not only the center of commercial and political activity but also the site of the temple. In the ancient world, temples marked the apex of heaven and earth. As such, Jerusalem is the place where Israel encounters God and the taproot from which God's blessings grow. Zechariah's visions, as they move toward the mythological center of the world and back out into the wider world, track the restoration of sacred space.

A close examination of the first vision of the horsemen in the glen (1:7-17) raises more questions than answers, but in general, it communicates that the apparent peace that dominates the Persian Empire (1:11) will now begin to permeate Jerusalem and the cities of Judah and will find its ultimate expression in the rebuilding of the temple ("my house," 1:16), where God will again be present to God's people. YHWH's anger will be redirected from the people of Judah to the nations. The time of suffering and punishment for Judah—seventy years, which accords with Jeremiah's prophecy (Jer. 25:9-12; 29:10)—is over, and it is time now for a message of comfort (1:14-17) (cf. Isa. 40:1-2).

That God is enacting a reversal of fortune on behalf of Judah is also evident in the second vision of the horns and the smiths (1:18-21). The angel identifies the four horns as the nations that scattered Judah and explains that these horns will be cut off by four heavenly blacksmiths, suggesting that God's agent will overthrow those who oppress Judah and that those nations will lose their power to dominate. Evident in this vision are features of proto-apocalyptic literature, including imagery of a final battle between God's agents (the smiths) and God's enemies (the horns) as well as the prophet's conviction that only direct divine intervention will allow for change to take place on earth. For Zechariah, Judah's restoration will only come about when the transcendent breaks into the ordinary realm of history.

The third vision of the surveyor (2:1-5) reveals that the population of Jerusalem will explode beyond the confines of the city walls. The absence of walls in the vision is not a sign of the city's vulnerability and of God's abandonment, as in Lam. 2:3, 7-9. Rather, Jerusalem's safety will be ensured by the abiding presence of God in the city and not by its defenses and walls. In the exposition that follows the vision (2:6-13), YHWH will reverse the circumstances of Zion and the nations (2:8-9), but YHWH's choice to dwell in Zion once again also has implications for "many nations," who will "join themselves to the LORD on that day, and shall be my people" (2:11).

▌ THE TEXT IN THE INTERPRETIVE TRADITION

Revelation's "four horsemen of the Apocalypse" (Rev. 6:1-8) likely takes its cue from the image of the four horses of different colors (1:7-10), and the figure of the interpreting angel features prominently in the New Testament (i.e., Luke 1:26-38) as well as in some contemporaneous Jewish traditions (1 Macc. 7:41; 2 Macc. 15:22; *2 Baruch (Syriac Apocalypse) 63:7; Jub. 42:11; 27:21*).

In some evangelical traditions, the image of "a brand plucked from the fire" (3:2) has become a powerful symbol to express the individual's struggle with evil and sin. The image is featured in the legends of John Wesley and in the so-called "Wesleys' Conversion Hymn," by Charles Wesley, which refers to "A slave redeemed from death and sin, / A brand plucked from eternal fire" (Coggins, 158–59).

▌ THE TEXT IN CONTEMPORARY DISCUSSION

Zechariah offers a radical vision of hope to communities in despair. For those who no longer believe that life can change, he renders the present temporary and relative in light of a divinely ordained future that is not structured according to any earthly form of logic. In calling for the people to repent (1:1-7), Zechariah provides his audience with a way to participate in and commit to God's unfolding future plans. Then as a witness to the secret designs of God in heaven, he unfolds a series of obscure but compelling visions. As he dramatizes God's moves to bring about the community's full restoration to God and to safety and prosperity, he shapes a countercultural community of hope. At the same time, precise timelines for God's intervention—the hallmark of many modern millennialist groups—are notably absent.

Zechariah 3:1—4:14: Visions of Leadership

▌THE TEXT IN ITS ANCIENT CONTEXT

The fourth and fifth visions (3:1-10; 4:1-14) suggest the restoration of Israel's central institutions: the priesthood and the monarchy.

In the fourth vision, Zechariah witnesses the accusation and cleansing of Joshua the high priest (Jeshua in Ezra and Nehemiah). The satan, a member of God's council who accuses Joshua, may represent Joshua's critics in the postexilic community. Alternatively, the vision of Joshua's cleansing may seek to alleviate anxiety about the guilt and worthiness of the community as a whole. The vision concludes on a note of uncertainty as the angel of YHWH issues a conditional promise that alludes to the failings of Judah's former leaders: "if you will walk in my ways and keep my statutes, then you shall rule my house and have charge of my courts" (3:7).

In the fifth vision, YHWH's presence is encoded in the specific modes and symbols of the temple, culminating with the image of the lampstand. The two olive trees that flank the lampstand likely represent the diarchy of priest and king. The remainder of the vision consists of the word of YHWH to Zerubbabel, governor of Yehud, promising that he will rebuild the temple, not by might but by God's spirit.

In the ancient Near Eastern world, temple building was a task for kings; therefore, images of Zerubbabel as the one who lays the foundation of the temple (4:9) activate messianic expectations. Many scholars have assumed that Zechariah views Zerubbabel as the Messiah based, in part, on the designation of him as "the Branch" (3:8), a term that refers to an ideal future ruler (Jer. 23:5; 33:15). However, Zerubbabel fades from the book without explanation. Perhaps the Persians removed him from power, or he was confined to a merely ceremonial role in the temple's rebuilding and founding ceremonies (Redditt). Or if Zechariah looked initially to Zerubbabel with messianic expectations, later his anticipation may have shifted toward an ideal Davidic leader (an unnamed Branch), who would implement justice on earth (Cook 1995).

▌THE TEXT IN THE INTERPRETIVE TRADITION

In the Targum of Jonathan, the account of Joshua's dirty clothes and their replacement sparks a haggadic treatment that draws on Ezra 10:18 to explain that Joshua's offense had to do with unacceptable marriages: "And Joshua had sons who had married wives who were not permitted for the priesthood" (*Tg. Zech.* 3:3; see also *Sanh.* 93a; see Coggins).

Fathers of the early church understood Joshua's cleansing in light of Christian doctrines of baptism, sin, and incarnation. For Gregory of Nyssa, the high priest Joshua is Jesus Christ (LXX renders the high priest's name as *Iēsous*, which is *Yeshua* in the MT), and the replacement of dirty garments with clean ones is a figure of the regeneration of the person that happens in and through baptism. Jerome connects the filthy garments with the sin that Jesus voluntarily takes on when he becomes human (Ferreiro).

▌The Text in Contemporary Discussion

This text provides an opportunity to discuss and challenge the common assumption that a prophecy is only "true" if it is later proven to have accurately predicted the future. Zechariah's prophecy imagines specific historical people, Zerubbabel and Joshua, in ideal leadership roles. Because these figures fade from history, should Zechariah's prophecy be viewed as a failure? Or is such particularity a risk all prophets must take lest Scripture be removed from the real world and become a "disembodied word" (Ollenburger)? While at times Zechariah surely supports particular "candidates" for office, in other instances, his imagination surpasses endorsement for particular human leaders. In the final form of the book, ideas about Zerubbabel stand in tension with references to the "Branch"; the messianic ideal both informs and serves to critique and challenge human leaders. The notion that prophecy is merely predictive limits the ways we might appreciate how the prophet's visions serve to restructure a community's worldview and revive its imagination about the ways God may be at work in their midst.

Zechariah 5:1—6:15: Visions of Purification

▌The Text in Its Ancient Context

Whereas the earlier visions are focused on YHWH's return to Jerusalem, Zechariah's final three visions are concerned with the elimination of impurity and reflect a movement outward from the temple, which stands at the center of Zechariah's world. The verb "to go out" appears thirteen times in this unit (Floyd; Stead). The presence of God's holiness requires the removal of corruption and, as such, reflects a priestly concern for purity in Zechariah. In order for Jerusalem to accommodate the presence of the returning holy God (8:3), the land itself must be become holy (2:16).

The vision of the flying scroll (5:1-4) addresses the threat of internal corruption and the perversion of justice ("false swearing" and "stealing"). The scroll continually monitors practices that threaten not only the health and security of the community but also God's willingness to be present in their midst. As the scroll flies about, it is able to detect potential threats to the people's well-being and immediately issue curses against thieves and liars that will remove them from the land.

The vision of the woman in the basket (5:5-11) features a woman called "Wickedness" who is carried off to Shinar (Babylon) in some sort of container (an *ephah*) by winged women. Precisely what sort of iniquity the woman represents is not clear. However, the image has a cultic dimension and implies the veneration of foreign, feminine deities (e.g., the Queen of Heaven, Jer. 7:18; 44:17-25; O'Brien). *Ephah* may refer to woven baskets as houses for deities, used in household shrines. However, as a unit of measurement, *ephah* also has an economic dimension and recalls the Persian king Darius's creation of standard weights as a means to collect taxes more efficiently. The concern behind the vision is to rid the land not only of individual sinners but also of communal practices Zechariah considers "wicked" in a cultic as well as an economic sense (Ollenburger).

The last of Zechariah's eight night visions is of four chariots (6:1-8). This final vision parallels the first of the four horsemen (1:7-11) and structurally returns back to the periphery of the world from the center. However, in the first vision, the horsemen have completed their patrol and the announcement of peace on earth prompts a lament related to the exile's continuation (1:12). By contrast, in the last vision, four chariots burst out from between two mountains of bronze (6:1), ready to patrol in the four compass directions (6:7). The chariots, associated with military armament, are identified as "the four winds of heaven" and indicate God's military omnipotence and readiness to engage all the nations in battle. With sacred space restored and the cosmic army marshaled, YHWH's spirit is set at rest in the north (6:8), alluding perhaps to the restoration of the exiles still in exile there (Petersen 1984).

Actions imagined as taking place on earth and in the present link the visions of the future with the here-and-now (6:9-15). Moving from vision to word, God commands Zechariah to collect silver and gold from the exiles (6:9) to make crown(s) for Joshua (6:11). Scholars debate whether the one who is called the Branch (6:12) refers to Joshua as the one charged to build the temple (Floyd, 405) or if the less specific designation "Branch" refers to a future ideal ruler (see 3:8; Cook 1995). The report implies a complementary, though perhaps subordinate, role for the priesthood ("a priest by his throne," 6:13). The chapter concludes with a vision of a harmonious, inclusive temple-building project (6:15) that contrasts with Ezra's account of the temple's construction as beset by conflict and delay.

▌THE TEXT IN THE INTERPRETIVE TRADITION

In Martin Luther's treatment of the sixth (flying scroll) and seventh (woman in the ephah) visions in his lectures on Zechariah, he claims Zechariah predicts the "treachery of the Jews" and details their punishment for failing to accept Jesus as "King and Savior." His shockingly negative characterization of the Jewish people and use of the Bible to condemn Judaism exemplifies the Christian anti-Jewish polemics common for at least a thousand years prior to his teaching (Schramm and Stjerna). Anti-Jewish sentiment continued to inform the interpretive rubrics of historical-critical biblical scholarship into the late nineteenth and twentieth centuries, when Protestant scholars tended to view priestly concerns about purity and impurity as a sign of the degeneration of Israelite religion. In the wake of the Shoah (Holocaust), Protestant biblical scholarship has become increasingly self-critical and self-reflective about the biases inherent in such readings.

▌THE TEXT IN CONTEMPORARY DISCUSSION

That Zechariah's vivid and evocative images are particularly open-ended has enabled centuries of their creative, often historically specific appropriation. The same creative potentiality in Zechariah's visions that enabled Christian readers to see Jesus in the Branch also led them to equate the Jews with a woman called Wickedness. Literature in the vein of Zechariah is a double-edged sword.

In the interpretive tradition, there has been a tendency to equate the woman in the ephah with contemporary "others" (e.g., Jews and women) and to use the text to justify the expulsion of that other from the community that sees itself as positioned to inherit the blessings promised in the book. The revulsion prompted by these interpretations could provide an opportunity for contemporary communities not to judge such readings, but to consider how their own assumptions about otherness function to structure the boundaries of their communities.

Zechariah 7:1—8:23: A Homily Contrasting the Past and the Present

THE TEXT IN ITS ANCIENT CONTEXT

The superscription in Zech. 7:1 situates the oracles that follow in the fourth year of the Persian king Darius's reign (518 BCE), two years after Zechariah received his visions. The reference to the completion of the laying of the temple's foundations (8:9) suggests that while the temple-building project is underway, it is not yet complete (completion dates to 515 BCE). The style of Zechariah 7–8 is comparable to that of Zech. 1:1-6 and has been linked to the "sermons" in Chronicles (e.g., 2 Chron. 30:6-9) and the teaching and preaching associated with the personnel of the Second Temple.

In general, this material is concerned to create a contrast between previous generations and the new community now living in Jerusalem. The ancestors' state of disobedience and punishment (7:7-12a) is contrasted to the peace-filled situation of the new community (8:4-8), which pivots on the announcement of YHWH's return to Jerusalem (8:3). YHWH's presence in Zion will lead to the reestablishment of a rich communal life, characterized by children playing and the elderly imparting wisdom (8:4-5). This vision of life restored is connected to the hortatory elements of the sermon (8:9-10, 16-17), which emphasize "neighborly" values (speaking truthfully, rendering right judgments, showing kindness and mercy, caring for the vulnerable, and not devising evil "in your hearts against one another").

The sermon's teachings on fasting (7:4-6; 8:18-19) can also be understood in light of the text's rhetorical creation of a contrast between the past and the present on the verge of the future. Fasts previously linked to mourning (7:3) "shall become seasons of joy and gladness, and cheerful festivals for the house of Judah" (8:19).

Although Zechariah does not refer directly to the visions that precede this sermon, his preaching reflects similar concerns and themes, including the return of YHWH to Jerusalem (cf. 1:16; 2:10-11 with 8:3, 8, 15), and a concern for the nations (cf. 2:11 with 8:20-23). But whereas the nations came to Jerusalem to be subjugated in 2:10-11, they come now to worship God.

THE TEXT IN THE INTERPRETIVE TRADITION

The images of a restored humanity in this material may have influenced Paul's understanding of Israel's relationship to the nations. In Paul's eschatology, the reunification of Israel and the nations, such as Zechariah imagines in 8:20-23, is a key feature of the new creation, marked by God's cosmic reign and Jews and gentiles worshiping God together (Gal. 3:26-29; Rom. 15:7-13; Sherwood). The ultimate restoration of humanity begins with Israel, but Israel's redemption cannot be realized apart from that of the gentiles.

THE TEXT IN CONTEMPORARY DISCUSSION

The way Zechariah configures the concept of universalism, with its resonances in Paul's thought, has implications for contemporary interreligious dialogue. The universalism in Zechariah is not unqualified; rather, it is rooted in the particular practices of the Jews (8:20-23). While the salvation of all people is essential for Zechariah's vision of the future reign of YHWH, the text does not depict humanity as an undifferentiated mass. Indeed, as in Paul, Israel's distinct theological heritage figures prominently in Zechariah's visions featuring the shalom of all.

Zechariah 9–11: War and Peace

■ THE TEXT IN ITS ANCIENT CONTEXT

Zechariah 9 makes use of and transforms the ancient ritual pattern of the Divine Warrior's "victory enthronement" (Hanson). In this pattern, YHWH as a Divine Warrior marches forth into battle against his enemies (9:1-7, 14). Elsewhere in the Hebrew Bible, these enemies represent the forces of chaos and take the form of monsters like the sea or Leviathan, human enemy armies, and even those perpetrating injustice within Israel. Following YHWH's victory over his foes, he enters his palace/temple where he takes his throne (9:8). YHWH's success in battle and subsequent enthronement are commemorated with victory shouts (9:9a), a procession (9:9b), sacrifices, and a banquet (9:15). The victory and enthronement of the Divine Warrior translates to the implementation of order, justice, and peace for his people.

When Zechariah 9 transposes and reimagines this pattern, God as Divine Warrior marches to Zion and reverses the current political realities for Israel. After routing the nations in battle, instead of taking his throne, YHWH encamps at his house as a guard (9:8). A human, rather than YHWH, is declared king, and while he is triumphant and victorious, he is also humble (9:9; cf. Ps. 72:2). Ringing with traditions of the ideal messiah, this king will end war for all time and in all places (9:10).

Symbols of blood play a role in the prophet's vision of restoration. The blood of the covenant in 9:11 sets apart Israel from the mass destruction of the nations (cf. Exodus 12, in which the blood on the Israelites' doorposts deters the angel of death during the plague of the firstborn). The blood that protects YHWH's people also serves to draw the people into ritual intimacy with God. As God and Israel partake of blood together in a banquet (9:15; cf. Exodus 24), the distance between Israel and God is bridged. Blood here evokes a rich and multivalent network of symbols to point to radical communion with God (Niditch).

Images of reversal dominate the next chapter (Zechariah 10). God indicts and vows to punish the leaders of Israel ("shepherds," 10:3), who have abdicated their responsibility to care for the people ("his flock, the house of Judah," 10:3); in turn, YHWH transforms the lowly into "the proud war-horse" (10:3), so that they may fight with God to scatter those who have persecuted them (10:4-5). God promises to gather, redeem, and strengthen the people whom God punished and scattered (10:6). Their restoration to God and to their land will represent an overwhelming reversal of the punishment of exile (10:8-12). This victory for Israel and the implementation of peace for the world has ecological consequences as well: the rain falls and vegetation flourishes (10:1).

The precise meaning of the narrative of the two shepherds (Zech. 11:4-17) is debated. The story appears to reverse the hopeful promises in Zechariah 9–10. God commands the prophet (?) to play the role of the unjust, greedy shepherd doomed to slaughter (11:4), and then vows that this shepherd will devastate the land. God then has the prophet symbolically break the covenant that God made with all the peoples (11:10). Although scholars have offered a number of different proposals with regard to the precise identity of these shepherds, generally speaking, "shepherds" are leaders; and as a Persian-period composition, it is likely that Zechariah is referring to Yehud's political leadership—governors who, though appointed by the Persian Empire, were Israelite.

▌ THE TEXT IN THE INTERPRETIVE TRADITION

The Gospel writers in the New Testament draw on Zechariah's image of the king riding on a donkey (9:9) to describe Jesus entering Jerusalem (Matt. 21:4-5; John 12:14-15). For them, the juxtaposition of power and humility captured in Zechariah's imagery is embodied in the person of Jesus Christ (Matt. 21:9; Mark 11:9-10; Luke 19:38; John 12:13). Zechariah's visions of peace (9:10), enabled by God's radical in-breaking to the world, resonate with the New Testament's understandings of the kingdom of God, made possible because of the incarnation, a particularly embodied instance of God's transcendence breaking in and becoming immanent on earth.

▌ THE TEXT IN CONTEMPORARY DISCUSSION

Contemporary readers are invited to grapple with Zechariah's suggestion that God approves of, and even participates in, acts of violence and aggression. While such theological claims may at first seem primitive to contemporary communities, the daily news continually reminds us that human beings are capable of great brutality and of justifying their acts of violence with "divine approval."

And yet, while glorified visions of God's violence are difficult to contend with, the text makes plain that it is God, not human beings, who will make war in order to end war. Zechariah does not encourage human beings to take up arms in order to initiate or enact the envisioned process of reversal. The Divine Warrior motif in (proto-)apocalyptic literature asserts that God as a warrior will break into history to deal personally with overwhelming evil and defend God's people against such evil. In this worldview, God is so infuriated by the presence of injustice and oppression that God physically appears to set things right and destroy evil once and for all.

The claim that God is more powerful than nations and empires and acts to temper their hubris and aggression flies in the face of the reality on the ground, and as such constitutes a powerful act of resistance. Nations and empires assert control over those they dominate by attempting to define the parameters of reality. One way of implementing such hegemonic control is to reshape myths to justify subtly the current reign as preordained, part of the structures of the cosmos. Proto-apocalyptic texts, such as Zechariah 9–11, present a counter-reality. The world may think the powerful nations are in control, but Zechariah asserts that their rule is temporary, even fragile. YHWH will appear with a vengeance to turn the current structures of power upside down, so that compassion, humility, and justice will reign in the lives of people who are currently suffering.

Zechariah 12–14: A Final Battle and a New Creation

▌ THE TEXT IN ITS ANCIENT CONTEXT

The superscription, "an oracle" (12:1), sets off this block of material (Zechariah 12–14) from that which precedes it. The repeated formula "on that day" (and its variant, "it will be on that day") introduces a variety of eschatological scenarios and also serves to structure the disparate material in these two chapters (Clark).

In 12:2-8, Jerusalem is at the center of the end-time battle waged by God against the nations. Zechariah uses a variety of metaphors to express the ways YHWH will use Jerusalem to execute YHWH's wrath and punishment against "the surrounding peoples." Jerusalem will be a "cup of reeling" (12:2), "a heavy stone" (12:3), and "a blazing pot" (12:6). God's promise to punish the nations physically and brutally does not lead immediately to Judah's restoration and safety. God's plan is to bring people hostile to Judah into the city to start a war there (12:3b) so that the nations will acknowledge that Jerusalem's strength comes from YHWH (12:5). God promises victory to Judah and Jerusalem (12:7).

Texts and traditions about David provide the comparisons for the "shield" God will provide for the inhabitants of Jerusalem (12:8) when God induces the nations to come against the city so that God can destroy them (12:9). The house of David also features prominently in the section on mourning that follows (12:10-14), but the thematic connections between these two halves of the chapter are difficult to discern as Zech. 12:10-14 is concerned that "the house of David" look on and mourn "the one whom they have pierced" (12:10). Some scholars argue that "the pierced one" is a royal figure, perhaps invoking the memory of Gedaliah's assassination (Jer. 41:1-3; Meyers and Meyers). However, the text provides few clues as to the precise identity of this one; rather, it focuses on eliciting feelings and actions of deep mourning from the people. Perhaps as a means of preparation for the new age, Zechariah calls the community to recognize and grieve for the one(s) on whom they have inflicted violence. It may be that "the spirit of compassion and supplication" God pours out on them enables them to view in a new light not only their own persecution but also their past involvement in the oppression of others. Alternatively, it may seek to present a particular manifestation of the suffering and mourning to be endured by the remnant as they await the coming reign of God.

As part of Zechariah's program of renewal, the city will be cleansed of its impurity with a salvation-flowing fountain (13:1-2). While this is a comforting image, the majority of the material in chapter 13 emphasizes a theme that will become a hallmark for apocalyptic literature, namely, the idea that a time of great suffering and testing for the faithful will precede the arrival of God's reign (Collins).

Zechariah's views of prophecy recall condemnations of false prophecy (Jer. 14:14; 23:16; 27:15; Ezek. 13:6-8) but go far beyond them to declare all prophecy to be deception (13:3-4). The order for parents to pierce their children who prophesy (13:3) recalls the physical afflictions of the one pierced (12:10), but it rings of brutality in the absence of mourning rituals to mark the violence. The preparation for God's new order entails a complete change in the religious order of business. In particular, the enforced censure of prophets entails a suspension of all attempts to discern God's will. The faithful will be utterly in the dark as to when the suffering will end, and they will be without divine reassurance about their fate.

In Zech. 13:7-9, the prophet returns to the theme that the coming ruler will suffer a sacrificial death (12:10—13:1). God calls on a sword to strike "my shepherd" and "the man who is my associate" (13:7) in order that the leaders' people (the sheep) will be scattered. Only a remnant will survive (a third of the population, 13:8) to be refined and tested (13:9). Religious leaders of all stripes, royal and prophetic, will be cleared away to make space for God alone to rule over the new order.

The book's drama culminates in Zechariah 14. The final battle in which all the nations will come against Jerusalem recalls chapter 12. However, in this final scene, there are no human leaders in view. The lack of references to the house of David, shepherds, royal figures, and prophets indicates that all leadership positions have been washed away. Chapter 14 exalts YHWH *alone* as king.

The chapter begins with, and intersperses throughout, graphic images of the intense suffering of the people in the city of Jerusalem (14:1-2, 12). As in 12:2-8, God enters the fray of battle, this time in giant human form, standing on the Mount of Olives, dividing the land (14:4) and shaking the earth with the force of an earthquake (14:5). In 14:10, the whole land will be turned into a plain so that the mountain of Zion will tower over all, aligning its physical prominence with its status as the holy mountain and the center of the world. The result will be the perpetual shalom and security of its inhabitants (14:11).

This radical act of divine intervention results in a radical reordering of creation. Polarities, like day and night (14:7) and holy and profane (14:21), are eliminated, while other divisions are implemented in the land itself (14:4) and in the course of the living waters flowing from Jerusalem (14:8; see also 14:13, 17). The book concludes with the temple's holiness extending beyond the temple altar to the courts and out into Jerusalem. Even everyday cooking pots become as holy as temple vessels (14:21).

Zechariah's radical eschatological vision of a new creation, which bridges priestly and apocalyptic modes of thinking, stipulates an equally radical program for cleansing the people and the land after generations of evil deeds (1:4; Cook 1995). Instead of human agents acting on God's behalf to govern all creation (e.g., Gen. 1:26-27), in Zechariah, it is God who will assume the duties of earthly governance (14:9). As a result, transcendence will no longer be an experience limited to the temple; rather, that transcendence will flow out from the temple and pervade the earthly realm. In Zechariah's imagination, this paradox of immanence and transcendence requires dramatic acts of purification.

▌ THE TEXT IN THE INTERPRETIVE TRADITION

Several allusions to Zechariah 12–14 appear in the Gospels to emphasize the belief that the Hebrew Scriptures foretold and prefigured Jesus' death and crucifixion. The pierced one in 12:10 is equated with Jesus in John 19:37. The striking down of the shepherd (13:7-9) figures in the story of the passion, in particular in the accounts of Jesus' abandonment by his followers at the time of his death (Matt. 26:31; Mark 14:27).

Allusions to the paired themes of messianic suffering and the redemption of Israel in Zech. 12:10 are also evident in rabbinic texts about Messiah ben Joseph, including *Aggadat Mashiah* and *Sefer Zerubbabel*. Expanding on Zech. 12:10, the targumic Tosefta to Zechariah identifies the one pierced as Messiah bar Ephraim, likely the same figure whom the Talmud later identifies as Messiah ben Joseph, said to die in an eschatological battle ("And they will look to me and inquire of me why the nations pierced Messiah bar Ephraim, and they will mourn for him"; Mitchell 2006, 223).

Images of the end times and the last battle in Zechariah 9–14, along with those in Revelation, figure prominently in the theologies of dispensationalism and millennialism. Martin Luther also believed that the events of Zechariah 14 applied to a future as yet unrealized and provided an account of the period of history beginning with the New Testament era and ending in the second coming of Christ. By contrast, John Calvin saw the promises of chapter 14 as fulfilled in the past through God's restoration of Israel to the land in the wake of the exile (Wolters).

■ THE TEXT IN CONTEMPORARY DISCUSSION

In a world saturated with religious violence, it is difficult to imagine how Zechariah might function in a theologically constructive way. And yet, the text might function positively if readers approach it, not as a model for how the world ought to be, but rather as a means to examine deeply held assumptions about the ways violence figures into rubrics of salvation. In the Bible, acts of brutality frequently precede redemption. Indeed, the crucifixion of Jesus himself, which is linked to an ultimate act of salvation, testifies to the pervasiveness of the biblical connection between destruction and renewal. Honestly confronting and grappling with the disturbing aspects of one's religious tradition can positively inform, even transform, the faith and practice of religious communities.

What disgusts many contemporary readers about biblical texts like this one is the graphic imagery used to depict the consequences of violence. The realities of war are not hidden or sanitized or explained in rational terms: women are raped (14:2), live human bodies rot like corpses (14:12), and neighbors will kill each other to survive (14:13). While Zechariah views violence and suffering as precursors to salvation, he does not gloss over the impact of war or rush to the happy ending. By contrast, modern warfare allows most of the United States' upper classes to ignore the cost to human bodies, which are regularly mutilated, broken, and blown to pieces. While we may be tempted to condemn Zechariah for being too violent, it is significant that the prophet makes us look when we would prefer to look away. Perhaps it is in the act of seeing suffering that we might find our way to redemption.

Works Cited

Clark, David. 1988. "Discourse Structure in Zech 9-14: Skeleton or Phantom?" in *Issues in Bible Translation*, edited by P. Steine, 64–80. UBS Monograph Series 3. London: United Bible Societies.

Coggins, R. J., and Jin Hee Han. 2011. *Six Minor Prophets through the Centuries*. Malden, MA: Wiley-Blackwell.

Collins, John J. 1998. *The Apocalyptic Imagination: An Introduction to Jewish Apocalyptic Literature*. Grand Rapids: Eerdmans.

Cook, Stephen L. 1995. *Prophecy and Apocalypticism: The Postexilic Social Setting*. Minneapolis: Fortress Press.

———. 2011. "Zechariah." In *The Oxford Encyclopedia of the Books of the Bible*, edited by Michael Coogan. New York: Oxford University Press. www.oxfordreference.com/view/10.1093/acref:o bso/9780195377378.001.0001/acref-9780195377378-e-57.

Ferreiro, Alberto, ed. 2003. *The Twelve Prophets*. Ancient Christian Commentary on Scripture, Old Testament 14. Downers Grove, IL: InterVarsity Press.

Floyd, Michael H. 2000. *Minor Prophets*. Vol. 2. Grand Rapids: Eerdmans.

Hanson, Paul. 1973. "Zechariah 9 and the Recapitulation of an Ancient Ritual Pattern." *JBL* 92:37–59.

Mason, Rex. 2003. "The Use of Earlier Biblical Material in Zechariah 9–14: A Study in Inner Biblical Exegesis." In *Bringing Out the Treasure: Inner Biblical Allusion in Zechariah 9–14*, edited by Mark J. Boda, and Michael H. Floyd, 1-208. London: Sheffield Academic.

Meyers, Carol L., and Eric M. Meyers. 1993. *Zechariah 9–14: A New Translation with Introduction and Commentary*. AB. New York: Doubleday.

Mitchell, David C. 2006. "Messiah bar Ephraim in the Targums," Aramaic Studies 4.2:211–28.

Niditch, Susan. 1983. *The Symbolic Vision in Biblical Tradition*. Chico, CA: Scholars Press.

———. 2011. "Good Blood, Bad Blood: Multivocality, Metonymy, and Mediation in Zechariah 9." *VT* 61:629–45.

Ollenburger, Ben C. 1996. "The Book of Zechariah." In *New Interpreter's Bible*. Vol. 7, *Introduction to Apocalyptic Literature, Daniel, the Twelve Prophets*, edited by Leander E. Keck, 733–840. Nashville: Abingdon.

Petersen, David L. 1984. *Haggai and Zechariah 1–8: A Commentary*. Philadelphia: Westminster Press.

———. 1995. *Zechariah 9–14 and Malachi: A Commentary*. Louisville: Westminster John Knox.

Redditt, Paul L. 2008. *Introduction to the Prophets*. Grand Rapids: Eerdmans.

Schramm, Brooks, and Kirsi Irmeli Stjerna. 2012. *Martin Luther, the Bible, and the Jewish People: A Reader*. Minneapolis: Fortress Press.

Sherwood, Aaron. 2012. *Paul and the Restoration of Humanity in Light of Ancient Jewish Traditions*. Leiden: Brill.

Sommer, Benjamin D. 1998. *A Prophet Reads Scripture: Allusion in Isaiah 40–66*. Stanford: Stanford University Press.

Stead, Michael R. 2009. *The Intertextuality of Zechariah 1–8*. New York: T&T Clark.

Wolters, A. 2002. "Zechariah 14: A Dialogue with the History of Interpretation." *Mid-America Journal of Theology* 13:42–55.

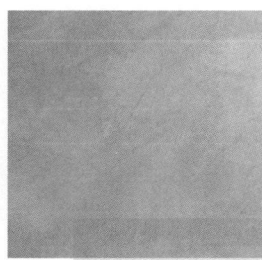

MALACHI

Richard J. Coggins and
Jin Hee Han

Introduction

It is universally agreed that Malachi is to be dated within what is often referred to as the "postexilic" period of Israel's history. It is perhaps better to think of this as the Persian or Second Temple period; "postexilic" seems to imply a universal exile of the community, whereas the great majority of the population remained in Palestine through the political turmoil of the sixth century BCE. By the time of Malachi's writing, however, this turmoil had died down; the book refers to a "governor" (*peḥâ* 1:8) whose position seems to be taken for granted as that of the established ruler. Since the governor is not named, one cannot establish a more precise date—attempts to date Malachi by reference to the various reforms described in Ezra and Nehemiah (see *b. Meg.* 15a) have largely been abandoned because of uncertainties relating to those books. The earliest reference to "the Twelve" as a collection is found in a deuterocanonical book (Sir. 49:10), so by then it seems that Malachi was established as part of a larger collection. It is widely held that the fifth century BCE is the most likely date, but any time during the period of Persian rule—that is, from the sixth century down to the conquests of Alexander the Great (c. 330 BCE)—is possible.

The uncertainty with regard to a precise historical setting has been one of the causes of a different approach to Malachi (and other prophetic collections) in recent study. The twelve Minor Prophets have usually been treated entirely independently of each other, implying that the "eighth-century prophets" such as Amos or Hosea would have had no connection with much later works such as Malachi. Even when historical approaches were still the norm, links were noted between Malachi and what immediately precedes it: Zech. 9:1 and 12:1, as well as Mal. 1:1, are all introduced by the word *maśśā*, usually translated "oracle," though there was no suggestion of identical authorship. A number of recent studies have maintained that one should take more seriously the idea of a "Book of the Twelve," noting links between the different components (see Nogalski 1993a; 1993b). On such a literary reading, Malachi is to be seen as the end point of a coherent literary collection rather than as an isolated unit. It is too early to say whether this approach will become more general; it should certainly be borne in mind as an alternative to more customary readings.

In any case, the fact that virtually all the collections of the twelve Minor Prophets place Malachi at the end has been important in traditional Christian interpretation. In Judaism, the Prophets are followed by the Writings, so that the overall structure is different. Protestant Christians, reading through their Bible, found Malachi immediately followed by the Gospel of Matthew, and it was natural to conclude that such passages as the hoped-for return of Elijah (4:5) were prefiguring the world of the New Testament.

It may be helpful to note that, whereas historical-critical scholarship has claimed to identify later additions to many prophetic collections, it is usually held that virtually the whole of Malachi is likely to come from one period. Malachi 4:4-6 to some extent stands apart as a kind of appendix, either to the book or to the Book of the Twelve as a whole, and there are a few breaks in the flow that will be noted below; otherwise, whereas some prophetic books can readily be divided into different "sense units," that is scarcely possible here. One possible way of dividing the book is offered below, but the book exists more naturally as a whole.

Malachi 1:1-5: God Loves Israel

▌ THE TEXT IN ITS ANCIENT CONTEXT

Is "Malachi" a personal name (1:1)? Many have supposed that the word (which does not occur as a personal name elsewhere in the Hebrew Bible) is best understood as "my messenger" (as in 3:1) and only came to be understood as a personal name when these oracles were taken to be a distinct collection (see 2 Esd. 1:40). Certainty is impossible; what is clear is that there is no basis for developing a "personality" approach such as used to be popular with many prophetic figures. However that may be, it is noteworthy that the message is addressed to "Israel." This is clearly no longer a reference to the northern kingdom of Israel and its inhabitants; Malachi is in the middle of the process that led to Israel being characteristically the name of a religious grouping. One feature of that process is brought out well in 1:2-5. Part of the language is appropriate for a political entity, with the reference to the futile rebuilding of ruins of Edom and "the borders of Israel" (1:4-5).

▌ THE TEXT IN THE INTERPRETIVE TRADITION

The Septuagint construes "Malachi" as a common noun and translates "his messenger," forming a link between 1:1 and 3:1 ("my messenger"). Most versions regard it as a personal name, and some suspect that the idea of his anonymity led to an unfortunate situation in which "these chapters have been taken less seriously than they deserve" (Baldwin, 221).

Malachi 1:2-3 makes a clear allusion to the stories in Genesis that set out the basis of the hostility between Jacob and Esau, the latter seen as the ancestor of Edom (Gen. 25:19—28:9). Whereas at an earlier period the main concerns of biblical scholarship were historical, and diligent efforts were made to find a plausible historical context involving a dispute between Israel and Edom in the Persian period, recent scholarship has to a much greater extent been concerned with drawing out literary linkages. In Jewish liturgy, the Torah lesson from Gen. 25:19—28:9 (*parashat toledoth*) is paired with Mal. 1:1—2:7 as the *haftarah* (reading from the Prophets) that connects God's election of Israel with the divine demand of faithfulness.

∎ THE TEXT IN CONTEMPORARY DISCUSSION

It is likely that a major concern for the modern audience is the assertion put into God's mouth: "I have loved Jacob but I have hated Esau" (1:2-3), a judgment whose difficulty is made even more acute by Paul's use of this passage for an elaborate theological reflection (Rom. 9:13). Those without any personal religious commitment may be content simply to observe that strong nationalistic feelings can be attributed to gods as much as to humans; religious believers will be more reluctant to think in this way of the one whom they worship. It has been proposed that "hate" here can be understood as "love less" (Kaiser 1984, 27), but there are no clear grounds for understanding the Hebrew verb (*śānā'*, "hate") in this sense. It may be relevant that the strong covenantal language found later in the book (Mal. 2:4-11) implies not only the election of Israel but also the implicit rejection of other communities. By contrast, in one popular introduction to Judaism, Malachi is cited for contending that "all nations have a share in God's goodness" based on the theology of "God as the One Father, the Creator of all" (Levine, 49).

Malachi 1:6—2:9: God's Demand of Proper Worship

∎ THE TEXT IN ITS ANCIENT CONTEXT

The prophetic charge of Israel's dishonoring of God (1:6a) unveils aberrations in the practice of worship (1:7-9). Their heinous offense is compounded by the priests' failure or refusal to recognize the wrong (1:6b-7) even as they sacrifice blemished animals (1:8). Although prophetic condemnations of the sacrificial cult are well known (e.g., Isa. 1:11; Amos 5:21-24), Mal. 1:6-10 differs from the others in that what is here condemned is the unacceptable quality of the offerings being made (see Lev. 1:3, 10). The prophet compares the unacceptable worship to the unlikely scenario of gifting the governor with a damaged good (Mal. 1:8), although there is no obvious parallel elsewhere in the Hebrew Bible to the presentation here of offerings to God and to the secular authorities being set out as matters of comparison. God demands penitence (1:9) and the cessation of the corrupt cult (1:10).

Malachi 1:11 seems to have been the subject of greater attention than any other in this prophetic book, and there is still no agreement as to how its implications are to be understood. What is clear is that a sweeping claim is being made as to the power and extent of the rule of YHWH of hosts. It may also be relevant to note the similarity between Ps. 50:1 and the beginning of Mal. 1:11. There, too, the universality of the rule of YHWH and its implications are set out; the claims of the Jerusalem cult and its priests to be the sole means of access to God's favor cannot be upheld. One may note also that three times in the verse stress is laid on the "name" of God; increasingly in

Jewish practice, any direct reference to God——or usage of the divine name itself—was avoided, and circumlocutions such as that found here became customary.

It is clear from Mal. 1:12 that a contrast with contemporary Jerusalem practice is intended. The remainder of the chapter continues the condemnation of the current worship being offered (1:12-14; see also 1:6-10). It is striking that both the quality of the offerings and the attitude of those making the offerings are strongly condemned. As noted above, whereas in other prophetic condemnations of the worship being offered it seems as if no form of sacrifice could be acceptable to God, here the implication is that better-quality offerings and a different mental attitude would be acceptable.

In 2:1-2, God gives a stern warning to the priests, who assumed an increasingly important and often contested role in the Judaism of the last centuries BCE. That there were divisions within the community as to the proper exercise of the priestly role is evident both from 2:1-9 and other writings of the period. The distinction between priests and Levites is not always clear in much of the Hebrew Bible. Although the reference to "the covenant with Levi" (2:4; "the covenant of Levi," 2:8) has no obvious parallel elsewhere, this is one of a number of passages in Malachi that suggest links with the Deuteronomic tradition rather than with the Priestly code. It may well be, though it cannot be proved, that the idea of what should be called "Scripture" was becoming established, and part of Malachi's concern was to draw out for the community of his own time the implications of earlier texts. This may also help to account for an unusual feature of the book—the prominence of the series of questions and answers, expressed as if the audience should know how to behave but are neglecting to apply that knowledge. In general, the themes tie in with the emphases of Deuteronomy, though it will be shown below that the view of divorce set out here is at odds with that found in Deut. 24:1-4.

■ THE TEXT IN THE INTERPRETIVE TRADITION

One widely held approach has been to interpret Mal. 1:11 in a Christian context and to see it as prefiguring the Catholic Mass; it was much used in the sixteenth century CE at the time of the Protestant Reformation in controversies relating to proper forms of worship. Much Old Testament (and here that expression is more appropriate than "Hebrew Bible") material has been understood as relating to events from a completely different period. This may be acceptable if one's approach is purely literary, although it is clearly far from historical-critical approaches.

Other interpretations of this verse may be more plausible if the aim is to discover a possible "original" intention. It could be understood as setting out a surely rather overstated view of what came to be known as the Diaspora; Jewish communities came to be established all round the Mediterranean world, though the evidence for this is later than any plausible date for Malachi. It is also worth bearing in mind that there are other texts which imply that pagan worship may be better than the state to which the Jerusalem temple had descended. Jonah's view of the sailors and the people of Nineveh would be an obvious example (Rudolph 1975, 263).

■ THE TEXT IN CONTEMPORARY DISCUSSION

Malachi's vision has also been construed as the worship of God worldwide (Kaiser 1996, 348). One modern scholar has called this "an instance of religious liberalism unparalleled in the Old

Testament," and adds that "the author would have undoubtedly repudiated the implications of this utterance in a calmer and more reflective mood" (Pfeiffer, 613). The thought, at one time quite widely maintained, that Mal. 1:11 is suggesting that all forms of worship are acceptable, has not found any recent advocates among critical scholars, but may provide a basis for common ground among those religious groups who are in the midst of schism and intra- or interconflict.

Malachi 2:10-16: Fidelity in Marriage

■ THE TEXT IN ITS ANCIENT CONTEXT

After the rather generalized condemnations of Mal. 2:1-9, matters become much more explicit in 2:10-16. The reference to the "daughter of a foreign god" (2:11) has elicited a wide variety of interpretations. One possibility is that in some quarters YHWH was thought to have a female consort, but this would have been a quite unacceptable view for Malachi. There is some evidence from earlier times to suggest such an understanding of YHWH (see Meshel), but none from this period, and the more usual view among commentators has been that the reference is either to marriage with foreign wives or the (perhaps surreptitious) worship of foreign deities. Certainty is impossible, and the extremely cryptic form of 2:12 does not help. There are not many major problems with the Hebrew text of Malachi, but this verse presents one such. Two words in Hebrew (*ʿēr* and *ʿōneh*) are translated by NRSV as "any to witness or answer," and a glance at different translations will show how uncertain the meaning is (for example, "the master and the scholar" in the KJV based on the Vulgate).

The terms of the rejection of divorce in 2:16 as something that YHWH detests are somewhat unexpected. The prophet condemns divorce in that it "serves to veil something that is amiss" (Petersen, 205). As noted above, some of the concerns link Malachi with Deuteronomy; here it seems as if there is a sharp disagreement with Deut. 24:1-4. There it appears that the possibility of divorce is taken for granted and the procedure for carrying it out is laid down; here (whether the third person of the Hebrew text or the first person favored by many translations including the NRSV is followed) it seems clear that the very possibility of divorce is rejected.

■ THE TEXT IN THE INTERPRETIVE TRADITION

In ancient versions, Mal. 2:16 is mostly interpreted as a concession of divorce. The Septuagint translates, "If you hate, send away." The Targum says, "If you hate her, divorce her." The text in a Qumran scroll (4Q82) is close to the Targum. Jewish scholars have been much exercised about the appropriate understanding of 2:16, but have mostly concluded that it is important that the woman so rejected should receive compassionate treatment. On the Christian side, the great seventeenth-century poet John Milton claimed to follow other contemporary interpreters in reading "he who hates let him divorce" (11), and justified this on the grounds that it was better for the woman to be spared any hard-heartedness (or worse) that might occur if she were in unwilling servitude.

◼ THE TEXT IN CONTEMPORARY DISCUSSION

Some refer to the apparent condemnation of divorce in Mal. 2:16 as a biblical teaching that prohibits divorce (see Sassoon, 25); it has even been called "a cosmic argument against divorce" (Lilly, 351), but it is not clear whether the denunciation is about cruelty (Hill, 258), intermarriage (Sweeney, 738), or breach of covenant in divorce (Block, 51). Some argue that this condemns divorce without justification prompted by dislike (Collins, 125). It may also be "the combination of . . . marriage to foreign women who worship 'foreign' gods and . . . 'faithlessness' toward one's own wife" (Wacker, 477).

Malachi 2:17—3:18 God of Covenantal Faithfulness

◼ THE TEXT IN ITS ANCIENT CONTEXT

The paragraph divisions in the Masoretic text suggest that Mal. 2:17 should be read along with 3:1-12. The combined section of Mal. 2:17—3:12 is marked by the question-and-answer form typical of Malachi, that much of the people's behavior remains unacceptable (2:17; see also 3:7-9). In English Bibles, Malachi 3 ends with a characteristic warning to the audience (3:13-18).

Whereas the last section of the book is divided into Malachi 3 and 4 in English Bibles, it is one chapter in the Hebrew, and thus forms the conclusion to the middle section of the Hebrew Bible, the *nĕbî'îm*, or Prophets. In English versions, this means that these chapters form the conclusion to the "Old Testament," and this may partly explain that they played a significant part in biblical studies before historical criticism became more or less the only approved approach. It is now almost universally accepted that the book of Daniel only reached its present form in the second century BCE, but when Daniel was taken as a sixth-century creation, Malachi was accepted as the last product of Judaism before what used to be described as the "intertestamental period."

"My messenger" in 3:1 translates "Malachi," and as is shown above it is likely that it was only at a later stage that this was taken to be a proper name (see 2 Esd. 1:40). The identity of this messenger is not revealed until Mal. 4:5, which is perhaps an explanatory gloss on 3:1. The figure expected is no mere bringer of a message (3:2-4). The prophet's words in 3:5 are typical of many prophetic condemnations of false practice, especially in religious matters. It may be that one can establish from 3:5 the particular problems affecting the community in Malachi's time, but to do this may be too specific—each of the evils condemned here could have been found at many different times in the people's history.

Following the affirmation of YHWH's continuing relationship with "the children of Jacob" (3:6), two rather divergent lines are pursued in 3:7-10. Malachi uses language typical of the Deuteronomistic tradition to warn the people against long-established practices regarded as sinful; they are to "return" to the requirements of the statutes laid down from of old (3:7). The verb *šûb*, here translated "return," is common throughout the prophetic collection (e.g., Isa. 1:27; Jer. 3:12; Hosea 6:1), and has been seen by some as supplying a connecting thread binding together the Book of the Twelve as a single coherent collection. It is much disputed whether it implies that at some point in the past the people really had been loyal and obedient, or whether a better translation would be "turn," implying something of a new start. In any case, following the promise of blessing for those who offer tithes and offerings (LXX "tithes and firstfruits," 3:8-10), the next verses have a rather different emphasis, expressing the hope of a universal affirmation of Israel in a way uncommon in the Old Testament prophetic speeches with their overwhelming message of doom (3:11-12).

In Mal. 3:13-15, the prophet returns to the more characteristic note of warning. The values espoused by at least some in the community are to be reversed. The idea of a book (or scroll) of remembrance in 3:16-18 is a new development as far as the Hebrew Bible is concerned, though it is not difficult to envisage how it emerged from such origins as the scroll found in Josiah's time (2 Kings 22).

▋ THE TEXT IN THE INTERPRETIVE TRADITION

Malachi 3:1 has been very important in Christian tradition. Each of the Synoptic Gospels uses this passage to bring out their understanding of the figure of Jesus; the messenger is John the Baptizer, seen here as a precursor of Jesus. Mark, usually taken to be the earliest of the Gospels, attributes the passage to Isaiah (Mark 1:2). Whether this is a simple error or it reflects the way in which "Isaiah" came to be regarded as *the* typical prophet cannot be decided here. In any case, the later Gospels strengthen the association with the prophetic tradition by attributing the citation to Jesus himself (Matt. 11:10; Luke 7:27).

The early Christian writers, except Theodore of Mopsuestia (d. 428) (415), were confident that in Mal. 3:2-4 the reference was to Jesus, but this vivid language was scarcely borne out by what was known of his earthly ministry. From an early stage, therefore, they came to be associated with an anticipated second coming of Jesus, and an understanding of this kind was common through much of Christian history, as is illustrated by the use of this passage in Handel's oratorio *Messiah*, which combines Mal. 3:1-3 with Hag. 2:6-7. This type of usage tended to play down the implications of Mal. 3:4, with its suggestion that the devastation would be followed by a speedy restoration of divine favor.

In later times, such a theme as "a book of remembrance" found in 3:16-18 became prominent, in the Dead Sea scrolls and the New Testament (Rev. 3:5), and of course through much of both Jewish and Christian history (see Daniélou, 198). Another matter that came to be of major significance in many religious traditions has been the distinction between the loyal members of the community ("the righteous"—those who serve God) and the rest ("the wicked"—those who do not). One is not far here from the themes of heresy and schism, which have occupied religious believers down the ages.

▋ THE TEXT IN CONTEMPORARY DISCUSSION

Malachi 3:6 found an unexpected contemporary application when the cricket World Cup played in India in 2011, with vast crowds gathering in Mumbai. Many religions were of course represented, and apparently a large Christian church near the ground had a big neon sign using this verse proclaiming "I am the LORD; I change not" (*Wisden Cricketers' Almanack* 2012, 791, has the reference;

it is not clear whether the sign had any effect!). More conventionally, this stress on the unchange-ability of the God worshiped by Jews and Christians has been used by apologists for those faiths, contrasting them with the fickleness of other forms of belief.

It is noteworthy that those condemned in 3:13-15 raise a question that has constantly arisen in philosophical and theological discussion to this day: Is there any point in following the words of a demanding God when those who are described as evildoers "not only prosper" but are also able to put God to the test with impunity? The claim is that it would be better to recognize that those who take matters into their own hands ("the arrogant") are really the blessed ones.

Malachi 4:1-6: The Day of Healing and Reconciliation

◼ THE TEXT IN ITS ANCIENT CONTEXT

The theme of a day of judgment characterized by the burning of the wicked (Mal. 4:1-3) may be a development of the "day of YHWH" referred to in Amos 5:18; Zeph. 1:14-17; and elsewhere. The final verses of the book (Mal. 4:4-6) are widely regarded as a kind of appendix, perhaps by the same author as the main part of the book, but more probably by a later editor. In any case, it functions as an appendix not just to the book of Malachi, but probably to the Twelve Minor Prophets as a whole, or even to the whole of the prophetic collection, which might include the "Former Prophets" (Joshua–2 Kings), as well as the material that has been customarily considered as "prophetic." The likelihood of its being the whole collection as the appropriate unit has been strengthened by the literary approach to this collection mentioned several times above.

Whereas in Mal. 4:4 the hearers or readers had been instructed to cast their mind back to God's past dealings with the people, in 4:5-6 the emphasis is clearly on the future. It becomes clear in 4:5 why there has been reference to the sending of Elijah, for this was a topic that became prominent later. It may be that he is singled out, not only because of the prominent role he played in the books of Kings, resisting the temptation of alien worship, but also because he is said not to have died but to have been "[taken] up to heaven by a whirlwind" (2 Kgs. 2:1), the obvious implication being that God had some further purpose in mind for him. One needs to bear in mind that to the best of the currently available knowledge there was no established belief in a future life for all at this period.

The final verse (4:6) is distinctly and surely deliberately ambiguous. Many modern translations, including the NRSV, have "children" here, in accordance with twenty-first-century expectations, but the Hebrew speaks of "sons"; in antiquity, the male members of the community were those who spelled out the demands of obedience to the torah. So the book, and the whole prophetic collection (covering from the Former Prophets of Joshua–2 Kings to the Latter Prophets of Isaiah, Jeremiah, Ezekiel, and the Twelve Minor Prophets) ends with the threat of a drastic curse.

◼ THE TEXT IN THE INTERPRETIVE TRADITION

The majority of Christian interpreters down the centuries have understood Mal. 4:1 as a reference to an anticipated time of final judgment. John Calvin took it to mean the first coming, and others regard it as the second coming (see Verhoef, 32). The KJV rendering of the end of 4:1 ("neither root nor branch") has become a standard way of describing the totality of judgment. The seventeenth-century English Long Parliament used the phrase "root and branch" to describe their desire to abolish episcopacy completely, and the situation eventually escalated to civil war.

The fate of the wicked is again the theme of 4:3, but the intervening, much more optimistic, verse (4:2) has been the source of a good deal of later reflection. In particular, the Gospels give no indication of the time of year at which Jesus was born, but his birth has come to be celebrated on December 25, following the winter solstice, and seen as the rising of a new sun of righteousness. Milton took up the theme in his *Ode on the Morning of Christ's Nativity*, and it is also found in the well-known Christmas hymn "Hark, the Herald Angels Sing," with its reference to Christ as "the sun of righteousness."

Malachi 4:5 offers the clearest reference within the Hebrew Bible itself to "the law of Moses." This may be a reference to the whole of the Pentateuch, but the most direct links are with Deuteronomy. As in Deuteronomy, "Horeb" is the name given to the holy mountain, rather than the more familiar "Sinai," and it was of course to Horeb that Elijah fled in 1 Kings 19 from the threat of revenge from Jezebel.

The New Testament Gospels clearly have in mind the expectation of a return of Elijah in Mal. 4:5-6; it is not clear whether the figure of the returning Elijah should be seen as John the Baptizer. Matthew 11:14 appears to accept this identification, and John 1:21 to deny it. In any case, it is noteworthy that in the account of what is usually termed the "transfiguration" of Jesus, Elijah is actually named before Moses (Mark 9:4). In Jewish tradition also, Elijah became important, with particular emphasis on his role in sustaining family life (*m. ʿEd.* 8:7; Danby 1933, 436–37); it is still a widespread custom to lay an extra place for Elijah at the Passover-tide meal.

The book (and the whole prophetic collection) ends with the threat of a drastic curse. Already by the time of the Greek translation (LXX), this was found unacceptable, and it was indicated that 4:4 should be read again after 4:6, to mitigate this threat. Some Jewish Bibles repeat 4:5 again in small print after 4:6, so that the book may end in the note of hope.

▮ THE TEXT IN CONTEMPORARY DISCUSSION

Depressingly familiar is the projected fate of those who are regarded as arrogant and evildoers in 4:1-3. By contrast, those who will fear the Lord are expected to experience healing with the return of Elijah. In light of 4:6, it is to be hoped that strong family traditions will ensure that Elijah's warnings will be taken to heart, so that the people may be proactive in seeking reconciliation and healing in broken relationships.

Works Cited

Baldwin, Joyce G. 1972. *Haggai, Zechariah, Malachi: An Introduction and Commentary.* TOTC. London: Tyndale Press.

Block, Daniel I. 2003. "Marriage and Family in Ancient Israel." *Marriage and Family in the Biblical World*, edited by Ken M. Campbell, 53–102. Downers Grove, IL: InterVarsity Press.

Coggins, Richard, and Jin H. Han. 2011. *Six Minor Prophets through the Centuries*. Blackwell Bible Commentaries. Chichester, UK: Wiley-Blackwell.

Collins, John J. 1997. "Marriage, Divorce, and Family in Second Temple Judaism." *Families in Ancient Israel*, by Leo G. Perdue, Joseph Blenkinsopp, John J. Collins, and Carol L. Meyers, 105–62. Louisville: Westminster John Knox.

Danby, Herbert, trans. 1933. *The Mishnah*. Oxford: Oxford University Press.

Daniélou, Jean. 1964. *The Theology of Jewish Christianity*. Vol. 1. London: Darton, Longman & Todd.

Hill, Andrew H. 1998. *Malachi: A New Translation with Introduction and Commentary*. AB 25D. New York: Doubleday.

Kaiser, Walter C., Jr. 1984. *Malachi: God's Unchanging Love*. Grand Rapids: Baker Books.

Kaiser, Walter C., Jr., Peter H. Davids, F. F. Bruce, and Manfred T. Brauch. 1996. *Hard Sayings of the Bible*. Downers Grove, IL: InterVarsity Press.

Levine, Ephraim. 1913. *Judaism*. People's Books 75. London: T. C. and E. C. Jack.

Lilly, Ingrid E. 2012. "Malachi." In *Women's Bible Commentary*, edited by Carol A. Newsom, Sharon H. Ringe, and Jacqueline E. Lapsley, 350–53. Rev. ed. Louisville: Westminster John Knox.

Meshel, Zeev. 1979. "Did Yahweh Have a Consort?" *BAR* 5:24–35.

Milton, John. 1645. *The Doctrine and Discipline of Divorce*. London: n.p.

Nogalski, James D. 1993a. *Literary Precursors to the Book of the Twelve*. BZAW 217. Berlin: de Gruyter.

———. 1993b. *Redactional Processes in the Book of the Twelve*. BZAW 218. Berlin: de Gruyter.

Petersen, David L. 1995. *Zechariah 9–14 and Malachi: A Commentary*. OTL. Louisville: Westminster John Knox.

Pfeiffer, Robert H. 1948. *Introduction to the Old Testament*. New York: Harper & Bros.

Rudolph, Wilhelm. 1975. *Micha, Nahum, Habakuk, Zephanja*. KAT 13/3. Gütersloh: Gütersloher Gerd Mohn.

Sassoon, Isaac. 2011. *The Status of Women in Jewish Tradition*. Cambridge: Cambridge University Press.

Schuller, Eileen M. 1996. "Malachi." *The New Interpreter's Bible*. Vol. 7, *Introduction to Apocalyptic Literature, Daniel, the Twelve Prophets*, edited by Leander E. Keck, 841–77. Nashville: Abingdon.

Sweeney, Marvin A. 2000. *The Twelve Prophets*. Vol. 2, *Micah, Nahum, Habakkuk, Zephaniah, Haggai, Zechariah, Malachi*. Berit Olam. Collegeville, MN: Liturgical Press.

Theodore of Mopsuestia. 2004. *Commentary on the Twelve Minor Prophets*. FC 108. Washington, DC: Catholic University of America Press.

Verhoef, Pieter A. 1987. *The Books of Haggai and Malachi*. NICOT. Grand Rapids: Eerdmans.

Wacker, Marie-Theres. 2012. "Malachi: To the Glory of God, the Father?" In *Feminist Biblical Interpretation: A Compendium of Critical Commentary on the Books of the Bible and Related Literature*, edited by Luise Schottroff and Marie-Theres Wacker, 473–82. Grand Rapids: Eerdmans.

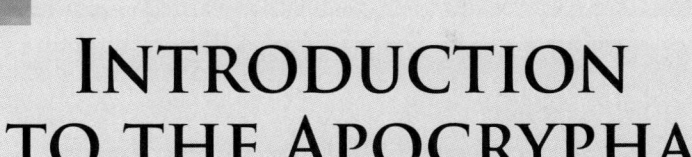

INTRODUCTION
TO THE APOCRYPHA

Eileen M. Schuller

Apocrypha is a term applied to various Jewish books of different genres and authors, written in Greek, Hebrew, or Aramaic, from about the third century BCE to the first century CE. These books are not part of the sacred Scriptures of Judaism today; hence they will not be found in a contemporary Jewish Bible (e.g., The Tanakh of the Jewish Publication Society). These books were, however, copied and transmitted by Christian scribes over the centuries. They have been accepted as sacred Scripture by the Roman Catholic and Orthodox churches, and have not been accepted as such by the Protestant churches; hence, they will be found in some contemporary Christian Bibles and not in others. Where they are included, they sometimes appear throughout the Old Testament, with other books of similar genre, and sometimes they are gathered together and placed between the Old and New Testaments (or, less frequently, after the New Testament). Over the centuries, their inclusion or exclusion has often been one of the more visible signs on a popular level of the differences between Catholics and Protestants ("our Bible is bigger/smaller than yours") and reflected at times very sharp polemics over who had the "right" biblical canon (that is, the authoritative list of books accepted as inspired sacred Scripture).

Over the last fifty or sixty years, there has been real shift in how the Apocrypha is approached, both within religious/church contexts and in the scholarly milieu. As the Apocrypha is translated and printed in more editions of the Bible and studied often in a religious studies context in universities, these books are becoming much more widely known. Although faith communities continue to have different views about their authority as Scripture, the value of these books "as significant documents of a most important era in religious history" (quoted in the preface to the Revised Standard Edition, 1957) is increasingly acknowledged, and they have become a significant component in the study of the beginnings of Judaism and Christianity.

We will begin by trying to understand why it is so difficult even to define the term and to draw up an agreed list of texts to be included in this category. Since each book of the Apocrypha is treated individually with its own introduction in the subsequent pages, here we will give only a general overview of the different genres and types of materials that are included in the Apocrypha. We will then conclude with some selective examples of what can be learned from these books and how they have been read and used over the centuries, both theologically and culturally.

Meaning and History of the Term

It is hard to give a short yet comprehensive definition of the term *Apocrypha* since the title has been applied to different collections both in antiquity and in modern times. Indeed, it is only quite recently that "the Apocrypha" has more frequently begun to be used as a singular noun as opposed to Apocrypha with a plural verb, emphasizing the individual books. In 1957, the RSV used the label "the Apocrypha"; the NRSV (1989) uses the designation "the Apocryphal/Deuterocanonical Books."

The word itself is Greek for something that is "hidden away" or "kept secret." Often the connotation is negative: something is kept hidden away because the contents of the books are false or at least not authoritative. (Thus Augustine and Athanasius use the term for books that were never part of the canon and that they considered heretical.) But something can be hidden because it is esoteric, knowledge that is designed only for an elite few. The term is often related to a passage in 2 Esd. 14:45-46 that distinguishes between twenty-four books (the traditional number in the Hebrew canon) that are accessible to everyone, and seventy other books ("Apocrypha") that "were written last" and were kept for the wise, "for in them is the spring of understanding, the fountain of wisdom and the river of knowledge." But there is no evidence that any of the seventy books referred to in 2 Esd. 14:46 overlap with what is presently known as the Apocrypha, and the Apocrypha as now defined is not kept hidden or secret.

The term in the sense that we are using it is very much influenced by the approach of Jerome, a Christian biblical scholar and translator who at the end of the fourth century CE was entrusted by Pope Damasus with preparing a revised Latin version of the Bible (the Vulgate) to replace the existing Latin translations (the so-called Old Latin). Jerome distinguished between the books that were in the Hebrew Bible as known by the Jews of his day and the additional books that were included in the major Greek (Septuagint) Christian Old Testament manuscripts of his day; these latter books he termed Apocrypha. (At times, he did include in this category still other books, such as *Shepherd of Hermas*.) Although Jerome translated the books of the Jewish Bible directly into Latin from their original Hebrew (rather than using the Greek translation), when it came to the Apocrypha, he translated only Tobit and Judith (noting in the prefaces that he had devoted only a single day to Tobit and a single night to Judith). He included the additions to Daniel and Esther but marked in the margins that these were not in the Hebrew Bible. Over time, the Old Latin translations of the rest of the Apocrypha were regularly included in Vulgate Bibles, usually without the notes and prefaces wherein Jerome had made his careful distinctions. With the wide acceptance of the

Vulgate, these books in Latin were read as part of "the Bible" in the Western church, as they were in the Eastern church, where they continued to be copied in Greek manuscripts.

The issue of the Apocrypha came to the fore again in the sixteenth century, when the Protestant Reformers decided to follow the canon of the Hebrew Bible, though for the most part, they did not totally deny a place to those books that were not included. Martin Luther translated these books (with the exception of 1 and 2 Esdras) into German in 1534 and put them in a separate section in his Bible with the heading "Apocrypha," that is, books which are not held as equal to holy Scripture, yet which are useful to read. The 1546 Geneva Bible, with an introduction attributed to John Calvin, made a stronger distinction between "Holy Scripture" and the Apocrypha, considered "profane books," and the latter were sometimes omitted entirely. In the Anglican tradition, these books were kept for "example of life and instruction of manner" but not "to establish any doctrine" (Thirty-Nine Articles); they continued to be heard frequently in church services since they were part of the lectionary of the Book of Common Prayer. After the publication of the King James Version in 1611, the archbishop of Canterbury in 1615 insisted that every Bible that was printed must include these books, though in fact within a few years many editions appeared that did not contain them. Later documents such as the 1647 Westminster Confession adopted a more negative stance: "the books commonly called Apocrypha, not being of divine inspiration, are no part of the canon of the Scripture; and therefore of no authority in the Church of God, nor to be otherwise approved, or made use of, than other human writings."

In this era of controversy over the biblical canon, the Council of Trent in 1546 drew up for the first time a specific and formal list of books that must be included in the Roman Catholic canon and "condemned" anyone "who does not accept these books in their entirety, with all their parts, according to the text usually read in the Catholic church, and as they are in the ancient Vulgate." In terms of their placement, in Catholic Bibles these books were not isolated but integrated, on the basis of genre and historical period; so, for example, Wisdom of Solomon and Ecclesiasticus (Sirach) come with the other Wisdom books after Song of Songs. Books concerned with the exile are grouped together in the following order: Lamentation, Baruch, and the Letter of Jeremiah. Since 1 and 2 Maccabees covered the latest historical period, they are placed at the end of the historical writings. The additions to Esther and Daniel are integrated into these books at relevant places in the narrative, and the additional stories about Daniel (Susanna, and Bel and the Dragon) become the final chapters, 13 and 14, of that book. Three works (Prayer of Manasseh and 1 and 2 Esdras) were not accorded status as canonical books and were put into an appendix after the New Testament in editions of the Vulgate published after the Council of Trent. (Over time, this appendix has disappeared from most Catholic Bibles.) In the terminology introduced by Sextus of Sienna in 1566, a distinction came to be made between "protocanonical" books (books of the Hebrew Bible for which there was no debate about status) and "deuterocanonical" books (those that had been debated).

In the following centuries, the Apocrypha section was often dropped from Protestant Bibles, sometimes for the pragmatic publishing reasons of saving space and cost, at other times in order to distinguish clearly between a Protestant and a Catholic Bible. Indeed, in the nineteenth century, Bible societies in various countries often debated and established formal policies about whether any of their funds could be used for the printing of these books. In 1957, the Apocrypha section of the Revised Standard Version was first published (the New Testament and Old Testament had been available since 1952), containing a rather sparse selection (the books included in the Roman Catholic canon plus 1 and 2 Esdras and the Prayer of Manasseh). The New Revised Standard Version (1989) included many more books in the Apocrypha (see discussion below), and it is in this form that the Apocrypha has become more widely known in both church and academic contexts. Responding to the desire to include these books but recognizing the different authority accorded to them, the "Guidelines for Interconfessional Cooperation in the Bible," published in 1987 by the Secretariat for Promoting Christian Unity (Roman Catholic) and the United Bible Societies (Protestant), agreed that they be published in a separate section.

Content of the Apocrypha

As implied above, there is no set content for "the Apocrypha," and there has been considerable fluidity in the books included in this category, dependent on the time and context. At minimum, the collection includes certain books that are always included in the Roman Catholic, Greek Orthodox, and Slavonic Bibles. These are sometimes counted as seven books plus additions to two books (Daniel and Esther), or as up to twelve books, depending on how the additions are arranged and counted: Tobit, Judith, Wisdom of Solomon, Ecclesiasticus or the Wisdom of Jesus Son of Sirach, Baruch, 1 Maccabees, 2 Maccabees, additions to the book of Esther (107 verses of narrative materials plus the prayers of Mordecai and Esther), additions to the book of Daniel (the Prayer of Azariah and the Song of the Three Young Men (or Three Jews), Susanna, Bel and the Dragon), and Letter of Jeremiah (sometimes included as chapter 6 of Baruch).

A wider version of the Apocrypha includes those books that are regularly part of Greek and Slavonic Bibles, but are not in the Roman Catholic canon (although as we have seen above, some are included in an appendix to the Latin Vulgate). The Orthodox churches have always set discussion about canon less in terms of conciliar decisions and specific lists of books, and more on which books are regularly read and quoted within the community, especially in a liturgical context. Orthodox Bibles, both Greek and Slavonic, include 1 Esdras, Prayer of Manasseh, Psalm 151, and 3 Maccabees; Slavonic Bibles regularly include 2 Esdras. Finally, 4 Maccabees is included because it appears as an appendix in Greek Bibles.

Thus two criteria are crucial for inclusion in the Apocrypha: (1) acceptance by churches (some, not necessarily all) as canonical and (2) inclusion in major fourth- to sixth-century Greek Christian manuscripts (Vaticanus, Sinaiticus, Alexandrinus) or in the Vulgate. Books such as *1 Enoch* and *Jubilees* meet only the first criterion insofar as these two books are accepted as canonical within the Ethiopic church. A work such as the *Psalms of Solomon*, which is included in a sort of appendix to Codex Alexandrinus, meets the second criterion, but this collection of psalms has not been accepted by any church body. The semiexception is 4 Maccabees, which is not canonical for any church but is printed as an appendix in Greek Bibles.

The Apocrypha both overlaps with and should be distinguished from other categories and descriptive titles that are used for related and semioverlapping collections. In the past, sometimes the designation "intertestamental literature" has been applied to books composed between the completion of the last books of Hebrew Bible and earliest of the New Testament books. These books were often grouped together and placed literally between the Old and Testaments, and could be considered to form a "theological bridge between the Testaments" (Harrington, 1). This term, however, is fading from use because of its ambiguity (many of these books may well predate Daniel, and parts of 2 Esdras are later than anything in the New Testament) and because the "inter-" terminology assumes the acceptance of the New Testament as part of the Bible.

From one perspective, the Apocrypha can be considered as part of the larger category of Pseudepigrapha. Many of the books of the Apocrypha are pseudonymous; that is, they are presented as the work of a figure of the past who is clearly not the real author. Thus the book of Baruch, though written probably sometime after 200 BCE, begins, "These are the words of the book that Baruch son of Neriah . . . wrote in Babylon . . . at the time when the Chaldeans took Jerusalem and burned it with fire." The Letter of Jeremiah, a postexilic work in Greek, starts, "A copy of a letter that Jeremiah sent to those who were to be taken to Babylon as exiles." Second Esdras, clearly written after the destruction of Jerusalem in 70 CE, situates itself in the time of the Babylonian conquest, "In the thirtieth year after the destruction of the city, I was in Babylon—I, Salathiel, who am also called Ezra" (2 Esd. 3:1). The royal figure who speaks as "I" in the Wisdom of Solomon continues the tradition already established in the Song of Songs and Proverbs of attributing wisdom works to King Solomon. However, the term *Pseudepigrapha* as introduced by Johann Fabricius in the early eighteenth century is used by many scholars to cover a much wider expanse of any nonbiblical Jewish literature from the Second Temple period, some pseudepigraphic in form (*1, 2,* and *3 Enoch, Testament of Abraham, Testament of Moses, Syriac Baruch, Psalms of Solomon*) and others not (*Jubilees, Biblical Antiquities, Life of Adam and Eve*). Sometimes, especially in European Catholic scholarship, the term *Apocrypha* is applied to this much larger and more amorphous collection of Jewish works (Charlesworth 1983; Bauckham, Davila, and Panayotov, 2013).

The Dead Sea Scrolls are standardly treated separately since this material was discovered only in 1947–1956 in caves near the northwestern shore of the Dead Sea. This collection of ancient manuscripts includes a number of the Apocrypha: four copies of Tobit in Aramaic and one in Hebrew (4Q196–200), a fragmentary Hebrew copy of Sirach (2Q18; in addition, a copy of Sir. 39:27—43:30 was found at Masada), one copy of the Letter of Jeremiah in Greek in Cave 7, and the Hebrew version of Psalm 151 (in 11QPs^a). Most of the Dead Sea Scrolls are either copies of the books of the Hebrew Bible (about one-quarter) or previously unknown works (rules, hymns, commentaries), some composed by a distinctive sectarian group (the Essenes or a related group) but others coming from "common Judaism" of the Second Temple period. What canonical status some of these books may have had for the communities that copied them is hard to ascertain; there are more copies of some books like *Enoch* and *Jubilees* than there are of many of the books of the Hebrew Bible, and *Jubilees* is quoted as an authority in a work like the Damascus Document.

The Apocrypha as applied to Jewish literature should be distinguished from the Christian "Apocrypha," that is, a large collection of Christian literature (especially narratives about specific figures such as the *Acts of Paul* and the *Acts of Thecla*) that did not become part of the New Testament canon. Finally, we should note that different traditions give different names to the same work, particularly to the Ezra literature, and this can often generate confusion about precisely what is included (e.g., 1 Esdras = 2 Esdras in Slavonic, 3 Esdras in appendix to Vulgate; 2 Esdras = 3 Esdras in Slavonic, 4 Esdras in Vulgate appendix; includes 5 and 6 Ezra).

Date and Genres of the Apocrypha

In terms of quantity of material, the Apocrypha is a substantial collection. It is about one-fifth of the length of the Old Testament and over two-thirds that of the New Testament (Goodman, 4). Although the books of the Apocrypha are all religious literature from the Jewish community written in the land of Israel and the Diaspora and in the Second Temple period (with the exception of 2 Esdras 1–2, 15–16, which contain somewhat later Christian material), it is often extremely difficult to establish with certainty the exact dates and places or even the original language of composition for individual works.

Some books such as 1 Maccabees, the first part of Baruch (1:1—3:8), and Sirach were certainly written in Hebrew. This is confirmed for Sirach by the fragments in Hebrew that have been found among the Dead Sea Scrolls, and Ben Sira's grandson in his prologue to his Greek translation explicitly reflects on the difficulty of capturing "what was originally expressed in Hebrew." It is likely that Tobit was originally written in Aramaic, but it was translated early on into Hebrew, since there is a Hebrew copy among the Dead Sea Scrolls. The book of Judith may have been written in Hebrew or in Aramaic. Yet all of these books in their totality survived only in Greek translation, and it is the Greek text from the fourth- to sixth-century-CE manuscripts (Vaticanus, Sinaiticus, Alexandrinus) that provides the basis for our modern translations. The exception is 2 Esdras, where translation must be made from the Vulgate. Greek was the original language of many books of the Apocrypha, including the Wisdom of Solomon, 2, 3, and 4 Maccabees, and Prayer of Manasseh. For the books written in Greek, it is often difficult to determine if they were composed in Alexandria or in another major city of the Diaspora. Antioch is often proposed, for instance, as the place of composition for 4 Maccabees, especially since the Maccabean martyrs, whose example is the foundation of the book, were especially venerated there.

For the most part, little can be known of individual authors, only a few of whom are known by name: Jesus son of Eleazar son of Sirach of Jerusalem identifies himself in Sir. 50:27; the name of the author of the unabridged work of five volumes, of which 2 Maccabees is a summary, is given as Jason of Cyrene (2 Macc. 2:19-23). The colophon at the end of the Greek version of Esther mentions "Lysimachus, son of Ptolemy, one of the residents of Jerusalem" (11:1), and it is generally thought that he was the translator of Esther into Greek.

The date of books that treat concrete historical events and persons can be established with some degree of precision or at least within certain boundaries, but for many books only a tentative date or range of dates can be proposed. (Dates of composition will be discussed in more detail in the commentary on individual books.) For example, the historical books 1 and 2 Maccabees were obviously written after the latest events described (134 BCE for 1 Maccabees, 163 BCE for 2 Maccabees). Sirach can be dated most precisely, since the book was translated into Greek by the author's grandson after his arrival in Egypt in 132 BCE (prologue to Sirach, "the thirty-eighth year of the reign of Euergetes"), and so his grandfather must have lived in Jerusalem around 180 BCE. Third Maccabees describes events in Egypt during the reign of King Ptolemy IV Philopator (221–203 BCE), but references to other facets of Egyptian Jewish life (a possible reference in 3 Macc. 2:28 to a poll tax inaugurated in 24 BCE) suggest the book was written considerably later than the events it purports to narrate. Books of prayers and wisdom admonitions are, of course, much more difficult to fit into a specific historical framework. Since Josephus knew and used books such as 1 Esdras, Greek Esther, and 1 Maccabees, this establishes a *terminus ante quem* before the late first century CE. It is generally accepted that 2 Esdras is one of the latest books; chapters 3–14 reflect on the destruction of Jerusalem in 70 CE, and chapters 1–2 and 15–16 are almost certainly additions by Christians authors, perhaps as late as the third century CE.

In terms of genre, historical or quasi-historical works predominate. First Esdras summarizes 2 Chron. 35:1—36:23 and reproduces all of Ezra plus Nehemiah 7:38—8:12. Only 1 Esd. 3:1—5:6 is "new" material, a court tale set in the time of King Xerxes but probably composed sometime later. First Maccabees is a type of theological interpretative history modeled after Deuteronomy–Chronicles. Second Maccabees is much more influenced by the Hellenistic genre of "pathetic history," in which highly charged and emotional language arouses the emotions or "pathos" of the readers. Third Maccabees, also in the Hellenistic style, has nothing to do with the Maccabean crisis of the mid-second century BCE in Judah but rather is a dramatic tale of the suffering and persecution of Jews in Egypt under the Ptolemies in the third century BCE. Fourth Maccabees, although set in the time of the Maccabean martyrs, is a philosophical treatise extolling the supremacy of reason over passion that could have been written in a number of different historical circumstances in the first century CE.

Other books are set in a historical context, but it is generally accepted that they are not intended to report history as such or to be used for recovering historical facts. These moralistic narratives are closer to our modern classification of novels/novellas (Judith, Tobit); some (like the stories in Daniel 1–6, Susanna, Bel and the Dragon) belong to a genre of "tales of the wise man in the court of the foreign ruler."

The wisdom tradition as exemplified in the biblical book of Proverbs is continued in Sirach, both in terms of proverbial sayings and themes (riches and poverty, fear of the Lord, women). However, there are new features, such as longer poetic units that develop a topic rather than individual proverbs, and new themes are introduced (the praise of the ancestors in chapters 44–50, the identification of personified Wisdom with Torah in chapter 24). The Wisdom of Solomon likewise treats standard wisdom themes, but with forms, vocabulary, and philosophical ideas, particularly concerning immortality, that are influenced by Hellenistic genres and philosophical concepts. The wisdom of 2 Esdras is a revealed wisdom, given in a series of seven revelations to Ezra in visions that are interpreted by an angel; this is the only example of a fully developed apocalypse in the Apocrypha.

Thus the books of the Apocrypha, in different ways depending on their genre, open up a window on Second Temple Judaism, both in terms of history and of religious and theological developments. For historical study, they cannot be used in isolation, but when they are combined with the Dead Sea Scrolls, the Pseudepigrapha, and the works of Philo and Josephus, we learn considerable information about this important period of history and religious development, certainly much more information than can be known from the Old and New Testament alone.

Selected Themes in the Apocrypha

On the one hand, it is misleading to treat the Apocrypha as if it were an intentional collection of books, put together because they share common themes or interests or purposes. As we have seen, this is a much more random collection of literature, very diverse in terms of when, where, and by whom individual books were composed. What came to be included in the collection was shaped predominately by issues of canon formation in the Jewish and Christian communities over the centuries. Yet there are certain themes and emphases that do seem to stand out. Other themes, some recurring frequently and some distinctive to particular books, will emerge in the commentaries on individual works.

Given the historical reality of empire and world powers, much of this literature is concerned either explicitly or implicitly with how to "respond to challenges of Hellenism and persevere as a minority culture in a Greek world" (deSilva, 16). An openness to and the adoption of the Greek language, new literary forms, and diverse philosophical ideas (e.g., immortality of the soul) stand along aside the conviction that there are beliefs and values that cannot be abandoned (monotheism, Torah, Sabbath, circumcision, dietary laws; see for instance 1 Macc. 1:54-64 or Tobit's deathbed instruction to his son in 4:5-19).

Beginning with one of the first modern studies of the Apocrypha (Johnson), the frequency and importance of prayer in this literature has often been recognized. The Apocrypha preserves independent prayers (Prayer of Manasseh, Psalm 151), as well as the extended prayers of both penitence and praise that were added to the Hebrew form of Daniel (Prayer of Azariah, Song of the Three Young Men) and Esther (prayers of Esther and Mordecai), the latter of which are particularly to be noted because the Hebrew version of the book has no address to God or even mention of the divine name. Both short prose prayers and longer poetic passages are scattered throughout the narratives of Tobit: the prayers of Tobit (3:1–6), Sarah (3:11–15), Tobias (8:5-7), Raguel (8:15–17); the hymn of Tobit in chapter13; Judith's prayer in chapter 9; the short petitions in 13:4, 7; the victory hymn in 16:1-17; and the penitential prayer of the high priest in 3 Macc. 2:2-20. Even when there is no actual prayer text given, 1 and 2 Maccabees presume that, in time of crisis and battle, the recitation of prayers and hymns are part of the preparation for warfare and the celebration of victory (1 Macc. 4:24, 40; 13:51; 2 Macc. 10:7, 38; 12:37). Although it is sometimes claimed that the introduction of frequent prayers, especially combined with an increased emphasis on angelic intermediaries, indicates that God has become "inaccessible in his holiness" (Kaiser, 3–4), these prayers can be seen rather as expressing a deep conviction of divine involvement that finds expression in a rich and active devotional piety. The prayers within narratives sometimes reflect liturgical practices that were in the process of development, especially in daily set forms of prayer (compare the blessing formularies that became the standardized introduction and conclusion for rabbinic prayers with the blessing formula at the beginning of some of the prayers in Tobit, e.g., "Blessed are you, merciful

God. Blessed is your name forever," 3:11; "Blessed are you, O God of our ancestors, and blessed is your name in all generations forever," 8:5.

Many of the apocryphal books touch on the "mystery of suffering" (Harrington, viii). While a book like Sirach keeps to the traditional view that there is no retribution after death and that sinners are punished in this life (Sir. 40:8-9), other books confront more directly the suffering of the righteous and look for a final vindication, sometimes in the immortality of the soul beyond death (Wisdom of Solomon) or through a direct divine revelation, as in the visions that Ezra sees of the restored Jerusalem or the man from the sea (2 Esdras 10, 13).

It has frequently been noted that women play an important and prominent role in many of these books. Two books, Judith and Susanna, are named after their central female characters, in addition to the book of Esther, where Queen Esther's role is enhanced by the addition of her prayer in the Greek version. Seventeen women are named in these books (Craven, 16), and there are significant women who are not given a name, most notably the mother of the seven martyred sons in 2 Maccabees 7 and 4 Maccabees. The Apocrypha contains some of the most negative material about women (such as Sir. 25:24, the first explicit statement blaming Eve for bringing death into the world). However, the Apocrypha also contains some positive statements about women. These range from the popularistic court tale (1 Esd. 4:13-32) that acknowledges that women are more powerful than the king or wine, indeed that "women rule over you," to the more theological reflections of Sirach 24 and Wisdom of Solomon 7–9, where rich female imagery is used to shape an exalted understanding of Sophia/Wisdom, who tells of her glory in the assembly of the Most High (Sir. 24:2) and who "in every generation . . . passes into holy souls and makes them friends of God and prophets" (Wisd. of Sol. 7:27).

The Use and Influence of the Apocrypha

It is often not clear to what extent individual books of the Apocrypha were known in Judaism after the Second Temple period. We have noted that Josephus used the additions to Esther, 1 Maccabees, and 1 Esdras (rather than the Hebrew Ezra-Nehemiah), but from the second century CE there was a move away from the Septuagint to using translations by Jews such as Aquila and Theodotion that did not include the Apocrypha or the additions to Daniel and Esther. When the rabbis discussed which Hebrew/Aramaic books "rendered the hands unclean" (*m. Yad.* 4:5), the polemic was around books such as Song of Songs and Ecclesiastes rather than books of the Apocrypha. Sirach was the one book quoted and often cited by name by the rabbis, even though it was acknowledged that it was not in the Hebrew Bible. It is often unclear whether the rabbis knew specific books per se or only traditions, such as those about the martyrdom of seven sons. Indeed, the rabbis sometimes focused on traditions not based on apocryphal books. For instance, the Hanukkah story of the oil in the temple that miraculously was sufficient to burn for eight days (*b. Shab.* 21b) is not found in 1 and 2 Maccabees.

During the Renaissance, Jewish interest was sparked in these books, and a translation of most into Hebrew was made in the early sixteenth century. Although historians have always drawn on the data in books such as 1 and 2 Maccabees, in recent centuries most of these books were not widely read by Jews, often being treated with suspicion as Christian literature. The Apocrypha will be part of the forthcoming major three-volume project, *Outside the Bible: Ancient Jewish Writings Related to Scripture*, initiated by the Jewish Publication Society to provide an up-to-date, readily accessible translation of extrabiblical texts for wide circulation in the Jewish and secular communities.

Since the Apocrypha was treated as part of the Old Testament for the most part in the Western and Eastern churches, it is not surprising to find numerous references and allusions in the New Testament and the church fathers. Again, it is often difficult to judge what is a direct quotation from an apocryphal book per se and when Christian authors are simply drawing on a common tradition or general vocabulary—for example, the reference to the martyrs in 2 Maccabees 6–7 and in Heb. 11:35-37, and similar terminology in the Wisdom of Solomon and the letters of Paul and the letter to the Hebrews (e.g., Heb. 1:1-3/Wisd. of Sol. 7.26; 1 Cor. 2:10-16/Jth. 8:14; Rom. 9:3; 10:1/Pr. of Man. 8–9).

The Apocrypha has exerted a significant influence on popular culture, in art, music, and drama, throughout the Middle Ages and into the modern era. The dramatic stories of Judith, Susanna, and the Maccabees have been particularly attractive and have been retold and reenacted in a variety of media: the *Canterbury Tales* (lines 3757–64); lesser-known Scottish ballads; medieval miracle plays; Henry Wadsworth Longfellow's poem on Judas Maccabeus; and Handel's oratorios *Susanna*, *Judas Maccabeus*, and *Alexander Balus*. A recent monograph has explored Judith studies across the disciplines, collecting examples of representations of Judith from the visual arts, music, and drama (see Brine, Ciletti, and Lähnemann). Equally rich studies could be done on the reception and reinterpretation of some of the other books of the Apocrypha.

Bruce Metzger collected some fascinating examples of the often-unrecognized influence of bits and pieces from the Apocrypha in the popular realm. For instance, many people quote the maxim, "Great is truth and strongest of all" (NRSV) or in the King James Version, "Great is Truth, and mighty above all things," without realizing that it comes from 1 Esd. 4:41. Similarly, when singing the Christmas hymn "It Came Upon the Midnight Clear," few people recognize that the identification of the hour of the birth is dependent on a passage in Wisdom of Solomon which declares that "the all-powerful word leaped from heaven" when "night in its swift course was now half gone" (18:14-15). And it was on the basis of 2 Esd. 6:42 and its interpretation of day three of the Genesis creation story that Christopher Columbus set out for India, confident that the seas could not be that vast since the waters were "gathered together in a seventh part of the earth" and six parts were dry land.

The Apocrypha becomes known to many churchgoers through the liturgy. In the Orthodox, Anglican, and Roman Catholic churches, selections from the Apocrypha are regularly read in the prescribed lectionary for Sundays, feasts, and weekdays; however, in the Revised Common Lectionary (an adaptation of the Roman lectionary), which is used in many Protestant churches, whenever a reading from Apocrypha is listed, an alternative from the canonical books is also provided. In lectionaries, the Wisdom of Solomon is the book that is used most frequently (on nine Sundays in the Roman Catholic lectionary). A passage from Wisdom of Solomon, "But the souls of the righteous are in the hand of God" (3:1), is sometimes popular as a funeral reading even in Protestant churches that do not otherwise use the Apocrypha. According to long-standing tradition, on feasts of Mary, the first reading is often a passage about Lady Wisdom from Wisdom of Solomon 7–9 or Sirach 24 or the canticle from Judith 16. In the daily Roman lectionary, substantial portions of Tobit, 1 and 2 Maccabees, and Sirach are read over consecutive days. The liturgical use of the Prayer of Manasseh and the Song of the Three Young Men makes these apocryphal prayers part of contemporary devotional practice.

Works Cited

Bauckham, Richard, James R. Davila, Alexander Panayotov, eds. *Old Testament Pseudepigrapha: More Noncanonical Scriptures*, 2013. Grand Rapids: Eerdmans.

Brine, Kevin R., Elena Ciletti, and Henrike Lähnemann. 2010. *The Sword of Judith: Judith Studies across the Disciplines*. Cambridge: OpenBook.

Charlesworth, James H., 1983. *The Old Testament Pseudepigrapha*. Garden City: Doubleday & Company.

Craven, Toni. 2000. "The Apocrypha/Deuterocanonical Books." In *Women in Scripture*, edited by Carol Meyers, Toni Craven, and Ross S. Kraemer, 12–16. Grand Rapids: Eerdmans.

DeSilva, David A. 2001. *Introducing the Apocrypha: Message, Context, and Significance*. Grand Rapids: Baker Academic.

Feldman, Louis H., James Kugel, and Lawrence H. Schiffman. 2013. *Outside the Bible: Ancient Jewish Writings Related to Scripture*. 3 vols. Philadelphia: Jewish Publication Society; Lincoln: University of Nebraska Press.

Goodman, Martin. 2012. *The Apocrypha*. Oxford Bible Commentary. Oxford: Oxford University Press.

Harrington, Daniel, J. 1999. *Invitation to the Apocrypha*. Grand Rapids: Eerdmans.

Johnson, Norma Burrows. 1948. *Prayer in the Apocrypha and Pseudepigrapha: A Study of the Jewish Concept of God*. Philadelphia: Society of Biblical Literature and Exegesis.

Kaiser, Otto. 2004. *The Old Testament Apocrypha: An Introduction*. Peabody, MA: Hendrickson.

Metzger, Bruce. 1957. *An Introduction to the Apocrypha*. New York: Oxford University Press.

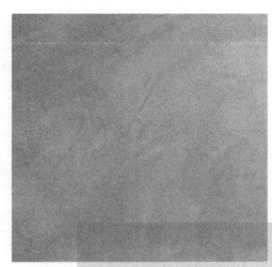

TOBIT

Micah D. Kiel

Introduction

The book of Tobit is a fascinating folktale about a family living in Nineveh during the Assyrian exile. It weaves many different threads, traditions, motifs, and characters into an entertaining tale that also has profound depth.

Historical Context

The book of Tobit makes no overt historical references that allow it to be dated with precision. Based on its original language (Aramaic) and theology (emphasis on unwarranted suffering), a date between 250–175 BCE seems the most likely. The place of its composition is also difficult to discern. Many recent treatments of the book suggest that it may have been composed quite close to, if not within, Jerusalem itself (Fitzmyer; Moore; Kiel).

Canonical and Theological Context

Tobit is a book within the deuterocanonical literature (sometimes also called the Apocrypha). As such, it is deemed canonical by Roman Catholics, but generally not by Protestants. The discovery of the Dead Sea Scrolls (DSS), however, has proved to be a watershed for our understanding of Tobit. Fragments of Tobit have been found among the DSS in both Aramaic and Hebrew, proving that it was written in Aramaic, not Greek. As a result, the philological criterion (that it should not be deemed canonical because it was not written in a semitic language) originally used to justify Tobit's proscription rests on shoddy footing.

Although not canonical for large segments of Christianity, the book of Tobit will prove salutary for anyone interested in studying Scripture. Many Christians, including early pillars of the faith (e.g., Origen, Clement), have read it as "Scripture." Tobit also contributes to an understanding of the biblical world. It is unique as the only text that envisions the Assyrian exile and deportation as its hypothetical historical referent. Tobit provides a more extended picture of quotidian Jewish family life than any other biblical book. Finally, the book of Tobit is a serious piece of narrative theology. Although enshrined in a folktale, it strives to say something profound in conversation with contemporaneous theological formulations. It intentionally engages Deuteronomy, Job, and Sirach as conversation partners. This is a book that had dipped its pen in many inkpots (Nickelsburg 1996, 340) and deserves a place at the table in canon-based theological discussions.

Tobit 1:1—3:17: Tobit and Sarah's Predicaments

◼ THE TEXT IN ITS ANCIENT CONTEXT

Tobit strives to live a righteous life while in exile, and he succeeds. His paradigmatic righteous activity is burying his kin properly. In Tobit 2, after another burial of one of his people, Tobit must sleep outside, where bird droppings and visits to physicians produce blindness. Tobit suffers: his wife mocks him; his family is suddenly destitute. As a result, he prays for release in 3:1-6. Tobit's prayer asserts his own guilt because of his association with the guilt of his forebears. He can find no way to conceive of his suffering other than that he brought it on himself. The prayer proffers a close connection between act and consequence.

After Tobit's prayer, the narrative flashes to a different city, where a similarly grieving Sarah laments over her demonic affliction (3:11-15). Sarah's prayer, however, brazenly asserts her own innocence in the face of her suffering. The narrative then provides a brief, dramatic glimpse of the heavenly realm. Both of these prayers, we are told, were received before the presence of God, and God sends Raphael to help.

These two prayers contain the two main issues of the book: The first is theodicy, or God's justice in the face of unwarranted suffering. The second is related to the first: a narrative dynamic in which the characters have a limited awareness of their own situations. Although both Tobit and Sarah face severe challenges, the reader knows quite a bit more about God's involvement in alleviating those challenges (in this case, dispatching Raphael to help and heal). This creates dramatic irony and, at the same time, foists on the reader questions about God and human experience: What do we know about God's ways? This is similar to the book of Job, in which the characters in the poetic chapters grope for a reason as to why Job suffers (while the reader knows that God's wager with *ha satan* was behind it the whole time). In Tobit, the characters are similarly in the dark as to the cause of their suffering, but so is the reader. It is not readily apparent why Tobit and Sarah suffer.

The episode in Tob. 3:16-17 bears some similarity to other Jewish literature of the Second Temple period. The prayers of both characters are heard "in the glorious presence of God," which in Greek is the exact description of God's throne in *1 Enoch* 104:1. The episode tells the reader how the story will end—with Tobit's sight restored and Sarah happily married to Tobias. God gives this mission to Raphael, whose name, "God heals," fits his role in the story. Raphael's mission in Tobit is similar to the apocalyptic text *1 Enoch*, in which he is dispatched to bind a demon and bury him in the desert, the same fate that Sarah's menace, Asmodeus, will suffer.

■ THE TEXT IN THE INTERPRETIVE TRADITION

Scenes from Tobit were popular in the history of art, especially in the late-medieval and Renaissance periods. In a time when most artists were restricted to painting only biblical scenes or those that their patrons wanted, available subject matter was quite limited. Tobit provides three specific details rare in biblical narratives: a fish, a named angel, and a dog. Many paintings from the book of Tobit have at least one of these three elements, often all three (e.g., Filippino Lippi's c.-1475 painting *Tobias and the Angel*).

The book also offers drama that many painters attempted to capture. Rembrandt's *Tobit and Anna with the Kid Goat* from 1626, for example, highlights several interpretive issues of the book. In the painting, Tobit, already blind, sanctimoniously folds his hands over his tattered clothing. Anna looms over him, goat tucked under her arm. A dog hides in the shadows. Tobit is annoyed at the goat's bleating, and in Rembrandt's interpretation, Anna is shoving the goat into Tobit's face, as if to make his suffering worse. It represents well the confrontational question Anna asks in the text: "Where are your acts of charity? Where are your righteous deeds? These things are known about you!" (2:14).

■ THE TEXT IN CONTEMPORARY DISCUSSION

The opening chapters of Tobit offer an interesting look at gender roles in both ancient and modern contexts. The interaction between Tobit and his wife devolves into a domestic spat. In the ancient context, it is quite possible that the author of Tobit viewed the title character's having to be supported by his wife as an addendum to his suffering (for an example of such thought, see Sir. 25:22).

Modern readers, especially feminist interpreters, read such a scenario differently. Amy-Jill Levine (105–19) has shown the broad disparity in how the two genders are treated in the book. Throughout, the patriarchs are paramount. In their respective prayers that respond to their situations (Tobit's blindness, Sarah's demonic menace), Tobit is the one who embodies the entire story of the nation of Israel, while Sarah does not. The arc of Tobit's story parallels that of the nation as a whole, while the wake of Sarah's affliction is limited only to the disgrace she may bring on her father's reputation (3:15).

Tobit 4:1—7:9: Wisdom Instruction, Disguised Angels, and Mettlesome Fish

■ THE TEXT IN ITS ANCIENT CONTEXT

In Tobit 4, Tobit gives his son a series of proverbial wisdom sayings as advice for life. Much of what we find here is sapiential boilerplate—sayings and themes similar to what one would find in Proverbs or Sirach. Two features of this material stand out. The first is its theological underpinnings. All of Tobit's advice is built on the basic assumption that God will reward righteous behavior: "almsgiving delivers from death and keeps you from going into the Darkness" (4:10); "If you serve God you will receive payment" (4:14). The second important feature is that the reader experiences such statements with irony. The one imparting this wisdom, Tobit, is a blinded, impoverished righteous person. Tobit's own words, in light of the events of the narrative as a whole, are shown to be ignorant. The wisdom instruction nevertheless seems to be taken seriously by the author, as it contributes to the complex view of God and retribution that the book embodies (see Macatangay).

In Tobit 5, the angel Raphael appears on the scene, disguised as a human being named Azariah. He agrees to accompany Tobias on his journey to retrieve the money his father had deposited in Rages of Media. Anna is distraught at the prospect of a dangerous journey for her son. Tobit's response, "Do not fear for them . . . for a good angel will accompany him," is another example of the author's penchant for irony.

As the boy and the angel start on their journey, they camp by the River Tigris. A huge fish leaps from the river and attempts to eat Tobias's foot. At Raphael's behest, Tobias grabs hold of the fish, which, as the plot unfolds, becomes a means of sustenance, deliverance, and healing. While birds defecating in Tobit's eyes, fish leaping from rivers, and demons afflicting a woman might all seem like entertaining elements of a well-told folktale, they are also a part of the author's narratological argument about the origin of Tobit's misfortune. We have already observed that Tobit's own explanations might not be sufficient, and telling a story in which the suffering is imposed on the righteous characters by outside forces might hint at a more sectarian origin for the experience of suffering and evil. Birds are seen elsewhere in Jewish literature as related to a demonic menace (*Jub.* 11:10-13; Mark 4:4, 15). The great fish may also be interpreted in a similar way. Many scholars (Nowell; Moore; Kiel) point to how the book of Tobit here evokes Israel's creation mythology in which God destroys a primordial foe as the means of creation (see Ps.74:12-17; Isa. 51:9-11). There are examples of such foes in apocalyptic literature that, like the fish in Tobit, get turned into food (e.g., *1 En.* 60:24; *2 Bar.* 29:4). Tobit, to be sure, is not fully an apocalyptic text, but in its ancient theological context, it seems to be appropriating some of the tenets of that worldview in attempting to address the complicated problem of suffering and evil.

▌ THE TEXT IN THE INTERPRETIVE TRADITION

The role of the angel Raphael in the book of Tobit has commonly been read as an anticipation or analogy to the incarnation of Jesus. Bede (d. 735) draws a close parallel between the two: both offered themselves as companions and played a saving role as the embodiment of that companionship (Voicu, 14).

As noted above, that throughout art history the fish and dog in Tobit have been found to be fascinating, so is true of many commentators on Scripture. Ambrose of Milan (d. 397), for instance, says that Raphael intentionally caused the dog to join them (although the text does not say this specifically), which was for protection, and thus those whom Ambrose admonishes should use their voices in defense of Christ (Voicu, 16). Bede reads the story of the fish directly through the lens of a completely developed Christian understanding of the devil. The fish is the devil, and Bede finds in this reading many parallels to the life of Jesus, particularly the passion (Voicu, 17).

■ THE TEXT IN CONTEMPORARY DISCUSSION

Two operas have been made of the book of Tobit in the twentieth century. The most recent of them (1999) is by English composer Jonathan Dove with a libretto by David Ian. A small chamber orchestra accompanies the singers. The opera depicts the experience of Tobit's blindness and Sarah's trouble from Asmodeus side by side. Staged music is able to accomplish this in a way that a written narrative cannot, as two characters, disparate in the original source material, can sing in harmony about their respective situations. This becomes a particularly effective interpretation of the story when the two afflicted characters can simultaneously sing of their desire for death. Both Edna (Sarah's mother) and Anna (Tobit's wife) sing together of their concern for their loved ones. Tobit and Sarah themselves slip into a duet that powerfully brings together their respective situations.

Tobit 7:10—10:13: Routing the Demon and Celebrating the Wedding

■ THE TEXT IN ITS ANCIENT CONTEXT

Tobit 7–10 narrates the resolution to the main characters' misfortune. Upon arrival in Ecbatana, Raphael and Tobias stay with Raguel. Tobias has heard of Sarah's affliction—some say that it was a demon (7:14)—but Raphael encourages him to pay no heed. Burning the heart and liver of the fish from the river will chase the demon away. This is exactly what happens as the narrative unfolds. Raphael binds the demon hand and foot in Upper Egypt, the wedded couple say a prayer, and they go to sleep.

Raguel, Sarah's father, does not show much hope. He expects to bury another potential son-in-law. He even sends a servant out to dig a hole for the body, another example of humor and irony in the book. This grave also recalls the opening chapters of the book, in which proper burial of the dead instigated the plot in the first place.

These middle chapters of Tobit provide one of the few pieces of literary evidence for ancient Jewish wedding practices, although even here the narrative does not reveal much. Ancient sources suggest an elaborate process to the betrothal period. When examining marriage broadly in the ancient Near East, a contract is often part of the process, and Tob. 7:13 offers the only specific example of such a contract in the entire Old Testament. There is some argument among scholars as to whether such contracts for marriage were used widely within ancient Judaism. In Tobit, the narrative itself condenses the betrothal period because the characters want immediate action—Raguel is keen to hand over his daughter, and Tobias himself refuses to eat or drink anything until the matter is settled (7:11). Thus the needs of the storyteller could explain some of the divergences from what was standard practice in the betrothal and marriage process. The feasting, it seems, was extensive: Raguel forces Tobias to stay for fourteen days of eating and drinking. Tobias, of course, is concerned about his worrying parents.

◼ THE TEXT IN THE INTERPRETIVE TRADITION

In his Hymns on Virginity (hymn 22; McVey, 354–60), Ephrem the Syrian (d. 373) interprets the story of Jesus' encounter with the Samaritan woman at the well in John 4 in a way that has been influenced by the story of Sarah from the book of Tobit. As Ephrem recounts the story, the woman at the well is not of questionable sexual repute. Like Sarah, her husbands have been killed before any sexual union, which is what led to a poor reputation: "Blessed are you, woman, because you saw that your husbands were dead, and your reproaches were many. Other men were afraid to take you [in marriage] lest they, like their counterparts, die" (strophe 4). The woman's current husband is only for show, and she lives chastely in that context. Ephrem's "exegesis" here is meant ultimately to avoid any impropriety on the part of Jesus. Jesus could not have approached a sinful woman, and so Ephrem turns her into a paragon of virtue and a victim of unfortunate circumstances, built on the example of Sarah. He says that the woman at the well has been called a harlot, but if she were, her "bad reputation would have wafted to Him" (strophe 5) and the interaction would have been impeded.

◼ THE TEXT IN CONTEMPORARY DISCUSSION

Given the importance of marriage in the construction of society and the debates regarding its definition, one might be surprised by how few biblical texts discuss marriage in a theological way. At weddings, readings are often taken from Genesis 2 (the two become one flesh) or John 2 (the wedding at Cana). Neither of these texts, however, is primarily about marriage. Tobit 7–8, however, might provide the most robust exposition of a theological understanding of marriage anywhere in the Bible. There are emphases that may not comport well with our modern context, such as the focus on endogamy (marriage of one's own kin) or the dowry. At the same time, the story narrated here is one where the marriage union is a dangerous step. Sarah and Tobias must step out in faith that the demon's curse can be overcome. The prayer on their wedding night is simple yet beautiful. They place their marriage within the long tradition of their ancestors, evoking Adam and Eve as those first to be united. Their prayer is simply to be together, with blessing and old age. While Tobit is not canonical for many Christians, a reading from Tobit 8 might provide a theological interpretation of marriage and give simple expression to hope for the future.

Tobit 11:1—12:22: The Journey Home and Raphael's Revelation

◼ THE TEXT IN ITS ANCIENT CONTEXT

In Tobit 11, Tobias and Raphael return to worried parents. Anna greets them first, while Tobit stumbles, blind, out the door. Tobias immediately spreads the gall of the fish on Tobit's eyes, his sight returns, and he blesses God and sees his son, the "light of [his] eyes" (11:14). The family then welcomes their new daughter-in-law into their home.

In Tobit 12, Raphael reveals his true identity as one of the seven angels who stands ready before the glory of the Lord (12:15). In this revelation, several of the prominent features of the book of Tobit cohere. At this point, the characters, Tobit in particular, suddenly learn that God's role in their ordeal has been different from that which they had assumed all along. God was working behind the scenes from the outset to alleviate their suffering. This means that with the return of Tobit's sight comes also new theological insight—that both the reasons for his suffering in the first place and what is required for restoration and healing are different than he had been assuming. Based on Tobit's previous statements (e.g., his prayer in Tobit 3), Tobit would have required renewed righteousness for his situation to change. What one finds, instead, is that restoration comes from an incursion by God's agent into human workings.

There are several points of contact here with *1 Enoch* that help further to place Tobit in an ancient theological context. Raphael's role in Tobit is quite similar to the one he plays in *1 Enoch*. In Tob. 3:16-17, Raphael is sent to heal the two characters (Tobit and Sarah), which parallels his being directed to "heal the earth" in *1 En.* 10:7. Also repeated in both Tob. 3:16 and 12:15 is Raphael's self-description as one of the angels who stand "before the glory of God," similar language to that used in *1 En.* 104:1. George Nickelsburg (1988, 67) has noted these similarities and posited similar origins for the traditions that undergird both Tobit and *1 Enoch*. This is just one of the many traditions from ancient Judaism with which the book of Tobit interacts. The author also clearly draws from wisdom traditions similar to Proverbs or Sirach (e.g., Tobit 4 and 14). Ahiqar, a figure known in wisdom circles from other ancient sources, makes two cameos as Tobit's relative. The author assumes that the reader will know the specifics of Ahiqar's tale (Macatangay, 173). The author also interacts with biblical texts, not only those quoted directly (Amos and Nahum), but also more subtly, with texts such as Job or Jonah. While this is a folktale, it is not simple. The breadth of its influences and subtle theological argument belies a depth that needs to be explored.

▮ THE TEXT IN THE INTERPRETIVE TRADITION

Although not quoted directly, the angelophany in Tobit 12 provides an important template for certain texts in the New Testament. In particular, the language used to describe Raphael's departure from the earth echoes some of the descriptions of Jesus' ascension in the New Testament. The clearest verbal echo is between Raphael's words in Tob. 12:20, "I am ascending to him who sent me," and those of Jesus in John 16:5, "but now I am going to him who sent me." The active verbs stand out when compared to most ascension scenes, which tend to narrate it with a divine passive construction—for example, "he was lifted up" in Acts 1:9 (Skemp, 54). Vincent Skemp makes a more specific argument that the angelophany in Tobit 12 is a "cultural intertext" for Luke's ascension scene in Luke 24.

▮ THE TEXT IN CONTEMPORARY DISCUSSION

I once had a student refer to the four-hundred-year gap of God's silence between the Old Testament and the New Testament. Tobit 12 might be a salutary spot to consider, at the very least, as to what can be learned about the intertestamental period as contextual information for those who are interested in the New Testament. Raphael's self-reference as one of the "seven angels who stand ready" is the earliest biblical reference to named angels, predating the references to Michael and Gabriel in the book of Daniel, which dates to the Maccabean period, by at least fifty to one hundred years. Specific interest in heavenly beings—both angels and demons—was increasing in the intertestamental period and on into the first century CE. The book of Tobit, at the very least, fills in some of the background to the development of such thinking and its theological and contextual underpinnings. One of the developments in this period of Judaism is an increasingly heavenly and enthroned God; texts describe God with otherworldly images rather than human metaphors. This makes God less accessible, and angelic intermediaries become necessary to mediate God's presence with the people and to achieve God's ends on the earth. Tobit becomes an important part of our understanding of this context both for early Judaism and nascent Christianity.

Tobit 13:1—14:15: The Future of Jerusalem, Tobit, Tobias, and Their Kin

▌ THE TEXT IN ITS ANCIENT CONTEXT

The final two chapters of Tobit are written in two different genres. Chapter 13 is a hymn that Tobit sings as a response to his situation. The hymn coordinates the fate of both Tobit and the people of Israel as a whole with God's future restoration of the city of Jerusalem. The first half of Tobit's song of praise finds similarities to kingship psalms and Moses' song in Exod. 15:1-18 (Fitzmyer, 304). The second half becomes more prophetic as it looks forward to a future restoration of Jerusalem, focusing on both the precious stones with which the future city will built (cf. Isa. 54:11-14) and the eschatological gathering of all nations at Jerusalem (cf. Isa. 60:1-4). By culminating Tobit's story with an eschatological hymn, the author argues that this new eschatological perspective is what is required in order to envision both the restoration of Tobit himself and the entire nation. The introspective, intracommunal explanations and hope for the future—marked by a close connection between act and consequence—are no longer apt. Instead, the restoration of Israel will coincide with God's plan for the entire world, all of which will be gathered in praise in Jerusalem. Tobit will be happy if a remnant of his people can survive to see such a thing.

In Tobit 14, the author turns to an entirely different genre of literature, a testament. This literature focuses on a patriarch on his deathbed, imparting wisdom and advice to his children before dying and being given a happy burial. Such a testament is similar to other biblical scenes, such as Jacob's address to his sons in Genesis 48–49. This genre of literature becomes important in some later apocalyptic forms as well, especially the *Testament of the Twelve Patriarchs* (also modeled on Jacob in Genesis 48–49) and the *Testament of Job*. The end of Tobit speaks of the destruction of Nineveh as something to look forward to, but at the time of the author, this is past history. Instead, the author writes in a more apocalyptic way about the future and how things will happen at their "appointed times" (14:4), which shows a deterministic view of time and specific language similar to parts of Daniel.

These final two chapters of the book of Tobit, in their respective genres, frame and interpret the events of Tobit's life. They suggest that, unlike Tobit's insistence early in the book, righteousness cannot guarantee blessing and a peaceful life. The experience of life under foreign rule—or suffering of some sort—has dismantled the underpinnings of such explanations. Instead, the fate of individuals and the nation as a whole are left more radically to God and God's freedom to act on behalf of the remnant of those who endure, faithfully, until the appointed times.

▮ THE TEXT IN THE INTERPRETIVE TRADITION

Tobit's description of a future Jerusalem in 13:9-17 in all likelihood influenced the author of Revelation in its own description of the city. The author of Tobit may have been influenced by a text such as Isa. 54:11-12; both of them in turn may have provided language and concepts for the picture of Jerusalem in Rev. 21:9-27. Most modern commentators on Revelation note Tobit as among the intertexts for the author of the Apocalypse.

▮ THE TEXT IN CONTEMPORARY DISCUSSION

The final two chapters of Tobit portray a change in perspective so drastic that they have long been considered by scholars to be extraneous to the core of the book. The sudden poetic turn to the fate of future Jerusalem and the gathering together of all nations at a rebuilt temple has suggested to some that it was written after the fall of the temple in 70 CE. The discovery of the fragments of Tobit among the Dead Sea Scrolls makes this impossible, as some of the fragments of Tobit 13–14 pre-date the destruction of the temple. Nevertheless, many scholars still maintain a distinction between the core story (about a family in the Diaspora) and an editorial frame that places that story in the "broader context of the history of Israel" (Collins, 25). A narrative approach to reading the book can find coherence between these sections without positing later redactors as the explanation. By showing a change in Tobit's perspective, the author may be intending to offer a new theological insight—that the explanations Tobit had previously offered are no longer valid. Instead, the author thinks a new eschatological perspective is needed in order for the individual and corporate suffering of the Jewish people to be alleviated. This is the very argument that underlies Raphael's role in the story—that a divine incursion into the human realm is necessary. A revelatory and eschatological perspective is exactly what was missing from Tobit's explanations all along.

What one finds, then, when reading this story, is a complex narrative argument. The author attempts to make a subtle, profound statement about how humans often find themselves stuck between traditional religious formulas and contradictory life experiences. The brilliance of the argument is that the author does not completely shun the traditional explanations, but instead shows how such explanations are of limited explanatory power. God is still free; humans are still dependent on God's willingness to continue to intervene on their behalf. Only by remaining open to what God will do in the future do humans properly understand their past, endure their present, and hope for the future.

Works Cited

Collins, John J. 2005. "The Judaism of the Book of Tobit." In *The Book of Tobit: Text, Tradition, Theology*, edited by Géza Xeravits and József Zsengeller, 23–40. Leiden: Brill.

Fitzmyer, Joseph A. 2003. *Tobit*. Berlin: de Gruyter.

Kiel, Micah D. 2012. *The "Whole Truth": Rethinking Retribution in the Book of Tobit*. London: T&T Clark.

Levine, Amy-Jill. 1992. "Diaspora as Metaphor: Bodies and Boundaries in the Book of Tobit." In *Diaspora Jews and Judaism*, edited by J. Andrew Overmann and Robert S. MacLennan, 105–19. Atlanta: Scholars Press.

Macatangay, Francis M. 2011. *The Wisdom Instruction in the Book of Tobit*. Berlin: de Gruyter.

McVey, Kathleen E. 1989. *Ephrem the Syrian: Hymns*. Mahwah, NJ: Paulist.

Moore, Carey A. 1996. *Tobit: A New Translation with Introduction and Commentary*. AB 40A. New York: Doubleday.

Nickelsburg, George W. E. 1988. "Tobit and Enoch: Distant Cousins with a Recognizable Resemblance." In *SBL 1988 Seminar Papers*, edited by David J. Lull, 54–68. Atlanta: Scholars Press.

———. 1996. "The Search for Tobit's Mixed Ancestry: A Historical and Hermeneutical Odyssey." *RevQ* 8:339–49.

Nowell, Irene. 1983. "The Book of Tobit: Narrative Technique and Theology." PhD diss., Catholic University of America.

Skemp, Vincent. 2005. "Avenues of Intertextuality between Tobit and the New Testament." In *Intertextual Studies in Ben Sira and Tobit*, edited by Jeremy Corley and Vincent T. M. Skemp, 43–70. Washington, DC: Catholic Biblical Association of America.

Voicu, Sever J., ed. 2010. *Apocrypha*. Ancient Christian Commentary on Scripture, Old Testament 15. Downers Grove, IL: InterVarsity Press.

JUDITH

Corrine L. Carvalho

Introduction

The book of Judith tells the fictional story of a Jewish widow who defeats an army through her looks and cunning. While the story has captured the imagination of artists throughout the centuries, it has been largely ignored or viewed as morally problematic by theologians.

Judith was probably written during the Hellenistic period, either under Greek rule or during the Hasmonean period (140–116 BCE; Hopkins). Specific dates have been offered, but none has garnered consensus, in part because the story's message transcends any particular historical setting. The book has been preserved in Greek, but the style of the Greek indicates it is a translation of either a Hebrew or Aramaic original. Judith was not preserved in the Hebrew version of the Tanak, but was included in the Septuagint. Because of this difference, it is considered canonical by Roman Catholic and Orthodox Christians (part of the historical books), but not by Jews or Protestants.

The story is set in a fictional past. The opening verse of the book deliberately confuses historical facts as a cue that the story is fictional. At various times, Christian scholars, perhaps influenced by its placement among the historical books, have searched for the historical veracity of the text, but this approach has now largely been abandoned. Because the historical backdrop of the narrative is deliberately distorted, it is impossible to state the narrative setting of the text. Even the geographical location of the story, a city named Bethulia, is unattested in any other Israelite text.

The book has two halves. Chapters 1–7, which depict an attack on the Israelite city of Bethulia, feature the evil general Holofernes and one of his subordinates, Achior the Ammonite, who warns Holofernes of his hubris. This is answered by chapters 8–16, which narrate the city's deliverance. The turning point is the introduction in 8:1 of Judith, who will venture into the enemy's camp to kill Holofernes. These two halves of the story are brought together at the end: Judith returns to Bethulia and Achior converts, while Holofernes's severed head looks on.

Judith 1:1—4:15: Introducing the Enemy

◼ THE TEXT IN ITS ANCIENT CONTEXT

The book opens with a seemingly historical notice, but one that clearly sets the book in a fictional past (1:1). It makes the Babylonian Nebuchadnezzar, who destroyed Jerusalem in 586 BCE, the king of the Assyrian city of Nineveh, a city destroyed by the Babylonians in 612 BCE. Both Assyria and Babylon had destroyed parts of Israel, but not at the same time. Historical distortions are a major feature of the book. By recalling Israel's great enemies here, the distortions project Bethulia's enemy onto a cosmic plane. Nebuchadnezzar is cast as an archvillain of a helpless city.

The conflict begins when Judea joins other nations in refusing to support the villain, insulting the honor of this dangerous enemy (1:11). Nebuchadnezzar vows revenge for this insult (1:12), commissioning Holofernes to attack the cities that have insulted him (2:4). Small details in chapters 2 and 3 give snapshots of the terrifying power of Holofernes's army (2:5, 15). They are likened to a swarm of locusts (2:20), who fill fields and ravines with the corpses of those they slaughter (2:8). Like Gog's army in Ezekiel 38, this is an enemy of cosmic proportion.

This cosmic nature is further stressed in 3:8, when Nebuchadnezzar is likened to a god who destroys the sanctuaries of other gods. After this point, Nebuchadnezzar recedes from the action, making him the literary parallel of Yahweh. The action of the rest of the narrative focuses on their envoys: a great general and a small-town widow, both of whom claim that they are serving their god.

Chapter 4 turns its attention to Bethulia, the only rebel land that has refused to capitulate. The city, otherwise unknown, is probably a fictional location. Its name, similar to the Hebrew word for "virgin," recalls a common epithet given to both Zion (Lam. 2:13) and Israel (Jer. 31:4). These first four chapters then use fictional places and mythical time in a story about a fully innocent Judean city attacked by the minions of an evil villain, who claims to be god.

◼ THE TEXT IN THE INTERPRETIVE TRADITION

There is not a vibrant history of interpretation of the book of Judith among theologians. In fact, the first full commentary of the book, by Rabanus Maurus, was not written until around 856 CE, although the earliest Christian reference is found in Clement of Rome. Jerome, who viewed Judith as apocryphal, scorned those who wanted to "accept a woman's book" (Brown). Later Christian exegetes, especially in the Middle Ages, read the book as an allegory.

◼ THE TEXT IN CONTEMPORARY DISCUSSION

The book's creative refashioning of history suggests the story is a kind of mythical realism, where the characters engage the symbolic aspects of Israel's cultural memory. Nebuchadnezzar, not just a foreign king, is the destroyer of Jerusalem. This rhetorical tactic is found in popular culture today. Movies such as *Abraham Lincoln: Vampire Hunter* (2012) or *Cowboys and Aliens* (2011) warp history in order to bring cultural symbols together in creative ways.

The book also plays with the symbolic meaning of space. Biblical scholars have begun to notice how spaces have a symbolic function. In the book of Judith, the city of Bethulia symbolizes the gendered city as vulnerable, innocent, and in need of the male God's protection. The book of Judith plays creatively with Israel's historical spatial symbols in order to exploit its theme of good's triumph over evil.

Judith 5:1—6:21: Achior the Ammonite

▊ THE TEXT IN ITS ANCIENT CONTEXT

The two characters who understand God's role in this story are Judith and Achior. These characters mirror each other in many ways (Roitman). Both are in dangerous positions while they are in the camp of Holofernes. Their vulnerability is augmented by their marginal social positions (Achior as a foreigner, Judith as a widow). When both of them speak the truth, it puts them at odds with prevailing authorities.

This section features Achior's speech to Holofernes in answer to his query of who would dare oppose him (5:5-21). Achior's answer consists in a thoroughly orthodox retelling of Israel's history. The fact that a foreigner provides the most conventional witness to Israel's past not only foreshadows his eventual conversion to Judaism but also marks him as a righteous foreigner, similar to Ruth the Moabite (Lacocque).

The Assyrians are outraged by both Bethulia's resistance and Achior's speech (5:22—6:4). Holofernes reasserts the divinity of Nebuchadnezzar (6:2). This overreaction to a city that is really no threat to the army shows that the issue is really Bethulia's failure to honor Nebuchadnezzar and accept their subordinate status. This is confirmed in the prayer of the Bethulians, which depicts the Assyrians as arrogant, and their own situation as one of "humiliation" (6:19).

▊ THE TEXT IN THE INTERPRETIVE TRADITION

Focus on the character of Achior became lively only in the second half of the twentieth century. Until the 1980s, most biblical scholars had a rather negative view of the narrative quality of the book of Judith. The general consensus was that the book was lopsided, since its main character was not introduced until chapter 8, making chapters 1–7 an overly long introduction to the book. This changed significantly with the work of Toni Craven, who demonstrated that chapters 1–7 were integral to the book's overall structure.

▊ THE TEXT IN CONTEMPORARY DISCUSSION

This new focus on Achior has led to an appreciation of how the book subverts expected power dynamics. While scholars have always noticed the book's inversion of gender categories, Achior's character demonstrates that the book also plays with other categories of privilege. Both Achior and Judith represent the "other," that is, those communities outside of the privileged circle of elite males within a patriarchal culture. Yet in this book, it is these two others who have the clearest understanding of who God is and, as a result, act with the most courage (Levine).

This text is written in the context of colonization; even if it was penned during the brief period of Israelite independence under the Hasmoneans, the imminent threat of colonization loomed large. The story projects both Achior and Judith as the ideal responses to colonizing threats, one that combines a recognition of the true cosmic power with the courage to stand up to evil.

Judith 7:1—8:36: Attack and Response

▌ THE TEXT IN ITS ANCIENT CONTEXT

Although Judith's introduction in 8:1 marks a turning point in the book, her reaction to the attack on Bethulia contrasts with the reaction of the rest of the citizens of the city, so the two elements are considered together here. As is true in any communal crisis, the tragedy elicits a variety of responses. The city's dire circumstances are highlighted by the detailed description of the advance of the army (7:1-18), the stopping up of the springs (7:17), and the plight of the whole city captured in the image of listless children and fainting youth (7:22).

The text contains three distinct reactions to the attack: the general population, who want to save lives at all costs (7:23-29), the civic leaders, who choose to wait and see how the situation unfolds (7:30), and Judith, who vehemently opposes both of these options (8:11-27). Although Judith's speech is the longest and most articulate position represented, all three responses invoke the question of sin and blame. The appropriate response depends on whether the attack is a punishment for prior sin to which the people should submit (7:28) or an unwarranted injustice from which God should deliver them (8:18-20). There is no prophetic voice in the text to tell them the correct interpretation, which is why the leaders suggest seeing if God delivers them (confirming their innocence) or allows the disaster to continue (affirming their sinfulness).

Judith's introduction tells the reader that hers is the authoritative voice in this debate. Every element of the text exalts her. She is wise, pious, beautiful, rich, honorable, and esteemed. The lengthy, if chronologically impossible, genealogy exalts her over every other character. She is the most eloquent character in the book, outshining even Holofernes and Achior in her verbal artistry. Her description of the autonomy of God shames her audience in their attempt to manipulate Yahweh. She understands that the fate of Bethulia has national implications, and she engages Israel's traditions in creative ways to depict the disaster as a test. Therefore, when she avers that this particular disaster is a test from God, the reader is ready to acquiesce.

▌ THE TEXT IN THE INTERPRETIVE TRADITION

Although the text introduces Judith as a pious widow, the artistic tradition has preferred to depict her after her transformation into a seductress. Medieval interpretations that viewed her as either a type of the Virgin Mary or as an allegory of chastity depend on her description here and at the end of the book.

▌ THE TEXT IN CONTEMPORARY DISCUSSION

Feminist scholarship on the book has renewed an interest in these opening descriptions of Judith. She has the longest genealogy of any woman in the Bible (Craghan). She seems to own property and conducts her affairs with full autonomy. She is an active character in the book who speaks in public to the city elders. Even before her heroic feat, she is a fascinating counterbalance to the usual way the Bible depicts women.

Judith 9:1—10:10: Judith Going Out

▌ THE TEXT IN ITS ANCIENT CONTEXT

Before Judith sets out to enact her plan, she prays for success (Eynde). The prayer introduces the theme of sexual violence that will dominate the rest of the book. The author has delayed the identity of Judith's tribe by not listing her tribal ancestor in the genealogy. This identification comes in her invocation of Yahweh as "God of my ancestor Simeon" (9:2). This delayed notice, which highlights the allusion to Simeon, is followed by a description of his revenge for Dinah's rape (Genesis 34). This rape is described not in terms of how Dinah experienced it, who is not even named in the prayer, but how it polluted, disgraced, defiled, and shamed her family. This shift to the communal ramifications justifies Simeon's, and subsequently Judith's revenge.

The sexual theme continues in 10:1-10 with the description of Judith's deliberate transformation of her performance of gender. She changes from a woman who mourns for her husband to that of a seductress. She does so knowing that her beauty gives her power over men.

▌ THE TEXT IN THE INTERPRETIVE TRADITION

Throughout the Christian tradition, theologians have tended to view Judith's manipulation of sexual attraction as a bad thing. Both traditional interpreters of the text who would prefer that Judith be a symbol of modesty, as well as some feminists who view her use of sexuality as a reinscription of patriarchal norms, are critical of this element in the text (Efthimiadis-Keith). Craven even suggests that the book does not make it into the Jewish canon because Judith herself "is simply too radical a woman for the tradition to memorialize" (Craven, 117).

▌ THE TEXT IN CONTEMPORARY DISCUSSION

Behind Judith's prayer is the reality that rape has been used a weapon of war throughout the centuries (Gafney). It is not surprising that this female character, who is about to confront the militarized enemy, should be reminding God to exact vengeance on rapists (Harrington). Rape and other forms of sexual violence are still used as military weapons today. Judith's prayer that God protect women and avenge sexual violence resonates with too many contemporary audiences.

Judith 10:11—12:9: Judith in the Enemy's Camp

▌ THE TEXT IN ITS ANCIENT CONTEXT

Judith's deliberative plan begins to unfold in this section of the book. Her success requires patience, and the ability to anticipate how the men in the camp will react. The details in the text are exaggerated.

One hundred men take her to Holofernes, whose tent is bejeweled. The general's entrance is grand, while her public acts of subservience are performed perfectly.

Once again, she gives an eloquent speech, but this time it drips with double meanings, ironic references, and cunning deception. Much of what she says seems true. For example, she reaffirms that God can punish Israel's sins through a foreign army (11:10), but she does not say that this particular situation is a test of their faithfulness. She states that she will not run out of food before God has accomplished his purpose (12:4), a purpose that the audience knows is the opposite of what Holofernes expects. She tells outright lies when she claims that the Bethulians are eating food dedicated to God (11:12-15).

Her hidden deception is matched by the ironic truth of the statements that the men in the camp make. For example, at the end of Judith's speech, Holofernes's servants declare, "No other woman . . . speaks so wisely" (11:21), without realizing that her words have just trapped Holofernes through a false sense of security. Perhaps the most ironic statement is found in 11:19, when the soldiers state that women like Judith are worrisome because they have the ability to "beguile the whole world."

Judith's beauty is a major element in this part of the story. The word is repeated seven times here (10:4, 7, 14, 19, 23; and 11:21, 23). While beauty in the Bible often makes a character vulnerable, Judith is able to use her beauty to accomplish her goals (Hopkins). While the threat that her beauty provokes (i.e., rape) has been alluded to in chapter 9, in chapter 10 she can use that beauty without becoming a loose woman (Proverbs 7), a whore (Ezekiel 16 and 23), or a seductive foreigner (Judges 16). To be sure, Judith's power rests in knowing that the Assyrian men would view her as all three of these, but the narrative makes it clear that this is all an act on her part.

▌THE TEXT IN THE INTERPRETIVE TRADITION

One of the biggest problems exegetes have had with the story of Judith is her use of deception. On the one hand, the story depicts her as the paradigm of virtue, through her observation of purity regulations and dietary restrictions, as well as her prayers and fasting. For many Christians, this seems incompatible with a victory wrought by outright lying. This assessment has again contributed to the fact that Judith has not been actively engaged in the theological traditions of Christianity.

▌THE TEXT IN CONTEMPORARY DISCUSSION

Advances in the use of sociological analysis have helped clarify how Judith's use of deception was viewed as an exemplary feature of her character (deSilva). Philip Esler in particular has noted that, within the collectivist context of ancient Mediterranean cultures, lying to an outsider, especially one who threatens the security of the insider group, is a sign of group loyalty (2002; 2011). In addition, lying is also an acceptable element of the trickster motif. In a group that does not have enough power to confront an oppressor, subverting their power through trickery can become a valued element of storytelling.

Judith 12:10—13:10: Judith in the Bedroom

■ THE TEXT IN ITS ANCIENT CONTEXT

The story reaches its dramatic climax in this section. The motivation for all of Judith's actions thus far is made clear to the audience. She has flattered Holofernes in order to garner his trust. She has gone out to pray regularly to establish an escape route. Even the purpose for her clothing comes into focus; she is literally dressed to kill.

While the whole narrative is rife with allusions to other biblical texts (Lacocque; Henten), this section echoes the story of Jael's execution of Sisera in Judges 4–5 (White). Both victims are generals of an army hostile to Israel. Both assume they are safe when alone with subservient women. Both women gain their trust when the men drink with them. Both men, feeling safe, fall asleep, a sleep that proves fatal. In both stories, there is a sexual undertone. While this is more explicit in Judith, the poetic version of Sisera's death in Judges 5 includes Sisera dying literally between Jael's thighs (5:27), while women talk about the reality of rape in war (Judg. 5:30).

God is offstage in both stories. Some scholars have pursued the fact that God is not a character in Judith (Day), since nowhere does Judith claim that her plan comes from God. Jael is even further removed from God: she is not even an Israelite. In fact, Judges offers no motivation for what she does. Yet the material surrounding both death scenes leads the audience to assume that these are acts of God (Judg. 4:9; Jth. 13:4-5; Eynde).

Perhaps the element that conveys most clearly that God is behind these acts, at least for the ancient audience, is the gender of the executioners. Deborah's oracle that foreshadows Sisera's death centers on the fact that he will die by the hand of a woman. In Judith, the phrase that Holofernes dies "by the hand of a woman" is repeated three times (9:10; 13:15; 16:6), showing that the killer's gender is significant. Since the killing of a warrior by a woman was shameful, the deaths of arrogant Sisera and Holofernes function as a kind of poetic justice.

■ THE TEXT IN THE INTERPRETIVE TRADITION

The most vibrant interpretive history of the book of Judith can be found in the artistic tradition, which has focused on either the actual beheading scene or the two women's return to Bethulia, bagged head in hand (Sölle). Nira Stone traces the Christian development of this type scene in three stages. In medieval art, Judith either represents the church or Mary. During the Renaissance, while she is often cast in nationalistic tones, Gentileschi's artwork in the early seventeenth century poignantly captures the threat of rape that permeates the book. Modern Christian art, Stone's third period, depicts Judith as a feminist heroine.

In medieval Judaism, the book of Judith, which medieval midrash associated with the Maccabean revolt, was used at Hanukkah (Moore). This association of Judith with Hanukkah is found in medieval Jewish art as well (Stone; Tilford). In post-Shoah art, she remains a Jewish heroine who sacrificed herself for her people and a symbol of resistance (Tilford).

The book of Judith has also been the subject of literary and musical retellings (Sölle). From early medieval German poetry to nineteenth-century operas to contemporary films, it is clear that the story of Judith strikes a chord with audiences across the centuries. Audiences can enjoy the suspense and irony of the text when it is freed from its biblical context. Art can play with the elements of the text that strike a universal chord, such as the thrill of the ironic undoing of unbridled claims to power.

■ THE TEXT IN CONTEMPORARY DISCUSSION

Psychological analyses of the deaths of Sisera, Shechem (Dinah's rapist), and Holofernes have exploited the sexual overtones of how each man died (Efthimiadis-Keith). Jael pierces Sisera's head with a tent peg, a symbolic reversal of rape. Shechem is slaughtered while recovering from circumcision, a ritual that Amy-Jill Levine likens to a symbolic castration (1992). Judith's decapitation of Holofernes also symbolizes castration (Stocker, p. 117). Through this interpretive lens, the book reflects male anxiety over women's sexual power. This fear is personified on the one hand with Holofernes's servant Bagoas, a eunuch, and, on the other hand with Judith, who is more masculine than all the men in the text.

Judith 13:11—16:25: Judith Triumphant

■ THE TEXT IN ITS ANCIENT CONTEXT

The final chapters integrate the themes that permeate the book. This section begins with the visual image of Judith pulling Holofernes's head out of her food bag. The text, however, is less interested in the dripping pate and more focused on Judith's assurance that she "committed no sin" in the commission of this execution (13:16), assuring them that the only body part involved in his seduction was her "face." The author is careful to distance Judith from a reverse rape of the evil general, which ironically reinforces the sexual overtones of the threat of violence found throughout the book.

While the two main heroes of the book represent the other, one of the notable features of these final scenes is the way this other becomes integrated into Bethulian society. Achior the Ammonite converts (14:10), Judith's maid becomes a free woman (16:23), and Judith returns to her life as pious widow (16:21-24). While some scholars seem bothered by the conversion of Achior, because of its prohibition in Deut. 23:3, this element parallels the view of foreigners in other postexilic texts, such as the book of Ruth and Isa. 56:6-8. Similarly, the whole book ends with a summary of Judith's life. This summary reintegrates her into Judean society. Once again, she becomes the honorable widow, living a chaste and pious life, for which she is greatly rewarded.

The ending of the book is satisfying because the fate of each character inverts the honor-shame rhetoric that upheld the colonizing power of the Assyrians. When the Bethulians see the severed head, they praise God, not for killing Holofernes, but for shaming the enemy (13:17). They simultaneously turn and honor Judith as they would a military hero (13:17-20; 15:9-10). It is the male soldier, Achior, who faints at the sight of the head and, when revived, bows down to Judith

(14:6-7). Even Bagoas proclaims that Judith's actions have shamed the supposed god Nebuchadnezzar (14:18).

The last time the audience hears Judith's voice is when she sings the victory song in chapter 16. Modeled after Judges 5, it gives a poetic version of the story of Judith, even referring to her in the third person. That story, however, is framed by her praise of God acting as a divine warrior (16:2), Judith serving as the divine weapon (vv. 5-6), and the battle as a cosmic fight (vv. 14-15). The final verse of the poem (16:17) reveals the purpose for the use of historical figures as symbols of a dehistoricized cosmic fight: the story is a warning to all of Yahweh's enemies of the fate they can expect if they dare attack Judea.

THE TEXT IN THE INTERPRETIVE TRADITION

The end of the story is not well represented in visual art. However, Judith's decision to remain celibate reinforces the early church's use of her as a symbol of virginity and chastity. This is seen most clearly in the works of Tertullian, Ambrose, and Jerome (Moore; Tilford).

THE TEXT IN CONTEMPORARY DISCUSSION

Many contemporary readers of the text resist the praise of Judith. In addition to her use of deceit, the way the text relishes her violence is problematic for some readers. The way the book itself carefully reintegrates Judith back into society shows that her actions were the result of dire circumstances.

It must be remembered, however, that this is a story that reflects the threat of colonization. It reminds readers of privilege that unjust claims to power and the exploitation of others invokes such desires for retaliation. It raises the question of whether armed revolution is always wrong and, even when it is deemed wrong, whether it allows for the fantasies of violent revenge to find expression. The story of Judith is one that can address many different audiences at many different times. Theology's snub of the book is countered by the artistic tradition, where moral taboos have less sway and the power of imaginative engagement with symbols of evil power and the triumph of good resonate for many people.

Works Cited

Brown, William P. 1999. "Judith." In *Dictionary of Biblical Interpretation*, ed. John H. Hayes, 647–50. Nashville: Abingdon.

Craghan, John. 1982. *Esther, Judith, Tobit, Jonah and Ruth*. OTM 16. Wilmington, DE: Michael Glazier.

Craven, Toni. 1983. *Artistry and Faith in the Book of Judith*. SBLDS 70. Chico, CA: Scholars Press.

Day, Linda. 2001. "Faith, Character and Perspective in Judith." *JSOT* 95:71–93.

DeSilva, David A. 2002. *Introducing the Apocrypha: Message, Context, and Significance*. Grand Rapids: Baker Academic.

Efthimiadis-Keith, Helen. 2010. "Judith, Feminist Ethics and Feminist Biblical/Old Testament Interpretation." *JTSA* 138:91–111.

Esler, Philip F. 2002. "Ludic History in the Book of Judith: The Reinvention of Israelite Identity?" *BibInt* 10:107–14.

———. 2011. *Sex, Wives and Warriors: Reading Biblical Narrative with Its Ancient Audience.* Eugene, OR: Cascade.

Eynde, Sabine van den. 2004. "Crying to God: Prayer and Plot in the Book of Judith." *Bib* 85:217–34.

Gafney, Wilda C. 2010. "Judith." In *The People's Companion to the Bible*, edited by Curtiss Paul DeYoung, Wilda C. Gafney, Leticia Guardiola-Sáenz, George E. Tinker, and Frank Yamada, 188–89. Minneapolis: Fortress Press.

Harrington, Daniel J. 2011. "Judith." In *Dictionary of Scripture and Ethics*, edited by Joel B. Green, 433. Grand Rapids: Baker Academic.

Henten, Jan Willem van. 1995. "Judith as Alternative Leader: A Re-Reading of Judith 7–13." In *A Feminist Companion to Esther, Judith and Susanna*, edited by Athalya Brenner, 224–52. London: T&T Clark.

Hopkins, Denise Dombkowski. 2012. "Judith." In *Women's Bible Commentary*, edited by Carol A. Newsom, Sharon H. Ringe, and Jacqueline E. Lapsley, 383–90. 3rd ed. Louisville: Westminster John Knox.

Lacocque, André. 1990. *The Feminine Unconventional: Four Subversive Figures in Israel's Tradition.* OBT. Minneapolis: Fortress Press.

Levine, Amy-Jill. 1992. "Sacrifice and Salvation: Otherness and Domestication in the Book of Judith." In *"No One Spoke Ill of Her": Essays on Judith*, edited by James C. VanderKam, 17–30. SBLEJL 2. Atlanta: Scholars Press.

Moore, Carey A. 1985. *Judith: A New Translation with Introduction and Commentary.* AB 40. Garden City, NY: Doubleday.

Roitman, Adolfo D. 1992. "Achior in the Book of Judith: His Role and Significance." In *"No One Spoke Ill of Her": Essays on Judith*, edited by James C. VanderKam, 31–45. SBLEJL 2. Atlanta: Scholars Press.

Sölle, Dorothee. 1994. *Great Women of the Bible in Art and Literature.* Macon, GA: Mercer University Press.

Stocker, Margarita. *Judith: Sexual Warrior, Women and Power in Western Culture.* New Haven: Yale University Press, 1998.

Stone, Nira. 1992. "Judith and Holofernes: Some Observations on the Development of the Scene in Art." In *"No One Spoke Ill of Her": Essays on Judith*, edited by James C. VanderKam, 73–93. SBLEJL 2. Atlanta: Scholars Press.

Tilford, Nicole. 2012. "Judith and Her Interpreters." In *Women's Bible Commentary*, edited by Carol A. Newsom, Sharon H. Ringe, and Jacqueline E. Lapsley, 391–95. 3rd ed. Louisville: Westminster John Knox.

White, Sidnie Ann. 1992. "In the Steps of Jael and Deborah: Judith as Heroine." In *"No One Spoke Ill of Her": Essays on Judith*, edited by James C. VanderKam, 5–16. SBLEJL 2. Atlanta: Scholars Press.

ESTHER (THE GREEK ADDITIONS)

Vivian Johnson

Introduction

The book of Greek Esther of the Septuagint innovatively adapts an earlier Hebrew version of the text by adding six additions (additions A–F) and a few marked theological notices (2:20; 4:8; 6:13). In rewriting and updating the story of Esther, the author of Greek Esther gives it an obvious religious tone, having God more directly involved in the action of the story. This feature contrasts sharply with the earlier Masoretic Hebrew text (MT), which does not mention the deity explicitly.

The adaptations Greek Esther makes to the MT speak to the challenges of Jews in coping with multiple and sometimes divergent loyalties in a foreign empire. Greek Esther, MT Esther, and another Greek version of the story, called the Alpha Text (AT) all reveal how Jews attempted "to forge an identity in exile that would allow them both to thrive in their wider societies and to retain their loyalties as Jews" (Koller, 8). Greek Esther seems interested in creating a portrait of Esther that would align with the times of its postexilic audience.

THE TEXT IN ITS ANCIENT CONTEXT

The marked religious tone occurs at the outset of Greek Esther where, in addition A, God takes center stage as the source of deliverance for the "righteous nation" against whom "every nation" wages war. This cosmic battle occurs in a dream Mordecai has in which God provides him foreknowledge of an impending threat. Mordecai's dream prefaces the content found in the MT, setting the entire story in a grand and universal framework. Indeed, addition B provides details of the Persian king's authorization of a pogrom against Jews, in which he singles out his Jewish inhabitants as contrary to "every nation." The king argues in his edict: "We understand that this people, and it alone, stands constantly in opposition to every nation, perversely following a strange manner of life and laws . . . doing all the harm they can so that our kingdom may not attain stability" (13:5). Thus he unleashes a horrific edict in which he orders the killing of all men, women, and children in a single day (13:6-7). Expanding the content of the royal decree in the MT deepens the need for divine intervention in Greek Esther.

Divine deliverance comes about only after the petitions from Mordecai and Esther for God to avert the annihilation of their people (addition C). Pious protagonists offer a paradigm for people living under hostile authority. Given that the book is named after Esther, her actions in particular come under scrutiny. The book of Greek Esther accentuates her piety, assures her adherence to orthodox Jewish practice, and asserts her sole reliance on the deity for deliverance. These qualities Esther exhibits in this version are noticeably absent in the MT.

Esther's prayer describes dire circumstances in which enemies cause them to undergo "bitter slavery" (14:8). Dissatisfied with the humiliation of their enslavement, Esther laments, they desire also to destroy them completely (14:8-9). Her supplication reinforces the cruelty of the royal decree with its order to destroy all Jews "without pity or restraint" (14:6). These additions evince the fragility of subjected peoples under imperial domination.

After her prayer, Esther exhibits great sangfroid, initially, when she appears before the Persian king in addition D. Her courage lapses at the sight of an angry king who is annoyed by her presence. Esther therefore faints and collapses right before him out of fear. The narrative of Greek Esther at this point reveals the limits of human initiative. Esther cannot achieve a successful outcome all by herself. She needs divine intervention desperately. God comes to her aid by altering "the spirit of the king to gentleness" (15:8). The added details of the MT not only heighten the suspense of the narrative but also underscore the need for divine action in the lives of the people.

Greek Esther affirms that God hears and responds to the needs of the Jewish people. Because God intervenes, the people are saved and addition E notes the reversal of the king's genocidal edict. In this decree, the writer of Greek Esther has the king himself declare God as sovereign, as one who rules over all things (16:17, 21), as one "who always sees everything" (16:4) and directs the kingdom for the Persians "in the most excellent order" (16:15).

Addition F, a colophon, notes the fulfillment of Mordecai's dream and identifies the symbolic elements of his earlier dream. This notice serves to confirm the efficacious nature of the strategy Mordecai and Esther took in their situation.

Although the story takes place in Susa, a city of the Persian Empire, it describes conditions relevant to any imperial context. Esther's deportment then serves as model for subsequent generations to follow as they straddled commitments to their religious heritage with those obligations demanded by the nation imposing its rule on them.

Greek Esther is often dated to the second to first centuries BCE, a precarious time for its Jewish audience. This period saw the heinous xenophobic acts of Antiochus IV (ruled 175–164 BCE), who outlawed Judaism and enforced Hellenism. According to one historian, his measures marked the beginning of Judaism as a persecuted religion (Scheindlin 1998). The story of Greek Esther, then, would resonate well with people experiencing the harshness of foreign domination, especially during this time in Jewish history. Esther describes complete abhorrence to courtly life even though she reigns as queen. She detests all the trappings of royalty and caustically remarks on having to adorn her head with the crown (14:16). Her life, she mourns, has existed without joy since she arrived at the Persian court. The Hebrew version of the story appears to be updated to intensify Esther's condition and uphold her as an exemplar of piety and orthodoxy. She offers a paradigm for how others could manage to live under hostile authority.

The story of Greek Esther befits the genre of literature called novella or short story (Harrington). It has similarities with apocryphal/deuterocanonical books like Tobit and Judith, whose compositions have the didactic purpose of communicating values and ideas that their composers deem important. Tobit, Judith, and Greek Esther all narrate the experience of Jewish characters that must navigate living under foreign rule and peril.

The fervent prayer that Esther offers in the book of Greek Esther encapsulates the pedagogical purpose of the work to show Jews how to live devoutly in unfavorable circumstances. In a few verses, Esther conveys her piety, her loyal observance to Jewish practice, and her complete reliance on the deity to prevent the obliteration of her people. This addition along with all the others that make up Greek Esther enhance its religious character by providing an ideal model for people to emulate as they attempted to maintain their religious convictions in adverse times.

■ THE TEXT IN THE INTERPRETIVE TRADITION

Greek Esther stands in the interpretive tradition of the book of Esther. It appears to be based on the Hebrew version appearing in the Masoretic Text (MT). Noticeably absent in the Hebrew story is the mention of God, and Greek Esther reinterprets the earlier narrative to give it a distinct theological emphasis.

In the Hebrew version of the book of Esther, the deity does not have an overt role in the narrative. Rather, the characters appear to achieve desired ends by their own human agency. Esther appears in this text as a Jewish woman who assimilates fairly well into Persian culture. Although she has strong ties with the Jewish community, especially Mordecai, she works within the system to achieve a favorable outcome for Jews in the Persian Diaspora. When the story of Esther is rewritten in Greek Esther, it resolves troublesome issues that the Hebrew version left open-ended. Did Esther, for example, abide by Jewish dietary restrictions? Did she have marital relations with the Persian king? Did she relish the lavish lifestyle of the Persian court? Esther's prayer addresses each of these concerns. She emphatically proclaims that she has kept *kashrut* and denies having eaten any food or consumed any libation at royal dining events (14:17). Her prayer suggests that she did assume marital sexual obligations with the Persian king, but states categorically that she detested it (14:15). As for her attitude toward living among Persia's most privileged citizens, she decries: "I hate the splendor of the wicked" (14:15).

Greek Esther also clarifies any ambiguity concerning the source of the deliverance. Saving activity lay in the divine realm. God, for example, "changes the spirit of the king to gentleness" (15:8) when Esther approaches the king unbidden to persuade him to revoke the lethal decree. Esther proclaims in her prayer that she has no one to help her but God and that he has been her only source of joy since she was brought to the Persian court (14:14, 18). At the prayer's end, she pleads for God to save her people from the impending threat (14:19).

While the basic story line remains the same, Greek Esther has in fact created a new narrative, where, as one scholar writes, "the scribal manipulation of the base text is so extensive that a recognizably new work is created" (Crawford, 14). Greek Esther takes the detail of the Hebrew story not including any mention of God as its springboard for a strong theological emphasis: Greek Esther mentions the deity more than fifty times. Although the name for the deity, "God" or "Lord," clusters in the additions, Greek Esther also includes the deity several times outside of the additions, integrating them into the main body of the story (2:20; 4:8; 6:1, 13). By rewriting the Hebrew version, Greek Esther does not leave open the possibility that the deliverance of the Jewish population in Persia derived from human ingenuity. Rather, it heightens the role of God and claims unequivocally that their deliverance depends on divine action (e.g., 13:15-17; 14:3, 5-6, 14, 19; 15:8; 6:1).

Greek Esther also reinterprets the story to explain and eradicate any objectionable content of the story. The seemingly unorthodox view of Esther becomes clearly orthodox, and while she may have had intercourse with the Persian king, she hated it. Thereby, her image as an assimilated Jew is recast as a Jewish woman who holds her traditions in the highest regard and observes her customs to the greatest extent possible in a threatening situation.

■ THE TEXT IN CONTEMPORARY DISCUSSION

As shown above, Greek Esther and the Hebrew version proffer different views of the story of Esther. Recent discussions on Greek Esther center on the relationship of this narrative to the MT and the AT. One commentator, for example, focuses on all three versions in order to demonstrate their points of similarity and divergence with regard to Esther's character (Day). Another scholar isolates one issue of the narrative, namely, the notice of Esther's keeping her identity secret, to offer a diachronic reading of how each story addresses concerns of the Jewish Diaspora (Halverson-Taylor). Both of these scholars argue that the AT plays a significant part in illuminating Jewish Diaspora issues.

All three versions of the story provide a different understanding of what it takes to have a successful life in an imperial context. While the dating of the AT remains equivocal, it is commonly placed earlier chronologically than the Hebrew. It portrays Esther as a woman whose Jewish descent poses little problem for her Persian neighbors. In the AT edition of Esther, it appears that her ethnicity is recognized throughout the story when the king is surprised that Haman would intend to harm Mordecai, a man from the same ethnic stock as Esther (AT 7:14). This interpretation of the book of Esther could reflect Diaspora communities that sought to meld their Jewish identity with those around them. Following Esther's example of a Jew working within the parameters of Persian policies could result, the AT suggests, in reaching high levels in the foreign government in order to effectuate positive change for Diaspora communities.

The Hebrew shares the cooperative spirit that the AT engenders. However, given that Esther has to keep her Jewish identity secret, it lacks the freedom of religious expression found in the AT

(Halverson-Taylor). A touch of suspense and tension is added with this detail (2:20). Notwithstanding her having to conceal her Jewish heritage, the Hebrew portrays Esther as an assimilated Jew whose winsome qualities facilitate her advance as a high-ranking authority in the Persian government. One critic argues that the Hebrew text of the book Esther, when compared to Greek Esther and the AT, has the widest appeal to audiences of the Jewish Diaspora because of her ability to handle her role as Persian queen and a Jewish leader with skill (Day). She holds these two potentially conflicting roles in delicate balance. By adeptly traversing the arenas of Persians and Jews, she offers another model to Jewish communities to work within the dominant political structure rather than against it.

Greek Esther contrasts sharply with the earlier Alpha and Hebrew texts with its anti-gentile stance. Esther has the strongest connection with the Jewish community in this version. While the Hebrew notes that Esther has to keep her identity a secret, Greek Esther builds on this tension with an apocalyptic preface (addition A), showing the extensive nature of Jewish persecution. The need for her to mask her Jewish roots appears urgent. In an increasingly perilous environment, Greek Esther conveys the import of strict adherence to divine law over that of the imperial overlord. Juxtaposed in the verse speaking of Esther's need to suppress her Jewish identity is the declaration that she maintained her "mode of life" by fearing God and keeping his laws (2:20). Thus, as one critic aptly asserts, the instance of Esther concealing her identity "becomes the occasion to vouch that she maintained the integrity of her identity by keeping the commandments" (Halverson-Taylor, 483).

Greek Esther escalates the sense of danger and could, as mentioned above, point to an audience experiencing persecution or discrimination at the hands of non-Jews. The model Greek Esther provides aligns with both the Hebrew and AT in that a Jew can attain high status in a foreign context and lead a successful existence. It however refocuses the attention to strict Jewish observance and dependence on God, to whom they owe their foremost allegiance.

Greek Esther does not hold canonical status in the Protestant tradition, and it is part of the deuterocanon of Catholic and Orthodox traditions. The attestation of three versions of the story of Esther assists in understanding how it could apply to different contexts of Jews grappling with living in the Diaspora. These stories could also apply to the same context but offer multiple views of how to go about negotiating one's life in an imperial setting. The scholar Linda Day reminds us that when a book became incorporated into a canon, all versions of the book held authority and not just one textual form (Day, 233). She encourages contemporary audiences to broaden "our concept of what can be considered authoritative," as it "opens the possibility for the two Greek versions of the book of Esther, as well as the Masoretic version, to be used by today's faith communities" (Day, 233).

All three versions of the story of Esther deal with how one should one live under imperial rule. In each narration, some acceptance to the imposed government and culture is assumed. The three versions of Esther, however, tackle the degree to which subjects accept the prevailing laws and traditions of the dominant society. Perhaps their ruminations can serve as resources for moderns living in cultures where ethnic traditions come into conflict with those of the dominant culture.

Works Cited

Crawford, Sidnie White. 2008. *Rewriting Scripture in Second Temple Times*. Studies in the Dead Sea Scrolls and Related Literature. Grand Rapids: Eerdmans.

Day, Linda. 1995. *Three Faces of a Queen: Characterization in the Books of Esther*. Sheffield: Sheffield Academic.

Halverson-Taylor, Martien. 2012. "Secrets and Lies: Secrecy Notices (Esther 2:10, 20) and Diasporic Identity in the Book of Esther." *JBL* 131, no. 3:467–85.

Harrington, Daniel. 1999. *Invitation to the Apocrypha*. Grand Rapids: Eerdmans.

Koller, Aaron. 2014. *Esther in Ancient Jewish Thought*. Cambridge: Cambridge University Press.

Scheindlin, Raymond. 1998. *A Short History of the Jewish People*. New York: Oxford University Press.

WISDOM OF SOLOMON

Emerson B. Powery

Introduction

The Wisdom of Solomon was written in Greek and, thereby, was not part of the Hebrew Bible. Its inclusion in the Septuagint and the Vulgate led to its incorporation into the Christian canon. Tracing their canonical traditions back to this earlier period, Roman Catholic and Eastern Orthodox communities still consider Wisdom part of the deuterocanonical collection. Protestants and Jews consider it part of the Apocrypha. Its emphasis on the immortality of the soul had a major influence on Christian theology in the early centuries of the Christian movement.

The Alexandrian author writes as a thoroughly Hellenized Jew who recognizes his immigrant status in a land in which his Egyptian and Greek neighbors mistreat many in the Jewish community (see 19:13-16). He addresses the community and encourages them to live out their faith, even as he employs Greek ideas to modernize Judaism for the new cultural setting. The teacher provides a clear objective in his final words, in a statement addressed to God: "you have not neglected to help [Israel] at all times and in all places" (19:22). As an immigrant in a land he now calls home, he refers to the "holy land" infrequently (see 12:3, 7) and without accompanying language of longing for that land. Rather, he trusts God to assist Israel "in all places." The idea of an Israelite living as an immigrant in foreign territory has many biblical antecedents (see Genesis 37–50; Esther; Daniel 1–6). At various points throughout the treatise, the author assumes the persona of King Solomon—the most internationally remembered figure in Israel's history—in order to detail a message on the origins and actions of wisdom universally available to all (see 7:1-22).

The Alexandrian wisdom teacher addresses three major themes. The first section (1:1—5:23) contrasts the godly with the ungodly, those who fail to follow torah and to do right as the sage teaches (see 1:1, 15; 2:11; 5:6, 18). Apparently, this latter group opposed the sage's challenge to traditional teaching, including his promotion of the concept of the immortal soul. With this idea, the

979

teacher questions established perspectives from the wisdom tradition, including how fertility (see 3:10-19) and longevity of life (see 4:7-12) are distinct signs of God's blessings.

The second section (6:1—10:21) reflects on wisdom's origin, characteristics, and actions. The sage, still assuming the persona of King Solomon, reimagines the specifics of Solomon's prayer for wisdom (8:21—9:18). Unlike the Solomon of old, this Alexandrian teacher connects wisdom to the language of torah in several instances (e.g., 2:11, 12; 6:4, 18; 9:5; 14:16; 16:6; 18:4, 9), even while maintaining wisdom's universal availability (6:9, 12; 7:23).

In the final section of the book, the sage contrasts Egyptians and Israelites through a creative midrash on the ancient exodus tradition (11:1—19:22). His retelling includes specific negative reactions to the issues of idolatry and animal worship (13:1—15:19), both of which stem from the sage's contemporary setting.

The treatise was written in the late first century BCE or in the first half of the first century CE. A few scholars have attempted to situate the book in the specific period of Caligula's reign, circa 38–41 CE (Winston, 23–24; Grabbe, 88). If the latter date is accepted, Philo of Alexandria and Paul of Tarsus are contemporary Jews whose writings provide significant points of comparison. As a book in the wisdom tradition, the Wisdom of Solomon is a late but comparable volume to other wisdom books, including Sirach, a volume translated into Greek in Egypt circa 120 BCE.

The "love of justice" our author advocates (see 1:1) will occasionally cause this interpreter to push back and read *against* the advice of this ancient sage. Justice is contextual, as this ancient literary classic exemplifies, so we must honor our calling for doing what is right in our own context, since those "who do what is right are in God's hands" (3:1 CEB).

Wisdom of Solomon 1:1-15: Seek Wisdom and Justice

■ THE TEXT IN ITS ANCIENT CONTEXT

The ancient Jewish author begins abruptly, without any opening formalities. Even the addressees (i.e., "rulers of the earth") are imagined. This sage was too far removed from the seats of power to address them directly. Rather, his audience is fellow Jews in the Alexandrian community, who found themselves increasingly isolated in a land that was becoming more hostile. These "leaders" should seek wisdom (i.e., God) and not put God to the test by committing unjust acts (1:1) or thinking illogically (1:3).

Like other ancient documents in the wisdom tradition, this sage emphasizes the discovery of wisdom as essential for faithful followers (1:4-6; cf. Sir. 1:1-8). The teacher is direct. Wisdom can only be found by those who act justly (1:1, 4) and speak reverently of, and to, God (1:6-11). The outer actions should match a person's inner thoughts. This type of "righteousness" will last forever (1:15). The theme that God's righteous children will live beyond death (1:12-15) is the author's contribution to the wisdom tradition. Many of his contemporaries would question the sage's new theological direction, preferring the older wisdom tradition, "for the fate of humans and the fate of animals is the same" (Eccles. 3:19).

For our author, however, "death" is an unnatural part of life, for which God is not responsible (1:13). This sage reads the Genesis narrative, apparently, as if death were not part of the original design.

▮ The Text in the Interpretive Tradition

Death's origins have attracted much reflection throughout history. Some ancient interpreters thought that righteous souls immediately rise to God while others linger in a nebulous arena separate from the divine (Clarke, 19). Others believed that the unrighteous "disintegrated at death" (Grabbe, 54). Scholars also debate whether the Alexandrian sage refers to a "spiritual" or a "biological death." Either way, the teacher appears not to have connected death and mortality to Adam's sin (see 10:1-2).

▮ The Text in Contemporary Discussion

Whatever specific situation surrounded the ancient teacher, the command to "love justice" (1:1) is universal. The contemporary person of faith should do what is just and right in the world. This is the way of the wise!

To encourage life-giving actions and policies should be standard practice for contemporary wisdom seekers. This coincides with the spirit of the ancient sage's advice that death did not originate with God (see 1:12-14). Rather than seeing death as a necessary *evil*, however, contemporary believers prefer to think (rightly) that death is a natural process of the life God grants.

Wisdom of Solomon 1:16—2:24: The Ungodly Lack Wisdom

▮ The Text in Its Ancient Context

Beginning in 1:16, the sage provides examples of the covenant the "ungodly" made with "death." Despite the label "ungodly," the reference to torah (2:12) indicates that the debate is an intrareligious one. In 2:1-9, the "beliefs" of the "ungodly" appear to draw on the ancient wisdom tradition of Qoheleth, the original Hebrew title for Ecclesiastes. Chapter 2 may be viewed as a brief summary of Ecclesiastes. "Let us enjoy the good things that exist" (2:6) since "our allotted time is the passing of a shadow" (2:5) echoes the ancient wisdom teacher, "There is nothing better for mortals than to eat and drink, and find enjoyment in their toil." (Eccles. 2:24). The Hellenistic Jewish teacher challenges this traditional view of life, death, and the hereafter (as represented in the biblical Wisdom literature itself).

While their confessions are similar to the traditional Israelite faith, their actions belie their intentions: "let our might be our law of right." The sage's opponents desire to attack the *dikaios* (or "the just one," 2:10, 12, 18), and by doing so "test" God (2:17) to see if God will intervene (2:18). To test (or tempt) God shows a lack of wisdom (1:2). They show themselves to be aligned with the "devil's party" by continuing to test and challenge just people (2:24).

▮ The Text in the Interpretive Tradition

Many early Christian interpreters (including Ambrose and Cyril of Alexandria) understood the phrase "God's child" (2:18) to be a reference to the Messiah, that is, Jesus who died at the hands of his Jewish contemporaries because he "opposes our actions" (2:12). But this Christocentric interpretation is not historically instructive for grasping the cultural moment of Judaism in Alexandria. If the "just one" was a reference to a specific person, then our sage probably had a local wise priest in mind who (also) taught the radical teaching of living forever.

■ The Text in Contemporary Discussion

Competing belief systems are becoming more common in the pluralistic society of the United States. Challenging this competitive framework is one issue for contemporary believers. How do we describe our neighbors? Do we disparage their attempts to wrestle with the divine? Are we like the ancient sage, who refers to his opponents as "ungodly" and disparages their attempts to hold on to older traditions in contemporary settings?

On the other hand, when is it time, as this ancient sage attempts, to challenge the theological (wisdom) tradition of the faith community? Isn't there a message for a time of reassessment of our own theological traditions? Isn't this what liberation theology, in its various guises (e.g., black theology, feminist theology, mujeristic theology, gay/lesbian theology), attempts to do?

Some interpreters suggest that the "righteous one" of 2:12 is representative of many persons who have died untimely deaths fighting for justice: "The pursuit and destruction of the just continues: it is the grist of the mills of history, empire after empire, army after army" (Berrigan, 31).

Wisdom of Solomon 3:1-19: Reward and Punishment after Death

■ The Text in Its Ancient Context

The sage begins this section (3:1) with a clear statement on the immortality of the godly (cf. 2:23), a fate that the ungodly will not share (3:10-13). The author describes the future state of the godly as one "at peace" (3:3) as they receive "good things" (3:5), and he envisions a meaningful future existence in which the godly will rule over the nations (3:8).

The use of "immortal" language occurs here for the first time in biblical literature. *Athanasia* literally means the opposite of "death" (*thanatos*; see 2:24). For the sage, Wisdom leads her children there (see 8:13, 17), by allowing the wise to do right in the world (see 4:1). More importantly, immortality will mean an ongoing relationship with God (3:9; O'Connor, 172).

Unlike his predecessor in the wisdom tradition (Ben Sira), the author of Wisdom uses the term *psychai* ("soul, life, human being") to refer to a person's earthly "life" (with Sirach) and as a reference for a person's future existence, as a "soul," after death. For Wisdom, a godly person's *psychai* "won't feel the pain of torment" (3:1), will "bear fruit" if barren (3:13), and won't be corrupted (4:11) because "God watches over God's chosen ones" (3:9 CEB).

With his understanding of immortality, the ancient sage calls into question the traditional perspective that God's blessings are visible on earth, including a long life and the presence of children. So the author attacks even the families of the unwise. Their unjust actions must mean that their family is dishonorable (3:10-12). In an honor-shame culture, a community's assessment of a person has a direct impact on that person's family and its communal arrangements (e.g., marriage, bartering). The godliness of "barren" women and "eunuchs"—those without physical descendants—are chief among the sage's examples. It is their godly lives that matter, not their failure to reproduce. It was widely believed that barrenness was due to sin (Winston, 131), but the wisdom tradition had already begun to question this belief (see Sir. 16:3). On the eunuch's spiritual status, the Alexandrian sage chose the prophetic tradition (see Isa. 56:4-5) over the Deuteronomic law (see Deut. 23:1). Reconceptualizing the afterlife allows the sage to challenge the theological idea that "offspring" provided one's future "immortality." In the traditional framework, without children, one's memory died forever.

■ THE TEXT IN THE INTERPRETIVE TRADITION

When the marginalized in a society discover that things on earth are not going according to plan or when they find themselves isolated from the political process, it is not uncommon to imagine a utopian space where they might have some control over their lives. "These promises reverse the reality in which the author's community currently lives" (O'Connor, 173).

■ THE TEXT IN CONTEMPORARY DISCUSSION

If God's life and love may be found in acts of justice and *not* in reproductive acts (see 3:13-17), then contemporary followers of wisdom might discover new ways to imagine the political dynamics of same-sex marriage and other gendered relationships in the contemporary church and world. Even those unable to reproduce naturally "will receive a precious gift" for fidelity to God and to others (see 3:14 CEB).

Wisdom of Solomon 4:1-20: Advantages of Godly Living

■ THE TEXT IN ITS ANCIENT CONTEXT

This section begins at 3:1, in which the author distinguishes between the "ungodly" (*hoi asebeis* at 3:10) and the "just one" (*ho dikaios* at 3:10), who represents those who do the right thing. The latter believes in life after death, the lens through which this Hellenistic Jewish teacher reinterprets the ancient tradition of wisdom on the blessings of fertility and longevity of life. In this ancient cosmopolitan culture, the author witnesses (and perhaps experiences) the prominence of infertility among local women including, perhaps, family members (4:1-7) and early deaths among honorable people in the community who thus never reach old age (4:1-20).

In chapter 4, the author uses the term "memory" (*mnēmē*) as an inclusio, to set this chapter apart (see 4:1, 19). He recognizes the long-standing role of memory as an ancient way of speaking about "life" beyond one's death (cf. 8:13; Eccles. 2:16; Prov. 1:12 LXX). Yet he moves beyond this idea to include a belief in the (good) soul living after present existence (see 1:15; 2:23). The final section (4:17) stresses God's judgment on the ungodly, including wiping out their "memory" (4:19). Apparently, he has in mind the group who murdered one of the contemporary priests in Alexandria (see 2:17-20).

■ THE TEXT IN THE INTERPRETIVE TRADITION

Although ancient patristic interpretation encouraged the association of the "prolific brood of the ungodly" (4:3 RSV) with the "heretics" of their day, recent scholarship rightfully struggles with this type of reasoning. Older wisdom tradition, in the vein of Job and Ecclesiastes, seems more sophisticated than wisdom's "naive" position that the offspring of the "ungodly" will amount to no good (Grabbe, 49–50). Daniel Berrigan uses even more forceful language: "Is the old canard here resuscitated, the sins of the fathers visited on the progeny? . . . Here, one thinks, wisdom fails the wise" (Berrigan, 62–63).

■ THE TEXT IN CONTEMPORARY DISCUSSION

Ancient dualism prevails. Bad things happen to bad people and its reverse, though not exactly in this life according to the Wisdom author!

Is it possible that the Alexandrian sage is *female*? Though this is unlikely, perhaps this male teacher had a barren wife, sister, or close family member. Either way, the sage attempts to lift the theological burden that was placed on infertile females. Infertility is not due to any religious or spiritual wrongdoing on the woman's part. The wise teaching offers a theological challenge to the long-standing religious tradition that childbearing was a sign of divine blessing.

Furthermore, the author questions another *traditional* teaching: longevity of life as a sign of God's blessing. The sage suggests that only the ones who act justly "will be at rest" (4:7); only they will "live a long life in a short span of time" (4:13 CEB).

Just as this Hellenistic teacher read against the grain of his theological heritage, so must later interpreters. The theme of the "useless" children of the ungodly (see 4:3-7) continues the specific issue begun in 3:16-19. Unfortunately, some contemporary Christians still believe that children are punished because of the "iniquity of the fathers" (see Exod. 20:5). This teacher seems not to question this tradition despite his willingness to reassess others. But we must do so in order to avoid the ideological warfare oftentimes imposed on our communities and on our children.

"Do not forget; forgetting is death before death" (Berrigan, 65).

Wisdom of Solomon 5:1-23: Reflections on the Final Judgment

■ THE TEXT IN ITS ANCIENT CONTEXT

The first section (5:2-14) describes the (re)action of the ungodly, more so than the godly (5:1), as the Alexandrian sage imagines a final judgment scene. Beginning in 4:19, the sage describes the loss of any memory of the ungodly: "it passes like the remembrance of a guest who stays but a day" (5:14). In traditional wisdom teaching, ancestors are expected to live on in their children's memory (see Prov. 20:7).

First, the sage imagines the thoughts of the ungodly at the final judgment when they will meet again the "just one" (*dikaios*, see 5:1) whom they murdered (cf. 2:12-20). The intent is to recall the figure in chapter 2, so the plurals in the NRSV—all the way through the passage—are misleading.

Second, the sage questions the value of "wealth" (5:8, *ploutos*), even though traditional wisdom thinking promotes wealth as a by-product of wisdom (see 7:11, 13; 8:18). It is still less valuable than wisdom itself (see 7:8; 8:5).

The second half of this chapter covers the rewards for the godly (5:15-16; cf. 3:5), before the teacher shifts into an unexpected discussion about apocalyptic warfare (5:17-20) and the role of the cosmos in the battle (5:20b-23). The arrival of God as a military warrior may have been borrowed from the earlier prophetic tradition (see Isa. 59:15-17; see below).

▌ THE TEXT IN THE INTERPRETIVE TRADITION

The Alexandrian sage's depiction of God's preparation for battle in a cosmic apocalyptic war has a history in the earlier biblical tradition and is picked up (from Wisdom?) in later Christian circles, as encouragement for believers as well.

Isaiah (see Isa. 59:15-17)	Wisdom of Solomon (see 5:17-20)	Ephesians (see 6:13-17)
"God"	"the Lord"	believers
———	———	Belt of truth
Breastplate of righteousness	Breastplate of righteousness	Breastplate of righteousness
Helmet of salvation	Helmet of impartial justice	Shoes to spread peace
Garments of vengeance	Shield of holiness	Shield of faith
Mantle of fury	Sword of anger	Helmet of salvation
	Sword of God's word	

▌ THE TEXT IN CONTEMPORARY DISCUSSION

"The arc of the universe is long, but it bends toward justice." The words of Martin Luther King Jr. seem to echo this ancient wisdom book. Many attempting to do what is right in the world have considered God/the cosmos/justice/wisdom on the side of their work. As the sage will state later, "the universe itself comes to the defense of those who do what is right" (16:17 CEB; cf. 16:15-19; 19:13-17). And we hope they are right!

Wisdom of Solomon 6:1-21: Rulers Should Seek Wisdom

▌ THE TEXT IN ITS ANCIENT CONTEXT

Addressing "kings" (6:1) recalls the opening address in 1:1 and continues the critique of "rulers" that began at 5:23. Though the sage imagines an audience of rulers, he has the people of his community in mind, especially those who oppose his views about "right" living and future rewards (see chapters 2–4). The fruits of following wisdom include living and ruling forever (6:18, 21).

While imagining kings, the sage offers the common theological perspective that all sovereignty originates with God (cf. Sir. 10:4-5; Rom. 13:1-7). Rulers must follow God's law, or else God will turn against them (6:4-5). Of course, no Egyptian ruler would feel obligated to follow Jewish law. But the sage's Jewish community would (Collins, 192). Furthermore, the teacher follows biblical tradition closely in advocating for God's judgment on those rulers who judge unjustly (cf. Job 12:17-20; 34:24-30; Ezek. 21:25-27). God has higher expectations for "rulers" than for the "lowly"

(6:6-8), a comparison that Sirach also makes (Sir. 10:14-16). The poor receive God's great mercy (Berrigan, 82).

In 6:12-21, the sage introduces the origins of wisdom, a discussion that will take up several chapters (see Wis. 6–9). The sage builds on the language of Proverbs 8 to explore the characteristics of Wisdom. Wisdom seeks those who seek her (cf. Prov. 8:17; Wis. 6:12-15). Moving beyond the tradition of Proverbs, however, those who desire her—in our sage's view—should follow torah (6:18). This chapter provides the clearest connection between torah and Wisdom in the book (6:4; 9:5; 14:16; 16:6; 18:4, 9).

▊ THE TEXT IN THE INTERPRETIVE TRADITION

The apostle Paul and the Alexandrian sage may be drawing on a common Jewish tradition on the relationship between God and civil authorities. Both agree that human sovereignty derives authority from God (cf. Wis. 6:3-8 with Rom. 13:1-8). But their similarities end there. For the Alexandrian sage, earthly rulers should follow God's law or else they lose divine covering. That is, God will act against them (6:4-5). On the other hand, Paul is less concerned with the way rulers govern than with those who fall under their civil authority (Rom. 13:1, 5).

▊ THE TEXT IN CONTEMPORARY DISCUSSION

What advice can the colonized give to the colonizer? "Your power stems from our God!" is one example. The colonized can presume that earthly authority is no true authority at all. They can hope for right treatment and justice in the land, demanding that God's law be followed.

On the other hand, is there only "wisdom" in the religious tradition (e.g., torah)? In our modern, secular state, those political leaders who frequently tend to govern from a religious (think "Christian") perspective tend to be more warlike and economically myopic, representing corporate interests rather than the wider democratic citizenry.

Wisdom of Solomon 6:22—8:1: A Treatise on Wisdom

▊ THE TEXT IN ITS ANCIENT CONTEXT

In chapters 6–9, attention shifts to Wisdom (cf. 6–9), which occurs twenty-five times (of its thirty uses) in chapters 6–10. At 6:22, the sage addresses the "origins" of wisdom, although the theme of immortality remains (see 6:18-19; 8:17).

Here in 7:5-6, the author again assumes the personification of "King Solomon" and discusses how he gained wisdom. This is a retelling of 1 Kgs. 3:5-15, in which King Solomon receives wisdom from God (7:7). The Solomon of old asked for a discerning mind to govern (see 1 Kgs. 3:9), a theme the sage examines more carefully in the following section (Wis. 8:9-15). Because of his original request, Solomon was also granted other gifts of wealth and fame (1 Kgs. 3:13; Wis. 7:11-12).

According to the sage, securing wisdom by prayer (7:7) differs from Solomon's dream in 1 Kgs. 3:5, in which he hears from YHWH. Perhaps the sage shared Ben Sira's general cultural condemnation of dreams, unless verifiably originating with God (see Sir. 34:1-8). The sage also moves beyond the biblical tradition in claiming Solomon's "friendship" with God (7:14, 27), a label that places Solomon on par with Abraham (see 2 Chron. 20:7) and Moses (see Exod. 33:11 LXX; Winston, 188). And Solomon's love for wisdom (7:10; cf. 6:17-18) may be an interpretive extension of Solomon's love for YHWH in the earlier account (cf. 1 Kgs. 3:3).

With wisdom comes *vast* knowledge (7:17-20): cosmology, astronomy, biology, botany, and more. Wisdom's "mobility" emphasizes that, as a spirit (see 1:6), it resides anywhere that is "pure" (7:23-24; Collins, 198). Wisdom and God are closely aligned, but they are not the same. For the sage, God guides wisdom (7:15).

If the sage has only the "traditional" prophets in mind (7:27), as those in whom wisdom resides, then he is similar to Sirach (see Sir. 1:1, 9; 46:13, 15; 48:1, 8, 22; 49:7, 10). If not, then the Alexandrian sage may be encouraging a continuing prophetic tradition through wisdom's presence.

▌ THE TEXT IN THE INTERPRETIVE TRADITION

In later Christian circles (e.g., Dionysius of Alexandria, Ambrose, Augustine) beginning with Hebrews, Christians will transfer the language about wisdom to the Christ figure (Voicu, 99–100). As wisdom is the "breath of the power of God," a "pure emanation," and a "reflection of eternal light" (7:25-26), so is Christ the "reflection of God's glory and the exact imprint of God's very being" (Heb. 1:3). The transfer of wisdom's characteristics to Christ will improve the popularity of the Wisdom of Solomon in early Christian circles.

▌ THE TEXT IN CONTEMPORARY DISCUSSION

Contemporary seekers of wisdom should appreciate the fictional Solomon's desire for wisdom above all else. To possess wisdom—or, rather, to be possessed by Wisdom—will enhance one's human journey beyond all other values (see 7:11).

Wisdom of Solomon 8:2—9:18: Solomon's Desire and Prayer for Wisdom

▌ THE TEXT IN ITS ANCIENT CONTEXT

The sage's character, "Solomon," personifies "Wisdom." He sought her as a "bride" (8:2), pursuing her since his youth. All true Wisdom seekers do this (cf. Sir. 51:13-22). Solomon brought her "to live with me" (8:9), so that they might share their lives together (8:16). Most significantly, Wisdom provided "good counsel" and assisted Solomon in governance (8:9-15). Solomon stresses this further when he describes the specifics of his prayer for Wisdom (9:5-8, 12). Wisdom is the only one who understands how God works in the world (9:9), and without her Solomon knew he would fail (9:13-18). So, Solomon loved Wisdom (cf. 7:10).

And, God "loves" Wisdom too (8:3), even as God loves those who seek Wisdom (7:28). Wisdom has an intimacy with God and thereby "knows God's secret ways" (8:4 CEB), working intimately with God in the affairs of the world. Initiation language (*mystis)* is used to describe Wisdom as an "initiate" in the knowledge of God. This same term (*mystis*) is used for the cultic initiate into the mystery religions (cf. 12:5). Those who seek wisdom and love it will find it (see 6:12), even as Solomon did (7:10). Other "rulers"—and all people—should also love right actions (1:1) and those who do work alongside Wisdom (8:7) to accomplish their goals. Since God loves Wisdom, God also loves those who do right (4:10).

Before describing his prayer, Solomon describes his preparation, since Wisdom only enters "holy beings" (7:27; 10:16). His own "good soul" entered a pure body (8:20; 9:15), which prepared the way for the reception of Wisdom. Inappropriate bodies may "weigh down" good souls (9:15). In the sage's Hellenistic theology, only the soul will resurrect (see 3:1; also, Collins, 186).

▮ THE TEXT IN THE INTERPRETIVE TRADITION

Biblical scholars have rightly recognized the female imagery of Wisdom that would not have been lost on the sage's readers. This is "Woman Wisdom," whose desire for relationship fits neatly into a Hellenistic setting in which Isis, the Egyptian goddess, is prominent (Tanzer, 293; Collins, 203–4; O'Connor, 175). With the sage's theological perspective, Jews need no longer look outside of Judaism for this type of intimate relationship. Wisdom (*sophia*) is so closely associated with God as God's "breath," "mirror," and "image" (see 7:25-26) that it is easy to claim that she and God are one: "To see her, therefore, is to see God. To relate to her is to relate to God. She is God, not a new god or a second god, but God poetically imaged as woman" (O'Connor, 178).

▮ THE TEXT IN CONTEMPORARY DISCUSSION

Contemporary discussions about God's *male*ness—with constant inconsiderate and unquestioned use of male pronouns—must deal with this ancient sage's attempts to imagine God's *female*ness. According to Wisdom of Solomon, God does nothing in the world except through *Sophia*.

Wisdom of Solomon 10:1-21: Wisdom Guides the Heroes of Israel

▮ THE TEXT IN ITS ANCIENT CONTEXT

Wisdom/Sophia language continues in chapter 10 (four times). The sage connects Sophia's actions to Israel's history and tells how Sophia guided (seven) heroes to do what was right. Wisdom not only led prominent heroes but also guided the people of Israel (10:15–11:14; cf. 18:20) from their bondage in Egypt. She may have "entered" Moses' soul (10:16; cf. 7:27), but the sage concentrates on her activity among all people (10:15-21). The sage uses the adjective *dikaion* ("just, right, fair") to define Wisdom's servants (10:4, 5, 6, 10, 13, 20), a term associated with the earlier theme of those who do what is right (see 3:1; 4:7; 5:1, 15).

There are a few surprises in this list. For example, apparently only Adam committed the "transgression" in the garden; there is no mention of Eve (see 10:1), although Sophia is present. The sage blames the flood on Cain's murder of Abel (10:2-4), although he knows the fuller Genesis tradition (see 14:6). Among the heroes, Jacob receives the most attention. Jacob's lesson about "holy things," though unclear, distinguishes his character's description (10:10). Wisdom teaches the knowledge of "hidden" things (see 7:21-22), since only she understands "heavenly things" (cf. 9:16-17). Perhaps this is a vague reference to Jacob's struggle with God in the "contest" of verse 12 (see Gen. 32:22-31), as the Revised Standard Version may capture ("knowledge of angels"). Here Wisdom represents God in that ancient struggle.

Compared to other lists of Jewish heroes (e.g., Sirach 44–50; 1 Macc. 2:49-64), this Alexandrian teacher highlights Wisdom's involvement and care in the lives of Israel's leaders. The heroes remain unnamed, since the sage's objective is to emphasize Sophia's role in their protection and salvation (Collins, 215).

■ THE TEXT IN THE INTERPRETIVE TRADITION

The author of Hebrews provides his own hero list, which shares parallels with Wisdom 10 (e.g., Noah, Abraham, Jacob, Moses). In Hebrews, names are specified, however, and the author emphasizes activities lived out by faith. Our Alexandrian sage focuses instead on the significant role Wisdom played in each of the unnamed representatives of Israel. In later Christian reflections on Wisdom 10 (e.g., Augustine), Christ will replace Wisdom's role as the one who, for example, "released" Adam from his "crime" (Voicu, 123).

■ THE TEXT IN CONTEMPORARY DISCUSSION

Jacob's struggle with Sophia in order to secure wisdom may model contemporary struggles to secure knowledge and wisdom in the modern world. It is an arduous task and not easily accomplished, but earned through diligent perseverance. At the end of the day, it may not simply be "godliness" alone, however, that allows one to succeed as the ancient sage believes (see 10:12). To be clear, those who do what is right are on Wisdom's path.

Wisdom of Solomon 11:1—12:2: The Role of Wisdom in Israel's Exodus from Egypt

■ THE TEXT IN ITS ANCIENT CONTEXT

Focusing less on Israel's individual heroes (chapter 10), the sage concentrates on Wisdom's contributions to Israel's history in the specific event of the exodus. The history of Israel's escape from Egyptian bondage would have had an immediate appeal for his Alexandrian audience, some of whom sensed hostility from their Egyptian neighbors (cf. 19:13-15). There is significantly less wisdom language in this final section (after 10:21, *Sophia* does not appear until 14:2, 5), though she is the implied subject at 11:1 (as the NRSV suggests). Referring to Moses as a "holy prophet" recalls the role of Wisdom as well (cf. 7:27). Despite some scholarly claims, the absence of "God" language in chapter 11 actually begins to shift the focus from Wisdom to God—as the primary acting agent (O'Connor, 183; cf. Clarke, 73; Collins, 180; Berrigan, 119; Tanzer, 294).

The sage views the worship of animals, which his contemporary neighbors practice, as a part of God's punishment for the Egyptians (11:15; cf. Rom. 1:23). God did not simply allow it; God initiated this misguided religious practice (11:15-17). The Creator of the world would have no difficulty forming the necessary creatures for this experiment, since God formed the original creations "out of formless matter" (11:17). The idea of preexistent matter was shared widely by other Jewish and Greek thinkers (e.g., Philo and Plato; see Grabbe, 65). This is *not* creation *ex nihilo*, which had only been expressed a few generations earlier (cf. 2 Macc. 7:28: "God made these things from nothing"; CEB). The sage supports the more widely held process of creation elsewhere as well (see 1:14; 2:23; 10:1; 11:17; 13:3).

In this passage, punishment is not the final word (11:20b—12:2). Rather, God's mercy is driven by God's love for all creation (11:24).

■ THE TEXT IN THE INTERPRETIVE TRADITION

Citing 11:17, Augustine claims—in his unfinished commentary on Genesis—that the "formless matter" was *also* created by God (Voicu, 131). This allowed later Christian thinkers to maintain the logic of a creation *ex nihilo* (cf. 2 Macc 7:28; Heb. 11:3).

■ THE TEXT IN CONTEMPORARY DISCUSSION

It is worth exploring the relationship between memory and religious discourse in light of its occurrence in this treatise (see 11:12). For example, the sage provides a biased retelling (i.e., a way to remember) of Israel's "goodness" and Egypt's "evil" as indicative of wisdom's presence with one group and not the other. Other uses of memory correlate. The memory of virtue will live on (4:1), while the memory of the ungodly will disappear (4:19); and "Solomon's" memory was preserved because of wisdom (8:13). What do we remember about our past, our histories, and the other? And what part of that memory are we willing to pass along to shape present relationships and communities?

Wisdom of Solomon 12:3-27: God's Treatment of the Gentiles

■ THE TEXT IN ITS ANCIENT CONTEXT

The sage continues his defense of God's mercy and fairness with God's treatment of the nations (12:8-18; cf. 11:23-26). Similar to Philo and Josephus, he justifies Israel's conquest of Canaan (Winston, 238). Canaanites had polluted the land. Yet God did not massacre them swiftly, allowing them an "opportunity to repent" (12:10; cf. 12:20).

The teacher concludes that the ancient practice of human sacrifice was the cause for God's anger (12:3-7). Only here, in Wisdom, does the author consider a special relationship between God and the "holy land" (12:3, 7), an expression rare in biblical literature (cf. 2 Macc. 1:7). On the other hand, this Alexandrian Jew does not express any desire himself to return to Judea. Unlike Ben Sira, the sage offers no preferential treatment to Jerusalem (19:22; cf. Sir. 24:8-12; Fuller, 34–35). The ambivalence of this immigrant is apropos.

His defense of God's mercy still allows room for proper judgment for the sage's Egyptian community. The sage begins here (12:23-27) an argument that will continue through chapter 15: God allowed the Egyptians to follow their own paths, which ended up in the ungodly worship of all sorts of creatures and animals.

■ THE TEXT IN THE INTERPRETIVE TRADITION

Has God been fair with the gentiles? According to the sage, God is sovereign yet fair and patient with wrongdoers. Divine patience is indicative of God's inevitable mercy, which Israel should also expect (12:19-22). Yet the sage's God is on Israel's side and not on the side of the majority population. This is the voice of the immigrant who has entered into another land; the sage echoes the voice of those who feel abused in foreign territory (cf. 19:13-15).

■ THE TEXT IN CONTEMPORARY DISCUSSION

The questions of theodicy, alluded to in 12:12, are age-old questions. In the sage's wisdom tradition, no one should question God. In the contemporary world, however, theodicy questions loom large. The sage provides one theological perspective: "You always do what's right" (12:15 CEB). Unfortunately, this kind of thinking may lead to the idea that whatever we see in the world is due to God's actions and is thereby "righteous." Many fundamentalists think this way. Others rightly question this approach, wondering whether "God" could be responsible for all of the destruction and chaos in the contemporary world, or, more likely, whether it was due to human machinations.

Wisdom of Solomon 13:1-19: Gentiles and Idolatry

■ THE TEXT IN ITS ANCIENT CONTEXT

In chapters 13–15, a lengthy digression, the sage attacks gentile religious practices. He wrestles with whether gentiles are guilty for their failure to acknowledge God and, therefore, should receive God's full judgment (12:27; 13:6-9). The sage claims (similar to Paul the apostle) that gentiles appreciated creation but failed to recognize its Creator (13:1; cf. Rom. 1:19-21). The outcome was the worship of created things, failing to recognize "a corresponding perception of their Creator" (Wis. 13:5).

This Jewish teacher stands in a long line of traditional opponents to idolatry (13:10-19; cf. Isa. 44:9-20; Jer. 10:1-16). In order to attack meaningless prayers to idols (Wis. 13:17-19), the sage explains the overtly human process of idol-making (13:11-16). Attacks on idolatry increased in the Hellenistic period (cf. 1 Corinthians 8; see Collins, 209). During his attack, the sage provides a window into why ancient people prayed: possessions, marriages, children, health, and safe travel (13:17-18). The sage does not condemn *why* gentiles pray, only *to what* they pray.

■ THE TEXT IN THE INTERPRETIVE TRADITION

The similarity between Wisdom 13 and Romans 1 has been widely discussed in scholarly literature. Whether Paul is dependent on the Alexandrian sage could only be determined if scholars were more certain about the historical circumstances surrounding Wisdom. The present consensus is that both authors share a common tradition and condemnation of gentile idolatry. Douglas Campbell has recently challenged this consensus, arguing that the words of Romans 1:18-32 are not Paul's position but his representation of an opponent's teaching in the Roman community who is closely aligned with the thinking of the Wisdom of Solomon.

▌THE TEXT IN CONTEMPORARY DISCUSSION

Why people pray today parallels the ancients of Alexandria. Possessions, marriage, children, health, and safety still resonate for many people. But where are the prayers on behalf of the other, those least like us? Where are the prayers for those who struggle for citizenship (i.e., immigrants), for those whose sexual identities cause political and theological debate (i.e., LGBT persons), and for those who seek religious solace through alternative means (i.e., Muslims)? Where are those prayers in the ancient world? And where are those prayers today?

Wisdom of Solomon 14:1-31: The Origin of Idols

▌THE TEXT IN ITS ANCIENT CONTEXT

The sage continues his attack on idolatry with a specific example: travel at sea. In the ancient world, sea travel was notoriously precarious (14:2-7), so prayers were plentiful (13:18). This wisdom teacher argues that God is the real protector of any voyage (14:3-4). The final references to "wisdom" in the book occur here (cf. 14:2, 5). The author links the "giants" to the flood (14:6), providing a closer reading of the Genesis narrative (see Gen. 6:1-4) than the earlier suggestion that Cain's actions led to the flood (see 10:3). The sage stands in a long line of biblical authors who view idolatry as the greatest offense to God (cf. Isa. 44:9-20; Jer. 10:1-16). According to Wisdom, God "hates" the idols and their designers (14:9).

The sage, then, offers two examples on the origins of idols: (1) a grieving father creates an image to remember a lost child (14:15-16); (2) an image is produced to remember the emperor (14:17-20). High infant mortality was commonplace in the first century, so many religious acts memorialized the tragic loss of the young (Winston, 274). Child veneration, however, was not common. In the second scenario, the emperor cult is initiated from the earlier practice (14:16-17), a practice perhaps common in the sage's experience. With "secret rites and initiations" surrounding the idol (14:15, 23), the sage seems to refer to the "mystery cults" of Egypt, perhaps those associated with the Isis cult.

Finally, there are other ramifications from these idolatrous practices (14:22-31), including the sage's charge that these religious rituals include murdering children (14:23; cf. 12:5), a common rhetorical attack in antiquity used against other religious groups. The "sacrifice" of a child may be more symbolic than real. Compare Paul's language of "death" for the practice of baptism (see Rom. 6:4-5). In the sage's mind, idolatry is the cause of all evil (14:27), a theme commonly shared by Jews.

▌THE TEXT IN THE INTERPRETIVE TRADITION

The language of 14:7—"blessed is the wood by which righteousness comes"—would have attracted Christian readers for other intentions than the sage's. Some scholars suggest that the verse is a later

Christian interpolation (Collins, 210n70). Others disagree (Winston, 267), preferring to locate the sage's use of wood as a reference to Noah's ark in the immediate context.

Early Christian theologians—for example, Epiphanius of Salamis and Augustine—will blame demons for the origins of idolatry. Epiphanius wrote that idols "are the products of wicked demons and of the human mind full of impulses to pleasure, since each of us is led to make his own passion an object of veneration" (*Ancoratus* 102.5–7; Voicu, 153). This moves beyond Wisdom, but may reflect Pauline thinking (see 1 Cor. 10:20).

▮ THE TEXT IN CONTEMPORARY DISCUSSION

In the ancient world, the sage follows a long tradition of recognizing idolatry as the one thing the God of love "hates" (see 14:9, 27). For many, idolatry is the cause of all that is evil in the world (see 14:27). What contemporary "idols," created by human hands, distort the image of God among us?

Wisdom of Solomon 15:1—16:1: God's Mercy toward Israel

▮ THE TEXT IN ITS ANCIENT CONTEXT

In chapter 15, the sage returns to the earlier theme of God's mercy toward Israel (cf. 11:20-26). The teacher links this mercy (at 15:3) to the theme of immortality (*athanasias*) that was prominent earlier in the book (cf. 3:4; 4:1; 8:13, 17). Knowing God (15:3) or wisdom (8:13, 17) will lead to immortality. The opposite of immortality is not sin for the Alexandrian sage. "Sin" has a more specific meaning in Wisdom. It refers to idolatry (see 11:16; 14:13) or the creation of idols that lead to the religious practice (15:13). So the sage's claim that "we will not sin" (15:2) is a statement of the unattractiveness of idol worship for the Alexandrian Jewish community (15:4-6; cf. 14:17-20). In the sage's theology, idolatry is the "origin of all evil" (14:27).

He reiterates how foolish it is to create idols themselves (15:7-13). Performing this egregious sin (15:13), that is, creating idols, for profit is no excuse (15:12). Even more foolish are those who worship these human-made creatures (15:14-16:1). The sage joins the common chorus of monotheists that idols have no life in themselves (15:17; cf. Ps. 115:4-8; 1 Cor. 8:7). The sage distinguishes between the lifeless idols and the humans who created them, whose own souls are loaned to them for the short period of their human existence (15:8, 11, 16), a popular idea in the Greco-Roman world (Winston, 286–87). His focused attack on idolatry does not ignore his particular critique of Egyptian animal worship (15:18—16:1; 11:15-20).

▮ THE TEXT IN THE INTERPRETIVE TRADITION

In early Christianity, a significant debate ensued as to whether souls preexist the created body in which they reside (so Origen) or are created at the same moment (so Tertullian, Jerome) when it enters the body. The language of "borrowed" souls (in 15:8, 16) seems to support Origen's position, which was later condemned. The latter position seems to be supported by 15:11, although early Christians disagreed whether the soul derived from one's parents (i.e., traducianism) or from God at the moment of one's birth (i.e., creationism, with respect to the soul).

◼ THE TEXT IN CONTEMPORARY DISCUSSION

The label "sin" has specific cultural contexts. For this Jewish teacher, there is no greater sin than idolatry (14:27). Just as ancient Jewish and Christian believers find idolatry to be opposed to the divine will, contemporary followers of God view racism as opposed to God's purposes. Racism is a theological problem, since people who think of other people as inferior make a direct statement about the Creator of all. So sin is not just theological but also cultural.

Wisdom of Solomon 16:2-29: God Protects Israel

◼ THE TEXT IN ITS ANCIENT CONTEXT

The author assures his listeners—using the classic story of the exodus—that God cares for Israel in their present surroundings in Egypt. Sometimes God's "wrath" (against Israel) appeared (6:5, 11), but it was only for brief moments of discipline. In light of the sage's attack on idolatry, the irony (and indirectness) of 16:5-8 should not be missed (Grabbe, 66). Under God's command, Moses created a bronze serpent (Num. 21:8-9) to symbolize God's salvation. The sage recognizes the potential conflict; people were "saved, not by the thing that was beheld, / but by you, the Savior of all" (16:7; cf. 16:12). Unlike Sirach (see Sir. 38:6-15), the sage emphasizes God alone as the agent of healing, not any mediating object (Wis. 16:12, 26).

The sage takes other liberties with the earlier biblical story in his retelling: the destructive role of fire (16:16-19, 22-23), the heavenly bread suiting each person's taste (16:21). The major point of this retelling is how nature took sides, operating in Israel's favor: "the universe defends the righteous" (16:17). This is a common theme throughout the book (see 5:17, 20; 16:24; 19:6). Finally, the sage stipulates the practice of praying twice daily, before sunrise and again at sunset (16:28). Ben Sira shares the example of early morning prayers (Sir. 39:5); the author of Daniel advocates praying thrice daily (Dan. 6:10).

◼ THE TEXT IN THE INTERPRETIVE TRADITION

A late contemporary of the sage, the author of the Gospel of John will also find a religious analogy in Moses' bronze serpent: "And just as Moses lifted up the serpent in the wilderness, so must the Son of Man be lifted up, that whoever believes in him may have eternal life" (John 3:14-15). For the Alexandrian sage, God's "word" is the salvific force (16:6, 26). For John, it is the "Son of Man" who is defined as the "word" (*logos*) who was "in the beginning with God" (John 1:2), in language reminiscent of the sage's conception of Wisdom: "All things came into being through him, and without him not one thing came into being" (John 1:3; cf. Wis. 7:22).

◼ THE TEXT IN CONTEMPORARY DISCUSSION

The sage expounds no greater wisdom than at 16:17: "for the universe defends the righteous." In another place and time, Rev. Martin Luther King Jr. put it this way: "the moral arc of the universe bends towards justice." Both sages make a theological assumption that the cosmos leans toward those who do what is right. King did not share with the ancient sage the view that right actions always come from "our" side, those who may be situated like us religiously, politically, or geographically. Unfortunately, the sage could not see through his own wisdom. For King, those who act *justly* can come from any walk of life and should be included in the beloved community.

Wisdom of Solomon 17:1-21: The Ignorance of the Ungodly

▌ THE TEXT IN ITS ANCIENT CONTEXT

The sage continues to address God (17:1), as if in a prayer (cf. 16:28). But here he concentrates his efforts on the ignorance of the ungodly (17:1-21), oblivious to their wrongdoing that gives them a false sense of hope (17:13). The author imagines psychological torment and emotional warfare on the enemies of Israel, and he offers a midrash on the fatal night of Israel's escape from bondage (17:5). His creative literary expression about this occasion is unmatched in biblical literature.

The darkness that overwhelmed them (17:2, 10, 14, 18, 21), despite the light that allowed others in the whole world to do its business (17:20), was based on the three-day darkness that covered Egypt (see Exod. 10:21-23). Darkness of this kind comes on those who presumably are not taught torah (17:1), who depend on magic (17:7; 18:13), and who let fear drive their ignorance (17:13, 15, 19).

The language of "holy nation" (17:2) is not common in Wisdom. Here "nation" (*ethnos*) refers to the *people* and not the *land* and is the only use of *ethnos* for Israel in the book (cf. 3:8; 6:2; 8:14; 10:5, 15; 12:12; 14:11; 15:15). The author prefers *laon hosion* ("holy people") throughout his account (see "holy ones," 4:15; 10:17; 18:1, 5, 9; and "your people," 9:7; 12:19; 16:2, 20; 18:7; 19:5, 22).

▌ THE TEXT IN THE INTERPRETIVE TRADITION

Samuel Cheon has argued that the Alexandrian teacher—whom he calls Pseudo-Solomon—was not interested in a careful explanation of the exodus account (Cheon, 109). Chapter 17 is an excellent case in point. Darkness was present in the biblical account (Exod. 10:21-23), but Pseudo-Solomon has interests beyond the text (e.g., ghosts, 17:3-4). As Cheon suggests, this sage was much more invested in applying the ancient story to his contemporary setting than explaining obscure elements of the biblical account.

▌ THE TEXT IN CONTEMPORARY DISCUSSION

The chapter reads like an ancient description of what we may classify today as clinical depression, a mood disorder in which feelings of sadness, loss, or anger inhibit common, everyday practices. The challenges of living peacefully in today's society can sometimes be hindered by fear, as the ancient sage writes: "For fear is nothing but a giving up of the helps that come from reason" (17:12). This kind of fear drives ignorance (17:13, 15, 19). As Ernest Clarke observes, "It is this psychological analysis of fear (17:11-13) which the writer developed in his exegesis of Exod. 10:23-4" (Clarke, 113).

Wisdom of Solomon 18:1-25: God's Deliverance from Egypt

▌THE TEXT IN ITS ANCIENT CONTEXT

The sage returns to God's protection of Israel (see Wisdom of Solomon 16). Just as darkness surrounded the enemy (18:4; cf. 17:2, 10, 14, 18, 21), so an incredible light brightened up Israel's path (18:1). The physical light of Exodus (Exod. 10:23) in the sage's retelling also becomes a metaphor for torah (18:4; cf. 5:6-7). In this way, the author introduces the law into the story (18:4), just as he included torah as the "symbol of deliverance" earlier (see 16:6). For the sage, the law was granted *before* Israel's departure from Egypt (18:9) and provided crucial guidance during Israel's journey in the wilderness. Later rabbis will promulgate the idea of a preexistent torah (before creation). Here, the sage alludes to torah's universal design through Israel (18:4).

The specific deliverance of Exodus is repeated here (18:5-9; cf. 16:2-29). Despite their enemies' request for forgiveness (18:2)—a scene absent from the original account (see Exod. 10:17)—God's annihilation of Egyptian children was inevitable (18:10-13). Egyptian magic hindered them from belief (18:13; 17:7), and their nightmares were fulfilled (18:14-19; 17:14-15).

Israel does not fully escape punishment and death either (18:20), as the sage focuses on a later period in Israel's wilderness journey (Num. 16:46-48). A priest was needed to fight the plague. Its punishment did not last long since their high priest—unnamed here as the heroes of chapter 10 were—intervened. The sage emphasizes the significant role of this ancient hero, Aaron (18:20-25). The high priest utilized prayer, along with incense, to intervene (18:21; Num. 16:48). He reminded God—who is implied as the "destroyer" here—of the divine promises and "covenants" (18:22), symbols the "destroyer" feared (18:24-25). Unlike Numbers, the sage is reluctant to name God directly throughout this section.

▌THE TEXT IN THE INTERPRETIVE TRADITION

Some scholars consider 18:4 as evidence of a missionary impulse in ancient Judaism (see Collins, 154). Martin Goodman has convincingly argued against any such inclination in Jewish Hellenistic literature. The Alexandrian sage probably did not view his teaching in this way—as encouragement to the Greeks and Egyptians to participate in Judaism—even if he understood torah and wisdom as having universal implications (see 6:24; 9:3). His teaching was directed at other Jews.

▌THE TEXT IN CONTEMPORARY DISCUSSION

God's destruction of the "enemy" is a theological problem in contemporary circles (Berrigan, 190), especially when innocent children are involved (18:5, 10, 12). The sage has his own theological dilemma, in that he reluctantly depicts God as striking Israel, as the indirect language of 18:20-24 suggests (cf. Num. 16:46-48). Some scholars highlight the absence of Lady Wisdom in this final segment, and the return of the God of violence (Tanzer, 294; Berrigan, 191).

Wisdom of Solomon 19:1-22: God Defeats Israel's Enemies

▌ THE TEXT IN ITS ANCIENT CONTEXT

After a long reflection on Israel's exodus from Egypt (starting in 11:1), the sage finally turns to the final destruction of the Egyptians, their drowning in the sea (19:1-5). The teacher highlights God's foreknowledge as an attempt to relieve God of any wrongdoing: "for God knew in advance even their future actions" (19:1; cf. 12:10-11). After all, it was nature again that protected God's people (19:6-12), a theme emphasized earlier (16:17, 24-25). Furthermore, these "sinners . . . justly suffered" (19:13) because of their mistreatment of the immigrants living among them (19:13-15).

The author's discussion of the immigrant is relevant to his own contemporary society. Some citizens treated strangers oddly from the very beginning (19:14)—an apparent allusion to the Sodomites of Genesis 19—while other citizens mistreated them after the immigrants had received the rights of citizenship (19:16). This latter group refers to the Egyptians and their oppression of their Jewish neighbors in Alexandria (Winston, 329). By implication, Egyptian mistreatment would again lead to their punishment.

The Alexandrian sage closes the treatise almost as abruptly as he began (19:18-22). First, as a teacher in the wisdom tradition, he reminds his audience of the importance of observation (19:18). What he observes is how nature defends those who do right, a theme discussed throughout the book (16:17, 24-25). More importantly, behind nature stands the Creator, whom the sage addresses in his closing words. The sage affirms God's faithfulness toward Israel (19:22; Sir. 51:3) in a closing doxology (Grabbe, 17).

▌ THE TEXT IN THE INTERPRETIVE TRADITION

The author writes as an immigrant who hopes to encourage the immigrant community in which he resides. There is also ambivalence in his perspective. On the one hand, he labels the mistreatment he experiences in the foreign land (19:14). On the other hand, he does not encourage the community to return home. In fact, he refers infrequently to Judea and does not express any longing to return there (12:3, 7). In the final verse of the book, he confesses trust in God to protect and guide Israel "in all places" (19:22).

▌ THE TEXT IN CONTEMPORARY DISCUSSION

Treatment of the stranger or immigrant is a common motif in biblical literature. This sage provides something profound—perhaps even unique—in biblical literature. Nature itself—as God's representative in the world scene—operates on behalf of the immigrant. Of course, in this instance, the author speaks as the immigrant and not as the host.

Works Cited

Berrigan, Daniel. 2001. *Wisdom: The Feminine Face of God*. Lanham, MD: Sheed & Ward.

Campbell, Douglas. 2009. *The Deliverance of God: An Apocalyptic Rereading of Justification in Paul*. Grand Rapids: Eerdmans.

Cheon, Samuel. 1997. *The Exodus Story in the Wisdom of Solomon: A Study in Biblical Interpretation*. Sheffield: Sheffield Academic.

Clarke, Ernest G. 1973. *The Wisdom of Solomon*. CBC. Cambridge: Cambridge University Press.

Collins, John J. 1997. *Jewish Wisdom in the Hellenistic Age*. OTL. London: T&T Clark.

Fuller, Michael E. 2006. *The Restoration of Israel*. Berlin: de Gruyter.

Goodman, Martin. 1994. *Mission and Conversion: Proselytizing in the Religious History of the Roman Empire*. Oxford: Clarendon.

Grabbe, Lester L. 1997. *Wisdom of Solomon*. Sheffield: Sheffield Academic.

O'Connor, Kathleen M. 1988. *The Wisdom Literature*. Message of Biblical Spirituality. Collegeville, MN: Michael Glazier.

Origen. *On First Principles*.

Tanzer, Sarah J. 2012. "Wisdom of Solomon." In *Women's Bible Commentary*, edited by Carol A. Newsom, Sharon H. Ringe, and Jacqueline E. Lapsley, , 404–9. 3rd ed. Louisville: Westminster John Knox.

Voicu, Sever, ed. 2010. "Commentary on Wisdom of Solomon." In *Apocrypha*, 34–175. Ancient Christian Commentary on Scripture, Old Testament 15. Downers Grove, IL: InterVarsity Press.

Winston, David. 1979: *The Wisdom of Solomon*. AB 43. New York: Doubleday.

SIRACH

Stacy Davis

Introduction

Sirach's author identifies himself in 50:27.

> Instruction in understanding and knowledge
>   I have written in this book,
> Jesus son of Eleazar son of Sirach of Jerusalem.

Most likely a teacher (Sir. 39:32-34), Ben Sira, as he is commonly called, left in written form the results of decades of oral instruction. Unlike most biblical books, Sirach's date can be determined from intertextual evidence. The praise of the high priest Simon (219–196 BCE) in Sirach 50 and the silence regarding the Maccabean revolt (175–164 BCE) suggest that Ben Sira completed his work in the 180s. His grandson translated the book from Hebrew to Greek after 132 BCE, "the thirty-eighth year of the reign of Euergetes" (prologue).

Catholic and Orthodox traditions recognize and include Sirach as part of their Hebrew Scriptures; Sirach appears between the Wisdom of Solomon and Isaiah in Catholic Bibles and between Wisdom and Hosea in Orthodox ones. Protestants do not consider Sirach canonical, although the book sometimes is printed in study Bibles, including the NRSV. Sirach was not included in the Jewish Tanak, but remained a part of Jewish tradition, cited in the Talmud and by Nachmanides (Koperski, 262).

Historical/Cultural Context

By the time Ben Sira was writing, in the first quarter of the second century BCE, the Greeks had controlled Palestine for 150 years; first by the Ptolemies and then the Seleucids. The Ptolemies had followed the Persian approach to governance—rule benevolently in exchange for timely tax revenue. Jewish communities paid their taxes and therefore lived peacefully. Peace notwithstanding, Jews supported the Seleucid rise to power under Antiochus III (223–187 BCE). He rewarded them with a three-year tax release. Temple workers specifically received some permanent tax relief. Religious freedom for Jews remained intact from Ptolemaic rule, although it disappeared shortly after Ben Sira completed his work (Di Lella 1992, 933; Perdue, 245). Culturally, Hellenization, or the adoption of Greek ideas and customs, was the word of the day. The extent of Ben Sira's acceptance and incorporation of Hellenization remains debatable, as the following section will indicate.

What was Ben Sira's view of Hellenization? Scholarly answers to the question vary and depend on an understanding of Sirach's purpose. Alexander A. Di Lella argues that Ben Sira's "purpose was not to condemn Hellenism as such, but rather to demonstrate to Jews and even gentiles of good will that true wisdom is to be found primarily in Jerusalem and not in Athens" (1992, 933). Leo G. Perdue suggests that Ben Sira "[attempts] . . . the forging of a somewhat uneasy synthesis between older Israelite and Jewish wisdom and Hellenistic *paideia*" (Perdue, 246). Sirach's breadth of topics lends itself to both arguments. While Ben Sira certainly reinforces belief in Israel's God and Jewish traditions, he also uncritically shows Hellenistic cultural influences, as his views about friendship and gender will indicate. As a whole, the book defends the writer's self-identification as a man "whose mind poured forth wisdom" (Sir. 50:27). Readers of Ben Sira's work "might make even greater progress in living according to the law" (prologue).

Literary Forms

Sirach contains several specific literary forms, including proverbs ("Birds roost with their own kind, / so honesty comes home to those who practice it" ([Sir. 27:9]), hymns, prayers, and what may be called teaching narratives, or stories designed to inform the reader how (and how not) to behave (see the discussion on table etiquette in Sir. 31:12-24). The proverbs and stories are scattered throughout Sirach, giving the author's point of view about themes such as wisdom, divine retribution, virtues, vices, and gender relations. While Sirach begins with a hymn, other hymns and prayers appear throughout the book.

Although the book uses clear literary forms, dividing the book into units is difficult at best. The number of large sections ranges from three to eight (nine including the conclusion following the hymn to the ancestors), and no consensus exists regarding the number of subsections, particularly in Sirach 1–38 (Di Lella 1992, 936–37; Perdue, 247; Clifford, 118–20). Additionally, Sirach has no linear thematic structure. The *Anchor Bible Dictionary* entry "Wisdom of Ben-Sira" (Di Lella 1992) sequentially divides the book's fifty-one chapters but then discusses the work thematically, with sections on the book's style, sources, and major theological themes. Richard Clifford follows the same approach. Burton Mack and Benjamin G. Wright III perhaps say it best: "The nature of the material in this large collection of wisdom proverbs and poetry prohibits neat organization and frustrates prolonged linear reading" (Mack and Wright, 1380). Yet the book's final form remains linear in some sense. The difficulty may be a consequence of Sirach's overall purpose. Alexander A. Di Lella notes that the book "is a kind of handbook of moral behavior for the early second-century BC Jew" (1992, 936). To that end, its purpose is similar to the easier-to-divide but still anthology-like Proverbs (Perdue, 77; Clifford, 43). With that in mind, this essay will approach Sirach thematically, form-critically, and linearly. The texts will be discussed in chapter-and-verse order, beginning with Sir. 1:1 and ending with 51:30. The following divisions, therefore, are neither definitive nor arbitrary; their purpose is to enable the reader to follow the linear pattern in which Sirach attained its final form, while noticing important and repeated ideas and themes in the book as a whole.

Sirach 1:1—10:31 Prologue and the Beginning of Wisdom

▉ The Text in Its Ancient Context

Ben Sira's grandson writes a brief prologue that explains both the purpose of his grandfather's work and offers an apology for any translation problems. Sirach as a whole is designed to help those who want to follow the torah and live well. The grandson, living in Egypt, worked tirelessly to translate the work from Hebrew into Greek.

The book itself then begins with a hymn. Ben Sira's hymns exemplify intertextuality, with allusions to Job, Genesis, and Proverbs (Perdue, 249, 259; Clifford, 122–23). The sage's opening hymn (Sir. 1:1-10) glorifies God as the Creator and therefore the source of wisdom (cf. Job 28). He concludes that "those who love [God]" will receive wisdom (Sir. 1:10). The hymns reinforce older traditions about God's majesty and the wonders of the created world. Yet they are also distinctive products of Hellenistic Judaism. Praising the God of Israel as the genuine and authoritative source of wisdom may be a response to *1 Enoch*'s apocalyptic claim that Enoch himself knows the universe's mysteries as well as a reaction to the Greek argument that such mysteries can be solved through scientific inquiry (Corley 2003, 269–85).

For Ben Sira, almost all proper behavior comes directly from fear of the Lord. A poem on the topic immediately follows the opening hymn to wisdom in Sirach 1, with the fear of the Lord being "the beginning . . . [the] fullness . . . the crown . . . [and] the root of wisdom" (1:14, 16, 18, 20). The ones who fear God enjoy length of days, riches, and good health (Sir. 1:12-13, 17-18).

Ben Sira then connects fear of the Lord to patience and steadfastness, both with God and with people. Followers of God must expect difficult times and not allow those times to weaken their resolve (Sir. 2:1-18). Additionally, they must honor their parents both as minor children and as adults, caring for elderly parents with love and patience (Sir. 3:1-16). Ben Sira argues that those who fear the Lord will be humble and obedient. The humble stick to their own tasks and concerns and do not exceed their own limits or capabilities by moving beyond the torah into mysticism or apocalypticism, the things that are "too difficult," "hidden," and "beyond you" (Sir. 3:21-23; Prockter, 245–52; Wright, 126). As a result, they are also wise (Sir. 3:17-29). The wise and humble not only care for family members but also for the poor and needy, blessing them with alms and offering justice when it is within their power to do so (Sir. 3:30—4:10).

As a wisdom text, Sirach's fifty-one chapters are full of the subject. But in some specific passages, Ben Sira offers praise of wisdom's advantages to those who seek it. The texts all take a gendered, heterosexual perspective regarding the acquisition and benefits of wisdom, which is feminine both in Hebrew (*ḥokmâ*) and Greek (*sophia*). According to Sir. 4:14-15, "Those who serve her [wisdom] minister to the Holy One; the Lord loves those who love her. Those who obey her will judge the nations, and all who listen to her will live secure." Both of these occupations, priest and judge, belonged to men in second-century Palestine. Wisdom is also the mother who teaches her sons how to prosper (Clifford, 126). Chapter 5 acts as a type of transition, in which Ben Sira offers a variety of pieces of wise advice. One must remain humble even if wealthy, repent speedily in order to avoid divine retribution, and be slow to speak and therefore avoid shame.

Ben Sira warns his readers that calmness of mind is the key to being a good friend and that not everyone who looks and acts like a friend deserves the title; some behave like friends when it is advantageous for them, but later reveal themselves as enemies (Sir. 6:7-13). Righteous, loyal friends are priceless (Sir. 6:14-15), and "those who fear the Lord will find them" (Sir. 6:16). Jeremy Corley argues that Ben Sira may have been familiar with ancient Greek and Egyptian ideas about friendship, especially from the Greek poet Theognis and traditions found in the Egyptian Papyrus Insinger. Corley concludes that "either he [Ben Sira] knows such works (directly or indirectly), or else he is familiar with at least their thought world" (2002, 213).

The lessons that Wisdom wants to teach her sons and the rewards she wants to bestow in Sirach 4 cannot be learned without patience (Sir. 6:19-22), perseverance (Sir. 6:24-31), and wise counsel (Sir. 6:34-36). As a transition to a lengthy list of dos and don'ts (mostly don'ts) in Sir. 7:1-9:9, Ben Sira reminds the reader to

> Reflect on the statutes of the Lord,
>   and meditate at all times on his commandments.
> It is he who will give insight to your mind,
>   and your desire for wisdom will be granted. (Sir. 6:37)

This insight should include the following important reminders: do not perform bad acts (Sir. 7:1-3); do not seek power (Sir. 7:4-7); do not break the commandments or neglect religious duties (Sir. 7:8-14); do not be lazy or arrogant (Sir. 7:15-17); do not mistreat a good friend, a good wife, a good slave, or a good farm animal (Sir. 7:18-23, 26); do not "show yourself too indulgent with [daughters]," but look out for their virginity and marry them off (Sir. 7:23-25); and do not neglect your parents, the priests, the poor, mourners, or the sick (Sir. 7:27-36). Additionally, one should avoid arguments with the rich and powerful as well as the sinful and foolish, respect the old and wise, stay away from lending, and keep one's thoughts to oneself (Sir. 8:1-19). The last rule applies to a man's relationships with women as well; the wise man will not allow a woman, whether a virgin, a prostitute, or another man's wife, to tempt him and therefore take away his strength (Sir. 9:1-7). The mention of different themes and ideas one right after another is similar to the structure of Proverbs 1–9, in which talk of wisdom is interspersed with practical advice about how to live well.

In spite of Ben Sira's warnings about the dangers of interpersonal relationships, friends do matter. To avoid false friends, the sage encourages his reader to

> Let your conversation be with intelligent people,
>   and let all your discussion be about the law of the Most High.
> Let the righteous be your dinner companions,
>   and let your glory be in the fear of the Lord. (Sir. 9:15-16)

Having this fear could make someone a competent leader one day, if it is God's will (Sir. 9:17—10:5).

For Ben Sira, vices include pride and anger, which can be avoided through remembrance of one's mortality. God dislikes and punishes pride (Sir. 10:7, 13-17), because

> the beginning of human pride is to forsake the Lord;
>> the heart has withdrawn from its Maker. (Sir. 10:12)

Additionally, Ben Sira suggests that pride makes little sense.

> How can dust and ashes be proud?
>> Even in life the human body decays.
> A long illness baffles the physician;
>> the king of today will die tomorrow. (Sir. 10:9-10)

Those who are born to die should not exalt themselves, and they should also restrain their anger. Only those who fear God deserve praise, regardless of their social status (Sir. 10:19-25).

Ben Sira returns to the theme of humility in this unit's final section. To be humble is to be honorable; Sir. 10:28 states that you should "honor yourself with humility, / and give yourself the esteem you deserve." This suggests that humility should not be confused with humiliation.

▌▌ THE TEXT IN THE INTERPRETIVE TRADITION

The Jewish canon excludes Sirach, but the praise of God for creation and the importance of wisdom remain fundamental parts of Jewish liturgy and tradition. Psalm 29, which is sung in some Conservative synagogues during the procession of the Torah, echoes Sirach's praise of God through a description of nature. Comparisons can also be made between Sirach and Christian tradition. The argument that wisdom is God's gift (Sir. 1:10) sounds like Paul's insistence on grace as God's gift in the book of Romans. Centuries later, the Catholic "Dogmatic Constitution on Divine Revelation," *Dei Verbum*, calls creation one source for such revelation (§3).

Sirach's admonition against repetitive prayers in 7:14 ("Do not repeat yourself when you pray") reappears in Matt. 6:7—"When you are praying, do not heap up empty phrases as the Gentiles do; for they think that they will be heard because of their many words." The author's response to such ineffective prayers is to give what Christians now know as the Lord's Prayer. Matthew's critique of lengthy prayers does not appear in Luke's citation of the prayer, and Luke condenses the prayer into two verses as opposed to Matthew's five. Both in Ben Sira's day and in the time of the first followers of Jesus, there appeared to be distaste for long-winded petitions, and Matthew's author specifically links such prayers to gentiles in a way Ben Sira does not.

The virtues Ben Sira describes appear as fundamentals in other religious traditions. Just as Sirach links right living to the fear of the Lord, the Qur'an connects proper behavior to obedience to Allah. In the instructions for the hajj, believers also should sacrifice properly designated animals (22:25-34, 36-37) and speak to the "humble whose hearts fill with awe whenever God is mentioned, who endure whatever happens to them with patience, who keep up the prayer, who give to others out of Our provision to them" (22:34-35). Allah's humble servants respond to others with compassion, pray regularly, use money moderately, and only worship God (25:63-68). The Qur'an also links friendship to the final judgment, and those who chose evil companions will regret their poor decision (25:27-29). By extension, unrighteous friends are not true friends at all, as Sirach 9 suggests. In Hindu tradition, deities and saints, represented by statues or photos, may receive food and incense offerings as signs of respect (Knott, 58, 60). Moderation pervades Buddhist teaching. Buddhists call the Noble Eightfold Path the Middle Path because of its insistence on moderation or finding happiness neither "through sensual pleasures" nor "through self-mortification" (Adiele, 162). Such moderate living includes no alcohol consumption, to give one example (Adiele, 163). While each religion applies the virtues in specific ways, Sirach's general ideas of humility, sacrifice, and moderation remain important spiritual practices and disciplines.

■ The Text in Contemporary Discussion

Michael Eric Dyson, a Baptist minister, uses religion and cultural criticism to define proper and improper pride in his volume for the New York Public Library and Oxford University Press series on the seven deadly sins. Using Aristotle and his own Christian tradition, Dyson argues that proper pride enables a person to appreciate fully their gifts and talents without vanity or apology. He concludes, "If thinking too highly of oneself is a sin, then the Aristotelian vice of thinking too lowly of oneself qualifies as well. At a minimum, it signifies a rejection of God's creation, even if the creature is the source of doubt about her worth. Thus, to take pride in one's person, one's achievements, one's moral worth . . . is to affirm and embrace the character of God reflected in one's own soul" (Dyson, 24). Improper pride manifests itself in racism and nationalism, both of which glorify accidental attributes at the expense of others who do not possess a particular skin color or passport stamp (Dyson, 43–57, 85–118). Dyson offers a view of pride that is less limiting that Ben Sira's insistence that pride "was not created for human beings" (Sir. 10:18).

Sirach's discussion of children's responsibilities toward their parents, however, resonates with religious and cultural ideas both in the West and the East. In a discussion of the Fourth Commandment ("Honor your father and your mother"), the *Catechism of the Catholic Church* states that "as much as they can, they [children] must give them [parents] material and moral support in old age and in times of illness, loneliness, or distress" (2218). The proof for such responsibility is Sir. 3:2-6, 12-13, and 16, which the catechism quotes directly. Whether Catholic or not, elder care remains a source of anxiety for adult children and a hugely profitable business in the United States. Businesses such as A Place for Mom offer assisted-living and nursing-home referrals, and children have an array of additional options for parental care, including in-home nursing care and attempting to do the work themselves. Yet such care comes at a great cost, not only in terms of money (often thousands of dollars a month) but also in terms of social stigma, particularly for those children who live with aging and infirm parents. Men who live with their mothers, for example, are not considered honorable. In contemporary musical group TLC's words, they are "scrubs," and even a woman who follows the catechism religiously stated to this author that such a man would never find a spouse. In Asian cultures, where for centuries it was assumed that parents would be supported by their children, the system is breaking down with devastating consequences.

The rate of elderly suicide in South Korea is "nearly four times the rich-country average" ("Poor Spirits"), particularly among the rural elderly, whose children have moved away and have not taken their parents with them. In India, where sons are expected to care for their mothers, the tension between mothers-in-law and daughters-in-law can be unbearable, with the mothers trying to rule the household and, more recently, the daughters fighting back. This pushback has resulted in the creation of charities to help elderly widows whose families have abandoned them. After centuries of daughter-in-law mistreatment, the mothers-in-law are now the mistreated ("Curse of the Mummyji"). While Sirach mentions the duties of children, adult children today are less willing to accept the parent-child hierarchy that the biblical text describes.

Sirach 11:1—16:23: A Balanced Life

■ THE TEXT IN ITS ANCIENT CONTEXT

Ben Sira warns that appearances deceive; therefore, the wise person will listen and think before making a judgment. Once a decision is made, however, the person should honor their obligations and work hard (Sir. 11:1-26). The reason is as follows:

> For it is easy for the Lord on the day of death
> to reward individuals according to their conduct. (Sir. 11:26)

The importance of proper decision making is connected to friendship. Finding true friends proves difficult (Sir. 11:29—12:18). Ben Sira notes that

> A friend is not known in prosperity,
>   nor is an enemy hidden in adversity.
> One's enemies are friendly when one prospers,
>   but in adversity even one's friend disappears. (Sir. 12:8-9)

Such friends should be chosen from one's own social station, lest a rich or powerful friend impoverish and humiliate the less wealthy and cultured acquaintance. Additionally, sinners and the righteous should not socially interact; just like the rich and the poor, they have nothing in common (Sir. 13:1-24).

And yet, anyone who holds their tongue and remains optimistic, rich or poor, can be counted as happy (Sir. 13:25—14:2). One way to be happy is to treat oneself and others well. To do otherwise is foolish, since all will die one day and cannot take their goods with them. Ben Sira argues,

> My child, treat yourself well, according to your means,
>   and present worthy offerings to the Lord. . . .
> Do good to friends before you die,
>   and reach out and give to them as much as you can.
> Do not deprive yourself of a day's enjoyment;
>   do not let your share of desired good pass by you. (Sir. 14:11, 13-14)

Such words remind the reader that the wise life need not be the ascetic life and sounds similar to Qoheleth's arguments a few centuries earlier and the Epicureans about a century before (Furley, 261, 263).

Ben Sira returns to the image of Woman Wisdom in chapters 14 and 15. The man "who camps near her house / and fastens his tent peg to her walls / [and] who pitches his tent near her" (Sir. 14:24-25) will find wisdom—"she will come to meet him like a mother, / and like a young bride she will welcome him" (Sir. 15:2). His rewards will include good reputation and joy (Sir. 15:5-6). But just like a bride, wisdom must be chosen. If people choose to disobey the commandments, they have only themselves to blame (Sir. 15:11-20). This belief in human choice appears famously in Deut. 30:15-20 and Josh. 24:14-15.

Like Proverbs, Sirach argues for the principle of divine retribution: God rewards the righteous and punishes the wicked. Because God sees all people, God will punish wrongdoers, whether few or many, and will bless the righteous; additionally, the ungodly may not live for long (Sir. 16:1-23). The lengthy discussion of retribution in chapter 16 reappears in shorter passages throughout the book.

■ THE TEXT IN THE INTERPRETIVE TRADITION

Wisdom's personification as female not only fits the gendered nouns of biblical language but also serves as a means of placing the biblical faiths within their historical context. Jews and Christians were surrounded by cultures that had goddesses as well as gods. To insist on the supremacy and exclusivity of one male deity was culturally odd. Making wisdom a feminine being in service of the divine, while not creating a consort for God, did at least offer some alternative to the constant glorification of God as "he." Judith Hadley notes that the worship of the Queen of Heaven condemned in Jeremiah 7 and 44 also may have been a response to male religious dominance (Hadley, 30–51). Today, Jews and Christians include female images in their liturgy and worship. Jewish congregations still sing the hymn *Lekha Dodi* to bring in the Sabbath, praised as the "bride, O Queen Sabbath" (*Lekha Dodi*). The hymn dates from the mid-sixteenth century. A synagogue in South Bend, Indiana, has bimah (altar) decorations that quote Prov. 3:18: "She [Wisdom] is a tree of life to those who lay hold of her." Catholic and Orthodox traditions venerate Mary as the Queen of Heaven and the Mother of God in mysteries of the rosary and on feast days. Medieval artwork of Mary's assumption into heaven and her coronation show the glorification of a woman in a male-centered heaven and earth.

■ THE TEXT IN CONTEMPORARY DISCUSSION

Claudia V. Camp notes the connections between friendship and economics in Sirach. Those who make friends with the poor will benefit when their friends' fortunes change (Camp 1991, 16). Such seemingly practical advice echoes the ancient idea of friendship as patronage, or a relationship between unequal parties (Malina, 100–102). What appears to be missing, however, is the concept of friendship as mutuality, when two people with common interests, ideas, or social standing develop and maintain a relationship. While Ben Sira hints at the joy of good friends, the hint almost disappears under the warnings about all the ways friendship can go off the rails. Recent scientific studies of female animals suggest that "affiliative, longlasting, and mutually beneficial relationships between females turn out to be the basic unit of social life" (Angier, 1–2). Faith Adiele says that she needs "reliable friends with whom I feel comfortable" (Adiele, 134), and she also may be saying something universal about "baboons, humans and other group-minded kinds" (Angier, 2). As an ancient man, Ben Sira could not have envisioned the ways in which friendship would evolve among women, and men, too—as the popularity of the word *bromance* to describe close male friendship indicates.

Sirach 16:24—19:30: The Two Ways

▌ THE TEXT IN ITS ANCIENT CONTEXT

Sirach 16–18 praises God's creation of the earth, with emphasis on humankind in general and Israel in particular. All of God's works are orderly and good, similar to the assessment of creation in Genesis 1. Distinctively, the hymn also supports the belief in divine retribution and encourages repentance. Leo Perdue notes that "Ben Sira is the first sage to bring sapiential teaching about creation into the normative traditions of Israelite faith that focused on salvation history" (Perdue, 262, see also 284).

Creation, however, will not be enjoyed by the immoderate. Ben Sira urges people to use care in financial decisions (almsgiving, saving resources, feasting) and personal interactions (sexual conduct, alcohol use; Sir. 18:15—19:3). Sirach's numerous passages about the tongue have a similar message: use sparingly. As the sage says,

> Never repeat a conversation,
>   and you will lose nothing at all. (Sir. 19:7)

People should avoid gossip or telling what they have heard, especially if the tale refers to someone close to them, lest they be guilty of spreading lies (Sir. 19:4-17).

Ben Sira's few comparisons of wisdom and folly both reinforce and disregard common Wisdom literature motifs. Sirach 19 insists that "the whole of wisdom is fear of the Lord" (19:20; cf. 21:11), a virtue that will be discussed later in this essay. Additionally, the wise will keep the commandments. Wisdom, however, cannot automatically function as a synonym for knowledge and intelligence, because both can be used for negative purposes. Fools know evil and/or behave unjustly (Sir. 19:24-28). And while Ben Sira personifies Wisdom as female, he does not do so with folly.

▌ THE TEXT IN THE INTERPRETIVE TRADITION

Themes from Sirach's warnings about wisdom and folly appear in the New Testament and rabbinic literature. Ben Sira's warning that "there is a cleverness that is detestable . . . exact but unjust" (Sir. 19:23, 25) finds a parallel in Paul's claim that "God's foolishness is wiser than human wisdom" (1 Cor. 1:25). Earthly wisdom may not be the same thing as righteousness, a much more important characteristic (Sir. 19:24; 1 Cor. 1:22, 26-27).

▍THE TEXT IN CONTEMPORARY DISCUSSION

Because Sirach does not personify folly, scholarship about Wisdom and Folly often focuses exclusively on Proverbs 1–9 (Estes, 151–69) or solely on Ben Sira's characterization of Woman Wisdom (Angel, 152–58). But other scholars have noted that Ben Sira's exclusion of Woman Folly is not unique; Qumran literature does not include her either, and Woman Wisdom appears infrequently (Goff, 20–38). In an intertextual comparison of Qoheleth, Ben Sira, and the opening chapters of Exodus, J. E. Owens argues that "Pharaoh is folly!" because he does not listen to counsel or act prudently (Owens, 235). Pharaoh's behavior in Exodus 5–10 contrasts with the wise man of Sirach 21 and 37. Whether personified or not, wisdom and foolishness are identifiable traits whose effects can be seen in ancient texts and contemporary life. Calling someone a fool today often conjures up the same images that Ben Sira describes—someone lacking knowledge and behaving badly. While Sirach limits its definition of the wise and foolish to men, today women too can receive either title, depending on the assessment of their actions. Wisdom and folly no longer reside solely in a man's world, as the musician Pink's 2006 song "Stupid Girls" humorously and profanely observes.

Sirach 20:1—22:26: The Importance of Proper Behavior

▍THE TEXT IN ITS ANCIENT CONTEXT

The wise know when to be silent, because poorly timed comments or outright lies produce nothing but trouble (Sir. 20:1-8, 20-26). A list of what the NRSV calls paradoxes (Sir. 20:9-19) interrupts the two-part discussion of speech and how to use words wisely. Most of these paradoxes are financial.

> There is the gift that profits you nothing,
> and the gift to be paid back double. . . .
> Some buy much for little,
> but pay for it seven times over. (Sir. 20:10, 12)

The ideal wise man, however, can avoid these paradoxes through proper living. This man speaks at the right time and avoids sinful acts and people (Sir. 20:27—21:7, 9-10). Returning to the importance of proper financial planning, Ben Sira warns that

> whoever builds his house with other people's money
> is like one who gathers stones for his burial mound. (Sir. 21:8)

Fools, unfortunately, cannot be educated or taught restraint; their mouths move constantly and say nothing useful, and they find themselves in the wrong place at the wrong time (Sir. 21:14-28). Fools include lazy people, who are compared to unclean stones and animal waste (Sir. 22:1-2). Before returning to his recurring theme of friendship, Ben Sira warns about badly behaved children, particularly daughters. Their birth is already "a loss" (Sir. 22:3) that can only be mitigated if they marry. In contrast,

An impudent daughter disgraces father and husband,
and is despised by both. (Sir. 22:5)

To avoid such disgrace, corporal punishment is in order (Sir. 22:6). Regarding equal social relations, in order to keep one's friends, one must be wise; such wisdom includes keeping their secrets and helping them during difficult times (Sir. 22:19-26).

▌The Text in the Interpretive Tradition

While the New Testament rarely personifies wisdom (Matt. 11:19 is one brief exception), Jesus' first followers valued the virtue. Parables condemn fools who do not prepare their souls for the final judgment and praise the wise who do (Matt. 25:1-12; Luke 12:13-21). The author of the book of James states, "If any of you is lacking in wisdom, ask God, who gives to all generously and ungrudgingly, and it will be given you" (1:5). Again, Ben Sira does not personify folly as female, but Revelation contains a good woman/bad woman binary. The "woman clothed with the sun" (Rev. 12:1) who gives birth to the Messiah contrasts with "the great whore who is seated on many waters" and is "clothed in purple and scarlet" (Rev. 17:1, 4).

▌The Text in Contemporary Discussion

In a culture now saturated with speech, written and verbal, Ben Sira's warnings about communication can easily go unheard. With Facebook, Twitter, talk radio, politically slanted news programming, and a proliferation of talk shows, thoughtless speech and constant chatter seem to be the new normal. But modern sages do exist. A college professor runs properfacebooketiquette.com, advising readers that knowing what to say and when enables them "to be . . . more comfortable, pleasant and happy [people]." Numerous sites are devoted to Twitter etiquette, and dummies.com warns that you should not "share information that you might regret making public." And the same noisy culture also offers examples of the benefits of silence, from the ashram visitors in *Eat Pray Love*, to the French Carthusian monks who hardly talk in the documentary *Into Great Silence*, to those who use quiet to protest hateful speech against LGBT students during the annual National Day of Silence. Ben Sira's observation that "honor and dishonor come from speaking" (Sir. 5:13) remains true today, and people still may choose whether to use their communication abilities for good or ill (Sir. 15:15-17).

Sirach 22:27—24:34: God Is Watching

▌The Text in Its Ancient Context

Sirach contains two petitions and a prayer of thanksgiving. Each of the book's three prayers has some connection either to a theme within Sirach particularly or the Hebrew Bible generally. Ben Sira's first prayer asks the following questions:

Who will set a guard over my mouth,
and an effective seal upon my lips,

> so that I may not fall because of them,
>   and my tongue may not destroy me? (Sir. 22:27)

> Who will set whips over my thoughts,
>   and the discipline of wisdom over my mind,
> so as not to spare me in my errors,
>   and not overlook my sins? (Sir. 23:2)

Assuming that his prayer is answered, God will save him from foolish words and unclean thoughts. The importance of controlling the tongue and limiting bad behavior reappears throughout the book. Ben Sira then warns against all manner of oaths,

> for as a servant who is constantly under scrutiny
>   will not lack bruises,
> so also the person who always swears and utters the Name
>   will never be cleansed from sin.
> The one who swears many oaths is full of iniquity,
>   and the scourge will not leave his house. (Sir. 23:10-11)

Additionally, sinful, undisciplined fools may be identified through their bad language (Sir. 23:12-15).

Other sinners think God is blind and forgetful and foolishly engage in fornication and adultery, but those men will be caught and punished (Sir. 23:16-21). So will a woman who produces children through adultery, "[disobeying] the law of the Most High" (Sir. 23:23). She and her children will be punished, and

> Those who survive her will recognize
>   that nothing is better than the fear of the Lord,
> and nothing sweeter than to heed the commandments of the Lord. (Sir. 23:27)

After describing foolish behavior, Ben Sira allows Wisdom to speak for herself in chapter 24. Scholars have noted the parallels between this chapter and Proverbs 8 (Skehan, 365–79; Perdue, 264; Rogers 1996, 148, 150–51; Clifford, 123; Hayward, 33–34). Yet Ben Sira offers innovation as well. Not only is Wisdom God's creation (Sir. 24:3), but she also rules the earth and its inhabitants (Sir. 24:6; Perdue, 268; Rogers 1996, 148–53). She resides, however, in the Jerusalem temple, smells like the fragrances used there, and joins herself to the Mosaic torah (Sir. 24:8-12, 15, 23). Ben Sira's poem emphasizes Second Temple Judaism's focus on Scripture as sacred and the importance of ritual practice (Perdue, 250, 271). The poem may also function as a defense of the temple against Jewish opponents like the Samaritans and the Essenes, and Hellenistic claims about Greece as the home of wisdom and philosophy (Hayward, 38–46). The most-sought-after woman on earth obeyed God's order and chose Israel as her man.

▮ THE TEXT IN THE INTERPRETIVE TRADITION

Sirach 22:27—23:1 asks God for deliverance from an out-of-control mouth. The author of James, while not praying for help, agrees in 3:1-12 with Ben Sira's assessment of the tongue as a tool of destruction, or "a restless evil, full of deadly poison" (James 3:9). Sophie Laws and Walter T. Wilson note that "the concern for such sins [of speech] is also prominent in wisdom literature" (Laws and Wilson, 2055). A number of Christian traditions include praying the Psalter as a spiritual practice, perhaps as a way to control one's speech. Previously limited often to clergy or those in religious orders, the Divine Office or the Liturgy of the Hours has become more common among Catholic and Protestant laity. Phyllis Tickle's *The Divine Hours* series is one example of the daily practice of utilizing the Psalms for their original purpose as prayers.

And in the Qur'an, just as in the Tanak and the Bible, adultery counts as a sin (17:32). Because God sees everything, women and men should "lower their eyes and guard their private parts" (24:30-31; cf. Sir. 23:18-20). Anthropologist Clifford Geertz argues that only through studying humans in particular can anything be said about humanity in general (Geertz, 52). The repetition of the same vices and their categorization as such across time and tradition suggests that certain states of being may be universal and perhaps even innate.

▮ THE TEXT IN CONTEMPORARY DISCUSSION

Most scholarly discourse about Sirach and Wisdom emphasizes the poem in chapter 24. Wisdom, the world traveler, makes her home in Jerusalem, a place greater than Greece; and she is described as superior to Isis, the premier Egyptian goddess (Hayward, 31–46; Rogers 1996, 141–56). Torah and Wisdom are connected, but Wisdom cannot be contained fully by anything, including torah (Rogers 2004, 114–21). Ben Sira may even give Wisdom masculine traits outside of chapter 24 (Camp 2005, 378, 386). Yet Ben Sira, while usually describing Wisdom as a woman, limits her benefits to men. Because of the parallels with Proverbs, another wisdom text written to instruct men, the limitation makes sense. But it need not be the last word. The Hebrew Bible contains examples of wise women, from Deborah the prophetess and judge to the prophetess Huldah and the wise women of Tekoa (2 Sam. 14:1-20) and Abel (2 Sam. 20:16-22). Their stories indicate that even within a patriarchal society, women too could be examples of the blessings of wisdom and help themselves and the men around them. If wisdom is a woman, then she has female and male devotees.

Sirach 25:1—29:28: Managing Social Relationships

▮ THE TEXT IN ITS ANCIENT CONTEXT

Harmonious domestic relations are praiseworthy (Sir. 25:1-11), but they can be difficult across gender lines. For the sage, women embody the worst type of evil and anger, and that warning begins his discussion of marriage and fatherhood, which fits perfectly in his patriarchal cultural context. He distinguishes first between good and bad wives. Good wives are quiet, organized, and chaste. If they happen to be physically attractive, then that is even better (Sir. 26:13-18). As with all good gifts, "the man who fears the Lord" receives her (Sir. 26:3); also, "a wife's charm delights her husband" (Sir. 26:13). But the husband with a bad wife will suffer. Such unattractive, loud, disobedient, and overbearing women torment their husbands, who should choose divorce if their wives refuse to behave (Sir. 25:16-26). And wives who support their husbands financially, drink excessively, or commit adultery are bad too (Sir. 26:7-9). While Sir. 26:10 mentions a "headstrong daughter," the text most likely refers to adulterous wives (Mack and Wright, 1413; Greenfield, 171).

Just as proper behavior comes from fear of the Lord, improper behavior comes from a lack of that fear. While Ben Sira hates to see strong men suffer from poverty (Sir. 26:28), he also claims that business and commercial transactions often lead to sin, because of the desire to acquire more (Sir. 26:29—27:1). He states,

> As a stake is driven firmly into a fissure between stones,
> > so sin is wedged in between selling and buying. (Sir. 27:2)

The passage could have ended there, but it does not; Ben Sira adds one more verse for the reader's information.

> If a person is not steadfast in the fear of the Lord,
> > his house will be quickly overthrown. (Sir. 27:3)

And being overthrown remains a possibility in life; such challenges show a person's worth, particularly when they speak (Sir. 27:4-7).

Ben Sira continues to remind the reader of the inevitability of divine retribution. According to him,

> If you pursue justice, you will attain it
> > and wear it like a glorious robe.
> Birds roost with their own kind,
> > so honesty comes home to those who practice it.
> A lion lies in wait for prey;
> > so does sin for evildoers. (Sir. 27:8-10)

Scholars have noted Sirach's repeated imperatives regarding the tongue, including an additional warning against swearing and combative language in Sir. 27:11-15. Alexander A. Di Lella notes that "the book contains more material on the use and abuse of the tongue/lips/mouth/palate (all organs of speech) than any other book of the Old Testament" (1996, 32). Linking speech to the ancient ideals of honor and shame, Ben Sira borrows ideas not only from other Hebrew wisdom texts but also Egyptian literature (Di Lella 1996, 37, 41).

And once again, poor control of the tongue will cost a person their friends. Failure to remain loyal, particularly through a public, verbal betrayal of a friend's confidence, guarantees the friendship's demise (Sir. 27:16-21). And for men at this time, reputation meant everything; its loss, particularly by a friend's deeds, would be unforgivable (Malina, 50–55).

The angry increase their sins (and the likelihood of negative divine retribution) and cannot expect God's forgiveness, since they refuse to forgive others (Sir. 27:30—28:11). Ben Sira asks,

> If a mere mortal harbors wrath,
> > who will make an atoning sacrifice for his sins? (Sir. 28:5)

The implied answer is no one, and the sage then reminds the reader of two eternal truths, death and the law.

> Remember the end of your life, and set enmity aside;
>> remember corruption and death, and be true to the commandments.
> Remember the commandments, and do not be angry with your neighbor;
>> remember the covenant of the Most High, and overlook faults. (Sir. 28:6-7)

This recollection leads a person away from anger and toward virtue.

Just like anger, negative speech regularly destroys individuals and communities (Sir. 28:13-18). In contrast, the righteous will be spared the destruction caused by the tongue (Sir. 28:19-23). Ben Sira advises the reader to take seriously the power of their lips.

> As you fence in your property with thorns,
>> so make a door and a bolt for your mouth.
> As you lock up your silver and gold,
>> so make balances and scales for your words.
> Take care not to err with your tongue,
>> and fall victim to one lying in wait. (Sir. 28:24-26)

In other words, watch your mouth.

And finally, watch your wallet (Sir. 29:1-28). While one should make loans, Ben Sira warns that some loans simply will not be repaid. The poor, relatives, and friends should be helped "for the commandment's sake" (Sir. 29:9), but guaranteeing another's debts is risky. The sage warns,

> Assist your neighbor to the best of your ability,
>> but be careful not to fall yourself. (Sir. 29:20)

It is better to be poor and have your own home than to rely on the hospitality of others, which could happen if one is too kind and therefore loose with one's finances.

▌ THE TEXT IN THE INTERPRETIVE TRADITION

Before modern feminist and nationalist movements, patriarchal views about wives and daughters dominated religious and social ideology and practice. In Hindu myth and Scripture, women's religious and domestic duties are synonymous; they care for their parents when single and their husbands when married (Knott, 44, 81–82). Although Buddhist texts such as *Anguttara Nikaya* 4.55 (see Bhikkhu 1997a) praise mutuality and harmony in marriage, other texts such as *Digha Nikaya* 31 assume that a woman belongs in the home (see Kelly, Sawyer, and Yareham). The Qur'an gives women the option of divorce if their marriages fail (4:128), but husbands can settle arguments by giving their wives the silent treatment or one slap (4:34). Times, however, have changed traditions. Hindu nationalist movements led women out of the home and into political life, later leading to increased activism on behalf of women's economic and domestic equality (Knott, 82–87). US converts to Buddhism resist and reject the traditions of segregated meditation centers and the androcentric practices and leadership assumed in Buddhist texts (see Gross). Muslim women also are experiencing similar transitions, placing ancient texts and traditions in conversation with modern realities (see Huq). Across geographical and religious space, women now speak for themselves, as opposed to men solely defining their roles and responsibilities.

Divine retribution remained a part of biblically based religions and non-Western traditions long after Ben Sira. The contemporary cliché that you reap what you sow comes from Paul in Gal. 6:7-8, although Stephen Travis describes the passage as an example of people receiving the results of their choices and not "retributive judgment" (Travis, 81). In the eighth-century Asauchiyama myth from Japan, a spirit kills a group of women who break a taboo and allow men to see them weave at night on a body loom (Palmer, 223–32). At the end of the medieval era, Rabbi Joseph Albo argued that divine retribution, especially in the next life, makes up an indispensable part of divine law (Ehrlich, 277, 282–83, 288). And after decades of apocalyptic preaching and natural disasters being interpreted as God's punishment for sin, the Christian Venetians decided to repent. As proof, in 1516 they created a ghetto for the Jews (Crouzet-Pavan, 163–79). In this case, a belief in divine retribution led to a specific social action with long-term ramifications.

Ben Sira's analysis of sins repeats itself in the other major world religions. Sirach 28:2 is in the Lord's Prayer (Matt. 6:12; Luke 11:4). Buddhist teaching warns that the angry may live a short life and "be reborn in a body which is ugly" ("Culakammavibhanga Sutta" 3.204). Lord Krishna states in the *Bhagavad Gita* that "there are three gates leading to this hell [separation from the divine and miserable human existence]—lust, anger, and greed (16.21; see Prabhupada). Thousands of years later, a young London blogger Farhanah Diman quoted the verse as an opening to a cautionary secular tale about perfectionism (Diman). The seriousness of particular bad acts remains a part of religion in general, regardless of the particular faith tradition.

Buddhists, Hindus, and Muslims place the same high value on silence and careful speech as Ben Sira. The Noble Eightfold Path asks Buddhists to engage in right speech, meaning no "lies, slander, verbal abuse, gossip" (Adiele, 162). According to Iti 1.25, "the person who lies, who transgress in this one thing, transcending concern for the world beyond: there's no evil he might not do" (Bhikkhu 2001). The author of a blog for Buddhist laypeople cites the passage in order to encourage truth-telling, stating that "one result of my own efforts to speak truthfully is that I speak less often than I used to" ("The Truth Will Set Us Free"). Like Buddhism, Hinduism also includes a vow of silence, *mauna*, which some observe through limiting speech at certain days and times. The benefits include getting rest and avoiding the consequences of negative and thoughtless words ("Silence Is Golden"). The Qur'an also encourages proper speech: "Believers, do not be like those who insulted Moses—God cleared him of their allegations and he was highly honoured in God's eyes. Believers, be mindful of God, speak in a direct fashion and to good purpose, and he will put your deeds right for you and forgive you your sins" (33:69-71). The faithful also should practice silence, because "God does not like bad words to be made public unless someone has been wronged: He is all hearing and all knowing" (4:148). Ben Sira's insistence on careful speech is an interreligious and cross-cultural commonplace.

■ THE TEXT IN CONTEMPORARY DISCUSSION

Buddhist Robert A. F. Thurman, in his volume on anger for the Seven Deadly Sins series mentioned above, uses the Buddhist wisdom teacher Shantideva's writings to describe anger and how to free oneself from it in an increasingly angry and hostile world. Because anger in Buddhist tradition is an addiction, rehabilitation is necessary to transform anger through mindfully practicing patience. One recognizes that irritating things will happen and that being angry about them will not make the irritations go away. One then learns to make peace with any human sources of those irritations. In a world where anger management classes can be part of a court-ordered punishment, usually because the defendant has committed a crime out of anger, Thurman's work is timely.

Sirach 30:1—42:14: Honor and Shame

■ THE TEXT IN ITS ANCIENT CONTEXT

Only when discussing food, wine, and party etiquette does Ben Sira's advice sound more secular than religious. Food should be enjoyed (Sir. 30:18-25), but one should not eat everything in sight at a dinner party (Sir. 31:12-18). Wine too is a blessing, as long as the drinker does not overindulge (Sir. 31:25-31). Ben Sira claims that moderation leads to good health.

> In everything you do be moderate,
> and no sickness will overtake you. (Sir. 31:22b)

The same rule applies at a party. Hosts should be attentive, but guests should limit their speech and their visit in order to have the best possible time (Sir. 32:1-13). Ben Sira's lengthy discussion of etiquette is interrupted by a warning against loving money (Sir. 31:1-11), which may be loosely connected to the money that one will spend on food and wine.

Similar to Sirach 7–8, Sir. 32:14—34:13 is a list of various wisdom ideals that are not necessarily connected to each other. The wise will trust in God's providence (Sir. 32:14—33:6). They will also know that God has made some days and people more important and special than others (Sir. 33:7-14). They will remain financially independent throughout their lives, treating all of their slaves well but not giving them too much time off (Sir. 33:20-33). And they will place their trust in God and not in their dreams (Sir. 34:1-8). In this discourse, Ben Sira offers himself as a model for others, having learned from older teachers (Sir. 33:16-17).

> Consider that I have not labored for myself alone,
> but for all who seek instruction.
> Hear me, you who are great among the people,
> and you leaders of the congregation, pay heed! (Sir. 33:18-19)

He also concludes that as a world traveler, he knows a great deal and is qualified to teach others (Sir. 34:9-13).

These qualifications, however, are nothing without fear of the Lord. Those who fear God will receive God's strength and protection (Sir. 34:14-20). Fearing God means doing what ought to be done, such as offering regular and generous sacrifices with joy (Sir. 35:1-13). Ben Sira insists,

> Do not appear before the Lord empty-handed,
> for all that you offer is in fulfillment of the commandment. (Sir. 35:6-7)

Imperfect animals or animals poached from the poor, however, will not be acknowledged (Sir. 34:21-27). Sirach's emphasis on the fear of the Lord appears not only in other Hebrew Bible texts but also generally in the ancient Near East (Perdue, 252; Clifford, 127). Ben Sira describes the fear of the Lord in terms of divine retribution from Deuteronomy; those who honor God will be blessed (Di Lella 1997, 188–204). Therefore, fear of God "is the fundamental attitude one needs to live wisely and thus enjoy all the good things of life" (Clifford, 121). Similar to *Jubilees*, Sirach links fear of the Lord to an occupation, specifically his own work as a scribe (Wright, 128–29).

Fear of the Lord is closely linked to divine retribution. God will respond to the mistreated and/ or vulnerable by punishing their oppressors (Sir. 35:14-26). Ben Sira then prays that God will do just that. In the prayer, theology and historical context come to the forefront. Ben Sira asks God to show divine power by protecting Israel against non-Israelites, rewarding faithful Jews and punishing their enemies. Such calls for divine retribution appear in all three divisions of the Hebrew Bible, including Deut. 28:1-14; Zephaniah 2–3; and Psalm 137. Not only will God's actions prove that God is the only deity (Sir. 36:5, 22), but they will also inspire the faithful Israelites.

> As you have used us to show your holiness to them,
> so use them to show your glory to us. (Sir. 36:4)

Additionally, the prayer "against foreign nations" (Sir. 36:3) may be a response to the second-century-BCE stress between Judaism and Hellenism that eventually led to the Maccabean revolt (Perdue, 245).

After his prayer, Ben Sira returns to practical advice. A man should use wisdom in picking the right wife, and the bachelor life is not to be trusted (Sir. 36:23-31). Using proper judgment and picking friends also go hand in hand. Sirach 37 warns that

> Every friend says, "I too am a friend";
> but some friends are friends only in name. (Sir. 37:1)

Such friends will not remain loyal during difficult times (Sir. 37:4). If one has a friend who remains constant even in difficulty, then one ought to show the same faithfulness in kind (Sir. 37:5-6). Regarding the warning in Sirach 37 that not all friends are true friends, Jeremy Corley notes, "This observation is a commonplace of ancient Greek writing" (2002, 72). Ben Sira's insistence that a friendship cannot survive public betrayal places the sage firmly "within a social system based on honor and shame" (Corley 2002, 202). Continuing with the theme of choice, one should not take advice from just anyone, but only from a follower of the torah, oneself, and God (Sir. 37:7-15).

Unlike the foolish, the wise think and speak carefully, bringing honor and blessing on themselves (Sir. 37:16-26). The connection of wisdom to moderate behavior and obedience to God appears in Prov. 1:7; 10:8, Eccles. 5:1-7; and Job 28:28, to name only a few examples. Unlike Proverbs, however, Sirach's Woman Wisdom has no corresponding Woman Folly as a rival. Instead, a fool is simply a man (Sir. 19:26-28; 21:19-20), and his opposite also is a man (Sir. 37:22-26).

Before offering another hymn, Ben Sira gives the reader additional practical advice. People should eat moderately; in case that advice is not followed, however, going to a doctor, who is a blessing from God, is a wise course of action (Sir. 37:27—38:15). Mourning, too, should be done in moderation, lest the mourner put themselves in an early grave (Sir. 38:16-23). Regarding occupations, those who work with their hands keep a community thriving, but they are not wise men. That honor belongs to scribes such as Ben Sira (Sir. 38:24—39:11).

Retribution and praise of the orderliness of creation reappear in Sir. 39:12-35. Not only are "all the works of the Lord . . . very good," but even troubles like famine are God's tools for punishing the wicked (Sir. 39:16, 28-31). The world is good and orderly, but it is also difficult, full of hard labor; such labor, however, will be even harder for sinners (Sir. 40:1-11). While the ungodly will neither live long nor enjoy financial blessings, the righteous will exist for all time because of their good deeds and reputation (Sir. 40:12-17; 41:5-14). Their lives, if blessed, will include a good wife, good friends, and food; they will neither beg nor shrink from their inevitable death (Sir. 40:18—41:4). Ben Sira's ideas about retribution resonate with other examples of Wisdom literature and non-Israelite historiography. The first lengthy passage in Proverbs warns that those who plot crimes

> lie in wait—to kill themselves!
>   and set an ambush—for their own lives!
> Such is the end of all who are greedy for gain;
>   it takes away the life of its possessors. (Prov. 1:18-19)

Proverbs concludes with the honors that competent wives and mothers receive as rewards for their work (Prov. 31:28-31). Job and his friends debate the legitimacy and effectiveness of divine retribution for twenty-eight chapters. Ecclesiastes insists on the absurdities and mysteries of life, but mentions divine retribution as well: "For to the one who pleases him God gives wisdom and knowledge and joy; but to the sinner he gives the work of gathering and heaping, only to give to one who pleases God. This also is vanity and a chasing after wind" (Eccles. 2:26). And belief in divine retribution was not limited to the Jews. Herodotus's *Histories*, written centuries before Sirach, argues in favor of the concept. While sometimes delayed or carried out by mortals, the gods' vengeance on the wicked is just and inevitable (Harrison, 101–22).

Ben Sira also warns that certain actions create shame—bad sexual behavior, lying, committing a crime, breaking a promise, bad manners, and gossiping (Sir. 41:15—42:1). In contrast, one should not be ashamed of the torah, proper judgment, sharing one's resources, earning a living, and keeping the household inferiors (women, children, and slaves) under control (Sir. 42:1-8).

And Sir. 42:9-14 distinctly describes daughters as a great source of potential shame. When unmarried, they may get pregnant or become old maids; when married, they may be sexually unfaithful and/or be infertile. The anxious father must "see that there is no lattice in her room, / no spot that overlooks the approaches to the house" as one way to protect his honor (Sir. 42:11).

Sirach's association of females with male dishonor appears both before and after the sage's time. Classical Athenian women must be domesticated through marriage, kept in the house as much as possible, and be sexually faithful at all times (Davis, 13, 36, 44). Written in the same century as Sirach, 2 Macc. 3:19, describing a state of emergency in which people gather outside to pray, notes that "some of the young women who were kept indoors ran together to the gates, and some to the walls, while others peered out of the windows." Ben Sira's warnings about controlling daughters reappear in *b. Sanh.* 100b, centuries later (Greenfield, 167–73). In opposition to the common identification of Eve with the woman in Sir. 25:24, Teresa Ann Ellis uses textual analysis to argue that the woman is Hesiod's Pandora (Ellis, 723–42), responsible for all the evil in the world (Davis, 25). And all women, in Ben Sira's worldview, have the potential to turn bad. Claudia V. Camp concludes, "It is as if, in Ben Sira's drive to master life amid anxiety and arbitrary reversals of fortune, women— especially as sexual beings—epitomize all that is potentially out of control" (1991, 36).

■ THE TEXT IN THE INTERPRETIVE TRADITION

Sirach 36:1-22, titled "A Prayer for God's People" in the NRSV, contains elements that appear in Jewish liturgy and tradition. While the texts that describe the Maccabean revolt are not part of the Jewish canon, the annual festival of Hanukkah commemorates the Jewish people's successful defense of their traditions and defeat of their Greek enemies. Ben Sira's prayer was answered. Purim, described in the book of Esther, is another yearly celebration of Jewish triumph over genocidal enemies.

Ben Sira's arguments about true versus false friends appear in Hindu, Buddhist, and Islamic traditions. The *Mahabharata* states that "a friend capable of listening to beneficial counsels, and also of doing good, is exceedingly rare"; one should therefore pick friends of good character, those "who continue unchanged (in their attachment) like a red blanket made of wool (which does not easily change its colour)" (Ganguli). Although the Third Noble Truth can be interpreted as a call to "detachment, [to] not needing people" (Adiele, 134), the Buddha insists in *Samyutta Nikaya* 45.2 that "admirable friendship, admirable companionship, admirable camaraderie is actually the whole of the holy life" (Bhikkhu 1997b). In another teaching, *Digha Nikaya* 31.15 and 21, the Buddha warns against "four enemies disguised as friends: the taker, the talker, the flatterer, and the reckless companion"; true friends, however, come in four types—"the helper, the friend who endures in good times and bad, the mentor, and the compassionate friend" (Kelly, Sawyer, and Yareham).

The Talmud, like Sirach, links wisdom to righteousness and restraint. One passage states: "A favourite saying of Raba was: The goal of wisdom is repentance and good deeds, so that a man should not study Torah and Mishnah and then despise his father and mother and teacher and his superior in wisdom and rank, as it says, The fear of the Lord is the beginning of wisdom, a good understanding have all that they do thereafter" (*b. Ber.* 17a; see Simon). Another saying reads: "Hence the Sages said: Silence is better for the wise, and how much more so for fools, as it is said, Even a fool, when he holds his peace, is counted wise" (*b. Pesah.* 99a; see *English Babylonian Talmud*). The previous passages, in abbreviated form, frequently pop in a Google search of "Talmud and wisdom," because of their ubiquity on Jewish websites and blogs. But Christians too have appropriated wisdom for various purposes. Elizabeth A. Johnson's classic *She Who Is: The Mystery of*

God in Feminist Theological Discourse links wisdom, or Sophia, to the Holy Spirit. And the revised Saint Mary's College (Notre Dame, IN) general education curriculum is called the Sophia Program because of the word's meaning and significance in a Catholic, all-women's college context.

■ THE TEXT IN CONTEMPORARY DISCUSSION

Scholars have recently noted Ben Sira's advice about party behavior. Sirach 32:10 reveals "the two-sided sense of shame. Controlled speech yields proper shame in the sense of modesty" (Camp 1991, 19). Moderate behavior brings praise—and perhaps future party invitations. Using Sirach to interpret Last Supper narratives, J. Bohnen concludes that in John, Jesus identifies Judas as the traitor through proper host etiquette; in Matthew, however, Judas identifies himself through poor guest etiquette (Bohnen, 259–83). Neither Camp nor Bohnen, however, mentions Sir. 31:21.

> If you are overstuffed with food,
>> get up to vomit, and you will have relief.

While Ben Sira writes before the development of *vomitoriums* in the Roman Empire (Prose, 25), the idea of bulimic behavior as a response to gluttony already had traction. This ancient practice is not modern bulimia nervosa (see "Bulimia Nervosa Fact Sheet"). But in a culture simultaneously obsessed with eating well and being thin (Miles, 99; Prose, 77–79), Ben Sira's advice raises a red flag. When "over half the females between the ages of eighteen and twenty-five would prefer to be run over by a truck than be fat" (Martin, 1), simply enjoying a meal, even a large one, without guilt or nausea may be the most moderate advice of all (Martin, 281–82, 285).

In a 2011 article, Bradley Gregory argues persuasively for the connection between Ben Sira's description of retribution in chapter 35 and the prayer for Israel in chapter 36. Since justice for the poor and oppressed Jews has been inexplicably delayed, Ben Sira prays that it will now come. Textually, Gregory's thesis holds. But in the modern era, historical events have challenged the theological implications of divine retribution, and no event more than the Holocaust. Job's question—why do the innocent suffer?—has been asked by survivors and all trying to understand what Jews call the horror. For Elie Wiesel, no satisfactory answer exists; as he writes in his classic text *Night*, his experiences in the camps destroy his faith in God. For those who choose to remain theists, divine retribution may seem far too simplistic. The idea that God will punish the guilty may sound like wish fulfillment. In the midst of suffering, God will make things right and orderly, even as the world appears to be out of sorts. And the Bible is full of this idea. Process theology, however, argues that while God is everywhere, human behavior, good and bad, creates consequences for other beings (see processandfaith.org). Human free will led to the abolitionist movement as well as the Holocaust. Choice also undergirds Deuteronomy's description of retribution (Deut. 30:15-20), so whether God can, does, will, or should override human agency remains unclear, both in the Bible and in contemporary theology.

Perhaps the most provocative prayer for modern readers in the book of Sirach is chapter 36. Theological us-versus-them language, common in the Hebrew Bible, deuterocanonical literature, and the New Testament, bore bitter historical fruit. Christian anti-Judaism and forced conversion of American indigenous peoples are two pieces of that fruit. Because the Psalms often lack religiously or culturally inclusive language, contemporary people of faith may have to write their own psalms. The Conservative Jewish "A Prayer for Our Country" (the United States) is one example, and it concludes with what can be described as a prayer from the prophet Micah.

> nation shall not lift up sword against nation,
>   neither shall they learn war any more. (Mic. 4:3)

The Bible can be a resource for modern prayer; as with all resources, selectivity may be necessary.

Ben Sira's discussion of daughters assumes the hegemony of marriage and male control of women's sexuality. But in the United States, single women have come into their own as an identity category, not just as daughters waiting to become wives. In the 2012 election, 68 percent of single women voted for President Obama, becoming the group equivalent of a swing state (see Scott). HBO has jumpstarted popular discourse in the last fifteen years. *Sex and the City* portrays four unapologetically sexual, thirtysomething women. No anxious guardian fathers appear; instead, the women seek protection via each other. *Girls* portrays four sexually active, twentysomething women with physically and/or emotionally absent fathers. But single women's empowerment is about more than sex. Because more women earn college degrees and therefore higher-paying jobs, marriage as an economic necessity is less of a cultural reality. And that leaves women free to develop relationships on their own terms, in "a place where single women can live and thrive as themselves" (Bolick). In Ben Sira's time, men should "marry down" (Camp 1991, 29). So, who did wealthy women marry? Today, the answer can be no one, and that answer marks an incredible and ongoing shift in gender relations.

Sirach 42:15—50:29: Songs of Praise

■ THE TEXT IN ITS ANCIENT CONTEXT

Sirach's fourth hymn expands the praise of creation, including the sun, moon, stars, and the rainbow. Thunderstorms and wintry weather also receive praise, because they are instruments of the all-knowing God. As a transition to his final hymn, Ben Sira writes,

> We could say more but could never say enough;
>   let the final word be: "He is the all." (Sir. 43:27)

The hymn in honor of our ancestors (Sirach 44–50) uses traditions and texts from the Torah and the Prophets. The sage honors great men in Israelite history, including patriarchs, priests, kings, prophets, and leaders, with the priests Aaron and Simon son of Onias receiving the lengthiest sections. The hymn concludes with a prayer for blessings on Israel and a reminder that "if they put them [Ben Sira's teachings] into practice, they will be equal to anything" (Sir. 50:29). Even as Ben Sira resists Hellenistic claims about the source of wisdom in other texts, he uses Hellenistic literary forms (the encomium in Sirach 44–50) to do so (Perdue, 245, 276; Clifford, 125).

■ THE TEXT IN THE INTERPRETIVE TRADITION

Just as Ben Sira honors the ancestors, there are prayers of blessing for the patriarchs and matriarchs during Shabbat services. Sirach 42–43 concludes that to see creation is to see God's glory. No direct textual references to Sirach appear in Paul or *Dei Verbum*, but the focus on creation and praise is a fundamental part of Christian hymnody, from Saint Francis's *Canticle of the Creatures* to Pierpoint's "For the Beauty of the Earth."

◼ THE TEXT IN CONTEMPORARY DISCUSSION

The most recent scholarship focuses on the final hymn in Sirach 44–50. The hymn's composition displays a numerical order designed to show God's orderliness (Corley 2007), and the ancestors receive praise for their piety and not merely their celebrity (Redmond). Feminist analysis, however, notes the gender(ed) trouble the hymn presents. Wisdom literature personifies Wisdom as feminine, reinforcing a heteronormative ideal to male students and readers—in other words, a male God gives a woman to obedient male followers. Ben Sira's description of wisdom will be no exception (Clifford, 126), but the connection he makes between wisdom and the priestly cult is even more male-centered. No woman appears in his final hymn. Claudia V. Camp argues that the hymn creates a "monument to the male textual body" (2002, 79) through its discussion of male ancestors and the male-dominated temple site. Ideally, Ben Sira desires an all-male space, but "Lady" Wisdom makes that impossible (Camp 2002). Camp warns that "this book [Sirach] is one of the most ideologically oppressive pieces of literature imaginable" (2002, 69). Precisely because Ben Sira is a man of his time, not all of his words, even the praise of God and men, fit comfortably in today's time.

Sirach 51:1-30: The Sage's Last Words

◼ THE TEXT IN ITS ANCIENT CONTEXT

Ben Sira concludes his work with a prayer and a poem. In the prayer, he thanks God for deliverance from enemies and "many troubles" (Sir. 51:3). Alexander A. Di Lella notes that the prayer, "a classical Hebrew poem" (1986, 407), borrows heavily from the Psalter and can easily be described as a psalm of thanksgiving (1986, 395–407). In the poem, Ben Sira claims that he has sought wisdom his entire life and therefore is capable of teaching those who need her. His students, if they apply themselves, will gain financial and spiritual rewards.

◼ THE TEXT IN THE INTERPRETIVE TRADITION

While Sir. 51:1-12 is not in the Psalms, both Jews and Christians regularly echo the text's praise of God for salvation from human enemies and troubles; such praises are part of synagogue liturgies and the Divine Office. The Qur'an makes a similar point; the believer should pray when in danger and "when you are safe again, remember God, for He has taught you what you did not know" (2:239).

◼ THE TEXT IN CONTEMPORARY DISCUSSION

Bing searches are not definitive, but they indicate that wisdom images are much less gendered than Sirach's. Wisdom does not appear as a woman whom one should desire; instead, it is a pithy one- or two-line statement on a poster. And desire has disappeared—wisdom does not seem to be sought for its own sake. Ben Sira would be disappointed.

Works Cited

Adiele, Faith. 2004. *Meeting Faith: The Forest Journals of a Black Buddhist Nun*. New York: W. W. Norton.

Angel, Andrew. 2007. "From Wild Men to Wise and Wicked Women: An Investigation into Male Heterosexuality in Second Temple Interpretations of the Ladies Wisdom and Folly." In *A Question of Sex? Gender Difference in the Hebrew Bible and Beyond*, edited by Deborah W. Rooke, 145–61. Sheffield: Sheffield Phoenix.

Angier, Natalie. 2012. "The Spirit of Sisterhood Is in the Air and on Air." *New York Times*. April 24, D1–D2.

Bhikkhu, Thanissaro, trans. 1997a. *Anguttara Nikaya: Samajivina Sutta: Living in Tune. Access to Insight*. www.accesstoinsight.org/tipitaka/an/an04/an04.055.than.html.

———. 1997b. *Samyutta Nikaya: Upaddha Sutta: Half (of the Holy Life). Access to Insight*. http://www.accesstoinsight.org/tipitaka/sn/sn45/sn45.002.than.html.

———, trans. 2001. *Itivuttaka: The Group of Ones (Iti 1-27). Access to Insight*. http://www.accesstoinsight.org/tipitaka/kn/iti/iti.1.001-027.than.html.

Bohnen, J. 2000. "'Watch How You're Eating': Judas and Jesus and Table Manners: An Intertextual Reading of John 13:26, Matthew 26:23 and Sirach 31:12—32:13." *Scriptura* 74:259–83.

Bolick, Kate. 2011. "All the Single Ladies." November. *The Atlantic*. http://www.theatlantic.com/magazine/archive/2011/11/all-the-single-ladies/308654/.

"Bulimia Nervosa Fact Sheet." 2012. *Office on Women's Health, U.S. Department of Health and Human Services*. www.womenshealth.gov/publications/our-publications/fact-sheet/bulimia-nervosa.html.

Camp, Claudia V. 1991. "Understanding a Patriarchy: Women in Second Century Jerusalem through the Eyes of Ben Sira." In *"Women Like This": New Perspectives on Jewish Women in the Greco Roman World*, edited by Amy-Jill Levine, 1–39. Atlanta: Scholars Press.

———. 2002. "Storied Space, or, Ben Sira 'Tells' a Temple." In *"Imagining" Biblical Worlds: Studies in Spatial, Social and Historical Constructs in Honor of James W. Flanagan*, edited by David M. Gunn and Paula M. McNutt, 64–80. Sheffield: Sheffield Academic.

———. 2005. "Becoming Canon: Women, Texts, and Scribes in Proverbs and Sirach." In *Seeking Out the Wisdom of the Ancients: Essays Offered to Honor Michael V. Fox on the Occasion of His Sixty-Fifth Birthday*, edited by Ronald L. Troxel, Kelvin G. Friebel, and Dennis R. Magary, 371–87. Winona Lake, IN: Eisenbrauns.

Catechism of the Catholic Church. 1995. New York: Doubleday.

Clifford, Richard J. 1998. *The Wisdom Literature*. Nashville: Abingdon.

Corley, Jeremy. 2002. *Ben Sira's Teaching on Friendship*. Providence: Brown University Press.

———. 2003. "Wisdom versus Apocalyptic and Science in Sirach 1, 1-10." In *Wisdom and Apocalypticism in the Dead Sea Scrolls and in the Biblical Tradition*, edited by F. García Martínez, 269–85. Leuven: Leuven University Press.

———. 2007. "A Numerical Structure in Sirach 44:1—50:24." *CBQ* 69, no. 1:43–63.

Crouzet-Pavan, Elisabeth. 1992. "Venice between Jerusalem, Byzantium, and Divine Retribution: The Origins of the Ghetto." Translated by Sharon Neeman. In *Jews, Christians, and Muslims in the Mediterranean World after 1492*, edited by Alisa Meyuhas Ginio, 163–79. London: Cass.

"Culakammavibhanga Sutta." 2000. In *366 Readings from Buddhism*, edited by Robert Van de Weyer, reading 3/19. Cleveland: Pilgrim.

"Curse of the Mummyji." 2013–2014. *The Economist*. December 21–January 3, 59–62.

Davis, Stacy. 1996. "Sex and Violence, Savagery and Madness: Women in Athens and Euripides' *Bacchae*." Senior Honors Project, the University of Tulsa.

Kelly, John, Sue Sawyer, and Victoria Yareham, trans. 2005. *Digha Nikaya: Sigalovada Sutta: The Buddha's Advice to Sigalaka*. *Access to Insight*. http://www.accesstoinsight.org/tipitaka/dn/dn.31.0.ksw0.html.

Di Lella, Alexander A. 1986. "Sirach 51:1-12: Poetic Structure and Analysis of Ben Sira's Psalm." *CBQ* 48:395–407.

———. 1992. "Wisdom of Ben-Sira." In *ABD* 6:931–45.

———. 1996. "Use and Abuse of the Tongue: Ben Sira 5,9–6,1." In *"Jedes Ding hat seine Zeit" Studien zur israelitischen und altorientalischen Weisheit Diethelm Michel zum 65. Geburtstag*, edited by Anja A. Diesel, Reinhard G. Lehmann, Eckart Otto, and Andreas Wagner, 33–47. Berlin: de Gruyter.

———. 1997. "Fear of the Lord and Belief and Hope in the Lord amid Trials: Sirach 2:1-18." In *Wisdom, You Are My Sister: Studies in Honor of Ronald E. Murphy, O.Carm., on the Occasion of His Eightieth Birthday*, edited by Michael L. Barré, SS, 188–204. Washington, DC: Catholic Biblical Association of America.

Diman, Farhanah. 2011. "'Hell has 3 gates—Lust, Anger, and Greed'—Bhagavad Gita." Blog post, March 22.

"Dogmatic Constitution on Divine Revelation: *Dei Verbum*." 1965. The Vatican. www.vatican.va/archive/hist_councils/ii_vatican_council/documents/vat- ii_const_19651118_dei-verbum_en.html.

Dyson, Michael Eric. 2006. *Pride*. The Seven Deadly Sins. New York: New York Public Library/Oxford University Press.

Ehrlich, Dror. 2011. "Does R. Joseph Albo Succeed in Proving the Dogmatic Necessity of Divine Retribution?" *JSQ* 18:277–89.

Ellis, Teresa Ann. 2011. "Is Eve the 'Woman' in Sirach 25:24?" *CBQ* 73:723–42.

English Babylonian Talmud. n.d. Tractate Pesachim. www.halakhah.com/pdf/moed/Pesachim.pdf.

Estes, Daniel J. 2010. "What Makes the Strange Woman of Proverbs 1–9 Strange?" In *Ethical and Unethical in the Old Testament: God and Humans in Dialogue*, edited by Katharine J. Dell, 151–69. New York: T&T Clark.

Furley, David John. 1998. "Epicurus." In *The Oxford Companion to Classical Civilization*, edited by Simon Hornblower and Antony Spawforth, 261–63. Oxford: Oxford University Press.

Ganguli, Sri Kisari Mohan, trans. n.d. "Santi Parva." In *The Mahabharata*. www.hinduism.co.za/friendsh.htm.

Geertz, Clifford. 1973. *The Interpretation of Cultures*. New York: Basic.

Goff, Matthew. 2010. "Looking for Sapiential Dualism at Qumran." In *Dualism in Qumran*, edited by Géza G. Xeravits, 20–38. New York: T&T Clark.

Greenfield, Jonas C. 1990. "Ben Sira 42.9-10 and Its Talmudic Paraphrase." In *A Tribute to Geza Vermes: Essays on Jewish and Christian Literature and History*, edited by Philip R. Davies and Richard T. White, 167–73. Sheffield: JSOT Press.

Gregory, Bradley C. 2011. "The Relationship between the Poor in Judea and Israel under Foreign Rule: Sirach 35:14-26 among Second Temple Prayers and Hymns." *Journal for the Study of Judaism* 42:311–27.

Gross, Rita M. July 2005. "How American Women Are Changing Buddhism." *Shambhala Sun*. www.shambhalasun.com/index.php?option=com_content&task=view&id=1319.

Hadley, Judith M. 2001. "The Queen of Heaven—Who Is She?" In *A Feminist Companion to Prophets and Daniel*, edited by Athalya Brenner, 30–53. 2nd series. London: Sheffield.

Harrison, Thomas. 1997. "Herodotus and the Certainty of Divine Retribution." In *What Is a God? Studies in the Nature of Greek Divinity*, edited by Alan B. Lloyd, 101–22. London: Duckworth.

Hayward, C. T. R. 1999. "Sirach and Wisdom's Dwelling Place." In *Where Shall Wisdom Be Found? Wisdom in the Bible, the Church and the Contemporary World*, edited by Stephen C. Barton, 31–46. London: T&T Clark.

Huq, Corine. 2012. *Rights and Wrongs: The Story of Women in Islam.* Women Make Movies. DVD.

Koperski, Veronica. 2003. "Sirach and Wisdom: A Plea for Canonicity." In *The Biblical Canons*, edited by J.-M. Auwers and H. J. De Jonge, 255–64. Leuven: Leuven University Press.

Knott, Kim. 2000. *Hinduism: A Very Short Introduction.* Oxford: Oxford University Press.

Laws, Sophie, and Walter T. Wilson. 2006. "James." In *The HarperCollins Study Bible*, edited by Harold W. Attridge, 2052–58. New York: HarperCollins.

Mack, Burton, and Benjamin G. Wright III. 2006. "Sirach." In *The HarperCollins Study Bible*, edited by Harold W. Attridge, 1378–451. New York: HarperCollins.

Malina, Bruce J. 1993. *The New Testament World: Insights from Cultural Anthropology.* Rev. ed. Louisville: Westminster John Knox.

Martin, Courtney E. 2007. *Perfect Girls, Starving Daughters: The Frightening New Normalcy of Hating Your Body.* New York: Free Press.

Miles, Sara. 2007. *Take This Bread: A Radical Conversion.* New York: Ballantine.

Owens, J. Edward. 2005. "'Come, Let Us Be Wise': Qoheleth and Ben Sira on True Wisdom, with an Ear to Pharaoh's Folly." In *Intertextual Studies in Ben Sira and Tobit: Essays in Honor of Alexander A. Di Lella, O.F.M.*, edited by Jeremy Corley and Vincent Skemp, 227–40. Washington, DC: Catholic Biblical Association of America.

Palmer, Edwina. 2007. "A Striking Tale of Weaving Taboos and Divine Retribution: A Reinterpretation of the Asauchiyama Myth in *Harima Fudoki*." *Asian Folklore Studies* 66:223–32.

Perdue, Leo G. 1994. *Wisdom and Creation: The Theology of Wisdom Literature.* Nashville: Abingdon.

"Poor Spirits." 2013. *The Economist.* December 7. http://www.economist.com/news/asia/21591211-loneliness-and-poverty-are-killers-poor-spirits.

Prabhupada, A. C. Bhaktivedanta Swami. 1972. *Bhagavad Gita.* www.asitis.com/16/.

Prockter, Lewis J. 1990. "Torah as a Fence against Apocalyptic Speculation: Ben Sira 3:17-24." In *Proceedings of the Tenth World Congress of Jewish Studies, Jerusalem, August 16–24, 1989: Division A: The Bible and Its World*, 245–52. Jerusalem: World Union of Jewish Studies.

Prose, Francine. 2003. *Gluttony.* The Seven Deadly Sins. New York: New York Public Library/Oxford University Press.

Qur'an, The. 2010. Trans. M. A. S. Abdel Haleem. Oxford: Oxford University Press.

Redmond, Eric D. 2001. "Prelude to the Praise of the Ancestors, Sirach 44:1-15. *HUCA* 72:1–14.

Rogers, Jessie F. 1996. "Wisdom and Creation in Sirach 24." *JNSL* 22, no. 2:141–56.

———. 2004. "'It Overflows Like the Euphrates with Understanding': Another Look at the Relationship between Law and Wisdom in Sirach." In *Of Scribes and Sages: Early Jewish Interpretation and Transmission of Scripture* Vol. 1, *Ancient Versions and Traditions*, edited by Craig A. Evans, 114–21. London: T&T Clark.

Scott, Beth. 2012. "Women and the 2012 Election." AAUW website. www.aauw.org/2012/11/7/women-and-the-2012-election/.

"Silence Is Golden." 1997. *Hinduism Today.* June. www.hinduismtoday.com/modules/smartsection/item.php?itemid=4881.

Simon, Maurice, trans. n.d. *Babylonian Talmud, Tractate Berakoth*. Edited by Isidore Epstein. *Come and Hear*. www.comeandhear.com/berakoth/berakoth_17.html.

Skehan, Patrick W. 1979. "Structures in Poems on Wisdom: Proverbs 8 and Sirach 24." *CBQ* 41:365–79.

Thurman, Robert A. F. 2005. *Anger*. The Seven Deadly Sins. New York: New York Public Library/Oxford University Press.

Travis, Stephen H. 2008. *Christ and the Judgement of God: The Limits of Divine Retribution in New Testament Thought*. Peabody, MA: Hendrickson.

"The Truth Will Set Us Free." 2013. *The Buddha's Advice to Laypeople* weblog entry. http://buddhasadvice.wordpress.com/2013/01/18/the-truth-will-set-us-free/.

Twitter for Dummies cheat sheet. www.dummies.com/how-to/content/twitter-for-dummies-cheat-sheet.html.

Wiesel, Elie. 1988. *The Night Trilogy: Night, Dawn, The Accident*. New York: Hill and Wang.

Wright, Benjamin G. 2009. "Jubilees, Sirach, and Sapiential Tradition." In *Enoch and the Mosaic Torah: The Evidence of Jubilees*, edited by Gabriele Boccaccini and Giovanni Ibba, 116–30. Grand Rapids: Eerdmans.

BARUCH

Karina Martin Hogan

Introduction

The book of Baruch is falsely attributed to Jeremiah's scribe and companion, Baruch son of Neriah. For most of its history, it was believed to be by Baruch, so it followed the book of Jeremiah in most manuscripts of the Septuagint and followed Lamentations (believed to be by Jeremiah) in the Vulgate. In reality, it was compiled centuries after the lifetimes of the historical Jeremiah and Baruch, probably in the mid-second century BCE. It has been called "a mosaic of older biblical passages" (Moore, 259), but it combines biblical traditions in innovative ways. Baruch is recognized as canonical by the Roman Catholic and Orthodox churches; it is classified as among the Apocrypha by Protestants.

The book consists of three originally separate compositions, with an introduction probably added by the compiler. The first half of the book consists of the prose introduction (1:1-14) and a lengthy prose prayer (1:15—3:8) that begins with a confession of sins and ends with a petition for deliverance, parallel to the prayer in Daniel 9. The second half of the book is made up of two poems, probably by different authors. The first (3:9—4:4), which imitates the language of Deuteronomy, Proverbs, and Job, is about the elusiveness of wisdom and ends by identifying wisdom with the Torah of Moses. The final part of the book (4:5—5:9) is a poem that alludes extensively to Isaiah 40–66 and part of it parallels *Ps. Sol.* 11, a noncanonical psalm. The various parts of the book are unified by the theme and setting of the Babylonian exile.

The prose portions of the book were almost certainly composed in Hebrew and were probably translated into Greek by the same person who revised the Septuagint translation of Jeremiah (Tov, 111–33). It is somewhat less certain, but still likely, that the two poems were written in Hebrew; if so, they were probably translated into Greek by a more fluent translator (Burke, 23–26). The other extant ancient versions (Latin, Syriac, Coptic, Ethiopic, Arabic, and Armenian) are derived from

1027

the Septuagint (Greek) version. The most likely historical setting for the composition of Baruch, despite its fictive setting in the Babylonian exile, is in the land of Israel, shortly after the Maccabean revolt (167–160 BCE), although scholarly opinions on the date of composition range from c. 300 BCE to after 70 CE (Steck, 285–303).

Baruch 1:1-14: Narrative Introduction

▌ THE TEXT IN ITS ANCIENT CONTEXT

The text confers authority on its putative author, Baruch, by giving him a lengthy genealogy (1:1; cf. Jer. 32:12). The book is presented both as a speech to the exiles in Babylon, including the exiled king Jeconiah (Jehoiachin), and as a letter to the people left behind in Jerusalem. In the book of Jeremiah, conversely, Baruch and Jeremiah are among those left behind in Jerusalem (though they were later taken to Egypt, according to Jer. 43:1-7), and Jeremiah writes a letter to the exiles in Babylon (Jer. 29:1-23). Baruch's location in Babylon "by the river Sud" (1:4; otherwise unknown) and "in the fifth year" (1:2) recalls the opening of the book of Ezekiel (Ezek. 1:1-2). The fifth year of the exile was 593 BCE, whereas Jerusalem was not actually destroyed until 586. Other anachronisms include the return of the temple vessels to Jerusalem by Baruch, along with a donation from the exiles (1:8-10); according to Ezra 1, this took place at the end of the exile (in 538). Further, Belshazzar is incorrectly identified as the son of Nebuchadnezzar (1:11), probably based on Daniel 5.

▌ THE TEXT IN THE INTERPRETIVE TRADITION

Baruch is the protagonist of two later Jewish apocalypses, *2 Baruch* and *3 Baruch*, and of a collection of legends about him and Jeremiah called *4 Baruch* or *Paraleipomena Jeremiou*. In none of these Pseudepigrapha, all preserved by Christians, does Baruch go to Babylon. *Second Baruch* ends with a letter (*2 Bar.* 78–87) that Baruch sent to the exiles in both Babylon and Assyria (the "nine and a half tribes" exiled from the northern kingdom). The tradition that Baruch went to Babylon himself is known from several rabbinic sources, though it is unlikely that they are directly dependent on the book of Baruch. In the Babylonian Talmud, Baruch is considered both a prophet and a priest (*b. Meg.* 14b) and the teacher of Ezra in Babylon (*b. Meg.* 16b). His presence in the exile is also attested in *y. Sanh.* 1:2, *Song Rab.* 5:5, and *S. 'Olam Rab.* 26.

▌ THE TEXT IN CONTEMPORARY DISCUSSION

The placement of Baruch in the Babylonian exile is significant because the exile of the Jewish people due to their sins is the theme that unifies the diverse parts of the book of Baruch. In contemporary theological discourse, exile can function as a symbol for alienation from the dominant culture. The message of the book is about maintaining Jewish identity and resisting assimilation, which has contemporary resonance. On the other hand, in 1:11, the exiles ask the people in Jerusalem to pray for King Nebuchadnezzar and his son, which suggests adaptation to a life under foreign domination (see also Ezra 6:10; Jer. 29:7). There is a tension throughout the book, as in contemporary Jewish experience, between exile as an existential necessity and a yearning for both literal and metaphorical return to the land of Israel.

Baruch 1:15—3:8: Penitential Prayer

■ THE TEXT IN ITS ANCIENT CONTEXT

This long prose prayer combines a communal confession of sins (1:15—2:10), in which God is referred to in the third person, with a petition for mercy and deliverance (2:11—3:8) addressed directly to God. This combination of confession and petition is typical of prayers contained in texts of Second Temple Judaism (Werline), but the closest parallel is the prayer in Daniel 9, which many scholars think is an older prayer incorporated by the author of Daniel 7–12. The confession of sins consists mainly of verbatim parallels with Daniel 9:7-14, but the mention of cannibalism of children in 2:3 is not found in Daniel's prayer. It is threatened in the Torah (2:2; cf. Lev. 26:29; Deut. 28:53) and alluded to elsewhere (2 Kgs. 6:28-29; Jer. 19:9; Lam. 2:20; 4:10; Ezek. 5:10) as the ultimate expression of social disintegration in times of war.

The prayer of petition parallels Dan. 9:15-19, but with many more expansions than are present in the confession of sins. Most of these expansions contain language drawn from Jeremiah; for example, the command to serve the king of Babylon and its accompanying threats (2:21-25) is a pastiche of phrases that are often repeated in Jeremiah. Even the long quotation attributed to Moses (2:29-35) consists mainly of phrases from Jeremiah. The idea that the dead cannot praise God (2:17)—as an argument for saving those who are near death (2:18)—is found in the Psalms (6:5; 30:9; 88:10-12; 115:17) and in Isa. 38:18. The concluding paragraph (3:1-8) summarizes the message of the whole prayer: Israel is in exile because of their sins and those of their ancestors, but they have repented and are imploring God's mercy, aware that their punishment is deserved.

■ THE TEXT IN THE INTERPRETIVE TRADITION

Although this prayer is part of an instructional letter from Baruch to the people living in the ruins of Jerusalem, Baruch also prays on behalf of the people in exile. Baruch does not play the part of intercessor for his people in Jeremiah, but he takes on that prophetic role here, and even more explicitly in the later books attributed to Baruch. In *2 Baruch*, Baruch prays for mercy on his people (48:1-24) and also advises his people, both in Jerusalem and in exile, to repent and pray for mercy (77:2-10; 84:10-11). In *4 Baruch*, both Baruch and Jeremiah are such powerful intercessors that God has to ask them to leave Jerusalem so that he can deliver it to the Chaldeans: their prayers are "like a firm pillar in the middle of it, and like an unbreachable wall encircling it" (1:2). Thus the penitential prayer in Baruch established his reputation as an intercessor and an advocate of repentance.

■ THE TEXT IN CONTEMPORARY DISCUSSION

The structure of the penitential prayer in Baruch can be found in penitential prayers in both Judaism and Christianity to this day: a communal acknowledgment of sins is followed by a recollection of God's forgiveness of his people's sins in the past and a petition for God's mercy in the present.

Such prayers can be useful reminders of the social dimension of sin: morality is not purely a matter between an individual and God, but involves taking responsibility for creating a more just society. The prayer in Baruch serves as a warning against self-righteousness and complacency, since Israel's history of continual disobedience (1:19) can be read as paradigmatic of human history. Human societies rarely live up to their ideals, and penitential prayer can be a vehicle for acknowledging collective failures and renewing a commitment to social justice.

Baruch 3:9—4:4: Wisdom Poem

▌ THE TEXT IN ITS ANCIENT CONTEXT

For this poem in praise of wisdom, the poet draws on several models in biblical Wisdom literature, but especially Job 28, a poem about the elusiveness of wisdom. The poem is connected to the previous prose portions of Baruch in that it addresses Israel in exile (3:10-11), in Deuteronomic language (3:9), explaining their predicament as the result of having "forsaken the fountain of wisdom" (3:12). The bulk of the poem (3:15-28) is devoted to the thesis that no one from other nations, no matter how rich or powerful, has been able to acquire wisdom. In 3:29-30, the poet alludes to Deut. 30:12-13 in order to introduce the association between wisdom and the divine gift of the Torah to Israel. Unlike Job 28, which declares the inaccessibility of wisdom to everyone but God, the wisdom poem of Baruch emphasizes the election of Israel, to whom alone God gave "the whole way of knowledge" (3:36; cf. 3:27). The next verse, "Afterward she appeared on earth and lived with humankind" (3:37), has been viewed by some scholars as a Christian interpolation, but it is consistent with the actions of personified Wisdom in Prov. 8:1-4, 31; Sir. 24:10-12; and Wis. 9:10-11.

The identification of wisdom with "the book of the commandments of God, the law that endures forever" (4:1), recalls Sir. 24:23, but whereas the Wisdom of Ben Sira maintains a more universal understanding of Torah-wisdom (Sir. 24:25-34), Baruch celebrates Israel's exclusive claim to the Torah as its advantage over other nations (Bar. 4:3-4). This difference in outlook may be attributed to the persecution of the Judeans under Antiochus IV Epiphanes, which happened just after Ben Sira wrote his book and probably shortly before the composition of Baruch (see introduction). Since that persecution aimed "to compel the Jews to forsake the laws of their ancestors," according to 2 Macc. 6:1, the Baruch poet may be appealing to ethnic pride in order to motivate his people to return to Torah observance.

▌ THE TEXT IN THE INTERPRETIVE TRADITION

This section of Baruch was very important in early Christianity for establishing a relationship between Wisdom and Christ. Baruch's reinterpretation (in 3:29-30) of the famous verses of Deuteronomy about the Torah being "very near to you" (Deut. 30:12-14) as applying to Wisdom made it possible for Paul (in Rom. 10:6-8) to read those same verses as referring to Christ. Therefore, a number of church fathers (including Irenaeus, Clement, Origen, Tertullian, Ambrose, and Hilary) understood 3:37 (3:38 in the Greek), about Wisdom appearing on earth, by analogy with John 1:14, to refer to the incarnation of the preexistent Christ (Tull, 420). While the subject of Bar. 3:38 in the

Greek is apparently Wisdom (feminine), in the Vulgate the subject has become masculine, apparently referring to Christ (or God).

◼THE TEXT IN CONTEMPORARY DISCUSSION

It is refreshing from a feminist perspective that this passage presents Wisdom as feminine but not eroticized (in contrast to Proverbs 1–9 and Sirach 51, for example), and that a feminine divine hypostasis could be identified with Christ in early Christianity. Nevertheless, the main message of the poem, that only Israel out of all the nations possesses wisdom, sounds disturbingly ethnocentric to contemporary ears. Clearly, it is possible to identify the Torah as the main source of Israel's wisdom (as Deut. 4:6-8 does) without claiming that Israel has exclusive access to wisdom, since Ben Sira manages to depict the Torah as a source of wisdom for the whole world (24:23-34). The contrast between Ben Sira and Baruch on this point (see "The Text in Its Ancient Context" above) is instructive, because it shows that extreme positions sometimes reflect the need to maintain group identity in the face of persecution or pressure to assimilate.

Baruch 4:5—5:9: Consolation Poem

◼THE TEXT IN ITS ANCIENT CONTEXT

The final section of Baruch is a poem of consolation and encouragement, which falls into three parts: An introductory address to Israel (4:5-9a), a discourse spoken by personified Zion (4:9b-29), and a prophetic speech addressed to Jerusalem, again personified (4:30–5:9). The introductory verses serve a similar function to the introductory verses of the wisdom poem (3:9-13): they explain why Israel is in exile, using language drawn from Deuteronomy (in this case, Deuteronomy 32, the Song of Moses). Whereas Deut. 32:16-18, which Bar. 4:7-8 is based on, applies maternal imagery to God, here the maternal role is assigned primarily to Jerusalem/Zion and God is presented as an involved (4:8) but angry father (4:6, 9).

The character of Zion that emerges in her speech (4:9b-29) is complex, combining features of the debased daughter Zion of Lamentations with the comforted and comforting mother Zion of Isaiah 49–55. At first, she addresses the "neighbors of Zion," asking them to "remember the capture of [her] sons and daughters, which the Everlasting brought upon them" (4:10, 14). The speaker's tone is a bit reproachful toward God, like that of Zion in Lamentations 2, but at the same time she acknowledges that it is actually her children (i.e., the inhabitants of Jerusalem) who are to blame for her bereavement (4:12-13). In the second half of her speech (4:17-29), she exhorts her children to "take courage" and "cry to God" (4:21) for deliverance from their enemies. The "neighbors of Zion" are invoked again, this time as proleptic witnesses to the salvation of God's people (4:24). Zion concludes by urging her children to "return with tenfold zeal to seek him" (4:28). Although the language of the poem evokes the Babylonian exile, the message makes sense in the aftermath of the persecution of the inhabitants of Jerusalem by Antiochus IV Epiphanes. In particular, the concern with the perception of Israel by her "neighbors" reflects the perspective of the Jews as a subject people dispersed throughout the Hellenistic empire.

The book of Baruch closes with a prophetic speech of consolation to Jerusalem/Zion (4:30—5:9). Answering Zion's lament about the ruthlessness of her enemies (4:15-16), the prophet (speaking for God) announces the downfall of her unnamed oppressors (5:31-35). This vengeful form of consolation is familiar from the prophets of the Babylonian exile and postexilic periods (e.g., Isaiah 47, Obadiah), but it was equally acceptable in the Maccabean period (e.g., Jth. 16:1-12, 17). The image of Jerusalem seeing her "children . . . gathered from east and west" (4:37; 5:5) is also drawn from exilic prophecy (see Isa. 43:5-6; 60:4), but it is the first of several verbal parallels with *Ps. Sol.* 11 (here, 11:2). The motifs in Bar. 5:1-4 of Jerusalem putting on God's glory as a garment and being given a new name have a parallel in *Ps. Sol.* 11:7-8 (cf. Isa. 52:1-2; 62:2, 12), and the sequence of images in Bar. 5:7-9 resembles *Ps. Sol.* 11:4-6. Scholars disagree about the direction of influence, but there is clearly some relationship between the two poems. At the same time, most of the imagery in both poems is found in Isaiah 40–66.

THE TEXT IN THE INTERPRETIVE TRADITION

Although it is not clear that it was directly influenced by Baruch, the apocalypse *2 Baruch*, written in response to the destruction of Jerusalem by the Romans in 70 ce, makes use of the personification of Zion as a mother (3:1-3; 10:16) and includes many of the same motifs as this poem. For example, *2 Bar.* 67–68 contrasts the present boasting of "Babylon" (= Rome) over Zion's defeat with the future glorification of Zion and downfall of their enemies (see *2 Bar.* 82). There is a brief mention of the ingathering of the exiles (78:7). Nevertheless, there is a new emphasis in *2 Baruch* on Zion as an eternal, heavenly city (4:1; 32:4; cf. Gal. 4:26; Heb. 11:16), a belief also found in two other apocalypses written around the same time, *4 Ezra* and Revelation. Those apocalypses are also in continuity with the consolation poem in Baruch in that they personify Jerusalem (as a mother in *4 Ezra* 10:7; as a bride in Rev. 21:2, 9), and they offer consolation for the destruction of the earthly Jerusalem by promising that the heavenly Zion will be revealed on earth in the end times (*4 Ezra* 7:26; 10:54; Rev. 21:3, 10).

THE TEXT IN CONTEMPORARY DISCUSSION

Like the wisdom poem, the consolation poem has appealing features for feminist readers: the feminine personification of Zion is not sexually degraded or abused, in contrast to some prophetic instances of it (e.g., Ezekiel 16, 23). She takes on some of God's parental role (4:8) and addresses her daughters as well as sons (4:10, 14, 16), frequently using the gender-neutral term for children, *tekna* (Tull, 421). Zion is a strong female figure, combining pathos with exhortation, who commands God's attention on behalf of her "children." God's response acknowledges that she embodies the collective moral agency of her people, when he urges her to "put on the robe of the righteousness that comes from God" (5:2). On the other hand, the consolation poem shares some of the wisdom poem's triumphalism, seeming to relish the suffering of Israel's enemies (4:25, 31-35). At least it allows a middle ground for the "neighbors of Zion," who serve as witnesses to Israel's suffering and redemption (4:14, 24). The poem's underlying Deuteronomic assumption (which it shares with the rest of the book of Baruch) that Israel is to blame for its historical suffering must be rejected in a post-Holocaust world.

Works Cited

Burke, David G. 1982. *The Poetry of Baruch: A Reconstruction and Analysis of the Original Hebrew Text of Baruch 3:9—5:9*. SBLSCS 10. Chico, CA: Scholars Press.

Moore, Carey A. 1977. *Daniel, Esther and Jeremiah: The Additions, A New Translation with Introduction and Commentary*. AB 44. Garden City, NY: Doubleday.

Saldarini, Anthony J. 2001. "The Book of Baruch: Introduction, Commentary and Reflections." In *The New Interpreter's Bible*. Vol. 6, *Introduction to Prophetic Literature, Isaiah, Jeremiah, Baruch, Letter of Jeremiah, Lamentations, Ezekiel*, edited by Leander Keck, 929–82. Nashville: Abingdon.

Steck, Odil Hannes. 1993. *Das apocryphe Baruchbuch: Studien zu Rezeption und Konzentration "kanonischer" Überlieferung*. Göttingen: Vandenhoeck & Ruprecht.

Tov, Emmanuel. 1976. *The Septuagint Translation of Jeremiah and Baruch: A Discussion of an Early Revision of the LXX of Jeremiah 29–52 and Bar 1:1—3:8*. HSM 8. Missoula, MT: Scholars Press.

Tull, Patricia K. 2012. "Baruch." In *Women's Bible Commentary, Third Edition*, edited by Carol A. Newsom, Sharon H. Ringe, and Jacqueline E. Lapsley, 418–22. Louisville: Westminster John Knox.

Werline, Rodney A. 1998. *Penitential Prayer in Second Temple Judaism: The Development of a Religious Institution*. SBLEJL 13. Atlanta: Scholars Press.

THE LETTER OF JEREMIAH

Patricia K. Tull

Introduction

The Letter (or Epistle) of Jeremiah (Ep. Jer.) is only extant today in Greek and its dependent translations, but several verbal confusions can best be explained as misreadings of an original Hebrew manuscript (Moore, 323). In the earliest Greek Bibles, it is found as an independent work following the book of Lamentations, but in the Vulgate and subsequent English translations, it was appended as the sixth chapter of Baruch, which, like Lamentations, was secondarily associated with Jeremiah. In the NRSV, where it appears immediately following Baruch and is numbered as chapter 6, it is nevertheless presented as a separate book.

The Letter of Jeremiah repeatedly asserts the absurdity of idol worship. Parodies of idols and idol worship are also found in the deuterocanonical Bel and the Dragon (Daniel 14), Wisd. of Sol. 13:10-19; 15:7-13, and the pseudepigraphic book of *Jubilees* (e.g., 12:2-5; 20:8-9). The parody in the Letter of Jeremiah is clearly influenced by the polemics against idolatry in Jer. 10:1-16 and elsewhere (see Deut. 4:27-28; Pss. 115:3-8; 135:15-18; Isa. 40:18-20; 41:7; 44:9-20; 46:1-7; Hab. 2:18-19). In fact, as will be seen below, it echoes many of their arguments. Its form as a letter written by Jeremiah to Judeans being taken captive to Babylon follows the tradition of Jeremiah 29, in which the prophet writes to those in exile. It is one of several Diaspora writings associated with Jeremiah and Baruch, epistolary writings intended to strengthen Jewish identity and unity (Doering, 44). These include Baruch and several other noncanonical writings now classified as Pseudepigrapha, Targum, and Qumran texts.

The letter consists of an introduction and ten further sections deriding the worth of Babylonian gods, which the writer equates with the human-made idols that represent them. Each of these arguments concludes with a variation on the exhortation in verse 16, "From this it is evident that they are not gods; so do not fear them" (see also vv. 23, 29, 65, and 69) or the rhetorical question in verse

40, "Why then must anyone think that they are gods, or call them gods?" (see also vv. 44, 52, 56, 64). The arguments do not build toward a case. Rather, topics are strung together in a manner described as "catchword and catchthought associations" (Roth, 20). For instance, discussion of priests' dishonest behavior in verse 28 precedes discussion of the ungenerous behavior of their wives (v. 28), which leads to description of their pollution by contact with women during unclean periods (v. 29), which leads to the objection against women serving in the temple at all (v. 30), which leads to the listing of behaviors of the male priests to which the writer objects (vv. 31-33) (Dancy, 199).

■ THE TEXT IN ITS ANCIENT CONTEXT

6:1-7: Introductory Words

The Vulgate and NJB number differently from the NRSV. In the Vulgate and NJB, the first verse of the Letter of Jeremiah is Bar. 5:9b, and the letter proper begins on verse 1. Internally, there are other variations in the numbering. This commentary follows the NRSV verses. Unlike the letter Jeremiah sent to captives in Jeremiah 29 instructing them to settle peaceably in Babylon, this one is delivered before the exiles leave Jerusalem, warning them of challenges they will meet in their new land. Whereas Jer. 29:10 warned of an exile of seventy years, Ep. Jer. 6:3 warns of an exile of up to seven generations. Commentators disagree over whether this is meant to reach to the writer's own timeframe, like the "seventy weeks" of years in Dan 9:2, or whether it simply indicates a very long time.

Throughout the book, beginning in verses 4 and 5, the word *theoi* ("gods") is used forty times to describe the figures of "silver and gold and wood." This usage, rather than the more common "idols," emphasizes the writer's equation of the Babylonian gods with the human-made objects representing them. Only in the final verse (see discussion below) does the word *eidola* ("idols") appear at all ("idols" in vv. 44 and 63 of the NRSV is a gloss for "them" or "these things").

6:8-73: Ten Arguments against Idolatry

Idols are helpless to act for themselves (6:8-16). The first of ten sections arguing the uselessness of Babylonian gods emphasizes their incapacity. Active verbs are all associated with craftspeople who produce them and worshipers who clothe and ornament them. Actions associated with the gods are negative: they cannot speak or defend themselves against rust, corrosion, violence, or theft. Even the weapons held by gods heighten their ineffectuality, since they are helpless to use these symbols of power. In verses 10-11, their attendants are accused of stealing from them.

The reductionistic argument being leveled against these gods—that they possess no reality beyond their manufactured representations—first appears here. It is the same argument that was made in Isaiah 40–46: the irrationality of worshiping objects that were made by humans (Isa. 40:19-20; 41:7; 44:11-17; cf. Jer. 10:9), objects that cannot move or act (Isa. 40:20; 44:18).

This section concludes, as subsequent ones will, with a refrain that repeats the point that what Babylonians are worshiping are not gods. Therefore, as the first and last several refrains exhort, they are not to be feared (see Jer. 10:5).

They suffer indignities without defending themselves (6:17-23). This second group of verses intensifies the argument. The gods are not even sound vessels, but are as useless as broken dishes (cf. Jer. 22:28; Hosea 8:8), their eyes filled with dust stirred up by their worshipers. They are locked up like criminals for their own protection. No matter how many lamps are lit for them, they cannot see (cf. Deut. 4:27-28; Pss. 115:3-8; 135:15-18), nor notice the soot blackening their faces. They are subject to destruction by insects and desecration by bats, cats, and birds. A refrain much like that in verse 16 concludes this section.

They are helpless when carried about (6:24-29). The arguments repeat themselves in variation here. Once again, the need to be cleaned is mentioned. They have no sensibilities—this time, no feeling. Though expensive, they cannot even breathe (cf. Ps. 135:17; Jer. 10:14; 51:17; Hab. 2:19). The need to carry them about is repeated (see v. 4 and Isa. 46:2; Jer. 10:5). Like the Philistine god Dagon in 1 Sam. 5:3-4, they fall to the ground and must wait for humans to right them. As in verse 18, where they were compared to prisoners, here also the writer's associations are damning: gifts brought to them resemble those given to the dead. Once again, the corruption of priests—and now their wives as well—is showcased, and the gods are even desecrated by unclean women.

They are unable to help humans in need (6:30-40a). What the gods cannot do dominates this section. All activity is attributed to women who feed them and priests who howl and shout at them. The gods cannot make or depose a king, bestow wealth or punish neglect, rescue from death or even from foes, or do anything a just God would do, such as to heal the disabled or help the helpless.

Prostitutes serve them (6:40b-44). Ironically, these gods, though mute themselves, are invoked to awaken tongues, which of course they cannot do. A ritual practice of cult prostitution inimical to Israelite practice and very similar to one related by Herodotus (*History* 1.199) is described.

They are made and managed by humans (6:45-52). Once again the gods' human-made construction and need for human protection are described.

They cannot help humans (6:53-56). An array of actions Scripture attributes to Israel's God are denied the Babylonian gods: They cannot appoint kings, bring rain, judge, or deliver—in fact, in case of fire, they cannot even save themselves.

Other human-made and natural objects are more valuable (6:57-65). In what may be the letter's most original statement, the claim is made not only that it is better to be a human king, but also that it is better to be a useful household utensil, a protective door, or a wooden pillar: even though standing still, they actually serve some purpose. Furthermore, elements of the heavens—sun, moon, stars, lightning, wind, clouds, and fire—likewise serve useful purposes, but these gods lack power to do anything of use.

They cannot do anything that others can (6:66-69).

It is better not to have idols (6:70-73). "Scarecrow in a cucumber field" here echoes Jer. 10:5. Commentators note significant distinctions in the final verse, the only verse to actually mention *eidola*, "idols," and the only verse to suggest that readers themselves might possess them.

■ The Text in the Interpretive Tradition

Most of what is known of later interpretation of this letter is the near silence with which it seems to have been received. Second Maccabees 2:2, written close to the end of the second century BCE, may allude to it: "The prophet [Jeremiah], after giving them the law, instructed those who were being deported not to forget the commandments of the Lord, or to be led astray in their thoughts on seeing the gold and silver statues and their adornment." A Greek fragment of verses 43-44 was found in Qumran cave 7. But the letter was neither included in the Jewish Bible nor widely discussed among early Christian writers. It may have influenced the second-century-CE *Apologia* of Aristides of Athens, which defends Christianity to Hadrian. Though brief passages were quoted by Tertullian and Cyprian, only the fourth-century Sicilian rhetorician Firmicus Maternus quoted it extensively (Moore, 324).

■ The Text in Contemporary Discussion

The Letter of Jeremiah raises the question, important in many religions, of the distinction between an idol and an icon. Iconic worship in the ancient world, both within and around Judea, was more subtle than this description of fetishism suggests. Babylonian inscriptions concerning the rites of idol initiation show goldsmith and carpenter ritually denying having made the statue, and the deity being invited to descend from heaven to indwell it (Jacobsen, 15–32). Such rituals indicate clearly the worshipers' awareness of the distinction between gold and god. To their worshipers, idols were understood to be wood and stone, and yet more as well. Parallels to the Jewish Torah scroll as more than mere parchment and ink, or the Christian Eucharist as more than mere bread and wine, might well be drawn. Every faith is vulnerable to ridicule, since its rituals reflect belief in unseen truths underlying perceived realities. The contemporary challenge in a multifaith world is to employ empathetic curiosity to seek to understand, rather than to denigrate, the faith of others. The depiction of another's belief as a straw figure, easily ridiculed and thus rendered nonthreatening, has in recent history gone hand in hand with arrogant theology, colonial domination, and interreligious violence.

Yet Ancient Judea did not stand in the same relationship to Babylon and subsequent foreign rulers in which contemporary Westerners stand to interfaith neighbors. Their overwhelming religious challenge was not so much getting along in a multicultural world as community survival in a world of other possibilities, possibilities made all the more attractive because of the participation of the powerful. Vivian L. Johnson has sympathetically described arguments similar to those in the Letter of Jeremiah that were made by leaders of her own Pentecostal faith, arguments used, as these were, to "thwart the attraction of other religions by presenting them as idolatrous" (Johnson, 311)—and, by extension, to counter the threat of assimilation to American popular culture by naming as idolatry secular attractions such as clothing, music, dancing, and consumerism.

Though we cannot, it would be instructive to know more about the debate through which the Letter of Jeremiah was excluded from Jewish Scripture, and the precise causes of its lack of attention among earliest Christians living in a Greco-Roman environment in which cultic figures remained important. Access to such a debate might more subtly have nuanced later similar views, such as those of the Reformers against Catholicism and those of Western missionaries encountering indigenous religions.

Works Cited

Dancy, John Christopher. 1972. *The Shorter Books of the Apocrypha: Tobit, Judith, Rest of Esther, Baruch, Letter of Jeremiah, Additions to Daniel and Prayer of Manasseh*. Cambridge: Cambridge University Press.

Doering, Lutz. 2005. "Jeremiah and the 'Diaspora Letters' in Ancient Judaism: Epistolary Communication with the Golah as Medium for Dealing with the Present." In *Reading the Present in the Qumran Library*, edited by Kristin de Troyer and Armin Lange, 43–72. Atlanta: Society of Biblical Literature.

Jacobsen, Thorkild. 1987. "The Graven Image." In *Ancient Israelite Religion: Essays in Honor of Frank Moore Cross*, edited by Patrick D. Miller, Paul D. Hanson, and S. Dean McBride, 15–32. Philadelphia: Fortress Press.

Johnson, Vivian L. 2010. "Letter of Jeremiah." In *The Africana Bible: Reading Israel's Scriptures from Africa and the African Diaspora*, edited by Hugh R. Page Jr., 310–11 Minneapolis: Fortress Press.

Moore, Carey A. 1977. *Daniel, Esther and Jeremiah: The Additions*. AB 44. Garden City, NY: Doubleday.

Roth, Wolfgang. 1975. "'For Life, He Appeals to Death' (Wis 13:18): A Study of Old Testament Idol Parodies." *CBQ* 37:21–47.

Tull, Patricia K. 2012. "The Letter of Jeremiah." In *The Women's Bible Commentary*, edited by Carol A. Newsom, Sharon H. Ringe, and Jacqueline Lapsley, 423–25. 3rd ed. Louisville: Westminster John Knox.

INTRODUCTION TO ALL ADDITIONS TO DANIEL

Lawrence M. Wills

The Greek and Latin versions of Daniel (and many versions dependent on them) contained three additions that were not included in the Jewish and Protestant canons of the Bible: the Prayer of Azariah and the Song of the Three Young Men (or Three Jews), Susanna, and Bel and the Dragon. The origins of these writings may be as old as the earliest parts of the Daniel tradition, composed anytime after the sixth century BCE. They may, like the other chapters of Daniel, have been composed in Hebrew or Aramaic, although no such ancient versions have been found. The latest they could have been written is the period of the incorporation of these chapters into the version of the book of Daniel in the Greek Bible, about the first century BCE. The additions were evidently written independently of each other, and some of them may not have originally been associated with the Daniel tradition (the names of Daniel and the three friends having been inserted at key points).

Prayer of Azariah and the Song of the Three Young Men

Lawrence M. Wills

Introduction

In Daniel 3, Daniel's three companions are thrown into the fiery furnace and emerge unharmed. The Prayer of Azariah and the Song of the Three Young Men (or Three Jews), inserted between Dan. 3:23 and 3:24, are the prayers uttered by these three. Similar prayers can be found in narrative works of the Bible (1 Samuel 2; 2 Samuel 22; Jonah 2; Judith 16; Additions to Esther 14:11-19). The theme of the Prayer of Azariah and the Song of the Three Young Men is communal confession, in a pattern of threat/prayer/redemption/praise of God, a well-established pattern in Israel from the exodus paradigm to the Deuteronomistic theology of the Historical Books. Yet it is important to take note of the differing themes of these texts before they were brought together (Nickelsburg, 26–27); the Prayer of Azariah and the Song of the Three Young Men differ in tone from each other, and in some ways from the tone of Daniel 1–6 as well.

The situation of Daniel and his friends is often likened to martyrdom, but what we find here is actually a subtly different paradigm. The young men do not die, although they are willing to testify bravely to their loyalty to God. This is rather a wisdom paradigm: the wise and righteous Jew who remains steadfastly loyal to God will be protected and saved; indeed, will somehow escape death (Wisdom of Solomon 2–5). It is important that originally Daniel was not a prophet but a wise courtier, and an intensification of the ideal sage found in the book of Proverbs.

◼ THE TEXT IN ITS ANCIENT CONTEXT

The form of the Prayer of Azariah (vv. 3-22) owes much to the psalms of national lament (e.g., Psalms 44, 74, 79, 80). In contrast to these, however, Azariah also *blesses* God for *punishing* Israel for its sins (vv. 3–5), reflecting the penitential theology found also in Daniel 9, Ezra 9, Nehemiah 9, and Baruch 1–3. This confession-of-sin motif, though plausible for the postexilic setting of the narrative, is different from the tone of the stories in Daniel 1–6; the latter depict "blameless" protagonists who have no apparent reason to confess their sins.

The contrite hearts of the three Jews will be accepted as a substitute for sacrifice (Horst and Newman, 190). The idea that sacrifices, though important, are yet not as important as devotion to God's moral and legal demands has a strong background among the prophets (Jer. 7:22-23; Hosea 6:6; Mic. 6:8), but here there is a new focus on the "contrite heart and humble spirit." This substitute sacrifice could be understood as the giving of the lives of the three men themselves, a sacrificial gift that they are prepared to offer. This would then link this scene with the martyrdom theme in Daniel 7–12 (Collins, 203). Alternatively, the sacrifice could also be the prayer itself (Horst and Newman, 186). At Qumran, some texts seem to emphasize the function of prayers and songs as a direct worship of God and a local substitute for temple liturgy.

The tone of the Song of the Three Young Men (vv. 28-68) is so different from the Prayer of Azariah that it is often suggested that they circulated separately before being inserted into Daniel 3. While Azariah is a penitential lament, the Song is a two-part communal confession of praise. In addition, in early Christian usage, the two parts of the Song were often divided between verses 34 and 35. The first part of the Song (vv. 29-34) is a royal enthronement hymn: God rules the heavens as a king would rule on earth (cf. Psalms 96–97). This part of the Song addresses God directly, but the second part (vv. 35–68) exhorts all creation to bless God (cf. Psalm 148). There is a downward progression from the highest cosmological powers and angels (vv. 36-41), elements of the atmosphere (vv. 42-51), to the earth and its creatures (vv. 52-59), and those who worship God (vv. 60–68). The second line of each verse was likely an antiphonal communal response (cf. Psalm 136). This section of the Song perhaps betrays an origin somewhat different from the wisdom and visions of the Daniel tradition; the command for the priests to bless God (v. 62) may suggest a temple setting for the song's composition. The servants (v. 63) are not likely prophets, as is sometimes the case, but priests or other orders of temple functionaries.

◼ THE TEXT IN THE INTERPRETIVE TRADITION

The quality of the poetry here was once disparaged. In a classic reference work, C. W. Bennett (630) characterizes Azariah and the Three Jews as "mostly secondary and imitative," but this anthological aspect actually renders these texts *more* a model for the common person, more a *liturgical* experience. In the words of more-recent scholars, "The words that echo the Torah should arise spontaneously on the lips of the faithful . . .; the prayers of the young men should be emulated by those in similar danger. . . . Such long, scripturalised prayers were depicted as performative exemplars" (Horst and Newman, 180).

These texts were reflected in the Jewish texts of 1 Macc. 2:59-60 and 3 Macc. 6:6-7, and in the Christian text of Justin Martyr's *Apology* 1.46. Verses 16-17, which relate the burning of the three as a substitute for sacrifice—their anticipated martyrdom—are perhaps the most important verses theologically. They simultaneously reflect new thinking on the significance of sacrifice apart from the temple, serving later as a metaphor for asceticism as sacrifice, and establishing a paradigm for martyrdom.

Among Christians, Azariah and the Song of the Three Young Men were separated and included as numbers 7 and 8 of the fifteen odes appended to the book of Psalms in some early Christian versions of the Bible. Both parts are sung in the Matins service in the Eastern Orthodox Church. The feast day of the three was the same as Daniel's, December 17, and they are commemorated on the two Sundays before the Nativity of Christ and on Holy Saturday. Like many texts of the Apocrypha, they also remained in use in the Lutheran Church; there the three, with Daniel, are commemorated as prophets on December 17. The fiery furnace is also featured in the Orthodox liturgy on Holy Saturday. Although Azariah and his companions are technically not martyrs because they do not die, and they anticipate that God will deliver them, the scene of the three Jews in the fiery furnace was also taken up in Christian art. Along with Jonah and the whale, it symbolized martyrdom and the hope of salvation. (See esp. the Catacomb of Priscilla in Rome, third–fourth centuries CE.)

■ THE TEXT IN CONTEMPORARY DISCUSSION

In contemporary ascetical theology, ancient prayers such as this are often adopted as a way of connecting to a deep tradition of prayer that transcends time and modernity. The fact that the three Jews appear in Christian theology as a type of martyrdom and resurrection only adds to the power of this book for a traditional reading in spirituality and ascetical theology. In addition, in response to present-day discussions of ethnic, racial, and sexual identity, many scholars now note the way some ancient texts shaped ancient Jewish notions of identity, especially prayers, hymns, and narratives such as those found in the Daniel tradition. These texts often respond to ethnic conflict and competition, and reveal a strong sense of how Jews are to understand their values and their place among other peoples.

Works Cited

Bennett, C. W. 1913. "Prayer of Azariah and Song of the Three Children." In *Apocrypha and Pseudepigrapha of the Old Testament in English*, edited by R. H. Charles, 1:625–37. Oxford: Clarendon.

Collins, John J. 1993. *Daniel*. Hermeneia. Minneapolis: Fortress Press.

Horst, Pieter van der, and Judith H. Newman. 2008. *Early Jewish Prayers in Greek*. Berlin and New York: de Gruyter.

Nickelsburg, George W. E. 2005. *Jewish Literature between the Bible and the Mishnah*. 2nd ed. Minneapolis: Fortress Press.

Wills, Lawrence M. 2006. "Ascetic Theology Before Asceticism? Jewish Narratives and the Decentering of the Self." *JAAR* 74, no. 4:902–25.

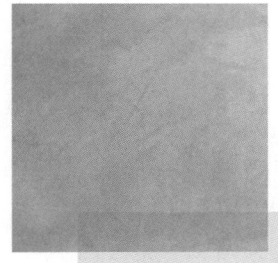

SUSANNA

Nyasha Junior

Introduction

The book of Susanna involves a married Jewish woman whom two elders attempt to coerce into a sexual encounter. When she refuses, they accuse her of adultery. Due to Daniel's intervention at Susanna's trial, she is acquitted, and the elders are punished. The book of Susanna is included in the Protestant Apocrypha and is considered to be deuterocanonical (literally "second canon") in the Roman Catholic and Orthodox canons. It is one of the three additions to the Greek book of Daniel, including the Prayer of Azariah and the Song of the Three Young Men (or Three Jews), and Bel and the Dragon. The book of Susanna is not found in the Jewish Tanakh. The text of Susanna was probably written during the late Persian or Hellenistic periods. Two ancient Greek texts, the Old Greek and Theodotion, provide the earliest texts of Susanna. For reasons now lost to us, the early Christian church chose to use Theodotion's version of Daniel (with additions) instead of the Old Greek version.

Verses 1-27: Susanna and the Two Elders

■ THE TEXT IN ITS ANCIENT CONTEXT

The book of Susanna is set in Babylon and appears to take place during the time of the Babylonian exile (c. sixth century BCE). The key character, Susanna, is a beautiful, God-fearing woman who is married to a wealthy Jewish man named Joakim. The primary conflict in the story takes place when two elders attempt to coerce Susanna into a sexual encounter with them. On a hot day, Susanna goes to bathe in her garden. She instructs her two maids to bring her toiletries, and while they are gone, two elders who serve as judges proposition her. Unless she has sex with them, they will claim that a young man was with her. She cries out with a loud voice and refuses, a significant detail in light of Deut. 22:24, which requires the death penalty for both the man and the woman if an engaged woman who is assaulted does not cry out when assault takes place in the city. The presupposition is that if an assault takes place in the city, someone will hear the woman's cries and come to her aid. A woman who does not cry out during an attack in the city is presumed guilty. When the people in Susanna's house hear the noise and come into the garden, instead of responding by assisting Susanna, they listen to the story offered by the elders (vv. 24-27). Susanna's cry is the last time she speaks in the text. She does not speak in her defense here or during the trial.

◼ THE TEXT IN THE INTERPRETIVE TRADITION

The story of Susanna, especially the bath scene, has a rich history in Christian visual interpretation. Representations of the Susanna story appear in catacombs and sarcophagi in early Christian art (Smith). Also, Susanna was a popular figure for painters and sculptors, especially during the Renaissance era (Clanton). The text does not specify that Susanna was in the bath or undressed when the elders confront her, but many artists depict Susanna as nude or in various states of undress, including sixteenth-century Italian painter Tintoretto, seventeenth-century Dutch painter Rembrandt van Rijn, and seventeenth-century Italian painter Artemisia Gentileschi. Yet, unlike the nudes of other artists who tend to eroticize the interaction of Susanna and the elders, Gentileschi's *Susanna and the Elders* (1610) depicts a fearful Susanna in a defensive posture with the two menacing elders leaning over the wall. Mary Garrard argues that this unusual portrayal of Susanna may be related to Gentileschi's personal experience of sexual trauma by her painting teacher Agostino Tassi. Gentileschi's sympathetic treatment need not be self-referential, but it is a distinctive artistic choice in contrast to the work of her contemporaries.

◼ THE TEXT IN CONTEMPORARY DISCUSSION

Given the attempted sexual encounter in Susanna, scholars often link the book of Susanna with other so-called seduction scenes such as the story of Joseph and Potiphar's wife in which Joseph refuses the demands of Potiphar's wife (Genesis 39) and the David and Bathsheba encounter (2 Samuel 11). Since the elders' proposition involves coercion, Jennifer Glancy questions the linking of Susanna with seduction texts and examines reasons why many interpreters do not regard the incident between Susanna and the elders as an attempted rape.

The book of Susanna does not label the interaction between Susanna and the elders. Nor does the story fit neatly within our contemporary legal definitions or social frameworks. Nevertheless, it illustrates how those in power attempt to take advantage of their position and authority, and such abuses of power remain problematic in our contemporary period. For example, in 1991, at the confirmation hearings for then Supreme Court nominee Clarence Thomas, Thomas's former employee Anita Hill testified at the hearings and alleged that Thomas had engaged in repeated, unwanted sexual advances toward her. Although Thomas denied Hill's claims, the televised hearings focused attention on the issue of sexual harassment in the United States. More recently, numerous abuse-of-power allegations have been made against various high-profile organizations such as the Boy Scouts of America, Pennsylvania State University, and the Roman Catholic Church.

Verses 28-64: Susanna's Trial

▌THE TEXT IN ITS ANCIENT CONTEXT

The day after the incident with the elders, Susanna is accused of adultery, tried, and condemned to death (see Lev. 20:10; Deut. 22:22). After being moved by the holy spirit of God, a young man, Daniel, comes forward to demand an examination of the charges against Susanna. According to Deuteronomy, at least two witnesses are necessary to convict someone of a crime (Deut. 19:15-16). Thus the charges against Susanna are allowed to stand because of the testimony of the two elders. Yet Daniel's skilled interrogation of the two men results in Susanna's acquittal. He notes that the Israelites have condemned Susanna without proper investigation (v. 48), which is required according to Mosaic law (Deut. 19:18). By separating the elders and questioning them individually, Daniel proves that the elders have lied and falsely accused Susanna. Since someone found to be a false witness will be punished in the same way as the person who was initially charged (Deut. 19:16-19), the elders are put to death "in accordance with the law of Moses" (v. 62).

▌THE TEXT IN THE INTERPRETIVE TRADITION

In his commentary on Daniel, Hippolytus of Rome, a third-century-CE Christian theologian and martyr, offers an allegorical reading of Susanna. He interprets Susanna as the church and her husband Joakim as Christ. The two elders are identified as two groups that oppose the church, those "of the circumcision" and the gentiles. Hippolytus contrasts Jezebel's adornment with makeup (2 Kgs. 9:30) with Susanna's adornment with faith, chastity, and sanctity. He admonishes believers to imitate Susanna.

▌THE TEXT IN CONTEMPORARY DISCUSSION

Susanna is typically regarded as a positive female character by many ancient and contemporary interpreters. Susanna is active and is named and speaks on her own behalf in courageously refusing the two elders. Yet, while Susanna's family praises her (in Theodotion's account), she is not present at the end of the story. She does not save herself. Instead, in the dramatic trial scene and interrogation, Daniel plays the role of hero (Glancy). Recent scholarship has noted important and overlooked issues of gender and ethnicity in interpreting Susanna. For example, Amy-Jill Levine notes the importance of women's bodies in biblical texts and explains how Susanna serves as a metaphor for the Diasporic community. Susanna is vulnerable and shamed but remains faithful. Similarly, the Diasporic community has experienced shame and faces threats to its continued existence.

The book of Susanna illustrates how those in positions of authority can take advantage of the vulnerable. Furthermore, it points out the ways in which even those with privilege can be vulnerable.

Although Susanna is married and enjoys status and wealth, the accusation of two men of advanced age and status places her at risk of being put to death without due process. Unlike Ruth, she is not a poor widow without the protection of the paterfamilias. Yet her husband and family do not speak on her behalf. Her community does not demand that the authorities properly examine the situation or ascertain the facts. The elders, who have taken advantage of other women (v. 57), serve in positions of power.

Among nonprofessional readers, Susanna is probably not as well known as other female biblical characters such as Miriam, Deborah, or Mary since Susanna is one of apocryphal/deuterocanonical books. Although this text is not well known, it offers relevant and poignant questions regarding the complexities of power and privilege.

Works Cited

Clanton, Dan W., Jr. 2006. *The Good, The Bold, and The Beautiful: The Story of Susanna and Its Renaissance Interpretations*. New York: T&T Clark.

Garrard, Mary. 1989. "Susanna." In *Artemisia Gentileschi: The Image of the Female Hero in Italian Baroque Art*, 183–209. Princeton: Princeton University Press.

Glancy, Jennifer A. 1993. "The Accused: Susanna and Her Readers." *JSOT* 58:103–16.

Hippolytus. 1994. "On Daniel." In *ANF* 5:177–94.

Levine, Amy-Jill. 1995. "'Hemmed In on Every Side': Jews and Women in the Book of Susanna." In *Reading from This Place*. Vol. 1, *Social Location and Biblical Interpretation in the United States*, edited by Fernando E. Segovia and Mary Ann Tolbert, 175–90. Minneapolis: Fortress Press.

Smith, Kathryn A. 1993. "Inventing Marital Chastity: The Iconography of Susanna and the Elders in Early Christian Art." *Oxford Art Journal* 16:3–24.

BEL AND THE DRAGON

Lawrence M. Wills

Introduction

Bel and the Dragon appears as chapter 14 of the book of Daniel in the Greek versions of the Bible (and those dependent on them). From the period of the exile on, Jews came to live in foreign lands ruled by powerful kings. Administration was carried out in the king's courts, where wise and well-trained scribes could rise to become powerful courtiers. The new genre of "court legend" appeared, which in narrative form treated the trials and triumphs of wise figures who counseled the king. These texts were exciting and highly entertaining, but they also encapsulated the affirmations of identity of the people who told them. Non-Jewish examples can be found in Herodotus and later Persian literature, and Daniel 1–6 is also composed of court legends, as are Esther and, at a local court level, Susanna. (The story of Joseph in Genesis 37–50 appears to be a forerunner.) Like Daniel 1–6, Bel and the Dragon begins in the reign of a famous monarch, but although Dan. 5:31 and 6:28 introduce a historically inaccurate king, "Darius the Mede," Bel gets the personages right: Astyages was the last king of the Medes, and Cyrus the Persian defeated him in 550 BCE.

■ THE TEXT IN ITS ANCIENT CONTEXT

The theme of this particular court legend is the parody of idols, which after the exile became a literary commonplace in a number of different genres in the Hebrew Bible (Pss. 115:4-8; 135:15-18; Isa. 40:18-20; 44:9-20; 46:6-7; Jer. 10:3-9; Hab. 2:18-19; Wisd. of Sol. 13:1—15:17; Epistle of Jeremiah; Nickelsburg, 24–27, 210–11). The message of the idol parodies is that the representations of the foreign gods are simply wood and stone, or in the case of the so-called dragon, a very mortal beast; the foreign peoples are foolish to revere them. The God of Israel, the truly "living God," rules history and is to be contrasted both with the "idols made with hands" and with the large snake. The "pitch, fat, and hair," for instance, that Daniel feeds the snake are not magical or miraculous but are everyday substances that evidently swell up in the serpent's stomach. The Jewish idol-parody narratives, both inside and outside the Bible, present a naturalistic exposé of the folly of idolatry. It was the nature of such polemic to affirm Jewish identity by exaggerating the distinction between the beliefs and practices of Jews and others, although the beliefs and practices were actually much more similar than these satires would indicate. After all, Jews provided food sacrifices for their God as well, and the other peoples held a much more sophisticated view of the representation of the gods than these texts suggest.

There are three parts to this story: the exposure of the priests of Bel (vv. 1-22), the destruction of the dragon (vv. 23-27), and the punishment and vindication of Daniel (vv. 28-42). The first two parts are "trickster tales," in which the brash courtier Daniel demonstrates the inferiority of idol worship. They are told humorously and ironically, even whimsically (Wills 1990, 129–38; Wills 1995, 40–67). In verse 18, for example, the king exclaims about Bel, "In you there is no deceit!" even though we have just learned that the priests of Bel and their families deceive everyone (except Daniel), and in the process eat all of the food laid out for the god. Some of the irony probes deeper theological issues as well. In verse 6, Cyrus applies the lofty theological idea of a "living God" to a god whose impressive deed is to gorge on vast quantities of food; lofty theological ideas are misunderstood on a mundane level (see v. 24). This sort of irony—lofty theological ideas misunderstood on a mundane level—is also explored in the Gospel of John (3:3-4; 4:10-15). The foreign kings are also often humorously depicted as being slow-witted. This conveys the message that the great empires were able to function solely through the efforts of the wise courtiers. Still, it is important to note that Cyrus the Persian, a positive king in Israelite history (Isa. 41:2-3; 45:1), is here sympathetic to Daniel's position; it is the Babylonian courtiers, a competing ethnic group, who persecute Daniel and unrealistically force the king's hand (cf. Dan. 3:8-12; 6:6-9).

The religious and political symbols in this story are crucial to its meaning. Bel is the East Semitic form of the Northwest Semitic Baal, meaning "lord," found also in the Hebrew Bible. In Babylonian mythology, Bel, "lord," almost always refers to Marduk, and is satirized, for instance, in Isa. 46:1. Bel and the Dragon is thus a narrative satire of Bel. Herodotus (*History* 1.183) includes information about a statue of Bel in Babylon eighteen feet tall made of gold, to which Nebuchadnezzar offered provisions of food and drink. Babylonians also believed that Bel/Marduk destroyed a mythological serpent or chaos monster (see Job 7:12; Ps. 74:13-14; Isa. 27:1), and serpents are a recurring motif in ancient Near Eastern mythology. Cyrus of Persia claimed to have been chosen by Bel, the Babylonian god, to liberate the Babylonians from their king (see Isa. 45:1-8).

By the end, Daniel's brashness has landed him in trouble, and the third part shows an adaptation of the trickster motif to the "higher wisdom" of the Daniel tradition: God will protect the wise and righteous worshiper. In legends and folktales, there is also often a "fitting end": the villain is executed by the very means he or she had originally devised for the protagonist (cf. Dan. 3:22, Esth. 7:8-10). It is not plausible that in the polytheistic empires a major deity like Bel would have been treated contemptuously in this way, but one may assume here a degree of poetic license that the audience also recognized. The structure of this court legend—the wise courtier suffers a fall from a position of honor, is persecuted by the non-Jewish courtiers, but is vindicated and reinstated—is similar to the plot structure of Daniel 3 and 6. The den of lions appears as well in both Bel and in Daniel 6, but neither exhibits a clear dependence on the other. Bel and the Dragon was thus probably not written for inclusion in the book of Daniel, but circulated independently, as an alternative telling of the "Daniel in the lions' den" motif.

◼ THE TEXT IN THE INTERPRETIVE TRADITION

There are no references to the additions to Daniel among the texts from Qumran or in the first-century Jewish authors Josephus or Philo, and as they were not canonical in the Jewish Scriptures, they are not commented on in rabbinic tradition. Although Bel and the Dragon is similar to Daniel 6—in both, Daniel is thrown into a lions' den—in Bel there is also a temporary intervention of the prophet Habakkuk (vv. 33-39); here the Daniel and Habakkuk traditions come together. As a result, in Christian art, there is a tradition of Habakkuk and Daniel together in the lions' den. Especially famous are a wooden panel in the door of the Basilica of Santa Sabina in Rome (c. 430 CE) and a sculpture by Gian Lorenzo Bernini (1655). While modern viewers of this art may assume that Habakkuk's image comes from the book by that name, it actually derives from Bel and the Dragon.

◼ THE TEXT IN CONTEMPORARY DISCUSSION

The story of Bel and the Dragon, like the court legends in Daniel 1–6 and Esther, emphasizes the challenge of remaining faithful to God and God's law in a broader world ruled by foreign kings. These ancient stories have postcolonial interest in that they depict a Jewish minority in a world controlled by great empires. In the modern world, where the rulers may be Jewish, Christian, Muslim, of some other faith, or of no faith at all, the image of one who will witness to his or her faith—or even to "freedom" or some other ideal—to the point of death is very strong. But in addition, such stories as this should be recognized for the way they construct and affirm the identity of the audience. The faith to be confessed is laid out, especially in the prayers and hymns, at the same time that the threats of the other peoples are depicted in sharp contrast. All of the narratives of the Daniel tradition, which were likely created separately, speak to the maintenance of identity in a threatening colonial world, and as global issues become more central in theological discourse, the postcolonial reading of Bel and the Dragon and the rest of the Daniel tradition will likely find an increased role as well.

Works Cited

Nickelsburg, George W. E. 2005. *Jewish Literature between the Bible and the Mishnah*. 2nd ed. Minneapolis: Fortress Press.

Wills, Lawrence M. 1990. *The Jew in the Court of the Foreign King: Ancient Jewish Court Legends*. Minneapolis: Fortress Press.

———. 1995. *The Jewish Novel in the Ancient World*. Ithaca, NY: Cornell University Press.

1 MACCABEES

Michael S. Moore

The first book of Maccabees depicts the aftermath of Alexander's fourth-century-BCE advance into Syria-Palestine. The story is told from an ideological perspective dominated by the pragmatic mindset of enfranchised Judean landowners resolutely opposed to the Hellenistic culture of acquisition that is invasively challenging their way of life (Schwartz 1993; Moore 2011, 168–201). Differing from other Jewish groups, these landowners view the world through stained-glass windows colored by outrage and disgust over anything "foreign," "oppressive," or "Greek."

1 Maccabees 1:1-64: Alexander's Aftermath

▌ THE TEXT IN ITS ANCIENT CONTEXT

The opening paragraph breaks down into two sections, one focused on *external* conflicts (vv. 1-9 and 16-64), the other on *internal* conflicts affecting the Jews trying to eke out a living in Yehud, a satrapy tucked away in the northwestern corner of the Persian Empire (vv. 10-15). Here the Macedonian conqueror Alexander appears not as "the Great," but as a rapacious colonialist hailing from the "land of the Kittim" (Hebrew code word for "northern foreigners"), a "foolish and childish" adolescent (Philo, *Cher.* 63) determined to "strike down" (Gk. *patassō*; see 1 Macc. 1:1) the Persian emperor Darius III and take over his kingdom. Where the Greek version of Daniel uses this verb to depict this West-versus-East conflict as a he-goat forcefully "striking" a helpless ram (*patassō*; see Dan. 8:7), 1 Maccabees uses it to create a grammatical construction designed to express emphasis, albeit translating it here into "clumsy, semitizing Greek" (Schwartz 1989, 380).

After the death of Alexander, his surviving lieutenants go to war with each other like wild dogs fighting over a fresh carcass, violently carving up his empire into several more-governable chunks (*CHJ* 2:45-52), forever revolutionizing Middle Eastern life through a development the writer of

1 Maccabees condescendingly describes as "the multiplication of evils" (1 Macc. 1:9). Other Jews, however, are not nearly so defensive about the Greeks or Greek culture. Capitulating to peer pressure from patrons and colleagues, the Jewish historian Josephus even goes so far as to describe Alexander's invasion as "the leading of God's will" (*Ant.* 2.348), while many of his countrymen fall all over themselves trying to enter with them into all sorts of "covenants" (Gk. *diathēkē*; 1 Macc. 1:11; Moore 2004). The author of 1 Maccabees summarily refers to such covenanters as "sons of lawlessness" (1 Macc. 1:11, another telltale Semitism, like "sons of disobedience" in Eph. 2:2), while others decide to leave Jerusalem and "wait things out" in xenophobic cocoons affixed to the northwestern bank of the Dead Sea (Moore 2011, 189–201). Against this pluralistic backdrop, the Jews in 1 Maccabees pick up weapons and fight, taking on the Greeks and their mercenaries while displaying in the process a form of patriotic nationalism quite unlike anything else within Second Temple Judaism.

▌ THE TEXT IN THE INTERPRETIVE TRADITION

Many contemporary critics see in 1 Maccabees a reliable witness to the impact of Alexandrian colonialism (Grabbe 2008b, 5–7), not only in its attention to sociohistorical detail, but also in its focus on the consequences of colonialism generally (Victor, 77–108). One of the more obvious of these consequences has to do with the ways and means by which various Jews imagine the function and purpose of circumcision, a complicated custom within the Middle East generally, but certainly within Judaism specifically (see Livesey). For example, where 1 Maccabees depicts this rite as a mark of allegiance to Hasmonean rule (1:15; a position echoed by Josephus, *Ant.* 12.265), the book of *Jubilees* interprets it as a mark of adherence to the Lord's "eternal ordinance" (*Jub.* 15:25-34). Where 2 Maccabees identifies it as a sign of pious sacrifice (6:10-17), 4 Maccabees champions it as a symbol of pious rationalism's supremacy over irrational emotivism (4:25). Where Josephus identifies circumcision as the most obvious symbol of monotheistic Judaism (*Ant.* 20.38–48), Philo more broadly classifies it as a symbol of divine-human fellowship (*QG* 3.46–52; *Migr.* 86–105). Given the breadth of this diversity, Paul's refusal to ascribe salvific power to the rite of circumcision inevitably challenges the beliefs of his rabbinic colleagues, thereby forcing him (1) to take a stand against what he perceives to be a stubbornly misguided religion driven by forces all-too-content to prioritize the trivial (the *flesh*) over the essential (the *spirit*; Gal. 3:3; Murphy-O'Connor); and (2) to refocus attention on that part of the human anatomy most in need of radical surgery (Rom. 2:29; citing Deut. 10:16).

▌ THE TEXT IN CONTEMPORARY DISCUSSION

As contemporary critics are making clear, the dynamic governing the process of group identity formation accelerates considerably whenever and wherever colonialism raises its ugly head (Tafjel). Prejudice and persecution continue to affect the lives of many today, particularly those who are perceived, for whatever reason, to be ethnically, linguistically, and/or religiously "odd" (Merskin, 3–105). Persecuted communities thus continue to gravitate, like the Maccabeans of old, to recognizable identity markers able to produce refuge and safety from the dangers of cultural assimilation and religious defilement. For example, as circumcision operated as a primary identity marker among colonialized Jews in the Second Temple period, contemporary Muslims gravitate to mosques requiring women to wear the hijab (headscarf), or to mosques championing the implementation of sharia law over against their more assimilated neighbors who permit the Jeffersonian separation of mosque and state (Jasser, 282). Again, certain sects of modern Judaism distinguish themselves from gentiles (and each other) by whether or not the men trim their sideburns "properly" (Becher, 286). Similarly, Christians gravitate to "contemporary" versus "traditional" worship, or to "welcoming-and-affirming" versus "welcoming-but-not-affirming" churches (Grenz). Each of these cases helps illustrate the kinds of decisions Second Temple Jews had to face with regard to circumcision, Sabbath observance, and other, less conspicuous forms of identity-marking. Regardless of religious *content*, each case illustrates the same anthropological *process* (Roy, 23–148).

1 Maccabees 2:1—9:22: The Maccabean Revolt

▮ THE TEXT IN ITS ANCIENT CONTEXT

The classic East-versus-West conflict portrayed in 1 Maccabees comes to a violent head when a country priest from the village of Modein (approximately twenty-one kilometers northwest of Jerusalem) finds his anger stretched to the breaking point and publicly assassinates a Greek tax official alongside an unnamed Judean villager who, in clear violation of the Mosaic code, caves in to the "pressure" of worshiping "other gods" (Gk. *katanagkazō*; 1 Macc. 2:15; see Exod. 20:1-6). This assassination sparks a grassroots revolt that the writer of 1 Maccabees associates with the spirit of Phineas, another priest driven by righteous indignation to "protect the law" via public assassination (Num. 25:6-13). The writer, in other words, is saying to his readers, "What Mattathias does is nothing new. He simply follows Phineas's example." The leaders of this grassroots revolt include the priest Mattathias and three of his sons—Judah, Jonathan, and Simon.

Whatever his intentions, however, Mattathias soon capitulates to a leadership model that is just as pagan, violent, and repressive as that practiced by his enemies. This is not the only instance of religious violence associated with Mattathias's name. For example, in lieu of offering Jewish children the *opportunity* of participating in the rite of circumcision, the text clearly states that Mattathias and his disciples zealously *force* it on many of them, going so far as to "strike down" anyone they consider unfit for duty (Gk. *patassō*; 1 Macc. 2:44; this is the same verb used to describe Alexander's "striking" of Darius in 1 Macc. 1:1). After Mattathias's death, then, it comes as no surprise that the son on whom he lays his mantle—Judah—quickly distances himself from such extremism, focusing instead on more immediate pragmatic concerns like military defense strategy (Klawans, 155) and international diplomacy (Mandell). To protect the homeland from further attack, Mattathias even organizes a militia and trains it to fight against the battle-hardened mercenaries perennially hired to keep the Jews "in line" (Bar-Kochva 1989). Lacing his training lectures with biblical stories of past victories, Mattathias makes sure to expose his students to those sections of the Bible he deems most able to inspire them sufficiently to fight for hearth and home (Berthelot). Succinctly put, the narrator of 1 Maccabees portrays Judah ben Mattathias as a "second David," and the account of his days as a guerrilla leader as an updated version of David's days as an "outlaw on the run" (Himmelfarb, 80).

THE TEXT IN THE INTERPRETIVE TRADITION

Where 1 Maccabees focuses on Mattathias's decision to "strike down" (again, Gk. *patassō*; see 1 Macc. 1:1; 2:44) the "lawless," tear down their altars, and circumcise their children "by force" (Gk. *en ischui*; 1 Macc. 2:46), Josephus highlights these same three projects (*Ant.* 12.278). Other than Josephus, though, few other texts have much to say about Judah or his activities (with the obvious exception of 2 Maccabees; see below). Preoccupied with other concerns, the Pharisaic rabbis remain conspicuously silent in the documents for which they are most obviously responsible (Targum, Mishnah, Talmud, Tosefta, Midrash), while the Nazarene library preserved in the Greek New Testament refrains from mentioning him at all. Should the Zealots be the most likely successors of the Maccabees (Farmer, 182–83, contra Josephus, *J. W.* 2.117–18), then the silence of this group seems somewhat less surprising. Why? Because zealot fringe groups have a long history of camouflaging their literary footprints (Sivan and Friedman).

THE TEXT IN CONTEMPORARY DISCUSSION

With a few exceptions, this silence remains in place until the twentieth century—the most violent century in human history. Apart from a few artistic compositions (e.g., Handel's 1746 oratorio *Judas Maccabaeus*), interest in Judah Maccabaeus used to be limited to the annual holiday seder around the candles of Hanukkah. Early in the twentieth century, however, some Jews (later called "Zionists") began to take an interest in Judah's life in their literary attempts to throw off the shackles of Teutonic oppression. In their zeal, they often blur the boundaries separating contemporary discourse from ancient narrative as they enlist others to follow their "impossible dream," the creation of a democratic Jewish state to shelter the survivors of the Holocaust. Lamenting the "contemptible role" Jews are forced to play in the 1930s, one writer expresses his astonishment that the world would allow something as barbaric as a "concentration camp" to imprison and destroy "a people which once had its Maccabees" (Pinsker, 87). Another dares to imagine, in this dark and lonely time, that a "wondrous generation of Jews" will someday "spring into existence," and that good people everywhere will someday support the creation of a new nation where "the Maccabeans will rise again" (Herzl, 102). Looking for ways to substantiate this hope, one enthusiastic student goes to the Psalter, where he imagines that the "sons of Adam" to whom the Lord gives "the earth" (Ps. 115:16) actually refers to "Maccabean warriors" destined to "acquire earthly life for themselves and their nation" (Klausner, 3:29).

Building on these sentiments, several Zionists began pushing hard for the next logical step: the development of a "Maccabean philosophy of military nationalism" into a workable model for transforming Arab Palestine into a functioning Jewish state (Jabotinsky). As is widely known, debate over the efficacy and propriety of such a philosophy continues to polarize the politics of the Middle East, repeatedly igniting what seems to most Westerners to be endless arguments both pro (Kahane) and con (Sprinzak). Perhaps no response is so poignantly eloquent, however, as that voiced by Holocaust survivor and Pulitzer Prize–winning novelist Elie Wiesel, who in his 1960 novel *Dawn* narrates the story of a troubled Holocaust survivor who, after surviving the horrors of the camps, soon finds himself forced to assume the role of a guerrilla fighter, thereby ironically prolonging his exposure to suffering and destruction and death. One of Wiesel's biographers tellingly describes this protagonist as "a twentieth century Maccabee struggling for the liberation of the . . . Jewish spirit" (Downing, 141).

1 Maccabees 9:23—12:53: Marginalizing Hebrew Religion

■ THE TEXT IN ITS ANCIENT CONTEXT

When Judah dies, his brother Jonathan inherits a tenuous situation in which a bureaucrat named Bacchides, the handpicked emissary of King Demetrius I (d. 150 BCE), stands on Judea's throat. In spite of this uncomfortable beginning, Jonathan soon turns the tables on Bacchides and the rest of his neighbors. In fact, this strategy becomes so successful, one might well compare his leadership style with that exercised by his ancestor Jacob—another wheeler-dealer able to summon up the savoir faire necessary to outfox his opponents (Genesis 27–35). Where Judah Maccabaeus has to bear the brunt of facing a united enemy, however, Jonathan's success hangs on how well he can manipulate his enemies into turning against one another. Where Judah helps Judea weather wave after wave of foreign attack, Jonathan negotiates with his hostile neighbors in ways designed to humiliate and embarrass them.

Marginalized and diminished by this politicking, the office of high priest loses considerable religious traction (VanderKam, 251–71). Compared to previous high priests, like the "tyrannical" Menelaus (2 Macc. 4:25) and the "ungodly" Alcimus (1 Macc. 7:9), Jonathan's decision to procure the office for himself looks relatively innocuous at first glance. He's worse than some, yet better than others. Yet whatever the social, economic, and political factors responsible for his decisions, the high priesthood significantly loses its "religious mediator" and "spiritual advisor" components, replacing them with those more aligned with the roles of "bureaucratic administrator" and "cultic figurehead" (Rooke, 266–302).

■ THE TEXT IN THE INTERPRETIVE TRADITION

Apart from Josephus's narrative of these events (*Ant.* 13.1–194), few writers have much to say about Jonathan or his contribution to the establishment of what soon becomes, under the leadership of his brother Simon, a full-fledged Hasmonean "state" (Goodblatt, 1–27). Even less can be said about the impact of the high priesthood on Judean religious life. Since Jonathan does not descend from the line of Aaron (Moore 1996), some hypothetically associate his name with the figure of the "wicked priest," the cryptic figure in the Dead Sea Scrolls who is so adamantly condemned by the puritan community of the Essenes (1QpHab 8:8). Whatever the validity of this association (Woude), the fact remains that the integrity of the office of the high priest takes a beating in this time period, a fact underlined by the lopsidedly negative depiction of it generated by the Nazarenes (Metzner).

On trial for his life, for example, Paul laments, "Brothers, up to this day I have lived my life with a clear conscience before God," after which Ananias the high priest orders those standing next to him to punch him in the face. At this Paul angrily responds, "May God strike *you*, you whitewashed wall! How dare you sit there, judging me according to the law, when contrary to the law you order me to be struck?" (Acts 23:1-5).

■ THE TEXT IN CONTEMPORARY DISCUSSION

Similar tensions continue to afflict the lives and families of modern religious leaders. Where Jonathan the high priest has to deal with the fallout generated by Hebraic-versus-Hellenistic religious models, postmodern believers have to deal with ministry models in which such specific intangibles that are unique to ministry as building a sense of community, growing within an ecclesiastical communion, and the inclusion of spirituality are covertly ignored, if not overtly ridiculed. As the present text shows, the relationship between religion and popular culture can be paradoxically complex. Religion can have a powerful impact on popular culture, but popular culture can exercise just as much influence on religious leaders and their priorities (Kyle). Whatever the direction of influence, it is becoming increasingly difficult to find "successful" pastors who are appreciated more for their commitment to a "suffering servant" ministry model than to a "televangelist" ministry model (Schultze). The media culture is just too strong for many religious leaders to resist, especially if they want to keep their jobs and support their families (Postman).

Globally, these tensions may be either directly or indirectly responsible for various kinds of puritan extremism (Juergensmeyer). Such analysis may be too simplistic (Berlinerblau), but no one can deny that just as Essenes rise up against Sadducees, so also do Taliban rise up against corrupt Sunni Muslims, Hasidim against Reform Jews, and US Anglicanism against Episcopalians.

1 Maccabees 13:1—16:24: Reestablishing a Nation

■ THE TEXT IN ITS ANCIENT CONTEXT

Like the Saul–David–Solomon sequence in Samuel–Kings and the warlord–monarchy–colony sequence within Hebrew history generally, the Judah–Jonathan–Simon sequence follows a recognizable pattern, one sociologists call "routinization" (Weber). Like his brothers, Simon registers a number of military, diplomatic, and cultural successes. But unlike his brothers, he receives for his efforts the largesse of a grateful people who reward him with honors and awards not unlike those conferred on other civic benefactors in the Hellenistic world. Conspicuously posted on bronze tablets, one of these awards proclaims Simon's civic achievements as well as several of his official titles, all bestowed on him by the "great assembly of the priests and the people and the rulers of the nation and the elders of the country" (1 Macc. 14:28). These include the titles of "governor" (*hēgoumenos*; Lucian, *Alex.* 44), "commander" (*stratēgos*, Aristotle, *Ath. Pol.* 4.2), "ethnarch" (*ethnarchos*; Origen, *De princ.* 4.1.3), "high priest" (*archiereus*, Herodotus, *Hist.* 2.37), and "friend of the king" (*philos basileōs*; see Richardson, 208).

◼ THE TEXT IN THE INTERPRETIVE TRADITION

To this list of titles, Josephus adds one more, "benefactor" (*euergetēs*, *Ant.* 13.214), one of the most important functionaries in every Greek *polis* (Gardner). Taken together, these titles identify Simon as a force to be reckoned with in the eastern Levant, a reality confirmed by the fact that the next generation of Hasmonean leaders comes through *his* seed, not that of his brothers. Public international recognition of Simon thus signifies a major development in Hasmonean history.

◼ THE TEXT IN CONTEMPORARY DISCUSSION

Sociologically, religious groups tend to develop according to the following sequence: sects develop into communities, which in turn develop into denominations (Troeltsch, 331–43). Exceptions occur, of course, but generally speaking, the "routinization" pattern holds just as true for Muslim (Brumberg, 98–151) and Jewish communities (Cohen, 6–7, 44–45) as it does for Christian communities (Goldstein). Never does it proceed *in reverso* because the "routinization of charisma" is a one-way street. What this means, practically speaking, is that all religious groups can benefit from understanding where they fit within this "routinization" sequence. Just as Judah is not the right candidate for the position given to his brother Simon, so not every congregation needs a high-powered entrepreneurial pastor to serve the Lord faithfully and effectively (Davis). And just as Jonathan is not the appropriate candidate for the position given to Simon, so not every congregation needs a postmodern radical thinker to fulfill the gospel mandate (Galli). Pastoral search committees, to cite only one group of contemporary constituents, need to understand how "routinization" works if they expect to find the right "fit" for the congregations in which they serve.

Works Cited

Bar-Kochva, Bezalel. 1989. *Judas Maccabaeus: The Jewish Struggle Against the Seleucids.* Cambridge: Cambridge University Press.

Becher, Mordechai. 2005. *Gateway to Judaism: The What, How, and Why of Jewish Life.* Brooklyn, NY: Shaar Press.

Berlinerblau, Jacques. 2012. *How to Be Secular: A Call to Arms for Religious Freedom.* Boston: Houghton Mifflin Harcourt.

Berthelot, Katell. 2005. "The Biblical Conquest of the Promised Land and the Hasmonean Wars According to 1 and 2 Maccabees." In *The Books of the Maccabees: History, Theology, Ideology*, edited by Géza Xeravits and József Zsengellér, 45–60. Leiden: Brill.

Brumberg, Daniel. 2001. *Reinventing Khomeini: The Struggle for Reform in Iran.* Chicago: University of Chicago Press.

Cohen, Michael. 2012. *The Birth of Conservative Judaism: Solomon Schechter's Disciples and the Creation of an American Religious Movement.* New York: Columbia University Press.

Davis, Marshall. 2006. *More Than a Purpose: An Evangelical Response to Rick Warren and the Megachurch Movement.* Enumclaw, WA: WinePress.

Downing, Frederick L. 2008. *Elie Wiesel: A Religious Biography.* Macon, GA: Mercer University Press.

Farmer, William R. 1956. *Maccabees, Zealots, and Josephus.* New York: Columbia University Press.

Galli, Mark. 2011. "What's Up with Hell?" *Christianity Today* 55:63–65.

Gardner, Gregg. 2007. "Jewish Leadership and Hellenistic Civic Benefaction in the Second Century BCE." *JBL* 126:327–43.

Goldstein, Warren S. 2011. "The Dialectics of Religious Conflict: Church–Sect, Denomination and the Culture Wars." *Culture and Religion: An Interdisciplinary Journal* 12:77–99.

Goodblatt, David. 2006. *Elements of Ancient Jewish Nationalism*. Cambridge: Cambridge University Press.

Grabbe, Lester L. 2008a. "The High Priest." In *A History of Judaism and the Jews in the Second Temple Period*. Vol. 2, *The Coming of the Greeks*, 225–29. London: T&T Clark.

———. 2008b. "The Relevance of Post-Colonial Theory." In *A History of Judaism and the Jews in the Second Temple Period*. Vol. 2, *The Coming of the Greeks*, 5–7. London: T&T Clark.

Grenz, Stanley. 1998. *Welcoming but Not Affirming*. Louisville: Westminster John Knox.

Herzl, Theodor. 1904. *A Jewish State*. New York: Maccabaean.

Himmelfarb, Martha. 2008. "'He Was Renowned to the Ends of the Earth' (1 Macc. 3:9): Judaism and Hellenism in 1 Maccabees." In *Jewish Literatures and Cultures*, edited by Anita Norich and Yaron Eliav, 77–98. Providence: Brown Judaic Studies.

Jabotinsky, Vladimir. 1923. "The Iron Wall." In *Israel and the Middle East: Documents and Readings on Society, Politics, and Foreign Relations, pre-1948 to the Present*, edited by Itamar Rabinovich and Jehuda Reinharz, 41–43. Waltham, MA: Brandeis University Press, 2007.

Jasser, M. Zuhdi. 2012. *A Battle for the Soul of Islam: An American Muslim Patriot's Fight to Save His Faith*. New York: Simon & Schuster.

Juergensmeyer, Mark. 2008. *Global Rebellion: Religious Challenges to the Secular State, from Christian Militias to al Qaeda*. Berkeley: University of California Press.

Kahane, Meir. 1972. *Never Again!* New York: Pyramid Books.

Klausner, Joseph. 1952. *Historya shel ha-bayit ha-sheni*. 5 vols. Jerusalem: Achiasaf.

Klawans, Jonathan. 2012. *Josephus and the Theologies of Ancient Judaism*. New York: Oxford University Press.

Kyle, Richard. 2006. *Evangelicalism: An Americanized Christianity*. New Brunswick, NJ: Transaction.

Livesey, Nina E. 2010. *Circumcision as a Malleable Symbol*. Tübingen: Mohr Siebeck.

Mandell, Sara. 1991. "Did the Maccabees Believe That They Had a Valid Treaty with Rome?" *CBQ* 53:202–20.

Merskin, Debra L. 2010: *Media, Minorities, and Meaning: A Critical Introduction*. New York: Peter Lang.

Metzner, Rainer. 2010. *Kaiphas. Der Hohepriester jenes Jahres: Geschichte und Deutung*. Leiden: Brill.

Moore, Michael S. 1996. "Role Preemption in the Israelite Priesthood." *VT* 46:316–29.

———. 2004. "Big Dreams and Broken Promises: Solomon's Treaty with Hiram in Its International Context." *BBR* 14:205–21.

———. 2011. *WealthWatch: A Study of Socioeconomic Conflict in the Bible*. Eugene, OR: Pickwick.

Murphy-O'Connor, Jerome. 1998. *Paul: A Critical Life*. Oxford: Oxford University Press.

Pinsker, Lev S. 1944. *Road to Freedom*. New York: Scopus.

Postman, Neil. 1985: *Amusing Ourselves to Death: Public Discourse in the Age of Show Business*. New York: Viking.

Richardson, Peter. 1996. *Herod: King of the Jews and Friend of the Romans*. Columbia: University of South Carolina Press.

Rooke, Deborah. 2000. *Zadok's Heirs: The Role and Development of the High Priesthood in Ancient Israel*. New York: Oxford University Press.

Roy, Olivier. 2010. *Holy Ignorance: When Religion and Culture Part Ways*. New York: Columbia University Press.

Schultze, Quentin J. 2003. *Televangelism and American Culture: The Business of Popular Religion*. Eugene, OR: Wipf & Stock.

Schwartz, Seth. 1989. "The 'Judaism' of Samaria and Galilee in Josephus's Version of the Letter of Demetrius I to Jonathan (*Antiquities* 13.48-57)." *HTR* 82:377–91.

———. 1993. "A Note on the Social Type and Political Ideology of the Hasmonean Family." *JBL* 112:305–9.

Sivan, Emmanuel, and Menachem Friedman, eds. 1990. *Religious Radicalism and Politics in the Middle East*. Albany: State University of New York Press.

Sprinzak, Ehud. 1999. *Brother against Brother: Violence and Extremism in Israeli Politics*. New York: Free Press.

Tafjel, Henri, ed. 2010. *Social Identity and Intergroup Relations*. Cambridge: Cambridge University Press.

Troeltsch, Ernst. 1992 (1912). *The Social Teaching of the Christian Churches*. Louisville: Westminster John Knox.

VanderKam, James C. 2004. *From Joshua to Caiaphas: High Priests after the Exile*. Minneapolis: Fortress Press.

Victor, Royce M. 2010. "Hellenism and Material Culture in Israel." In *Colonial Education and Class Formation in Early Judaism: A Postcolonial Reading*, 77–108. London: T&T Clark.

Weber, Max. 2009 (1922). *The Theory of Social and Economic Organization*. Edited and translated by Talcott Parsons. New York: Free Press.

Woude, A. S. van der. 1982. "Wicked Priest or Wicked Priests? Reflections on the Identification of the Wicked Priest in the Habakkuk Commentary." *JJS* 33:349–59.

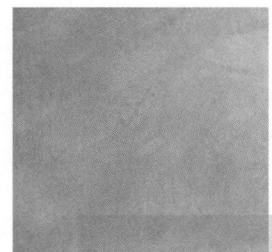

2 MACCABEES

Michael S. Moore

Introduction

The second book of Maccabees covers much the same historical ground as the first, only from a perspective much more intentionally Hellenistic, focused on the life of the guerrilla warrior Judah Maccabaeus and his efforts to save Judea from the colonialist oppressions of Judah's Greek ruler, King Antiochus IV Epiphanes (d. 164 BCE).

2 Maccabees 1:1—2.32: An Invitation to Diaspora Jews

▌ THE TEXT IN ITS ANCIENT CONTEXT

Two prefatory letters introduce this document, one addressed to Alexandrian Jews from their cousins in Jerusalem, the other to a Jewish scholar named Aristobulus—a tutor of Egyptian king Ptolemy VII—from Judah Maccabaeus and the Jerusalem Council. The purpose of these letters is to invite Egyptian readers up to Jerusalem to celebrate the Festivals of Tabernacles and Hanukkah. Underneath the pleasantries, however, the primary goal of these letters is to encourage Egyptian Jews to come over and participate in a purification ceremony designed to cleanse the Jerusalem temple from years of gentile defilement (1 Macc. 4:41-51), thereby providing for these émigrés the opportunity to either affirm or reaffirm their loyalty to *this* shrine over all others (Frey).

Fleshing out the rationale for these invitations, the author, who describes himself as the "epitomizer" of a much larger five-volume history (Gk. *epitomein*; 2 Macc. 2:23), relates two legends to "prove" to his Diaspora cousins that the sacred fire to be used in this purification ritual is not a "strange fire"; that is, it will not have the same deleterious effect on them as does the "strange fire" in Lev. 10:1 on Aaron's sons Nadab and Abihu. The first legend claims that this fire comes directly from Solomon's temple, having been propitiously saved from extinction by their priestly ancestors before the Babylonian invasion and destruction (2 Kgs. 24:1-17). The second legend then claims that Nehemiah rediscovers this sacred fire in a hidden cistern after it has transformed into a thick, oily liquid (2 Macc. 1:20-21; Lange).

THE TEXT IN THE INTERPRETIVE TRADITION

Two socioreligious concerns drive these invitations, each grounded in the ideological world of priestly torah reflection (Knohl, 8–40). First, the Palestinian Jews responsible for issuing the invitations believe that full protection from cultic defilement can only occur at one divinely designated place (Deut. 12:5; Philo, *Spec. Laws* 1.66–70). Second, they believe the Jerusalem temple to be that place. This view is challenged in one of the Dead Sea Scrolls (the *Halakic Letter*, 4Q394–99) and the Greek New Testament (Matt. 12:6; Luke 21:5-6), but reaffirmed and promoted in one of the longest of the Dead Sea scrolls, the *Temple Scroll* (11Q19 45:10). The focus of this ideology tends to blur, however, as Jerusalem's festival celebrations transform the city into an international circus attended by Diaspora Jews eager to replace the rituals of torah with the indigenous ritual traditions of their adopted countries (see John 2:13-21; Acts 2:5-11).

THE TEXT IN CONTEMPORARY DISCUSSION

Similar concerns influence contemporary religious behavior. First, whether or not postmodern Westerners will admit it, "defilement" continues to be a very real problem, whether for believers or nonbelievers, monotheists or polytheists, religionists or secularists, Christians or Jews (Kristeva, 56–89). Anthropologists have long known that unimpeded defilement tends to breed cultures of despair (Douglas) that are myopically focused on death and denial instead of life and renewal (Mjaaland), even when "suffering and evil, on the one hand, and the indelible memory of hope on the other" combine to expose, however faintly, the possibility of an antidote (Moltmann, 141). Engaging the problem of defilement seriously—that is, through healthy ritual (Ramshaw) instead of rhetorical hypocrisy (Molnar), escapist demagoguery (Aslan), or worse, perverse ideology (Heschel)—can be difficult for many Westerners to imagine, much less recognize or embrace. Even when the spiritual survival of a generation is at stake (Solzhenitsyn), Westerners can delude themselves into thinking that purification from defilement is solely a private, individual affair. From a biblical perspective, however, true purification cannot be imagined apart from active participation in the "fellowship of the Spirit" (2 Cor. 3:17-18; Phil. 2:1-6).

A second concern is that in spite of all their good intentions, the Protestant Reformers are largely responsible for fostering a religious legacy more attuned to the polyphonic melodies of sociopolitical pluralism than the concordial harmonies of sacral unity (Littell, 102–28), thereby invalidating for many the possibility "of a religiously pluralistic, yet Christian, confessional political order" (Kozinski, 113–14). Today most "Protestants" (a quaint holdover term) devote little attention to questions of religious unity (Putnam and Campbell, 1–36) or spiritual development (Foster) because many are far more preoccupied with questions of particularized romance and consumptive politics. Paul's query to the Corinthians has therefore lost none of its sting: "Do you not know that you [plural] are God's temple and that God's Spirit resides (author trans.) in you [plural]?" (1 Cor. 3:16).

2 Maccabees 3:1—7:42: Martyrs and Martyrdom

■ THE TEXT IN ITS ANCIENT CONTEXT

According to the summary prayer in 2 Macc. 8:2-4, colonialist oppression affects Judean life in three areas: the *temple*, the *city*, and the *people*. Since ancient temples served both economic and religious functions, it's not surprising to find at the beginning of 2 Maccabees a nasty narrative focused on a vicious socioeconomic conflict dividing temple employees. One of the temple captains—a Benjamite named Simon—openly challenges the methods by which his boss, the high priest Onias III, manages "the administration of the city market" (2 Macc. 3:4), basically accusing him of so much corruption. Delighted to learn of this conflict, some Greek bureaucrats quickly manipulate it to their advantage in pursuit of their primary goal: the confiscation of temple funds (Moore 2011, 173–77).

Greek geographer Pausanias (d. 180 CE) observes that every Hellenistic "city" (*polis*) must have a "municipal office," a "marketplace," a "public fountain," a "theater," and a "school" (*gymnasion*; *Descr.* 10.4.1; see Moore 2013). Thus Jason's attempt to build a *gymnasion* in Jerusalem may represent nothing more than a good-faith attempt to integrate Jewish life into Hellenistic culture (Dequeker). Regardless of his motives, however, the author of 2 Maccabees will have none of it, condemning this development in no uncertain terms, labeling it a primary example of foreign "corruption" (2 Macc. 4:7).

Where the Aramaic book of Daniel condemns Babylonian oppressors for their persecution of innocent Hebrews, 2 Maccabees dramatically focuses attention on one particularly violent Greek oppressor, Antiochus IV Epiphanes, and his penchant for torturing Jewish civilians by the most hideous means imaginable (Shepkaru). The epitomizer gives three examples. In the first example, Antiochus's henchmen parade two Jewish mothers through the streets of Jerusalem before throwing them to their deaths, along with their nursing infants, from the top of the city wall. Their crime? Circumcising their children in accordance with the Mosaic law (Gen. 17:12-14). The second example addresses an occurrence in which Antiochus's men try to force an elderly gentleman named Eleazar to violate torah by eating pork (Lev. 11:7-8), only to hear him refuse via a most eloquent testimonial to the many spiritual advantages of submitting to a "noble death" (2 Macc. 6:24-28). In the third example, seven brothers and their mother perish in one of the most drawn-out, grisly scenes in all the Bible, a depiction as horrifying and revolting as the rape-murder-dissection scene that concludes the book of Judges (Judg. 19:1-30).

■ THE TEXT IN THE INTERPRETIVE TRADITION

Martyr stories like these eventually coalesce into a literary trajectory on which sit the philosophical speeches of 4 Maccabees (deSilva), the Talmud's account of Rabbi Akiba's execution (Boustan, 58–61), the Greek account of Polycarp's execution (McCready), the Latin account of Perpetua's passion (Heffernan), the Arabic account of the earliest Muslim martyrs (Afsaruddin), and the Gospel accounts of the passion (Boff). Whether the Nazarenes "prolong and supersede" an indigenously Jewish martyr tradition (Frend, 31) or draw from a broader Greco-Roman martyr tradition in their understanding of the passion is difficult to determine, but it is less difficult to see how intentionally all these stories focus on a common desire to bear "witness" (Gk. *martyria*) to the power of God in the midst of injustice, even when such witness leads to torture and death (Rouwhorst).

■ THE TEXT IN CONTEMPORARY DISCUSSION

For obvious reasons, martyrdom is never something widely embraced by the majority, whether that majority be Jewish (Sprinzak), Christian (Hefley and Hefley), Muslim (Kurzman), or agnostic (Mitchell). Most difficult today is the problem of definition. What, exactly, *is* "martyrdom"? How much truth *actually* adheres to the oft-cited proverb, "One man's terrorist is another man's martyr"? Is martyrdom always "religious" in nature? Does it always possess the element of transcendence, or does each act of "martyrdom" depend on the life circumstances of this or that particular "martyr"? If "a poet immortalizes himself through his poetic art, and a moral teacher through his wise sayings," do martyrs achieve fame by transfusing "invaluable fresh blood" into the groups with which they are most obviously identified (Atkins, 550)? Does martyrdom consist only of self-infliction, or can it also include elements of "collateral damage"? To be specific, does Jesus of Nazareth's voluntary decision to suffer and die on a Roman cross truly compare to Mohamed Atta's voluntary decision to pilot American Airlines flight number 11 into the north tower of the World Trade Center on September 11, 2011? If so, how does one explain why Jesus goes so far out of his way to protect everyone around him from bodily harm, both enemies as well as friends?

2 Maccabees 8:1—15:39: Faith under Pressure

■ THE TEXT IN ITS ANCIENT CONTEXT

Responding to the systematic injustices perpetrated by Antiochus and his court, 2 Maccabees claims that God will miraculously intervene to save his people whenever and wherever God sees fit. Three angels miraculously shield the Jerusalem temple from foreign attack (2 Macc. 3:25-28), five angels miraculously protect Judah Maccabaeus from foreign attack (2 Macc. 10:29-31), and an angelic horseman successfully rides with Judah into battle against foreign mercenaries (2 Macc. 11:8). Overt theological commentary sometimes perforates these texts to explain these divine interventions, using statements like "the wrath of the Lord turned to mercy" (2 Macc. 8:5) or "the Lord no longer showed mercy to him" (2 Macc. 9:13). Though never simply relying on the "miracle option," Judah Maccabaeus often asks the deity for help (2 Macc. 8:16-21; 10:25-27; 12:5, 15, 28, 36; 13:10-12; 15:8-11), especially after "seeing" the prophet Jeremiah giving him a "holy sword" (*hagian rhomphaian*; 2 Macc. 15:16) in a "waking vision" (*hypar*; 2 Macc. 15:11; n.b. the same word association in Homer, *Od.* 19.547).

The epitomizer of 2 Maccabees also wants his readers to know that Judah's opponents, like foreigners throughout Hebrew history (Moore 1998), can confess the supremacy of Israel's God and be blessed, especially after being humbled by the terrifying experience of divine intervention. Struck down by such an experience, the taxman Heliodorus immediately vows eternal loyalty to Israel's deity, addressing him as "Lord" and "Savior" while the Jewish high priest benevolently administers his "atonement" (Gk. *hilasmos*; 2 Macc. 3:33; see 1 John 2:2). So available is this blessing, even Antiochus IV Epiphanes experiences attitudinal transformation when the Lord "strikes" him (Gk. *pattassō*; 2 Macc. 9:5) with an "incurable and invisible plague" (cf. the use of *pattassō* in 1 Macc. 1:1; 2:44). Not only does the king's "conversion" make it possible for him to realize and experience the torture he previously inflicts on others, but it also destroys his plan to turn Jerusalem into a "cemetery of Jews" (2 Macc. 9:4), replacing it instead with a positive communiqué declaring the city's inhabitants "equal to the citizens of Athens" (2 Macc. 9:14-15).

▊ THE TEXT IN THE INTERPRETIVE TRADITION

Where 2 Maccabees emphasizes the phenomenon of miraculous intervention, 3 and 4 Maccabees stretch this emphasis to the point of preferential reliance (Eve, 244). The Talmud also weighs in with "miracle stories" of its own. For example, when a pious man considers repairing a breach in his fence but refrains from taking action because the job might carry over to the Sabbath, a "miracle occurs" (Heb *nēs naʾăśeh*, lit. "is made") when a caper bush sprouts into existence ex nihilo at the spot of the breach, thereby providing him with enough income to replace that which might otherwise have been lost (*b. Shab.* 150b). Again, when a widower with an infant child suddenly develops the biological capability to nurse it, one rabbi labels this a "miracle" (Heb *nēs*), attributing it to the man's "superiority" (*gĕdōl*). Another rabbi, however, disagrees, attributing it rather to his "inferiority" (*gĕrōʾâ*). Weighing both opinions, still another rabbi states what eventually becomes the rabbinic *via media*: Miracles can and do "happen" (*mitḥārîś*), but only rarely do they "produce" (*ʾăbārû*, lit. "thicken into") any real benefit to their recipients (*b. Shab.* 53b). Discussions like these illustrate how many pre-Enlightenment Jews try to explain their understanding of the natural-versus-supernatural polarity, championing neither while denying neither (Chajes).

Miracle stories in the Greek New Testament operate more from a desire to affirm God's interventional power—as in 2 Maccabees—than to explain the natural-supernatural polarity, as in Talmud (Kahl). Where the Fourth Gospel describes Christ's miracles via the Greek word *sēmeia* ("signs"; John 2:11; 4:54; 20:30), the Synoptic Gospels avoid this term, preferring instead the Greek word *dynameis*, or "deeds of power" (Matt. 11:20-23; Mark 6:2; Luke 10:13). Why? Because the Nazarenes believe that Jesus of Nazareth—not this or that angelic figure—is the final, primary conduit of divine power on earth (Schenck).

▊ THE TEXT IN CONTEMPORARY DISCUSSION

Western children of the European Enlightenment tend to bristle at this kind of discussion because many of us suffer deep resistance to the possibility that anything (or Anyone) can be perceived by something other than the five senses (Craig), much less consider the possibility that a supernatural, personal, and loving God can and will visit his creation to protect, rescue, and/or salvage his loved ones from the scourge of defilement. Yet if the force responsible for what physicists call "the big bang" is, in fact, a divine Creator, does it make any sense to imagine this person "running up and down the corridors of the hotel he created like a bewildered bellhop trying to find the right key" (Rogers, 16)? The contents of 2 Macc. 8:1—15:39 give food for thought that might be able to address such skepticism.

Works Cited

Afsaruddin, Asma. 2006. "Competing Perspectives on *Jihad* and 'Martyrdom' in Early Islamic Sources." In *Witnesses to Faith? Martyrdom in Christianity and Islam*, edited by Brian Wicker, 15–32. Burlington, VT: Ashgate.

Aslan, Reza. 2010. *Beyond Fundamentalism: Confronting Religious Extremism in the Age of Globalization*. New York: Random House.

Atkins, Stephen E., ed. 2011. *The 9/11 Encyclopedia*. New York: ABC-Clio.

Boff, Leonardo. 2011. *Passion of Christ, Passion of the World*. Maryknoll, NY: Orbis.

Boustan, Ra'anan S. 2005. *From Martyr to Mystic: Rabbinic Martyrology and the Making of Merkavah Mysticism*. Tübingen: Mohr Siebeck.

Chajes, Jeffrey H. 2007. "*Entzauberung* and Jewish Modernity: On 'Magic,' Enlightenment, and Faith." In *Early Modern Culture and Haskalah: Reconsidering the Borderlines of Modern Jewish History*, edited by David B. Ruderman and Shmuel Feiner, 191–200. Göttingen: Vandenhoeck & Ruprecht.

Craig, William Lane. 2000. "Naturalism and Cosmology." In *Naturalism: A Critical Analysis*, edited by William Lane Craig and J. P. Moreland, 215–52. London: Routledge.

Dequeker, L. 1993. "Jason's Gymnasium in Jerusalem (2 Macc 4:7–17): The Failure of a Cultural Experiment." *Bijdragen* 54:371–92.

DeSilva, David. 1998. *4 Maccabees*. Sheffield: Sheffield Academic Press.

Douglas, Mary. 1966. *Purity and Danger: An Analysis of Concepts of Pollution and Taboo*. London: Routledge.

Eve, Eric. 2002. *The Jewish Context of Jesus' Miracles*. Sheffield: Sheffield Academic Press.

Foster, Richard. 1998. *Celebration of Discipline*. San Francisco: HarperSanFrancisco.

Frend, W. H. C. 1965. *Martyrdom and Persecution in the Early Church*. London: Blackwell.

Frey, Jorg. 1999. "Temple and Rival Temple: The Cases of Elephantine, Mt. Gerizim, and Leontopolis." In *Gemeinde ohne Tempel*, edited by Beate Ego et al., 171–204. Tübingen: Mohr Siebeck.

Heffernan, Thomas J. 2012. *The Passion of Perpetua and Felicity*. New York: Oxford University Press.

Hefley, James C., and Marti Hefley. 2004. *By Their Blood: Christian Martyrs from the Twentieth Century and Beyond*. Grand Rapids: Baker Books.

Heschel, Susannah. 2008. *The Aryan Jesus: Christian Theologians and the Bible in Nazi Germany*. Princeton: Princeton University Press.

Kahl, Werner. 1994. *New Testament Miracle-Stories in Their Religious-Historical Setting*. Göttingen: Vandenhoeck & Ruprecht.

Knohl, Israel. 2007. *The Sanctuary of Silence: The Priestly Torah and the Holiness School*. Winona Lake, IN: Eisenbrauns.

Kozinski, Thaddeus J. 2012. *The Political Problem of Religious Pluralism, and Why Philosophers Can't Solve It*. Lanham, MD: Lexington.

Kristeva, Julia. 1982. *Powers of Horror: An Essay on Abjection*. New York: Columbia University Press.

Kurzman, Charles. 2011. *The Missing Martyrs: Why There Are So Few Muslim Terrorists*. New York: Oxford University Press.

Lange, Armin. 2007. "2 Maccabees 2:13-15: Library or Canon." In *The Books of the Maccabees: History, Theology, Ideology*, edited by Géza Xeravits and József Zsengellér, 155–67. Leiden: Brill.

Littell, Franklin H. 2007. *From State Church to Pluralism: A Protestant Interpretation of Religion in America*. New Brunswick, NJ: Aldine Transaction.

McCready, Wayne O. 2005. "Martyrdom: In Accordance with the Gospel." In *Religious Rivalries and the Struggle for Success in Sardis and Smyrna*, ed. Richard S. Ascough, 141–55. Waterloo, ON: Wilfrid Laurier University Press.

Mitchell, Jolyon P. 2012. *Martyrdom: A Very Short Introduction*. New York: Oxford University Press.

Mjaaland, Marius Timmann. 2011. "Suicide and Despair." In *Kierkegaard and Death*, edited by Patrick Stokes and Adam Buben, 81–100. Bloomington: Indiana University Press.

Molnar, Thomas Steven. 1987. *The Pagan Temptation*. Grand Rapids: Eerdmans.

Moltmann, Jürgen. 1968. "Resurrection as Hope." *HTR* 61:129–47.

Moore, Michael S. 1998. "Ruth the Moabite and the Blessing of Foreigners." *CBQ* 60:203-17.

———. 2011. *WealthWatch: A Study of Socioeconomic Conflict in the Bible*. Eugene, OR: Pickwick.

———. 2013. "Civic and Voluntary Associations in the Greco-Roman World." In *The World of the New Testament: Cultural, Social, and Historical Contexts*, edited by Joel B. Green and Lee Martin McDonald, 149–55. Grand Rapids: Baker Academic.

Putnam, Robert, and David Campbell, 2010. *American Grace: How Religion Divides and Unites Us*. New York: Simon & Schuster.

Ramshaw, Elaine. 1987. *Ritual and Pastoral Care*. Philadelphia: Fortress Press.

Rogers, Adrian. 1997. *Believe in Miracles, But Trust in Jesus*. Wheaton, IL: Crossway.

Rouwhorst, Gerard. 2005. "The Emergence of the Cult of the Maccabean Martyrs in Late Antique Christianity." In *More Than a Memory: The Discourse of Martyrdom and the Construction of Christian Identity in the History of Christianity*, edited by Johan Leemans, 81–96. Leuven: Peeters.

Schenck, Kenneth L. 2009. "The Worship of Jesus among Early Christians: The Evidence of Hebrews." In *Jesus and Paul: Global Perspectives in Honor of James D. G. Dunn for His 70th Birthday*, edited by B. J. Oropeza, C. K. Robertson, and Douglas C. Mohrmann, 114–26. London: T&T Clark.

Shepkaru, Shmuel. 2006. *Jewish Martyrs in the Pagan and Christian Worlds*. Cambridge: Cambridge University Press.

Solzhenitsyn, Alexander. 1976. *Warning to the West*. New York: Farrar, Straus & Giroux.

Sprinzak, Ehud. 2000. "Israel's Radical Right and the Countdown to the Rabin Assassination." In *The Assassination of Yitzhak Rabin*, edited by Yoram Peri, 96–128. Palo Alto: Stanford University Press.

1 ESDRAS

Daniel L. Smith-Christopher

Introduction

As with many characters of the Hebrew Bible (e.g., Jeremiah, Baruch, Esther, Daniel), Ezra has been the subject of continued interest in late Jewish works, only some of which (e.g., 1 Esdras) appear in editions of the Septuagint (Bird, 34). Sara Japhet points out that Josephus makes use of 1 Esdras in combination with Ezra-Nehemiah in his biblical "summaries," despite the work being absent from significant discussion in Jewish sources. First Esdras was used more widely in early Christian traditions, but as Michael Bird, Japhet, and Jacob Myers all note, not without significant criticism.

The most important initial observation about 1 Esdras is the relation of the work to 2 Chronicles, Ezra, and Nehemiah. Thus, any commentary, however brief, must begin with some form of the following chart:

1 Esd. 1:1-22	2 Chron. 35:1-19
1 Esd. 1:23-24	*unique* to 1 Esdras (summary of Josiah's reign)
1 Esd. 1:25-33	2 Chron. 35:20-27
1 Esd. 1:34-58	2 Chron. 36:1-21
1 Esd. 2:1-15	Ezra 1:1-11
1 Esd. 2:16-30	Ezra 4:6-24 (out of the sequence in MT Ezra)
1 Esd. 3:1—5:6	*unique* to 1 Esdras (the three youths/guards)
1 Esd. 5:7-46	Ezra 2:1-70
1 Esd. 5:47-66	Ezra 3:1-13
1 Esd. 5:67-73	Ezra 4:1-5
1 Esd. 6:1-22	Ezra 5:1-17
1 Esd. 6:23-34	Ezra 6:1-12

1 Esd. 7:1-15	Ezra 6:13-22
1 Esd. 8:1-27	Ezra 7:1-28
1 Esd. 8:28-67	Ezra 8:1-36
1 Esd. 8:68-90	Ezra 9:1-15
1 Esd. 8:91-96	Ezra 10:1-5
1 Esd. 9:1-36	Ezra 10: 6-44
1 Esd. 9:37-55	Neh. 7:73—8:12

While Bird (3–16, 22–26) has recently reviewed text-critical issues, it is generally agreed that the three most significant literary issues raised by 1 Esdras (Japhet, 752) are as follows:

1. The story of the three guards (3:1—5:6). Zipora Talshir (1999, 6) is surely correct to suggest that this long story must be central to 1 Esdras as a unique work, as it represents the single most important difference with the canonical versions.

2. The editorial comment in 1:23-24 with regard to the reign of Josiah leads to the question: Is Ezra to be compared with Josiah—thus explaining why we begin with Josiah and end with Ezra as an inclusio (Bird, 18)?

3. The rearrangement of the material that appears in the MT at Ezra 4:6-24 so that it comes immediately following the material found in the MT at Ezra 1 apparently magnifies the problems facing the returning community, and shifts the list of returnees under Jeshua and Zerubbabel to later in the book of 1 Esdras.

1 Esdras 1:1-58: Passover and Temple Restoration

▌ THE TEXT IN ITS ANCIENT CONTEXT

The opening narrative of the book, paralleled in 2 Chron. 35:1-19, focuses on the Passover celebration under Josiah. The emphasis is on large-scale preparations, the meticulous care given to the ritually appropriate steps, and the beneficence of the Persian king in providing meat to the people from royal herds (2,600 sheep, 300 calves, etc.). Central to the opening lines, however, is the restoration of the ark in the temple. The Passover, in other words, is the occasion for the renewal of the temple itself and its role among the people. Josiah is explicitly compared to David and Solomon, but Josiah's celebration exceeded all the kings of Israel (1:20-21). Nevertheless, the theme from Jeremiah that the exile was God's response to royal and priestly corruption is strongly maintained. Blame is shared among "leaders and priests" (1:49).

▌ THE TEXT IN THE INTERPRETIVE TRADITION

Talshir (1999) concludes that the work does indeed begin with this note of praise for Josiah (against those who propose a "lost" beginning). Myers (28–29) suggests that the emphasis on Josiah's righteousness draws a stronger contrast with the sins of the people faced by Ezra at a later age. Bird, however, suggests that beginning with Josiah magnifies Ezra's accomplishments at the end—what Josiah could not fully accomplish, Ezra does (Bird, 18)! It is interesting that 1:50 features a reference to a single "messenger." Was this understood to be a particular reference to Jeremiah, and thus a verification of Jeremiah's promise of seventy years (Jeremiah 29)?

◼ THE TEXT IN CONTEMPORARY DISCUSSION

Like many discussions of the monarchy, the sheer power and wealth of the central administration ought not be overlooked. The benevolence of Josiah raises ambiguous issues with regard to the privileges of the central power. On the one hand, the text attempts to praise generosity; on the other hand, it highlights the rather shocking excess of the king's holdings. The wealthy always attempt to divert attention from their greed by emphasizing their generosity and philanthropy. The praise of the generosity of the wealthy is the public face of bitter oppression and misappropriation of resources. A healthy skepticism is in order when reading any monarchy, especially in ancient Israelite experience. While Bird suggests that there is a "distinct absence of Judean militancy" in the attitude toward foreign rule in 1 Esdras (Bird, 19), it is also true that verses 34-58 contain no recognition of the *validity* of foreign strength or sovereignty (cf. John 19:11).

1 Esdras 2:1-30: Cyrus and the Restoration

◼ THE TEXT IN ITS ANCIENT CONTEXT

First Esdras, like Ezra, summarizes the story of Cyrus's giving the Israelites permission to rebuild their temple. In the text, Cyrus himself piously says he has been instructed by the God of the Israelites to do so. The captured temple vessels are returned, money is raised, and a delegation is headed by a certain "Sheshbazzar." However, opposition back in the land is strong. Jerusalem is called a "rebellious city," and the local Persian officials seem to express concern that the city itself is being revived, and not merely the temple.

◼ THE TEXT IN THE INTERPRETIVE TRADITION

Talshir (2001, 105) notes that the entire Persian period is summarized quickly, emphasizing the direct fulfillment of Jeremiah's prophecy. Furthermore, 1 Esdras presents a linear view of history rather than the somewhat jumbled perspectives of Ezra 1–4. It is widely noted (e.g., Myers, 37) that the biblical image of Cyrus, emphasizing his piety and kindness toward the Judeans, is consistently maintained in the Bible, and is especially contrasted with more negative treatment by later Persian rulers. The discussion about the later ruler Artaxerxes, therefore, is reminiscent of a pharaoh "who did not know Joseph" (Exod. 1:8). Consistent with this, 1 Esdras uses the work stoppage to create a dramatic pause in the narrative to introduce the tale of Zerubbabel.

◼ THE TEXT IN CONTEMPORARY DISCUSSION

While it is often suggested that the reports of Cyrus are intended to show God's concern and care, a perspective informed by the experience of colonized and/or minority peoples may suggest the reality of constant Imperial red tape, the need to appeal to authorities for everything, and the threats of constant harassment. Here, as in the Daniel stories, opposition to the Hebrew community then creates occasions for a test of Judean character and faith.

1 Esdras 3:1—4:63: Speaking Truth

▌THE TEXT IN ITS ANCIENT CONTEXT

The contest among members of Darius's court, found only in this text, is "the literary summit of the document" (Bird, 142). Darius is introduced as the most powerful man on the earth, with an emphasis on all the people under his rule. Whatever else the story is intended to communicate, it cannot be understood apart from this carefully constructed description of the worldly power of the emperor! The youths write their answer to the question: What is strongest? The answers of the three are (1) wine, (2) the king, and (3) women, but ultimately truth! The three youths appear to seek rewards; they wish to share in the power of Darius and the opulence of his rule and wealth. This is an important element for later in the story. Zerubbabel does not accept the offer of power or wealth, but instead asks for the restoration of Jerusalem and the freedom of the people from harassment and interference of local officials. The story contrasts the God of truth and wisdom to the power of the Persian officials. Cleverness, faithfulness, and wisdom (e.g., truth) prevail over brute strength (see Prov. 11:14; 24:6).

▌THE TEXT IN THE INTERPRETIVE TRADITION

The story clearly intends to magnify the role of Zerubbabel, who secures more from Darius than either Ezra or Nehemiah in the MT (Talshir 1999, 47). There is no doubt who is responsible for Darius's change of heart; it is the blessed brilliance of Zerubbabel in facing down, Daniel-like, the challenge of a ruler. Indeed, Talshir proposes, finally, that Zerubbabel's persona is constructed from "pieces" of the Nehemiah tradition and is clearly intended to replace him in the story of the Persian-period restoration (1999, 56–57). It seems hardly a coincidence that the same ruler who favored Daniel (Daniel 6) is here shown as favoring Zerubbabel. However, was this story written for its present position in the book of 1 Esdras? It has a clear beginning and ending, and no connections with the material surrounding it, and is an entirely different kind of literature from the rest of 1 Esdras (Talshir 1999, 58–59). Bird emphasizes "Hellenistic characteristics" (143–44), and suggests that the final element, "Truth," was added to "religionize a philosophical discussion" (145). Finally, Stacy Davis strongly challenges the values of the story as once again seeing women as "powerful only insofar as they can manipulate men" (201) and furthermore notes feminist critique of this story beginning already with Mary Wollstonecraft in 1792 (Davis, 201; cf. Schuller, 236).

▌THE TEXT IN CONTEMPORARY DISCUSSION

"Strength" is understood as closely related to the emperor's power of privilege. The argument for wine centers on how wine makes one forget their lowly state and ignore their proper place! A person might "forget kings and satraps," and "talk in talents" (comparing money to words). The second argues for the importance of the king himself, but the argument is entirely centered on the violent power of the ruler to make war. Zerubbabel's answer is the height of irony. Because men do all manner of things to please women, they are considered even more powerful than the king himself. But then, out of the blue, Zerubbabel shocks the reader with a direct reference to the sexual enslavement of the emperor to his concubine—who is even named! Zerubbabel's courageous challenge to the king is reminiscent of Nathan's challenge to David, and even more, to Daniel's laughter—whose name means *laughter*—at Nebuchadnezzar for believing that an idol consumed food (the story of Bel). In short, Zerubbabel is mocking the ruler of the world. Zerubbabel then rounds on the king with a fourth power—the God of Truth! That God and truth are seen together is clear from the close association between the creator and truth in verses 33-41. Bird certainly understates when he wonders if this tale reflects "Deuteronomistic misgivings about Kings" (162).

1 Esdras 5:1-46: The List of Returnees

◼ THE TEXT IN ITS ANCIENT CONTEXT

This is another copy of the famous "Golah List" ("List of Exiles") that also appears in both Ezra 2 and Nehemiah 7. Leaders are named first, followed by very large "families" named for either an ancestor or a village/town name. This is followed by priests, Levites, and temple servants, and then an interesting series of references to certain groups that could not establish their lineage, suggesting that there was some controversy surrounding who is legitimately to be included in this roll.

◼ THE TEXT IN THE INTERPRETIVE TRADITION

There has been considerable controversy about what this list actually intends to portray—a census of the "true Israel" living in Judah at a particular time? A utopian list of the number of people who returned with Zerubbabel in a kind of "exodus" entourage heading back to the land? The large numbers in the first section (families and villagers) furthermore raise questions about what is actually being enumerated here since the numbers seem too large for simple "families." Klein (1643) suggests that the list may have been intended to show that the community is composed almost entirely of returnees, which he notes does "not conform to historical fact."

◼ THE TEXT IN CONTEMPORARY DISCUSSION

Official lists of population always serve an authoritarian goal (cf. 2 Samuel 24) because lists are intended to exclude as much as include—as the controversies around some of the members clearly state. Census information is power, and control. Often the powerful want lists to control financial assistance provided by the state (e.g., carefully excluding people from tribal/indigenous membership [even "authenticity"] in countries that conquered an indigenous people for their land, sorting "legal" from "illegal," and thus "legitimate," etc.). If the people can be enticed into fighting among themselves, all the better for the powerful. In short, we seriously mistake the significance of this list if we do not read it in the context of the interference and harassment by the Persian administration.

1 Esdras 5:47-73: Temple Building

■ THE TEXT IN ITS ANCIENT CONTEXT

The text returns to the narrative provided in Ezra about the beginnings of the building of the temple. Notable in this discussion is the local opposition. Although it is implied that some of the "people of the land" joined in, the force of the text seems to be aimed at excluding those whose offer to help was considered interference. In response, then, the local officials write their protests to the emperor, which temporarily halts the work. Having introduced the story of the three youths, the reason for another work stoppage seems awkward here, but it is forced on the editor by the materials borrowed from Ezra-Nehemiah.

■ THE TEXT IN THE INTERPRETIVE TRADITION

As Talshir notes (2001, 320–21), 1 Esdras expands on the opposition activities that led to a halt of the building project—referring to "cutting off supplies," "hindering the building," "plots and demagoguery and uprisings"—and implies that this opposition activity prevented progress throughout the reign of Cyrus and into the reign of Darius (completely skipping the reign of Cambyses). Most of this detail is not found in Ezra. Resumption of worship at the altar, suggests Myers (70), reflects the "zeal" of the returned community.

■ THE TEXT IN CONTEMPORARY DISCUSSION

The exclusionary practices of the group from the Diaspora are particularly notable. The motivation for their opposition is not developed, leaving readers to presume that the locals were not serious in their original offer to help. But it is the Judean community whose members have planted the seeds of conflict here. This will lead directly to the mixed-marriage crisis, another form of the conflict over who is the "true Judean" in this context. Isaiah 56 and the story of Ruth both attest to the continued debates about who is an acceptable member of the "inner circle," the "legitimate community." Infighting among indigenous peoples is a sad legacy of imperial disappropriation.

1 Esdras 6:1-34: Darius Commands the Temple's Completion

■ THE TEXT IN ITS ANCIENT CONTEXT

Although 1 Esdras usually follows the *Vorlage* of Ezra-Nehemiah closely, it is interesting that the differences tend to favor the Persian officials. Their inquiries about the building of the temple in Ezra seem gruff and official, whereas in 1 Esdras their questions are rendered a bit more gracious (see 6:5). Still, names are taken (another list), and inquiries are made. When the Judean leaders claim that they have royal permission from Cyrus, Darius not only confirms this but also adds additional threats to any who would further interfere.

▌The Text in the Interpretive Tradition

Talshir (2001) notes that Zerubbabel's name is added to the discussion with Persian officials, but further notes the awkward inconsistencies of following the Ezra material too closely. According the story of the three youths, it was Zerubbabel's cleverness that earned Darius's favor, and Zerubbabel then had full support for rebuilding Jerusalem and the temple. Here, however, Darius knows nothing of the building until a search is made in the archive. This seems to be further indication that the story of the three youths was rather roughly forced into place, and the editor then strangely does not correct the other textual problems created by aligning closely with the older Ezra-Nehemiah materials.

▌The Text in Contemporary Discussion

Is this apparent contradiction a real problem? Has Darius forgotten his clever Jewish advisor so quickly? If so, then there are dramatic parallels with the image of absentminded Ptolemy in 3 Maccabees, who constantly forgets his previous decisions with regard to the Jews in his realm, or even with the frequent *re*introductions of Daniel in Daniel 1–6. Are we to be reminded of the inconsistency, the untrustworthiness, and the sheer fickle nature of imperial rule?

1 Esdras 7:1-15: Passover and Purification

▌The Text in Its Ancient Context

After the successful completion of the temple, chapter 7 narrates a return to normal. The Passover is being celebrated again, precisely where we began the narrative of 1 Esdras. There is a sense, therefore, that the community has restored the righteousness (if not power) of Josiah. Although the hints of opposition to local peoples remain, the image suggests a community in restoration. The addition of the narratives about Ezra in chapters 8 and 9, however, suggests that this is a calm before another storm.

▌The Text in the Interpretive Tradition

Most commentators note the significance of the temple in later biblical texts, and here also "glorification" of the temple is "characteristic" of 1 Esdras (Myers, 78–79; Bird, 17). Further, R. J. Coggins notes that the total absence of Nehemiah glorifies Ezra himself (55). Temple personnel, and especially the high priest, of course, rise to a central role in Jewish life after the exile, well into the Roman period. Japhet, however, also notes the abbreviated nature of the celebrations in comparison to Ezra and Chronicles, particularly noting the absence of singing or music, which was a "hallmark of Second Temple ceremonies" (764). Bird notes the importance of referring to the twelve tribes in 7:1-9, implying the restoration of the whole of Israel, which is further emphasized by the otherwise odd reference to "Assyria"—that is, the restoration includes those carried away by Assyria in 722 BCE from the north (Bird, 226, 230).

■ THE TEXT IN CONTEMPORARY DISCUSSION

The transformation here is notable. The Hebrew people are passing from a small nation (among many other "nations" and "peoples" in the immediate area) to a minority in a larger imperial context. Similar to many modern experiences of minorities, the changed status heightens tension over issues of identity, resources, and relations to other peoples.

1 Esdras 8:1-96: Under Persian Rule

■ THE TEXT IN ITS ANCIENT CONTEXT

Once again, the text emphasizes an unusually positive relation with the Persian rulers (8:4) when compared to Ezra-Nehemiah (also Myers, 79), hinted at by small changes (e.g., not so many punishments threatened in 8:24, friendly relations with the king in 8:25-27). Indeed, in 8:80-81, the Persians give food and help, which is associated with the "favor" of the king, and not the steadfast love of God "before the King" (Ezra 7:28). Furthermore, there are not even threats from ambushes in 1 Esdras, suggesting limited Persian authority (cf. Ezra 8:31).

■ THE TEXT IN THE INTERPRETIVE TRADITION

The varied discussions about the heritage, descent, and thus status of the group accompanying Ezra back to Palestine is a matter of frequent analysis (Coggins, 60–65; Myers, 96–97; "his caravan . . . representative of the whole people," Japhet, 765). After a long, more positive introduction, the text turns on the issue of mixed marriage and Ezra's horrified response (Smith-Christopher). What is less often noted in the many discussions of these events, however, is the text's use of ancient ethnic markers to recall Joshua's conquests (8:69), implying previous rights to land as well as traditional hatreds (e.g., Perizzites, Jebusites, Canaanites; see Josh. 12:8).

■ THE TEXT IN CONTEMPORARY DISCUSSION

Who is the "authentic" member of a community? Divisions created by apportionment of economic benefits is a tactic with a long legacy in colonialism. Communal tensions are exploited by foreign powers to "divide and conquer": tempers flare, attitudes harden, and communities divide into factions. The Maori of New Zealand were deftly divided into allies and opposition, as was India under British occupation, and Native American tribal groups of the eastern United States in the seventeenth and eighteenth centuries, and even the Japanese American internees during the Second World War.

1 Esdras 9:1-55: Restoring the People

■ THE TEXT IN ITS ANCIENT CONTEXT

The final "purification" of the community involves the infamous dismissal of foreign wives. When Ezra is informed of the defilement of the "holy seed" (Ezra 9:2), he launches into one of the many examples of the postexilic prayer form typically identified as "the penitential prayer" (1 Kings 8; Daniel 9; Ezra 9; Nehemiah 9; Baruch; see Werline). This confessional prayer form emphasizes communal guilt from the past as well as the present, and pleads for God's help in the present. The placement of this episode as the final chapter of 1 Esdras tends to emphasize that the community is now fully prepared to face the future—its community rebuilt, at home, and purified. Bird comments that after rebuilding the shrine, rebuilding the people "must accordingly follow" (231).

■ THE TEXT IN THE INTERPRETIVE TRADITION

Coggins refers to chapter 9 as "a particularly lame conclusion" (70), but Myers and Bird have both tried to take the issue of mixed marriage seriously as a social and religious threat (Myers, 98; Bird, 257, who even refers to foreign "contamination" [!], 272). Similarly, Japhet (766) notes that the significance of the mixed-marriage crisis is magnified in comparison to Ezra-Nehemiah: "The implication is self-evident: the only way for Israel to atone for this sin is to purify themselves, to detach themselves completely . . . from the peoples of the land" (767). Much has been made of the notion that law is given the "last word" in 1 Esdras—a law given to the redeemed and purified, and not in order to redeem or purity them (Bird, 233).

■ THE TEXT IN CONTEMPORARY DISCUSSION

First Esdras 9 ultimately shows a community unified by its own moral traditions, but at the horrific price of a rejection of "the other"—for example, minorities, different ethnicities, different people. "Unity" (like "patriotism") is too often achieved by vilifying minorities or outsiders (Bird, 256, even refers to "traditional enemies," a sobering phrase). The caution here, however, is that it is a moral law backed up by the authority of a state, and indeed the threat of violence from that state. Since Constantine's authorization of Christianity, the church has too often succumbed to the temptation of backing its authority with the use of power and violence. Indeed, both Islam and Judaism similarly face temptations of mixing religion and power. First Esdras is thus a cautionary tale for virtually all modern readers, and commentators have been altogether too sanguine about its portrayal of national and/or religious revival.

Works Cited

Bird, Michael F. 2012. *1 Esdras: Introduction and Commentary on the Greek Text in Codex Vaticanus.* Septuagint Commentary Series. Leiden: Brill.

Coggins, R. J. 1979. *The First and Second Books of Esdras.* CBC. Cambridge: Cambridge University Press.

Davis, Stacy. "1 Esdras." In *The People's Companion to the Bible*, edited by C. P. DeYoung, W. Gafney, L. A. Guardiola-Saenz, G. Tinker, and F. M. Yamada, 200–201. Minneapolis: Fortress Press.

Japhet, Sara. 2001. "1 Esdras." In *The Oxford Bible Commentary*, edited by John Barton and John Muddiman, 751–70. New York: Oxford University Press.

Klein, Ralph. 2003. "1 Esdras." In *The New Interpreter's Study Bible*, edited by Walter J. Harrelson, 1633–54. Nashville: Abingdon.

Myers, Jacob. 1974. *I and II Esdras: Introduction, Translation and Commentary.* AB. New York: Doubleday.

Schuller, Eileen. 1992. "The Apocrypha." In *The Women's Bible Commentary*, edited by Carol A. Newsom and Sharon H. Ringe, 234–43. Louisville: Westminster John Knox.

Smith-Christopher, Daniel. 1996. "Between Ezra and Isaiah: Exclusion, Transformation, and Inclusion of the 'Foreigner' in Post-Exilic Biblical Theology." In *Ethnicity and the Bible*, edited by Mark Brett, 117–42. Leiden: Brill.

Talshir, Zipora. 1999. *I Esdras: From Origin to Translation*. Atlanta: Society of Biblical Literature.

———. 2001. *1 Esdras: A Text Critical Commentary* [Septuagint and Cognate Studies 50]. Atlanta: Scholars Press.

Werline, Rodney A. 1998. *Penitential Prayer in Second Temple Judaism: The Development of a Religious Institution*. Atlanta: Scholars Press.

Prayer of Manasseh

Christopher Frechette

Introduction

Manasseh ruled Judah from either 698 or 687 until 642 BCE, and the accounts of his reign in both 2 Kings 21 and in 2 Chronicles 33 condemn him for causing Israel to do more evil than any of the other nations had done. Of the two accounts, only the former cites his offenses as the cause of the destruction of Jerusalem by the Babylonians in 586 BCE, and only the latter tells of the king's repentance; it describes how God has Manasseh taken captive to Babylon by the Assyrians because of his idolatry; once there, the king humbles himself and entreats God, who hears his prayer and restores him to rule in Jerusalem, where he then corrects his prior idolatry by enacting cultic reforms. The narrative does not provide the wording of the king's prayer. Yet close parallels between the Prayer of Manasseh and the situation described in the narrative suggest that this text was understood to be that wording, and from its earliest attestations the prayer bears a superscription attributing it to Manasseh.

The earliest known versions of the Prayer of Manasseh are in Syriac and Greek, but it is uncertain whether either of these, or perhaps an unknown Hebrew or Aramaic version, represents the original. The earliest Hebrew version, preserved in a tenth-century manuscript from the Cairo Genizah document, is considered a translation (Davila). The prayer is included in the following ancient texts: the odes appended to the Psalter in versions of the LXX from as early as the fifth century CE; an appendix to some Syriac copies of Chronicles; and a conflation of the two biblical accounts of the reign of Manasseh found in two Christian handbooks from the third–fourth centuries CE: the *Didascalia* (ch. 7) and the *Apostolic Constitutions* (2.22). The prayer was likely composed between the second century BCE and the third century CE. Its central theme, that God allows grievous sinners to repent, is at home in both Christianity and Judaism, and although Jewish authorship of the prayer cannot be ruled out, it may provisionally be considered a Christian work (Davila).

Some evidence suggests that the prayer was composed for inclusion in the Christian handbooks (Nickelsburg). The prayer appears in the Eastern Orthodox canon and in modern editions of the LXX, but Jewish, Protestant, and Catholic canons do not include it.

■ THE TEXT IN ITS ANCIENT CONTEXT

While sharing several elements with Psalm 51, which is the most elaborate treatment of repentance among biblical psalms of an individual, the Prayer of Manasseh presents God's capacity to forgive in even more emphatic terms. Both prayers are attributed to a king, but the contrast is dramatic: for Psalm 51, it is Israel's archetypal king, David; for the Prayer of Manasseh, it is the archvillain of Israel's kings. The Prayer of Manasseh begins by addressing God as "Lord almighty, God of our ancestors, of Abraham and Isaac and Jacob and of their righteous offspring," and as the Creator who has mastery over chaos, symbolized by "sea" and "abyss" (vv. 1-3). Assuming the ancient worldview that sees transgressions against God as violations of divinely established social harmony, the prayer describes God's capacity to restore that order by destroying those who commit such violations (vv. 4-5). Yet it affirms that God is merciful beyond measure and has established an alternative means of restoring order: repentance (vv. 6-7). Claiming access to that repentance, the speaker confesses being an unworthy sinner, whose sins are "more numerous than the sands of the sea," and who consequently is weighed down with "many an iron shackle" (vv. 8-12). The speaker then asks to be forgiven and preserved from eternal punishment by God, here named not as "God of the righteous" but as "God of those who repent" (v. 13). In support of this petition, the speaker declares that in God's forgiving the undeserving speaker, the goodness of God will become manifest in him, who will in turn praise God continually, as do all the heavenly host (vv. 14-15).

Like a number of so-called penitential prayers from early Judaism, for example, Ezra 9, the Prayer of Manasseh would have given those who prayed it a voice with which to appeal to God as one who receives and responds mercifully to those who repent. Moreover, its implied context in the narrative of 2 Chronicles affirms that God indeed responds mercifully to such prayers. Although in many "penitential prayers" the people speak as a corporate body linked to prior generations in their transgressions, it is an individual taking responsibility for personal guilt who speaks here; the significance of this difference deserves further investigation (Newman).

■ THE TEXT IN THE INTERPRETIVE TRADITION

The Prayer of Manasseh had considerable influence in early Christianity but is much less conspicuous in Jewish traditions. The ancient Christian handbooks cited above place it within an exhortation to bishops to enact well their ministry of healing and reconciling of the faithful. Thomas Aquinas quoted lines 6-7a of the prayer in arguing that the sacrament of penance could be repeated (*Summa Theologiae* 3 q. 84 a. 10). The prayer is cited by several patristic authors in exhortations to penitence, and there is abundant evidence for its liturgical usage during the patristic period from the fifth century onward; it is included, for instance, in the liturgy of Jerusalem and in the Coptic, Ethiopian, and Mozarabic Psalters (Rose). However, it was not included among the canticles in the Roman office (1911) or the Liturgy of the Hours (1971). Some of the earliest printed German Bibles include the prayer at the end of 2 Chronicles, and although Martin Luther considered it apocryphal in his Bible, he circulated it in a variety of contexts (Bream).

■ THE TEXT IN CONTEMPORARY DISCUSSION

Perhaps the greatest challenges that the Prayer of Manasseh poses for modern readers concern its depictions of God's capacity to destroy sinners in anger and of the speaker's self-abasement. However, interpreting such portrayals within their cultural context and in light of the prayer as a whole can disabuse the reader of the assumption that this prayer addresses a misanthropic God who requires that sinful people abandon their dignity in order to gain forgiveness. Here, as in many biblical and other ancient Near Eastern texts, divine anger is portrayed as erupting in response to violations of the social harmony intended by God, which includes all aspects of human behavior. Since, in the biblical view, a key purpose for which God established that harmony is to provide a place in which people can thrive in relationship to God, portraying God as angry over violations of that harmony actually affirms God's fundamental care for humanity. At the same time, the prayer accents not the angry destruction of the sinner but repentance and forgiveness, as being the preferred means by which God allows order to be restored after it has been violated. The speaker's claims of unworthiness and hyperbolic confessions of sin need not be taken as reflections of the speaker's value in an objective sense. In their ancient Near Eastern context, such expressions constituted an affective mode of speaking understood to convey sincerity.

Works Cited

Bream, Howard N. 1986. "Manasseh and His Prayer." *Lutheran Theological Seminary Bulletin* 66 no. 4:5–47.

Charlesworth, James H. 1983–1985. "Prayer of Manasseh." In *The Old Testament Pseudepigrapha*, edited by James H. Charlesworth, 625–37. Garden City, NY: Doubleday.

Davila, James R. 2007. "Is the Prayer of Manasseh a Jewish Work?" In *Heavenly Tablets: Interpretation, Identity and Tradition in Ancient Judaism*, edited by Lynn. R. LiDonnici and Andrea Lieber, 75–85. Leiden: Brill.

Newman, Judith H. 2007. "Form and Function in the Prayer of Manasseh." In *Seeking the Favor of God*. Vol. 2, *The Development of Penitential Prayer in Second Temple Judaism*, edited by Mark J. Boda, Daniel K. Falk, and Rodney Alan Werline, 105–25. Atlanta: Society of Biblical Literature.

Nickelsburg, George W. E. 2001. "Prayer of Manasseh." In *The Oxford Bible Commentary*, edited by John Barton and John Muddiman, 770–73. New York: Oxford University Press.

Rose, Andre. 1988. "La prière d'Azarias (Dan 3.26–45) et le cantique de Manassé dans la tradition chrétienne et dans la liturgie." In *Liturgie, conversion et vie monastique: Conférences Saint-Serge, XXXVe semaine d'études liturgiques, Paris, 28 juin–1er juillet 1988*, edited by Achille M. Triacca and Alessandro Pistoia, 293–305. Rome: C.L.V. Edizioni liturgiche, 1989.

PSALM 151

Christopher Frechette

Introduction

Psalm 151 comes to us in shorter and longer versions, both of which divide into two parts, each narrating events of David's youth (1 Samuel 16–17). Part A celebrates David, who began by making music and tending flocks, but whom God anointed as ruler. Part B recounts the young David's legendary victory over the Philistine warrior. Among the ancient versions of this psalm, the longer is preserved only in the Hebrew text of the *Great Psalms Scroll* from Qumran, in which part B is separated from part A by a superscription. The LXX contains the shorter version, on which the Syriac, Latin, and Ethiopic are dependent. This version combines in a single unit part A, which is much shorter (twelve phrases) than the Hebrew (twenty-eight phrases), with part B (five phrases) in a single psalm. That the Hebrew manuscript of part B is missing about eight lines (each with a capacity for three or four phrases) after the initial two phrases indicates that this part would have consisted of much more text. Both versions were likely based on a prior Hebrew version dating to before 200 BCE. It seems probable that even though the LXX version may have left out some parts of that prior version, some significant portions of the Hebrew were likely expansions on it (Smith).

The Jewish, Protestant, and Roman Catholic canons do not include Psalm 151. Both the LXX and the *Great Psalms Scroll* position Psalm 151 at the very end of the collection of psalms, and its superscription in the LXX identifies it as "outside the enumeration" of the Psalter. With a more flexible understanding of canonicity than in the West (Pentiuc), Eastern Orthodox Bibles include it but with a lesser level of canonicity than the 150 psalms, following Athanasius's consideration that it is not *kanonizomenōn* ("canonized") but rather *anaginoskomenon* ("readable").

◼ THE TEXT IN ITS ANCIENT CONTEXT

The shorter version of Psalm 151 highlights the wonder of how God selected David, a youth of humble origins, to defeat the Philistine and thereby remove the shame experienced by Israel. Such an emphasis would have encouraged the Jewish people living under a succession of empires with a message that God can choose the humble to remove the shame brought about by foreign powers. The LXX superscription identifies this psalm as an "afterword" to the Psalter that serves to attribute the entire Psalter to the David, God's unlikely chosen warrior, and so to frame it as prayers of resistance (Zenger).

In the longer version, part A conveys the reciprocal character of the relationship between David and God. After describing David's making of pipe and lyre, the Hebrew includes eight phrases in which David honors God, none of which are present in the Greek. This section provides a counterpart to the subsequent section that tells of God's hearing David and then, in eight phrases, selecting and anointing him as ruler over God's people. Thus the longer version emphasizes that it is David's honoring of God, particularly through music, that provides the key to understanding God's honoring of David by selecting him to be Israel's archetypal king. Portraying God as taking notice of David's musical worship and responding favorably to it would have encouraged Jews living under empire to hold fast to their own liturgical practices under cultural pressures to abandon them. Furthermore, elaborating on the ideal king's honoring of God makes clear that the authority to rule remains fundamentally grounded in the ruler's subordination to God. Portraying the king exercising power as the humble and conscientious servant of the deity is well attested among ancient Near Eastern cultures; although we may see in such portrayals a device for legitimating rulers who presided over hegemonic institutions, such texts could also serve to bolster an expectation that rulers exercise authority justly.

◼ THE TEXT IN THE INTERPRETIVE TRADITION

Psalm 151 has enjoyed a place in Coptic, Armenian, and Ethiopian liturgy. The Coptic liturgy employs it on the night of Holy Saturday; the Armenian liturgy, at Pentecost. In the Ethiopian liturgy, it is read on the night of Good Friday, and parts of it occur in the ritual for the enthronement of the king. Although Psalm 151 is printed in some Eastern Orthodox liturgical books, currently it is with the understanding that it not be read during liturgies.

◼ THE TEXT IN CONTEMPORARY DISCUSSION

The emphasis of the psalm's longer version on reciprocal relationship between God and ruler underscores the fundamental tenet that those who claim divine authority for the exercise of power must act within proper relationship to God. This version thus serves to confront tendencies among those who exercise such power to act unjustly or in self-interest. The prominence given to honoring God through music affirms the value of liturgical worship for cultivating such proper relationship with God.

Both versions emphasize David's restoring Israel's dignity by killing the Philistine, who had not only threatened violence against Israel but also further offended the people's dignity with his cursing. Two distinctions are helpful to assist contemporary readers in understanding the role of killing in this text. First, the central concern is God's care for the dignity of the people, and killing the offender is a means employed to restore it. The association between parts A and B, present in both versions, makes clear that the restoration of dignity results from God's empowering the humble David, who was committed to proper relationship with God. Second, it is important to distinguish between taking the account as a model for behavior and employing it for its capacity to convey symbolically and dramatically God's concern for the dignity of those who are violated (Frechette). David effectively confronts the offender by killing him, and according to the ancient worldview, killing in this situation was legitimate. However, modern psychology reveals that the ability of those who have been violated to reclaim their dignity does not depend on the fate of the perpetrator. Yet, being violated can cement within a person perceptions of lack of dignity and of abandonment by God in such an emotionally intense way that these perceptions can prove resistant to reinterpretation. As a phase in one's recovery process from such violation and without harming anyone, reading dramatic narratives such as Ps. 18:1-19, in which God confronts the offender, can be helpful as a symbolic means of asserting that God judges the violation to be wrong and upholds the victim's dignity. The present psalm can support such a symbolic confrontation of violations against human dignity.

Works Cited

Frechette, Christopher G. 2014. "Destroying the Internalized Perpetrator: A Healing Function of the Violent Language against Enemies in the Psalms." In *Trauma and Traumatization in Individual and Collective Dimensions: Insights from Biblical Studies and Beyond*, edited by Becker, Jan Dochhorn, and Else K. Holt. Studia Aarhusiana Neotestamentica 2. Göttingen: Vandenhoeck & Ruprecht.

"Introduction au psaume 151." 2011. No author cited. In *La Bible: Notes intégrale, traduction oecuménique, TOB*, 2065–66. 12th ed. Paris: Éditions du Cerf.

Pentiuc, Eugen J. 2014. *The Old Testament in Eastern Orthodox Tradition*. New York: Oxford University Press.

Smith, Mark S. 1997. "How to Write a Poem: The Case of Psalm 151A (11QPs^a 28.3–12)." In *The Hebrew of the Dead Sea Scrolls and Ben Sira: Proceedings of a Symposium Held at Leiden University, 11–14 December 1995*, edited by T. Muraoka and J. Elwolde, 182–208. Leiden: Brill.

Zenger, Erich. 2011. "Excursus: Psalm 151 LXX as Afterword to the Septuagint Psalter." In Frank-Lothar Hossfeld and Erich Zenger, *Psalms 3: A Commentary on Psalms 101–150*, 665–69. Translated by Linda Maloney. Hermeneia. Minneapolis: Fortress Press.

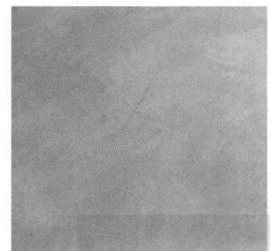

3 MACCABEES

Introduction

The book 3 Maccabees is included as a canonical work in Orthodox and Armenian collections of Scripture, and is considered noncanonical in Protestant and Catholic traditions. Originally composed in Greek by an anonymous Jewish writer living in Alexandria sometime after the Battle of Raphia (217 BCE), and perhaps as late as the reign of the Roman emperor Caligula (37–41 CE), 3 Maccabees constitutes three main episodes involving the Ptolemy-Seleucid conflict and persecution of the Jews of Alexandria.

The title of the work is something of a misnomer, since the narrative of 3 Maccabees does not involve any members of the Hasmonean family and its historical setting is well before the Maccabean Revolt (167–164 BCE). Nevertheless, it was grouped with the books of 1 and 2 Maccabees in early manuscripts, and presents a plot line that is thematically similar to them. In genre, it can be compared to other Maccabean literature, the books of Esther and Daniel, and the *Letter of Aristeas*, especially in the way that it presents an account of royal conflict and Jewish persecution with a degree of historical verisimilitude.

The literary style of 3 Maccabees, which has been described as "bombastic" and "pretentious," fits within the range of Hellenistic Jewish writings of the period (Croy, xiii–xiv). While the author employs some conventions of Greek style in the composition, he appears less interested in style than in religious and nationalistic propagandizing.

Scholars generally agree that the beginning of the work is missing. The extant version of 3 Maccabees opens abruptly with an account of the Battle of Raphia between Antiochus III and Ptolemy IV Philopator, moves to a narrative about the latter's persecution of the Jews of Alexandria, and ends with a story about a gruesome plot to slaughter apostate Jews and purify those who have remained faithful to the covenant community. The work as a whole is intended to uphold the authority of torah and the sacredness of the Jerusalem temple—either in the face of an immediate persecution or in memory of one—and to affirm the status of Israel as the covenant people. The author's theology shows no apparent signs of interaction with the apocalyptic eschatology and messianic hope then current in Palestine (and, to a lesser extent, in the Diaspora), advocating instead for a traditionally Deuteronomic understanding of divine favor and retribution.

3 Maccabees 1:1—2:24: Historical Prologue

▪ THE TEXT IN ITS ANCIENT CONTEXT

Third Maccabees begins with a terse account of the Battle of Raphia, a confrontation between Ptolemy IV Philopator and Antiochus III ("the Great") in 217 BCE. This event is recorded also by Polybius (*Histories* 5), whose lengthier account accords with the general shape and details of 3 Macc. 1:1—2:24. The perspective of the author of 3 Maccabees differs from that of the ancient Roman historian; for the former, the historical details are the raw materials out of which he fashions a narrative that is not primarily a work of historiography, but one that is polemical and apologetic at its core, arguing that Jews should not trade their ancestral faith for acceptance in Greco-Roman societies.

The characters in this account are for the most part known from other sources: Philopator, Antiochus, Arsinoë, Dositheos son of Drimylus, and Theodotus—all of these figure into Polybius's rendering of the episode, and some are mentioned by Josephus. The author of 3 Maccabees, however, is interested in these characters primarily insofar as their roles can be manipulated to serve his purposes. The victory of Philopator over Antiochus, for example, provides the occasion for the Ptolemaic king to become "eager" to visit the Jews in Jerusalem and to worship their "faithful" God (see below). Dositheos (whose existence is also likely attested in *P. Hibeh* 90) is introduced as one of the "apostate" Jews who, as a group, are scorned and executed in the conclusion to the work.

The rest of the prologue is taken up by an account of Philopator's attempt to enter the Jerusalem temple. Here the author juxtaposes the pious and humble Jews with the arrogant, haughty king, deploying maudlin appeals to emotion in order to underline the importance of maintaining the covenant obligations. This episode may reflect a real event (it is recorded elsewhere that Philopator visited other sacred sites of Coele-Syria in his postvictory tours), though it is unlikely to have transpired in the way 3 Maccabees narrates it. The author is possibly drawing from a parallel story in 2 Maccabees, a story in which controversy arises out of a pagan king's desire to enter the temple (2 Macc. 3:1-40; cf. Josephus, *Ant.* 11.329–39; 2 Macc. 5:11-21; Josephus, *Ant.* 14.67–72; Philo, *Embassy* 203; Josephus, *Ant.* 18.252–309). This section concludes with a prayer by the high priest Simon II, who presided over Jerusalem during the last fifth of the third century BCE. Simon's prayer follows a series of dramatic escalations of suspense—young maidens rushing forth, mothers and nurses abandoning newborn children, and so on—serving thus as the climactic reversal of the plot's movement. Using language and structure reflecting "a type common in postexilic Judaism (Ezra 9; Nehemiah 9; Daniel 9; Bar. 1:15–3:8) that reviews salvation history and emphasizes the righteousness of God and sinfulness of Israel" (Collins, 1756), Simon's prayer brings about God's intervention in the story. According to the narrative, Philopator falls paralyzed and mute and then slinks away in defeat.

▌THE TEXT IN THE INTERPRETIVE TRADITION

Sara Raup Johnson aptly notes that scholarly interpretations of the date of 3 Maccabees fall into two main categories, each of them with consequences for how to understand the message of the work as a whole. Those who have viewed 3 Maccabees as a pre-Roman Hellenistic composition (prior to 30 BCE) have tended to "stress the possibilities for peaceful compromise found in the story," while those who ascribe it a date in the early Roman period "stress the elements in the story that depict the Jews as a persecuted minority" (Johnson, 2683). She writes that "both interpretations are possible, and ultimately readers must decide for themselves whether the text works more effectively as a model for life in a time of compromise, or life in a time of crisis and conflict." This view no doubt represents the various ways 3 Maccabees functioned for later readers attempting to navigate their own experiences of cultural difference, persecution, and assimilation, and may help to explain why this text was transmitted despite its questionable canonical status.

▌THE TEXT IN CONTEMPORARY DISCUSSION

Third Maccabees reframes historical events in order to address questions of religious identity and piety. This is a tendency found in other biblical texts, and appears to be a perennial theme in religion more broadly. While this particular passage does not figure explicitly into contemporary discussions, it represents a continually relevant problem: How is the telling of history used to shape culture and self-understanding? Should history writing be about the politics of identity, or should it strive for some more objective truth about the nature of human affairs?

A more contemporary example might be the way the history of the United States is sometimes framed as a story of moral progress and of the instantiation of "Judeo-Christian values" in national life. History then becomes the theater for a series of ideological claims that serve to shore up the identity of certain contemporary groups—often at the expense of others. One thinks, for example, of the revisionist history of evangelical author David Barton, who draws on the reconstructionist and racist theology of R. J. Rushdoony in his glorifications of the American past. Whom does this kind of historiography serve? While the overall goals of Barton and the author of 3 Maccabees are clearly very different, they share the tendency to intermix history-telling with religious propaganda.

3 Maccabees 2:25—6:15: Ptolemy IV Philopator's Persecution of the Jews

▌THE TEXT IN ITS ANCIENT CONTEXT

Philopator was apparently not adequately chastened by his experience entering the Jerusalem temple. According to 3 Maccabees, he went to Egypt and added to his nefarious deeds, most especially by setting out to restrict the Jews from worshiping at their religious sites, registering and "branding" them, and relegating them to the status of slaves (2:25-30). Alternatively, they could choose to participate in the "mysteries" of Dionysius and receive the same political rights as citizens of Greek descent. This moment in the narrative introduces the possibility that some Jews will become apostate and align themselves with the king—which is what the story as a whole attempts to circumvent (see below). These apostates thus serve as a counterexample to the kind of religious fidelity that 3 Maccabees advocates.

The registration (*laographia*) of the Jews was to include branding by fire with an image of the Dionysian ivy leaf—representing the family god of the Ptolemies—and, perhaps, the payment of a special tax (see 2 Macc. 6:7). It was not uncommon in the history of the Roman Empire for Jews to be subject to special laws and taxation (see especially the *fiscus Iudaicus* of the first century CE and following; see Josephus, *J. W.* 7.218; Suetonius, *Life of Domitian* 12.1–2; Cassius Dio, 65.7.2, 67.14.1–2), but this practice is otherwise unattested in pre-Roman Greek law.

Philopator's warning of servitude is reminiscent of the exodus story, perhaps deliberately invoking the paradigmatic account of liberation for a new time and place: Jews in Egypt threatened with slavery by a king whose aims are frustrated by divine intervention. As the narrative unfolds, the Jews are imprisoned and several chapters in this section recount the changing moods and designs of Philopator, who is presented alternately as a madman and as someone whose intentions can easily be undermined by the divine will.

This section as a whole emphasizes the various ways in which God (or "providence") frustrates the plans of Philopator to persecute the Egyptian Jews. First, the registration in the hippodrome fails for lack of time, paper, and pens. In response, Philopator issues the strange order to unleash a large number of intoxicated elephants on the Jews assembled in the hippodrome. Philopator then reverses his disposition—which, according to 3 Maccabees, is yet another instance of divine intervention-—and castigates Hermon (whose name is reminiscent of Haman, who plays a similar role in the book of Esther) for seeking to carry out the elephant plan too diligently. Another reversal by Philopator then heightens the drama, as he charges Hermon once again to execute the genocide. Here the capricious and moody character of the king perhaps intentionally plays on a trope found elsewhere in early Jewish texts: that of the mad king (see Daniel 4; *Prayer of Nabonidus* [4QPrNab]).

The episode involving drunken elephants is unlikely to have transpired exactly as described (see Josephus, *Ag. Ap.* 2.52–55, in which there is a similar scene involving not Philopator but Ptolemy Physcon). Elephants were often used in war and in games and other public performances in the Greco-Roman world. While it is highly implausible that Philopator could have actually assembled five hundred elephants, and the number simply appears to have been symbolic for a very large quantity, "the rhetorical force of the number is unmistakable: the Jews faced a calamity of mind boggling proportions" (Croy, 84). If the number of elephants was exaggerated, other sources attest that their drunkenness remains an intriguing possibility (Josephus, *Ag. Ap.* 2.53–55; 1 Macc. 6:34).

With his plans to kill the Jews foiled several times, and with those in attendance at the banquet growing unruly, Philopator additionally resolves to invade Judea and destroy the temple in Jerusalem. While he never undertook such an attempt, this notice serves to heighten the drama of the narrative and connect the current episode with earlier parts of the work. Here the text refers to Philopator as a "Phalaris in every way," invoking the image of the sixth-century-BCE ruler of Acragas (Sicily) whose name was synonymous in antiquity with savage tyranny (Polybius, *Hist.* 12.25.1–5; Diodorus Siculus, *Bib. hist.* 9.19, 13.90, 19.108; Lucian, *Phal.* 1.11–12)

At the climax of suspense, this section of 3 Maccabees concludes with an intercessory prayer by Eleazar, in which that figure calls forth Daniel and Jonah as exemplars of Jewish redemption from death by beast and the three companions in Babylon as examples of fidelity in the face of persecution and death (Daniel 3; cf. the Prayer of Azariah and the Song of the Three Young Men). The identity of this Eleazar is unknown; in most manuscripts, he is described as a "priest," though elsewhere he is simply one of "the Jews." His supplication is structurally and thematically reminiscent of the prayer of Simon II at the end of chapter 1, referencing also Israel's salvation history and God's reputation among the gentiles as reasons for his saving mercies to work once again. It is worth noting that the beginning of his prayer calls to mind a standard Jewish daily prayer known as the *Amidah*, the opening of which also appeals to the God of Abraham, Isaac, and Jacob and recounts the saving acts of God in history. The themes of the prayer align with the basic Deuteronomic sin-punishment/repentance-deliverance theology found in some biblical texts.

◼ THE TEXT IN THE INTERPRETIVE TRADITION

While some German biblical scholars aligned with the ideology of the National Socialist German Worker's Party and produced scholarship that exhibited antisemitic tendencies (see, for example, Kittel's *Theological Dictionary of the New Testament*), 3 Maccabees was not apparently used directly to support the Nazi program of Jewish extermination. Nevertheless, some of the most chilling lines from 3 Maccabees—lines that would be echoed more than two millennia later by leaders of the Nazi Party in the 1930s and 1940s—come in the decree issued by Philopator in chapter 3: "we have given an order that as soon as this letter reaches you [royal functionaries in the provinces], you are to send to us those who live among you, together with their wives and children, with abusive and harsh treatment, bound on all sides in iron chains, for an irremediable and ill-fated slaughter befitting enemies. For we have come to understand that, when these people have been punished together, the affairs of our state will be perfectly established for us in stability and the best order for time hereafter" (3 Macc. 3:25-26; translation from Croy, 13).

◼ THE TEXT IN CONTEMPORARY DISCUSSION

Perhaps the most salient aspect of this passage for contemporary reflection is the registration and marking of Jews—or any ethnic group—for "special" treatment. Third Maccabees thus represents perhaps the earliest source attesting to what will later become an enduring practice in Roman, European, and some Islamic societies, culminating in the yellow "Jude" badges of the German Third Reich in the twentieth century. This passage thus represents an opportunity for dominant groups to consider ways in which minority religious communities might be similarly "marked" and oppressed or marginalized (or perhaps the ways in which groups that "mark" themselves with outward signs of religious observance might receive different treatment from others in positions of power).

3 Maccabees 6:16—7:23: Reversal, "Conversion," Revenge, and Homecoming

■ THE TEXT IN ITS ANCIENT CONTEXT

King Philopator finally arrives at the hippodrome to witness the spectacle he has ordered, and his appearance provokes an outcry of terror on the part of the captive Jews. But suddenly angels of the Lord intervene and the elephants "forget" their mission (because of their inebriation? or because of the terrifying angels?), thus mirroring the amnesiac mania of the king in all his earlier reversals. The angels represent a common theme in early Jewish—especially apocalyptic—literature of the Hellenistic era, namely, that God's redemptive plans are brought about by the work of heavenly intermediaries. The fact that these particular angels remain invisible to the assembled Jews is striking, leading at least one interpreter (Grotius) to suggest that "God did not want the Jews, who were already traumatized, to be further frightened by the angels" (Croy, 103). Here the story finds parallels in other early Jewish literature in which angels come to the rescue of Jews in heavy-hitting displays of supernatural power (see the parallel story in Josephus, *Ag. Ap.* 2.53–55; cf. 2 Macc. 3:25-29; Wis. 17:3; Herodotus, *Hist.* 6.117).

In 3 Maccabees, this reversal serves as the pivot point between Philopator's earlier forgetfulness and his present inability to remember that he himself was responsible for the situation now culminating before him. Both the king and the elephants turn on those executing the plan against the Jews, and the king is safeguarded, presumably, so that he can repent and then vindicate the Jews in their triumph. Perhaps not surprisingly—the theme is found elsewhere in biblical and early Jewish literature—the entire scenario provides the occasion for a "foreign" king to pay homage to the God of the Jews and to "confess" that he owes his own prosperity and authority to none other than Israel's God. While such a scenario is historically unlikely, it fits the propagandistic purposes of the story.

The feasting and celebrating then becomes the prerogative of the Jews, who, having barely escaped death (Hades), take the place of Philopator's previously favored guests. Only now, as if to emphasize that this is indeed a "festival of deliverance," the celebration takes place in the hippodrome itself (3 Macc. 6:31; cf. Luke 9:14). The author of 3 Maccabees apparently wishes also to commemorate the celebration of this deliverance in repeated ritual observance (cf, e.g., Esther 9:20-32; 1 Macc. 4:56; 2 Macc. 10:5-8), though there are no signs that this was ever instituted in early Jewish practice.

According to 3 Maccabees, Philopator issues a letter at this point for the Jews to take with them on their journeys home. Here the irony of the story reaches a climax: the king accuses his (former) companions of having designed the treachery against the Jews who had only ever shown "steadfast good will," and he grants the Jews safe passage on account of their standing as children of "the most high God." It is implausible that such a letter would have been written, and yet it represents an effort on the part of the author to lend verisimilitude to the story (cf., e.g., Ezra 1; 1 Macc. 8:23-30; 10:25-45; 2 Macc. 9:19-27; Gk. Esther 13:1-7). The presentation of a foreign king praising the God of Israel has parallels in other texts of the period, such as in Dan. 4:34-37.

In a dramatic denouement, the Jews who have been freed by Philopator do not depart until some final business is settled. The author of 3 Maccabees wishes to make another point—and perhaps, in the end, this is the central goal of the composition—namely, that those who previously converted or acquiesced to the king's demands ought to be put to death. In this way, the end of the work circles back toward its beginning, so that only those who steadfastly resisted the temptations of assimilation to Greek religion and society would live on to enjoy the deliverance from the hippodrome and the return to their homes. Here, then, is another dramatic irony: Philopator's "conversion" turns him against the very Jews who earlier had acquiesced to his demands. What is more, it is the faithful Jews who petition the king for the right to slaughter the apostates, and thus divine clemency is juxtaposed to human desire for retribution and purification.

◼ THE TEXT IN THE INTERPRETIVE TRADITION

While 3 Maccabees does not appear to have much of an interpretive afterlife in Jewish and Christian traditions, it attests to a theme that is prominent in contemporary and later discourse: that of apostasy. Later Jewish traditions make examples out of apostates such as Elisha ben Abuyah (*y. Hag.* 2:1), and there is epigraphic evidence that the practice of Jewish defection was not uncommon around the Mediterranean world for a long period of time (Wilson, 44–65). Stephen Wilson aptly notes that defection and/or conversion are always two sides of the same coin, but that accounts of apostasy are "generally not interested in both sides at once" but seek to assure their audiences that "leaving the fold" is a poor option (Wilson, 134).

◼ THE TEXT IN CONTEMPORARY DISCUSSION

Perhaps especially in the Hellenistic Jewish Diaspora communities (such as in Egypt), assimilation was a social and religious problem that was negotiated in various ways by different individuals and groups. Some chose to embrace Greek culture, religion, and authority, and others to resist it. Thus the question of whether and how much to assimilate was a central fact of life for Jewish people in the Hellenistic age, and it gave rise to both external and internal conflicts. While the depiction of the released captives happily slaughtering three hundred of their apostate kinfolk is surely not historically factual, it is an apt literary expression of the inherent tensions of Jewish existence during this period.

Some contemporary scholars have suggested that the conditions inviting assimilation in Hellenistic settings may be compared to those of the modern period. Elias Bickerman, for example, draws a parallel between the enticements of Hellenistic "belonging" and those of nineteenth-century European societies in which Jews left or modified their traditional practices in favor of more modern ones (see Wilson, 25). In this way, the beginnings of Reform Judaism can be seen as a response to the conditions of contemporary Western life—an attempt to align Jewish life with the ethical, intellectual, and cultural values of modernity.

Works Cited

Croy, N. Clayton. 2005. *3 Maccabees*. Leiden: Brill.

Collins, John J. 1993. "3 Maccabees." In *HarperCollins Study Bible with the Apocryphal/Deuterocanonical Books*, edited by Wayne A. Meeks, 1752–67. New York: HarperCollins.

Johnson, Sara Raup. 2013. "3 Maccabees." In *Outside the Bible: Ancient Jewish Writings Related to Scripture*, volume 3, edited by Louis H. Feldman, James L. Kugel, and Lawrence H. Schiffman. Philadelphia: Jewish Publication Society, 2681–2707.

Wilson, Stephen G. 2004. *Leaving the Fold: Apostates and Defectors in Antiquity*. Minneapolis: Fortress Press.

2 ESDRAS (4, 5, AND 6 EZRA)

Robin Darling Young

Introduction

The early second-century Jewish apocalypse called Ezra (Greek and Latin, *Esdras*) records and interprets the distress of a Jewish community probably in Roman Judea three decades after the Roman general Titus conquered the country and destroyed Jerusalem in the war of 66–71 CE. Yet, like other apocalyptic books, it claims to have been written far earlier, under prophetic inspiration. Its purported author was the Ezra who returned from Babylon in 457 BCE to build a new city and temple and to enforce Jewish law among its inhabitants, just as the biblical books of Ezra and Nehemiah report. Although that earlier Ezra was not a prophet but a scribe and priest, the apocalyptic genre transformed an ancient leader into a visionary sage and a prophet of the later Roman destruction, showing how the scribe responsible for the rebuilding of Jerusalem in the 450s BCE actually knew two destructions and two reconstructions of the city and its temple: first, he witnessed the destruction under the Neo-Assyrians; and second, he foretold its destruction under the Romans with a reconstruction promised for the near future. Cyrus financed the first rebuilding; the second did not happen in antiquity.

No traces of a Hebrew text survive, and no later Jewish literature is known to have used it. The Greek text was not quoted after Clement of Alexandria (d. c. 220 CE). A Latin version was frequently copied and quoted, and a Syriac version survived in only one manuscript. Other ancient versions—Ethiopic, Georgian, Arabic, and Coptic—probably came from the lost Greek version, and the Armenian was probably translated from the Syriac (Stone 1990).

The standard name for the original Jewish Ezra apocalypse is 4 Ezra, so enumerated because two earlier scriptural books have the title "book of Ezra." In Bibles translated into English, 4 Ezra does not appear in its original form, remaining as the long, middle section of a larger book called 2 Esdras. Second Esdras, in turn, is the expanded version of 4 Ezra; translated from Latin, it appears in the Apocrypha section of English Bibles. The reason for this expansion of 4 Ezra is conjectural; at some point before 900 CE, an unknown copyist added two later oracular texts, each having a different origin; the copyist then put them on either side of the earlier 4 Ezra, giving the title of the new, expanded version, 2 Esdras.

The book of 2 Esdras appears in modern Bibles (Protestant and Catholic) because, beginning with Ambrose (340–397), bishop of Milan, the medieval Western church considered it inspired Scripture. Jerome disagreed, calling it a "book of dreams" and omitting it from the Vulgate, but biblical manuscripts retained the work until the sixteenth century. Columbus thought it predicted that New World voyages could lead to Jerusalem and a final triumphant Crusade to retake the Holy Land. Anabaptists and other dissenters were attracted to its apocalyptic eschatology. Spanish Catholic authors used the text to justify their New World colonies.

Such European interest lasted despite Renaissance textual scholars' doubts about its authenticity. Protestant Reformers rejected it because it was not part of the Hebrew Scriptures. Because the Church of England accepted 2 Esdras and the other apocryphal biblical works of the Vulgate, the King James Version includes 2 Esdras in the Apocrypha, as does the Revised Standard Version.

In editions of the Catholic Bible from the sixteenth century, 2 Esdras also remains apocryphal. The Council of Trent, responding to Protestant criticisms of church tradition, did not include 2 Esdras in its list of canonical Scriptures but did not remove it, along with other disputed books. After Catholic scholars' debates, 2 Esdras was removed from the Sixtine Vulgate of 1590, but restored in the Clementine Vulgate (1592); it appears in the Apocrypha of the Douay-Rheims English translation of the Vulgate. Only the Slavonic Bible of the Russian Orthodox Church still contains 2 Esdras in its canon, but calls it 3 Esdras. The smaller, Jewish text of 4 Ezra, however, has been retained in Ethiopian and Armenian Bibles; although it exists in the Syriac Peshitta in one manuscript, it has long been noncanonical in that tradition. It was not included in the Septuagint, and does not appear in Greek or Eastern Orthodox Bibles. For many readers of the Bible, then, 2 Esdras is unfamiliar.

Second Esdras combines three works. Its longest part is a core of fourteen chapters containing seven distinct discourses. The title 4 Ezra emphasizes its continuity with the Jewish traditions about Ezra, beginning with the canonical book of Ezra. Its seven episodes have four conversations between the putative author, Ezra/Shealtiel and the angel Uriel, and three are visions—apocalypses—granted to the visionary Ezra, revealing the future restoration of Jerusalem by a conquering Messiah, and the return of the dispersed tribes.

The bookends of 4 Ezra are Christian works composed to adapt the Jewish work for Christian use. The first, now called 5 Ezra, dates from the second century CE. It numbers two chapters, and functions as a preface. It recounts Ezra's genealogy, and an account of his prophetic call (1:4), lists God's spurned favors to Israel and subsequent rejection, and refers to Israel as a mother who then receives new children, the "nations that hear and understand" (2:34). The second bookend of 4 Ezra is usually called 6 Ezra, and it is an appendix concerning persecution and martyrdom. It envisions a cosmic battle, the protection of the people faithful to God, and the deliverance of God's elect at the end of time; it is now believed to date from the third century. In neither bookend is there a developed Christian teaching, but the use of typology and the theme of Israel's rejection, as well as the preservation of the book in Christian circles, point toward a Christian author who has cleverly reoriented the book to Christian polemic against the Jews.

Fourth Ezra thus has been interpreted against itself by the later addition of this preface and conclusion. As the last Jewish apocalypse of its era, it was the most explicitly messianic of any Second Temple Jewish text outside apocalyptic works in the New Testament. Yet Ezra's Messiah is not like Jesus; he is a militant conqueror who fights against the enemy and then dies. The remnant of Israel preserved by that Messiah turns for preservation to renewed and augmented Scriptures. The Jewish Christians who added to 4 Ezra the two later bookends of 5 and 6 Ezra forced the original Jewish text to serve their arguments against the Jews who did not accept Jesus. They thought that the Jews' alleged failures explicitly to obey God's law and in rejecting Jesus as Messiah made them subject not to God's rescue, but to rejection. Ironically, they turned 4 Ezra into 2 Esdras, one of the earliest anti-Jewish works in the Christian tradition, turning an apocalypse conveying hope for Jewish restoration into a condemnation of the Jews and an assertion of Christian triumph.

2 Esdras 3–14 (4 Ezra): An Apocalyptic and Prophetic Tapestry

▌ THE TEXT IN ITS ANCIENT CONTEXT

In its ancient context, chapters 3–14 of 2 Esdras form an elaborate work in the prophetic-apocalyptic tradition, intermingled with elements of the earlier wisdom tradition. It dates from after 71 CE, that is, from the Roman war against, and conquest of, Judea. Like other non-Christian Jewish apocalypses from the period, such as *2 Baruch*, the *Apocalypse of Abraham*, and parts of the *Sibylline Oracles*, it represents one Jewish reaction to the event. The disastrous rebellion against Roman rule led to a brutal imperial military campaign that led to the burning of the temple, the slaughter of thousands of Jewish subjects of Rome, and the exile and/or death of many of those who had survived the battles of the five-year war. The loss of the Jewish community—its people, books, holy sites, and rituals—gives the unknown author the occasion to assume the identity of an earlier Jew who was not a prophet, but a scribe and community leader. Ezra the scribe and hereditary member of the priesthood helped lead the Jewish community that had returned from Babylon in the late fifth century BCE; thus his restoration of the community around the Second Temple and the law gave him the status of a founder of Israel in succession to Abraham, Moses, and David/Solomon. As Shealtiel, he was son of Jehoiakin king of Judah (1 Chron. 3:17) and thus a successor to Israelite royalty.

This section (4 Ezra) is constructed as a prophecy from that older, historical Ezra, who reports in the prologue (2 Esd. 3:1) that he was "troubled" in Babylon "because I [fore]saw the desolation of Zion and the wealth of those who live in Babylon." Like the contemporary book of Revelation, it makes Babylon a symbol of Rome and its rule, thus contrasting God's faithful to their brutal oppressors. The author relied on his readers to understand that he was appropriating the identity of the earlier Ezra in order to issue prophetic denunciations, as well as consolation, to the Jewish people. Ezra speaks in the first person all the way through the text; in this, he resembles not only Paul but also the visionary of the book of Revelation.

Not only the prophetic mode appears in 4 Ezra; Lamentations also inspires a long complaint about human weakness, including the presence of an "evil heart" that is present in human beings from Adam, which makes it difficult to obey the divine law. In 4 Ezra, the "angel that had been sent to me, whose name was Uriel," becomes the *angelus interpres* questioning Ezra in return, illustrating his points with parables. Uriel resembles a heavenly messenger like the angels who converse with Ezekiel, Daniel, and Zechariah, in the noncanonical book of *Enoch*, and in later rabbinic and Christian works (such as the *Shepherd* of Hermas). As one of the priestly line, Ezra thus is an example of the association of angels with priests of the temple, a relationship having to do with the offering of sacrifice. In conversing with Uriel, Ezra gains in wisdom, and thus one recent interpreter has argued that the book is a combination of wisdom-traditions and apocalyptic discourse.

The final chapter of 4 Ezra is the commissioning of the prophet as a scribe. It takes an esoteric turn: first, Ezra receives divine instructions to withdraw for forty days and commit his own visions to writing with the aid of five well-trained scribes. Ezra dismisses the people of Israel whom he was commissioned to lead with instructions to "rule over your minds and discipline your hearts" (2 Esd. 14:34). For forty days, Ezra withdraws to a field. "A voice" calls Ezra to give him a special drink, in a cup containing a liquid like water, but with the color of fire. Then "my heart poured forth understanding, and wisdom increased in my breast" (14:40). Ezra's mouth is opened and his spirit retains its memory, and five scribes sit for forty days, taking down his dictation, in letters they do not understand; they "ate their bread at night" (14:42) but spend each day writing out what Ezra dictates. In the end, "the Most High" instructs Ezra to reveal twenty-four books he wrote first to both the worthy and unworthy, but to keep the seventy written last for "the wise among your people. For in them is the spring of understanding, the fountain of wisdom, and the river of knowledge" (14:46). The genuine apocalypse of Ezra (4 Ezra) thus ends with an endorsement of secret wisdom and Ezra's ascent (Hogan 2008).

Second Esdras 3–14 (4 Ezra) has much in common with the concerns of other Jewish authors of the first century—not only with the author of *2 Baruch* but also with those of the letters, Gospels, and apocalypse of the New Testament. The "evil heart" afflicting humanity since Adam has parallels in Paul (particularly in Romans); its insistence on following the law in continuity with Mosaic injunction recalls the Gospel of Matthew; its interest in the Messiah links it with all four Gospels; and its concern for the eschaton and the restoration of Jerusalem links it with Revelation (Longenecker 1991).

■ THE TEXT IN THE INTERPRETIVE TRADITION

Second Esdras, or for that matter 4 Ezra, had a long but limited influence on the interpretive tradition of European Christianity. Clearly related to the literary compositions of prior apocalypses, some of which are in the canonical Old Testament, it also participates in the wisdom tradition as exemplified in the book of Job, and it is most closely related to the works of first-century Judaism, including the New Testament. Ezra's instruction about the small number of the saved resembles Paul's views in Galatians and Romans. His seven apocalyptic visions mirror, or perhaps inspired, those in the book of Revelation. His conversations with the archangel Uriel resemble Enoch, a book still read in the first century; over all, *2 Baruch* mirrors it. Finally, his dependence on the judgment and combat scenes in Daniel echoes themes in the Gospel of Matthew, as does his recourse to the gathering of disciples to transmit esoteric teaching. Because 4 Ezra was not preserved in the post–Second Temple Jewish tradition, it seems to resemble more closely the trajectories of early Christianity; but in the first century, Jewish and Christian worlds of discourse overlapped; therefore, a full treatment of 4 Ezra should resemble studies of the New Testament texts as Jewish literature (Najman and Young).

The early Christian tradition shows interest in the text. Fourth Ezra (in a now-lost Greek version) has been quoted by Clement of Alexandria and called "the prophet." He also seems to be quoted by Cyprian and Tertullian from the Latin text, as well as from Commodian. Ambrose of Milan quoted 4 Ezra/2 Esdras frequently, and a tradition of respect for the text developed in Spain, where it was preserved and quoted as an authority. In particular, because it refers to the presence of lost tribes in a distant land, it was taken to indicate the existence of the New World. But although such a tradition is of interest to scholars of the text, it shows only that 2 Esdras had a durable but extremely narrow authority in the Latin West; originating in an apocalyptic literary tradition, its influence remained relegated to that current in the theological tradition of the West.

▌THE TEXT IN CONTEMPORARY DISCUSSION

Although 2 Esdras holds great interest for scholars of first-century Judaism and Christianity and for those interested in medieval textual traditions and the reception of prophetic discourse in medieval and early modern Europe, it seems to have had little attraction initially for those contemporary communities that read the Old Testament. Hence, it is not often thoroughly compared with the contemporary Christian texts with which it shares so many theological points of view. This is especially true of its most thorough commentary to date (Stone 1990). Ironically, its esotericism seems to have worked to make it relatively inaccessible. Yet a consideration of 2 Esdras offers the opportunity to address the growing tradition, in the second and third centuries CE, of the hostile appropriation of Jewish Scriptures that marked the Christian community from Justin Martyr's *Dialogue with Trypho* forward. But 2 Esdras can be a resource for the appreciation of a first-century Jewish messianism centered not on Jesus of Nazareth but on the hope for the military defeat of Rome and that looked toward a renewed reverence for the Law, both as a set of books and as pattern for conduct. Thus readers of the New Testament could appreciate the text as a contemporary of and a contrast to the other first-century Jewish texts of that book.

In addition, 2 Esdras raises other questions fruitful for exploration: What is the ongoing role of prophecy and denunciation/consolation, as encouraged by the reading of this book? How is the doctrine of election received in the Christian tradition to which 2 Esdras has been joined? How does the text's conception of an "evil root" relate to the teaching of original sin, itself now as problematic as the doctrine of the end of the world articulated in the book's visions?

Following Michael Stone's massive commentary on the text, some interpreters have focused on a "psychological approach" (Hogan 2008) to Ezra 4—for instance, interpreting the woman/Zion as a symbol of the author's transformation from mourner to prophet and sage (Humphrey 1995);

or as a projection of the author's own dilemma (Daschke); a literary expression of the struggle for identity (Burkes); and the interpretation of dreams (Flannery-Dailes). Collins also emphasizes the psychological approach as an interpretation of apocalyptic (reassurance, not literal prophecy). But like Longenecker, Brandenburger, and Harnisch, Karina Martin Hogan reads 4 Ezra as a "literary representation of a theological debate external to the author, a debate between two schools of wisdom at around 100" (2012).

Second Esdras is a work of high drama containing many of the theological concerns of ancient Judaism and Christianity but posing many of the same problems to nonliteralist modern interpreters and readers, who must choose between allegorizing the texts or reducing them to curiosities.

2 Esdras 1–2; 15–16 (5–6 Ezra): Rethinking Israel's Restoration

▐ The Text in Its Ancient Context

In reinterpreting the text of 4 Ezra, the additions of 5 and 6 Ezra reflect the teachings of two separate communities that had turned away from the idea of the literal, political restoration of Israel. Extant only in the Latin tradition, these are therefore Western additions. For the author of each text, the real Messiah sent to rescue the remnant was one whom not the gentiles, and not the Jews, followed. These additions represent a thorough repudiation of 4 Ezra's conviction that some—a remnant—of the Jewish community will continue to obey the law and be vindicated at the end of Ezra's revelatory experiences. In particular, the two chapters of 5 Ezra (2 Esdras 1–2) may represent the origins of the *Improperia*, a series of antiphons and responses formerly appearing in the Good Friday liturgy in Roman Catholic and other traditions, by which Christ mourns his rejection by Israel.

Second Esdras 1–2 (5 Ezra) commences with a fictive genealogy of the prophet Ezra, and an account of his prophetic commission. There follows a series of accusations against Israel (1:5-23) gathered from earlier prophetic utterances in the canonical prophets. The remainder of the chapter asserts the rejection of Israel and the substitution of the gentiles ("the people who is to come") for Israel as the recipients of both the covenant and the promises of God. Finally, the membership in the patriarchal religion ("of Abraham, Isaac, and Jacob . . .") is transferred to "a people who is coming from the East" (1:38). Here the text may recall traditions about the Persian *magoi* recorded in the Gospel of Matthew, where the Persians stand for the future faith of the gentile kingdoms.

The second chapter of 5 Ezra (2 Esdras 2) begins with a direct, traditionally prophetic statement, "Thus says the Lord," and records that Israel no longer deserves its inclusion in the kinship group loyal to God: "Let their names be blotted from the earth because they have despised my covenant" (2:7). The kingdom of Jerusalem will be prepared for the gentiles; the promises are transferred to the gentiles; and a new law will be given from them. Finally, the chapter makes of Ezra a second Moses, brought up to Mt. Horeb, where he has a vision of the Christian martyrs and the Son of God, and is commissioned to "go and tell" his vision more widely (2:33-48).

The original context of 5 Ezra, then, was probably a community of Jewish Christians that had separated from the synagogue only recently. Because it incorporated 4 Ezra, it cherished the traditions of Second Temple Judaism, but condemned those Jews who did not think that Jesus was the Messiah, and insisted that God had transferred his care to the gentiles who were ready to inherit Jewish Scripture, adjusted to point typologically to Jesus. Thus the text brings 4 Ezra closer to the views of the book of Revelation or the Gospel of John. There is no condemnation of scribes or Pharisees, but an implicit rejection of early rabbinic endorsement of the written and oral laws (Bergren 1990).

Because 6 Ezra (2 Esdras 15–16) was meant to modify and extend the conclusion of 4 Ezra, it reinforces the apocalyptic sections of the central and original text with a series of eschatological images. God commissions Ezra in the first verses to speak "in the ears of the people the word of the prophecy . . . and cause them to be written on paper, for they are faithful and true" (2 Esd. 15:1-2). The last clause may reflect Revelation 20, and its evocation of warring nations in very general terms—Egypt, Syria, Babylon, and Asia—also echoes earlier prophetic discourse in the canonical Old Testament prophets. The rest of 6 Ezra underlines the chaos and destruction coming in the last days, illustrating the chaos of the end of the world by recounting the calamities coming upon "my people." There next will be a respite from calamity; at the conclusion of this prophecy, the author recalls God's work of creation and predicts that the God who has made human beings will know how to judge them on the Day of Judgment. Finally, the text predicts persecution of a kind that points to the end of the second century: the wrath of "a great multitude" causes persecutors to "drag some of you away and force you to eat what was sacrificed to idols" (2 Esd. 16:68). This persecution tests which of the new people of God are faithful. The ones "who keep my commandments and precepts" will be rescued from the tribulation (Bergren 1998).

▌The Text in the Interpretive Tradition

The additions of 5 and 6 Ezra signal the implicit recognition of the text's origins, among the earliest Christians who received and used the text. Since 4 Ezra clearly differed from developing Christian teachings about Jesus and the church, it needed to be altered slightly to be used in community settings—thus the Christianizing adjustments that appear, and that make Ezra a prophet of Christianity, much like John the Baptist, or like Enoch in his Christian reception.

▌The Text in Contemporary Discussion

Recent scholarly discussions of 5 and 6 Ezra have shown their function in claiming the larger text for a Christian community and its scriptural tradition. They are treated as part of 4 Ezra in discussions of the ongoing use of the text in medieval and Renaissance Christianity, but their semicanonical status limits their interest largely to scholars of Christian rewritten Scriptures (Hogan, 2008).

Since 5 and 6 Ezra (2 Esdras 1–2, 15–16) together constitute a Christian addition to the original, Jewish work ascribed to Ezra the scribe, contemporary discussion could take two directions. The first direction would separate the two additions, since they are thought to come from different time periods; the second would treat them together as part of the Christian appropriation—and in this case a hostile appropriation—of an originally Jewish work.

In the first direction, it could be observed that the first addition (5 Ezra) seems to add Christian material to an originally Jewish chapter (1), to make up an apocalyptic prediction of persecution and triumph. This first addition, written in around 200 CE, comes from an era when apocalyptic prophecy had not been marginalized in early Christianity; but the second addition, possibly composed in the third century, marginalizes prophecy and anticipates heavenly reward for those suffering distress. This direction of discussion could ask about the ongoing production of prophecy in Christianity and would be concerned with matters of authority and legitimacy in Christian communities as eschatological anticipation became embarrassing or illegitimate.

In the second line of discussion, the text could be queried as to its anti-Jewish invective. How is a Christian community to handle such invective when it appears as canonical Scripture? This approach raises questions about inspiration and mutual reprobation that, while disturbing in the present, could be a fruitful subject of discussion in a period in which discussions between Jews and Christians have become more frequent.

Works Cited

Bergren, Theodore A. 1990. *Fifth Ezra: The Text, Origin and Early History*. Atlanta: Scholars Press.

———. 1998. *Sixth Ezra: The Text and Its Origin*. New York: Oxford University Press.

Coggins, R. J., and M. A. Knibb. 1979. *The First and Second Books of Esdras*. New York: Cambridge University Press.

Michael D. Coogan, ed. *Oxford Annotated Bible*. 3rd ed. Oxford: Oxford University Press.

Hamilton, Alastair. 1999. *The Apocryphal Apocalypse: The Reception of the Second Book of Esdras (4 Ezra) from the Renaissance to the Enlightenment*. Oxford: Clarendon.

Hogan, Karina Martin. 2008. *Theologies in Conflict in 4 Ezra: Wisdom Debate and Apocalyptic Solution*. Leiden: Brill.

———. 2012. "2 Esdras." In *The Women's Bible Commentary*, edited by Carol A. Newsom, Sharon H. Ringe, and Jacqueline E. Lapsley, 370–75. 3rd ed. Louisville: Westminster John Knox.

Humphrey, Edith M. 1995. *The Ladies and the Cities: Transformation and Apocalyptic Identitiy in Joseph and Aseneth, 4 Ezra, the Apocalypse and the Shepherd of Hermas* (Journal of the Pseudepigrapha Supplement Series). Continuum International Publishing Group.

Longenecker, Bruce. 1991. *Eschatology and the Covenant: A Comparison of 4 Ezra and Romans 1–11*. Sheffield: JOST Press.

———. 1995. *2 Esdras*. Sheffield: Sheffield Academic.

Myers, Jacob M. 1974. *1 and 2 Esdras*. AB 42. Garden City, NY: Doubleday.

Najman, Hindy. 2014. *Losing the Temple and Recovering the Future: An Analysis of 4 Ezra*. Cambridge: Cambridge University Press.

Najman, Hindy, and Robin Darling Young. Forthcoming. *Fourth Ezra: A Commentary on The Syriac Text*. Berlin: de Gruyter.

Stone, Michael E. 1979. *The Armenian Version of IV Ezra*. Armenian Texts and Studies 1. Philadelphia: University of Pennsylvania Press.

———. 1990. *Fourth Ezra: A Commentary on the Book of Fourth Ezra*. Minneapolis: Fortress Press.

Stone, Michael E., and Matthias Henze. 2013. *4 Ezra and 2 Baruch: Translations, Introductions, and Notes*. Minneapolis: Fortress Press.

Thompson, Alden Lloyd. 1977. *Responsibility for Evil in the Theodicy of 1V Ezra*. Missoula, MT: Scholars Press.

4 MACCABEES

Samuel I. Thomas

Introduction

Fourth Maccabees is an early Jewish composition written in Greek and included as an appendix in some manuscripts of the Septuagint, eventually becoming canonical in the Georgian Orthodox tradition. The composition was grouped with other books about the Maccabees (Hasmoneans) despite its lack of any explicit mention of the family of Mattathias and Judas Maccabaeus; this is probably because 4 Maccabees retells much of the martyr narrative of 2 Maccabees 6–7, recasting the language and purpose of the story for a new setting under Roman rule. Given its focus on martyrs, the text played an important role in early Christian theologies of martyrdom, perhaps early enough to have a direct influence on some New Testament compositions.

The author of 4 Maccabees seems principally concerned to present Jewish torah piety as a prime vehicle for the triumph of reason over the passions, thereby reflecting a theme common to Hellenistic philosophical ethics. For this reason, among others, commentators have often dated the composition to the mid- to late first century CE, during which time the literary style and philosophical outlook of the author would fit well within its context. While both Jerome and Eusebius attribute the work to Josephus, contemporary scholars argue that the author is an unknown Diaspora Jew writing from Antioch or Alexandria.

David deSilva characterizes the literary features of 4 Maccabees as "epideictic rhetoric including elements of different genres such as encomium, sermon, diatribe" (deSilva, xxi), and the philosophical perspective reflects a relatively sophisticated awareness of Greek structures of argumentation and oratorical topics. In particular, the author draws on the form of the funeral oration in his presentation of the lives of the martyrs—a presentation that constitutes the bulk of the narrative. Despite the author's immersion in Hellenistic intellectual trends and literary forms, he advocates a life guided by traditional observance of the torah.

Fourth Maccabees is not well attested in later (rabbinic) Jewish tradition, perhaps because of its popularity among Christians by the second century CE. The only Jewish text that may show familiarity with 4 Maccabees is *Lamentations Rabbah* 1:16, which refers to the martyrdom of Miriam bat Tanhum and her sons (see 4 Macc. 5:29). In contrast, 4 Maccabees was influential in the early church, with citations or allusions in the letters of Ignatius, the *Martyrdom of Polycarp*, Origen's *Exhortation to Martyrdom*, *Perpetua and Felicity* (Eusebius, *Hist. eccl.* 5.1), *Martyrdom of Montanus and Lucius*, Tertullian's *On Patience*, and the sermons of John Chrysostom, Gregory of Nazianzus, and Ambrose of Milan. The text is also included in the Sinaiticus and Alexandrinus codexes, which serve as the basis for most modern critical editions of the Septuagint.

4 Maccabees 1:1—3:18: Introduction

▌ THE TEXT IN ITS ANCIENT CONTEXT

The author of 4 Maccabees opens his exordium with an appeal to pious reason as the "absolute master of the passions." The author informs the audience in advance that in order to demonstrate the truth of this claim, it will be necessary to know his procedural method: first, he will expound the hypothesis, and then he will prove it by recourse to a story about the moral excellence of people who died in order to uphold their faith.

The framing of the work in this way reflects the literary conventions of the time, and with specific uses of language ("most philosophical," "passions," "reason," "self-mastery," etc.) the author invokes a set of concepts common to Greek virtue ethics. This author, however, wishes to reframe the discussion of rational virtue in terms of the Jewish scriptural tradition. He both draws on schools of thought represented by the Stoics, Peripatetics, and others, and at the same time cautions that Greek "philosophy" is itself not adequate without pious adherence to torah. The author of this work avoids specific references to Greek figures or stories, and instead draws all of his examples of virtue and reason from the Jewish tradition.

In its rather lengthy introduction, 4 Maccabees provides the interpretive lens by which to understand the examples of the martyrs, whose stories constitute the main body of the work. While the author purports to define the nature of the "passions" and of "reason" in this section, he does little more than provide a catalog of their common characteristics. In any case, for this author, reason is a faculty of the mind that, along with "right thinking," leads a person to wisdom. All this is made possible by the right kind of education (*paideia*, an important term in Greek philosophical discourse), a notion that will return later in the composition in relation to the torah.

It is fitting to the period that the author attempts to integrate Jewish wisdom with Greek traditions regarding the four cardinal virtues of prudence (*phronēsis*), justice (*dikaiosynē*), courage (*andreia*), and moderation (*sōphrosynē*), claiming that torah, as the embodiment of wisdom, is the way to foster each virtue in the life of the sage (see Wisd. of Sol. 8:7; Philo, *Leg.* 1.71). Indeed, wisdom in its cardinal forms is "knowledge of divine and human matters and the causes of these," and comes from "the instruction gained from the Law" (4 Macc. 1:15-18).

According to the introduction to the work, knowledge of the law leads primarily to prudence, which is ultimately a kind of ethical restraint. As an example of this virtue, the author has recourse to David's mastery of his thirst, by which he overcame the desires of the body with "the nobility and goodness of reason" (4 Macc. 3:18). Here we find a reflection of a well-attested theme in Hellenistic literature, namely, the "mind-body" dualism found also in Philo, the letters of Paul, and elsewhere. But here, too, the author of 4 Maccabees exceeds other accounts of David's thirst (for example Josephus, *Ant.* 7.12.4) in the way he embellishes and transforms the story to suit the purposes of his argument.

■ THE TEXT IN THE INTERPRETIVE TRADITION

It is difficult to know in many cases whether the introduction to 4 Maccabees has influenced other texts and traditions of early Judaism and Christianity. Perhaps because of its marginal status in scriptural collections, 4 Maccabees as a whole has not elicited much commentary beyond late antiquity.

The author of 4 Maccabees was indebted—and made his own contribution—to the Jewish wisdom tradition of the late Second Temple period. In the introduction to the work, one may discern the influence LXX Proverbs, Ben Sira, and the Wisdom of Solomon may have had on the concept of "pious reason" in 4 Maccabees. This is especially true with respect to the development of the association between wisdom and torah (Prov. 8:22-30; Sir. 1:26; 24:23; Wis. 6:17-20; 9:9; 4 Macc. 1:16-17; 2:21-23; cf. Collins, 23–61), a development that reaches full expression in the opening lines of *Genesis Rabbah* several centuries later. In this commentary on Genesis, the rabbis make explicit the association between wisdom and torah, and deduce therefore that the torah was the blueprint for all creation.

While the direction of influence is difficult to determine, there are close affinities between 4 Macc. 1:1—3:18 and several New Testament compositions (see deSilva, xxxii–xxxviii). This is particularly evident in the Pastoral Epistles, in which self-mastery is crucial to rightly order oneself to desires and achieve piety and faith (cf., e.g., 4 Macc. 1:1, 31-32; 2:1-6; 2 Tim. 2:22; 3:6; Titus 2:12; 3:3). The explicit uses of this text in later Christianity seem limited to the passages regarding martyrdom.

■ THE TEXT IN CONTEMPORARY DISCUSSION

While the introduction to 4 Maccabees has not elicited extensive commentary in the contemporary world, it addresses certain themes that continue to be relevant today. What is the relationship between "faith" and "reason"? Is there such a thing as an appropriate demand to remain dedicated to a way of life even in the face of death? During a time of prosperity and consumerism, what might it mean to restrain "desires" in the service of wisdom and the ethically good life?

Fourth Maccabees also carries a challenge to the present age of borrowing, debts, and deficits. Drawing on LXX Deut. 15:2, 8-9, the author teaches the importance of reducing debts in order to avoid the accumulation of wealth and in favor of the well-being of the community. Fourth Maccabees thus offers "remedies against the human tendency toward greed" so that "mastery of the passions is part of the means by which justice in human relations can be secured" (deSilva, 98). In an era of a widening gulf between rich and poor—individuals and nations—it is appropriate to ask: What would the world be like if human communities took these admonitions to heart?

4 Maccabees 3:19—7:23: Antiochus IV and the Martyrdom of Eleazar the Priest

■ THE TEXT IN ITS ANCIENT CONTEXT

The narratives of the martyrs occupy most of the rest of 4 Maccabees, and serve as the "narrative demonstration" (3:19) of the author's opening argument about reason, the passions, and the life of torah observance. After an introduction (3:19—4:26), this section recounts the martyrdom of Eleazar, a story based on the presentation of this figure in 2 Maccabees.

Fourth Maccabees 3:19—4:26 reflects an adapted and stylized version of a story known from other sources, beginning with an account of the idyllic and peaceful rule of the high priest Onias III (204?–175 BCE), who was the last of the Oniad family to inherit the high priestly office (VanderKam, 188). Second Maccabees also refers to the reign of Onias III as a time of "unbroken peace," when "the laws were strictly observed because of the piety of the high priest Onias and his hatred of wickedness" (2 Macc. 3:1-3). Beginning the episode of Eleazar's martyrdom in this way serves the dramatic purposes of the author by setting up the contrast with what is to follow—political intrigue, subterfuge, and persecution.

The story of Eleazar is set during the time of the Seleucid ruler Antiochus IV Epiphanes (here mistakenly called the son rather than the brother of Seleucus IV), whose reign is well known for its persecution of Jews in Jerusalem and for creating the conditions for the Maccabean revolt. The activities of Antiochus were despised and resisted by a number of early Jewish groups and writers, including the authors of 2 Maccabees and Daniel.

The account in this section of 4 Maccabees, however, differs from 2 Maccabees in some important details. For example, 2 Maccabees reports that it was one Heliodorus—and not Apollonius—who attempted to seize funds from the temple treasury (2 Macc. 3:7-8; cf. 3 Macc. 1:8—2:24), a discrepancy that may derive from the fact that 4 Maccabees is interested more in the mechanics of his "narrative demonstration" than in historically accurate details (deSilva, 116). In any case, a common theme in the "temple-robbing" narratives in early Jewish literature is the drubbing of the temple invader followed by his supplication according to standard Jewish forms of prayer.

This story revolves around a crucial question for Jews of the third and second centuries BCE: Embrace Hellenism or reject and resist it? Like other writers dealing with this period in Jewish history, the author of 4 Maccabees uses particular characters to represent, on the one hand, advocates of the appropriation of Greek culture into Judaism of the period (e.g., the Simon of 4 Macc. 4:1, Jason the High Priest, Antiochus IV) and, on the other, those who resisted the incursions of Hellenism for the sake of tradition and piety (e.g., Onias III, the Maccabees). The story of the martyrs is thus offered here as part of the author's commentary on this period, and as the main ideological vehicle of his "narrative demonstration."

In 4 Maccabees, Jason the high priest, who is portrayed as a usurper, is responsible for the decay of a more traditional way of Jewish life. But while Jason may have taken measures to remake Jerusalem into a Greek *polis*, it was in fact not Jason who undertook to abolish the temple cult but his successor Menelaus (2 Macc. 6:1-5; cf. 4 Macc. 4:20). The attribution of the latter action to Jason serves the author's larger aims, however: in the narrative logic of this episode, it is the suspension of the temple cult that makes necessary the "sacrifice" of the martyrs for the sake of the preservation of the covenant between God and Israel (deSilva, 121–22).

The work of the martyrs in 4 Maccabees serves as a "demonstration" of the basic Deuteronomic principle that collective infidelity to the covenant (i.e., in the form of Hellenization, worship of foreign gods, etc.) would result in punishment, and that corporate obedience leads to restoration. Thus Eleazar and the other martyrs provide the examples of fidelity that would prompt a renewed covenantal harmony should they be emulated by the rest of the community.

In what follows in this section, 4 Maccabees offers its own unique intervention in its presentation of the rhetorical contest between Antiochus IV and Eleazar—a scene that doubtless is not historical, however compellingly narrated it may be. Fourth Maccabees refers to Antiochus IV as a "tyrant" (e.g., 5:1; 14; 6:1), a term that is used deliberately to contrast him with Eleazar and to suggest that the confrontation between those two was a confrontation between tyranny and innocence; this term may also connect 4 Maccabees here with other "resistance literature," such as the early Christian martyrologies (see deSilva, 125).

One of the most distinctive aspects of Jewish identity in the Greco-Roman world was in the sphere of dietary practices. Non-Jewish commentators often took note of this distinction in a derogatory way in order to marginalize Jews and establish Judaism as a kind of superstition (in contrast with the "noble" and "lofty" religion and philosophy of the Greeks and Romans). Dietary and other religious practices served also to fuel a major controversy between the Antioch and Jerusalem factions of the earliest Christian church (Galatians 2–3; Acts 15).

Fourth Maccabees presents the violation of the Jewish food laws as the main vehicle for apostasy, especially since it is the wicked king Antiochus who seeks to persuade them (via Eleazar) to eat pork as a sign of their recognition of the superiority of the Greek way of life. The debate between Eleazar and Antiochus thus revolves around the question of the relationship between obedience to the Jewish law and the use of reason in pursuit of the "natural law" of the Greek philosophers.

To counter Antiochus's argument regarding the "necessity" of obeying his command, Eleazar argues—it seems for the sake of his audience—that the only "necessity" is to obey God by observing the torah. This rhetorical strategy (on the part of the author, who speaks here through Eleazar) connects with and animates a number of Greek philosophical virtues, most especially those of courage and piety, as well as the notion of the ultimate freedom of the ones who resist tyranny by remaining true to principle. This latter idea reflects a characteristically Stoic outlook in which the true sage renounces worldly comfort or success in favor of a life (or death, as it were) of integrity and honor.

The heady exchange between Antiochus and Eleazar on matters of religion and philosophy may seem strange in view of the gruesome scenes of torture and death that follow. Yet there is a connection between the two: the structure and logic of the debate seems to invite a ghastly display of piety insofar as this becomes necessary as a consequence of Eleazar's rhetorical victory. The greater the suffering of the martyrs, the greater their integrity; the more graphic the detail, the more compelling their witness—a witness that underscores Eleazar's greater embodiment of *both* Jewish and Greek virtues. In fact, here 4 Maccabees departs considerably from its base text in 2 Maccabees in its embellished account of the torture and death of the martyrs, causing some interpreters to become uncomfortable with its vivid description.

At the end of this section, the author returns to his main thesis by way of a narrative intermission. The martyrdom of Eleazar confirms the notion that pious reason—or the use of steadfast reason as the foundation for piety—allows one to overcome the passions (fear, pain, pleasure, etc.) in moments of trial. Eleazar is given an encomium in a manner consistent with Hellenistic conventions, and he is presented in this eulogy as the ideal sage—and as the model for those who would come after him.

▌▌ THE TEXT IN THE INTERPRETIVE TRADITION

Fourth Maccabees—and in particular the account of Eleazar's martyrdom—seems to have been influential in the presentation of later Jewish and Christian martyr figures. While the question of whether 4 Maccabees had direct influence on writings in the New Testament is debated (and unlikely in most cases), 4 Maccabees does provide some important parallel material regarding certain first-century-CE ideas and themes. This is especially true with respect to attitudes about torah observance (Galatians 2–3; 5–6) and the "noble death" of those who suffer for the sake of others (e.g., Mark 10:45; Rom. 3:24-25; 1 Tim. 2:6; Heb. 9:1—10:18; Phil. 2:5-11), though other conceptual and linguistic parallels exist (see deSilva, xxxii–xxxiii).

The description of the death of Eleazar in 4 Maccabees evinces a theme found in other early Jewish and Christian texts: that of an obedient individual (or several individuals) whose voluntary suffering and death prompts the favor of God to the benefit of others (cf. the LXX interpretation of Isa. 52:13—53:12 and 39:5-7; 2 Macc. 8:5; Heb. 10:5-10; 1 Pet. 2:21-25). This idea—and surely the presentations of the martyrs in both 2 Maccabees and 4 Maccabees—also informs early Christian martyr accounts such as the letters of Ignatius of Antioch (*Eph.* 21.1; *Smyr.* 10.2) and the diaries of Perpetua and Felicitas, among others. It is also possible that the *Martyrdom of Habbib* relies on 4 Maccabees in the way Habbib "makes a claim for recognition before God for not fleeing the torments when he was able to do so" and insists on the just punishment of the tyrant (deSilva, xxvii; *Martyrdom of Habbib* 36; 4 Macc. 6:27).

▌▌ THE TEXT IN CONTEMPORARY DISCUSSION

The exchange between Eleazar and Antiochus represents the tension between the (then) dominant culture's view of Judaism and the case for the Jewish way of life from an insider perspective. This "debate" also attests to the fact that assumptions about identity are always and everywhere shaped by one's vantage point and by power and social position.

Fourth Maccabees deals with a problem that spans many ages and cultures. How should religious minorities deal adequately with the tension that arises between adherence to customary beliefs and practices and living in a dominant culture that emphasizes different values? What are the demands—and the limits—of conformity to imperial life? Fourth Maccabees argues that it is better and more reasonable to adhere to a traditional culture than to acquiesce to the pressures of assimilation. What forms might this kind of resistance take in contemporary life, especially when it comes to the kinds of pressures that religious minorities face? Conversely, what obligation do traditional, religious communities have to demonstrate the reasonableness and nobility—that is, the acceptability—of their traditions within the larger social and cultural systems?

The martyrdoms of Eleazar and others in 4 Maccabees have the effect (in the narrative) of destroying the power of the ruler through self-restraint and martyrdom coupled with the sophisticated political rhetoric of honor and shame. David deSilva puts it well: "The underlying question [in the debate between Eleazar and Antiochus]: is what truly is compelling. Is it the force of law or power and the concern for temporal well-being on which they depend in order to work, or concern for maintaining one's integrity in regard to the values one holds inviolable?" (deSilva, 133). Fourth Maccabees depicts an act of nonviolent resistance to oppression, serving thus as an ancient example of a perennial impulse that also finds expression in the contemporary world—Gandhi, Martin Luther King Jr., and the writings of Gene Sharp readily come to mind.

The martyrdom of Eleazar has also served in recent years as an example of the construction of masculinity in the ancient world. Drawing on gender studies and poststructuralist approaches, for example, Stephen Moore and Janice Anderson have argued that the classical virtue of courage—*andreia*, which can be translated as "manliness"—is the principal virtue that 4 Maccabees wishes to lift up for emulation. At the end of the encomium of Eleazar, the author of 4 Maccabees declares that "some persons appear to be dominated by their emotions because of the weakness of their reason," but that "only the wise and courageous [*ho sophos kai andreios*] is master of the passions" (4 Macc. 7:23). The text thus inverts the notion that manliness is related to physical or coercive power and roots it instead in self-mastery—a masculine ideal that applied also to women (see the martyrdom of the mother, 4 Macc. 15:23, 28-30; 16:3-4; see below for further discussion).

4 Maccabees 8:1—14:10: The Martyrdom of the Seven Brothers

■ THE TEXT IN ITS ANCIENT CONTEXT

Both the torture and the rhetoric are heightened in the narrative about the seven brothers. While 2 Maccabees 7 once again serves as the point of departure for this martyrdom account, here the author of 4 Maccabees elaborates and embellishes the story to serve his own rhetorical purposes. It is not implausible that something like this episode may have occurred in antiquity, but in keeping with his grandiose style the author is not primarily concerned here with historicity.

In the ancient Greek world, youth was often associated with a certain brashness and lack of control over impulses and passions (see Aristotle, *Rhet.* 2.12). How much more significant, then, that these seven youths submit themselves to the pious reason shaped by their education in torah! This is rhetorically forceful for the added reason that the young men were offered enticements from Antiochus—positions, land, wealth—that may have been hard to come by for nonestablishment Jews of second-century-BCE Jerusalem.

Antiochus proceeds to torture each of the brothers one by one, and 4 Maccabees narrates the methods and implements used in gruesome detail (a rhetorical technique known as "vivid description," or *ekphrasis*) with the express aim to make the audience squirm with discomfort (4 Macc. 14:9). Some of the instruments of torture are known from other ancient Greek sources, while others are not. The text seems to assume that the audience would have been familiar with these contraptions, most of which were dedicated to inflicting acute pain at extremities and joints (see deSilva, 162–64, for a detailed discussion).

In keeping with the theme of 4 Maccabees generally, each brother embodies the triumph of pious reason over the temptations to acquiesce, appealing also to the reward that is greater than any Antiochus has to offer—that of an afterlife that honors their ancestors and vouchsafes immortality (e.g., 4 Macc. 9:1-9). This theme is reflected also in Plato's depiction of Socrates' last moments in the *Gorgias* (*Gorg.* 527A–B), and in Jewish Wisdom and apocalyptic literature of the age (Wisd. of Sol. 1:16-5:23; 6:17-20; *T. Mos.* 9:6-7). Fourth Maccabees also connects the theme of honoring ancestors to the example of Abraham, who preferred "sacrifice" over disobeying God (4 Macc. 9:21; 13:12; 14:20; 15:28; 16:20).

Toward the end of this section, 4 Maccabees strongly evinces the theme of "brotherly love," or *philadelphia*, which is a kind of virtuous friendship discussed also in Aristotle's *Nicomachean Ethics* and other classical sources. The ties that bind these brothers include their education in the Torah, their association with a larger community of the faithful, and their shared moral excellence. This fraternal bond helps to heighten the sense of sacrifice and lend it an aura of the paradoxical: their passionate, mutual affection became the very force that compelled them to obey "reason" and to resist the demands of the tyrant (13:19—14:1).

▌▌ THE TEXT IN THE INTERPRETIVE TRADITION

The brutal treatment of the seven brothers in 4 Maccabees becomes a template for the presentation of later (Christian) martyrs. The *Martyrdom of Polycarp*, for example, contains a graphic depiction of the hero's torture and death (though in this case by burning, stabbing, and other bodily insults) and gives Polycarp a similar justification for choosing martyrdom: that he will be eternally rewarded while his persecutors will be forever caught in the fire of judgment (*Mart. Pol.* 11; cf. 4 Macc. 9:7-9; 10:11; 13:14-15).

Fourth Maccabees clearly influences subsequent Christian martyrologies. Some of the most interesting legacies of the narrative about the seven brothers and their mother include its concept of martyrs as "athletes" and "devotees" and even "contestants" of piety and virtue (Origen, *Exhortation to Martyrdom* 23; *Passion of Saints Perpetua and Felicity* 10.1-4; cf. 4 Macc. 12:11-14; 13:27; 17:15). The athletic metaphor here is apt, given the emphasis on endurance, victory, and the ultimate vanquishing of the heroes' foes.

▌▌ THE TEXT IN CONTEMPORARY DISCUSSION

The most striking aspect of this section of 4 Maccabees is its vivid portrayal of torture. While this may be understandable from a rhetorical point of view—the author wished to underscore the severity of the brutality so as to heighten the readers' respect for the self-sacrifice and religious integrity of the brothers—it is unsettling to imagine these torments actually taking place. This is especially the case when we recognize that the perpetrator in this text (Antiochus) was a functionary of the "rational" imperial regime and that the victims were among the persecuted and caricatured religious minorities of the time.

Torture has long been a staple in the official (or unofficial) treatment of enemies of any state. It is, in essence, treatment of the dominated body toward its coercive capitulation to the will of the dominator. Refusal to capitulate is the last refuge of the martyr—or the one who would become a martyr to the people he or she represents. In this way, "martyrdom" is always defined and narrated by those who experience their own reality to be one of persecution—and it can thus be a way to claim moral power for the otherwise powerless. Accounts like this—indeed, perhaps all martyrdom stories—call one to recognize that experience and perspective are important dimensions in the creation of martyrs, and that there is often a polemical edge to martyrdom discourses.

In an age of terrorism, school shootings, and waterboarding, it is fitting to ask: What are the conditions of "martyrdom" today? Is torture a necessary component, or is anyone who dies for a belief a martyr? From whose perspective is torture a legitimate exercise to induce compliance? And finally, whose martyrdom counts as martyrdom?

4 Maccabees 14:11—18:19: The Mother of the Seven

▉ THE TEXT IN ITS ANCIENT CONTEXT

The author of 4 Maccabees combines ancient Greek gender stereotypes with examples from nature in his presentation of the mother of the seven martyrs. This figure, whose depiction derives also from 2 Maccabees (7:20-41), provides the climactic example in the author's "narrative demonstration" of reason over the passions. While the mother is not named in any of the earliest sources, rabbinic traditions call her Hannah or Miriam bat Tanhum, later Greek sources name her Solomone, and Syriac texts refer to her as Mart Simouni (Young, 67).

It was generally assumed in ancient Greek contexts that there was a "natural" correspondence between men/reason and women/passion, and that the former held pride of place over the latter (for a classic formulation, see Aristotle, *Pol.* 1.13). If the (male) children were able to overcome the passions with reason, goes the argument in 4 Maccabees, how much more remarkable that a woman—and a mother—would do so (cf. Xenophon, *Oec.* 7.24). This, then, is the ultimate effect of torah piety: it allows even a woman to become "like Abraham" in faithfulness, bracing her also to experience the appalling deaths of her sons.

Fourth Maccabees contrasts the expected "this-worldly" and "fainthearted" response of a mother who has lost everything (16:5-11) with that of the mother of the seven martyrs, whose steadfast purpose was to "rebirth" them for an immortality accomplished by witnessing to the faith. Fourth Maccabees even draws on the Septuagint (Greek) translation of Deut. 33:3 to make the argument that the martyrs have found their eternal home with God.

In this section, 4 Maccabees uses the language of martyrdom ("witness") in an explicit way, while also adapting the imagery of athletic contests to the trial of the mother and sons (17:11-16). Here the heroes are "athletes of the divine legislation," a trope that has echoes in other early Jewish literature and that derives from ancient Greek ideas about the practice and endurance of the virtuous sage (see, e.g., Philo on the Essenes, *Prob.* 88–91; Josephus, *Ant.* 18; 20). Here, as in Greek and Roman athletic games, the "athletes" have spectators whose presence serves to heighten the drama and to provide additional energy and legendary status to the heroes.

Fourth Maccabees presents the mother's suicide as the only honorable way for her to meet her end (cf. Plutarch, *Mulier. virt.* 15 [*Mor.* 240C–263C]; and the depiction of Hecuba in Euripides' *Trojan Women* 1282–83). In this way, she avoids improper handling by the soldiers and accomplishes both the preservation of her womanly chastity and the expression of her manly courage—which, in the view of the author, is the highest possible attainment of virtue.

The final passages in this section (17:7—18:5) represent the author's closing perorations, written in a style reminiscent of Hellenistic honorary inscriptions and *epitaphios logos* (see deSilva, 242–44). The final exhortations use the self-sacrifices—the victories of pious reason—of the martyrs to encourage the audiences of 4 Maccabees to continue their witness to the integrity of the Jewish way of life.

▌The Text in the Interpretive Tradition

Traditions involving the mother of the seven are plentiful. She is first mentioned only briefly in 2 Maccabees, and thus the elaborations of her account in 4 Maccabees appear to serve as the primary basis for later interpretive presentations.

The only known Jewish tradition associated with the mother of the seven comes from *Lamentations Rabbah*, an early interpretive work on the biblical book of Lamentations. This midrash throughout juxtaposes Athens and Jerusalem, elevating the latter fallen city above the former in prestige and piety—and perhaps for this reason invokes motifs from 4 Maccabees. In a passage depicting the martyrdom of Miriam bat Tanhum and her seven sons under the rule of Roman emperor Hadrian (117–138 CE), *Lamentations Rabbah* adapts 4 Maccabees to a later persecution under a different ruler—one closer in time and cultural context to that of the early rabbis. This midrash, like 4 Maccabees, likens the mother to Abraham and even promotes her above him. The mother says, "You built one altar [for Isaac] and did not sacrifice your son, but I built seven altars and sacrificed my sons on them. And for that matter, yours was a trial, but mine was a fact" (*Lam. Rab.* 1.16 N; Henten and Avemarie, 150). The comparison with Abraham is found also in early Christian traditions (e.g., *Martyrdom of Montanus and Lucius* 16.3–4).

If 4 Maccabees asserts any influence on New Testament writings, the Epistle to the Hebrews seems the most likely candidate. Hebrews and 4 Maccabees share thematic emphasis upon the role of (self-)sacrifice as it relates to atonement, the centrality of faith, and the eternal rewards for the righteous. The two texts even evidence several verbal parallels that may indicate a direct relationship (e.g., 4 Macc. 17:4; Heb. 3:6, 14).

■ THE TEXT IN CONTEMPORARY DISCUSSION

Depictions of gender and virtue in 4 Maccabees have special importance in contemporary discussions of this text. The most obvious point of contemporary controversy would be the way 4 Maccabees incorporates Greco-Roman assumptions about "the sexes"—namely, that women are associated with the body and the passions and men with reason and piety, and that the latter has higher status than the former. This dichotomy is also put to use, for example, by the *Gospel of Thomas* (114: "every woman who will make herself male will enter the kingdom of heaven") and Philo (e.g., *QE* 1.8; see Tobin, 32), and it has a long history in Western ideas about sex, gender, and their relation to language and social and economic life (Boyarin).

The point of view of 4 Maccabees is challenged by a modern feminist tradition that (arguably) begins with Elizabeth Cady Stanton's *The Woman's Bible* and, later, Simone de Beauvoir's *The Second Sex*, and continues through many different trajectories of feminist criticism. Beginning in the 1960s, feminist theologians such as Mary Daly and Rosemary Radford Ruether began to challenge patriarchal and paternalistic assumptions about sex and gender, proposing new and compelling ways to read the Bible that drew from the full scope of feminist theory.

Moore and Anderson argue that the theme of gender and virtue in 4 Maccabees "denigrates women's biology and constructs female gender negatively" (Moore and Anderson, 269), and they seek to offer a critical reading of the text that deconstructs its gender assumptions. They note, too, that not only is the mother's victory masculinized in 4 Maccabees, but also Antiochus's defeat is "feminized" insofar as he gives in to his passions and becomes a "failed man" (252–64). Mary Rose D'Angelo sees the sudden emergence of the father of the seven sons in 4 Macc. 18:9-19 as another sign of the author's worldview—he represents the "family values" of piety and reason, and thus takes his "rightful" place as the primary teacher of torah (D'Angelo, 156–57).

4 Maccabees 18:20-24: Conclusion

Fourth Maccabees concludes by rehearsing its main points and closes with a doxology reminiscent of other ancient texts (Heb. 13:21; 2 Tim. 4:18). In the Hebrew Bible generally, the phrase "to be gathered to one's fathers" conveys a notion of death that rests on the metaphor of burial—literally to be buried in the family tomb and deposited in Sheol, and to be remembered as one among the ancestors. In 4 Maccabees, the promise of gathering and memory is framed in terms of eternal life, reflecting the widespread Jewish adoption of Hellenistic ideas about immortality during the late Second Temple period. Thus the work closes on a note that reiterates its central idea: eternal life is preferable to temporary satisfactions, and it is made possible by steadfast commitment to pious reason—and to a life of honor and religious integrity.

Works Cited

Boyarin, Daniel. 1998. "Gender." In *Critical Terms for Religious Studies*, edited by Mark C. Taylor, 117–35. Chicago: University of Chicago Press.

Collins, John J. 1997. *Jewish Wisdom in the Hellenistic Age*. Louisville: Westminster John Knox.

D'Angelo, Mary Rose. 2003. "*Eusebeia*: Roman Imperial Family Values and the Sexual Politics of 4 Maccabees and the Pastorals." *BibInt* 11:139–65.

DeSilva, David. 2006. *4 Maccabees: Introduction and Commentary on the Greek Text in Codex Sinaiticus*. Leiden: Brill.

Henten, Jan Willem van, and Friedrich Avemarie. 2002. *Martyrdom and Noble Death: Selected Texts from Graeco-Roman, Jewish, and Christian Antiquity*. London: Routledge.

Moore, Stephen D., and Janice Capel Anderson. 1998. "Taking It Like a Man: Masculinity in 4 Maccabees." *JBL* 117:249–73.

Tobin, Thomas H. 1983. *The Creation of Man: Philo and the History of Interpretation*. CBQMS 14. Washington, DC: Catholic Biblical Association of America.

VanderKam, James. 2004. *From Joshua to Caiaphas: High Priests after the Exile*. Minneapolis: Fortress Press.

Young, Robin Darling. 1991. "The 'Woman with the Soul of Abraham': Traditions about the Mother of the Maccabean Martyrs." In *Women Like This: New Perspectives on Jewish Women in the Greco-Roman World*, edited by Amy-Jill Levine, 67–81. Atlanta: Scholars Press.